D1827329

1 MONTH OF
FREE
READING

at

www.ForgottenBooks.com

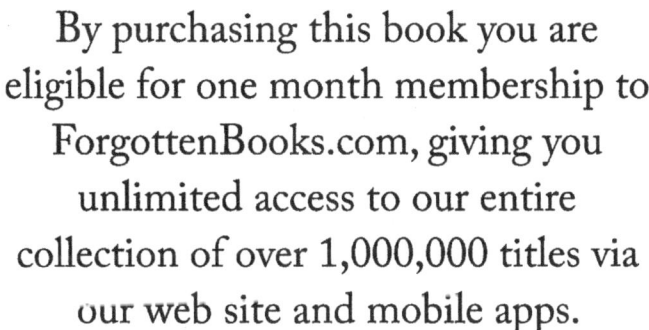

By purchasing this book you are eligible for one month membership to ForgottenBooks.com, giving you unlimited access to our entire collection of over 1,000,000 titles via our web site and mobile apps.

To claim your free month visit:

www.forgottenbooks.com/free907188

ISBN 978-0-265-90287-5
PIBN 10907188

This book is a reproduction of an important historical work. Forgotten Books uses state-of-the-art technology to digitally reconstruct the work, preserving the original format whilst repairing imperfections present in the aged copy. In rare cases, an imperfection in the original, such as a blemish or missing page, may be replicated in our edition. We do, however, repair the vast majority of imperfections successfully; any imperfections that remain are intentionally left to preserve the state of such historical works.

W. W. REILLY & CO.'S

OHIO STATE

BUSINESS DIRECTORY:

CONTAINING

THE MERCANTILE FIRMS, MANUFACTURING ESTABLISHMENTS, MECHANICS, PRO-
FESSIONAL MEN, TOGETHER WITH THE BANKING INSTITUTIONS, POST
OFFICES AND ALL THE MISCELLANEOUS DEPARTMENTS
WHICH CONTRIBUTE TO THE WEALTH AND
PROSPERITY OF THE STATE.

FOR 1853-4.

CAREFULLY CORRECTED AND ARRANGED.

ALSO, AN

ADVERTISING DEPARTMENT.

To be Revised and Continued.

CINCINNATI:
MORGAN & OVEREND, PRINTERS.
1853.

1870, July 13.
Gift of
John W. Quincy,
of New York.

PREFACE.

WE have been induced to prepare and publish the present volume, in accordance with the settled convictions of our own minds, that the business interests of the State of Ohio demanded the publication of a work which would present, at one view, its Mercantile, Manufacturing, and Commercial resources, and present to professional and business men, in every city, town, and village, a medium of acquaintance with each other; which conviction has been confirmed, as we have progressed with the work, by the almost universal approbation and support which it has received from an intelligent public throughout every portion of the State, manifested by the hearty co-operation of numbers of gentlemen of almost every occupation, in aiding our special agents in obtaining the necessary statistics, and in becoming themselves local agents in their own vicinities, for procuring and furnishing such information as would enable us to compile a correct list of every business and profession. The agents, wherever they presented the prospectus, received almost the universal support of business men, being far greater than was anticipated by the proprietors.

In addition to the list of Post-Offices in the State of Ohio, promised in our prospectus, we have inserted a Map of the State, laid off in Townships, on which all the Railroads now in operation, as well as those in process of construction, are correctly laid down. We have also prepared and inserted a neat Map of the city of Cincinnati.

In reference to the arrangement of the work, it will be perceived that every business, as well as the counties in the State, are arranged in alphabetical order. Other plans will doubtless suggest themselves, as being preferable to the one we have adopted, but we think, on reflection, it will be conceded that its convenience, as a book of reference, has been promoted by the present arrangement; inasmuch as all that is necessary to be known, in order to find the location of any business or professional man in the State, is to know what is his occupation, then by referring to the Index, it will be seen on what page of the Directory that business is to be

(iii)

The Gift of
John W. Quincy,
of New York.

13 July, 1870.

John H Quincy
98 William St
January 25, '56
New York

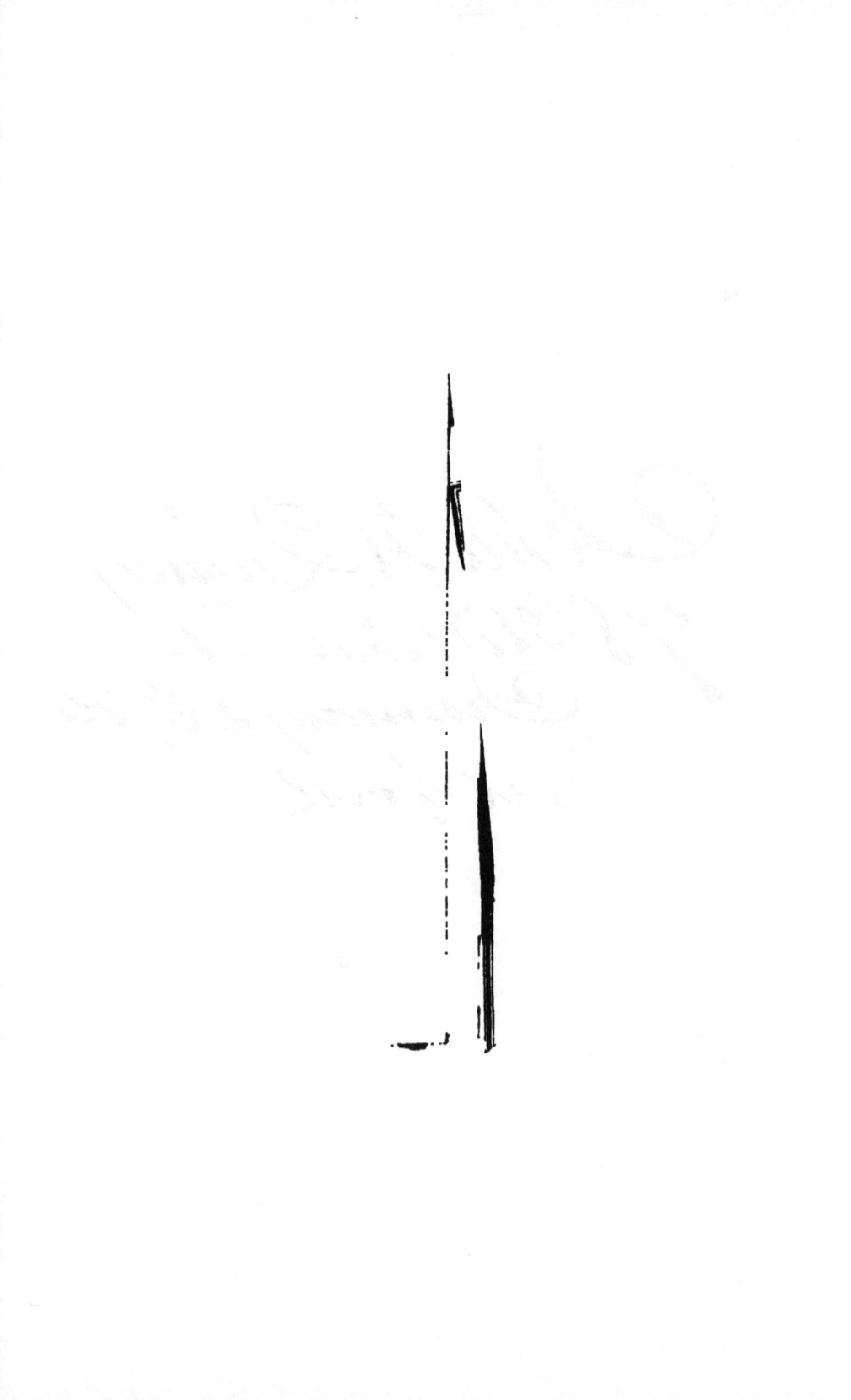

1853.

W. W. REILLY & CO.'S

OHIO STATE

BUSINESS DIRECTORY:

CONTAINING

THE MERCANTILE FIRMS, MANUFACTURING ESTABLISHMENTS, MECHANICS, PRO-
FESSIONAL MEN, TOGETHER WITH THE BANKING INSTITUTIONS, POST
OFFICES AND ALL THE MISCELLANEOUS DEPARTMENTS
WHICH CONTRIBUTE TO THE WEALTH AND
PROSPERITY OF THE STATE.

FOR 1853-4.

CAREFULLY CORRECTED AND ARRANGED.

ALSO, AN

ADVERTISING DEPARTMENT.

To be Revised and Continued.

CINCINNATI:
MORGAN & OVEREND, PRINTERS.
1853.

1870, July 13.
Gift of
John W. Quincy,
of New York.

PREFACE.

WE have been induced to prepare and publish the present volume, in accordance with the settled convictions of our own minds, that the business interests of the State of Ohio demanded the publication of a work which would present, at one view, its Mercantile, Manufacturing, and Commercial resources, and present to professional and business men, in every city, town, and village, a medium of acquaintance with each other; which conviction has been confirmed, as we have progressed with the work, by the almost universal approbation and support which it has received from an intelligent public throughout every portion of the State, manifested by the hearty co-operation of numbers of gentlemen of almost every occupation, in aiding our special agents in obtaining the necessary statistics, and in becoming themselves local agents in their own vicinities, for procuring and furnishing such information as would enable us to compile a correct list of every business and profession. The agents, wherever they presented the prospectus, received almost the universal support of business men, being far greater than was anticipated by the proprietors.

In addition to the list of Post-Offices in the State of Ohio, promised in our prospectus, we have inserted a Map of the State, laid off in Townships, on which all the Railroads now in operation, as well as those in process of construction, are correctly laid down. We have also prepared and inserted a neat Map of the city of Cincinnati.

In reference to the arrangement of the work, it will be perceived that every business, as well as the counties in the State, are arranged in alphabetical order. Other plans will doubtless suggest themselves, as being preferable to the one we have adopted, but we think, on reflection, it will be conceded that its convenience, as a book of reference, has been promoted by the present arrangement; inasmuch as all that is necessary to be known, in order to find the location of any business or professional man in the State, is to know what is his occupation, then by referring to the Index, it will be seen on what page of the Directory that business is to be

(iii)

found, and by commencing at the heading, and running through the different counties, as they are alphabetically arranged, the object of the research will doubtless be found.

We congratulate ourselves on the accomplishment of our great aim, to make the work as perfect as time, money, and labor could make it. In doing this, we have had from ten to thirty men employed for different periods during the last four months, and in its issue, nothing has been spared to produce the work as quickly as it could be done, to get the matter correct before publication. Some may have thought it slow in its issue, but every one who will reflect, for a moment, on the immense labor necessary to procure statistics from eighty-eight counties, divided into nearly seventeen hundred post-offices, in addition to which was the arranging and compiling this matter in the order in which it is now presented, must be convinced that no unnecessary delay has occurred. In reference to the fullness of the list, we would observe, that out of nearly seventeen hundred post-offices in the State, we have received returns from all but a very few, and these are chiefly offices where there are no villages. Many places have had to be taken the second and third time, in consequence of the loss of matter through the mails, yet the publication was delayed until they were received. We feel no hesitation in saying that no work of the kind has been published upon which so much money has been spent, and the work made so perfect. Although it would be impossible to get every name in every town, yet each place has been canvassed by good men, who have acted toward us and our business in good faith.

Trusting our work will be appreciated according to its merits, we respectfully submit it to all who may be interested in the matter it contains.

                                        W. W. REILLY & CO.

Cincinnati, 1853.

INDEX.

(v)

[The names of the Post-Masters have been omitted in consequence of the numerous changes made.]

POST-OFFICE.	COUNTY.	POST-OFFICE.	COUNTY.	POST-OFFICE.	COUNTY.
Abbeyville	Medina	Armstrong's Mills,	Belmont	Beech Land,	Licking
Abbotsville,	Darke	Arnheim,	Brown	Belfast,	Clermont
Aberdeen,	Brown	Arrowsmith's,	Defiance	Bell,	Highland
Achor,	Columbiana	Ashbury,	Perry	Bell Air,	Belmont
Adams,	Seneca	Asherey,	Hancock	Bell Brook,	Greene
Adams' Mills,	Muskingum	Ashland c. h.,	Ashland	Bell Centre,	Logan
Adamsville,	"	Ash Ridge,	Brown	Bellefontaine c. h.,	"
Adario,	Richland	Ashtabula,	Ashtabula	Belle Point,	Delaware
Addison,	Gallia	Ashville,	Pickaway	Belle Vernon,	Wyandott
Adelphia,	Ross	Athens c. h.,	Athens	Belleville,	Richland
Ai,	Lucas	Attica,	Seneca	Bellvue,	Huron
Aid,	Lawrence	Atwater,	Portage	Belmont,	Belmont
Akron c. h.,	Summit	Auburn,	Geauga	Belpre,	Washington
Albany,	Tuscarawas	Auglaize,	Van Wert	Bennington,	Morrow
Albion,	Ashland	Augusta,	Carroll	Benton,	Holmes
Alert,	Butler	Aurelia,	Washington	Benton Ridge,	Hancock
Alexander,	Athens	Aurora,	Portage	Bentonville,	Adams
Alexandersville,	Montgom.	Austin,	Ross	Berea,	Cuyahoga
Alexandria,	Licking	Austinburgh,	Ashtabula	Berkshire,	Delaware
Alfred,	Meigs	Avon,	Lorain	Berlin,	Holmes
Allen Centre,	Union	Avon Lake,	"	Berlin Centre,	Mahoning
Allen's,	Miami	Ayersville,	Defiance	Berlinville,	Erie
Allensburgh,	Highland	Bainbridge,	Ross	Berlin X Roads,	Jackson
Allensville,	Jackson	Baker's,	Champaign	Berne,	Monroe
Allentown,	Allen	Bakersville,	Coshocton	Berwick,	Seneca
Alpha,	Green	Ball,	Knox	Bethany,	Butler
Alton,	Franklin	Baltimore,	Fairfield	Bethel,	Clermont
Alum Creek,	Delaware	Bantam,	Clermont	Bettsville,	Seneca
Alum Run,	Monroe	Bare's,	Monroe	Beverly,	Washington
Amanda,	Fairfield	Barlow,	Washington	Bevis' Tavern,	Hamilton
Amboy,	Ashtabula	Barne's,	Richland	Big Island,	Marion
Amelia,	Clermont	Barnesville,	Belmont	Big Plain,	Madison
Amesville,	Athens	Barry,	Cuyahoga	Big Prairie,	Wayne
Amherst,	Lorain	Barryville,	Stark	Big Lick,	Hancock
Amsterdam,	Jefferson	Bartlett,	Washington	Bird's Run,	Muskingum
Anderson's Store,	Morgan	Bascom,	Seneca	Birmingham,	Erie
Andover,	Ashtabula	Bashan,	Meigs	Bissell's,	Geauga
Andrews,	Morrow	Batavia c. h.,	Clermont	Black Creek,	Holmes
Ankenytown,	Knox	Batesville,	Guernsey	Blachysville,	Wayne
Annapolis,	Jefferson	Bath,	Summit	Black River,	Lorain
Anselm,	Gallia	Baxter's,	Muskingum	Black Swamp,	Sandusky
Antioch,	Monroe	Bay's Bottom,	Gallia	Bladensburgh,	Knox
Antrim,	Guernsey	Bazetta,	Trumbull	Blanc,	Lucas
Antwerp,	Paulding	Bealsville,	Monroe	Blanchard Bridge,	Hancock
Apple Creek,	Wayne	Beamsville,	Darke	Blanchester,	Clinton
Apple Grove,	Meigs	Bear Creek,	Montgomery	Blendon,	Franklin
Appleton,	Licking	Beaver,	Pike	Bloomfield,	Morrow
Archer,	Harrison	Beaver Dam,	Allen	Bloomingburgh,	Fayette
Arcole,	Lake	Beckett's Store,	Pickaway	Bloomingdale	Jefferson
Arlington,	Hancock	Bedford,	Cuyahoga	Bloomington,	Clinton

POST-OFFICE	COUNTY	POST-OFFICE	COUNTY	POST-OFFICE	COUNTY
Bloomingvill .,	Erie	Cable,	Guernsey	Chesterville,	Morrow
Bloomville,	Seneca	Cadiz c. h.,	Harrison	Cheviot,	Hamilton
Blue Ball,	Butler	Cadwallader,	Tuscarawas	Chickasaw,	Mercer
Blue Cre·k,	Adams	Cairo,	Starke	Chili,	Coshocton
Blue Rock,	Muskingum	Calain,	Monroe	Chillicothe c. h.,	Ross
Boardman,	Mahoning	Calcutta,	Columbiana	Cilo,	Clermont
Boetia, ·	Mercer	Caledonia,	Marion	Chippewa,	Wayne
Boke's Creek,	Union	California,	Clermont	Christiansburgh,	Champai'n
Bolen's Mills,	Athens	Calvary,	Athens	Church Hill,	Trumbull
Bolivar,	Tuscarawas	Cambridge c. h.,	Guernsey	Cincinnati, c. h.,	Hamilton
Bonn,	Washington	Camden,	Preble	Circleville, c. h.,	Pickaway
Boston,	Summit	Campbell,	Lawrence	Claridon,	Geauga
Bourneville,	Ross	Campbellsport,	Portage	Clark's,	Coshocton
Bowersville,	Greene	Canaan,	Wayne	Clarksburgh,	Ross
Bowling Greene,	Wood	Canaanville,	Athens	Clarksfield,	Huron
Bowsherville,	Wyandott	Canal Dover, .	Tuscarawas	Clarkson,	Columbiana
Braceville,	Trumbull	Canal Fulton,	Starke	Clarksville,	Clinton
Bradyville,	Adams	Canal Louisville,	Coshocton	Claysville,	Guernsey
Branch Hill,	Clermont	Canal Winchester,	Fairfield	Clayton,	Montgomery
Brandon,	Knox	Canfield c. h.,	Mahoning	Claytona,	Morgan
Brandt,	Miami	Cannonsburgh,	Hancock	Clear Creek,	Fairfield
Bremen,	Fairfield	Cannon's Mill,	Columbiana	Clement,	Hancock
Brennersville,	Preble	Canton c. h.,	Starke	Cleveland c. h..	Cuyahoga
Bricksville,	Cuyahoga	Captina,	Belmont	Cleves,	Hamilton
Bridge Creek,	Geauga	Cardington,	Morrow	Clifton,	Greene
Bridgeport,	Belmont	Carey,	Wyandott	Clinton,	Summit
Bridgeville,	Muskingum	Carey's Academy,	Hamilt'n	Clintonville,	Franklin
Bridgewater,	Williams	Carlisle,	Lorain	Clio,	Greene
Briar Hill,	Mahoning	Carroll,	Fairfield	Clover,	Clermont
Brighton,	Lorain	Carrolton c. h.	Carroll	Clyde,	Sandusky
Brimfield,	Portage	Carthage,	Hamilton	Coal Grove,	Lawrence
Brinton,	Champaign	Carysville	Champaign	Coal Run,	Washington
Bristol,	Morgan	Cass,	Hancock	Coberly's,	Union
Bristolville,	Trumbull	Casstown,	Miami	Cochran's Landing,	Monroe
Brock,	Darke	Cassville,	Harrison	Cochranton, ·	Marion
Broken Sword,	Crawford	Castalia,	Erie	Coddingville,	Medina
Bronson,	Huron	Castine,	Darke	Coe Ridge,	Cuyahoga
Brookfield,	Trumbull	Catawba,	Clark	Cokesburgh,	Licking
Brooklyn,	Cuyahoga	Cedar Valley,	Wayne	Coitsville,	Mahoning
Brownhelm,	Lorain	Cedarville,	Greene	Cold Spring,	Harrison
Brown's Grove,	Hamilton	Celina,	Mercer	Cold Water,	Mercer
Brown's Mills,	Washington	Central College,	Franklin	Colerain,	Belmont
Brown's Store,	Warren	Centre,	Montgomery	Cole's Mills,	Delaware
Brownsville,	Licking	Centre Belpre,	Washington	Collamer,	Cuyahoga
Brunersburgh,	Defiance	Centreburgh,	Knox	College Corner,	Butler
Brunswick,	Medina	Centrefield,	Highland	College Hill,	Hamilton
Bryan c, h.,	Williams	Centreton,	Huron	Collinsville,	Butler
Buckeye,	Putnam	Centreville,	Montgomery	Columbia,	Hamilton
Buckeye Cottage,	Perry	Chagrin Falls,	Cuyahoga	Columbiana,	Columbiana
Buckeye Furnace,	Jackson	Chambersburgh,	Montgom.	Columbus c. h.,	Franklin
Buck's,	Columbiana	Champion,	Trumbull	Columbia Centre,	Licking
Bucyrus c. h.,	Crawford	Chandlersville,	Muskingum	Concord,	Lake
Buffalo,	Guernsey	Chaneyville,	Morgan	Concordia,	Darke
Buford,	Highland	Chapel Hill,	Perry	Congress,	Wayne
Bundysburgh,	Geauga	Chardon c. h.,	Geauga	Conine,	Licking
Buena Vista,	Holmes	Charlestown,	Portage	Conneaut,	Ashtabula
Burbank,	Wayne	Charloe,	Paulding	Conotton,	Harrison
Burlingham,	Meigs	Chatfield,	Crawford	Constitution,	Washington
Berlington .	Lawrence	Chatham,	Licking	Contreras,	Butler
Burton,	Geauga	Chauncey,	Athens	Convenience,	Fayette
Butler,	Richland	Cherry Valley,	Ashtabula	Cook's Corners,	Erie
Butlerville,	Warren	Cheshire,	Gallia	Coolville,	Athens
Butternut Ridge,	Sandusky	Chester c. h.,	Meigs	Cooper,	Wayne
Byesville,	Guernsey	Chester X Roads,	Geauga	Cope's Mills,	Jefferson
Byington,	Pike	Chesterfield,	Lucas	Copley,	Summit
Byron, .	Greene	Chester Hill,	Morgan	Copopa,	Lorain

POST-OFFICE.	COUNTY.	POST OFFICE.	COUNTY.	POST-OFFICE	COUNTY.
Cork.	Ashtabula	Dry Ridge.	Hamilton	Fairfield	Greene
Cornersburgh,	Mahoning	Dublin,	Franklin	Fair Haven,	Preble
Corsica,	Morrow	Duck Creek.	Trumbull	Fair Mount,	Miami
Corwin,	Montgomery	Dudley,	Hardin	Fairport,	Lake
Coshocton, c. h.,	Coshocton	Duff's Forks,	Fayette	Fairview,	Guernsey
Cottage Mills,	Franklin	Dukes,	Putnam	Fallsburgh,	Licking
Covington,	Miami	Dumontville,	Fairfield	Farmer,	Defiance
Cranberry,	Allen	Dunbarton,	Adams	Farmersville,	Montgomery
Cranesville,	Paulding	Duncan's Falls,	Muskingum	Farmington,	Trumbull
Crawford,	Wyandott	Dundee,	Tuscarawas	Fayetteville,	Brown
Croghan,	Putnam	Dungauon,	Columbiana	Fearing,	Washington
Crossanville,	Perry	Dunkinsville,	Adams	Federalton,	Athens
Cross Roads,	Madison	Dunlap,	Hamilton	Feed Spring,	Harrison
Croton,	Licking	Dunlevey,	Warren	Feesburgh,	Brown
Croxton,	Jefferson	Durand,	Henry	Felicity,	Clermont
Cuba,	Clinton	Durbin's Corners,	Williams	Fidelity,	Miami
Culver Creek,	Delaware	Dysous,	Guernsey	Fillmore,	Washington
Cumberland,	Guernsey	Eagle,	Hancock	Fincastle,	Brown
Cumminsville,	Hamilton	Eagleville,	Ashtabula	Five Mile,	"
Cuyahoga Falls,	Summit	East Claridon,	Geauga	Finley c. h.,	Hancock
Cynthiana,	Pike	East Clarksfield.	Huron	Fitchville,	Huron
Dallas,	Highland	East Cleaveland.	Cuyahoga	Fitz Henry,	Seneca
Dallasburgh,	Warren	East Fairfield,	Columbiana	Flat,	Pike
Dalton,	Wayne	East Greenville,	Starke	Flat Rock,	Seneca
Damascoville,	Columbiana	East Lewiston,	Mahoning	Fletcher,	Miami
Damascus,	Henry	East Liberty,	Logan	Flint's Mills,	Washington
Danville,	Knox	East Liverpool,	Columbiana	Florence,	Erie
Darby,	Franklin	East Monroe,	Highland	Florida,	Henry
Darby Creek,	Madison	Easton,	Wayne	Flushing,	Belmont
Darby Plains,	Union	East Orange,	Delaware	Fort Ancient,	Warren
Darbyville,	Pickaway	East Palestine,	Columbiana	Fort Jefferson,	Darke
Darke,	Darke	East Plymouth,	Ashtabula	Fort Jennings,	Putnam
Darrtown,	Butler	East Richland,	Belmont	Fort Recovery,	Mercer
Dawkin's Mills,	Jackson	East Rochester,	Columbiana	Fort Seneca,	Seneca
Dayton c. h.	Montgomery	East Springfield,	Jefferson	Foster's Mill,	"
Deardorff's Mills,	Tuscara.	East Townsend,	Huron	Four Corners,	Huron
Deavertown,	Morgan	East Union,	Wayne	Fowler,	Trumbull
Decatur,	Brown	East Westville,	Mahoning	Fowler's Mill's	Geauga
Decatursville,	Washington	Eaton c. h.,	Preble	Franconia,	Putnam
Deep Cut,	Mercer	Eckmansville,	Adams	Frankfort,	Ross
Deerfield,	Portage	Eden,	Trumbull	Franklin,	Warren
Deerfield Village,	Warren	Edenton,	Clermont	Franklin Furnace,	Scioto
Deer Lick,	Williams	Edinburgh,	Portage	Franklin Mills,	Portage
Deersville,	Harrison	Edwardsville,	Warren	Franklin Square,	Columbiana
Defiance,	Defiance	Elizabeth,	Lawrence	Frazeysburgh,	Muskingum
De Kalb,	Crawford	Elizabethtown,	Hamilton	Frease's Store,	Starke
De La Palma,	Brown	Elkton,	Columbiana	Frederick,	Mahoning
Delaware c. h.,	Delaware	Elliottsville,	Jefferson	Fredericksburgh,	Wayne
Delphos,	Van Wert	Elliott's X Roads,	Morgan	Fredericktown,	Knox
Delta,	Lucas	Ellsworth,	Mahoning	Fredonia,	Licking
Democracy,	Knox	Elmira,	Lucas	Freedom,	Portage
Demos,	Belmont	Elyria, c. h.,	Lorain	Freelands,	Muskingum
Denmark,	Ashtabula	Emery,	Lucas	Freeport,	Harrison
Dent,	Hamilton	Euoch,	Monroe	Fremont,	Sandusky
Dille's Bottom,	Belmont	Enon,	Clark	French Grant,	Scioto
Dinsmore,	Shelby	Enterprise,	Preble	Friendship,	"
Dodsonville,	Highland	Essex,	Lucas	Fryburgh,	Allen
Domestic,	Williams	Etna,	Licking	Fulton,	Hamilton
Donnel's,	Allen	Euclid,	Cuyahoga	Fultonham,	Muskingum
Donnellsville,	Clark	Euphemia,	Preble	Furnace,	Erie
Dorset,	Ashtabula	Eureka Mills,	Greene	Gahanna,	Franklin
Dover,	Cuyahoga	Evansburg,	Coshocton	Galena,	Delaware
Downington,	Meigs	Evansport,	Defiance	Galion,	Crawford
Doylestown,	Paulding	Ewing,	Hocking	Gallatin,	Allen
Dresden,	Muskingum	Ewington,	Gallia	Gallia Furnace,	Gallia
Dry Fork,	Hamilton	Fairfax,	Highland	Gallipolis c. h.,	"

POST-OFFICE	COUNTY.	POST-OFFICE	COUNTY.	POST-OFFICE.	COUNTY.
Gambie,	Knox	Hanging Rock,	Lawrence	Hyattsville,	Miami
Ganges,	Richland,	Hanna's Mill's	Mahoning	Hygeia,	Hamilton
Garder,	Morgan	Hanover,	Licking	Iberia,	Morrow
Garrettsville,	Portage	Hanoverton,	Columbiana	Independence,	Cuyahoga
Gates' Mills,	Cuyahoga	Hardin c. h.,	Shelby	Inland,	Summit
Gavers,	Columbiana	Harlem,	Delaware	Inverness,	Columbiana
Geneva,	Ashtabula	Harlem Spring,	Carroll	Iron Furnace,	Scioto
Genoa X Roads,	Delaware	Harmar,	Washington	Ironton,	Lawrence
Georgesville,	Franklin	Harmony,	Clark	Irville,	Muskingum
Georgetown c. h.,	Brown	Harpersfield	Ashtabula	Irwin Creek,	Jefferson
German,	Darke	Harrietsville,	Monroe	Ithaca,	Darke
Germano,	Harrison	Harrisburgh,	Franklin	Jackson c. h.,	Jackson
Germantown,	Montgomery	Harrison,	Hamilton	Jacksonboro',	Butler
Gettysburg,	Preble	Harrisonville,	Meigs	Jackson Furnace,	Jackson
Gibson,	Pike	Harrisville,	Harrison	Jacksontown,	Licking
Gibsonville,	Hocking	Harshmansville,	Montgom.	Jacksonville,	Darke
Gilboa,	Putnam	Hartford,	Trumbull	Jacobsburgh,	Belmont
Gilead,	Wood	Hartland,	Huron	Jamestown,	Greene
Gillespieville,	Ross	Hart's Grove,	Ashtabula	Jasper,	Pike
Girard,	Trumbull	Hartville,	Starke	Java,	Lucas
Glasgow,	Columbiana	Harveysburgh,	Warren	Jeddo,	Jefferson
Gnadenhutten,	Tuscarawas	Hastings,	Richland	Jefferson c. h.,	Ashtabula
Gohanna,	Franklin	Hastingsville,	Columbiana	Jeffersonville,	Fayette
Good Hope,	Fayette	Hayesville,	Ashland	Jelloway,	Knox
Gorham,	Lucas	Hebbardsville,	Athens	Jerome,	Union
Goshen,	Clermont	Hebron,	Licking	Jeromeville,	Ashland
Grafton,	Lorain	Henby,	Montgomery	Jersey,	Licking
Graham's Station,	Meigs	Hendrysburgh,	Belmont	Jerusalem,	Monroe
Grand Prairie,	Marion	Henrietta,	Lorain	Johnson's Corners,	Summit
Grand View,	Washington	Herring,	Allen	Johnsonville,	Trumbull
Granger,	Medina	Hibernia,	Franklin	Johnstown,	Licking
Granville,	Licking	Hickory,	Carroll	Johnsville,	Montgomery
Grape Grove,	Green	Hickerson's X Roads,	Morg.	Jolly,	Washington
Gratiot,	Muskingum	Hicksville,	Defiance	Jonesville,	Monroe
Gratis,	Preble	Higginsport,	Brown	Junction,	Paulding
Graysville,	Monroe	High Hill,	Muskingum	Junior,	Scioto
Great Bend,	Meigs	Highland,	Highland	Kalida c, h.,	Putnam
Greenbush X Roads,	San'ky	Hill Creek,	Williams	Keene,	Coshocton
Greencastle,	Fairfield	Hill Grove,	Darke	Keith's,	Morgan
Green Creek,	Sandusky	Hillhouse,	Lake	Kelley's Mills,	Lawrence
Greene's Store,	Lawrence	Hillsboro' c. h.,	Highland	Kelloggsville,	Ashtabula
Greenfield,	Highland	Hinckley,	Medina	Kennou,	Belmont
Greenford,	Mahoning	Hiram,	Portage	Kennonsburgh,	Guernsey
Green Hill,	Columbiana	Hiramsburgh,	Morgan	Kenton c. h.,	Hardin
Greensburgh,	Trumbull	Hockingport,	Athens	Keystone,	Jackson
Greensburgh X Roads,	San.	Hog Creek,	Allen	Kilgore,	Carroll
Green Spring,	Seneca	Holmesville,	Holmes	Killbourne,	Delaware
Greentown,	Starke	Homer,	Licking	Killbuck,	Holmes
Greenville c. h.,	Darke	Homerville,	Medina	Kimbolton,	Guernsey
Greenwich,	Huron	Hope,	Franklin	Kingston,	Ross
Groveland,	Fulton	Hopedale,	Harrison	Kingston Centre,	Delaware
Groveport,	Franklin	Hopewell,	Muskingum	Kingsville,	Ashtabula
Groton,	Huron	Hopkinsville,	Warren	Kinsman's,	Trumbull
Guilford,	Medina	Hoskinsville,	Morgan	Kirkersville,	Licking
Gustavus,	Trumbull	Houston,	Shelby	Kirtland,	Lake
Gustine,	Adams	Howland,	Trumbull	Kossuth,	Auglaize
Guysville,	Athens	Hubbard,	"	Knox,	Knox
Hagerstown,	Preble	Hudson,	Summit	Knoxville,	Jefferson
Hale,	Hardin	Hulls,	Athens	Kyger,	Gallia
Hall's Valley,	Morgan	Humphrey's Villa,	Holmes	Laceyville,	Harrison
Harmony,	Clarke	Hunter,	Belmont	La Fayette,	Madison
Hallsville,	Ross	Huntersville,	Hardin	La Grange,	Lorain
Hamburg,	Preble	Huntington,	Lorain	Laing's,	Monroe
Hamersville,	Brown	Huntsburgh,	Geauga	Lake,	Starke
Hamilton c. h.,	Butler	Huntsville,	Logan	Lamartine,	Carroll
Hampden,	Geauga	Huron,	Erie	La Mira,	Belmont

POST-OFFICE.	COUNTY.	POST-OFFICE.	COUNTY.	POST-OFFICE.	COUNTY.
Lampsville,	Belmont	Loss Creek,	Crawford	Marysville c. h.,	Union
Lancaster c. h.,	Fairfield	Lottridge,	Athens	Mason,	Warren
Langsville,	Meigs	Lovett's,	Adams	Massilon,	Starke
La Porte,	Lorain	Loudonville,	Ashland	Masterton,	Monroe
Lattas,	Ross	Louisville,	Starke	Maumee City c. h.,	Lucas
Laura,	Miami	Loveland,	Clermont	Maxwell,	Delaware
Laurel,	Clermont	Lowell,	Kent	Maybees,	Jackson
Lavena,	Lucas	Lowell,	Washington	Mayfield,	Cuyahoga
Lawrence,	Washington	Lowellville,	Mahoning	Meadow Branch,	Jackson
Leatherwood,	Guernsey	Lower Lawrence,	Wash.	Meadow Farm,	Muskingum
Leavitt,	Carroll	Lower Newport,	"	Mecca,	Trumbull
Lebanon c. h.,	Warren	Lower Salem,	"	Mechanicsburgh,	Champ'n
Ledlie's,	Meigs	Lowry,	Athens	Mechanicstown,	Carroll
Lee,	Athens	Loydsville,	Belmont	Modary,	Putnam
Leesburgh,	Highland	Lucas,	Richland	Medina c. h.,	Medina
Lee's Creek,	Clinton	Lucasville,	Scioto	Medway,	Clark
Leesville,	Carroll	Lucerne,	Knox	Meig's Creek,	Morgan
Leesville X Roads,	Craw'd	Lumberton,	Clinton	Meigsville,	"
Leipsic,	Putnam	Lyme,	Huron	Meiners,	Seneca
Leistville,	Pickaway	Lynchburgh,	Highland	Mendon,	Mercer
Lenox,	Ashtabula	Lyons,	Lucas	Mentor,	Lake
Le Roy,	Medina	Lyra,	Scioto	Mercer,	Mercer
Le Sourdsville,	Ashtabula	McArthurstown,	- Athens	Merritt's,	Morrow
Letart Falls,	Meigs	McCombs,	Hancock	Mesopotamia,	Trumbull
Letimberville,	Marion	McConnellsville c. h.,	Morg.	Metamora,	Lucas
Level,	Warren	McCutchenville,	Wyandott	Mexico,	Wyandott
Levering,	Knox	McEwen's X Roads,	Mor'w	Miami,	Hamilton
Levi,	Jackson	McGhee's Store,	Jackson	Miamisburgh,	Montgomery
Lewis,	Brown	McKaig's Mill's,	Columb'na	Miamisville,	Clermont
Lewisburgh,	Preble	McKay,	Ashland	Middlebourne,	Guernsey
Lewiston,	Logan	Macedon,	Mercer	Middle Branch,	Starke
Lewisville,	Monroe	Madison,	Lake	Middleburgh,	Cuyahoga
Lexington,	Richland	Madisonburgh,	Wayne	Middlebury,	Summit
Liberty,	Montgomery	Madisonville,	Hamilton	Middle Creek,	Monroe
Liberty Corners,	Crawford	Magnolia,	Starke	Middlefield,	Geauga
Liberty Hall,	Warren	Maguire,	Morgan	Middle River,	Allen
Liken's,	Crawford	Mahala,	Adams	Middletown,	Butler
Lima c. h.,	Allen	Mahoning,	Starke	Mifflin,	Ashland
Limaville,	Starke	Malaga,	Monroe	Milan,	Erie
Lincoln,	Morrow	Mallet Creek,	Medina	Milford,	Clermont
Linnville,	Licking	Malta,	Morgan	Milford Centre,	Union
Lindenville,	Ashtabula	Malvern,	Carroll	Millfordton,	Knox
Litchfield,	Medina	Manchester,	Adams	Mill Brook,	Wayne
Lithopolis,	Fairfield	Manhatten,	Lucas	Mill Dale,	Defiance
Little Beaver Bridge,	Col'na	Mansfield c. h.,	Richland	Millers,	Lawrence
Little Hockhocking,	Wash.	Mantua,	Portage	Millersburgh c. h.,	Holmes
Little Mill Creek,	Delaware	Mantua Centre,	"	Millersport,	Fairfield
Little Sandusky,	Wyandott	Maple,	Brown	Millerstown,	Champaign
Little Scioto,	Marion	Maple Grove,	Knox	Millfield,	Athens
Little York,	Montgomery	Mapleton,	Starke	Mill Grove,	Morgan
Liverpool,	Medina	Marathon,	Clermont	Millville,	Butler
Lock,	Knox	Marblehead,	Ottawa	Millwood,	Knox
Lockbourne,	Franklin	Marble Furnace,	Adams	Millersville,	Guernsey
Lockington,	Shelby	Marengo,	Morrow	Milo,	Defiance
Lockport,	Williams	Maria Stein,	Mercer	Milton,	Mahoning
Lockville,	Fairfield	Marietta c. h.,	Washington	Miltonsburgh,	Monroe
Locust Corner,	Clermont	Marion c. h.,	Marion	Miltonville,	Wood
Locust Grove,	Adams	Marit's,	Morrow	Minerva,	Starke
Lodi,	Medina	Marlborough,	Starke	Minster,	Auglaize
Logan c. h.,	Hocking	Marseilles,	Wyandott	Mississinawa,	Darke
Loganville,	Logan	Marshall,	Highland	Mitchell's Salt Works,	Jeff.
Log Cabin,	Morgan	Marshallaville,	Wayne	Mogadore,	Summit
London c. h.,	Madison	Martinsburgh,	Knox	Mohawk Valley,	Coshocton
Londonderry,	Guernsey	Martin's Ferry,	Belmont	Mohican,	Ashland
Long Bottom,	Meigs	Martinsville,	Clinton	Monroe,	Butler
Loramie's,	Shelby	Marvin's Mill,	Hancock	Monroe Centre,	Ashtabula

POST-OFFICE.	COUNTY.	POST-OFFICE.	COUNTY.	POST-OFFICE.	COUNTY.
Monroe Mills,	Knox	New Athens,	Harrison	Nimisila,	Summit
Monroeville,	Huron	New Baltimore,	Starke	Nimmons' X Roads,	Mor'w
Monterey,	Clermont	New Bavaria,	Henry	Nonpareil,	Knox
Montezuma,	Mercer	New Bedford,	Coshocton	Norristown,	Carroll
Montgomery,	Hamilton	New Berlin,	Starke	North Benton,	Mahoning
Montgomery X Roads,	Wood	Newberry,	Geauga	North Bloomfield,	Trumbull
Montpelier,	Williams	New Bremen,	Auglaize	North Camden,	Lorain
Montra,	Shelby	Newburgh,	Cuyahoga	North Dover,	Cuyahoga
Montville,	Geauga	New Burlington,	Clinton	North Eaton,	Lorain
Moon's,	Fayette	New California,	Union	North Fairfield,	Huron
Moorefield,	Harrison	New Carlisle,	Clark	Northfield,	Summit
Moore's Salt Works,	Jeff.	New Castle,	Coshocton	North Georgetown,	Colum's
Moorland,	Wayne	New Chambersburg,	Col'na	North Hampton,	Clark
Morgan,	Ashtabula	New Comerstown,	Tusc'wa	North Industry,	Starke
Morgan's Fork,	Pike	New Concord,	Muskingum	North Jackson,	Mahoning
Morgansville,	Morgan	New Corwin,	Highland	North Lewisburgh,	Cham'n
Morning Sun,	Preble	New Cumberland,	Tuscar.	North Liberty,	Knox
Morristown,	Belmont	New Franklin,	Starke	North Lima,	Mahoning
Morrow,	Warren	New Garden,	Columbiana	North Newberry,	Geauga
Moscow,	Clermont	New Gottingen,	Guernsey	North Norwich,	Huron
Moscow Mills,	Morgan	New Guilford,	Coshocton	North Perry,	Lake
Mount Blanchard,	Hanc'k	New Hagerstown,	Carroll	North Ridge,	Hancock
Mount Carmel,	Clermont	New Harrisburgh,	"	North Ridgeville,	Lorain
Mount Eaton,	Wayne	New Haven,	Huron	North Rochester,	"
Mount Ephraim,	Guernsey	New Holland,	Pickaway	North Royalton,	Cuyahoga
Mount Gilead,	Morrow	New Hope,	Brown	North Sheffield,	Ashtabula
Mount Healthy,	Hamilton	New Jasper,	Greene	North Springfield,	Summit
Mount Heron,	Darke	New Lebanon,	Montgomery	North Star,	Darke
Mount Holly,	Warren	New Lexington,	Perry	North Union,	Washington
Mount Hope,	Holmes	New Lisbon c. h,	Colum'na	North Uniontown,	Highland
Mount Liberty,	Knox	New London,	Huron	North West,	Williams
Mount Olive,	Clermont	New Lyme,	Ashtabula	Norton,	Delaware
Mount Perry,	Perry	New Madison,	Darke	Norton Centre,	Summit
Mount Pisgah,	Clermont	New Market,	Highland	Norwalk c. h.,	Huron
Mount Pleasant,	Jefferson	New Metamora,	Washington	Norwich,	Muskingum
Mount Rose,	Summit	New Middletown,	Mahon'g	Nottingham,	Harrison
Mount Sterling,	Madison	New Moscow,	Coshocton	Nova,	Ashland
Mount Union,	Starke	New Palestine,	Clermont	Number One,	Wayne
Mount Vernon c. h.,	Knox	New Paris,	Preble	Oakfield,	Perry
Mount Washington,	Ham.	New Petersburgh,	Highland	Oak Hill,	Jackson
Mowrystown,	Highland	New Philadelphia c. h.,	Tus.	Oakland,	Clinton
Mouth of Yellow Creek,	Jef.	New Pittsburgh,	Wayne	Oak Ridge,	Hancock
Muchinippe,	Logan	New Plymouth,	Vinton	Oberlin,	Lorain
Mulberry,	Clermont	Newport,	Washington	Oceola,	Crawford
Munnaville,	Coshocton	New Portage,	Summit	Ohio City,	Cuyahoga
Muskingum,	Muskingum	New Princeton,	Coshocton	Ohlstown,	Trumbull
Mutual,	Champaign	New Prospect,	Wayne	Old Hickory,	Wayne
Nairn,	Scioto	New Richland,	Logan	Olena,	Huron
Nankin,	Ashland	New Richmond,	Clermont	Olentangy,	Crawford
Napoleon c. h,	Henry	New Rochester,	Wood	Olive,	Morgan
Nashport,	Muskingum	New Rumley,	Harrison	Olive Branch,	Clermont
Nashville,	Holmes	New Salem,	Fairfield	Olivesburgh,	Richland
Navarre,	Starke	New Somerset,	Jefferson	Olmstead,	Cuyahoga
Nebo,	Jefferson	New Springfield,	Mahoning	Omega,	Pike
Neelysville,	Morgan	Newton,	Muskingum	Oneida Mills,	Carroll
Nelson,	Portage	Newton Falls,	Trumbull	Ontario,	Richland
Nelsonville,	Athens	Newtonville,	Clermont	Orange,	Mahoning
Neptune,	Mercer	Newtown,	Hamilton	Orangeville,	Trumbull
Nettle Lake,	Williams	New Vienna,	Clinton	Oregon,	Warren
Neville,	Clermont	Newville,	Richland	Orwell,	Ashtabula
Nevin,	Highland	New Washington,	Crawford	Osnaburgh,	Starke
New Albany,	Mahoning	New Westville,	Preble	Ostend,	Washington
New Alexander,	Columbiana	New Winchester,	Crawford	Ostego,	Muskingum
New Alexandria,	Jefferson	Ney,	Defiance	Ottawa,	Ottawa
New Antioch,	Clinton	Nicholsville,	Clermont	Oury's,	Hamilton
Newark c. h.,	Licking	Niles,	Trumbull	Ovid,	Franklin

POST-OFFICE.	COUNTY.	POST-OFFICE.	COUNTY.	POST-OFFICE.	COUNTY.
Owensville,	Clermont	Pleasantville,	Fairfield	Richwood,	Union
Oxford,	Butler	Plymouth c. h.,	Richland	Ridge,	Coshocton
Paddy's Run,	"	Poasttown,	Butler	Ridgeland,	Henry
Painesville c. h.,	Lake	Point Isabel,	Clermont	Ridgeville,	Warren
Paintersville,	Green	Point Pleasant,	"	Ridgeville Corners,	Henry
Palermo,	Carroll	Poland,	Mahoning	Ridgeway,	Muskingum
Palestine,	Pickaway	Polk,	Ashland	Riga,	Lucas
Palmyra,	Portage	Pomeroy,	Meigs	Riley Centre,	Sandusky
Panama,	Defiance	Pontiac,	Huron	Ringgold,	Morgan
Pancoastburgh,	Fayette	Poplar,	Crawford	Rio Grande,	Gallia
Parcher's Corners,	Lucas	Poplar Ridge,	Darke	Ripley,	Brown
Paris,	Starke	Portage,	Wood	Ripleyville,	Huron
Parisville,	Portage	Port Clinton,	Ottawa	Risdon,	Seneca
Parkman,	Geauga	Porter,	Delaware	River Styx,	Medina
Park's Mills,	Franklin	Portersville,	Perry	Rives,	Richland
Parma,	Cuyahoga	Port Homer,	Jefferson	Rix's Mills,	Muskingum
Patriot,	Gallia	Portsmouth c. h.,	Scioto	Robison's,	Darke
Patterson,	Delaware	Port Union,	Hamilton	Rochester,	Warren
Pattonsville,	Hocking	Port Washington,	Tuscar.	Rock House,	Hocking
Paulding,	Paulding	Port William,	Clinton	Rockport,	Cuyahoga
Pekin,	Carroll	Pottersville,	Mahoning	Rockxford,	Tuscarawas
Pendleton,	Putnam	Powhatten Point,	Belmont	Rockville,	Adams
Penfield,	Lorain	Pratt,	Shelby	Rocky Hill,	Jackson
Peninsula,	Summit	Prattsville,	Athens	Rocky Narrows,	Monroe
Pennsville,	Morgan	Preston,	Hamilton	Rodney,	Gallia
Peoli,	Tuscarawas	Pricetown,	Highland	Rogersville,	Tuscarawas
Perin's Mills,	Clermont	Princeton,	Butler	Rokeby,	Morgan
Perote,	Ashland	Princeton,	Highland	Rollersville,	Sandusky
Perry,	Lake	Prospect,	Delaware	Rome,	Ashtabula
Perrysburgh c. h.,	Wood	Providence,	Lucas	Rootstown,	Portage
Perryton,	Licking	Puebla,	Brown	Roscoe,	Coshocton
Perryville,	Ashland	Pulaski,	Williams	Rose,	Carroll
Peru,	Huron	Pulaskiville,	Morrow	Rosedale,	Madison
Petersburgh,	Mahoning	Putnam,	Muskingum	Roseville,	Muskingum
Phalanx,	Williams	Pyrmont,	Montgomery	Ross,	Butler
Pharisburgh,	Union	Quaker Bottom,	Lawrence	Rosseau,	Morgan
Phelps, .	Ashtabula	Quincy,	Logan	Rossville,	Butler
Philanthropy,	Butler	Quinn's Mills,	Clinton	Round Head,	Hardin
Philipsburgh,	Jefferson	Raccoon Island,	Gallia	Row's,	Ashland
Philo,	Muskingum	Radnor,	Delaware	Royalton,	Fairfield
Pickerington,	Fairfield	Rainsborough,	Highland	Ruggles,	Ashland
Pierpont,	Ashtabula	Randolph,	Portage	Rural,	Clermont
Pierpont Centre	"	Rapids,	"	Rush,	Tuscarawas
Pioneer,	Williams	Ratcliffsburg,	Vinton	Rush Creek,	Union
Pike,	Perry	Ravenna c. h.,	Portage	Rushville,	Fairfield
Piketon c. h.,	Pike	Raymond's,	Union	Rushsylvania,	Logan
Pilcher,	Belmont	Reading,	Hamilton	Russell,	Geauga
Pine Grove,	Gallia	Red Lion,	Warren	Russell Place,	Lawrence
Piqua,	Miami	Reedsburgh,	Wayne	Russellville,	Brown
Pisgah,	Butler	Reed's Mills,	Jackson	Rutland,	Meigs
Pittsburg,	Darke	Reedtown,	Seneca	Sabina,	Clinton
Pittsfield,	Lorain	Regnier's Mills,	Washing.	Saint Charles,	Butler
Plain,	Wayne	Rehoboth,	Perry	Saint Clair,	Columbiana
Plainfield,	Coshocton	Reiley,	Butler	Saint Clairsville c. h.,	Bel.
Plainville,	Hamilton	Renwick,	Morgan	Saintfield,	Muskingum
Plato,	Lorain	Republic,	Seneca	Saint Henry's,	Mercer
Pleasant,	Putnam	Republican,	Darke	Saint John's,	Allen
Pleasant Dale,	Wyandott	Reynolds,	Licking	Saint Joseph,	Williams
Pleasant Grove,	Clermont	Reynoldsburgh,	Franklin	Saint Louisville,	Licking
Pleasant Hill,	Miami	Riblets,	Richland	Saint Mary's c. h.,	Mercer
Pleasant Mount,	Harrison	Richfield,	Summit	Saint Paris,	Champaign
Pleasant Plain,	Clermont	Rich Hill,	Muskingum	Salem.	Columbiana
Pleasant Ridge,	Hamilton	Richland,	Richland	Salineville,	"
Pleasant Run,	"	Richmond,	Jefferson	Salisbury,	Meigs
Pleasanton,	Athens	Richmond Centre,	Ashtabula	Salt Petre,	Washington
Pleasant Valley,	Morgan	Richmond Dale,	Ross	Samantha,	Highland

2

POST-OFFICE	COUNTY	POST-OFFICE	COUNTY	POST-OFFICE	COUNTY
Sampson,	Darke	Southington,	Trumbull	Tawawa,	Shelby
Sandusky c. h.,	Erie	South Kirtland,	Lake	Taylor,	Richland
Sandy,	Columbiana	South New Castle,	Gallia	Taylorsville,	Montgomery
Sandyville,	Tuscarawas	South Olive,	Morgan	Tedrow,	Lucas
Sarahsville,	Morgan	South Perry,	Fairfield	Temperanceville,	Belmont
Sardinia,	Brown	South Ridge,	Ashtabula	Terre Haute	Champaign
Sardis,	Monroe	South Salem,	Ross	Texas,	Henry
Savannah,	Ashland	South Solon,	Madison	Thinener,	Gallia
Saybrook,	Ashtabula	South Thompson,	Geauga	Thompson,	Geauga
Scio,	Harrison	Sparta,	Morrow	Thornville,	Perry
Scioto,	Scioto	Speer's Landing,	Shelby	Thurman,	Gallia
Scioto Bridge,	Delaware	Spencer,	Lorain	Tiffin c. h.,	Seneca
Sciotoville,	Scioto	Springboro',	Warren	Tippecanoe,	Harrison
Scott,	Adams	Spring Dale,	Hamilton	Tiro,	Richland
Scroggafield,	Carroll	Springfield c. h.,	Clarke	Tiverton,	Coshocton
Seal,	Wyandott	Spring Hill,	Champaign	Toledo,	Lucas
Seddo,	Jefferson	Spring Lake,	Williams	Townsend,	Sandusky
Sego,	Perry	Spring Valley,	Greene	Tradersville,	Madison
Selma,	Clark	Stafford,	Monroe	Tranquility,	Adams
Senecaville,	Guernsey	Starr,	Hocking	Tremainville,	Lucas
Seven Mile,	Butler	State Line,	Trumbull	Tremont,	Clark
Seven Mile Prairie,	Darke	Staunton,	Fayette	Trenton,	Butler
Sewellsville,	Belmont	Sterling Bottom,	Meigs	Triadelphia,	Morgan
Shade,	Athens	Steuben,	Huron	Trimble,	Athens
Shaler's Mills,	Knox	Steubenville c. h.,	Jefferson	Troy c. h.,	Miami
Shalersville,	Portage	Stillwater,	Tuscarawas	Trumbull,	Ashtabula
Shane's Crossings,	Mercer	Stillwell's,	Butler	Tully,	Van Wert
Shanesville,	Tuscarawas	Stockport,	Morgan	Tupper's Plains,	Meigs
Shannon,	Muskingum	Stone Creek,	Tuscarawas	Turkey Foot,	Henry
Sharon,	Morgan	Stoner,	Seneca	Tuscarawas,	Tuscarawas
Sharon Centre,	Medina	Stonerstown,	Muskingum	Twenty Mile Stand,	Warren
Sharonville,	Hamilton	Stony Ridge,	Wood	Twinsburgh,	Summit
Sharp's Fork,	Athens	Stout's,	Adams	Tymochtee,	Wyandott
Shauck's,	Morrow	Stow,	Summit	Tyrone,	Coshocton
Sheffield,	Lorain	Strait Creek,	Brown	Uhrichsville,	Tuscarawas
Sheffield Lake,	"	Straitsville,	Perry	Underwood's,	Morrow
Shelby,	Richland	Strasburgh,	Tuscarawas	Union,	Montgomery
Shenandoah,	"	Stratford,	Delaware	Unionopolis,	Auglaize
Shepherdstown,	Belmont	Streetsboro',	Portage	Union Plain,	Brown
Sherman,	Huron	Strongsville,	Cuyahoga	Uniontown,	Belmont
Sherodsville,	Carroll	Suffield,	Portage	Unionville,	Lake
Shober's Mills,	"	Sugar Grove,	Fairfield	Uniouville Centre,	Union
Short Creek,	Harrison	Sugar Tree Ridge,	Highland	Uuison,	Delaware
Shreve,	Wayne	Sugar Valley,	Preble	Uuity,	Columbiana
Shunk,	Henry	Sullivan,	Ashland	Updegraff's,	Jefferson
Sicily,	Highland	Sulphur Spring,	Crawford	Upper Sandusky c. h.,	Wy't
Sidney,	Shelby	Summerfield,	Monroe	Upshur,	Preble
Silver Run,	Meigs	Summerford,	Madison	Urbaua c h.,	Champaign
Simmons,	Lawrence	Summit,	Summit	Utah,	Lucas
Sinking Spring,	Highland	Sunbury,	Delaware	Utica,	Licking
Six Corners,	Richland	Sunday Creek X Roads,	Per.	Vail's X Roads,	Morrow
Skeels' X Roads,	Mercer	Sunfish,	Monroe	Valentia,	Shelby
Sligo,	Clinton	Swan,	Hocking	Van Buren,	Hancock
Smithfield,	Jefferson	Swan Creek,	Gallia	Vandalia,	Montgomery
Smith's,	Gallia	Swanton,	Lucas	Vanlue,	Hancock
Smith's Mills,	Morrow	Sycamore,	Wyandott	Van's Valley,	Delaware
Smithville,	Wayne	Sylvania,	Licking	Van Wert,	Van Wert
Smyrna,	Harrison	Sylvia,	Hardin	Vaughnsville,	Putnam
Snooksville,	Defiance	Symmes' Corner,	Butler	Venice,	Erie
Snow Hill,	Clinton	Symmes' Creek,	Muskingum	Vermillion,	"
Solon,	Cuyahoga	Tabor,	Tuscarawas	Vernon,	Trumbull
Somerset a. h.,	Perry	Tallmadge,	Summit	Veto,	Washington
Somerton,	Belmont	Tampico,	Darke	Vienna,	Trumbull
Somerville,	Butler	Tappan,	Harrison	Vienna X Roads,	Clark
South Bloomfield,	Pickaway	Tariff,	Butler	Viuton,	Gallia
South Charleston,	Clark	Tarlton,	Pickaway	Wadsworth,	Medina

ERRATA, AND NAMES TOO LATE FOR INSERTION.

Agents—Insurance.

Lake County.

Benson H. J. — *Painesville.*
Bartlett C. S.
Everett Geo.
Mathews John S.
Mathews Wm.
Shepard H. F.

Agents—Patent.

Champaign County.

Townsend Ross — *North Lewisburg.*

Agents—Real Estate.

Lake County.

Mathews Wm. — *Painesville.*

Medina County.

Canfield & Kimball — *Medina.*

Van Wert County

Gilliland Robert — *Van Wert.*

Agricultural Implement Dealers.

Wayne County.

Johnson James — *Wooster.*

Agricultural Implement Manufacturers.

Starke County.

Russell C. M. & Co. — *Massillon.*

Ashes—Pearl Manufacturers.

Putnam County.

Marshall R. M. & Co. — *Pendleton.*

Seneca County.

Simmons William — *Republic.*

Attorneys at Law.

Ashtabula County.

Wilder Horace — *Conneaut.*
Farmer J. Q.
Randall B.
Graham Wm. T.

Coshocton County.

Irvin James — *Coshocton.*
Simmons John T.
Spangler David
Humrickhouse T. S.
Mathews James
Stone W. M.
Hillier A. R.
Campbell Thomas
Sample William
Flagg Thomas F.
Titball J. C.
Lanning Richard — *West Carlisle.*

Cuyahoga County.

Beavis B. R., 106 Superior — *Cleveland.*

Guernsey County,

Rinehart James — *Senecaville.*
Wisher John R.
Raney Joseph M.
Dilley Benjamin F.
Thompson James

Highland County.

Barrere Nelson — *Hillsboro'.*
Keys William
Lilley Robert
McDowell Joseph J.
Scott William
Smith James A.
Thompson James H.

Huron County.

Hunt Benj. F. — *North Fairfield.*
Foote Marcus

Lake County.

Perkins Wm. L. — *Painesville.*
Smith C. B.
Wilder E. Z.

Medina County.

Bostwick N. H. — *Medina.*
Castle ——
Floyd H. W.
Mead Whitman
Olcott Charles

Noble County.

Taneyhill Richard H. — *Batesville.*

(xxi)

Seneca County.

Lang William   *Tiffin.*
Lewis J. P.
Rawson A.
Brown G. M.

Tuscarawas County.

Belknap S. A.   - *Rockford.*

Washington County.

Buell C. F.   *Marietta.*
Dodge G. W.
Millard C. E.
Town ——

Auctioneers & Commission Merchants.

Lake County.

Steele G. W.   *Painesville.*

Medina County.

Selkirk E. L.   *Medina.*
Randall A.
Marks H.

Axe Manufacturers.

Lake County.

Edgerton E.   *Painesville.*

Axe Helve Makers.

Lake County.

Thornton S.   *Painesville.*

Bakers.

Lake County.

Sharpe, Bro's. & Wilson   *Painesville.*

Lorain County.

Rose & Lee   *Oberlin.*

Medina County.

Ossinger U.   *Medina.*
Setterly F.

Wayne County.

Black D.   *Wooster.*
Trimble Joseph B.

Bedstead Manufacturers.

Lake County.

Belnap, Mansfield & Co.   *Painesville.*

Medina County.

Ainsworth J. T.   *Medina.*
Davis A.
Little & Asire
Seaton R. P.

Morrow County.

Cravath S. P.   *Chesterville.*
Cunningham Robt.

Seneca County.

Chamberlin Henry   *Republic.*
Kessler George E.

Beef and Pork Packers and Dealers.

Hamilton County.

Magill James, n. w. cor. Race and Canal.
                           Cincinnati.

Blacksmiths.

Allen County.

Bentley J. & Co.   *Croghan.*
Cox Robert

Ashtabula County.

Collins M. H.   *Conneaut.*
Clark E. A.
Couch Joel
Davis H.
Fredericks J.
Guthrie James
Gilbert Giles
Stone E. A.
Taylor Joel

Carroll County.

Baker Abraham   *Kilgore.*
Hosterman Peter
Shilling Jacob

Champaign County.

Heller John   *North Lewisburg.*
Winder Henry

Coshocton County.

Smith Thomas   *Coshocton.*
Hutchison Robert
Miller Peter
Fretts A
Orr Wm. & Joseph   *Warsaw.*
Bills Wm. & Benj.
Hardsock John   *Walhonding.*
Loverns Lusk

Guernsey County.

Webster Wm.   *Leatherwood.*
Heartley David
Sprout James

Hardin County.

Freeman Wm. B.   *Huntersville*
Runser Andrew
Hagerman Samuel

Huron County.

Wright Zenos   *North Fairfield.*
Slater G. & S.
Trembly M.

Knox County.

Hortifee Daniel   *Bladensburg*
Hortifee Daniel, Jr.

Hortifee Wilson *Bladensburg.*
Mercer Levi

Lake County.

Andrews Oscar *Painesville.*
Briggs S. B.
Croft, Bagley & Co.
Hall J. R.
Sherwood E. N.
Titus H. A.
Woodhead F.

Lorain County.

Disbrow George *Amherst.*
Dean S. K.
Reynolds Joseph

Medina County.

Merrill R. W. *Medina.*
Beedle S.
Huff & Ensworth

Meigs County.

Haines Samuel *Langsville.*
Rathburn Elijah *Rutland.*

Monroe County.

Hamilton & Barackman *Graysville.*

Morrow County.

McCracken J. & O. *Chesterville.*
Lambert S. & H.

Noble County.

Gebhart Samuel *Batesville.*
Douden Thomas
Weihr Elias
Ball Thomas
Haines Aaron *South Olive.*
Hughey Robert
McAlley John *Kennonsburg.*
Moore Elijah

Preble County.

Beckner Aaron *Hagerstown.*
Bringman Elias

Putnam County.

Tweedel R. *Pendleton.*
Bagley J.
Green W. S.
Killen J. A.

Ross County.

Counts Andrew *Richmonddale.*
McConaha George

Seneca County.

Stewart James A. *Republic.*
Wilkinson E. P.

Tuscarawas County.

Roby H. & Co. *Rockford.*
Pharas Wm. & Co.

Wayne County.

Caswell D. H. *Wooster.*
Campbell Jerrod

Leggett John *Wooster.*
Reeves O. M.

Boiler Makers.

Belmont County.

Theaker, Mitchell & Co. *Bridgeport.*

Cuyahoga County.

Williams A., cor. Front and Meadow sts.
Cleveland.

Bookseller & Publisher.

Hamilton County.

Howe H., 111 Main *Cincinnati.*

Booksellers and Stationers.

Coshocton County.

Dreyer & Co. *Coshocton.*

Lucas County.

Sawyer, Ingersoll & Co. *Toledo.*

Medina County.

Curtiss G. R. & A. L. *Medina.*
Bissell D. J.

Boot and Shoe Dealers.

Hamilton County.

Webster E. G. & Co., cor. 5th and Lodge,
Cincinnati.

Huron County.

Stevens J. G. *North Fairfield.*
Allen Amasa

Starke County.

Burke W. H. & Co. *Massillon.*
Sausser & Daugler
Nettleton J.
Young M. & Co.

Wayne County.

Metz Jacob *Wooster.*
Bartol G. & J.
Wood Samuel

Boot & Shoe Manufacturers.

Allen County.

Long Abraham *Croghan.*
Mecum Jacob

Carroll County.

Blackledge Joseph *Kilgore.*
Hamilton H.
Lucas Samuel

Clinton County.

Eastham Robert S. *Bloomington.*
Turner Isaac

Guernsey County.
Garrett C.   *Leatherwood.*
Wilson George
Davis —
Robison John
Marshall Ezra

Hamilton County.
Webster E. G. & Co., cor. 5th and Lodge   *Cincinnati.*
Waldman Jacob, 37 Lower Market

Lorain County.
Betts William A.   *Amherst.*

Noble County.
Cisney P.   *Kennonsburg.*
Burlingame Russell   *Batesville.*
Nace Uriah H.

Preble County.
Howell Lewis   *Hagerstown.*

Ross County.
Davis J. & Co.   *Richmonddale.*
Puffer R. H. & Son
Randall Keeler

Wayne County.
Montgomery John   *Moorland.*
Hughes J. W.   *Wooster.*
Foglesong David
Shuchers E.
Horn J.
Bartol G. & J.
Metz Jacob
Wood Samuel

Bridge Builders.

Muskingum County.
Douglas, Smith & Co.   *Zanesville.*

Brokers—Exchange.

Columbiana County.
McClymonds John   *New Lisbon.*
McCoy Thomas
Dickinson S. W.   *East Palestine.*

Lawrence County.
Chides & Boyd   *Ironton.*

Wayne County.
Wright Anthony   *Wooster.*

Butterscotch Manufacturer.

Hamilton County.
Stevens R. St. Clair, 47 e. 3d   *Cincinnati.*

Cabinet, Chair, & Furniture Manufacturers & Dealers.

Carroll County.
Phillips D   *Kilgore.*
Hursh John

Clinton County.
Suttle John   *Bloomington.*

Guernsey County.
Marsh S. & Co.   *Leatherwood.*

Hamilton County.
Diehl Jacob, (Ag't, Cabinet Mak's Union), 217 Walnut   *Cincinnati.*
Helmkamp H. & F., 13 e. Liberty
Constine A., 69 w. Fifth

Meigs County.
Braley Ruel   *Langsville.*

Wayne County.
Smith Harrison   *Wooster.*
Baumgardner Peter

Carpenters and Builders.

Clinton County.
Lamb Isom   *Bloomington.*
Lamb Joseph
Harris James

Guernsey County.
Hogue Z.   *Leatherwood.*
Scott P.

Hamilton County.
Jones & Reister, 267 w. 5th   *Cincinnati.*

Knox County.
Stevens John   *Milfordton.*

Preble County.
Chrisman Joshua   *Hagerstown*

Ross County.
Crumit C. G.   *Richmonddale.*
Downs John W.
Bramblet Wm.
Mackey James
Sigler John

Shelby County.
Coe & Joslin   *Sidney.*
Smiley & Wilker
Bush Samuel A.

Wayne County.
Miller Michael & Co.   *Wooster.*
Marks George
McKeal John
Atkins D.
Clark Captain
Ryan M.

Carpet Weavers.

Crawford County.
Reichart H.   *Bucyrus.*
Slaybaugh Samuel
Slaybaugh & Co.

Carriage Makers.

Clinton County.
Wood John N.   *Bloomington.*

Hamilton County.

Mulligan, Shields & Co., 421 W. Row
Cincinnati.

Wayne County.

Hanna Wm. W. *Wooster.*
Wilhelm J.
Blackburn J. M.

Chair Makers.

Morrow County.

Rice E. *Chesterville.*
Trusdell James

Chemist and Geologist.

Hamilton County.

Wright Chas. Wm., n. e. cor. 3d & Race
Cincinnati.

China, Glass, and Queens-ware Dealers.

Hamilton County.

Kolbe & Wenner, 326 W. Row *Cincinnati.*

Highland County.

McFadden & Co. *Hillsboro'.*

Muskingum County.

Lents Henry *Zanesville.*
McFadden A.

Cigars—Importers of.

Hamilton County.

Block E. & Co., 34 Sycamore *Cincinnati.*
Hoffheimer H. & A., 28 Broadway
Louis A., 22 Columbia

Cigars—Manufacturers.

Hamilton County.

Faehr Henry, 438 Main *Cincinnati.*
Schmidt & Sack, 535 Vine

Wayne County.

Kaufman Jacob *Wooster.*

Clothiers, and Ready Made Clothing.

Starke County.

Dellwigk Charles *Massillon.*

Wayne County.

Childs William *Wooster.*
Rollman Isaac
Powers Thomas
Strause M. & Co.
Pierson & King
Kreps David

Cocoa, and Chocolate Manu-facturers.

Hamilton County.

Lambe & Co., 130 Columbia *Cincinnati.*
Wernert J. B. & Goettheim, 596 Main

Coffee-House.

Hamilton County.

Bertsen Deidrich, cor. Race & Columbia
Cincinnati.

Confectioner.

Wayne County.

Femekes & Harver *Wooster.*

Coopers.

Carroll County.

Hosterman D. *Kilgore.*

Hamilton County.

Johnson James, New bet. Syc. & Broad-way *Cincinnati.*

Corset Manufacturer.

Hamilton County.

Shepherd J., 100 w. 5th *Cincinnati.*

Dentists.

Wayne County.

McDowell Robert *Wooster.*
Coulter Thomas

Dental Furnishing Store.

Hamilton County.

Wardle S. & Co., 256 Walnut *Cincinnati.*

Distillers.

Hamilton County.

Sterling S. & Co., cor. Race and Water
Cincinnati.

Druggists.

Belmont County.

McConahey & Kelly   Bridgeport.

Dry Goods—Retail Dealers.

Hamilton County.

Lewis Frank & Co., 38 and 40 e. 4th
                              Cincinnati.
Grassow J. F., 513 Vine

Dry Goods, Groceries, and Variety Stores.

Belmont County,

Gray, Junkins & Co.   Bridgeport.

Ross County.

Harbert & Crumit   Richmonddale.
Tomlinson James

Engine (Fire) Builders.

Hamilton County.

Newman & Prichard, 172 Elm Cincinnati.

Engine (Steam) Builders.

Belmont County.

Theaker, Mitchell & Co.   Bridgeport.

Engravers.

Hamilton County.

Barth F., Vine bet 12th & 13th Cincinnati.
Morrison & Crouther, 74 w. Fourth

Fancy Goods—Dealer.

Hamilton County.

Koller & Wenner, 396 W. Row Cincinnati.

Founders—Iron.

Hamilton County.

Semple R. S. & Co.   Cincinnati.

Muskingum County.

Douglas, Smith & Co.   Zanesville.

Grocers and Commission Merchants (Wholesale).

Belmont County.

Anderson George W.   Bridgeport
Atkinson D. B. & Co.
Gray, Junkins & Co.
Harden, Branum & Co.
Holloway & Warfield
Rhodes & Oglebay

Groceries and Provisions—Retail.

Hamilton County.

Feldwisch J. H., 36 and 38 Hughes
                              Cincinnati.

Hats, Caps, and Furs.

Hamilton County.

Kling & Theis, 260 Main   Cincinnati.

Inspector of Leaf Tobacco.

Hamilton County.

How Joseph, Pearl bet. Vine and Race
                              Cincinnati.

Lumber Dealers.

Belmont County.

Nueland & Nelson   Bridgeport.

Machinists.

Belmont County.

Theaker, Mitchell & Co.   Bridgeport.

Hamilton County.

Newman & Prichard 172 Elm   Cincinnati.

Wayne County.

Crawford & McCurdy   Wooster.

Marble Workers.

Hamilton County.

The Stone Company, cor. High & Miami
Canal   Cincinnati.

Wayne County.

Yarnell & Eberhardt   Wooster.

Merchant—Forwarding and Commission.

Belmont County.

Anderson Geo. W.   *Bridgeport.*

Metallic Burial Cases—Manufacturers of.

Hamilton County.

Davis W. C. & Co., cor. Main and Ninth. *Cincinnati.*

Ornamental Plaster Work.

Hamilton County.

West Cyrus, 130 Vine   *Cincinnati.*

Painters—House, Sign, and Ornamental.

Coshocton County.

Coe & Maaw   *Coshocton.*
Dewey A. W.

Cuyahoga County.

Pereira J. D. & G., 47 Ohio   *Cleveland.*

Lake County.

Single J. S.   *Painesville.*
Perry J.
Croft Wm.

Medina County.

Davis A.   *Medina.*
Peterson F.
Rhoades E.
Loomis S.
Ferm P. O.

Putnam County.

Whitam R.   *Pendleton.*
Keen G. T.

Seneca County.

Elliott Captain   *Republic.*
Pierce Charles

Warren County.

Smith T. L.   *Morrow.*

Wayne County.

Paws & Co.   *Wooster.*

Paints, Oils, Varnishes, and Dye Stuffs.

Franklin County.

Denig G. & Sons, cor. High & Rich   *Columbus.*
Fahrenholtz Wm., cor. High and Rich
Gere & Abbott   do   do   do
Little R. P.,   do   do   do

Paper Hangings—Importers, Manufacturers & Dealers.

Hamilton County.

Gottmann P. & H., 455 Main   *Cincinnati.*
Holmes S. & Son, 189   do

Pencil (Black Lead) Manufacturers.

Hamilton County.

Cohen Sim., 260 w. 6th   *Cincinnati.*

Physicians.

Allen County.

Ewing Silas   *Croghan.*
Eaton Horace P.
Springer George

Ashtabula County.

Kellogg L. D.   *Conneaut.*
Raymond D. W.
Hall A. C.
Bean A. A.
Junis J.
Southwick W. L.
Morris J. F.

Carroll County.

Creal Joseph   *Kilgore.*

Champaign County,

Butcher J. M.   *North Lewisburg.*
Hyde O. S.
Marsh David
Williams John
Reames Wm.

Clinton County.

Davis A. T.   *Wilmington.*
Jones A.
McArthur A. T.
Williams Isaac C.   *Bloomington.*

Coshocton County.

Cass A. S.   *Coshocton.*
Seppe E.
Harris J.
Delemater D. F.
Lee Samuel
Nicholas Jesse   *Walhonding.*
Blackman H.   *Warsaw.*
Lawson David
Stanton William

Cuyahoga County.

Tear J., 88 Erie street,   *Cleveland.*
Hornby Dr., 125 do
Woodward A., cor. Kinsman and Cross

Guernsey County.

Woods William   *Leatherwood.*
Roman Thomas J.
Wright M. K.
Sidel Jacob

Huron County.

Webb E. H.   *North Fairfield.*
Campbell & Skinner
Tuller E. R.
Payne Wm.
Bronson Abraham

Knox County.

Hayes William   *Milfordton.*
Cunningham John   *Bladensburg.*
Scott A. C.

Licking County.

Hale S.   *Fredonia.*
Kellogg Joseph

Lorain County.

Bryant J. C,   *Amherst.*

Medina County.

Tolman L. D,   *Medina.*
Smith A. C.
Spillman H.
Munger P. E.
Keitel F.

Noble County.

Judkins Carolaus   *Batesville.*
Hoover Isaac L.
Joseph James M.
Statler W. B.

Gibbs E. N.   *South Olive.*
Ogle Miles

Ross County.

Evans W. T.   *Richmonddale.*
Myers D. C.

Wayne County.

Kohn J. S.   *Moorland.*
Metzger D.   *Wooster.*
Day & Wilso
Shaffer M.
Wolford H. S.
Long H. C.
Gay S. F.
Weaver J.
Weaver D.
Pobison J. D.

Piano-forte Manufacturers.

Hamilton County.

Skiff & Trayser, Walnut bet. Front and 2d
                              Cincinnati.

Piano Manufacturer.

Portage County.

Griffin O. H.   *Ravenna.*

Planing Mills.

Hamilton County.

Horsley & Ehler, Front bet. W. Row and
  John   *Cincinnati.*
Hughes & Foster, s. e. cor. John and
  Augusta

Medina County.

Ainsworth J. T.   *Medina.*

Platers—Silver & Brass.

Hamilton County.

Barth F., Vine bet. 12th & 13th   *Cinsin.*
Morrison & Crouther, 74 w. 4th

Logan County.

Covert Joseph   *Bellefontaine.*

Plow Manufacturers.

Cuyahoga County.

De Witt & Co., Merwin　　*Cleveland.*

Printers—(Book & Job).

Ashtabula County.

Allen D. C.　　*Conneaut.*

Coshocton County.

Dille H. A.　　*Coshocton.*
Rich S. M.

Cuyahoga County.

Medill J. & J. C., Forest City Office
　　Cleveland

Franklin County.

Geary John & Co., 9 and 4 Buckeye block
　　Columbus.
Reinhart & Feiser, Westbote Office

Montgomery County.

Clasflin L. F. & Bro.　　*Dayton.*
Dubois B. P. & Co.

Wayne County.

Foreman, Johnson & Booth　　*Wooster.*
Marchand Jacob
Brawnick George

Provision Dealer.

Wayne County.

Myers A. H.　　*Wooster.*

Pumps (Force & Lift) Manufacturers.

Hamilton County.

Newman & Prichard, 171 Elm　*Cincinnati.*

Rasp & File Manufacturer.

Cuyahoga County.

Parkin John, 28 Lorain　　*Ohio City.*

Refrigerator Manufacturers.

Hamilton County.

Johnston J. & J. M., 3d bet. Plum and W.
　Row　　*Cincinnati.*

Restaurant.

Hamilton County.

Piepenbring F., 54 Broadway　*Cincinnati.*

Saddle & Harness Makers.

Guernsey County.

Gleaves James S.　　*Leatherwood.*
McRane E. H.

Noble County.

Mercer David　　*Batesville.*
St. John Martin

Wayne County.

Eckert C. H.　　*Wooster.*
Robison W. H.
Shorltz Jacob
Mohn B. & F. & Co.　　*Moorland.*

Saleratus Manufacturer.

Knox County.

Wright B. P.　　*Democracy.*

Salt Manufacturer

Meigs County.

Braley Ruel　　*Langsville.*

Sash, Door, and Blind Manufacturers.

Portage County.

Brown & Tracey　　*Ravenna.*

Meigs County.

Braley Ruel　　*Langsville.*

Saw Mills.

Guernsey County.

Hutchinson E.　　*Leatherwood.*
Sherman Levi

Hamilton County.

Dudley J. M., junction Front & Sixth
                                    Cincinnati.

Shelby County.

Maxwell S.   *Sidney.*
Walker H.

Ship Carpenters & Joiners.

Hamilton County.

Horsley & Ebler, Front bet. W. Row and
John   *Cincinnati.*

Silver Ware Manufacturers.

Hamilton County.

Kinsey E. & D., 24 w. Fifth   *Cincinnati.*

Spoke, Felloe, & Hub Manu-facturers

Portage County.

Hitchcock & McClain   *Ravenna.*

Stove and Grate Manufac-turers.

Hamilton County.

Semple R. S. & Co.   *Cincinnati.*

Stove, Grate, and Tin Ware Dealers.

Wayne County.

McClure C. & J.   *Wooster.*
Carr Hubbard
Howard Harvey

Tailors & Drapers.

Ross County.

Mitchell & Elliott   *Richmonddale.*

Tallow, & Neat's-Foot Oil Dealer.

Hamilton County.

Whitaker Jacob, Deer Creek   *Cincinnati.*

Tanners & Curriers.

Ross County.

Harbert John   *Richmonddale.*
Heath Ira P.

Wayne County.

Sanderson William   *Wooster.*
Robison W. H.
Immel David
Leciter William

Tin, Copper, & Sheet-Iron Workers.

Hamilton County.

Fais Peter, 190 Vine   *Cincinnati.*

Portage County.

Rawson S.   *Ravenna.*

Wayne County.

McClure C. & J.   *Wooster.*
Carr Hubbard
Howard Harvey

Tobacconists.

Hamilton County.

Faehr Henry, 438 Main   *Cincinnati.*
Schmidt & Sack, 535 Vine

Umbrella & Parasol Manu-facturers.

Starke County.

Harsh A. & Z.   *Massillon.*

Upholsterers.

Muskingum County.

Smith Wm. & Co.   *Dresden.*
Slyder Lewis   *Zanesville.*

Variety Stores.

Wayne County.

Kaufman G. W.   *Wooster*
James J. O.

Vinegar Manufacturers.

Hamilton County.

Elbreg & Ruhl, 395 Broadway *Cincinnati.*

Wine & Liquors—Importers and Dealers.

Hamilton County.

Hoffheimer H. & A., 28 Broadway
Cincinnati.

Starke County.

Willenborg H. & Co. *Massillon.*
Dickey & Barkdull

Wooden & Willow Ware.

Wayne County.

McConohay J. E. & Co. *Wooster.*

Wool Dealer.

Wayne County.

Crandal A. C. *Wooster.*

OHIO STATE
BUSINESS DIRECTORY.

Agents.

AGENTS—ADVERTISING.

Hamilton County.
Parvin S. H., 68 w. Fourth   *Cin.*

AGENTS—EXPRESS.

Livingston, Fargo & Co.'s Line.

Butler County.
Lowes J.   *Hamilton.*
Locke E.

Champaigne County.
McCord James   *Urbana.*

Clark County.
Mattox A. & Co.   *Springfield.*

Cuyahoga County.
Cole John E.   *Cleveland.*

Erie County.
Thayer C. P.   *Sandusky.*

Franklin County.
Cornell E. J.   *Columbus.*

Greene County.
Stark A. W.   *Xenia.*

Hamilton County.
Clark F., e. 3d   *Cincinnati.*

Hardin County.
Davis A. M.   *Kenton.*

Knox County.
McEwen T. C.   *Mount Vernon.*

Logan County.
Gardner & McCullough   *Bellefontaine.*
Runkle R. A.   *West Liberty.*

Lorain County.
Stone —   *Oberlin.*

Lucas County.
Fargo C.   *Toledo.*

Montgomery County.
Hay R. B.   *Corwin.*
Alexander J. Jr.   *Dayton*

Muskingam County.
Ross A. C.   *Zanesville.*

Richland County.
Beach J. L.   *Mansfield.*
Patterson J.   *Shelby.*

Seneca County.
Don Benham F   *Tiffin.*

AGENTS—GENERAL.

Crawford County.
Scroggs J.   *Bucyrus.*

Cuyahoga County.
Taylor R.   *Chagrin Falls.*
Palmer John H., 4 Bank   *Cleveland.*
Shaw S. B., 68 Superior

Greene County.
Fairchild William B.   *Xenia.*
Winans James J.

Summit County.
Weld James W.   *Richfield.*

AGENTS—INSURANCE.
(See also Insurance Companies.)

Adams County.
McFerren J. W.   *West Union.*
Stevenson R.   *Manchester*

Ashtabula County.
Fitch O. H.   *Ashtabula.*
Sherman & King
Cook J. R.
Grinold R. W.
Fassett Henry
Hall J. H.   *Conneaut.*

Athens County.
Brown H. T.   *Athens.*

3

(33)

Auglaize County.

Andrews George W.   *Wapakoneta.*

Belmont County.

Glover M. J. W.   *St. Clairsville.*
Cowen D. D. T.

Brown County.

Elliott William N.   *Higginsport.*
Wylie William F.   *Ripley.*
Shan William M.
Baird Chambers

Butler County.

Miller & Brown   *Hamilton.*
Lewis John
Miller William H.
Hume A. F.
Wilson J. W.
McFarland N. O.
Heaton D.   *Middletown.*

Clark County.

Freeman L. D.   *Springfield.*
Osborne Joseph
Cooper David
Spencer William M.
Wick Theodore O.

Clermont County.

Dunam P. J.   *New Richmond.*
Ballard W. F.   *Loveland.*
Sheldon Thomas   *Bantam.*
Lowe John W.   *Batavia.*

Clinton County.

Bosworth Charles M.   *Wilmington.*
McKay A.

Columbiana County.

Clarke James   *New Lisbon.*
Martin Levi
Pritchard Benjamin
Baker George   *Wellsville.*

Crawford County.

Pitzzel J.   *Poplar.*
Butterfield O. W.   *Bucyrus.*
Casey Aaron
Clark W. R. S.
Plants J. S.
Ruhl A. A.
Scroggs J.
Sims John

Cuyahoga County.

Brayton & Mason, Exchange building   *Cleveland.*
Carlton O. O., 69 Superior
Coe S. S., on Dock
Garrett & Briggs, Herald buildings
Hays & Moore, cor. Bank and Superior
Martin Levi, Seneca block
Senter George B., Dunham block
Shaw S. B., 68 Superior
Stratton H. D., Main

Darke County.

Putnam David   *German.*
Wilson William M.   *Greenville.*

Defiance County.

Gilson R. H.   *Defiance.*
Taylor D.

Erie County.

Haynes E. H.   *Sandusky City.*
Gibbs & Butler
Godfrey J. W.
Cheesbrough A.
Godfrey John W.
Leonard O.
Camp J. G.
Camp J. A.
Gibbs R. J.
Pinto J. A.

Franklin County.

Adams Demas, Jr.   *Columbus.*
Jenkins Warren
Patterson John
Stockton Thomas
Van Rensselaer K. H.
Tuttle J. R.
Flowers T. C.

Gallia County.

Hale G. H.   *Gallipolis.*

Geauga County.

Philips Alfred   *Chardon.*
Canfield E. V.
Rodgers A. L.
Darfee L. E.
Hathaway J. N.
Paine J. O.
Dayton R.   *Troy.*
Church George   *Thompson.*
Perkins L.   *Auburn.*

Greene County.

Harris Francis   *Xenia.*
Merrick Charles R.
Nesbitt Benoni

Hamilton County.

Burgoyne John, s. w. cor. Front & Main   *Cincinnati.*
Carter T. H., 3 e. Front
Church William F., 6 e. Front
Copelin George W., n. w. cor. Front and Main
Chew A. S., 14 e. Front
Dobbs T. D., 8 Main
Davis J. J., 4 Main
Ferry Francis, 19 e. 4th
Foster John, 52 w. 6th
Hickenlooper A., 8 Front
Hallam P. H., 24 e. Front
Harris S. W., 24 e. Fourth
Hartwell J. W., 4 Main
Knapp M. L., 30 w. 3d.
Law John S., cor. 3d & Sycamore
Moody John B., 282 Main
Phipps W. T., 4 College buildings

Reeves John, 3 e. Front   *Cincinnati.*
Robbins W. B., 6 Front
Spencer H. E., cor. Main & Front
Stewart R. & Son, 16 Front
Urner B., Front, bet. Main & Sycamore.
VanBuren A. H., 4 Main
Wood & Copelin, 9 Front
Wing Thomas B., 101 Walnut
Waters Byron, Reeder's Building.
Arnold Montgomery   *Harrison.*
Beattie Thomas
Coates John
Converse William F.
McMackin James
Williams Owen

Hancock County.

Porter Andrew J.   *McComb.*

Hardin County.

Hurd L. C.   *Kenton.*
Bain James
Curtis A. W.
Thomson David
Coulson Servell
Carey W.
Jamison R. G.

Harrison County.

Phillips B. W.   *Cadiz.*
Bowles Thos. O.
Dewey C.

Highland County.

Brown James.   *Hillsborough.*

Huron County.

Kennan J.   *Norwalk*
Foster John H.
Stewart G. T.

Jefferson County.

Elliott James   *Steubenville.*
Worrell J. R.
Mason G. M.
Thompson T.
Andrews M.
McFeeley E. H.

Knox County.

Davis J. S.   *Mount Vernon.*
Muenscher Joseph
Smith W. H.
Turner William
Doolittle Philo.   *Fredericktown.*

Lake County.

Moore J. G.   *Painesville.*
Perkins W. L.

Lawrence County.

Johnson W. W.   *Ironton.*
Neal H. S.

Licking County.

Teneyck H. B.   *Newark.*
Buckingham J.
Woodbridge T. H.

Lorain County.

Burke S.   *Elyria.*
Bagg S.

Lucas County.

Baker & Latimer   *Toledo.*
Bennett & Nye
Bissel E. Jr.
Clark A. G.
Dodd H. H.
Eagle Henry E.
Hill, Perigo & Pratt.

Madison County.

Freeman J. F.   *London.*
Lacy J. T.
Smith H. W.

Mahoning County.

King John H.   *Canfield.*
Quillation M.   *Youngstown.*

Medina County.

Austin B. D.   *Leroy.*
Blake H. G.   *Medina.*

Miami County.

Wood S. H.   *Piqua.*
Elliott W.
Ewing J. M.
Mitchell M. P.
Furnas R. W.   *Troy.*

Montgomery County

Bartlett W. C., Third   *Dayton*
Collins F., Main
Craine J. W.
Kelley J., Third
Sullivan S. M.

Muskingum County.

Bennett & Eaton   *Zanesville.*
Rollo W. E.
Perley A. W.
Crosby J & J.
Crosby Joseph
Dillon Isaac

Pickaway County.

Ballard O.   *Circleville.*

Portage County.

Smith Henry   *Ravenna.*

Preble County.

Gane G. W.   *Eaton.*
Chadwick M. B.
Bursen John
Collins Saml.   *Camden.*
Higgins Saml.   *New Paris.*

Richland County.

McQuin David A.   *Lexington.*
Johnson William   *Mansfield.*
Young D. B.
Young D. H.

Morrow J.   *Belleville.*
Howard C.
Walker Joel

Ross County.

Waddel T. F.   *Chillicothe,*
Schutte D. A.
Safford W. H.
Pinto H. M.
Gillmore C. W.
Lewis Edward

Scioto County.

Dugan Thomas   *Portsmouth.*
Lodwick James
Mc Dowell J.
Ross S. R.
Smith J. A.
Terry L. G.

Seneca County.

Higgins M. L.   *Tiffin.*
Lee J. C.
Noble W. P.
Reime E. W.

Stark County.

Evans W. F.   *Canton.*
Goodman T.
Shellenberger J. B.
Focke Frederick   *Massilon.*
Bacon D. W. C.
Fletcher & Logan

Summit County.

Codding Robert F.   *Coply.*

Tuscarawas County.

Taylor O. P.   *New Philadelphia.*

Union County.

Clark R. C.   *Mayseville.*

Van Wert County.

De Puy P.   *Van Wert.*

Vinton County.

Bingham E. F.   *McArthur.*
Plyley J.P.

Warren County.

Evans David   *Waynesville.*

Washington County.

Crawford Robert   *Marietta.*
Shipman S.
Nye W. S.
Temple L.
Broth J. M.
Putnam D.

Wayne County.

Bonewitz S. R.   *Wooster.*
Foreman & Johnson
Lehman Henry

Williams County.

Foster Edward   *Bryan.*

Norris P. W.   *West Unity*
Simon & Wyatt   *Bryan.*

Wood County.

Hall J. A.   *Perrysburg.*
Tury W.
Wright Albert D.

AGENTS—MERCANTILE AND LAW.

Hamilton County.

Bradstreet J. M., 73 w. 3d.
    Cincinnati.
Douglas B. & Co., 84 Main.

Washington County.

Jewel R. L.   *Harmer.*
Newton John

AGENTS—MISCELLANEOUS.

Oith Jas. S. (Sale of Woolen Goods), No.
26, e. 2d.   *Cincinnati.*
Buchanan R. (Covington Cotton Factory),
Columbia e. of Main.
Bait & Hickcox (Goodyear's India Rubber
Fabrics), No. 2, Main.
Ray, Keith & Co. (St. Louis Sugar Re-
finery), 54 Walnut.
Calhoun James (Queen City Varnish
Co.), Walnut, bet. Front and Colum-
bia.
Ackley W. E. (Land Agent), 140 Walnut.
McDowell Malcolm (Troy Iron and Nail
Factory), 29 Congress.
Gould Wm. (Pale Ale and Porter), 98 Co-
lumbia
Wood Seely (American Tract Society),
163 Walnut.
Skinner & Franklin (General)
Wilson & Slader (Oatmeal, Pearl Barley,
and Hominy), n. e. cor. Eighth and
Walnut.
Matthews Jas. & Co. (Nails, Window
glass, Cotton Yarns, etc.), 53 Walnut.
Wells L. T. (Cincinnati Type Foundery),
cor. Vine and Centre.
Post R. (American and Foreign Publi-
cations), 10 w. 3d.
Weightman A. F., 18 e. 3d.
Cooper S. S. (Brookville Cotton Factory),
39 Main.
Hartwell J. W. (Lockland Paper Mills),
2 Walnut.
Weed G. L. & Scott (Young Men's Bible
Society and American Sunday School
Union), w. Fourth.
Thos. B. Smith (House Agent and Street
Broker), Smith's buildings, cor. Court
and Walnut.

AGENTS—PATENT.

Cuyahoga County.

Barry S. S. & Co., 44 Bank,   *Cleveland.*
Burridge & Brainard, 4 Herald Block.

Hamilton County.

Benson M., cor. 3d & Sycamore, *Cin.*
Knight Geo. H. & Bro., 6 Public Landing.
Easton E., 25 e 4th.

Highland County.

Smith J. J. *Hillsboro'.*

AGENTS—REAL ESTATE.

Adams County.

Evans E. P. *West Union.*
Billings John K.

Allen County.

Roberts J. B. *Westminster.*

Butler County.

Wilson J. W. *Hamilton.*

Columbiana County.

Beaumont Jabez *New Lisbon.*

Cuyahoga County.

Bartholomew E., Forest City Block, *Cleveland.*
Hays & Moore, cor. Bank & Superior.
Palmer John H., 4½ Bank.
Pyfer & Co., 6, do
Garret & Briggs, Herald Building.
Root Elias S., 10 Seneca Block.
Seymour B. *Ohio City.*

Darke County

Garst H. C. *Greenville.*

Defiance County.

Gilson R. H. *Defiance.*
Sheffield & Taylor

Erie County.

Whitney T. *Sandusky City.*

Franklin County.

Smith & Mills *Columbus.*
Baker & Armstrong
Smith Joseph F.

Greene County.

Fairchild W. B. *Xenia.*
Winans James J.

Hamilton County.

Denniston J. J., 54 w. 3d *Cincinnati.*
Dennis W. B., s. e. cor. 4th & Vine
Graves Thos. H., 207 W. Row
Gregg & Harvey, s. e. cor. 3d & Walnut
Herron Andrew C., 4th bet. Walnut & Vine
Hale W. B., 123 Walnut
Hickman J. L., 150 do
Jones & Co., 118 do
Jackson —
Jones Wm., Vine bet 4th & 5th
Lanpbear Edward, 3 Mechanics' Institute
Linn and Brown, 2 Mechanics' Institute
Masters J., 11 Art Union building
Reeder A. L., 52 6th
Shepherd & Miller, 144 Walnut
Sutton E., 138 Vine
Smith C. J. W. & Winters, 221 Vine

Waggoner John, 56 6th *Cincinnati.*
Wellers, 202 Plum
Paige H., 10½ 3d

Hardin County.

Robinson J. S. *Kenton.*
Hind L. C.
Stilligs E.

Harrison County.

Scott & Bingham *Cadiz.*

Henry County.

Jackson Wm. J. *Napoleon.*

Knox County.

Cochran W. S. *Mount Vernon.*

Lake County.

Sterling L. *Willoughby.*

Lorain County.

Burke & Lake *Elyria.*
Lockwood & Bagg
Vincent John M.

Lucas County.

Baker & Latimer *Toledo.*
Bennett & Nye
Hill, Perigo & Pratt
Clark A. G.
Allen N.

Mercer County.

Hunter Wm. *Celina.*
Riley J. W.

Pickaway County.

Crouse G. B. *Circleville.*

Portage County.

Tappan Francis W. .... *Ravenna.*

Richland County.

Meredith John *Mansfield.*

Starke County.

Dresel Otto *Massillon.*

Union County.

Curry & Robinson *Marysville.*

Warren County.

Hammell E. *Waynesville.*
Sanders D. A. *Morrow.*

Washington County.

Putnam Douglas *Harmar.*
Ward Wm. *Marietta.*

Williams County.

Foster Edward *Bryan.*
Norris P. W. *West Unity.*
Simon & Wyatt *Bryan.*

Wood County.

Cook A. *Perrysburg.*
Way Wm. V.
Mefford D. M.
Spunk & Muny
Bell S. H.

Huntington E.   *Perrysburg.*
Bates John

Agents—Steamboat.

Hamilton County.

Athearn & Hibbard, Front bet. Broadway &
  Sycamore   *Cincinnati.*
Bishop J., cor. Vine & Wharf
Campbell, Russell & Co., 3 Cassily's Row
Irwin A. & Co , 22 Broadway
Jack, Collier & Co., 46 e. Front
Latham & McBurnie, 20 Public Landing
McFall & Cullum, 5 Water
Michael D. C., 5 West Front
Paul & Murdock, 7 Water
Rogers & Sherlock, 2 Broadway
Taylor & Odiorne, 48 Public Landing

Agricultural Implement Manufacturers and Dealers.

Clark County.

Warder & Brokaw   *Springfield.*

Cuyahoga County.

De Witt & Co., cor. West & Merwin
Stair J. & Son, 6 Ontario   *Cleveland.*

Franklin County.

Gill Wm A. & Co., Broad   *Columbus.*

Knox County.

Headley David S.   *Fredericktown.*

Licking County.

Pepper N. C.   *Newark.*

Lorain County.

Bullock J. W.   *Elyria.*

Montgomery County.

Thresher E., Keoway   *Dayton.*
Kittridge & Co., Basin

Pickaway County.

Bierce W. W. & Co.   *Circleville.*

Summit County.

Gardiner & Walker   *Akron.*

Ale and Porter Bottlers.

Hamilton County.

Bonn Joseph, 49 Green bet. Race & Elm
Niehaus Joseph, 138 Woodward *Cincin.*

Amusements—Places of.

Hamilton County.

Frank's Museum, Sycamore ab. 3d *Cincin.*
National Theatre,   belw. 4th
New Lyceum, cor. of Vine & 6th

Apple Butter and Mince Meat Manufacturers.

Hamilton County.

Hunt John, Ann bet. Plum & Western Row
                Cincinnati.

Architects.

Ashtabula County.

Udell C.   *Jefferson.*

Cuyahoga County.

Harris Edward, Pulte's Block *Cleveland*
Husband John J., 34 Bank
White Henry,   10   do

Franklin County.

Schlapp P. A., High   *Columbus.*
Lakin J. Q., Sugar A

Geauga County.

Smith H. A.   *Newbury.*

Hamilton County.

Tinsley & Son. 15 Walnut   *Cincinnati.*
Walter & Wilson, n. w. cor. Walnut & 6th
Powell Lemuel,   do   5th
Rogers Isaiah, cor. Vine & Baker
Howe Hammond   do
Bayless Wm. H., n. e. cor. 9th & Elm
Reddish Stephen   do
Hamilton J. R., 69½ w. 6th
M'Clure J., City Buildings, 9th
Husband J. J., cor. 4th & Vine,
Love Robert,   do   Race
Palmer Seneca, n. w. cor. 5th & Walnut
Sawyer Joseph, cor. 4th & Vine

Lucas County.

Scott F. J.   *Toledo!*

Portage County.

Harris S. D.   *Ravenna.*
Skinner J. N.

Ashes—Pot and Pearl Manufacturers.

Allen County.

Heaton J.   *Deep Cut.*
Harbert W. H.   *West Newton.*
Hazlet John
Cunningham J. & J.   *Hog Creek.*

Ashland County.

Parker W. W.   *Ruggles.*

Ashtabula County.

Norris R. D.   *Hart's Grove.*
Morgan H.

Crawford County.

Chilcote N. C.   *New Washington.*
High V.

Cuyahoga County.

Robbins A. & Sons   *Solon.*
Rose John   *Coe Ridge.*
Usher
Stanley W. P. & Co., 54 & 56 St. Clair
                Cleveland.

Darke County.

Arnold John Y.   *New Madison.*

Defiance County.

Evans & Lindenberger	*Defiance.*
Coy & Snyder	*Evansport.*
Denman Syllinger & Co.	
Partee John & Co.	*Brunnersburg.*

Fulton County.

Wilden J. G.	*Elmyra.*
Hollington R. A.	
Maisen A. & R.	

Geauga County.

Chase A. H.	*Russel.*
Stafford A. & Harpham	*Bainbridge.*
Mead D. W.	*Thompson.*
Brown R. & Co.	*Hamden.*
Thompson & Co.	*Middlefield.*

Hardin County.

McConnel F. M.	*Kenton.*

Henry County.

Waterman G. W.	*Florida.*
Eastman G. C.	*Napoleon.*

Lorain County.

Bolton George	*Oberlin.*
Goodwin A.	*Copopa.*

Madison County.

Crabb —	*West Jefferson.*

Mahoning County.

Bartlett Enos	*Petersburgh.*

Marion County.

Tyler Hiram	*Prospect.*
Parks David	

Medina County.

Howes A.	*Sharon Centre.*
Higbee J.	*Lodi.*
Ainsworth —	

Mercer County.

Prouty Simon	*Celina.*
Collins Moses	*Mercer.*

Morrow County.

Doty John M.	*Lincoln.*

Portage County.

Bostwick D.	*Edinburgh.*
Youtz Samuel	*Ravenna.*
Osborn Russell	*Mantau.*
Risbridger William & George	*Deerfield.*
Hull A.	

Richland County.

Ramsey John	*Ontario.*

Seneca County.

Hart H. W.	*Reedtown.*
Kistler Abraham	*Green Spring.*
Peatt Benjamin	

Trumbull County.

Kibbee A. D.	*Farmington.*

Union County.

Wood W. W.	*Marysville.*

Raymond N. & Co.	*Raymond's*
Taylor A.	*Watkins'*
Skeels H.	*Pharisburg.*

Van Wert County.

Conn R. & Co.	*Van Wert.*
Englsright S.	
Clark, Perry & Co.	
Webber John & Co.	*Auglaize.*

Williams County.

Arnold B. L.	*Spring Lake.*
Boyers, Jacobs & Co.	*Bryan.*
Boyanton A. W.	*Pulaski.*
Crissey & Gilbert	*Montpelier.*
Knapp & Benson	*Spring Lake.*
Luke J.	
	West Unity.

Stough William	*Pulaski.*
Tomlinson G. H.	*Center.*

Wood County.

Ross & Key	*Perrysburg.*
Lock L. C. & Co.	*Bowling Green*

Wyandot County.

Shawhan R. W.	*Carey.*
Stephens D. & Co.	
Robbins Alonzo	*Upper Sandusky.*
Beidler Peter P.	

Attorneys and Counsellors at Law.

Adams County.

Billings John K.	*West Union.*
Buck W. C.	
Cockerill Joseph C.	
Collings J. W	
Diboll A. C.	
Evans Edward P.	
Graham David B.	
McCauslen Thomas	
McFerran J. W.	
Ouraler H.	
Bryan Daniel M.	*Duckiasville.*

Allen County.

Baxter Samuel A.	*Lima.*
Lamison C. H.	
Nichols & Waldroff	

Ashland County.

Curtis A. L.	*Ashland.*
Fulton J. S.	
Gates & McCombs	
Hill George W.	
Johnson, Kenney & Porter	
Kellogg & Allison	
Parker George H.	
Slocum & Osburn	
Smith & Sloan	
Cowen William	*Perrysville.*

Ashtabula County.

Edwards A. M.	*Harpersfield.*
Giddings L.	*West Williamsfield*

Meigs O.   *Rome.*
Woodbury E. B.   *Kelloggsville.*
Woodbury Hamilton
Booth Charles   *Ashtabula.*
Fitch O. H.
Sherman & King
Cook J. R.
Grinold R. W.
Jones S. P.   *Jefferson.*
Giddings & Jones
Simonds & Cadwell
Chaffee & Woodbury
Oliver J. L.
Allen William R.
Pond Selden   *Windsor.*
Gibbs G. A.
Wight J. N.   *Andover.*
Leonard M. A.   *Pierpont.*
Lee Eusebius   *New Lyme.*
Turner A.   *Geneva.*

Athens County.

Welde John   *Athens.*
Jewett Leonidas
Smith L. L.
Constable R. E.
Brown H. G. & H. T.
Johnson J. D.
Golden Read
Wilson Horace
Knowles Samuel
Brown O. W.

Auglaize County.

Andrews George W.   *Wapakoneta.*
Barr Christian
Crane William M.
Craig Joseph B.
Dumbroff M.
Walkup John
Williams John S.
Cowan O. W.   *Saint Mary's.*
Mott Samuel
Plunkett Jos.

Belmont County.

Arrick Clifford   *Saint Clairsville.*
Carroll O. O.
Cowen Benjamin S.
Cowen D. D. T.
Glover M. J. W.
Hibben John
Jennings David L.
Kelley St. Clair
Kennon E. E.
Kennon William S.
Kennon William
Kennon William, Jr.
Newport John W.
Peck Daniel
Pennington M.
Shannon Wilson
Simpson William P.
Swaney O. J.
Weir & Tallman
Coleman Pierson   *Demos.*
Davenport John   *Barnesville.*
Dunbar John, Jr.   *Sewellsville.*

Stevens Joshua, Jr.   *Shepherdstown*

Brown County.

Devore David G.   *Georgetown*
Ellison Andrew
Fishback & Bower
Johnston S. W.
King George W.
King John W.
London D. W. C.
Marshall & White
Mullen T. J.
Penn Harrison L.
Sellers Preston W
White O. A.
Evans S. E.   *Ash Ridge.*
Mc Adams William   *De La Palma.*
Livengood Nathan
Baird O.   *Ripley.*
Wylie William F.
Campbell O. F.
Thomas D. M.   *New Hope.*
Lowrey James B.   *Aberdeen.*
Underwood J. M.

Butler County.

Brown W. E.   *Hamilton.*
Campbell Hon. L. D.
Clark James
Chase Valentine
Furrow L. M.
Hume A. F.
Hittel J. H.
Lewis J. R.
Millikin Thomas
Millikin J. B.
Miller William H.
Robertson Isaac
Scott & McFarland
Smith Charles K.
Vance & White
Vanderver T.
Wilkins Thomas H.
Wilson John W.
Moore Thomas   *Rossville.*
Doughty L. D.   *Middletown.*
Peck H.
Heaton D.
Smith William H.   *Oxford.*
Mollyneaux W. J.
Cox A. P.   *West Chester.*

Carroll County.

Atkinson Robert J.   *Carrollton.*
Crosier Robert J.
Davis James M.
Eckley Ephraim
McLave Robert
Ramsey Alexander S.
Tripp John H.
Knight Robert E.   *Leesville.*
McCarty R.   *Leavitt.*

Champaign County.

Blanchford A. R.   *Urbana.*
Corwin M. B. & J.
Denels J. D
Geiger Levi

Jones & Dewell   *Urbana.*
Young & Ludson

Clermont County.

Ashburn Thomas Q.   *Batavia.*
Clark & Lewis
Denison George W.
Fishback & Swing
Howard William
Jamieson Milton
Lowe John W.
Logan R. C.
Penn & Johnson
Swing George L.
Talley Henry N.
Goodall C.   *Mount Pisgah.*
Carver L. W.   *Felicity.*
Dowdry S. F.
Hastings Peter H.
McElfresh George
Elstune Isaac   *Mulberry.*
Temple O.   *Mount Carmel.*
Witham M.   *Withamsville.*
Dunam P. J.   *New Richmond.*
Tritt J.

Clinton County.

Baldwin W. H.   *Wilmington.*
Corwine F.
Fuller W. & B. W.
Fisher W. B.
Foos Griffith
Hinkson & Telfair
Harlan R. B.
Doan & Linton
White & Wright
McKay A.
Thatcher Thomas   *Cuba.*
Baldwin W. H.   *Blanchester.*

Columbiana County.

Sloan George M.   *Hanoverton.*
Smith J. L.
Smith J. B.
Brewer Anson L.   *New Lisbon.*
Clarke John
Gilman John M.
Lee & Gilman
Mason, Potter & Woods
Vance Joseph E.
Wadsworth Seth L.
Wisden & Vanatta
Orr & Beaumont.
Upham William K.
Brooks Joseph J.   *Salem.*
Edwards E. M.
Kannett Thomas
Batten Ara H.   *East Rochester.*
Reilly James W.   *Wellsville.*
Trainer J. L. H.
Thomas Uriah.

Crawford County.

Adams Franklin   *Bucyrus.*
Allen & Kerr
Kendig Jacob
Plants Josiah S.
Summers A., Jr.
Swegart D. W.
Clements James   *Leesville Cross Roads.*

Frong John   *Leesville Cross Roads.*

Cuyahoga County.

Axtell & Prentiss, 10 Seneca block   *Cleveland.*
Bishop, Backus & Noble, Phenix Build's
Bingham F. W., 63 Superior
Briggs James A., Herald building
Clark A.
Coe Amos, 5 Water
Cross & Parks, Franklin building
Crowell Hon. J., Forest City building
Davidson R., William's block
Foot & Hoyt, 44 Superior
Foot & Newton, over Commercial Bank
Griswold & Payne, Kelley's block
Granniss J. C., Parson's block
Hay & Palmer, 8 Superior
Hitchcock J. R., 4 Johnson's block
Husband William O., 34 Bank
Johnson Henry N., 10 Seneca block
Lynde & Castle, 15 Superior
Mason & Estep, 34 Superior
Mather S. H., 4 Bank
Mather S. L., Public Square
Noble S. J., Empire building
Prentiss S. B. & J. F., 6 Johnson's block
Parsons R. C., Parson's block
Palmer David B., 80 Superior
Platt H. P., 63   do
Porter D. M., 129   do
Van Ness W. W., Melodeon building
Sherman & Hay, 80 Superior
Stetson Charles, over Merchant's Bank
Slade William, Jr., Forest City block
Tilden & Paine, Empire building
Treat S. W., 80 Superior
Vail J. C., 5 Water
Willey & Carey, 15 Superior
Williamson & Riddle, 65 Superior
Wyman George, 63 Superior
Canfield Jason, cor. Pearl & Detroit   *Ohio City.*

Dennis & Hunt
Ainger W. W.   *Chagrin Falls.*
Blakesley C. T.
Knox A.
Bosworth Perry   *North Royalton.*
Adams Joseph   *East Cleveland.*
McReynolds A.   *Euclid.*
Haight A. B.   *Newburgh.*
Henry J. R.   *Coe Ridge.*
Hatch L. O.   *Bedford.*
Barnum G. T.   *Rockport.*
Wood George R.

Darke County.

Allen William   *Greenville.*
Beers David
Beers John
Beers Theodore
Bell Hiram
Collins William
Calkins Charles
Calderwood A. R.
Frisell J. W.
Lumbard L.

Wilson W. M.
Jaqua ——
Best W. C.   *Poplar Ridge.*

Defiance County.

Carter William   *Defiance.*
Holgate William C.
Leland E. H.
McCord S M.
Phelps Edwin
Phelps Edward
Sessions H.
Sheffield William
Slevin Patrick
Taylor D.
Willson George H.
Wells W. W.

Delaware County.

Allen J.   *Delaware.*
Barnes James A.
Buck J. E.
Critchfield L. J.
Crawford James W.
Finch Sherman
Fuller D. T.
Humbell James R.
Hall George W.
Little L. W.
Penell Thomas W
Ranney Isaac
Reid W. P.
Sweetser Charles

Erie County.

Beecher Lewis S.   *Sandusky City*
Bigelow J. G.
Camp & Leonard
Converse & Giddings
Cogswell F. W.
Finch John
Goodwin H.
Hendry A. W.
Lane, Stone & Lane
Lewis Samuel
Mackey John
Minor Samuel
Miner A.
Root Joseph M.
Sloane Rush R.
Sadler E. B.
Tucker & Miller
Wildman H.
Wheeler George A.
Homan M.   *Huron.*
McLaurin S. H.
Campbell C.   *Birmingham.*
Striker A. H.
Taylor S. F.   *Milan.*
Andrews E.
Peckett J. W.
Hopkins P. R.
Emmons B.

Fairfield County.

Leonard Jesse   *West Rushville.*
Hunter & Fink   *Lancaster.*

Ewing Thomas, Hon.   *Lancaster.*
Brazee & Tallmadge
Martin J. D. & C.
Van Trump P.
Ewing P. B.
Schleich N.
Medill Wm. Hon.
Borland Charles
Shaffer C.
Creed W. P.
Garrahty John
Shaw V. E. & J.
Weaver George
Whitman H. C.
Lyle D.   *Millersport.*
Guesey E.   *Sugar Grove.*
Ream J. A.

Fayette County.

Rush Nelson   *Washington.*
Kerr S. F.
Jones David M.
Edwards J. M.   *Bloomingbury.*
McCoy A. M.

Franklin County.

Andrews S. C., High st.   *Columbus.*
Andrews S. W., State
Backus E., High
Brush S., High
Butler E., State
Carrington H. B., High
Convers George L., State
Cradlebaugh John, High
Dresel Otto
Dennison William, Jr., High
English and Martin, State
Gieger Joseph H., State
Gilbert & Baldwin, State
Harris S. R.
Jamerson W., High
Mathews & Rankin, State
Martin W. T., Friend
Motters H. D., State
Noble Henry C., High
Parsons George M., do
Sparrow Thomas
Smith Joseph F., Town
Swayne & Bates, State
Swann & Andrews, High
Stamberry H.,   do
Thomas W.,   do
Thrall W., Friend
Wambaugh H. M., High
Ware H. M.,   do
Wilcox P. B.,   do
Wilcox J. A.,   do
Shields R.   *Reynoldsburg*
Wright James E.   *Dublin*

Fulton County.

Carmicle Allen   *Ottokee*
Hill Amos
Handy Martin
Reid John H.
Upham L. H.   *Delta*
Leggett & Hall

Gallia County.

Albin David — *Gallipolis.*
Cushing A.
Cushing F.
Drouillard S. B.
Menoger E. S.
Nash Samuel E.
Perry Lemuel
Vinton Samuel F.
Clark John N. — *Smith's.*
Lewis Joshua
Strach F. T.
Holcomb Anselm T. — *Vinton.*
Holcomb Edward T.
Symmes William
Bradbury Joseph — *Kyger.*

Geauga County.

Abell B. F. — *Troy.*
Durfee L. E. — *Chardon.*
Forrist William O.
Hathaway J. N.
Phelps Alfred
Thrasher A. H.
Wilber William
Ford Seabury — *Burton.*
Deeky A. S.

Greene County.

Barlow Moses — *Xenia*
Boyd John
Elsberry & Sexton
Gatch Moses D.
Gest Joseph G.
Howard K. F.
Liggett James
Mouger Edward
Nesbitt Benoni
Partington Richard
Winans James J.
Harlan Aaron — *Yellow Springs.*
Forlong Andrew — *Zimmerman.*

Guernsey County.

Bushfield & Buchanan — *Cambridge.*
Evans N.
Leech Robert
Morton John
Wagstaff William R.
Ferrell Joseph — *Washington.*
Casey J. K. — *Cumberland.*
Foster John M.

Hamilton County.

Abraham Joseph, Hart's Building — *Cincinnati.*
Anderson Lars, cor. Pike & Symmes
Anderson Charles, 23 w. 3d
Antes M. R., 115 & 117 Main
Applegate J. W. & J. O., n. e. cor. Wal. & 4th
Bassford T. Jr., 40 w. 4th
Bateman W. M., n. w. cor. Court & Main
Bates & Scarborough, 8 & 9 Law Build'gs
Bell Peter, Court bet. Main & Walnut
Birney & Pierce, 114 Main
Birney James, s. w. cor. 3d & Sycamore
Blackburn John

Bonte J. H. O., s. w. cor. 3d & Syc. *Cin.*
Boyle James, s. e. cor. 9th & Western Row
Bradstreet J. M., 73 w. 3d.
Brooke Hunter, 2 Law Buildings
Brown Oliver B., s. w. cor. Main & Court
Brown D. L., 227 Vine
Brown & McGroarty, 10 w. 3d
Bryant & Probasco, s. w. cor. Court & Main
Burnet Jacob, Jr., 148 Main
Bushnell & Scott, 141 do
Butler A. C., 148 do
Carey Samuel F.,
Caldwell & Burrows, 1 Court Square
Carroll R. W., 282 Main
Carpenter Samuel S., 23 w. 3d
Chase & Ball, Chase's Buildings
Chambers F. T., 14 Law Buildings
Clemmer J. H., n. e. cor. Main & 7th
Coenzler J., cor. Walnut & Court
Collet J., 141 Main
Coffin & Mitchell, 117 Main
Collins Isaac, 23 w. 3d
Conklin Trueman, s. e. cor. 9th & W. Row
Conklin O. M., 128 Walnut
Colton F., 101 Main
Conover J. F., 25 Main
Cox Joseph, n. w. cor. Walnut & 5th
Crapsey J. T., cor. Walnut & Court
Crosa Nelson, n. e. cor. 3d & Hammond
Curwen M. E., Chase's Buildings
Dennis J. J., Lee's do
Dickson W. M., 3d, bet. Main & Sycamore
Dodd Edwin D., 14 e. 2d
Douglass John G., n. e. cor. 4th & Walnut
Douglass Peter, Broadway
Dutton Aaron R., 13 Law Buildings
Eaton & Jones, 10 Law do
Edwards Edwin, 39 w. 3d
Egly J. E., Eagle Buildings
Emerson William D., Clerk's Office
Fales Stephen, 117 Main
Furguson E. A., Court
Ferguson William, 3d bet. Main & Sycamore
Foren W. F., Lee's Buildings
Fosdick W. W., n. e. cor. 4th & Walnut
Fox & French, 3 & 4 Manchester Build'gs
French Lewis, Bacon's do
Frost George W., 8 Manchester do
Freon Joseph, n. w. cor. Main & 8th
Gaines Henry, n. e. cor. Walnut & 5th
Gaines Theo., 3d bet. Main & Sycamore
Gallagher Thomas J., 1 Law Buildings
Garrard Israel, Reeder's Buildings
Getzendanner J H., Commercial Buildings
Gholson, Miner & Colller, 12 Manchester Buildings
Gibbons Joseph G., 10 Law Buildings
Gilbert A. W., 3d bet. Main & Sycamore
Gitchell James M., 28 w. 6th
Goodman & Colton, 103 Main
Graves S., 205 Western Row
Grames & Morse, s. e. cor. 3d & Walnut
Groesbeck & Thompson, 23 w. 3d
Gwynne L. M., n. e. cor. Main & 7th
Haines Ezekiel S., 57 w. 3d
Hamilton R. S., 144 Walnut

Handy Robert D., 13 Law Buildings, *Cin.*
Harris C. C., n. w. cor. Court & Main
Hart Samuel M., Hart's Buildings
Hartwell Shattuck, 95 Walnut
Hartz A., Lee's Buildings
Hayes R. B., 6 Law Buildings
Henderson T. J., n. w. cor. Main & 3d
Henry Evan J., s. w. cor. 3d & Sycamore
Hill A. P., Court bet. Main & Walnut
Hilton G. H., cor. Walnut & Court
Hilts Charles, Lee's Buildings
Highway S. M., 14 Law Buildings
Hodgson W. E., 126 Walnut
Hollister George B., n.w. cor. Court & Main
Holt Robert S., n. w. cor. Main & 3d
Hopkins W. H., 6 e. 5th
Hopple M., 3d bet. Main & Sycamore
Hubbard E. S., 7 Manchester Buildings
Hoy John F., 28 w. 6th
Irwin J. C., 120 Main
Johnston William, 282 Main
Jones J. H., 11 e. 3d
Jones William D., 23 w. 3d
James Charles P., Chase's Buildings
Jones & Ware, 103 Main
Jolliffe John, 120   do
Ketchum & Headington, Hart's Buildings
Kirby Clinton,
Kimberland William, 8 & 9 Law Buildings
King, Anderson & Herron, 23 w. 3d
Leake J. B., 7 Law Buildings
Lewis & Butler, 148 Main
Lincoln Timothy D., 8 e. 2d
Logan Thomas A., Law Buildings
Long Alexander, 250 Main
Lord & Wright, 23 w. 3d
Lowe J. W., n. w. cor. Court & Main
Lytle William H., 57 w. 3d
McCormick Joseph, 141 Main
McClymon J. B., 10 w. 3d
McDougal Joseph J., n. w. cor. 3d & Syc.
McDowell W. C., 6 Law Buildings
McElroy George W., Lee's   do
McGuffey Alexander H., 120 Main
McClean John, Reeder's Buildings
Meline James F., 3d bet. Race & Vine
Miller F. W., 57 w. 3d
Mills & Hoadly, 2 Law Buildings
Moorman J. B., 18 w. 9th
Morris, Tilden & Rariden, n. e. cor. Court
  & Main
Mosher Lafayette, n. w. cor. Court & Main
Murdoch Charles C., Lee's Buildings
Mussey John, 8 Manchester   do
Newhall E. R., Meline's   do
Nesmith & Pugh, Hart's   do
Nixon John S., 43 w. 3d
Norton E. P., Meline's Buildings
O'Conner T. A., Lee's   do
Oliver A. L., 57 w. Third
Oliver & Adams, Reeder's Building
Paddock Alexander, 23 w. Third
Parker James, 7 Manchester Buildings
Parkhurst & Still, 95 Walnut
Pendry John L., 57 w. Third
Pendleton George H., 23 do
Pendleton Edmund, 8 Manchester B'ld's.

Phillips W. Jr., 6 bet. Main & Walnut, *Cin*
Piatt & Piatt, 6 w. 6th
Pierce Chas. C., n w. cor. Third & Syc.
Pomeroy Chas. S., Law Buildings
Pruden A. J., Court House
Pugh Geo. E., Hart's Buildings
Pugh Job, Eagle   do
Pugh & Pendleton, 8 e. 3d
Richardson W. M., Chase's Buildings
Reddington D., s. w. cor. W. Row & 7
Rice & Harrison 176 Race
Riddle Adam M., 256 Main
Roll E. C.,   do
Riley James, 59 Main
Roger W. H., n. w. cor. Court & Main
Sage George R., Manchester Buildings
Safin James, Lee's   do
Scarborough W. S., 2 Law   do
Sullivan & Holcomb, 3   do
Skinner J. R., n. w. cor. 3d & Sycamore
Slough J. P., 256 Main
Snow Henry, St. John's Buildings
Smith, Corwine & Holt, n. w. cor. Main &
  Sycamore
Spencer O. M., 39 w. 3d
Sprague J. R., Walnut, bet. Pearl & 3d
Stewart John M., 28 w. 6th
Stille John, Eagle Buildings
Stone & Collett, 308 Main
Stone R. H., Court near Main
Soden & Nielson, 360   do
Storer & Gwynne, Hart's Buildings
Strait & Hollister, n. w. cor. Court & Main
Sullivan & Holcomb, Law Buildings
Sullivan P. J., n. w. cor. 3d & Sycamore
Taft, Key & Mallon, 1 & 2 Manchester
  Buildings
Tapscott J. M., Eagle Buildings
Telfair W. B., 43 w. 3d
Thompson Egbert A., 25 w. 3d
Thorpe W. Coleman, 128 Walnut
Todd Alexander, 39 w. 3d
Thresher Thos. F., Chase's Buildings
Tuttle E. W., n. w. cor. 3d & Walnut
Van Hamm Wash., 7 Law Buildings
Van Hamm Alexander, Bacon's Build'gs
Van Every M., 57 w. 3d
Van Matre Daniel, 232 Main
Walker, Koebler & Force, Chase's B'ld'gs.
Warden & Warden, 141 Main
Warden & Paddock, 23 w. 3d
Warren J. B., Probate Judge
White James S., St. John's Building
White Oliver D., s. e. cor. 9th & W. Row
Williamson M. T., Eagle Buildings
Williamson G. T., n. e. cor. 4th & Walnut
Wilson J. M., n. e. cor. 5th & Walnut
Wiseman J. A., n. w. cor. Court & Main
Woodbury Geo. W., Lee's Buildings
Woodruff T., n. w. cor. 6th & Walnut
Worthington & Matthews, Worthington's
  Buildings
Williams P. T., s. e. cor. 5th & Walnut
Wright D. T., w. 3d
Zinn & Bateman, n. w. cor. Court & Main
Zimmer Leo, 1 Court Square
Asby John   *Harrison*

Tibbs Alvin G.,   *Harrison.*
Burnett Isaac G.   *Walnut Hills.*
Moore Robert   *Cheviot.*
Roll E. C.   *Cummingsville.*

Hancock County.

Bigelow & Patterson   *Finley.*
Brown & Blackford
Coffenberry Audrew
Coffenberry James M.
Goit & Parker
Morrison & Gribben
O'Neal & Whitely
Rosette John E.

Hardin County.

Coulson S.   *Kenton.*
Gatch & Thompson
Hurd L. C.
Stillings E.
Smith Sam.
Stevens J. C.
Walker W. L.
Kemp G. W.
Camp B.

Harrison County.

Bingham J. A.   *Cadiz.*
Bastwick S. W.
Forsythe L.
Garton W. C.
Lenton Lewis
Lemmon A.
Peppard S. G.
Rowles T. C.
Shotwell S. B.
Scott Isaiah
Turner Allen C.
Thomas J. S.
Sharon Joseph

Henry County.

Durbin James   *Texas.*
Caldwell James O.   *Napoleon.*
Moe W. H.
McBane S. R.
Sheffield E.
Tyler J. H.

Highland County.

Sloan & Collins   *Hillsboro'.*
Mathews A. G.
Price & Beach
Stevenson R. B.
Scott Danl.
Beeson R.   *Leesburgh.*
Irion Silas
Hockett Amos
Rees David
Dickey A. S.   *Greenfield.*
Hocket Amos   *Belfast.*
Huett Allen O.   *New Petersburg.*
Ellis Thos.

Hocking County.

Groghan Raymond   *Logan*
Roberts W. O.
Saunders H. R.

Holmes County.

Armor & Walker   *Millersburg.*
Anderson Robert
Bancroft & Given
Everett G. W.
Huston John
Hoagland & Gilbert
McKinley D. M.
Taggart Chas. D.
Reed W.
Voorhees & Ankeny
Stillwell Asher   *Humphreysville.*
McFarland R.
Cain James   *Nashville.*

Huron County.

Curtis Alfred S.   *Norwalk.*
Kellogg Oscar E.
Kennan J.
Lattimer & Bishop
Osborn John R.
Roberts B. F.
Stewart Gideon T.
Sawyer Franklin
Strong T. R.
Safford G. H.
Stone & Patrick
Wilbeck John
Worcester & Penneweil
Winslow H. W.   *Bellevue.*

Jackson County.

Dungan Levi   *Jackson.*
Hoffman R. C.
Johnson E.
Stanley T. R.
Mackley D.   *Oak Hill.*

Jefferson County.

Andrews Martin   *Steubenville.*
Collier Danl. L.
Elliott James
Forsythe Levi C.
Lloyd W. R.
McCook Geo. W.
Mason Geo. W.
Moody R. S.
Meredith John R.
Means Thos.
Miller John H.
Marsh Rosswell
Sherrard Robert
Stokely Saml.
Stanton Edwin M.
Shane John
Tappan Eli T.
Trainer John H.
McCleary J. C.   *Warrenton.*

Knox County.

Curtis & Scribner   *Mount Vernon.*
Curtis & Devin
Cotton E. W.
Davis J. C.
Dunbar W.
Harle J. E.
Jackson Philip

Irvine Clark   *Mount Vernon.*
Israel & Galusha
Mc Intire & Lockwood
Mitchell M. H.
Miller & Adams
Morgan & Chapman
Norton A. B.
Sapp & McClelland
Sapp, Delano & Smith
Shafer S.
Stockton J. C.
Vance & Smith
Windom & Norton
Kelley E.   *Millwood.*

Lake County.

Matthews W.   *Painesville.*
Tinker A. L.
Doolittle J. T.
Bissel B.
Sterling L.   *Willoughby.*
Komar C. J.
Smith S. M.   *Kirtland.*
Rising C. B.

Lawrence County.

Colvin S. P.   *Ironton.*
George John S.
Golden F.
Hawley C. G.
Johnson William W.
Neal H. S.
Nigh Elias
Sprigg Singleton
Leet Ralph

Licking County.

Arven W. W.   *Newark.*
Buckingham & White
Blackman H. C.
Case L.
Follett Chas.
Greene James
King & Wood
King W.
Smythe & Sprague
Stanbury, Wright & Kibler
Stanbury W.
Teneyck H. B.
Thrapp P. V.
Veneyck H. B.
Wintumute John
Rodgers A. E.   *Granville.*
Ladone James
Jones F. A.
Smith E.   *Kirkersville.*

Logan County.

Bennett Ezra   *Bellefontaine.*
Canby Richard S.
Casad Anthony
Corwin & Shelby
Howard J. P. M.
Hubbard & Kernan
Lawrence & West
Pollock John
Robb Thomas

Smith Ypsilanti A.   *Bellefontaine*
Stanton & Allison
Strain Lewis L.
Walker James
Warren Marvin
Underwood J. B.
Hayes O.   *West Liberty.*

Lorain County.

Bliss Philemon   *Elyria.*
Boynton Elbridge G.
Burke & Lake
Chapman B. B.
Coon John V.
Doolittle Charles H.
Garvey E. C. R.
Lockwood & Bagg
Myers Joshua
Vincent John M.
Warner E. L.
Washburn & Smith
Putnam Schuyler
Sheldon L. A.   *La Grange.*
Norris A.   *Wellington.*

Lucas County.

Cook Daniel F.   *Maumee City.*
Lemmon R. C.
Young Samuel M.
Abbott Caleb F.   *Toledo.*
Allen Edson
Baker & Latimer
Bassett & Kent
Bennett Henry
Bissell Edward, Jr.
Braly & Gliddon
Clark Albert G.
Commager & Lemmon
Dodge Charles
Dorr Charles M.
Dunlap Thomas
Espy John C.
Fitch & Mc Bain
Galpin P. G.
Harris Ahial C.
Hall W. H.
Hill, Perigo & Pratt
Hosmer Hezekiah L.
Manor John J.
Morton & Lee
Nye Edmund D.
Rouse Birdsey W.
Young & Waite

Madison County.

Fisher Z. T.   *London.*
Freeman J. F.
Harrison R. A.
Lacy J. F.
Smith H. W.
Weldon Lawrence   *Somerford.*

Mahoning County.

Blocksom B.   *Canfield.*
Canfield E. G.
Church J. W.
Gilson S. W.

King John H. — *Canfield.*
Lewis J. H.
Newton E.
Ruggles Chas.
Wilson D. W.
Young G. J.
Powers R. J. — *Youngstown.*
Hutchins F. E.
Sanderson T. W.
Furguson Wm.
Moore Wm.
Price Robert — *Milton.*

Marion County.

Bertrams J. & S. H. — *Marion.*
Bowen and Durfee
Bowen Ozias
Bunker P.
Durfee Bradford R.
Hume John F.
Williams & Hume
Guthrey J. D. — *Wilson.*

Medina County.

Canfield & Kimball — *Medina.*
McElhinny H.
Reynolds E. W.
Canfield H.
Mills C. T.
Brace A. — *Litchfield.*
Camp I. J. — *Sharon Centre.*
Dickenson A. — *Wadsworth.*
Pardee Aaron
Lake C. A. — *Lodi.*
Hibbard H. H. — *Homerville.*

Meigs County.

Cartwright John — *Pomeroy.*
Heckard Martin
Horton V. B.
Plants T. A.
Earhart Jacob S.
Irvin Thos.
Merrill Arthur — *Rutland.*
Simpson Nathan
Hutton Elijah — *Ledlies.*

Mercer County.

Hunter Wm. — *Celina.*
Le Blond F. C.
Riley J. W.
Sheldon G. James

Miami County.

Johnson & Jones — *Piqua.*
McKinney S. S.
Janvier J. T.
Jas. H. Hart
Wilber N. F.
Wood S.
Aylesworth G. H. — *Troy.*
Burgess G. D.
Grovener D.
Gibbs David
Morris & Smeltzer
Parsons E.
Sellers & Ross
White M. B.

Davis Saml. — *West Milton.*
Jones W. B.

Monroe County.

Archbold Edward — *Woodsfield.*
Davenport Samuel
Hollister Nathan
Hollister Simpson
Hunter William F.
Okey John W.
Ross Archibald
Sinclair John
Wire Daniel H.

Montgomery County.

Ackerman John J. — *Dayton.*
Baggott James H.
Bartlett William O.
Du Bois B. P.
Collins F.
Conover Wilbur
Crane Joseph G.
Craighead Samuel
Davies Edward W.
Forsyth Eli J.
Gunckel L. B.
Hart Ralph S., (Judge)
Haynes & Howard
Holt George B.
Houk George W.
Howard John
Huesman Lewis
Iddings Daniel W.
Jordan J. A.
Kelley P.
Kennedy Gilbert
Knox J. B.
Lovell Josiah
Lowe John G.
Lowe Peter P.
Lyman O. A.
McKinney Wm. J.
Malambre George W.
Nead D. P.
Odlin & Lowe
Piper William H.
Scott A. M.
Smith Thomas J. S.
Stoddard Henry
Strong Hiram
Sullivan Stith M.
Vallandigham C. L.
Walker Moses B.
Wood Youngs V., (Probate Judge)
Elliot H. — *Germantown.*
Bolten Samuel — *Miamisburgh.*
Clay Adam

Morgan County.

Davis H. W. — *McConnelsville*
Evans E. E.
Hanna John E.
Hanna James L.
Linn D. B.
Rich V.
Robertson H. S.
Shivel D. B.
Tipton T. W

Tompkins C. B.   *McConnelsville.*
Wood F. W.
Glenn Wm.   *Meigs Creek.*
Lutgen James H.
Glenn —   *Bristol.*
Crew Thos.   *Chester Hill.*

Morrow County.

Burns & Beebe   *Mount Gilead.*
Dunn & Gurley
Erwin S.
Leonard J.
Mitchell R. B.
Olds & Dalrymple
Stinchcomb and Brumbach
McThomas W.   *Cardington.*

Muskingum County.

Ball Wm. H.   *Zanesville.*
Blocksom A. C.
Brush Edward
Buell John M.
Chapman Saml.
Converse Chas, C.
Eastman E. B.
Goddard & Eastman
Guile N. A.
Granger Moses M.
Harper & Harper
Jewett & Oneill
James Geo.
Marsh & Ball
Oneill John
Searle Covington W.
Seborn F. A.
Taylor Thos. I.
Copeland Howard   *Dresden.*
Converse C. C.   *Putnam.*
Chapman S.
Monroe J. H.

Noble County.

Spriggs B. F.   *Mount Ephraim*
Rothrock J. H.   *Olive.*
Bratton E. A.   *Sarahsville.*
Belford Jabez
Frazier William H.
Okey William C.
Pettay Daniel
Priestly William

Ottawa County.

Magruder J. H.   *Port Clinton.*
Wilcox S. N.
Ansley W.

Paulding County.

Latty A.   *Paulding.*
Snooks J.   *Antwerp.*

Perry County.

Costigan Jacob   *Somerset.*
Gallagher Thomas J.
Hickman & Wilson
Maginnis T. J.
O'Neill John H.
Sherrard James

Spencer Eli A.   *Somerset.*
Spencer William
Muzzy L. F.   *New Lexington.*
Smith Eli
Worley & Boling
Olive D.   *Sego.*

Pickaway County.

Bremingan William   *Circleville.*
Crouse Charles B.
Doan G. W. & Co.
Hall Jeremiah
Hedges Henry R., Senr.
Jones & Smith
Knox Thomas J.
Miller J.
Olds Chancy N.
Olds Marcus L.
Wyman Julius L.
Rennick & Page

Pike County.

Fitzgerald J.   *Piketon.*
Collings James
McCauslin A. W.
Reed Wm. H.

Portage County.

Brown O. P   *Ravenna.*
Conant P. B.
Conn M. W.
Lyman Darius
Strawder Samuel
Ranney John L.
Taylor E. B.
Stuart M.
Jeffries N. L.
Tappan F. W.
Willard Horace   *Palmyra.*
Tyler Joel W.   *Franklin.*

Preble County.

Gilmore & Bolens   *Eaton.*
Banta & Clark
Hubbard & Foos
Harris Joel W.
Chawick & Drayer
Marsh Felix
Mitchell V.
Larsh B. F.
Gans G. W.
Freeman Irvin E.   *Lewisburg.*

Putnam County.

Budd Azariah   *Kalida.*
Mackenzie James
Monroe Alonzo
Day E.   *Gilboa.*

Richland County.

Bartley & Price   *Mansfield.*
Brinkerhoff & Shupe
Carhart H. Clay
Gass & Davis
Kirkwood & Burns
Purdy & Johnston
Smith & Hedges
Young & Poe

Andrews T. B.	*Butler.*
Ramsay John	*Ontario.*
Fleming Joseph	*Newville.*
Stanton J. G.	
Wolf S.	*Richland,*
Beekman John W.	*Plymouth.*

Ross County.

Boys Alex. S.	*Chillicothe.*
Briggs Robert M.	
Clark Milton L.	
Clark & Wallace	
Cook S. S.	
Dickey & Briggs	
Douglas Luke	
Gilmore Charles W.	
Gilmore William E.	
Hurst Thomas P.	
Keith John H.	
Keith & Van Ham	
Lewis & Safford	
Lewis Edward	
McClintock & Smith	
McClintock William T.	
McCoy Samuel F.	
McLain Jas. S.	
Massie Henry	
Miller Joseph	
Miller & Anerman	
Safford William H.	
Scott Thomas	
Scott Thomas T.	
Shever Theodore	
Sill Joseph	
Smith Amos	
Taylor J. L.	
Taylor & Massie	
Van Ham Alex.	
Wallace Samuel L.	
Wake Thomas	
Wople Alfred	
Feter George D.	*Bainbridge.*

Sandusky County

Bartlett B. J. & Son	*Fremont.*
Buckland & Everett	
Edgerton O.	
Finefrock T. P.	
Greene & Mugg	
Glick Geo. W.	
Haynes Geo. R.	
Ward & Heaton	
Ray William	*Clyde.*

Scioto County.

Crichton A., Jr.	*Portsmouth.*
Davis J. W.	
Glover Eli	
Hutchins W. A.	
Jordan E. W.	
Moore O. F.	
Nabb George W.	
Peck W. V.	
Ramsay Benjamin	
Tracy Charles O.	
Tracy Samuel M.	
Turner George	

4

Lindsey Peter T.	*Iron Furnaced.*
Searles F. O	*Lyra.*

Seneca County.

Gibson William H.	*Tiffin.*
Hall Luther A.	
Hord John K.	
Johnson William M.	
Noble W. P. & H.	
Pennington & Lee	
Pillars James P.	
Hedges William	
Steiner John J.	
Stem Leander	
Tunison T. O.	
Watson Cooper K.	
Seney George E.	
Wilson Joel W.	
Lamareux John L	*Attica.*
Moore —	*Republic.*
Welch J. W.	*Stoner.*

Shelby County.

Conklin & Thompson	*Sidney.*
Good P. G.	
Hale M. C.	
Martin William J.	
Smith Edmusd	
Walker S. B.	

Stark County.

Beldon George W.	*Canton.*
Beirce Alexander	
Brown & Myers	
Frease Joseph	
Frease W.	
Hazlett Isaac	
Leiter Benjamin F.	
Pool Joseph	
Shaefer Louis	
Stark & Evans	
Lahm S. & J.	
Humphrey Lyman	*New Baltimore.*
Bradshaw & Wales	*Massillon.*
Carter D. K.	
Folger R. H.	
Keith & Underhill	
Logan & Fletcher	
Pease A.	
Pease S.	
Dresel Otto	
Cunningham William M.	*Canal Fulton.*
Rinehart C. H.	
Morse J. G.	*Limaville,*
Borden Amos	*Mahoning.*

Summit County.

Berry Abel B.	*Akron.*
Bierce Lucius B.	
Bliss & Pleasants	
Bryan Constant	
Carpenter J. S.	
Dodge William M.	
Hammond Rollin O.	
Humphrey, Upson & Edgerton	
Nash & Goodhue.	
Otis & Wolcott	
Oviatt Edward	
Schuyler Philip N.	

Tilden & Hadley	*Akron.*	Clark & Plyley	*McArthur.*
McClure & McKinney	*Cuyahoga Falls.*	Wilson & Cully	
Wolcott A. E.			
Humphrey Hon. Van R.	*Hudson.*	**Van Wert County.**	
McMillen S. C.		De Puy Perrin	*Van Wert.*
Whedon Harvey		Edson Charles P.	
Hand Seneca L.	*Middlebury.*	Gilliland Robert	
Hunsberger Abraham	*Inland.*	Roberts Caleb	
Humphrey Isaiah	*Peninsula.*	Rose Obadiah W.	
Weld James W.	*Richfield.*	Spears Richard C.	
McNiel William	*Bath.*	Brown S. E.	*Delphos.*
		Huber Noah	

Trumbull County.

Asper J. F.	*Warren.*	**Warren County.**	
Birchard & Sutliff		Corwin R. G.	*Lebanon.*
Brown George F.		Dunlevy A. H.	
Buel J. R.		Mickle W. S.	
Crowell John		McBurney A. G.	
Curtis B. F.		Oneal J. K.	
Hoffman B. F.		Probasco John	
Hutchins John		Sabin James	
Leggitt M. D.		Smith Geo. J. & J. M.	
McLain T. J.		Stokes G. W.	
Palm Jefferson		Stokes H. M.	
Perry Albert		Smith Lawrence	
Porter John		Vanhavligin F. S.	
Ranney R. P		Williams James M.	
Ranney J. L. & H. C.		Ward J. D.	
Reice Philo E.		Wallace J. D.	*Morrow.*
Rice T. M.		Dodds J. A.	*Mason.*
Smith C. W.		Hutchinson E.	
Sutliff & Tuttle			
Webb Thomas D.		**Washington County.**	
Harrington Charles A.	*Greensburgh.*	Clark & Ewart	*Marietta.*
Bright William J.	*Hartford.*	Green Davis	
Ferris N. S.		Maxwell F.	
Jones L. C.		Nye D. S. & W. S.	
McKay George C.	*Johnsonville.*	Rhodes Chas.	

Tuscarawas County.

Bartolson & Shotwell	*New Philadelphia.*	Whittlesey W. A.	
Belden & Hoag		Welch & Rhodes	
Hance Joseph C.		Barber David	*Harmar.*
Hardesty P. J.			
Helnick W.		**Wayne County.**	
Stambaugh & McIlvain		Avery Edward	*Wooster.*
McMath W.		Bonewitz S. R.	
Patrick Andrew		Cox Levi	
Patrick J.		Dean E. & E. V.	
Ready A. T.		Foreman E.	
Starkweather & Mitchener		Given W.	
Harmount S.	*Canal Dover.*	Glusgoon James C.	
Robinson John J.		Hottery Lucas	
Stocknell Hosea T.		Johnson Thos. S.	
Warner Wright		Jeffries John P.	
Wilhelm A.		Johnson H. C.	
Myers A. W.	*Sandyville.*	Jones Ohio F.	
		Lehman Henry	
Union County.		McSweeney John	
Allen J. B.	*Marysville.*	Orr W. M.	
Clark Ransom C.		Pardee E.	
Coats John B.		Parsons C. C.	
Cole & Porter		Rex Geo.	
Curry & Robinson			
Doughty Jackson C.		**Williams County.**	
		Blakeslee S. E.	*Bryan.*
Vinton County.		Dobbs J.	
Bingham E. F.	*McArthur.*	Foster Edward	
Hewitt B. P.		Lantz John P.	

Morrow John K.
Simon John A.
Treat S. A.
Wyatt J. B.
Hunter W. A. *West Unity.*
Morrison T. S. O.
Parker J. O.
Willett M. H.
Dewolf John G. *Montpelier.*

Wood County.

Cook Asher *Perrysburg.*
Jefferson Sylvanus
Mefford David M.
Spink & Murry
Way W. V.
Hinsdale Geo. P. *Gilead.*

Wyandot County.

Atkinson M. J. *Upper Sandusky.*
Beeley & Dennison
Kirby Moses H.
McKelley Robert
Mott O. R.
Sears J. D.
Smith P. B. *Careys.*
Tyler Peter A. *McCutchensville.*
Brockley Michael

Auction Tobacco Warehouse.

Hamilton County.

Love Thos. Rufus, cor. Pearl & Race Cin.

Auctioneers & Commission Merchants.

Clark County.

Compton J. H. *Springfield.*

Columbiana County.

Arter Geo. *New Lisbon.*
Rogers Geo. A.
Wisden Simon

Crawford County.

Cramer Henry *Bucyrus.*

Cuyahoga County.

Abrams, King & Co. Ontario, *Cleveland.*
Outter O. & Son, 8 Bank
Mollen O., 12 Water
Moore H., 118, 120 Superior

Defiance County.

Eldridge W. F. *Defiance.*

Franklin County.

Glazier V. R. & Co., cor. Town & 4th *Columbus.*
Smith B. E., High

Geauga County.

Paino J. C. *Chardon.*

Hamilton County.

Blunt E. B., 23 w. 5th *Cincinnati.*
Brashiers G. & Co., 57 Main
Cooper James, 23 w. 5th

Johnson & Graff, 168 Main *Cincinnati.*
Hewson & Holmes, 83 & 85 Walnut
Hayden S. F. & Co., 235 Main
Kellogg A., 25 e. 3d
Kissick James, 223 Main
McDermot & Co., cor. Court & Walnut
Palmer S. D. & Co., 13 & 15 e. 3d
Reese & Read, 17 5th
Reese & Read, 227 Main
Rodgers S. O.,
Woodruff O. S., s. e. cor. Walnut & 5th
Yorke & Bryson, 30 Main
Black Peter *Pleasant Ridge.*
Bonham Hezekiah
Hartpense D. E. *Harrison.*

Hardin County.

Thomas A. *Kenton.*
Furney H.

Jefferson County.

Sutton Isaac *Steubenville.*
Bruce —

Madison County.

Clark B. F. *London.*

Montgomery County.

Rouser Samuel, N. Market *Dayton.*
Rouser & Arnold, Third

Portage County.

Fowler Abel *Ravenna.*
Sawyer John B. *Franklin.*

Richland County.

Littler J. W. *Mansfield.*

Scioto County.

McDowell & Chandler *Portsmouth.*

Seneca County

Brink S. W. *Tiffin.*

Starke County.

Zerbe J. *Massillon.*

Summit County.

Wright J. J. *Akron.*

Union County.

Malen Wm. O. *Marysville.*

Vinton County.

Matthews E. *McArthur.*

Williams County.

Ely Ralph G. *West Unity.*
Scomel Wm. O. *Pulaski.*

Wyandot County

Roberts James G. *Upper Sandusky*

Awning Manufacturers.

Hamilton County.

Alcorn & Vandvier, 100 Sycamore *Cincin*
Gordon George, Fifth bet. Sycamore & Main
Ryling John, 22 Eighth

Axe Manufacturers.

Cuyahoga County.

White H. & Sons   Chagrin Falls
McGregor James   Ohio City.

Knox County.

Boyle Aaron   Brandon.

Lawrence County.

Scott, Brother & Co.   Ironton.

Portage County.

Joiner Alvin   Nelson.
French Isaac & Co.   Ravenna.

Axe Helve Manufacturers.

Geauga County.

Hopkins Wm. A.   Parkman.

Van Wert County.

Davis J. O.   Van Wert.

Wyandot County.

Hunter Samuel   Upper Sandusky.

Bagging Manufacturer.

Hamilton County.

Tucker E. F., 505 e. Front   Cincinnati.

Bakers.

Belmont County.

Wright John   St. Clairsville.

Brown County.

Hannise Jacob   Higginsport.
Kiehl Joseph   Ripley.
Ekermeier W.

Butler County.

Clute A.   Oxford.
Cooper J. W.
Swartz John   Hamilton.
McCandles & Bridge
Brewer J. H.
Shorr C.
Schuler Geo.   Rossville.
Holdeffer J.
Huber Philip
Foster G.   Middletown.
Stevens A.

Champaign County.

McCord S. K.   Urbana.

Clark County.

Stinman E.   Springfield.
Winger C.
George Geo.
Styner G.

Clermont County.

Folandine Wm.   New Richmond.
Parr John

Clinton County.

Hinis Nathan   Wilmington
Vantup Thos.

Columbiana County.

Lee John   Wellsville
Oster M. P.
Watson John   New Lisbon

Cuyahoga County.

Cramer & Sliney, 145 River, 76 Dock
                         Cleveland.
Gorham & Aplin, 16 Superior
Lyon L. L., 187 River, 77 Dock
Light C. H. & Co., 64 Ontario
Ray R. J. & Co., 34 Ontario
Mitchell Alexander, cor. Ohio & Kinsman

Defiance County.

Wisenberger F.   Defiance.

Erie County.

Motch Joseph   Sandusky City.
Wisbaden S.
Frieburg S.
Newmir John

Franklin County.

Bentz F.,   High   Columbus.
Butler C. P. L.   do
Drury & Werley   do
Leadley Mark   do
Robins & Lathimer do
Stellzer G. & Co. do
King William   do

Gallia County.

Litchenfelt C.   Gallipolis.

Greene County.

Austin & Smith   Xenia.
Davidson J.

Hamilton County.

Altvogt P. W., Linn bet. Clark & Cathe-
  rine   Cincinnati.
Amrerhen B., 35 Elder
Atkins & Son, 205 Elm
Bennett & Littleford, 30 Lower Market
Brooks —, 8 Walnut
Bailie John, 60 Front
Bennett —, 89 Court
Burt F., 121 Locke
Boyce W., cor. Race & Pearl
Buce A., W. Row bet. Everett & Mason
Brickley & Smith, 369 W. Row
Blair Joseph. s. w. cor. Clinton & John
Burbeck A. C., Catherine bet. Rittenhouse
  & Cutter
Brice —, s. e. cor. John & 6th
Belser & Co., cor. 5th & W. Row
Cooper Robt. A., 84 & 86 Lower Market
Craig J., 172 Congress
Cavagna J., 5th near Walnut
Crossley & McCartney, 444 w. 5th
Decker C., Harrison Road w. of Brighton
Dunholter H., 244 w. 6th
Elter W., 31 Hamilton Road

Friedborns A., 2 Hamilton Road *Cincin.*
Friedlious J., 86 Court
Fields R. B., 5th bet. Vine & Race
Frank L., 461 Elm
Getty R., 15 Sycamore
Gunkel E., 205 Vine
Honhouser J. B., 6 Hunt
Hahneman O., 549 Vine
Hoffman J.. cor., Plum & Liberty
Heckle J., 701 Elm
Hesling H. J., cor. Linn & Clinton
Jinkins R., s. e. cor. Catherine & Fulton
Kepling H. J., s. e. cor. Clinton & Linn
Kurtz A., 8th bet. John & Mound
Keeley W. J., 186 6th
Kuhn V., 84 Buckeye
Kinsey Henry, 546 w. 5th
Luers J. B., cor. Sycamore & 5th
Lanther G., 65 Court
Laterkin C., 82 Hunt
Lang John, cor. B. Miller & 7th
Lewis J., 420 w. 4th
Muir T.. s. e. cor. John & Catherine
Merrill R. J., cor. Walnut & Front
Muller J., 609 Vine
Mack H., 54 Liberty
Nuzel J., 150 Front
Presho W., 180 Front
Rock A., 451 Sycamore
Smith & Brickley, 256 w. 6th
Seiter C., cor. 8th & Elm
Spreen C. F. & Co., 228 w. 6th
Simon S., 330 Western Row
Schoch Andrew,
Smith H. W., 256 Main
Schivene J.,342 Hamilton Road
Schilt George, 133   do
Taylor J., 4th bet. Park & Smith
Vasmeyer J. H., cor. Front & Plum
Vorwald T., 500 Main
Wheeler M. G., 134 Front
Wehrman C. H., s. w. cor. Locust & Everett
Welsh J. , 211 w. 6th
Wagnor V., 74 Hamilton Road
Zimmerman J. 413 Vine
Walker D.   *Fulton.*
Burner J. B.
Singleton H.   *Walnut Hills.*
Huth George   *Mt. Healthy.*
Bender Lewis   *Harrison.*
Johnson Adam
Kolb George
Schurman Rudolph   *Reading.*
Sener Louis
Keely Washington   *Cheviet.*

Hardin County.
Aston W. D.   *Kenton.*

Huron County.
Ingles J. F.   *Norwalk.*
Dewalett A. J.
Graves J. R.

Jefferson County.
Seabold Lewis   *Steubenville.*
Pierce B

Ingraham N.   *Steubenville.*
Stanley Charles
Boyer John

Knox County.
Boyd J.   *Mount Vernon.*
George J.

Licking County.
Cross Gilbert   *Newark.*

Logan County.
Railton J.   *Bellefontaine.*

Madison County.
Weeber Peter   *London.*

Mercer County.
Marvelious L.   *St. Mary's.*
Fox L.

Miami County.
Kruck J.   *Piqua.*
Rexford E. M.
Crook John
Latin E. & Co.
Mentel M.   *Troy.*
Ackley J. B.
Johns D.

Montgomery County.
Bohlender V., 2d street   *Dayton.*
Lehman H. G., 4th
Wyatt H , 3d
Wyatt & Nickum, 2d
Davis & Brother   *Miamisburgh.*

Morgan County.
Shaffer & Blakenbeiler   *McConnelsville.*
Hageman O.

Pickaway County.
Duncan & Sherman   *Circleville.*
Mader J. F.
Wolfley J.

Pike County.
Ormsby James   *Piketon.*

Portage County.
Taylor S. A.   *Ravenna.*

Preble County.
Stannah & Beller   *Eaton.*
Wilson & Co.
Homer John F.
Crouse Jacob
Bruce, Houk & Co.

Ross County.
Shafer A.   *Chillicothe.*
Staphler David
Sculley A.
Lasman George
Lasman Hiram
Sants & Co.

Scioto County.
Steward Hugh   *Portsmouth*
Sulcman O.
Timmonds M. & S.

Seneca County.

Black G. W.   *Tiffin.*
Boss Charles F.
Engelfried L.
Huffman James

Trumbull County.

Bedford J.   *Warren.*
Brooks O. J.
Delph P.
Dunlap J. D.
Lowry J.

Tuscarawas County.

Schoch Charles   *New Philadelphia.*

Union County.

Wilkinson J. M.   *Marysville.*

Vinton County.

Malone James   *McArthur.*

Warren County.

Collins & Barnhurst, S. & A. *Waynesville.*
Endres Philip   *Morrow.*

Washington County.

Hall W. & Co.   *Marietta.*
Wildt J. & Co.
Smith E. G.   *Harmar.*

Wyandot County.

Keller Harrison   *Upper Sandusky.*

Bankers.

Cuyahoga County.

Mygatt & Brown, 6 Bank st.   *Cleveland.*
Sturges & Hale, American Hotel building
Wright W. W. & Co. Superior

Hamilton County.

Almy & Wilcox, 53 w. 3d st.   *Cincinnati.*
Burnet, Shoup & Co., cor. Walnut & 3d
Ellis & Morton, n. e. cor.   do
Gilmore & Brotherton, 31 Main
Groesbeck J. H. & Co., w. 3d
Goodman T. S., 101 Main
Hatch & Langdon, s. w. cor. Main & Court
Ingalls W., Agt (West.B'k) 7 Burnet House
Dunlevy, Atwood & Co., 34 w. 3d
Manchester P. B., s. w. cor. 3d & Syc.
Milne George & Co., 3d bet. Main & Wal.
McMicken & Co., 3d bet. Walnut & Vine
Rowe, Stanhope S. & Co., 25 3d
Ramsey James B., 4th near Walnut
Sanford B. F., n. e. cor. Walnut & 4th
Smead, Collard & Hughes, 141 Main
Wood & Dunlap, 15 w. 3d
Wheeler A. J., cor. 3d & Main

Bankers & Exchange Brokers.

Hamilton County.

Burt A. G., 12 w. 3d street,   *Cincinnati.*
Bascom & Bird, 28   do

Conway W. A., 36 e. 3d   *Cincinnati.*
Carpenter A. B. & Co., 4th near Sycamore
Dye John S., s. e. cor. Walnut & 3d
Green R. C., cor. Sycamore & Pub. Land.
McKinney & Gilbert, cor 3d & Sycamore
McCammon W. & Co., 43 w. 3d
Mann Isaac, 117 Walnut
Outcalt J. & Co., 5 & 6 w. 3d
Page H., 10½   do
Saunders David A., 90   do
Thompson A. B., 38   do
Towle & Co., 4 College buildings
Wright George S. & Co. 26 w. 3d

Hocking County.

Culver R.   *Logan.*
Officur S. P.

Marion County.

Durfee R. R.   *Marion.*
Reed J. S.

Muskingum County.

Wheeler M. D.   *Zanesville.*
Sturges, Buckingham & Co.

Bank Note Engravers.

Hamilton County.

Toppan, Carpenter, Casilear & Co., Odd
    Fellow's Hall   *Cincinnati.*
Rawdon, Wright, Hatch & Edson, s. e. cor.
    Main & 4th
Shipley H. H. & Bro., 22 West Fourth

Barbers and Hair Dressers.

Butler County.

Anderson   *Hamilton.*
Jones Franklin
Anderson A. J.
Francis Henry   *Rossville.*
Miller F.   *Middletown.*

Champaign County.

Russell Wm.   *Urbana.*
Hanly J.

Clark County.

Piles R.   *Springfield.*
Piles Wm.
Coles T. T.
Davis C.
Adams Isaac   *New Carlisle.*

Erie County.

Garrett N.   *Huron.*
Scott J. B.   *Sandusky City.*
Bock M. G.
Roberts & Carren

Hamilton County.

Brischo J., 95 w. 5th   *Cincinnati.*
Brunk P., 490 Walnut
Bohlender G., 424 Vine
Barnard Wm., 280 Wes. Row
Caffrey Wm. A., 343 5th
Davis Wm., 14 e. 8th
Eberle F. H., 151 Front

Evans S., 26 Ludlow *Cincinnati.*
Feinthel C. H. & Co., 82 Columbia
Ferguson A., Burnet House
Frey J., 668 Vine
Goff & Cousins, Court bet. Walnut & Vine
Hart —, 148 Walnut
Hunster Wm. H., 244 3d
Holmes & Jones, 26 Court
Herrold A., 16 13th
Hagenfritch H., 500 Vine
Huntser A . cor. 6th & Mound
Judah J., 256 Main
Johanner J. P., 543 Vine
Johnson Wm., 253 6th
Luzius Philip, 61 Court
Lanfer M., 594 Main
Margna V., 92 Columbia
Mabis H., 596 Vine
Mandel C., 291 Wes. Row
Pilson Wm., 263 w. 6th
Ross D., 205 Wes. Row
Schmidt Michael, 40 Front
Stenser Geo., 30   do
Schrichart H.
Saal F., 579 Race
Thickside W., 9 w. 6th
Thomas R., 324 Wes. Row
Peterson W. *Pendleton.*
Betscher J.
Attig P. *Fulton.*
Dilg Charles *Harrison.*
Hawkins Joseph
Cox James *Carthage.*

Logan County.

Andross William *Bellefontaine.*
Johnson Wm.

Miami County.

Smith R. *Piqua.*
Howard—
Anderson T. *Troy.*
Clark Wm. B.

Montgomery County.

Coms Isaac, Main *Dayton.*
Clinton M., First
Davis J. J. & C., 2d
Dister Peter, N. Market
Greene John, 3d
Koch J. W.
Piner J.
Techuner Joseph, 2d
Wise J. A., 3d

Seneca County.

Scott W. A. *Tiffin.*
Wingfield John

Warren County.

Lawrence Wm. *Morrow.*
Jones James

Basket Makers.

Clinton County.

Hannon R. *Cuba.*

Geauga County.

Rodgers H. *Chardon.*
Williams L. *Troy.*

Hamilton County.

Ottignon J. P., 83 Court *Cincinnati.*
Cryer Thomas *Pleasant Ridge.*

Knox County.

Brewn George, Senr. *Democracy.*

Portage County.

Glass Mathias *Randolph.*
Springer Henry *Streetsboro'.*
Finch Solomon *Rootstown.*
Cox Wm. *Deerfield.*
Reeder Alvin *Paris.*

Williams County.

Barrens Joseph *Bryan.*
Hornett Wm.
Jones Cass *West Unity.*

Wyandot County.

Inman A. B. *Carey.*
Swarty Jacob *Upper Sandusky.*

Bathing Houses.

Franklin County.

Reichert E., High *Columbus.*

Hamilton County.

Briscoe J., 5th w. Vine *Cincinnati.*
Coleman A. B., Burnet House
Hunster A., cor. 6th & Mound
Johnson J., 6th bet. Plum & Wes. Row
Ophoff & Jackson, 137 Sycamore
Williams G., Broadway
Watson W. W., 3d bet. Main & Walnut

Union County.

Rathbun Charles *Marysville.*

Bed Pin Manufacturers.

Hamilton County.

Armstrong C. G. & W. H. *Plainville.*

Bedstead (Patent) Manufacturers.

Hamilton County.

Knoetmann J. F. & Bro., 6th bet. Sycamore & Broadway *Cincinnati.*
Boyd Henry, n. w. cor. 8th & Broadway
Clawson & Mudge, 2d bet. Vine & Race
Penny Richard H. *Harrison.*

Miami County.

Bains J. *Troy*

Mercer County.

Hight & Kirkpatrick *Celina.*

Muskingum County

Mohler & Smith *Zanesville.*

Portage County.

McElwain & Turnham　　　　*Ravenna.*
Lane Gustavus
Griffin A. B. & O. H.
Hought Z.　　　　*Sheleraville.*
Stedman Wm. & Co.　　　　*Randolph.*
Knowlton A. & T. & Co.　　　　*Franklin.*
Stedman Isaac N. & Co.　　　　*Aurora.*
Demmers John　　　　*Freedom.*
Lee E.　　　　*Nelson.*
Knapp J. & Sons　　　　*Charleston.*
Smith Danl. S.　　　　*Paris.*

Williams County.

Fulton Joseph　　　　*Bryan.*
Henry Thomas
Konepper Jeremiah
Wrea Alex.
Yates Wm.

Beef and Pork Packers and Dealers.

Brown County.

Liggett A.　　　　*Ripley.*
Wiltshire Geo.　　　　*Aberdeen.*

Butler County.

Markle John L.　　　　*Dartown.*
Sanderson John　　　　*Hamilton.*

Cuyahoga County.

Rose E. & B., 24 Ontario　　　　*Cleveland.*
Sholl William H.

Hamilton County.

Child John R., Sycamore bet. 6th & Court
　　　　Cincinnati.
Davis Wm. W., 40 Front
Davis Chas. & Co., Syc. bet. 8th & 9th
Davis John H. & Co., s. e. cor. Court & Broadway
Davis S. & Co., s. w. cor.　　　　do
Dominic Geo. & Bro., 25 & 27 Water
Evans & Swift, cor. 9th & Sycamore
Gardner, Phipps & Co., n. w. cor. 9th & Broadway
Hieatt & Gerard, B'dway bet. 9th & Court
Johnson & Pence, 9 Sycamore
Kirby Wm. & Robert, Poplar bet. John & Linn
Lewis Henry, s. e. cor. Canal & Sycamore
Laycock Wm., 23 & 25 Canal
McKeehan & Evans, cor. Sycamore & 9th
Miller & Brown, s. e. cor. Syc. & Court
Maguson Peter, cor. Canal & Sycamore
Mitchell & Flanagan, cor. Everett & Plum
Morrison & Duncan, n. w. cor. Cutter & David
Nye Henry, Broadway bet. Court & Hunt
Neff Wm., cor. Canal & Vine
Neff Wm. C., cor. Canal & Vine
Stagg Warren, e. s. Syc. bet. Court & 9th
Stagg & Shays, Court & Sycamore
Shays John & Co., Walnut near Court
Spencer —, cor. Mason & Plum
Smith, Kissane & Magill, cor. Race & Canal

Schooley John, 114 Court　　　*Cincinnati.*
Shaw John A., 4 Canal
Thomas N. W. & Co., s. w. cor. Canal & Walnut
Todd M. M. R., cor. Vine & Court
Thomas J. K., 59 Canal
Trowbridge & Beatty, s. w. cor. Race & Canal
Vonsteik —, Court
Witte H. & F., 15 & 17 e. Front
Bramble A. L.　　　　*Mount Healthy.*
Mewhinney David　　　　*Montgomery.*
Ross James J.
Stites H.　　　　*Columbia.*

Harrison County.

McFadden S. & H.　　　　*Cadiz.*
Hogg & Milligan
Paul Saml.　　　　*Green.*
Watson Joshua　　　　*Harrisville.*
Leion J. & T.　　　　*Short Creek.*

Jefferson County.

McGowan D. & Son　　　　*Steubenville*
Dohrman & Collier

Montgomery County.

Reiser Jacob　　　　*Dayton.*
Cassady M.　　　　*Miamisburg*
Deckert Samuel
Platt J. F.

Preble County.

McWhinney James　　　　*New Westville.*
McWhinney Harvey　　　　*West Florence.*

Bellows Manufacturers.

Cuyahoga County.

Smith E. T.　　　　*Dover.*
Voas & Ward, Champlain　　　*Cleveland.*

Hamilton County.

Darling Jeremiah, George bet. Smith & John　　　　*Cincinnati.*
English S. & Sons, 106 e. Columbia
Hamilton S. R., 2d bet. Broadway & Sycamore

Richland County.

Cocher C.　　　　*Mansfield.*

Belt (Riveted) Manufacturers.

Hamilton County.

Seymour Jeffery, 41 Walnut　　*Cincinnati.*
Thompson & McNail, cor. Front & Butler

Billiard Table Manufacturers.

Hamilton County.

Brunswick J. M., n. w. cor. Walnut & Canal　　　　*Cincinnati.*

Bird Dealer.

Hamilton County.

Clabe J., w. 6th　　　　*Cincinnati.*

Bird-cage Makers.

Hamilton County.
Bromwell & Melish, 181 Walnut   *Cincin.*

Bitters and Sirup Dealers.

Hamilton County.
Levi & Brothers, 215 Walnut   *Cincinnati.*

Blacking Manufacturers.

Hamilton County.
Butler & Brother, Patterson Alley bet. Main
  & Walnut   *Cincinnati.*
Titcomb R., 158 5th

Union County.
Kezartee Ira   *Marysville.*

Blacksmiths.

Adams County.
Cook George   *Eckmansville.*
Eckman William
Aldred Alfred   *Makalo*
Crumme John
Blentlinger John   *Stouts.*
Blentlinger A. J.
Freber J. T.   *Dunkinsville.*
Pettitt J.
Pemberton Silas   *Locust Grove.*
Zoll J. & J.
Hunt Levin
Beam Joseph   *Bradysville.*
Fink J. C.   *West Union.*
Patten M. S.
Santee S.
Sprinkle David   *Dumbarton.*
McNeil Peter
Phillips Lenox
Potter Enos   *Marble Furnace.*
Carter T.   *Gustine.*
Leebb G.
Palmer J   *Lovetts.*

Allen County.
Flaugher S.   *Deep Cut.*
Jones John   *West Newton.*
Owen David
Scott Abraham
Bolender S. D.   *Allen Town.*
Conrad Rufus   *Middle River.*
Evans William H.
Evans Job
Mollenhour Henry
Swisher Joseph
Ward O. F.   *Cranberry.*
Ward James   *Donnells.*
Rothe Christian   *Westminster.*

Ashland County.
Woodbury R. C.   *Sullivan.*
Chandler Hiram
Frost Isaiah   *Ruggles.*
Innis Adam

Burgan James   *Savannah.*
Marshall William
Rumfield Philip
Sponceller William
Fulkerson R. P.   *Ashland.*
Hildebrand Jacob
Jackson William
McCleland Alexander
Hootman Christopher H.   *Jeromeville.*
Rogers John P.
Danner Sylvester   *Loudonsville.*
Dill Thomas
Hannan William
Wiley John
Helbert Peter   *Mohecan.*
Zeigler H. & J.   *Perrysville.*
Nixon F. C.

Ashtabula County.
Phillips O. L.   *Richmond Centre*
Sunbury C. T.
Adams R.
Grover Luther   *Lenox.*
Fowler A.
Spencer D.   *Eagleville.*
Barnum C. P.
Remick Henry   *New Lyme.*
McLaughlin A.   *Cherry Valley.*
Belknapp & Jones   *Geneva.*
Looms S.
Swan L.
Preston D.   *Austinburg.*
Sargent J.
Bates J.
Williams D.
Spencer D.
Longley William S.
Turner Charles   *Kelloggsville.*
Peters O. S.
Moon A. F.
Johnson S. S.
Upson E. C.   *East Plymouth.*
Mann B. P.
Culver H. F. & J.   *Jefferson.*
Crocker L.
Preston Z.
Worthing S. S.   *Trumbull.*
Johnson Henry
Quirk John
Amsden Samuel   *Jefferson.*
Gillis J.
Scoville A.   *Ashtabula.*
Wilsey E. H.
Scoville George B.
Luce A. B.
Watrons Nelson
Goodall C.
Winslow Jonathan   *Hart's Grove.*
Turner John
Nevison E.
Ford P.
Lindsey M.
Johnson S. S.
Peters O.
Moon A.
Couch & Shipard
Sanford H. F.

Cone S. | *Rome.*
Cone H.
Dilden J. | *Pierpont.*
Schamlin John
Gaylord Henry
Headley Francis | *Cork.*
Miner J. T. | *Lindenville.*
Barber Reuben
Gillett L.
Morley Wm A.
Barnes W. C. | *Harpersfield.*
Phillips James B.
Wilcox D.
Phillips Jacob

Athens County.

Whitehurst J. | *Chauncey.*
Dodds C. | *Amesville.*
Patterson J.
Ross G.
Conn Wm.
Johnson Wm. | *Albany.*
Drake Dennis
Pierson Wm.
Lincoln B. A. | *Nelsonville.*
Roberts W. P.
Nelson Daniel
Abbott William | *Shad.*
Sweeney D. P.
Wilson James
Bearbout Benj. | *Canaanville.*
Cox Allison | *Lowry.*
Wilson Peter B.
Young Alexander
Young Wm.
Young John
Wolfe Samuel | *Pleasanton.*
Adams & Crippen | *Athens.*
Tedron E.
Walker J.
Drake D. | *Lee.*
Pierson Wm.
Johnson Wm.
Martin David G.
Bebout S. | *Guysville.*
English Wm. H. | *Hibardville.*

Auglaize County.

Herpst Charles | *Wapakoneta.*
Craft Joseph
Winemiller Michael
Craft George | *St. Mary's.*
Skoonover Thomas
Drees John M. | *Minster.*
Gocke Henry
Rechtin Gersh.
Schemel Th. H.
Tippie Jas. & M. B. | *Kossuth.*
Porter James W. | *St. John's.*
Leeman James
Beech Samuel

Belmont County.

Dove Pinkney | *Hendrysburgh.*
Chessell George
Wells Richard C.

Applegate Lewis & Co. | *Demos.*
Deoffenbaugh John
Jones L. C.
Embree Mordecai | *Colerain.*
Kasely John
Taylor Isaac
Evans Jesse | *Barnesville.*
Francis John
Moore Wm. R.
Garret John
Lowman Elias B. | *Bell Air.*
Reese John
Wheatley —
Barlow Perry | *Union Town.*
Bartholomew Geo.
Hirst Oliver | *Flushing.*
Kirk M. & J.
Leinard David
Pickering Jefferson
Vanmeter John
Craft J. & Wicks | *Loydsville.*
McColaster Charles
Hetherington Richard | *Dillies Bottom.*
McGrew Alexander
Wallace William
Jenkins Andrew & Sons | *Lampsville.*
Butler Joseph | *St. Clairsville.*
Hoover Jacob
Kittlewell William
Rose George
Scovern Henry
Green John | *Shepherdstown.*
Carrier A. | *Morristown.*
Davidson R.
Swany F.
Lewis Theodore | *Hunter.*
Stidd Charles
Broomhall Wm.
Carter E. P. | *Armstrong's Mills.*
Hoops Daniel | *Pilcher.*
Waters Enos
McCaffery Wm. | *Belmont.*
Jobe Samuel
Secrist Joseph
Burdett M.
Jackson S.

Brown County.

Tearsley Saml. | *Higginsport.*
Pense Joseph
Belle J. M. | *Ripley.*
Hendry J. M.
Thompson James & John | *Decatur.*
Early John | *Hamersville.*
Parlmer F. | *Newhope.*
Varley H. & J. | *Puebla.*
Mower P. | *Russellville.*
Pitzer F.
Stevens W. W.
Pearce James | *Feesburg.*
Conover Thos. S. | *De La Palma.*
Kratzer James | *Union Plane.*
Cowen & Lamonda | *Fincastle.*
Alexander John
Robbins W. M.
Dent R. | *Sardinia.*

Dunn Henry — *Sardinia.*
Shepherd D.

Butler County.

Dilley P. C. — *Bethany.*
Elliott S. R.
Akres B.
Oseby Wm.
Avey Wm. — *West Chester.*
Stephenson Joshua
Jones Paul
Middleton James — *Pisgah.*
Smith Joseph
Hercules James
McKinney George
Murphey E. & Bonaker — *Collinsville.*
Kirkpatrick John
Smith Chas. — *Dartown.*
Mee David
Grismore Adam
Cooper Nelson B.
Squier Jeremiah — *Blue Ball.*
Berry Philip — *Hamilton.*
McGreery P.
Clark, Lane & Co.
Hocheimer A.
Stevenson Wm. — *Reesville.*
Schlarb J.
Mills J.
Rife J. P.
Smoyer J.
McWitty Saml. — *Middletown.*
Sutphin J.
Hedden W.
McAdams R.
Kennedy J.
Aarons John
Roberts G. W. — *Saint Charles.*
Beaver M. — *Symmes Corner.*
Hulsbarger F.
Hulsbarger John
Carroll John
Gilleland B. F. — *Venice.*
Dancer S. J.
Demey James R. — *Monroe.*
Willes C.
Cart S. — *College Corner.*
Stark A.
Mee Isaac — *Somerville.*
Connaroe J.
Smith W. J. & Atchley
Bookwalter B. & J. — *Seven Miles.*
Nathans H.
Berk Henry — *Trenton.*
Ball D. R.
Weaber George
Smock A. F.
Vanscoyke & Weaver
Green T. B.
Stokes S. & J. — *Jacksonsburg.*
Dine A. J.
Weston J.
Milholland G. W. — *Alert.*
Rowe S. P.
Gray Jas. T. — *Riley.*
Davis Saml.
Dingfelter John

Proctor Enoch — *Contreras.*

Carroll County.

Gatchall J. & A. — *Harlem Springs.*
Graves Martin
Morrison Alexr. — *New Hagerstown.*
Kesler Philip — *New Harrisburg.*
Adams Columbus — *Scroggsfield.*
Davis William — *Norristown.*
Baxter William — *Carrollton.*
Combs & Crosier
Gould J. S.
Gould R. P.
Knox Otho — *Hickory.*
Thompson Eli & Co.
Herron Robert P. — *Ross.*
Maffet William
Marshall Alexander
Perdue R. J. — *Oneida Mills.*

Champaign County.

Widner & Shimer — *Christiansburg.*
Overton S. B.
Groves A.
Minnich G. W. — *Westville.*
Benoker Noah
Gray H. — *Urbana.*
Hurd John
McLelland J.
Stone Isaac — *Mutual.*
Wright A.
Marsh J. D. — *Woodstock.*
Smith & Stodard
Conner James
Alsted John — *Caryshill.*
Gordon Thos.
Breckles S. H. — *St. Paris.*
Shaffer Aaron — *Terre Haute.*
Ely John

Clark County.

Hardman & Akin — *Enon.*
Kock & Pottle
Arthur M. — *Selma.*
Hanniberry —
Morgan Wm. P.
Floyd Henry — *Springfield.*
McGarr J.
Roller J.
Simmons Danl.
McGorin J.
Bolan J.
Dickey R. G. — *Catawba.*
Goff H. G.
Stipes T.
Bennett James — *South Charleston.*
Nicholls E. T.
Peters Samuel J.
Sprague Charles
Coulter J. C. — *New Carlisle.*
Hatten Thomas
Long William
McLure T. J.
Landacre Lawrence
Sorter William

Clermont County.

Hulshulte Henry — *New Richmond.*

Mockabee U. C.	*New Richmond.*
Reeves Wm. K.	
ickerson & White	
ole A. B.	*Nicholsville.*
Melvin James	
McMurchy A.	
Vaughn E.	*Goshen.*
Smith E.	
Athey Thos. M.	*Felicity.*
Johnson A. & Wm.	
Hendrix E. B.	
Griffith —	*Bethel.*
Thornton O. & Co.	
Beck J. D.	
Laveny Martin	
Anderson M.	*Mt. Carmel.*
Johnson F.	
Danberry Spencer	*Batavia.*
Leonard Aaron	
Worstell Isaac	
Tice Stephen	
Larkin John W.	*Neville.*
Becket Solomon	*Amelia.*
Phillis Thomas	
Hillen John	*Withamsville.*
Jones A. B.	
Jones John W.	
Hunter George	
Kelloy Daniel	
Miller John A.	
Witham Wm. D.	
Leming & Fick	*Mulberry.*
Lever H. G.	*Miamisville.*
Beard William	*Milford.*
Coboral Thomas	
Conley John	
Lapham & Terwillager	
Howe John	*Chilo.*
Wyatt Thomas	*Mount Pisgah.*
Cushard Wm. H.	*Moscow.*
Pigman W. G. & Co.	
Dunsanson Robert	*Clover.*
Hall Alexander	*Loveland.*
Dean J. B.	*Rural.*
Perin S.	*Perin's Mills.*
Douh J. S.	*Laurel.*
Norris Wm.	
Peterson Jesse	*Bantam.*
Wilson Josiah	
Smith Robert	
Newberry Chas. H.	
Ely John L.	
Burnett Wesley	
Belts Andrew	*Newtonsville.*
Needham George	
Dudley W. C.	*West Woodville.*
Kelsey Thomas	
Blymer Solomon	*Locust Corner.*
Hall Elijah	
Williams James	

Clinton County.

Smith Jas.	*New Burlington.*
Miller H.	
Green H. M.	
Price G.	*Cuba.*
Stevenson G. H.	*Westboro.*

Brown R.	*Westboro.*
Garman H.	*Lumberton.*
Hayworth L.	*Port William.*
Hayworth M.	
Holloway D.	
Kinbrough Ira	*Sligo*
Andrew C.	
Bundy W.	*Blanchester.*
Seaman W.	
Taylor W.	
Goodwin R.	
Clelland L.	
Bowermaster F. A.	*New Antioch.*
Brown T. E.	*New Vienna.*
Dellon T.	
Dellon J.	
Southard B.	
Cox V.	
Cory J.	
Perrine E.	
Shoewalter L.	*Sabina.*
Marsh J. D.	*Martinsville.*
Vance John W.	
Templin W. S.	
Caat E. W.	
Smith Amos	
Cashatt Thos.	
Perren Elias	
Dillon John	*Wilmington,*
Whall Absalom	
Moore Thos.	

Columbiana County.

Kitzer John	*New Chambersburgh.*
Paxson Jesse	
Humphrey Joseph	*East Rochester.*
Gillingham John	*Salem.*
Hise Jesse	
Silvers Albert	
Smith William	
Dresbaugh Philip	*Bucks.*
Mc Millen —, Sr.	
Calhoun Adam	*East Liverpool.*
Detrick George	
Purington J.	
Tregor Peter	
Grosehoutz John	*St. Clair.*
Tawney John	
Norris J.	*West Point.*
Clouse Noah	*Columbiana.*
Freed Morgan	
Havel David	
Kridler Abraham	
Miller George	
Enos Woods	
Baumgardner F.	*Unity.*
Ertsinger D.	
Chandlin Peter	*East Fairfield.*
Rowland Thos.	
Woods John H.	
Douglass Andrew	*Inverness.*
March Samuel	*Cannon's Mills.*
Brown James	*Elkton.*
Crow David	
Nuzum William	
Scott David	
Hollough Wm.	*Wellsville.*

Lawrence John   *Wellsville.*
Pacy John
Adams J. & A.   *New Lisben.*
Brown George W,
Lamborn Samuel
Mann Samuel
Riest John
Shawke Jacob
Shawke Samuel
Shawke Joseph
Stackberger Frederick
Wilson Jesse
Greate John   *East Palestina*
Kriner Andrew
McCready James
Meek Matthew
Johnson David   *Salineville.*
Thompson Ralph
Graham James   *New Garden.*
Saffell James
Ashford A.   *Calcutta.*
Garwood L.
Ball Guy   *North Georgetown.*
Davis Benj.
Gorman John
Lupton Daniel
Watson & Johnson
Williams J.
Ritter John   *Franklin Square.*
Zimmerman Wm.
Coulson Mahlon   *Green Hill.*
Speakman Layton

Coshocton County.

Randels Benjamin   *Evansburgh.*
McCaskey Wm.   *Clarks.*
Loveless Alexander   *Bakersville.*
Mauk John
Bixler Robert
Swigart Anderson   *Chili.*
Todd Wm.
Ramer C. G.   *Keene.*

Crawford County.

McGuire & Bebout   *Leesville Cross Roads.*
McGuire —,
Gasser Frederick   *Poplar*
Jones Roswell
Donnenwirth Geo.   *New Washington.*
Bang Henry   *Wellerville.*
Arter Samuel   *Liberty Corners.*
Cariss John, Jr.   *Sulphur Spring.*
Magner Robert
Stern William
Bashou Elias   *Bucyrus.*
Kelley & Thomas
Kent N.
Lindsey David
Norton Jefferson
Rexroth John
Shawke Thomas
Stubbs John
Wingart Jacob
Hanan John   *De Kalb.*
Rex William

Cuyahoga County.

Aumick J.   *East Cleveland.*

Lincoln A.   *East Cleveland.*
Curtis J. H.   *Dover.*
Porter D. W.
Smith J. C.
Chase A.   *Chagrin Falls.*
Chase O.
Church H.
Brannd W. A.
Gray R.
Bissell Sherman   *Solon.*
McFee Daniel
Williams Porter
Avery E. P.   *Brecksville.*
Tyler Stephen J
Beckley Samuel   *Coe Ridge.*
Perry Harry
Matthews Thomas   *Bedford.*
Warner E. G.
Way J. L.
Baldwin H.   *Warrensville.*
Lewin William
Salsbury H.
Thayer M.
Thayer S.
Clark Silas   *Berea.*
Runnion E. T.
Dorland D.
Squin Stephen
Wemple M.   *Collamer.*
Sheehen Daniel
Rumsdale Olney
Masters E.   *Ohio City.*
Brewer William   *Euclid,*
McNeal J. & J.
Finney J.   *Newburgh.*
Knapp N.
Bennett Jacob   *Mayfield.*
Shuart William
Hanscom Alva   *Gates' Mills.*
Akers John   *North Royalton.*
Randall Y.
Clark James   *Brooklyn.*
Rudel P. & G.
Throut Peter
Buskirk Wm.   *Independence.*
Fosdick M. Q.
Fox O.
Palmer M. F.
Penhale & Gabriel, cor. Seneca & Michigan   *Cleveland.*

Darke County.

Robbins S.   *Ithica.*
Ryan M.
Shaver H.
Emerick —,   *Hillgrove.*
Thorp J.   *Port Jefferson.*
Harding James   *Tampico.*
Zecek Michael   *New Madison.*
Harter Elias
Shriver John B.
Reeves E. R.
Worley David
Miller Stephen
Throp J.   *Port Jefferson.*
Teford Geo.   *German*
Davis J. A.

Barger Jacob — *Sampson.*
Shields Isaac — *Poplar Ridge.*
Oswalt Wm. — *Greenville.*
Ormsby Saml.
Rice Jeremiah
Harris John — *Republican.*
Robinson Thos.
Reshner D. W. — *Beamsville.*
Reele Jacob
Harmon Jacob — *Poplar Ridge.*
Shields Isaac
McCollister Wm. H. — *North Star.*
McCollister James
Reader Levi C. — *Mississinewa.*

Defiance County.

Berup John — *Defiance.*
Bruner M.
Corwin J.
Garrett Thos.
Houtz M.
Stotler B.
Reisinger David S. — *Mill Dale.*
Koons F. A. — *Brunersbury.*
Dowe —,
Crowl John — *Mill Dale.*

Delaware County.

Davis Wm. — *Delaware.*
Chester Nathan
Burnes Thos.
Britton J. K.
Thompson E. R.
Kroninger J. K. — *Stratsford*
Brewmiller J.
Seegfried Benj.
Seegfried John
Harrison F. A. — *Galena.*
Scofull C. G.
Cook Stephen
Bailey D. B. — *Vans Valley.*
Ketchum John
Selanders Saml. — *Waldo.*
Brown James
Watters B. C. — *Harlem.*
Adams John — *Delaware.*
Jaycox Ephraim — *East Orange.*
Byers Geo. — *Norton.*
Smith John
Jones E. — *Padnor.*
Jones David L.
Marley John M.
Collins D.
Stanton D. B. — *Sunbury.*
Muker L. C.
Standish Wm. A. — *Unison.*

Erie County.

Kleedy Isaac — *Florence.*
Akers John J.
Dwelly George W. — *Venice.*
Dean H. & D. — *Sandusky City.*
Schwein P. & Co.
Rice C.
Loomis P. K. — *Berlinville.*
Manning B.
Young R

Sayre A. — *Bloomingville.*
Rainey James — *Furnace.*
Bradford Wm.
Willard A. L.
Standish B. — *Milan.*
McMillen H.
Terrill S.
Burt R.

Fairfield County.

Petty Anselm — *Pickerington.*
Whitsell Washington
Whitsell Philip
Smith George — *Pleasantville.*
Spitler Joel
Abright D. & Son — *West Rushville.*
Fisher Ephraim — *New Salem.*
Hupp James
Church A. — *Bremen.*
Chamberlain J. — *Rushville.*
McBride J. W.
Baker & Kealer — *Amanda.*
Spitler J.
Hunter A. & Son — *Lancaster.*
Flood J. C.
Hennick S.
Garret B.
Smith S.
Guseman —
Guseman G. & A
Doner C.
Fetters D.
Lawrence John — *Clear Creek.*
Kirkwood G.
Peters A.
Bomgardner H. — *Sugar Grove.*
Cranston Joseph
Miller F.
Coffman N. W. — *Lithopolis.*
Livelsburger Wm.
Runkle George
Zwayer O.

Fayette County.

Bostwick Adley — *Pancoastburg.*
Young James
Timmons A.
Wendell Peter — *Washington.*
Hammond Geo. — *Bloomingburg.*
McCoy A. M.
Weller & Muzer — *Washington.*
Sial George
Hartman Paul
Hurtt J.N.
Douden Thomas — *Moons.*
Arrich Jas. A.
Johnson P. P. — *Staunton.*

Franklin County.

Althouse Isaac, Front street, — *Columbus.*
Boston J. H., Rich
Cutler Robert, High
Hempsted E. R., Cherry Alley
Heintz, Kuchner & Co., Friend
Harrison Wm., High
Holts J. S., Friend
Hunt John, High

Litchford Frederick, Front *Columbus.*
Marples J., High
O'Donnell J., Front
Newman —, do
Shewry Charles, High
Tressenrider J. & Son, Broadway
Waggoner Levi, Front
Wise J., 4th
Sandusky Samuel, do
Shirey Lewis *Groveport.*
Shirey M.
Beiber & Coyert *Reynoldsburg.*
Beals George
Evans William
Rush & Banister
Ferguson & Tiler *Clintonville.*
Bechtoldt F. *Hibernia.*
Nichols A. J.
Cavendish John *Hope.*
Huff H. H.
Curry O. T. *Harrisburg.*
Piffit Isaac
Shenafelt Wm.
Berger B. G. *Central College.*
Dickey M. T.
Martin M. D.
Hoyt Stephen *Worthington.*
Martin Isaac
Martin Charles
Derr George *Canal, Winchester.*
Leidy Michael
Cannon & Williams
Kemerrer Eli
McClelland Silas
Zarbaugh Jacob
Zarbaugh Peter
Koker M. *Lockbourn.*
Sands & Alberry *Dublin.*
Fogalsang Charles
Tedewick William
Beunm Samuel *Gahanna.*
Ridenour George, Jr.
Ogden Joseph A.
Wellen John *Ovid.*

Fulton County.

Lipe J. *Elmira.*
Abbely A.
Abbely J.
Masters B.
Casler M. *Delta.*
Brown & Andrews
Nachtrich J.
Stites Isaac *Ottokee.*
Mikesell Thomas
Monroe James

Gallia County.

King Henry *Rodney.*
Atkinson Wm. R. *Adamsville.*
McCarty Oran
Long John *Pine Grove.*
Sexton John
Sims Charles W.
Sproase John
Newman H. *Raccoon Island.*
McComber W. H. H. *Ewington.*

Billings Lewis *Gallipolis.*
Gates Moses & Son
Bailey John *Patriot.*
Waddell Geo. & Bro.
Castle Isaac *Kyger.*
Lewis Halsey

Geauga County.

Foster E. D. *Munson.*
Rider Wm.
Robinson B. M.
Hayden A.
Davis W. S.
Hasen W.
Robinson L. N. *Hamden.*
Calkins J.
Sumner John H. *Thompson.*
Sumner N. G.
Cottam James
McArthur J. C.
Allen Silas
Stinson J. D.
Mailand E. B.
Moorehouse E. *Huntsburg.*
Loomis N.
Morehouse David
Clark A.
Curtiss John *Auburn.*
Peabody George
Gilson O.
Rathborn H.
Hough Lawrence *Burton.*
Conrad George *Troy.*
Tinkham A.
Gould S.
Bassett J. S.
Hollenbeck H. *Middlefield.*
Centton A. & J. *Burton.*
Mathews J. B. *Chardon.*
Bourn R. R.
Olmstead George
Foot E.
Bustin Joseph *Chester.*
Ames Mason
Wisner John
Frain Thomas
Judd E. R. *Chardon.*
Darling George
Rockefillon J. M.
Stibbins M. *Claridon.*
Stibbins Horace
Stanhope G.
Morehouse O.
Wilson W. S. *Bainbridge.*
Baldwin C. H.
Chase Wm.
Chase P.
Gilbert R. *Russell.*
Deming David *Newbury.*
Miller H.
Owen G. S.
Knapp Lewis *Parkman.*
Ensign E. B.
Glendening Wm.
Cook H. W.
Pickett Lewis
Fuller Lewis

Oook H. — *Parkman.*
Philips Wm. L.

Greene County.

Coxen Levi — *Xenia.*
Harbogast Chas.
Jones Washington
Jones G. W.
Jones William
Pottel George
Pottel David
White James
Scofield A. D.
Griner George — *Fairfield.*
Martin A.
Stive Edward — *Zimmerman.*
Cox J. B. — *Spring Valley.*
Adams John S. — *New Jasper.*
Adams James
Dean Alfred
Sitler Peter
Confarr John — *Clifton.*
Milburn J. — *Cedarville.*
Owens & Huffins
Owens J. S.
Cosler Isaac — *Byron.*
Cox S. W. — *Yellow Springs.*
Franklin Hiram
Hursh Jacob
Job D. A.
Wharton James — *Clio.*
Seamons T. J. — *Paintersville.*
Seamons Jacob
Redduck Abner
Conklin Carpenter
Thomas James
Mallow John
Andrew John
Murphy Jacob V.
Budge & Layman — *Jamestown.*
McCord James
Adams John

Guernsey County.

McCortle W. — *Cumberland.*
Ousick M.
Barton John — *Washington.*
Kirk John
Stewart Chas.
Dick Jonathan — *Londonderry.*
Madden James
Collins Jacob — *Byesville.*
Booth L. & E. — *Winchester.*
Barten Wm.
Johnson S. L.
Dutro Solimon — *New Gottingen.*
Dilley Abraham
Gleaves Joseph — *Fairview.*
Bell John
Bell James
Millburne James
Fulton Samuel A. — *Claysville.*
Neeland J.
Wagstaff & Smith — *Cambridge.*
Atkinson & Smith
Park Joseph
Zahniser M.

McConahey Robert — *Cambridge.*
Davis James
Goodie Joseph — *Kimbolton.*
Kearnes H. A.
Duncan R. M.
Snyder J. & T. — *Millersville.*
Hogue J.
Williams A.
Knowles S.
Dilley Robert — *Senecaville.*
Waller J.
Rogers B.
Buchanan J.

Hamilton County.

Bellew P., 66 Vine street, — *Cincinnati.*
Boggs Samuel, 126 Columbia
Bewman John, 65 e. 3d
Boake J., 66 Canal
Buckley Wm., cor. Hamilton Road and Brighton
Beinke J., s. w. cor. Linn & Hopkins
Beinke F., 173 Hopkins
Butter E., 585 Western Row
Crowder J., Front bet. Lawrence & Pike
Corber H., 66 Front
Caldwell James, 51 e. 2d
Daniels Peter, 524 w. 8th
Echelmeier W., 19 Hamilton Road
Fobe M., 540 Vine
Frost C., 127 Hamilton Road
Fink H., Vine, above Hamilton Road
Gilbert J.,
Grawson —, Linn bet. Richm'd & Kemble
Gessell J., 91 Hamilton Road
Hamlin & White, cor. Ludlow & Lawrence
Houseman F., cor. Hunt & Syc.
Hirst & Co., cor. Front & Freeman
Hueber C. F., Linn bet. Clark & Catherine
Heller H., Kemble bet. John & W. Row
Keppa Henry, Hunt bet. Spring & Pendleton
Krazer Joseph, 166 Hamilton Road
Lewis H., 6th bet. Butler & Pike
McDonald J., 516 e. Front
McCormick J. & Co., 142 West 3d
Magerle J., cor Walnut & Liberty
Norris J. C., 6th bet. Broadway & Sycamore
Pearson Abel, Lawson's Alley bet 4th & 5th
Purser John, 48 e. 2d
Radcliffe C., Butler bet. Congress & Front
Ryan & Wesley, Court near W. Row
Rortly John, Linn bet. Richmond & Catherine
Shore J. G., 170 Front
Simms Wm., 94 Columbia
Stephens J. L., 202 e. Front
Sanders G., 133 Congress
Stephens J., cor. Canal & Sycamore
Stoll John, 150 Court
Sibbernagle M., 60 Liberty
Schmidt C., 636 Vine
Schimmed F., 664 do
Saddler D., 114 w. 5th
Sweet B., 631 do
Tuttle John N., W. Row bet. 9th & Court
Wendt H. & T., 108 Columbia

Williams W. & D., Lock near 6th *Cincin*
Wolfington & Budke, Pearl bet. Vine & Race
Winall G. W., 62 Canal
Zout H. C., Bremen bet. 12th & 13th
Amiot F. *Pendleton.*
D ake F. K. *Fulton.*
S ac y E. *Walnut Hills.*
Wheeler Wm. H.
Wood Enos *Columbia.*
Warwick D.
Ferguson E. *Carthage.*
Hearth & Son
Shinkle & Lober
Southwell Thos.
Thomas James
Obrien Edward *Reading.*
Whitehead E.
Ashley Daul. *Cheviot.*
Granard B.
Hope Robert
Miller John M.
Toune David U. *Dunlap.*
Hearn Stephen *Dent.*
Stoughton Eli
Boyer Andrew *Dry Ridge*
Oarson E. W.
Patton Chas.
Dom P. *Mount Healthy.*
Roberson Cuthbert
Robinson W.
Smith Benjamin *New Burlington.*
Wiggins Josiah
Sampson Wm. *Montgomery.*
Bowen P. M.
Smith James
Erwin Thomas *Pleasant Ridge.*
Roosa James
Swift Thomas
Barbin Joseph *Harrison.*
Campbell W. & J.
Ross Alvin W. B.
Williams Ambrose
Eckman Jacob *Cleves.*
Lawton A. *Elizabethtown.*
Ferris Isaac *Mt. Washington.*
Mullen James
Mundell D. W.
Barnes Alvey T. *Miami.*
McCullough John G.
Canfield David *Plainville*
Compton Joseph B. *Springdale.*
Covert Richard
Tozzer William *Cummingsville.*
Williams David
Barrow Archibald *Newtown.*
Brown Thomas
Hahn Stephen
Sparks James
Jones Martin R. *Sharonville.*
Monger William
Tullis John

Hancock County.

Liter David & Co. *Van Buren.*
Shine Christian *Arlington.*
Elden J. W. *Mt. Blanchard.*
5

Pickett Wm. *Mt. Blanchard.*
Shoemaker A.
Wolford Godfrey
Ballard P *Benton Ridge,*
Ebaugh William *Ashery.*
Hollowell Charles
Boyles Hugh *McComb.*
Coleman Levi
Kooken A. B. *Canonsburg.*
Pool J. W.
Wilker Jacob
Biggs George *Finley*
Church William
Firman Edmund
George Jesse
Koons Jonas
Shipman Parker
Swap Charles

Hardin County.

Pool Wm. & J. *Kenton.*
Day, Pugh & Co.
Smith C.
Steiner John
Letson & Dehart
Cloe J. & Marshall *Roundhead.*

Harrison County

Seaquine Elijah *Cadiz,*
Slemmons Mathew G.
Quinn Thos. *Deersville.*
Steel Andrew S. *Freeport,*
Welling Wm. *New Rum ey.*
Woodburn E. S. *Germano.*
Leazine Riley *New Athens.*
Lott Henry *Short Creek.*
Croskey John *Green,*
Cox Jacob *Feed Spring.*
Eslick John

Henry County.

Sisler Peter *Florida*
Groshner Jacob
Goldenstern Wm.
Vanhorn Isaac *Napoleon.*
Mann E. & L.
Lines Henry *New Bavaria*
Giesy David *Texas.*
Harrison John

Highland County.

Wright & Hiatt *Highland,*
Woodmansee G. W. & J.
McDonald G. W.
Davis John
Jones John *Greenfield*
D pay Wm.
Chustin Wm.
Shalford Wm. & Son
Wigginton Saml.
Sanderson & Wigginton
Patterson Chas.
Baten & Saylor *Belfast Town*
McClure R.
Mathews Andrew
Swhishelm Saml
Ivon Robert
Keller W. *Dedesnville*
Bussey T. B.

Dunkinson A.　　　　　*Buford.*　| Eddy Joseph　　　　　*Greenwich.*
Ogden Sidney　　　　　　　　　| Cotant Z. B.
Riley J. L.　　　　　*Mowrytown.*　| Yarick D.　　　　　*Four Corners.*
Petory James　　　　　　　　　| Partelo & Cleveland　　*New Haven.*
Stewart John　　　　*New Merkt.*　| Mills M. & J.
Few Wm.　　　　　　　．　　| Cady & Richards　　　*Bellevue.*
Jackson Gideon　　　　　　　　| Carver D.
Burns & White　　*Sugartree Ridge.*　| Tucker John
Fisher Joseph　　*New Petersburg.*　| Owens Martin　　　*North Norwich.*
Goldsberry F.　　　　　　　　| Jenkins David
Jarnagon D. S.　　　　　　　　| Butts John　　　　　*Norwalk.*
Spolin Jacob　　　　　　　　| Pantlind C. S.
Stoneback Saml.　　　　　　　| Oneal & Flaharty
Worley Martin　　　　　　　　| Tidswell J. & Co.　　　*Fitchville,*
Lamb R.
Smith A　　　　　*Marshall.*　| **Jackson County.**
Smith & Pennyweight　　　　　| Davis John　　　　　*Oakhill,*
Ream Jacob & Co.　　*Centrefield.*　| Davis Owen
Webster Wm. P.　　*Allensburg.*　| Lewis Danl.
Saum Geo.　　　　　　　　| Webb Guilford　　　*Berlin.*
Behrr Danl.　　　　*Greenford.*　| Lyle & Miller　　　*Allensville.*
Clinker Josiah　　　　　　　　| West John W.　　*McGee's Store.*
Dubbs Henry　　　　　　　　| Hatten John　　　　*Jackson.*
Brown James　　　　*Semantha.*　| Gilland T.
Smith R.
McDaniel Wm.　　　　　　　| **Jefferson County.**
Strader S.　　　　　*Dallas*　| Springer Levi　　　*Steubenville.*
Bentley C. M.　　　　*Leesburg,*　| Huff C.
Williams David　　　　　　　| Harris & McDonald
Nevin J. R.　　　）　*Hillsboro'.*　| Heborn & Myers
　　　　　　　　　　　　| Buck & Whitacre
　　　　　　　　　　　　| Hawkins J.
Hocking County.　　　　　| Davis R.
Dalton William　　*Rock House.*　| Crawford James B.　　*Richmond.*
Braddock M. J.　　　　*Logan.*　| McGreger John
Braddock John　　　　　　　| Nickles Albert
Cook James　　　　　　　　| Cashell O. R.　　*East Springfield,*
Angle Josiah　　　　　　　　| Malin J.
Jones Giles　　　*Gibisonville.*　| Groves John　　　　*Annopolis.*
Ogle H.　　　　　　　　| McKinney E.
Rodgers John　　　　　　　| Watson James　　　*Mt. Pleasant.*
Willemin Eli　　　　　　　| Jones & Chambers
　　　　　　　　　　　　| Smith R. B.
　　　　　　　　　　　　| McClerg D.　　　　*Knoxville,*
Holmes County.　　　　　| Josephs M.
Lowe David　　　　*Holmesville.*　| Woods Saml.　*Mouth of Yellow Creek.*
Riley & Burrell　　　　　　　| Boner C.
Moore & Dowty　　　　　　　| Rolstan James E.　　*Elliotsville,*
Richardson A.　　　　*Benton.*　| Triest Valentine　　*Wintersville.*
Richardson Wm. J.　　　　　　| Linsey James
Slarack Jacob　　*Walnut Creek.*　|
Look John　　　　　　　　| **Knox County.**
Schott A.　　　　　*Winesburg.*　|
Bachtel H.　　　　　　　　| Bishop Stephen　　*Mount Vernon,*
Kingsley John　　　　　　　| Eble & Neal
Wiggins S.　　　　*Nashville.*　| Furlong M. C.
Brown F.　　　　　　　　| McCreary Lot　　　*Levering,*
Repp P.　　　　　　　　| Pierson Silas
　　　　　　　　　　　　| Madie William　　　*Lucerne,*
Huron County.　　　　　| Harry James　　*Fredericktown.*
．Fuller Lyman　　　*Steuben.*　| Huff J. R.
Cook A.　　　　　　　　| Moore George
Burk L. D.　　　　　　　| Coleman H.　　　　*Brandon,*
Furguson John　　*East Townsend,*　| Ide B. S.
Lester Wm.　　　　　　　| Ankeny Joseph　　*Ankenytown*
Oakley W.　　　　　　　| Gilbert John　　　*Monroe Mills*
Daniels & Hendrickson　*Clarksfield.*　| Parmenter S. A.
Bodwell Edwin　　　　．　　| Phillips Thomas

Bell Robert	Democracy.
Riley Levi	
Shipley James	
Jump Henry A.	North Liberty.
Lanis Jacob	.
Reach Hugh	
Ward James	
Horn Josiah	Millwood.
Lybarger Asa	
Lybarger Richard	
McMillen John	.
Mix Wm. B. & Levi	Jelloway.
Brown Samuel	
Mosteller D.	Mt. Liberty.
Swords A.	
Shell J.	

Lake County.

Burr C.	Madison.
Allen A.	
Wisner P.	
Weightman C. B.	Kirtland.
Hanson O. R.	
Simon O.	
Ives Hiram	North Perry.
Blanchard James	
Owen Geo.	
Owen H.	
Harper Orrin	
Graves J. K.	Wickliffe.
Stratten E.	Perry.
Kenny Geo.	
Rockfellow J. C.	Concord.
Wilson A.	
Stickney Jonathan	
Williams B.	
Jungle Thos.	
Hambleton B. F.	Pennsville.
Yocum Wm. S.	
Williams Enoch	
Williams Isaac	
Worrell Geo.	

Lawrence County.

Clark Geo.	Ironton.
Thomas R.	
Wait & Bush	
Perdy Wm.	Burlington.
Hedeker M.	Hanging Rock.
Arnold Drury	Russell's Place.
Journey S.	Millers.
Weekline Jacob	Waterloo.
Snell Alfred	Green's Store.
Carter J. H.	Quaker Bottom.
McGill J. W.	
Chapman Edmund	
Chapman Calvary	
Clonniger L. E.	

Licking County.

Smith Saml.	Linnville.
Switezer Jacob	
Wilson Thos.	
Beach Eli & Co.	Etna.
Ammie & Jolly	
Fluke & Bissett	Brownsville.
Burns W. F.	
Seary John	Jacksontown.

Brown Thos.	Jacksontown.
Vanhorn R. P.	
Mantonga A.	Granville.
Mantonga M.	
Linnett Chas.	
Wilson Alex.	Newark.
Tilson J.	
Jones & Darrah	
Goodwin & Line	
Ingham Wm.	
Stuart T.	
Tyhurst & Mitchell	
Williams Geo.	
Boyd N. H.	Croton.
Clark W.	
Speer J.	
Baily J.	
Houck T.	
Wilcox C.	
Cooley H.	
Snyder W.	
Nichols A.	Perryton.
Miller J.	
Brown Thos.	
Grove S. D.	Johnstown.
Clarke C. C.	
Clark Wm.	
Barnum A.	
Austin A. H.	Kirkersville.
Jones K.	
Evans N.	St. Louisville.
Greene David	
Bowlwin Wm.	

Logan County.

McMillin John	Logansville.
Reinhart George	
Rogers Isaac A.	Huntsville.
Underwood John	
Ritchey & Fowler	
McChesney Robert	New Richland.
Howe H.	East Liberty.
Pugsley J. T.	
Sprague —,	
Baker & Underwood	Rushsylvania.
Elliott Moses	
Stillwell Samuel	
Bair Isaac	Bellefontaine.
De Witt & Wood	
Emory & Bro.	
Miller A & D.	
Powers —,	
Wilson & Wright	
Bishop E. T.	Zanesfield.
Cline Elias	
Downs Daniel	
Hines Jacob	
Stimel Wm.	
Rogers & Miller	Lewistown.
Retter L.	Quincy.
Gessner C.	
Karr J.	

Lorain County.

Franklin Daniel	Rochester Depot
Litchfield B. K.	
Bearup John	Huntington

Nimox Chester   *Huntington.*
Nooney Wm.
Walts Jacob
Helm Henry   *La Grange.*
Noble Geo. W.
Paine William
Jones Allen   *Oberlin.*
Penfield T.
Clark Wm.   *Copopa.*
Gabriel J.
Hewitt J.
Snell H.
Gillet Octavus   *Brighton.*
Hastings Nathan
Basnard J. W.   *Pittsfield.*
Chaney W. J.
Whitney A. W.
Larned Curtis   *North Camden.*
Osborn Edward
Whitney Wm. E.
Hillgur J. W.   *Avon Lake.*

Lucas County.

McKennan James   *Providence.*
Dailey Robert   *Riga.*
Welch C. C.
Fletcher A.   *Lyons.*
Anderson C. B.   *Whiteford.*
Hahnon J.   *Toledo.*
Kirk Geo. V.
Waite A. B.
Wall Valentine

Madison County.

Gerard J. M.   *London.*
Jones & Atkins
Jones & Ingham
Boland —
Bettyer Francis   *Lafayette.*
Snyder Jacob
Watkins Aaron   *Midway.*
Huffman J.
Lebright Wm.   *California.*
Thomas —   *South Solon.*
Ward John H.   *West Canaan.*
Kilberry Armenas
Curry James   *West Jefferson.*
Carter Eli
Burrows James
Olney George
McNeal Jacob
Clark Alexander   *Mt. Sterling.*
Wright Benjamin   *Danville.*
Dickinson & Morgan   *Somerford.*
Fairbanks Orin   *Pleasant Valley.*

Mahoning County.

Kriner John   *Petersburgh.*
Seiter Wm.
Barnhart John
Mock Joseph
McFaden John   *Youngstown.*
Wilder P. N.
Groot Charles
Wilson Wm.
Wire S.   *New Middletown.*
Mutts Jacob.

Gutterba J.   *New Middletown*
Zook James
Price Wm.   *Coitsville*
McGechen T.
Witmer Jacob   *East Lewistown*
Metzler Christian
Roland Wm.   *Orange*
Marburger E.   *North Jackson.*
Klinginsmith S.
Snider J.
Behm Daniel   *Green Village.*
Olinker Josiah
Callahan Geo.
Shumaker John   *Frederick.*
Stevens David   *Hanna's Mills.*
Nicholls Wm. H.   *Milton.*
Nicholls T. H.
Bradley B. R.
Lybold Calvin
Plaw John   *New Springfield.*
Snoke George
Dritzler C.   *North Lima.*
Witmer David
Malsbury Isaac   *Damascoville.*
Girl Isaac   *Pottersville.*

Marion County.

Edgington S.   *Cochranton.*
Gray J.
Waters N. B.   *Prospect.*
Water Samuel
Watkins Thomas
Butts Geo.
Curby John
Clark & Brown   *Marion.*
Jones N.
Monser D.
Smith L.

Medina County.

Richards S. R.   *Leroy.*
Cotton J.
Stinson Wm.
Blakeshe E.
Stranghan C. A.   *Litchfield.*
Pfifer George
Doan E.
Smolk Thos.   *Mallet Creek.*
McIntyre Harvey
Scott O.
Hawks R. S.   *Sharon Centre.*
Warner & Bailey   *Liverpool.*
Leatherman M.   *River Styx.*
Tyler Solomon   *Wadsworth.*
Traver H.
Deiter H.
Stoller J.
Hanahoe J.
McIntyre Henry   *Abbeyville.*
Sildns Henry   *Lodi.*
Dorr Wm.
Crooks J. L.   *Hinckley.*
Forriat Geo.
Webber Geo.
Fourner J.
Hays Geo. W.   *Weymouth.*
Cushman Samuel W.

Hawks R. S.	*Sharon Centre.*	Penn Owen	*Antioch.*
Henshie & Huxley		Young Isaac	
McGentry Daniel H.	*Chatham Centre.*	Estle D.	*Sardis.*
Jameyson A.		Hustead Sanford	
Crosby Silas		Brown James	*Masterton.*
Hazzen James	*Coddingville.*	Roberts John	
Ellis G.	*Homersville.*	Smith J. R.	*Malaga.*
Miller J. A.		White & Matchett	
		Tipton John	
Meigs County.		Tipton Elihu	*Jerusalem.*
Venehiher J.	*Downington.*	King G. W. & Alfred	*Bealsville.*
Mackaels Joseph		Wolf John	*Sunfish.*
Church A.	*Silver Run.*	Dorl Wm.	
Willock A.		Litten Wm.	
McKown John	*Latert's Falls.*	Himes John	*Miltonsburgh.*
Stivers Geo.	*Pomeroy.*	Zabrey Christian	
Humphrey H. E.		Martin John	*Stafford.*
Martin Robert		Shaklee Solomon	
Schriber Peter		Hicks J. W.	
McKnight J.		Gehring Isaac	*Baresville.*
Mercer County.		**Montgomery County.**	
Frenary H.	*Celina.*	Ebert A., 5th	*Dayton.*
Kesler John	*Mercer.*	Edmond M., 3d	
Whitley C. B.	*Shane's Crossings.*	Hagan C.	
Runkles G. W.	*Recovery.*	McKey A., Jefferson	
Studor Joseph	*St. Henry's.*	Raymond Wm., 3d	
Leseny Daniel	*Fort Recovery.*	Shack Jacob	
Morningstar Jacob		Sifferman N.	
Breadlove Giles	*Montesuma.*	Brusnam D.	*Little York.*
Frank George	*Coldwater.*	Lawrence Joseph	
Runckles Joseph	*Macedon.*	Arnett & Butt	*Farmersville.*
		Kisling John	
Miami County.		Anderson & Miller	*West Baltimore.*
Layman J.	*Fletcher.*	Eckhart Samuel	*New Lebanon.*
Hill John		Riger John	
Howell J.		Compton John	*Clayton.*
Walts D.	*West Charleston.*	Hoobly Frederick	
Swindler J. H.		Kimmell J.	*Johnsville.*
Foster R. T.	*Piqua.*	Koogle J.	*Germantown.*
Mason G. C.		Boyer M.	
Quail James		Conover J.	
Coffer J.		Huff & Brigle	
Norris R. W.		Grouser & Miller	
Hardin Brook H.		Fisk Joseph	*Miamisburg.*
Yantiss & Orbison	*Troy.*	Conoon C. S.	
Gampher & Teegel		Kaufman J. B.	
Daily W.		Hinkle Henry	*Taylorsville.*
Rogers C. P.	*Casstown.*	Reed Thomas	*Vandalia.*
Ivester G.		Burnett Hezekiah	*Liberty.*
Detrick J. N.		Young Wilford	
McKee W.		Friedlein Solomon	
Lenon D.		Kindle J. B.	*Centreville.*
Kreighbann John	*West Milton.*	Reeder H. W.	
Covert & Irwin		Alexander Andrew	*Chambersburg.*
Minch David	*Pleasant Hill.*	Clunk John	
Colby Wm. A.		Ross James	
Sultzbaugh C.	*Hyattsville.*	Arnold & Gilbert	*Centre.*
Kesler P.		Hart William	
		Dietrich David	*Harshmansville.*
Monroe County.		Knisly Joseph	
Hall Thomas.	*Woodsfield.*	Ricker John	
Neal Barnet			
Rodgers Joseph		**Morgan County.**	
Smith Japheth		King G. G.	*Chester Hill.*
Huffman & Brown	*Laing's*	Patterson E.	
Jackson Aaron		Mercer Thos.	

Finloy John — *Triadelphia.*
Tanner William
Hoops Israel — *Chaneyville.*
Humphrey Isaac — *Malta.*
Wetherell Joseph
Furgason George
Vanfassen William — *Meigs Creek.*
Fouts B. F.
Townsend R.
Adams William
Cormel H.
Ellis Ira — *Pleasant Valley.*
Bullock Moses.
Craig Victor — *Meigsville.*
Brown William P.
Freeman George
Best William — *Hickerson's Cross Roads.*
Cain Walter
Dunaway John A. — *McConnelsville.*
Powell George
Lewis Valentine — *Stockport.*
Sidwell Jesse
Scott Benjamin
Hanson Reuben — *Neelysville.*

Morrow County.

Underwood Solomon — *Underwood's.*
Simmermaker George — *Iberia.*
Munday Elimus — *Merengo.*
Fluckey John — *Cardington.*
Randolph James
Cox Emanuel — *Shauk's*
Hetrig Jacob
Walker Ephraim
Spenser Isaac — *Woodview.*
Corwin Ephraim — *Pulaskiville.*
Corwin Stephen & Jackson
Craine A. — *Vail's Cross Roads.*
Stiffler Adam
Kirkpatrick George — *Corsica.*
Johnston J. C.
Olapham Thomas — *Nimmon's Cross Roads.*
McClintock J.
Twiss O. P.

Muskingum County.

Buckingham A. — *Nashport.*
Edwards D.
Conoway James — *Ostego.*
Cowden William
Dempster John P. — *Norwick.*
Rodgers A.
Conaway John — *Frazeysburg.*
Walker John
McKinney & Co. — *New Concord.*
Bell B.
Wilson R. M.
Milhollen & Co.
Dempster B. — *Duncan's Falls.*
Trimble Edwin
Muncy Levi
Keys A. R. — *Fultonham.*
McNeir F.
Stonburner J.
Bail John V. — *Shannon.*
Johnson C. — *Hopewell.*
Rudolph E. — *White Cottage.*

Keeys J. G. — *White Cottage*
Bogus H.
Gibson J. — *Stovertown*
Smart Joseph G. — *Gratiot*
Vermilion George
Morrison M. — *Chandlersville*
McKinney M.

Noble County.

Phillips Job. — *Berne.*
Wolf Solomon
Shirk Absalom A. — *Mount Ephraim.*
Ullman Peter — *Harrietsville.*
Silken John
Noble & Davison — *Sarahsville.*
Stewart William M.
Orr John — *Gardner.*
Windows Geo. — *Olive.*
Davis F.

Ottawa County.

Saltsgiber S. — *Elmore.*
Smith F. F. & Co. — *Port Clinton.*
Eichle Lewis
Clemons M. — *Marblehead.*
Beed Rock John

Perry County.

Filler Jacob — *New Lexington*
Longwell George
Smith James
Nyswander & Fisher — *Thornville.*
Rousculp & Morehead
Brown Samuel — *Rehoboth.*
Hull John
Laird James — *Mount Perry.*
Hoakerly John W. — *Sunday Creek Cross* [*Roads.*
Statlar P. P.
Coyle John — *Chapel Hill.*
Coolman George — *Somerset.*
Coolman Jacob
McKeaver James
Wilson J. P.
Green Moses — *Straitsville.*
Edington James
Boor George — *Sego.*

Pickaway County.

Hudson Benjamin — *Circleville.*
King A.
Knox William
Moody & Williamson
Moyst Moses
Price Samuel
Wilter Jacob
Adams Peter — *Tarlton.*
Lewis Vernon
Smith & Grove
Wingler G. W.
Cheatum & Allen — *Darbyville.*
Tipton Isaac
Burnley John C. — *Baskett's Store.*
Purcell Cyrus
Davis James H. — *Williamsport*
Williams Thomas
Keira John — *Camp Charlotte.*
Coffman Daniel — *Palestine.*

Matlock Nehemiah — *Palestine.*
Meeker D. — *South Bloomfield.*

Pike County.

Davey J. E. & J. P. — *Cynthiana.*
Briant Daniel
Greenfield Wm.
Tucker J. — *Jasper.*
Mitchell & Bennett — *Waverley.*
Gikler, Bunshin & Co.
Tucker John — *Jasper.*
Gall R. E. — *Beaver.*
Spangler Philip
Burgess N.
Treber John — *Byington.*
Parker Samuel
Rockwell A. — *Gibson.*
Austin Nelson
Bumgarner A.
Adams H. — *Piketon.*
Patterson Wm.
Bechamp M.
Rinefrank N.
Williams W. D. — *Omega.*

Portage County.

Stowe E. & W. — *Edinburgh.*
Godard J.
McCully John
Kelley James
Douthait Thos.
Plum George — *Streetsboro'.*
Nash John
Taylor John W. — *Aurora.*
Plum E.
Thompson L.
Norway Charles — *Shalersville.*
Skiff Ezra
Archer James — *Franklin.*
Russell Almon
Clark N. D. & Co. — *Ravenna.*
Kelley Isaac & Sons
Wells Wm. — *Randolph.*
Donald John
Hamilton Robert
Horning Andrew
Ryners John — *Atwater.*
Strong Michael
Selby B., Jr. — *Paris.*
Williams John
Knapp & Vinton — *Charleston.*
Longhead R.
Root Joseph F. — *Mantua.*
Hardie B. L.
Mitchell R. C.
Roberts Joseph C.
Plum S.
Mell Jacob — *Deerfield.*
Coller R.
Notman G.
Lewis John — *Nelson.*
McClentick M.
Messenger Alonzo
Daniels C. & L.
Wood Charles — *Rootstown.*
Burnham Daniel
Case Horace — *Palmyra.*

Tuttle George — *Palmyra.*
Davis Wm.
Williams Wm. W.
Jones O. & Orson — *Brimfield.*
Furry Henry
Atwood Joshua — *Freedom.*
Whitney Wm.
Francis James
Rials John

Preble County.

Singer Solimon — *Lewisburg.*
Kumler H. P.
Weist Andrew — *Camden.*
Carroll C.
McKinstre John
Fleming & Lockwood — *Eaton.*
Kline & Co.
Neal John
Sort John
Miller George
Bonodaile A. — *Fairhaven.*
McDanel H.
Blackford J. — *New Westville.*
Aker Daniel W.
McGriff Jas. — *Eaton.*
Ginger G. W. — *Gettysburg.*
Means J. D.
Naeff & Weaver — *Enterprise.*
Hirick Solomon
Covert S. — *Hamburg.*
Aydlotte Jonathan — *West Florence.*
Crane Wm. — *Morningsun.*
Stack Geo.
Pugh John
Wasson S. — *New Paris.*
Smith G. & T.
Oharra W.
Mikesell Geo. — *West Elkton.*
Vandiver John
Overpeck John M.
Pickett B. N.

Putnam County.

Bennett Charles — *Medary.*
Denard John — *Leipsic.*
Conn J. — *Gilboa.*
Coffill J.
Leiter A.
Oram N. F.
Coulter L. M. — *Kalida.*
Fuller O. D.
Wells J.
Burris R. & D. — *Buckeye.*
Bachtel & Shoudel
Seisker J. T.
Krown Moses — *Vaughnsville.*

Richland County.

Hiles William — *Shelby.*
Mickey H.
Slaybangh J. F.
Hissong David — *Butler.*
Miller Martin
Bushong Henry — *Shenandoah.*
Jackson William
Adams J. & Co. — *Mansfield.*
Patterson Thos. — *Lexington.*

White John — *Lexington.*
Armstrong Alfred — *Barnes.*
Barnes E. W.
Butt George
Day D. B.
Reimer Ferdinand
Jarvis Samuel — *West Windsor.*
McFleming Wm.
Beach George — *Olivesburg.*
Egner B. H.
Dunn James — *Belleville.*
High C. W.
Newlon H. — *Lucas.*
Moffett S.
Moffett & Runkle
Dickson Henry — *Adario.*
Dancer Josiah

Ross County

Donahue A. C. — *Clarksburgh.*
Gone J.
Jones John D.
Harrington H.
Lime Chas. — *Chillicothe.*
Miller J.
Gartner A. & G.
Keller John
Garsuck John
Burkline J.
Satchell Wm. W. — *South Salem.*
Hesten Henry
Moonan & McGinnis
Metzler M. — *Hallsville.*
Crites Lewis
Strawser Jacob
Day Abraham — *Gillespieville.*
Walker S. S.
Moots George
Kates J. D. — *Kingston.*
Harvey & Davis
Rinehart James
Prother Nelson — *Bourneville.*
Max Nicholas
Dikes Wm.

Sandusky County.

Nehfer A. — *Woodville.*
Bunham & Whitman
Faler J.
Wales J. G. — *Exeter.*
Granger Thos. — *Clyde.*
Perry A. G.
Cookson Israel — *Greensburg Cross Roads.*
Ickes Saml.
Waters James — *Rutland Ridge.*
Steiner Joseph
Peters Henry
Wilcox S. — *Townsend.*
Bailey Wm.
Shults Danl.
Rice Barney
Lanning S. — *Fremont.*
Myers P.
Canfield D.
Grimes Geo.
Miller Martin — *Rollersville.*
Long David

Scioto County.

Ball John — *Portsmouth.*
Burgal & Metzger
Fox David
McFarlin B. & J. J.
Schafer S.
Smith John
Wertz Wm.
Howell Jonathan — *Lyra.*
Weaver William
Copen — — *Iron Furnaces.*
Evans John
Hook Andrew
Pool Daniel
Riddlebargger Jacob
Tarington Nathan
Lucas E. — *Wheelersburgh.*
Mack Augustus — *Friendship.*
Thompson James

Seneca County.

Childs J. A. — *Attica.*
McCasley Wm.
Ringle John
Crooks & Co. — *Adrian.*
Duivil Frederick
Feathers Adam
Caldwell John B. — *Berwick.*
Henry Daniel
Pecher Daniel
Apple C. — *Bloomville.*
Estep J.
Silverwood H.
Fabing John — *Bettsville.*
Farver John
Housberger Joseph — *Tiffin.*
Jackson M.
Sebel M.
Reiley William
Rouker Joseph
Strous & Pew
Iseler John — *Bascom.*
Wagoner Jacob
Dutton Thomas — *Green Spring.*
Gorman Peter
Sharp O. B.
Hawk & Rockefellow — *West Lodi.*
Probasco John

Shelby County.

Black George — *Houston.*
Day David
Johnson & Armstrong — *Pratt.*
Hannell & Woocox
Dryden J. C. — *Sydney.*
Kingseed & Boyer
Meyer M.
McManamy James — *Dinsmore*
Wainer Joseph
Hale Samuel — *Hardin.*

Starke County.

Bilezea A. — *Louisville*
Myers R.
Myers S.
Wolfly S.
Bowers J. W. — *Lake.*

Smith R.   *Lake.*
Boop J. G.   *Minerva.*
Hoops William
Rea William
Miller Jeremiah   *West Brookfield.*
Reinehl Solomon
Capada Jacob   *Waynesburg.*
Kline John
Krumlauf Jacob
Zents John W.
Auwerter Henry   *New Franklin.*
Weyer Anthony
Barnhart & Youngblutt   *Canton.*
Beechel P.
Combs J.
Donnamiller B.
Hahn P.
Mack & Engle
Phillips G.
Brown John.   *East Greenville.*
Reichard Jacob
Stausbury Jacob
Sell Jesse   *Paris.*
Can U. R.   *New Berlin.*
Mesmer Charles
Strape Peter
Fenwick John   *Marlboro'.*
Stimmel Henry
Righter & Rakestraw   *Mount Union.*
Kemp G G.   *Magnolia.*
Creyton Abraham
Morrison John J.
Kelley William   *Mapleton.*
Lohr Jacob.
Shine Jacob
Beans Warren   *New Baltimore.*
Harper William
Mettz Emanuel
Smith Theobald   *Hartville.*
Snyder Peter P.
Kreighbom Peter
Bense George, Junr.
Gray George   *Limaville.*
Willet Richard
Clay William P.   *Massillon.*
Madison N.
Penewell F.
Richards W.
Masinheimer C.   *Mahoning.*
Miller —

Summit County.

Belden Charles   *Middlebury.*
Cotter A. L.
Myers George   *Clinton.*
Spangler Wm.
Stotlar John
Augstadt David   *Inland.*
Darious Lewis
Siess Joseph O.
Diehl Daniel   *Nimisilla.*
Kellor David
Blakeslee W. B.   *Richfield.*
Olmsted H.
Parmalee E.
Phelps Sheldon
Legget J.   *Montrose.*

Sloon Robert   *Montrose.*
Alexander R.   *Northfield.*
Cross J. D.
Tucker E.
Ranny M.   *Macedonia Depot.*
Beila S. & Cos.   *Eden.*
Sheffleton Geo.
Coffman Norris   *Copley.*
Murray Wm. D.
Null John
Mann Philip.
Dean Lester
Tubba George
Jackson William   *Bath.*
Peach Hiram
Johnson D. B.

Trumbull County.

Bennett H.   *Mecca.*
Bennett A.
Barton A. A.
Gilmore J.   *Johnsonville.*
Boon William
Wier S. J.
Woalley Frank
Barnes John R.   *Southington.*
Ripple William
Brainard Erastus   *Gustavus,*
Kinleyside David
Roberts Reuben
Darling R. C. & Bro.   *Warren.*
Earnest John
Miller Robert
Wagoner Eli   *Ohlstown.*
Will Hieronimus
Arnold A. J.
Brown W. & J.   *Newton Falls.*
Stimpson —   *Orangeville.*
Wilson Nathaniel
Lethler Samuel   *Girard,*
Rall William
Taft H. L.   *Farmington.*
Dabney Charles
Gillett Amos
Chapman Levi
Belden H. M.
Fries Sylvester
Wilder Alonzo
Miller Noah
Miller S. B.
Jackson Emerson
Spencer James   *Brookfield.*
Clark L. W.
Benner Peter
Cratsley Frederick
Messersmith Benjamin
Messersmith Abraham
Denison John S.   *Church Hill*
Robinson John
Denison Calvin
Ellet A. B.
Mansell —
Bushnell & Crayton   *Hartford*
Drewney & McMullen
Hull Osman

Tuscarawas County.

Clark & Co.   *Bolivar*

Fetters A.	*Bolivar.*	
Kirkpatrick O.	*Sandyville.*	
Rinehart George		
Clark John Y.	*Winfield.*	
Dunlap John R.		
Rease Eli	*Deardorff Mills.*	
Toomy Samuel		
Wyler Joseph		
Daugherty John	*Albany.*	
Morlan William		
Chambers J. V.	*New Cumberland.*	
Stoody David		
Demuth & Peter	*Gnadenhutten.*	
Miller Joseph M.	*Peoli.*	
Hochstettler Christian	*Ragersville.*	
Lanzer A. & Co.		
Shaffer Martin		
Blair R.	*New Philadelphia.*	
Burton R.		
Dorsey E.		
Young J.		
Raiff A.		
Korns H.		
Lindenberry A.		
Hormel C.	*Canal Dover.*	
Renkert Jacob		
Grumlich E.		
Shook F.		
Speese Geo.	*Tuscarawas.*	
Snider P.		

Union County.

Campbell Wm.	*Marysville.*
Cooder John	
Peacock Thos.	
Turner Thos.	
O'Donahoe Stephen	*Allen Centre.*
Butz Solomon	*Watkins.*
Yanties Jonas W.	*Wilkins.*
Burrows Enoch	*Milford Centre.*
Colver Standish	
Kenada Oliver	
McKeever J.	
Stranahan Wm.	
Phillips W. & C.	
Walley John	*New California.*
Butterfield John	*Pharisburg.*

Van Wert County.

Clark John W.	*Van Wert.*
Howard James	

Vinton County.

Arnold A.	*McArthur.*
Lowry Harmon	
Lottridge M. F. & Co.	
Miller & Lyle	*Allensville.*
Cannady —,	*Mount Pleasant.*
Avey Andrew	*Prattsville.*
Betts G.	*Reed's Mills.*
St. Clair J.	

Warren County.

Warwick J.	*Springboro'.*
Poebles Stephen	
Ross John	
Ross David	

Hopkins J. R	*Springboro'.*
Wright M.	
Rich John	*Twenty Mile Stand.*
Hoff Jackson	
Quimby Danl.	
Dugal John	*Oregon.*
Bursk Jacob	*Mason.*
Collins Henry	
Fox B.	
Cortleyow A.	
Bursk Danl.	
Gustin B. J.	*Red Lion.*
Veibons James M.	*Edwardsville.*
Henry Enoch	
Henry Wm.	
Mell Jacob	*Deerfield.*
Collar R.	
Craig Wm.	*Haysville.*
Leazer John & Co.	
Baker & Son	
Elsten J. L.	*Dallasburg.*
Kling Lewis	*Dunlevy.*
McComas Thos. T.	*Waynesville.*
Hartsock Levi	
Taylor G. J.	*Hopkinsville.*
Tufts S. G.	
Parker Saml.	*Morrow.*
Packer Wm.	
Stewart James	
Runyan Henry	*Butlerville.*
St. John Hiram	
Clingan Edward	*Mount Holly.*
Coffman Jacob	
Everhart John	
Randall Jesse	*Harveysburg.*
Ham Wm.	
Harris D.	
Oyler C. P.	

Washington County.

Reckard & Fawcett	*Marietta.*
Picksley Chas.	
Swift John	
Dibly Christopher	
Richards G.	
Hutchinson D.	*Harmar.*
Scott John	
Wells J.	
Gandy James	*Centre Belpré.*
Conley James C.	
Baily E.	
Davis E.	
Townsend Levi	
Zollers Abraham	*Lower Salem.*
Ewings James	
Deuchers D.	*Ostend.*
Harvy S.	
Moyers M.	
Newton Mark	*Coal Run.*
Hughey Robert	*Reynier's Mills.*
Black John	
Jack David	
Watters J.	
Cook M. G.	*Newport*
Cartwright & Gregory	
Smith John	
Gilchrist & Bell	*Bartlett*

Morrow Chas.   *Bartlett.*
Chutes Wm. B.   *Wesley.*
Fish Abner
Anderson Ira
Eaton G.   *Jolly.*
Switzer H.
Bower Moses   *Watertown.*
Wells Ira
Haines A.   *Lowell.*
Britton Josiah   *Benn.*
Lee Samuel   *North Union.*
Lee Ellis

Wayne County.

Webb Chas.   *Dalton.*
Keller Saml.
Tanner A
Cox Eli
Lawrence D.   *Edinburgh.*
Woodruff A.
Knox A. & D.   *Fredericksburg.*
Porter H.
Hurly T.
Mowry Wm.   *Reedsburg.*
Starn Mathias
Overholt & Shannon   *New Prospect.*
Berkey Jacob
Plum Geo.
Grimes Isaac   *Burbank.*
Feasel Silas
Shibler Joseph   *Smithville.*
Hunchherger Jacob
Mellinger Geo.
Iugram & Pinkley
Secrist John
Bair Danl. W.   *East Union.*
Bohney John
Shultz Nicolas
Nogel John   *West Lebanon.*
Baird John   *Number One.*
Fink John
Parmenter W.   *Old Hickory.*
Robison John   *Shreve.*
Castle Henry
Darrah Levi
Huffman C.
Looter Danl.   *Marshallsville.*
Winegardner Conrad
Beck Joseph

Williams County.

Arnold George   *Bryan.*
Arnold Henry
Clampit John   *Pulaski.*
Crowl John   *West Unity.*
Garrison Wm.   *Bryan.*
Sheridan Wm.
Thompson John S.
Iler Danl   *Montpelier.*
Landeman & Gleason   *Pulaski.*
Sheffler Benj.
Pifer George   *West Unity.*
Richardson J. H.
Stoner Henry   *Montpelier.*
Wanemacher W.   *Williams Centre.*
Yocum J.

Wood County.

Cranker Peter   *Perrysburg.*
Myers B. F.
Riser Nicholas
Troy & Woods   *Bowling Green.*
Wolker John
Droke John
Womer Elliott   *Weston.*
Skinner John
Rico Wm.
West B.   *Portage.*
Morris John W.   *Gilead.*
Sterling Thos. J.
Brakeman Hiram   *Montgomery Cross Roads.*
Dimmock R.
Brooks Chas. & Bro.

Wyandot County.

Gruble George   *McCutchensville.*
Augustine Isaac
Freet Saml.
Freet James H.   *Tymoctee.*
Lytle H. D.   *Carey.*
Shaw Cornelius   *Crawfordsville.*
Pool Harris   *Upper Sandusky.*
Trager & Cover
Wooley C. V. D.   *Little Sandusky.*
Basom D. F.   *Sycamore.*
Hiteshew L.
Gaunter & Murphey   *Mexico.*
White Jesse
Eaton & Harroh   *Marseilles.*
Stover J. M.

Blank Book Manufacturers.

Cuyahoga County.

Cobb J. B. & Co., 46 Superior street   *Cleveland.*
Sanford A. S., 17   do

Franklin County.

Lilley M. C., High street   *Columbus.*
Riley Joseph H. & Co., do
Scott & Bascon, cor. do & Pearl

Hamilton County.

Cropper C., 23 e. 3d   *Cincinnati.*
Applegate & Co., 43 Main
Ernst Jacob, 112   do
Tumy J. C. & H. L., 43 do
Moore, Anderson, Wilstach & Keys, n. e. cor. 4th & Main
Morgan E. & Co., 111 Main

Jefferson County.

Jewett Wm. T.   *Steubenville.*
McDowell S. W.

Muskingum County.

Hopkins T. C. & Co.,   *Zanesville*

Scioto County.

Stephenson J. & Co.,   *Portsmouth.*

Bleachers & Pressers of Hats and Bonnets.

Columbiana County.

Alford Abby   *New Lisbon.*
Dutch Hannah
Miller M A.
Northcroft —
Russell & Hamilton Misses
Starr Sarah
Watson Mrs.

Defiance County.

Cole Mrs. E. E.   *Defiance.*
Richardson Mrs. E. M.

Hamilton County.

Rapp Z., 599 Main street,   *Cincinnati.*
Winter T., 268 do
Weston S., 231 Race
Millson J., 164 w. 6th
Slocum A. R., 29 w. 7th
Millson J., 212 Vine
Diamond T., 133 Western Row
Kunk G. H., Linn bet. Clark & Hopkins
Bice Mrs., 7th bet. Baymiller & Freeman

Boarding Houses.

Belmont County.

Ramage Mrs.   *St. Clairsville.*

Butler County.

Rendall Stephen   *Dartown.*
Egan L.   *Hamilton.*
Potter Mary   *Middletown.*

Clark County.

Kelly M.   *Springfield.*
Murat F.
Dalie M.

Clermont County.

Mochabee M. C.   *New Richmond.*

Columbiana County.

Campbell Alexander   *Wellsville.*
Lawrence Joseph

Crawford County.

Crabb Misses   *Bucyrus.*

Defiance County

Cheney Mrs. A.   *Defiance*

Erie County.

Murphey Peter   *Sandusky City.*
Hall Wm.
Magle G.
Shelp Joseph
Sullivan M.
Hertel J.
Kernan Patrick
Ward P.

Franklin County.

Cook Mrs., Town street,   *Columbus.*
Daymade Wm., Broadway

Gibbons N., High   *Columbus*
Griffith J. B , do
Hyke W. H., Broadway
Low Mrs. Mary, Sugar Alley
Nelson F., High
Rawson —, Friend
Smith N. W., High

Hamilton County.

Alpha Dr. H., 123 w. 5th street,   *Cincin.*
Arnetz Peter, 92 Court
Arnold Wm., s. e. cor. 9th & Walnut
Braecker F., 5th bet. Walnut & Vine
Buche F., 24 Front
Bromley Thos., 203 w. 5th
Buckley F., 265 Western Row
Baur C., 29 w. Front
Castner J., 337 Elm
Carding J., cor. Vine & Walnut
Coleman Mrs., 201 w. 5th
Carter Mrs.,   do
Carr Michael, Landing bet. Main & Wal.
Curry J.,   do
Devitt P., 49 5th
Davenport B., 129 w. 5th
Deveny J., 105 5th
Drescher Charles, Court bet Walnut & Vine
Dunham Mrs., 144 5th
Davit J. B., Landing bet. Main & Walnut
Ehrenfried H., 185 Vine
Freeley James, Landing bet. Wal. & Vine
Fullerton L., 99 n. 2d
Furguson Mrs., 103 do
Gavin M. 59 Water
Gibson J., Landing bet. Main & Walnut
Hammer L., 90 Court
Howard John, 204 5th
Henry James, 52 Water
Johnster Mrs., 411 Race
Jones A., 107 w. 5th
Jones Mrs., 128 5th
Kerr Mrs., 109 w. 5th
King S , 235 6th
Kelley J., 591 Western Row
Knussman M., 160 Hamilton Road
Keown J., 22 Water
Killkenny A., Landing bet. Wal. & Vine
Love Mrs. J., 141 Longworth
Layton Thos., Fulton
Lennangham P., 65 Water
Longshore A., cor. Walnut & Water
Long John, cor.   do   & Landing
Lewis Mrs. E., 5 7th
Linch Mrs. A., 152 Longworth
Mabis C , 61 Court
Mapes J. M., 322 Western Row
Mehan E., 292   do
Martin John, Walnut bet. 5th & 6th
McCollough Mrs., Fulton
McDonald —, 15 Water
McShea H., Landing bet. Walnut & Vine
Murphey John, 24 Sycamore
Nimagern P., 27 Cassily's Row
Pearson M. B., 63 Court
Ryan Mrs. B. A., 138 Longworth
Ryland W. T., 90 Sycamore
Schwegman J., Sycamore near Front

Smith H., 55 w. Front street, *Cincinnati.*
Shaley Mrs., 68 do
Swan Mrs. J. A., 123 w. 5th
Sashton Mrs E., 215 Elm
Shornberger Mrs., 171 5th
Tangerman F., Landing bet. Wal. & Vine
Thompson J , 22 Sycamore
Turner Mrs. J., 27 Longworth
Watson S., 55 Sycamore
Wesselling W. & Co., cor. Vine & Water
Woodington Mrs., 105 n. 2d

Harrison County.
Mc Cue Thos. *Cadis.*

Jefferson County.
Russell Mrs. *Steubenville.*
Abercrombie Mrs. E.

Mercer County.
Allen G. W. *Celina.*
Prouty Simon

Montgomery County.
Beckman M., 2d *Dayton.*
Edelman J. A., N. Market
Shubert A., 2d
Symes Mrs., do

Portage County.
Taylor S. A. *Ravenna.*
Sheffield J. W.
Seffingwell —
Adams Hiram
Freeman S. R.

Seneca County.
Noonan J. F. *Tiffin.*

Boat Builders.

Athens County.
Burgess A. M. *Nelsonville.*

Brown County.
Crosby J. & Son *Ripley.*

Clermont County.
Guinn Wm. & Bros. *Moscow.*

Cuyahoga County.
Locklin B. B. *Ohio City.*
Vaughn J. M.

Franklin County.
Watson Jonathan *Groveport.*

Gallia County.
Coffman James M. *Raccoon Island.*
Morton Henry

Hamilton County.
Westover & Co., Landing *Cincinnati.*
Gunninger J. do
Kiersted Green, bet. Ludlow & Lawrence.
Lithurbury John, *Fulton.*
Hambleton S. F.

Hocking County.
Montgomery William *Logan.*

Lucas County.
Johnson Samuel *Maumee City*
Pitt & Sprangler
Warford M. F.
Ludwing Isaac *Providence.*
Straight George W. *Manhatten.*

Miami County.
Heagan P. *Piqua.*

Monroe County.
Hurd William T. *Sunfish.*
Maseny Lewis *Baresville.*

Morgan County.
Bell J. R. *McConnelsville.*
Chendle E. H.

Muskingum County.
Brown & Jones *Putnam.*
Manly James G.

Pike County.
Spinger J. P. *Waverly.*

Summit County.
Barnhart & Fayerweather *Boston.*

Tuscarawas County.
Cahill Clement *Canal Dover.*
Lock Joshua

Wood County.
Jenenson Chas V. *Perrysburg.*
Purvis Thos. J.

Boiler Makers.

Columbiana County.
McCollister T. & J. Williams *Wellsville.*

Cuyahoga County.
Morris H. C , River St. *Cleveland*
Frankland J. & Co., Front

Franklin County.
Ambos & Lennox *National Bridge [Columbus.*
Boyler Peter

Hamilton County.
McLean Washington & Co., Congress e.
 of Ludlow *Cincinnati.*
McLean & Shaddinger, cor. Ludlow &
 Congress
West & Dumont, Pike bet. Congress &
 Front
Hirschaler P. & Co., 151 Front

Book Binders.

Clark County.
Smith J. D. *Springfield*

Cuyahoga County.
Ingham W. A. *Ohio City*

Sandford A. S., 17 Superior   *Cleveland.*

Erie County.

Miller J.   *Sandusky City.*
Kies L.

Franklin County.

Lilley M. C., High   *Columbus.*
Riley Joseph H. & Co.
Smith & Cox, cor. Pearl & State
Scott & Bascom, cor. Pearl & High

Greene County.

Harris Francis   *Xenia.*

Hamilton County.

Bardes L. C., 169 Main   *Cincinnati.*
Baker & Donnington, 271 W. Row
Cropper C., 23 e. 3d
De Forrest, — 3d bet. Walnut & Vine
Ernst Jacob, 112 Main
Hincles A. J., 27 w. 2d
Hayman —, Main bet. 8th & 9th
Kreuzburger & Co., Main bet. 12th & 13th
Morgan E. & Co., 111 Main
McCormick James, W. Row bet. 8th & Kemble
Moore, Anderson, Wilstach & Keys, n. e. cor. 4th & Main
Pfefer —, Main bet. Court & Canal
Smith Wm. B. & Co., 58 Main
Smith & Fairman, 141 Main, up stairs
James —, Walnut bet. 4th & 5th
Turner Saml B., 115   Main
Tumy J. C. & H. L., 43   do

Hocking County.

Anderson William   *Gibisonville.*

Huron County.

McArdle J. P.   *Norwalk.*
Newman & Rose

Jefferson County.

Jewett Wm. T.   *Steubenville.*
McDowell S. W.

Mahoning County.

Frithey Chas.   *Canfield.*

Miami County.

Lummerville F.   *Troy.*

Montgomery County.

Odell J. W., Main   *Dayton.*

Muskingum County.

Hopkins T. C. & Co.   *Zanesville.*
Cox H. J. & Co.
Elliott H.

Richland County.

Ide D. M.   *Mansfield.*
Tichnor B. C. & Co.

Scioto County.

Stephenson J. & Co.   *Portsmouth.*

Seneca County.

Wolf William   *Tiffin.*

Starke County.

Tittle J.   *Canton.*

Washington County.

Williams J. M.   *Marietta.*
Crawford & Co.

Booksellers & Publishers.

Cuyahoga County.

Jewett, Proctor & Worthington, 138 Superior   *Cleveland.*
Knight E. G. & Co., 59 Superior

Hamilton County.

Applegate & Co., 43 Main   *Cincinnati.*
Baker & Donnington, 271 W. Row
Derby H. W. & Co., 145 Main
Crittenden W. L., agent, 305 Walnut, office Christian Publication Society
Ernst Jacob, 112 Main
Hart J. & Co., 41 & 43 Columbia
Harding N. S. & Co., 131 Main
James J. A. & U. P., 169 & 170 Walnut
Methodist Book Concern, s. e. cor. Main & 8th.
E. Morgan & Co., 111 Main
Onken Otto, 6th bet. Vine & Race
Smith W. B. & Co., 56 & 58 Main
Truman & Spofford, 111   do
Ward & Taylor, 10 e. 4th

Booksellers & Stationers.

Ashland County.

Potter H. H.   *Ashland.*

Ashtabula County.

Spring R.   *Geneva.*
Allen Wm. R.   *Jefferson.*

Belmont County.

Cressinger S.   *Saint Clairsville.*
Williams John H.

Champaign County.

French E. & Co.   *Urbana.*

Clark County.

Wright A. R.   *Springfield.*
Black Robert

Clinton County.

Antrum Joseph   *Wilmington*

Columbiana County.

Graham David P.   *New Lisbon.*
McMillen Joel   *Salem.*
Trescott J. & Co.

Crawford County.

Failor Joseph   *Bucyrus.*

Cuyahoga County.

Baer & Cotter, 168 Superior   *Cleveland*
Cobb J. B. & Co., 46   do
Jewett, Proctor & Worthington, 138 Supa.
Knight E. G. & Co., 59 Superior
Kramer H. & Co., 38   do

Merrill E. H., 21 Prospect   *Cleveland.*
Parsons C. H., Forest City Block
Sanford A. S., 17 Superior
Tooker & Gatchell, 102 do
Ingham W. A., cor. Det't & P'rl   *Ohio City.*

Defiance County.

Allen O. H.   *Defiance.*

Erie County.

Derby C. L.   *Sandusky City.*
Remele & Russ

Fairfield County.

Connel B.   *Lancaster.*
Searls John
Scott H.

Fayette County.

Millikan Richard   *Washington.*

Franklin County.

Burr & Randall, High   *Columbus.*
Riley Joseph H. & Co., High
Sykes J.,   do
Pearson H. B.,   do
Scott & Bascom, cor. High & Pearl

Geauga County.

Smith & Woodard   *Chardon.*

Greene County.

Barr David   *Xenia.*
Harris & Co.

Guernsey County.

Moss J. R.   *Antrim.*
Hyatt & Atkins   *Cambridge.*

Hamilton County.

Adams Eli, 7 w, Fourth   *Cincinnati.*
Applegate & Co., 43 Main
Bradley C. F. & Co., 147 Main
Bly F., 160 Vine
Buehler Edward, 129 w. 5th
Bailey Frederick, W. Row bet. 5th & 6th .
Derby H. W. & Co., 145 Main
Dennis L., 5th bet. Smith & Park
Ernst Jacob, 112 Main
Eggers J. & Wilde, 317 Main
Eggers & Co., 21 w. 4th
Edwards & Goshorn, 130 Main
Garret G., 277   do
Harding N. S. & Co., 131   do
Harpham S., 254 W. Row
Hartwell W. D., 192 5th
James & Co., 115 Main
Kile G. W., 69 6th
Lyon & Patterson, 46 6th
Mahoney John B., 167 Sycamore
Moore, Anderson, Wilstach & Keys, 28 4th
Mendenhall E., Walnut bet. 4th & 5th
McArthur A., 364 W. Row
McCormick James,   do bet. 8th & Kemble
O'Hea John, 311 W. Row
Ouken Otto, 6th bet. Vine & Race
Phillips H. Clime, 11 Broadway
Pearson H. & Co., 17 e. 4th

Pease S. W., 28 6th   *Cincinnati*
Perry & Benson, cor. 3d & Main
Richter Theodore, 556 Vine
Smith W. B. & Co., 58 Main
Thorpe John D., 74 w. 4th
Theobald & Theurkauf, 41 Court
Titcomb R , 158 w. 5th
Truman & Spofford, 111 Main
Watson & Sargeant, 169   do
Fuller Edgar E.   *Harrison.*

Hancock County.

McKee & Spear   *Finley.*

Hardin County.

Ashton E. & C.   *Kenton.*

Harrison County.

Beall John   *Cadiz.*
McCollough Wm.   *Deersville.*

Highland County.

Bowles John   *Hillsboro'.*

Huron County.

Beers J. M.   *Steuben.*
Newman C. E.   *Norwalk.*
Crosby J. M.

Jefferson County.

McDowell S. W.   *Steubenville.*
Slack J. R. & Co.

Knox County.

Cunningham Wm. M.   *Mt. Vernon.*

Lake County.

Holmes S. W.   *Painesville.*
Bartlett C. S.

Lawrence County.

Hanssche J. G.   *Ironton.*

Licking County.

Sanford E.   *Newark.*

Logan County.

Wilson C. R.   *West Liberty.*
Hartley & Bro.   *Bellefontaine.*
More L. G.

Lorain County.

Fitch James M.   *Oberlin.*
Plumb Wm. H.
Parsons C. H.   *Elyria.*

Lucas County.

Holt C. P.   *Maumee City.*
Nye & Johnson   *Toledo.*

Mahoning County.

Parker Rufus   *Poland.*

Marion County.

Allen C. & Son   *Marion.*

Miami County.

Kyle Barton   *Troy.*

Montgomery County.

Bomberger & Co., 2d street,   *Dayton.*
Claflin L. F. & Co., 3d
Ellis Erastus, Main
Osborn D.,   do
Paine Edward, do

Morrow County.

Emery S. L.   *Lincoln.*

Muskingum County.

Fracker D. S.,   *Zanesville.*
Reed W. W. & Sons
Fletcher A.
Perley A. W. & Co.

Pickaway County,

Barclay H.   *Circleville.*

Portage County.

Hall L. W.   *Ravenna.*
Little Benjamin

Preble County.

Campbell John V.   *Eaton.*
Ellis, Mitchell & Co.

Richland County.

McMillen J. F. & Co.   *Shelby.*
Tichnor B. C. & Co.   *Mansfield.*
Dubois A. C. & Sons   *Plymouth.*

Ross County.

Whitmore & Saxton   *Chilicothe.*
Jones E.

Scioto County.

Keys & Parker   *Portsmouth.*
Stephenson J. & Co.

Seneca County

Converse & Kenower   *Tiffin.*
Newman & Gross.

Starke County.

Fast J. J. & Son   *Canton.*
McCall R. H.
Sterrhoff P.
Bacon D. W. C.   *Massilion.*
Busher William

Summit County.

Bender J. L.   *Inland.*
Beebe & Elkins   *Akron.*
Laurie & Barnan

Trumbull County.

Adams George   *Warren.*
Brown J. F.
Porter Wm. N.

Tuscarawas County.

Hazlett W. L.   *New Philadelphia.*
Mathews E. P.

Wayne County.

Howard Geo.   *Wooster.*
Baumgardner J. H. & Co.
Zimmerman & Co.

Wyandot County.

Weisz Darius   *Upper Sandusky.*

Book Trade Sales,

(CONDUCTORS OF).

Hamilton County.

Hayden & Hubbard, s. e. cor. Walnut
& 5th   *Cincinnati.*

Bolting Cloths,

(DEALERS IN).

Hamilton County.

Burrows J. H. & Co., 27 w. Front st. *Cin*
Cochran Robert, 41 Walnut
Bradford T. & Co., 59 & 64 do

Boot & Shoe Dealers.

(WHOLESALE & RETAIL.)

Belmont County,

Mitchell Henry   *St. Clairsville.*
Ryan R. B.

Clinton County.

Akin John B.   *Clarksville*

Cuyahoga County.

Black John, 54 Superior   *Cleveland.*
Brew Wm , 98   do
Bratenahl & Brothers, Vineyard & Block
Crittenden J H. & Co., 9 Superior
Cook W. P. & Co., Water near Main
Gerlach J., 72 River
Gross L., 131 Superior
Hopper John, 24 Ontario
Lindsley C H., 111 Superior
Masury, Dole & Co., 68
McGuire P. F., 17 Ontario
Ogram & Lord, 136 Superior
Ranney Sylvester, 81
Seaman & Smith, 84
Seymour & Orowell, 39 Bank
Seymour C. W. & Co., 107 Superior
Snider A., 102 River
Tuttle E. M., 7 Seneca
Wolke H., 1 Clothier's Block
Whitley George, cor. Superior & Seneca
Simonds D. H., 24 Ontario
Sexton C. C., 4 Columbus Block
Eggleston & McFarland   *Chagrin Falls.*
Pratt & Waldron
Robinson J.
Saunders David   *Ohio City.*
Meid Thomas S.

Fairfield County.

Work, Son & Work   *Lancaster.*
Reed Robert
Robinson & Trout

Fayette County.

Backenstoe & Robinson   *Washington*

Franklin County.

Constans J. W., High street, *Columbus.*
Crawford J., do
Fay, Cyrus & Son, do
Kelton, Bancroft & Co., do
Kimball H. H., do
Richards Wm. & Co., do
Stanton S. B., do
Van Slyke L. G., do
Wetmore P. M., do
Wick Andrew, do

Hamilton County.

Cheney J. S., 7 Pearl street, *Cincinnati.*
Comstock, Wilcox & Co., 14 & 16 do
Evans W. F., 13 Lower Market
Gates John, 54 Pearl
Hopper M. S., 24 Lower Market
Hart Wm. & Co., 49 & 51 Pearl
Johnson, Prichard & Co., 32 do
Neff, Ambrose W. & Co., 65 do
Reeves, Stephens & Co., 126 Main
Robbins & Pomeroy, 71 do
Simpkinson H., 5 Lower Market
Simpkinson J. & A., 25 do
Sharp Thos. & Co., 10 do
Thorne W. F., 74 do

Hancock County.

Glanner John *Finley.*
Pray William K.

Highland County.

Pike N. M. *Greenfield.*
Merchant & Hays
Haslam James *Mowrytown.*

Huron County.

Ells A. G. & Co. *Fitchville.*

Jefferson County.

Troth & Scott *Steubenville.*
Bailie W. L.
Barrett Wm. H.
Halsted R. H.

Knox County

Miller T. E. & Co. *Mount Vernon.*
Smith Walter
Hammond G. A. *Fredericktown.*
Lane William

Licking County.

Reynolds S. J. & Co. *Newark.*
King & Weaver

Medina County.

Overheur Joseph *River Styx.*

Meigs County.

Smith H. B. & Brother *Pomeroy.*

Monroe County.

Ferrier David *Sunfish.*

Morgan County.

Devol & Corner *McConnelsville.*
Howard & Stone
6

Muskingum County.

Troutman Benj. *Otsego.*
Bradford A.
Day James *Norwich.*
Aplin E. A.
Harder C. R. *Putnam.*
Shaw & Russell *White Cottage.*
Mann & Cochran *Zanesville.*
Rogers H.
Thompson J. M.
Lyon C. W.
Filley M. B.

Pike County.

Dunham B. C. & Co. *Piketon.*
Ware D.
Hempstead H. & Son

Preble County.

Graves M. *New Paris.*
Crampton J. C.

Ross County.

Wilson N. *Chillicothe.*
Hand S. O.
McDougal T. & Co.
Jack Jacob *Kingston.*

Scioto County.

Bell R. & Co. *Portsmouth.*
Kehoe M. & Son
Lloyd & Gharky
Lloyd R. & Co.

Trumbull County.

Cranage W. & B. *Warren.*
McConnell James & Co.
Johnson William *Girard;*
Gaylord William *Newton Falls.*
Sampson A. J.
Bachelor S.

Warren County.

Hale W. H. *Waynesville.*

Wayne County.

Petrick J. J. N. *Fredericksburg.*

Boot & Shoe Manufacturers.

Adams County.

Lang A. M. *Manchester.*
Couly P. T.
Beard W. B. *Stouts;*
Tarleton W. *Locust Grove.*
Lannum D.
Tener Samuel
Miller William *Eckmansville.*
Wittenmere Jackson
Mathias James *Dunbarton.*
Upp H.
Burwell N. *West Union.*
McConnel Alexander
Shelton Robert *Bradysville.*

Allen County

Harper James *Lima.*
Penton John

Railing Isaac ... *Lima.*
Wall Hudson
Welch William *Deep Cut.*
Wicks J.
Carr D. *Allentown.*
Morris J.

Ashland County.

France H. *Roweburg.*
Danniels Samuel *Ruggles.*
Harney James
Brant H. *Hayesville.*
Fox D.
Krabill H.
Bailey Eli *Savannah.*
Harris Eliphalet
Kirkland Henry W.
McDonald Jonathan
Lutterbaugh John *Ashland.*
Oswalt Levi
Wasson William
Wasson & Stubbs
Robb O. & V. *Jeromeville.*
Williams J. M.
Doerrer J. F. *Loudonville.*
Steiber Adam
Coulter T. W. *Perrysville.*
Gharst William *Mohecan.*

Ashtabula County.

Gaskill B. & J. *Richmond Centre*
Warren A. & Co. *Eagleville.*
Randolph Wm. *Cherry Valley.*
Clark S.
French J. V. A. *Geneva.*
Turner J. N.
Knapp J. L.
Knapp L.
Palmer J. *Austinburg.*
Cushman E. E
Merrill A. O.
Cushman L.
Baker F.
Pierce J. B.
Pierce F. B.
Leonard O.
Rockwell J. W. *East Plymouth.*
Rose S. M. *Jefferson.*
Moyer S.
Young D.
Marsh John S.
Lucas John S.
Wood Charles
Curtis H. *Trumbull.*
Marwin J.
Marwin Geo.
Skillicorn — *Ashtabula.*
Nutall J.
Smith Geo. B.
Sykes F. W.
Hills E
Chase M. & Son *Hart's Grove.*
Sanborn T.
Cook S. M.
Burlingham C. M. *West Williamsfield*
Woodworth O.
Scott G. *Rome.*
Miller T.

Stevens Ira & Co. *Pierpont*
Scoville D. & Co.
Neeley James *Cork*

Athens County.

Edwards W. M. *Chauncey*
Picket W.
Larry T. *.*
Atkin S.
Wedge A. C. *Coolville.*
Chester & Woodworth *Millfield.*
Guinn J. *Amesville.*
Sullivan G. W.
Lindsey W. C. *Albany.*
Banks Wm.
Brown John M. *Nelsonville.*
Owen William
Chalker G. W. *Canaanville.*
Menser John
Dowler Richard
Norris Joseph
Nichols Wm. *Lowry.*
Bobo Thos.
Gennard Moses
Gudgen H. D. *Pleasanton.*
Davis J. *Athens.*
Davis George
Peters G & J.
Banks Wm. *Lee.*
Lindsey Wm. C.
Jewell Wm. *Guysville.*
Heath L.
Chalker G. W.

Auglaize County.

Sifert J. M. *Wapakoneta.*
Roth A.
Buckle A.
Crozier J *St. Mary's*
Haverbeck Anthony *Minster.*
Hus Theodore
Knostman Henry
Ripploh Henry
Schuhmacher Anthony
Vallo Henry
Vagedes Anthony
Idner Jacob *Kossuth.*
Miller Daniel *St. John's.*

Belmont County.

Bumgarner Harvey *Uniontown.*
Bethel George C. *Flushing.*
Smith John B.
Walker Richard
Widdoes John
Vanlaw George *Loydsville.*
Craig Patrick *Dillies Bottom.*
Duvall D. H.
Cutchall Henry
McGuire Ebenezer
Verbeck Jacob
Chyland H. M. B. *St. Clairsville.*
Jones Wilmeth
Metcalf E.
Mitchell Henry
Patton George
Young Thomas

Griffith M. B. — *Shephardstown.*
Hallowell Jeremiah
Foster T. — *Morristown.*
Foster J.
Lynch R.
Miller O. — *Sewellsville.*
Oliver Thomas
Palmer William
Tracy G.
Tracy T.
Green William H. — *Belmont.*
Hedge A.
Mayhew A.
Biles F. — *Armstrong's Mills.*
Brewer Howard
McFarland Elias — *Hunter.*
Hicks Abel
Heaney Robert — *Hendrysburgh.*
Ralston Robert
Mayhugh Lloyd — *Demos.*
McGuire Joseph
Stonebraker Ephraim
McCoy J. D. — *Martin's Ferry.*
Henning Wm. — *Barnesville.*
McGill John
Reed William
Reed John
Uncles F. E.
Jacobs John N. — *Bell Air.*
Westlake Benjamin
Westlake Daniel
Westlake George

Brown County.

Roth Peter — *Higginsport.*
Molier Peter
Thompson James — *Ripley.*
Herzog Jacob
Hensel A.
Williams J. & Co.
Jolley S.
Thompson Solomon — *Decatur.*
Campbell James
Reed C. W. — *Georgetown.*
Jones S. M.
Slayton W. — *Newhope.*
Mitchell & Sharp — *Aberdeen.*
Prine H. & Son — *Russelville.*
Yates W. T. — *Feesburg.*
Swope Wm.
Upp Geo. W. — *Fincastle.*
Talley Timothy — *Fine Mile.*
Rainey J. R. — *Sardinia.*
Scott G.
Delwitter J.

Butler County.

Prewitt Wm. — *Bethany.*
Gress C. W.
Perrine Henry — *Westchester.*
Darr Hiram — *Dartown.*
Haenrick Jacob
Meil Jacob E. — *Blue Ball.*
Stern J. M. — *Oxford.*
Brooks D.
Johnson W. H.
Ellis J.

Rider H. F. — *Hamilton.*
Griesel D.
Onler P.
Wiley Peter
Fisher A.
Menche G.
Kehler J.
Schevenh J.
O Conner James
Beck Daniel — *Rossville.*
Meyer E.
Sell M. F.
Emely G. W. — *Middletown.*
Sheal J.
White J.
Greenlee & Goodwin — *St. Charles.*
Shuler F. — *Symmes' Corner.*
Woodruff Wm. — *Ross.*
Mason Jacob
McClure C. A. — *Monroe.*
Ward J. M. — *College Corner.*
Shaw Robert
Leistner A. — *Trenton.*
Wachter Samuel
Reister F.
Funk John
Becker O.
Berry James
Mister M. — *Seven Mile.*
Morris D. — *Somerville.*
McNeeley H.
Lamark G.
Miller M.
Edwards B.
Butts D & J. — *Jacksonsburg.*
Wilson F. E.

Carroll County.

Johnston John J. — *Harlem Springs.*
Richards Otho
Brand William — *New Hagerstown.*
Price John W.
Perry S G. — *New Harrisburgh.*
Marsh Reuben R. — *Norristown.*
Helfrich Jacob — *Carrollton.*
Ruckenbrod J. S.
Wilson Thomas
Gladden J. B. — *Hickory.*
Ray John — *Sherodsville.*
Soneman Benjamin
Beckley Conrad — *Oneida Mills.*
Gregory John

Champaign County.

Mann A. T. & Co. — *Mechanicsburg.*
Jones & More — *Christiansburg.*
Gibbs Samuel — *Westville.*
Howard K.
Colwell W. V. — *Urbana*
White J.
Ward G. H.
Sampson Wm.
Hall D. H. — *Woodstock.*
Chapman J. & Co.
Hakerman Eli — *Careysbill.*
Flaners Wm.

Wirick Samuel	*St. Paris.*
Seeley R. H.	
Jenkins M. L.	*Terre Haute.*
Jenkins David	
Fabes Josiah	
Reames J. R.	*North Lewisburg.*
Limes Harmon	
Hunter John	

Clark County.

Nove John	*Tremont.*
Crosby Hiram	*Enon.*
King Johnston R.	
Maple Davidson	
Keys T.	*Selma.*
Marshall Jas.	
Marshall J.	
Brown & White	*Springfield.*
Ludlow G. & C.	
Mayo & Co.	
Lohner & Heil	
Starrett H. F.	
Homer R.	
Rogers James	
Schulte A.	
Luking E. H.	
Neil & Pearson	
Ewin John	*Catawba.*
Shanks E. M.	
Highwood & Roe	*South Charleston.*
Aspinall Frederick	*New Carlisle.*
Earl Charles	
Greer William	
Shermer Joseph.	

Clermont County.

Moser Adam	*New Richmond.*
Zingle J. R.	
Kelvey M.	
Zimmer Anthony	
Luts John	
Jackson Stephen	
Muller J.	
Lindsey Ira	
Elliot Oliver P.	*Nicholsville.*
House & Edwards	*Felicity.*
Sargent Wilson	
Miller Louis	
Sargent O. S.	
Crowell & Sims	*Bethel.*
Sims J. W.	
South E. A.	
Lindsey D.	
Conolly J.	*Mt. Carmel.*
Ketchum A. J.	
Carter Jno.	*Batavia.*
McCann D.	
Rhodes Jno. A.	
Zurmhle John	
Dorsey Dennis	*Neville.*
McLaughlin John	
Rust Paul E	
Edwards Marrion	*Amelia.*
Pease Wm. B.	
Pumpelly Bernard	
Lane Daniel A.	*Centre.*
Park Lemanda	

Wilmington Joseph H.	*Cratre*
Mellan John F.	*Milford*
Hughes A. M.	*Miamisville*
Leming Jeremiah	*Mulberry*
Ackley James	*Moscow*
Reynolds M. S. & Co.	
Rust J. H.	
Sapp & Young	
McClure H.	*Mount Pisgah*
Cubberly M.	*Rural.*
Perry J.	
Pebernot John	*Loveland.*
Hunt William H.	*Perin's Mills.*
Dudley Moses	*West Woodville.*
De Vellis Michael	
Foote Amos B.	
Smith George W.	*Bantam.*
West James	
Aorris Abbot	*Locust Corner.*
Mattox Elijah	

Clinton County.

Grant John	*New Burlington.*
Hollingsworth D.	
Lewis J.	*Cuba.*
Dale Rev. J.	
Carson J. L.	*Westboro'.*
Vanzant J.	*Port William.*
Arnold A. J.	
Cohagan J.	*Lumberton.*
Carter & Hazard	*Sligo.*
Douglass John N.	
Sever J. T.	*Blanchester.*
Allen John	
Hobson Eli	*New Antioch.*
Holmes J.	*New Vienna.*
Holmes John	
Miller J.	
McKee S.	
Garrett J.	*Sabina.*
Bloom Wm.	*Martinsville.*
Rother August	
Martin Wm.	*Wilmington*
Ashcroft Wm. E.	

Columbiana County.

Deal C. W.	*Wellsville.*
McCloud Daniel	
Mertes C.	
Shearman O. P.	
Cole John	*New Lisbon.*
Nelson George W.	
Todd William	
Low Salathiel	*East Palestine.*
Low Henry	
Paxson L. A.	
Duffy James	*Salineville.*
Farmer George	
Johnson Isaac	*New Garden.*
Walton A. B.	
Bradiah T. F.	*Calcutta*
Buskirk Wm.	
Redman Samuel	*North Georgetown*
Varnes Daniel	
Davison John	*Franklin Square*
Estell E. J.	
Ginther Samuel	*East Rochester*

Behner John	*New Chambersburgh.*
Behuer Jacob	
Meyer J. H.	
Shaffer Adam	
Whitacre Martin	*Green Hill.*
Eldridge Enos	*Salem.*
Hudson & Taylor	
Trescott J. & Co.	
Harkins R. J.	*Bucks.*
Willinton J.	
Dobbs John	*East Liverpool.*
Gause Andrew	
Hill John M.	
Taylor James	
Brubaker William	*Columbiana.*
Miller George	
Stouffer David	
Voglesang John	
Clunk M.	*West Point.*
Norris H.	
Todd L.	
Hooker Jacob	*Saint Clair.*
Marriner Robert	
Myers George	
Early Samuel	*Unity.*
Hoffstott William	
Molenkopf John	
Smith J. M.	
Hartman James	*East Fairfield.*
Huffman George	
Duffy Hugh	*Inverness.*
Mehaffy Jonathan	*Cannon's Mills.*
Moore John	*Elkton.*
McClain Leonard	

Coshocton County.

Cunning John	*Chili.*
Cunning Albert	
Graham Miller	
McCollum Thos.	
Schoonover Isaac	*Bakersville.*
Lewis Samuel	
Eutly Jacob	
Harbaugh John	*Clark's.*
Coy Alonzo	*West Bedford.*
Elliott Andrew	*Keene.*
Carroll George	
Carroll Thomas	
Akens James	
Shaw H. N.	*Coshocton.*
Saffer H.	
McFarlin Wm.	
Wells W.	
Zucksouk T.	
Summers Wm.	

Crawford County.

Castle E.	*Leesville Cross Roads.*
Hund John	
Slorp J.	
Bentley L	*Poplar.*
Detray J. B.	
Martin M.	
Bauer Peter	*New Washington.*
Blum Jacob	
Knodel Daniel	
Michelfelder John	

Davis James K.	*Wellerville.*
Horman Henry	*Liberty Corners.*
Kaler George	
Like John	
Perse Samuel	*Sulphur Spring.*
Cramer John	*Bucyrus.*
Holler J. G.	
Kirkland Samuel	
Margraff H.	
Messner John	
Morris John	
Reck & Shimpf	
Shuler Charles	
Shuler Frederick	
Welz A.	
Miller O.	*Lykens.*
George S.	
Hart Ephraim	*De Kalb.*

Cuyahoga County.

Blake J. M.	*Euclid.*
Amos H.	*Newburgh.*
Fish M.	
Skidmore & Co.	*Mayfield.*
Chase W.	*Gates' Mills.*
Chase O.	
Sarles A.	*North Royalton.*
Smith J. W.	
Dunchey William	*Independence.*
Demilt D.	*East Cleveland.*
Merrill Charles	
Lilley L.	*Dover.*
Eggleston & McFarland	*Chagrin Falls.*
Pratt & Waldron	
Robinson J.	
Barnard Wm. W.	*Solon.*
Bull Pitkin S.	
Cate Moses O.	
Dunwell S. A.	
Morrell John	
Pratt Zenos	
Ballow Isaac A.	*Brecksville.*
Crossman Robert	
McWade William	
Williams George	
Suard Stephen	
Earl J.	
Graham S.	*Warrensville.*
Shoots J.	
Wood H.	
Heath William	*Bedford.*
Heston H.	
Robison Neuman	
Austin N. H.	*Coe Ridge.*
Gage Stevens	
Hendricks Lucius	
Perry Daniel	
Short Lewis	
Williams Lyman	
Meeker Enoch	*Collamer.*
Burton Curtis	
Taylor Seymour	
Wallace John	
Wyman P.	*Berea.*
Carman William	
Black John, 54 Superior	*Cleveland.*
Gross L., 131 do	

Brew W.. 98 Superior   *Cleveland.*
Hopper John, 24 Ontario
Linnsley O. H., 111 Superior
McGuire P. F., 17 Ontario
Ogram & Lord, 136 Superior
Ranney S., 81   do
Seymour & Crowell, 39 Bank
Whitley George, cor. Seneca & Superior
Wolke H., 1 Clothier's Block
Saunders Daniel   *Ohio City.*
Meid Thomas S.

Darké County.

Wert Peter   *Ithica.*
Werts D K.
Leas William   *Fort Jefferson.*
Wolf Alfred
Lemberger J.
Douglass John   *Hillgrove.*
Reeves Lewis
Mendenhall S. T.   *Woodington.*
Smith S. R.   *New Madison.*
Jacobs John
Crocker M. L.
Leace & Mills   *Fort Jefferson.*
Burgess Joseph   *German.*
Gier J. F.
Garrett John   *Sempson.*
Miller John & G. W.   *Greenville.*
Birely & Bildermere
Slussen John   *Beamsville.*
Barts E.
Beanblossom Solomon
Johns Wm.

Defiance County.

Grass John   *Defiance.*
Hese C & Co.
O'Connell Wm.
Phillips J. W.
Metz John   *Milldale.*
Nagle Frederick   *Brunersburg.*

Delaware County.

Day J. & J.   *Delaware.*
Jones & Dunlap
Slough R.   *Stratsford.*
Keiser S.
Heller John
Hedrick Levi
Shaw S. D.
Libald Jacob
Pierson L.   *Galena.*
Arnold Alex.
Wheaton M.
Eldridge R. C.
Schenck W.   *Vans Valley.*
Freeman Lewis
Partridge J.   *Waldo.*
Reuzenberger Wm.
Reuzenberger Thos.
Good B.   *Harlem.*
Spooner James   *East Orange.*
Palmer James
Jones John   *Delaware.*
Loyd A. L.   *Padnor.*
Bomford R.

Thomas David O.   *Padnor*
Brown J. G.
Bayley Israel   *Norton*
Musselman Henry
Norton Jerome
Mentenger G. A.   *Sunbury.*
Sparks & Cowin

Erie County.

Click L.   *Sandusky City.*
Doll F.
Dahm F.
Damen & Filder
Esch B.
Ferry Austin
Grnig W. & Son
Haley J.
Kuhn J.
Lobstein J.
Lundy W.
Moss A.
Phillips J.
Rohrbacker M.
Rupreckt J.
Schlegel G.
Wetzler A.
Wigand O.
Bartlett H.   *Huron.*
Paule J.
Wunderlee A.
Wott J.   *Birmingham.*
Robertson Wm.   *Florence.*
Dervil J. S.   *Berlinville.*
Bartholomew G. W.   *Furnace.*
Bassett Nathan
Bradley C.   *Milan.*
Hough J. & P.
Stoddard H.
Young C. K.

Fairfield County.

Kramer William   *Pickerington.*
Kurfus George
Williams Elias
Blackwell David   *Pleasantville.*
Fitzer P.
Brattime J. L.   *New Salem.*
Fix George
Dilger John   *West Rushville.*
Marris Henry
Marris Thomas
Sugart & Parks'
Stiles & Widner   *Bremen.*
Angle & McFee   *Rushville.*
Hutchins J.
Sheety David   *Amanda.*
Work, Son & Work   *Lancaster.*
Reed Robert
Lahman J.
Miller J.
Embeck William
Robinson & Trout
Kiefaber P.   *Clear Creek.*
Vandemark C.
Grimm G.
Merary & Groah
Mensing M.   *Sugar Grove*

Wonn J. E. *Sugar Grove.*
Edwards W. H. *Lithopolis.*
Bowser Michael
Pifer S.
Rumel V.

Fayette County.

Svenger John *Pancoastburg.*
Kuneaster L. B.
Ball M. *Bloomingburg.*
Gordon Geo W.
Blair Wm. H. *Moons.*
Blair James
Govel John
Holbrook James *Staunton.*
Ferry David

Franklin County.

Adams John, Friend street, *Columbus.*
Brown A. C., High
Brooker R. P., Front
Blanchard R., High
Brevitt John, do
Cooper A., do
Constans J. W., 1 State
Crawford John, 133 High
Deshler —, Broadway
Emory G. P., High
Fassig M. & F., do
Frelenbusch G., do
Freyer & Danterman, Front
Gast A., High
Horiger G., do
Hendrick & Beck, do
Johnson H., do
Kimball H. H., do
Langguth Charles, do
Leibold A., Friend
Lusch M., 3d
Mangold John, High
Mealheim J., Town
Peifer J., Friend
Sager William, High
Sheridan James, Town
Schroll G. P, 172 High
Scott Charles, Broadway
Sullivan D, do
Steichele C, High
Ury J., Friend
Van Slyke L. G., High
Wick Andrew, do
Woolbert M., 3d
Berget Jacob *Groveport.*
Champ Geo. P.
Crook George
Edwards E. W.
Conkun H. *Reynoldsburg.*
Smith Timothy
Webb E.
Frost J. *Clintonville.*
Samers J.
Benedict N. *Hope.*
Bishop Joseph
Pierson Thompson
Barthman V. *Harrisburg.*
Swingvod S.
Noble A. H. *Worthington.*

Walling Joshua *Worthington.*
Havens T. O. *Central College.*
Mullen Henry
Bollenbaugh Peter *Canal Winchester.*
Goitel Nicholas
Trine Reuben
Learn J. *Ovid.*
Sisco Abraham
Vicerry Peter
Woodruff Archibald *Gohanna.*
Sneider George
Harlow Jones *Dublin.*
Wells John
Wing Jesse

Fulton County.

Haneywell B. *Elmira.*
Beaverson S.
Krouse F.
Reager F.

Gallia County.

Foster Travis *Adamsville.*
Davis William
Rowley Isaac *Pine Grove.*
Rowley Franklin
Grey Jackson *Kyger.*
Hampton Taylor W.
Morgan John C. *Patriot.*
McCafferty Thomas *Gallipolis.*
Doges John

Geauga County.

Roberts Wm. *Chardon.*
Weaver A.
Marsh Michael
Brunson James
Munsell R. P.
Griswold A. W.
Smith Edward
Wilson Gilbert
Burr H.
Orcutt J. *Auburn.*
Maynard Wm
Parris Wm. *Chester.*
Herrick D. L.
Shaw B. N.
Pool A. R. *Troy.*
Marey D. W.
Hawkins O.
Hildreth Thomas
Munson H. *Huntsburgh.*
Clark Z.
Dunkee Wm. H. *Montville.*
Busquin M. S.
Whitney J. R.
Thompson Z. *Middlefield.*
Russell Samuel
Hitt C. *Thompson.*
Goodrich Charles
Jackson Wm.
Cook Z.
Scott Ira
Hale A.
Harris Joseph *Munson*
Sutton N. & J.
Eldridge S.

Walker B.   *Parkman.*
Bucking T.
Popplewell Benj.
Williams J. E.
Pease J.
Corwin J. W.   *Newbury.*
Clark H.
Parr L.
Jones H.   *Russell.*
Page James R.
Thompson Thos.   *Bainbridge.*
Johnson L.
Briggs A.
Pitkin T. W.   *Claridon.*
Davis J.
Harrison Jacob
Gaylord S.   *Burton.*
Tucker Asa
Tucker Alfred

Greene County.

Allen John   *Xenia.*
Bodine J.
Kump George
Neal & Pearson
Alspough John   *Fairfield.*
Smith J. B.
Smith J.
Buck Henry   *Zimmerman.*
Sachem R. W.   *Spring Valley.*
Neald J. M.
Bigelow B. A.   *New Jasper.*
Carroll William
Smith John
Johnson S.   *Clifton.*
Prevost Samuel
Shaffer A.
Paris N.   *Cedarville.*
Wilson D. S.
Schauer & Wilson   *Byron.*
Ball P.   *Yellow Springs.*
O'Herron Patrick
Ellis Arnett   *Paintersville.*
Ellis Simeon
Ellison Arthur
Noland James
Adams & McKindry   *Jamestown.*
Smith Samuel
Way Thomas

Guernsey County.

Sigman Geo.   *Cumberland.*
Elliott John
Cairnes J. G.
Rodd J. & Brother
Sescallet W. H.   *Washington.*
Sawn E.
Roach J.
Clements H.
Rankin J.   *Londonderry.*
Andress Saml.
McCoy Wm. H.   *Winchester.*
Travis N.
Scott S.
Smith Wm.   *New Gottingen.*
Ross R. C.
Coultrup D. S.   *Fairview.*

Darling A. W.   *Fairview,*
Gleaves Saml.
Gardner Matthew
Gardner H.
Humphrey John
Bernard Wm.
Teener Jas. F.   *Dyson's.*
Saverley Jas.
Ogg Moses   *Claysville*
Wallar B. B.
Patterson H.
Moreland J.   *Cambridge.*
Ogier W. & D.
Talbert N. & Co.
McIlyar Wm.
Thompson D. G.
Temple Thos.   *Kimbolton.*
Temple Thos. D. & J. B.
McNutt Nathaniel
Jones Robert S.
Morrow E.   *Millersville.*
Fleming F.
Dilley & McGaw   *Senecaville.*
Hutchinson R. M.

Hamilton County.

Ahler J. H., 402 Sycamore   *Cincinnati.*
Arhman James, 549 W. Row
Berger J., 221 6th
Baker John, 5th near Plum
Baumer E., 217 7th
Brodfueher G. H., 58 6th
Bertman C., 383 Main
Burger Philip H., 234 do
Brooks M., 5th e. of Walnut
Buter B., 144 e. Front
Brinkman J. H., 112 Hunt
Bolinger P., Clinton bet. Cutter & Lynn
Buhrmann G. L., 45 Wade
Burke E., 299 W. Row
Burke T. 219 do
Berling H. H., Hamilton Road bet. Main
    & Piatt
Becht F. J., 502 Vine
Brachemier A., 516 do
Bucker J. F., 104 13th
Barlage J. H., 378 Broadway
Bodine E. & V., 245 W. Row
Blanke H., 18 Jefferson
Buckner G., cor. Elm & Liberty
Berming C., 102 Buckeye
Conard P., 54 Hamilton Road
Conrad J., W. Row bet. Court & Catherine
Clinton H., 102 Front
Cook J. H., 458 5th
Conner M., 25 8th
Cous F., 11 Levee
Cheney J. S., cor. Sycamore & Columbia
Crook & Goodall, 268 Main
Collins Henry, 144 5th
Carter & Robertson, 230 5th
Deters J. H., 41 3d
Davis J. R. & Son, 22 w. 5th
Deters G. H., 4 Levee
Digman Francis, 6th bet. Butler & Pike
Duffel C., 37 Ludlow

Dorras James, 59 8th   *Cincinnati.*
Duke Joseph, 27 8th
Daniels H., 184 6th
Duste J. H., 35 Race
Dutchemin J., 354 6th
Dunlap & Son, 267 W. Row
Doever G. W., W. Row near 6th
Ellman John, Bremen bet. 12th & 13th
Eckelmann —, 6 n. 5th
Eshelby James, 10 6th
Eveslage H., 171 5th
Engerser H., 94 Court
Ewell W. H. S., cor. W. Row & Catherine
Fries Sylvester, 10 Walnut
Fisher W. J., 275 W. Row
Fogel J., 628 Vine
Feien G., 46 Woodward
Grampp M., 47 Liberty
Gray J., 545 Vine
Gerland H., 482 w. 3d
Gerdink J. G., 460 Main
Groeniger T., 544 do
Griffin Peter, Vine near 4th
Griesting J. D. & G., 38 5th
Giese F., 10 Levee
Guy C. C., 63 Lower Market
Groskerpe H., 3 Congress
Halley G. W., 190 5th
Hellman F. H., Main near Abigail
Horman G. & Lake, 76 Court
Holthas Bennett, Vine
Horstschneider J., 165 5th
Hermann C., 325 Plum
Hart Wm. & Co., 49 & 51 Pearl
Hayden A. W., 67 Lower Market
Hercenrother F., 6 Walnut
Hudson James, 223 Main
Hutter H. H., 235   do
Hatlay H., s. w. cor. Pearl & Vine
Holthouse B. H., 27 Vine
Hart W. & Co., 18 w. 5th
Hocker G. & F., 5 Levee
Hilson H., 15 Levee
Handley C., 7 Congress
Hoffman H., 39 Ludlow
Hamman H., 543 Sycamore
Hempel N., 662 Main
Holbrock J. H., 439
Hughes J. H., 206 Elm
Haldy P., 290
Hurmann —, 378 w. 5th
Hollenbeck M., 188 Everett
Hohff N., Harrison Road bet. Freeman & Riddle
Halmer K., cor. Vine & 12th
Haebermehl G., 452 Vine
Hirschfeld H., 488   do
Harnold J., 638   do
Heilmann J. B., 497 Race
Hindermann H., cor. Race & Liberty
Helmich H. H., Bremen bet. Liberty & 15th
Halmer P. H., 15th bet. Bremen & Vine
Hunmann S., 420 Walnut
Hoffman J., 486   do
Heckmann J., 512   do
Henscher H., 7th bet. Outter & Linn
Herbers J. B., 84 Hopkins

Hollalein C. H., 271 Clinton   *Cincinnati.*
Hogan D., cor. John & Elizabeth
Hofman K., 90 Hamilton Road
Heckmann F., 22 Jefferson
Ilrath J., 22 e. Front
Ichler David, 344 Main
Jausseer W., 170 Everett
Kuhlman C., 371 Elm
King James R., Catherine bet. Fulton & Outter
Koble P., 23 Hamilton Road
Kramer X., 124   do
Krames J., 666 Elm
Kliman J, 99 Clay
Klute J. H., 485 Walnut
Korlbrand D., 418 Vine
Krainer C., 669   do
Killers J., 67 Wade
Klusman G., 525 Sycamore
Korte F. H., Burgoyne bet. Main & Sye.
Kallmeyer L., 583   Main
Kerman E., 279   do
Kalmeir G. & Bro., 357 do
Koch H. & H., 284   do
Kurts J. A., 109 Court
Kalmeir G. & H., 16 e. Court
King Wm. H., 67 6th
Lamping J. H., 191 6th
Lange J., 100 Court
Loring Wm., 242 3d
Leaon A., 141 5th
Lowenstein H., 365 Main
Leininger J. G., 315 Vine
Lampe F., 545 Main
Lamb J. W., 220 6th
Linert J., 200 Plum
Lambers H., cor. Congress & Ludlow
Lapking H. W., 303 6th
Luherman H. H., 536 Race
Lehmkuhle A., 102 Clay
Liemp G., 81 Spring
Lumley R., W. Row bet. 8th & Kemble
Lange J. A., 8th bet. Baymiller & Linn
Moermann J. J., cor. Main & Public Landing
McCollough H., 28 Broadway
Markert G., 37 Hamilton Road
Melle B. H., 482 Walnut
Mannieve H., 461 Sycamore
Maltby Edward, 45 Front
Mair T., Mohawk bet. Hamburg & Vine
Miller —, 655   Vine
Meier N. H., 537   do
Monenger G., 429   do
Moreman J. J., cor. Main & Public Landing
Meyers B., 478 5th
Morehouse A. H., 486 Main
Meyer H., 588   do
McGrath G., 12 8th
Martin J., 212 Walnut
Moss L. A., 375 Vine
Martin & Koehler, 175 Main
Mann L & C., 79 Lower Market
Meirs J. H., 10 Walnut
Martin John 18 e. 5th
Martin Saml., 3d bet. Walnut & Vine

Moorman B. J., 39 7th   *Cincinnati.*
Nieter G., 13 6th
Nienaber J. H., 49 Plum
Neiters J., 438 5th
Niemann G., 89 Spring
Oelfken J. C., 398 Broadway
Obrien Geo., 72 3d
Oberle J., 8 Pike
Pfuster Fred., 351 Main
Patton J . Butler near Congress
Paschen W., 705 Main
Pittenger A., 296 5th
Port Johannes, Hamilton Road bet. Piatt
   & Freeman
Pillen H., 32 Green
Plogman F., 457 Walnut
Peck S. R., Ludlow bet. Front & Landing
Pounath H., Clark bet. Cutter & Ritten-
   house
Quinon S., 151 Congress
Reed John, 88 5th
Renneker J., 8 9th
Rothert L , 3d bet. Walnut & Vine
Rice A., 7 Levee
Romer J., 179 E. Front
Rowe J., 578   do
Remme H. W., 468 Main
Rice J., 108 6th
Rorde C. F., cor. Mound & Longworth
Rehe Henry, 68 Front
Roth John, Hamilton Road bet. Ham-
   burg & W. Row
Ruter B., 144 Front
Rerring & Co., 7th bet. Baymiller & Linn
Rider F., 102 13th
Roth J., 340 Hamilton Road
Smith J., Catherine bet. Fulton & John
Stoll Henry, John bet. Kemble & Richm'd
Shneider C., Linn bet. Clark & Catherine
Sanderson Joseph, 21 Broadway
Shoner P., cor. Vine & Hamilton Road
Stritel J. H., 62 Findley
Seiler T., 170 Clay
Strickner F., 59 do
Schutte R., 57 12th
Sauer M., 633 Vine
Sinning N., W. Row bet. Liberty & Ever-
   ett
Seep H., 70 12th
Spreckermann —, 393 Race
Schutte B., & Co., 402 Fifth
Segers Geo., 48 Front
Schutte J., 22 Woodward
Stall F., 509 Main
Steinbrecher J., 71 8th
Shiff Isaac, 183 Vine
Schemer J., 28 e. Front
Stair John, 9 Congress
Straus S., 40 Front
Sliker V., 49 & 83 Lower Market
Sullivan T., 120 Walnut
Straus D., 335 Main
Straus M., 436 do
Schuk D., 36 e. Front
Troy S., 128½ 3d
Treman Chas., 69 Sycamore
Thorne W. F., 74 Lower Market

Theirle W., 607 Main   *Cincinnati.*
Troy Wm., cor. W. Row & Perry
Teipel P., 166 6th
Treasurer J., 413 W. Row
Theising F., 9 12th
Tippe W., 9 Buckeye
Utley H., cor. Walnut & Front
Ullfelder L., 262 5th
Vornholt J. H., 3d bet. Smith & Park
Valdam H., 479 Walnut
Verhr G., 71 Greene
Witt George, cor. W. Row & 8th
Worth S., 112 Clinton
Wertham D., 255 Main
Weindel J., 89 Hamilton Road
Wittekind J., 101   do
Weber M. R., 105   do
Wellman H. H., 50 Clay
Winkle D., 370 Broadway
White W., 76 Front
Wildman G. H., 166 Everett
Wellenkamp J. D., 593 Race
Weiler G. F., 17 Greene
Waditer J. H., 59 Race
Winkel W., 95 Canal
Wilken A. W., 57 5th
Wahlborn —, 499 John
Williams J. M., 356 5th
Wirthin F., 548 e. Front
Wormser & Benedict, 199 Elm
Wallman B. J., 345 5th
Westcott M. A., 10 w. 6th
Wegmann F., 8 Levee
White W., 76 e. Front
Weitheim D., 255 Main
Wallwork J., 214 6th
Warrington O. S., 169 5th
Durham Howard   *Mt. Healthy.*
Smith G. W.
Ahrens A.
Jordan G. B.
Ohm H.
Reweider Saml. S.
Addis S.
Conover C.   *Montgomery.*
Askew David
Smethurst Lloyd
Hamilton Joseph   *Pleasant Ridge.*
Hatter John
Simkinson Wm.
Kaiser Henry   *Harrison.*
Keen Robert A.
Lancaster & Gibbs
Shermer Philip
Wilson Monroe
Wise Henry
Argo E.   *Cleves.*
Veil —
Bolander Luke   *Elizabethtown.*
Kleinfelder A.   *Mt. Washington.*
Wolf G.
Gibbons John   *Plainville.*
Hageman B. H.   *Cummingsville.*
Hoffman John
Carrigan James
Moore Wm. R.
Stryker A. A.   *Springdale.*

Armstrong H. & J.	*Newtown.*
Beattie Charles	
Waggoner H.	
Suer C.	*Columbia.*
Schilling J.	*Pendleton.*
Werber V.	*Fulton.*
Green R.	
Roseboom S. D.	
Rabergh J.	
Frese H.	
Leisure O.	
Wagner N.	*Walnut Hills.*
Aydelott Wm.	*Sharonville.*
Edmeads Thos.	
Whallon Horatio	
Dempsey Thos. H.	*Carthage.*
McAuley C. D.	
Rowe James	
Thayer Caleb	
Thayer Stephen	
Williams T.	
Conrad N.	*Cheviot.*
Covert John	
McReynolds H.	
Rapp H.	
Wills Thomas	
Edwards M. M.	*College Hill.*

Hancock County.

Reigle Philip	*Arlington.*
Brown R.	*Benton Ridge.*
Saunders J.	
Crawford Abner	*Cass.*
Smith Gideon	
Ardinger P. D.	*Finley.*
Glaimer John	
Manwarring R. D.	
Wilkinson C. G.	
Purse M.	*Canonsburg.*
Stoults John	
Howk David	
Burnett Seth S.	
Mitchell William	*McComb.*

Hardin County.

Campbell Saml.	*Kenton.*
Snodgrass & Gillmore	
Duns J. J. & Co.	*Roundhead.*
Wise Matthew R.	*Huntersville.*
Runyer John	
Jones Saml.	

Harrison County.

Slemmons Saml.	*Cadiz.*
Phillips Thos. & Son	
Phillips John	
Banister James	
Hamilton Francis	
Real John	
Smith John	*Deersville.*
Arkle Christopher	
Towlen M. M.	*Harrisville.*
Harris Isaac	*Updegroff.*

Henry County.

Long John	*Florida.*
Yockey —	*Napoleon.*

Miller Frederick	*New Bavaria.*
Spengler F.	
Schall Henry	

Highland County.

Wilkins John	*Highland.*
Rhea & Kelley	
Plummer Eli	
Scott Wm.	*Greenfield.*
Loush Philip	
Douglass D. & W.	
Griffith James	*Belfast Town.*
Saylor Jacob	
Caplinger Jeremiah	
Campbell Wm.	
Orebaugh A.	*Dodsonville.*
Baker M.	
Spence Preston	*Buford.*
Winestone C.	
Stine J. C.	*New Market.*
Tinor Chas.	
Bruce Moses	
Pearce M.	*New Petersburg.*
Vanpelt Isaac	
Maddox Amos	
Thurman David	
Ross H.	*Sugartree Ridge.*
Futts J.	
Burnett Ephraim	*Marshall.*
Main David	
Thayer Wm. T.	
Smith Peter	
Anderson Samuel	*Centrefield.*
Lucas J. B.	
Loyd James	
Pettitt Wm. D.	*Greenford.*
Kelly John D.	
Glover Robert	*Samantha.*
Ashmore A. R.	
Kerns John	
Winter Wm. C.	
Orr A W.	*Dallas.*
Griffith John	*Leesburg*
Kelley R. T.	
Binager J.	
Guthrie James	
Kesler Andrew	*North Uniontown.*
Griffith Reese	*Hillsboro'.*
McKee Saml.	
Vanpelt J.	

Hocking County.

Mattox & Harper	*Rock House.*
Carroll & Mettler	
Avey Alexander	*Logan.*
Kanode O.	
Miller P.	
Roads & Fritter	
Work John W. & Co.	
Miller Jacob	
Nail John	
Keller George	*Gibisonville.*
Kinser John J.	
Roby Barton	
Vorhees Clarkson	
Swetland J. G.	*Swan.*
Everet Darius	

Holmes County.

Morgan John	*Holmesville.*
Wiseman John	*Benton.*
Smith John	
Grevener Peter	*Berlin.*
Leaf John	
Howalt Henry	*Walnut Creek.*
Miller Aaron	
Wyler C.	*Winesburg.*
Kesler John	
Schnider Jacob	
Bruney John B.	
Vogle Geo.	*Millersburg.*
Hull E. H.	

Huron County.

Young J. J.	*Steuben.*
St. John M.	*East Townsend.*
St. John A. W.	
Smith John	
Porter James	*Clarkfield.*
Porter Henry	
Barnum Wm. L.	
Willow B.	*Four Corners.*
Shivel John	*Newhaven.*
Ames & Rutledge	
Lighter A.	*Bellevue.*
Herrell P.	
Porter James S.	*Clarkfield.*
Husted E. E.	*Norwalk.*
Smith E. H.	
Northrop B. H.	
Brown N.	
Ells A. G. & Co.	*Fitchville.*

Jackson County.

Dyer A. J.	*Berlin.*
Savage Joseph	
Beals J. N.	*Allensville.*
Belford B. & A.	
Steele S. C.	*Jackson.*
Hadway P. D.	

Jefferson County.

Alexander James	*Steubenville.*
Bailie W. L.	
Drury Thos.	
Dougherty Wm.	
Hudson J.	
Hunkill W.	
Kimble John	
McDonald J.	
Troth & Scott	
Wheeler H.	
McViece Hugh	*Richmond.*
Tobe John	
Stout Francis	
Parter Richard	*East Springfield.*
Cloman John	*Annapolis.*
Barr Wm.	
McHugh Wm. & D.	*Mt. Pleasant.*
Sinemore J. C. & Spencer	
Bone Benj.	
Peters A. & Son	*Knoxville.*
Miles J.	
Hurd Timothy T.	*Wintersville.*

Sanborn H. M.	*Wintersville.*
Fisher Wm. R. & Co.	
Fisher Geo. L.	

Knox County.

Magill S. W.	*Mount Vernon.*
McReady D.	
Mealey T. F.	
Small S.	
Taylor Edward	
Voorhies Silas	
Weaver C.	
Payn E. & J.	*Danville.*
Carr John	*Fredericktown.*
Cox W. B.	
Hammond A. G.	
Lane William	
Leasure John	
Snow A.	
Thrapp & De Puy	
Shafer, Rufus & Bro.	*Brandon.*
Condon J. W.	*Ankenytown.*
Winchell Henry	*Monroe Mills.*
Treakle Samuel	*Democracy.*
Long O. D.	*North Liberty.*
Long Henry	
Neff John	*Millwood.*
Pain Thomas	
Smith Wm. & J. N.	
Beeman William	*Jelloway.*
Collins Jacob	
Ramy A. W.	*Mount Liberty.*
Clegborn James	
Osborn James	
Baltzell Joseph	*Bladensburg.*
Baltzell A.	
Ross James	
Hullinger H.	
Hall Samuel	

Lake County.

Eddy & Kilborne	*Painesville.*
Holmes L. W.	
Wells L. K.	
Benedict R. S	
Beebe R. H.	
Gardner & Hitchcock	*Madison*
Wood E.	
Wheeler Alfred	*Perry.*
Vanness Caleb	*North Perry.*
Rowland R.	
Coburn T. G.	*Concord.*
Joyce P.	
Burr David	

Lawrence County.

Bishop & Perley	*Ironton.*
Evans R. O.	
Hopkins M. C.	*Hanging Rock.*
Osmer A. & F.	*Burlington.*
Smith —	
Keeny William S.	*Russellsplace.*
Beckett M. K.	
Buskirk Uriah	*Millers.*
Jack William	
Becket Lafayette	*Quaker Bottom.*
Wilgus James	

Licking County.

Tipton Joshua	Linnville.
Richter E.	
Holtzmar H.	Etna.
Arendt S. H.	
Stalman A. O.	
Houser George	
Bixler John	Brownsville.
Hindle John	
Morris J.	
Rodgers Jason	Jacksontown.
Maple Wm.	
Messmer Jacob	
Swift F.	
Pierson J. N.	Granville.
Walker A.	
Snyder J. F.	
Vanderwort —	
Miller A. L.	
Smith John	Newark.
Werle S.	
Edwards J. & Co.	
Preston J. Q.	
Vandyne J. B.	
Peetrie Jacob	
Cole J.	Homer.
Carey W.	
Vasburg H.	
Francis J.	Perryton.
Hall E.	
Taylor L.	
Liggett T. N.	
Walker D.	
Mesel E.	Croton.
Samson L. B.	
Egglestou J. F.	
Martindale John	Johnstown.
Deroolf S. A.	
Graves J. M.	Fallsburg.
McQueen John	
Walters A.	St. Louisville.
Smith S. H.	Kirkersville.
Tipton Robert T.	Fredonia
Higley Edwin	
Barlow H.	

Logan County.

Beck Daniel	Logansville.
Herren J. B. & W. T.	Huntsville.
Milleson Jonathan	
Tarbutton Wm. E.	
Cocklin Christian	New Richland.
Ferree Uriah	
Patterson Thos.	
Hathaway E.	East Liberty.
Heath J. D.	
Uline William	Rushsylvania.
Deby George	
Williams Wm.	
Anderson D. & M.	Bellefontaine.
Davidson A.	
Gano, Butler & Co.	
Downs Noah	Zanesfield.
Horn John	
Keys William	
Robinson John A.	
Waltner A.	

Young & Monroe	Lewistown.
Leach J.	Quincy.
Leigh O.	
Dodson J.	
Walborn E.	

Lorain County.

Hovey Alvin S.	North Camden.
Clemens Isaac	Rochester Depot.
Hickok F. T.	Huntington.
Mack & Bro.	
Perkins John	
Sage M. L.,	
Phelps J. D.	La Grange.
Matthews S. H.	Oberlin.
Scott Thomas	
Howard J.	Copopa.
Irist A.	
Wilbur E.	
Wheeler J.	
Berkly John H.	Brighton.
Hagart A.	Pittsfield.
Jourdan S.	
Young David	
Goodrich William	Braconheim.
Cogswell M. W.	Elyria.
Robinson W. D.	
Sheffield Charles	
Quark Thomas	

Lucas County.

Cook C. L.	Emery.
Kimball Joseph	Riga.
McBride James R.	
Tripp C. D.	
Redding George	Toledo.
Myers J.	
Kaufman J.	
Ruggles D. W. & S.	
O'Brian C.	
O'Neal T.	
Wilcox H.	
Pauly C.	

Madison County.

Bolds Thos. & Son	London.
Kemister John	
Davy Henry	Danville.
Wright A. F.	
Hubbard William	Mt. Sterling.
Stanford William	
Alter Charles	West Jefferson.
Voheers Andrew	
Willoughby James	Newport.
Eaton William	Somerford.
Freeman John	California.
Waltrous Henry	
Scranton Albert	Rosedale.
Simpson & Millans	Lafayette.
Converse Loran	Pleasant Valley.
Gossard James H.	Midway.
Watson E.	
Bethards J.	
Norman Isaac	
Hamilton A.	

Mahoning County.

Norris Ira	Canfield.

Strouse Chas.   *Cornersburg.*   Whitman A.   *Chatham Centre.*
Strouse J. D.   Cook Saml.
Schnabel G. J.   *Petersburg.*   Prentiss Barney   *Medina.*
Kuesal A.   Blackford T.
Marks J.   Blanott & Jones
Henny J. G.   *Youngstown.*   Siphort & Morse
Webeler Fred.   Freeman R. T.
Squares J. R.   Garrett E. H.
Squares John
Wilcox B. G.   *Berlin Centre.*   **Meigs County.**
Fisher Wm.   Sullivan Wm.   *Downington.*
Stilson Saml. O.   *Beardman.*   Bosworth J.
Stilson J. D.   Cook M.
Livingston R. R.   *New Middletown.* Calvert Wm.
Miller J.   Childers Saml.   *Apple Grove.*
Rohrbach Andrew   Sidler J.
Sharbaugh George   *East Lewistown.* Childers Saml. R.   *Letert's Falls.*
Winning John   Whiteside Thos.   *Pomeroy.*
Hudson Moses   *Coitsville.*   Smith Thos.
Weaver J. B.   *North Jackson.* Flanagan Danl.
Bell J. W.   Dilcher Henry
Wilderson Saml.   Duttenhaver Adam
Fey Chas.
Pettitt W. D.   *Green Village.*   **Mercer County.**
Beans B.   Clark A. P.   *St. Mary's.*
Kelley John   Sanchie George
Bloom David   *North Lima.*   Burnsides A.   *Celina.*
Haas Solomon   Moore J. T.   *Shane's Crossing.*
Kudesell Jerome   Cherington Isaac   *Menden.*
Stanley Isaac   *Damascoville.*   Roop Thos.   *Fort Recovery.*
Peters John   *New Springfield.* Potter Henry   *Montezuma.*
Smith Geo. F.   Towuville George   *Macedon.*
Wehagon H.   *New Albany.*
Preston Geo.   **Miami County.**
                                                  Everett M.   *Fletcher.*
                                                  Dued J. H.
         Marion County.   Lehman Danl.   *Covington.*
Ball Allen   *Cochranton.*   Collins George B.   *West Charleston.*
Sherman C. W.   *Prospect.*   Null J.
Marstelle H.   Plumb F.
Richman Ira   Hauk G.   *Piqua.*
Holderbrand John   Meyer & Lines
Rainey & Thew   *Marion.*   Medaris W.
Thew & Ellis   Beeder T.
Fetter & Gagle   Reser A.
Cone J. W.   Byrne & Gill
Shultz & Dutt   Bartel A.
Terpany S.   Jacob J.
                                                  Bartel James
         Medina County.   Sunderland White   *Troy.*
McBride A.   *Sharon Centre.* Harramau W. S.
Hagerling O.   *Liverpool.*   Kreider J.
Wood J.   Beckweith & Markly
Houk H. M.   Gorsuch E.   *Casstown.*
Dewey R. B.   *Wadsworth.*   Merritt A.
Hulben D.   Scully D.   *Pleasant Hill.*
Warner E. & B. B.   Birch Henry
Nice Isaac   Brown H. J.   *West Milton.*
Horner John   *Lodi.*   Randall & Low
Merrifield P.
Beck Peter   *Weymouth.*   **Monroe County.**
Bishop S.
Bishop O.   Diehl Christian   *Woodfield.*
Woodruff A.   *Hinckley.*   Thomas Daniel M
Cowell Wm   Monroe James S.   *Antioch.*
Woodruff S. P.   Swartwood Hugh
McBride A.   *Sharon Cen're.* Swartwood Levi
Robinson F.   *Chatham Cen. re.* Chapman Gideon   *Lainga.*

Thomas Reuben	*Sunfish.*	Swank & Smith	*Centre.*
Thomas Gardiner		Opdyke Perry	*Little York.*
Thomas O. S.		Richards John	
Seibert F.		Griffith Alfred	*West Baltimore.*
Seibert J.		Scofield J. W.	
Howell J.		Clay Adam	*Miamisburg.*
Lobmire Henry	*Bealsville.*	Shell John	
McCullough Alex.		Wolf & Heckerman	
Griffith Reese L.	*Jerusalem.*	Bechtol P.	*Germantown.*
McGuire Samuel	*Malaga.*	Troup David	
Blackledge R. J.		Auchenbaugh & Isenhomer	
Kronhart Casper & John			
Janeway James		**Morgan County.**	
Sheats Henry	*Miltonsburgh.*	Bowell Isaac	*Chester Hill.*
Steel W. & Co.	*Stafford.*	Worrell Z.	
Hawkins & Magill		Maris Lewis	
Isamborth Casper	*Baresville.*	Bricker Peter	*Malta.*
Wolf Henry		Silling Wm.	
Barker Isaiah	*Graysville.*	Hambleton W. D.	*Rousseau.*
Joy Jesse		Buckley Joseph	
		Adrean Amos	*Meigsville.*
		Thornberg —	
Montgomery County.		Devol & Corner	*McConnelsville.*
Biddleman J., Main	*Dayton.*	Howard & Stone	
Brickford D , First		Robb Joel	
Buvinger L., Third		Bailey R. W. H.	
Crider George, Second		Corey H. H.	*Stockport.*
Darrow W. H. & Co., Main		Rainey Smith	
Fanning & Co., Second		Vanfassen A.	
Flinn C. D., Green		Matson Aaron	*Pennsville.*
Hand J., Wayne		Ralph Nelson	
Hockwall Geo., Main		Hutton J. M.	*Neelysville.*
Ingram & Lutz, do			
Jeffers A., do		**Morrow County.**	
Johantzen P., Jefferson		Wortman Joshua	*Underwoods.*
Lindsey L., Main		Cyphers Barry	*Iberia.*
McCutcheon J.. Third		Reed James	
McCauley W., Main		Carpenter Aaron	*Marengo.*
Morey & Co., Jefferson		Morehouse Silas	
Meider A., Spratt		Crawford James	*Cardington.*
Moorehouse & Son, Main		Ensign T. H.	
Miller A. S., Fifth		Keen H.	
Nugent O., Third		Richards & Ramsower	
Phillips A.. do		Wilson Isaac J.	
Powell J.. Main		Bachelor Benjamin	*Shauk's.*
Reed J. F., First		Holt Michael	
Schreik C . Jefferson		Spear John	*Woodview.*
Schroder W., Fifth		Benedict Gideon	*Lincoln.*
Vanderson & Wilson, Market		Emery Homer O.	
Weekel J. G., Third		Wilson David S.	
Glass Frederick	*Clayton.*	Gleason John	*Pulaskiville.*
Steel John A.		Peterson Silas	
Stillwell Morgan		Masker D. J.	*Nimmon's Cross Roads.*
Williams George M.		Dicks Eli	*Vail's Cross Roads.*
Burwick John	*New Lebanon.*	Enseyn & Snieb	*Mt. Gilead,*
Tobias James		Squires —	
Hollenbach W.	*Farmersville.*	Struble Jesse	*Chesterville.*
Holp P.		Mather James	
Buchenaw Charles	*Harshmansville.*	Swingley William	
Dodds & Weber	*Alexandersville.*	Jarvis Eli	
Conover J.			
Dell John	*Liberty.*	**Muskingum County.**	
Kalter Paul		Hull C. W.	*Nashport.*
West Joseph	*Centreville.*	Mitchell S. H.	
Jean Samuel	*Chambersburg.*	Mitchell G. D.	
Randle J. A.		Cassingham F.	*Frazeysburg.*
Wenly S. W.		Cassingham James	

White J. D.   *Duncan's Falls.*
Murdock James
Dean Jonathan   *Putnam.*
Ewing H. G.
Harden C. R.
Ziegler J.   *Fultonham.*
Southard Wm.
Southard J.
Muller E.
Rusk J. L.
Warner R.
Floyd M.
Turley J. H.   *Hopewell.*
Stewart R. L.
Cook W.
Terry Wm.   *Shannon.*
Krouse C.
Wather L.   *White Cottage.*
Shaw J.
Bonner H. J.   *New Concord.*
Guthrie Wm.
Finley John
Swingle C.   *Stovertown.*
Dutton A. B.   *Gratiot.*
Wise Peter
Wilson Abel
Morgan J.   *Chandlersville.*
Lepage P.
Randolph S. B.

Noble County.

Robinson John W.   *Berne.*
Ferguson Christopher   *Mount Ephraim.*
Rhodes George
Stevens John
Tribly Michael
Dickson H.   *Sarahsville.*
Scott J. P.
Smith J. W.
Headley J. & Benj.   *Olive.*
McHugh —   *South Oliv.*

Ottawa County.

Shafer Chas.   *Elmore.*
Saltzgiber F.
Sylvester J. W.   *Port Clinton.*
Gill A.

Perry County.

Falder Francis   *New Lexington.*
Kelley & Dean
Lloyd H. M.
McMahan John
Dunwody Jacob   *Thornville.*
Forgrave Robert
Groff Ignatius   *Rehoboth.*
Thomas John
Warthan Henry
Yates Elijah
Rust James   *Mount Perry.*
Rusk John
Bruner Jacob   *Somerset.*
Freeman William
Greiner Leonard
Hubner Charles
McAvon Samuel
Walker Joseph

Wiler John   *Somerset.*
Coyle Peter   *Chapel Hill.*
Huffman D.   *Sego.*

Pickaway County.

Darst & Co.   *Circleville.*
Hamilton T.
Kaiser J.
Miller P.
Millet A.
Myres J. & B.
Purfurst F.
Ludwig & Bashford   *Tarlton.*
Moore William
Rodgers & Johnson   *Darbyville.*
Hill Henry B.   *Beckett's Store.*
Harmount John   *Williamsport.*
Leiby James
McElroy John
Bethards Frank   *Palestine.*
Harrington Peter
Russell John
Kellogg J. S.   *South Bloomfield.*

Pike County.

Stratton Lorenzo   *Waverly.*
Boxerman H.
Schriver Henry
Kokensparger G.   *Beaver.*
Rinkman & Shy   *Gibson.*
Kellison A. & J.   *Piketon.*
Buchart John
Theabald Jacob
Barnett J. E.   *Omega.*
Snodgrass John

Portage County.

Hyde Lawrence   *Edinburgh.*
Meeker C. W.
McGrew W. & F.   *Streetsboro'.*
Lacy Isaac J.   *Aurora.*
Burroughs & Dacon
Gillis & Durham   *Ravenna.*
Beans Moses
Young John
Bouche A.
Rockwell D. L. & Co.   *Franklin.*
Gillett Nathan
Travis L. & Co.
Husted N. P.
Lynn James   *Atwater.*
Johnson Wm.
Barton Ira   *Shalersville.*
Burroughs John
Osborn W.   *Suffield.*
Mantel Christian
Stone Samuel   *Paris.*
Osborn A.
Meeker C.
Colton Solomon   *Charleston.*
Palmer S.
Mahan Andrew
Mattison M.   *Mantua.*
Pepper John & Thos.
Brown Jacob
Jones J. & W.
Betts J.   *Deerfield.*
Betts C.

Murrell Joseph · — *Deerfield.*
Stowell, Williams & Co. — *Nelson.*
Hutchins P. K.
Horrington S.
Barlow A. H. & J. C. — *Rootstown.*
Kiser George
Caris George
McCain Robert
Lewis F. — *Palmyra.*
Tod Gideon
Ober James
Abels Ebenezer
Williams John & Co.
Bierce O. — *Freedom.*
Bryant L.
Hall Ambrose

Preble County.

Hume E. — *West Alexandria.*
Karn M.
Ruple John
Homan Peter — *Lewisburg.*
Sheller A.
Sturr Thos. J. — *Camden.*
Hittle Perry
Simpson C. J.
Lockwood E. P. & J. L. — *Eaton.*
Miller M.
Guild Wm.
Long J.
Pierce C. — *Fairhaven.*
Kane A.
King Samuel — *New Westville.*
Wilcoxen George
Gill Wm. — *Eaton.*
Shafer C. & S. — *Gettysburg.*
Rollins Thos. J. — *West Florence.*
Burnett Watson — *Morningsun.*
Harris Joseph

Putnam County.

Bell George — *Leipsic.*
Landis F S.
McConnel John E.
Patterson Robert
Winkler Casper
Conley J. — *Gilboa.*
Conley P.
Conley J. B.
Feril J.
Miller S. R. — *Kalida.*
Mohlman H. — *Buckeye.*
Mormon J.
Rumpe H.
Iler John
Yancy D.
Conaway Joseph — *Vaughnsville.*
Sloane William
Morrison A. — *Pendleton.*
Lukemiller John

Richland County.

Fought C. — *Shelby.*
Horner J.
Klees N.
Beal George — *Butler.*
Garber Daniel

7

Scott George — *Butler.*
Garber J. — *Ontario.*
Ritenon W. H. — *Shenandoah.*
Valentine John
Miller & Niese — *Mansfield.*
Robinson T. J.
Smith H. R.
Baughman Jacob — *Lexington.*
Donahill Z.
Dudley Asa
Rhodes Levi
Fleming John — *Barnes.*
Stoat Frederick
Wise Philip
Broach Peter — *West Windsor.*
Williams Josiah R.
Martin Moses — *Olivesburg.*
Osier John M.
Cutting & Cross — *Bellville.*
Dean John T.
Shafer M. C.
Waggoner S.
Oline Henry — *Adario.*
Huston Oursey
First J. — *Lucas.*
Case & Seeley — *Plymouth.*

Ross County.

Muniphred Josiah — *Clarksburgh.*
Eskridge G. W.
Aman C. — *Chilicothe.*
Rollman G. M.
Smith Peter
Young P.
Laughlin J.
Bahr J.
Geng J.
Binton John
Peters P.
Ogleavee J.
Howard John
Schafer A.
Aid T.
Wilson N.
Bitter H.
Brodman J.
McDougal T. & Co.
Marsh M. N.
Hauser C. — *South Salem.*
Puffenberger Henry — *Hallsville.*
Long John — *Gillespieville.*
Meeker John
Lennex W. — *Kingston.*
Hoover John
Wait Wm — *Bourneville.*
Hartfield James

Sandusky County.

Gramling E. — *Woodville.*
Seaman J. H.
Oline Peter — *Greensburg Cross Roads.*
Miller John W.
Willis Wm. — *Townsend.*
Farrand Wm. W.
Hull O. D. — *Fremont.*
Door P.
Evans James — *Rollersville*

Miller Simon   *Rollersville.* | Parker William   *Republic.*
Shively Danl. | Detray & Ley
                                              | Hall A. A.

Scioto County.

Bell R. & Co.   *Portsmouth.*

Shelby County.

Baker Jacob | Griffin Abraham   *Houston.*
Brown J. | Wicks J.
Branch A. G. | Cannon C. W.   *Pratt.*
Bertram H. | Drake Fielding
Brediger F. | Woodruff J.
Cook Henry | Gillispie M.   *Sydney.*
Eicher A. & Co. | McCabe D.
Gutman M. | Niewonger N.
Lloyd R. & Co. | Riniker J.
Worts P. & Co.

Starke County.

Garlick & Goldsberry   *Lucasville.* | Elson H.   *Waynesburg.*
Moore Cornelius   *Iron Furnaces.* | Elsass Peter
Chaffin Phinehas   *Lyra.* | Glesner Joseph
Chaffin D. | Kent Philip
Brooks C.   *Wheelersburgh.* | Shaeffer J. & H.
Moore C. | Moles L. B.   *West Brookfield.*
Rood James | Hutton George   *Minerva.*
Adamonge John   *Friendship.* | Prints John
                                              | Stockman John

Seneca County.

                                              | Gastil John   *Lake.*
Van Pelt R.   *Stoner.* | Myers D. W.
Lace & Eastlick   *Melmore.* | Myers M. D.
Nelson & Odor | Zellers J.
Newton James F. | Howl John   *Louisville.*
Couch Rufus   *Adrian.* | Samuel J.
Eaton Jared | Griffith James   *West Brookfield.*
Gear Eli | Humberger J. B.
Tyler William | Hahn Simon   *New Franklin.*
Emich Frederick   *Berwick.* | Hutton Joel
Shuenson Conrad | Mengus Levi
Snider John | Zimmerman John
Zender Joseph | Buckins & Son   *Canton.*
Briner Jacob   *Bloomville.* | Kimball & Co.
Eisenberger Wm. | Lynch A.
Hathaway Wm. W. | Webb W. J.
Sheerer H. | Johnson James   *East Greenville.*
Shirkey Frederick   *Bettsville.* | Holt D. R.   *New Berlin.*
Stickler Jacob | Kolb Nicholas
Bartel D.   *Tiffin.* | Schultz John N.
Houck John | Orubaugh Wm. B.   *Mount Union.*
Keibler B. | Hoiles Joshua
Neise S. | Brown William   *Marlboro'.*
Robinson E. W. | Brown Milton
Scott, Denser & Co. | Paxson E. W.
Shamwell F. | Birkemmeyer Joseph   *Magnolia.*
Snyder J. | Palmer G. W.
Sullivan D. O. | Berry Edward   *Hartville.*
Wagner A. | Shaffer John
  Ione A. A.   *Reed Town.* | Beans James G.   *New Baltimore.*
  Ione Charles | Bradfield Wm. J.
Chaney John   *Bascom.* | Sausser & Dangler   *Massillon.*
Price Michael | Burke Wm. H. & Co.
Weaver Henry | Nettleton J.
Huber Jacob   *Green Spring.* | Young M. & Co.
Daniels George | Koch D.   *Canal Fulton.*
Roath Lewis | Burg S.
Kelsey Daniel | Upson Noah   *Limaville.*
Phailen Allen | Schuler Adam
Coffman Matthew

Summit County.

Ross David
Dunn David   *West Lodi.* | Tinker S.   *Middlebury.*
Show George H.   *Republic.* | Upham W. R.

Winterstein J.	*Middlebury.*	
Hamlin J.	*Cuyahoga Falls.*	
Plum H. & Co.		
Porter S. B.		
Savage Geo.		
Shaffer Levi	*Western Star.*	
Shaffer Jacob		
Hinkston N. & J. C.	*Hudson.*	
Quay J. A.		
Burgent J	*Inland.*	
Haring H.		
Leapard Adam		
Ream G. D.		
Stamm J. P.		
Tate Jesse C.	*North Springfield.*	
Collins C. A.	*Akron.*	
Christy J. H. & Co.		
Outler J. M. & Co.		
Lauder John		
Painton W. S.		
Robertson & Co.		
Sanborn A. J.		
Limbach George	*Clinton.*	
Denions Michael	*Nimisilla.*	
Sour Jonathan		
Goodell P. D. & Co.	*Richfield.*	
Weld H. S.		
Seeley A. L.	*Montrose.*	
Cranford S.	*Tallmadge.*	
Limberner J.		
Upton W.		
Post Giles	*Northfield.*	
Healy Alanson H.		
Wilson —	*Macedonia Depot.*	
Weager William	*Eden.*	
Taylor J. M.		
Smith Lewis	*Summit.*	
Scudder Walter	*Copley.*	
Frederick —		
Foster Martin	*Bath.*	
Taylor Alonzo F.		

Trumbull County.

Butler J.	*Mecca.*
Smith C.	
Allyn Peter E. G.	*Johnsonville.*
Dawson John	*Southington.*
Rice Joseph J.	
Nims Charles	*Gustavus.*
Bridle J.	*Warren.*
Greer George	
Milliken C. J.	
Thorp J. S.	
Floyd —	*Orangeville.*
Shotwell —	
Johnson William	*Girard.*
Willicoth Andrew	
Young Eli	
McIntyre Hugh	*Church Hill.*
Wages Israel	
Denison James	
Plott Frederick	
Williams Alfred	*Brookfield.*
Conklin Charles	
Ross Elijah	
Happer Ged.	
Frazier B.	

Buttles F.	*Farmington.*
Crane Ira R.	
Norris Increase	
Young Eli	
Ooble William	*Ohlstown.*
Bachelor S.	*Newton Falls.*
Gaylord William	
Sampson A. J.	

Tuscarawas County.

Alick Peter	*Winfield.*
Snyder J. W.	
Kusick Joseph	*Peoli.*
Eggenberg John	*Gnadenhutten.*
Huebner August	
Huebner Anthony	
Hofer Samuel, Jr.	
Eckert John	*Ragersville.*
Zink P. T.	
Jimeson W.	*New Philadelphia.*
Broad C.	
Gress & Korderly	
Nicholas P.	
Rumell E.	
Atkins W.	
Gerrold P.	
Oswald George	*Canal Dover.*
Sholly Charles	
Clapp S. S.	
McDannel John	
Montag N.	
Reall J. C.	

Union County.

Bouser Jacob	*Marysville.*
Hendric Curry	
Miller James	
Nugent H. J.	
Zuemer J.	
Henderson F. E.	*Raymond's*
Wiswell Theodore I.	
Bell Silas	*Watkins.*
Barrows W. E.	
Finney R.	
Wilkins Charles E.	*Wilkins.*
Downer N.	*Milford Centre.*
Riddle & Hill	
Gump James	*New California.*
Irwin Lackey	*Coberly's.*

Van Wert County.

Coffin J. B. & Co.	*Van Wert.*
Profit Philip	
Brickner G. W.	*Delphos.*

Vinton County.

Tomlinson Henry	*McArthur.*
Duffie Charles	
Robo Jared	
Shockey William	
Hays Arnold	
Sweatland Joel	*Mount Pleasant*
Belford Benj.	*Allensville.*
Dill Benj.	*Reed's Mills.*
Seymour Wm. & Son.	*New Plymouth.*

Warren County.

Coles R. — *Franklin.*
Ireland T.
Hemphill H.
Hughes Charles — *Springboro'.*
Elbert H.
Hicks Wm.
Baner J.
Mathews M. — *Ridgeville.*
Sisco Moses — *Waynesville.*
Brown J. J.
Clendenen Francis — *Twenty Mile Stand.*
Kitchel E. C. — *Mason.*
Crawford John
Morgan John
Henry James — *Red Lion.*
Cunningham J.
Schmidt John C. — *Edwardsville.*
Rust Joseph — *Dunlevy.*
Keys J. E. — *Waynesville.*
Briscoe Edward — *Hopkinsville.*
Cooper & Barber — *Deerfield.*
Harford John — *Morrow.*
Meeks John
Daniels Wm.
Corcoran John
Foot Wm. — *Lebanon.*
Applegate B.
Burdett F. S.
Lefler J. C.
Baldwin J. C. — *Hopkinsville.*
Coats J.
Frost Wm. — *Lebanon.*
Macy & Hormel — *Harveysburg.*
Ward Wm. M.
Roll David — *Butlerville.*
Ely John
Higgins Joseph
Sisco Samuel G. — *Mount Holly.*
Sisco John
Griffith E.

Washington County.

Fisher John — *Marietta.*
Theis Jacob
Gros Jacob
Emlich F.
Jennings John
Cain & Co.
Slocomb, Bigelow & Co.
Stewart W. H.
Birney & Jennings — *Harmer.*
Naylor J.
Dee S.
Colbert, O'Neal & Co. — *Centre Belpre.*
Clark J. D.
Clark Isaiah
Byron S.
Downer Sanford
Harris H.
Teufall Moses — *Coal Run.*
Booth J. — *Ostend.*
Cady C. C.
Stanley James — *Lower Salem.*
Marsh David
Porter Rufus
Morse M. R.

Watters M.
Bosworth J. H. — *Regniers' Mills, Newport.*
Crandall J. T.
Phipps S. W. — *Bartlett.*
Rubal Joseph
Paff C.
Lendersmith J. — *Wesley.*
Swasey James
Hilderbrand John
Chalk L. — *Jolly.*
Ward B.
Cromner C. — *Lowell.*
Henderson J. M.
Morris J. C.
Riley J. D. — *Watertown.*
McCowan Wm. L.
Jeniker C.
Alger John — *Decaturville.*
Wyer Garret
Payne Joseph
Newell Daniel

Wayne County.

Dickie James — *Dalton.*
Netroer J. C.
Spencer Jacob — *Fredericksburg.*
Rheum W. C.
Griffeth T. R.
Peters H. F.
Butler A. G. & Co. — *Chippewa.*
Hindman C. — *Edinburgh.*
Sowers P.
Hoot N. — *Reedsburg.*
Hines John
Weaver John
Yeagley Danl.
Day John A. — *New Prospect.*
Frank J.
Cotton Wm.
Towaley John — *Burbank.*
Hart Hiram
Harter J. M. — *Smithville.*
Reed & Co.
Drabenstalt John
Catterman Michael — *East Union.*
Bond Saml.
Nober J. — *West Lebanon.*
Bowers Jacob
Hoffman F. — *Number One.*
Roth Christian — *Shreve.*
Sabin Albert
Ewing Wm.
Poulson Wm.
Sitcott John
Hotter Wm. W.
Perry Abraham
Booth C. — *Marshallville.*

Williams County.

Ager James — *Williams Centre.*
Britafield S.
Edwards N. — *West Unity.*
Hoot Abraham
Low John — *Bryan.*
Miller Jacob
Ozier Wm. — *West Unity.*
Rockwell D. L.

Shober Jacob   *Bryan.*
Urea Solomon
Sisson O.   *Montpelier.*

Wood County.

Parks J. J.   *Perrysburg.*
Webb Thos. S.
Oroft John
Benty Jacob
Fairbanks D. A.   *Portage.*
Guyer Gabriel E.   *Gilead.*
Reed N. A.   *Miltonville.*

Wyandot County.

Belstle Christian C.   *Upper Sandusky.*
Hohwald C.
Hitchcock —,
Hennick A.   *Sycamore.*
Blom & Grummell   *Mexico.*
Stoley M.   *Marseilles.*
Phillips Wm.
Adams S.
Lowmaster J.   *McCutchensville.*

Bottle Manufacturers.

Portage County.

Purdy & Fenton   *Suffield.*

Bowl (Wooden) Manufacturers.

Cuyahoga County.

Fairchild J. W.   *Berea.*
Pickard Jonathan

Box (Cigar) Manufacturers.

Hamilton County.

Brooks Thos., 56 w. 2d.   *Cincinnati.*
Clinker J. H., 9th near Elm

Box (Packing) Manufacturers.

Hamilton County.

Brooks Thos., 56 w. 2d   *Cincinnati.*
Hinkle P., Front bet. John & Smith
Johnston J. & J. M., 3d bet. W. Row & Plum
Walters S., 120 W. Row

Box (Paper & Fancy) Manufacturers.

Hamilton County.

Vornholt J. F., 315 Main   *Cincinnati.*
Franklin Max, 65 Lower Market
Jordan D. B., s. e. cor. Main & 5th
Friedman Wm.. n. e. cor. 7th & Main
Lohnsbach G., 5th bet. Vine & Race

Muskingum County.

Baily L. & Co.   *Dresden.*
Elliots H.   *Zanesville.*

Bran Separators—Manufacturers of.

Butler County.

Hughes Stephen B.   *Hamilton.*

Brewers.

Ashland County.

Lepper G.   *Ashland.*

Auglaise County.

Luckmann John G.   *Mineler.*

Butler County.

Sohn J. W.   *Hamilton.*
Dinkfelter H.

Champaign County.

Humphrey T.   *Urbana.*

Clark County.

Brain J. J. W.   *Springfield.*
Burroughs & Dyke   *New Carlisle.*

Clermont County.

Kratzer J. A.   *New Richmond.*

Coshocton County.

Slea F.   *Coshocton.*

Crawford County.

Marck John   *Bucyrus.*
Wingart Christopher

Cuyahoga County.

Hamilton & Tutberry, Michigan *Cleveland.*
Hughes J. M., 3 Canal Block
Ives Samuel C., 109 Canal
Mack J. M., Elm near Main   *Ohio City.*

Defiance County.

Amen Daniel   *Defiance.*

Delaware County.

Anthony Fred.   *Delaware.*

Franklin County.

Hoster L. & Co., Front   *Columbus.*
Schlegel George & Co.

Greene County.

Kyle & Barber   *Xenia.*

Hamilton County.

Baner & Class J. & Chas., 465 Vine   *Cin*
Billiods Fred , 184 Hamilton Road
Fortmann F., cor. 12th & Main
Fortman Francis, cor. Syc & Abigail
Glossner & Brothers, 436 Vine
Harris David, Syc. bet. 3d & 4th
Houser M., cor. Race & 13th
Jonte P., cor. Syc. & Abigail
Klotter G., cor. Main & Hamburg
Kaler G., 90 Buckeye
Klopf Martin, 284 Hamilton Road
Klotter Geo. & Co,,   do   near Mohawk Bridge

Shults & Bro., 485 e. Front   *Cincinnati.*
Schaller & Schiff, 4th bet. John & Smith
Walker John, 391 Sycamore
Weymond P., Harrison Road bet. Davison
  & Brighton
Duntz Christian,   *Harrison.*

Hardin County.
Holsworth Joshua   *Kenton.*

Highland County.
Mahill Christian   *Hillsboro'.*

Huron County.
Robey J. S. & R.   *Monroeville.*

Jefferson County.
Bailie Joseph   *Steubenville.*

Lucas County.
Berger & Rall   *Maumee City.*

Miami County.
Fisher & Kochler   *Marion.*
Irmer C.

Monroe County.
Walters & Stencil   *Miltonsburgh.*

Montgomery County.
Houghton W., Third   *Dayton.*
Harris J. W., Jefferson
Swint George, Main
Schenck & Rohrer   *Germantown.*
Sehrander Charles   *Miamisburg.*

Muskingum County.
Closman John   *Zanesville.*
Achaner —,

Preble County.
Wisemiller Jacob   *Eaton.*

Richland County.
Long John   *Mansfield.*

Ross County.
Gediesen R.   *Chillicothe.*

Scioto County.
Muhlheusser T. H.   *Portsmouth.*
Layher John

Starke County.
Scholder Henry   *Waynesburg.*
Seedsorf Philip   *Lake.*
Graff C.   *Canton.*
Neighmann C. C.
Melchoir P.
Somers H.

Summit County.
Marshall Viall & Brother   *Middlebury.*

Tuscarawas County.
Orater Frederick   *New Philadelphia.*

Warren County.
Irvin John W.   *Waynesville.*

Washington County.
Grittle Jacob   *Marietta.*

Wayne County.
Burkhalter J.   *Smithville.*

Wyandot County.
Fry Henry   *Upper Sandusky.*

Bricklayers.

Allen County
Orayne Joseph   *West Newton.*

Ashland County.
Harris William M.   *Savannah.*

Belmont County.
Bartholomew John   *Uniontown.*
Abel George   *Bell Air.*
Bailey Charles H.   *Saint Clairsville.*
Hosleton John
Thompson —
Clark J.   *Morristown.*
Clark W.
Wiley W.

Clark County.
Barringer Wm.   *Enon.*
Oraig John S.
Drummond John
Grogg George
Holt William   *Selma.*
Murphy J. C.
Gunn Lewis   *South Charleston.*
Johnson A. M.
Acres Gideon   *New Carlisle.*
Sheets William

Clermont County.
Hitch William   *Neville.*
Cox James   *Mulberry.*
Lucey J. W.
Luckey James
Sears George   *Loveland.*
Ann J.   *Laurel.*
Clark M.   *Bantam.*
Clark Wm.
Clark Z.
McIntosh Alexr.
Smith William

Columbiana County.
Hunter S.   *East Palestine.*
Mite A.
Bander Fredr. & Abm.   *North Georgetown.*
Fisher Andrew
Fryfogle Benjn.
Woolf Peter
Yengling John
Hunter John   *East Rochester.*
Gonnare Anthony   *Salem.*
Bricker Reason
Forney Jesse   *Unity.*
Jenkinson R.

Coshocton County.
Davis H.   *Coshocton.*

Crawford County.

Valentine Joseph — *Poplar.*
Valentine James
Carroll William — *Bucyrus.*
Cunning William
McClure H. W.

Cuyahoga County.

Spencer J. L — *Coe Ridge.*
Woodworth Theron — *Collamer.*
Woodworth Enoch
McIlrath Alexander
Taylor J. R., Euclid bet. Perry & Hudson — *Cleveland.*

Darke County.

Beard John — *New Madison.*
Downing J.
Eubank Thos.

Defiance County.

Allen H. — *Defiance.*
Bridenbaugh F.
Crunkilton A. B.

Fairfield County.

Kuhm Michael — *West Rushville.*

Franklin County.

Beck F. — *Columbus.*
Beck L.
Boyd John
Bradley Joseph
Cashman John
Campbell D. B. — *Groveport.*
Wallace J.
Landon Calvin — *Hope.*
Montgomery Calvin
Day Lyman — *Blendon.*
Loomis H. — *Central College.*
Dellinger Jacob — *Canal Winchester.*
Myers Ezra
Myer Henry

Greene County.

Leslie & Orowl — *Xenia.*
Rader John & Bros.
Rogers Amil

Hamilton County.

Bills, Lewis & Co., Court nr. Race — *Cincin.*
Bowers Wm., Piatt near Dayton
Kirman W., 128 Hopkins
Craven Wm., 271 Richmond
Hopper Garret — *Mt. Healthy.*
Garretson O.
Spahr Joseph
Johnson Ransaler
Liclear Michael — *Mt. Washington.*
Pool —
Bogunshots Michael — *Harrison.*
Looker Allison
Shubridge George
Baird Jas. H. — *Miami.*
Roberts Wm.
Burnes John A. — *Cummingsville.*
Reider William

Burkholter Solomon — *Reading.*
Bush Joseph — *Cheviot.*
Craven J.
McManama A. B.
Vail Samuel

Hancock County.

Crites Jacob — *Finley.*
Powell Jacob
Routson John
Stannard Asa

Hocking County.

Bragg Josiah — *Logan.*
Funcannan Henry
Rathburn Wm.

Jefferson County.

Neas & Co. — *Steubenville.*
Morgan J.
Huntsman N.
Thompson Caleb — *Annapolis.*
Shultz Saml.
Miller S. J. — *Mt. Pleasant.*
Mercer C. D.
Smith John

Knox County.

Gardner Joseph — *Mt. Vernon.*
Hearbel T.
Jennings John
Leach Chas. & Bro.
Smith Solomon
Smith William
Scarborough John
Beers James — *Fredericktown.*
Henderson James
Struble Daniel

Lawrence County.

Murdock Thos. — *Ironton.*
Newton John
Shepherd A. O.
Walker Wm.
White S.
Bickel A. — *Hanging Rock.*
Shepard M. L. — *Millers.*

Logan County.

Bush John — *Rushsylvania.*
Hatcher Daniel
Stilwell Thomas
Bane & Son — *Bellefontaine.*
Selden Hugh
Walters W. W. & Bro.
Watson J. R.
Courter Alexander — *Zanesfield.*
Courter George
McVaugh Jesse
Reames J. M.
Chambers Wm. — *Quincy.*
Neher M. C.
Neher E.

Lorain County.

Gerrish N. — *Oberlin.*
Smith E.

Strouse Chas.   *Cornersburg.*
Strouse J. D.
Schnabel G. J.   *Petersburg.*
Knesal A.
Marks J.
Henny J. G.   *Youngstown.*
Webster Fred.
Squares J. R.
Squares John
Wilcox B. G.   *Berlin Centre.*
Fisher Wm.
Stilson Saml. O.   *Beardman.*
Stilson J. D.
Livingston R. R.   *New Middletown.*
Miller J.
Rohrbach Andrew
Sharbaugh George   *East Lewistown.*
Winning John
Hudson Moses   *Coitsville.*
Weaver J. B.   *North Jackson.*
Bell J. W.
Wilderson Saml.
Fey Chas.
Pettitt W. D.   *Green Village.*
Beans B.
Kelley John
Bloom David   *North Lima.*
Haas Solomon
Kudesell Jerome
Stanley Isaac   *Damascoville.*
Peters John   *New Springfield.*
Smith Geo. F.
Wehagon H.   *New Albany.*
Preston Geo.

Marion County.

Ball Allen   *Cochranton.*
Sherman O. W.   *Prospect.*
Maratelle H.
Richman Ira
Holderbrand John
Rainey & Thew   *Marion.*
Thew & Ellis
Fetter & Gugle
Cone J. W.
Shultz & Dutt
Terpany S.

Medina County.

McBride A.   *Sharon Centre.*
Hagerling O.   *Liverpool.*
Wood J.
Houk H. M.
Dewey R. B.   *Wadsworth.*
Hulben D.
Warner E. & B. B.
Nice Isaac
Horner John   *Lodi.*
Merrifield P.
Beck Peter   *Weymouth.*
Bishop S.
Bishop O.
Woodruff A.   *Hinckley.*
Cowell Wm
Woodruff S. P.
McBride A.   *Sharon Cen're.*
Robinson F.   *Chatham Cen. re.*

Whitman A.   *Chatham Centre.*
Cook Saml.
Prentiss Barney   *Medina.*
Blackford T.
Blanott & Jones
Siphert & Morse
Freeman R. T.
Garrett E. H.

Meigs County.

Sullivan Wm.   *Downington.*
Bosworth J.
Cook M.
Calvert Wm.
Childers Saml.   *Apple Grove.*
Sidler J.
Childers Saml. R.   *Letert's Falls.*
Whiteside Thos.   *Pomeroy.*
Smith Thos.
Flannagan Danl.
Dilcher Henry
Duttenhaver Adam

Mercer County.

Clark A. P.   *St. Mary's.*
Sanchie George
Burnsides A.   *Celina.*
Moore J. T.   *Shane's Crossing.*
Cherington Isaac   *Menden.*
Roop Thos.   *Fort Recovery.*
Potter Henry   *Montezuma.*
Townville George   *Macedon.*

Miami County.

Everett M.   *Fletcher.*
Dued J. H.
Lehman Danl.   *Covington.*
Collins George B.   *West Charleston.*
Null J.
Plumb F.
Hauk G.   *Piqua.*
Meyer & Lines
Medaris W.
Beeder T.
Reser A.
Byrne & Gill
Bartel A.
Jacob J.
Bartel James
Sunderland White   *Troy.*
Harraman W. S.
Kreider J.
Beckweith & Markly
Gorsuch E.   *Casstown.*
Merritt A.
Scully D.   *Pleasant Hill.*
Birch Henry
Brown H. J.   *West Milton.*
Randall & Low

Monroe County.

Diehl Christian   *Woodfield.*
Thomas Daniel M
Monroe James S.   *Antioch.*
Swartwood Hugh
Swartwood Levi
Chapman Gideon   *Lainge.*

Thomas Reuben   *Sunfish.*
Thomas Gardiner
Thomas O. S.
Seibert F.
Seibert J.
Howell J.
Lohmire Henry   *Bealsville.*
McCullough Alex.
Griffith Reese L.   *Jerusalem.*
McGuire Samuel   *Malaga.*
Blackledge R. J.
Krouhart Casper & John
Janeway James
Sheats Henry   *Miltonsburgh.*
Steel W. & Co.   *Stafford.*
Hawkins & Magill
Isamborth Casper   *Baresville.*
Wolf Henry
Barker Isaiah   *Graysville.*
Joy Jesse

Montgomery County.

Biddleman J., Main   *Dayton.*
Brickford D., First
Buvinger L., Third
Crider George, Second
Darrow W. H. & Co., Main
Fanning & Co., Second
Flinn C. D., Green
Hand J., Wayne
Hockwall Geo., Main
Ingram & Lutz, do
Jeffers A.,   do
Johantzen P., Jefferson
Lindsey L., Main
McCutcheon J., Third
McCauley W., Main
Morey & Co., Jefferson
Meider A., Spratt
Moorehouse & Son, Main
Miller A. S., Fifth
Nugent C., Third
Phillips A., do
Powell J., Main
Reed J. F., First
Schreik C., Jefferson
Schroder W., Fifth
Vandenson & Wilson, Market
Weekel J. G., Third
Glass Frederick   *Clayton.*
Steel John A.
Stillwell Morgan
Williams George M.
Burwick John   *New Lebanon.*
Tobias James
Hollenbach W.   *Farmersville.*
Holp P.
Buchenaw Charles   *Harshmansville.*
Dodds & Weber   *Alexandersville.*
Conover J.
Dell John   *Liberty.*
Kalter Paul
West Joseph   *Centreville.*
Jean Samuel   *Chambersburg.*
Randle J. A.
Wenly S. W.

Swank & Smith   *Centre.*
Opdyke Perry   *Little York.*
Richards John
Griffith Alfred   *West Baltimore.*
Scofield J. W.
Clay Adam   *Miamisburg.*
Shell John
Wolf & Heckerman
Brechtol P.   *Germantown.*
Troup David
Auchenbaugh & Isenhomer

Morgan County.

Bowell Isaac   *Chester Hill.*
Worrell Z.
Maria Lewis
Bricker Peter   *Malta.*
Silling Wm.
Hambleton W. D.   *Rousseau.*
Buckley Joseph
Adrean Amos   *Meigsville.*
Thornberg —
Devol & Corner   *McConnelsville.*
Howard & Stone
Robb Joel
Bailey R. W. H.
Corey H. H.   *Stockport.*
Rainey Smith
Vanfassen A.
Matson Aaron   *Pennsville.*
Ralph Nelson
Hutton J. M.   *Neelysville.*

Morrow County.

Wortman Joshua   *Underwoods.*
Cyphers Barry   *Iberia.*
Reed James
Carpenter Aaron   *Marengo.*
Morehouse Silas
Crawford James   *Cardington.*
Ensign T. H.
Keen H.
Richards & Ramsower
Wilson Isaac J.
Bachelor Benjamin   *Shauk's.*
Holt Michael
Spear John   *Woodview.*
Benedict Gideon   *Lincoln.*
Emery Homer O.
Wilson David S.
Gleason John   *Pulaskiville.*
Peterson Silas
Masker D. J.   *Nimmon's Cross Roads.*
Dicks Eli   *Vail's Cross Roads.*
Enseyn & Snieb   *Mt. Gilead.*
Squires —
Struble Jesse   *Chesterville.*
Mather James
Swingley William
Jarvis Eli

Muskingum County.

Hull C. W.   *Nashport.*
Mitchell S. H.
Mitchell G. D.
Cassingham F.   *Frazeysburg.*
Cassingham James

Brokers—Exchange.

Allen County.

Roberts J. B. *Westminster.*

Ashland County.

Orall Luther & Co. *Ashland.*

Crawford County.

Miller A. A. *Bucyrus.*

Coshocton County.

Johnson Wm. K. *Coshocton.*
Ricketts Thos. O.
Brown J. M.

Cuyahoga County.

Brayton & Mason, Exchange Building *Cleveland.*
Lewis G. F., cor. Superior & Union
Lyman & Atwater do
Morrison J. do
Pyfer P. M. & Co., 6 Bank
Wicks, Otis & Brownell, do
Williams Geo. & Co., 18 Spruce
Wright W. W. & Co., Franklin House Block
Morrison A. & Co., 8 Detroit *Ohio City.*

Franklin County.

Bartlett & Smith, High *Columbus.*
Martin E., do
McCormick F. A., do
Johnston S., do
Donaldson L. & Co., cor. State & High

Gallia County.

Henking Charles *Gallipolis.*

Greene County.

Drake & Porsman *Xenia.*
Nunnemaker & Allen

Highland County.

Smith W. R. *Hillsboro'.*

Jefferson County.

McCollough Wm. *Mouth of Yellow Creek.*

Knox County.

Britton Lewis *Millwood.*

Licking County.

Franklin E. & Son *Newark.*
Sturges & Co.

Logan County.

Smith Y. A. *Bellefontaine.*

Morgan County.

Goodline, McClain, Bell & Co. *McCon-[neleville.*

Richland County.

Patterson & Co. *Mansfield.*

Scioto County.

Dugan & Mackoy *Portsmouth.*
Kinney & Tracy
Kinney P. & Co.

Seneca County.

Shawhan B. W. *Tiffin.*

Starke County.

Greer William H. *Magnolia.*
Cecil J. R. & Co. *Massillon.*

Summit County.

Smith Luther *Montrose.*

Trumbull County.

Harsh H. & Co. *Warren.*
Merriam & Co.

Tuscarawas County.

Vinton & Co. *New Philadelphia.*
Simpson J.
Sargeant A. W.
Braucher Joseph *Canal Dover.*

Warren County.

Evans D. *Waynesville.*
Sanders D. A. *Morrow.*

Brokers—Insurance.

Hamilton County.

Chapman W. S., 6 w. Front *Cincinnati.*

Broom Manufacturers.

Belmont County.

Hall William *Bellair.*
Bramhall P. *Morristown.*
Wiley W.

Butler County.

Jackson A. M. *West Chester.*
Jackson Wm.
Taust James
Vanhise Nehemiah *Pisgah.*
Ousom John N. *Rily.*

Clermont County.

Gray William *Bantam.*
Moss William

Columbiana County.

Fuller Horace *Wellsville.*

Coshocton County.

Smith Oliver *Coshocton.*

Cuyahoga County.

Gilbert L. *Chagrin Falls.*

Defiance County.

Robinson Tracy B. *Brunersburg.*

Franklin County.

Howard E. D. *Central College.*

Geauga County.

Bassett J. A. *Chardon.*
Vaughn C. A.
Hastings Z. R. *Auburn.*

Hamilton County.

Johnson R. *Mt. Healthy.*

Allis E.   *Carthage.*
Bullard J. M.
Curtis E.
Curtis L.
Burns T.   *Dunlap.*
Struble & Huey

Mahoning County.

Davidson Wm.   *Boardman.*
Vatter Wm.
Stanford T.
Simon A.
Meeker M.
Kisstner C.

Miami County.

Hafer George L.   *West Charleston.*
Page John   *Piqua.*
Hutchins Josiah   *West Milton.*
Jones David

Portage County.

Rogers Joseph   *Randolph.*
Stahl John   *Deerfield.*
NcNabb Alex.
Beardsley M.   *Charleston.*
Waller G. & M.   *Palmyra.*

Preble County.

Johnson Levi   *New Paris.*
Mauzy J. H.
Marshall R.

Richland County.

Cooley Austin   *Belleville.*

Summit County.

Beals Thomas   *Copley.*

Warren County.

Pening E.   *Franklin.*
McLain J.
McCauley Wm.   *Mason.*
Tompkins Wm.

Washington County.

Dutton Jas.   *Marietta.*
Stanley George   *Fearing.*

Brush Manufacturers.

Hamilton County.

Miles W. H., 7 w. Fourth *Cincinnati.*
Mintzer E. L., 211 Walnut
Butcher & Co., 11 Main
Tiptons J., 16 w. 8th
Herbert C., 479 W. Row
Fresh M., 104 Bremen
Claassen C. & Co., Main bet. Webster & Orchard
Keopff G. F., 39 Ham. Road bet. Main & Walnut

Montgomery County.

Mehlberth B., 3d   *Dayton.*

Butchers & Meat Dealers.

Ashland County.

Miller John   *Ashland.*

Ashtabula County.

Phillips James   *Ashtabula.*
Sessions H.

Auglaize County.

Marts J.   *Wapakoneta.*

Belmont County.

Butler Absalom   *Hendrysburgh.*
White Thomas   *Bellair.*
Muth John
Craft Stacey   *Saint Clairsville.*
Craft John
Darrah William
Darrah John
Parker Thomas
Fawcett Frank   *Belmont.*

Brown County.

Shafer John   *Higginsport.*
Zimmerly Jacob   *Ripley.*
Helpling Joseph
Delebaugh John

Butler County.

Johnson Jesse R.   *West Chester.*
Hiram & Conard   *Dartown.*
Cooch & Bagley, J. & J. E.
Straub & Noe   *Hamilton.*
Warwick J. M.
Howard J. F.   *Middletown.*
Bailey & Beck
Dillman & Barger   *Trenton.*
Boughman —
Debolt B.
Craig J.

Carroll County.

Baur Boniface   *Oneida Mills.*

Clarke County.

Cramer Joseph   *New Carlisle.*
Wilson Erastus

Clermont County.

Watkins Wm.   *New Richmond.*

Clinton County.

Antrum John   *Wilmington.*
Hazard James

Columbiana County.

Bright Elijah   *Wellsville.*
Byers Frederick   *New Lisbon.*
Helman Jacob D.
King Frederick
Rogers George S.
Springer David

Crawford County.

Feising Frederick   *Bucyrus.*
Foreman P. & T.
Hoffman M.

Cuyahoga County.

Champney & Co., C'rcial Market *Cleveland.*

Defiance County.

Shipley & Co.   *Defiance.*
Wilhelm A.

Erie County.

Darling Geo. H.   *Milan.*
Lockwood S. H.

Franklin County.

Bellar Asa   *Columbus.*
Benigans F.
Born Conrad
Cowling E., Friend
Cox William, Rich
Davis Oliver, Nat. Road
Derrick Peter, Friend
Dolter Paul, South
Emmet Philip, Friend
Feltz Charles, Front
Fuchs William, South
Gault James, Friend
Horch John, New
Imes John F., Friend
Kidd A., High
Knadlear Jos. & C. Borns, Friend
Kimmerly T.   do
Lang J. M.   do
Lerh Henry   do
Lewis Joseph, Locust Alley
Rickley R. S., Nat. Road
Chamberlin S.   *Reynoldsburg.*
Leathers Charles   *Canal Winchester.*

Geauga County.

Gorton B. B.   *Claridon.*
Bosley R.
Frost John   *Munson.*

Greene County.

Parks & Allen   *Clifton.*

Hamilton County.

Bogen G. & P. & Co., Harrison Road bet.
    Davison & Riddle streets,   *Cincinnati.*
Carter F. A., 573 Western Row
Cooper W. W., n. e. cor. Smith & 5th
Foley Samuel, cor. Park & 4th
Fenuion R. H., 212 w. 6th
Gerstader S., 33 Ham. Road
Har Jack, 152 Front
Harhn Max, 616 Vine
Hopperton J., 254 w. 6th
Katus F., cor. Elm & Ham. road
Luis Jacob, 210 Walnut
McDermott —, 27 8th
Marshall & Co., 202 w. 6th
Meyer Chas., 38 Ham. road
Muller C., cor. Pleasant & Liberty
Porter G., 195 w. 6th
Rush R., 450 w. 5th
Waetman W., 509 Sycamore
Wittiche A., 565 Main
Winter Perry, Hamilton Road bet. Piatt &
    Freeman
Ziegle J. G., 256 Western Row
Wise P.   *Fulton.*
Jordan E.   *Mt. Healthy.*
Ridenbaugh John
Orist Ebenezer   *Montgomery.*
Cochran O. O.

Gable John   *Harrison.*
Hais S.
Oyler Samuel
Vantress Wm.
Croseley Josiah   *Mt. Washington.*
Moore Geo.   *Cheviot.*
Moore John

Hardin County.

Hulls T.   *Kenton.*
Ohand G. W.

Harrison County.

Shauk Samuel   *Cadis.*

Hocking County.

Roth John   *Logan.*

Huron County.

Thorne & Heale   *Bellevue.*
Joint William

Jefferson County.

Huscroft Wm.   *Steubenville.*
Richardson Wm.
Huddel A. & D.
Solomons Samuel
Wilcoxon Samuel
Gracey George
Bullock J.
Mantle J.
Barr John
Karum Philip   *Annapolis.*
Kithcart Joseph   *Mt. Pleasant.*

Knox County.

Beach Allen   *Mount Vernon.*
Bechtel Joseph
DeWitt John
Irwin James
Thompson & Beach
Work David
Morrow James   *Fredericktown.*

Lake County.

Elias J.   *Painesville.*
Woodman & Masher
Huntoon & Carter

Lawrence County.

Kirker W. W.   *Ironton.*
Roberts Roberts

Licking County.

Watkins Wm.   *Brownsville.*
Youngman C.
Corsen Wm. A.   *Newark.*
Graves & Hoover   *Croton.*
Allen W. G.

Logan County.

Carter K. G.   *Huntsville.*
Holland D. B.   *Zanesfield.*
Pope William

Lorain County.

Bacon C. F.   *Oberlin.*

Madison County.

Farrar Henry   *London.*

Stutson Jennet   *West Jefferson.*
Johnston Abraham

Medina County.

Pursell J.   *Wadsworth.*
Oatman L.   *Medina.*
Tuller George

Monroe County.

Lynch John K.   *Woodsfield.*
Mason Russel

Montgomery County.

Lawson A.   *Chambersburg.*
Smith J.
Keifer George, Third   *Dayton.*
Conrad C. M., Fifth
Stickline James, N. Market
Mell David   *West Baltimore.*
Bowser Jacob   *Germantown.*
Emerick Levi
Miller John   *Miamisburg.*
Moyer Michael
Shuster Christian

Morgan County.

Robison J.   *Meigsville.*
Fogle Robert   *McConnelsville.*
Wylie M.
Lockey Wm.
McConnell John

Morrow County.

Manahan Aaron   *Underwood's.*

Muskingum County.

Bendure George   *White Cottage.*
Thomas Wm. H.   *Gratiot.*

Perry County.

Fowler & Brown   *New Lexington.*

Pickaway County.

Carlisle & Throne   *Circleville.*
Walters & Hoselton

Portage County.

Beckweth & Sabin   *Ravenna.*
Carter & Brother
Newberry & Broomfield   *Franklin.*
Phelps John   *Atwater.*
Shain Alex.   *Randolph.*

Preble County.

Show David   *Eaton.*
Show Joseph

Richland County.

Lippard P.   *Shelby.*
Layver Philip   *Mansfield.*
Marks George
Moore James
McQuinn John   *Lexington.*
Whiteford Cornelius
Fisher Daniel   *Belleville.*
Smith J. A.

Ross County.

Baker Abraham   *Chilicothe.*

May & Bartlett   *Chilicothe.*
Reed & Carlisle
Frazer A. & Co.
Marfield J. & Co.

Sandusky County.

Meyers John   *Fremont.*
Weigstine & Fancks

Scioto County.

Bennett W. H.   *Portsmouth.*
Young & White
Coons C.
Humel P.
Lanager M.
Tombs George
Welch & Lawson

Seneca County.

Grudgings Daniel   *Republic.*

Starke County.

Weisner George   *East Greenville.*
Harmon Benjamin   *New Baltimore.*

Summit County.

Treep & Hart   *Middlebury.*
Musser William   *Inland.*
Siess Benjamin
Hammond Elijah   *Richfield.*
Humphrey N. M.

Tuscarawas County.

Hammond S.   *Canal Dover.*
Helmstaffer C.
Walters George
Crasland S.   *New Philadelphia*

Warren County.

Thorne John L.   *Waynesville.*
Tea B. L.   *Morrow.*
Roach John
Shawhan James

Washington County.

Wood F.   *Marietta.*
Wood J.
Morse J.
Armstrong H.
Wood Jas.   *Harmar.*
Wood Francis
Cooper J. B.

Wayne County.

Swan Chas. J.   *Number One.*
Johnson John

Wood County.

Sander John   *Perrysburg*
Needer John

Wyandot County.

Martin Wm.   *Upper Sandusky*
Miller Henry
Johnson Wm.

Butter & Eggs—Wholesale Dealers.

Columbiana County.

Watt John   *New Lisbon.*
Myers Samuel
Patrick James   *Salem.*
Fisher H.   *Unity.*

Hamilton County.

Coates & Co., Elbow Miami Canal *Cincia.*
Cowgill & Goodall, 29 Sycamore
Gould G. W., 9th bet Main & Sycamore
Golden —, 201 w. 6th
John J. C., cor. 9th & Main
Jones A. & Son, 107 5th
Russell C. S., 199 W. Row
Swasey & Wise, cor. Columbia & Broad-way
Townsend O., 45 Columbia
Wydman S., 155 5th

Licking County.

Merriman A. & Co.   *Granville.*
Irwin J, G. & Co.

Medina County.

Bissell D. J.   *Medina.*
Bissell Benjamin
Collier Lemuel   *Leroy.*

Portage County.

Loomis & Dickinson   *Ravenna.*

Buttons—Bone & Horn Manufacturers.

Hamilton County.

Heol J. H., Pearl bet. Elm & Plum *Cincin.*

Lorain County.

Terrell & Smith   *North Ridgeville.*

Cabinet, Chair & Furniture Manufacturers & Dealers.

Adams County.

Coner L. L.   *Manchester.*
Cluxton D. D.
Gregory E. R.   *Stouts.*
Toll William   *Locust Grove.*
McColm William Q.   *Eckmansville.*
Woodrow Alexr.   *West Union.*
Lafferty & Co.
Harshall Thos.
Carl William

Allen County

Smith J. C.   *Deep Cut.*
Gibson G. A.   *Westminster.*
Walcott J. M.
Huffer Simeon   *Donnell's.*
Auchmutz George   *Cranberry.*
Kerlin James

Ashland County.

Kettlewell Charles   *Savannah.*
Frankeberger William

Stem Erastus   *Savannah.*
Grubb Jacob   *Ashland.*
King Philip
Kriefbaum Jacob
Horn George W.   *Jeromeville.*
Rice John
Gilbert Henry   *Loudonsville.*
Winters Philip
Shafer D.   *Perrysville.*
Oldroyd Johnson   *Mohecan.*

Ashtabula County.

Cornis Ogdon   *Kelloggsville.*
Young M.
Mattison L.
Stone T. H.   *Jefferson.*
Ducro & Brothers
Fay Wm. H.
Savage J.   *Ashtabula.*
Culley J. C.
Boyles John
Nevison Thos.   *Hart's Grove.*
Franklin Wm.   *Pierpont*
Foster M. J.   *Lindenville*
Woodworth H.   *Conneaut.*
Hart P.
Hathaway J. R.
Beach S.

Athens County.

Puters B.   *Amesville.*
Ellison Wm.
Holler M.
Clouse J. W.   *Albany.*
Howe John R.   *Nelsonville.*
McCollum Isaac
Roberts J. G.   *Shad.*
Bartlett W. D.   *Athens.*
McGill Wm.
Dell John
Clouse James   *Lee.*
Bellows G. B.

Auglaize County.

Steinger Sebastian   *Wapakoneta.*
Austin J. M. & Co.   *St. John's.*

Belmont County.

Jackson John   *Demos.*
Hibbard Hiram   *Barnesville.*
Riley David
Riley Nathan
Morley Amos   *Bell Air.*
Arnold Putnam   *Uniontown.*
Cannon Erasmus   *Flushing.*
White B. & J.
Brewer John P.   *Loydsville.*
Murray John P.   *Dillies Bottom.*
Faris William   *St. Clairsville.*
Rice Thomas
Broxton T.   *Morristown.*
Roseborough D.
Stevens J., Junr.   *Shepherdstown.*
Chalfant Ephraim   *Belmont.*
Hall W.   *Armstrong's Mills*
Price John H.   *Hunter.*
Travis Moses

Brown County.

Casset Dennis	*Higginsport.*
Sparks & Lane	*Ripley.*
Bryant John	*Hamersville.*
Parlmer H.	*Newhope.*
Pasthtlewait L.	*Russellville.*
Main J. W.	
Marsh Wm. H.	*Fincastle.*
Bradley J. T.	
Pangbum & Stamm	*Sardinis.*
Cabrin Ira	
Sweet Benjamin	*Five Mile.*

Butler County.

Constinger Joseph	*Bethany.*
McMillen D. B.	*Blue Ball.*
Osborn H.	*Oxford.*
Gath S.	
Clonph J. P.	
Duffield R. E.	*Hamilton.*
Koonsman G. B.	*Roseville.*
Deleplane Joshua	
Smallwood Daniel	*Middletown.*
Wilson Thos.	
Hill C.	*Millville.*
Long John	*Monroe.*
Shideler L.	*College Corner.*
Harper James	
Conley J.	*Somerville.*
Fisher & Shiffer	*Seven Mile.*
Gardner John	*Trenton.*
Daup Conrad	
Gilland C. K.	*Reily.*

Carroll County.

Hixson Abner	*New Hagerstown.*
McLaren John W.	
Gantz Abraham	*Norristown.*
Crumrine Peter	*Carrollton.*
Reehm David	
Thompson John	
Coyan Addison	*Oneida Mills.*

Champaign County.

French Noah	*Christiansburg.*
Decious J.	*Westville.*
Smith J. & A.	
McCord J. P.	*Urbana.*
Patrick Wm. & E. B.	
Collwell R. R.	
Sweet C.	
Lyon John	*Mutual.*
Death D. A.	*St. Paris.*
White B.	
Smith S.	
Haines Samuel	
Reynolds John	*North Lewisburg.*
Reynolds & Shully	

Clarke County.

Kurtz Conrad	*Enon.*
Shipman, Mussy & Filbert	*Springfield.*
Phelps John	
Coles W.	
Wood John G.	
Baumgarner P. L.	*Catawba.*
Fry H.	

Warner William L.	*South Charleston.*
Kinert & Taylor	*New Carlisle.*

Clermont County.

Garrison J.	*New Richmona.*
Hoover Stephen	
McClung David	*Williamsburg.*
Bricker R.	
Israel Benjamin	*Bethel.*
Orsborn David	
Bryan & South	*Felicity.*
Simmons John H.	
Pierce E.	
Ellis Jesse	*Batavia.*
McCune James	
Robinson John W.	*Amelia.*
Buchanan Robert	*Moscow.*
Fletcher John	
Stewart P. G.	*Perin's Mills.*
Nichols E.	*Laurel.*
Doughty Levi	*Bantam.*
Sears A. P.	*West Woodville.*
Leich J. M.	

Clinton County.

Linsey Wm.	*New Burlington.*
Ellis A. & J.	*Port William.*
Borton John	*Lumberton.*
Johnson L.	*Westboro'.*
Winfield H.	*Sligo.*
Supinger Robert	*Blanchester.*
Mitchell W. F.	*New Antioch.*
Hale T. E.	*New Vienna.*
Hines J.	
Leeke J.	
Myers H.	
Newman James	*Martinsville.*
Gorman Jas. M.	
Hunt John	
Marble Daniel	*Wilmington.*
Marble W. J.	
Marble R. B.	
McGuger Eli	

Columbiana County.

Aughingough Henry	*Wellsville.*
Thatcher Geo. W.	
Eells Erastus	*New Lisbon.*
Eells George W.	
Hessin Henry	
Hellen & McGarry	
Hays John	*East Palestine.*
Haldeman John	*Salineville.*
Sheckler Simon	
Temple M. D.	*New Garden.*
Chesholm Robert	*North Georgetown.*
Miller Anthony	
Ruhl George	
Budd C. J.	*Franklin Square.*
Thomas Jacob	*New Chambersburgh.*
Thomas Alfred	
Colestock Daniel	*East Rochester.*
Henchellnood George	*Salem.*
Henchellnood John	
Stratton Edward	
Kuhl John	*Bucks.*
Bennet H.	*West Point.*
Beard Jacob	*Columbiana.*

Brubaker Samuel   *Columbiana.*
Crawford & Simkins   *East Fairfield.*
Tullis Thomas   *Elkton.*
Tullis Seth

Coshocton County.

Shipler Peter   *Clark's.*
Mizer Philip   *Bakersville.*
Jones Asbury
Porter David
Need George
Stanley William
Rinehart M.
Ringor James   *Chili.*
Himebaugh Wm.
Ross John   *Keene.*
Nieless Benjamin   *Warsaw.*
Nosker George
Waggoner Jacob   *Coshocton.*
Sells B. F.

Crawford County.

McLane Alexander   *Leesville Cross Roads.*
Swank David   *Poplar.*
Honey Christian   *New Washington.*
Balser Henry   *Liberty Corners.*
Parson George
Bolinger S. & Spore   *Sulphur Spring.*
Fulton A.   *Bucyrus.*
Howenstine & Wise
Lightner D. R.
Miller Henry
Smith & Welling
Spors S. S.   *Chatfield.*

Cuyahoga County.

Bauder Levi, 70 Public Square, *Cleveland.*
Bauder C. L., 35 Prospect street
Body F. J., 51 Pittsburgh
Fuldheim M., 42 Ontario
Goodull David J., cor. Pittsburgh & Huron
Gardner & Vincent, 48 Water
Griffin & Brinker, 54   do
Hart William, 59   do
Henry J., cor. Kinsman & Cross
Lathrup H., 50 Detroit
Shepard D. A. & Co., 31 Water
Schults & Co., 38 Bank
Strong Homer   *Ohio City.*
Combs, Longstreet & Co.
Brown H.   *Chagrin Falls.*
Goodman T. J.
Russell H.
Morse G. H.   *Bedford.*
Peck S.
Powel F.
Frost E. C.   *Coe Ridge.*
Knight George   *Collamer.*
Davids J. J. E.   *Berea.*
McCarron H. W.

Darke County.

Boley Lewis   *Ithica.*
Fleming James & J. M.   *New Madison.*
Martin Wm.   *German.*
Cowgill & Son   *Republican.*

Longnecker John   *Beamsville.*
Holloway John

Defiance County.

Ayres A. A.   *Defiance.*
Holloway Anson
Price Edward
Fellers Peter   *Brunersburg.*
Kuhn J. J.

Delaware County.

Manser Wm.   *Delaware.*
Welch A. A.
Reichart J. J.
Taylor J. E.   *Waldo.*
Smith Saml.
Minich Saml.
Thomas Truman   *Sunbury.*
Marble N.

Erie County.

Thorpe, Norcross & Thorpe   *Sandusky [City.*
Edson T.
Meyers B.
Zullinger C. W.
Guild J. G.
Sanderson S. M.   *Berlinville.*
Stevens J.   *Milan.*
Stine G.
Seaman G.

Fairfield County.

Sharp John & Samuel   *Pickerington.*
Cowan John   *West Rushville.*
Fix John   *New Salem.*
Eckhart & Smith   *Lancaster.*
Dodson T.
Franklin B.
Foster D.
Fishell D. K.
Riffel D.
Thomas John   *Clear Creek*
Long L.
Guley M.   *Sugar Grove.*
Andrew James   *Lithopolis.*
Smith John

Fayette County.

Brown W. T.   *Pancoastburg.*
Heagler Geo.   *Washington.*
Stengel M.
Burnett Jesse
Johnson Edwin   *Moons.*
Heller Wm.   *Staunton.*

Franklin County.

Fischer J., Front   *Columbus.*
Halm M., High
Reitz John, do
Shumacher F., Friend
Stark G. P., High
Schoedinger & Co., Rich
Smith Philip, High
Shettingger Philip
Willard & Howlett, Front
Shaffer Moses   *Groveport.*
Zinn Abram

Fogle George   *Reynoldsburg.*
Graham A. T.
Morton A. M.
Jack Chas. & Hugh   *Hope.*
Ogden Charles
Taylor George   *Worthington.*
Benadum Joseph   *Canal Winchester.*
Hunsucker Abraham
Staux Lewis

Fulton County.

Wilt George W.   *Elmira.*
Theobold L. D

Porter M.   *Delta.*

Gallia County.

Brandyberry Wm.   *Adamsville.*
Skerrit William
Fillmore Charles D.   *Pine Grove.*
Irwin John
Weatherbolt Elias
Hayward Solomon   *Gallipolis.*
McIntyre Reuben
Skees James
Simmerman H. P.   *Patriot.*
Cogshell Daniel   *Kyger.*
Johnson James H.

Geauga County.

Munsell Wm. G.   *Chardon.*
Teed J. B.
Johnson Daniel   *Burton.*
Phinney H.   *Russell.*
Jones E. C.   *Parkman.*
Harrinden F. J.
Gouldwood A. C.
Pomeroy E.   *Huntsburg.*
Hammond G. H.   *Hamden.*
Colson L.   *Troy.*
Rich F. C.   *Chester.*
Ross H.   *Auburn.*

Greene County.

Jones J.   *Xenia.*
Shearer & Smith
Cost Peter.   *Fairfield.*
Colands Stephen
DeWitt H.   *Spring Valley.*
Torrence J.
Jeffreys U. & J.   *Cedarville.*
Studavant & Tracy
McCulloch Samuel   *Yellow Springs.*
Shunk Adam

Guernsey County.

Atchison John   *Cumberland.*
Crosgrove & Casey
Johnson George
Robinson Wm.   *Washington.*
Tounk Henry
Wilkins Wm.   *Londonderry.*
Moore Wm.
Morrison J.   *Antrim.*
Thompson Saml.
Morrison J.   *Winchester.*
Meyer Christian   *New Gottingen.*
Lemmon Jas.   *Fairview.*
McCune John

8

Johnson O. W.   *Fairview.*
Parkhill John
Hunter J. C.   *Cambridge.*
Nelson James
Lindsey John
Bumgardner John   *Kimbolton.*
Bumgardner David
Powers Wm.
Daugherty R.   *Millersville.*
Morrison J. & Co.   *Senecaville.*
Anderson J. H.

Hamilton County.

Bailey John, 39 e. Front   *Cincinnati.*
Barlage & Steinman, 227 w. Fifth
Baumeister & Goldschmidt, 66 Sycamore
Bergman J. D., 541 Main
Bosse Henry, 59 w. Fifth
Boyd Peter, 72 w. Eighth
Crane Lemuel M., 81 Sycamore
Coolidge John K., 51 & 53 Vine
Oramsey W., 125 w. 5th
Crowell & Plattenburg, 6th bet. Vine & Race
Duncan L. M. & Bro., Columbia bet. Walnut & Vine
Dobell E. B., 68 Lower Market
De Camp John, cor. Front & Pike
Davis John B., 21 w. 6th
Duchscher Pierre, 123 w. 5th
Doring J. H., 170 Hamilton Road
Ellerman John, 67 w. 5th
Feith Nicholas, 81 do
Gaus & Knupfer, 50 Hamilton Road
Goodrich E., 280 w. 5th
Geyer John, 8 e. 4th
Henshaw G., 85 Sycamore
Hang Jacob T., 541 Race
Hackman G., 93 Court
Hoffman & Schmidt, Court near Walnut
Hessa C. H., Wade bet. Plum & W. Row
John S. J., 23 e. 4th
Johnston C. D , 51 & 53 Vine
Jones T. C., 229 w. 5th
Knostmann J. F., 52 w. 9th
Kraumer & Co., 11 Franklin
Kramer & Co., 535 Main
Kalmbach D., 551 Vine
Lieblers T., 79 Spring
Lefontan S., 322 Elm
Louge John M., 77 w. 5th
Morehouse Wm., 134 Sycamore
Mullen Jonathan, 132   do
Mitchell & Rammelsberg, 23 & 25 e. 2d
Netherman Casper, 27 Ham. Road
Neather Augustus, s. w. cor. 5th & Home
Overbeck G., 102 Hunt
Osborn B., 339 Elm
Remmert Henry, 5th bet. Walnut & Vine
Schmid H. B., 442 Walnut
Simon J., 444   do
Schasbartt Frederick 603 Vine
Smith & Hawley, 64 Sycamore
Suydam —, Front e. of Broadway
Schuller F., 337 Walnut
Shaw Aaron, 18 e. 4th
Tynan B., 3 w. 5th

Tetur H. F., Hamilton Road bet. Piatt & Main *Cincinnati.*
Volger P., 558 Vine
Wessen C. J , 350 w. 4th
Wrampelmoerer & Otto. cor. Canal & Plum
Wrampelmeier & Otto, 215 w. 5th
White Barton, 126 Sycamore
Zaiser Wm., 41 Hunt
Crosly S. *Pendleton.*
Miesenfield J. *Fulton.*
Curry H. R. *Walnut Hills.*
Gearhart C. *Mount Healthy.*
Paiu James G.
Glisson S. *Dunlap.*
Bratzel George *Harrison.*
Slote & Bonham

Hancock County.

Coleman Herman *Van Buren.*
Peirce Gad & Co.
Subers Paul F. & Co
Zorbauch John
Howe A. *Mt. Blanchard.*
Hullsinger George *Benton Ridge.*
Diffenderffer R. *Canonsburgh.*
Tubolet Jacob
Collins J. *McComb.*
Todd William

Hardin County.

Stanford, Brandaugh & Co. *Kenton.*
Damon Luther
Kennett & Markle
Dom Peter
Thompson Jacob *Roundhead.*
Snow L. *Sylvia.*

Harrison County.

Fry Wm J. *Cadiz.*
Hunter Joseph R.
Gillespie John.
Moore Aaron *Deersville.*
Anderson James *Harrisville.*

Henry County.

Andrew H. & J. *Florida.*
Rogers Joseph
Yarmill Thos. *Napoleon.*
Ferguson —
Durbin Wm. *Texas.*

Highland County.

Hodson Lewis *Highland.*
Mitchner John
Daughters Elias
Roan John *Greenfield.*
Kelly Wm.
Boyd & Anderson
Cohran R. *Belfastown.*
Sloan Wm.
Leaman Robert *New Market.*
Holmes S. *Sugartree Ridge.*
Woods H. *New Petersburg.*
Meridith E.
Williams John *Marshall.*
Morris John *Centrefield.*
Ashenfelter Henry *Allensburg.*

Roller Saml.
Clark Thos. G. *Greenford*
McGee E. R. *Samantha*
Hawkins Wm. H.
Moore Robert *Dallas.*
Bentley A. *Leesburg.*
Henley John
Doggett Washington *Hillsboro'.*

Hocking County.

Butin A. H. *Logan.*
Eversole & Butin
Kanode Henry
Johnson Alfred *Swan.*

Holmes County.

Beall Alfred *Holmesville.*
Drunett F. *Benton.*
Kuon Conrad *Walnut Creek.*
Faith Anderson
Winch M. *Winesburg.*
Mullett A.
Inner G.
Harpster & Farras *Millersburg.*

Huron County.

Husted H. *Clarksfield.*
Henry M.
White Chas.
Billinger A. *Bellevue.*
Moore D.
Eickhorn L.
Hoyt W. R. *Norwalk.*
Sharp J. V.
Farley R.

Jackson County.

Howell N. T. *Jackson.*

Jefferson County.

Ammon David *Steubenville.*
Walker J.
Walker R.
Donaldson A.
Childs Samuel *Annapolis.*
Findlay Thos. B.
Humphreyville Wm. B. *Mt. Pleasant.*
Kelley John *Knoxville.*

Knox County.

King J. *Mt. Vernon.*
Lewis M. & D. *Lucerne.*
Chamberlain Thos. *Fredericktown.*
Sargent G. W.
Greene James *Democracy.*
Hibbart Wm.
Miller John
Rockwell J. W.
Armuthut D. *North Liberty.*
Fry Charles
Wimland E.
Fish Saml. R. *Millwood.*
Lamborn Linly
Sago A. B. *Mt. Liberty*

Lake County.

Talcott A. *Madison*
Thompson R.

Belnap, Mansfield & Co. *Painesville.*
Harris Milo

Lawrence County.

Hall William *Ironton.*
Young William *Hanging Rock.*
Hughes Silas *Millers.*

Licking County.

Garrison Peter & Saml. *Linnville.*
Tracy H.
Garrison David
Flowers John *Etna.*
Green John B.
Sylvester John Z. *Granville.*
Bancroft G. P.
Roney B. H. *Newark.*
Beemer J. H. *Homer.*
Payne N. H. *Croton.*
Green H. S. *Perryton.*
Duke Wm. *Johnstown.*
Smith Chas. *Kirkersville.*

Logan County.

Quick John *Huntsville.*
Hyndman C. F. *New Richland.*
Sergent T. *East Liberty.*
Hall James *Rushsylvania.*
Kirkpatrick J. *Bellefontaine.*
Bishop T. S. *Zanesfield.*
Little M. E.
Little Wm. H.
Seaman Benjamin
Shinn D. A.
Means George *Quincy.*
Means Alexander
Welsh Maxwell

Lorain County.

Brown Henry *La Grange.*
Cook Ambrose *Huntington.*
Bedortha S. *Oberlin.*
Gager Stephen *North Camden.*
Niepfoot Henry *Elyria.*
Stratton James *Amherst.*

Lucas County.

Lamb Chas. A. *Maumee City.*
Peckham J. D.
Clappick J. *Toledo.*
Johnson D.
Melick B.
Stockman T. L.

Madison County.

Dungan Wilson *London.*
Smith F. L. *Mt. Sterling.*
Orr Hugh *South Solon.*
White William J. *West Canaan.*
Bradley Jonas *West Jefferson.*

Mahoning County.

Witherell John *Canfield.*
Arnold A. G.
Dustware Abraham *Cornersburg.*
Musser Jacob *Petersburgh.*
Sholl J. E.
Headley Henry *Youngstown.*
Hazen J. B.

Langhridge John *Youngstown.*
Kaisor John *Berlin Centre.*
Faas C. *New Middletown.*
Thoman Henry *East Lewistown.*
Yoder Peter B.
Kunkle O. & J. *North Jackson.*
Houselman Wm.
Lancaster John
Augdon Wm. J. *Poland.*
Cocker & Boies
Roller Samuel *Green Village.*
Wasser Jacob
Hasness Martin *North Lima.*
Good Moses

Marion County.

Carter O. *Wilson.*
Gillispie N.
Gart John *Prospect.*
Gart Joseph
Jameson D. *Marion.*
Hineman F.

Medina County

Caskey James *Sharon Centre.*
Tubles L. *Liverpool.*
Hendricks Amos *River Styx.*
Prentice Geo. *Lodi.*
Weaver Henry
Stewart P. C. *Hinckley.*
Miller Moses *Weymouth.*
Wilder W.
Runtz M. *Homerville.*
Plattner C.
Davis A. *Medina.*
Ainsworth J. T
Little & Osire
Seaton R. P.

Meigs County.

Gatchel Abraham *Pomeroy.*
Bartlett R. H.
Probst John C.
McPheter J. D. *Ledlies.*
Cline Alex.

Mercer County.

Hight & Kirkpatrick *Celina.*
Resler Wm. *Mendon.*
Hunter Shanesville *Shanesville.*
Studen B. *Macedon.*

Miami County.

Abbott Wm. *Piqua.*
Muchman R.
Brotherton & Abbott
Dealty Wm.
Morvin R.
Harthin M.
Bennett & Davis
Bains J. & J. *Troy.*
Thompson G.
Baugh & Eyer *Casstown.*
Pence J.
Kindelsberger S.
Marshall & Fuller
Swain & Long

Moses H.   *West Milton.*
Miller Jacob
Ice Joseph
Updegraft A.   *Brant.*
Curtis H. M.
Vorhees A.   *Pleasant Hill.*
Deeter S. R.
Duncan H.

Monroe County.

Perry William G.   *Woodfield.*
Wheeler Jacob
Mitchell & Mahoney   *Laing's.*
White & Henthorn   *Antioch.*
Cathel P.   *Rocky Narrows.*
Davis Joseph
Swobe John A.   *Miltonsburgh.*
Mankey Henry
Imax & Carter   *Malaga.*
Smith & Slusher
Girsell Simeon
Sinclair J. B.   *Bealsville.*
Morris Jesse
McConnel Alexander   *Sunfish.*
Steele James R.   *Plymouth.*
Pepper G. W.   *Graysville.*
Dye John R.

Montgomery County.

Weaver Martin   *Liberty.*
McCracken Jacob   *Centreville.*
Davenport & Shomo   *Centre.*
Boyer William, Third   *Dayton.*
Conklin J. O., Main
Elliot James, do
Hartel J., Second
McLear G. S., Wayne
Omer M., Main
Spakn A., do
Haskins Augustus   *Clayton.*
Haskins Aaron
Shell George
Karr Jacob   *West Baltimore.*
Basore D.   *Farmersville.*
Stiver John
Brough Benjamin   *Miamisburgh.*
Doebling Henry
Pansing Henry
Zimmerman Henry
Artze Joseph   *Germantown.*
Boyer George
Hawkins B. G
Heister George

Morgan County.

Shoop Wm.   *Chester Hill.*
Hunnicutt Wm. P.
Lee A. T.
Palmer J. J. & Wm. O.   *Malta.*
Brown John   *Meigs Creek.*
Newlan David   *Rousseau.*
Warner Wm.   *Elliott's Cross Roads.*
Pinkerton R. A.   *McConnelsville.*
Pinkerton, H. R.
Harris John & Son

Morrow County.

Gruber Henry   *Iberia*
Doty Peter   *Marengo.*
Paine E.   *Cardington.*
St. John A.
Rusler John   *Shauk's.*
Weibling William   *Woodview.*
Weibling John
Stackhouse D. J.   *Pulaskiville.*
Beard C.   *Nimmons' Cross Roads.*
Fogle Thomas   *Corsica.*
Strong & Nixon   *Chesterville.*

Muskingum County.

Whitaker Israel   *Norwich.*
Vaughn A. B.   *Frazeysburg.*
Furner Henry   *Dresden.*
Thompson & Love
Fauley A.   *Fultonham.*
Benjamin David   *Hopewell.*
Grunmon J. & W.   *Concord.*
Wolfe J. E.   *Chandlersville.*
Cassidy & Co.   *Zanesville.*
Mohler & Smith.

Noble County.

Enoch David   *Berne.*
Camden John P.   *Mount Ephraim.*
Magill William   *Harrietsville.*
Corwin James   *Sarahsville.*
Dougherty Wm. F.
Cunningham George   *Gardner.*
Powell James H.   *Batesville.*
Robinson James M.

Perry County.

Davenport George   *New Lexington.*
Hatcher & Gruber
Donelly Thomas   *Rehoboth.*
Gordon Wm. T.
Elder Charles   *Somerset.*
Elder Joseph
Fulton Robert
Jackson William
Page Robert
Adams John   *Chapel Hill.*
Deaver H. J.
Goulding H.

Pickaway County.

Myers G. W.   *Circleville*
Puncher M.
Robison Frank
Mayes & Myers & Co.   *Tarlton.*
Roby G. W.
Ambrose G. W.   *Darbyville.*
Dornsife David

Pike County.

Suple Isaac   *Piketon.*
Ware Wm.
Ragon John D.

Portage County.

McElwaine & Turnham   *Ravenna.*
Lane G.
Griffin A. B. & O. H.
Knowlton A. & T. & Co.   *Franklin.*
Houpt B.   *Shalersville.*

Stedman Isaac N.	*Aurora.*
Pierson E.	*Edinburgh.*
Goddard V.	
Winans Alex.	*Atwater.*
Lee Ebenezer	*Nelson.*
Demmers John	*Freedom.*
Hoyer Joseph	*Deerfield.*
Suttle Isaac	*Palmyra.*

Preble County.

Gitzer John	*West Alexander.*
Mehaffic A.	
Schlingman D.	
Gardiner Benj. F.	*Camden.*
Shaeffer John M.	
Hughes Jarrett	*Eaton.*
Morgan Thomas	
Morgan Robert	
Harshman John	
Simpson J.	
Bloomfield W. A.	
Tykle F.	*Fairhaven.*
Gift D.	
Bowen J. H.	*New Westville.*
Stubbs Eli	*West Elkton.*
Hasletine & Walker	*New Paris.*
Cullon James	

Putnam County.

Horner John	*Leipsic.*
Edgington J.	*Gilboa.*
Hoagland & Brooks	
Sterling S.	*Kalida.*
Soaper W. T.	*Buckeye.*
Hasson E. A.	*Vaughnsville.*
Frey Henry	*Pendleton.*

Richland County.

Saltzgaber S.	*Shelby.*
Suter S.	
Blymer & Myers	*Mansfield.*
Heldman J. A.	
Niman James	
Stow John	*Lexington.*
Endlow Andrew J.	*Barnes.*
Johnson James	
Ward Profit B.	*Olivesburg.*
Cowan H.	*Belleville.*
Lainhart Wm.	
Lafevre C. A.	
Lobach John	
Phillips Jacob	
Enlow A. J.	*Lucas.*
Pettingee William	*Adario.*

Ross County.

Ware J. M.	*Frankfort.*
Siep David	*Chilicothe.*
Hess L.	
Kirkpatrick Wm.	
Hamilton John	*South Salem.*
Heap George	*Hallsville.*
Zimmerman John	*Kingston.*

Sandusky County.

Chamberlin J. W.	*Woodville.*
Steurnen J. W.	*Fremont.*
Sindlebunck J.	*Fremont.*
Miller J.	
Smith D.	*Rollersville.*
Chaner Jesse	

Scioto County.

Grassman H.	*Portsmouth.*
Williams W. E.	
Boyd James L.	*Wheelersburgh.*

Seneca County.

Orall John B.	*Attica.*
Huddleson John H.	
Philo Adams P.	
Cleckner Philip	*Adrian.*
Springer John	
Covert Orra	*Berwick.*
Kalmus Francis	
Betts Daniel	*Bettsville.*
Fry John	
Campbell Wm. & Co.	*Tiffin.*
Feize John	
Myers J.	
Seller & Limp	
Smith M.	
Thompson D.	*Green Spring.*
Donk Frederick	
Chamberlin Henry	*Republic.*
Kessaler George E.	
Bogart M. F.	

Shelby County.

Young H. D.	*Houston.*
Dewees C. M.	*Pratt.*
Robbins & Dickerson	
McVay Jason	*Sidney.*
Murray George	
Reed W. P.	
Powell William	*Hardin.*

Starke County.

Johnson Eli	*East Greenville.*
Reeves John	
Smith Jacob	*Paris.*
Walton William	
Doering John C. (Agent.)	*Marlboro'.*
Dukes John	*Magnolia.*
Mock Zacheus	
Loehr Jacob	*Mapleton.*
Loehr Samuel	
Somers Daniel	
Shallenberger Jacob	*New Baltimore.*
Nidich Michael W. H.	*Hartville.*
Pontious Moses	
Fisher A.	*Canal Fulton.*
Shunk A.	
Yost A.	*Louisville.*
Wolf John	*Lake.*
Wolf W.	
Wolf James	
Gleasner Jacob	*Waynesburg.*
Ross William	
Voight Henry	
Kurtz Charles E.	*Minerva.*
Pitney O. J.	
Haas George B.	*Canton.*
Nicholett J.	
Prince Bramenderffer	

Fickes Ralph | East Greenville
Heath Jesse
Heath Albert
Russell C. M. & Co. | Massillon.
Bahney J. P.
Rice Asa
Baldwin N. | Limaville
Wyner A. B.
Scranton Ralph | Mahoning.

Summit County.

Barber Geo. W. & Co. | Middlebury
Viall Eli A.
Brown S. | Cuyahoga Falls.
Mc Konkey A.
Muchter Jonas | Western Star
Cutshaw Samuel | Inland.
Spitlar Christian
Randolph Rezin | Bath
Stump David | Nimisilla.
Jones Morgan | Clinton.
Brooks C P. | Richfield
Ellsworth T. E.
Hart Thomas
Costella John | Summit.
Richardson Alexander | Copley.
Starr D. B.
Warren H.

Trumbull County.

Gilmore D. B. | Warren.
Graft Theodore
Mackey Robert
Truesdale A.
Van Wormer A.
Coe Dwight | Hartford.
Davis T. C.
Hall Elijah
Townsend George T. | Girard.
Bolls Stephen H. | Farmington.
Kennedy C. D.
Crawford, Green & Co. | Newton Falls.

Tuscarawas County.

Mc Gonagle M. | New Cumberland.
Steen James
McGee Fielding | Albany.
Cockerill Henry | Sandyville.
Snyder J. M. | Peoli.
Richards John V.
Peter C. B. | Gnadenhutten.
Eckhardt Chas. F. | Canal Dover.
Burg John
Kreiter John
Yantes A.
Demuth J. | New Philadelphia.
Matlock M.
Cribbs G.
Gentch G.
Gross Henry | Tuscarawas.
Seuft Ernest

Union County.

Applegard & Patridge | Marysville.
Frank Wm. H.
Moony Abraham
Foote Reuben | Allen Centre.

Burge James | Wilkins.
Snodgrass James R. | Milford Centre.
Hanes O. P. | Coberly's.

Van Wert County.

Armentrout & Lown | Van Wert.
Coffin & Morse
Garfield E. A. | Delphos.

Vinton County.

Sprague L. | McArthur.
Allen A.
Finney Alvin | New Plymouth.

Warren County.

Clutch U. & Son | Franklin.
August, Veusterer & Miller | Edwardsville.
Keller J. A.
Timpler Richard
Bowman & Miller
Semans W. W. | Hayesville.
Younglin D.
Hawyer Joseph | Deerfield.
Keys J. W. & J. | Waynesville
Creswell David
Johnson J S. | Hopkinsville.
St. John Hiram | Butlerville.
Wilson Thos. | Harveysburg.
Hamn Geo.

Washington County.

Fuller A. & S. | Marietta.
Griggs S.
Drape Stephen | Centre Belpre.
Longley Saml.
Decker A. | Ostend.
Barnes R.
Dilley R. P. | Regnier's Mills.
Palmer James
Palmer A.
Helebricht W. | Jolly.
Shafer G.
Leasure Wm. F | Watertown.
Lake Thos.
Palmer Luther | Boun.
Palmer A.

Wayne County.

Herr D. H. & Co. | Dalton.
Kosier Geo.
Reuter L. | Edinburgh.
Cheney William
Lindsey John | Fredericksburg.
Mennez B. A.
Hilterbrant Benj. | Reedsburg.
Amstutz F. | New Prospect.
Shook John
Beelman J. & E. | Smithville.
Zimmerman John
Epler Chas.
Blythe David | West Lebanon.
Stineburg Saml. | Shreve.
Culbertson J.
Spear & Beistle | Wooster

Williams County.

Kunkle Alex. | Bryan
Cunningham Levi

Henry Thos.   Bryan.
Knepper Jeremiah
Over Jacob
Schmachtenbarger Benj.
Urea Alex
Johnson L.   West Unity.
Newcomer Wm.
McDowell James   Williams Centre.
Ritchee David
Mason Isaac   Montpelier.
Spake R.
Cothran S. G.

Wood County.

Brown Abner   Perrysburg.
Crook Wm., Jr.
Brassey K.
Lord Caleb   Bowling Green.
Conway James   Weston.
Borbour James
Ketchum E. A.
Hanford D. C.   Miltonville.

Wyandot County.

Elkins Enoch   Upper Sandusky.
Sensney John W.
Criswell G. W.
Sulligen —,
Man & Hoke
Grussell Michael   Carey.
Dusbrough Anthony   McCutchensville.
Durbornw J. H.
Hill & Pettitt   Sycamore.
Cozier Daniel   Marseilles.

Candle Manufacturers.

Hamilton County.

Gross & Dietrick, 5 w. Front & 744 W.
    Row   Cincinnati.
Bille G. H., Canal near Liberty
Proctor & Gamble, W. Row above Liberty
Rose Charles D., 109 Canal
Stephens J. C, cor. Broadway & Liberty
Sheerer A. D. & Co., Lock bet. 4th & 5th
Shillito George, Maple w. of W. Row
Werk M & Co., 11 Main
Ford William   Fulton.

Montgomery County.

Keliperel F., Wayne   Dayton.

Morgan County.

Richardson George   McConnelsville.

Cane & Umbrella Makers.

Hamilton County.

Fox Jacob, 9 W. Row   Cincinnati.
Kreke M., 207 Vine
Kratz Conrad, 184 Walnut
Mason E H., 52 w. Fifth
Richard F. R., 14 e. Canal
Rosensal H., 516 Main
Sleeper I. & Bro., 167 Main
Seyppel Ferdinand, 427 Vine

Cap Makers.

Erie County.

Remmele G.   Sandusky City.

Montgomery County.

Lutzenberger C., 3d   Dayton.

Car-Axles & Locomotive Tires (Manufacturers of).

Hamilton County.

Winslow A. S., 9 & 11 w. 2d   Cincinnati.
Wolf D., Congress w. of Ludlow

Car (Railroad) Manufacturers.

Clarke County.

Hatch & Wicker   Springfield.
Winger & Anderson

Columbiana County.

Geisse P. F.   Wellsville.

Delaware County.

Muzzy L.   Delaware.

Erie County.

Wetheral W. W.   Sandusky City.

Franklin County.

Ridgway & Kimball   Columbus.

Hamilton County.

Keck G.   Fulton.

Knox County.

Cooper C. C. & Co.   Mt. Vernon.

Lawrence County.

Merrill J. M. & Co.   Ironton.

Medina County.

Russell John   Medina.
Dean Z.

Montgomery County.

Thresher E., Keoway   Dayton.

Starke County.

Davenport Russell & Co.   Massillon.

Carpenters & Builders.

Adams County.

Robison W. S.   Stout's
Bowie Nathaniel   Ecknansville.
Menely Geo. G.
McAdow Joseph   Dumbarton.
Thurman Joseph
Young Charles   Locust Grove.
Zoll W.
Smith & Murfin

Allen County

Beeber G. P.   Deep Cut.
Mead Stillman   West Newton.
Howe William A.

Bett & Swisher   *Middle River.*
Hatterman Amos
Hotchkiss Calvin
Miller George
Wagoner John
Auchmutz Robert   *Cranberry.*
Kidd William
Smith J. S.   *Westminster.*
Underwood B. L.
Fenton William   *Croghan.*
Fenton Samuel
Fisher Charles
Shaffer John
Wilson William

Ashland County.

Gault Samuel   *Savannah.*
Alleman Harmon   *Jeromeville.*
Earnest John
Rollins Charles   *Loudonsville.*
Rowland C. F.
Mumper Joseph   *Mohecan.*
Smith Jacob T.
Quick A. N.   *Perrysville.*

Ashtabula County.

Heath Wm. W.   *Richmond Centre.*
Parsons M. M.
Cornell D. R.   *Cherry Valley.*
Higbee H. H.
Bassett S.
Randolph A.
Dodge M. M.   *New Lyme.*
Willis G. M.
Chapin M.   *Lenox.*
Wickham John
Atkins J.
Orowell Wm.   *Geneva.*
Morse J. D.
Williams B.   *Austinburg.*
Winchester F. W.
Webb F.
Myers H.
Markham A.
Baldwin J. M.
Blood Z.
Ward Saml.   *East Plymouth.*
Harper Edward
Smith Frederick
Ballon Sanford
Udell C.   *Jefferson.*
Hunt H. S.
Cowell S. B.
Loomis H. S.
Sikes A. F.
Hoskins S. D.
McAdams H. F.
Sanders E. P.   *Trumbull.*
Morland David
Alexander J.
Johnson H.
Foot Julius
Brainard S. R.
Leslie John
Wilson M.
Ballard James   *Ashtabula.*
Gates L. D.

Cortle H. B.   *Ashtabula.*
Perigo S.
Loveland Geo. C.
Allen David
Smith Harvey
Smith T.
Young L. E.   *Hart's Grove.*
Read C. M.
Bulfinch L. D.
Marsh R.
Johnson E.
Bill J.
Avery A. A.
Fairchilds W. C.
Smith J. M.   *Monroe Centre.*
Oheaney H.
Huntley E. W.
Barber A.
Frock Henry   *South Ridge.*
Daniels Stephen
Hall E.   *Rome.*
Hungerford & Co.
Darling James   *Pierpont.*
Hopkins S. B.
Kinne A.
Follett Francis
Franklin A.
Marvin Alex
Withenbury Benj.   *Andover.*
Strickland Simon
Marsh D. B.
Blanchard W. M.
Wight Benj. P.
Boothby Nathaniel
Rockway Saml.   *Lindenville.*
Andrews J. C.
Hart David
Hayes Albert
Parker S. E.
Brakeman L. L.   *Cork.*
Evans E. W.
Mills Alfred
Hibbard S. S.
Mills Chas.
Evans Edward   *Harpersfield.*
Evans O.
Bates David H.
Smith E. P.   *Conneaut.*
De Wolf O.
Lloy A.
Reid D. S.
Wade J.
Baker Geo.
Woodworth M.

Athens County.

Dood A.   *Amesville.*
Mullen A.
Ogg A. F.
Diffenbaugh M.
Spalding J.
Beckley Walter   *Albany.*
Beckley John
Hall John
Hull John   *Nelsonville.*
Basson John
Williams Wm. G.

Hide C. T.	*Nelsonville.*	Anderson George W.	*Loydsville.*
Mintun T. L.		Eavins William	
Cooley G. L.		Walters William	
Bosson Thos.		Campbell Samuel	*Dillies' Bottom.*
Sweasey H.		Craig Wilson	
Tracey Wm.		Fish Samuel	
Selby John L.	*Canaanville.*	Fish Henry	
Durant A.		Lewis John	
Davis Peter		Walters Andrew	
Branch C.	*Lottridge.*	Alexander Andrew	*St. Claireville.*
Griffith John		Billingsley James	
Herren Wm.	*Lowry.*	Clark Isaac	
Spear Robert		Crawford E. D.	
Herron Andrew		Elerick J.	*Morristown.*
Allen Wm.		Fields J.	
Baty Wm. A.		McKelvy R.	
McNeal Robert		Sharon S.	
Hand George W.	*Pleasanton.*	Hoover G. T.	*Shepherdstown.*
Warren G. F.	*Athens.*	Ager S.	*Sewellsville.*
Miller Samuel		Frizzell Nimrod	
Davis Thos.		Sewell Peter	
Childs Oliver		Taylor Barnet	
Stedman J. C.		Gatton R.	*Armstrong's Mills.*
Stedman A.		McCoy Charles W.	*Hunter.*
Beckley W.	*Lee.*	Hosman John	
Beckley John		Frost Andrew	
Hall Reuben			
Baccus Aaron		**Brown County.**	
Scott T. A.	*Hibardville.*	McCall Albert	*Higginsport.*
Freedline A.		Bear Saml.	
Perrell Irvin	*Guysville.*	Kinner Jacob	
		Gaddis David & Wm.	*Ripley.*
Auglaize County.		Palmer Leander	
		Palmer Harvey	
Robbins Jonathan	*Wapakoneta.*	Goldberry B.	
Allen Wm.		Anderson Nathan	
Craft Wm.		Cary & Lowry	
Showan J. N.		Beach E.	
Adelmeyer B. H.	*Minster.*	Collins Scott	
Bresbrink B.		McNish Wm.	
Goehr Anthony		Logan W. B.	*Russellville.*
Haemelgarn Henry		Tucker W.	
Meiners Dieterich		Ayres J.	
Oldiges Wm.		Hunter Thos.	*Feesburg.*
Von Handorf B.		Riggs John	*De La Palma.*
Deniston Milton	*Kossuth.*	Hebblethwaite Benj.	*Union Plane.*
Rogers E.	*St. John's.*	Brunaugh Daniel	*Five Mile.*
Beever A.		Austin John	
Beever N.		Runyan S. D.	*Sardinia.*
Walck A.		Wells Wm. W.	
		Hamilton M.	
Belmont County.			
		Butler County.	
Combs Edward	*Hendrysburgh.*		
Ridgaway Richard		Anderson Wm.	*Bethany.*
Spran Philip		Anderson S.	
Mayhugh Wm.	*Demos.*	Miller Saml. C.	*West Chester.*
Stonebraker Jeremiah		Perrine Wm	
Long Philip	*Bellair.*	Tubs P. N.	
Oglebee John M.		Hercules C.	
Kyser Thomas		Williamson W.	
Spangler Jacob M.		Phillips Jacob	
Sponsler Oliver M.		Steele Joseph	*Collinsville.*
Wilson Joseph		McKay & McCanlas	*Hamilton.*
Brandenburgh Jacob	*Flushing.*	Myers Peter	
Kirk R. C.		Lowes J.	
Milburn Leander		Coppage J.	*Rossville.*
Palmer William		Schuler Titus	
Wood Elias			

Slack R. G.   *Middletown.*
Park C.   *Millville.*
McLoskey James
McLoskey John
Zinn G.
Huston K.
Talbot J.   *Symmes' Corner.*
Talbot Isaac
Hill J.
Hillsted Asbery
Jones E.   *Ross*
Stewart W.
Perrine & Butterfield   *Monroe.*
Carri Saml. P.
Bennett G. W.   *College Corner.*
Shideler L.
Harper J.
Prichard J.
Gilbert P. H.   *Seven Mile.*
Nourse E. B.   *Somerville.*
Alexander J.
Decamp W. & Son
Macy E. & J.
Peak J.
Blossom E.
Vansickle J. C.   *Trenton.*
Carle P.
Moore David
Snider Daniel
Weaver Wm.
Snook M. J. & S.   *Contreras.*
Barton Thos.
White John
Proctor J. A.

Carroll County.

Burier William   *Harlem Springs.*
Burier George
Johnston John
Martin George H.
Thompson Morgan
Wiggins A.
Barnes Henry   *New Hagerstown.*
Tope Stephen
Fouts George   *Carrollton.*
Hampson G. Y.
Hoops Enos
Shultz Jacob
Ball Nathan   *Sherodsville.*
Barrick Samuel
Scott Crawford R.   *Rose.*

Champaign County.

Howell Andrew   *Christiansburg.*
Long F. C.
Pearson C.
Corwin J. R.
Collins John
Leffell D.
Willey A.   *Urbana.*
Ripley & Thomas
Morrow Isaac
Mathews S.
Hubble Sanders
Judd W. S.
Greenbeo J.

Runyan S. C.   *Mutual.*
Oben J.
Mathews Henry   *Caryshill.*
Canon John
Hatterman Saml.
Haise James   *North Lewisburg.*
Black Joseph
Shaffer Wm.
Reames Wm.

Clarke County.

Baker George W.   *Enon.*
Boice Leonard
Gallagher John
Jenkins Abraham
Ross Elijah
Sheldon Theodore
Baldwin N.   *Selma.*
Berry T.
Myers & Darst   *Springfield.*
Davidson J.
Keshner & Crouch
Lock J. B.   *Catawba.*
Skillman John
Wingate T.
Edwards Edward   *South Charleston.*
Reed & Leidigh
Eshelman John   *New Carlisle.*
Myers & Mourit
Sanderson Lemuel
Stafford James E.

Clermont County.

Leming R. B.   *Mulberry.*
Shinard S. J.
Bell William   *Milford.*
Clark L. A.
McGill David
Bayless John   *Moscow.*
Camera Lewis
Scott William
Blair John   *Mt. Pisgah.*
Calhoun O.
Calhoun J.
Wilton Joshua
Wilton James
Crawford Jackson   *Clover.*
McHenry Wm.
Crooks Henry   *Loveland.*
Loveland James
Mitchell Thos.
Jordan S.   *Rural.*
Friend Wm. T.   *West Woodville.*
Scott Thos. D.
Lyon T. J.
Fordice Aaron
Ely George   *Bantam.*
Scull Thomas
White David
Homan David
Blair Charles
Doughty Edward
Dell Joseph
Sargent S. G.   *Laurel*
Nichols E.
Bainum B. H.
Stairs William

Rogers J. F.   *Laurel.*
Aldrage J. L.
Beckenham S.   *New Richmond.*
Watson James.
Carr Alexander   *Bethel.*
Frazee James
Richards J. H.
Goff D. M.   *Batavia.*
Moore E. A.
Rust William
Tice Lewis
Broadwell H.   *Mt. Carmel.*
Harris & Manning
Jones D.
Buvinger Edward   *Neville.*
Cord John
Johnson Joseph
Kain Joseph H.
Gelvin Sanford A.
Solenberg Eli
Wheeler John B.
Potter Jacob   *Amelia.*
Short John
Whiting Franklin
Davis Otho   *Withamsville.*
Henry George
Henry Wm. R.
Meguier John
Nordike Joseph
Shafer Isaiah
Witham Gideon V.
Lefebre James   *Miamisville.*
Lefebre P.
Robinson Ansco
Wasson E.
Whitset —
Blymer John   *Locust Corner.*

Clinton County.

Wood A. T.   *Westboro'.*
Fisher J.
Darby Wm. A.
Smith J. W.
Lee E. C.
Reiley W. S.   *Sligo.*
Moore Saml.
Schooley Isaac
Hamilton E.
Brown H.   *Blanchester.*
Carlisle H.
Adear A.
Carlisle F.
Read W. P.
Cooper John
Thatcher Wm.   *New Antioch.*
Marble David
Veley T.   *New Vienna.*
Johns A.
Bowers C. C.
Bowers G.
Swarts J. L.
Dixon C. A.
Moore G. F.
Stephens J.
Duncan T. F.
Riser Danl.   *Martinsville.*
Davis John

Wear R. C.   *Martinsville.*
Piqua Andrew
Roush J. T.
Posey John B.   *Wilmington.*
Bowaman John
Cromwell Saml.
McCool John

Columbiana County.

Burnett & Davis   *Wellsville.*
Embry James
Frazier Wm.
House John
Fassett & King
Perbes Jno. & James
Putnam Isaac
Rawlston Robert
Starr Thos.
Totan Alex.
Rawlston David
Adams George W.   *New Lisbon.*
Armstrong John
Adair Martin
Adams James C.
Burns James C.
Chambers William
Cromser Benj. F.
Ewing William
Hudson Jesse
Scott James
Huston J. C.   *East Palestine.*
Huston G.
Huston J.
Beard John   *Salineville.*
Milbourn David
Shechler Jacob
Parker Jonah H.   *New Garden.*
Rakestraw Milton
Robinson A. H.
Grim M.   *Calcutta.*
Murray J.
Raugh Samuel
Bartley John   *North Georgetown.*
Bartley Francis
Morrolf John
Shivley Daniel
Shivley Solomon
Whiteleather John
Whiteleather Andrew
Deronda John   *Franklin Square.*
Manhill Michael
Smith Jabez
Bragan Joshua   *East Rochester.*
Crowl John
Emmons David
Aspey Joshua   *New Chambersburgh.*
Thomas Jacob
Thomas Alfred
Rubicam Jonathan   *Green Hill.*
Wickersham Joseph
Hall Robert   *Salem.*
Hillman B.
Hillman & Grimery
Keen & Kirkbride
Tompkins Wm.
Webster Lawrence
Fogg Shepard   *Bucks.*

Clackner O.	*Bucks.*	
Hawley Caleb		
King Nathan		
Mitchel Eden		
Bucher Milton	*East Liverpool.*	
Carey Joseph		
Engles George		
Grim Michael		
Miller William		
Tumbleson George		
McKim T. J.	*West Point.*	
Smith J. L.		
Stewart S.		
Hamill Wm. D.	*Saint Clair.*	
Simmons Wm. H.		
Smith Jacob		
Wollam Thomas		
Paton Joseph	*East Fairfield.*	
Williamson L.		
Early Elijah	*Unity.*	
Hadly J. D.		
Orissinger D.		
Ranch Peter		
Wetzel Joseph		
Wetzel Peter		
Wetzel Charles		
McCann Henry	*Hanoverton.*	
Brown George		
Henry William		
Nicholas Charles		
Baker Thomas	*Elkton.*	
Stewart Samuel		
Dickey Alfred		

Coshocton County.

Christy Thomas	*Chili.*	
McCaskey George		
Swarts David	*Bakersville.*	
Hayes John		
Shanks George		
Evens James		
Baker J. A.		
Baker John		
Hour H.	*Clark's.*	
Weatherwax J.		
Davidson James		
Foster & Dougherty	*Evansburgh.*	
Rinehart Charles		
Maxwell Sylvester		
Sunderlin John		
Farwell Seth	*Keene.*	
Massey A.		
Grimes Hiram		
Stringfellow George	*Walhonding.*	
Stringfellow Benjamin		
Chapin D.	*Coshocton.*	
Elliot Jacob		
Welch William R.		
Wells Thomas		
Babcock B.		
Hay George		
Mason S. F.		
Richards Ab'm.		

Crawford County.

Bresler John	*Leesville Cross Roads.*	
Hice Henry		

Malery P.	*Leesville Cross Roads.*	
Parks Robert		
Sawyer Simon		
Culver Sylvester	*Poplar.*	
Martin Talleyrand		
Osborn Warner		
Sweet Benjamin		
Alt John	*New Washington.*	
Baer Moses T.		
Demuth John		
Gary F. W.		
Hill J.		
Wiegandt Jacob		
Striker Christian	*Wellerville.*	
Bair Adam	*Bucyrus.*	
Henthorn D. H.		
Lamerson Thomas		
Nare S. P.		
Shull John		
Snyder John		
Stoll George & Brothers		
Stoner & Messis		
Salickman Wm.		
Yost John F.		
McLaughlin John	*Lykens.*	
Fox H.	*DeKalb.*	

Cuyahoga County.

Fish L.	*Brooklyn.*	
Gates C. & R.		
Harrison T.		
Shurtliff N.		
Brewer D.	*Chagrin Falls.*	
Harpham G.		
Pitt S. D.		
Walters R. R.		
Walton P. R.		
Cannon James H.	*Solon.*	
Hill Ira		
Perkins William		
Sawry Abel W.		
Wheeler William		
Fitzwater David	*Brecksville.*	
Miller Chesman		
White Julius		
Wright William		
Ames John	*Coe Ridge.*	
Frost E. C.		
Hyde E. J.		
Morgan George		
Nelson Newell		
Rice F. J.		
Stearns T. E.		
Stearns Edmond		
Tichenor J. L.		
Allen Enoch	*Bedford.*	
Benedict J. S.		
Benedict J. O.		
Benedict N. P.		
Robinson N. H.		
Spafford A. J.		
Adams J.	*Warrensville.*	
Hubbel L.		
Salsbury A.		
Thacher J.		
Warren Wm.		
Adams Darius	*Collamer.*	

Ruple J. R.   *Collamer.*
Beers Daniel
Lewis George R.
Minor John
Minor Marvin
Allerton J. C.
Morton O. H. P.
Allerton A. B.
Leroy Seymour
Curtiss J. W.   *Berea.*
Seger P. H.
Phelps Roger
Putler J.
Crocker John
Hancock Daniel
Wyman J.
Nelson S. & N.   *Ohio City.*
Black R., cor. Kinsman & Ohio *Cleveland.*
Blackburn & Thompson, 70 Champlain
Brooks S. C. & E. W., Division
Corlett & Cubborn, 97 Prospect
Hills Charles A., 48 Parkman
Henninger J., 83 St. Clair
Piper A. J., 17 Rockwell
Sturtevant Brothers, 71 Champlain
Thomas E., 91 Kinsman
Black & Alexander, 47 Ohio
Schofield William, Erie
Gayton James, 32   do
Bartlett M. W.   *Euclid.*
Binghardt H.   *Newburgh.*
Ingersol A.
Marble H.
Thomas C.
Sherwood O.   *North Royalton.*
Mather George   *East Cleveland.*
Slaght Joseph
Walters B. C.
Schofield John   *Independence.*
Scoville Leroy A.
Richardson Ira G.
Campbell E. D.   *Brooklyn.*
Fish B.
Fish O.

Darke County.

Arnold Sam'l.   *Hillgrove.*
Creveston John
Minchin Thos.
Heaton Joseph
Davis D. T.   *Tampico.*
Davis E. H.
Mackey W.   *Concordia.*
Harriman M. T.   *New Madison.*
Wakeland Chas.
Harter E.
Henderson Nathan
Biddle Wm.
Bullinger Henry
Hullinger J. & Dan'l.   *Fort Jefferson.*
Harding Sam'l.   *German.*
Shorp John
Baker A.   *Sampson.*
Ullery Leonard   *Greenville.*
Ullery Geo.
McGinnis W.
Hathaway B. R.

McGinnis Mathew   *Greenville.*
Hart M. F.
Johns J. P.   *Beamsville.*
Johnson James
Oliver D.
Harmon A.   *Poplar Ridge.*
Harman Wm.
Folkorth Henry
Roll O.
Caldwell P.   *North Star.*
Bard J. H.   *Mississinawa.*
Hartman W. W. —
Jaslin J. B.
Bigham Joseph.

Defiance County.

Elder James   *Defiance.*
Hall H. B.
Marcellus D. W.
Miller Wm.
Oliver David
Lovejoy D. D.   *Farmer Centre.*
Robinson Hiram   *Milldale.*
Waters Loren
Sloan Ezra
Bridenbaugh William   *Brunersburg.*
Bridenbaugh John

Delaware County.

Giffin & Penny   *Delaware.*
Cadwalader R.
Cadwalader M.
Wachter & Harter
Jones R. N.
Word S. R.   *Stratzford.*
Anderson Sam'l.
Dutcher J. B.
Anderson E.
Ducker J. H.
Zimmerman J.
Null Wm.
Colfiesh J.
Stearns M.   *Galena.*
Stough Sam'l.
Beekman John
Henry J.
Doyle Oliver   *Vans Valley.*
Rose S. C.
Francis M.   *Waldo.*
Barnhart David
Minich Sam'l.
Taylor Eli
Thompson James
Nichols J. W.
Smith B. F.   *Williamsville.*
Chambers H.
Waters Charles
Haws B. A.   *Louis Centre.*
Jaycox John   *East Orange.*
Evans Robert   *Padnor.*
Griffeth Thomas D.
Jones Thos. P.
Rowland Thos. W.
Thomas T.
Lewis D. R.
Watkins Wm.
Baxter David

Davis D.   *Padner*

Winter Ralph
Winter Wm.
Winter Valentine
Lidick Joseph
Spalding J.   *Norton.*
Smith Jeremiah
Newkirk Henry   *Unison.*
Standish John M.

Erie County.

Woodley F.   *Venice.*
Miller G.   *Sandusky Ci'y*
Melvin Wm.
Enrick Henry
Blake L.   *Berlinville.*
Blake E.
Green G. W.
Lowry Wm.   *Furnace.*
Bassett Miles
Whitney S. T.
Schneider J.   *Milan.*
Ferguson
Ashley O.
Canfield A.
Ninnes H.
Smith J.
Rinehart O.
McCulloch J.

Fairfield County.

Alspaw John   *Pickerington.*
Hieⁿand Michael
Emrick Jacob   *West Rushville.*
Berry Enoch   *New Salem.*
Baker D.   *Rushville.*
Baker M. D.
Bailey R.   *Lithopolis.*
England Amos
Foltz David
Olive —.
Shenck N.   *Sugar Grove.*
Hansley A.
Hansley H.
Guley M.
Maheney N.
Rudolph D.
Dennes E.
Woodward J. M.
Jackson E.
White S.
Walker James   *Clear Creek*
Hoffman Ambrose
Denton S.   *Lancaster.*
Kendall B. F.
Orman Henry

Fayette County.

Lanam Richard   *Washington.*
Higgins F.
Crone B A.
Freeman R. J.
Garris Conrad   *Bloominghurg.*
Worrell Geo W.
Burton James W.   *Moon's.*

Franklin County.

Reeder William   *Clintonville.*
Selby L H.
Toney Wm.
Arnold Geo. W.   *Hope.*
Hamaker Saml.
Landon Jarvis
Landon Wellington
Landon Noble
Hutches Nathan   *Blenden.*
Vincent N. & W.
Wythe Parker
Barber Solomon   *Central College.*
McCatchan R. R.
Strong N. R. S.
Clark A. C.   *Worthington:*
Metcalf Ira
Pinney Horace
Whip George P.
Wright Charles
Hubbaugh Jacob   *Canal Winchester.*
Koole John
Kramer Peter
Kramer Levi
Miller William
Shaffer Harrison
Shaffer Henry
Wilson William
Bailey Knowlton   *Darby.*
Kain William
Todd & Baldwin   *Ovid.*
Smith George   *Gohanna.*
Hays Z.   *Dublin.*
Hutchinson G. E.
Brake —,   *Columbus.*
Biddel Thomas
Biddel Joseph
Bosserman John
Boswell J & Son
Boswell Wm.
Boswell J.
Bower John
Brake Jacob
Bridge Joseph
Brooks James
Brown A. J.
Burgraff George
Butler Henry
Butolf T. S.
Carlisle A.
Chrisley J.
Clark J.
Cloud R. W.
Hid. T. R.
Leakin J Q.
Miner William
Rawson H C.
Price Samuel
Sheldon Richard
Tyler A.
McFillen G.
Vandemark G.
Gallagher B.   *Groveport.*
Garos S.
Shockley D. C.
Willi Augustus

Zinn Moses   *Groveport.*
Burton Walter   *Reynoldsburg.*
Cooper A.
Cookus James
Rush George

Fulton County.

Grice John   *Elmira.*
Rogers Solomon
Wissler D. C.
Baumgardner S.
Litty P.
Ashlyman Chas.
Luy Wm.
Abbott S.   *Delta.*
Harrison B.
Thayer Chas.
Johnson Theodore

Gallia County.

Hamilton George   *Raccoon Island.*
Roberts Maxey   *Pine Grove*
Russell J. C.
King Calvin   *Kyger.*
Rupe Mathias
Folden William   *Patriot.*
McClaflin Orin

Geauga County.

Magumeigal Samuel   *Chardon.*
Adgate John W.
Hedges Alfred
Smith A.   *Auburn.*
Norton J. W.
Chilson Joseph   *Chester.*
Cummins D.
Williams E. B.
Pratt F.   *Troy.*
Hopkins M.
Grish John B.   *Hambro.*
Burk J. A.   *Middlefield.*
Belden M.
Hart R.   *Montville.*
Moore Chas. C.
Pratt N.   *Parkman.*
Waterman B. D.
Woodard D.   *Munson.*
Stone H. B.
Granger John
Keeny R. W.
Way E. W.   *Newbury.*
Cutter John
Ward E. M.
Briggs P.
Odell Chas.   *Russell.*
Manchester John
Foot Ira   *Bainbridge.*
Kennedy Wm.
Downing J. S.
Nettleton M.   *Burton.*
Carl on A.
Moffit M.   *Clariden.*
Preston R.
Gould H.
Skinner George   *Chardon.*
Hedges A.
Munsill G.

Stone Samuel.   *Huntsburg.*

Greene County.

Barnes Henry   *Xenia.*
Crandle N.
Crow A. S.
Crandle & Morse
Foreman D. R.
Furgeson & Davis
Drees & Scott
Giff & Wolf
Jones & Johns
Manor & Babb
Shephard & Taylor
Griner John   *Fairfield.*
Hebble H.
Tritt Til
Bullock Wm. H.   *New Jasper.*
Fields Thomas
Good John
Allison W.   *Clifton.*
Trumbull A. E.
Woodward W.
Barr James   *Cedarville.*
Boos J.
French J. K.
French H. G.
Gowdy W. C.
Jackson & Barber
Burns Benjamin   *Byron.*
Barnhisel B.   *Yellow Springs.*
Creswell Launcelot
Flory Valentine
Hammond John
Huffman W. B.
Dunwiddie Samuel   *Clio.*
Ellis Joseph   *Paintersville.*
Sever Jesse
Christopher A. J.   *Jamestown.*
Smith Joshua
Boop George
McLaughlin George
Tucker Stephen

Guernsey County.

McKinley W.   *Cumberland.*
Dolman Wm.
Coulter S. P.
Sigman John
Waller F. A.
Allen Joseph
Thomas J.   *Winchester.*
Shipman J.
Padgit S.
Johnson J.
Johnson E.
Garber Samuel   *New Gottingen.*
Sottlemire H. J.   *Cambridge.*
Snitt Z. C.
Gallion A.
Adair James
Jackson Israel
Scott Thomas
Walker John C.   *Kimbolton.*
Sverist Fred   *Buffalo.*
Shaw Thos.   *Senecaville.*
Morrison J.

Kays M.   *Senecaville.*
Booth H.
Spring J.
Stewart C.

Hamilton County.

Blair & Custard, 102 Walnut   *Cincinnati.*
Bindley James, Front bet. Pike & Butler
Bagley J., 7th bet. Broadway & Sycamore
Behmyer D., 146 w. 3d
Barrett D. R., 46 Betts
Baldwin Joseph, 304 Elm
Brading J. V., 14 Ham. Road
Cameron R. & W., s. w. cor. W. Row & Clark
Cotterell & Goldsworthy, s. e. cor. Plum & Court
Clark B., 148 w. 6th
Darling J., 322 w. 6th
DeCamp & Hand, Geo. bet. Smith & John
Davis S., 324 w. 5th
Ellick J., 583 Sycamore
Glasgow Hugh, 169 Vine
Handy & Brother, 431 Broadway
Hoffman & Schmidt, Court near Walnut
Holker & J. McCamon, s. w. cor. Clinton & Cutter
Hopkins F., 114 w. 5th
Kirby C., n. e. cor. Elizabeth & Fulton
Livezy J. W., Hammond bet. 3d & 4th
Lathrop & Joyce, 121 w. 2d
Lowder John, 7th bet. Cutter & Linn
Morton & Co., 61 Front
Morrow T. W., 141 do
Morgan —, 371 Vine
Mapon—, cor. Deer Creek & 5th
Mills R., 328 W. Row
Magill C. W. & W. W., Richmond bet John & Fulton
Miller M. H , Race bet. Finley & Ham. Road
Males S., 96 Everett
Merret & Compton, 517 W. Row
Mills Samuel E., Ev'ret. b. W. Row & John
McCleary J., Everett bet. Linn & Cutter
Morton Thomas, 100 w. 6th
Newman & Byron, Colum. bet. Elm & Race
Neill S. B., 151 Broadway
Peirson D., 260 Longworth
Solar & Jacox, Front bet. Lawrence & Pike
Settle W. B., 10 7th
Stewart Wm. H. & Bro., Plum bet. Canal & Court
Slack Jas. & Wm., n. e. cor. J'n & Chesnut
Stout J., 478 Race
Stilley James, George bet. Smith & John
Stewart W. H., 345 Plum
Thompson & Wance, 150 w. 8th
Vandergon —, Congress bet. Ludlow & Lawrence
Weaver Saml., Public Landing
Warrington George, 3d bet. Smith & Park
Woolf S., 210 W. Row
Trimmer A.   *Pendleton.*
Barr S.   *Fulton.*
Wheeler A. C.
Lowry H. J. & W.   *Walnut Hills.*
Billingsley A. E.   *Sharonville.*
Booram D.

Ritter F. C.   *Sharonville.*
Bonnel Jonathan   *Carthage.*
Hays W. G.
Hefferman J.
Riggs J. J.
Stevens John
Thayre O.
Walker A.
Cady P.   *Reading.*
Wachendorp J. H.
Charles D.   *Mt. Healthy.*
Dom B. P.
Gorman H. C.
Lowe G. D.
Immel Joseph
Agnew Daniel W.   *Pleasant Ridge.*
Holt John
Kenton Henry V.
Ross William F.   *Harrison.*
Rice & Thompson
Stokes Richard M.
Wait Richard
Noblaw —   *Cleves.*
Rosecrans Wm.
Simpers R. R.
Gudgeon James   *Mt. Washington.*
Harris James
Mundell John
Cox Michael   *Miami.*
Hesider Daniel
Miller S. C.
Taber J. W.
Thompson J. M.
Gerard Abner   *Plainville.*
Price Hezekiah
Carle Abraham   *Springdale.*
Naylor B. H.
Forward Rollin   *Cumminsville.*
Hayward Joseph
Tozzer William
Brown Charles   *Newtown.*
Clarke P. F. G.
Doughty Jonah
Gerard Jonathan
Ade William   *Cheviot.*
Barker Samuel
Blaco John
Brown Benjamin
Craver P.
Gain John
Harwood M.
Mantor A. C.
Nugent Thomas
Barkus William   *Dunlap.*
Barkus J.
Hughs J.
Pipher J.
Struble G.
Thomas D. B.   *College Hill.*

Hancock County.

Bell James   *Mt. Blanchard.*
Coleman J. C.
Elder Abner
Hammond Henry
Howard Thomas
Hammond T. G.

Mantz G. W.	Mt. Blanchard.	Henline —,	Napoleon.
Myers Thompson		Glass J.	
Patterson Joseph		Conaway —,	
Pickett Joseph		Zetter Jacob	New Bavaria.
Wiseman Harvey		**Highland County.**	
Wiseman L. D.		Smith Levi	Highland.
Smith Wm. W.		Adams John	
Smith John		Falkinburg Jas. A.	
De Garmo James	Benton Ridge.	Duff John J.	
Farmer Henry		Cox J. N.	
Jones Henry		Shrock John	Greenfield.
Miller William		Boyd & Anderson	
Campbell R. W.	Cass.	Murdock H.	
Newsburn David		Gray James	
Terrel David C.		Perry James	
Gibson Thomas	Ashery.	Perry John	
Martin Joshua		Crooks Alex.	
Reeder Anderson		Townsend Thos.	
Wight Hiram		Campbell John	
Fabur John	Arlington.	Murrey James	
Tiffany Luther		Hay Isaac	Mowrytown
Waugh J. W.	Canonsburgh.	Watson Robert	
West J.		Shafer Isaac	Dodsonville.
Berry George	Finley.	Fite Cyrus	Buford.
Clifford Lewis		Fiscus John	
Engleman John		Tenor Jacob W.	New Market.
Guise Jesse		Nutt John	
Klamroth Wm.		Wilson Alex.	
Miller Alexander		Hewey A.	
Shuggart G. F.		Kelso John	Marshall.
Wheeler Jesse		Dick C. G.	
Yerger Simon		Dunlap James	
Bryan Jacob	McComb.	Creed Austin	
Condit Harvey G.		Main Jacob	
Kelley Thomas P		Main Danl.	
Porter James		Cook James F.	Greenford.
Todd John W.		Wasser Jacob	
		Shaffer Jacob	
Hardin County.		Keelor H.	Dallas.
Maston John	Kenton.	Clark Thos. G.	Samantha.
Mustard John		Hawkins Wm. H.	
Hill Wm.		McKee E. R.	
Mellinger W.		Wailey R. B.	Leesburg.
Schoonover Chas.		Sweney C. C.	
Reise Henry		Coalter John A.	
Rinehart A.		Doggett John W.	Hillsboro'.
McElroy Geo.	Huntersville.	**Hocking County.**	
McElroy Jacob		Gavane L. S.	Rock House.
Hitchcock Isaac		Hickox C.	
Wilson Wm		Scoville E. A.	
		Shaw S. S.	
Harrison County.		Ball William	Logan.
		Butin Jacob	
McCrary Thos.	Cadiz.	Butin James	
Bryan Geo. W.		Craig F. J.	
Benedict Levi	Germano.	Leonard P.	
Hilton J. H. T.	Feed Spring.	McClintock W. H.	
Wagstaff Andrew		Kitchen A.	
Utterback R. B.		Risley David	
		Gibison Joel	Gibisonville.
Henry County.		Hartley Isaac	
Sapp L.	Florida.	Parks Perry	
Bullen B. T.		Rainsburger George	
Austin J.		Root Isaac	
Banks H.		**Holmes County.**	
Low H. N.	Napoleon.	Berlett J. & D	Holmesville.
Hartman —,			
Cooper S.			

9

Gorrell John	*Holmesville.*	Reed Wm.	*Richmond,*
Gorrell Wm.		Beebout F.	
Watson Thos.		Grim A.	
Butter John	*Benton.*	Baker A.	
Monfort Peter	*Berlin.*	Beicker W. F.	*East Springfield,*
Lamon George		Shultz John	*Annapolis*
Riven O.		Walker B. & Son	*Mt. Pleasant.*
Homer J.		Gill John	
Buyzard Jacob	*Walnut Creek.*	McMasters Wm. F.	
Gross H.	*Winesburg.*	McFall John	*Mouth Yellow Creek.*
		Ross Wm. B.	*Elliottsville.*
Huron County.		Hall Joseph	*Wintersville.*
King John G.	*East Townsend.*		
Kinney E.		**Knox County.**	
Cooley Seth	*Clarksfield.*	Clark & Hubbell	*Mt. Vernon.*
Signor Jacob		Giles & Emory	
Bains F.		Johnston James	
Scott Isaac		Fowler L. N.	
Spuryer John		Murphey Israel	
Worden J.		Randolph —,	
Fox G.		Roberts John	
Fox A.		Rumsey James	
Fellows W.		Rathel Parrett	
Pixley J.		Smith Russel	
Studwell George	*Greenwich.*	Haiesler James	*Fredericktown.*
Trusedale James	*Four Corners.*	Hillis A. B.	
Johnson L.		Kellum S. M.	
Buck J.	*Bellevue.*	McMount O. G.	
Spaulding O.	*North Norwich.*	Strong S. D.	
Wheeler H.		Woodruff S. W. & Co.	
Randolph John	*Norwalk.*	Ellis W.	*Brandon.*
Miller O. R.		Rouse E.	
Brewster Wm.		Nickols Jona	*Democracy.*
Hoyt P. B.		O'Brian W. E.	
Kozee Wm.		Wimer James	
Jamison G.		Frederick P. E.	*North Liberty.*
Hurlburt H. S.		Frederick O. P.	
Hurlburt G.		Stow Newlan	
		Worley William	
		Heillis E. B.	*Fredericktown.*
Jackson County.		Mount Charles G.	
Taumine L.	*Oakhill.*	Woodruff S. W.	
Morgan Wm.		Coleman Frederick Jr.	*Jelloway.*
Jones Benj.		Miller J. P.	
Mackley John		Strong J. C.	
Bonborger C.	*Allensville.*		
Wilcox Nathan		**Lake County.**	
Radcliffe & Brown	*Berlin.*		
Caughey & Boyce		Talcott M.	*Madison.*
Thrapp C. W.	*McGee's Store.*	Kimball A.	
Walters R. Z.		Ware E. L.	
Radcliffe David	*Jackson.*	Woodworth H.	
Farran Jas.		Morse H. H.	*Kirtland.*
		Bryant D. S.	
Jefferson County.		Bryant A. L.	
Alig & Leighthizer	*Steubenville.*	Green R. B.	
Abraham J.		Witter Wm.	
Boyles John		Crary E. W.	
Broker R.		Wight John	*North Perry.*
Copeland John		Barrows A.	
Doyle John		Wolverton Benj.	
Hamilton —,		Ward H.	
McKinney J.		Jones Wm. H.	*Wickliffe.*
Oneal John		Smith Marcus	*Painesville.*
Thompson Wm.		Weed Julius	
Walker J.		Carter W. P.	
Riley John		Hickok F. S.	
Duncan Danl.	*Richmond.*	Morse J. F.	

Lawrence County.

Hamilton & Barr	*Ironton.*
Mackey A. G.	
Rogles & Buchanan	
Shore G. & J.	
Winters Thomas	
Judd Chester	*Burlington.*
Thomas T.	
Hoskinson M.	*Hanging Rock.*
Olinefelter T	
Clark A.	
Hall Zack.	
Gibbs Ashley	*Millers.*
Rolfe Elijah	
McClure David	
Drown G. W.	
Campbell A. J.	*Russell's Place.*
McIntire J. J.	*Quaker Bottom.*
Brown F. G.	
Judd J. Cotton	
Magee Ephraim	
Magee Warren	
Boggs Allen	*Aid.*

Licking County.

Stevens W. T.	*Linnville.*
Orr Isaac	
Winter Isaac	*Etna.*
Shaff Jacob	
Neff Henry	
Sutherland B. F.	
Garlan S. B.	*Brownsville.*
Emery B.	
Butler Joseph	*Jacksontown.*
Shadrick R. A.	
Kemper Joseph	
Bashaw R.	
Warden J. H.	*Granville.*
Ellsworth B. F.	
Sheldon J. R.	
Legg Andrew	*Newark.*
Smith J.	
Richardson & Boss	
Braddock John	
White M.	
Wilkins R.	
Burgess J.	
Moore T. G.	*Croton.*
Spencer G.	
Spencer H.	
Frank T.	
Trimble J.	
Fowler D.	
Sperry M.	
Shacklett H. D.	*Perryton.*
Leatherman G.	
Whitman Edward	*Johnstown.*
Duke H.	
Close R.	
Smith John	*Kirkersville.*
Wagy John	
Smith Wm.	
Burt E.	
Stover Benj.	
Nisley Isaac	

Armintrout A.	*Kirkersville.*
Dixon Wm.	
Peas Hanson	*Fredonia.*
Bellows S.	
Bellows A.	

Logan County.

McAllister Samuel	*Huntsville.*
Morrow Moses K.	
Kramer Louis	
Stanfield Wm. H.	
Murphy Joseph A.	*New Richland.*
Scott J. M.	
Elliott David	*Rushsylvania.*
Moore William	
Oder Benj. & George	
Patterson Andrew	
Patterson Francis	
Adams S.	*Bellefontaine.*
Irwin & Winans	
Morgan George	
Howell & Short	
Patterson & Keiger	
Reed Robert	
Ricer J.	
Rheub & Arnold	
White & Good	
Wilson & Smith	
Cleaveland Jed.	*Zanesfield.*
Everingham Wm.	
Everingham H.	
Garwood D. L.	
Scott Joshua	
Unangst Peter	
Wonder Samuel	
Cooper T. B.	*Lewistown.*
Westfall R. N.	
Askron Isaac	*Quincy.*
Daniels T. T.	
Patton Shepherd	
Patton John	
Patton James	
Short C.	
Van Hofn —	
McConaha Saml.	

Lorain County.

Stranahan W. W.	*Oupope.*
Wooll J.	
Bennet John	*Brighton.*
Dunbar H. B.	
Hall Theophilus	
Jones E. D. G.	
Strong Frederick	
Marshall William	*Pittsfield.*
Pulver John	
Rowel John	
Rowel C. B.	
Worcester Emmerson	
Worcester D. M.	
Waters David	
Adams John	*Sheffield.*
Garfield Haley	
Smith Perry	
Downing Charles	*North Camden.*
Lee John	
Twining J. N.	

Viles William	*North Camden.*
Hart Henry	*Brownhelm.*
Stoddart Henry	
Brooks H. J.	*Elyria.*
Hamilton Wm. P.	
Jacobs J. J.	
Wilber James	*Amherst.*
Baker O. T.	*Huntington.*
Barker Orlando	
Bray H.	
Bickley Ami	
Bower W. O.	
Martin John	
Miller Samuel	
Wright Peter	
Young John S.	
Gott Edwin	*La Grange.*
Gott E. S.	
Hastings J. B.	
Merriam S. J.	
Knapp Luman	*Rochester Depot.*
Mann Asa	
Hill L. A.	*Oberlin.*
Compton John	
Morris L. A.	
Turner T. P.	
Bears N.	*Copopa.*
Darling O.	
Fuller R. N.	
Isbell F.	
Pelton J.	
Powell O. G.	

Lucas County.

Hoerner Lewis	*Providence.*
Dilgert Henry	*Rigs.*
Faxon H. A.	
Faxon W. R.	
Miller Lawrence	
Clark Sanford	*Lyons.*
Davies Chapin	
Porter Samuel	*Whiteford.*
Holloway Oriston	*...*
Green Elijah	
Curtiss D. B.	
Segur O D.	
Torrance O.	
Collum W.	
Stevens Joseph	
Browning Samuel	*Toledo.*
Cheeny William O.	
Crane Joel W.	
Church Q. A.	
Freeman J. P.	
Freeman M. B.	
Huffman William	
Jones Joseph	
Lewis Lyman W.	
Plough David	:
Rudd Harrison	
Rousey O. O.	
Saxton H.	
Shepherd J. F.	
Shirts Andrew	
Swift —	
Warner George B.	
Wagner Samuel	

Madison County.

Wright James	*Lafayette-*
Blair Nathan	*Loudon.*
Gould William	
Rea James	
Rouse Thomas	
Vincent & Latspeich	
Smith F. L.	*Mt. Sterling.*
Trout Peter	*California.*
Trout Andrew	
Defebaugh Joseph	
Arnett E. V.	*West Jefferson.*
Bartow William	
Case Geo. E.	
Davison Samuel	
Jones Thos. & Chas.	
Winget D. O.	*Darby Creek.*
Hynes T.	*Midway.*
Tomlinson V.	
Scott George	
Hazzard J.	
Watkins William	

Mahoning County.

Lunsey Wm.	*Youngstown.*
Morteller O.	
Bumpsted M.	
Phillips James	
Truesdel Col. R.	
Holeman E.	*Berlin Centre.*
Kirk Isaac W.	
Stogdill Geo.	*North Jackson.*
Eckenrode Daniel	
Camp A.	
Harner David	
Shafer Wm.	
Shafer Edward	
Poorman Philip	*Green Village.*
Cook James L.	
Hapley Sam'l.	
Shaffer Jacob	
Simpson B.	*Hanna's Mills.*
Winans Jacob	
McKinsey Hiram	*Milton.*
Smith Noah	
Dalley Henry	
Simpson B.	
Hampton Jason	*Damascoville.*
Glenn Wm. S.	*North Lima.*
Stafford Sam'l.	
Lower Jacob	*New Springfield*
Smith Jesse	
Dotterer Isaac	*New Albany.*
Vallance David	
Haycock M.	*Pottersville.*
Brosing Sam'l.	

Marion County.

Smallwood J. M	*Wilson.*
Smallwood A. M.	
Mills J.	
Hockenbury J.	
Hockenbury D.	

Medina County.

Wright H. B,	*Leroy.*
Nye W. F.	

Phillips Isaiah *Leroy.*
Wright G. C.
Newton J. R.
Fletcher M. *Mallet Creek.*
Mead Dan'l.
Peiree Thompson
Herick Nelson
Tiffany Elijah
Bates Leonard
Hopkins Wm. *Sharon Centre.*
Ferryman O.
Keller A.
Hill H. *Liverpool.*
Tubbs E. & S.
Arnold T. C.
Dennis Henry *River Styx.*
Ruby Wm. H.
Robbins L. D. *Wadsworth.*
Hurd N. L.
Battles Caleb
Coyne W. C.
Prentice Wm. W. *Lodi.*
Tuttle L.
Clark J. M. *Hinckley.*
Goodwin H.
Andrews Wm. B.
Wilkinson Jas. T
Prichard M.
Wilcox E. H.
Churchhill T. A. *Weymouth.*
Allen David
Ripley S. O. *Chatham Centre.*
Packard Jonathan
Switzer D.
Brick John
Plattner O. *Homerville.*
Towalle D.
Giar H. W.
Bawbell T. *Medina.*
Harris L.
McClure A.
Peelsifer S.
Rhodes S.
Green B.

Meigs County.

Dudley D. *Downington.*
Halliday N.
Page J. N.
Reeves S.
Wagner A. *Apple Grove.*
Pilchard L.
Loter James.
Knapp Chas.
Wagner Alfred *Letart Falls.*
Morten & Davis *Pomeroy.*
Winkleblack R. L.
Stephens F. W.
Whee Henry
Eiselstine Leonard
Weyesmiller John
Simpson Jacob
Smart Caleb
Crosbie H.
Crosbie Peter
Wadman Benj.
Barclay Peter

Rowe Chas. *Ledlies*
Edmonson John

Mercer County.

Hight Chas. *Celina.*
McGunnis T.
Mazier T. W.
Sutton Ira
Johns H. L.
Greer G. W. *Mercer.*
Judkins James *Coldwaters*

Miami County.

Durm A. *Fletcher.*
Frazier J. N.
Walts J. *West Charleston.*
Jacobs J.
Clark F. G. *Troy.*
Vandegrift & Boner
Houser Isaac
Baugh & Eyer *Casstown.*
Pence J.
Kindelsberger S.
Marshall & Fuller
Swain & Long
Baker Stephen *Brant.*
Eargood Millard
Wheeler O. *Hyattsville.*
Favorite S. D.
Coffman J. W. *West Milton.*
Everitt S. H.
Hollingsworth W. K.
Hollingsworth Thomas
Hickman John
Kinzey David
Coppock Calvin
Spence Sam'l.

Monroe County.

Brooks William *Woodsfield.*
Davis William
Gray Walter
Henthorn William
Okey Arthur
Okey Henry
Smith Samuel G.
Armstrong William *Antioch.*
Davis Absalom
White James
Vanlaw Reason *Rocky Narrows.*
Watson Jacob
Watson John B.
Bowers John *Masterton.*
Crawford Alexander
Crawford James
McPeek Phineas
Meredith R.
Brown Wm. J. *Sunfish.*
McConnel Alexander
Noffsinger & Sill *Malaga.*
Morton Barzillai *Plymouth.*
Tanner Samuel
Clevenger Amos
Brock G. *Baresville.*
Noll J. P.
Finney E. M. *Graysville.*

Montgomery County.

Crawford J., St. Clair	*Dayton.*
Comius J. M., Sixth	
Davis E., Ludlow	
Decker Howel & Co., Fifth	
Foster J. C.,　　　do	
Jilson J., St. Clair	
Peter Thomas, Third	
Schaffer G. W., First	
Steel William,　do	
Thomas H.,　　do	
Ware Thomas, Jefferson	
Wareham & Bolsley, St. Clair	
Bols D.	*Farmersville.*
Bull Solomon	
Bollenbach H.	
Katro Oliver	
Oldfather H.	
Karr Jacob	*West Baltimore.*
Bright Samuel	*New Lebanon.*
Brown Henry	
McCully David	
Wike John	
Ebbert Frederick	*Germantown.*
Kindig Elias	
Kindig Samuel	
Kolb David	
McClure Samuel	
Garlick Jacob	*Miamisburgh.*
Gephart Moses	
Groby Henry	
Groby David	
Weaver Martin	*Liberty.*
Kunkle John	*Chambersburg.*
Sullivan Alexander	
Cox & Olinger	*Centre.*
Miller & Hudybaker	
Smith Christian	
Williamson Wm. H.	
Wike John	*Hershmansville.*
Wike Jonathan	
Claywell James	
Rauser John	

Morgan County.

Palmer Joseph	*Chester Hill.*
Palmer Jonathan	
Welch J.	
Vernon James	
Pettit Wm.	*Triadelphia.*
Hampton David	*Chaneyville.*
Tappan Wm. H.	*Malta.*
McAslin Sam'l.	
Fouts Isaac	*Meigs' Creek.*
Fuller John M	
Bishop Joshua	*Pleasant Valley.*
Wells Alex.	*Meigsville.*
Kidd James	
Fouts Lemon	*McConnelsville.*
Lutton James	
Hesket Harvey	
Porter Jonathan	
Adams James T.	
Jett John P.	
Ouster D. C.	

McCarty A.	*McConnelsville.*
Robinson Alex.	
Concklin John B.	
Bradley Benj.	
Fouts Thos.	
Brown J. R.	
Rainey James	*Stockport*
Bowles S.	
Cheadle P.	
Ourry John R.	*Pennsville*
Coulson Jesse	
Breneman Reuben	
Roberts John	
Johns A. T.	
Johns Robert	
Wiley Marshall	
Deweese Aaron	
Deweese Joseph	
Stilions Stephen	*Neelysville.*
Herron M.	

Morrow County.

McCloud J.	*Underwood's.*
Miller Obadiah	
Smithson Joseph	
Blair W. P.	*Iberia.*
Reed James	
Simpson William	*Marengo.*
Wood Amos	
Estlack A. W.	*Cardington.*
Hall N. H.	
Lee Isaac	
Moxwell L.	
Sloan H.	
Allman Silas	*Lincoln.*
Brooke Mordecai	
Halfhill Moses	
Hays William	
Hyde Russell	
James Ludwell	
Sipe Jacob	
Stiuer David	
Underhill John	
Wood Jonathan	
Doherty A.	*Nimmons' Cross Roads.*
Harrester John	*Corsica.*
Roberts Charles	
Corwin Samuel	*Vail's Cross Roads.*
Chase Daniel	
Hardesty R. J.	
Jimmerson John	*Chesterville.*
Woodward E.	
Ogilvie H.	
Conger James	
Bain John	
Strong James	
Struble Joseph	
Ogden John	

Muskingum County.

McCall T.	*Otsego.*
Trimble R.	
Wortman Samuel	
Ruckle John	*Frazeysburg.*
Large Andrew	*Putnam.*
Collins Joseph	
Cook John B.	*Norwich.*

Ervin James   *Norwich.*
Shipman Levi
Ziegler D.   *Fultonham.*
Hatcher J. E.
Chilcoat S.
Axline Wm.
Powell R.
Baker A.
Ensminger S.
McFarland R.
Moore R.
Mathews D.
Holmes Joseph   *Hopewell.*
Liggit John
Anderson A.
Madden George   *New Concord.*
Brown Alex.
Arnold Saml.
Nelson John
Robinson W.   *White Cottage.*
Bentley Wm.
Sowers Henry   *Stovertown.*
Lacock Edward   *Gratiot.*
Bowers John
Landes Thos.
Taylor J.   *Chandlersville.*
Renouff N.

Noble County.

Gladfelder William   *Batesville.*
Gatchell F. D.
Camden John P.   *Mt. Ephraim.*
McConnell Austin
Morrison John H.
Pool Joseph
Willis Cyrus
Cook T. R.   *Sarahsville.*
Davison Robert
Drum W. R.
Nichols H.
Phelps C.
Dudley James   *Gardner.*
Tilton Freeman
Cunningham George   *South Olive.*
Mitchell Henry
Parker John S.
Hagerty Nicholas E.   *Kennonsburg.*
Mendenhall Thomas

Ottawa County.

Wright G.   *Elmore.*
Wright A.
Rice H. J.
Rice J. F.
Cook Jesse
Brown J.
Grainline Jacob
Thorn G.   *Port Clinton.*
Knight J.
Batter L.
Couchain B.
Larsh S.
Bredhuff Henry   *Marble Head.*
Malona James

Paulding County.

Cress Geo.   *Paulding.*

McCreary Robert   *Paulding.*
Pritchard Andrew

Perry County.

Battan John   *New Lexington.*
Brown Barnard
Feigley Samuel
Kelley Trimble
Oatley Jabez
White A. M.
Drake Ralph   *Sunday Creek Cross Roads.*
Golden John
Hoak Samuel
Thorp Lemuel
Bruner George   *Somerset.*
Chilcote Ensor
Maning Edgar
Martin John
May Wm. & Alex.
Swinehart Samuel
McDonald P.
Olive D.   *Sego.*
Fulton Wm.
Edwards Oliver   *Straitsville.*

Pickaway County.

Border Jacob   *Circleville.*
Cook & Wilmore
Cook & Valentine
Earhart A.
Hartz Charles
Hamil & Peters
Jewel & Cook
May George
Peters & Upp
Pedrick A. & J.
Richter Sandford
Robins Mathias
Williams Thomas
Callihan F.   *Tarlton.*
Miller J. F.
Ambrose & Miller   *Darbyville.*
Wheeler Isaac
Fretwell John W.   *Beckett's Store.*
Baughman Jacob   *Williamsport.*
Reed Joshua

Pike County.

Ashenfelter Wm.   *Cynthiana.*
Collins J. R.
Bridebaugh John   *Waverly.*
Houser Jacob
Miller Levi
Miller George
Snyder T. J.
Cochran Wm. S.   *Gibson.*
Rinsley Danl.
Ware John   *Piketon.*
Ware John E.
Hawk T. A.
Kellison Richard
Groves Geo.
Kouch Joseph
Corwine A. & B. F.   *Omega.*

Portage County.

Stratton D. & E.   *Atwater.*
Bow A.

Craig Saml. & Wm.   *Atwater.* | Taylor T. M.   *Gettysburg.*
Case T. & H.   *Randolph.* | Sackman Jacob
Waldo Henry   *Aurora.* | Willkin Wm.   *West Florence.*
Lord David | Juday J.   *Hamburg.*
Clark James   *Streetsboro'.* | Crisler A.
Wing B. A. & T. A. | McDaniels S.
Musser Wm.   *Shalersville.* | Juland S.   *New Paris.*
Ramsey John S. | Sawyer & Myers
Shook E. W. | Liftwick A. W.
Anderson B. F.   *Franklin.* | Little T.
Allen G. | Raybum J.
Dean E. O. | Austin B.
Botsford E. W.   *Edinburgh.* | Samuels McOager   *West Elkton.*
Jones Thos. | Maddock John
Egbert Thos.   *Suffield.* | Fouts John
Yerrick Jacob & John | Hornaday Nelson
Patterson H. & L. L.   *Paris.* | Hulls John
Calkins John D. |
Carlisle S. & J. | **Putnam County.**
Brown E. B.   *Charleston.* | Burkholder J. R.   *Leipsic.*
Hall E. & C. L. | Clark D.
Alford Saml.   *Mantua* | Long Samuel
Sanford S. | Sigler Joel
Carleton Levi | Strain John A.
Keys F. | Watters Henry
Mason C. A.   *Deerfield.* | Watters Saml.   *Medary.*
Greenemyre A. | Watters Saml., Jr.
Taylor John   *Nelson.* | Bowers A. J.   *Gilboa.*
Daniels F. | Brown G. W.
Tuttle Isaac   *Palmyra.* | Galloway J. W. S.
Jones Richard | Wynkoop Wm.
Hollis John | Wynkoop J.
Gurley A. D. & A.   *Rootstown.* | Sebough S. T.   *Buckeye.*
Austin G. & J. S. | McCurdy Milton
Bows Oliver | Lee Jonathan
Chapman — | Alteknise J.
Stanford O. | Elwell Joseph   *Vaughnsville.*
Hart M. & S.   *Freedom.* | Garner Geo. S.
Hopkins George | Monroe James
Altman Wm.   *Brimfield.* | Alkire G. W.   *Pendleton.*
Mallory A. & B. | Augustin D.
Carnahan Wm. & Co.   *Ravenna.* | Brown D.
Bostwick D. & H. N. | Nigh J.
Tribon Wm. |
Miller Robert | **Richland County.**
                                | Dickerson M.   *Shelby.*
Preble County. | Funk M.
Tomson & Cotterman   *Lewisburg.* | Gamble & Funk
Scanling John   *Camden.* | Johns & Shupe
Runkle John | Livensparger Geo.
Huffman Saml. | Smith George
Elliott Nathaniel | Wheeler D.
Hewit J. | Andrews John E.   *Butler.*
Nelson Moses   *Eaton.* | Dilts John
Ammerman J. R. | Hernug Simon
Crume A. D. | Perry Gilbert
Walker Danl. | Nelson James   *Shenandoah.*
Lockwood S. H. | Crabb Abraham   *Olivesburg.*
Coons G. W. | Daniels Henry
Hoover George   *Fairhaven.* | Houston Robert
Glover Silas | Swineford Israel
Larsh W. C. | Troup Philip   *West Windsor.*
Biggs H. P. | Charles Wm. F.   *Barnes.*
Truax Wm.   *New Westville.* | Richmond John
Watt L. A. | Welshlager Samuel
Nelson Moses   *Eaton.* | Workman John
Burley Joshua | Moore Hugh   *Lexington.*

Snider David	*Lexington.*
Spencer David	
White Wm. P.	
An S. & C.	*Mansfield.*
Bell John	
Courtney Wm.	
Fisher David	
Crouthers Samuel	
McClarren Barney	
McCoy & Downing	
Shefler & Conley	
Weber Saml.	
Wolf Barney	
Brichards E.	*Belleville.*
Donald Samuel	
Howard Otis	
Howard J. B.	
Lash J. L.	
Lobach John	
Whittin Riley	
Wills Richard	
Algers S.	*Richland.*
Delaney J.	
Muring John & Peter	
Markes & Baugher	*Lucas.*
Baker David	

Ross County.

Phillips W.	*Chillicothe.*
Cook S. & J.	
Lyons Josiah	
Hills G. E.	
Reed Henry	
Shaw & Haakins	
Warwick Nelson	
Long & McAdon	
Flood & Hoadley	
Sample Jeremiah	*South Salem.*
Pummel H.	
Morton Wm. R.	
Latta Saml. C.	
Scott R. A.	
McGinnis Alex.	
Harrel Wm.	*Halleville.*
Browning H.	*Bourneville.*
Kearnes Pat.	
Flora J.	
Frederick Daniel	*Kingston.*
Franks Isaiah	
Gillespie Wm.	

Sandusky County.

Yarba John	*Woodville.*
Cook J. J.	
Real J.	
Sealy Wm.	*Clyde.*
Weeks Wm.	
Elliott Henry	
Weaver A.	
Lyttle John	*Greensburg Cross Roads.*
Mapes Joseph	
Harvy M.	*Rutland Ridge.*
Yutter John	
Holbrook Silas	*Townsend.*
Levisee John L.	
Terry M,	
Day Wm B.	

Willis Wm.	*Townsend.*

Scioto County.

Creese David	*Portsmouth.*
Deeds Hiram	
Foster Archibald	
Fuller & Carey	
Jackson & Fryer	
Leglar George	
McIntire Daniel	
McCollister & Dawley	
Misman Andrew	
Purdum J. W.	
Rockhold & Gills.	
Drake Elias	*Iron Furnaces.*
Hawkins Edmond	
Luther John	
Page John	

Seneca County,

Bier Levi	*Attica.*
Keifer Charles	
Kelly Benjamin	
Shiry John	
McBride O. P.	*Adrian.*
Ragan John	
Row Samuel	
Bland William	*Berwick.*
Christlip Geo. S.	
Dick Noah	
Kerr Wm. F.	
Martin George	
Needham Thomas	
Phillips Joseph	
Sailor Jeremiah	
Kershner J.	*Bloomville.*
Zimmerman F.	
Betts Charles	*Bettsville.*
Betts Oran	
De Witt P.	*Tiffin.*
Berkey & Meyers	
Lour George	
Meyers John	
Patterson & Groff	
Small Geo. C.	
Dewaldt Nicholas	*Bascom.*
Miller John	
Miller Isaac	
Miller Michael	
Nicholas Benjamin	*Green Spring.*
Norris Thomas	
Baughman George	
Heath Cozentine	
Vontassel Frederick	
Critchfield Asa	
Sharp William	
Lapham Robert	*Republic.*
Rhoads Joseph	
Covert Jehiel	
Sweatland Joel	

Starke County.

Davis Hiram	*Waynesburg.*
Gleaner Daniel	
Koons Solomon	
Mays Andrew	
Mays John W.	
McLowell Samuel	

Graybill Samuel	*West Brookfield.*	
Graybill Jacob		
Graybill D.		
Hackett A.		
Gibson Abraham	*Minerva.*	
Kerstetter Jacob		
Myers Jeremiah		
Zemborver John		
Bolender John	*Lake.*	
Bolender Levi		
Bolender Daniel		
Heffenfinger M.		
Richards A. K. B.		
Slack Levi		
Wonders Peter D.	*New Franklin.*	
Coulter James	*East Greenville.*	
Duck Benjamin		
Luty Abraham		
Nesbit James		
Roan Christian		
Roan William		
Wible John		
Disler Jacob	*New Berlin.*	
Pepper Silas		
Reemsnyder Daniel		
Shook John		
Borton Levi	*Mt. Union.*	
Hair J. M.		
Hoiles C. L.		
Schmachtenberger Samuel	*Mapleton.*	
Kriny George		
Shearer David		
Shearer Jacob		
Miser Henry		
Coates Jesse	*Marlboro'.*	
Ellyson Dempsy		
Esting Michael		
Morgan Thomas		
Orr & Smith		
Beans James	*New Baltimore.*	
Brumbaugh Conrad	*Hartville.*	
Madlam William		
Weary William		
Gibbs Samuel S.		
Kramer Andrew		
Ulerick Isaac		
Mong & Snyder	*Massillon.*	
Drew John		
Shearer H.		
Zimmerman —		
Seaman U.		
Seeley D. B.		
Stanard A. V.	*Limaville.*	
Sluyghter Henry		
Flitcroft L. D.	*Mahoning.*	
Young W.		
Roath L.		

Summit County.

Buel D. C.	*Northfield.*	
Darling George		
Darling James		
Ingledon W. P.		
Palmer H. H.		
Foster L.	*Macedonia Depot.*	
Morris Joseph		
Lanford Hezekiah		

Withered George	*Macedonia Depot.*
Angell Calvin	*Copley.*
Barnett Henry	
Chapman J. H.	
Hohn Samuel	
Carr Shafer	*Bath.*
Currier H. L.	
Ferguson Robert	
Thomas George	
Weaver Jonathan	*Clinton.*
Parsons H. K.	*Tallmadge.*
Hayes W.	
Richardson J. & E. A.	
Anderson Michael	*Inland.*
Hammel Levi	
Warner William	
Weston John	
Clark James	*Richfield.*
Pricket Samuel	
Sheldon G. C.	
Thomas John	
Garthwait C.	
Boughton Noble	*Montrose.*
Evans Philip & Brothers	
Huntley Ira	

Trumbull County.

Boothe D. P.	*Greensburgh.*
Boothe Peter	
Horton William	
Crosby E. D.	*Southington.*
Stroup David	
Timmerman James	
White Henry R.	
Kauffman J.	*Warren.*
Soule J.	
Soule J., Junr.	
Hampson J.	
Hampson Robert	
Longmore David	
Rand Wm. R.	
Burns William	*Johnsonville.*
Moury Isaac	
Allison John C.	*Girard.*
Prindell Horatio N.	
Daws Adrian	*Orangeville.*
Palmer Sheldon	
Kennedy J. D.	*Farmington.*
Reynolds S.	
Bundy E.	
Stetler John	
Urich David.	
Loveland Hiram	
Armitage J. C.	
Taylor Philip	*Brookfield.*
Clark Seth	
Clark Smith	
Mills Frank	
Tribby Arthur	
Clark James	*Church Hill.*
Lease Enos	
Sutton William	
Denison John	
Gilkey Solon	*Hartford.*
Ford David	
Davis Robert	
Hart Calvin	

Coe Dwight   *Hartford.*
Beal John   *Ohlstown.*
Ohl John
Ohl Michael
Palm Cyrus
Williams Calvin   *Vienna.*
Williams Ransom
Holcomb C. J
Hull Lucius

Tuscarawas County.

Henderson Henry   *Winfield.*
Myers Joseph
Sholtey H. J.   *Deardorf's Mills.*
Woodar John M.   *Albany.*
Winsch Jonathan   *Gnadenhutten.*
Cunning Richard   *Ragersville.*
Gonter John W.
Gonter Jacob M.
Hays Thomas
Link Michael J.
Penrod Tobias
Rager Jacob
Stough Simon
Frazier T. J.   *Canal Dover.*
Orites George
Lind F.
Lind Jacob
Bippus Jacob
Neidlinger Jacob
Lahm Philip
Knisely J. B.   *New Philadelphia.*
Exline J.
Young W.
Sluthour J.
Long J.
Myler R.
Young J.
Albert W.
Knoff J.
Mitchell H.
Irwin A.
How S.
Oaseleer G.
Carlisle W.
Guyton Augustus   *Peoli.*
Randall Ellis H.
Eberhart J.   *Rockford.*
Eberhart O.
Herran Wm.
Beans Thomas

Union County.

Ammerine Wesley   *Marysville.*
Caves William A.
Drake William
Rice & Grummons
Teas Thomas
Wells William H.
Duvall A.   *Watkins.*
Oemens Joseph   *Milford Centre.*
Lambert J. H.
Monroe L. P.
Snodgrass Samuel
Webster Lester
Mitchell Jacob   *New California.*
Ressler Samuel

Dovana Joseph   *New California,*
Hobbs J. M.   *Coberly's.*

Van Wert County.

Armentrout Wm.   *Van Wert.*
Evers D.
Glenn —
Long James
Moulton —
Nail W.
Slain —
Thorn Jacob
Maisch George
Roach A. & Bro.
Fox E.
Rose Perry
Zimmerman A.

Vinton County.

Crist, Lowry & Ullom   *McArthur.*
Dillon & Sprague
Allen & Sniff
Bradbury J.
Wilcox Nathan   *Allensville.*
Doss Austin L.   *Prattsville.*
Dye H.   *Reed's Mills.*
Tench J. H.
Nunemaker J.
Walters R. Z.

Warren County.

Thompson J. H.   *Oregon.*
Terry Jonathan
Whitaker D.   *Mason.*
Willoughby E
Heaton E.
Hastings R.
Miller B.
Allen A.
Garrard Joseph   *Red Lion.*
Garrard Wm.
Decker Henry
Williams Wm. M.   *Edwardsville.*
Peacock L. S.
Barrick John L.   *Deerfield.*
Mason Cyrus
Gilbert Ira
Grenamier J.
Were Wm.   *Dallasburg.*
Carey S. S.   *Dunlevy.*
Merritt A.   *Wayneaville.*
Keys Wm.
Prince H. W.
Hainey William   *Hopkinsville.*
Starkey G. W.   *Morrow.*
Stanley W. A.
Snyder Henry
Hamilton John
Gilham Wm.
Oraver David   *Lebanon.*
Mikeswell Benj.
Starkey Simon B.   *Butlerville.*
Vanderburg Henry   *Harveysburg.*
Orew J. H.
Buckles John   *Mount Holly.*
Buckles Jacob
West B. R.

Washington County.

Hill Jacob	*Marietta.*
Hill Samuel	
Gird —	
Neadham —	
Leonhart L. & J.	
Adams & Son	
Towsley & Lord	
Rumbold J.	*Harmar.*
Morten E.	
Thompson —	
Fogle George	*Centre Belpre.*
Kirkpatrick Alex.	
Stubbs Jason	
Decker A.	*Ostend.*
Barnes R.	
Hovey B. B.	*Lower Salem.*
Hovey G. S.	
Capman Jonathan	
Twigs Andrew	
True Moses	
Whetstone Jacob	
Chapman R.	
Scott M. E.	*Regniers' Mills.*
Smithson R. E.	
Britton John	*Fearing.*
Athey Solomon	
Mullen James	*Beverly.*
Barr Ellis	*Wesley.*
Barfield Isaac	
Fairbanks E.	
Davis James	
Steed Z.	*Lowell.*
Schriener T.	
Place Walter	*Decaturville.*
Twiggs Andrew	*Bonn.*
Twiggs Josiah	
Kidd F. T.	
Imuel Conrad	
Olose H. L.	
Garretson Joel	*North Union.*

Wayne County.

Hutchinson Wm.	*Fredericksburg.*
Hutchinson J.	
McCartney S. C.	
McMillen J. P.	
Hileman John	*Reedsburg.*
Buffenmier Peter	
Ryland Wm.	
Wertz Levi.	
Beard Enoch	
Emery David	
Cassidy W.	
Weldoy Henry	*New Prospect.*
Kindig John	
Robb John	
Robb Franklin	
Bruce Calvin	*Burbank.*
Atkinson D. M.	
Darley John	*Shreve.*
Bevington Saml.	
Everley Geo.	
Moore Wilson	
Schlett Chas.	*Marshallville.*
Wimer Martin	

Hennebarger M.	*Marshallville.*
Detzler Joseph	
Keefer Jacob	
Halter Ambrose	
Emerson S. F.	*Canaan.*
Emerson Daniel	
Vandoorn T. Z.	

Williams County.

Arnold Chas.	*Bryan.*
Bombarger Daniel	
Connin J.	
Cunningham Levi	
Fulton Joseph	
Fulton J., Jr.	
Knepper Jeremiah	
Kunkle Alex.	
Over Jacob	
Schmachtenbarger Benj.	
Urea Alex.	
Young John	
Allegear H. S.	*West Unity.*
Cline Jeremiah	
Ely Isaac	
Megarrah Wm.	
Marshall John	
Mann E.	
Rockwell G.	
Spencer D.	
Smith G. O.	
Wise George	
Bell James	*Centre.*
Brittan F.	
Polick J.	
Teems Jacob	
Walker H.	
Dalrymple Daniel	*Pulaski.*
Harrington L. B.	
Myers George	
Ried Ephraim	
Dillon John	*Montpelier.*
Spake R.	
Mason Isaac	
Mason Albert	

Wood County.

Courson W. H.	*Perrysburg.*
Miller J.	
Curtis Mark	
Vass Alex.	
Jolly Thos.	*Bowling Green.*
Dolleyhoyn Wm.	
Whitehead John	
Smith J. D.	
Evers John	
Drurey Allen	
Conway James	*Weston.*
Borbour James	
Skinner John	
Rice Wm.	
Van Blurcum A.	*Portage.*
Ortury P.	
McMillen John	
Elder John	
Cloyt E. P.	
Alcorn Alex.	*Gilead.*
Davis A. C.	

Davis H. *Gilead.*
Fuller Alfred B.
Bossard Saml.
Snively Isaac B.
Saye Orrin
Brook John *Montgomery Cross Roads.*
Friesbie Theodore
Pain Henry A. *Miltonville.*

Wyandot County.

Rodgers Matthew *Upper Sandusky.*
Sigler A.
Sigler Josiah
Jenkins John H.
French Noah
Spangle Joseph
Peterson D. H.
Graham David
Ayres Wm.
Smith Saml.
Murphey Henry
Whinery Stephen
Houke Henry *Carey.*
Gear Jacob O.
Sweatland Hiram
Houke John
Kennedy James *Marseilles.*
Huntley Chas.
Chamberlain —,
Cooper John *Mexico.*
Ingman E. O.
Fisher Michael M.
Shafer Wm. *McCutchensville.*
Voght Henry

Carpet—Rug, Oil Cloth & Matting, Wholesale & Retail Dealers.

Cuyahoga County.

Beckwith T. S. & Co., 65 Superior *Cleveland.*
Branch & Moulton, 69 do
Outter & Taylor, 55 do
Raymond S. & Co., 63 do

Franklin County.

McCoy W. A. & J. O., High *Columbus.*
Osborn & Stewart, do
Stanton S. B., do
Aston Isaac O., do

Hamilton County.

Falls H., 19 e. 4th *Cincinnati.*
Maxwell George, 26 w. 5th
Ringwalt J. C. & Co., 174 Main
Shillito J., 12 e. 4th
Tolbert & Nold, 30 Lower Market

Scioto County.

Elden Wm. & Co. *Portsmouth.*
Towel J. F. & Co.

Carpet Weavers.

Ashland County.

Weaver J. *Roseburg.*

Belmont County.

Birch S. A. *Morristown.*
Maxwell Wm.
Sweeny T. *Armstrong's Mills.*

Butler County.

Laget A. *Middletown.*
Jotter Jacob *Monroe*

Carroll County.

Anschutz P. H. *Carrollton.*

Clark County.

Moyall James *New Carlisle.*
Myers Jacob

Clermont County.

Bryant Mrs. *Amelia.*
Cleveland Mrs.

Columbiana County.

Bartler Joseph *North Georgetown.*
Will William
Horsfall Henry *New Lisbon.*
Eckler Henry *New Chambersburg.*

Darke County.

Young John *Fort Jefferson.*

Defiance County.

Kettinger Viet *Brunersburg.*

Franklin County.

Ayrhart Peter *Canal Winchester.*
Brelsford Samuel *Columbus.*

Hamilton County.

Bailey G., No 349 W. Fifth *Cincinnati.*
Gottman H. G., 661 Vine
Nurre Henry, n. e. cor. 12th and Clay
Weir J., 143 W. Fifth
Smith J. J. *Fulton.*
Merrell Mrs. *Harrison.*

Harrison County.

Davis John *Cadis.*

Henry County.

Heaton Mrs. *Napoleon.*
Sabins Mrs.

Highland County.

Sulser Henry *Greenfield.*

Jefferson County.

McMillen S. *Steubenville.*
Lawrence David *Mouth of Yellow Creek.*

Licking County.

Tobin J. *Newark.*

Mahoning County.

Burry Dan'l. *Cornersburg.*
Bower L. *New Springfield.*
Welk George
Buyard Jacob *North Lima.*

Medina County.

Baldwin Miss H. *Medina*
Bean Mrs.

Montgomery County.

Turner William, Fifth   *Dayton.*
Sheaner Michael   *New Lebanon.*

Pickaway County.

Hemon James   *Circleville.*

Pike County.

Fouth Jacob   *Piketon.*

Richland County.

Baughman John   *Lexington.*
Etner Reuben
McNall John
Mosser John   *West Windsor.*
Masters Margaret   *Belleville.*

Ross County.

Heiser Wm. L.   *Chillicothe.*
Burns J.

Tuscarawas County.

Campbell J.   *New Philadelphia.*
Wilson R. B.

Vinton County.

Elliott Edward   *McArthur.*

Warren County.

Beard Wm.   *Dunlevy.*

Wayne County.

Brumman David   *Shreve.*
Lichty Benj.   *Martinsville.*

Carriage Manufacturers.

Allen County

Steever Jacob   *Middle River.*

Ashland County.

Williams A. R.   *Sullivan.*
Tubbs Henry
Houck O. B.
Cummings T.
Wickham Jeremiah   *Savannah.*
Scott Moses C.
Leach & Sprangle   *Ashland.*
Myers Christian
Horn Henry   *Jeromeville.*
Beard Henry   *Mohecan.*
Chapel R. A.   *Perrysville.*

Ashtabula County.

Webster H.   *Richmond Centre.*
Rutter M.
McLaughlin H.   *Cherry Valley.*
Clark J. V. D.
Knapp L. O.   *Geneva.*
Loomis H.   *Jefferson.*
Amsden P. S.
Johnson H. N.
Benham Wm. G.   *Ashtabula.*
Turner Israel
Phillips J.
Kellogg ——
Pinney P. & Son   *Hart's Grove.*
Root U. O.
Peters F.

Ford A. H.   *West Williamsfield.*
Ford B.
Clark A. B.   *South Ridge.*
Kinney A.
Dunbar Hugh   *Andover.*
Smith Philo
Wheeler Wm. N.   *Harpersfield.*
Wright Chester
Custin M.
Gleason Alanson
Dykeman A. J.
Dodge H. B.
Clark A. B.   *Conneaut.*
Fenton A.
Kinney A.
Brewer E. F.
Smith ——

Athens County.

Kigg Wm. N.   *Albany.*
Socie M. D.   *Nelsonville.*
Ring J. L. & Co.   *Athens.*
Lordy Randall
Cooley A.
Cockril Elijah
Rigg Wm. N.   *Lee.*
Johnson Geo.
Durant G.   *Guysville.*

Belmont County.

Jones John M.   *Hendrysburgh.*
Lingo William   *Demos.*
Krim Simon   *Flushing.*
Walker Isaac
Davis Shepherd   *Saint Clairsville.*
Graham Thomas M.   *Shepherdstown.*
Day Henry H.   *Belmont.*

Brown County.

Kellogg Horace   *Ripley.*
Gibson H. C.   *Newhope.*
Keethler John   *Puebla.*
Still J. C.
Curren J.   *Russellville.*

Butler County.

Burley & Brother   *Blue Ball.*
Morganthaler C.   *Hamilton.*
Conover & Keene
Harris Wm. H.   *Saint Charles.*
Jotter P.   *Monroe.*
Thompson H. D.   *Ross.*
Crume W. R.   *College Corner.*
Howe E.
Bookwalter B. & J.   *Seven Mile.*

Champaign County.

Rodgers Chas.   *Christiansburg.*
Rodgers John
Ganson W. H.   *Urbana.*
Jamison D. C.
Marsh J. D.   *Woodstock.*
Creighbaum ——

Clark County.

Baker A. & M.   *Enon.*
Driscoll E.   *Springfield.*
West David
Olstot & Toland
Merritt Edward   *South Charleston.*
Baker P. E. & Co.   *New Carlisle.*

Clermont County.

Bainum David	*Laurel.*
Melvin James	
McMurchy A.	
McNutt J. D.	*Williamsburg.*
Moyer H.	
Walker Wm	
Sims Samuel B.	*New Richmond.*
Gelvin L.	*Goshen.*
Hall J. H.	
Thornton & Co.	*Bethel.*
Crossley George	*Felicity.*
Mullen W. E.	
Bowers James	
Jones & Wilmington	*Withamsville.*
Phillips E. D.	*Mt. Carmel.*
Bragdon Jotham	*Amelia.*
Stirling W. B. C.	
Dillius Boyd	*Neville.*
Allen F. H.	*Milford.*
Beard William	
Hitch James F.	*Clover.*
Chambers John	*Moscow.*
Hughes Edwd. & Son	
Dickinson Y.	*West Woodville.*

Clinton County.

Smith & Grant J. & J.	*New Burlington.*
Conklin Thos.	*Lumberton.*
Toy John	
Slack J. W.	*Sligo.*
Longshore J. H.	
Luckey James	*New Antioch.*
Brewer J.	*New Vienna.*
Dennis J.	
Stolks S.	
Hixon S.	
Cleever James	*Wilmington.*
Shinwalters Westly	

Columbiana County.

Boyers Alexr.	*Wellsville.*
Goodman D. S. & Co.	
Ella & Myers	*New Lisbon.*
Adam Gottlieb F.	
Hamilton David	
Fording John	*New Garden.*
Liber Charles	
Taylor Joel B.	
Sheets George	*Salem.*
Woodruff David.	
Fitzpatrick John	*Columbiana.*
Williamson William	
Winch John	

Coshocton County.

Geese Samuel	*Chili.*
Gonser David	
Walsh William	*Keene.*
Carroll Robert	

Crawford County.

Dinkle Lewis	*Bucyrus.*
Norton Jefferson	
Miller John	
Sheckler Hugh	*Bucyrus.*
Trish John	
Yost A.	

Cuyahoga County.

Burnett Joel	*Chagrin Falls.*
Rowe R.	
Russell S.	
Curtiss J. H.	*Dover.*
Scoughton David	*Solon.*
Marsh Luther	*Brecksville.*
Thomas John L.	
Cleveland James C.	*Bedford.*
Cleveland Charles	
Higgins William	*Coe Ridge.*
Black & Smith, Pittsburgh	*Cleveland.*
Burrows G W. do	
Drumm John, 61 Seneca	
Gray & Smith, Michigan	
Holden & Brown, 56 Ontario	
Hulbert A. W., 72 do	
Lowman Jacob, cor. Vineyard & Long	
Potter Andrew, 1 Kinsman	
Rapparlie John, Michigan	
Wright & Myers, Pittsburgh	

Darke County.

McEwen H. H.	*Ithica.*
Millett W.	
Snider G. W.	*Hillgrove.*
Moyer A. S.	*German.*
Best J. B.	*Poplar Ridge.*
Greenawalt Jacob	*Greenville.*
Ormsby Saml.	

Defiance County.

Corwine J.	*Defiance.*
Dunshee A. E.	
Knowles James	
Thompson George	*Milldale.*

Delaware County.

McElroy John	*Delaware.*
Covill Manley	
Hedrick Joseph	*Stratsford.*
Kroninger J. K.	
Libald John	
Null Jacob	
Lunger John	*Waldo.*
Bishop C.	
Francis M.	
Watters B. C.	*Harlem.*

Erie County.

Schneeke F.	*Sandusky City.*
Standish B.	*Milan.*

Fairfield County.

Crain Milton W.	*Pickerington.*
Patterson Wm.	*West Rushville.*
Dodson Daniel	*Bremen.*
Deets & McCall	*Lancaster.*
Shutt William	
Zink A.	
Moody W.	
Farrow M.	
Keyser M.	

Odell R.   *Sugar Grove.*
Hawkens D.
Philips Joseph

Franklin County.

Booth E. & H. F., Gay   *Columbus.*
Chadwick W. B., cor. Pearl & Rich
Cutler Robert, High
Ohio Stage Manufactory, J. G. Jones, Gay
Kesler Henry, Gay
Shannon J. A., Front
Abbott Ira   *Reynoldsburg.*
Clark J.
Grimm L.
Longshore T.
Norris T.
Armstrong Thos., Jr.   *Hibernia.*
Bush Isaac   *Worthington.*
Cook Peter
Mattoon William
Scanland James
White C. S.
Nicodemus Henry   *Canal Winchester.*

Geauga County.

Rodgers Wm.   *Chardon.*
McCarty C.
Parsons George
Rodgers N. E. & W.
Collins Norman
Parsons G. K.
Norris Moses R.
Troumper Jacob   *Claridon.*
Fowler & Carlton   *Burton.*
Hollister H.   *Bainbridge.*
Smith A. Russell
Baker Wm.   *Newbury.*
Center George
Whaley J.
Pike Wm.   *Munson.*
Haskill J.
Shattick George
Rider L. F.
White C.   *Perkman.*
Smith A.
McIlwain C.
Alderman F.
Freeman L.
Worts A.   *Montville.*
Smith R.   *Huntsburgh.*
Nichols W. F.   *Middlefield.*
Hays E. J.
Staunton H.   *Hamden.*
Sumner, Ormsly & Co.   *Thompson.*
Miller E.   *Troy.*
Conrad J. D.
Colson N.
Gould H.   *Chester.*
Callon Jerome

Greene County.

Coxen Levi   *Xenia.*
Morehouse & Davis
Boots E.   *Spring Valley.*
Parry D. S.   *New Jasper.*
Huffman Josiah   *Cedarville.*
McSyfers Asa   *Jamestown.*

Guernsey County.

Buckanon & Johnson   *Cumberland.*
Conwell J.   *Washington.*
Hurst Wm.
Johnson D.   *Antrim.*
Maynard W.   *Cambridge.*
McGrew F.   *Millersville.*
Orr J.

Hamilton County.

Barnes H., 5th bet. Sycamore & Broadway
                             Cincinnati.
Bruce I. & B. & Co., 75 Walnut
Butter E., 585 Western Row
Cameron & Mills, Freeman near 5th
Curtiss —, 670 w. Front
Dalton Joseph, 610 Main
Davis & Frey, Vine above Ham. Road
Fera, Hesing & Co., 48 w. 12th
Gosling John W., s. w. cor. Syc. & 6th
Gryden H. P. & Co., 55 e. 5th
Miller George C. & Sons, 7th bet. Main &
                               [Walnut
Marsh William E., s. w. cor. 7th & Main
Murdock, Porter & Marks, 16 & 18 e. 8th
Mueller & Vogelbach, 548 Vine
Oviatt & Sperry, 25 e. 5th
Pummell W., 214 w. 7th
Pummell & Paine, 197 do
Palmer J. R., Bank near W. Row
Roberts J., 91 w. 6th
Snodgrass H., Hamilton Road bet. Main
                               [& Piatt
Tooker J. M., 14 7th
Veerkamp Bernard, 470 Walnut
Ward L. M. & J., W. Row bet. 4th & 5th
Wilts John, Sycamore bet. 7th & 8th
Jackson W. R.   *Columbia.*
Iferd A. & Co.   *Pendleton.*
Wheeler Wm. H.   *Walnut Hills.*
Dom P.   *Mt. Healthy.*
Crain Hiram   *Montgomery.*
Bowen P. M.
Knight Charles
Bower S. B.   *Pleasant Ridge.*
Clark J. T.
Hamor John
Campbell Wm. & J.   *Harrison.*
Evans Joseph C.
Brown J. H.   *Newtown.*
Lantz Daniel
Richardson J. D.
Hagemann A. S.   *Sharonville.*
Phillips John R.
Miller & Voorhees   *Reading.*
Myers F.

Hancock County.

Liter John   *Ashery.*
Tevinney James
Hall J. B. & Co.   *Finley.*
Koous Edward & Co.

Hardin County.

Pugh D. & Co.   *Kenton.*

Harrison County.

Williams Joseph — *Cadiz.*
Foreman Aaron

Highland County.

Wright & Hiatt — *Highland.*
Woodmansee G. W. & J.
Daniels Lyman — *Greenfield.*
Cunningham J. R. — *Belfast Town.*
Huffman Daniel
Fidler J. & J. — *Hillsborough.*

Hocking County.

Frash Frederick — *Logan.*
Gross J. B.
Hamer B.

Huron County.

Cook A. — *Steuben.*
Burk L. D.
Cady M. — *East Townsend.*
Lamb Nathan
Tucker A.
Trumble Wm.
Hadley, Fuller & Co. — *Norwalk.*
Miller & Butts
Platt David H. — *North Fairfield.*
Smith S. S.

Jefferson County.

Brister J. & H. M. — *Steubenville.*
Murphy J.
Reed Wm. — *Mt. Pleasant.*
Hansberry L.
Eldridge David

Knox County.

McCracken B. — *Mount Vernon.*
Sanderson Wm.
Vanlieu Augden — *Levering.*
Coleman Isaac — *Brandon.*
Pattison M. J.
Gibson William — *Fredericktown.*
Moore John G.
Cole Aaron — *Democracy.*
Fults Benjamin
Kirkpatrick Samuel

Lake County.

Thompson C. C. — *Willoughby.*
Fairchild L. S.
Bird T. E. — *Painesville.*
Croft & Bagley

Licking County.

Sinnett & Graves — *Granville.*
Huggins J. L.
Ball, Ward & Co. — *Newark.*
Bush & McLelland — *Homer.*
Moore John G.
Wiant James
Evans H. — *Perryton.*
Hull T. J.
Snyder B. — *Croton.*
Cady C. C. — *Johnstown.*
Stowell H.

10

Gesner W. T. — *Johnstown.*
Gardner A. A.

Logan County.

Jackson George W. — *Huntsville.*
Emery & Brother — *Bellefontaine,*
Miller A. & D.

Lorain County.

Mungar & Whiton — *Huntington.*
Noble George W. — *La Grange.*
Gaston M. T. — *Oberlin.*
Goodsfread A. — *Elyria,*
Stow W. A.
Weyler P. M.
Reynolds Nelson — *Amherst.*

Lucas County.

Chatfield L. N. — *Emery.*
Harris Wm. H.

Madison County.

Fay P. S. — *London.*
Morlan John C.
Kauffman George — *Lafayette.*
Hughes Smiley — *Mt. Sterling.*
Ogden Absam — *West Jefferson.*
Olney George
McCauley Edward
Nuth A. — *Midway.*

Mahoning County.

Swank Mathias — *Canfield.*
Selter Christian — *Petersburgh.*
Brothers John & Co. — *Youngstown.*
Wilson & Co.
Razen Wm.
Bartlett Chancy L. — *Berlin Centre.*
Haines J. H. — *Orange.*
Monsell Wm. B. — *North Jackson.*
Case Stephen — *Milton.*
Delong James W.

Medina County.

Strauchan C. A. — *Lichfield.*
Warner & Bailey — *Liverpool.*
Briggs E. — *River Styx.*
Beach Geo. & Co. — *Wadsworth.*
Warner J. J.
Gilbert A. W. — *Lodi.*
Gaylord Wm. B.
Rose Thos. — *Homerville.*
Parker S. S. — *Medina.*
Drake C. W.
Kimmell & Baldwin
Olcott A.

Mercer County.

Winters Jacob — *Celina.*

Miami County.

Buckingham J. L. — *Piqua.*
Foster & Crosier
Stockton J. C. — *Troy.*
Lewis E. D. & Thos. — *Casstown.*
Chamberlain A. C. & J.
Williams John H. — *Pleasant Hill,*
Rhodehamel Benj.

Montgomery County.

Brandenburge David	*Vandalia.*
Bennett & Tucker, St. Clair	*Dayton.*
Cohen J., Fifth	
Conover & Smith, Third	
Golding & Hammond, do	
Noleen & Freed, Second	
Phillips W. W., Third	
Rough R., do	
Woodmouse S., St Clair	
Musselman Christian	*New Lebanon.*
Billmire Samuel	*Germantown.*
Schaeffer George W.	
Weaver Daniel	
Hibbart J.	*Miamisburgh.*
McConnell & Bookwalter	

Morgan County.

Bingham John	*Stockport.*
McGwigan S.	

Morrow County.

Brocklesby Wm.	*Underwood's.*
Garwin & Peck	*Cardington.*
Dennis Emanuel	*Woodview.*
Huffman Samuel	
Davis & Mitchell	*Chesterville.*
Trusdell Stephen	

Muskingum County.

Hoose J. O.	*Hopewell.*
Dunlap John	*Shannon.*
Wilking Henry	
Goslin Bernard	*White Cottage.*
Conwell Jonathan	*Gratiot.*
Huntington C. & J.	*Zanesville.*
Barret & Elberson	
Palmer Davis	
Vanhorn R.	

Perry County.

Nyswander Frederick	*Thornville.*
Hammond William	*Rehoboth.*
Oull H. & P.	*Somerset.*
Grimm Jacob	

Pickaway County,

Bander William	*Circleville.*
King A.	

Preble County.

Smith Wm.	*West Alexandria.*
Smith Stephen	
Guild Charles	*Camden.*
Kline & Lockwood	*Eaton.*
Flemming & Snow	
Whitfield W. T.	
Art John	
Collins Chas.	*West Florence.*
Collins Luther	

Putnam County.

McBride J. G.	*Gilboa.*
Wagner J. H.	

Richland County.

Funk D. W.	*Shelby.*
Kerr J.	

Rogers J.	*Shelby.*
Christofel Jacob	*Mansfield.*
Platt George	
Strop Jacob	
Harvey Francis	*Lexington.*
Lowry George	
Reilly Vincent B.	*West Windsor.*
Bailey George	*Belleville.*
Fugard J. F.	
Moffett T. G. & Son	*Lucas.*

Ross County.

Leslie & Irwin	*Frankfort.*
Wissler & King	*Chillicothe.*
Bonzer J.	
Reynolds E. D.	*Hallsville.*
Ranck John	
Miller David A.	*Bourneville.*
Browning Joseph	
Walker Sam'l.	
Rinehart James	*Kingston.*
Kauck Jacob	
Hunt Wm.	

Sandusky County.

Moulten F.	*Woodville.*
Wales J. C.	*Exeter.*
Rafford F. H.	*Fremont.*
Keiffer B.	
Oacks John	
Moore Sam'l.	

Scioto County.

Burket J. & Co.	*Portsmouth.*
Murry, Ward & Stephenson	

Seneca County.

Childs J. A.	*Attica.*
Rehring & Whitman	
Hakes N.	*Adrian.*
Shear John	
Weber J.	
Van Nest Peter	*Tiffin.*
Gardner Joseph	
Flaugher Jacob B.	
Kelly W. W.	*Reedtown.*
Kelly Anson	
Olds M. T.	*Republic.*
Collins Osborn	

Shelby County.

Fink & Birnel	*Sydney.*

Starke County.

Oddo E.	*Louisville.*
Serheney F.	
Crip & Taylor	*Minerva.*
Montgomery Josiah	
Hamilton R. B.	*Waynesburg.*
Pool Samuel	
Richards Samuel	
Ream E.	*Canton.*
Lattimer R.	
Estep Isaiah	*Paris.*
Miller Joseph	
Lynde Frederick	*Marlboro'.*
Mendenball Stephen	
Miller David	

Coates Hays	*New Baltimore.*
Archer George	*Massillon.*
Bohannen William	
Clay William P.	
Potter J. B.	*Canal Fulton.*
Houk A.	

Summit County.

Avery Amos	*Middlebury.*
Collins O. A.	
Steel J. W.	
Radcliffe J.	*Cuyahoga Falls.*
Rumrill Geo.	
Moore & Doxser	*Western Star.*
Noe E. N.	
Hurn Daniel	*Hudson.*
Markellin John	
Blakelee J.	*Tallmadge.*
Oviatt & Sperry	
Lancaster Joseph	*Nimisilla.*
Shook John	
Carr Calvin	*Richfield.*
Cowles Oliver	

Trumbull County.

Lindsley Benjamin	*Johnsonville.*
Tyler George	
Eldred Judah	*Southington.*
Ormbury Johnston	
Beleton H. C.	*Warren.*
McNeal R.	
Wisell Eli K.	
Craton, Bushnell & Co.	*Hartford.*
Murray H. W.	
Tracey Aznel & Co	
Miller Lent L.	*Girard.*
Wilson William	
Goist Samuel	*Church Hill.*
Bell James H	
Denison John	
Fox Henry	*Brookfield.*
Fox John	
Stewart James	
Erwin David	*Ohltown.*
Campbell John	
Kenedy Samuel J.	
Russell Abraham	
Moore James	

Tuscarawas County.

Lackey William	*New Cumberland.*
Stoody Daniel	
White Joseph	*Gnadenhutten.*
Bartells J. & Co.	*New Philadelphia.*
Rogers & Co.	
Brunk Michael	*Canal Dover.*
Myers Emanuel	
Sponsler David	
Yantes A.	

Union County.

Loe Rolen	*Marysville.*
Plum David	
Colver Standish	*Milford Centre.*
Dealing Charles	
Sheiderer George	
Whitmore Jared	

Van Wert County.

Strothers A. R.	*Van Wert.*

Warren County.

Langsdon Wm.	*Springboro'.*
Hopkins T. J.	
Butler Wm. E.	
Morten J.	
Conover P.	*Franklin.*
Parker T.	
Stanton J.	
Scott James	*Twenty Mile Stand.*
Presly M.	*Red Lion.*
Olinger Sam'l.	
Dawson C.	*Mason.*
Stout S.	
Waltch Peter	
Sides S.	
Jarvis R.	*Hayesville.*
Letcher J.	
McClellan R. & W.	
Day M. L.	*Deerfield.*
Frazer J. A.	*Dunlevy.*
Fairholm J. V.	*Waynesville.*
Losey W. P.	*Morrow.*
Chamberlin Lewis	*Lebanon.*
March & Brothers	
St. John Hiram	*Butlerville.*
Walters Geo.	
Hormel James H.	*Harveysburg.*
Varner E. F.	
Lippencott J. H.	

Washington County.

Parker L. M.	*Marietta.*
Bartlett John	*Harmar.*

Wayne County.

Fenton S.	*Dalton.*
Scott Levi	
Baughman S.	
Drabenstall J.	*Smithville.*
Sonders B.	
Stainer W.	
Sheller D.	
Lightfoot Sam'l.	*East Union.*
Hanna W. W.	*Wooster.*
Wilhelm John	

Williams County.

Crocker V.	*Bryan.*
Jones John B.	
Saddoris John	
Welden O. T.	
Grim Joseph	*Pulaski.*
Gutheree D. D.	
Miller John M.	*West Unity.*
Platt Thos.	*Montpelier.*

Wyandot County.

Finch & Berringer	*Upper Sandusky.*
Hunter Sam'l.	
Myers Wm.	*Carey.*
Parkers Wm.	*Crawfordsville.*
Houst Thos. Henry	*McCutchensville.*
Kiens Michael	*Mexico.*

Carriage Trimmers.

Clermont County.
White & Barnhard   *Bantam.*

Columbiana County.
Clark Charles   *New Lisbon.*
McGraff —

Franklin County.
Bergstresser Daniel   *Canal Winchester.*

Geauga County.
Knowles C.
Wilber W.   *Chardon.*
Hays O.   *Auburn.*
Fowler & Carlton   *Burton.*
White A. W.   *Parkman.*

Greene County.
Carey H. & W. T.   *Xenia.*

Hamilton County.
Alward Henry   *Harrison.*
McClain John F.

Harrison County.
McKennon Wm.   *Cadis.*

Morrow County.
Hughes Edward   *Chesterville.*

Pickaway County.
Lybrand G. W. H.   *Tarlton.*

Portage County.
Mason Henry   *Atwater.*
Curtis James   *Ravenna.*
Merwin Wm.   *Aurora.*
Brainard J. C.   *Randolph.*
Norton S. D.   *Shalersville.*
Boyd Wm.   *Nelson.*

Lake County.
Leckman S. O.   *Painesville.*

Medina County.
Rettig J. H.   *Medina.*
Chidester Wm. B.
Parker S. S.

Wyandot County.
Beals Sylvanus   *Upper Sandusky.*

Carvers & Designers. (Wood.)

Hamilton County.
Anderson A. W., No. 128 w. Col.   *Cincin.*
Fry H. & W., 144 w. Third
Morrison Thos. G., 217 w. Fifth

Montgomery County.
Croome G. L., Ohio Block   *Dayton.*
Lambert Joseph, Third

Chair (Railroad) Manu-
facturers

Franklin County.
Hayden P., Broad   *Columbus.*

Hamilton County
Clark W. H. & Co., 128 Vine   *Cincinnati.*
Granger, Draper & Co., Walnut above 3d
Winslow A. S., 9 & 11 w. 2d

Chair Manufacturers.

Ashland County.
Crose Benjamin   *Ashland.*

Ashtabula County.
Stone T. H.   *Jefferson.*
Bordwell W. A.   *Lindenville.*
Putney Loren   *Conneaut.*
Allen Richard

Athens County.
Socie M. D.   *Nelsonville.*

Belmont County.
Robe D. F.   *Demos.*
Crawford Samuel   *St. Clairsville.*
Sambert & Wright

Brown County.
Flick Wm. R.   *Hamersville.*
Denney D.   *Fincastle.*
Moore C. B.   *Sardinia.*

Butler County.
Osborn H.   *Oxford.*
Gath S.
Clough J. P.

Carroll County.
Shisler John   *New Hagerstown.*

Champaign County.
Morse Geo.   *North Lewisburg.*

Clark County.
Phelps J.   *Springfield.*

Clermont County.
Brawner John   *West Union.*
Bunton John R.   *Williamsville.*
Edwards Sylvester
Glasgow John W.
Hunt John
Kelly Henry C.
Taylor Adam
Thompson A. J.
Thompson S. C.
Witham L. D.
Witham Jefferson C.
Wilmington Levi
Gorden David   *Mulberry.*
Robb Peter   *Milford.*
Gardner W. W.   *Nicholsville.*
Smith J. W.   *Pleasant Grove.*
Hoover Stephen   *New Richmond.*
Davis M. H.
Tompkins James   *Laurel.*
Corbin J. S.
Dudley O. & Son   *Williamsburg.*
Stockton V.
Boulware A. V.
Van Briggle S. & Co.   *Felicity.*

Pattison John — *Felicity.*
Fagan David
Joslin Peter
Kelly Henry C. — *Withamsville.*
Jones & Wilmington
Leeds J. E. — *Mt. Carmel.*
McMahan N.
Stagg & Kelly

Clinton County.

Griffith Wm. B. — *Wilmington.*
Frazier Saml. W.
Sewell Wm.

Columbiana County.

Shields James H. — *New Lisbon.*
Eakins John — *Calcutta.*
Nelson Amos — *New Garden.*
Rogers Samuel
Blythe Thomas — *East Liverpool.*
Beard John — *Columbiana.*
Brubecker Samuel
Boies D. — *Unity.*
Eakin John — *Cennon's Mills.*

Coshocton County.

Dewey J. & G. — *Coshocton.*

Crawford County.

Tippin Michael — *Sulphur Springs.*
Brown S. G. — *Bucyrus.*
Fulton A.
Yost A.

Cuyahoga County.

Pratt, French & Co. — *Newburgh.*
Hitt W. J. — *Gates' Mills.*
Goodell Peter — *Brecksville.*
Wheelock, Church & Co. — *Bedford.*
Monroe Edmond — *Collamer.*
Hart, William & Co., 39½ Bank — *Cleve-[land.*
Bauder L., opp. Court House
Combs, Longstreet & Co. — *Ohio City.*

Darke County.

Odell J. — *Ithica.*
Walker R.
Walker J.
Shaver H.
Ryhn H. M. — *New Madison.*
Achey J. C. — *German.*

Fairfield County.

Lawyer Jackson — *Pickerington.*

Fayette County.

Tracy Solomon — *Moons.*

Franklin County.

Fitzwater Joseph — *Columbus.*
Benadum Joseph — *Canal Winchester.*
Markley George

Gallia County.

Harrison John — *Rodney.*
Shepard John B. — *Gallipolis.*

Geauga County.

Atkins Wm. — *Thompson.*
Fuller Ira
Ston & Gridley — *Montville.*
Spencer R. — *Claridon.*

Guernsey County.

Johnson David — *Antrim.*
Reed John — *Cambridge.*
Stanley A. W.
Salmon R. D.
Hatton J. H. — *Senecaville.*

Hamilton County.

Closterman Henry, s. w. cor. Smith & Augusta — *Cincinnati.*
Crane Lemuel M., 81 Sycamore
Geyer John, 8 e. Fourth
Johnston C. D., 51 & 53 Vine
Johnston & Mitchell, 2d bet. J'n & Smith
Lefontain S., 322 Elm
Mullen Jonathan, 132 Sycamore
Smith & Hawley, 64 — do
White Barton, 126 — do
Bratzel George — *Harrison.*
Martin J. F. — *Newtown.*

Hardin County.

Bogardus & Rowe — *Kenton.*
Kennett & Markle

Harrison County.

McConnell Michael — *Cadiz.*

Highland County.

Elder A. G. — *Greenfield.*
Roads Jacob
Allmore T.
McClure S. — *Centrefield.*

Hocking County.

Cupp Charles — *Gibisonville.*
Cupp Jacob

Holmes County.

Gerrick C. — *Winesburg.*

Huron County.

Childs Chas. — *Steuben.*
Ruggles & Burr — *North Fairfield.*
Truxell Addison

Knox County.

Jacobs Joseph — *Mt. Vernon.*
McDowel Daniel
McFarlan Daniel
Breese Edson — *Fredericktown.*
Hart Jacob — *Democracy.*
Koch Daniel — *North Liberty.*
Loos William
Johnson Ephraim — *Millwood.*
Youngblood William — *Mt. Liberty.*

Licking County.

Duke L. H. — *Johnstown.*

Logan County.

Dickey J. — *East Liberty.*

McAden T. F.   East Liberty.
Nevan John   Bellefontaine.
Easton William   Zanesfield.
Mulhem E. R.

Lorain County.

Butler L. W.   Oberlin.
Bowen Obadiah   North Camden.

Mahoning County.

Edwards P.   Canfield.

Marion County.

Saiter S.   Marion.

Medina County.

Tubbs L.   Liverpool.
Barrett James   Lodi.
Miller Moses   Weymouth.
Hickcox Henry
Davis A.   Medina.
Ainsworth I. T.

Miami County.

James Benj.   Troy.

Monroe County.

Shotwell Thomas   Woodsfield.
Bowman Joshua   Antioch.
Steele Stephen   Plymouth.

Montgomery County.

Conklin & Stork, First   Dayton.
Hatfield G. A.   do
Stonebarger A. & J. do
Cotterman Elias   Miamisburgh.
Tickle Walter

Morgan County.

Patterson M.   Chester Hill.
Maris J.
Cornelius James   Malta.
Berry R. W.
Blain Wm.   McConnelsville.
Burgess Clarkson   Pennsville.

Muskingum County.

Smith Wm. & Co.   Dresden.
Marpool Enoch   White Cottage.
Thorp George
Lawyer John   Gratiot.
Lawyer Wm.
McCutchen J. B.   Chandlersville.
Mohler & Smith   Zanesville.

Noble County.

Morrison Kelita   Sarahsville.
Wilson J. B.   Olive.

Pickaway County.

Puncher M.   Circleville.
Davisson, Gossim & Co.   Tarlton.

Perry County.

Lane D. C.   New Lexington.
Fairman Amos   Rehoboth.
Huston James & Co.   Somerset.

Portage County.

Lane Edward   Nelson.
McElwaine & Turnham   Ravenna.

Preble County.

Johnson I. L.   Eaton.
Harshman John
Sterling A.   Hamburg.
Richey & Son   New Paris.
Putman & Hinman

Putnam County.

Shenard William   Gilboa.
Keen E. H.   Pendleton.

Richland County.

Wickersham Wm.   Shelby.
Palmer A. R.   Mansfield.
McCain John   Lexington.
Bailey Hiram   Belleville.
Bixby Simon
Heckarel John
Marks Jacob   Lucas.

Ross County.

Bowdish J. H..   Chillicothe.

Sandusky County

Roush Michael   Greensburg Cross Roads.

Seneca County.

Chamberlin H.   Republic.
Kessler G. E.
Campbell & Blakeney   Tiffin.
Fiege John
Lemp Henry
Myers John

Starke County.

Kurtz Charles R.   Minerva.
Pitney O. J.
Wertenberger Daniel.   New Franklin.
Haas George R.   Canton.
Ware J. H.   Limaville.

Summit County.

Wilcox C. C.   Middlebury.
Nice Jonas   Western Star.
Stripe Wm.   Inland.
Porter Joseph   Bath.

Trumbull County.

Coe Dwight   Hartford.
Davis T. C.
Hall Elijah
Hall E.   Orangeville.

Tuscarawas County.

Miksch Amos   Gnadenhutten.
Krebs Christian   Ragersville.
Ax P.   New Philadelphia.
Demuth J.
Matlock M.
McElroy J.

Union County.

Courteney Jacob   Marysville.

Van Wert County.

Swineford Simeon — *Van Wert.*
Young Alpheus

Vinton County.

Drake Wm. R. — *McArthur.*
Finney Alvin — *New Plymouth.*

Warren County.

Scofield J. C. — *Mason.*
Scofield Wm.
Scofield James
Githins Geo. — *Waynesville.*

Washington County.

Sprague E. W. — *Lowell.*

Williams County.

Connin Alex. — *Bryan.*
Perkins F.
Young Chas.
Yates Wm. B.
McDowell James — *Centre.*
Ritchie D.
Sissen R. — *Montpelier.*
Hunter H.
Stokes George — *West Unity.*

Wood County.

Brown Abner — *Perrysburg.*
Crook Wm.
Brassey K.
Teeller E. — *Weston.*

Charcoal (Refined) Manufacturers.

Hamilton County.

Coats Paxson, W. Row bet. Front & Col. *Cincinnati.*
Loder A. W., 271 Main

Cheese Dealers.

Geauga County.

Randall, Cook & Co. — *Chardon.*
Wilkins, Young & Co.
Wilbz Wm.
Lukin J. P. — *Claridon.*
Field C. C. & C. S.
Farmers' Co.
Union Co.
Kyle, Wilkins & Co. — *Huntsburgh.*
Foote —— — *Middlefield.*
Thompson P. T. & E.
Bishop H. L.
Parkman E. B. — *Parkman.*
Tilden J. S. & A. P.
Converse & Wilmot — *Auburn.*
Mayhew John
Stevenson & Russell — *Chester.*
Farmers' Co. — *Munson.*
Tolls W. R. & H. S. — *Burton.*

Portage County.

Prentiss O. — *Ravenna.*
Gillett S. A. & E. A.

Stedman & Loomis — *Randolph.*
Harmon C. & C. R. — *Aurora.*
Granger Sam'l.
Farmers' Co.
Pease & Son — *Streetsboro'.*
Jenkins & Peck
Bostwick D. — *Edinburgh.*
Foster J. W. — *Mantua.*
Bradley T. C. & H. G.

Cheese Box Manufacturers.

Ashtabula County,

Ryder N. — *Austinsburg.*
Miller J. O. — *Rome.*
Miller E. B.
Palmer Dan'l. — *Lindenville.*
Bell Wm.

Cuyahoga County.

Hilt W. J. — *Gates' Mills.*
Bull & Tucker — *Solon.*
Chamberlain L. & Sons
Reaves Horace E.

Trumbull County.

Wolcott J. H. & L. B. — *Farmington.*
Dana O.
Reynolds S.

Cheese Paper Manufacturers.

Trumbull County.

Roberts S. — *Warren.*

Chemist, Analytical and Consulting.

Hamilton County.

Locke Joseph M., 14 O. M. Col. *Cincinnati.*

Chemical Laboratories.

Hamilton County.

Baum J. C., 53 Dunlap — *Cincinnati.*
Graselli Eugene, Frt. e. of Water Works.
Harwood & Marsh, Ham. R. w. of Dunlap.
Hill Francis D., 99 Walnut
Mirrieless Brothers, cor. Eighth and Deer creek Road
Snedewend & Bunce, Miami Canal above Liberty

Chimney Top Manufacturers.

Hamilton County.

Fairclough F., cor. Richmond and Linn *Cincinnati.*
Martin T., Catherine, bet. Linn and Rittenhouse
Merrell & Leonard, Race bet. 15th and Liberty

China, Glass, and Queensware, Wholesale & Retail Dealers.

Clark County.

Fisher M. W. — *Springfield.*

Cuyahoga County.

Brooks O. A. & Co., 109 Superior *Cleveland.*
Fogg J. & W. P., 105   do
Gardner A. S., 134   do
Huntington & Brooks, 30 Water
Lewis C. & Co.   *Ohio City.*
Tyler & Whitney

Erie County.

Kilbourn L. H.   *Sandusky City.*

Franklin County.

Foster N. & G., High   *Columbus.*
Westwater J. M. & W. do

Greene County.

Jones M. Luther   *Xenia.*
Hivling & Williamson

Hamilton County.

Aldrich Otis, No. 181 Main   *Cincinnati.*
Bare & West, 22 Pearl
Beste H. A., cor. Main and Franklin
Bloomsten L., 198 w. Fifth
Orents J., 192 w. Sixth
Orail M., 254 w. Fifth
Dickson & Lebetter, 217 Main
Franklin Benjamin, 195 Elm
Huggins, Brother & Anderson, 91 Main
Hunnewell, Hill & Co., 87   do
Huntington John C. & Co., 21 e. Fourth
Hackman John F., 214 w. Fifth
Harker G., 236 w. Sixth
Huntington & Brooks, 47 Pearl
Ihle Michael, 522 Main
Kistner Edward, 341 do
Krainig Frank, 78 Court
Lilley William, 92 w. Fifth
Monkhoff Christian F., 321 Main
Morton Thomas, 102 w. Sixth
Nixon Joseph, 60 Lower Market
Rintz S., 248 w. Sixth
Sampson & Co., No. 92 Main
Stackhouse George, 44 w. Fifth
Whitehead & Co., 34 Main
Wiest G. F., Canal Market
Wiser Isaac, 116 w. Fifth

Jefferson County.

Beatty & Steelman   *Steubenville.*
Dorhman P. & Co

Knox County.

Arnold G. B.   *Mount Vernon.*

Lucas County.

Stebbins H. & A. T.   *Toledo.*

Mercer County.

Bruner O.   *St. Mary's.*
Johnson W. N. & J.
McLaughlin G. W.

Montgomery County.

Jewel George, Second   *Dayton.*
Perine J.   do
Wolf & Barlow   do

Ross County.

McKell Wm.   *Chillicothe.*

Scioto County.

Purcell James   *Portsmouth.*
Towell J. F. & Co.
Elden Wm. & Co.

Churn Manufacturers.

Columbiana County.

Starr James   *New Lisbon.*

Geauga County.

Seeland H.   *Munson.*

Richland County.

Howard Otis   *Belleville.*

Warren County.

Holaway & Morgan   *Franklin.*

Cigars—(Importers of).

Hamilton County.

Adae C. F. & Labrot, 16 w. Front,   *Cin.*
Barber D. S., 10 Broadway
Besuden Henry, 93 Walnut
Davis N. H. & G. H., 13 Sycamore
Fatman A. & Co., 12 Main
Feltman Henry & Co., 30 Front
Feust F. W., Apollo Buildings
Hill Samuel V., 5 Main
Jacob J., 25 Congress
Johnson G., 148 Vine
Little R. A. & Co., 50 Main
Lewis & Depuy, 22 Broadway
Muhl George, 60 6th
Neilson & Churchill, 23 Main
Neuman E. & Co , 128 Sycamore
Nuelsen Francis, 233 Main
Pieper John H. & Co., 322 do
Racine & Constant, 86 & 88 e. Columbia
Richard F. R., 14 e. Court
Tewes Charles F., Burnet House
Vetterlein B. & Co., n. w. cor. Columbia &
                      . [Broadway

Cigars—(Dealers in).

Hamilton County.

Adae & Labrot, 16 w. Front,   *Cincin.*
Becker C. F., 77 w. 3d
Outair J. & Batchelder, 237 Main
Cooper William, 72 Front
Dorr & Arnold, 6 w. 6th
Davis A. H. & G., 13 Sycamore
Dill B. M. & Co., 3d bet. Walnut & Main
Dieckman & Co., Hughes near Liberty
Fatman A. & Co , 12 Main
Feltman Henry & Co., 30 Front
Feust C. H , 583 Main
Feust F. W., Apollo Building
Fuldner P. H., 88 Clinton
Gellenbeck G., 503 Main
Gruhler & Co., 226 Western Row
Groene J. H. F., s. e. cor. Race & Cclum.

Hill Samuel V., 5 Main   *Cincinnati.*
Hirsch & Strauss, 209 Walnut
Jeenier Peter, 98 Court
King & Daley, 33 Sycamore
Leuchtenburg J. F., 626 Western Row
Lamb H., W. Row bet. Liberty & Everett
Landwher F., 110 Liberty
Metz B. & E., 340 Main
Meyen Antony, 348 do
Martin H., 12 Front
Mills J. F., s. w. cor. Main & 6th
Mosler G., 177 w. 5th
Muhl George, 60 6th
Malonee E., 177 Front
Menzel J., 449 Walnut
Marthens & Ordman, 293 Main
Nulsen & Mersmann, 17   do
Nuelsen Francis, 233   do
Neilson & Churchill, 23   do
Neumann E. & C., 128 Sycamore
Orlopp M. A., 42 4th
Pieper John H. & C., 322 Main
Richard F. R., 14 e. Court
Sherrick M., 225 Western Row
Steinocker H. E., 8th bet. Freeman & Bay-
           |miller
Shrader H. F. & Co., 249 Western Row
Tewes Charles F., Burnet House
Von Der Heide H., 12 Sycamore
Wedekind Julius, 6th bet. Plum & W. Row
Weishampt J., 148 Front
Winklar J., 381 Vine
Wolff S., 38 Broadway Hotel
Williams Simeon B., 88, 90 & 92 Pearl
Wesjohan H., 100 e. Columbia

Cigars—(Manufacturers of).

Belmont County.

Alban —   *St. Clairsville.*
Trimble T.   *Morristown.*

Brown County.

Allen John   *Ripley.*

Butler County.

Lander D. B.   *Hamilton.*
Wikel Saml.   *Middletown.*
Doney W.   *Seven Mile.*

Clark County.

Koutz F.   *Springfield.*
Steele & Morrow

Clermont County.

Kain W. L.   *Williamsburg.*
West Thos. O.
Talman James   *Bethel.*

Columbiana County.

Albert E. P.   *Wellsville.*

Crawford County.

Slaybaugh George   *Bucyrus.*

Cuyahoga County.

Harrison Justus   *Coe Ridge.*

Deitz George, 9 Water street,   *Cleveland.*
Richardson Mark, 10 Miller's block
Schriber James, Canal
Walter Alexander W., 33 Superior
Keppler Frederick A., 20   do
Downing W. W., 19 Seneca

Defiance County.

Buhnemann John   *Defiance.*

Erie County.

Starck F. T.   *Sandusky.*
Fromman S.
Wehrly A.

Franklin County.

Klie Charles, State street   *Columbus.*
Mayer M., Friend
Neagle John, High
Maltin & Wilth, do
Wotring Charles, do
Baldwin L.,   do

Geauga County.

Knowles C. S.   *Chardon.*
Cowles W. W.
Pool P.
Bassett J. A.
Warren G.

Hamilton County.

Baker C., 320 Plum   *Cincinnati.*
Dieckmann H., Hughes near Liberty
Dorr & Arnold, 6 w. 6th
Feller Charles, 14 Front
Garland William, 14 Walnut
Herman H., 420 Vine
Lade J., Ham. Road bet. Main & Piatt
Mosler G., 177 w. 5th
Mauer Toney, 535 e. Front
Mosler H., 100 w. 6th
Miller Charles, 588 Elm
Neilson & Churchill, 23 Main
Nuelsen Francis, 233   do
Nulsen & Mersmann 17   do
Norton & Myre, 226 w. 5th
Otten F., 504 Vine
Pipher J. & G., 10 Lower Market
Pauck Henry W., cor. W. Row & Everett
Petarrman J., 68 Findley
Roschenkemper H., 323 w. 5th
Renaw W., 645 Vine
Rhienbergen A., 509 Vine
Stark E., 247 w. 6th
Schafstall C. F., 78 do
Stuntebeck H. H., 295 Elm
Seive H., 625 Main
Weis L. & Co., 233 Walnut
Wedekind Julius, 6th bet Plum & W. Row

Harrison County.

Bancroft George   *Cadiz.*

Holmes County.

Wortz G. M.   *Winesburg.*
Gangnagle N. F.
Buyson A.
Achenberger N.

Jefferson County.

Fiechtner John   *Steubenville.*
Evans John
Sharp Saml.
Bair Wm.
Lorenzo C. A.

Knox County.

Kindrick R.   *Mt. Vernon.*

Licking County.

Switezer Isaac   *Linnville.*
Klots S. R.   *Brownsville.*
Baldwin & Vaness   *Newark.*

Lucas County.

Brooks S.   *Toledo.*
Engefer A.
Hide Henry
Quinche C. S.

Medina County.

Smith John   *Wadsworth.*

Miami County.

Williams J.   *Troy.*

Montgomery County.

Strader S. P.   *Alexandersville.*
Lehman D.
Springer P., 3d   *Dayton.*
Bach Frederick   *Miamisburgh.*
Riechard Peter
Schew Jacob

Pickaway County.

Doughterly & Parker   *Circleville.*
Juppenlaz J. G.

Portage County.

Simonson A. & Co.   *Streetsboro'.*

Preble County.

Harbaugh Theodore   *Eaton.*
King John O.
Lockwood Saml.

Richland County.

Barbour J. S.   *Mansfield.*

Ross County.

McCormick & Simmons   *Chillicothe.*
McCormick C. C.

Scioto County.

Ranshehouse Wm. F.   *Portsmouth.*
Doehr J. & F.

Starke County.

McGrevey John   *Louisville.*
Moyer Conrad
Pecher John
Martin & Klett   *New Franklin.*

Warren County.

Mason Frederick   *Edwardsville.*
Cox John   *Hayesville.*

City Post.

Hamilton County.

Browne John W. S., 2 Mechanic's Insti-
    tute   *Cincinnati.*

Clocks—Manufacturers of.

Franklin County.

Brannan G., 3d   *Columbus.*

Hamilton County.

Blakeslee E , 220 Main   *Cincinnati.*
Keller Stephen, Court bet. Main & Walnut
Smith T., 12 e. 5th
Trotter J., 241 w. 5th

Clocks (Town & Church) Manufacturer of.

Hamilton County.

Verdin M., 396 Vine   *Cincinnati.*

Clocks—Dealers in.

Coshocton County.

Osborn T.   *Keene.*

Geauga County.

Cook, Randall & Co.   *Chardon.*

Hardin County.

Chapman H.   *Kenton.*

Harrison County.

Lofland John   *Cadiz.*

Holmes County.

Shrock & Cook   *Millersburg.*

Licking County.

Sprague H. S.   *Newark.*

Muskingum County.

Arnold Henry   *Gratiot.*

Pike County.

Pearce Joseph   *Cynthiana.*
Reed & McCord

Portage County.

Button Wm.   *Franklin.*

Preble County.

Chambers Jacob.   *Eaton.*

Seneca County.

Cram Moses   *Republic.*

Cloth Dressers.

Allen County.

Flack Lewis W.   *Croghan.*

Crawford County.

Clapper S.   *Bucyrus.*
Lantzinheiser H.

Defiance County.

Barnum S. B.   *Defiance.*
Stevens & Crosier

Noble G. O.   *Panama.*

Morrow County.

Dillingham Samuel   *Lincoln.*

Richland County.

Wiggins N. S.   *Shelby.*

Trumbull County.

Soule H. C.   *Newton Falls.*

Cloths Cassimeres & Vestings, Wholesale Dealers in.

Cuyahoga County.

Denker P. J. & Son, 5 Water   *Cleveland.*
Isaacs & Loeb, 42 Bank

Hamilton County.

Duhme H. H., 74 5th   *Cincinnati.*
Goodheart & Ackerland, 66 Pearl
Heidelbach, Weitheimer & Klaw, 56 do
Marks Henry & Co., 12 do
Rickel William, 334 Main

Clothiers & Ready-made Clothing.

Adams County.

Lafferty J. W.   *West Union.*

Allen County.

Curtis & Howard   *Lima.*
Evans E.

Ashland County.

Burgan L.   *Ashland.*
Bushnell Tully C.
Risser P. & J.
Lontzy Jacob   *Loudonville.*

Ashtabula County.

Willard & Wells & Co.   *Ashtabula.*
Mansfield John

Athens County.

Zener David   *Athens.*
Blackstone W. K.

Belmont County.

Sligman Philip   *Barnesville.*
Frint John L.   *St. Clairsville.*
Thomas Benjamin

Brown County.

Stroube & Ellis   *Higginsport.*
Osborn W. S.   *Ripley.*
Fenton B.
Friedman & Ranshein
Reed C. W.   *Georgetown.*
Jones S. M.
Blair Wm. & Co.   *Newhope.*

Butler County.

Miller Jacob   *Hamilton.*
Brown & Myers
Schober J.
Bruck J. P.

Falconer J. H.   *Rossville.*
Becker & Henn
Leibee Jacob   *Middletown.*
Oglesby & Barnitz
Golden S. & Co.
Wickoff Jas.
Conklin W. D.
Harris & Wolverton

Champaign County.

Carlton J. L.   *Mechanicsburg.*
Stadler & Brothers   *Urbana.*
Talbott J. G. & Co.

Clark County.

Baker Miller   *Enon.*
Hill & Murray   *Springfield.*
Mann Isaac
Wolfson Israel
Wolf Isaac
Kaufman M.
Phillips & So
Norton & Shepherd
Conway S. & Son   *Catawba.*
Harr Abraham   *New Carlisle.*
Morehead T. T.
Tilton —,

Clermont County.

Donham Isaac   *New Richmond.*
Layfield & Co.
Perine H. R.   *Williamsburg.*
Moore N.
Lonegar Wm.   *Milford.*
Williams Otho
Hitch & Hammond   *Clover*

Clinton County.

Probasco Wm. H.   *Wilmington.*
Leming E. T.
Vogle —,

Columbiana County.

Evans & Co.   *Wellsville.*
Frohman M. & Co.
Fugate William   *North Georgetown.*
Hepburn John   *New Garden.*
Thornburg Clayton
Hissey Allen   *Columbiana.*
Lamb & Donges

Crawford County.

Bowman J. P.   *Bucyrus.*
Converse H.
Tailor A.
Heavenrich S.
Rothchild Joseph
Seal & Hoffer

Cuyahoga County.

Borges J. F., cor. Superior & River   *Cleveland.*

Carpenter J. S. & Co., 13 do
Cohen E., 2 Clothiers' Block
Cauffman D., 30 Merwin
Davis George A., cor. Superior & Water
Denker J. P. & Son, 5 & 7 Water
Detmer G. H. & Co., 86 & 88 River

Dickson & Montgomery,78 Sup'r. *Cleveland.*
Dugan James, 4 Union
Englehart Joel, 1 Clothiers' Block
Elfiein J. G. F., 35 Superior
Hexter & Brother, 15 do
Heiman Louis, 24 Bank
Hagerling H., 10 Superior
Isaacs & Loeb, 42 Bank
Isaacs A. & G., 3 Clothiers' Block
Kenny William, 8 Union
Koch C., 76 Superior
Kramer H. & Co., 38 do & 7 Merwin
Kramer J. G., 11 Merwin
Kuenholt J. & Co., 13 Water
Loeb A. & C., Superior
Loeb Samuel, 1 Oviatt's Block
Morse T. W. & Co., 7 & 8 Superior, 3 Ex.
  Buildings
Riiglander & Bloch, 23 Superior Lane
Roemer H. & H., 6 Union
Robinson C. H., 88 Superior
Starkweather E. B. & Co., 5 do
Schwab A., 5 Union
Schwab Moses, 14 Superior
Schloss M., Merwin
Suhr William, 92 River
Wageman & Bergman, 12 Superior
Zeimer Valentine, 2 Union
Althen M., 41 Superior
Janes Jason   *Brecksville.*
Whitaker L. P. T.   *Bedford.*

Darke County.

Oppenhcmer Joseph   *Greenville.*
Wolenstine & Co.

Defiance County.

Falk L.   *Defiance.*
Weismantle ——
Zellers A.

Delaware County.

Glasser M. & J.   *Delaware.*
Lower E.
Jones & Dunlap Wm. & A.
Storrer John   *Waldo.*

Erie County.

Smith & Lapp   *Huron.*
Cohen, Godderman & Co.   *Sandusky City.*
Bowman L.
Billstein A.
Wheeden J.
Cohen A.
Huichammer G. H.
Krondel Joseph
Heckster M.
Latham W. V.
Hart George

Fairfield County.

Springer & Trout   *Lancaster.*
Smith G. H.
Coulhan ——
Hite J.
Frank J.

Fayette County.

Levingstine & Holburg   *Washington.*
Wiles L. & Co.
Stitt & McLaughlin   *Bloomingburg*

Franklin County.

Amburg & Co., High   *Columbus.*
Anson & Bro.,   do
Aranson & Bro.,   do
Burkley V.,   do
Breitonstoll H., 104 do
Burkley & Lunz, corner High and Rich
Coit H. & D. S., High
Hess & Brother,   do
Kacel & Shumacher, do
Mack & Co.,   do
Nusbaum Samuel,   do
Nusbaum J.,   do
Wetmore W. P.,   do
Bernheimer & Brother, 72, 73, High
Goodman J. & Co.,   do
Gundersheimer A. & Co.,   do
Gundersheimer J. & Co.,   do
Dierling Jacob   *Canal Winchester.*

Gallia County

Parker & Sons   *Cheshire.*
Cohn & Frank   *Gallipolis.*
Frank M & H.
Morrison John
Smith J. B.
Veysier B.
Frank H.

Greene County.

Mitchell J. E.   *Cedarville.*
More John   *Xenia.*
Straus Solomon

Guernsey County.

Watson & Seilix   *Cumberland.*
Mayor & Brother   *Washington.*
Stein Lewis   *Cambridge.*

Hamilton County.

Aub, Block & Frenkle. 54 Main *Cincinn'ti.*
Amburg & Strachel, 209   do
Amburgh & Co., cor. Sycamore and Front
Buerkle & Weizenecker, n. w. cor. Main
  and Eighth
Brown L. M., 98 Main
Bowman Mayers, 415 Main
Bamberger P., 333   do
Berman D., 7 Broadway
Bing N., 269 Main
Bing M., 268 do
Bernheimer & Brothers, 184 Main
Cohen, Guiterman & Co., 391 do
Enneking B., 2 Cassilly's Row
Elsas Jacob, 18 Pearl
Enneking F., 355 Main
Fechheimer, Goldsmith & Co., 72 Main
Fisher, George & Co., 29 Lower Market
Fleischtheil ——, 6 Sycamore
Friedman & Miller, 42 do
Frank H., 29 Broadway
Grantman H., Levee bet. Main and Walnut
Goodhart & Fishel, 21 Lower Market

Goldburg & Lorwensten, 52 Pearl
Cincinnati.
Goodheart & Ackerland, 66   do
Goodman & Vornholy. 307 Main
Harris A., s. e. cor. Fifth and Main
Harmon, Mack & Co., 191 Main
Heft & Cohen, 359   do
Heinsheimer J. H. & Co., s. w. cor. Main
  and Seventh
Heidelbach, Seasongood & Co., s. e. cor.
  Main and Third.
Hollstein L., 14 Sycamore
Hirsch P. D., 40 Main
Harris A. & P., 86 do
Heidelbach, Wortheimer & Kaw, 56 Pearl
Harwig & Clocke, s. e. cor. Court and Main
Hattenbach G., cor. Main and Water
Hammann C., 72 Court
Havenrich S., 511 Vine
Himmelreigh S., 265 W. Row
Hattenber Solomon, 7 Cassilly's Row
Joseph Richard, C. & Co., s. e. cor. Pearl
  and Walnut
Katzenberger, Straus & Co., 106 Main
Kaufman S., 417   do
Kornblith J. & M., 148   do
Klemse & Busher, 367   do
Kleinsmand E. & Co., 15 Broadway
Klienshmidt F. E., 3 Cassilly's Row
Leopold & Goodheart, 159 Main
Labold H. & M., 36 Front
Lockwood Brothers, 73 Pearl
Liebstein Isaac, s. e. cor. L. Market and
  Sycamore
Limon G. & Co., 6 Main
Leinsbiemer B., 305 do
Luhen & Rikoff, 363 do
Lyens L., 27 Broadway
Luken J. B. & Trame, 5 Cassilly's Row.
Luning J. & H., 110 Columbia
Landower A., 471 Vine
Lohman C. H. & Co., 279 Main
Menderson Frohman, 104 Main
Monheimer J., 68   do
Marienthal & Block, 203   do
Mack & Brothers, 211   do
Milius & Brothers, 42 and 43 Front
Mayer & Cohn, n. e. cor. Front and Main
Meyer J. B., 9 Cassilly's Row
Max M., 317 W. Row
Maue F. & Co., 269 Main
Nebb George & Co., 70 Broadway
Newhouse G., 19   do
Price Jacob, 46 Main
Price L. & Co., 23 Broadway
Rosenberg A., 272 W. Row
Sprague T. W. & Co., 113 Main
Stadler & Brother, 231   do
Springer L. H., 49 Front
Stiens A. H., 46 Sycamore
Simon Joseph, (Agent), 37 Broadway
Schradeki M. & P., 397 Main
Stix & Kronsdroh, 347   do
Schlebbe John T., 343   do
Schroeder B. & Co., 311 Main
Suer J., 10 Cassilly's Row
Sutkamp J., 12 do   do

Stein Henry, 3 Front   *Cincinnati.*
Star E. 15   do
Trost Isaac & Brother, 45 Front
Troustine A. & J. & Co., 58 Pearl
Ulmer A., 467 Vine
Ulmer A., 54 Sycamore
Workum L. P., 94 Main
Wolf A. J. & Co., 76 do
Weiller Salimon, 167 do
Wolf A. J. & Co., 247 Main
Wertheimer J. P., 243   do
Wolf ——, 32 Front
Wald, Hacks & Bergman, 53 Pearl
Wertheimer J. H., 289 Main
Wise Leopold, 8½ Sycamore
Weaver George, 12 Walnut
Wolf & Hoet N. & J. M., 74 Broadway
Witt W. B., 249 W. Row
Emery Edward   *Dry Ridge.*

Hancock County.

Campbell Charles J.   *Finley.*
Ford Joseph D.
Ottinger Jonas

Hardin County.

Fry George   *Kenton.*
Miller & Wingate
Letson H.
Wolfson J.

Highland County.

Holburg F.   *Greenfield.*
Spiegel Abraham   *Hillsboro'.*
McCorkle T. A.

Hocking County.

Kaufman William   *Logan.*

Holmes County.

Cohn Benj.   *Millersburg.*
Hoxworth J.

Huron County.

Curtiss A. W.   *Wakeman.*
Little & Follett   *Bellevue.*
Nathans & Openheimer
Jenny & Peeters   *Norwalk.*
Hexter Levi
Henry W.

Jefferson County.

Shwabaker S.   *Steubenville*
Block Henry
Frohman E. & Co.
Gutermann F.
Dougherty & Brother

Knox County.

Jackson & Newell   *Mt. Vernon.*
Oppenheim S.
Rosenthal H.
Weaver J. H. & Co.
Wolff A.
Beach D. C. & Co.   *Fredericktown.*
Mosier & Griffith

Lake County.

McFarland & Pfouts   *Kirtland.*
Williams & Malby

Cullen John & Co.   *Painesville.*
Fisher N. M.
Morrell S. P. & Co.
Wolff L.

Lawrence County.
Wise H. & Bro.   *Ironton.*
Davison & Ferguson   *Hanging Rock.*

Licking County.
Miller Joseph   *Newark.*
Marganthau & Brother

Logan County.
Hays & Swan   *West Liberty.*
Lyon & Kizer
Mierfelt H.
Ordway & Low
Criswell & Gilmore   *Bellefontaine.*
Knapp O. S.
Scanlan P. & Bro.
Slicer W.

Lorain County.
Titus, Hanch &. Co.   *Grafton.*
Merwin & Mason   *Elyria.*
Thorp Hoyt O.   *Oberlin.*

Lucas County.
Eddy E. D.   *Toledo.*
Fink W. S.
Heinsheiner D. & Co.
Higgins M.
Kraus & Roemer
Kraus Jacob
Mack & Thomas
Mulhenny John
Orr James
Tirey Thomas
Vischer O.
Wood O. D.

Madison County.
Chamberlain V. S.   *London.*
Evans J. B.
Winchester A. & Son
Willson & Dunn   *Midway*
Bliss O. H. & Co.   *West Jefferson.*
Handcock E. S.
Parks James
Simpson A.   *Lafayette.*
Snyder John
Crabb B.   *West Jefferson.*

Mahoning County.
Kyle John G.   *Canfield.*
Edwards P.
Theobald David   *Youngstown.*
Cuse & Duncan   *Poland.*
Dietrick Peter   *Green Village.*
Swats George
Kitsel F.

Marion County.
Merrill J. & Co.   *Marion.*
Ullman J.
Harmon H.

Medina County.
Bergy John   *River Styx.*
Boyer W. F.   *Wadsworth.*
Palmer H. F.   *Lodi.*
Poe & Musser   *Medina.*
Coppas S. D.
Brown J.

Meigs County.
Piper G. L.   *Letart Falls.*

Mercer County.
Barrington & Bro.   *St. Mary's.*
Brucker & Vieter

Miami County.
Lebensberger & Lebolt   *Piqua.*
Zeigler N.
Fredlick & Brother
Frederick M.
Wertnemer J.   *Troy.*
Cromer J.

Monroe County.
Ferrier David   *Sunfish.*

Montgomery County.
Willis & Grauel   *Liberty.*
Beckman P., Third   *Dayton.*
Bess Casper, Second
Franklin & Kline, N. Market
Fries Valentine, Second
Herman H., Main
Kropp & Roth, Third
Lebensburger & Lebolt, Main
McDaniel J.,   do
Marks & Whitehammer, do
Schaefer S.   do
Scaffer J., Third
Walker Wm., Main
Ebel Jacob   *Miamisburg.*
Gephart A., Jr.
Hoover —,
Rice & Solomon

Morrow County.
Rosenthal H. & S.   *Cardington.*

Muskingum County.
Oppenheimer L. & H.   *Zanesville.*
Beitman S.
Vogel Michael & Co.
Rutter B.
Shiff A.
Mayer & Cohn
Moch Elias
English J. O.

Pickaway County.
Cogen D. & Co.   *Circleville.*
Hirsh & Levy
Levy Henry
May H.
Gephart G. O.
Weil Nathan
Weils L. & Co.

Perry County.

Delong A. J.   *Somerset.*
English L. C. & Co.

Portage County.

Fairchilds W.   *Edinburgh.*
Holden Wm. L. & O. O.   *Franklin.*
Wilson & Gray   *Deerfield.*
Day & Wahn
Beecher Henry   *Nelson.*
Sprague J.
Day Henry L.   *Ravenna.*
Alcorn J.
Holt P.
Dalrymple L.
Greenfielder Chas.
Seymour F. W.

Preble County.

Coffman Saml.   *Eaton.*

Richland County.

Sipe D.   *Shelby.*
Shatzer & Frazier
Liebenthal M.   *Mansfield.*
Miller M. L.
Rosenbaum M.
Greaber Samuel   *Newville.*
Billstun S.   *Plymouth.*
Burgoyne P. F.
Deveny John & Co.

Ross County.

Mackey & McBull   *Frankfort.*
Orabb J. H.
Light J. & Co.
Hoffman A.   *Chillicothe.*
Shrader J. F.
Rubel N. & Son
Henly Wm. B.
Huffman J. & Co.
Sulzbacher Henry
Ketner E.
Wolfe & Bereman
Davis M.
Frederick Saml.   *Kingston.*

Sandusky County.

Drybauch J.   *Fremont.*
Kridler Wm.
Durnham —

Scioto County.

Brandis & Deitsch   *Portsmouth.*
Seidenbach M.
Seidenbach L.
Starr E.
Hart M.   *Haverhill.*

Seneca County.

Faulhorer Philip   *Stoner.*
Watson J. S.
Pratt Hiram   *Melmore.*
Eaton Jared   *Adrian.*
Reeme W. R.   *Tiffin.*
Schwarzenberg M. H.
Schwarzenberg & Dryfoos

Hobbs William   *Tiffin.*
Baker B. F.   *Republic.*
Harkness & McKee

Shelby County.

Amann X.   *Sidney.*
Bracken & Wear
Meyers M. & Cc.
Smith & Shultz

Starke County.

Erb & Umstead   *Navarre.*
Wygandt E.
Boegel H. H.   *Waynesburg*
Brownwell J. G.
Rutter J. G.
Ream A. J.   *Paris.*
Straus & Funkenstine   *Massillon.*
Hookway F.
Dillenberry D.
Bender John
Bell John

Summit County.

Hayes M.   *Akron.*
Hoffman S. B.
Kenther S.
Koch & Levi
Latimer L. M. & Co.
Marshall S. S.
Sanford J. P. & Co.

Trumbull County.

Hofstater J.   *Newton Falls.*
Shell J.

Tuscarawas County.

Black Gilbert   *Bolivar.*
Farwell James C.   *Canal Dover.*
Kohl John A.
Montag Valentine

Van Wert County.

Campbell H. & Co.   *Van Wert.*
Todd W. & Bro.
Lehman G.   *Delphos.*
Moore P. B.

Vinton County.

Elrick J. W.   *McArthur.*

Warren County.

Hemphill & Teneicke   *Franklin.*
Sharf G.
Cook M.   *Waynesville.*

Washington County.

Lamm & Brothers   *Marietta.*
Leophold M. L. & Co.
McCleod J.
Gruffort Chas.
Kramer J. G. & Brother

Wayne County.

Childs Wm.   *Wooster.*
Kreps Daniel
Allison M.
Pierson & King

Wyandot County.

Reed P. L.   *Upper Sandusky.*
Owen John
Lumbert J. M.   *Marseilles.*

Coach Smiths.

Hamilton County.

Hirst & Co., cor. Front & Fr'man *Cincinn.*

Coal Dealers.

Adams County.

Anderson Saml.   *Manchester.*

Athens County.

Somers J. F.   *Nelsonville.*
Bland & Juniper
Paston L. P.
Steenrod O.
Beesman I. F.
Judson L.
Shepherd S. M.
Butt J.
Harper B. F.
Johnson J.
Coe Jackson
Stem A.
Robbins Joseph
White H.
Hayden P.
Shannon Thos.

Belmont County.

Austin Lycurgus   *Bell Air.*
Barnard William
Cummins James
Davis Nelson
Hetherington Jacob
Horn Thornton A.
Lake Evan
O'Neal Robert H.
Omet & Shrum
Rodefer John
Ryan Joseph
Todd Martin L.

Butler County.

Hutchinson E.   *Hamilton.*

Clinton County.

Stevenson G. H.   *Westboro'.*

Columbiana County.

Chamberlain R.   *East Palestine.*
Kuntz Abraham   *New Chambersburgh.*
Pippit Henry
Vanhorn John
Wallace John

Cuyahoga County.

Brayson & Mason, (Agents,) Rail Road
Pier   *Cleveland.*
Crawford & Price, Rail Road Pier
Dickinson C., Champlain & Canal
Hays John, Rail Road Pier
Murfey William A., do
Pendleton J. C., (Agent,) Head Merwin

Porter Edwin, Canal   *Cleveland.*
Tod, Rhodes & Co., Rail Road Pier
Winch T. & Co, Government Pier
Hays & Moore, R. Road Pier
Howell & Doane   *Ohio City*

Hamilton County.

Ashcraft J., Front bet. Lawrence & Pike
Bigley N. J. & Co., s. e. cor. W. Row &
  Water   *Cincinnati.*
Bigley N. J. & Co., n. e. cor. 5th & Mound
Brooks John, cor. 3d & John
Brooks John, 5 Masonic Hall
Bertram A., 242 e. Front
Brown Wm. & Sons, 674 w. Front
Brown G. & Son, s. w. cor. Plum & Court
Cochnower John, Broadway abv. Court
Cochnower John, cor. Lock & Front
Cochnower John, do. 8th & Mound
Cochnower John, do. 3d & W. Row
Cochnower John, 461 W. Row
Dodsworth T. & M., cor. Law'nce & Front
Dodsworth T. & M., do. Ludlow & Front
Dodsworth T. & M., do. Liberty & Miami
  Canal
Deloiac Wm. T., L'n bet. Clark & Hopkins
Gordon Robert & Co., 6th e. Broadway
Guild & Marshall, s. e. cor. Plum & Water
Guild & Marshall, cor. P'k & W. W. Canal
Gosiger & Schuerman, cor. Wood & 3d
Gorrell J. W., 183 Plum
Hubbell N. S., cor. 3d & Ludlow
Hubbell N. S., do. 5th & Park
Kuhn & Buchanan, cor. 2d & Elm
Kuhn & Buchanan, do. Front w. Smith
Maxon & Baker, (Measurers,) 181 Front
Patton C., 81 Front
Ross A., 7th bet. Baymiller & Freeman
Sanders & Baldwin, cor. Canal & Walnut
Vanberger Henry, (Agent,) cor. W. W.
  Canal & 5th
Wood E. B., Plum n. of Mason
Walker William, n. e. cor. Race & Court
Walker William, cor. W. W. Canal & 5th
Rucker S. C.   *Fulton.*
Shepard J. Z.   *Columbia.*

Jefferson County.

Nissly Saml.   *Mouth of Yellow Creek.*
Groff Jacob
Roberts Edward

Lawrence County.

Campbell J., (Agent)   *Ironton.*

Mahoning County.

Crawford & Murray   *Youngstown.*
Todd & Ford
Thornton Jesse

Meigs County.

Holland A. A.   *Silver Run.*

Montgomery County.

Beaver B. N., St. Clair   *Dayton.*
Wike J. N., Mill

Trumbull County.

Morris David　　　　　　　*Girard.*
Todd David

Tuscarawas County.

McIlvain & Robb　　　*New Philadelphia.*
Everett & English
Korns D. & Co.
Patrick J. U. & Co.
Robison & Co.
Gribble J.
Williams P.
Simeral M. & Co.

Summit County.

Harris & Houts　　　　　　*Tallmadge.*
Upron D.
Becher F. & Co.　　　　　　*Clinton.*

Coffee Houses.

Adams County.

Cooley Jas. H.　　　　　　*Manchester.*
Morlatt J. P.　　　　　　　*West Union.*

Belmont County.

Eyre L. A.　　　　　　　*St. Clairsville.*
Hessey Charles

Brown County.

Hennise Jacob　　　　　　*Higginsport.*
Tice Jacob

Butler County.

Smith David　　　　　　　*Oxford.*
Earhart J.　　　　　　　　*Hamilton.*
Sloocum Thos.
McGehan G.
Basey Jas.

Clark County.

Bergerbaugh H.　　　　　　*Springfield.*
Shrader M.

Cuyahoga County.

Cozzens A., Forest City House Block
Smith Richard, Canal Basin　*Cleveland.*

Delaware County.

Miller Martin　　　　　　　*Delaware.*
Howard E.
Heller A.

Erie County.

Butts F.　　　　　　　　*Sandusky City.*
Huke Wm.
Hagy G.
Boyer N.
Hugler John
Bauer J. B.
Baumeister J.
Unglenk F.
Myers Wm.
Blanch J.

Franklin County.

Schuntzer —, Broad　　　　*Columbus.*
11

Hamilton County.

Aleman M., 98 Ham. road　　*Cincinnati.*
Ahlero B., cor. W. Row and Liberty
Abrams J., Court bet. Walnut and Main
Arbuckle William, 20 é. Fourth
Aigler H., 32 e. Front
Brenninger S., Front near Landing
Brockman R., cor. Sixth and Vine
Boman Louis, Broadway near Front
Bagot Walter, 430 Main
Baxter Archibald, cor. Wal. and Fourth
Burnett A., Vine bet. Sixth and Seventh
Bauman J., 17 Levee
Bilcer A., 26　　do
Berna John, 39 Pike
Bohrer A., 606 e. Front
Birkett J. A., 562 e. do
Bloom F., 526　　do
Brataler C., 226　　do
Broughkaus H., 114 Hunt
Bracker F., Fifth bet. Walnut and Vine.
Bonacum E., n. w. cor. Third and W. Row
Bushing & Barnhorn, 60 Court
Bass Thomas, 68　　　do
Bierschwale A., 216 W. Row
Buckel G. M., 56 Clay
Brugleman C., 477 Walnut
Bobl S., 412 Vine
Buehl J., 677 do
Batchlor F. Y., 30 W. Row
Bricher G., n. e. cor. Elm and Green
Bards J., 290 Ham. road
Bolinger T., 22 do　do
Baner C., 29 W. Front
Beeks J., Landing bet. Main and Walnut
Brown & Lardy P. & B. H., Landing bet.
　Walnut and Vine
Brunse A., 66 Lower Market
Beckhouse M., 48 do　do
Carruthers W., cor. Wood and Fifth
Carr M., Landing bet. Main & Walnut
Curry J.,　do　　do　　do　　　do
Cavallie Louis, 13 Broadway
Corders D., cor. Twelfth and Walnut
Cates M.. 704 Front
Connell Daniel, 22 Cassilly's Row
Copy J. & C., Ninth e. of Main
Casserly M., 20 Levee
Campbell P., 35 Ludlow
Canongè L., 154 Sycamore
Churley J., cor. Broadway and Landing
Cunningham A., 18 Levee
Drescher Charles, Court bet. Vine and
　Walnut
Daum M., 14 e. Front
Dodt C., 100 Hunt
Dunlap Robert, 193 Court
Dilg F., 478 Vine
Doll G., 58 Liberty
Dull F., 612 Vine
Dick F., 630　do
Doll J., 681　do
Dinger A., 661 do
Davis John A., 119 Sycamore
Davit J. B., Landing bet. Main & Walnut
Elk A., 72 Ham. Road
Engert G. M., 106 Buckeye

Eichenlaub G. F., 605 Vine   · *Cincinnati.*
Eid Francis J., 74 Court   ·
Ehrenfield H., 185 Vine
Frame H. & Co., 18 Lower Market
Faildeldi A., 12 e. Front
Frohliger S., cor Sec. and Lawrence
Fey S., 621 Vine
Flick F. J., 593 do
Firnkass M., 8 Buckeye
Fox H. L., 363 Ham. Road.
Freely James, Landing between Main and Walnut
Foote W. H., cor. Fourth and Sycamore
Gardner C., Fifth e. of Main
Gosling H., 21 Fifth
Gavin M., 59 Water
Gibson J., Landing bet. Main and Walnut
Gas J., 634 Vine
Gerhard Kotter, 78 Western Row
Gilden C., 199 Sixth
Grossman D. & Co., 514 Walnut
Graff F. X., 514 Vine
Glaser J., 82 Court
Geise H. A., 167 w. Fifth
Gaiser J., 28 Levee
Gerson ——, 183 Walnut
Gifford W. W., 61 e. Front
Grimmelsman ——, 672 w. Front
Holster & Nabe, cor. Main and Landing
Haddix William, 163 Court
Hackman H., 287 Main
Husman A., 563   do
Horn ——, 34 Broadway
Hobleman C., 55 Main
Hall J., 143 Walnut
Haching J. C., cor. Vine and Fifth
Heuermann John, s. e. cor. Vine & Fifth
Halligan James, 21 Levee
Harrison John, 23 do
Hartleb Charles, 24 do
Hullman J. H., 137 e. Front
Horsley Henry, 38 e. Front
Husband W., 418 do do
Hallican James, 21 Cassilly's Row
Hofschulte Wm., 79 Court
Hughan J., 203 w. Fifth
Horncomp F., 145 w. do
Hemkof D. W., 431 Main
Haar Frenzybonder, 183 Canal
Heindrick A., 461 Walnut
Homan F., cor. Vine and Canal
Houseman B., 372 Sycamore
Hebenstrict A., 52 Liberty
Hummel J., 606 Vine
Hana Charles, 493 do
Hobneck J., 401 do   [Riddle
Heinback A., Har. Road bet. Freeman and
Hudson Wm. S., 289 W. Row
Hageman Adam, 464 Linn
Hans Bier, 623 W. Row
Heckel G. M., s. e. cor. Bremen & Liberty
Hans J., 359 Ham. Road
Hisemstap John, 20 do
Hofer J., 44 Findley
Henry James, 52 Water
Heans J., 57 Sycamore
Jacobs P., 617 Vine

Johnston John, cor. Ludlow and Front
                   Cincinnati.
Inderiden A., 18 Thirteenth
Knobe B., 187 Vine
Kling George, 109 e. Second
Kyte J., 117 Locke
Krumser J., 43 e. Front
Kelley J., 179 w. Fifth
Kiefer Jacob, 20 Eighth
Koengstein D., 56½ W. Fifth
Ketcham J. C., cor. W. Row and Front
Krieger J. H., cor. Front and Elm
Kleine H., 490 Main
Kiefer D., 97 Canal
Kirchner L., 216 Walnut
Koking B., 14 Thirteenth
Klefot Frederick, cor. Syc. and Abigail
Klingler J., Mercer bet. Walnut & Vine
Kuhn W., 411 Vine
Klein F., Har. Road between Riddle and Davison
Kesler Joseph, 583 W. Row
Kipps John, 116 Ham. Road
Kelch Mrs. C., 29 w. Front
Keown J., 22 Water
Kellem Mrs. M., Landing bet. Main and Walnut
Kilkenny A., Land. bet. Walnut & Vine
Kochler J., 48 Sycamore
Kauhlman G.,   do
Kuldman J. F., 116 Columbia
Laughlan Peter, Landing bet. Walnut and Vine
Lennaughan P. K., 65 Water
Laughlin P., 64   do
Longshore A., cor. Walnut & Water
Long John, cor. Walnut and Landing.
Landfrit A., 659 Vine
Lantser L., 599   do
Lamping B., 193 Sixth
Lubberman George, 23 Thirteenth
Landeuweschl A., 67 Liberty
Lackmann H., 404 Fifth
Leonhart G., 41 Congress
Lephert Lowry, 40 Pike
Lutz J., 453 Main
Layman John H., 520 Main
Meiers R., s. w. cor. Vine and Water
McCristal & Bracken, 13 Levee
Murphy J., 16   do
NcQueeny T., 19   do
McCullon, O. M. C., 30 e. Front
McCue ——, 10   do do
Macklin H., 44 Congress
Menger M., cor. Congress & Pike
Morscher G., 107 e. Second
McConnell J., 35 e. Front
Martin ——, 75 Court
McKay C., 160½ Third
Middendorf Bernard, 177 Water
Montgomery J., 122 Third
Maerose & Berthelsman, 550 Main
Mawn W., cor. Longworth and Smith
Meyer J. H., 582 Walnut
Mohn J., 408 Vine
Muhler P., 395 do
Mugel P., W. Row bet. Main and Liberty

Miller John, Ham. Road bet. W. Row and
   Liberty   *Cincinnati.*
Murry P., 293 W. Row
Mulligan H., cor. Clinton and John
Mollory P., cor John and Richmond
Meier H., 28 Elder
Moser J., 94 Buckeye
Moores C., 152 Ham. Road
Muller J., 348 do do
Morelle J., Vine st. Hill
McDonald A., 15 Water
Murphy William, Landing near Main
McShea H., Landing bet. Walnut & Vine.
McAulty P., do do do do
McGinty P., do do do do
McCann J., do do do do
Murphy John, 24 Sycamore
Martin L., 44   do
Martin Robert, Sixth bet. Walnut & Vine.
Moore A., cor. Liberty and Main
Manison & Thorp, 200 Sixth
Noble A., 119 Sycamore
North A., 446 w. Third
Neemer F. J., 112 Columbia
O'Connell Daniel, 22 Levee
Parr Adam, 556 w. Sixth
Pfau P. H., 83 Sycamore
Prehner Frederick, cor. Wade and John
Peter A., 263 Clinton
Prager A., 545 Race
Phillips A., 22 Liberty
Peters Meinard, Front bet. Broad. & Lud.
Pippert & Hecket, 613 Vine
Ruby John, Front bet. Butler and Canal.
Richof W., 46 e. Front
Reif A., 106 Hunt
Rentz J., 47 e. Front
Rourke Wesley, 685 w. Front
Ranchler A., 575 w. Fifth
Rab L., 54 Vine
Roese W., 99 Ham. Road
Roll W., 154 do do
Ruane T., Landing near Main
Ryland W. T., 90 Sycamore
Rothairt Frank, s. w. cor. Vine and Pearl
Stonestreet J., 29 Fifth
Schmidt A., 27 w. Front
Smith H., 55 do do
Smith George, 142 Ham. Road
Snyder C., 76   do do
Schattle J., 514 Elm
Sander H , 19 Greene
Sargant C., 251 W. Row
Somer F., 104 Liberty
Sockstedar F., 361 Ham. Road
Staunsz M., 137   do
Steininitz M., 557 Vine
Smidt A., W. Row bet. Wade & Everett
Scitser G., 356 W. Row
Seamen J., 334 do
Sapf J., 480 Vine
Stephen C., 490 Vine
Struve H. W., 488 Main
Smith A. F., 598   do
Schramm J., 615   do
Stockman F., 62 Court
Stokes J., W. Row bet. 4th and 5th

Smith Henry, 95 Court   *Cincinnati.*
Strohm J., 175, e. Front
Schufman F., 90 Columbia
Slotman & Wisfieke, 69 w. Third
Selves & Roth, Third bet. Main & Syc'ore
Schott F. R., 349 Walnut
Saweil Barney, 4 Levee
Schwegman J., Sycamore near Front
Spencer & Flagg, 17 w. Sixth
Tuffle C. & Co., 104 Walnut
Tufel Joseph, 347   do
Fushmit C., 164 e. Front
Tinger E., 36 do do
Thurwachter J., 53 Court
Thurwachte J., 502 Walnut
Tippenhauer J., cor. Plum and Liberty
Tiler John, Vine st. Hill
Tangeman F., Landing bet. Walnut and
   Vine
Thompson J., 22 Sycamore
Thomann P., 53 Main
Thompson Sandy, 19 e. Third
Vincent E. J., s. w. cor. Sixth and Elm
Vierling Francis, 36 Fifth
Walker ——, 7 Sycamore
Watson S., 55   do
Whitman J. J., s. cor. Wade and John
Wakeman J., s. w. cor. eighth and Carr
Weis Peter, 192 Clinton
Weil J., cor. Race and Fourteenth
Wittenb H. H., 544 Race
Whernbarger Peter, 357 Ham. Road
Waltz C., 635 Vine
Weber J. A., 567 do
Witmer G., cor. Clay and Allison
Wagner H., 447 Walnut
Wust J., 64 Court
Worthington & Van Buren, 12 Court
Weichelman John C., 130   do
Wood L , Pearl
Watts William, 216 W. Row
Wells John, 341 Fifth
Wetzger John, 515 e. Front
Wentworth L. A., 492 e. Front
Wolf & Mack, 173 do do
Winkum Peter, 42 do do
Watkins James, s. e. cor. Syc. and Front.
Wesseling W. & Co., cor. Vine and Fifth
Westjohan H. H., 8 Levee
Weingartner F. J., cor. Wood and Fifth
Wisman Joseph, 58 Lower Market
Zins J., 592 Elm
Zoller J., 63 Main
Zimmerman J., s. w. cor. Walnut & Fifth
Zap J., 464 Walnut
Peterson P.   *Pendleton.*
Rice G.
Jonas J. A.
Casay J.   *Fulton*
Smith W. F.
Williams George   *Miami.*
McMakin George   *Cumminsville.*
Nett & Co.
Jones J. J.   *Lockland.*

Licking County.
Morath M.   *Newark*
Haynes H. H.

Logan County.

Lewis H.   *Huntsville.*
Shrop A.   *Bellefontaine.*
Snyder John L.   *Logansville.*

Marion County.

Lobrick P.   *Marion.*
Kraner John

Medina County.

Hobart Geo.   *Medina.*
Selkirk E. L.

Monroe County.

McAnaspy Richard   *Woodsfield.*

Montgomery County.

Clark D. J., N. Market   *Dayton.*
Oron George, Second
Ingram J. F., N. Market
Leffel & Richards, Mill
Mesler George, Third
Morrel H.   do
Schieble F., N. Market
Stiblins J. M., Jefferson
Zinck C., Sixth
Zinck J.   do

Portage County.

Severence O. F.   *Ravenna.*
Taylor S. A.
Sayer John

Scioto County.

Dreyfuss P.   *Portsmouth.*
Gramm Moses.

Seneca County.

Graff M. Y.   *Tiffin.*

Coffee Mill Manufacturers.

Franklin County.

Sites Andrew, Friend   *Columbus.*

Coffee & Spice Mills.

Cuyahoga County.

Downing W. W., 19 Seneca   *Cleveland.*

Hamilton County.

Dixon & Darst, Sycamore bet. 7th & 8th
                           Cincinnati.
Harrison Eaton & Co., 99 & 101 Walnut

Ross County.

Rose & Brothers   *Chillicothe.*

Collar (Patent Horse) Manufacturers.

Cuyahoga County.

Briggs Joseph W., cor. Ontario & Prospect
                           Cleveland.

Colleges (Commercial).

Babbitt & Nugent, 162 Superior *Cleveland.*
Folsom E. G., 105 Sartwell's Block

Hamilton County.

Bacon's Commercial College (R. S. Bacon,
  Principal), n. w. cor. Wal. & 6th *Cincin.*
Bartlett's Commercial College (R. M. Bart-
  lett, Principal), s. e. cor. Walnut & 4th
Cincinnati Mercantile College (John Gun-
  dry, Principal), n. w. cor. Walnut & 5th
Head & Clarkson's Commercial College
  (J. E. Head, Principal), s. e. cor. Main
  & Fourth

Montgomery County.

Barnaby S. B., Glegg's Buildings *Dayton*

Colleges (Law).

Hamilton County.

The Law School of Cincinnati College
  (Hon. Chas. P. James, President), Walnut bet. 4th & 5th   *Cincinnati.*

Colleges Literary.

Cuyahoga County.

Cleveland University (Rev. Asa Mahon,
  President),   *Cleveland.*

Hamilton County.

St. John's College (Chauncey Colton, Presi-
  dent), s. w. cor. Walnut & Gano *Cincin.*
St. Xavier's College (Rev. John De Bliek,
  President), Syc. bet. 6 & 7th.
Wesleyan Female College (Rev. P. B.
  Wilbur, President), Vine bet. 6th & 7th
Farmers' College (F. G. Carey, President),
                           College Hill.
Female Seminary ——,

Colleges (Medical).

Cuyahoga County.

Cleveland Medical College (John Delamater, M. D., Dean),   *Cleveland.*
Western College of Homœopathic Medicine (Chas. D. Williams, M. D., Dean),

Franklin County.

Starling Medical College, (S. M. Smith,
  M. D., Dean),   *Columbus.*

Hamilton County.

Cincinnati Med. & Surgical College, (A. H.
  Baker, M. D., President), cor. Western
  Row & Longworth,   *Cincinnati.*
Eclectic Medical Institute, (Jos. R. Bu-
  chanan, M. D., Dean), n. w. cor. Court
  & Plum
Medical College of Ohio, (L. M. Lawson,
  M. D., Dean), 6th bet. Race & Vine
Miami Medical College of Cincinnati,
  (Geo. Mendenhall, M. D., Dean), n. w.
  cor. 5th & W. Row
Physo-Medical College, (Botanic ; A. Cur-
  tis, M. D., President), Walnut bet. 4th
  & 5th

Colleges—Dental.

Hamilton County.

Ohio College of Dental Surgery, (James
Taylor, M. D., Dean), College street bet.
6th & 7th *Cincinnati.*

Composition & Metal Roof Manufacturers.

Brown County.

Palmer L. M. *Ripley.*

Hamilton County.

Dunn William & Co., 3d near Vine *Cin-*
Howard L. & Co., 173 Main [*cinnati.*
Mann & Co., Columbia bet. Walnut & Vine
McGeorge James, Race bet. 3d & 4th
Page, Beckley & Co., 90 w. Pearl
Warren S. M. & C. M., Pearl bet. Vine &
Race

Confectioners & Candy Manufacturers—Wholesale.

Hamilton County.

Alley S. A., 290 w. 5th *Cincinnati.*
Burnett Alfred, 164 w. 5th
Demand M., 224 Walnut
Hall P., 52 Main
Hedger R., 336 Main
Howe S. D., 1 College Hall, Walnut
Myers & Co., 40 Main
Myers John R., 221 do
Stevens J. A. & Co., 320 Main
Smith G., 343 Walnut
Wolfe W. W., 156 w. 6th

Licking County.

Spear J. R. *Granville.*
Carter F. M.

Pickaway County.

Wittich G. F. *Circleville.*

Richland County.

Clapp E. *Mansfield.*

Scioto County.

Dresher A. *Portsmouth.*
Freshell John

Warren County.

Hoy B. B. , *Waynesville.*

Confectioners & Fruit Dealers.

Brown County.

Doerler Cornelius *Ripley.*
Shan J. H.
Kendall O. D.

Butler County.

Stillwalt John *Hamilton.*
Brawer John
Freeman A. C. *Middletown.*

Champaign County.

McCord J. K. *Urbana.*

Clark County.

Hall & Paden *Springfield.*

Clermont County.

Degolyer A. *Loveland.*

Columbiana County.

McKinnell Wm. *Wellsville.*
Lease J. W. *Salem.*

Cuyahoga County.

Gorham & Aplin, 16 Superior *Cleveland.*
Heisel N., 13 Water
Light C. H. & Co., 64 Ontario
Mould H. & Son., 32 Superior
Williams, Babcock & Hurd, 83 do
Crandall William M., *Ohio City.*

Erie County.

Buyer N. J. *Sandusky City.*
Miller A.
Prenatt J.

Fairfield County.

Smith J. C. *Lancaster.*

Franklin County.

Ambor P. & Co., High *Columbus.*
Butler C. P. L. do
Drury & Werley do
Leadley Mark do
Snider A. & Co. do
Someler George do
Stage & Frisbie do
Winger Frank *Worthington.*
Beers Uriah Jr.

Gallia County.

Laiblain Charles *Gallipolis.*

Geauga County.

Crampton G. *Burton.*

Greene County.

Austin & Smith *Xenia.*
Davidson J.
Klein Jacob
Milbourn Wm.
Snell R. T.
Collier James *Yellow Springs.*
Kesler S. T.

Guernsey County.

Graham B. B. *Cumberland.*
Niswander J. *Cambridge.*
Cook A. E.
McIlyar Mrs. E.
Allen John

Hamilton County.

Brezola James, 81 Pearl *Cincinnati.*
Bugguina Peter, Court bet. Main & Walnut
Bacciocco J., 124 w. 5th
Bacciocco S., 176 do
Bausman Henry, n. w. cor. Plum & 5th
Burnett T. N., 412 w. 5th
Behle Frederick, 198 Clinton
Candolpho Stephen, 209 Elm
Cavagna Bartholomew, 31 w. 5th
De Voto A., 243 w. 4th

Doorly C., 241 w. 6th   *Cincinnati.*
Demand L., s. e. cor. Court & Elm
Down J., 292 Elm
Ferry James, 212 w. 7th
Fisher William, 80 6th
Fisher A., 463 w. 5th
Garebaldi James, n. e. cor. Plum & 5th
Gillard William, 238 Vine
Gayler August, 456   do
Harter M., 308 Main
Herberding F., 331 Walnut
Hall J. W., 374 w. 5th
Ingersoll J. M., 403 W. Row
Johnson Miss, W. Row below 5th
Kurtz A., 8th bet. Mound & John
Lagory Joseph, 346 w. 5th
Lanone A. & Boggiano, 60 w. 5th
Lewis J., 136 Columbia
Longinoth J., 140 w. 8th
Littlebury T., 264 w. 6th
Maluppina John, 142 Walnut
Miller J. H., 76 Main
Massa Nicholas, n. e. cor. Race & 8th
Moore N., 260 Race
McDonald G., 300 w. 5th
Malespina J., 285 W. Row
Nolan N., 277   do
Ottenheimer H., cor. Vine & Centre
Orreto Joseph, 96 Pearl
O'Brien N., cor. 6th & John
Padesta P., 295 W. Row
Podesta John, 427 Main
Punghoff J. H., 317 Vine
Richeimer M., 295 Main
Reatter Francis, 160 Front
Rittweger P., 282 W. Row
Schmidt T., s. w. cor. Race & 6th
Smith Oliver, 577 W. Row
Stookey Isaac, 264 Main
Schwegman C., 385 do
Scintti M., 130 w. 4th
Todd J. & Co., 35 5th
Thomas John, 180 Front
Wessling Henry, n. e. cor. Race & 9th
Witt H., 315 W. Row
Williams W., 146 w. 6th
Young N., 204 w. 6th
Helmig H.   *Fulton.*
Walker D.
Singleton —   *Walnut Hills.*
Johnson Adam   *Harrison.*
Yost Frederick

Highland County.

Bour Valentine   *Hillsboro'.*
Hurtt Abel

Jefferson County.

Kirck Saml.   *   *Steubenville.*
Harter Wm.
Blackburn J.
McCauley John
Penell J.
Boyer John
Pollock Eliza
Patterson Wm.
Dillon B.

Feist M. & Co.   *Steubenville.*
Jackson J.   *Warrenton.*

Knox County.

George J.   *Mt. Vernon.*
Relf John

Lake County.

Byes H. N.   *Painesville.*

Licking County.

Marshall & Chandler   *Newark.*

Medina County.

Letterly F.   *Medina.*

Montgomery County.

Dunn S., N. Market   *Dayton.*
Espy J. M. & Bro., Third
Kiefer J. A., Second
Omer J. P., Main
Stedman Isaac, do
Davis & Bro.   *Miamisburgh.*

Muskingum County.

Mell Francis   *Dresden.*
Dutton F. F.   *Gratiot.*
Nevitt Thos. F.   *Zanesville.*

Pickaway County.

Greeno & Ward   *Circleville.*
Wittich G. F.

Portage County.

Little Benj.   *Ravenna.*
Cone J. W.   *Franklin.*

Preble County.

Homer John   *Eaton.*

Ross County.

Kaizer John   *Chillicothe.*
Klein Philip

Scioto County.

Treshell John   *Portsmouth.*
Bentley J. H.

Seneca County.

Black G. W.   *Tiffin.*
Huffman J. C.

Summit County.

Bitman William   *Akron.*
Weibezhan & Brothers

Trumbull County.

Anderson & Rupp   *Warren.*
Bishop D.

Union County.

Winget David P.   *Marysville.*

Warren County.

Hay B. B.   *Waynesville.*

Washington County.

Wildt J. & Co.   *Marietta.*
Soyes L.

Cousuls—Foreign.

Hamilton County,

Adae C. F. (Wurtemburg, Bavaria, Hanover, Oldenburg, and Nassau), 16 w. Front *Cincinnati.*
Meline J. F. (France, Belgium, Sardinia, Sweden, and Norway), 99 w. 3d
Rowcroft Charles (Great Britain), Ludlow bet. Arch & 4th
Stanislaus Louis (Prussia, etc.), s. w. cor. Court & Walnut

Coopers.

Adams County.

Golaspa D. H.	*Manchester.*
Wilson C.	
Mahaffey Samuel	*Dunkinsville.*
Cannon B. N.	*Locust Grove.*
Copeland Joseph R.	
Fritts J.	
Funk A.	
Cook John	*Eckmansville*
Cooper John C.	
Maddox Harrison	*West Union.*
Myers Nicholas	

Allen County.

Bowers Stephen	*Cranberry.*
Parker Isaac	
Hinton Joseph	*Croghan.*

Ashland County.

Harlin Henry	*Mohecan.*

Ashtabula County.

Summers Geo.	*Richmond Centre.*
Summers A.	
Peck Silas	*New Lyme.*
Markham E.	
Higbee J. M.	*Cherry Valley.*
Dodge J.	*Lenox.*
Bowers E. N.	*Geneva.*
Cormer E.	
Hill John	*Windsor.*
Hill Lewis	
Merritt Martin	
Johnson Reuben	*East Plymouth.*
Manley Warren	*Ashtabula.*
Manley J.	
Childs D.	
Peas J. F.	*Hart's Grove.*
Packard C.	
Coffin F. A.	*Rome.*
Shutz Adam	*Conneaut.*
Graham Thos.	

Athens County.

Watts Theodore	*Canaanville.*
Ward James	
Selby John	
Day Elias	*Shad.*
Maynard C.	
Williams Luther	
Williams A.	
Johnston James	*Lowry.*
Felroe James	

Brooks Benj.	*Lowry.*
Robinett H.	
Konkhite A.	*Guysville.*
Dudy G. B.	*Hull's.*

Auglaize County

Bonfig Casper	*Wapakoneta.*
Balgenars Wm.	*Minslet.*
Berting Charles	
Bude & Meyer	
Dillmann Her.	
Frieling John	
Gillis John	*Kossuth.*

Belmont County.

Piggott Geo. W.	*Hendrysburgh.*
Archer John	*Bellair.*
Brown Andrew	
Brown Elijah	
Kenady Stephen	
Kenady Peter	
Dennis John	*Uniontown.*
Parish George	
Blanchard Isaac	*Flushing.*
Branson Jacob	
Fisher John	
Mitchell Isaac	
Norris John	
Hilles Nathan	*Loydsville.*
Umbenhom Michae	
Campbell Lewis R.	*Dillies' Bottom.*
Campbell Wm. P.	
Campbell John B.	
Campbell James P.	
Coleman Leonard	
Dunlap William	
Pellell Poland	
McManus Jacob & Bro.	*Shepherdstown.*
Ricketts Nathan & Sons	
McAvoy J.	*Armstrong's Mills.*
McAvoy E. E.	
Landers J.	
Wade W.	

Brown County.

Thomas Saml.	*Higginsport.*
Dinman Jesse	
Sidowell H.	*Ripley.*
Liggett A.	
Ridgeway C.	
Kleinknicht C.	*Decatur.*
Applegate Thos. & Son	*Hamersville.*
Shannon Wesley	*Five Mile.*
Willey Levi	*De La Palma.*
Ross John	
Winters J. E.	*Fincastle.*
Sellman E. A.	
Temple N.	
Morrow A.	
Patton Richard	*Five Mile.*

Butler County.

Glardon L. P.	*West Chester.*
Brahan John	
Whittlesy Wm.	
Fitzimmons Michael	
Davis Willis	*Dartown.*

Cooch Thos. D.   *Dertown.*
Smith Wm.
Lauber Anthony   *Hamilton.*
Vorheis Jacob   *Middletown.*
Enyart W.
Stowe Wm.   *Ross.*
Armstrong S.   *Somerville.*
Norris B.
Gundy J. V.   *Seven Mile.*
Duck Theodore   *Trenton.*
Stainbrook F.
Fike K.
Gardner J. T.
Phres Robert   *Jacksonburg.*

Carroll County.

Belding G. B.   *Sherodsville.*
Jennings Peter
Jennings Henry

Champaign County.

Snyder James   *Christiansburg.*
Chew J.   *Urbana.*
Hedges Joseph
Guinnes & Sheffield

Clark County.

McKinley & Neff   *Tremont.*
Barton William   *Enon.*
Miller Peter
Stilwell Thomas
Swart Joseph
Sweeney Charles
Holloway J. B.   *Selma.*
Devolt H.   *Springfield.*
Buffington ——   *Catawba.*
Gare P.
Lloyd James
Wingfield R.
Scourse John   *New Carlisle.*

Clermont County.

Gibson David   *New Richmond.*
Durham Joseph
Alcorn Wm.
Silver J.
Gilbreth A.   *Point Pleasant.*
Cooper Joseph
Ellis Sam'l. & Son   *Williamsburg.*
Morehead W. R.
Temple R.   *Mt. Carmel.*
Stratton Aaron   *Neville.*
Bryant George   *Amelia.*
Young Reece
Butler Charles
Brunaugh & Buchanan
Monjar James
Fitzwaters Samuel   *Miamisville.*
Fitzwaters John
Woodlif P. Y.
Kugler John   *Milford.*
Elstune Isaac   *Mulberry.*
Clark Wm. A.   *Moscow.*
Vannosdall O. H. P.   *Mount Pisgah.*
Robbins Daniel
Cochran Aquilla
Lindsey Edward, Jr.

Perin S.   *Perin's Mills*
Simkins D.   *Belfast.*
Vance J. C.
Anderson John   *Laurel.*
Fee G. G.
Wallace A.
Winans Silas D.   *Bantam.*

Clinton County.

Grant John   *New Burlington.*
Anderson W.   *Westboro'.*

Columbiana County.

Haze Cyrus   *New Chambersburg.*
Slents James
Atterholt R. B.   *Bucks.*
Brandon Moses
Mitchel Thomas
Orr & Sons   *East Liverpool.*
Ewing John   *Saint Clair.*
Hart Samuel
Wollam Edward
Klechner Peter   *Columbiana.*
Baight Jacob   *Unity.*
Forney D. J.
Unger B.
Enny H.   *Cannon's Mills.*
Ewing & McClarain   *Wellsville.*
Warner ——   *New Lisbon.*
Peters ——
Smith Abraham
Smith Washington
Dessellem John S,   *Salineville.*
Paisley George
Shaffer David
Hay B. S.   *New Garden*
Wood Azariah
Grim Joseph   *North Georgetown.*
Jackson Levi
McKee Fisher
Whiteleather Joseph
Frederick J. C.   *Franklin Square.*
Weaver John

Coshocton County.

Thompson Wm. C.   *Chili.*
Licklain David   *Walhonding.*
Holmes Jackson
Huff John & Co.   *Coshocton.*

Crawford County.

Rentz Sebastian   *Poplar.*
March Joseph   *New Washington.*
Keltner S.   *Bucyrus.*
Nofsker H.
Russell J.

Cuyahoga County.

Sibley Rufus   *Solon.*
Bacon H.   *Bedford.*
Miner D. K.
Hanchit H.   *Warrensville.*
Hewit J.
Parmer F.
Taylor A.
Gregor Alexander   *Collamer.*
Shay ——

Scoville S. S.	*Collamer.*
Stafford G. T.	
Reed Henry	
Lardner R. & Co.	*Cleveland.*

Darke County.

Hutton J. W.	*Ithica.*
McGrue W.	
Sanderly P.	
Graham J. H.	*Hillgrove.*
Clark Jonathan	*Concordia.*
Craig H.	
Little Robert	
Tilson Luther	
Frank Solomon	*German.*
Black A.	
Werts Wm.	*Sampson.*
Roth Peter	*Greenville.*
Layman Peter	*North Star.*
Longnecker J.	
King F.	
Houston Stephen J.	

Defiance County.

Graper D.	*Defiance.*
Lehman J.	

Delaware County.

Hoover J. W.	*Galena.*
Bancroft A.	
Hoff B.	*Van's Valley.*
Swallow A.	
Fuller Alvin	*Unison.*

Erie County.

Green Asa	*Venice.*
Grow Jacob	
Franklin & Gardner	*Sandusky City.*
Reynolds A. S.	
Martin J.	*Milan.*
Collins J.	
Jenkins & Sanford	

Fairfield County.

Kilgore William	*West Rushville.*
Kline J.	*Amanda.*
Bell H.	*Lancaster.*
F. Tatger	
Cluts Lewis	*Sugar Grove*
Clark E.	
Clark S.	
Smith J.	
Haynes Samuel	*Clear Creek.*
Bechtell David H.	
Bowers C.	
Shaver James	

Franklin County.

Seliger W.	*Columbus.*
Merrick & Bretsford	
Brown S.	*Worthington.*
Gilbert Esra	
Jaycox James	
Brantner J.	*Lockbourn.*

Gallia County

King A.	*Raccoon Island.*
Hooper S.	*Kyger.*
Loundes S. D.	

Geauga County.

Blood James	*Parkman.*
Jaques J. W.	*Burton.*
Ellenwood S.	
Stickney E.	
St. John H.	*Chardon.*
Holliday O.	*Bainbridge.*
Henry O. P.	
Spears W. A.	
Smith Sam'l.	*Huntsburgh.*
Garrett S.	*Montville.*
Stout Jonas	*Thompson.*
Webster H.	
Wagoner Samuel	*Chester.*
Odell A.	*Auburn.*
Reed W.	

Greene County.

Curl Joseph	*Xenia.*
Curl William	
Jackson Samuel	
Manor John	
McCrary Francis	
McClelland F.	
Traster Robert	
Kinney J.	*Spring Valley.*
McCoy S. W.	*Clifton.*
Turner Levi	*Jamestown.*
Wright John	
Erwin Joseph A.	
James Richard	*Clio.*

Guernsey County.

Johnston J. S.	*Winchester.*
Shamblin C.	*Fairview*
Tinsman Sam'l.	
Tinsman Thos.	
Downing J.	
Boothe Robert	*Kimbolton.*

Hamilton County.

Adamson Robert, 91 Front	*Cincinnati.*
Buckton & Forster, 47 Columbia	
Derrell F., 89 e. Canal	
Francis A. W., 93 Eighth	
Gilson & Replogle, 525 Plum	
Hemmelcon H., 410 Sycamore	
Hainug William, 94 Ham. Road	
Jonte P. N., 486 Race	
Meyer Adam F., Laurel bet. Cutter and John	
Prows S., cor. Liberty and Front	
Richards John, 274 Sycamore	
Richards J., Ninth bet. Main and Syc.	
Schillinger W., Jr., 44 e. Second	
Thomas R., 28 w. Fifth	
Westing H., 27 and 28 e. Eighth	
Piner Z. M.,	*Pendleton.*
Davidson Wm.	*Harrison.*
Teller John	
Zane Delt	*Cumminsville.*

Hunkins John L.   *Mount Healthy.*
Kinney Lawrence
LaBoyteaux Wm.
LaBoyteaux Wm. S.
LaBoyteaux Sam'l.
McGill J. L.
Stevens Charles
Marsh S. C.   *Dunlap.*
Marsh E.
Pickens J.
Pinney J.

Hancock County.

Albright Alexander   *Cass.*
Smith John

Hardin County.

Oane & Co.   *Kenton.*
McCampbell Chas.
Gardner Caleb   *Sylvia.*

Harrison County.

Simonton John   *Cadiz.*
Monders Jacob   *Harrisville.*

Highland County.

Yank Davis   *Dodsonville.*
Wilkelm Elias   *Greenford.*
Callahan N. P.
McNeal Harvey   *East Monroe.*

Hocking County.

Colter Wm.   *Logan.*

Holmes County.

Trager Noah   *Walnut Creek.*
Statsbauch John   *Winesburg.*
Statsbauch M.

Huron County.

Ellis Martin   *Clarksfield.*
McKirn Wm.   *Bellevue.*
McKirn B. F.
Sprague J. R.   *Fitchville.*

Jefferson County.

McFerren Richard   *Richmond.*
Evans George   *East Springfield.*
Funston J. D.
Clair Thos.   *Knoxville.*
Jarvis Joshua   *Mouth of Yellow Creek.*

Knox County.

Miller Charles   *Mt. Vernon.*
Taylor Samuel
Harbin E.   *Fredericktown.*
Roberts B.
Shira Rudolph   *Ankenytown.*
Corbus J. G.   *Democracy.*
Oake Samuel   *Monroe Mills.*
Oake Erastus
McMahon Andrew
Spindler Clark
Spindler Wm.
Chapman E. B.   *Millwood.*
Smith Caleb
Boggs Alexander   *Bladensburg.*
Hull David

Hartifer William   *Bladensburg.*
Hayden David
Smith Levi

Lawrence County.

Bryan W. H.   *Burlington.*
Haskell James   *Haskellville.*
Knight William   *Millers.*
Condon J. W.   *Quaker Bottom.*
Johnson J. H.
Neff Adam
Pease C. M.

Lake County.

Lawrence D. C.   *Kirtland.*
Aschraft J. D.
Carrell H.
Waste B.
Butterfield W.   *Perry.*
Curtis Wm.
Warner A.   *North Perry.*
Curtis Wm. F.
Butterfield J. W.
Shepard H. F.   *Painesville.*
Durand L.

Licking County.

Gillespie Wm.   *Brownsville.*
Williamson W.
Burton C.
Burton R.
Payne B.
Yearly Wm.
Burton C. F.
Ditter G.
Dodd N.   *Jacksontown.*
Pond A.   *Granville.*
Gardner M.
Scott Wm.
Williams Thos. D.
Smith E.   *Newark.*
Link Adam
Saums Gideon   *Homer.*
Hayden Saml.   *Perryton.*
Colman J.   *Croton.*
Miller James   *Johnstown.*
Gardner George
Town N. B.   *Kirkersville.*
Brackett Josiah   *Fredonia.*

Logan County.

Cadwallader Wm.   *Huntsville.*
Campbell Wm.
Reed Thomas
Trimble Wm. & D.
Brotten G.   *Bellefontaine.*
Davis E.
Edsall Andrew   *Zanesfield.*
Garber James
Vanaka Wm.
Vanaka Geo.
Dratt Andrew   *Quincy.*
Dratt Peter
Jourdan J.
Holmes J.

Lorain County.

Sweet John   *Huntington.*

Leonard E.	*Oberlin.*
Jemerson J.	*Copops.*
Orabon N.	
Smith Melvin	*Brighton.*
Wallace N. A.	*Elyria.*

Lucas County.

Gordon Truman	*Riga.*
Johnson George G.	
Sanderson David	
Frany D. W.	*Whiteford.*
Beach William	
Phelps W. J.	
Kimble Jerome	
Disbro Peter	
McCracken L.	*Toledo.*

Madison County.

Rains Presley	*London.*
Dean James	*West Jefferson.*
Morse Joseph	
Carter John	
Crabb B. & Co.	
Stutson & Umpstead	

Mahoning County.

Rohr Christian	*Petersburgh.*
Rohr Henry	
Thorn Wilson	*Boardman.*
Dowler Thos.	
Titus S. G.	
Simons George	
Knecht Chas.	
Callahan N. P.	*Green Village.*
Willhelm Elias	
Templin Richard	
Orwig Danl.	*Milton.*
Orwig John H.	
Orwig Saml.	
Cox Saml.	*New Albany.*
Toot Jacob	

Marion County.

Weaver John	*Prospect*
Eversole David	
Robison W.	

Medina County.

Obrien James	*River Styx.*
Snell J. M.	*Wadsworth.*
Dickinson J. L.	
McGulliard James	
Knoll John N.	*Lodi.*
Stevens Perry	
Wetherbee B. K.	*Chatham Centre.*
Codding Geo M.	*Coddingsville.*
Drake J. L.	
Codding W. M.	
Point Geo.	

Meigs County.

Day James C.	*Apple Grove.*
Willis Henry	
Willis John	
Willis Jeremiah	
Grant Oliver	*Salisbury.*
Minick Wm. S.	

Dickerson John	*Ledlies.*
Stewart John	

Miami County.

Wood C. A. & A.	*Piqua.*
League Wm.	
Vogel George	
Hudson B. F.	
Spawn Danl.	
Cheeber Chas.	
Upton & Daniels	
Martin W.	*Troy.*
Williams Saml.	
Linson J. M.	
Williams J.	
Hardecre B.	*Casstown.*
Beck J.	
Coffman Jesse	*West Milton.*
McCord Wm.	
Long Joseph	
Porter John	
Coate Thos.	
Brown John	*Brant.*

Monroe County.

Long Michael	*Woodfield.*
Boughner A. W.	*Sunfish.*
Mathews Andrew	
Whitsell Joseph	
Blanker & Stancil	*Miltonsburg.*
Henderson William	*Baresville.*
Kast George	
Cline Perry	
Cline G. W.	*Sardis.*

Montgomery County.

Sponseller George	*West Baltimore.*
Grubb William	*New Lebanon.*
Grubb Henry	
Bear George	*Clayton.*
Cline Michael	
Heverling Henry	
Heverling Andrew	
Stouffer Henry	
Dubs Samuel	*Miamisburgh.*
Hueit Simon	
Liess Jacob	
Miller Joseph	
Widaman Benjn.	
Clingman A.	*Harshmansville.*
Snyder A.	
Patten Uriah	*Liberty.*
Shivitts Christian	
Wiley Ephraim & Son	*Centre.*
Conway Adam, First	*Dayton.*
Cathcart J., 6th	
Eichelberger T. D., 5th	
Gardner J. R., Head Basin	
Gorsuch Abraham, First	
Wiggins H., Canal	
Stork H., First	
Henderson A.	*Little York.*
Quilling John	
Reed Martin	
Ritchison Danl.	
Davidson O. R.	*Germantown.*
Beam Martin	

Lease Dease — *Germantown.*
Lesly Levi
Roplagh F. G.

Morgan County.

Roberts Saml. — *Triadelphia.*
McCarty Thos.
Pickerel Wm.
Adams Francis — *Meigs' Creek.*
Paxton J. K.
Rich & Wood — *McConnelsville.*
Head Cornelius
Johnson Henry
Offord Alex.
Broomhall J. H. — *Stockport.*
McCoy J.
Geddis J.
Cramblet Henry — *Pennsville.*
Neeley W. — *Neeleyeville.*
Hanson Saml.

Morrow County.

Ligget John — *Cardington.*
Morton E. M. — *Nimmons' Cross Roads.*

Muskingum County.

Palmer T. K. & Co. — *Nashport.*
Barnes Lewis — *Norwich.*
Pickeral Wm. — *Hopewell.*
Pickerel R.
Holmes A.
McLain John — *White Cottage.*
Williams James
Eakins David — *Stovertown.*
Payne George — *Gratiot.*
Miner Frederick

Noble County.

Gibson Joseph — *Sarahsville.*

Ottawa County.

Hubbard Wm. — *Elmore.*

Perry County.

Kennedy J. D. — *New Lexington.*
Hiles & Co.
Croft John — *Mt. Perry.*
Daymud Jacob
Caywood Thomas — *Somerset.*

Pickaway County,

Maiden John — *Circleville.*
Anderson James — *Beckett's Store.*
Myers William
Risk James

Pike County.

Wiltshire E. — *Waverly.*
Ellington W.
Ellington J.
Goddard C.
Bateman Robert
Bateman O.
Saxe George

Portage County.

Moulton H. — *Brimfield.*

Hatch Henry — *Freedom*
Hubbard Q.
York James
Husted Danl.
Stutberger John — *Atwater.*
Stanton E. M. — *Streetsboro'.*
Shanklin C. M.
Kneeland J. — *Shalersville.*
Osterhold Benj.
Coe A. B. & S. A. — *Edinburgh.*
Bond Jonas
Bostwick Wm. R.
Archer Isaac — *Franklin.*
Hinds Erastus
Hutson Wm. — *Paris.*
White O. B. — *Mantua.*
Odell Benj.
Woods J. F.
Manley Danl. — *Nelson.*
Taylor Wm.
Baldwin T. — *Palmyra.*
Wilcox Benj.
Bradshaw Wm. — *Rootstown.*
Sapp Moses
Snell J.
Hallock G.

Preble County.

Brennan John — *Camden.*
McDonald A.
Smiley Wm.
Collins Saml.
Kreichboam Jacob — *Eaton.*
Harper Wm.
McCoy Joshua
Craiger John — *Fairhaven.*
Reed J. C. — *Gettysburg.*
Glassford Alex.
Brower George — *West Florence.*
Smith Wm. — *New Paris.*
Trammel J.
Medaw J.

Putnam County.

Depker Henry — *Buckeye.*
Radabaugh J. M.
Cooley W. — *Pendleton.*
Mellinger J. J.

Richland County.

Croshy J. C. — *Shelby.*
Flint G. W.
Groscost A.
Wilson William — *Ontario.*
Burgoyne Alfred — *Shenandoah.*
Grubaugh Jonathan — *Barnes.*
Smith George F.
Smith William O.
Johnson Daniel — *Lexington.*
Bedcar Martin & Co. — *Mansfield.*
Austin & Hirst — *Belleville.*
Miles J. O.
Brantner Levi — *Lucas.*
Zediker John

Ross County.

Belford Wm. — *Chillicothe.*
Deets D.

Nengeon J.   *Chillicothe.*
Oull Chas.
Mash Titus
Dickson James
Holstein Leonard   *Halleville.*
Wort John

Sandusky County

Clough N.   *Clyde.*
Starks L. D.
Stark James   *Townsend.*
Stark J. B. W.
Phillips A.   *Fremont.*
Johnson Jacob
Spade Geo. W.

Scioto County.

Gunn Saml.   *Portsmouth.*
Wynn William

Seneca County.

Smith Martin   *Adrian.*
Dysinger D.   *Bloomville.*
Brook Daniel   *Tiffin.*
Haynes Henry
Mitchell Samuel
Bradt Richard   *Green Spring.*
Hutcheson Joseph
Allen E.   *Republic.*

Shelby County.

Bailey James E.   *Sidney.*
Bailey Charles
Drain M. & Son
Davis George W.   *Hardin.*
Weymer Charles W.

Starke County.

Hahn Florence   *Waynesburg.*
Detrick John   *Minerva.*
Packer Samuel
Sell Andrew   *New Franklin.*
Shitsley Wm.
Bowers John F.   *East Greenville,*
Gittinger Abraham
Peters Abraham
Gutsball Henry   *New Berlin.*

Summit County.

Schenkenberger F.   *Tallmadge.*
Crandall W. A.   *Richfield.*
Hancock Alonzo
Lee C. E.
Lootz Ephraim   *Montrose.*
McConkey Samuel
Robinson Joseph
Ferrell J. H.   *Northfield.*
Olds W. F.   *Macedonia Depot.*
Arnold Josiah   *Copley.*
Robinson Joseph
Wagoner William
Nico Valentine
Green Lyman   *Bath.*
Hale Luther
White Thomas

Trumbull County.

Crawford J.   *Warren.*

Nettlefield Wm.   *Warren.*
Simmons Wm. L.
Johnson Henry   *Farmington.*

Tuscarawas County.

Roberts H. S.   *Peoli.*
Espich C. F.   *Ragersville.*
Madison Joseph
Waltz & Stevens   *New Philadelphia.*
Therrett M.
Sedgwick S.
Funk J.
Blickensderfer John   *Canal Dover.*
Weaver John
Showaker Wm.
Snyder W.
Snyder Frederick
Weitzenberger H.
Bechtel J.
Kailer Jacob
Otto Jacob
Weitsel Jacob
Dutell Angustus
Lohm James
Gieser Frank

Union County.

Henderson W. C.   *Watkins.*
Woodburn W.
Blain John   *Milford Centre.*
Maynard Samuel

Vinton County.

Myrick F. & J.   *McArthur.*
Murray William   *Pratteville.*

Warren County.

Lipencott S.   *Franklin.*
Woodward J.
Grifner H.
Robertson Daniel   *Oregon.*
Ward James   *Fort Ancient.*
Earnhart Jesse   *Red Lion.*
Keister S.   *Hayesville.*
Knaub J.
Cadwalader A.   *Waynesville.*
Humphrey Lewis
Dyer S. E.   *Morrow.*
Cameron James
Shields Samuel
Sims Geo. M.   *Mount Holly.*
Huffman E.
Randle R.
Merlatt John W.

Washington County.

Fuller Isaac   *Marietta.*
Walters A.
Willis Henry   *Centre Belpre.*
Oneal O.
Brookover Asa
Barrett John
Bellows John
Bellows Elias
Henderson Edward
Henderson W.
Smith Sam'l.

Bellows George   *Centre Belpre.* Krammer J., 632 Vine   *Cincinnati*
Hall A.   *Coal Run.*   Robson W. & G. W., Front bet. Pike and
Collins J. G.   *Fearing.*   Butler
Collins Isaac   Shaddinger Geo. A., Congress bet. Broad
Reynolds J.   *Newport.*   way and Butler
Bosworth S.
Willie R.   ### Meigs County.
Bowmen Peter   *Wesley.*   Thrush Sam'l.   *Pomeroy.*
Tott Alfred
Myers John   *Watertown.*   ### Montgomery County.
Wilson J. S.   *Lowell.*   Ach A., Second   *Dayton.*
Collins H.
                                          ### Portage County.
Wayne County.   Cluto John   *Ravenna.*
                                          Rawson S.
Beard Wm.   *Dalton.*   Prentiss O.
Pile Levi   *Edinburgh.*   Pitkin O. A.
Fair Christian   *Reedsburg.*   Bethel & Dodge   *Franklin.*
Dennis Wm.   *Burbank.*   Lamb O.   *Mantua.*
Dice Michael   *East Union.*
Gephart Lewis   ### Scioto County.
Cowel O.   *Shreve.*   Byerly & O'Neill   *Portsmouth.*
Botdorff Dan'l
Kiester Leonard   ## Cord, Fringe, and Tassel
Shelman Wm.   ## Manufacturers.
Munhull John
                                          ### Hamilton County.
Williams County.   Fletcher S., 195 Elm   *Cincinnati.*
Hadkins James   *Bryan.*   Hambo S., 236 Vine
Ward Sam'l.   Hoffmeister Ferdinand, 80 w. Court
Lanty S.   *Pulaski.*   Pickering J. M., 6 e. Fourth
                                          Pohlman Geo. W., 15 e. Fourth and 63 w.
Wood County.   Fourth
Smith J. J.   *Perrysburg.*   ### Montgomery County.
Bowsprit Chas.   Kesler J., Jefferson   *Dayton.*
Beach David
Simons P.   ## Cork Cutters.
Baldwin John
Marver S.   *Weston.*   ### Hamilton County.
Marver G.   Fisher & Isaac, 9 e. Franklin *Cincinnati.*
Poland Oliver   Laning & Peticolas, cor. e. Fifth and Mia-
Careys Joseph   mi Canal
Nearing E.   *Miltonville.*
Haynes A.   ## Cotton Goods Manufacturers.

Wyandot County.   ### Clark County.
Shoemaker Wm. & Alex.   *Corey.*   Conradt J. A.   *Springfield.*
Emerson N.   *Mexico.*   ### Hamilton County.
Damon Nicholas   *McCutchensville.* Fosdick S. & Co., cor. Smith and Third
                                                                        Cincinnati.
Copperas Manufacturers.   Geisendorff J. O., cor. Congress & Canal
                                          Gould, Pearce & Co., cor. Fifth & Locke.
Jefferson County.
                                          ### Jefferson County.
Fisher John   *Steubenville.*   Warner G. E. & J. H.   *Steubenville.*
Roberts M.
                                          ### Miami County.
Coppersmiths.   Chase R. R.   *West Milton*

Columbiana County.   ### Montgomery County.
Briggs Mahlon   *New Lisbon.*   Brown Henry L. & Co., Third   *Dayton*
Thompson John   Phillips T. A., Canal
Baker Jacob   *East Palestine.*
                                          ### Muskingum County.
Hamilton County.   Hazlett W. R., Agent Zanesville Cotton
Deckebach H., 171 Court *Cincinnati.*   Mill Co.   *Zanesville.*
Kiersted & Hoffman, junction Front and   Galigher Wm., Agent Muskingum Cotton
    Columbia   Mill Co.

Cotton Yarn, Candlewick, and Cotton Batting Manufacturers.

Hamilton County.

Ernst W. H., 517 W. Row   *Cincinnati.*
Fosdick S. & Co., cor. Smith & Third
Gould, Pearce & Co., cor. Fifth & Lock.
Geisendorff J. C., cor. Congress & Canal.
Stearns & Foster, 179 Clay

Montgomery County.

Harrington J., Upper Hydraulic   *Dayton.*

Coverlet Weavers.

Ashland County.

Weaver J.   *Rowsburg.*

Belmont County.

Birch S. A.   *Morristown.*
Maxwell Wm.
Sweeny T.   *Armstrong's Mills.*

Butler County.

Laget A.   *Middletown.*
Jotter Jacob   *Monroe.*

Carroll County.

Auschutz P. H.   *Carrollton.*

Clark County.

Moyall James   *New Carlisle.*
Myers Jacob

Columbiana County.

Bartler Joseph   *North Georgetown.*
Will William
Horsfall Henry   *New Lisbon.*
Eckler Henry   *New Chambersburg.*

Crawford County.

Heshe Henry   *Poplar.*
Reichart H.   *Bucyrus.*
Slaybaugh Samuel
Slaybaugh & Co.

Darke County.

Young John   *Fort Jefferson.*

Fairfield County.

Moncriff A. B.   *West Rushville.*
Phlegen ——   *Lithopolis.*

Franklin County.

Ayrhart Peter   *Canal Winchester.*

Highland County.

Sulser Henry   *Greenfield.*

Jefferson County.

McMillen S.   *Steubenville.*
Lawrence David   *Mouth of Yellow Creek.*

Licking County.

Tobin J.   *Newark.*

Lorain County.

Lashels G. W.   *Huntington.*

Mahoning County.

Burry Daniel   *Cornersburg*
Bower L.   *New Springfield.*
Welk George
Bayard Jacob   *North Lima.*

Medina County.

Baldwin H.   *Medina.*
Bean Mrs.

Montgomery County.

Olein Mathias   *Liberty.*
Turner William   *Dayton.*
Sheaner Michael   *New Lebanon.*

Morrow County.

Van Buskirk Jacob.   *Woodview.*

Pickaway County.

Hemon James   *Circleville.*

Pike County.

Fouth Jacob   *Piketon.*

Richland County.

Mosser John   *West Windsor.*
Baughman John   *Lexington.*
Etner Reuben
McNall John
Masters Margaret   *Belleville.*

Ross County.

Heiser William L.   *Chillicothe.*
Burns J.

Seneca County.

Brinkman Henry   *Bascom.*

Starke County.

Hoke George   *West Brookfield.*
Jenion J.
Reed Wm.
Berthalemy Jacob   *New Berlin.*
Meckel J. S.
Singer John   *Mapleton.*
Walk Jacob M.

Summit County.

Steurnagle Andrew   *Inland.*

Tuscarawas County.

Campbell J.   *New Philadelphia.*
Wilson R. B.

Warren County.

Beard William   *Dunlevy.*

Wayne County.

Brumman David   *Shreve.*
Lichty Benjamin   *Martinsville.*

Wyandot County.

Duddleson O.   *Upper Sandusky.*
Fox John   *McCutchensville.*

Cradle (Grain) Manufactu'rs.

Ashtabula County,
Seymour Norman   *East Plymouth.*

Clermont County.
Tompkins James   *Laurel.*

Holmes County.
Bay Henry   *Benton.*
McCully J.

Cultivator Manufacturers.

Coshocton County.
Shields John   *West Bedford.*

Cuppers and Leechers.

Hamilton County.
Gafeny, Owen O. B., n. w. cor. Sixth and
  Walnut   *Cincinnati.*
Kohl John S., 316 Main
Liedel Peter. Sixth bet. Plum & W. Row
Luzius Philip, 61 Court
Dilg Charles   *Harrison.*

Curled Hair Manufacturers.

Hamilton County.
Forgey J. P. & Co., 12 and 14 Columbia.
      Cincinnati.

Cutlery Manufacturers and Dealers.

Butler County.
Murdock J.   *Rossville.*

Hamilton County.
Bender Henry, 402 Vine   *Cincinnati.*
Eyman C., 493 Main
Haugh T., 207 Plum
Hollinshade & Newell, cor. W. Row and
  Clinton
Kesall T., cor. Seventh and Baymiller
Lilley William, Fifth bet. Vine & Race
Lanx V., n. e. cor. Liberty & Vine
Luther John, 16 e. Fifth
Rees William Z., 70 w. Sixth
Schrichton G., 456 Main
Weiser Isaac, 116 Fifth

Daguerrean Artists.

Ashland County.
Enseminger E.   *Ashland.*

Belmont County.
Aduddell Geo. M.   *Barnesville.*
Neel John B   *Uniontown.*

Butler County.
Webster J. L. M.   *Hamilton.*
Slack J. N.   *Rossville.*
Waldron W. S.   *Middletown.*

Clark County.
Winter W. W.   *Springfield.*

Clermont County.
Simmons & Anno   *Laurel.*

Clinton County.
Marble C.   *Wilmington.*
Holmes Wm.   *New Vienna.*

Columbiana County.
Peabody A. J.   *Unity.*

Coshocton County.
Hulsbizer Godfrey   *Walhonding.*

Cuyahoga County.
Crobaugh S., 6 Ontario street   *Cleveland.*
Johnson & Fellows, cor. Superior & Bank
North William C., Melodeon Buildings
Short Mrs. S. P., Miller's block

Defiance County.
Southworth B. F.   *Defiance.*

Delaware County.
Mendenhall J. Z.   *Delaware.*
Badger H. L.   *Galena.*
Carpenter D.

Erie County.
Phelps J. M.   *Sandusky City.*
Vail A.
Frisbie J. M.
Potter F.   *Milan.*

Franklin County.
Bambrough Wm., High street,   *Columbus.*
Fischer A.   do
Lindell H.   do
Lumley A. T.   do
Mason A. P.   do
Winchester D. D. do

Geauga County.
Bisbe C. A.   *Charden.*
Wheelock —

Greene County.
Charters J.   *Xenia.*

Hamilton County.
Bishop & Cornelis, n. w. cor. Main & 5th
      Cincinnati.
Ball J. P., 10 w. 5th
Bartons —, 20 do
Davis —, 14 do
Faris T., cor. 4th & Wal. Melodeon b'ding
Farnsworth —, 32 5th
Fithian —, 24 4th
Fontayne & Porter, 2 w. do
Hawkins E. C., Vine near 4th
Hunt & Weeks, 32 w. 4th
Potter —, 131 Main
Ross D. A., 244 w. 6th
Shewell E., s. w. cor. Walnut & 5th
White S. M., 112 5th
McCracken J. C.,   *Harrison*

Hardin County.

Thomas Mrs. Nancy   *Kenton.*

Harrison County.

Davis H.   *Cadis.*
Thompson Saml.   *Harrisville.*

Highland County.

Bredwell James W.   *Greenfield.*
Tucker Caleb H.   *Hillsboro'.*

Holmes County.

Parker W. J.   *Millersburg.*

Jefferson County.

Delano D. C.   *Steubenville.*
Weiser G. W.

Knox County.

Collins Edwin   *Mt. Vernon.*
Stewart —
Keller —   *Fredericktown.*

Lake County.

Clapsadle F.   *Painesville.*

Licking County.

Weicks R. E.   *Newark.*
Benham B. H.
Case S. & Co.   *Croton.*

Logan County.

Gano R. M.   *Bellefontaine.*

Lorain County.

Brokaw D.   *Oberlin.*
Culver —   *Copopa.*
Ryder J. F.   *Elyria.*

Madison County.

Crabb Oliver P.   *West Jefferson.*
Ewing William   *Lafayette.*

Medina County.

Golden Wm. R.   *Lodi.*
Whitmore J.   *Medina.*
Deming Miss G. S.

Miami County.

Davis Isaac   *Piqua.*
Day Y.   *Troy.*

Montgomery County.

Anderson W., 3d   *Dayton.*
Barnaby J. B. do
Bisbee & Robertson, Main
Deardorf P.   do

Morgan County.

Guthrie Miss Anna   *McConnelsville.*

Morrow County.

Concling Jacob   *Chesterville.*

Muskingum County.

Archbold E.   *Zanesville.*

Pickaway County.

Nelson H. T.   *Circleville.*
12

Perry County.

Huston & Barnd   *New Lexington.*

Portage County.

Mathews W. B.
Larkum A.   *Ravenna.*
Lake O. L.   *Freedom.*
    Nelson.

Richland County.

Kingsburry H. K.   *Mansfield.*
Phelps C. D.   *Belleville.*

Ross County.

Fontayne & Poster   *Chillicothe.*

Sandusky County.

Wiles A. D.   *Fremont.*

Scioto County,

Wocester Samuel   *Portsmouth;*
Shewell E.

Seneca County.

Griswold M. M.
McDonald & Co.   *Tyfin.*
Fay F. B.

Starke County.

Fletcher Abel   *Massillon.*

Summit County.

Miller S. S.   *Akron.*

Trumbull County.

Holloway H. W.   *Warren.*
Le Roy F. L.

Tuscarawas County.

Walling O. B.,   *Canal Dover.*

Union County.

Bouser Henry   *Marysville.*

Washington County.

Maxwell A. D.   *Marietta.*
Brewster —   *Harmar,*

Wayne County.

Wykes J. W.   *Wooster.*

Daguerreotype Stock—Importers & Dealers.

Hamilton County.

Smith Peter, 36 5th near Walnut, *Cincin,*

Dentists.

Allen County.

Satterthwait B. A.   *Lima*

Ashland County.

McDowell Joseph   *Ashland*

Ashtabula County.

Walker J. W.   *New Lyme*
Nutt J. K.   *Eagleville.*
Gillman H. F.   *Conneaut.*

Brown County.

Woodward C. N.   *Ripley.*
Hamel J. G.
Grove J. M.   *Russellville.*

Butler County.

Keeley George W.   *Oxford.*
Clippenger S.   *Rossville.*
Gunkel W. P.   *Middletown.*
Booth R. D.
Fellbrick D.   *Millville.*
Corson John   *Jacksonsburg.*

Carroll County.

Myers R. D.   *Carrollton.*

Champaign County.

Howell Joseph   *Urbana.*
Godfrey N. P.
Palmer J. G.

Clark County.

Mount A. A.   *Springfield.*

Clermont County.

Weaver J. A.   *Batavia.*
Simkins Isaac   *Belfast.*

Columbiana County.

Bowell C. T.   *Wellsville.*
Price N. L.   *East Liverpool.*
Parker Thornton G.   *New Lisbon.*
Shishler Jacob   *North Georgetown.*
Harris J.   *Salem.*
Whinny John C.
Hurd S. P.   *Hanoverton.*

Cuyahoga County.

Johnson W. R.   *Chagrin Falls.*
Pierce B.
Strickland & Horton, 125 Superior street, *Cleveland.*
Robinson & Ambler, Superior block
Slosson & Atkinson, 123 Superior
Short S. P., Miller's block
Lukens J., 94 Prospect

Darke County.

Munday Wm. B.   *Ithica.*
Williams George

Defiance County.

Kilmer W. H.   *Defiance.*

Delaware County.

Beaunean —   *Delaware.*

Erie County.

Aiken J. C.   *Sandusky City.*
Delano M. F.
Dryer L. T.   *Milan.*

Fairfield County.

King H. W.   *Lancaster.*
Crider H. L.
Scott H.

Franklin County.

Fowler John, High street,   *Columbus.*
Ide W. E.,   do
Riley W. W.   do
Switzer G., Friend
Todd H., High

Gallia County.

Payne Joseph   *Gallipolis.*
Sterneman C. R.

Greene County.

Payne G. L.   *Xenia.*
Taft J.
Watt George

Guernsey County.

Burian R. E.   *Washington.*

Hamilton County.

Allon & Van Emmon, 90 w. 4th,   *Cincin.*
Barnes G., 116 Vine
Bonsall G., 118 w. 6th
Crane & Handy, 152 Walnut
Darling E. G., 120 w. 6th
Duncan W. C., 156 do
Gray S. C., 79 w. 4th
Hamlen S. L., 3 do
Hunter Wm., 296 Vine
Haremberg C., Linn bet. Cath. & Clark
Hewitt H. C., 63 Plum
Knowlton P., 60 w. 4th
Leslie —, n. w. cor. Walnut & 7th
Lane Chas. A., 272 Vine
Leslie James, 181 Walnut
Ludlow W. B., 243 Elm
Meredith J., 68 w. 6th
Medary G. W., 158 do
Owen J., 36   do
Rogers M., 4th e. of Main
Richards H. C. J., 58 w. 6th
Richardson J., W. Row bet. Mason & Green
Sexton C., 284 Walnut
Taylor J. & J., 59 w. 4th
Wickersham L., 317 w. 8th
Wardel S. & Co., 256 Walnut
Wickersham O. J., 342 w. 5th
Wheeler B. D., 152 w. 6th
Carnahan G. A   *Mount Healthy.*
Scott W. A.   *Harrison.*

Hardin County.

Atkinson J. E.   *Kenton.*

Harrison County.

Moffitt John   *Cadis.*
Orellen J. C.
Hurford Joseph   *Short Creek.*

Highland County.

Compton S. F.   *Hillsboro'.*
Hunt N.

Hocking County.

Rose B. A.   *Logan.*

Huron County.

Giddings S. B.   *Bellevue.*

Fray L. W.   *Bellevue.*
Berry S. H.   *Norwalk.*

Jefferson County.

Sample A. W.   *Steubenville.*
Morrison H.
Morrison J. B.   *East Springfield.*
McKinley J.

Knox County.

Kelsey C. M.   *Mount Vernon.*
Reeves A. J.
Thompson Hugh   *Fredericktown.*

Lake County.

Parmely J.   *North Perry.*
Doolittle J.   *Painesville.*
Moore J. G.
Huntington S. P.
Smith E. E.

Lawrence County.

Sloan E. C.   *Ironton.*

Licking County.

Harrington S. P.   *Newark.*

Logan County.

Harris D. W.   *West Liberty.*
Penock W. C.   *Bellefontaine.*
Aylworth B. H.

Lorain County.

Knowlton Cyrus B   *Grafton.*
Culver A.   *Copopa.*
Ingersoll Wm. B   *Elyria.*
White D. C.

Lucas County.

Estile J.   *Toledo.*

Mahoning County.

Thomas H.   *East Lewistown.*

Medina County.

Whitmore J.   *Medina.*
Cameron J.
Shaffer & Foss

Meigs County.

Maddy C. N.   *Pomeroy.*

Miami County.

Hall W. P.   *Piqua.*
Lee H. A.
Berger ——
Brooks R.
Hall Dr.   *Troy.*

Montgomery County.

Sheets Andrew   *Union.*
Walters David   *Centre.*
Bradley ——, Main   *Dayton.*
Conway E., Ludlow
Pease W. A., Main
Talbert & Willard, Main

Gauckle G. W.   *Germantown.*
Gillespie P. P.   *Johnsville.*

Morgan County.

Robertson Chas.   *McConnelsville.*
Barker Wm. H.
Coulson E. G.   *Pennsville.*

Muskingum County.

Granger O. S.   *Norwich.*
Young & Hobbs   *Zanesville.*

Morrow County.

Swingley George P.   *Chesterville.*

Pickaway County.

Clark E. C.   *Circleville.*

Pike County.

Hempstead H. Jr.   *Piketon.*

Portage County.

Spelman B. L.   *Ravenna.*
Harris A. A.
Willis J. G.   *Streetsboro'.*

Preble County.

McManus John G.   *Eaton.*

Richland County.

DeCamp Moses   *Mansfield.*
Whitcomb N. D.   *Bellville.*

Ross County.

Dunlap J. L.   *Chillicothe.*

Sandusky County.

Parker L. B.   *Fremont.*

Scioto County.

Gibbs B.   *Portsmouth.*
Spry J. W.
Work B.

Seneca County.

Atwood John   *Republic.*
Show G. H.
Beilharz C. C.   *Tiffin.*

Starke County.

Beatty G. S.   *Canton.*
McAbee J. N.
Reynett Henry   *New Berlin.*
Ohldester E.   *Massillon.*
Jeffries D. W.

Summit County.

Carter J. E.   *Akron.*
Wells A.

Trumbull County.

Hollaway H. W.   *Warren.*
Palmer C.
Bourgh J. C.
Woodin D.
Morse D.   *Greensburgh.*

Tuscarawas County.

Hewitt J. W.,   *New Philadelphia.*
Janes W. W.

Union County.

Kezartee Ira   *Marysville.*

Warren County.

Vandyke O. W.   *Mason.*
Robb J. R.   *Waynesville.*
Nott H. K.   *Morrow.*
Roach John T.   *Rochester.*

Washington County.

Tenney J. A.   *Marietta.*
Burger E. G.

Wyandot County.

Wersy Darius   *Upper Sandusky.*

Dentists' Foil, and Gold Leaf Manufacturers.

Hamilton County.

Leslie Jas., 181 Walnut   *Cincinnati.*
Neele Wm., Walnut bet. 3d and 4th

Distillers and Manufacturers of Liquors.

Auglaize County.

Vocke John H.   *Minster.*

Brown County.

Thomas John   *Higginsport.*

Butler County.

Marshall Wm. H.   *Dertown.*
Callender Wm. A.   *Hamilton.*

Clark County.

Spence J.   *Springfield.*
Staley Elias   *New Carlisle.*
Voorhis Daniel P.

Clermont County.

Beck B. G.   *New Richmond.*
Gibson David
Roberts & Cheeseman   *Neville.*
Buckingham M.   *Miamisville.*
Kugler John   *Milford.*
Perin Samuel.   *Perin's Mills.*

Coshocton County.

Young Barnhard   *Walhonding.*
Love Thos. & Co.   *Coshocton.*

Delaware County.

Van Brinner Thos.   *Delaware.*

Erie County.

Jenkins & Sanford   *Milan.*

Franklin County.

Howlet P. L.   *Canal Winchester.*

Greene County.

Morris V. L. & Co.   *Spring Valley.*

Hamilton County.

Lowell, Fletcher & Co., cor. Vine & Front
Pike S. N. & H., 18 & 20 Sycamore *Cincin.*
Boyle S. S., 57 & 59 2d
Oliver D. W., 68 & 70 Water
D'Homergue Jno. & Co., cor. R'ce & W'ter
Jones J. G., 11 Canal
Oberheu E. & F., 112 Court
Krueskamp & Meyer, do above Race
Cloud & Dair   *Harrison.*
Schotts J.   *Miami.*
Dodsworth M.   *Cumminsville.*
Hughes J.   *Dunlap.*
Pinney J.

Hardin County.

Leffort & Pfeuffer   *Kenton.*
Davis A. J.

Huron County.

Perkins E. B.   *Monroeville.*
Zahm Lewis & Co.
Chapman F.
Karkness & Co.   *Bellevue.*
Joslin R. D.   *Norwalk.*

Jefferson County.

Mears Robert   *Steubenville.*

Licking County.

Coming S.   *Newark.*

Miami County.

Smith E. & G.   *Hyattsville.*

Montgomery County.

Harshman and Brothers   *Harshmansville.*
Harris William
Dryden Jos. H.   *Alexandersville.*
Pease Perry
Farquher William   *Little York.*

Muskingum County.

Orane & Jones   *Dresden.*

Pike County.

Esamiti & Davis   *Waverly.*

Preble County.

Smith & Shields   *New Paris.*

Ross County.

Clemson Wm. F. & Co.   *Chillicothe.*

Scioto County.

Miller John   *Lucasville.*

Shelby County.

Maxwell S.   *Sidney.*

Summit County.

Davis J. & Co.   *Cuyahoga Falls*

Warren County.

Watts & Mounts   *Morrow.*
Pence E. H.   *Mt. Holly.*
Pence John W.

Dress & Mantua Makers.

Belmont County.

Dillon Misses.	St. Clairsville.
Hutchinson Mrs. A.	
McShaver Mrs.	
Nagle Mrs.	
Orr Miss E.	

Clark County.

Morgan Miss	Springfield.

Cuyahoga County.

Jones Mrs.	Coe Ridge.

Franklin County.

Barker Miss, 3d	Columbus.
Berry Mrs., High	
Chears Mrs. do	
Corwin Mrs., 3d	
Crowl Mrs., Rich	
Culbertson Mrs., High	
Donnell Mrs. do	
Hopkins Miss M. J., Broad	
Jordon Miss, High	
Leaman H. & B. do	
Watson Mrs., 3d	
Winders Mrs., Town	
Russell Mrs. do	

Greene County.

Dockroy Mrs.	Xenia.
Walsh M. & E. Misses	
Young Mrs.	
Zertman Misses	Jamestown.
Hales Mrs.	
Mead Mrs.	

Hamilton County.

Alcorn Mrs., 383 W. Row	Cincinnati.
Corliss Mrs. L. V., 24 e. 4th	
Deniel Mrs. M. A., 221 Walnut	
Doyle Miss, 149 W. Row	
Dempsey Miss, 182 w. 6th	
Edwards Mrs., 8th bet. Baymiller & Linn	
Fisher Mrs., 32 Jackson	
Fisher Mrs., 229 Race	
Gilden E., 42 e. 6th	
Henry Mrs., 278 W. Row	
Heuver Miss, 473 Race	
Knott Miss A., 107 Court	
Kerr Mrs. M. A., 292 W. Row	
Leary Mrs. J. O., 10 e. 6th	
Levi Miss E., 20 e. 4th	
McKonkey Mrs., John bet. Kemble & Richmond	
McNulty E., 348 W. Row	
Mulliner Miss, 106 w. 5th	
Massey Mrs. E. J., 296 do	
Noon Mrs. E., 241 w. 4th	
Nelson Mrs., 415 Betts	
Shepner Miss, John bet. Kemble & R mond	
Wilson Mrs. Ann, 230 Water	
Wilhelm Mrs., W. Row	
Weighler Mrs., 5th bet. Smith & Park	
Bartlow Mrs.	Cumminsville.
Were Mrs.	

Knox County.

Haiealer Mrs.	Fredericktown.

Pickaway County.

Sweyer Mrs. M.	Circleville.

Lorain County.

Smith Miss M.	Oberlin.

Seneca County

Orwig Miss Rebecca	Tiffin.
Orwig Mrs. Hannah	
Melio Miss Mary	
Thayer Miss E.	
Underhill Mrs. O.	

Summit County.

Brewer Miss Sarah	Copley.

Druggists, Wholesale and Retail.

Adams County.

Frow John	Scott.
Hood John P.	West Union.

Allen County.

Kincaid Rob't & Wm.	Lima.
Sanford Samuel	

Ashland County.

Millington Wm.	Ashland.
Sampsel N. S.	
Anderson A. R.	Loudonsville.
Griffith J. W. & Co.	Perrysville.

Ashtabula County.

Spring R.	Geneva.
Gibbs E. L.	Windsor.
Allen Wm. R.	Jefferson.
Willard, Wells & Co.	Ashtabula.
Ely A. L.	Lindenville.
Fenton S. P.	Conneaut.
Webster Jas. L.	

Athens County.

Osmer Abraham	Canaanville.
Johnson & Pickering	Athens.
Perkins John	

Auglaize County.

Young T. J.	Wapakoneta.
Stump & Pelham	
McLain J.	St. Mary's.
Kishler J. W.	

Belmont County.

Schooley & McGrew	Martin's Ferry.
Folger Wm. H	Barnesville.
Mott H. H.	
Odell H. F.	
Bracken John	Flushing.
Alexander Humphrey	Saint Clairsville.
Collins James W.	

Brown County.

Holden & Delleway	*Higginsport.*
Hunter & Maddox	*Ripley.*
Granthon & Fulton	
Walker T. H.	*Georgetown.*
Heterick J. W.	
Ellis S.	*Aberdeen.*

Butler County.

Garver & Wiggs	*Oxford.*
Fithian & Rea	
Porter & Barnett	
Morrison E.	*Hamilton.*
Dobbs H.	
Howells H. G.	
Jacobs & Brown	
Kennedy & McElevee	*Rossville.*
Smith P. G.	
Hyndman & Peck	*Middletown.*
Clark J. Q.	
Kimball Edward	*Monroe.*

Carroll County.

Clark Emmor	*Norristown.*
Boegel C. A.	*Carrollton.*
Stephenson Benjamin	

Champaign County.

Ball T. L. & Brother	*Mechanicsburg.*
Keyes E.	
Dinkins A. J.	*Christiansburg.*
Huffman & Nelson	*Urbana.*
Mosgrove & Moore	

Clark County.

Ludlow J.	*Springfield.*
Park Wm.	
Brown S. & Co.	
Kindelberger & Schindler	
Conway S. & Son	*Catawba.*
Clark & Conwell	*South Charleston.*
Hubbard Lucien	*New Carlisle.*

Clermont County.

Beakert H. & S.	*New Richmond.*
Stinchfield D. L.	
Gilmore Hugh	
Walker A. S.	*Williamsburg.*
Hines A.N.	*Felicity.*
Frizell & Molen	
Fee W. W.	*Bethel.*
Penn J. S.	*Batavia.*
Henry William	*Miamisville.*
Johnson & Moore	*Moscow.*

Clinton County.

Hadley W. O. & E.	*Clarksville.*
Carpenter J.	*Wilmington.*
Morry & Ellis	
Hall & Bundle	

Columbiana County.

Baker George	*Wellsville.*
Walter N. U. & Co.	
Gragg & Nace	*New Lisbon.*
Scott R. & Co	

Chamberlain R.	*East Palestine.*
Dennis Robert	*New Garden.*
Chepman & Wright	*Salem.*
Williams E. W.	
Ogden B.	*East Liberty.*
Estle John A.	*Columbiana.*
Keener T.	*Unity.*

Coshocton County.

Irwin, Simmons & Co.	*West Bedford.*
Elliott J. S. & W.	*Keene.*
Canwell G. E.	*Coshocton.*
Hackeson R. L.	

Crawford County.

Hare H. R.	*Bucyrus.*
Johnston & Jones	

Cuyahoga County.

Benton Horace, cor. Detroit and Pearl	*Cleveland.*
Cary H. G. O., cor. Merwin & Canal Basin	
Churchill F. E , cor. Euclid & Ontario	
Fisk William, 11 Superior	
Gaylord & Co., 30 do	
Hayward, Woods & Co., Superior	
Huntington O. E. 99 do	
Hensch & Raebel, 31 Ontario	
Keeler J. C., 54 Seneca	
Kingsley E., 37 Ontario	
Lyon W. & Co., 73 Superior	
MacKenzie C. S., 34 do	
Palmer & Sackrider 73 do	
Parsons H., 2 Columbus Block	*Ohio City.*
Wenham A. J., 9 Merwin	
Zwinger A , 55 Ontario	
Collins & Curtiss,	*Chagrin Falls.*
Cutler S. D.	
Waldron William	
Tarbell L.	*Bedford.*
Adams L. L.	*Collamer.*

Darke County.

Millett J.	*Rhica.*
Schmidt Wm.	*Greenville.*
Knox Robert	

Defiance County.

Allen O. H.	*Defiance.*
Caston & Paige	

Delaware County.

Dickinson B. & Co.	*Delaware.*
Hendrew & Westfield	
Lamb & Wetmore.	

Erie County.

Lewis B. B.	*Huron.*
Johnson L. B.	
Elliott V. F.	*Vermillion.*
Fuller T. S.	*Birmingham.*
Wheeden & Rhodes	*Sandusky City.*
Lange F. R.	
Belden A. R.	
Morton George R.	

Fairfield County.

Kauffman Geo. & Co.   *Lancaster.*
Krider M. Z.
Slocum E.
Dyson Jos.   *Sugar Grove.*
Walker R. B.   *West Rushville.*

Fayette County.

Stewart H. C.   *Bloomingburg.*
Brown & Worley   *Washington.*
Allen O. A.

Franklin County.

Cook J. & R. T.   *Columbus.*
Denig G. & Sons, cor. High and Rich
Denig R. M., Town
Fahrenholtz Wm., cor. High and Rich
Little R. P.   do
Samuel S. E. & Co.,   do
Roberts G. & Co.,
Swain John   *Dublin.*
Snow G. R.   *Worthington.*

Fulton County.

Trobridge J. C.   *Delta.*

Gallia County.

Sisson N. B.   *Pine Grove.*
Hannan Wm. F.   *Swan Creek.*
Shallcross Joseph
Sams J. & P. A.   *Gallipolis.*
Maguet & Bailey

Geauga County.

Cook B. & A.   *Chardon.*
Ayres & Parsons

Greene County.

Dille, Willis & Co.   *Cedarville.*
Bratton W. S.
McGuire & Crighton   *Xenia.*
Patton & Vigus
Grimes W. H.   *Yellow Springs.*
Torrence J. M.   *Jamestown.*

Guernsey County.

Cooper H. T.   *Cumberland.*
Draper Chas.
Foreman & McConnell   *Washington.*
Rice & Chanes
Warfield J. W.   *Fairview.*
Ogier & Clark   *Cambridge.*
Green & Nyce
McDonald —

Hamilton County.

Abbott & Ferris, cor. 7th & Mound streets
          Cincinnati.
Arons W. C. & Co., n. e. cor. 8th & Vine
Armstrong L. L., s. w. cor. 7th & Broad-
          [way
Allen & Co., cor. Main & 5th
Allen Geo. M., cor. Main & 6th
Burdsal & Bro., n. w. cor. Main & Front
Burdsal Saml., Main opp. Court House
Barkhaus —, n. w. cor. Main & 7th
Burdsal C. S. & Co., 298 Main

Bishoprick Henry, n. w. cor. Wal. & 5th
          Cincinnati.
Blake M., 204 5th
Bockius J. M., n. e. cor. 6th & Mound
Brown —, cor. Catherine & Fulton
Brand F., s. w. cor. Race & 15th
Bottger Wm., cor. Vine & Findley
Cox John S., Race near 12th
Chapman Wm. B., s. w. cor. 6th & Vine
Crichton D., s. e. cor. 5th & Broadway
Doughty & Dixon, n. e. cor. Main & 5th
Darling J., cor. 5th & Mill
Duncan A. P., s. w. cor. 8th & John
Davidson J. S, cor. Linn & 7th
Eberling D., 405 Vine
Eckstein Fred., cor. Main & 4th
Emerson E. S., s. e. cor. Broadway & Low.
          [Market
Fletcher Robert, n. e. cor. Syc. & Lower
          [Market
Fifield David E., s. e. cor. 12th & Elm
Forshas S. W., 5th bet. John & Smith
Fritsch Chas., 581 Western Row
Fibich S., Linn bet. Betts & Lawrence
Gordon & Co., cor. 8th & Western Row
Griffith S. A. & Co., 51 Broadway
Grasselli E., 436 e. Front
Greene Caleb B., 19 Lower Market
Howells, Patton & Co., 16 & 18 Main
Holroyd H., cor. Main & 9th
Hiller G. A., 76 Broadway
Harrison W. H. & Co., 23 4th
Hill F. D., s. e. cor. Race & 5th
Huebner A., cor. Vine & Canal
Halenbeck H. G., n. w. cor. Clinton & Cut.
Heckler John Y., 223 Front
Helman & Williams, n. e. cor. 6th & West.
          [Row
Johnston J. R., s. e. cor. Walnut & 8th
Junghams Chas., n. w. cor. 3d & Mill
Karmann W., cor. Smith & 5th
Kohn A., cor. Main & Western Row
Kurzbach F., Vine bet. 14th & 15th
Kent A., cor. Elm & 6th
Koerbitz F., cor Vine & Greene
Kirk & Briggs, 200 Walnut
Keeshan John, n. w. cor. Walnut & 6th
Kost J. & Co., 45 e. 4th
Kinsey O., 232 6th
Light Geo. S., cor. Sycamore & 2d.
Langebeck —, Main bet. 12th & 13th
Merrill W. S., n. w. cor. Plum & Court
Muller G., cor. Spring & Abigail
Merrill A. S., cor. Western Row & 6th
Massard & Brother, s. w. cor. Court & Vine
Merrill Wm. S. & Co., 94 Pearl
Meers R. L., cor. 8th & Dublin
Marsh T., s. e. cor. W. Row & 6th
McCready R., s. w. cor. Walnut & Front
Moody John B., 282 Main
Parvin D. A., junction of 2d e. of Front
Parr J. C., 554 5th
Reskirt J. & C., 21 Pearl
Rehfuss L. & Kolb, cor. Vine & 5th
Rahn Dr., e. Front
Renz Theodore, 319 6th
Ronayne Justin, cor. W. Row & Chesnut

Reinlein P. A., cor. 8th & Freeman streets
Cincinnati.
Spach G., cor. Vine & 14th
Schenck J., cor. John & Clark
Smith C. A. & Co., n. w. cor. Vine & 4th
Scoville A. L. & Co., 60 w. 3d
Scott John, n. w. cor. Broadway & 7th
Smidt Chas., cor. Main & Liberty
Snedewend & Bunce, Miami Canal
Salter T., Broadway bet. 2d & Congress
Turner Saml., cor. Main & Orchard
Tower E. C., Walnut near Front
Tafel Albert, cor. Walnut & Court
Vansant R. R., cor. Elm & Front
Wilson J., 337 Main
Whittemore J. R., 86 Broadway
Wagner A., cor. Main & Woodward
Young W. McK., s. w. cor. Race & Front
Zeller Abia, n. e. cor. Main & Columbia
Fuller E. E. *Harrison.*
Coffin Goldsmith *Sharonville.*
Hair, B. W.
Peck J. P. P.
Parvin S. J. *Reading.*
Gilbert Henry *Lockland.*
Carnell H. D. *Cheviot.*
Watkins John L. *Cleves.*

Hancock County.

Goucher H. B. & Co. *Van Buren.*
Dixon David *Finley.*
Langworthy Albert

Hardin County.

Ashton E. & C. *Kenton.*
Moore & Goodin
Stanley A. F. *Sylvia.*

Harrison County.

Beall John *Cadiz.*
McBean & Knox

Highland County.

Tarrie John *Lynchburg.*
Robison & Norten *Greenfield.*
Smith & Brown *Hillsboro'.*
Weodrow Joshua
Perrin Lyman

Hocking County.

Bishop G. & Son *Logan.*
Collius Enoch
Culver R.
Hilt Daniel R. *Ewing.*

Holmes County.

Snediker J. H. *Nashville.*
Boyson A. *Winesburg.*
Saunders H. G. *Millersburg.*

Huron County.

Cook T. M. *Monroeville.*
White H. E. *Clarksfield.*
Dimich W. B. *Bellevue.*
Denny John F. *Norwalk.*
Wooster N. & Sons

Jackson County.

Miller J. H. C. *Jackson.*
Clewers R. G.

Jefferson County.

Sinclair J. *Steubenville.*
Morrison R. D.
Hening & Melvin
Marsh & McCutcheon
Fancutt Henry B. *Mt. Pleasant.*

Knox County.

Abernethy M. & Co. *Mt. Vernon.*
Lippitt B. B.
Russell W. B. & Co.
Tuttle S. S. *Fredericktown.*
Conway W. *Mt. Liberty.*

Lake County.

Cook & Co. *Madison.*
Nichol John *Kirtland.*
Moody S. *Painesville.*
Kelley S. H.

Lawrence County.

Moxley & Barbour *Ironton.*
Shaw Joseph P.

Licking County.

Woolf Palmer & Co. *Linnville.*
Basley & Boyd *Utica.*
Prichard A. P. *Granville.*
Wilson J. N. *Newark.*
Paige & Ingram
O'Conner D. N. *Homer.*
Stinson B. C. *Alexandria.*
Follett Alfred *Johnstown.*
Belt & Richardson *Kirkersville.*

Logan County.

Fuller S. W. *West Liberty.*
Garwood D. H.
McCandless & Magruder *Bellefontaine.*
Hard & Chubb
Hartley & Son
Johnson J.
Moore L. G.
Scarff J. C.

Lorain County.

Brooks Levin *Grafton.*
Grout Wm. *North Camden.*
Roberts & Henry *Oberlin.*
Wooster Wm. F. *Elyria.*
Griswold & Mauville
De Witt R. C.

Lucas County.

Burritt & Hooker *Maumee City.*
Carroll Jay *Lyons.*
Ashley Jas. M. & Co. *Toledo.*
Daniels Thomas
Linsley S. & Co.
Winans C. E.

Madison County.

Jones & Brother *London.*
Smith & Jones
Stutson J. *West Jefferson.*

Mahoning County.

Prentice W. M.	*Canfield.*
Holcomb & Tomson	
Sexton J. K.	*Youngstown.*
Manning John	
Parker Rufus	*Poland.*

Marion County.

Johnson & Reed	*Marion.*
Gailey J. D. & Co.	

Medina County.

Carpenter J. H.	*Litchfield.*
Elder R. W.	
Hoag M.	*Lodi.*
Curtiss L. A. & G. R.	*Medina.*
Cameron J.	

Meigs County.

Hayman S. H.	*Apple Grove.*
Davis J.	*Salisbury.*
Lasher Wm. V.	
Reed D. & Bro.	*Pomeroy.*

Mercer County.

Lain John M.	*St. Mary's.*
Hetchler K.	
Frits Chas.	
Williamson E. T.	*Celina.*
Campbell J. M. & Co.	*Fort Recovery.*

Miami County.

Latchford Thos.	*Covington.*
Ashton W. B.	*Piqua.*
Abernathy H.	
Staritt J.	
Youart Jas.	*Troy.*
Holden E.	
Brooks J. M.	
Darst H. H.	*Casstown.*
Booher & Hoagland	*Hyattsville.*

Montgomery County.

Butler Calvin	*Centre.*
Coblentz Isaac, Main	*Dayton.*
Comstock H. W., Fifth	
Dietrick & Olden, Main	
Glover N. A., Third	
Keorner C., Second	
Laughstedt H., Third	
Newal A. do	
Walters J. A. do	
Wenschoff W. do	
Wilkes Thos., Main	
Eichelberger J. T.	*Miamisburgh.*
Unger & Wilson	*Germantown.*
Zellerd Wm. & Co.	

Morgan County.

Huestis Isaac	*Chester Hill.*
Cornelius James	*Malta.*
Kirk A.	*Meigs Creek.*
Green Israel	*McConnelsville.*
Barker & McKue	

Morrow County.

Angell & Miller	*Cardington.*
Wooster & Park	

Welland J.	*Mt. Gilead.*
Burges O.	
Brown Wm. S.	*Chesterville.*

Muskingum County.

Griffee Richard.	*Frazeysburg.*
Adams Saml.	*Dresden.*
Cary H. G. O.	
Dillon E.	*Putnam.*
Benjamin D.	*Hopewell.*
Blocksom Geo. W.	*Zanesville.*
Watkins B. T.	
Graham W. A.	
Eastman & Bigelow	

Noble County.

Capell James F.	*Sarahsville.*

Paulding County.

Mason John	*Junction.*

Perry County.

Skinner & Foncannon	*New Lexington.*
Pierce C. A.	
Magruder & Johnson	*Somerset.*
Moeller O. H. & Co.	

Pickaway County.

Griswold & Ballard	*Circleville.*
Olds Joseph H.	
Troup and Fickard	
Davisson N. A.	*Tarlton.*
King Henry	

Pike County.

Allen E. R.	*Piketon.*

Portage County.

Hatch O.	*Ravenna.*
Swift J.	
Cone J. W. & Co.	*Franklin.*
Earle Thos.	
Coles Isaac	*Palmyra.*
Sprague J.	*Nelson.*

Preble County.

Coblentz J. P.	*Lewisburg.*
Bohn John H.	*Camden.*
Minshall E. & Son	*Eaton.*
Brookins J. P. & Co.	
Gilmore W. H.	*Fairhaven.*
Boyd E.	*West Florence.*
Showalter J.	*New Paris.*

Putnam County.

Hipkins J. H. D.	*Gilboa.*

Richland County.

McMillen J. F. & Co.	*Shelby.*
Moore Geo. W. & Co.	
Dell John	*Mansfield*
Stocking Z. S.	
Sturges & Bigelow	
Weagly A. R.	
Eells S. W.	*Belleville.*
Lee J. C.	
Wooster Henry W.	*Plymouth.*

Ross County.

Robins Chas.	*Bainbridge.*
King F. G.	
Fulton R. & Co.	*Frankfort.*
Guiher A.	
Lemsing & Safford	*Chillicothe.*
Dennis Dr.	
McKee D.	
Tritshler F.	
Denig G. W.	

Sandusky County.

Janjer D. F.	*Woodville.*
Buckland S. & Co.	*Fremont.*
Wooster John	

Scioto County.

Jones H. G. & A. B.	*Portsmouth.*
McVey Jas. L. & Co.	
Shackleford & Orichton	
Tyrrell & Wood	*Iron Furnaces.*
Vangters T. G.	*Friendship.*
Moseley T. N.	*Wheelersburg.*

Seneca County.

Freeman Benj. N.	*Attica.*
Jaeck F.	*Tiffin.*
St. John J. L. & Co.	
Sprague G.	
Hamilton William L.	*Republic.*

Shelby County.

Frazer J. F.	*Sidney.*
Haggott & Gamble	
Thompson H.	

Starke County.

Leeper J. L.	*Navarre.*
Couch John R.	*Waynesburg.*
Tritt H. & Co.	*Minerva.*
McCall R. H.	*Canton.*
Mealey S. A.	
Bueher Wm.	*Massillon.*
Watson J. & Co.	
Hall William	*Canal Fulton.*

Summit County.

Heath F. S. & Co.	*Cuyahoga Falls.*
Sill E. J. & Co.	
Graham J. L.	*Hudson.*
Commins J. D.	*Akron.*
Beebe & Elkins	
Ives L. J.	
Weimer & Steinbecher	
Clark S. S.	*Richfield.*
Munson & Hall	
Wright Amos	*Tallmadge.*

Trumbull County.

Kibbee C. W.	*Bristolville.*
Powers J. A.	*Mecca.*
Campbell J.	*Newton Falls.*
Moore M. M.	*Vienna.*
Moore A.	

Tuscarawas County.

Reichenbach & Co.	*Port Washington.*
Williams W. H.	*Uhrichsville.*
Baer John	*Canal Dover.*
Reichenbach Theo.	
Hazlett W. L.	*New Philadelphia.*
Himes P. W.	
Smith J. J.	

Union County.

Cassil & Barbour	*Marysville.*
Johnson John	

Van Wert County.

Hines P. J.	*Van Wert.*
Talbott Smith	*Delphos.*

Vinton County.

Will J. K.	*McArthur.*
Reynolds H. & Co	

Warren County.

Wright Wm.	*Franklin.*
Evans O., Jr.	
Trabern Asa	*Waynesville.*
Cadwallader J. T.	
Foster C. A.	*Morrow.*
Anderson & Glenny	*Lebanon.*
Klingling & Co.	
Wright E. B.	
Roach Geo.	*Harveysburg.*
Scroggs John W.	

Washington County.

Cotton & Buell	*Marietta.*
Perkins C. B.	
Chamberlin L.	*Harmar.*
Crandall J. T.	*Newport.*
Lyons John & Co.	*Beverly.*
Olines Wm.	

Wayne County.

Cahill R. & E. W.	*Dalton.*
Hart George	*Reedsburg.*
Roberts E. J.	
Ott John & G.	*Marshallville.*
Baumgardner J. H. & Co.	*Wooster.*
Zimmerman J. & Co.	
Knepper Samuel	
Spink & Weed	

Williams County.

Kent Thos.	*Bryan.*
Thorne Jas.	*West Unity.*

Wood County.

Peck & Robinson	*Perrysburg.*
Smith Henry	

Wyandot County.

Sigler John	*Upper Sandusky.*
Wilcox & Sweatland	*Carey.*
Chesney Wm. M. & J. M.	*Marseilles.*

Dry Goods—Importers.

Hamilton County.

Stedman, Maynard & Co., 17 Pearl Street *Cincinnati.*
Carney, Swift & Co., 25 Pearl Street
White Peter A. & Co., 61 do   do
Wentworth & Brothers, s. e. cor. Main and Fourth
Acton & Woodnutt, 69 Pearl
Heidelbach, Seasongood & Co., s. e. cor. 3d and Main

Dry Goods—Wholesale Dealers.

Hamilton County.

Blackley & Simpson, 11 Pearl st.   *Cincin.*
Boylan & Co., 190 Main
Cooper Geo., 225   do
Day & Matlock, 57 Pearl
Ellis John W. & Co., 23 do
Epply Adam, 29 Lower Market
Gallagher & Ernst, 128 Main
Jones, Brothers & Co., 19 Pearl
Jenkens Geo. S. & Co., s. e. cor. Pearl and [Vine
King, Corwin & Co., 8 & 10 Pearl
Kuhu, Rindskopf & Co., n. e. cor. Walnut [and Pearl
Ritchie C. & J., 69 & 71 Lower Market
Stedman, Maynard & Co., 17 Pearl
Squire E. S., 39 and 41 Lower Market
Sachs & Brothers, s. w. cor. Syc. & Lower [Market
Simon B. & M. & Co., n. e. cor. Main and [Lower Market
Slevin J. & J., 146 Main
Sharp Thos. & Co., 10 Lower Market
Trounstine A. & J. & Co., 58 Pearl
Taylor, French & Wynne, 9   do
Watts & Colburn, 63   do
Wentworth & Bros., s. e. cor. Main & 4th
Wynne, Haines & Co., 30 Pearl

Dry Goods—Wholesale & Retail Dealers.

Cuyahoga County.

Alcott & Horton, 57 Superior street *Cleveland.*
Beebe A. M., 37 Bank
Best & Freeman, 93 Superior
Beckwith T. S. & Co., 65 do
Brooke & Whitney, 41 Bank
Branch & Moulton, 69 Superior
Cameron Alexander, 128 do
Outter & Taylor, 55   do
Dudley Brothers, 82   do
Emery & Co., 43 Bank
Freedman S. & Brothers 160 Superior
French & Co., 91   do
Greene S. C., 67   do
Hilliard, Hays & Co., 29 and 34 Water
Hyman S., 172 Superior
Hoffman & Kupfer, 18 Ontario

Harney T., 164 Superior street *Cleveland.*
Ivison Edward, 72 do
Judd & Coffin, 75 do
Lambert F. J. & Co., 76 Public Square
North, French & Sterling, cor. Bank and [Centre
Noyes A. B., 97 Superior
Perry A. M., & Co., 140 do and 12 Seneca
Quinn & Robbins, 71   do
Raymond S. & Co., 63   do
Rouse, Post & Co., 61   do
Sexton C. C., 4 Columbus Block
Spangler B. L., 47 Superior
Stern M. & Co., 89   do
Warren W., 45   do
Rettberg, Doelts & Hausman, 166 do
Lewis C. & Son, 34 Detroit   *Ohio City.*
Tyler & Whitney 28 do

Franklin County.

Bain P.   *Columbus.*
Brown A. C.
Fay, Cyrus & Son, High
Coit H. & D. S.,   do
Gooding M., 55   do
Headley, Taylor & Co., do
Kelton, Bancroft & Co., do
McDonald J. R. & Co., Town
McCoy W. A. & J. C. & Co., High
Osborn & Stewart, 100   do
Richards Wm. & Co.,   do
Stanton S. B.,   do
Stone A. P. & Co.,   do
Stone D. & Co., 143   do
Stone John & Co.,   do
Sessions & Harris,   do
Taft D. H.,   do
Wetmore P. M.,   do

Hamilton County.

Alexander James, 12 5th street,   *Cincin.*
Cameron & Co., 68 do
Crawford John, 82 do
Heidelbach, Seasongood & Co., s. e. cor. [Main & 3d
Hyman, Moses & Son, 50 5th
Jenkins Geo. S. & Co., s. e. cor. Pearl and [Vine
Lee Wm. & Co., 76 w. 4th
LeBoutillier J. & Brothers, 11 e. do
Nevins J. B. & Co., cor. W. Row & 7th
Shillito John & Co., 12 e. 4th
Schwartze & Agin, 8 5th
Stix Louis & Co., 78 do
Trum & Meyer, s. cor. Vine & Court
Walker J. H. & Co., 20 5th
White Geo., 56 & 58   do
Wright & Co, n. w. cor. Broadway & Low. [Market

Jefferson County.

Spear Wm.   *Steubenville.*
Coehoan John & Brother
Garrett H. G.

Muskingum County.

Haslett Theodore   *Zanesville.*
Blair, Thompson & Co.

Black John S.   *Zanesville.* | Assur Alex., 129 w. 5th   *Cincinnati.*
Wilcox J. | Alms A., 571 Vine
Irwin & Johnson | Blake & Swing, 66 5th
Grigbys & Johnson | Bush M., 400 Broadway
Black Peter | Brey L., 259 W. Row
| Bakes S., cor Richmond & Fulton

Dry Goods—Retail Dealers.
Brockington J. C., 272 w. 5th
Brey L., 188 w.   do

Belmont County.
Bachman M. E., 148   do
Bonner & Co., 154   do
Adams D. S.   *St. Clairsville.* | Betty & Williamson, 98 do
Campbell Wm. S. | Bogen Mary, 214 w. 6th
Carothers E. R. & Co. | Busken J. H., 234 w. 6th
Grove Jacob E. | Cones W., 261 6th
Grove John A. | Crigler M. F., 15 Lower Market
Kline Samuel | Cobb Z. B., cor. Stone & 5th
Patton John | Cocherine G., 361 W. Row
Troll Conrad | Castill T., 30 5th
| Conahan Miss C., 194 w. 5th

Butler County.
Caldow William, 5th bet. Vine & Race
Colirs H. F., 501 Vine
Howell & Dye   *Hamilton.* | Chesseldine Chas.. cor W. Row & 6th
Watkins J. | Duhme H. H., 74 5th
Springer J. | Deppes J. H., 101 Woodward
Miller & Kleine | Downard M. A., 150 4th
Trabor Joseph   *Rossville.* | Dopke J., 498 e. Front
Curtis N. G. | Dalton J., 212 5th
Trabor W. H. & J. R. | Doan J. S., 442 5th
Bridenback A. & A. | Evans C., 571 W. Row
Rosman J. & N. | Eveslage J., 470 Main
Leibee Jacob   *Middletown.* | Fihe John, 585 Race
Oglesby & Barnity | Fust S., 104 5th
Golden S. & Co. | Fairchild Wmilliam, south west cor. 5th
Conklin W. D. | & Park   u
| Forbes Josiah, 551 W. Row

Clark County.
Gibbes H., 205 Plum
Hedrick J.   *Springfield.* | Greason S. E., 33 Race
Anderson Wm. | Guilford J., 363 6th
Murray Peter | Hill & Johnson, 70 Pearl
Baldwin & Bacon | Heffman W. G., 434 Main
Hall Henry R. | Henson & Brother, 475 do
Snyder H. G. & S. P. | Haap Adam, W. Row bet. Main & Piatt
McCreight J. C. | Heid K. L., 150 w. 5th
Foos John | Hand Ellis, 268 w. 6th
Harbaugh G. H.   *t* | Haire, Nugent & Co., 269 W. Row
Norton & Shepherd | Hallenberger C. H., 143 Everett
Swoope & Crosstand | Hurley C., 363 W. Row.
| Holby J., 369   do

Columbiana County.
James E., 206 w. 5th
Jackson R., 385 W. Row
Hull Levi   *Wellsville.* | Kemball M. S., 107 w. 5th
McIntosh & Smith | Kruse J. F., 506 Walnut
Stewart & Hibbets | Krumburg T. H. & Vogt, 489 Main
Wells A. | Krumburg M., 485   do
Williams J. & W.   *East Fairfield.* | Kaumann H. W., 499   do
Young Saml. & W. L. | Lenz Michael, 178 w. 5th
| Luthenkoff J. O., 248 w. 6th

Greene County.
McComas R. P., 575 W. Row
Morrison Wm., 229   do
Allison & Townsley   *Xenia.* | Mooning E., 499 Elm
Gordon & Miller | Mental V., 295 W. Row
Hivling & Co. | Mills & Wright, 397 W. Row
Hivling & Williamson | Menke Gerhard, 213 Front
Jones M. Luther | Messeck L., 186 W. 5th
Merrick C. L. & Co. | Moorman B. H. & Co., 480 Main
Millan D. & E. | Moore Miss J., 252 w. 5th

Hamilton County.
Assman H. F., W. Row Bet. Richmond | Moore Miss J., 252 w. 5th
  & Kemble   *Cincinnati.* | Oespers P., 36 Hamilton Road

Oppenheimer Jones & Co., 257 W. Row
O'Conner & Brother, 22 w. 5th *Cincinnati.*
Rideman J., 475 Vine
Rinckoff A. A., 517 Race
Reeves & Speers, 162 w. 5th
Regan & Sampson, 150 5th
Rosenstiel S., 108 5th
Rambo Francis, 41 Race
Scott F., 347 W. Row
Sullivan W., 257 Main
Stewart A., 230 6th
Sudler J. F., 222 w. 6th
Shutteres M., 524 Race
Shrover H. P., 110 13th
Smith H. & A., 90 w. 5th
Smith & Co., 216 & 218 w. 5th
Swarts Isaac, 505 Vine
Streife T., 95 Hamilton Road
Ulrich A. C., 339 W. Row
Wright & Co., n. w. cor. Br'dway & Lower
    Market
Wood Geo. M., n. e. cor. Vine & 5th
West J. G., 458 Walnut
Weisenecker A., 388 Vine
Wesseman R. H., 577 Main
Wassenick W., 675 Vine
Windeller J. J., 513   do
Wright & Co., 90 Broadway
Wright W. H., 510 Sycamore
Winters T., cor. Catherine & Linn
Wellman L. B., 118 Clinton
Williams W. G., 248 W. Row
Wentworth R. P., 112 w. 5th
Woods G., 170   do
Woods H., 264   do
Wright W. H. & Brother, s. e. cor Syc. &
    Liberty
Wellman H. B., 132 5th
Wallman & Schmidt, 174 5th
Waldron J. E., 250 w. 6th
Walters & Lane, 262 W. Row
Williams J. 261 Main
Wolf J. F., 68 Hamilton Road
Zullman A. H., 22 13th
Dennis C. H.   *Columbia.*
Kincely A. & D.
Sandman G. & Co.
Allrath C.   *Reading.*
Carr Mrs.   *Lockland.*
Emery Edward   *Dry Ridge.*

Jefferson County.

Patterson J. S.   *Steubenville.*
McMechan John
Kerlin Wm. B.
Allen J.
Parks Jas.
Coehoan John & Brother.
Garrett H. G.
Conn Alex.
Dougherty & Brother
Sterling & Dunlap

Lorain County.

Johnson & Kelley   *Oberlin.*
Kinney & Carpenter
Ryder O. R.

Miami County.

Morrow T. S.   *Piqua.*
Harbaugh W. H.
Scott Wm.
Culbertson R.   *Troy.*
Brandriff R.
Douglass & Brothers

Montgomery County.

Babbitt & Hammond, Main   *Dayton.*
Curtis D. M., Fifth
Gump A., Second
Hatch E. N., Main
Herchelrode & Bunstin, do
John, Vandover & Co., do
Keifer & Conover   do
Perine H. V., Third
Perine J., Second
Perrine & Dart, do
Phillips & Son do
Prugh, Joice & Rike, Third
Schaffer F.   do
Schaefer J., Main
Shoup B. F. & Co., Jefferson
Shuey & Ayers, Main
Vanausdale C.,   do
Whitmore J. W., Third
Winter V., Main

Muskingum County.

Haslett Theodore   *Zanesville.*
Blair, Thompson & Co.
Pelmer Fred.
Dume Chas.
Gattzell N.
Filley M. B.
Black John S.
Wilcox J.
Irwin & Johnson
Northrop F. W.
Moore James
Black Peter
Gingaley & Johnston

Pickaway County.

Weils L. & Co.   *Circleville.*

Richland County.

Townsend A. & Co.   *Mansfield.*

Ross County.

Carlisle A. & H. N.   *Chillicothe.*
Smart R. B. & Co.
Reeves O. T.
Woodron T.
Steele & Wright
Limle E. G.
Adams D. & Co.
Marfield & Luckett
Davis M.
Montgomery D.
Wegerley & Dustman
Rowe James
Stewart Joseph
Spence A.
Douglas Wm. H. & Son
Bennett & Brothers

Miller C. J. & Co.   *Chillicothe.*
Miller Wm. & Co.
Warner A. H. & D.
Carson Wm.
Long R. & Son
Douglas & Shull

Scioto County.

Brodbeck Stephen   *Portsmouth.*
Brunner R.
Elder Wm. & Co.
Hall W. & Son
Jefferson B. S.
Lodwick J. & Sons
Pursell James
Salter Wm., Jr.
Towell J. F. & Co.

Starke County.

Brownwell J. O   *Canton.*
Bucher J. R.
Danner John
Estep J. B.
Farmers' & Mechanics' Store
Hartman J.
Harter & Co.
Hoffman J. & Co.
Hurford H. P. & Bro.
Kimball & Co.
Raynolds J. F. & Co.
Reehman & Co.
Rohrer & Dewalt
Sickafoose G. W.
Wickadall M.
Ryder A.   *Massillon.*
Rawson L. & S.
Lind & Weirick
Sausser & Dangler
Bayliss James
Focke & Brother
Cummins & Co
Reed T. P. & Co.
Humberger A.
Burgesser S.

Trumbull County.

Anderson & Haskill   *Warren.*
Fight J.
Hoyt E. E. & Co.
Iddings & Morgan
Kibbee J. H. & Co.
Moser S. & C.
Parks & Wentz
Smith & McCombs
Stiles & Son

Tuscarawas County.

Adams Ira   *Uhrichsville.*
Miller Hiram
O'Donnell & Forbes
Sterling John
Wolf A. & E.

Dry Goods, Groceries, and Variety Stores.
Adams County.

Brown Wm. B.   *Wheat Ridge.*
Patton George A.

Black David   *Wagoners' Ripple.*
Chaney M.
Drennen Minor
Hempelman Jacob
Huye Jonathan
Penwitte David
Scott John
Zortman Henry
Naylor David   *Mahala.*
Eakins Isaac   *Dunbarton.*
Wittenmyer Isaac
Wood J. N.
Wittenmyer Daniel
McMillan James   *Gustine.*
Fulton David   *Lovett's.*
Yanky A. W.
Greenby W. M.   *Bradysville.*
Pence M.
Ellison A. B. & J.   *Manchester.*
McColm James
Case R. B. & Co.
McCutchen John T.
Stableton Wm.
McCormick G. S.   *Stout's.*
Stout Wm., Jr.
DeBruin H. J.   *Scott.*
De Bruin J. H.
Dixon A. & Son
Bowman, Adams & Co.
Frow John
Chambers P. G. & J.   *Dunkinsville.*
Dunkin J. & H.
Read J. A.
Black D. S.   *West Union.*
Chambers & Co.
Culbertson Samuel
Hood James, Sen.
McCarren Andrew
Rape & Mider
Sparks Salathiel
Wilson Samuel
Downing & Murphy   *Locust Grove.*
George H. & W.
Wilson J. T.   *Tranquillity.*
Young Wm. & J. F.   *Youngsville,*
Young & Tillcott
Pettit George   *Rockville.*
Williamson John
Worthington Henry
Morrison John   *Eckmansville.*
Walker James

Allen County.

Anderson & Jacobs   *Lima.*
Binkley & Grawel
Holmes Branson P.
King J. W.
Saint Levi
Root J. S. & Co.
Taylor & Cowels
Overmyer G. W.   *Deep Cut.*
Webb N. H.
Gutman N. A.   *Fryburg.*
Roth Conrad
Brown Wm. H.   *West Newton.*
Haslett John
Hutchins William   *Middle River.*

Brewer Enoch	*Allentown.*	Palmer W. D.	*Austinburg.*
Morrison Robert	*Hog Creek.*	Bushnell S. S.	*Kelloggville.*
Sager N.	*Herring.*	Bushnell C. L.	
Orope A.	*Westminster.*	Smith Isaac	
Gilbert Hollis	*Cranberry.*	Warren & Cook	
Vance William	*Croghan.*	Farmers' Union Co.,	
Thompson Erastus		Burge Josiah, Ag't.	
		Adams & Tudo	*Windsor.*
Ashland County.		Farmers' Co., Norris G. G., Ag't.	
		Cook P. W. & A. P.	
Porter, Hall & Fox	*Sullivan*	Mann Wm. W.	*East Plymouth.*
Wright J. J.		Price O. H.	*Trumbull.*
Musgrave & Drayton	*Polk.*	Daun S. D.	*Jefferson.*
McHose M. A. & Co.	*Rowsburg.*	McIntyre & Kellogg	
Eshleman & Hamilton		Goodale A. H. & J. A.	
Lee Edward	*Ruggles'.*	Bailey A.	
Parker Wm. W.		Wood T. F.	
Cox T. J. & Co.	*Hayesville.*	Hunter M. A.	
Hayes & Kinninger		Warren A. & Co.	
Scott & Hayes		Allen Wm. R.	
Cook Thos. O.	*Savannah.*	Willard, Wells & Co.	*Ashtabula.*
Cowie & Williamson		Hubbard & Canous	
See H. S. & Co.		Root & Morrison	
Lee Josiah	*Albion.*	Brown Geo.	
Spencer W. & Co.		Hall Stephen	
Finley A.	*McKay.*	Tickner H. & H. L.	*West Williamsfield.*
Freeman A.		Stearns Chas.	*Hart's Grove.*
Bushnell Tully O.	*Ashland.*	Norris R. D.	
Clugston & Burns		Morgan Hiram	
McCombs Judson	,	Bushnell O. L.	*Monroe Centre.*
Miller J. & G.		Morgan H. & Son	*Rome.*
Squires & Porter		Norten R.	*Andover.*
Risser P. & J.		Morley Wm. H. & Son	
Hargrave R. & Son	*Jeromeville.*	Lundy B. W. O.	
Hargrave B. F.		Mead P.	
McMahan R.		Jennings Wm. D.	*Pierpont.*
Wilson John		Wick Calvin O.	*Lindenville.*
Haskell N.	*Loudonville.*	Judson Parmetre & Co.	
McMahan & Yarnell		Secheverell G. H.	*Cork.*
Taylor & Larwill		Martin & Moreley	*Harpersfield.*
Stroug & Krenerick		Cleveland Daniel	
Younker John		Secheverall G. H.	
Coulter T. W	*Petrysville.*	Cleveland J. B.	*Conneaut.*
McNall Wm.		Cleveland Cyrus	
Tyler Major	*Mohecan.*	Gould L.	
Bemenderffer Joseph		Hall Charles	
Finley Abner		Howard Silas	
		Judson & Cheney	
		Lyon Robert	
Ashtabula County.		Osborne Milo	
		Reid John	
Wilcox F. M.	*Richmond Centre.*	Webster D. N.	
Sheldon S. O.		Webster B. G.	
Brower A.		Warren A.	
Barber M.			
Smith F. B.	*Raplenville.*	**Athens County.**	
St. John H. L. & Brother	*New Lyme.*		
Beckwith A. R.		Harper E. D.	*Chauncey.*
Plumb S. & H.	*Lenox.*	Fuller & Walker	
Ray J. M.		Sharp R.	
Bushnell J. L.	*Cherry Valley.*	Pruden B.	
Stephens & Fitch	*Geneva.*	Figley R.	*Woodyards*
Mills E. & Co.		Haning P.	
Morgan & Brothers		Roberts G. W.	*Trimble*
Watrous A.	*Austinburg.*	Black G	
Pulin Wm.		Wakeman Samuel	
Smith F.		Frame, Lord & Co.	*Coolville.*

Davis & Hicks	*Coolville.*
Self S.	
Curfman George	*Calvary.*
Brown H.	*Millfield.*
Andrews M. L.	
Keever W. C.	*Hockingport.*
Ray C. P.	
Williams G. & A.	
Kenney Samuel H.	*Pleasanton.*
Murphy F. P.	
Buntrum Franklin	
Warner N. O.	*Canaansville.*
Johnson B.	
Pruden S. B.	
Norris, Gold & Co,	
Walker G., Jr.	*Amesville.*
Fulton R. A.	
Patterson, Glazier & Co.	
Mitchell & Fulton	
Paston L. D.	*Nelsonville.*
Paston E. S.	
Paston W. W.	
Vanwormer ——	
Mansfield E. P.	
Somers J. F.	
Cable Chas.	
Ashton C. A.	
Robbins & Chesire	
Stacy & Wilkins	*Hull's.*
Wilkins & Stacy	*Shad*
Mayhugh James	*Lowry.*
Denna Daniel	
Ballard J. & Sons	*Athens.*
Kessinger A. & J. L.	
Robinson J. & Co.	
Carley & Pickering	
Hatch H.	
Irving John & Co.	
Golden William	
Constable R. A.	
Norton J. H.	
Carpenter F. L.	
Steigner R. D.	
Stewart E.	
Atkinson M.	
Dickey & Wells	*Lee.*
Gabait & Johnson	
Voorhes John	
McClain Thos. A.	
Stone & Cather	*Guysville.*
Perrill & Root	
Buckley Aratus	
Hill & Walker	*Hebardville.*
Brennon & Wilson	

Auglaize County

Young T. J.	*Wapakoneta.*
Martin R. D.	
Reisbarger J.	
Smith Caspar	
Shawber John	
Merkley F.	
Bernet J. A.	
Leblond F. C.	*St. Mary's.*
Rieche S.	

Bushe & Dieker	*St. Mary's.*
Bliss & Kelsey	
Bruner O.	
Adelmeyer B. H.	*Minster.*
Athmer, Bernard & Co.	
Bensmann Her.	
Eiting John	
Heinemann John H.	
Kooper B. A.	
Nienburg B. H.	
Nuxall Clemens	
Kramer Angela	
Spreke Francis	
Vocke John H.	
Von Handorf B.	
Willoh J. B.	
Dellinger & Nye	*Kossuth.*
Carman & Howbard	
Westfall & Whitens	
Brandon & Hill	*New Bremen.*
Backhoof ——	
Garmoosen ——	
Kenings & Ketler	
Koolhorst ——	
Preston & Son	
Schmidt ——	
Weimeier William	
Bilter Daniel	*St. Johns.*
Blum & Myers	
Neil John	
Vantress Benjamin	
Waggoner Andrew	

Belmont County.

Brooks John W.	*Hendrysburgh.*
Murphy Hamilton	
Mettan & Keiger	
Tidball William	
Ward & Arrick	
Cope & Horton	*Colerain.*
Maule Joshua	
Nicholson & Street	
Cole & Foreman	*Demos.*
Mutson Aaron	
Pryor Albert	
Wilson Charles R.	
Allan James	*Martin's Ferry.*
Holliday T. J.	
Park David	
Pratt & Maguire	
Rice Hyde B.	
Hogue W. & S.	*Somerton.*
Koontz J. & J.	
Miles M. P. & Son	
Dorsey L. T. & Co.	*Captina.*
Bailey Stephen	*Barnesville.*
Brown Henry R.	
Bradfield John	
Davenports & Talbott	
Eiseman & Davis	
Eiseman Joseph	
Frazier & White	
Gardner Wm. H.	
Hager & Sons	
Holloway & Jones	
Horkheimer Simon	

Horkheimer Isaac	*Barnesville.*	Dunham G. & Son	*Georgetown.*
Anderson A. W. & J. S.	*Bellair.*	Kay Z.	*Hamersville.*
Calhoon Samuel		McGohan J. W.	
Fulton Thomas		Moore G. W. & Brother	
Hammond A & T.		Neal Wm.	
Dunbar William	*Uniontown.*	Redman J.	
Holloway J. & Co.		Boyle J. & Wm.	*Fayetteville.*
Martin, Irwin & Co.		Tallier & Ashton	
Bethel Geo. O. & Co.	*Flushing.*	Ashton T.	
Holloway L. M.		Hank N.	
Holloway D. & Co.		Seegar A.	
Holloway Isaac		Heiroheimer & Meinheimer	
Hollingsworth Elihu		Havrer A.	
Ely Jacob	*Loydsville.*	Hoover J.	
Gregg A. & J.		Murry J. H.	
Lodge Hiram		Derance B.	
Taggart Henry	*Shepherdstown.*	Feeld J.	
Duvall & Campbell	*Dillies' Bottom.*	Acklin & Bradford	*Aberdeen.*
White Thomas		Power J. O.	
Kemp & Thrasher	*Lampeville.*	Ellis & Slagle	
Campbell W. S.	*St. Clairsville.*	Campbell S.	
Ryan R. B.		Moore E. S.	
Clark R. S.	*Morristown.*	Day G. W.	*Puebla.*
Hanauer S. & Bro's.		Tweed & Kirker	*Russellville.*
Hogan William		Shaw R. & Son	
Gregg & Metcalf		Mitchell S. K.	*Ash Ridge.*
Cannon & Alexander	*Sewellsville.*	Potts A.	
Waddell & Ball		Clark Wm. W.	*Lewis.*
Wright & Fawcett	*Belmont.*	Weeks Wm.	*De La Palma.*
Thornbury W.		Allison John	
Grove John A.		Holman James	
Paterson W. & A.		Brown Joseph	
Haric A.		Pettit Saml.	*Five Mile.*
Waters Thompson	*Pilcher's.*	McKibbon W. S. & H.	*Feesburg.*
Armstrong A.	*Armstrong's Mills.*	Barker Wm. M.	
Hendershot Jacob		Trout David	
Bentley Wm. Jr.	*La Mira.*	Lewis Edwin	*Union Plane.*
Orison & Boyer	*Hunter.*	Salisbury John	
Grove & Miller		Morrow A.	*Fincastle.*
		Manker S. L.	
Brown County.		Ouney Benson	
Holden & Delleway	*Higginsport.*	Kettering Godfrey	*Arnheim.*
Strobe & Ellis		Davis Wm. O.	
Anderson Robert		Brown L.	
London Alfred		Huckberger John	
Benington J.	*Ripley.*	McIntire James	*Sardinia.*
Evans, Wylie & Co.		Davis Thos.	
Snider & Johnson		Graham John	
McMillen R. & Son		Kincaid Robert	
Cradit M. & Co.		Rigg & Bare	
Fenton S. & Brother			
Murphey D. H.		**Butler County.**	
Noland & Devore		Williamson Peter	*Bethany.*
Shan O. F.		Rose Nathaniel	
Pool & Bennet		Pearson L.	
Stevenson & Sham	*Decatur.*	Vanhise James	*West Chester.*
Luedaker Jas.		Davis J. S.	
Eckinan B.		Wharton Z.	
Salisbury T. D.	*Georgetown.*	Conover David	*Pisgah.*
Evans G. D.		Vanhise Wm. W.	
Galbreath W. T.		Davis Johnson	*Collinsville.*
O'Hara C. P. & Co.		Brown Wm.	
Evans S. W.		Steele James M.	
Vorhees L. R.		Stephens & Irwin	*Darrtown.*
Evans & Voorheese		Kyger G. & M.	
Dunham G.		Antvein & Kemp	*Poast Town.*
Dunham F. W.		Butler R T. & Co.	*Winton.*

13

Logan & Marrison	*Blue Bell.*	Latimer & Forbes	*New Hagerstown.*
Iler Dr. A. H.		Walters William	
Kumler E.	*Oxford.*	Highland S. A.	*New Harrisburgh.*
Hills R. E.		Potter John	
Peyton F. H.		George Robert & Son	*Scroggsfield.*
Brown S. R. & Co.		Tiernan Peter	*Norristown.*
Smith C. K.		Allen Samuel	*Leavitt.*
Bond Thos.		McLaughlin W. W. & Co.	
Stewart R. E.		Atkinson J. & Co.	*Carrollton.*
Evans J. L.	*Paddy's Run.*	Cameron James	
Robinson H. H.		Cumming & Bracken	
Boyd A.	*Reily.*	Huston James	
Gray Arthur		Sidger H. A.	
Bartlow C. & Son		Thompson William	
Halbrook B. H.	*Hamilton.*	Carr Amos	*Leesville*
Hiser John		Hunt John L.	
Clark D. M.		Roby H. & Pretsman	
Waterson & Seward		West John	
Brown & Myers		Barber D. R.	*Hickory.*
Kennedy L. & A.		Zollars Daniel	*Sherodsville.*
Wallace Geo.		Hull & Buss	*Oneida Mills.*
Getz & Fisher		Scott R. G.	*Kilgore.*
Skinner J. O.		Oreal W. B.	
Stewart S. R.	*Saint Charles.*		
Squire & Scudder	*Princeton.*	**Champaign County.**	
Beal B. J. Z.		McCarble S. S.	*Mechanicsburgh.*
Salisbery J. S.	*Millville.*	Rathburn L.	
Beaty J. C.		Owen W. B.	
Stillwell & Son	*Stillwells.*	Williams R. D. & Co.	
Lake & Blackburn	*Symmes' Corner.*	Dye J. H. & Son	
Boal T. & J.	*Ross.*	McGinley F. E. D.	
Dick & Reese		Quick & McCollough	*Christiansburg.*
Frost I. & J.		Goodrich B. F.	
La Turett Peter P.	*Monroe.*	Howell M.	
Bennett N. O. & W.		Fitzpatrick & Talbot	
Hammill J. L.		Hunter David	*Westville.*
Kelley & Emmerson	*Middletown.*	Robbins John	
Thompson E.	*College Corner.*	Brown Alfred & Co.	*Urbana.*
Ridenour Jonathan M.		Guynne E.	
Brown B. H.		Weaver & Brother	
Linn & Young	*Somerville.*	Braud & Purcell	
Cook & Brother		Stadler & Brothers	
Davis D.		Hill & Sloan	
Beall B. C.	*Seven Miles.*	Eaker J. B.	
Watson & Phares		McDonald D. & H.	
Rose S. D. & Co.	*Trenton.*	Marsh H.	
Beahring & Koch		Talbott J. G. & Co.	
Gunkle Danl.		Ross, Hill & Co.	
Peterson George		McCord J. O.	
Hunt A. A. & H. C.		Johnson E.	*Woodstock.*
Thomas Wm. B.	*Jacksonburg.*	Harbach W. H.	
Gary J. D.		Clark S. B. & C. K.	*Mutual.*
Kelley John		Spencer J. W. & Co	
Metz M. & Co.	*Port Union.*	Bailey S. B.	
Dearmand K.		Bonenock Saml.	*Careyskill.*
Miller Benj. F.	*Contreras.*	Coventon & Alexander	
Hand O. W.		Dick Elisha	
Gray Saml.	*Reily.*	Cretcher & Edes	*Springhills.*
Gaston & Conklin		Mayne G.	
Steele Robert	*Jericho.*	Smith J. A.	
Antrim J. & T.	*Poast Town.*	Batdorf Jacob	*St. Paris*
Barklow W.		Klapp Jeremiah	
		Frank Jonathan	
Carroll County.		Black & Coverstone	
Heidy Samuel	*Harlem Springs.*	Talbott J. G. & Co.	
Ross S. J.	*Malvern.*	Derikson Danl.	*Terre Haute.*
Vail Sidney.		Boggs Wm. G.	*North Lewisburg.*

Gwymes & Jennings	*North Lewisburg.*
Lyon, Callender & Co.,	
Parker & Taylor	

Clark County.

Brandenburgh H.	*Donnelsville.*
Liffell James	
Overpach & Heath	*North Hampton.*
Weever Newton	*Tremont.*
Gay & Son	
Gasten Robert	*Enon.*
Ohlwine Charles	'
Johnson S. S.	*Selma.*
Jones W. W.	
Wallace J. R.	*Springfield.*
Spencer Wm. M.	
Funk John	
Black & Bro.	
Osborne J.	
Cartmell Wm. H. & J. L.	*Catawba.*
Chaney T. S.	
Conway S. & Son	
Creamer Joseph D.	
Diehl A. G. & Co.	*South Charleston.*
Haughey & Edwards	
Holmes & Jones	
Pringle & Brothers	
Rankin & Houston	
Dever & Murray	*New Carlisle.*
Muzzy & Johnston	
Taylor Jonathan	
Taylor E. G.	
Warwick A. S.	
Crowl Henry	
Burns J. J.	*Medway.*
Stiles D. J.	

Clermont County.

Porta Robert	*New Richmond.*
Watkins Wm.	
Layfield & Co.	
Bainum James H.	
Shannon E. R.	
Davis M. H.	
Sturgis Wm.	
Gowdy & Butler	
Ricker Benj.	*Pleasant Hill.*
Sly William	*Nicholsville.*
Nichols W. B.	
Mitchell Isaac	*Point Pleasant.*
Cooper John	
Duncan James	
Friedman Frank	
Cheseldine P. & D.	*Williamsburg.*
Sharp & Stockton	
Sinks & Peterson	
Lane S.	*Mt. Carmel.*
Elstun M.	
Cumbach H. H.	
Perdinette F.	
Kugler John	*Milford.*
Dart Albert	
Dennison James	
Lafferty Mary	*Monterey.*
Foster M.	
Smith J. C.	
Sourd A.	

Vaughan C. H.	*Goshen.*
Holmes Daniel	
Parker & Son	*Neville.*
Rust & Fee	
McMath David	
Jones & Wilmington	*Withamsville.*
Kelly Henry C.	
Fee O. P. S. & D. E.	*Felicity.*
Goodwin & Fee	
Parrish & Shriver	
Powell & Knowles	
Richards & McClain	
Burke M. T.	*Bethel.*
Johnson John S.	
Sinks & Quinlan	
Bohm Chas. & Bro.	*Batavia.*
Dustin J. S.	
Kain T. & Co.,	
Hunt Jesse	
Hatfield J. D.	*Olive Branch.*
Vanosdal J. R.	*California.*
Jones Robert	*Edenton.*
Thacker Cornwall	
Thompson John W.	
Holtes & Bro.	*Point Isabel.*
Tivis & Freese	
Doughty Collins	*Amelia.*
Coombs & Wheeler	
Fairfield Cyrus	
Griffin & Seargeant	
Hymer John B.	
Jernegan David	
Short Cornelius	
Anderson Peter	*Owensville.*
Dimmitt Ezekiel	
Juen Francis X.	
Ulrey William	
Ely Samuel	*Mt. Olive.*
Buckingham Mark	*Miamisville.*
Robinson Moses	
Sparks David G.	*Mulberry.*
Foote C. D.	*Chilo.*
Noland G. B.	
Prather W. F. & Co.	
Fee Wm. M.	*Moscow.*
Fisher B. F.	
McLaughlin A. J.	
McNash & Keys	
Powell & Fee	
Smith & Son	
Hayford Cyrus P.	*Mt. Pisgah.*
Wheeler & Coombs	
Hitch & Hammond	*Clover.*
Ballard W. F.	*Loveland.*
Degalyer L. F.	
Smith J. M.	
Smith, Moore & Co.	*Rural.*
Perin Harvey	*Perin's Mills.*
Spence E.	
Moleux Francis	
Johnston James S.	*Belfast*
Smith Isaac	
Simmons B. H.	*Laurel*
Fisher S. M.	
Fee Daniel	
Ely Benjamin	*Bantam.*
Ely John F. M.	

Slade William — *Bentam.*
Doughty Collins
Slade Ezekiel
Weaver Samuel
Carr A. & P. G. & Co. — *West Woodville.*
Sourd C.
Hibbetts Nathl. M. — *Newtonsville.*
Johnson James
Powell John T. — *Pleasant Grove.*
Younge William
John James — *Locust Corner.*
Clark & Blymer
Geskin John

Clinton County.

Harris E. — *Snow Hill.*
Johnson Wm.
Baum Henry
Leonard B. — *Oakland.*
Leonard Joseph
Mulford E. M. — *Westboro'.*
Garner & Hockett
Slone & Hudson
Slone & Hammer
Slone W. W. & Co.
Hadley Jacob — *Sligo.*
Ginton & Faquei
Carter & Hazard
Grant John — *New Burlington.*
Hollingsworth David
Arnold John
Johnson R. B. — *Cuba.*
Wilson S. J.
James J. C. — *Lumberton.*
Constant W. W. & Co.
Farmon R. D. — *Port William.*
Ellis A.
Hardesty E. G.
Hadley & Leinton — *Clarksville.*
Harris & Wilson
Harlin Wm.
Gardner J.
Temberlake J.
Bryan & Brother — *Lees' Creek.*
Rhonnus C.
Pierce W. T.
Baldwin S. — *Blanchester.*
Baldwin W. H. & Co.
Baldwin J. B. & Co
Kelsey J. & K.
Ousick W.
Carver John — *New Antioch.*
Wilson Wm. C.
Wilson Alex. — *Wilson's Station.*
Amberg A. S. — *New Vienna.*
Sandfelder & Mathews
Edwards & Nobb
Crawford J. F.
Hadson J.
Moyers J.
Mathews G. W.
Bowen H.
Bentley B. — *Sabina,*
Hallam John
Betts & Co. — *Martinsville.*
Hiatt & Kugler

Fulton Robert — *Martinsville.*
Haynes Asa
Amberg & Williams
Johnson W. D.
Baum Henry & S.
Bruce Henry H. — *Bloomington.*
Bevan Abel
Jenkins Alfred & Son
Hibbon Thos. — *Wilmington.*
Hall Saml. H.
Strattan Stephen T.
Hadley John O.
Hibbon Wm.
Fife Wm. O.
Smith & Shepherd
Stuckle A. E. & J.
Harrison D. C.
Morgan Wm. J.
Morgan David
Bevan Abel — *Decaturville.*
Funcet Wm.
Fanner Saml.

Columbiana County.

Faucett J. & W. T. — *Salem.*
Fetters John
Johnson & Horner
Heaton Jacob
Scattergood T. & Son
Schilling J. & L.
Street Zadock
Thomas & Greiner
Tomlinson & Stratton
Kensey S. & Co. — *East Liverpool.*
Price Richard
Smith Wm. G.
Thompson J. & Co.
Miller J. — *West Point.*
Culbertson David — *St. Clair.*
Laughlin Thomas
Mackall James
Allen Jesse N. — *Columbiana.*
Greenmire Jacob
Icenhour & Allen
Stouffer Daniel
Wallace Joseph
Martin John — *Glasgow.*
Orr Wm. B.
Augustine D. — *Unity.*
Baker M.
Sillaman J. & B.
Milner & Coburn — *Inverness.*
McGillivray George
Sloan Geo. — *Hanoverton.*
Atwell C.
Arter & Nicholas
Arter J. R.
Cope L. S. — *Wellsville.*
Fraser D. K.
Smith W.
Stewart Jas.
Todd W.
Estill James A. — *New Lisbon.*
Helman C. H. & Co.
Hessen Horace P.
Pitcairn & Huston
Paul, Pritchard & Co.

Shults M. & F.   *New Lisbon.*
Springer & Co.
Travis J.
Brewster John T.   *East Palestine.*
Chamberlain R.
Craig Andrew
Young S. & Son
Farmer & Lacock   *Salineville.*
Hoey A. & J.
Robins & Irwin
Graham James   *New Garden*
Dawson A. M.   *Calcutta.*
Thompson J. & Brothers
Fugate Stephen   *North Georgetown.*
Woolf Samuel
Clapsaddle John   *Franklin Square.*
Deborest Barton
Emmons & Colestock   *East Rochester.*
Emmons Jacob
Ruth William & Co.   *New Chambersburg.*
Laughlin Matthew   *Little Beaver Bridge.*
Pitcairn Robert   *Bucks.*
Kemble George   *Elkton.*
Huffman Adam & Co.
Armstrong Andrew, Jr.

Coshocton County.

Bell J. C. & Co.   *New Bedford.*
Burgut David
Church B. S.   *Tiverton.*
Forker & McKee   *West Carlisle.*
Morgan & Butler
McFarlin James   *West Bedford.*
Jones T. P. & S.
Lillie & Wilson
Moore, Brown & Norris
Wolf P. C. & Co.   *Evansburg.*
Davis C. F.
Johnston J. R.
Richmond J.
Tidball Samuel   *Clark's.*
Foley Patrick
Ringer A. & J.   *Chili.*
Helmriech S. & P.
Everhart N
McFadden Wm.   *Bakersville.*
McFadden Joseph
Frick J. A.
Snyder Simon
Crantz E.
Neglespough E.
Boyd Richard   *Keene.*
Kiney John
Renfrew A.
Elliott J. S. & W.
Burns Samuel   *Walhonding.*
McCormick Geo.
Crowley, Williams & Strome   *Warsaw.*
Bonnet, Denmor & Strome
Hay R. & H.   *Coshocton.*
Millerner A. N.
Ricketts T. C.
Meeke H.

Crawford County.

Kuhn Andrew   *Leesville Cross Roads.*
Lewis J. M.

Neuman John   *Leesville Cross Roads.*
Mulford Joh   *Poplar.*
Chilcote N. C.   *New Washington*
High Valentine
Sheets John A.
Sims Wm. D. & Son   *Wellerville.*
Kaler John   *Liberty Corners.*
Warner Emanuel
Martin Saml. E.   *Lykens.*
Gillispie Thomas   *Sulphur Spring.*
Ziegler & Perse
Bowman J. P.   *Bucyrus.*
Boyer E. & B.
Converse H.
Converse Loring
Failor A.
Marshall & Monnett
Meriman E. R.
Rupp & Moderwell
Widman A. P.
Fox C. & G.   *De Kalb.*
Webber & Cartright   *Chatfield.*
Nefzger S. & C.

Cuyahoga County.

Bishop & Farr   *Euclid.*
Foote A. M.
Moses C.
Burke H.   *Newburgh.*
Miles E. & Co.
Shattrick A. M.
Wakeman D.   *Mayfield.*
Webster & Eggleston   *Gates' Mills.*
Redrup Joseph   *North Royalton.*
Teachont & Bosworth
Babcock Charles H.   *Brooklyn.*
Poe A. W.
Brainard J. K.   *Independence.*
Gleason & Shales
Clark E.
Hildreth D. R.   *East Cleveland.*
Hoyt & Dusenberry
Bradley & Noble   *Strongsville.*
Pomeroy & Gallup
Strong W. H.
Strong W.
Wells L.
Farr Edwin   *Dover.*
Phinny Edwin
Phinny Calvin
Collins & Curtiss   *Chagrin Falls.*
McFarland L.
Peet L. L.
Willey & Wait
Williams & McFarland
Wollcott E. P.
Breck & Humphrey   *Brecksville.*
Odell, Price & Co.   *Solon*
Robbins A. & Sons
Smith C. B.
Cannon T. H.   *Bedford.*
Comstock A. H.
Hathaway L. D.
Hillman, Robison & Co.
Burk J.   *Warrensville.*
Gribben J.
Halsted H.

Hanchit H.   *Warrensville.*
Romp William   *Coe Ridge.*
Aldrich & West   *Collamer.*
Currier S. & Son
Foote Herschel
Case W. J.   *Berea.*
Evans Alva.
Johnson Thomas
Phinney B.   *Rockport.*
Tyler & Whitney   *Ohio City.*
Sims C. & Co.

Darke County.

Sull & Davis   *Castine.*
Hays Z. C.
Shawk & Hoove.
Thomas J. & J.   *Ithica.*
Huffer A.
Davidson & McKee   *Hillgrove.*
Nishwitz & White
Mendenhall W. B.   *Woodington.*
Brodrick S. O.   *Tampico.*
Higgins & Co.   *Concordia.*
Townsend Wm.   *Abbottsville.*
Waldo C. C.   *New Madison.*
Thomas David
Bloom & Bacon
Bowen & Gray
Warner & Sowers   *Fort Jefferson.*
Avery & Dickey   *German.*
Norris J. G.
Harter J. M.
Leas & Brother   *Sampson.*
Gower Danl.   *Poplar Ridge.*
Workman & Dailey   *Greenville.*
Swishler D. K.
Compton J.
Turpin Thos. P.
Garst H. C.
Vanmater John
Alexander & McWhinney   *Republican.*
French W. W.
Bowen & Townsend
Dill John H. C.   *Greenville.*
Robinson A.
Stuck Henry
Turpin Geo.
Dill J. H. C.   *Beamsville.*
Warrenfells F.
Ward David
Plessinger Jacob
Grisson Cyrus   *Seven Mile Prairie.*
Grisson C.   *Mississinawa.*

Defiance County.

Ayers A. A.   *Defiance.*
Brown G. R.
Coston & Paige
Evans R.
Evans P. & Lindenberger
Falloon & Groff
Hilton H.
Spague & Warren
Stilwell J. M.
Tuttle J. & Co.
Noble L. C.   *Panama.*

Edgerton A. P.   *Hicksville.*
Hilton & Bruner   *Brunersburg.*
Foot & Powell   *Farmer Centre.*
Kenkey & Mills
Coy & Snider   *Evansport.*
Denman & Sullinger
Bradley George
Comparet & Bro.   *Hicksville.*
Blain James W.

Delaware County.

Welch W. L. & Co.   *Delaware.*
Welch & Williams W. L. & H.
Lamb & Wetman
Campbell, Little & Co.
Pettibone Thos.
Watkins J. H.
Hills C. & Co.
McCune J.
Turner & Mickey
Latimer S.
Sherman & Maynard   *Galena.*
Allen H.
Lenington Arnold & Co.
Rose John   *Vans Valley.*
Stroub Andrew   *Waldo.*
French J. M. & Co.
Hull L. S.
Tull J. C.   *Harlem.*
Tompkins James
Jarvis H. J.   *Williamsville.*
Hyde U. H.   *East Orange.*
Mendenhall J. H.   *Delaware.*
Elmore John
Gooddale & Co.
Morten Thos.   *Radnor.*
Norten J. J. & Co.
Curren S.   *Norton.*
Myers Hale & Co.   *Sunbury.*
Kimble, Fickner & Co.
Stark A. J. & Co.
Wilcox C. & Co.
Seymore & Co.
Mealey Michael   *Patterson.*
Root Edwin   *Unison.*
Osborne E. L.   *Maxwell.*
Martin R.
Stark G. N.   *Kingston Centre.*
Dunham E.   *Kilbourne.*
McMaster Hiram
Scott Seymore
Leonard A. H.
Benson & Hiatt   *Bellepoint.*
Liggett James

Erie County.

Adams H. L.   *Sandusky City.*
Barney T. Y.
Converse Chas.
Everitt Drake & Co.
Hubbard & Shepherd
Lyon L. L. & Co.
Monroe & Peck
Pearl Wm.
Stevenson John W.
Whitney J. D. & F.
West T. D. & Co.

White Henry A.	*Sandusky City.*	Miller G. C.	*Millersport.*
West W. T. & A. K.		Weakly John H.	
Wells, Lewis & Co.	*Furnace.*		
Ayres S.	*Milan.*	**Fayette County.**	
Barney Geo.		Southward A. B.	*Bloomingburg.*
Brass A.		Gibson Wm. G.	
Graham J.		Southward H. B. & Co.	
Hamilton James		Kinney Wm. M.	
Hopkins D. C.		Boice David E.	
King Z.		Pearson H. K.	*Jeffersonville.*
Lockwood J. C.		Popejoy J. J.	
Lockwood F. & R.		Hill Wm.	
McClure W.		Blizard J. W.	*Pancoastburg.*
Moury A. P.		Bailey John R.	
Stuart M.		Sayres Henry	*Convenience.*
Burgess S.	*Huron.*	Orr John	*Washington.*
Skinner H.		Yeonean & Finegan	
Minard O. T.		Allen Joseph	
Hinkley & Brother		Heagler Z. W.	
Smith & Lapp		Van Deman J. L.	
Furton O. S.	*Vermillion.*	Melvin George	
Lenard O. A.		Bell & Thompson	
Pitten J. S.		Campbell Lenox	
Jackson & Co.		Blakemore W. H.	
Cobb A.	*Birmingham.*	Henkle Moab	
Pierce Bennett		Plumb J. & Sons	
Griggs L. S.		Wilson Wesley	*Moon's.*
Minurd H. W.		Waln Henry	
Lommis C.		Jinkins Wm. H.	
Squire V.		Craig T. & W.	*Staunton.*
Darling & Harley	*Florence.*	Vanpelt Chas.	
Heywood R. H.	*Venice.*		
		Franklin County.	
		Squires & Hawthorn	*Central College.*
		Wilson D. & Co.	
Fairfield County.		Headley & Eberly	*Groveport.*
		Chapman & Smith	
Curtiss William	*Pickerington.*	Algier Amon	*Reynoldsburg*
Pickering Jacob, Jr.		Miller H. E.	
Ijams William	*West Rushville.*	Osborn & Johnson	
Shaw John		Rhoads & Hutson	
Hane P.	*Pleasantville.*	Weaver & Hunt	
Mithoff A. & E.	*Lockville.*	Hauck H.	*Clintonville.*
Laudon O. P.	*New Salem.*	Armstrong J. S.	*Hibernia.*
Ashbaugh & Beery	*Bremen.*	Beams & Baughman	*Hope.*
Rodehafer Daniel		Browning Isaac	
Lewis W. B.	*Rushville.*	Horlocker, Baughman & Co.	
Nourse J. G.		McCurdy John	
Reid G. W.		Hays Addison	*Blendon.*
Holderman David & Co.	*Amanda.*	Amburgh A.	*Harrisburg.*
Sunderman J. H.		Bell J. B.	
Vanhise David & Co.		Miller H.	
Wise W. T.	*Lancaster.*	Safrit T. W.	
Hendley J. C		Safrit J.	
Julien & Foresman		Harrington N.	*Alton.*
Little & Dresback		Putnam S. H. & Co.	
Reber & Kutz		Groham William	*Dublin.*
Rising & Lyons		Sells G. W.	
Reinman & Martin		Thompson A.	
Willock J. G.		Weaver & Artz	
White & Julien		Zoller Holeob	
Beck Jacob		Ferguson John	*Georgesville*
Hamlin G. F.	*Clear Creek.*	Ferguson James	
Hedge Samuel O.		Bradfield James	
Strayer J. E.	*Sugar Grove.*	Brown Sidney	*Worthington*
Kinser C.		Snow G. R.	
Gregg J.	*Lithopolis*	Fuller & Thompson	
Porter & Martin			
Brabst D.			

Wilcox & Barker   *Worthington.* | Guthrie J. H. & D. Q.   *Swan Creek.*
Wright Potter | Handley William
Bartlett & Fry   *Canal Winchester.* | Hannan Joseph T.
Benadum A. D. | Boswell Wm. S.   *Kyger.*
Benadum A. D. & Co. | McDaniel Matthew
Carty Jacob | Tate David
Tallman, Allen & Co. | Deletomb & Heisner   *Gallipolis.*
Tallman, Stevenson & Co. | Menager, Blackford & Co.
Cherry & Stimmel   *Lockbourn.* | Carell F., Jr.
Miner & Converse | Sanns John, Sen.
Young Thomas   *Gahanna.* | Weibert C. C.
Dickinson J.   *Ovid.* | Kerr Wm. S.
Fisk M. & W. | Regnier Julius
Fisher A. B. | Langley Wm. H.
                                           | Langley S. T. & R.
                                           | Greene C. D
Fulton County. | Miller Wm. C.
                                           | Holliday & Waddell
Hollington R. P.   *Elmira.* | Vanden Martin
Luts John | Decker S. H.
Marks & Brown | Newton & Cubboye
Darly S. B. | Veyseir B.
Maisen A. & R. | Carter & Townsend   *Patriot.*
Day Hosea   *Ottokee.* | Wombledorf S. B.
Welch James H.
Reynolds Ransom   ## Geanga County.
Walters O. & Co.   *Delta.*
White Allen | Randall, Cook & Co.   *Chardon.*
Alman C. C. | Squire Saml. & Son
Gates J. T. | Wilber Wm.
Cullan & Clark | Young Allison
Culver W. W.   *Metamora.* | Wilkins, Young & Co.
Morey J. & Co.   *Lyons.* | Bruce W. W. & E.
Willey —— | Parsons & Ayres
Hibbard M. D. & Son   *Tedrow.* | Ranney L & Co.
Watters J. | Dayton R., (Agt. Troy Farmers' Co.)
Allman A. J.   *West Swanton.* | *Welshfield.*
Harter & Harter | McBride James   *Hamden.*
Day Hosea   *West Barre.* | Wilber & Vaughn
Clark G. & Co. | Alvord & Garritt   *Montville.*
                                           | Kile, Wilkins & Co.   *Huntsburgh.*
Gallia County. | Thompson P. T. & E.   *Middlefield.*
                                           | Bishop H. S.
Evans Thomas   *Thurman.* | Foote ——
Newson Junius L. | Bowe Russell   *Parkman.*
Rickabaugh John | Baldwin & Co.
Steele, William | Parkman E. B.
Wynne Abel | Tilden J. S. & A. P.
Sheret M.   *Rodney.* | Farmers' Co.   *Troy.*
Holcomb E. T.   *Vinton.* | Mayhew John   *Auburn.*
Holcomb & Matthews | Converse & Wilmot
McCumber L. A. | Treet A. M.   *Bainbridge.*
Edmiston Andrew   *Ewington.* | Stafford & Harpham
Edmiston & Cherington | Bennett H. P.   *Russell.*
Matthews Noble S. | Philbrick S. P.   *Chester.*
Gates & Co.   *Cheshire.* | Stevenson & Russell
Gates & McGrath | Lyman E. O. & Co.
Guthrie C. L. | Farmers' Co.   *Munson*
Bentley, Campbell & Co. *Gallia Furnace.* | Mathews A.   *Newbury*
Davis Jacob   *Adamsville.* | Dickinson F.
Beaman R. & L. | Fuller James
Kelly & Baldridge | Boughton G. & Co.   *Burton.*
Reynolds Wm. | Tolls W. R. & H. S.
Reynolds H. C. & S. G. | Field C. O. & C. S.   *Claridon.*
Rickabaugh & Reynolds | Lukins J. P.
Hebbard, Walker & Co.   *Pine Grove.* | Farmers' Co.
Payne G. J. | Union Co.
Graham, Cole & Co.   *Raccoon Island.* | Smith & Woodard
Hall N

Greene County.

Dunlap, Plowman & Co.	Cedarville.
Frazier & Reid	
Nesbit J. C.	
Orr John	
Walker & Currie	
Barnes, Goe & Andrews	Xenia.
Chalmers J. C.	
Conwell S. D. & Co.	
Ewing John	
McMillan J. C. & Co.	
Thorpe W. G. & Co.	
Bennett S. E.	Fairfield.
Burrows J. A.	
Herr & Batdorf	
Buck J. H. & J.	Zimmerman.
Barrett & Walton	Spring Valley.
Morris T. L. & W. & Co.	
Watson & Sands	
Anderson John	Clifton.
Lewis Bennet	
Huston James	New Jasper.
Schauer & Wilson	Byron.
Brown James A.	Yellow Springs.
Knox John B.	
Stewart & Brother	
Carman W. J.	Clio.
Oglesbee Jonathan	Paintersville.
Jenkins A.	
Boteler & Syfers	Jamestown.
Syfers J. Co.	
Johnson J. F. & Co.	
Baker William G.	
Wickersham Edward	

Guernsey County.

Craig & Clark	Washington.
Potts Stephen	
Endley L. & Co.	
Coldwell Martin & Co.	
Craig & Bryant	
Totten J.	
Burt, Berry & Co.	Cumberland.
Hurd James L.	
Stephens John	
Bye Jonathan	Byesville.
Dillon, Pickering & Co.	Middlebourne.
Robinson Wm.	
Strong & Linn	Winchester.
Brown S.	
Stockdale J. & S. & Co.	Antrim.
Clark & Craig & Co.	
Sankey A.	
Stewart John	Londonderry.
Lindsey S. B.	
Sayre Ira	New Gottingen.
Freeman Thos.	
Mullen & Ballard	
Foresber Isaac	
Heidelbach G. W.	
Hare Joseph	Fairview.
Brown & Smith	
Martin & Carlisle	
Plattenburg Geo.	
Dyson Thos. A. & Co.	Dyson's.
Johnson J.	Claysville.

Harrison Wm. G.	Claysville.
Perry John	
Smith H. & J. P.	Cambridge.
McDonald Wm. & Co.	
Shaffner A. P.	
Rainey & Clark	
Craig Samuel	
Naftel T.	
McCracken W.	
Hyatt & Atkins	
Mackey N. & Brother	
Luccock N. & Sons	Kimbolton.
Brown Joshua	
Ledlie Andrew	
Roseman, Orme & Co.	Millersville.
Meredith W. F. & J.	
Jenkins F.	
Umstot, Nichols & Co.	Senecaville.
Brown G. W. & Co.	
Alexander & Baldridge	
Hall John & Son	Leatherwood.
Webster Joseph G.	
Rimer John & Co.	

Hamilton County.

Runyan Joseph M.	Cleves.
Dunn Amos B.	
Davis D. E.	
Mills Isaac D.	Elizabethtown.
Ewing Richard	
Husten James	Pleasant Run.
Taber J. W. & Co.	Miami.
Temple T. D.	Plainville.
Wright F. C. & J. F.	Mt. Healthy.
Hoffuer E. W.	
Sayre A. R.	
Carnahan W. S.	New Burlington.
Mewhinney David	Montgomery.
Slaback Samuel	
Sweet S. B.	
Cosbey A. L.	
Bodine H.	Newtown.
Crosley John W.	
Felter David E.	
McGill W. R.	
Close & Peterson	Springdale.
Hilts Anthony & Son	
Service Abraham	
Watson William	
Wilmuth Geo. W.	
Gutsviller Frederick	Mount Airy.
Liuchinger Martin	
Memmel John M.	
Bacon J. W.	Carthage
Dempsey T. H.	
Foreman Mary	
Sheehan & Bonnel	
Southard M. R.	
Bowen & Edingfield	Sharonville.
Cornell T. S.	
Reick John	
Carnell & Stranger	Cheviot.
Carver Charles	
Statem D.	
Matson M.	Dunlap.
Pinney Joseph	
Dorr Peter	Miltonsburgh.

Dressel Christian — *Miltonsburgh.*
Oblinger John B.
Durham W. B. — *Mt. Washington.*
Garriot & Scudder — *Harrison.*
Hasson & Rittenhouse
Jarard Abner
Pharas William
Rifner J. & M.
Mooney Stephen W. — *Pleasant Ridge.*
Brown James — *Reading.*
Ireland Anthon
Ralston Isabel
Brown & Garriott — *Lockland.*
Brown & Brothers
Markland Thomas — *Dry Ridge.*
Markland Noah L.
Sinclair John

Hancock County.

Cook Chester — *Mt. Blanchard.*
Lake A. M.
Smith J. & Co.
Taylor & Bell
Ensminger J. H. & Co. — *Van Buren.*
Heller W. L. & Co.
Vails E. B. & O. — *Arlington.*
Goit & Beardsley — *Benton Ridge.*
Gilbert Aquilla — *Blanchard Bridge.*
Beach S. N. — *Ashery.*
Weskett John
Barney W. Z. & Co. — *McComb.*
Ballard F. — *Canonsburg.*
Church C. & Co.
Ewing T.
Wheeler Wm. H. & Co. — *Finley.*
Henderson & Patterson
King & Zeigler
Newell Hugh
Hyatt Alex. H.
Wilson James H.
Goit Edson
Goit E. & Co.
Vaneman & Balentine
Dixon D. & Co.

Hardin County.

Ingman G. P. — *Kenton.*
Miller & Wingate
Bumbager & Johns
Carey Wm.
Russell R. G.
McConnell F. M.
Taylor & Stanford
Root J. S.
White Jas. M. — *Roundhead.*
Kemble John F. & Co.
Seymour & Chaise — *Sylvia.*
Worley A. W.
Wilson J. J. & W. H. — *Huntersville.*
Johnston S. M. & Co.

Harrison County.

McFadden S. & H. — *Cadis.*
Hogg Wm. & Co.
Burtch A. H.
Stewart James

Wood Joseph P. — *Cadis*
McCormick John
Crabb & Shotwell
Moore Alex.
Watson J. P. — *Harrisville.*
Nicholson Thos
Lewis Isaac — *Short Creek.*
Watson Wm. H.
Paul Saml. — *Green.*
Richardson John
Hobler & Mikeswell — *Germano.*
Stenger Wm.
Wert & Gulshall — *Rumley.*
Oroskey A. F. — *Newmarket.*
Cramblit John T. — *Deersville.*
Pittis Robert T. & Son
Pittis Robert, Jr.
Finney Wm. G.
Green Thos. — *Freeport.*
Smith Thos.
Shriber A. J. — *Moorefield.*
Brown T. J.
Atkinson B. F. — *Cassville.*
Snyder Saml. — *Cold Spring.*
Stuart, Prier & Co. — *Feed Spring.*
Strouse Saml.
Lee Wm. — *New Athens.*
Kennerd Levi
Atchison Wm.
Kennerd Marshall

Henry County.

Dodd & Haley — *Napoleon.*
Powell John
Stedman & Mearly
Stout Adam — *Florida*
Frease J. & J.
Scofield J. E.
Harley David
Smith & Durbin — *Texas.*
Crosby O. C. & G. P.
Crockett L. & Co. — *Shunk.*

Highland County.

Spargru & Montgomery — *Rainsboro'.*
Spargru & Johnston
Dewitt John & Co.
Hundley Jesse S. — *Lynchburg.*
Hundley Jas.
Marsh & Campbell G. & C.
Johnson & Dennison A. & J. R.
Cranmore Henry S.
Stratton & Stephens — *Highland.*
Ellis & Stephens
Johnson & Swearington
Applegate & Nutt
Scott & Faris — *Pricetown.*
Colvin John
Smart Hugh — *Greenfield.*
Bell Chas. & Son
Dunlap & Hyre
Boyd & Wasson
Caldwell & Miller
Sellers Geo. W.
Bell Josiah
Leake James J.

Wright & Brothers	*Belfast Town.*	Simes Jeremiah	*Rock House.*
Blair J. W. & Son		Dille, Brice & Moore	*Pattonsville.*
Wittenmyer Danl. G.	*Buford.*	Lewis Israel	*Star.*
Evans Benj.		Flowers Jacob	*Ewing.*
Duvall John & Co.		Linn Canada	*Gibisonville.*
Shafer Jonas	*Dodsonville.*	Shulties John	
Ovebaugh Adam		Stearnes & Watsonburgh	
Shafer Joseph		Holland John	*Swan.*
McIntire & Rainey	*Mowrytown.*	Davis J. B. & Co.	
Picard J. C.			
Colvin Isaac	*Newmarket.*	**Holmes County.**	
Leamon Saml.			
Hethrington James	*Sugartree Ridge.*	Hutchison J. & W.	*Holmesville.*
Holmes N.		Karr & Gorrell	
Lewis A.		Mayer B.	*Berlin.*
Hetherington C.		Shuble J.	
Glasscock & Mead	*Petersburg.*	Lemman Wm.	*Benton.*
Pearce & Hiatt		Divvers & Burkholder	
Trounstine & Kiefer		Clement J. C.	*Nashville.*
Grove James M.		Bodenhamer H.	*Walnut Creek.*
Rockhold David		Joss N. F.	*Winesburg.*
Hughs & Carlisle J. & J.	*Marshall.*	Miller H.	
Amen & Elliot		Smith Geo. F.	
Grabill Abraham		Beall & Drake	*Killbuck.*
Barnes Wm. W.	*Centrefield.*	Buzzard M. M.	*Nashville.*
Hughey & Town		Liggett D. J.	
Hawkins James	*Allensburg.*	Landiker P & Co.	
Roller Wm. & Co.	*Greenford.*	Barnes P.	*Humphreyville.*
Pernell A.		Bailey John	
Peal J. & J. D.	*Samantha.*	Cherryholmes J.	*Millersburg.*
Gardner M. & E. S.		Brumbaugh C.	
Roads Isaac F.	*Dallas.*		
Easter Solomon		**Huron County.**	
McKeen John	*Leesburg.*	Peakins A. B.	*Monroeville.*
Livingston J. L.		Fish Edwin	
Eldrick B.		Steel H. K. & Co.	
Irion J. & Co.		Squares Douglass	
Templin Jas. S.		Harper & Patterson	
Johnson E. P. & Brother		Smith Isaac & Co.	
Quinn J. H.		Prentiss A. W.	
Bayhan Franklin	*North Uniontown.*	Prentiss & Hoover	
Barrere Benj. & Co.	*Hillsboro'.*	Smith & Child	*Steuben.*
Clayton D. M.		Bunce E. J.	*Wakeman.*
Dill Saml.		Hall L. S.	
Evans & Patterson		Hosfred & Andrews	
Evans A. S.		Lawson G.	*East Townsend.*
Tallis D. J.		Hyde W. S.	
Hibben Saml. E.		Humphrey W. & D	
Inskeep J. Q.		Tyler H. P.	*Clarksfield.*
Lawrence Geo. W.		Stevenson D.	
Moore Abner		Jones A.	
Nugent Wm.		Curry J. L.	*Greenwich.*
Trimble John T.		Fowler J. T.	
Woodrow J. J.		Cotant & Brother	
Bamber Thos. C.	*East Monroe.*	Cook E. W.	*Four Corners.*
		Owen H. N.	*North Norwich.*
		Ranson L. E.	
Hocking County.		Chapman & Woodward	*Bellevue.*
		Weller Chas.	
Collins Enoch & Co.	*Logan.*	Brooks W.	
Collins & James		Amsden & Co.	
Culver Reuben		Summers Edward	
Friesner Daniel		Harkness & Co.	
Ijams William & Co.		Summers J. G.	
Rempel F. F.		McWhorton J.	*Centreton.*
Rochester J. & Sons		Beardsly H. & Co.	*Norwalk.*
Carnes John	*Rock House.*	Rose & Gager	
Jardner G. G. & Co.			

Boughton & Inacho   *Norwalk.*
Patrick S. & Son
Williams Theodore
Olmstead M.
Vedder Thos.
McDonald W. H. & Co.
Curtiss J. O. & Co.   *Fitchville,*
White & Martin
White D.
Siillman, Edwards & Co.   *North Fairfield.*
States & Johnson
Eastman A. R.
Moulton H. L.

Jackson County.

Hughes & Jones   *Oakhill.*
Morris & Edwards
Johnson John J.
Greene, Benner & Co.   *Keystone.*
Miller Peter   *Allensville.*
Miller Marcus
Wilcox J.
Neal & Rowell   *Berlin.*
Austin & Brown
Spence L. W. & Brother
Stevenson S. A.
McGee Wm.   *McGee's Store.*
Jackson, Furnace Co.   *Jackson Furnace.*
Price & Taylor   *Jackson.*
Stemberger M. & Co.
Hoffman D.
Owens M.
Long E.
Dyer James
Martin John M.
Ewing Peter
Adams H. H. & Co.
Dickason & Co.
Nelson John
Bunn & Waterhouse
Fullaton & Cado
Leach D. P.

Jefferson County

Hogg John   *Mt. Pleasant.*
Maxwell James
Jones Lemuel
McGee Wm. T.
Dilworth W. W.
Gaston H. F.   *Knoxville.*
Douglass J. M.
Gaston H. F.   *Port Homer.*
Bailey Alex.   *Mouth of Yellow Creek.*
Merchant Thos.   *Moore's Salt Works.*
McCoy David   *Elliottsville.*
Elliott John O.
Fisher ——,   *Wintersville.*
Hall David
Anderson Lewis   *Steubenville.*
Beatty W. H. & Co.
Barr J.
Cummings M. M.
Cummings G. M.
Downess John
Fisher John & Co.
McCartey Wm.
McCormick D.

Nash Wm. D.   *Steubenville.*
Rowen Wm.
Kirkpatrick Wm. & Co.   *Warrenton.*
McAdams John
Goudy A. & Son
Humphrey & Ewards
Baylens J. P.
Sweazey & Gillespie
Thompson S. R.
Shannon Thos.
Grimes W. & Co.   *Annapolis.*
Betz B. E.
Dungan & Marsh   *Richmond.*
Jones Joseph
Crew Wm. H. & Co.
Starr Geo.
McCollough John   *East Springfield*
Lindsey Saml.
Porter Alex.
Jackson E.

Knox County.

Bryant C. G.   *Mt. Vernon.*
Cooper, Eichelberger & Co.
Curtiss Mark
Hill & Mills
Hutchinson James
Miller J. W.
Norton A. Banning
Kirk R. C. & Co.
Sperry G. & Co.
Stoughton A. N.
Vore Elliott C.
Ward L. B.
Warden & Burr
Woodbridge Jas. E.
Miller T. E. & Co.
Beam Wm.
Faucett Josiah   *Levering.*
Ketchem R. D.
Levering John
Levering Columbus
Hildreth W.   *Danville.*
Sapp S. W.
Hammond J.   *Millwood.*
McCloud R.
Shaw G.
Conger Joseph   *Lucerne.*
Lewis Aaron
Barnes A. & R.   *Martinsburg.*
Burkholder Isaac
Mercer William
Patterson & Bricker   *Brandon.*
Greegor H. W.   *Ankenytown.*
Bartlett C. T.   *Fredericktown.*
Hooker & Ink
Howes W. J.
Massey J. B. & Co.
Strong & Mickey
Struble D. & W. J.
Tuttle & Smith
Hicks James   *Democracy.*
Wright B. P.
Boynton Henry   *Monroe Mills.*
Arnold W. & P. & Co   *North Liberty.*
Pearce Joseph W.
Pinkley C. & Co.   *Jelloway.*

Vincent S. M. & Bro.   *Jelloway.*
Bryant O. G.   *Mt. Liberty.*
Black —,
Berry Peter   *Bladensburg.*
Loverage James
Morquead O. L. E. D.

Lake County.

Sharp O. H.   *Willoughby.*
Boyce J. H. & Co.
Losey H.
Skiff George
Bates L. P. & Son
Smart Saml
Flanders J. G.   *Fairport.*
Spear J. & Co.
Paige & Willard   *Madison.*
Sheaner & King
Cook & Barnes
Damon D. & A.   *Kirtland.*
Williams G. H.
Shorman J.
Voree S. & J.   *Wickliffe.*
Allen G. W.   *Painesville.*
Booth & Harper
Cowles G. R.
Faucher & Congdon
Gillett & Childs
House J. & Son
Lockwood & Seymore
Mathews J. S.
Munson & Prime
Rockwell T.
Williams & Curtis
Wilcox A.

Lawrence County.

Campbell. Ellison & Co.   *Ironton.*
Kelly & Falwell
Merrill J. M. & Co.
Shingleton J. & Sons
Ward S.
Israel W. P., Agent Coalgrove Co. *Coal-*
                                [grove.
Davison R O.   *Hanging Rock.*
Hamilton & Martin
Kyle John
Shinnowit Frank
Williams & Co.
Davison Joseph   *Burlington.*
Johnston & Drury
Wilson S.
Langdon Elisha   *Russellsplace.*
Neal Manoah
Clark John & Son   *Miller's.*
Darling Isaac
Knight William
Morrison L. D.   *Quaker Bottom.*
Proctor Jacob & A. S.
Riley James
Wilgus Charles
Waters Charles A.
Haskell James   *Haskellville.*
Massie & Tagg   *Waterloo.*
Lewis Samuel
Nelson B.

Sylvester —,   *Aid.*
Kelley W. H.   *Kelley's Mills.*
Jones D. A.   *Elizabeth.*
Hooper William
Davison R.   *Campbell's.*
Willard, Peters & Co.
Johnston Benjamin   *Green's Store.*

Licking County.

Condit J. B.   *Johnstown.*
Condit R. B.
Reed A.
Wright S. S.
Alesworth J. C.
Scofield F. A. & Co.   *Kirkersville.*
Whitaker J. R. & Co.
Wells Wm.   *Fallsburg.*
Wyeth Joseph B.   *Fredonia.*
Curier Saml.
Peas & Bowers
Elliott C. H. & Co.   *Etna.*
Nelson James
Wolf R. S.   *Linnville.*
Richter E.
Knowlton L. W. & Co.   *Utica.*
Chapman S. & Son
Moore & Rogers
Rankin & Brown   *Brownsville.*
Griner J. C.
Gray G. M.   *Jacksontown.*
Cully Thos. & Co.   *Hebron.*
Lyon James
Wintrode Jacob
Harvey James
Wright S. & Co.   *Granville.*
Green H. R.
Humphrey D.
Bancroft H. L.
Parsons R.
Shields Joseph   *Newark.*
Stone J. N. & Co.
Seymour & Coman
Newkork M. & Co.
Darlinton R.
Wilson G. A. & Co.
Woodbridge & Co.
Baldwin Wm M.
Streeper W.
Corning S.
Dennis A. W. & Brother
Postlewait Thos. H.   *Homer.*
Williams Edwin
Seymour J. W.   *Croton.*
Winslow W.
Dewes John   *Alexandria.*
Murrell E.
Sherman J.
Boudinot H. & Co.
Phillips Wm.   *Perryton.*
Field D.

Logan County.

Cadwallader Wm.   *Huntsville.*
Gotze John & Co.
Hogge & Boyd
Shafer Hezekiah
Fuson J. M. & Bro.   *West Liberty.*

Hanger & Crane   *West Liberty.*
Hays & Swan
Lyon & Kizer
Merriweather N.
Montgomery W. K.
Taylor & Miller
Dorwin J. H.   *Logansville.*
Todd John
Youngman R. F
Chapman A. S. & J. O.   *New Richland.*
Maxwell & Co.
Davis & McClain   *East Liberty.*
Hamilton & Perry
McClain & Son
McColloch John   *Rushsylvania*
Rumer & Fulton
Stevenson Wm.
Westhammer H.
Allen Homer   *Bellefontaine.*
Brown, Taylor & Co.
Dorwin P.
Gardner, McCulloch & Co.
Gardner Andrew, Jr.
Miller & Dunham
Peterson & McCulloch
Taylor & Hodge
Cleveland & Smith   *Zanesfield.*
Sands & Brown
Davis & Crew
Darnall Wm.   *Lewistown.*
Renick Jas. H. & Co.
Bailey J. & E.   *Quincy.*
Joseph Wm. & D.
Johnson Wm. H.

Lorain County.

Carpenter B. G.   *Huntington.*
Gibbs L. C.
Horr R. A.
Hart Wm.   *Grafton.*
Bacon Horatio   *Rochester Depot.*
Robinson W. A.
Terrell & Smith   *North Ridgeville.*
Phelps J. D.   *La Grange.*
Teachont & Robbins
Hitchcock W. G.   *Pittsfield.*
Churchward & Bastard   *Copopa.*
Fuller & Clark
Stranahan & Hockins
Jones S. P.   *Brighton.*
Case Isaac G. & Co.   *Sheffield.*
Park A. A.
Carpenter R. & J. T. & Co.   *North Camden.*
Williams J. W. & J. D.
Case J. L. & Co.   *Avon Lake.*
Sherbondis ——
Case Isaac L.   *Sheffield Lake.*
Parks A. A.
Bacon John C.   *Brownhelm.*
Goodrich John
Mussey & Fuller   *Elyria.*
Starr & Co.
Cowles Owen
Coleman & Perry
Tillotson A. J.

Lucas County.

Allen John O.   *Maumee City.*
Boyd W. P. & Co.
Drummond Quincy
Frost & Backus
Merrill G. B.
Moore John A.
Moore E. C. & Co.
Post E. C.
Ranney O. D.
Williams Daniel
Dodd E. & Son   *Waterville.*
Morehouse L. L. & Co.
Reed A. P.
Clymer Samuel   *Providence.*
Roach & Wilson
Steedman & Mead
Hart Henry   *Lyons.*
Phillips B. F.
Willey Job
Bradley Levi W.   *Whiteford.*
Dewey W. F. & Son
Huling W. H.
Stout D. B.
Warren H. D. & Co.
Bell & Deveau   *Toledo.*
Church, Hays & Co.
Ketchum & Co.
Berdan & Keeler
Granger & Brothers
Hall J. S. & W. R.
Hobart S.
Hough T. H.
Leavitt D.
Maples S. H. & Co.
Reidmuster Otto
Segur W. P.
Stoddard S.
Schneman John
Wilkins W. H.

Madison County.

Melvin Joseph V.   *Somerford.*
Prugh A. G.
Simpson A.   *Lafayette.*
Snyder John
Carpenter & Harrington   *West Canaan.*
Lane Luther
Stephens John
White William J.
Worthington & Lane
Fox Isaac   *Tradersville.*
Evans John B.   *London.*
Kinney John & Co.
Fellows & Ross
Shenklin A.
Smith John M.
Warner Henry & Sons
Gedtner P. E. & J.   *Pleasant Valley.*
Crabb Benjamin
Hill George
Converse Charles
Griffin Foster   *Rosedale.*
Curry & Thomas   *South Solon.*
Noland & Snyder
Moore & McCafferty   *Mt. Sterling.*

Robison J. W. & Co.	*Mt. Sterling.*
Swetland & Riddle	
Willson & Dunn	*Midway.*
Allen Vincent	
Otarrage & Mervin	*Danville.*
Parks James	*West Jefferson.*
Stutson T. J.	
Hancock E. S.	
Hubbard Sterling	
Bliss O. H. & Co.	
Stutson James	
Florence & Brother	*California.*
Johnson J. J.	

Mahoning County.

Fusselman John C.	*Ellsworth.*
Hise Wm.	*Canfield.*
Holcomb & Tomson	
Church D. J.	
Mygott C. S.	
McBride, Steward & Co.	*Lewelville.*
McCombs C.	
Davidson J. B.	
Brown J. & Co.	
Hunter & Watson	
Wilkinson & Wilkes	
Swisher O. H. P.	*Petersburgh.*
Harrah & Hanna	
Elder J. R.	
Keller, Stumbaugh & Co.	*Youngstown.*
Wells Thos. H.	
McErwin S. B.	
Brennerman & Andrews	
Wick & Munning	
Winchell & Heiner	
Armes & Murrey	
Wick P. & Brother	
Jacobs Philip	
Jacobs A. D.	
Bennett S. F.	
McCalla & Teegarden	*Berlin Centre.*
Linton S. & Co.	
Maddox, Raymond & Co.	*Frederick.*
Mattock & Raymond	
Brainard Calvin C.	*Boardman.*
Ernst S.	*New Middletown.*
Halm T. & J.	
Thoman & Northrop	*East Lewistown.*
Roller Wm. & Co.	*Greenford.*
Pennell A.	
Jacobs A. D. & Co.	*Coitsville.*
McAughtry Joseph	*Orange.*
Porter & Hoover	
Welker Peter & Jacob	*North Jackson.*
Anthony & Flaugher	
Anderson David	
Leslie John G. & Co.	*Poland.*
Richardson H.	
Little Wm. & Co.	
Hall T. R.	
Duncan & McClelland	
Roller Wm. & Thos. W.	*Green Village.*
Pennell A.	
Porter Wm.	*Brier's Mills.*
Porter Wm.	*Milton.*

Clark J. Q. A.	*Milton.*
Linton Saml.	
Smith Geo.	*New Springfield.*
Taylor C.	
May Wm.	
Buyard G. & Co.	*North Lima.*
Buyard & Hinkle	
Fetzer Philip	
Haycock & Barber	*Pottersville.*
Harzon ——	
Ware Asa	*Damascoville.*
Crew John	
Dalzell Martin	

Marion County.

Wheeler, Delong & Co.	*Wilson.*
Roberts H.	
Banning & Davis	
Carter C.	
Drown P. A.	*Cochranton.*
Mathers A. D.	*Prospect.*
Johnson S. L.	
Field J. A. & Co.	
Wyatt John	
Barnes Geo. W. & Co.	
Spaulding L. & Co.	*Marion.*
Patten R.	
Patten & Wallace	
Runyan A. C.	
Reed J. S. & Co.	
Hardy Wm. M.	
Fisher & Reed	
Bain & Williams	
Davids J. E.	
Ault J. & Co.	
Sloan & Dockwood	

Medina County.

Austin B. D	*Leroy.*
Cargo David	
Nickerson Hiram	*Litchfield.*
Wells J. A.	
Loomis O. C.	
Howes A.	*Sharon Centre.*
Chatfield Wm. & Co.	
Burt & Golbraith	*Liverpool.*
Walker E.	
Smallman F.	
Teachont & Lewis	
Montgomery R. M.	*River Styx.*
Colborn C. J.	
Walker H. J.	*Abbeyville.*
Pardee J. & Co.	*Wadsworth.*
Blocker S.	
Higbee J.	*Lodi.*
Lewis E.	
Wetmores F. P. & W. L.	*Hickley.*
Easton J. N.	
Simmons Geo.	
Damon H.	
Towsley L.	
Wilcox J. L. & J. R.	*Weymouth.*
Stover Z. & John	*Coddingville.*
Dyer & Son	*Chatham Centre.*
Gardner, Packard & Co.	

Beeman D. O. & A. C.	*Homerville.*
Newton A. G. & Co.	
Bronson H.	*Medina.*
Peak A. L.	
Blake & Warner	
Bradley & Bevet	
Albro J. H.	
Firman A. M.	

Meigs County.

Hays W. O.	*Downington.*
Heming M.	
Rice Jacob	*Silver Run.*
Paine B.	*Rutland.*
Simpson N. & Co.	
Barrett S. H.	
Holt H.	
Roberts & Tidd	*Long Bottom.*
Stewart J. H. & Son	
Cornwell J.	
Alderman C.	*Apple Grove.*
Parr W. H.	
Hayman S. H.	
Wilson H. R. & Son	*Salisbury.*
Cooper G. W.	
Stedman E. H.	
Watkins A. P. T.	
Barlow A. M.	
Wildon S. M.	
Reed Jacob	
Hayman H.	*Letart Falls.*
Swallow H. H. & Wm. M.	
Hayman J. & Son	
Braley Ruel	*Langsville.*
Edwards Elias S.	*Pomeroy.*
Crawford T. O. & Co.	
Ralston James	
Stivers Washington	
Branch O. & Co.	
Rennington W. H.	
Loubner Andrew	
Neutzling Jacob	
Hoffman Peter	
Rasp Geo.	
Kats C. A. & Brothers	
Darst Peter	
Strider James M.	
Schriber Peter	
Bentz & Mase	
Horton W. B.	
Allison G. W.	
Hutchinson Saml.	*Ledlies.*
Crowell B. A.	

Mercer County.

Harbison John H. & Co.	*Mendon.*
Bliss & Kelsey	*St. Mary's.*
Bosche & Dicker	
Leblond & Brother	
Pauk & Bieber	
Lemhuhl H.	*Celina.*
Brandon & Hole	
LeBlond G. & T. C.	
Brandon Wm.	
Neckle Benj.	*Neptune.*

Harly Wm. & Co.	*Mercer.*
Davis James	
Collins Jacob	*Shanesville.*
Hedges Wm. B.	
Harluson J. H.	*Mendon.*
Johnson L.	*Macedon.*
Nichols Wm.	
Smith Wm.	
Brothers Gotlieb	*Cold Water.*
Bundsler David	*Fort Recovery.*
Hill & Co.	
Campbell & Co.	
Beardslee & Cecil	
Smith & Beardslee	
Roemer Joseph	*St. Henry's.*
Muckler Jacob	*Chickasaw.*
Rundley Chas.	
Burck & Dean	*Montezuma.*
Gotlieb & Sachs	*Coldwater.*
Johnson Luke	*Macedon.*
Winterman H.	
Rolmer Bernard	*St. Henry.*
Rolmer Joseph	
Rolmer Henry	

Miami County.

Beamer & Bennett	*Fletcher.*
Dukemineer J.	
Bercount & Duncan	
Shullaberger & Mikesell	*Covington.*
Lehman Jacob	
Ronston Leonard & Co.	
Shellaberger M. R.	
Carlton C. W.	
Ward Jonas	
McCabe H. H.	*West Charleston.*
Reiter & Co.	*Piqua.*
Strong W. Y.	
Whipple J. B.	
Mendenhall W. M.	
Larger J. B.	
McKnight J. M. & Co.	
Furnas R. W.	*Troy.*
Smith & Drury	
Kreider J.	
Evans & Jay	
Knoop D. & Son	*Casstown.*
Clark & Baldwin	
Low A.	*West Milton.*
Davis Saml.	
Nishwitz Geo.	
Hart J. & A.	
Harb Wm.	
McPherson & Hoagland	*Hyattsville,*
Ootral & Hartman	
Krise H.	
Wilcox & Milligan	
Hyatt M.	
Leiter J. K.	*Pleasant Hill.*
Patty John	
Mikesell Wm. H.	
Hoffner M. & Son	*Brant.*
Dunham A.	
Blessinger Geo. W.	
Yount John J.	*Fidelity*
Helmick Alex.	

Yence Abraham — *Fidelity.*
Bowman Joseph

Monroe County.

Davenport John A. & Geo. H. — *Woodsfield.*
Diehl Peter
Holland Horace
Jones Samuel P.
Kirkbride John M.
Koebler Nicholas & Co.
Gillespie George — *Laing's.*
Hopton Edward
Marailliot A. S.
Mitchell Jacob N.
Kincaid Joseph — *Antioch.*
Mitchell Thos., Sr.
Penn Thos. O.
Shotwell Thos. & Allen
Brannen & Rhodes — *Sardis.*
Hornbrook Edwin
Shumard Thos. P.
Patton & Martin
Barnett J. W. — *Stafford.*
Hawkins Reuben
Steel William
Pancoast & Headley — *Rocky Narrows.*
Garlington Thomas — *Masterton.*
Valentine Nathaniel & Co.
Pollock, Suter & Anshuts — *Sunfish.*
Thomas Thaddeus
Baldwin Levi
Ohase Robert
Smith James R.
Porter William
Ray James H.
Bidenham J. F. — *Malaga.*
Kotzebue H. O.
Moore Elijah
Brown Isaac — *Jerusalem.*
Armstrong, Mooney & Co. — *Bealsville.*
Wisner J. & Co.
Gratigny Lewis, Jr.
Hutchison W. H. & Co.
Beall Citizen
Troll & Wollenweeber
Dresel Christian — *Miltonsburgh.*
Dorr Peter
Oblinger J. B.
Benninghaur Theo. — *Lewisville.*
Buchanan William
Hamilton Jacob
Powell Isaac — *Graysville.*
Lamping T. A.
Lankerd J. A. — *Baresville.*
Thompson George
Voegtly Martin

Montgomery County.

Simmons J. — *Harshmansville.*
Snodgrass J.
Salcamp Wm. — *Vandalia.*
Sebold J. B.
Jackson H. — *Chambersburg.*
Moxton J.
Dodds M. M. — *Alexandersville.*

Baker Peter — *Alexandersville.*
Bryant O.
Dewey & Co.
Black G. A.
Markee Perry — *Liberty.*
Patten Samuel
Boyer & Eby — *Union.*
Fetters & Hoover
Sheets Daniel
Maxwell N. V. — *Centreville.*
Strong & Anderson
Arnold & Sigafoos — *Centre.*
Davis & Williamson
Swank & Baker
Reid & Mundheuk — *Pyrmont.*
Tasur Daniel
Cohn P., 2d street, — *Dayton.*
Clegg S., Jr., 3d
Baker Chas., 2d
Green John — *Farmersville.*
Shafer P. B.
Dye J. D. — *West Baltimore.*
Karr Jacob
Schnorf Milton O.
Myers Emanuel — *New Lebanon.*
Studybaker & Cloppert — *Clayton.*
Turner & Bro.
Boyer, Fritchey & Co. — *West Baltimore.*
Stump, Gunkel & McKean — *Germantown.*
Schench & Beard
Liggett & Son
Kern J. F.
Kemp George
Oblinger Gabriel
Heckerman & Stephenson — *Miamisburgh.*
Huiet Simon
Weaver & Perry
Deckert Samuel
Hoff William
Hoff D. E.
Riechard Peter
Schoeder Jacob
Platt J. F.
Curls Daniel — *Taylorsville.*
Sullivan Samuel
Olwin D. B. — *Johnsville.*

Morgan County.

Stanton & Penrose — *Chester Hill.*
Wright John D.
Vanlaw Thos. E. & Co.
Williams C. A. & Co.
Hodgin Elias
Pettit Francis — *Triadelphia.*
Jenkins & Adams — *Meigs Creek.*
Talley John F.
Pugh Wm. H. — *Malta.*
Conner G. L. & Co.
Black & Simpson
Sprague W. P. & Co.
Dawes Henry
Sands & Smith — *Morganville.*
Nelson Wm. D.
Stephens Elijah — *Bristol.*
Jenkins & Murray

14

Cool & Hedge   *Bristol.*   Munch Wm. & Co.   *Putnam.*
Deaver W. P.   *Deavertown.*   Seamans & Hainer
Jones T. B.   McCoy & Dodge
Gift A. S. J.   Fauley A & Sons   *Fultonham.*
Krider Jacob   Camon I. W.
Box John   *Wood Grove.*   Colvin Saml.   *Hopewell.*
Glassford James B.   *Rousseau.*   Richey Joseph
Drake David B.   Terry Wm.   *Shannon.*
Hester Wm.   *Pleasant Valley.*   Rankin & Wilson   *White Cottage.*
Wells Benj. & Co.   *Meigsville.*   Ungerrach Jacob
Israel B.   Dugan John & A.   *Newton.*
Barker O. L & Co.   *McConnelsville.*   Winegarner J. R.   *Gratiot.*
Gregg Joshua   Sims Simeon
Kelley & Seaman   Bowers Martin
Simpson & Black   Stevens J.   *Chandlersville.*
Stone John B. & Co.   Chapman N.
Shepard & Adams   •   Britain J.
Sill & Robinson   Harris Wm. B.   *Zanesville.*
Whissen Amas F.   Oppenheimer L. H.
Waterman D. B.   Dume Chas.
Williamson Saml.   Bainter Henry
Rogers T. & Son   *Stockport.*   McCoy & Dodge
McDermot John   Culbertson D. M.
Thomas D. E. & Brother   Guthrie W. B. & Co
Penrose John   *Pennsville.*   Grigsbys & Johnson
Spurrier John & Son   Cox H. J. & Co.
Triplett E. C.   *Neelysville.*   Gibbons J. & E.   *Ridgway.*
Neeley Thos.   Betts Wm.
Scott David   Lyman Wm.   *Nashport.*
                                             Claypool A. F.
Morrow County.   Brook Z. R.
Lazenby James & Co.   *Underwoods.*   McAdams E. A G.   *Adams' Mills.*
Cass & Myers   *Iberia.*   Smith H. A.
Colborn William   Beeker Caleb   *Otsego.*
Davis James   Marshall Wm.
Shunk & Riblet   Kinsey & Maxfie o   *Norwich.*
Arm-trong & Brother   *Cardington.*   Maxfield H. & Son
Brockway & Phelps   Walsh Wm.
Glidden T. P. & Co.   Henderson Wm.   *Frazeysburg*
Godman —   Norris John
Hite Israel   Harper & McDonald   *New Concord*
Likins & Brother   Speer Alex.
Starr & Bull   Cunningham & Wylie
Creigh & Cooper   *Shauk's.*   Kelley N.
Laveving Morgan   *Woodview*   McNutt J. & Co.
Galleher N. J.   *Pulaskiville.*   Coulter, Bonner & Co.
Doty John M.   *Lincoln.*   Britton, Cooper & Co.   *Duncan's Falls.*
Bachman Henry   *Corsica.*   Harkins R. J. J.
Cator Arthur S.   Adams E. & G. W.   *Dresden.*
Harrison Joseph   *Ninmons' Cross Roads.*   Ingalls John N.
Barnhard N.   Harone A.
House G. E. & Co.   *Mt. Gilead.*   Leggett B, A.
Reygen D. G. & Co.   Bainter John H.
Swetland & Hilt   Crane & Jones
Bartlett Z. D. & Co.
Beatty J. & Co.   -   ## Noble County.
Burgess O.
Bartlett W. F. & G. V.   *Chesterville.*   Boyd S. J.   *Berne.*
Shire W. & C. P.   Mott M. & Co.
Brown, Ayers & Co.   Cooper Charles   *Mt. Ephraim.*
Hance William   Morris Isaac Q.
                                             Ulrich Harmer
Muskingum County.   McKee & McCune   *Olive.*
                                             Wehr J. & J.
Guthrie & Co.   *Putnam.*   Benninghause & Werneke   *Harrietsville,*
Large Wm. P.   Anderson J. P.   *Sarahsville.*
Wiles L. & P.   Fowler John

Patterson D. W.   *Sarahsville.*

Round H. J.

Young & Vanmeter

McIntyre Wilson F.   *Gardner.*

Davis Joseph   *South Olive.*

Mott & Heidelhiemer

Ward Edward   *Kennonsburg.*

Rhinehart & Johnson

Bidenhorn & Baninghouse   *Batesville.*

Hare & Inskeep

McPherson & Simmons

Hendershitt & Co.

Ottawa County.

Kelley & Beach   *Elmore.*

Tyler J. S.

Powers John

Hull & Bell

Kingliam James   *Port Clinton.*

Smith S. A.

Cawell H. S. & Co.

Howard & Burke

Paulding County.

Curtis H. N.   *Antwerp.*

Snook W. H. & J. S.

Curtis H. N.   *Cranesville.*

Mason John   *Junction.*

Naver H.

Columla D.

Hickerson A. H.   *Paulding.*

Hickerson A. H. & Co.

Perry County.

Barud & Eckler   *New Lexington.*

Eckles & Burkhead

Forquer & Donally

Huston R. E.

McGreevy J. J.

Montgomery John

Munch, Buckingham & Co.

Skinner & Davis

Wilson & Kelley

Granger Oliver H.

Cusaac William   *Thomville.*

Jefferson, Miles & Co.

Johnson James

Hammond Jacob   *Rehoboth.*

Hichcock Israel

Sims & Holmes   *Mt. Perry.*

Kloons Samuel *Sunday Creek Cross Roads.*

McDonald John, Jr.

Williams B. T.

Anderson William   *Portersville.*

Brown Dixon   *Somerset.*

Delong A. L.

Fink & Dittoe

Hood C. C.

McCristal James

McMahan & Brown

Moelle W. F. & Co.

Scott M. F.

Gileny Thomas   *Chapel Hill.*

Greer Thomas

Supples H. & E.   *Straitsville.*

Huston Samuel

Pickaway County.

Baker W.   *Circleville.*

Crouse F.

Darst J. & J.

Delaplane & Bro.

Driesbach & Huffonan

Einsel & Driesbach

Franklin J. L.

Groce & Helman

McCoy James

McOrea & Co.

Pierce D.

Rodgers, Adams & Co.

Wolfley, Gregg & Shuze

Ballard O. & Co.   *Tarlton.*

Creager E.

Nye A. & H. C. & Co.

Lybrand A.

Carpenter & Thompson   *Darbyville.*

Carpenter & Weimmer

Beckett James A. & Co.   *Beckett's Store.*

Vanhoutin & Martin

Davis E. S.   *Williamsport.*

Delaplain & Bros.

Rose Abraham D.

Shoemaker Charles   *Camp Charlotte.*

Whisler T. P.

Zill William

Neff George   *Palestine.*

Darst J.   *South Bloomfield.*

Delaplane S. L.

Stebbins R.

Pike County.

McCague J. W. & J.   *Cynthiana.*

Copeland Chambers

Reed P. J.

Truesdell & Haynes W. & H.   *Jasper.*

Reed & Brothers

McMillin & Ragon   *Omega.*

Day Thos.

Blain John

Emmitt, Davis & Co.   *Waverly.*

Gross & Carolus

Hibbons J. R. & Son

Kuntzman Jacob   *Beaver.*

Penn A.   *Byington.*

Humphrey John

Cartwright H.

Galford John W.   *Gibeon.*

Rinkman A.

Moore & Chenoweth   *Piketon.*

Dunham, Jones & Co.

Donehoe & March

Becker, Rust & Boyd

Portage County.

Gillett S. A. & R. A.   *Ravenna.*

Prentiss O. & J. C.

Day Henry L.

Howell, Witter & Co.

Seymour F. W.

Day S.

Bostwick John H.   *Campbellsport.*

Alderman & Bush   *Atwater.*

Hough B.

Beldin J.	*Randolph.*	Ewing M. E.	*Gilboa.*
Dickinson Walter		Hipkins T. H. B.	
Farmers' Co.	*Aurora.*	Hughes & Mapel	
Harmon C. & C. R.		Lowry R. J.	*Leipsic.*
Abel & Thompson	*Streetsboro'.*	Huyck & Blaker	*Medary.*
Horr A.	*Shalersville.*	Bochmer H. J	*Fort Jennings.*
Bostwick D.	*Edinburgh.*	DeLacenay Lewis	
Button Wm. D.	*Franklin.*	Greene E. W.	*Pleasant.*
Earle Thos.		Taylor Wm. & A. T.	*Kalida.*
Parmele Elisha		Douglass Robert	
Reynolds S. S.		Lee M. & Son	
Rent, Grennell & Co.		Rice C. H.	
Welch Danl.	*Suffield.*	Coulter & Crow	
Price John	*Paris.*	Kemper B. H.	*Buckeye.*
Davis & Thomas		Lapold B.	
Foster J. W.	*Mantua.*	Musman B.	
Bradley H. G. & T. C.		Cox & Allen	
Nooney H. A.		Lee J.	
Wilson & Gray	*Deerfield.*	Garner W. W. & T. F.	*Vaughnsville.*
Day & Wann		Marshall R. & Co.	*Pendleton.*
Beecher Henry	*Nelson.*	Bagley N. H.	
Pixley E. J.			
Sprague J.		**Richland County.**	
Thomas John	*Palmyra.*	Anderson & Davis	*Shelby.*
Lewis F.		Evans J. C. & Co.	
Parsons & Root	*Windham.*	Leyman H.	
Clark & Barnes	*Freedom.*	McConnell M. & Co.	
		Hackedorn & Co.	*Ontario.*
Preble County.		Holland R.	
		Stought & Evans	
Gale John H.	*West Alexandria.*	Geary Joseph	*Butler.*
Coffman Andrew		Lamley Wm.	
Alexander P.		Robison & Jones	
Baer John D.		Hall Edward	*Shenandoah.*
Baer George		Avery C. L.	*Mansfield.*
Horn Geo. & Son	*Lewisburg.*	Endly Henry	
Hoover A.		Hedges E. & C.	
Potter Ezra	*Camden.*	Strong W. L. & Co.	
Craig Isaac		Strong F. W. & Co.	
Myers Benj.		Sturges, Grimes & Co.	
Vanausdal C. & Co.	*Eaton.*	Weldon, Robinson & Co.	
Minor O. & W. H. H. B.		Wigle J. H. & Co.	
Marsh & Lockwood		Adams John & Son	*Lexington.*
Epply A. & J. B.		Beverstock A. B.	
Presely & Pinkerton	*Fairhaven.*	Dalamater John	
Hawes Edward		McCrary John	*West Windsor.*
Lough D. A.		Beverstock J. A.	*Olivesburg.*
McKown J. P.	*New Westville.*	Houston R. & R.	
McWhinney James		Cross Silas	*Belleville.*
Cox S. B.	*Gettysburg.*	Cutting & Cross	
Duffield A.		Jackson B.	
McWhinney J. H.	*West Florence.*	Moore & Brown	
McWhinney Saml.		Morrow John	
Adams S. R.	*Hamburg.*	Strong & Mickey	
Adams M. C.		Brown Caleb	
Adams L.		Greaber Samuel	
McWhinney LeRoy		Morrison James	
Coffman J. H. & Son	*Enterprise.*	Skilling J. D.	
Brown Joseph	*Morning Sun.*	Squire & Porter	*Richland.*
Steele John		Mickey & Swaney	*Lucas.*
Vanneman G. W.	*New Paris.*	Tucker Norman	
Crampton J. C.		Foulks Henry	*Adario.*
Purviance A. & D. L.		Powers & Kinney	*Plymouth*
Wheeler and Randall	*West Elkton.*	Culp & Croninger	
Hornaday & Hallowell		McDonough Robert	
		Hornbeck & Co.	
Putnam County.		Spenser & Wright	
Creighton & Co.	*Gilboa.*	Starr S. H. & Co.	

Ross County.

Rockhold E.	Bainbridge.
Fitzwilliams Wm.	
Cobb C. B.	
Brown J. P.	
Giffin & Terrill	
Mark & March	Lattis.
Haynes T. F. & W. M.	
Shepherd J.	Frankfort.
Anderson & Tulleys	
Roseboom G.	
Rittenhouse Wm.	
Jones Wm.	
Betts & Knox	Clarksburg.
McClintick S. & Co.	
Clark Saml.	
Smith G. W.	
Lawrence H.	
Godfrey E.	
Bush, Dean & Co.	South Salem.
Benner & Pricer	
Sloan J. M.	
Buchwalter S. D.	Hallsville.
Ponsler & Grafton J & F.	
Drusbach J. B. & M. B.	Yellow Bud.
Carr J. D.	Gillespieville.
Motter A.	
Ratcliffe Simon	
Cushion, Wood & Co.	
Griffin Saml.	
Smith, Prother & Co.	Bourneville.
McCracken Robert P.	
Hoys J. A. & Co.	Kingston.
May J. & J. M.	
Woods Chas.	

Sandusky County.

Powers Chas.	Woodville.
Blinn John H.	
Teyman A. R.	
Wales J. C.	Baxter.
Beerry P. B.	Clyde.
Ames Jonathan	
Brownwell H. A.	Greensburg Cross Roads.
Smith, Crockett & Co.	Rutland Ridge.
Olmstead J. S.	Fremont.
McLellan & McGee	
Moss Joseph	
Haynes J. P. & Son	
Clenet & Garvin	
Ziegler M. N.	
Gurdorf A.	
Nims O. L.	
Betts Danl.	
Eisenhour & Coles	
Smith D.	Rollersville.

Scioto County.

Davidson Thos.	Haverhill.
Smith Charles	
McGilligan Thos.	Lucasville.
Muckilrath Hugh	
Nolls Sylvester	
Brodbeck P.	Portsmouth.
Gaylord & Co.	
Barbier Eugene	Scioteville.
Barrett Thornton	
Marshall Elias	Scioteville.
Chaffin P. & Son	Lyra.
Chaffin D. S.	
Collett A. M.	
Bennet John	Iron Furnace.
Collis Royal T.	0
Gephardt Lewis	
Hamilton, Wesley & Bro.	Friendship.
Bruner Samuel N.	Wheelersburgh.
McConnel J. & Son	

Seneca County.

Graham J.	Attica.
Miller Samuel	
Molts M. R. & Geo.	
Rininger Wm	
Schuyler & Schombirt	
Foster Chas. W. & Son	Steiner.
Hales Joel	
Hays David	
Bernard E.	Adams.
Arnold H. & L. D.	Melmore.
Arnold & Gray	
Burns, Stevens & Co.	
Crowell, Burns & Co.	
Cook E. H.	Adrian.
Ewing & Co.	
Swagart J.	
Bibler C. & L.	Berwick.
Campbell John	
Curtis & Bibler	
Hoffman Geo. W.	
Sailor S. & J.	
Hunsicker J. C.	Bloomville.
Seitz & De Witt	
Miller & Cessna	Bettsville.
Wehley & Wagoner	Berwick.
Baldwin & Co.	Tiffin.
Barber J. S.	
Crumb Robert	
Groff M. Y. Co.	
Holt W.	
Martin L.	
McNeil H.	
Shriver & Sneath	
Scott W. D.	
Shepherd S. W.	
Coonrod U. P.	
Spayth W. O.	
Reeme J. W.	
Sullivan M.	
Baldwin & Co.	
Taylor George	
Graff & Co.	
Walker & Ourand	
Dugan P.	
McNeal M.	
Martin Lewis	
Wertz Henry	Bascom.
Spencer H. & Co.	Reedtown.
Williams B. D. & Co.	
Smith, Crockett & Co.	Green Spring.
Finch E. B.	
Brown & Burns	West Lodi.
Easterbrook Wm.	
White Lyme	

Simmons Wm.   *Republic.* | Miller & Keplinger   *New Franklin*
Baker B. F. | Snyder G. H. & Co
Harkness & McKee | Snyder Jacob
Ogden G. M. | Welty & Jarvis   *Frease's Store.*
                                           | Beachtel & Pierson   *New Berlin.*
Shelby County. | Mohler & Young
                                           | Brooke, Scott & Leek   *Marlboro'.*
Maillat J. B.   *Houston.* | Hambleton & Trisk
McDermit Wm. | Barkdull E. J. & Co.   *Magnolia.*
Layrisse Peter   *Wynant.* | Fertig G. W. & Co.
Meller James   , | Walser J. W.
Pilliod Francis | Criswell William   *Mapleton.*
Ailes A. V. & Co.   *Montra.* | Baird, Stephens & Co.   *New Baltimore.*
Howell Geo. W. | McClun T. P.
Maharin J. & J. | Lewis J. & A. Co.
Knox & Simpson   *Pratt.* | Houghton & Brown   *Hartville.*
Ogden John | Shollenberger Peter
Thirkield S. & J. H. | Robinson J.   *Massillon.*
Blake & Hawkey   *Sidney.* | Black William
Fry J. O. | Russell John
Fry R. L. | Williams & Greene   *Limaville.*
Howe J. B. | Hellman J.
Lamb & Zinn | Schilling Jacob
McCord & Co. | Milhous V. & Co.   *Mt. Union.*
McCullough S. | Pettis J. M.
Neal John | Hamlin Stephen   *Mahoning*
Ogden P. A.
Rodgers & Brothers
Starrett Charles   ### Summit County.
Thirkield & Burrows
Wright John   *Hardin.* | Curtiss Elijah   *Middlebury.*
Lenox N. B. | Moore & Sawyer
Rose H.   *Leckington.* | Pease S. & Son   *Cuyahoga Falls.*
Simons B. F. & Co. | Becker A.
Burns W. O. S. | Comstock O. J. & S.
                                           | Dow & Co.
                                           | Harrison J. B. & Co.
Starke County. | Inskeep John
                                           | Newman S.   *New Portage.*
Bell P. V.   *Navarre.* | Baker, Weaver & Wholf   *Clinton.*
Hawk J. | Price John C. & Co.
Roff E., Agent Farmers and Mechanic's | Robinson John
                            [Association | Wellhouse Wm.
Wert & Burgert | Dunham F. A.   *Western Star.*
Augustine G. P.   *Waynesburg.* | Brewster A. A.   *Hudson.*
Gray R. R. | Buss John
Reynolds E. & J. | Hart & Brother
Rupe George   *West Brookfield.* | Smith J. W. & Co.
Sibbalow M. | Carter H. S. & Co.   *Tallmadge.*
Hames & Foster   *Minerva.* | Hunsberger John   *Inland.*
Hibbets & Boory | Abbey G. N.   *Akron.*
Morledge & Perdue | Edson J. D. & J. M.
Pool Joseph & Co. | Fuller H.
Feather & Glaser   *Lake.* | Hall P. D. & Co.
Joseph M. & M. | Henry M. W.
Woods J. B. | Hibbard A.
Faiver L.   *Louisville.* | Keys F.
Fry John W. & Co. | McCurdy Geo. T.
Lawrence & Mathias | May H.
Gremes & McCleery   *Paris.* | Stacy, Johns & Co.
Koons Lewis | Stephens J. W. & Co
Martin Rudolphus | Sumner O. A. & Co.
Philipe Daniel & Son | Sumner J. A & Co.
Adolph George | Wesener J. E.
Frick George | Zwisler J. W.
Marsh Edward | Sisler John   *Nimisilla.*
Wise J. H. & Co.   *Greentown.* | Comstock & Chaffin   *Peninsula.*
Woods J. B. | Curtiss Charles
Feathers & Glasser

Ewing, Weld & Co. *Richfield.*
Wood Baxter
Hubbard Archibald *Montrose.*
Edson Julius D. *Boston.*
Wood Frederick
Woodman J. H. *Northfield.*
Decker N.
Odell, Price & Co.
Pearce J. S. *Eden.*
Nash Frederick *Copley.*
Gaylord Flavius
Higgins Thomas *Bath.*
Jagger Elmus H.
McFarland Moses

Tuscarawas County.

Armstrong William *Port Washington.*
Killgore G.
Knight John
Rounbaugh John
Vinton M. M.
Boyd M. A. *New Cumberland.*
McGregor Wilson
Horn Thomas *Cadwallader.*
McGuire John
McMath James
Jenkins Jane
Rosman & Parsons
Bell P. V. & Dawson *Deardorff's Mills.*
Chapman Amon
Spangler Walter R.
Correll & Delaney *Winfield.*
Winkelpleck Adam
Dickson J. & Co. *Sandyville.*
Laffer P. P. & Co.
Keyser Henry *Bolivar.*
Smith J. V.
Shanell Abraham *Gnadenhutten.*
Hanold J. & Hursey *Peoli.*
McPherson, Shaw & Co.
Bimeler J. M, Agent Zoar Community
[*Zoar.*
Eckert Charles A. *Ragersville.*
Snyder Jacob S. & Co.
Steese & McClean *New Philadelphia.*
Chapin J. P.
Roby & Dixon
Minich & Warner
Graham & Dye
Greenleaf & Seaton
Terrell J. & Co.
Welty & Hayden *Canal Dover.*
Burnett Edmund
Deardorff Jesse S.
Deardorff & Maus
Benson H. V.
Oswald George
Sterling Jacob S.
Ream H. & M. V. *Shanesville.*
Good D. M.
Bates Albert
Minnick J. *Tuscarawas.*
Knisely H. J.
Walker T. W. & Gartrell *Rockford.*

Trumbull County.

Crandle N & Co. *Girard.*

Gilbert & Morris *Girard.*
Keibler A. D. *Farmington.*
Crane Ira R. & Son
Lane E. T.
Clark G. W. *Church Hill.*
Chew & Case *Brookfield.*
Miner Joel
Arms F. O.
Abbott & Higgins *Newton Falls.*
Merwin A. & O.
Spencer & Hart
Tew William
Brown Benj. *Ohlstown.*
Christy George L.
Booth U. K. *Vienna.*
Scovill Smith
Corey F. H. *Bristolville.*
Thompson Jas. O. & Co.
Mason H. H. *Niles.*
Robison, Battles & Grist
Ward James & Co.
Hurd Hiram *Southington,*
Abell & Son *Mecca.*
Powers M.
Hickok J. C.
Jackson J. W., Ag't. Farmers' Co., *John-*
[*sonville.*
Waller, Rice & Co. *Greensburgh,*
Cramer John *Hubbard.*
Hine Samuel
Jacobs & Jackson
Barnes & Horner *Gustavus.*
Fitts Geo. W. & Co.
Horner Jas. T.
Collar H., Agent Mesopotamia Farmers'
Co. *Mesopotamia.*
Mears S. & L. W.
Williams & Easton
Christy Mathias *Hartford.*
Hayes & Plumb
Woodford George L.
Hurlburt & Coe *Orangeville.*

Union County.

Rathbun O. & Co. *Marysville.*
Snider P. & Co.
Warner & Co.
Skinner W. H.
Hammond E. *Raymond's.*
Manchester P.
Raymond N. & Co.
Thompson James *Watkins.*
Bruck E. *Richwood.*
Hastings L. H.
Fullington & Garwood *Milford Centre.*
Neal Henry
Reynolds E. L.
Stout & Bewersmith *Jerome.*
Andrews William
Wells J. N.
Buck Henry *New California.*
Kessler Samuel
Tunks S. A. & A. G. *Pharisburg.*
Skeels H. & L.
Mitchell Wm. D. W. *Boke's Creek.*
Price T. R.
Miller Rees *Byhalia.*

Van Wert County.

Baker A. W.	*Van Wert.*
Conn R. & Co.	
Crafts George S.	
Vance E. & Co.	
Wells E. R.	
Hollister, Bliss & Lytle	*Delphos.*
Jones Evan B.	
Moore P. B.	
McCune & Woolson	

Vinton County.

Will J. K.	*McArthur.*
McLain T. A.	
Dodge J. & E.	
Davis & Payne	
Dowd O.	
Hawk J. S.	
Martin & Shockey	
Reynolds H. & Co.	
Shades Francis	
Miller Peter	*Allensville.*
Wilcox Joseph	
Miller Marcus	
Franee Jehiel	*Reed's Mills.*
Moore H. B. & Co.	
Hampton E.	
Hines & Hard	
Wilson J. B. & Co.	
Murray S. S.	*Wilkesville.*
Thompson & Co.	
Carr —	
Stoddard H. W.	*Prattsville.*
Davis & Payne	*Mt. Pleasant.*
Holland John	
Chapman Amos	*New Plymouth.*
Eggleston S. D. & C. C.	
Chapman Warren	
Gregory Jackson & Co.	

Warren County.

Thirkield Brother & Co.	*Franklin.*
Evans & Adams	
Thomas D. N.	
Wright M. & J.	*Springboro'.*
Stansel J.	
Gilpin A.	
Miller & Voorhees	
Graham Saml.	*Ridgeville.*
Russum C. P.	
Hadden & McClelland J. M. & W. B.	
	Waynesville.
Harris J. H. & Co.	
Allen T. L.	
Rogers S. W.	
Mills M.	
Johnson A. E.	
Drew A.	*Twenty Mile Stand.*
Foster James H.	
Terry Danl.	*Oregon.*
Sherwood Jonathan	
Bennett R. H.	*Mason.*
Dodds Wm. S.	
Murphey J. C.	
Wickoff P. W. & G.	
Leitch Wm.	

Todd J. S.	*Red Lion.*
Ballard W. H.	
Gustin J.	
Ivins & Powell	*Dunlevy.*
Hill F. G.	*Dallasburgh.*
Hill Wm. J. & Co.	
Mason John	*Edwardsville.*
Hill P. W.	
Peters Joseph	
Whitaire J. M.	
Severs L.	
Day & Wann	*Deerfield.*
Wilson H. & Co.	
Johnson B. & E.	*Waynesville.*
Plunkett John M.	*Hopkinsville.*
Butterworth & Linton	
Ford Jas.	
Foster J. H.	
Boke R.	*Lebanon.*
Noble & Lewis	
Adams Wm. & Co.	
Gilvest J. P.	
Skinner & Foster	
Rapp & Saucer	
Siminton John	
Hart Z.	
Blackburn Wm.	
Egbert & Piles	
Wood & Pharis	
McCurdy & Pharis	
White Henry	
Parcel Richard	
Hyman Martin	
Hopkins & Mounts	*Morrow.*
Fairchild Lewis	
Smith Saml.	
Snyder Thos J.	
Moore O. P.	
Smith J. M.	
Ogden S. E.	
Gilmore R. B.	*Rochester.*
Mulford H.	
St. John Hiram	*Butlerville.*
Morgan Henry	
Vaughan Wm.	
Pence E. H.	*Mt. Holly.*
Pence John W.	
Craft Josiah	
Antrum A. L. & Son	*Harveysburg.*
Thompson Reuben	
Haines & Dakin	
Smith J. P.	

Washington County.

Campbell Daniel & Co.	*Centre Belpre*
Gilbert & McConnell	
Lewis Parker & Co.	
Chidister —	
Shevilier Wm.	
Skeen S.	
Rea Wm.	*Ostend.*
Riggs H. R.	
Harvey J. P.	
Oady J. C.	
Boyd Chas. A.	*Regnier's Mills.*
Darrow Wm.	
Delong Isaac H.	

Smithson John	*Regnier's Mills.*	Schwab & Coplins	*Lowell.*
Davis Joseph		Wolf H.	
Dana & Holdren	*Newport.*	Spease V.	
Edgerton Luther		Ryan M.	
Bradfield & Barnes		Winsor Augustus	*Watertown.*
Talbot & Brother	*Bartlett.*	Richards Thos. E.	
Fairris & Henry		Jones Thos.	*Decaturville.*
Smith Harvey		Heeft J.	
Smith John S.		McNamara T.	
Smith James		McMeans —	
Withington M.		Kidd & Darrow	*Bonn.*
Bowen C. & Co.	*Waterford.*	Lambert B.	*North Union.*
Hughes George		Morland A.	
McCollum Saml. & Co.	*Beverly.*	Wickman W. W.	
Thendas, Hoge & Co.		Coles D. B.	
Seiley S. F.			
Truesdell John		**Wayne County.**	
Brophy John	*Marietta.*	Cleppinger & Cameron	*Dalton.*
Bosworth, Wells & Co.		Hoover M. & A. S.	
Burke John		Gondy John	
Curtiss & Brothers		Clark A.	*Chippewa.*
Dana James & Co.		Franks A.	
Holden N.		Graham & Hower	
Holden J.		Guilhouse E. & Co.	
Marshall John		Rautson S.	
Ross Andrew		Cummins & Co.	*Fredericksburg.*
Shipman C. & S.		McCormick & Moore	
Turner S. R.		Clark & Number	*Edinburgh.*
Taylor James		Jameson A. H. & J. K.	
Thomas W. B. & Co.		Biggs John	
Watters A. B.		Armstrong W. B.	*Big Prairie.*
Woodbridge D.		Stoner A.	
Woodbridge & Wescott		Kisen J. S.	*Reedsburg.*
Wells W. & T. K.	*Harmar.*	Swarts Jeremiah	
Jewel & Co.		Sullinger John	
Rolf D. & Co.		Martin D. C.	
Barter L. & D.		Stewart & Hoover	*Burbank.*
Tomlinson & Mansfield		Eby & Howe	
Amlin J. M. & Co.		Krysher & Son	*Smithville.*
Vinton Wm.		Ely & Willaman	
Williams & Brother		Allman Tipton	*East Union.*
Bosworth & Wells	*Lower Salem.*	Allman T.	*Number One.*
Kueck Frederick		Gandy John	*West Lebanon.*
Magee H.		Benjamin E. A.	*Old Hickory.*
Hill Danl.		Marsh W. N.	
Thorld Silas	*Coal Run.*	Stibbins & Pollock	
Slater Ellis		Jones D. K.	*Shreve.*
Devol Chas.		Ott John & G.	*Marshallville.*
Harrison Wm.	*Fillmore.*	Latimer P.	
Ballard Z. B. & Co.		Gibbins F. W.	
Lake James B.		Childs Wm.	*Wooster.*
Fish Alex. & Co.	*Wesley.*	Robison & Co.	
Smith C.		Jones & Gillis	
Dunbar S.		Frost H. J. & Co.	
Cook & Gage		King D. H. & Co.	
Sheets A. & Co.	*Grandview.*	Jones J. N. —	
Talbott, Williamson & Co.		Lanvell John	
Collins J. H.		Winebrenner & Baker	
Fand P.		Alison M.	
Koontz J.	*Jolly.*	Power & Leeberger	
Campbell, O'Neal & Co.	*Belpre.*	Spink & Robb	
Regnier J. B.	*Lowell.*	Grey J.	
Magee J.			
Williamson Jas.		**Williams County.**	
Williamson Robert		Ayres Abner	*West Unity.*
Smith John		Blinn & Letcher	
Fleek & Sprague		Juileat G. W.	

Mattison Thos.   *West Unity.*
Rings & Benson
Tressler A. J.
Boyanton A. W.   *Pulaski.*
Griswold J.
Stougt Wm.
Boyers Jacob & Co.   *Bryan.*
Orall David
Kent Thos & Co.
Will John
Bowman David   *Williams Centre.*
Ruse & Tharp
Tomlinson G. H.
Grissey & Gilbert   *Montpelier.*
Mallory C. W.
Platt James
Sheriden Wm.   *Lockport.*
Edington S.   *Bridgewater.*

Wood County.

Hall J. A.   *Perrysburg.*
Peck E. D. & Co.
Beach S. N. & Co.
Hollister B. F. & Co.
Ross & Key
Hood Wm.
Huston Wm.
Locke L. C. & Co.   *Bowling Green.*
Pike Mrs. T. M.
McCroy & McFadden   *Portage.*
Van Blarcum John
Haskins & Johnson
Larkey Geo. & Co.   *Gilead.*
Clymer Samuel
Hughes & Camp   [*Roads.*
Ensminger & Mogle   *Montgomery Cross*
Kelley Joseph
McCrary Samuel   *Woodbury.*
Bronson James
Childs J.   *New Rochester.*

Wyandot County.

Beidler P. B.   *Upper Sandusky.*
Beery Isaac H. & Anthony
McJunkins J. & Co.
Roberts James G.
Sigler H. C.
Wheeler J.
Worth G. C.
Brinkerhof & Wilson   *Sycamore.*
Suffell, Pride & Co.
Brayton Wm.   *Crawfordsville.*
Beebe Sheldon
Mailon E.
Dow, Stephens & Co   *Carey.*
Shawhan R. W.
Reinecker James H.   *Wyandot.*
Straw/Danl.   *Brownstown.*
Worth S. M.   *Little Sandusky.*
Campbell Alex.   *McCutchensville.*
Freet Henry
Davis & Morton   *Marseilles.*
Kennedy & Long
Potter Wm. S.
James James E.   *Whartonsburg.*

Debolt S.   *Mexico.*
Bernard Aaron

Dyers (Silk, Cotton, and Woolen).

Cuyahoga County.
Williams George S., 83 Water *Cleveland.*
Jackson J. B., 71 Pearl   *Ohio City.*

Erie County.
Comstock T. C.   *Sandusky City.*

Franklin County.
Kinseller M., High   *Columbus.*
Robertson George do

Hamilton County.
Teasdale W., 265 Walnut   *Cincinnati.*
Job H., 135   do
Peel & Sons, 274   do
Walker R., Congress near Broadway
Harmeur J., 231 Walnut
Harmeier J., 44 e. Sixth
Knodle E., 425 Vine
Hammitt D. S. & Co., 221 Western Row
Hesselbach F., 45 w. Twelfth
Curtis R. B., 244 Elm

Highland County.
Grant F.   *Hillsboro'.*

Jefferson County.
Wyatt Jas.   *Steubenville.*

Montgomery County.
Howard N., Third   *Dayton.*

Washington County.
Pitton A.   *Marietta.*

Earthenware Manufacturers.

Belmont County.
Mehollen & Batson   *Uniontown.*

Clark County.
Hicks W. J.   *Springfield.*
Foreman Joseph   *New Carlisle.*

Columbiana County.
Philip J. R.   *Wellsville.*
Ridder D.
Croxall & Brothers
Bane Taylor   *New Lisbon.*
Brouse Philip
Russell William
Buck Jacob   *Bucks.*
Ball & Morris   *East Liverpool.*
Brunt & Bloor
Goodwin John
Harker, Thompson & Co.
Harrison & Brothers
Harvey, Green & Co.
Larkins, Newell & Co.
Salt & Mear

Walley & Co. *East Liverpool.*
Woodward, Blakely & Oo.
Keister Isaac *Columbiana.*

Defiance County.

Speaker Lucas *Brunersburg.*

Franklin County.

Jenkins A., Front *Columbus.*

Greene County.

Nesbit Nathaniel *Xenia.*

Hamilton County.

Brumley W., cor. Freeman and Ham. Road
Cincinnati.
Eichenlaub V., 649 Vine
Lessell Peter, 99 Hunt
Lewis J. H., 683 Vine
Scott George & Co., w. Front
Seamans & Hainer, 14 and 16 w. Water
Schuck Jacob, 651 Vine
Derrough William *Fulton.*
Jackson J. & E. *Harrison.*

Knox County.

Blue William H. *Bladensburg.*
Harris Jesse
Griffith Abraham

Lucas County.

French E. P. *Emery.*

Montgomery County.

Gephart & Isor *Germantown.*
Winebrenner D. *Miamisburgh.*
Bright Samuel D. *Liberty.*
Ross H. J. *Centreville.*

Muskingum County.

Hawson & Son *Zanesville.*

Richland County.

Hisey William *Shenandoah.*

Starke County.

Ross J. H. *Waynesburg.*

Tuscarawas County.

Riggs Alfred *Sandyville.*
Schwendiman John *Ragersville.*
Gibbs W. *New Philadelphia.*

Eating Houses.

Cuyahoga County.

Haley & Wellman, 46½ Bank *Cleveland.*

Defiance County.

Richardson M. *Defiance.*
Shipley & Co.

Franklin County.

Boyer H., Fourth *Columbus.*

Hamilton County.

Brenan James H., 100 Main *Cincinnati.*
Devitt P., 49 w. Fifth
Davis John N., 113 Sycamore
Fales & Wheeler, 130 do

Portage County.

Taylor S. A. *Ravenna.*
Leffingwell J. W.

Richland County.

Beckel J. *Shelby.*
Coltman S.
Cross D.
Gamble E. D.
Knobloch & Klesa

Ross County.

McGee R. L. *Chillicothe.*
Clark E. B.

Scioto County.

Gramm Moses *Portsmouth.*
Willis & Ripley

Union County.

Wilkinson J. M. *Marysville.*

Vinton County.

Nichols Geo. W. *McArthur.*
Shockey J. J.

Edge Tool Manufacturers.

Butler County.

Smith C. J. *Hamilton.*

Crawford County.

Stem William *Sulphur Spring.*

Cuyahoga County.

White H. & Sons *Chagrin Falls.*
Halsey Charles, Columbus near Centre
Cleveland.
Marble F. B , cor. Seneca and Champlain
McGregor James *Ohio City.*
Powell & Co., Detroit

Franklin County.

Ohio Tool Co., State Avenue *Columbus.*

Hamilton County.

Thiesing & Evens, 319 Main *Cincinnati.*
Schaeffer & Cobb, 28 Pearl
Smith C J. & Co., 206 Main
Seybold C., 207 do
Kolp J., 260 Broadway
Cunningham A. & Co., Lock bet. 5th & 6th
Galbreath Jas., 7th bet. Main & Walnut,
Siewers C , Eighth bet. Broadway & Canal
Berthoud J. H & T. Busse, 16 Canal
Isphordina & Stumpe, cor. Clay & 13th
Berckhemer C., 62 w. Thirteenth
Hattersly G., cor. Mohawk & Hamburg
Tuttle John N., W. Row bet. 9th & Court
Holliday Thos., 197 W. Row

Lake County.

Edgerton E.   *Painesville.*

Montgomery County.

Benjamin T.   *Dayton.*

Portage County.

French Isaac & Co.   *Ravenna.*
Joiner Alvin   *Nelson.*
Waters R. N. & Co.   *Charlestown.*

Summit County.

Wright W.   *Cuyahoga Falls.*
Hinman Z.   *Tallmadge.*
Blakelee J.
Siess J. O. & Co.   *Inland.*

Trumbull County.

Brainard O   *Warren.*
Bushnell Eli & Co.   *Hartford.*

Enameled Work Manufacturers.

Hamilton County.

Taylor F. & Co., 275 Fifth   *Cincinnati.*
Horton & Macy, 210 and 212 do and s. w.
   cor. Elm and Pearl

Engine (Fire) Builders.

Hamilton County.

Westover & Co., Front bet. Ludlow and
   Lawrence streets,   *Cincinnati.*
Cummings Saml. do, bet. Pike and Butler
Latta, Shawk & Co., Race bet. 4th and 5th

Engine (Steam) Builders.

Ashland County.

Fairchild Asahel   *Ashland.*

Ashtabula County.

Castle H. P.   *Geneva.*
Ryder N.   *Austinburg.*

Columbiana County.

Geisse P. F.   *Wellsville.*
Sharp, Davis & Co.   *Salem.*
Sharp Thomas
Taylor Samuel O.
Woods Enos   *Columbiana.*

Crawford County.

Wingart J. & H.   *Bucyrus.*

Cuyahoga County.

Craig W. S., Division street   *Cleveland.*
Frankland J. & Co , Front
McCleland & Co., Phenix Foundry
Searls Albert G , River
Cuyahoga Locomotive Works

Erie County.

Moss Saml.   *Sandusky City.*

Franklin County.

Ambos & Lennox, National Bridge *Columb.*

Greene County.

Gowdy John B.   *Xenia.*

Hamilton County.

Niles & Co., e. Congress st.   *Cincinnati.*
Anshutz, Martin & Co., e. Front bet. Ludlow and Lawrence.
Harkness, Moore & Co., do
Goodloe James, 14 Congress e. of B'dway
Pollock J. S., Columbia bet. Race and Elm
Burge & Johnston, Pearl bet. Elm & Plum
Latta, Shawk & Co., Race bet. 4th and 5th

Huron County.

Seymour & Coburn   *North Fairfield.*

Knox County.

Buckingham C. P. & Co,   *Mt. Vernon.*
Cooper C. C. & Co.
Braington, Speakman & Co. *Fredericktown*

Lake County.

Anderson & Genung   *Painesville.*

Lawrence County.

Merrill J. M. & Co.   *Ironton.*

Licking County.

McCune & Ebersole   *Newark.*

Meigs County.

McAboy Wm.   *Pomeroy.*
Depew John C.

Muskingum County.

Blandy H. & F.   *Zanesville.*
Hoadley John

Pickaway County.

Bright M. & Co.   *Circleville.*

Richland County.

Hall & Allen   *Mansfield.*
Moody J. W.   *Belleville.*

Ross County.

Welch Wm.   *Chillicothe.*

Seneca County.

Watson & Hall   *Republic.*

Starke County.

Walton M. & A.   *Marlboro'.*
Russell E. M. & Co.   *Massillon.*
Hart & Brown
Partridge H. & R.

Summit County.

Webster & Taplin   *Akron.*

Warren County.

Crispen & Kelley   *Waynesville.*

Wayne County.

Wathey Wm.   *Dalton.*
Harrison H. R.   *Wooster.*

Engineers (Civil).

Crawford County.

Dixon Lot *Bucyrus.*

Cuyahoga County.

Pillsbury & Callan, 3 Williams' Block *Cleveland.*
Case H. H., Columbus Block *Ohio City.*

Franklin County.

Case William P. *Columbus.*

Hamilton County.

Gilbert A. W., College Hall *Cincinnati.*
Leopold Otto G., cor. 4th and Vine
Scowden T. R., at Water Works
Knight Geo. H. & Brother, 6 Pub. Landing

Lake County.

Rotter J. A. *Painesville.*
Kerr Danl.
Harvey M. S.

Medina County.

Mead Whitman *Medina.*

Starke County.

Roan George W. *East Greenville.*

Engravers

Map, Historical, Portrait & Copperplate in general.

Belmont County.

Anderson Hugh *St. Clairsville.*

Cuyahoga County.

Brainard & Burridge, Herald Block *Cleveland.*
Hopkins J. E., 73 Superior.
Goodman John, 4 Ontario

Erie County.

Wappenstein J. *Sandusky City.*

Franklin County.

Felch J. M. *Columbus.*

Hamilton County.

Middleton & Wallace, 115 Walnut *Cincin.*
Jewett Charles A., cor. 3d & Walnut
Gibson Geo. & Co , 101 Main
Reed Edwin O., 36 w. Third
Booth T. D., 148 Main
Jones George F., do
Garrett J. W. B., 2 w. 4th
Shipley H. H. & Bro., 22 do
Hall Charles F., do
Barth S., Vine bet. 12 & 13

Harrison County.

Jarvass Jacob *Cadiz.*

Lake County.

Single J. F. *Painesville.*

Muskingam County.

Hosking P. W. *Zanesville.*

Ross County.

Taylor N. H. *Chillicothe.*

Trumbull County.

Porter William F. *Warren.*

Engravers (Wood).

Hamilton County.

Frazer & Denis, 120 Main *Cincinnati.*
Grosvenor H. C., n. w. cor. Walnut & 4th
Telfer J. R., 3d story Gazette Building
Hutenreith L., 78 13th
Perry C. H., 347 Race
Shipley & Stillman, 6 w. 4th
Seyppel Ferdinand, 427 Vine
Wagner Wm. W., 6th near Walnut

Medina County.

Whitmore J. *Medina.*

Montgomery County.

Croome Geo. L. *Dayton.*

Union County.

Groome Geo. L. *Marysville.*

Expresses.

Hamilton County.

Adams & Co., 54 e. 3d *Cincinnati.*
American Express Co. (Livingston, Fargo & Co.), 11 e. 3d

Fancy Goods—Importers.

Hamilton County.

Ihle Michael, 522 Main *Cincinnati.*
Kekeler & Brothers, 38 w. 4th
Schrader Henry, 66 Main
Schultze F. & Co , 64 do
Smith Peter, 36 e. 5th
Wagner Ferdinand, 90 Main, upstairs

Fancy Goods—Dealers.

Delaware County.

Barlow Misses *Delaware.*

Franklin County.

Clark & Co., High *Columbus.*
Dunbar R. D., do
Savage John T., Jr., do
Shapley & Hall do
Snowden P. T., do
Riley Joseph H. & Co., do

Hamilton County.

Allan J., 22 e. 4th *Cincinnati.*
Berry & Berry, 192 Main
Beale John & Co., 26 Pearl
Blake & Swing, 66 5th
Cheseldine G. R., s. e. cor. Main & Lower Market
Calvert Geo. H., 63 & 65 w. 6th
Cady D. H. & Barrow, n. e. cor. Walnut & 5th
Dougherty & Smith, 81 Lower Market
Dorr & Arnold, 4 & 6 w. 6th

Drum Michael, 79 Vine   *Cincinnati.*
Duhme H. H., 74 w. 5th
Dickson —, 146   do
Epply Adam, 29 Lower Market
Franklin Max, 65   do
Ferray A., 162 Vine
Goodhart & Fishel, 21 Lower Market
Garret G., 277 Main
Gibbes H., 205 Plum
Hopper M. S., 24 Lower Market
Jorgensen Geo., 77   do
Ihle Michael, 522 Main
Keckeler & Brothers, 38 w. 4th
Lakeman Daniel, 160 w. 5th
Maggini Joseph A., 246 do
Menken S., 62   do
Ogborn W. E. & Co., 35 & 37 Pearl
Pinney S. A., 51 Lower Market
Pickering J. M., 126 w. 5th
Sterrett B., 8 Lower Market
Spencer R., 53   do
Sharp John (Agent), 86 do
Smith Peter, 36 w. 5th
Sheppard J. W., 20 w. 4th
Schlessinger B., 270 w. 5th
Taylor, French & Wynne, cor. Main & Pearl
Todd J. & Co., 188 Walnut & 35 w. 5th
Williams J. B. & Co., 35 Lower Market
Wagener W., 73 Main

Perry County.
Moeller Mrs. Sarah   *Somerset.*

Pickaway County.
Hirsch & Levy   *Circleville.*

Ross County.
Smart R. B. & Co.   *Chillicothe.*
Montgomery D.
Bennett & Brothers
Davison R. & J.

Scioto County.
Brodbeck Stephen   *Portsmouth.*
Brunner R.
Lodwick J. & Sons
Pursell James
Salter Wm., Jr.

Fanning Mill Manufacturers.

Athens County.
Nebb A. J.   *Hebardville.*
Northrop W.

Brown County.
Stewart O. J. & Co.   *Newhope.*

Champaign County.
Howell David   *Christiansburg.*

Clinton County.
Hunt Jesse & James   *Martinsville.*

Columbiana County.
Harness Abraham   *New Lisbon.*

Starr James   *New Lisbon.*
Martin Robert   *East Fairfield.*

Defiance County.
Stevens & Crozier   *Defiance.*

Guernsey County.
Brown Robert   *Londonderry.*

Huron County.
Green John   *Norwalk.*

Logan County.
Carter E. L.   *Zanesfield.*

Lorain County.
Bullock J. W.   *Elyria.*

Miami County.
Martin J. R.   *Casstown.*

Morgan County.
Stinchcomb J.   *Triadelphia.*
Stinchcomb A.

Muskingum County.
Crane B.   *Chandlersville.*

Richland County.
Moore & Brown   *Belleville.*

Seneca County.
Miller Jacob   *Tiffin.*
Sneath Wm. O.

Summit County.
Palmer A. & Brother   *Middlebury.*

Vinton County.
Bliss Henry   *Mc. Arthur.*
Crist J.

Washington County.
Wilcox W.   *Marietta.*

Williams County.
Boyanton Joseph   *Pulaski.*
Willett H.   *West Unity.*

Feed Dealers.

Cuyahoga County.
Cottrell L. Dow, Mechanics' Block   *Cleve-*
Kimball & Westcott, 43 Seneca   [*land.*

Franklin County.
McAlister M., High   *Columbus.*

Hamilton County.
Alferds & Niling, 454 Vine   *Cincinnati.*
Barkalow W. F., Poplar bet. John & Linn
Burk William, W. Row bet. Laurel & Betts
Claypoole J., Front bet. Ludlow & L'rence
Crist J. M. & H. C., 599 W. Row
Dierkers John D., cor. Webster & Sycamore
Erkenbrecker A., Lock bet. 5th & 6th
Fenger John & Co., cor. 8th & Canal
Fox L., 360 Ham. Road
Geisse B. H. & Co., 71 Hunt

Huel & Schlager, 666 Vine   *Cincinnati.*
Hoppe & Grave, Race above 12th
Harminic H., 8th bet. Baymiller and Linn
Johnson E., W Row bet. 5th & Longworth
Kelley & Sowers, Baymiller bet Kemble & Richmond
Nordlohne & Lammers, 601 Elm
Neenneny B., Vine Street Hill
Orth T., cor. W. Row and Everett
Ripley G., W. Row bet. Main & Piatt
Ripley G., John below 5th
Ripley George, Vine above Ham. Road
Stone L. & M., 32 and 36 Vine
Scudder & Chambers, s. w. cor. Clinton & Linn
Stedman A. B., 159 Clinton
Secrest H., 359 W. Row

Fishing Tackle Dealers.

Hamilton County.

Cady & Barlow, n. e. cor. 5th and Walnut
Martin John B., 214 Walnut   *Cincinnati.*
Smith P., 36 w. 5th
Winter John, 80 w. 3d

Flax Dealers.

Geauga County.

Cook B. & A.   *Chardon.*
Ayres & Parsons
Wilber Wm.
Randall, Cook & Co.
Stephenson & Russell   *Chester.*
Armstrong B.   *Claridon.*

Preble County.

Denny A.   *Eaton.*
McCabe L. T.

Flax Mills.

Geauga County.

Armstrong B.   *Claridon.*

Montgomery County.

Estabrook F., Upper Hydraulic   *Dayton.*

Summit County.

Wetmore Henry   *Cuyahoga Falls.*

Flour Dealers.

Ashland County.

Reznor, Risser & Co.   *Ashland.*

Belmont County.

Dorsey Michael   *Captina.*
Lockwood B. & Sons   *Dillies' Bottom.*
Lockwood J. M.
McGrew A.

Cuyahoga County.

Cottrell L. Dow, Mechanic's Block   *Cleveland.*
Kimball & Westcott, 43 Seneca

Gallia County.

Guthrie O. L.   *Cheshire.*

Hamilton County.

Armstrong & Krafeldt, 7 Canal street   *Cincinnati.*
Dubois J., s. e. cor. Walnut and Canal
Elstner & Son, Broadway e. of 9th
Fosdick F. & Co., 56 Columbia
Foster E., 7th bet. Smith & Mound
Gelleubeck & Dutman, 426 and 428 Main
Grace J. W., 15 Walnut
Groene J. H. F., s. e. cor. Race and Columb.
Hauck & Pengemann, 19 Canal
Osborne John H., 128 w. 4th
Pierce & Palmer, 432 Main
Taylor J., 4th bet. Smith & Park

Scioto County.

Row & Son   *Portsmouth.*
Ross S. R.
Conway B. F. & Co.
Dameren O. A. M.
Terry, Davis & Smith
Robinson & Sons

Union County.

Kelsey B. F.   *Marysville.*

Wyandot County.

Nelson Geo. P.   *Upper Sandusky.*
Kennedy, Long & Irwin   *Marseilles.*

Flouring & Grist Mills.

Adams County.

Clark S. E.   *Manchester.*
Patterson Moses J.   *Scott.*
Horner Bennett
Suffran Samuel   *Marble Furnace.*
Buck R.   *West Union.*

Allen County.

Thomas S. H.   *Deep Cut.*
Orall D.   *Westminster.*
Fisher Charles   *Croghan.*
Stump John

Ashland County.

Sullivan Steam Mill Co.   *Sullivan.*
Reznor, Risser & Co.   *Ashland.*
McMahan R. & Co.   *Jeromeville.*

Ashtabula County.

Palmer Wm. D.   *Austinburg.*
Dodge Danl.   *Trumbull.*
Brown N.
Harmon Edwin   *Ashtabula.*
White C. W.   *South Ridge.*
Farnham F.
Ransom John   *Harpersfield.*

Athens County.

Kincade Wm.   *Canaansville.*
Pruden Samuel
Burche Wm.

Ouner & Dustman   *Athens.*
Kessinger A. & J. L.
Pruden S. B.
Herrold Joseph

Auglaize County.

Ayres J.   *Wapakoneta.*
Holt H. S.
Herzing P. V.   *St. Mary's.*
Bushe & Rickley
Vocke Jno H.   *Minster.*

Belmont County.

Brooks & Shaffer   *Hendrysburgh.*
Rhodes Ebenezer
Dorsey Michael   *Captina.*
Bamford Joseph   *Bellair.*
Dunlap S H. & J.
McMurray Joseph
Wallace Richard
Branson Jacob   *Flushing.*
Holloway D.
McCartney James   *Uniontown.*
Lockwood B. & Sons   *Dillies' Bottom.*
Lockwood J. M.
McGrew A.
Lamp Henry   *Lampsville.*
Mack Henry   *St. Clairsville.*
McMillen Ira
Armstrong A.   *Armstrong's Mills.*
Duncan Ira B.   *Belmont.*
McNichols & Curtis
Simson John T.

Brown County.

Thomas John   *Higginsport.*
Holden B. F.
Clark Wm.
Thompson J. F.
Smart Joshua
McKegg & Co.   *Ripley.*
Ridgeway & Crotier   *Uniontown.*
Carr Barney
Blair R. R.   *Newhope.*
Clark Wm. W.   *Lewis.*
Abbott G. W.   *Fincastle.*
Webber & Marhoffer   *De La Pulma.*
Weaver & Co.   *Five Mile.*

Butler County.

Hunter & Irwin   *Hamilton.*
Russell E. P.
Elliott W. A.   *Rossville.*
Shelaberger J. M.   *Middletown.*
Kinkle & Mumma
Eichelberger Wm.
Edmonds B.   *Somerville.*
McKinney J.   *Trenton.*

Carroll County.

Hardesty Geo. & Thos.   *Malvern.*
Patterson James   *Scroggsfield.*
Pearch John   *Sherodsville.*
Fishil James G.   *Oneida Mills.*
Davis Ephraim P.

Champaign County.

Brown & Willy   *Urbana.*

Wiley, Brown & Co.   *Urbana.*
James J. H.
Smith J. & S.   *Woodstock.*

Clark County.

Seitz Andrew   *Tremont.*
Kneisley & Bohn
Filler & Bogg   *Springfield.*
Strouss John
Christie & Page
Barnet Samuel
Warder & Brokaw
Cartmell J. H.   *Catawba.*
Chance John
Woodward Wm.
Brubaker J. & H.   *New Carlisle.*
Oable Saml.
Keplinger Isaac
Stafford William
Staley Elias

Clermont County.

Beck E. G.   *New Richmond.*
Gibson David
Roberts & Cheeseman   *Neville.*
Kugler John   *Milford.*
Buckingham M.   *Miamisville.*
McLaughlin A. J.   *Moscow.*
Paxton, Eveland & Co.   *Loveland.*
Prescott G   *Rural.*
Perin Saml.   *Perin's Mills.*
Bassett & Jones   *Bantam.*
Snyder & Weaver

Clinton County.

Jackson Elihu   *Bloomington.*
Pitcher & Furnas   *New Burlington.*
Mitchner J.   *Port William.*
Benton J.   *Sligo.*
Thacher J.
Hixon H. B.   *New Vienna.*
McPherson J.
Jurenial M.
Nordyke C.
Brunson & Carey   *Martinsville.*
Pike & Davis
Linton Mathan   *Wilmington.*
Burton Peyton

Columbiana County.

Crowl Jacob   *New Lisbon.*
Pettit Austin
Taylor Wilson   *East Palestine.*
Farmer & Kirk   *Salineville.*
Dellenbaugh John   *North Georgetown.*
Stratton J.
Davis Bayles   *East Rochester.*
Pim Isaac
Allison G. W.   *Salem.*
Smith E. K.
Nichols Stace   *Columbiana*
Nold Jacob
Smith Andrew
Milbourn Jacob & Co.   *New Chambers-*
        [burg.
Oaskey J. M.   *West Point.*
Glenn A.

Souder M.   *West Point.*
Wines H.
Culbertson David   *St. Clair.*
Wollam John
McCoy Alexander   *Cannon's Mills.*
McGelvay Philip
Crawford Edward
Sloan Geo.   *Hanoverton.*
Fox S.
Arter J. R.
Kemble Wm.   *Elkton.*
Caldwell James T.
McMillen Enos
Crawford Edward
Schooley John
Simkins Nathan

Coshocton County.

Winklepleck David   *Chili.*
McVey J. S.   *Walhonding.*
Rector Nicholas & Porter   *Warsaw.*
Strome Christian & Frederick

Crawford County.

Wooster & Longwell   *Poplar.*
Bucyrus Mill Co. ——,   *Bucyrus.*

Cuyahoga County.

Webb S. S.   *Newburgh.*
Gates Halcy   *Gates' Mills.*
Wilson F.   *Mayfield.*
Gates C. & R   *Brooklyn.*
Harnes Charles   *Brecksville.*
Wyatt Ezra
Young C. L.
Lawrence Sidney   *Coe Ridge.*
Robison & Egbert   *Bedford.*
Floyd, T. C. (Agent, cor. Vineyard and C'n'l   *Cleveland.*
Harvey H., Canal
Hutchinson S. R. & A. S., Merwin

Darke County.

Moore & Shultz   *New Madison.*
Turner & Bro.   *Greenville.*

Defiance County.

Brown Wm. A.   *Defiance.*
Ball J. A.   *Panama.*
Coy & Snyder   *Evansport.*

Delaware County.

Howard C. & Co.   *Delaware.*
Slough & Wootving
Rinehart J.   *Galena.*
Idleman J. J.   *Waldo.*
Lewis E.
Johnson H.   *Harlem.*
Dunlap & Van Brinner   *Delaware.*

Erie County.

Squire V.   *Birmingham.*
Heywood R. H.   *Venice.*
Swigart J.   *Sandusky City.*
Merry E.   *Milan.*

Fairfield County.

Brown Peter & Co.   *Sugar Grove.*
,15

Stukey Joseph   *Sugar Grove.*
Ream D.

Fayette County

Millikan C.   *Washington.*
Moon Thos.   *Moon's.*
Stafford W.

Franklin County.

Lee Theron   *Central College.*
Colvin William   *Blendon.*
Chaney & Son   *Canal Winchester.*
Fisher George
Loucks Samuel
Farnam D. L.   *Lockbourn.*

Fulton County.

Johnston George W.   *Elmira.*

Gallia County.

Guthrie C. L.   *Cheshire.*
Giles & Davis   *Adamsville.*
Watson Samuel
Wood Wm. M.
Menoger Peter   *Gallipolis.*
Neal H. H.
Bingham Samuel   *Kyger.*
Buxton D. V.
Tate James

Geauga County.

Mitchells M.   *Chardon.*
Armstrong H.   *Claridon.*
Bosleys Joshua   *Thompson.*
Pinderson D. & E.   *Newbury.*
Fuller James
Branch E.   *Munson.*
Ford M.
Converse J. P.   *Parkman.*
Gilmore J.   *Burton.*

Greene County.

Morris T. L. & Co.   *Spring Valley.*
Johnson W. O.   *Clifton.*
Brewer P. J.   *Yellow Springs.*
Lannon John
Kendal Joseph & J. H.   *Jamestown.*

Guernsey County.

Grimes Elijah   *Byesville.*
Allison & Marling   *Cambridge,*
Meharry M.
Secrest S.
Brown, Frame & McCleary   *Kimbolton.*
Robins Peter D.   *Buffalo.*
Smith St. Clair   *Leatherwood.*
Galloway Enoch

Hamilton County.

Bradbury O. S., n. e. cor. 8th & Broadway
Elstner J., 294 Broadway   *Cincinnati.*
Erkinbucker A., Lock bet. 5th & 6th
Fagin Lewis, 33 Lock
West O. W. & Co., junction 3d & Front
Hill & Rogers   *Mt. Healthy.*
Moore L. W.
Godfrey John   *Harrison.*
Miley John

Oilley Joseph   *Cleves.*
Martin Joseph
Matson John D.
Short John C.
Hesider Wm. C.   *Miami.*
Armstrong M. D.   *Plainville.*
Armstrong Nathaniel
Armstrong Thos.   *Newtown.*
Meeker & Myers   *Sharonville.*
Patterson & Co.   *Lockland.*
Shepherd & Co.
Pinney J.   *Dunlap.*
Fithian Joseph   *Cheviot.*

Hancock County.

Fahl G.   *Mt. Blanchard.*
Miller Nathanial
Missan John
Funk Martin   *Arlington.*
Carlin S. & P.   *Finley.*
Huber Benjamin
Laurel Joseph   *McComb.*

Hardin County.

Davis A. J.   *Kenton.*
Leffort & Pfeuffer

Harrison County.

Wilson Wm. W.   *Cadiz.*
Thompson Joseph
Gray Warfel
Dickerson Joshua
Richardson John   *Green.*
Hebeling John   *Short Creek.*
More & Hilton   *Deersville.*

Henry County.

Warsner & Parry   *Florida.*
Stamp A. & G.   *Texas.*

Highland County.

Ball Wilson   *Mowrytown.*
Bennett Thos.   *Marshall.*

Hocking County.

Crownover H.   *Rock House.*
Boordman Samuel   *Logan.*
Dewees Jas. & Wm.
Kinman Nathan

Holmes County.

Randolph Saml.   *Benton.*

Huron County.

Yeaman A.   *Clarksfield.*
Stiles Saml.
Lawrence & Hugby   *Bellevue.*
Scott B.   *Fitchville.*

Jefferson County.

Means J. & Son   *Steubenville.*
Dotts Wm.   *Annapolis.*
Wooster John C.   *Mouth of Yellow Creek.*

Knox County.

Norton D. S.   *Mt. Vernon.*
Adams & McGrew   *Fredericktown.*
Haiesler George

Strong Lewis   *Fredericktown.*
Struble John D.
Young N. M.
Snyder H.   *Ankenytown.*
Boynton & Davis   *Monroe Mills.*
Davis Jacob   *Democracy.*
Walkey John
Denny James   *Bladensburg.*
Fowls Eli

Lake County.

Irvin James   *Kirtland.*
Parmely J.   *Perry.*
Stickney Jonathan   *Concord.*
Williams H.
Levins W.
Cole H.   *Painesville.*
Geauga F. Co.

Lawrence County.

Rodgers, Parker & Co.   *Ironton.*
Fudge David   *Russell's Place.*
Hallock Lewis
Kelley W. H.   *Kelly's Mills.*
Griffith & Co.   *Campbell*
Frampton Martin   *Burlington.*
Ingles James   *Aid.*

Licking County.

Rankin & Brown   *Brownsville.*
Case .:.   *Granville.*
Hilyer J. & Co.
Buckingham A. D.   *Newark.*
Ross D.   *Croton.*
Stone James   *Kirkersville.*

Logan County.

Anstine Henry   *Huntsville.*
Stewart Samuel
Woodward Jonathan
Webb & Co.   *East Liberty.*
Fisher William   *Bellefontaine.*
Joseph W. & D.   *Quincy.*

Lorain County.

Stedman M. W. & C. Sprague *Huntington.*
Chapman E. J.   *La Grange.*
Holtalander L. & Co.   *Oberlin.*
Sabin George   *Copopa.*
Curtis W. L.   *Sheffield.*
Brown & Hawley   *Brownhelm.*
Miles —

Lucas County.

Dix W. B. & Co.   *Maumee City.*
Forsyth H. H. & Co.
Mirwin R. P.
Young S. M. & Co.
Cadwill A. D. & Co.   *Whiteford.*

Madison County.

Link David   *Somerford.*
Roberts Charles   *London.*
Willson Wm. D.   *West Canaan.*
Cartmell John   *West Jefferson.*
Crabb & Parks
Stutson & Olmsted
Chrisman Joseph   *London.*
Wood Wm. D.   *Kiensville.*
Wood Col. W. D.   *Mt. Sterling.*

Mahoning County.

Holcomb J. H.	Canfield.
Henter, Watson & Co.	Lowellville.
Baldwin, Hamilton & Co.	Youngstown.
Morse H. K.	Poland.
Ripley Wm.	
Tod J. J.	Milton.

Medina County.

Moses Rufus	Litchfield.
Andrews D.	Sharon Centre.
Parmely A. S. & Co.	Liverpool.
Pardee Allen	Wadsworth.
Gifford J.	
Stiles J.	Weymouth.
Heacox Wm.	
Chapin Levi	Medina.

Meigs County.

Nye M.	Salisbury.
Grant John	
Fetus Z.	
Young O.	Apple Grove.
Harpold Henry	
Harpold Wm.	
Murdock & Nye	Pomeroy.
Vale & Kepler	
McMaster William	Langsville.

Mercer County.

Rickley & Bosche	St. Mary's.
Keedy & Bennett	
Herzing P. V. & Co.	
Riley & LeBlond	Celina.
Hamilton J.	Mendon.
Rhodes J.	Shanesville.
Laughridge Joseph	Macedon.
Arbaugh George	
Blake R.	Fort Recovery.

Miami County.

Shattuck B. F. & Co.	Fletcher.
Worey & Yager	Piqua.
Burton & Hulseman	
Young & Yager	
Barr & Daniel	
Mayo Henry	Troy.
Burton W.	Casstown.
Burton J.	
Weimer J. S.	West Milton.
Weddle J. K.	
Byrkeit Solomon	
Harper Saml.	
Herr J. K. & B.	Hyattsville.
Croomer & Morrison	

Monroe County.

Barnes George	Woodsfield.
Clingan Robert	
Ford Stephen	
Ford Thomas	
Hollister Jeremiah	
Steed George	
Winland John	
Beard William	Rocky Narrows.
Holtsclan Wm.	

Williams J. & Brothers	Baresville.
Niahberly Jacob	

Montgomery County.

Harshman & Bros.	Harshmansville.
Harris Wm.	
Dryden Joseph H.	Alexandersville.
Pease Perry	
Snider Peter	
Lamme David	
Weldy Joseph	
Bellaman Eno	
Hikes John	Little York.
Beckel D., Upper Hydraulic	Dayton.
Eichelberger D. & S., do	
Moter R. E., 6th	
Pease H., 3d	
Wallaston S. & S., 5th	
Costenberger J., do	
Gerhard William	Taylorsville.
Clark Nelson	Miamisburgh.
Marsh & Marlatt	

Morgan County.

Seaman Milton	Malta.
Gillespie John	
Bay J. C.	Meigsville.
Sammons John	
Ong R.	
Magers, Parker & Co.	
McConnell Jas. A.	McConnelsville.
Shepard & Martin	
Marple C. H.	Stockport.
Hoggin E.	

Morrow County.

Goodman John C. & Co.	Cardington.
House & Cook	

Muskingum County.

Claypool Levi	Nashport.
Hutchinson & Wylie	Norwich.
Kerr J. D. & Co.	Frazeysburg.
Sturges J. D. & B.	Duncan's Falls.
McAdams E. & G.	Dresden.
Brown & Smith	
Machan K. G.	
Beaumont & Hollingsworth	Putnam.
Mathews A.	White Cottage.
Powell Joseph	Newton.
Watson Chas. F.	
Cassel & Galigher	Zanesville.
Pratt John R.	
Beaumont & Hollingsworth	

Noble County.

Burton Joseph	Kennonsburg.
Morris James	

Ottawa County.

Scott Jacob	Port Clinton.

Perry County.

Granger H. C.	New Lexington
Cunningham John W.	Mount Perry.
Taylor Walter B.	

Pickaway County.

Allen George	*Circleville.*
Dunkle K. H.	*Tarlton.*

Pike County.

Emmitt & Davis	*Waverly.*
Havens Chas. & Reuben,	*Gibson.*
Blosser Joseph	
Wells Richard	
Brown John H.	
Thorp David	*Piketon.*
Moore N. S.	
Slane & McCallister	*Omega.*

Portage County.

Whittlesey G. B. & Co.	*Ravenna.*
Parmely L. & Sons	
Dickinson W. & Co.	*Randolph.*
Davenport H.	*Aurora.*
Smith Jas. & Co.	*Shalersville.*
Centre Mill Co.	*Franklin.*
Huggins & Rent	
Hall Martin & Co.	*Suffield.*
Fritch John	
Allison M.	*Charleston.*
Smith H. N.	*Mantua.*
Lazarus Peter	*Deerfield.*
Laughlin H. & C.	
McConnaughey & Trotter	

Preble County.

Bolens Jas.	*Lewisburg.*
Carroll N. W.	*Camden.*
Barnett & Whitesides	
Hall Wm. & Son	
Barnett David	
Bruce Chas.	*Eaton.*
Smith S.	*New Paris.*
Woofter D.	
Tood & Weist	
Higgins S. S.	
Stubbs J. & J. H. & Co.	*West Elkton.*

Richland County.

Calwell Robert	*Lexington.*
Robinson L. R. & Co.	*Mansfield.*
Langum James	*Belleville.*
Leichty & Willis	
Markey & Bowers	
Mickey & Strong	
Baker & Marks	*Lucas.*
Larue A.	
Masdon W.	

Ross County.

Linbeck Benj.	*Chillicothe.*
Selvy Wm. & Co.	
Holcomb & Co.	
Jones D. K. & Co.	
Proth'r F'no	*Bourneville.*
Conner J. C.	

Sandusky County.

Draton, Chamberlain & Co.	*Townsend.*
Chamberlain John	
Morgan & Downs	*Fremont.*
Moore James	*Rollersville.*
Farmers, Union Milling Co.	

Scioto County.

Damaren C. A. M.	*Portsmouth.*
Robinson & Sons	
Terry, Davis & Smith	
Chaffin Reuben	*Lyra.*

Seneca County.

Cunningham Geo. W.	*Tiffin.*
Shoemaker R. M.	
Russell D. P.	*Republic.*

Shelby County.

Maxwell B. W.	*Sidney.*
Stowell W. P.	
Walker H.	
Maxwell S.	

Starke County.

Hawk J.	*Navarre.*
Stump & Chapman	
Ross J. N.	*Waynesburg.*
Haldeman L.	*Minerva.*
Cummins & Co.	*West Brookfield.*
Walton Eli	*New Franklin.*
Butcher Ephraim	
Cameron D. R.	*Magnolia.*
Elson A. R.	
Akey & Wharton	*Limaville.*
Bevington Thomas	*Mount Union.*

Summit County.

Allen & Co.	*Akron.*
Beech & Co.	
Chamberlin & Co.	
Rawson & Co.	
Fritz & Miller	*Montrose.*
Spafford M.	
Miller Christian	*Coply.*
Oviatt Aaron	
Wagoner Wm.	
Harris Henry	*Bath.*

Trumbull County.

Jackson & Otis	*Johnsonville.*
Lane Silas A.	
Baldwin J. & H.	*Girard.*
Clark Ralza	*Orangeville.*
Van Gorder A.	*Warren.*
Van Gorder J. L.	
Pierce Ellis	*Farmington.*
Beam John F.	*Newton Falls.*
Du Bois & Tew	

Tuscarawas County.

Bimiler J. M. (Agent Zoar Community),	*Zoar.*
Sagent Levi & Co.	*Ragersville.*
Blake W. M.	*New Philadelphia.*
Hayden N.	*Canal Dover.*
Snyder & Frebly	
Welty & Hayden	

Union County.

Belts Andrew & Daniel	*Allen Centre.*
Elwell T. H. & Co.	*Milford Centre.*

Van Wert County.

Gleason Joseph	*Van Wert*
Zigler J. & W.	

Vinton County.

Hutson J. N.	*McArthur.*
Kaler Joseph	
Aiken S. C.	
Bolen —,	

Warren County.

Balentine & Death	*Franklin.*
Conover, Vandiveer & Co.	
McKay A. H. & J. F.	*Waynesville.*
Wright & Bailey O. J. & E.	
Sherwood & Terry	*Oregon.*
Scott J.	*Hayesville.*
Boyd J. & J.	
Smith D.	
Rhodes J. W.	*Deerfield.*
Vandervort J.	*Hopkinsville.*
Lee John	*Morrow.*
Ross Geo. P.	*Mt. Holly.*
Crockett M.	
Brinker Wm. R.	

Washington County.

Cram J. O.	*Marietta.*
Harmar Manufacturing Co.	*Harmar.*
Boyle Frederick	*Lower Salem.*
Allen A.	
Alden & Matthews	
Worren Geo.	*Fearing.*
Robinson Geo.	
Hilderbrand David	*Fillmore.*
Huston S.	
Hosmer, Arthur & Co.	*Beverly.*
Cook Silas	*Watertown.*
Ross James	
Allen A.	*Bonn.*

Wayne County.

Folts & Nevill	*Dalton.*
Brenizer D	*Smithville.*
Plank John	
Shreve Henry	*Shreve.*
McConkey Thos.	
Robison D.	*Wooster.*
Stibbs R. B.	

Williams County.

Lewis Wm.	*St. Joseph.*
Miller Saml.	*Lockport.*
Ruse & Tharp	*Williams Centre.*
Stephens W. A.	*Pulaski.*
Miller John	*Montpelier.*
Shaffer John	
Jobes John	

Wood County.

Peak E. D. & Son	*Perrysburg*

Wyandot County.

Tarry J. T.	*Tymochtee.*
Rummell Francis	*Upper Sandusky.*
Fehl John	*Marseilles.*
Carter Wm.	*McCutchensville.*

Forge and Iron Works.

Summit County.

James Wright	*Cuyahoga Falls.*

Forge (Patent Portable) Manufacturer.

Hamilton County.

Hunt Davis S., 45 Sycamore	*Cincinnati.*

Fork, Hoe, and Shovel Manufacturers.

Starke County.

Doering John O. (Agent)	*Marlboro'.*

Summit County.

Becker A.	*Cuyahoga Falls.*
Campbell S. D.	
Griffith, Willetts & Co.	
Inskeep John	
Joly A. & Co.	

Foreign Fruits—Wholesale Dealers.

Franklin County.

Finch W. M., Broad	*Columbus.*
Stage & Frisbie, cor. High & Friend	
Butler C. P. L. do do do	

Hamilton County.

Pearson & Devin, cor. Walnut & Water	*Cincinnati.*
Von Der Heide H., 53 Main	
Warren J. T. & Co., 12 Sycamore	

Founders (Bell).

Hamilton County.

Coffin G. W. & Co., Second bet. Broadway and Ludlow *Cincinnati.*
Hanks George L., Columbia e. of Ludlow
Powell William, Fifth bet. Elm & Plum
Thorburn Rob't. T., 53 w. Front

Founders (Brass).

Ashtabula County,

Castle H. P.	*Geneva.*

Cuyahoga County.

Farnan Walter, Division	*Cleveland.*
Schwartzenburg J., Seneca	

Hamilton County.

Coffin G. W. & Co., Second bet Broadway and Ludlow *Cincinnati.*
Cummings Samuel, Front bet. Pike and Ludlow
Hanks George L., Columbia e. of Ludlow
Haven Jas. L. & Co., 319 Main
Kirkup, Potts & Co., Front e. of Deer Creek Bridge
Leuchtweis August, 12th below Vine
Powell William, 5th bet. Elm and Plum
Ruthven John, Columbia bet. Elm and Race
Rolson Clinton, 154 Front
Reynolds, Kite & Tatum, cor. John and Water

Sheld E. M., 75 e. Front   *Cincinnati.*
Thorburn R. T., 53 Front
Westover & Co., Front bet. Ludlow and
   Lawrence

Montgomery County.

Altic D., Canal   *Dayton.*

Founders (Iron).

Allen County.

Smith A. N. & Co.   *Lima.*

Ashland County.

Fairchild Asahel   *Ashland.*
Mansfield & Co.
Tillson & Moltrup   *Loudonville.*

Ashtabula County.

Stanton Harvey   *New Lyme.*
Castle H. P.   *Geneva.*
Hall & Crosby   *Ashtabula.*
Butler & Co.

Athens County.

Smith & Wheeler   *Athens.*

Brown County.

Quinnon E.   *Ripley.*
Boyle Wm.

Butler County.

Owens, Ebert & Dyer   *Hamilton.*

Carroll County.

McGuire E.   *Carrollton.*

Champaign County.

French C. & Co.   *Urbana.*
Guinnes & Wilcox

Clark County.

Leffell, Cook & Blakeney   *Springfield.*

Clermont County.

Andrews & Iven   *Marble Furnace.*

Columbiana County.

Geese P. F.   *Wellsville.*
Geese & Page
Lider & Morrison
Treenick Henry   *New Lisbon.*
Call P.   *Salineville.*
Cope N. & O.
Taylor H.   *New Garden.*
Fugate Stephen   *North Georgetown.*
Suyder & Woodruff   *Salem.*
Hune, Haltzman & Co.   *East Liverpool.*
Holmes & Sheets   *Columbiana.*
Woods & Rook
Thompson S. J.   *East Fairfield.*

Coshocton County.

McMickle & Shannon,   *Coshocton.*
McGinny & Brown

Crawford County.

Wingart J. & H.   *Bucyrus.*

Cuyahoga County.

Morton C. E.   *Chagrin Falls.*
Williams J. W.
Johnson H.   *Bedford.*
Craig W. S., Division   *Cleveland*
Frankland J. & Co., Front
McCleland & Co., Phœnix Foundery
Searls Albert G., River
Woolson & Hitchcock
Merchant Silas, 168 River
Ford & Otis, west of Depots

Darke County.

Taylor John & Samuel   *Greenville.*

Defiance County.

Stevens & Crozier   *Defiance.*

Erie County.

Messer D. T. & C. J.   *Sandusky City.*
Griffith & Olds
Wells, Lewis & Co.   *Furnace.*

Fairfield County.

Devall G. & Co.   *Lancaster.*
Beery & Jenkins
Clark, Wright & Co.

Franklin County.

Ambos & Lennox, National Bridge
   Columbus.
Gill John L., Broad
Ridgway J.

Gallia County.

Carrell F.   *Gallipolis.*
McLaughlin & Brown

Geauga County.

Rider Wm.   *Munson.*
Fisher & Co.   *Auburn.*
Gilmore M.   *Burton.*

Greene County.

Gowdy John B.   *Xenia.*

Guernsey County.

Prouty Russell   *Cumberland.*
Allright B. A. & F. W.   *Cambridge.*

Hamilton County.

Ashcraft & McCammon, Plum bet. Wade
   and Liberty   *Cincinnati.*
Bevan J. & Co., cor. Vine & Centre
Burrows J. H. & Co., 23 w. Front
Burge & Johnston, Pearl bet. Elm & Plum
Campbell, Ellison & Co., 12 e. 2d
Davis W. C. & Co., cor. Main & 9th
Greenwald & Bonsall, cor. 5th and Lock
Greenwood Miles, n. e. cor. Walnut and
   Canal

Griffey David, Congress bet. Ludlow and Lawrence   *Cincinnati.*
Haven James L. & Co., 319 Main
Harkness A. & Son, Front bet. Lawrence and Pike
Holabird A. B. & Co., Front w. of Smith
Horton & Macy, 5th bet. Elm & Plum
Lyon & Bell, cor. Lock and 3d
Martin, Anshutz & Co., e. Front bet. Ludlow and Lawrence
Niles & Co., 222 e. Front
Pollock Jas. S., Columbia bet. Race and Elm
Penniman & Elmer, 5th and W. W. Canal
Reynolds, Kite & Tatum, Water bet. W. Row and John
Todd James & Co., cor. Smith and 7th
Tunnicliffe & Co., e. Front bet. Pike and Butler
Williams & Adams, Pearl bet. Vine and Race
Woolf Charles, n. e. cor. Canal & Syc.

Hancock County.

Wolf & Wilhelm   *Finley.*
George Jesse

Harrison County.

Pool David   *Cadiz.*

Henry County.

Evans Jeremiah   *Texas.*

Highland County.

Bitler & Clayton   *Hillsboro'.*

Hocking County.

Belt R.   *Logan.*

Holmes County.

Armstrong & Hill   *Millersburg.*

Huron County.

Seyer & McKinney   *Clarksfield.*
Johns & Riley   *Newhaven.*
Haskell J. & G.   *Bellevue.*
Baker J. W.   *Norwalk.*
Perkins N.
Waterous Danl.
Morehouse G.

Jefferson County.

Means & Co.   *Steubenville.*
Sharp & Craig

Knox County.

Buckingham C. P. & Co.   *Mt. Vernon.*
Cooper C. C. & Co.
Braington, Speakman & Co.   *Frederick-*
                                        [town.
Rarkins D. L.

Lake County.

Wilder & Brother   *Painesville.*
Geauga F. Co.

Lawrence County.

Campbell, Ellison & Co.   *Ironton.*

Merrill J. M. & Co.   *Ironton.*
Peebles, Wood & Co.   *Hanging Rock.*

Licking County

Woodcock J. W.   *Brownsville.*
Lennel & Clemmons   *Granville.*
McCune & Ebersole   *Newark.*

Logan County.

Hamilton & Asher   *East Liberty.*
Scott J. S.   *Bellefontaine.*

Lorain County.

Curtis Chester   *Huntington.*
Prichard & Downey   *La Grange.*

Lucas County.

Porter Samuel   *Toledo.*
Michell Edward   *Maumee City.*
Winslow A. C.

Mahoning County.

Predmore J. & C.   *Youngstown.*
Wells Edward
Allen & Woodruff   *Poland.*
Bell J. P. & J. M.   *Milton.*
Tod J. J.

Marion County.

Smith J. & L.   *Marion.*

Medina County.

Prichard C.   *Liverpool.*
Farnsworth E.
Ainsworth J. T.   *Medina.*

Meigs County.

McAboy Wm.   *Pomeroy.*
Depew J. C.

Miami County.

Alexander, Rouser & Evans   *Piqua.*
Bowdel, Clark & Co.
Shillen & Brother   *Troy.*

Montgomery County.

Lockwood N. L., 1st street,   *Dayton.*
Pease W. H., 3d
Westerman & Stout, Canal
Thompson C. & Son, do
Hoover D. H.   *Miamisburg.*

Morgan County.

Dunsmore, Guthry & Co.   *Malta.*
Dickerson David   *McConnelsville.*
Fisher C. P.

Muskingum County.

Johnson Wm.   *Dresden.*
Douglas, Smith & Co.   *Zanesville.*
Potts & Cox
Hoadley John
Blandy H. & F.
Wheeler B.

Perry County.

Moiller O. H.   *Somerset.*

Pickaway County.

Bright M. & Co.   *Circleville.*

Portage County.

Gardner G. S. & Co.   *Ravenna.*
Betts H.   *Deerfield.*
Ferry L.   *Nelson.*
McMillin R.

Richland County.

Clark Thomas   *Shelby.*
Hall & Allen   *Mansfield.*
Liter & Argo
Moody J. W.   *Belleville.*

Ross County.

Welsh William   *Chillicothe.*
Kennedy & Bonner
Barlion Geo.

Sandusky County.

Norton F. J.   *Fremont.*
Lansdale A. H.   *Rollersville.*

Scioto County.

Fox Charles   *Iron Furnaces.*

Seneca County.

Kellogg S. F.   *Attica.*
Loomis Jno. D. & Co.   *Tiffin.*
Watson & Hall   *Republic.*
Swift & Ogden

Shelby County.

Edwards, Carlisle & Co.   *Sidney.*

Starke County.

Speaker William   *Minerva.*
Jones Robert   *Waynesburg.*
Wyandts & Putman   *Frease's Store.*
Ball, Aultman & Co.   *Canton.*
Buckers H. & Co.
Laird M & J.
Walton M. & A.   *Marlboro'.*
Everhart Christian   *New Baltimore.*
Russell C. M. & Co.   *Massillon.*
Hart & Brown
Partridge H. & R.
Bliler & Helt   *Canal Fulton.*

Summit County.

Bill F.   *Cuyahoga Falls.*
Bills & Chamberlain
Hunt C. & Co.
Webster & Taplin   *Akron.*

Trumbull County.

Jameson & Blair   *Warren.*
Morley T. H. & Co.
Fell N. A.   *Orangeville.*

Tuscarawas County.

Baker Philip   *Canal Dover.*
English J., (Agent)   *New Philadelphia*

Van Wert County.

Hoover C. H. & Co.   *Delphos.*

Warren County.

Crispen & Kelley   *Waynesville.*

Washington County.

Franks Owen   *Marietta.*

Nye A. T. & Co.   *Harmer*
Harmer Manufacturing Co.
Gilbert Geo. N. & Co.   *Centre Belpre.*

Wayne County.

Burton J. & Sons   *Edinburgh.*
Harrison H. R.   *Wooster.*
McDonald, Laughlin & Co.

Wood County.

Brown, Smith & Co.   *Perrysburg.*

Frame (Picture & Looking-Glass) Makers & Gilders.

Cuyahoga County.

Jones & Co., 58 Superior st.   *Cleveland.*
Sargeant Samuel, 7 Water
Adams George H., 6 Miller's Block
Worley J., cor. Ontario and Champlain

Franklin County.

Holmes N., Town street,   *Columbus.*

Hamilton County.

Blakesley Edward, cor. 7th and North sts.
                               Cincinnati.
Bown & Hartigan, 16 e. 4th
Burt & Hallowell, 7 Masonic Row, 3d
Bonte & Moorhead, 159 Vine
Cridland Thos. W., 167 do
Fry H. W., 144 3d
Haspe A., 20 w. Court
Holmes Wm., 119 w. 5th
Hornblow W., 12 w. 6th
Perry William H., 3d bet. Sycamore and
      Broadway
Wiswell E., Front bet. Mill and Wood
Wiswell Wm., Jr., 129 Main

Jefferson County.

Hawkins W.   *Steubenville.*

Montgomery County.

Cridland T. W., 3d   *Dayton.*

Fulling Mills.

Allen County.

Flack Lewis W   *Croghan.*

Belmont County.

Sweeny E.   *Armstrong's Mills.*

Butler County.

Deevis Richard R.   *Middletown.*

Coshocton County.

Wirts Geo. D. & Edward   *Bakersville.*

Fairfield County.

Fehr H. & F.   *Clear Creek.*

Guernsey County.

Moore Thomas   *Leatherwood.*

Fur Dealers.

Cuyahoga County.

Harrison Justus — *Coe Ridge.*
Benedict L. & Co., 6 Superior — *Cleveland.*
Dockstader R. & N., 19 do
Fuller A. & Co., 95, and 97 do
Mack John G., 66 do
Simonds D. H., 24 Ontario
Worthington & Stair, 15 Superior

Fairfield County.

Fellers D. — *Lithopolis.*
Sallers Wm.
Sallers H.

Franklin County.

Osborn George & Son — *Blendon.*

Hamilton County.

Baker L. H. & Co., s. w. cor. Main and 4th — *Cincinnati.*
Burkle John G., s. w. cor. Main and 8th
Camp O. B., 123 Main
Chace J. H. & Co., 71 Pearl
Dodd William & Co., 144 Main
Jarvis & Fairchild, 149 do
Kepler H., Main bet. 6th and 7th
Sherwood & Co., 67 Pearl
Vansant, Hiblert & Marconnier, 77 Main
Whitcher William O. & Co., cor. Main and Pearl

Holmes County.

Ryan E. P. — *Berlin.*
Edwards Thos.

Summit County.

Farrar John, Senr. — *Hudson.*

Furniture Dealers.

Brown County.

Tweed W. W. — *Ripley.*

Cuyahoga County.

Hill J. P. — *Cleveland.*

Darke County.

Dorman David — *Greenville.*
Brubaker John
Bauer Augustus

Delaware County.

Crawshaw James — *Waldo.*

Erie County.

Bourne & Furry — *Sandusky City.*

Franklin County.

Burr John, Broad — *Columbus.*
Hughes & Beebe, 112 High
Dryer J. G. & Co. do
Halm M., 148 do

Greene County.

Medsker D. — *Xenia.*
Monroe George

Hamilton County.

Anderson L. D., 28 & 30 Water — *Cincinnati.*
Blinn & Blume, 41 3d
Block L., 284 W. Row
Carter W. M., 5th bet. W. Row & John
Constine Abraham, 131 & 133 w. 5th
Dismond J., 209 W. Row
Farell Thomas, 46 Congress
Freiberg J., 139 w. 5th
Fitzgibbon P., 345 W. Row
Fay William, 234 Elm
Geat J. C., 59 Broadway
Greene E., 153 w. 5th
Hallewell J., 260 do
Hamburger S. & Brother, 73 Court
Newberg H., s. w. cor. Main & 8th
Oakes H., 161 w. 5th
Ortman H., 97 Court
Shnier A. B., 217 Walnut
Stone E., 275 W. Row
Tamers J. G. H., 517 Main
Turner J. P., 188 w. 6th

Hardin County.

Kennett & Markle — *Kenton.*

Holmes County.

Harpster & Farra — *Millersburg.*

Jefferson County.

Donaldson A. — *Steubenville.*
Burchfield —
Houston J. B. — *Warrenton.*
Stenesifer Henry
Oliver Wm.

Knox County.

Houghton M. — *Mt. Vernon.*
McCormick & Preston

Lawrence County.

Gillen & Brother — *Ironton.*

Licking County.

Robbins & Swan — *Newark.*
Brooks C.
Moore B.

Pickaway County.

Myers G. W. — *Circleville.*

Portage County.

McElwaine & Turnham — *Ravenna-*
Lane G.
Griffin A. B. & O. H.
Knowlton A. & T. — *Franklin.*

Ross County.

Stewart Wm. — *Chillicothe.*
Robinson T. W.
Hoffman Geo.

Scioto County.

Alexander & Co. — *Portsmouth.*
Nickells J. B. & S. P.
Walt J. H.
Williams W. E.

Summit County.

Crantz Constant   *Akron.*
Gilbert J. F.
Sanford D. G.

Washington County.

Dana L. D.   *Marietta.*
Taylor E. M.

Gas Apparatus—Manufacturers.

Cuyahoga County.

Farnan Walter, Division   *Cleveland.*

Hamilton County. •

Baker & Von Phul, Main n'r Levee *Cincin.*
Goodin & Mahon, 411 Main

Jefferson County.

Miller D.   •   *Steubenville.*

Gentlemens' Furnishing Stores.

Cuyahoga County.

Carpenter J. S. & Co., 13 Superior *Cleve-*
Cohen E., 2 Clothier's Block   [*land.*
Davis Geo. A., cor. Superior & Water
Hagerling H. 10   do   n
Hancock & Pychon, Weddell House Block
Isaac A. & G., 3 Clothier's Block
Loeb S., 1 Oviatt's Block
Morse F. W. & Co., 7, 8 Superior, 3 Exchange Buildings
Powers S. A., 51   do
Robinson, C. H., 88   do
Schwab Moses, 14   do
Seamen Henry, 40   do
Smith, Silas, 7 Bank
Starkweather E. B. & Co., 5 Superior
Beverlin John   *Ohio City.*

Franklin County.

Goodman J. & Co., High   *Columbus.*
Gundersheimer A.   do
Hess E. & Co.,   do
Mack & Co.,   do

Hamilton County.

Avis J. J., 146 Walnut   *Cincinnati.*
Baker, McCracken & Co., Walnut above 3d
Buchman & Rindskoff, 70 Main
Cady M., 213, Walnut
Coopper Mrs. M., 223 W. Row
Evens P., 127 Main
Goodheart & Ackerland, 66 w. Pearl
Hathaway John A. & Co , 11 w. 6th
Heidelbach, Wertheimer & Klaw, 56 w.
Leslie James Y., 14 w. 5th   [Pearl
Leslie Robert, 34 Broadway
Lowman J. & Bro., 108 Main
Martin G. J., 3 w. 4th
Maue F. & Co., 269 Main
Philley H., 44 w. 6th
Richardson James, 4 e. 4th

Shepherd J., 100 w. 5th   *Cincinnati.*
Smith Raymond, 58 Broadway
Smith Isaac F., 10 e. 5th
Stockton O., 213 W. Row
Williams C. M., n. w. cor. 5th & Vine

Montgomery County.

Brotherton J. G., Main   *Dayton.*

Washington County.

Crawford C. W.   *Marietta.*

Gilt Mouldings, etc. — Importers of.

Hamilton County.

Rickel William, 334 Main   *Cincinnati.*

Glass Manufacturers.

Hamilton County.

Gray & Hemingray, Hammond, bet. 3d &
4th   *Cincinnati.*

Jefferson County.

Beatty & Steelman   *Steubenville.*

Muskingum County.

Lippitt A. & Co.   *Zanesville.*
Nicholson A. J. & Co.
Dunlap, Burns & Co.   *Putnam.*

Portage County.

Kent, Wells & Co.   *Franklin.*

Glass Door-Plate Manufacturers.

Hamilton County.

Cooper S. M., cor. 5th & Home *Cincinnati.*

Glass and Emery Paper Manufacturers.

Hamilton County.

Amringer J. Von, 9 Sycamore *Cincinnati.*

Glaziers.

Cuyahoga County.

Preston George   *East Cleveland.*
Adams E. E.   *Collamer.*
Hall Zilea
Adams Geo. H. Superior   *Cleveland.*
Denham Thomas, 80 Public Square
Downie John, Superior
Worley J., cor. Ontario & Champlain
Stevens C. C.   *Ohio City.*

Hamilton County.

O'Niel J., 198 Elm   *Cincinnati.*
Porter Allen A., 199 Plum
Saunders & Baldwin, 5th bet. Elm & Plum
Schafer J., 149 Everett
Trener & Misener 145 Walnut
Kear B.   *Fulton.*
Powell Wm. B.   *Harrison.*
Ryan George

Logan County.

Matthews John T.   *Huntsville.*

Lorain County.

Kenaston D.   *Oberlin.*

Medina County.

Davis A.   *Medina.*

Starke County.

McMaster Robert   *Massillon.*
Seaton F. & Co.
Snider & Deits

Summit County.

Evans E. S.   *Cuyahoga Falls.*
Lawson W. A.
Lee P. J.

Trumbull County.

Bartlett Lucius   *Johnsonville.*
Winters Coradon

Tuscarawas County.

Hall Trueman G.   *Canal Dover.*
France Henry
Stansbury John
Scott John
Lahm Frederick
Williams S.
Ditto John
Ditto Joseph   *New Philadelphia.*
Carlisle & Son

Glove and Mitten Makers.

Columbiana County.

Orr William   *New Lisbon.*

Mahoning County.

Davis & Cotton   *Berlin Centre.*

Glue Manufacturers.

Ashtabula County.

Shoal Jacob   *Kelloggsville.*
Smith Geo. B.   *Ashtabula.*

Franklin County.

Sanders & Barr   *Columbus.*

Hamilton County.

Degen Philip, Ham. Road near Mohawk Bridge   *Cincinnati.*
Forgey J. P. & Co., 12 and 14 w. Col'bia.
Giesler Francis, 110 Findley
Goas John H., Miami Canal above Findley
James & Brother, M.   do   near   do
Mensing & Smith   *Harrison.*

Holmes County.

Smith C.   *Winesburg.*

Gold Pen Manufacturer.

Hamilton County.

Shepherd G. W., 30 w. Sixth   *Cincinnati.*

Grain Cradle Manufacturer.

Columbiana County.

Enticken Thos. L.   *Franklin Square.*

Knox County.

Rigby W. H.   *Fredericktown.*

Morrow County.

Salsbury G. L.   *Cardington.*

Starke County.

Smith John   *New Franklin.*

Grain and Grass Harvester—Manufacturer of

Fairfield County.

Van Fossen D.   *Lancaster.*

Grain Separators—Manufacturer of

Seneca County.

Hoffman George W.   *Berwick.*

Grindstone Manufacturers.

Cuyahoga County.

Crane R. B.   *Berea.*
Finch J. W.
Wallace R.
Whitney Geo. W.
Wallace James

Muskingum County.

Beard Joseph   *White Cottage.*

Grocers and Commission Merchants (Wholesale).

Clark County.

Harrison R. D. & J. T.   *Springfield.*

Columbiana County.

Lawson & Wells   *Wellsville.*
Martin M.

Cuyahoga County.

Bailey R. B., 190 River   *Cleveland.*
Beckman H., 84   do
Blossom O. S. (Agent), cor. James and Merwin
Bradburn C. & Son, 67 River
Burgess L. F., cor. River and Superior
Boas S., 188 River
Cummings J. M. & Co., 135 River, 97, 98 Dock
Denzer & Treat, cor. Champl'n & Vine'rd.
Gaylord & Co., 30 Superior
Gordon W. J., 73 River
Hilliard, Hayes & Co., 33, 34 Water
Hanna, Garretson & Co., Merwin & River
McDowell H. C. & Co., 10 Merwin
Morgan, White & Co., Dock

Nicola F., 52 Ontario   *Cleveland.*
Rielly Robert, cor. Merwin and Canal.
Roeder Henry, cor. Division & Columbia
Wick Chas. D.. 192 River
Wamelink L. B., 70, 72 Superior
Wylie George W., River near C. C. & C.
  R. R. Depot
Wenham Arthur J., 9 Merwin
Perry A. M. & Co., 149 Superior, 12 Sen'a
Williams, Babcock & Hurd, 83 do

Erie County.

Wetherell J. W.   *Sandusky City.*
Buyer N. J.
Porter S. P. & Co.

Franklin County.

Brooks J. & W. B., cor. High and Rich
                         Columbus.
Decker & Hibbs, 146 High
Finch Wm. M., Broad
Fisher Isaac & John, High
Frazea & Co., Broadway
Hanes & Wheeler, High
Main R., 65   do
Miller & Co.,   do
Stage & Frisbie, cor. High and Friend
Tuttle & Long, Broad
Van Sickle E. R., High
Weaver & Main   do
Fay Cyrus & Sons, do
McCoy W. A. & J. C. do
Stanton S. B.,   do

Gallia County

Ford & Drouillard   *Gallipolis.*
Henking & Cadot

Greene County.

Austin & Smith   *Xenia.*
Hivling & Williamson

Hamilton County.

Butler Joseph C. & Co., cor. Main and
  Columbia   *Cincinnati.*
Bell James B. & Co., n. w. cor. Main & 6th
Brown & Brothers, 238 Main
Bailey M. & Son., 61 Walnut
Bain M. 139   do
Bricket H. M., 134   do
Baldwin H. W. & Co., 72 Pearl
Borden James U., 32 Lower Market
Babbitt & Knapp, s. w. corner 5th and
  Broadway
Bakewell Thomas W., 6 w. Front
Cleneay John & Co., 51 Walnut
Canfield & Moffett, 68 and 70 do
Carter E. S. & Co., 76 Lower Market
Coffin L & G., 36 Court
Donaldson A., 31 e. Front
Dickson, Biggs & Co., 26 Main
Dean & Wayne, 51 2d
Emmerson Henry, 47 Walnut
Ferguson John, n. e. cor. Ludlow and
  Front
Ficken John, 28 Lower Market
Fosdick S. & Co., 56 Columbia

Fisher & Emerson, 51 Main   *Cincinnati.*
Gilpin & Sherlock, Canal bet. Main and
  Sycamore
Holmes & Conwell, 34 Walnut
Holt & Clark, 227 Walnut
Hofer F. & Co., 29 Columbia
Hewson & Holmes, 83 and 85 Walnut
Hoaes & Frazer, cor. Main and Front
Harrison & Hooper, 61 Main
Jones, Lovett & Robbins, 68 Pearl
Kestner G. F., n. e. cor. Main and Canal
King & Dailey, 33 Sycamore
Kattenhorn A., 361 Main
Kennett & Dudley, 14 Public Landing
Keys, Maltby & Co., 21 and 23 Columbia.
Mehner Louis, 34 Lower Market
Mackentope Bernard, n. w. cor. Vine and
  Columbia
McGinty A. T., n. w. cor. Vine and Water
Meader N. R., 50 Lower Market
Minor, Andrews & White, s. w. cor. Main
  and Columbia
Messick & Co., cor. Syc. and Columbia
McGechin Thomas, s. e. cor. Main and 6th
Montgomery J. C., 292 Main
McNair James & Co., n. e. cor. Main and
  7th
Mathews James & Co., 53 Walnut
McKee James M. & Co., 14 Main
Manning Samuel & Co., 251 do
McFall & Cullum, 5 Water
Mills P. F., 245 Main
McKenzie, Craft & Co., 20 and 22 Main
Owen Allison, 29 and 31 e. 3d
Oberhen E. & F., 112 Court
Poor & Co., 225 Walnut
Pullen, Hatfield & Brown, 19 Columbia
Porter Thomas & Sons, 66 Walnut
Raper & Brothers, 25 Main
Ridgely & Brother, 81 Walnut
Rauth Francis, 80 Lower Market
Reese & Reed, 17 5th
Richardson A. G., cor. Walnut and Colum.
Racine & Constant, 86 and 88   do
Smielan John, 62 Lower Market
Sommer & Meyer, 23   do
Springer & Whiteman, Columbia bet. Main
  and Walnut
Smith & Graham, 4 and 5 Commerc'l Row
Stem. Baker & Co., 49 Walnut
Thirkield, Thompson & Co., 49 Main
Tweed & Andrews, 31 and 33 Pearl
Thompson & Taaffe, 13   do
Taylor R. M. W., 45 Walnut
Warner & Craford, 36 Walnut
Wendland C. L., cor. Vine and Front
Wann & McBirney, 53 Columbia
Wilcox S. T., n. e. cor. 5th and Broadway
Ward William M., 8 Main
Woods Wells, 55 Pearl
Yost Henry, 65 Walnut

Jefferson County.

Vevis B. W.   *Steubenville.*
Hull R. C. & Co.
Frazier & Drennen
Dohrman & Collier

Mears Robert   *Steubenville.*
McGowen D. & Son

Knox County.

Davidson A. E.   *Mt. Vernon.*
Miller J. W.
Potwin Geo. B.
Weaver J.

Lawrence County.

Murdock & Rodgers   *Ironton.*

Licking County.

Cooper E.
Richter F.   *Newark.*
Jewett & Marble
Lott J. & H.
Mooney John L.

Lucas County.

Church, Hays & Co.   *Toledo.*
Hine & Dillon
Ketchum H. V.

Madison County.

McMillan & Welden   *London.*

Muskingum County.

Thompson F. A.   *Zanesville.*
Crosby J. & J.
Applegate & Mathews
Monroe J. H.
Summers H. J. & Co.
Davis W. H. & Co.
Martin & Price
Ragut James
Bratshaw J. B. H.
Stevens John
Alter John
Dixon A.

Pickaway County.

McQueen James & Co.   *Circleville.*

Richland County.

McFall E. & Co.   *Mansfield.*

Ross County.

McClintick James   *Chillicothe.*
Holcomb & Co.
Allston & Peitsmeyer
Clark J. & Son
Poland Wm.
Allston & Garfield
Smart D.
Marfield & Lenkett

Scioto County.

Brown W. S.   *Portsmouth.*
Cutler W. S. & Co.
Davis Jas. W. & Co.
Damarin Chas. A. M. & Co.
Gilbert M. & G.
Martin W. P.
Oakes & Buskirk
Ross S. R.
Conway & Co.

Seneca County.

Buskirk Henry A.   *Tiffin.*

Starke County.

Dickey & Barkdull   *Massillon.*
Watson J. & Co.
Atwater D. R.
Oberlin & Beatty
Willenbarg H.
Harbaugh D.

Tuscarawas County.

Forbes & Dunning   *Uhrichsville.*
Fertig Samuel   *Canal Dover.*
Shane F.

Union County.

Wood & Buxton   *Marysville.*

Washington County.

Woodbridge & Wescott   *Marietta.*
Hall W. H. & Co.
Hall, Mathews & Co.
Crawford R.
Bosworth, Wells & Co.

Wayne County.

Knepper Samuel   *Wooster.*

Grocers, Forwarding & Commission Merchants (Wholesale).

Hamilton County.

Athearn & Hibberd, 5 e. Front *Cincinnati.*
Andrew & Wilson, cor. Congress & Kilg'r
Andrews Robert, 58 w. Front
Baker & Co., 29 Main
Bartlett B. & Co., 23 w. Front
Brown & Ray, s. e. cor. Sycamore & Court
Bishop, Wells & Co., Front e. of Main
Babbit, Good & Co., Front near Sycamore
Bruce, Morgan & Co., 26 w. Front
Barr & Cadien, 25 Columbia
Banning D. & P. W., 32 Walnut
Bartlett, Stockton & Co., 38 do
Buckles J. C. & Judge, e. Front
Campbell, Russell & Co., 3 Cassilly's Row
Chenoweth J. S. & Co., 25 e. Front
Cohoon & Perrin, 33 & 35 Walnut
Cunningham Wm. & Co., 21 Sycamore
Copen & Bassett, 69 Water
Cinnamon & Kerr, 11 do
Dugan T. S. & Co., 27 Main
Graham & McCoy, 50 Walnut
Gilbert, Jones & Ogborn, 5th and W. W. Canal
Holmes & Conwell, 34 Walnut
Hosea & Frazer, Main and Front
Hull Julius, Canal bet. Main & Sycamore
Jack, Collier & Co., 46 Public Landing
Johnston J. V., 63 Walnut
Langley, Manser & Kincaid, 25 Front
Latham & Woods, 20 Public Landing
Lehmer James D., s. w. cor. Walnut and Second

McBride & Hammar, 52 Walnut *Cincinnati.*
McCleary Andrew & Co., 19 Canal
Nye Henry, Broadway bet. Court & Canal
Ogden Henry A., C. H. & D. R. R. Depot
  and Little Miami R. R. Depot
Richardson, Gardner & Stone, 30 w. Front
Rawson, Wilby & Co., 8 w.   do ·
Ross & Ricker, 16 and 17 e.   do
Stone B. T. & Co., 18 Columbia
Sontag C., 10 w. Front
Sprigman & Brown, 21 and 23 w. Front
Skinner & Franklin, 9   do
Taylor & Odiorne, 48 e. Front
Traber & Aubery, 7   do
Townsend E. B. & Co., 18 w. do
Wright Wm. S. & Co., 16 do

Grocers, Produce & Commission Merchants (Wholesale).

Hamilton County.

Adae & Labrot, 16 w. Front   *Cincinnati.*
Boss Christian, 72 Lower Market
Brooks F. F., 1 and 3 Water
Beattie & Frazer, 51 Front
Bates Richard, 43 Walnut
Bailey C. P., 25   do
Bronson, Warren & Co., 62 Walnut
Briscoe & White, 12 Lower Market
Colter Aaron A., s. e. cor. 7th & Main
Clisby & Patrick, 12 Front
Cody P., 9 & 10 Water
Coffin D. H. B., 17 Lower Market
Cowguill & Smith, 27 & 29 Sycamore
Conklin A. & Co., 23 Walnut
Cunningham & Moore, cor. 9th and Main
Cox R. S., 624 W. Row
Davis George F. & Co., 11 Sycamore
Davis S. P. & Co., s. w. cor. Court and
  Broadway
Dickinson & Co., 35 Walnut
Empson J. H., 72 Lower Market
Fletcher C., 20 & 22 w. Front
French & Hine, 27   do
Fiedeldey John C., 54 & 56 Lower Market
Gilpin Thomas & Co., s. e. cor. Main and
  Canal
Gray George A., 14 and 16 Water
Glenn Wm. & Sons, n. e. cor. Walnut and
  Columbia
Gardner, Phipps & Co., n. w. cor B'adway
  and 9th
Gould G. W., 9th bet. Main and Sycamore
Goelx John, 69 Court
Groene J. H. F., s. e. cor. Race & Columbia
Harper, Winall & Co., 12 Columbia
Harding L. L. & Co., 28 & 30 e. 2d
Hieatt & Gerard, cor. Broadway and Canal
Johnson H., cor. Vine & Landing
John James C., 9th bet. Main & Sycamore
Manning J., 62 Water
McMillen & Watson, 21 Water
Miller & Co., 20 Public Landing
Michael D. C., 5 w. Front
McKenzie, Craft & Co., 20 and 22 Main
Overaker George, 7 Main

Paul & Murdock, 7 Water   *Cincinnati.*
Poland & Henry, 38 and 40 2d
Porter Thos. & Sons, 66 Walnut
Russell John B., 26 Sycamore
Rockey Henry, 21 e. Front
Rounebaum J. H., 36 Lower Marker
Rechtin G. H., 70   do
Richardson A. G., cor. Walnut and O'bia
Ruffner & Murphy, n. e. cor. 8th & W'nut
Sprigman & Brown, 21 & 23 w. Front
Siebern J. N. & Brothers, 8 Lower Market
Stall & Meyer, n. w. cor. Lower Market &
  Sycamore
Straight & Deming, 31 Sycamore
Spining, Wilson & Brown, 215 Main
Swasey John & Co., 23 and 25 Sycamore
Swasey & Wise, s. w. cor. Broadway and
  Columbia
Spalding & Giraldin, 8 and 10 Columbia
Sheehan P., n. w. cor. Court and Br'dway
Stilwell J. D., 39 Walnut
Skiff J. A., 30   do
Stone L. & M., 32 and 36 Vine
Seifert Francis, 72 5th
Smith J. W. & Son, 9th bet. Main and
  Sycamore
Snyder Frederick, 99 Canal
Schultz Charles, 2   do
Thompson R. F., 290 Main
Tweed, Sibley & Wright, 40 Walnut
Tudor F. F., 27   do
Townsend O. & Co., 45 Columbia
Todd J. & Co., 35 5th
Thomas N. W. & Co., s. w. cor. Canal and
  Walnut
Walbridge J. D., Canal
Wesjohan H., 100 e. Columbia
Williams, Moore & Posey, 290 Main
Wilshire, Bristol & Co., 17 Sycamore

Groceries and Provisions (Retail Dealers).

Adams County.

Dunbar David   *Manchester.*
Dunbar John S.
Cooley Oliver H.
Wikoff Melk   *Stout's.*
Kerr Hiram
Reynolds W. T.
Blair W. L.   *Scott.*
Jackman Mrs. Elizabeth   *West Union.*
Lafferty J. W.
Campbell James B.   *Bradysville.*

Allen County.

Alferd & Hazeltine   *Lima.*
Collins S.
Curtis & Howard
Myers & Wolf
Ansbach John   *Deep Cut.*
Bradford L. S.
Harvey M. E.
Swaney S.
Wery J. H.   *Fryburg.*

Myers Daniel	*Middle River.*
Moore G. G.	*Donnell's.*
Fullerton A.	*Cranberry.*
Lawrence William	*Hog Creek.*
Grubbs Abraham	*Croghan.*

Ashland County.

Eaton George	*Ruggles.*
Stamets J.	*Rowsburg.*
Melon G. C.	*Polk.*
Smith Thomas	
Heifner J. P.	*Hayesville.*
Kithcart J.	
Earl Silas	*Savannah.*
Culbertson Wm.	
Henry John H.	
Johnson Elijah	*Albion.*
Barnes J. W.	*Ashland.*
Freer J. & R.	
Jacobs Anthony	
Miller Michael	
Walick & Coffin	
Black P. J.	*Loudonville.*
Shuch Frederick	
Dunham Thomas	*Jeromeville.*
Hoffman John	
Ridgely Elias	
Baughman George	*Perrysville.*
O'Hara H.	

Ashtabula County.

Allen Joseph	*Geneva.*
Gibbs E. L.	*Windsor.*
Brainard Abner	*Trumbull.*
Jones E.	
Warren A. & Co.	*Jefferson.*
Allen Wm. R.	
Prentice & Gleason	*Ashtabula.*
Heuckley H.	
Word J. C.	
Gleason C. C.	*Harpersfield.*
Belding O.	
Keys A. C.	*Conneaut.*
Jobes H.	
Spring M. G.	

Athens County.

Hartley Saml.	*Trimble.*
Dupler Saml.	
Pilcher Wm. F.	*Coolville.*
Williams E. H.	*Hockingport.*
Beane George	*Pleasanton.*
Johnson B.	*Canaanville.*
Gallotin E. D.	*Nelsonville.*
Shannon Thos.	
Harmon Christian	
Grethers J. L. & J.	*Athens.*
Root Wm.	*Guysville.*

Belmont County.

McPherson L. D.	*Hendrysburgh.*
Reynolds Oliver	
Wills L. M.	
Cole E.	*Demos.*
Barnes E. S.	*Somerton.*
Edwards & Shouse	*Martin's Ferry.*
Fenimore John	

Heberling Henry	*Martin's Ferry.*
Meddles John	
Turner Joseph	
Turner & Bendell	
Wallace & Geiger	
Weeks Edwin	
Brown John	*Barnesville.*
Crew James	
Folger Wm. H.	
Gardner Wesley	
Jewett James	
McCune John	
Mott H. H.	
Odell H. F.	
Jefferson John	*Bellair.*
McMurry J.	
O'Neal Robt. H.	
Krim & Vanmeter	*Flushing*
Vanlaw Isaac W.	*Loydsville.*
Griffith M. B.	*Shepherdstown.*
Ainger M.	*St. Clairsville.*
Armsuster A.	
Boroff William	
Darrah William	
Eyre E. A.	
Hessey Charles	
Hubbard O. G.	
Johnson Isaac D.	
Palmer John	
Thompson James	
Young Elihu	
Wright John	
Campbell Wm. S.	
Ryan R. B.	
Boring J. W.	*Morristown.*
Brown O.	
Gardner G.	
Hauauer S.	
Mitchell J. R.	
Mitchell J.	
Swan F. M.	
Tompkins B.	
Fawcett M. T.	*Belmont.*
Vanfossen N.	
Shafer P.	*Armstrong's Mills.*
Faro Reece C.	*Hunter.*

Brown County.

King & McConaghay	*Higginsport.*
Friedly Lewis	*Ripley.*
Maddox J. F. & J.	
Gregg Stephen	
Liggett F. T.	
Hook Z. & J. W.	
Hemphill S. & Co.	
Jolly & Shaw	
Carter J.	
Armstrong W. M.	
Parker D. F.	
Gray, Lewis & Co.	
Drake & Russell	
Troutman Lewis	
Beihn H.	
McKinley E. & Son.	
Biehn G. M.	
New H.	
Brafford J. W.	

Reed C. W.	*Georgetown.*	**Champaign County.**	
Jones S. M.		Davis J.	*Mechanicsburg.*
Brose J. G.		Keyes & Jones	
Shane A. F.		Sutton & Baker	
Gates J. & Co.	*Aberdeen.*	Gorsuch E.	*Christiansburg.*
Scott J. S. & Co.		Riddle John	
Worstell J. H.		Smith J. & A.	*Westville.*
White N.		Cox Patrick	
Mervin J. H.		Colwell & Berry	*Urbana.*
Allen D. D.		Brown J. M.	
Conover W. N.	*Maple.*	Smith Wm.	
Beck Joseph P.		Geiger & Son	
Trisley James		Bacon P. J. D.	
Rishforth G.	*Russellville.*	Moore George	
Edwards & Smith		Kenton Wm. M.	
Richards P.	*Fincastle.*	Hull D. W.	
Butler County.		Wiley & Son	
Mollyneaux S.	*Oxford.*	Bailie J.	
Lathrop D.		Miller L.	
Spidle P.		Powell T.	
Wooley J.	*Paddy's Run.*	Collins J. & O. P.	
Booty James C.	*Melville.*	Clark E. G.	*Woodstock.*
Salesbery Saml.		Sprague M.	
Jacobs & Young	*Hamilton.*	Goul J.	*Mutual.*
Huston C. W.		Hill John	*Careyskill.*
Davis & Dyes		Bell G.	*Springkills.*
Lander D. B.		Craig A.	
Dilge H.		Forrey J.	
Leppart H.		Stineman Jacob	*St. Paris.*
Schumm C.		Runkle Eli	
Brook J. P.		Amy Elisha	*North Lewisburg.*
Lemp A.		**Clark County.**	
Lashorn J.		Liffel Peter	*Donnelsville.*
Hunter & Son		Fulck Christopher	
Johnson & Weil	*Rossville.*	Littlejohn Jonathan	*North Hampton.*
Schugen & Waltner		Hughell Lewis	
Huffman M.		Wallace S. H.	*Tremont.*
Kimbol & Reiley		Carter David	
Longfellow Geo.		Conklin Joseph S.	*Enon.*
Garver J. L.		Bormet J.	*Springfield.*
Suler J.	*Middletown.*	Barcafer J. P.	
Peck D. H. & Conimer		Raffensperger D.	
Hilt J. D. & Co.		Detrick J.	
Ginnes G.		Miller Charles	
Sulphin & Simpson		Anderson J.	
Wheelen G. W.	*Millville.*	Icenbarger Geo.	
Tilhardt J.		Frankenburg & Muzzy	
Kensinger John	*Ross.*	Berger W. H.	
Berrow George		Huben Danl. V.	
Wilkinson B. F.	*College Corner.*	Siebert George	
Morris R. F.		Loucks G. A.	
Peters D.	*Somerville.*	Sagar S.	
Torbert A.		Rockway & Miller	
Buckle Jacob	*Trenton.*	Stewart J. C.	
Spitle Jacob	*Jacksonsburg.*	Bean B.	
Knox T. W.	*Port Union.*	Tallmadge S. S.	
Carroll County.		Compton J. H.	
Thomson J. R. & J. B.	*Harlem Springs.*	Murat F.	
Wiand Israel		Dalie M.	
Beths Charles	*Malvern.*	Eby Wm.	
McCauley Isaac	*New Harrisburg.*	Evans Wm.	
Clark Emmor	*Norristown.*	Frankhouse J.	
Bell James S.	*Carrollton.*	Thornton Jas.	
Meister Balser		Clark S.	
Shelden Cyrus		Steele M. S.	
Adair John W.	*Leesville.*	Smith G. A.	

Loak John	*Catawba.*	Horsfall Henry	*New Lisbon.*
McManamay ——		Hoover Wm. S.	
Harrington & Reeder	*South Charleston.*	Ham David	
Heiskell John		Helman Samuel	
Nolan George		Miller David F.	
Coleman A. G.	*New Carlisle.*	Morrison Freeman	
Harman John		Morrow John A.	
McGuire O.		Nelson George W.	
Ross J. W.		Richards Samuel	
		Watson John	
		Weikart George	

Clermont County.

		Andrew Philip	*New Garden.*
Wibbels J.	*New Richmond.*	Hepburn John	
Aston James		Bandy A. L.	*North Georgetown.*
Smith Henry		Grossman Daniel	
Schumacker Henry		Huffman Ladolph	
Wetzel Frederick		Salander John	
Elmer William		Summers George	
Sturges William		Bunn Stephen	*East Rochester.*
McMillen A. G.	*Williamsburg.*	Shabe Conrad	*New Chambersburg.*
Williams Chas.	*Milford.*	Amens Nimrod	*Green Hill.*
Conrad John		Allen H. H.	*Salem.*
Shumard Thos.		Bassett Wm. T.	
Belt R.	*Goshen.*	Betz Wm.	
Frybarger M.		Eggman James	
Butts Wm.		Grove Samuel	
Brush J.	*Felicity.*	Thompson John	
Fee, Miller & Co.		Willington Jason	*Bucks.*
Judd & Sargent		Keck George	*East Liverpool.*
Kain T. & Co.	*Batavia.*	Moore & Allison	
Kline A.		Till Caleb	
Ware R.		Walpert B.	
Elstune Isaac	*Mulberry.*	Armstrong Samuel	*Columbiana.*
Stuart & Buchanan	*Moscow.*	Davis Richard	
Hamilton A.	*Chili.*	Keener T.	*Unity.*
Bartlow C.	*Rural.*	Brisbane James	*East Fairfield.*
		McGillivray John	*Inverness.*

Clinton County.

Coshocton County.

Hasard A.	*Sligo.*	Fleming J. E.	*New Bedford.*
Black Alex.	*New Burlington.*	Willen ——	
Starr Allen	*Port William.*	Rodgers Evan	*Tiverton.*
Biven A.		Henderson A.	*Evansburgh.*
Connell John	*Lamberton.*	Norman J. & J.	
Kelley Saml. C.	*Clarksville.*	Kent Enoch	*Keene.*
Nichols Mrs. E.		Dickey Robert	
Howmans A. & J.	*Blanchester.*	King John, Jr.	
Proud Thos.	*Sabina.*	Dunley Thos. B.	*Warsaw.*
Bromhall Wm.	*Wilmington.*	McDermot David	
Caul & Harlan		Linebough Noah	*Walhonding.*
Woodruff Saml.		Buxton N. W. & Co.	
Hale Joseph		Purdy B. C.	
Wraith Thos.		Rickeut H.	*Coshocton.*
		Frickey F. X.	

Columbiana County.

		Faclar George	
Best W. R.	*Wellsville.*	Thomas George	
Blackburn H.		Traxler J. F.	
Bowers M.		Oraway A.	
Cooper R. D.		Swaggert F.	
Denham Alex.		Lemaster H.	
Garringer G. W.		Dewey J. & G.	
Gun & McLeon		Hoover S.	
Hull Levi			
Patterson J.			
Rogers Wm.		**Crawford County.**	
Stevens O. M. & Son		Redich Nicholas	*Leesville Cross Roads.*
Stewart & Hibbets		Teel John C.	
		Tuttle Daniel	*Poplar.*

16

Williams Alvin   *Poplar.*
Derr John M. •   *New Washington.*
Dietche Peter
Pratt Wm. H.
Clark Martin   *Wellerville.*
Read Samuel   *Liberty Corners.*
Heiby Michael   *Sulphur Spring.*
McIntire James
Bowman J. J.   *Bucyrus.*
Hesche F. G.

Cuyahoga County.

Brainard & Snow, cor. Ontario and Pros-
    pect   *Cleveland.*
Blackmer R. H. & Co., 36 Davison
Bond Henry, 126 Superior
Bramley J. P., 11 St. Clair
Coonrad & Newell, Canal Basin
Cramer & Silkey, 76 Dock 145 River
Cushing & Mead, River and Dock
Dunn & Smith, 94 Superior
Farley John, 53 Detroit
Folsom G., 50   do
Gorham & Alpin, 16 Superior
Johnson & Short, 38 Ontario
Koenigsloew A. H., 28 Merwine
Kyser James, 72 Superior
Light C. H. & Co., 64 Ontario
Lyon L. L., 77 Dock 147 River
Machen H. P. L., 106 Superior
Mead T. W., cor. Ontario and Prospect
Miller J. H., 20   do
Mitchell Joseph, Canal Basin
Mitchell Alexander, cor. Ohio and Kins-
    man
Pollock David, 92 Superior
Reeve William F., cor. Ontario and Pub.
    Square
Rouse B. F., 173 Superior
Rose W. E., 22 Ontario
Ray J. R. & Co., 34 do
Sanborn C. & G. L., 7 do
Stair J. & Son., 6   do
Smithknight L. & Co., 3 Mechanics' Block
Sullivan P. O., 94 Water
Tomblyn J., 12 Ontario
Winer G. W., Canal Basin
Williams, Babbock & Hurd, 83 Superior
Spring J & H.   *Euclid.*
Bergin W.   *Newburgh.*
Orth Geo.   *Brooklyn.*
Selzer D.
Green William V.   *Independence.*
Rowan John
Earl J.   *Chagrin Falls.*
Gates William
Handy J.
Kellogg P.
Nettleton L.
Tarbell L.   *Bedford.*
Halsted H.   *Warrensville.*
Adams L. L.   *Collamer.*
Meeker R. C.
Lewis C. & Son   *Ohio City.*
Tyler & Whitney
Carr Francis
Myrick, Crosby & Co.

Lacy William, Columbus Block *Ohio City*
Cox John
Treat L.
Keina James
Turner A. P.
Nelson S. W., 58 Detroit

Darke County.

Orouse Geo.   *Castine.*
Klinger & Brothers   *Ithica.*
Watson B.
Mears J.
Culbertson John   *Hillgrove.*
McLittle R.   *Concordia.*
Espy Thos.   *New Madison.*
King John V.   *Greenville.*
McKhann James
Bertch J. C.
Doty A. R.
Lechlider J. C.
Fielding G. W.
Oavison Matthew
Swhisher A.
McConnell Elijah
Humphrey John
Finkbone John   *North Star.*

Defiance County.

Corn & Woolsifer   *Defiance.*
Gorman M. & H.
Marcellus D. W.
Stover S.
Wilhelm A.
Wisenberger J.
Wisenberger F.
Abell G. B.   *Milldale.*
Coy Eli   *Panama.*
Helfrich & Wolsifer   *Brungsburg.*

Delaware County.

Little & Le Duc E. W. & L.   *Delaware.*
Duden & Ely
Little S. W.
King & Evans R. & J. C.
Spinger H.
Slough Richard   *Stratsford.*
Williams, Andrews & Co.
Coleman Jacob   *Waldo.*
Nedleton Wm.   *Williamsville.*
Coleman Valentine   *Norton.*
Jones Thos. J.   *Delaware.*
McFarlin Wm. Z.
Benson Jacob   *Bellepoint.*
Jones Joseph

Erie County.

Alpin H.   *Sandusky City.*
Alder & Brown
Baubac Jacob
Balzaphel M.
Bear Nathan
Blosier C. A. & Co.
Bird Geo.
Oady Wm. & Co.
Olausius John
Deeley W. E.
Daniel M.

Farena John	*Sandusky City.*
Frohman H.	
Fing Wm.	
Hathaway R.	
Hadley O.	
Hosmer S. S.	
Hull Francis	
Hall Wm.	
Kugler John	
Lamb & Eck	
Lytle A. & Co.	
Lammers John	
Lotz Henry	
Miller A.	
Murphey Peter	
Magle Geo.	
Niebling A.	
Parsons & Derr	
Porter S. & Co.	
Radcliff H. P.	
Simpson W. A.	
Stead & Tucker	
Schelb D.	
Thompson Wm.	
Unckrich Geo.	
Warner Geo.	
Wallace L.	
Wolf L.	
Wetherel J. W. & Co.	
Walter J. W.	
Young M. M. & Co.	
Woodworth John	*Bloomingville.*
Bartholomew G. W. & Co.	*Furnace.*
Sears N. M.	*Milan.*
Stine C.	
Edridge C.	
Frees V.	
Dorr C.	
Sprague Geo.	*Huron.*
Dew Thos.	
Phelps James	
Lawrence P.	
Rice R. A.	
Durud S.	*Vermillion.*
Mainch P.	
Spears J.	
Blackman J.	*Florence.*
Squires J.	*Birmingham.*
Reed T.	
Shepherd W. H.	*Venice.*
Thomas Henry	

Fairfield County.

Beers James	*Pickerington.*
Hays William	
Walker R. B.	*West Rushville.*
Greeke John	*Pleasantville.*
Wilson T. O. & Co.	
Hoye John	*Lockville.*
Thrash M.	
Carpenter H. M	*New Salem.*
Hilliard & Stuart	*Bremen.*
Tobin & Blosser	
Kalb E.	*Rushville.*
McBride J. W.	
Lerch & Hyle	*Amanda.*

Lyons J.	*Lancaster.*
Kinkead & Doty	
Wygum Geo.	
Wilhite Geo.	
Beery Samuel	
Hunter Henry	
Giani & Brandt	
Kreamer O. W.	
Gabeline H.	
Zink & Bish	
Cranmer Joseph	
Becker E.	
Massey J.	
Church J.	
Beery H.	*Sugar Grove.*
Dyson Joseph	
Nopp A.	
Billings M.	*Lithopolis.*
Beecher F.	
Piper S.	
Mays —,	*Clear Creek.*
Hyde Daniel	

Fayette County.

Lindsey R. R.	*Bloomingsburg.*
Gray E.	*Jeffersonville.*
Moore Isaac W.	*Pancoastburg.*
Heckill Noah	*Convenience.*
Moore & Wibliver T. & G.	
Vanpelt John	*Washington,*
Dahl & Baughn	
Dahl D. & H.	
Moon R. P.	
Evans Richard	
Ely J. F.	
Bainter Jacob	*Moon's.*

Franklin County.

Beall S. W., Friend street,	*Columbus.*
Bergin B., Broadway	
Backus C. & L., High	
Baner Peter, Friend	
Butler John, cor. do. and High	
Burnett W. F., High	
Cochran N., do	
Dailey John, cor. Front & Rich	
Dickson & Willard, Long	
Eldridge Ira, High	
Felch A. S. & Co., do	
Frankinberg A., do	
Garrett Wm. M., do	
Gibbard Charles, cor. North and 3d	
Harton J. C., Broadway	
Heints Adam, cor. Friend and 4th	
Hetteshimer W., Front	
Hoyl William L., Town	
Hymrod & White, High	
Hunt Mrs., do	
James J., Broadway	
Krayer C. F., High	
Kientc George, Broadway	
Kammer P., Pike	
Murphy Peter, High	
McNeal J. W., 4th	
Myer M., Friend	
Reel G. W., High	
Robinson G. M., do	

Robertson George, High   *Columbus.*
Robins & Lattimer, do
Setler John, cor. 3d and Gay
Sells T. A. & Co., 4th
Sawyer C., cor. High and Gay
Augustus S. W., cor. High and Town
Statton John, Broadway
Schreiner Henry, Friend
Stanring Jas. H., High
Shafer George,   do
Tipton & Tarbor, cor. Spring and High
Tressenrider B., cor. 4th and Town
Ury P., Pike
Kidd A., High
Van York John, Jr., do
Wetmore P. M., do
Weiver S., cor. do and Friend
Woodbury D. T. & Co., High
Zettler Jacob, Friend
Marks M. D. & Co., High
Turner W. L., cor. 4th and Town
Brook Samuel, High
McBeth Joseph, do
Hellesheimer V., Front
Perrin P.,   do
Conn John   *Groveport.*
Stephenson & Rainier
Hepson Richard   *Hope.*
Beatty Wm. S., Jr.   *Harrisburg.*
Strubelt J.
Filler Eli   *Dublin.*
Davis William
Hay A. J.
Watson H. S.
Freatwell James A.   *Georgesville.*
Brown Sidney   *Worthington.*
Hunt Jasper
Wilcox Salmon
Chandler Albion   *Canal Winchester.*
Schoch John M.
Sarber J. A.   *Lockbourn.*
Bowman J.

Fulton County.

Marsh J. N.   *Delta.*
Wilcox Ezra   *Ottokee.*
Culver W. W.   *Metamora.*

Gallia County.

Potter William   *Vinton.*
Bierly Joseph   *Rodney.*
Clark William   *Pine Grove.*
Parker S. M.
Frank M. & H.   *Gallipolis.*
Frost Solomon
Bailey & Cherrington
Hern Allison
Kuhn John L.
Litchenfelt C.
Beard James
Baltzell John
Baxter Zenos

Geauga County.

Cook B. & A.   *Chardon.*
Smith & Woodard
Avery B. F.

Bishop J. A.   *Newbury.*
Heath W. H.
Austin A.   *Montville.*
Barnett David   *Thompson.*
Proctor John
Strong Z.
Hunniston J. L.   *Chester.*

Greene County.

Barber & Brother   *Cedarville.*
Huffine George
Shigley & Brother
Allison & Townsley   *Xenia.*
Bull William
Curl J. P.
Dean D. A. & Bro.
Edsall E. H.
Hoyle James
Jones M. Luther
Klein Jacob
Moody John
Pierson Lewis
Rockhill S.
Sellers John N.
Shehan T.
Smith & Austin
Smith J. J.   *Fairfield.*
Byrd A. J. & Co.   *Spring Valley.*
Sanders J.
Houghton Saml.   *Clifton.*
Simonton & Smith   *Yellow Springs.*
Mullen James   *Paintersville.*
Johnson R. H.
Alexander & Co.   *Jamestown.*
Deardorff Jacob
Torrence J. M.
Neal Thomas

Guernsey County.

Powers R. W.   *Byesville.*
Finnefrock Jacob   *Middlebourg.*
Henry D. S.
Kirkpatrick A.
Hanna H. H.   *Winchester.*
Hill Andrew   *Londonderry.*
Edson D. B.   *Fairview.*
Humphrey John
Bernard Wm.
Duff Alex.
Deering John   *Dyson's.*
Davis W. K & J. V.   *Cambridge.*
Corbet Joseph
Davis J. W.
Niswander J.
Cook A. E.
McIlyar Mrs. E.
Allen John
Kincaid W.   *Millersville.*
Fleming F.
Foreman H.   *Senecaville.*
Craft E.
Johnson T. M. & B. J.   *Leatherwood.*
Vance James
Sidel Joseph

Hamilton County.

Ashman William, 4 Mulberry st.   *Cincin.*

Ahlers Frederick, 679 Vine st. *Cincinnati.*
Alleld F. W., cor. John and Kemble
Aue F., cor. Clark & Rittenhouse
Ackerstaff J., 432 Sycamore
Auston James S., n. e. cor. 5th and Elm
Arndt D., cor. Lock and 6th
Burgoyne Joseph, 507 Sycamore
Belldin F., cor. 5th and McAllister
Bentce H., 34 Lock
Billerback O. A. cor. Congress and Butler
Bewley T., 42 5th
Byrne E., 126 3d
Bergen F., 547 Main
Brackerhoff A., 519 do
Bone J. S., 15 Front
Brockhaus B. W., cor. Mound and Longworth
Bushknap Joseph, n.w. cor. Plum and Wm.
Boston Israel, 219 Elm
Byma J., cor. 9th and Elm
Burnett E., W. Row bet. 4th and 5th
Barr John, cor. Elm and George
Bellinger & Shaw, 359 w. 5th
Bryce William, cor. Race and Pearl
Beckman H., 101 Clay
Broyer C., 173 do
Bransiger C., cor. Bremen and 15th
Bodi G. W., cor. do and Liberty
Beril George, cor. Betts and Linn
Bolson John, cor. John and Everett
Bellinger J., Kemble bet. John and Fulton
Bowlaley J. N., cor. Everett and John
Billods G., Vine street Hill
Cammen Fred, n. e. cor. Elm & Findley
Cambel Mrs., s. w. cor. John & Catherine
Cornable L., cor. 8th & Linn
Cook Wm., 196 Clinton
Coulters A., 31 Canal
Cook Henry, 369 5th
Cartman Thos., 587 5th
Coleman John, 49 Plum
Clark Patrick, 23 8th
Cruse F. H., 507 Main
Cline A., 36 Butler
Conklin C. S., n. w. cor. Plum & Water
Coffin Z. B., 32 5th
Cavagna B., 5th bet. Main & Walnut
Drum Mrs., cor. 7th & North
Dewein J. N., 537 e. Front
Drake C. G., n. w. cor. Race & 5th
Denne & Meyer J. F. & F., cor Jackson and 12th
Davis James, 195 George
Dunham C., cor. Linn and Clark
Degraw A., cor. John & Clinton
Dodd J., 260 W. Row
Deppin John, 613 do
Distler J., 481 Ham. Road
Delinton P., 717 Elm
Esman Ernst, 24 Ham. Road
Eversman H. H., cor. Cutter & Richmond
Emenhort H., 507 Race
Enyart J. L., Ham. Road bet. Main and Piatt
Ellis F. & H., 37 Water
Ehenger E., 550 e. Front
Fengen John & Co., cor. Canal and 8th

Frommeyer J. F., 540 Sycamore *Cincin.*
Fackler J., 581 do
Fries J. & Co., 123 Court
Frank A. W. & Co., n. w. cor. Race & 6th
Fitzgerald J., 211 W. Row
Fruchtmicht H., 504 Walnut
Frecker F., cor. Jackson & 13th
Frimble Geo., 569 Vine
Frank S. H., cor. Vine & Canal
Fogarty James, Ham. Road bet. Piatt and Freeman
Fichilberger J., 108 Liberty
Freine Joseph, cor. Race and Greene
Fibbe B., 413 Race
Foot F. H., cor. Richmond and Baymiller
Frank G. A., 387 W. Row
Gers H. H., n. w. cor. Greene and Pleasant
Gray Wm., 372 W. Row
Gets Fred, cor Bremen & 14th
Grieve G., 665 Vine
Grass A., 503 do
Grieve J. H., 382 Broadway
Gardner R., 308 Longworth
Griesehop E., 480 w. 5th
Goforth N. P., 230 Elm
Germann John B., 467 Main
Greeiwe H., 382 Broadway
Gold Peter, cor. 2d & Ludlow
Hart James, 211 Broadway
Hughes Wm., 502 Sycamore
Hobbs H., cor. Vine & 9th
Hooker J. J., n. e. cor. Vine & 6th
Hamilton F. G., 22 5th
Hazlett J., 13 Front
Hornsman M., 132 Front
Haas N. & G., 614 Sycamore
Harzog T., 24 Harrison
Hubble & Conley, 226 Main
Henry Mrs., s. e. cor. Smith & Plum
Hill Arthur, 321 Elm
Handy Robert J., cor. Elm & 9th
Hall Wm., 459 5th
Hall Wm., cor. Mill & 4th
Hagerdonn J. & Co., 560 Walnut
Hut H., 70 Hunt
Hoffman J., 565 Vine
Houstedt H., 497 do
Harvy E., cor. W. Row & Betts
Heitman F. H., 611 Race
Hoppe D., cor. Race and 12th
Hopkins E., cor. Hopkins and Cutter
Hanbold F., 141 Everett
Holland J. R., cor 8th and Baymiller
Hilp J., s. w. cor. John and Kemble
Hash M., cor. John & Catharine
Herpenstandt Joseph, 137 Everett
Harvig J. V., Maple bet. Piatt & Linn
Holden R. A., 393 Main
Hager John, 60 Ham. Road
Hauk J., 691 Elm
Holder G., cor. Linn & Poplar
Johnson J., 230 Sycamore
Jones A. & Son, 107 5th
Joyce John, 58 Water
Jones E. W., 513 w. 5th
Jackson G., 353 W. Row
Krise C. & Co., s. w. cor. Pl'sant & Lib'ty

Keith J., cor. John & Chesnut *Cincinnati.*
Koch J. H., Clark bet. Rittenhouse & Linn
King John H., cor. Liberty and Freeman
Kreger J., 7th bet. Cutter & Linn
Kramer C., cor. Laurel and   do
Korte G., 615 Race
Kunz John, cor. Clinton & Locust
Killduff P., cor. John and Elizabeth
Kronlace H., 384 Sycamore
Knapka F., 357 5th
Kusgoerd H. & A., cor. Park and 3d
Karnes A., 238 6th
Kattenhorn J. H., cor. Lock and Smith
Kurthamp H., cor. Congress and Butler
Keith & Sanderlin, n. w. cor. 4th and Race
Keshan Wm. 150 Vine
Kerr A., 569 e. Front
Lawson J., cor. Elm & 2d
Lightbody J. M. F., cor. Smith & 3d
Linch D., 220 W. Row
Landenkutter —, 106 Abigail
Langhorst W., 526 Race
Linn Wm., cor. Piatt and Poplar
Lambur H., cor. Catherine and Linn
Menks J., 641 cor. Elm and 12th
Muller A., 78 Buckeye
Morman & Hatke, cor. Poplar & Buckeye
Mulhauser F., 275 Ham. Road
Mohrhaus B., 540 Plum
Morrison W., cor. Linn and Kemble
Myer P., cor. Rittenhouse and Catherine
Miller T., cor. Cutter and David
Mahnken H., Linn bet. Catherine and
  Clark
Martin Mrs. N., 128 Clinton
Mix Z., cor. Cutter and 7th
McGoldrick E., cor. Mound and 6th
Mahlhoop F., 491 Race
Masman L., 99 Woodward
Myers H., 115   do
Miller J. H., 62 Webster
McDonald Thos., 6th bet. Elm and Plum
Muse H., 122 Longworth
Murrey James, 644 Fifth
Martin & Co., n. w. cor. 6th and Elm
McDermott Mrs. Mary, 134 Water
Macke H. H., 24 Woodward
Meier F., 569 Main
Moulster C., 598 e. Front
McCormick M., Dublin near Locke
Masty J., cor. Ludlow and Third
Moulton C., n. e. cor. W. Row and Third
Moran Patrick, 170 Front
Murphey Pat., 109   do
Marshall Wm., n. e. cor. Front and Plum
McGinty A. T., n. w. cor. Vine and Water
Magill F. & G., 70 Walnut
McCawley Saml., 61 5th
McCann J. H., 55 7th
Nowry H., 23 Greene
Nordman G. F., 24 Buckeye
Newton M. A., s. w. cor. Elm and 12th
Oalage E. F., 497 Elm
Oberline G. H., cor. Liberty and Freeman
Orr Wm., Ham. Road bet. Freeman and
  Brighton
Osborn J., cor. Smith and Longworth

O'Hara P. H., w. 4th   *Cincinnati.*
O'Brien Chas., 21 8th
Osteng John D., 466 Main
Orr Mellville, n. e. cor. Plum and 6th
O'Conner —, 124 e. 8th
Postler John, Vine above Ham. Road
Poochat George, 411 W. Row
Pugh H. & J. D., cor. Cutter and Laurel
Price T., cor. Smith & 6th
Peepough M., W. Row bet. 4th and 5th
Peters A., cor. Walnut and Allison
Pelkers C., 73 Plum
Peebles Joseph R., n. e. cor. Race and 5th
Pugh J. W., cor. Plum and Water
Peters G. E., 112 Front
Pengemar J. T., 399 Sycamore
Puttman J. H., 196   do
Quinn R., 419 4th
Rennckemp Lewis, 627 W. Row
Reif F., 126 Ham. Road
Roehm G., s. e. cor. Pleasant and Liberty
Renniker Henry, 116 Betts
Robertson Geo., cor. Betts and Cutter
Rotteman B., 577 Race
Ryall Thos., cor. Hopkins and Freeman
Rodart H., 104 Abigail
Robbin H., 50   do
Reiter & Busching, 410 Sycamore
Rabbe J. H., 450 Vine
Reinhard D., cor. Har. Road & Brighton
Rose S., 461 5th
Roach Michael, 13 8th
Rump Henry, 169 Court
Raste Albert, 231 Sycamore
Smith G. W., 402 Broadway
Sterritt D. B., 425 Sycamore
Stone L. & M., 32 Vine
Shaw T., 5 Congress
Smith Spencer, 697 e. Front
Stiles Benj., 664   do
Stockman H., cor. Baum and 6th
Schraer J., Pike bet. Congress and Front
Strunck H., 19 8th
Schrifer H., 25 Liberty
Smith S. W. & Co., 29 Water
Seeger Wm. & Co., 322 5th
Synch M. D., 220 W. Row
Schulte E. H. W., 26 Lower Market
Skaats G., 641 w. Front
Straukamp T. W., 480 w. 3d
Scott W. R., 208 Elm
Sandman H., 258 5th
Stuve H., 366 Broadway
Schettleelkott J. L., 116 Woodward
Smith G. W., cor. Broadway & Wood'ard
Stevens G. H., 65 Hunt
Schawrer J., 634 Vine
Schultz J., 553   do
Shafer J., 362 W. Row
Sander H., cor. Race and Liberty
Stalkamp H., cor. Greene and Bremen
Scudder & Chambers, cor. Clinton & Linn
Secrist J. M., n. w. cor. John & Chestnut
Sutton C., 140 Hopkins
Schroerlucke H., cor. Everett and Locust
Samon J., 8th bet. W. Row and John
Schmier L., cor. Richmond and Fulton

Secrist J. H., cor. Fulton and Richmond, *Cincinnati.*
Smith W., n. e cor Catherine and Linn
Smith P., cor. Catherine and Baymiller
Sloan J., cor. John and Richmond
Scharhnren H. H., cor. Everett and Linn
Spillian J., 118 Everett
Stiedel Geo., s. w. cor. Linn and Poplar
Schutte J., 72 Buckeye
Schnitger J. M., 108 do
Slatling John, 113 Ham. Road
Shenenbecker Jas., 106 do
Stegner H., n. e. cor. Elm and Liberty
Trussell M., cor. John and Wade
Taylor W., cor. Linn and Bank
Thompson ——, cor. Main and Court
Thomas C. W., 30 Buckeye
Thierman J. H., cor. John and 8th
Thaw W. R., cor. John and Everett
Terman John, 8th bet. Carr and Harriet
Tice John, cor. John and 6th
Tembald G., cor. Freeman & Ham. Road
Tomlin & Ripley, cor. John and 5th
Tomes J. G., 28 13th
Thompson N., 448 5th
Tait G., 196 6th
Trobridge Wm. A., 139 Court
Trenchard E. P., cor. W. Row and Everett
Trumpe J. A., 699 e. Front
Tounies C. F., 189 Front
Todd J. & Co., 35 5th
Teck Jacob, 127 Congress
Ulain Joseph, cor. Hopkins and Cutter
Voggt F., 472 Sycamore
Voll M., cor. Plum and Longworth
Wilson & Slader, cor. Walnut and 8th
White D. A., 34 e. 5th
Wesseman R. H., 577 Main
Woodruff Wm. H., 113 Canal
Wendland C. L., 70 Front
Weidmyer F. G., 276 w. 3d
Wolcott A. G., s. e. cor. Plum and 6th
Wilson J. & G., 294 6th
Wiekershaw C., cor. Smith and 4th
Weise Joseph, 573 5th
Wewell H., 172 5th
Wellman M., 422 Vine
Wilson T., 337 W. Row
Wam Joseph, cor. Cutter and Hopkins
Wilkymacky H., Hopkins bet. Cutter and Linn
Warnken G., 147 Clinton
Wines C., cor. John and 7th
Wicker H., cor. 7th and Mound
Weller C., 8th bet. Cutter and Linn
Walsh J., cor. John and Catherine
Weaver & Howell J. & W. F., cor. Clinton and Cutter
Wortman F., 566 Elm
Wetzer L., 405 do
Wiechman H., 164 Everett
Zurmehlen J. & H., 57 Wade
Zeiglar Philip, 94 Betts
Kemper S. D., *Walnut Hills.*
Marsh S.
Singleton H.
Krouts G.

Meeker D. S. *Montgomery.*
Daubenhieer Wm. E. & Co. *Harrison.*
Bender Lewis
Bowlby Geo. W.
Hendrickson C. W.
Vandree & Pearson
Penny Richard H.
Brookhart John *Newtown.*
Gothlin Charles *Cumminsville.*
Keller Christopher
Knowlton E.
Myer Charles
Roll Isaac
Craig William *Mount Airy.*
Dun F.
Shiving John
Sillner Valentine
Stenger Christof
Fye John *Sharonville.*
Feltus John *Carthage.*
Strabaugh Wm.
Helmkamp Henry *Reading.*
Schurman Rudolph
Sener Louis
Johnston James *Miltonsburgh.*
Johnston Vance
Strong Z. *College Hill.*
Cooke J. J.
Popham Charles *Cleves.*
Watkins John L.
Bolander Luke *Elizabethtown.*
Grah H. *Miami.*
Basson Hector *Mount Healthy.*
Sandman G. & Co. *Columbia.*
Knicely A. & D.
Conklin B. C.
Rogers J. D. *Pendleton.*
Bebb D. B. & Co.
Hopkins Wm. & Co.
Streeter J. *Fulton.*
Edwards J.
Stone C. F.
Broadwell M. L.
Hooker Wm. J.
Wainwright T. C. & Co.
Wainwright & Augur
Finton Wm.
Degraw D.
Naylor Wm.
Shurreer J. L.
McGarry Mrs.
Scott C. W.
Rainey Wm.
Wells A.
King J.
Duft M.
Hogan J.
Prowt T. L.
Trimp J. A.

Hancock County.

Heller V. U. *Van Buren.*
Stott Wm.
Pardee G. W. *Mt. Blanchard.*
Markle Joel *Arlington.*
Vanetta James
Corwin John L. *Benton Ridge.*

Schuck Peter   *Ashery.* | Gillean —, | *Logan.*
Monesmith John   *Cass.* | Gimble Frederick
Brooks G. W.   *McComb.* | Kinney Thos. W.
Calbert James | Reheen Mrs.
Adams Lewis   *Finley.* | Beckley & Crook
Rusman Peter | Crownover H.   *Rock House.*
Davis Isaac | Dyson E.   *Pattonsville.*
Rice & Cooper | Hartley Isaac   *Gibisonville.*
Lamb Henry | Shulties John
Karst Frank
Neibling James M.

Hardin County.

                                           | **Holmes County.**
                                           | Jones J. W.   *Holmesville.*
Jamison R. G.   *Kenton.* | Sharp J. W.
Stevens John | Taylor T. A.
Letson John | Reed Geo.   *Nashville.*
Bockway & Shartser | Lenaman C.   *Benton.*
Trager & John | Renkenberg F.   *Walnut Creek.*
Davis A. M. | Bruny M.   *Winesburg.*
Black & Co.   *Roundhead.* | Troyer S.
Bruce Wm. & George | Garber A.
Baker Christian   *Sylvia.* | McDowell A. J.
Boslow P. C. | McDowell James C.   *Killbuck.*
Gordon Geo. W.   *Huntersville.*| Vogle V.   *Millersburg.*
Kayl A. L. | Stoll John
                                           | Watson J. & Co.

Henry County.

Eastman G. C.   *Napoleon.* | **Huron County.**
Rowan J. P. | Turner James   *Monroeville.*
Arnold J. L.   *Florida.* | Price Wm.
Schneider Joseph | Williams & Co.
Dutting C.   *New Bavaria.* | Terry Noah
Bauman John | Suthleph Benj.
Smith & Durbin   *Texas.* | Robey J. S. & R.
Crosby O. C. & G. P | Flickingen Wm.
                                           | Robbins & Wright   *Steuben.*
High'and County. | Wheeler C. B.
                                           | Center A. J.
Mackerley H.   *Rainsboro.* | Westfall J. N   *Wakeman.*
Ravenscroft H. | Freeman J.
Morrow Wm. A.   *Lynchburg.* | Church John   *East Townsend.*
Hunnelly W. C. | Perry J.   *Greenwich.*
Savage John   *Highland.* | Culver R. M. & Co.
Haisting John   *Pricetown* | Peirce Lewis   *Four Corners.*
Hess A. | Ruth Saml.   *Newhaven.*
Wright & McMillin   *Greenfield.* | Moore Wm. V. B.
Furhour A. J. | White O. H   *Bellevue.*
Bredwell J. | Layor John
Davis James | Moore C.
Bender F. | Biddings F.
Mader John | Chandler L. L.
Depay John | Smith —,   *North Norwich.*
Abors John   *New Petersburg.* | Vanhorn W. D.   *Centreton.*
Dilts Danl. | Pennewell S.   *Norwalk.*
McDaniel John   *Samantha.* | Morton G.
Wright John H. | Graves J. R.
Stevens C. J.   *Leesburgh.* | Rose & Gager
Higgins John W.   *Hillsboro'.* | Pearce & Slocum
Turnipseed Jacob | Yale Moses
Miller David | Venus S.
Higgins S. D. | Bush Isaac   *Clarkfield.*
Wilson Wm. | Lorier A.   *Fitchville.*
Doggett Elmore | Barnum & Berry   *North Fairfield.*
Hart & Chapman
Reynolds Henry   *East Monroe.* | **Jackson County.**
                                           | Brown B.   *Jackson.*
Hocking County. | Brooks C. E.

Frash Jacob   *Logan.*

French B.   *Jackson.*
Noell P.
Flowers Wm.
French A.

Jefferson County.

Abercrombie Mrs. E.   *Steubenville.*
Biles J. W.
Carter B.
Collins M.
Day J. F.
Doyle J. C.
Dohrman P. & Co.
Fickes G.
Gilmore T.
Henry J.
Holmes Saml.
Junkins M. O.
McCollong C.
McAlhaney G. W.
McMillen S.
Owesney Valentine
Orr John
Orr John, Jr.
Petters J. B.
Rohn H.
Spencer J.
Simpson Wm.
Turnbull M.
Wade Mrs. M.
Irwin James   *Warrenton.*
Kimball M. C.
Glazeuer Garret   *Annapolis.*
Glen Thos.   *Richmond.*
Vangilder M.
Parter Adam   *East Springfield.*
Elliott Stephen   *Moore's Salt Works.*

Knox County.

Graff J. A.   *Mt. Vernon.*
Sproule & Watson
George James
Andrews James
Britton Lewis   *Millwood.*
McMaken W. T.
Dayton M. N.   *Martinsburg.*
Davis Moses M.
Smith & Sanders
Eddy James   *Fredericktown.*
Elliott James
Love & Stephens
Freeman Luther   *Brandon.*
Bishop John   *North Liberty.*
Bishop Stephen
Mix J. L.
Pinkley Joseph   *Jelloway.*
Conway W.   *Mt. Liberty.*
Smith H. H.   *Milfordton.*

Lawrence County.

Clark D. M.   *Ironton.*
Cole H. & L.
Murphy M. & P.
Berkley J. H.   *Hanging Rock.*
Hall Robert
Stuart J. W.

McKnight John   *Millers.*

Lake County.

Durban Wm.   *Willoughby.*
Atkinson Thos.
Fifield H. A.   *Fairport.*
Babcock J.
Beetler M. B.
Boud Ezra   *Kirtland.*
Nichol John
Whitney A.   *Perry.*
Whiting A.   *North Perry.*
Durand H.   *Painesville.*
Ladd S. T.
Morrell S. B.
Stevens G.
Stocking S.
Stull J.
Sharpe & Brothers
Shepard H. F.
Wells L. K.
Whitney H. & Co.

Licking County

Orr Wm.   *Linnville.*
Bower John
Ferrill Chas.
Zellers George   *Etna.*
Dennis Z.
Kearns John   *Utica.*
Pierson J. H.
Brown J. C.   *Brownsville.*
Ditter George
Clark J. H.   *Jacksontown.*
Neal James
Woolron & Cutting   *Hebron.*
Lyon & Kelsey
Balthus & Cutting
Carter L.   *Granville.*
Sennett A.
Ayers J.   *Newark.*
Cross Gilbert
Davis Thos.
Irwin H. W.
Abraham J.
Towne A. L.
Tompkins D. C.
Jenkins L.
Henderson J. D.
Warden & Weaver   *Homer.*
Rice J. C.
O'Conner D. N.
Shacklett J. C.   *Perryton.*
Pork Saml.
Smith J.
Adams A.
Seymour C. A.   *Croton.*
Greene Josiah   *Johnstown,*
Harris Perry   *St. Louisville.*
Ritter Stephen
Belt J.
Bell & Richardson   *Kirkersville*
Wright John
Smead S.   *Fredonia.*

Logan County.

Dickson Wm.   *Huntsville.*

Elder & Co.   *Huntsville.*
Fleming James
Quick Wm.
Wishart Thos.
Broadwell J.   *West Liberty.*
Cheatham R. H.
Dunn G. F.
Hunter N.
Tallman T. W.
Humphreys John   *Logansville.*
Heath & Gifford   *East Liberty.*
Blaylock Edward   *Rushsylvania.*
Carter B. P.
Davis & Munsol
Buddon J. & M.   *Bellefontaine.*
Conner F H.
Cook Robert
Detrick A.
Downs William
Greig E. G.
Harper P.
Milliner Wm.
Miller J. B.
Moratty M.
Morrison Isaac
Short & Preston
Thrift & Brother
Williams A.
Stafford & Garwood   *Zanesfield.*
Thompson Amos
Conly Andrew   *Lewistown.*
Joseph John
Young George
Piatt & Bunker   *Quincy.*
Roads & Wolfe
Webb J.
Osborn A. S.
Gano & Smith
Chambers M.

Lorain County.

Lang J. B. & Co.   *Huntington.*
Fisher Carlos   *Grafton.*
Titus, Hanch & Co.
Blair Wm. H.   *Rochester Depot.*
Leach H. C.
Peck L.   *North Ridgeville.*
Loomis C. O.   *La Grange.*
Beecher & Co.   *Oberlin.*
Roberts & Henry
Rose & Lee
Thompson & Elliott
Watson John
Austin R.   *Elyria.*
Clark Charles
Potter S. O.
St. John Benjamin   *Amherst.*

Lucas County.

Clark T. L.   *Maumee City.*
Denny E. & M.
Dyer E. R.
Farnsworth Lott
Geiger John
Nelis Matthias
Plant A. H. & Co.

Pool Michael   *Maumee City.*
Wolfinger J. & J.
Marston & Gillett   *Waterville.*
Webb John
Eastwood L.
Thorp Peter   *Whiteford.*
Brigham & Parmelee   *Toledo.*
Brown & Wilkison
Brown W. O.
Dority John
Edwards P. & Co.
Fifield J. & Co.
Flinn W. & J.
Fleming W. & Co.
Hollenbant M.
Hauk E. S.
Holt F.
Hunkers —
Howard & Connelly
Heck J.
Johnson M. R.
Moross P. C.
McWayne & Co.
Metz C.
Mahon B.
Nichols Thomas
Peabody W. H.
Phillips H. & Co.
Raymond S. A.
Ream John
Shawl Charles
Stahl F.
Simmons R. A.
Shawl & Deifel
Shonocker M.
Turner George
Waite A. B.
Williams & Co.
Yost Peter

Madison County.

Kemp J. C.   *London.*
Smith & Jones
Tinder Benjamin
Bloomer J. & H.   *Midway.*
Hamilton A.
Wright Augustus   *Danville.*
Sherly William   *Newport.*
Nutt William H.   *Mt. Sterling.*
Timmons E.
Curry & Co.   *South Solon.*
Noland John
Melvin Joseph   *Somerford.*
Nibarger Anderson
McNeal Jacob   *West Jefferson.*
Miller N. L. H.
Stutson Jennet

Mahoning County.

Adams Henry P.   *Elsworth.*
Edsall Oreill   *Canfield.*
Schmick Wm.
Holland Nathan
Rohr Adam
Kyle John G.
Edwards P.
Goucher M.   *Lowellvil'e.*

Gleghorn Wm.   *Lowellville.*
Smith Henry
Conrad John   *Petersburgh.*
Coats D. C.   *Youngstown.*
Wallace R. M.
Winsworth John
Ashworth Mrs.
Cover Jeremiah   *New Middletown.*
Bensenboch George
Stickets Conrad   *East Lewistown.*
May Danl.   *Poland.*
Cracraft John
Smith J. H. & N.   *Milton.*
Wisner & Linton
Hudson Andrew
Zoolin Henry   *New Albany.*
Chescolan A. F.
Beard Solomon

Marion County.

Williams George   *Wilson.*
Sherman & Co.
Stultes A.
Dodd J.
Anderson J.
Avery A.   *Prospect.*
Adams Edward
Seibert John   *Marion.*
Lewis W. B.
Munzinger M

Medina County.

Wheeler A.   *Litchfield.*
Ford A.   *Mallet Creek.*
Burne G. N.
Moore Wm. S.   *Lodi*
Clause H.   *Homerville.*
Shook & Hobart   *Medina.*
Beswick A.
Selkirk E. L.
Hobart Geo.
Coffin N. H.

Meigs County.

Allen E. P.   *Downington.*
Holmes G. W.   *Salisbury.*
Womeldorf Geo.
Fultz Jacob
Eagle —
Smith S. S.

Mercer County.

Bruner O.   *St. Mary's.*
Johnson W. N. & J.
McLaughlin G. W.
Williamson & Ham
Rich Saml.
Fronts G.
Lakamp H.
Sulter A.
Mervelious H.
House M.
Mervelious L.
Fox Lewis
Nickel Benj.   *Neptune.*
Craig A. J.   *Celina.*
Brush Wm.

Brandon Wm.   *Celina.*
Blake J. G.   *Fort Recovery.*

Miami County.

Simmons Wm. T.   *Fletcher.*
Fahnestock James   *Covington.*
Lehman Saml.
Shafer George   *West Charleston.*
Collins G. B.
Davis, Defries & Co   *Piqua.*
Clark & Bollinger
Schmidtlapp J.
Miller & Wise
Barton E. H. & W. S.
Bell & Morrow
Sawyer & Jackson
Brown M. L.
Beecher J.
Miles R.
Hitchel —
Dicker —
Zeigenfelder Chas.
James J.
Heltzermean D. J.
Licklider A.
Mayo A.   *Troy.*
Douglass —
Calder R.
Rieder M.
Zuganfelter S.
Wasserman J.
Zeigenfelter G.
Zeigenfelter O.
Fuller W. T.   *Casstown.*
Williams L. D.   *West Milton.*
Armstrong James
Booker & Wittmer   *Hyattsville.*
Kauffman O. M.
Singer M.   *Brant.*
Williams R. F.   *Pleasant Hill.*
Ross J.

Monroe County.

Baker Martin   *Woodsfield.*
Steel John
Mishenack Jacob   *Sardis.*
Stewart William   *Masterton.*
Schwing George   *Rocky Narrows.*
McCormick T. B.   *Stafford.*
Morgan Mrs.   *Sunfish.*
Kiger T. C.
Cain Marion
Mallory Wm. H.
Wheeler Solomon V.
Luppes Theodore
Blackledge R. J.   *Malaga.*
Fowler Thomas S.
Bender Jacob   *Lewisville*
Marshall Christian
Fisher Jacob   *Caresville.*
Frick F.
Harman Samuel
Beaver & Okey   *Graysville.*
Hall Jonathan

Montgomery County.

Murphy J.   *Chambersburg.*

Shepherd Sarah	*Alexandersville.*
Byerly J. K.	*Liberty.*
Berry Benjamin	*Centreville.*
Stover George	*Little York.*
Baker J. G., Wayne	*Dayton.*
Baker J. H. do	
Berns H., John	
Baufman Thos., N. Market	
Bennet & Glen, do	
Brown J. do	
Bimm J. & Bro., First	
Clark E. & J. F., Jefferson	
Clark A., N. Market	
Croom & Toby do	
Coblentz J. R., Main	
Deaver William, First	
Dibck L., 5th	
Eastbrook & Phillips, First	
Emerick & Oblinger, 3d	
Folherth A. R. H., 2d	
Foster H. C., Main	
Gekhart A. K. do	
Gilbert B. & Son, First	
Grouse W. Main	
Groves & Morehouse, N. Market	
Gustin & Staley, Main	
Gerdes H., First	
Glegg W., 3d	
Hauitsch J., 2d	
Holden & Claflin, N. Market	
Hilgefoot Henry H., Jefferson	
Holtse J., 2d	
Heing L., 3d	
Holz P., Jefferson	
Himes —, First	
Johnson & Garver, Main	
Kenney J., 2d	
Kaufman J. E. & H. J., 2d	
Kenedy & Bro., 3d	
Karr W., First	
Lemmermill H., 5th	
Larkin Wm., 5th	
Leonard G. P., Jefferson	
McGee & Harshman, Main	
Miller J., 5th	
Morris S. M., 3d	
Mueller M. do	
Nauerth Geo., 2d	
Nissgen John, Main	
O'Brien Edward, 2d	
Piscard Eugene do	
Post Charles do	
Potter & Engle, Main	
Pruden A., Mill	
Powers E., N. Market	
Plagermaish J., Jackson	
Reilmier Henrich, First	
Reynolds J. M., 5th	
Schaeffer Joseph, Main	
Smith & Oldwin do	
Smith William, 3d	
Schomacker W., John	
Stephens A., N. Market	
Scholls J., Main	
Shepherd H., Jefferson	
Unger G., N. Market	
Viot N., 3d	

Wilt J., 5th	*Dayton.*
Fockler J.	*Clayton.*
Schauff Isaac	*West Baltimore.*
Matchett J.	*Johnsville.*
Lowe & Koogle	*Germantown.*
Bason P.	
Christine Benj.	
Grouser C. D.	
Schaeffer L.	
Spade Horace	
Brooks William	*Miamisburg.*
Friar J.	
Huiet Henry	
McElwee George	
Swatztrouber Jacob	

Morgan County.

Hann & Hall	*Malta.*
Miller Edward	
Rogers & Johnson	
Rounson Adam	
Saylor John	*Bristol.*
Brown Wm.	*Elliotts Cross Roads.*
Johnson John K.	*Meigsville.*
Kerns Isaac	
Hammond & Mummy	*McConnelsville.*
Richardson & Chambers	
Goodline & McCarver	
Brady Amos	
Edwards John C.	
Farra Saml.	
Brown Epping	
Lawrence I. P.	
Johnson & Nash	
Elwood James	*Stockport.*
Wood Joshua	
Morris Danl.	

Morrow County.

Williams Andrew	*Underwood's.*
Kirk W. & J. S.	*Iberia.*
Fidler Jacob	*Cardington.*
Lentze John	
Prophet John & Son	
Tinker John	
Pim William H.	*Shauk's.*
Burch James E.	*Woodview.*
McFarland Joshua	*Pulaskiville.*
Moore Samuel	*Nimmon's Cross Roads.*
Reader Milton	*Corsica.*
German A.	*Mt. Gilead.*
Rhodes J.	
Storer J.	
Pharis & Morgan	*Chesterville.*
Fogle B. F.	

Muskingum County.

Johnson B.	*White Cottage.*
Mitchell G. D.	*Nashport.*
Colville J. W. & Co.	
Bradford A.	*Otsego.*
Noble Wm. D.	*Norwich.*
Whitaker Reuben	
Launder James	
Jenkins O. & Son	*Frazeyeburg.*
Tumbler John	
Vantasel John	
Dunn James	

Dungan Cameron — *New Concord.*
Fuller Elijah
Hughes M. A.
Irvin & Mason — *Duncan's Falls.*
Price A. B.
Adams Benj. — *Dresden.*
Hardey Henry
Osburn Thos.
Shutts Henry
Henderson & Balch
Smallwood Wm. H.
Loyed Wm.
Kennett H. Y.
Dorsey O.
Mell Francis
Crane & Jones
Drake Wm. W. — *Putnam.*
Manley James
Dewar Thomas
Dunlap Burns & Co.
Ganer J. D. — *Hopewell.*
Chappelean C.
McCracken David — *Gratiot.*
Rutlege Wm.
Elbert John H.
Walls F. — *Chandlersville.*
Crosby J. & J. — *Zanesville.*
Summers H. J. & Co.
Haffy Philip
Brannan & Walsh
Moore J. P.
Martin & Price
Brennan & Cavanaugh
Cooper G. W. & Co.

Noble County.

McElroy Wm F. — *Berne.*
Smith Gustavus A. — *Mt. Ephraim.*
Thurlo Wesley — *Olive.*
Morris T. W.
Howard Jeremiah — *Harrietsville.*
Lloyd Sarah
Dilly & McGarry — *Sarahsville.*
Gliddon Sidney — *Gardner.*
Friels J.
Parker Thomas — *South Olive.*
Judkins & Taneyhill — *Batesville.*
Avick George

Ottawa County.

Eoff Geo. W. — *Elmore.*
Day David M.
Ludlow Lewis — *Marble Head.*
Thelton Mathias

Paulding County.

Jones T. J. — *Antwerp.*
Barnhard — — *Junction.*
Russell John
Kessler David

Perry County.

Carlos C. — *New Lexington.*
Chappellaer J. H.
Kelley N. T.
Riley & Phillips
Sumers C. T.

Beverly W. L. — *Thornville.*
Yorger Enoch
Donelly Edward — *Rehoboth.*
Warthan Henry
Cox T. B. — *Somerset.*
Gallen James
Kelley Daniel
Levett A.
Hodge Leander
Kuntz Reuben
Kuntz Henry
McEntire John
Russell William
Westerman J.
McGovern Mathew — *Chapel Hill.*
Snider George
Addison J. — *Sego.*
Hammot S.

Pickaway County.

Bradford G. G. & N. T. — *Circleville.*
Duncan and Sherman
Diffenderffer S.
Juppenlatz J. G.
Kelstadt M.
King C. A. & J. L.
Mader J F.
Moran Martin
Stein George
Sullivan Wm.
Witlick F. F.
Weils L.
Yates David — *Darbyville.*
Bitlers C. F. & S. — *Tarlton.*
Saylar & Housel
Smith & Grochenour — *Beckett's Store.*
Welch John
Barnes & Wiley — *Williamsport.*
Mitchel David
Betharda Frank — *Palestine.*
Borden J. W. — *South Bloomfield.*
Jenings J.

Pike County.

Barnes & Kilgore — *Waverly.*
Row Jacob
Tellart Jacob
Tool Frederick
Martin W.
Parker Thos. G. — *Byington.*
Ware D. — *Piketon.*
Hempstead H. & Son
Brown J. R. & C.
Smith Joseph
Daniels & Smith
Moore & Greene
Loughbum A.
Richards C A.
Collings Daniel

Portage County.

Taylor S. A. — *Ravenna.*
Sutherland T. C.
Smith H. W. & Co.
Leffingwell J. W.
Harbrouck Peter
May Geo. — *Randolph*

Sawyer John B.   *Franklin.*   Hull Wesley   *Lucas.*
Baird H. & W.   Wooster Henry W.   *Plymouth.*
Frank John   *Suffield.*   Root Ira
Keister, Howells & Co.   Rogers H. W. & Co.
Ray John W.   *Paris.*   Reshon Lewis
Jones David
Pierce Hiram   *Nelson.*   **Ross County.**
Reed D.   *Rootstown.*
Hunt John S.   *Freedom.*   Crooks A.   *Bainbridge.*
Deull Z. T.   *Carleville.* Moeller J. E.
                                           Benn J. W.
       Preble County.   Bayler H.   *Lattis.*
                                           Carder Wm.   *Frankfort.*
Herdman E. & Son   *West Alexandria.*   Guiher & Ferril
Waters & Johnson   Reeves John   *Clarksburgh.*
Bowers John   Clifford J. D. & Co.   *Chillicothe.*
McKinzie D. S.   *Lewisburg.*   Wolfe Jacob
Maner J. F.   Bader M.
Francis & Brother   *Camden.*   Hellmuth A.
Longnecker J. J.   Klein Jacob
Oldham Wm.   Zimmerman A.
Spinable John W. & Co.   March G. B.
Stannah & Beller   *Eaton.*   Hirn J.
Cunningham R. S.   Welch W.
Brosier & Campbell   Miller M.
Wilson & Co.   Phillips C. & Co.
Homer John F.   Sculley James
Crouse Jacob   Hoffman Peter
Bruce, Houk & Co.   Devrall Thos
Mack & Owens   *Fairhaven.*   Hoddy J. & J.
Campbell & Fisher   *New Westville.*   Bodamer A.
Fox J. S.   Campbell & Wentworth
McMacken A.   *Hamburg.*   Shilder Michael
McWhinney Matthew   *West Florence.*   Cory Isaac
Morton S. W. & J.   *New Paris.*   Starr C.
Reinheimer P.   Gait John
McOown W.   Mathias J.
Johnson L.   Fry George
                                           Harminger M.
        Putnam County.   Dalrymple D.
                                           Wolf Jacob
Corrin P.   *Gilboa.*   Briggs John
Hardishell & Rinehart   *.*   Keller John
Kisaberth P.   Armstrong Geo.
Coates Elisha H.   *Leipsic.*   McFarlin Saml.
Jones J. B.   *Pleasant.*   Aikin J. & Co.
Bell Wm.   *Buckeye.*   Kramer & Hammer
Fife W. H.   *Vaughnsville.* Albertin A.
Martz Walter   Collins G. W.   *South Salem.*
Odeawiller L.   *Pendleton.*   McKinsey H.
                                           Cook Benj.   *Yellow Bud.*
       Richland County.   Dresbach J. B. & M. B.
                                           Kroell Henry C.   *Halleville.*
Moore Geo. W. & Co.   *Shelby.*   Dunning & Hedges   *Yellow Bud.*
Fox Alfred   *Shenandoah.*   Cook Alex.
Dickson James   *Mansfield.*   Griffith & Pontious   *Kingston.*
Hickox & Kirkwood   Nye Jacob
Hooker J. R.   Lindsey T. J. N.
Jackson J. A.   Dean Dickinson
Krile & Rhodes   Oorlman Wm.   *Bourneville.*
Hazelton John   *Lexington.*   Swisher Henry
Inglehart Peter   Robbins & Barnes
Joues Geo.   *West Windsor.*
Van Tilburg & Starrett   *Olivesburg.*
Bailey B. F.   *Belleville.*   **Sandusky County.**
Reeves John
Simpson A.   Smith N.   *Woodville.*
Cole John   *Newville.*   Pillows & William
Boone Thomas   *Richland.*   Scott J.
Craigh Thomas

Harkness D. E.   *Clyde.*
Taylor G. W.
Forbs & Starks
McCleary Jacob
Finch Eli   *Rutland Ridge.*
Anson A.   *Townsend.*
Willis Wm.
Baron Benj.
Stuber J. & J   *Fremont.*
Tillotson Tyler
Sebring J. F. R.
Dougherty J.
Clere P.
Sharp Isaac
Shunk M. A.
Dungan C.
Lesher J.
Lane D.
Snyder Jacob   *Rollersville.*

Scioto County.

Barker B.   *Portsmouth.*
Behrens J.
Brodbeck V.
Clemens Daniel
Clade Peter
Camden W. P.
Cook Henry
Englebrecht F.
Gunn P. C.
Hyatt C. C.
Krause Geo.
Kricker M.
Lawson F.
Martin U.
Maule H.
Miller Charles
Miller Wm.
Musser Wm.
Patton & Tate
Thompson & Noel
Tillow John
Timmonds M. & S.
Whitney W. G.
Willson & Morrow
Powers Ezekiel & Co.   *Sciotoville.*
Burgess Joseph & Son   *Friendship.*
Reed Rodney   *Wheelersburg.*

Seneca County.

Compton John   *Attica.*
Shouff John
Mitchell & Britton   *Stoner.*
Riley, Stewart & Buchtel
Newton James F.   *Melmore.*
Curtis J.   *Adrian.*
Gantz J.
Gray Charles
Wing J. W.
Adam Peter   *Berwick.*
Ruch C.
Nick Michael
Zender Joseph
Bets H. M.   *Bloomville.*
Dysinger T.
Lewis John T.   *Bettsville.*

Bainer Geo.   *Tiffin.*
Black G. W.
Buskirk H. A.
Boos Charles
Bloom F.
Benner George
Graff & Co.
Feige & Emick
Holt E. N.
Lesser John
Leidy J. H.
Mitchell & Dildine
Raizks A.
Rank Alonzo
Rease Baltzer
Reame P. H.
Six & Repp
Sheets F. & J.
Snyder Danl. M.
Schreiner Lawrence
Wehel Xavier
Wortmiller J.
Oserholdt D. D.   *Bascom.*
Trobasco Ephraim   *West Lodi.*
Harkness D. E.   *Green Spring.*
Wickwire James
Haxten G. W.   *Republic.*
Witter Isaac
Childs C.
Slaughter F.
Eckman D.
Pearce J. O.
Smiths & Co.
Myers T.
Eastman P. O.

Shelby County.

Bannon James   *Houston.*
Maniere John   *Wynant.*
Haney & Smith   *Pratt.*
Haney, William & Co.
Munch William
Burrows E.   *Sidney.*
Kelsey G. S.
Lennox James   *Dinsmore.*
Bowers Mathias
Lennox C. P.   *Hardin.*

Starke County.

Allman D. & P.   *Navarre.*
Bennett F.
Boli F.
Frimize J.
Gribel H.
Scholder C. H.
Stroble G.
Couch John R.   *Waynesburg.*
Crevise Joseph, Jr.
Hamilton James M.
Hoops Marshall   *Minerva.*
Miluer & Scott
Tritt H. & Co.
Umstetter Daniel   *Lake.*
Bailey Peter   *Louisville.*
Hartman J. J.
Moyer Conrad
Rodabaugh A.

Slusser & Holwick   *Louisville.*
Williard B. L. P.
Wintz J. N.
Oyer Martin   *Paris.*
Lininger W. J.   *Greentown.*
Hahn Samuel   *New Franklin.*
Sager George   *Frease's Store.*
Sager Isaac
Adams J. B.   *Canton.*
Bollett Joseph
Foglesong Christopher
Foglesong L.
Heckman J.
Hippee George
Maline J.
Miller J.
Oberly C.
Patton & Trump
Patton & Saxton
Sowers E.
Stearl G.
Wernet J. B.
Winterhatter F. J.
Doll Joseph   *East Greenville.*
Johnson Abraham   *New Berlin.*
Hetzel Henry
Paxson Ezra W.   *Marlboro'.*
Machamer J. B. & J.   *Hartville.*
Sible N.   *Massillon.*
Sible A.
Lehman L.
Albright F.
Albright E.
Lockwood J. S.
Zerbe J.
Kitsmiller W. G.   *Canal Fulton.*
Hall William
Whitmyer M.
Bobst D.
Campbell James   *Limaville.*
Petree William
Barnaby J.   *Mount Union.*
Johnson C.

Summit County.

Bartholomew Perry   *Middlebury.*
Gilbert J. C.   *Cuyahoga Falls.*
Haynes J.
Lewis Isaac
L'Hommedieu J. & Co.
Patterson J.
Rouse Geo.
Sax H. R.
Hanes ——   *New Portage.*
Pearce Wm.
Wheeler Wm.
Zimmerman Z
Stelbeng Adolph   *Clinton.*
Wagner Nicholas
Everett C. W.   *Hudson.*
Whedon John
Markle Adam   *North Springfield.*
Aultman S. J.   *Inland.*
Bitman M.   *Akron.*
Bitman B.
Cramer Henry
Dussel J. B. & Co.

Fisher H.   *Akron.*
Gardiner James
Grether George
Grether J. M.
Hanscome D. & C.
Kirchner J.
Kolb J.
L'Hommedieu & Jones
McCall J.
Mason J.
More George
Mushross M.
Mussle J.
Pierce Job
Schumacher S.
Smith C.
Shaffer & Winters
Vaughn L. & Co.
Wheeler H. H.
Wheeler B. F.
Case N.   *Macedonia Depot.*
Allen Robert   *Boston.*
McBride Wm.
Osborn W. B., (Agent)   *Summit.*

Trumbull County.

Curtis G. P.   *Greensburgh.*
Petton & Gibbs
Andrews & Finney   *Johnsonville.*
Webb J. L.
Brisbane Leslie   *Hubbard.*
Pennell Wm.
Thomas Henry   *Gustavus.*
Anderson James   *Girard.*
Rupp & Anderson
Walter John
Hoxie ——   *Orangeville.*
Lane Lester   *Hartford.*
Meikle Thos.
Anderson & Rup   *Warren*
Dunlap J. B.
Greene William
McManus M
Martin E.   *Newton Falls.*
Smith J.

Tuscarawas County.

Albright J. M.   *Bolivar*
App Daniel
Taylor Abraham
Fowler L. D.   *Sandyville*
West Andrew
Rhodes Joseph   *Deardorff's Mills.*
Hunt John   *Uhrichsville.*
Laport George
Shilling Jacob
Fleming William   *Cadwallader.*
Taylor & Beard   *New Cumberland.*
Steen James
Wilson Boyd
Carr Richard B.   *Port Washington.*
Doyle Eli
Eis Peter
Haas Adam   *Ragersville.*
Kunts Peter
Breitenstein L.   *Canal Dover.*
Hare S.

Kaiserman S.   *Canal Dover.*
Boyer Valentine
Herbold John
Shane F.
Fertig Samuel
Vorherr A.
Lippe Wm.
Bennet J. F.
Hoffman John J.
Knablock F.
Dangleiser A.
Heck & Co.   *New Philadelphia.*
Winspear J.
Knisely J.
Thompson J.
Rinehart J.
Ichhart J.
Messerly L. & Co.
Gentch G.
Rex A.
Carver John   *Tuscarawas.*
Sprankle Jacob   *Shanesville.*
Kratz Jacob
Demin F.   *Rockford.*

Union County.

Hawkins & Judy   *Marysville.*
Houston Christopher
Jaquies William   *Raymond's.*
Lyons William   *Richwood.*
Miles George
Douglass John   *Milford Centre.*
Gill W. P.
Morrow John

Van Wert County.

Dougherty Isaac   *Van Wert.*
Engleright Saml.
Glenn Wm.
Howard Jesse B.
Kyle W. H.
Webber John & Co.   *Auglaize.*
Howell A. G.   *Delphos.*
Phelah Peter
Barnhiser & Phillips

Vinton County.

Bliss H.   *McArthur.*
Dunkle & Brother
Stinchcomb N. M.
Nickle Geo. W.
Shockey J. J. & Co.
Miller M.   *Allensville.*
Tarr S.   *Reed's Mills.*
Binkley J. B.   *New Plymouth.*

Warren County.

Francis & Barklow   *Franklin.*
Schenck J. C. & Co.
Dechant F.
Dial W.
Rickard & Copler
Vorris Platt
Wilkison R. & Co.
Thayer S. & Son
Huffman T. B.
17

Knour Wm.   *Franklin.*
Leak A. & G.   *Waynesville.*
Thomas G. W. & C. H.
Kemp Benj.
Creswell David
Irwin John A.
Collins & Barnhurst
Whorton Thos.   *Corwin.*
Sanders John   *Twenty Mile Stand.*
Harner Peter   *Oregon.*
Cunningham P.   *Fort Ancient.*
Frazee Wm.
Durain Lewis   *Morrow.*
Endres Philip
Harner P. P.
Starry James   *Butlerville.*
Lancaster John W.   *Harveysburg.*
Stone Henry

Washington County.

Bosworth, Wells & Co.   *Marietta.*
Brenan H. & Son
Bacon Wm.
Crawford R.
Gram A.
Dutton J. & Co.
Fisher W. H.
Fonbergens Henry
Guitteau A. L.
Gray W. J.
Hall W. & Co.
Hall, Matthews & Co.
Hagberling Philip
Kneck & Holat
Richards John
Rowson & Bower
Richards J.
Sham N. H.
Talbot Wm.
Wildt Joseph
Woodbridge & Woacott
Rumbold & Arnold   *Harmar.*
Spalding & Dow
Mackey John B.   *Coal Run.*
Crandall J. T.   *Newport.*
Hutchinson Wm.   *Centre Belpre.*
Gashorn Edward
Townsend L. & Co.
Amlin John D.   *Fearing.*
Kendall Patrick   *Beverly.*
Hutchison Wm.   *Belpre.*
Dunbar S.   *Decaturville.*
Jones Thomas
Athey W.   *Benn.*
Johnson S.

Wayne County.

Fleck D.   *Dalton.*
Detrick J. J. N.   *Fredericksburg.*
Heath & Orr
Dowell Wm.
Armstrong W. B.   *Big Prairie.*
Stoner A.
Lightfoot Saml.   *East Union.*
Kirkendall S.
Harsh Henry   *New Prospect.*
Beach Wm. B. H.

Grindle Abraham   *Reedsburg.*
Swartz Jeremiah
Sullinger John
Heizer John   *West Lebanon.*
Bysel Fred.
Power M.   *Shreve.*
Reihnold Geo.   *Marshallville.*
Ott John & G.
Wilson Solon O.   *Moreland.*
Rossiter George
Brumpter Jacob   *Wooster.*
Redich J.
Young Peter
Young Lanis
Young Wendell
Row M.
Fawcett John
Sorg Christian
Jackson Cyrus
James J. C.

Williams County.

Arnold P. G.   *Bryan.*
Foster Wm.   *West Unity.*
Johnson Henry   *Williams Centre.*
Rodebaugh D.
Sissen & Clark   *Montpelier.*
Oothran Saml. G.

Wood County.

Baird George W.   *Perrysburg.*
Cholett John
Cooper & Atkinson
Needer John
Nufer Anthony
Fronklyn Francis   *Bowling-Green.*
Gunn Wm.   *Portage.*
Lansdale Isaac & Bro.   *Montgomery Cross*
                         Roads.
Harmon Henry
Childs J.   *New Rochester.*

Wyandot County.

Christian Anthony   *Upper Sandusky.*
Groff Jeremiah
Jenkins & French
Morrison J. & J.
Tiffany P.
Brown Wm.   *Crawfordsville.*
Straw David   *Carey's.*
Zuck Charles
Willard Franklin   *Wyandot.*
Standtclift M.
Munger, Duwees & Co.   *McCutchensville.*
Brackley M.
Fox & Lambert   *Marseilles.*
Shilling Joseph
Dudley M.
Kennedy H.
Goodman Daniel   *Mexico.*

Gun-Barrel Manufacturers.

Jefferson County.

Rendyls Bernard   *Steubenville.*

Montgomery County.

Wilt J., Upper Hydraulic,   *Dayton.*

Starke County.

Schneider F. A.   *Canton.*
Ritzel P. N.

Guns, Pistols and Rifles—
(Importers of).

Hamilton County.

Fletcher Henry, W. Row bet. Everett and
    Wade streets,   *Cincinnati.*
Hudson W. L., 234 Main
Kittredge B. & Co., 134 do
Pappenheimer & Dreyfoos, 36 Pearl

Gun, Rifle and Pistol Manu-
facturers.

Franklin County.

Cullman Charles, High street,   *Columbus.*
Siebert Christian,   do

Hamilton County.

Griffiths & Seibert, 279 Main   *Cincinnati.*
Hudson W. L., 238   do

Gunsmiths.

Ashtabula County.

Nutt Rollin   *Eagleville.*
Hall Perry   *Ashtabula.*
Frisbee J.   *Cork.*

Athens County.

Jarvis Lewis   *Athens.*
Augustine Saml.
Knowlton W.   *Lee.*

Auglaize County.

DeWitt —   *Wapakoneta.*
Smith Wm.   *St. Mary's.*
Dunlap H. C.   *Kossuth.*

Belmont County.

Folger Wm. H.   *Barnesville.*
Neel George   *Uniontown.*

Brown County.

Thomas Oratio   *Higginsport.*
Hughstead A.   *Ripley.*
Norris Wm.
Farver Wm.

Champaign County.

Sample B.   *Urbana.*

Clark County.

Beebe R.   *Springfield.*
Clippinger Joseph   *New Carlisle.*

Clermont County.

Lipphardt Charles   *New Richmond.*

Clinton County.

Noggle Washington	*New Burlington.*
Moon J H.	*Martinsville.*
Carey John	
Moon C. C.	
Haga Jesse	
Vanderburgh Wm.	*Wilmington.*

Columbiana County.

Small Samuel	*New Lisbon.*
Jones John	*Salineville.*

Coshocton County.

Shepler Peter, Jr.	*Clark's.*
Jinney B.	*Coshocton.*

Crawford County.

Harman Jonas	*Sulphur Spring.*
Cronenberger A.	*Bucyrus.*
McClure J. M.	

Cuyahoga County.

Andrews E. W., 19 Ontario st. *Cleveland.*
Hattersley H.. 41 Superior
Jennings Richard, 43 Pittsburgh

Darke County.

Wolf L. F.	*Ithica.*
Zeek A.	*New Madison.*

Defiance County.

King N.	*Defiance.*
Nagle John	*Brunersburg.*

Erie County.

Robinson J. H.	*Sandusky City.*

Fairfield County.

Claspill G. W.	*Lancaster.*
Bodenhimer W.	
Gibbs J.	

Fayette County.

Burgess Saml.	*Staunton.*

Geauga County.

Strong James	*Claridon.*

Greene County.

Rogers L.	*Xenia.*

Guernsey County.

Free Joel	*Cumberland.*
Boetcher C.	*Cambridge.*
Hosack E. L.	*Kimbolton.*
Brumley S.	*Senecaville.*

Hamilton County.

Powel G., 97 Walnut street, *Cincinnati.*
Slossmeister C., 512 Vine
Krug Goodlip, 538 do
Stofel W., 36 w. 12th
Fletcher Henry, W. Row bet. Everett and
Wade
Everson Lewis *Harrison.*

Hancock County.

Vandeburg O. B.	*Finlay.*
Lannart Henry	

Hardin County.

Bird N.	*Kenton.*
Weaver N.	

Harrison County.

Righter John G.	*Cadiz.*

Highland County.

Webb Geo. G.	*Greenford.*
Webb James	

Hocking County.

Hudson E. L.	*Logan.*
Stalter Wm.	

Huron County.

Benderritter J.	*Bellevue.*
Bartley R.	*Norwalk.*

Jackson County.

White H. W.	*Jackson.*

Jefferson County,

Teaff Jas.	*Steubenville.*
Thompson Thos.	*Richmond.*
Gorsuch J. M.	*Mt. Pleasant.*

Knox County.

Carpie P. F.	*Mount Vernon.*

Lake County.

Morse C.	*Painesville.*

Licking County.

Zartman J.	*Newark.*
Morath L.	
Umbarger Saml.	*Kirkersville.*

Logan County.

Moxley M.	*Bellefontaine.*
Hornback Wm.	*Quincy.*

Lorain County.

Kelsey Wm.	*Huntington.*
Parker Thomas	*Oberlin.*
Clark M.	*Elyria.*

Lucas County.

Burdo Peter	*Maumee City.*
Vickars Jonathan	

Mahoning County.

Kneppenberger S.	*Cornersburg.*
Bennett S. F.	*Youngstown.*
Snyder Frederick	*East Lewistown.*
Miller S.	*Damascoville.*

Medina County.

Heisington O. & Son	*Leroy.*
Pierce H.	*Liverpool.*
Rose D.	
Wood Mason	*Chatham Centre.*
Anson Geo.	*Medina.*

Miami County.

Weldy D.   *West Charleston.*
Norris R. W.   *Piqua.*
Lenour H. R.   *Troy.*

Montgomery County.

Thomas John & Son   *Centre.*
Schnieder M., Second   *Dayton.*
Stutaman J. G., First
Clark Nelson   *Miamisburgh.*

Morgan County.

Ball Joseph T.   *Malta.*
Coleman B. B.   *McConnelsville.*

Morrow County.

Eldin M.   *Cardington.*
Gray Lorin   *Lincoln.*

Muskingum County.

Fondersmith Saml.   *Gratiot.*
Hale M.   *Chandlersville.*

Noble County.

McKitrick John   *Berne.*

Paulding County.

Shafer Elias   *Paulding.*

Perry County.

Foncannon M. B.   *New Lexington.*
Kirlin John
Humberger A.   *Somerset.*
Swinehart Andrew

Pickaway County.

Floyd T.   *Circleville.*

Portage County.

Forker Israel   *Ravenna.*
Topping A.
Crane Ashley   *Shalersville.*
Loudonslanger John   *Suffield.*
Smith Alfred   *Nelson.*
Long John   *Deerfield.*
Shattoo L.
Purrington John   *Rootstown.*

Preble County.

Burns H.   *Lewisburg.*
Ginger L.   *New Paris.*
Flemin S. M.

Putnam County.

Sigler Thos.   *Leipsic.*

Richland County.

Rickers J.   *Mansfield.*
Laferty Smith   *Belleville.*

Ross County.

Sleret E.   *Chillicothe.*
Millen Geo.   *South Salem.*
Day Wm.   *Gillespieville.*
Walker Wm.   *Bourneville.*

Sandusky County.

Smith David   *Rollersville.*
Smith Danl.

Scioto County.

Shermon A. P.   *Portsmouth.*
Zeigler H. D.

Seneca County.

Gross H. & C. B.   *Tiffin.*
Smith Louis
Heitzer Lewis

Starke County.

Vernier Lewis   *Louisville.*
Clark John   *West Brookfield.*
Kittinger Levi   *East Greenville.*
Labo Gustavus   *Mapleton.*

Summit County.

Newton Samuel   *Middlebury*
Pricket Frederick   *Richfield.*

Tuscarawas County.

Ax William   *Deardorff's Mills.*
Wright Benjamin   *Pcoli.*
Shuyler V.   *New Philadelphia.*

Trumbull County.

Paine Stephen L.   *Farmington*

Union County.

Brigham J.   *Jerome.*
Lehman G. F.

Vinton County.

Rose E.   *New Plymouth.*

Warren County.

Bunnel M.   *Ridgeville.*
Fondersmith J.   *Mason.*
Turk James   *Morrow.*
Norman Benj.

Washington County.

Pratt Elisha   *Marietta.*
King, Sylvestus & Co.   *Bartlett.*
Riley Wm. L.   *Watertown.*

Wayne County.

Troxle John   *Reedsburg.*
Franks & Watt   *New Prospect.*
France Joseph   *Shreve.*

Williams County.

Dickson Joseph   *Montpelier.*
Kimble David

Wood County.

Koch Edward   *Bowling-Green.*

Wyandot County.

Gump J.   *Upper Sandusky*

Hair Cloth Manufacturer.

Hamilton County.

Hatterly G., cor. Mobawk and Hamburg
                           Cincinnati.

Hair Curled) Manufacturers.

Cuyahoga County.
Wisdom, Russell & Co.   *Cleveland.*

Hamilton County.
Forgey J. P. & Co., 12 & 14 Columbia
        Cincinnati.

Hames Manufacturers.

Clermont County.
McMullen Wm.   *Goshen.*
Hitch B. F.   *Bantam.*
Smith William

Cuyahoga County.
Colson Chandlers   *Brecksville.*
Colson Lyman
Dustin Farley

Defiance County.
Haskell E. P.   *Defiance.*

Franklin County.
Hayden P., Broad   *Columbus.*

Geauga County.
Kingsbury Benj.   *Troy.*

Summit County.
Sanford Benjamin   *Montrose.*

Trumbull County.
Buel Warren   *Johnsonville.*
Dunbar Daniel
Humphrey J. W.
Lord Samuel

Hardware & Cutlery—Wholesale & Retail Dealers.

Adams County.
Stevenson Edward   *Manchester.*

Allen County.
Hurlbutt Samuel   *Lima.*

Ashland County.
Hohenahill S.   *Rowsburg.*
Schell W. P.   *Hayesville.*
Leither H. & Co.   *Ashland.*

Ashtabula County.
Krick P. W.   *Conneaut.*

Brown County.
Bennington, Snyder & Kellogg   *Ripley.*

Butler County.
Howard R. L.   *Rossville.*
Skinner John C.   *Hamilton.*

Champaign County.
Mann A. L. & Co.   *Mechanicsburg.*
Morgan & Baker
Riddle J. & Brother
Patrick J. H.   *Urbana.*

Clark County.
Rungon W.   *Springfield.*
Field W. T. & Co.
Klinefelter J.
Doty & Rinehart

Clermont County.
Hobson William   *New Richmond.*
Pigman A. S.   *Neville.*
Dustin J. S.   *Batavia.*

Clinton County.
Penny G. J.   *Wilmington.*

Columbiana County.
Cope H. & S.   *Wellsville.*
Small Samuel   *New Lisbon.*
Chepman & Wright   *Salem.*

Coshocton County.
Harbaugh S.   *Coshocton.*
Harrison J. C.

Cuyahoga County.
Bingham W. & Co., Superior   *Cleveland.*
Clark James F., 4   do
Colwell & Co., 35 Ontario
Hoyt, McArthur & Co., 45 Bank
Luetkemeyer & Schmidthusen, cor. Sup'r.
    and Vineyard
Morley & Raynolds, 8 Superior
Murfey & Latham, 2   do
Tennis John & Co., 48   do
Wells H. K , 34 Bank
Worthington Geo. & Co., cor. Superior and
    Water
Clark James F., 4   do
Crawford & Reynolds
Hedenberg J. H.   *Ohio City.*

Darke County.
Ullery & Weston S. & A.   *Greenville.*

Delaware County.
Potter C. D. & Co.   *Delaware.*
Chamberlain & Avery C. C. & J. C.

Erie County.
Mass A. H.   *Sandusky City.*
Mass M. V.
Whitney J. D. & Co.
Daniels & Co.
Barney F. T.

Fairfield County.
Bope P.   *Lancaster.*
Effinger, White & Latta

Franklin County.
Gere & Abbott, 161 High   *Columbus.*
Kilbourne & Kuhns   do.
McCune J. M. & Co., 63   do
Peck Stephen L.   *Worthington.*

Gallia County.
Rupp G. H. & Co.   *Vinton.*

Greene County.
Cary H. & W. T.   *Xenia.*

McAlpin Henry　　　　　　　*Xenia.*
Syfers Jacob　　　　　　*Jamestown.*

Hamilton County.

Booth R. W. & Co., n. e. cor. Walnut and
　Pearl　　　　　　　　*Cincinnati.*
Booth John P., 93 Main
Coombs, Ryland & Blackwell, 90 Main
Dury F. W., 243 W. Row
Eymann C., 493 Main
Gano, Howell & Brothers, 122 Main
Herder Gustav., 338 Main
Hollinshade & Newhall, cor. W. Row and
　Clinton
Kruse L., cor. Main & Woodward
Kensall T., cor. 7th and Baymiller
Latimer, Cox, Colburn & Lupton, 74 Main
Lawrence D. M., 198　　　　　do
Lender & Lohn, 376　　　　　do
Lawton J., 312　　　　　　　do
Lang R., 7th bet Cutter and Linn
Lohn J., 533 5th
Lilley Wm., 5th bet. Vine and Race
Mead, Selden & Co., 15 Pearl
Neff, Peter & Sons, 59 Pearl
Neff, Brother & Co., s. w. cor. Main & 2d
Neave T. & Sons, 65 & 67 Main
Neave & Free, 33　　　　do
Openhein Saml. S., 263 cor. W. Row and
　George
Pappenheimer & Dreyfoos, 36 Pearl
Rohrkasse H. & Co., s. e. cor. Main & 9th
Rosboom & Thomas, 210 Main
Rohrer Geo. B. & Co., s. w. cor. W. Row
　and 5th
Smith C. J. & Co., 206 Main
Seybold C., 207　　　do
Stagaman F., 19 Lower Market
Thiesing E. & Evans, 389 Main
Tyler, Davidson & Co., 140 & 142 do
Wayne Joseph W., 196　　　do
Wieser Isaac, 116 5th
Wayne Anthony, 69 Main
Wayne J. L., 124 Main

Hancock County.

Lamb David　　　　　　　　*Finley.*
Spinning & Stansberry

Hardin County.

Ashton W. & F.　　　　　　*Kenton.*
Moore & Goodin

Highland County.

Kenkead R. C.　　　　　　*Greenfield.*
Marlay J. K.　　　　　　　*Hillsboro'.*

Hocking County.

Homyhans Charles　　　　　*Logan.*

Holmes County.

Hebron & Uhl　　　　　　*Millersburg.*

Huron County.

Perkins E. P.,　　　　*Monroeville.*
Oline John　　　　　　　*Norwalk.*

Jackson County

White H. W.　　　　　　　*Jackson.*

Jefferson County.

Stier D. W.　　　　　*Steubenville.*
Kilgore & Rex
McGowan D. & Son
Bebout Wm.　　　　　　*Warrenton.*

Knox County.

Curtis & McCormick　　*Mt. Vernon.*
McCormick John
Weaver Adam

Lake County.

Adams, Moody & Co.　　*Painesville.*
Marshall S. & Co.

Lawrence County.

Duke & Kingsbury　　　　*Ironton.*
McLane J. & Co.

Licking County.

McCune John & Co.　　　*Newark.*
Dennis & Bro.

Logan County.

Hunter N.　　　　　*West Liberty.*
Williams J. & H. N.
Allen J. N. & Co.　　*Bellefontaine.*
Whitehill D. M.
Walburn E.　　　　　　　*Quincy.*

Lucas County.

Card J. F. & Co.　　　　*Toledo.*
Eddy A.
Whitaker J. H.
Whitney J. M.
Bendix Martin H. & Co.

Madison County.

Dungan John　　　　　　*London.*

Marion County.

Williams & Bain　　　　*Marion.*

Medina County.

Brown H. W.　　　　　　*Medina.*

Mercer County.

Bruner O.　　　　　　*St. Mary's.*
Johnson W. N. & J.
McLaughlin G. W.

Miami County.

Wood Saml.　　　　　　　*Piqua.*
Morrow J. A. & Co.
Geyer F.
Simpson & Defries
Hart & Harter　　　　　　*Troy.*

Montgomery County.

Braclin James, Main street,　　*Dayton.*
Langdon & Bro., do
Loomis J. D. & Co., 3d
Rittinge O. & Co., do
Rogers & Fowler, Main
Heckerman & Stephenson　*Miamisburgh.*
Huiet Simon

Weaver & Perry *Miamisburg.*
Frank M. P. *Germantown.*

Morgan County.

Morris Geo. *McConnelsville.*
Thompson S.

Morrow County.

Rosenthal Simeon *Cardington.*

Muskingum County.

Dorney Owen *Dresden.*
Fillmore E. E. *Zanesville.*
Potwin O. W. & Co.
Robinson R. P.

Perry County.

Tolbet John *Somerset.*

Pickaway County.

Groom J. O. & Co. *Circleville.*
Wright J.

Portage County.

Richardson E. T. *Ravenna.*
Fraser Wm.
Pierce Hiram *Nelson.*

Preble County.

Rinehart Perry *Eaton.*
Marsh & Lockwood

Richland County.

Endley & Shepherd *Mansfield.*
Granger W. S.
Runyan B. S.

Ross County.

Shutte D. A. *Chillicothe.*
Denuing, Campbell & Co.
Allen & Evant

Sandusky County.

Canfield & Mitchell *Fremont.*

Scioto County.

Davey T. N. *Portsmouth.*
Kinney H. R.
Murray D. N.

Seneca County.

Gross John G. & Co. *Tiffin.*
Naylor & Pettinger
Wolf J. G. & Co. "

Shelby County.

Edgar D. & J. *Sidney.*
Johnston James

Starke County.

McQueen & Mallin *Minerva.*
Lester J. Y. *Canton.*
Loughan J. C.
Saxton J. A.

Kelly J. S. & Co. *Massillon.*
Reed & Fraley
Focke & Bro.

Summit County.

Farrar J. N. *Hudson.*
Neal Major
Crautz Chas. & Co. *Akron.*

Tuscarawas County.

Harger Madison *Canal Dover.*
Sterling John & Co.

Warren County.

Butler Chas. & Co. *Franklin.*

Washington County.

Bosworth, Wells & Co. *Marietta.*
Nye A. T.
Lamott L. A.
Woodbridge & Westcott

Wayne County.

Foltz H. & S. *Dalton.*
Wickey Chas. *Marshallville.*
McBride John K. *Wooster.*
Kauke John H.
Conrad & Davis

Hardware (Saddlery & Coach) Dealers.

Cuyahoga County.

Whitelaw & Marshall, 36 Superior street
Cleveland.

Franklin County.

Hayden P., Broad street, *Columbus.*

Hamilton County.

Clark S. & S. S., 180 Main st. *Cincinnati.*
Macknet L., 6th bet. Main & Sycamore
Wilson & Hayden, 17 & 19 w. Columbia

Warren County.

Reeder & Shertzers , *Franklin.*

Hats, Caps & Furs—Manufacturers & Wholesale & Retail Dealers.

Ashland County.

McClain Jacob *Savannah.*
Campbell M. W. *Ashland.*

Athens County.

Wright O. *Amesville.*
Webb W. H. *Athens.*

Brown County.

Caldwell J. J. *Ripley.*

Butler County.

Beardsley B. *Hamilton.*
Thorp Chas.
West S. *Rossville.*
Bowman D. F. *Middletown.*
Craig James *Somerville.*

Carroll County.

Adair John N.   *Leesville.*

Champaign County.

Keller Wm. E.   *Urbana.*
Talbott D.

Clark County.

Birdseye P.   *Springfield.*
Coter P.
Mayo W.
Bancroft & Pool
Wise Thomas   *New Carlisle.*

Clermont County.

South Benj. H.   *Williamsburg.*

Columbiana County.

Clark Samuel S.   *New Lisbon.*
Murray William   *Calcutta.*
Beans Israel   *Salem.*
Bradfield & Gibbons

Crawford County.

Scroggs John   *Bucyrus.*

Cuyahoga County.

Benedick L. & Co., 6 Superior   *Cleveland.*
Dockstader R. & N., 19 do
Fuller A. & Co., 97   do
Lederman A., 47 Ontario
Mack John G., 66 Superior
Paddock T. C., 39 do
Ruffini E., 23 Ontario
Simonds D. H , 24 do
Warner & Co., 26 Superior
Worthington & Stair, 15 do
Sexton C. C , 4 Columbus Block

Darke County.

Mitchell & Casadd   *Greenville.*

Erie County.

Ferry Austin   *Sandusky City.*
Keech O. C.

Fairfield County.

Fielding R.   *Lancaster.*
Smally M.

Franklin County.

Richards Wm. & Co., High   *Columbus.*
Rudisill J. E.   do
Stanton S. B.   do
Smith J. B., 82   do
Gillett & Co.   do

Gallia County.

Connell John S.   *Gallipolis.*

Geauga County.

Merrill H.   *Chardon.*

Greene County.

Ornmbaugh Samuel   *Xenia.*
Neinkirk Benjamin

Guernsey County.

McKelvey Wm.   *Cumberland.*

Hamilton County.

Alley B. R., 41 Broadway   *Cincinnati.*
Baker L. H. & Co., s. w. cor. Main & 4th
Boelens J., 72 6th
Crambach M., 226 6th
Camp C. B., 123 Main
Chace Ira H. & Co., 71 Pearl
Dunn Joseph, 10 w. 8th
Dodd G. C., 54 w. 5th
Dodd Wm. & Co., 144 Main
Deho Wm., Linn bet. Clark and Cutter
Erwin James, 236 Main
Ferdinand Heury, 209 6th
Forchheimer & Gutmann, 60 & 62 Main
Grantman H., 260 Main
Homish B. B., 206 6th
Isaacs & Franklin, 64 Pearl & 77 Main
Jorgensen Geo., 77 Lower Market
Jarvis & Fairchild, 194 Main
Kling Jacob, Vine bet. 14 & 15th
Kerr G., 127 w. 5th
Kohlbrand F., 410 Main
Meyberg & Hellman, 185 Main
Moore J. A., 342   do
Mason E. & Co., 52 w. 5th
Muller O., 492 Vine
Otter & Schoer, 304 Main
Plummer Hiram, 212 do
Pye J. R., 48 5th
Plasphol J. H., 481 Main
Rawe James, 264 W. Row
Robbins & Pomeroy, 9 Pearl & 71 Main
Rielag F , 67 Court
Rielag F. & J., 273 Main
Ulmer F., 280 Main
Van Sant Hibbert & Marconnier, 77 Main
Williams T. J., 371 Main
Weyl & Shappach, 180 6th
Whitcher William C. & Co., cor. Main &
  Pearl
Hand —   *Harrison.*
Ryland James

Hardin County.

Harnean George   *Renton.*

Highland County.

Pike N. M.   *Greenfield.*
Eldrick B.   *Leesburg.*
Stone B.   *Hillsboro'.*

Hooking County.

Spibey John   *Logan.*

Huron County.

Abbott Wm. O.   *Norwalk.*
Raitt Danl. G.

Jefferson County.

Davison J. G.   *Steubenville.*
Leach J. & Son
Gray R.   *East Springfield.*
Smith William   *Annapolis.*
Childs Samuel

Knox County.

King William L.   *Mt. Vernon.*
Rumer M. H.
Voorhies S. F. & Co.

Lake County.

Massey Wm. *Painesville.*

Licking County.

King & Weaver *Newark.*
Miller John

Logan County.

Starr Samuel *Bellefontaine.*

Lorain County.

Scott Anor *Elyria.*
Merwin J. B. & Co.

Lucas County.

Tolman J. & Son *Toledo.*

Mahoning County.

Norris Ira *Canfield.*

Medina County.

Ellinger D. *Wadsworth.*
Jackson P. *Hinckley.*
Manville J. *Medina.*

Miami County.

Thomas J. *West Charleston.*
Thomas H.
Morten Thos. *Piqua.*
Bireley M.

Montgomery County.

Brown H. M., Main *Dayton.*
Cramer H., do
Crider George, Second
Favourit E., do
Moore J. P., Main

Morgan County.

Spence H. *McConnelsville.*
Gilbert B.
Scott John

Muskingum County.

Allen J. B. *Zanesville.*
Galigher & Brother

Perry County.

Spibey James *Somerset.*

Pickaway County.

Miller John *Circleville.*
Wentworth A.

Portage County.

Twitt James & Co. *Ravenna.*

Preble County.

Smith J. H. *Camden.*
Hock W. *Eaton.*

Putnam County.

Landis F. S. *Leipsic.*
Winters W. W., Jr.

Richland County.

Keech Charles *Mansfield.*
King H. L.
Weagley A. K.
Clark E. *Belleville.*

Ross County.

McGinnis & Brother *Chillicothe.*

Scioto County.

Glover S. C. *Portsmouth.*
McComb W.

Seneca County.

Leiner Charles *Tiffin.*

Shelby County.

Irwin D. *Sidney.*

Summit County.

Clapsaddle M. *Akron.*

Trumbull County.

Nichols Levi *Warren.*
Wood John A.
Catlin George *Newton Falls.*

Tuscarawas County.

O'Donnell D. *New Philadelphia.*
Perley E. G. *Canal Dover.*
Wilson Chas.

Warren County.

Mayer J. *Hayesville.*
Deem S.
Lagrain C. *Deerfield.*
Brown Jeremiah *Waynesville.*

Washington County.

Stewart W. H & Co. *Marietta.*
Soule B.

Wayne County.

Wilson J. *Fredericksburg.*
Pierson & King *Wooster.*
Miller Levi
Nachtrieb & Co.

Williams County.

Patterson Wm. *Bryan.*
White Saml.

Hatters' Stock and Trimmings—Dealers in.

Cuyahoga County.

Dockstader R. & N., 19 Superior *Cleveland.*

Franklin County.

Gillett & Co., High *Columbus.*

Hamilton County.

Isaacs & Franklin, 64 w. Pearl & 77 Main *Cincinnati.*
Sherwood & Co., 67 w. Pearl

Hide and Leather Dealers.

Belmont County.
Vanlaw George   *Loydsville.*

Butler County.
Lohn J. W.   *Hamilton.*
Anderson & Snively   *Rossville.*

Brown County.
Ross Israel   *Puebla.*

Carroll County.
Young John W.   *Carrollton.*

Clermont County.
Kinley Thos.   *New Richmond.*
Grant J. R.   *Bethel.*

Columbiana County.
Riddle J. A.   *Wellsville.*

Coshocton County.
Elliott Andrew   *Keene.*
Sprague W. W. & Co.
Sprague John
Lity John & Co

Cuyahoga County.
Chase O.   *Gates' Mills.*
Bratenahl Brothers, Vineyard Block   *Cleveland.*
Cooke W. P. & Co., Water near Main
Crittenden J. H. & Co., 9 Superior
Seaman & Smith, 84   do

Darke County.
Taylor Joseph   *Greenville.*

Erie County.
Bouton A. & Co.   *Sandusky.*

Franklin County.
Kimball H. H., High   *Columbus.*
Ridgeway T.   do
Stanton S. B.   do

Greene County.
Allen John   *Xenia.*
Conwell B. G.

Hamilton County.
Baldwin L. F., 116 Main   *Cincinnati.*
Beitmann Chas., w. 6th
Cronin T. & Co., 27 Water
Dole J., cor. Everett and Plum
Easton S., 232   Main
Ehlen J. H., 356   do
Forbus John F., 254   do
Kessler H., 278   do
Lumsden S & W., 216 do
Leist John, 315   do
McCabe A., 352   do
Palmer M. D., 7   do
Paul Josiah, 166½   do
Thornton J. & C., 9   do
Thorne W. F., 74 Lower Market

Taylor A. M. & Co. Columbia *Cincinnati.*
Veith J., 421 Vine
Widmer C A. & Co., 240 Main

Jefferson County.
Spencer J. C.   *Steubenville.*
Ellott Wm. & Co.
Hutton J. & W.   *Warrenton.*

Knox County.
Hendrick H. & H.   *Mt. Vernon.*
Ogilvie Henry
Williams Nahum
Merring & Morris   *Fredericktown.*
Woodruff T. H. & Co.

Lake County.
Holmes L. W.   *Painesville.*
Childs Asa
Case E.

Lawrence County.
Osner A. & F.   *Burlington.*
Stumbo James   *Aid.*

Licking County.
Preston J. Q.   *Newark.*
Lantz Michael

Logan County.
Anderson D & M.   *Bellefontaine.*

Lucas County.
Cook C. L.   *Emery.*
Coghlin & Brooks   *Toledo.*
Smith J. B.
Stephens A.

Madison County.
Hancock E. S.   *West Jefferson.*
Phifer George   *London.*
Long Benjamin

Mahoning County.
Smith Walter   *Ellsworth.*

Miami County.
Worley J.   *Piqua.*

Montgomery County.
Edmonson E., Second   *Dayton.*
Johnson Levi, Main
Shade Josh., Third

Muskingum County.
Moorehead W. C.   *Zanesville.*

Pickaway County.
Hayser John   *Circleville.*

Portage County.
Heckman F.   *Ravenna.*
Frazer Wm.
Newberry F.
Enos Wm. A.
Gillis & Durham
Rockwell David L.   *Franklin.*
Mason Lewis   *Atwater.*
Donalds A. P.   *Randolph.*

Lewis F. — *Edinburgh.*
Atchinson, Roof & Co. — *Suffield.*
Converse E. S. — *Mantua.*
Kisseck John
Merriman C. & Brother — *Deerfield.*
Frisby N. T. — *Nelson.*
Baldwin A. T. & Co. — *Palmyra.*
Heckman Eli & John — *Brimfield.*

Richland County.

Kindel Emanuel — *Mansfield.*
Ritter Joseph
Coleman P. T. — *Lexington.*
Whitford Cornelius
Dean & Bissel — *Belleville.*
Flaherty Nicholas
Carpenter Wm. B. — *Newville.*

Ross County.

Harman O. — *Chillicothe.*
Lowman B.

Scioto County.

Kehoe M. & Son — *Portsmouth.*
Lloyd R. & Co.
Robinson, Sons & Co.
Kinney Washington
Kinney Chas. & Co.

Seneca County.

Orobaugh & Ernest — *Attica.*
Porter Hugh A.
Scott Denzer & Co. — *Tiffin.*
Houck J.

Union County.

Sherwood S. — *Watkins.*

Warren County.

Henly Moses — *Waynesville.*
Hale W. H.

Washington County.

Skinner, Rolston & Co. — *Marietta.*
Moss M. C.
Vinton Wm — *Harmar.*

Hoisting Wheel and Capstan Manufacturer.

Hamilton County.

Weeks John — *Fulton.*

Hominy and Pearl Barley Manufacturers.

Hamilton County.

Burnet & Brother, Canal bet. Main and Walnut streets, — *Cincinnati.*

Hoop-Pole Dealers.

Hamilton County.

Copen & Bassett, 69 Water — *Cincinnati.*
Steelman Hosea, do bet. Vine and Race

Logan County.

Cadwallader Wm. — *Huntsville.*
Campbell Wm.

Hose (Riveted) Manufacturer.

Hamilton County.

Seymour Jeffery, 41 Walnut — *Cincinnati.*

Hosiery Manufacturers.

Hamilton County.

Brown D. & R., 253 Main — *Cincinnati.*
Wuest Jacob, do bet. Court and Canal
Wust G., 228 Walnut

Hosiery and Glove Dealers.

Hamilton County.

Buchman & Rindskopf, 70 Main — *Cincin.*
Ogborn W. E. & Co., 35 and 37 Pearl
Taylor, French & Wynne, cor. Main and Pearl
Brown D. & R., 253 Main
Beale John & Co., 26 Pearl
Shohl & Bettmann, 80 5th
Leslie James Y., 14 w. 5th
Williams C. M., n. w. cor. 5th and Vine
Raymond M. A., 18½ e. 4th
Webb J. & J., 166 5th
Webb J. & Son, 184 do
Dickson —, 146 do
Wood Geo. M., n. e. cor. Vine and 5th
Gibbs H., 205 Plum
Perry George F., 220 w. 5th
Stockton O., 213 W. Row

Hotels and Public Houses.

Adams County.

Dening, Daniel, Manchester House, — *Manchester.*
Cropper M. V., Cropper House
Taylor John — *Locust Grove.*
Leedon T. J.
Morlett Field — *West Union.*
Wood Nancy

Allen County.

Huff A J. — *Hog Creek.*
Lampher Jacob
Yazel William — *Donnell's.*

Ashland County.

Gorham J. M. — *Sullivan.*
Gray Joseph — *Savannah*
Andrews Austin — *Ashland*
McNulty M. A.
Slocum Elias

Ashtabula County.

Wood B. A. — *Kelloggsville.*
Lilley Geo.

Strong Walter — *Jefferson.*
Prentice & Prentice
Hall O. K. — *Ashtabula.*
Bartrum Wm. L.
Murry S.
Williams J. B.
Tyler Lorenzo
Shears Platt
Chuve Geo. — *Harts' Grove.*
Palmer A. B. — *South Ridge.*
Blakely H. — *Conneaut.*
Randolph P.
Thompson G.
Dunn O.
Holbrook K. L.
Keith Z.
Drake J.
Palmer A. B.

Athens County.

Koots D. — *Chauncey.*
Smith Wm. — *Albany.*
Dickson O.
Steenrod Lewis — *Nelsonville.*
Smith Wm. — *Lee.*
Dickson Catherine

Auglaize County.

Kruse J. B. — *Minster.*
Vocke John H.

Belmont County.

Creigh John D. — *St Clairsville.*
Johnson Thomas
Neiswanger Isaac
Norton John H.
Overbaugh Joseph
Smith James S.
Wells Abner
Alexander B. — *Morristown.*
Hoover D.
Lippincott J.
Watson J. F.

Brown County.

Johnson O., Union Inn, — *Higginsport.*
Sallee Thos., Higginsport House
Williams W. W., Bank Hotel, — *Ripley.*
Patterson Wm., Galt House
Troutman Lewis, Lafayette House
Porter John, Ripley Hotel
Pittenger R. W. — *Decatur.*
Stevenson Joseph
Bryant J. — *Hamersville.*
Moyer Philip

Butler County.

Davis E. — *Bethany.*
Avey Daniel — *West Chester.*
Mee David — *Dartown.*
Kouster Frederick
Johnson John L
Cone P. H. — *Oxford.*
Adams M.
Deinser M. — *Hamilton.*
Snyder Chas., Buckeye House

Hesseling B., Pearl st. House — *Hamilton.*
Frederick T., Kenton Hotel
Hough G., Hamilton Hotel
Hesling H., Schidtman House
Donges C., Wm. Tell Hotel
McGhear J. M., R. Road House
Lohmann J. W., Lohmann House
Shertz P., Miami House — *Rossville.*
Beaver Danl.
Rothenbush C., Butler House
Humback J., Straub House
Mitchell C. C., U. S. Hotel — *Middletown.*
Foster A.
Knowlton Z. — *Ross.*
Knox A. D.
Buell R.
Hoaglan Abraham — *Monroe.*
Ridenour Wm. H. — *College Corner.*
Andrews Jacob — *Somerville.*
Sheafer H. W. — *Trenton.*
Debolt H. S.
Buehl John O.
Potter Wm.
Deuscher H. P.
Smith Jacob
Keepers Wm. H. — *Jacksonburg.*
Mounts J. C.. — *Port Union.*

Carroll County.

Patton James — *Carrollton.*
Cameron William — *Kilgore.*
Hosterman Peter

Champaign County.

Gorsuch E., Addison Hotel, *Christiansburg.*
Corbly J. C., Western Hotel
Taylor S., Ohio House — *Urbana.*
Blanchard B., Exchange Hotel
Hamilton J., Hamilton House
Lyons Jacob — *Mutual.*
Chamberlin John
Winder Aaron — *North Lewisburg.*

Clark County.

Hagenbuck J. — *Springfield.*
Swonp E.
Akin Wm. H., Anthony House
Homberger S., American House
Teegarden D.
Good H. M., Western Hotel
Hunt James — *Catawba.*
Armstrong David — *South Charleston.*
Parsons Hiram — *New Carlisle.*

Clermont County.

Herbert Wm., Franklin House, *New Rich-
    [mond.*
Garrison J., Fulton House
Brumer Philip, Dutch Hotel
Kain J. W. — *Williamsburg*
Faris E. L.
Perrine J. A. — *Bethel.*
Morris T. J.
Thompson W. R.
Jamieson J., Batavia Hotel — *Batavia.*
Johnson Jos. S., Clermont House

Taylor John H.   *Amelia.*
Woodlif R. Y.   *Miamisville.*
Vooris T.   *Loveland.*
Stewart W. P.   *Perin's Mills.*

Clinton County.

Arnold John   *New Burlington.*
Cornell John   *Lumberton.*
Kimbrough Thos.   *Sligo.*
Nordyke B.   *New Vienna.*
Kopp Joseph   *Sabina.*

Columbiana County.

Bradfield N. U. & Co., United States
  House   *Wellsville.*
Orozer S., Missouri House
Hamilton O. M., City Hotel
Sargent Matthew, Sargent House
Whitacre T. W., National House
Byrns John   *New Lisbon.*
Morrison John
Seetin James
Watson Samuel
Hamilton Jas. R   *East Palestine.*
McMillen James
Densmore Thos.   *North Georgetown.*
Sturgeon S. L.
Bunn Stephen   *East Rochester.*
Clark Eli   *New Chambersburgh.*
McCoy Henry
Phillips E., Farquhar House   *Salem.*
Ritter William, Franklin House
Walton J. C., Western Hotel
Devers William   *East Liverpool.*
Shobert Joseph
Williams Jesse   *East Fairfield.*
Rose D.   *Inverness.*
Armstrong Andrew   *Elkton.*

Coshocton County.

Groham R.   *Clark's.*
Fisher John
Gamble James, Walhonding House
  Walhonding.
Robison John, American House

Crawford County.

Richards Isaiah   *Liberty Corners.*
Good J. G.   *New Washington.*
Tuttle Daniel   *Poplar.*
McKee Jas. G., Sulphur Spring House
  Sulphur Spring.
Black S., Oregon House   *Bucyrus.*
Marshall W. J., National Hotel
Warner H., American   do

Cuyahoga County.

Atkinson Wm., Farmers' Hotel, River near
  Landing   *Cleveland.*
Button Chester, University House, cor.
  Pittsburgh and First
Butts O. S. & Son, Weddell House, cor.
  Bank and Superior
Coon H. L., St. Clair House, cor. St. Clair
  and Water
French Lewis, Commercial House, 24, 26,
  28, 30 Seneca

Haltnorth F., William Tell House, Bath
  opp. R. R. Depot   *Cleveland.*
Harris H. B., City Hotel, 22, 24, 26 Seneca
Kellenberger Geo. A., Waverly House cor.
  Ontario and Prospect
Kiesel William, Pavilion House, 22 Water
Milford Wm., American Hotel, 45 Supe'r.
Patrick C. & Son, Franklin House, 25 do
Portser M., St. Charles Hotel, cor. Mervin
  and James
Richardson J. W., U. States Hotel, 146,
  148 River
Ross J. R., New England Hotel, cor. Mer-
  win and Superior
Smith W. A. & H. C., Forest City House,
  cor. Public Square
Thompson George, Rail Road Hotel, cor.
  River and Front
McLean Alexander   *Ohio City.*
Condit J. P.   *Euclid.*
Farr A.
Bergin W.   *Newburgh.*
Miles A. H.
Hatch Simeon   *Brooklyn.*
Lockwood S. S.
Birge S.   *Brecksville.*

Darke County.

Grovesner Saml.   *Fort Jefferson.*
Purvian John S.   *Concordia.*
Powell B.   *New Madison.*
Shields Patrick   *Sampson.*
John S. P.   *Beamsville.*

Defiance County.

Southworth B. B., American House
  Defiance.
Strubell M., Washington Hotel
Strait R.
Thomson George   *Milldale.*
Ladd Ira W.   *Panama.*
Bunnell B.   *Hicksville.*
Kintigh Wm. F., Tiffin House   *Evansport.*
Fay E. G., Travelers' Home   *Brunersburg.*
Cleland L., Our House

Delaware County.

Hunt H. H., American House   *Delaware.*
Shereb Martin, Shereb House
Cornwell A., Delaware Hotel
Armstrong J.   *Waldo.*
Curren David

Erie County.

Walker H.   *Berlinville.*
Russell C.   *Birmingham.*
Rice Charles, Bay City House
  Sandusky City
Rice Daniel, Portland House
Patterson W. R., St. Lawrence House
Ebersol David, Pennsylvania   do
Belford S. W., Travelers' Home
Andress C. L., Verandah House
Anderson James, City Hotel
Smith B. & Co., Townsend House
Burkinshaw W., Steamboat House
Thomas Enoch, Rail Road   do

Reummell Carl   *Sandusky City.*
Mullany William, American Eagle House

Fairfield County.

Degroff George   *Pickerington.*
Houck William
Rockey J.   *Amanda.*
Warrall N. J.
McFadeon James   *Sugar Grove.*
Vandyke E.
Sager Charles   *Clear Creek.*
Hite W. W.   *Lithopolis.*
Parr J.

Franklin County.

Allen John, Capitol House, High *Columbus.*
Davis Wm., Broadway House, Broad
Evans J., Railway Hotel, High
Ellis J. C., Farmers' & Mech. Hotel, Broad
Guy W., Douglass House   do
Glass C., Eagle Hotel, High
Kelsey Wm., American Hotel do
Mewfley A., Columbus House, Friend
Beiber M., Franklin House, High
Neil R. E., Neil House   do
Pounds J. D., Montgomery House, do
Reel G. H., Scioto Hotel, Canal
Smith J. & Son, U. S. Hotel, cor. High &
   Town
Simonton H., Buckeye House, Broad
Snider Joseph, Bloom House, Third
Chapter Philip, Franklin House
Overmine B., Farmers' Inn
Simpson W., Western House
Landon Noble, Sen., Albany House, *Hope.*
Hoover Samuel, Franklin House,
Schoch John M.,   *Canal Winchester.*
Hutchinson Z.,   *Dublin.*
Coffman F.

Fulton County.

Gleason Thos.   *Delta.*
Russell R. P.
Pease A.   *Ottokee.*
Taylor Henry

Gallia County.

Smith Geo. B.   *Rodney.*
Sloan Wm. B., American House *Gallipolis.*
Hoy Charles, U. S. Hotel
Frost Solomon
Goodno D.

Geauga County.

Stacking D. W.   *Chardon.*
Brush Joseph
Folsom J. R.   *Hamden.*
Church Calvin   *Thompson.*
Austin A.   *Montville.*
Austin B.
Thompson E.   *Middlefield.*
Allen ——   *Parkman.*
Foster G. W.   *Troy.*
Ethridge D. G.   *Auburn.*
Burnett D.   *Russell.*
Damons ——   *Chester.*
Shaw B. N.

Chase C. L.   *Munson.*
Center Reuben   *Newbury.*
Parker Amos
Jones O. A.
Gould H.   *Burton.*
Gaylord O.
Ensign T. W.   *Claridon.*
Hathaway James

Greene County.

Barnes Oliver, Ewing House, *Xenia.*
Eichelberger John, Hivling House
Snell R. T., Snell House
Stark A. W., Railroad House
Lamme J., Spring Valley Hell
                           Spring Valley.
Confar John   *Clifton.*
Diffenbaugh M. A.
Swaynie Joseph   *Yellow Springs.*
Adams J. R., Jamestown Hotel *Jamestown.*
McDowny J., American House

Guernsey County.

Beemis J.   *Cumberland.*
Draper John
White William
McConnell John   *Londonderry.*
Brown Robert
Clobaugh J.
Barber Samuel   *Fairview.*
Gleaves David
Bradshaw Wm.
Buckey John   *Kimbolton.*
Denoon Emanuel   *Leatherwood.*
Scott David

Hamilton County.

Achey Henry, Waverly House, cor. Main
   and Canal   *Cincinnati.*
Boechert B., Indiana Hotel, 620 Main
Buttermiller J., Court bet. Main & W'lnut
Cromwell J. H., Broadway Hotel, cor.
   Broadway & Columbia
Coleman A. B., Burnet House, cor. Vine
   and 3d
Dennison & Son, Dennison House, 5th bet.
   Main & Sycamore
Dubois W. S., s. s. 5th bet. Race & Elm
Farlow B., Central Hotel, cor. Elm & 6th
Garrison J. W., Madison House, 19 Main
Henrich & Blettner, Canal Hotel, 443 do
Horn G., Farmers' Rest, 229 6th
Hessing A. C., Farmers' Hotel, cor. Race &
   Court
Keown J., 22 Water
Longshore A., cor. Walnut & Water
Livering & Bicknell, Rail. R. Hotel, s. e.
   cor. Broadway & Landing
Mount L. & Co., Henrie House, 3d bet.
   Main and Walnut
Marsh Wm. E., Galt House, s. w. cor. Main
   and 6th
McDonald A., 15 Water
McAnaulty P., P. Landing bet. Walnut &
   Vine
Murphey John, 24 Sycamore

Marchant Isaac, Black Bear Tavern, cor.
Sycamore & 9th   *Cincinnati.*
Nicholas Wm., 500 Elm
Porter J. F., Brighton House, Forks Hamilton & Harr. Roads
Ross A. L., Ross House, s. e. cor. Walnut and Court
Rockenfield J. A., Evans Hotel, cor. B'adway & Lower Market
Rinkle J., Harrison Road
Sweeney J. W., Walnut St. House, Walnut bet. 6th & 7th
Schmidt A., W. Row bet. Everett & Wade
Schmidt A., 27 Front
Schwegman J., Sycamore near Front
Wetherbee, A., Gibson House, Walnut bet. 4th and 5th
Wetherbee A., U. S. Hotel, s. w. cor. Walnut & 6th
Winne K., Winne House, s. e. cor. Broadway & 3d
Wibel F., Revere House, 78 Broadway
Whitman J. J., cor. John & Wade
Watson S., Watson House, 55 Sycamore
Wetherbee, Bledsoe & Co , Woodruff H'se, Sycamore bet. 3d and 4th
Wagmann J. W., Lewistown House *Fulton.*
Weaver M., Fulton House
Holloway J.
Worley W.
Erchrick C., Sportsman's Hall
Vankirk J. D.   *Mt. Healthy.*
Auten John, American House   *Pleasant*
Scudder Wm., Scudder House   [*Ridge.*
Feil August   *Harrison.*
Garard David
Heil Valentine
Heterick B.
Miner Henry
Schmidt Titus
Wolf M.   *Mt. Washington.*
Stephens T. J., Mill Creek House   *Cum-*
Dohman F., Farmers' Hotel   [*minsville.*
Mills D. D.   *Sharonville.*
Vail T. S.
Collins John   *Reading.*
Woodruff Catharine
Duls John   *Lockland.*
Fenton Richard   *Cheviot.*
Jones J.
Metzener B.
Michael George
Remlinger J.
Howe —, Columbia Hotel   *Columbia.*
Mack H. H., Farmers' Hotel
Meismann H., Phœuix do
Belser John   *Carthage.*
Bickham Thos. D.
Shites J.   *Dunlap.*
Grant J.   *College Hill.*

Hancock County.

Carr Jacob   *Finley.*
Reed Eli S.
Schwab A. W.
Smith Alexander

Hardin County.

Shurr John, Jr., American House   *Kenton.*
Furney L., Mansion House
Eglin B., Kenton   do
Moore John   *Roundhead.*
Nevil Samuel

Harrison County.

Barnett Wm., Mansion House   *Cadis.*
Vincent Chas. O., National do
Edney R. J., Union Inn   *Deersville.*
Bleckum G. W., American House *H'risville.*
Potts Samuel, Eagle   do   *Germano.*
Crovkey A. F., Rail Road do *New Market.*
Lacey John L., Laceysville do   *Laceysville.*
White Joseph   *Feed Spring.*

Henry County.

Honning Chas.   *New Bavaria.*
Spink John C.   *Texas.*
Stamp B. F.
Shophell Jeremiah

Highland County.

Hughs A. S.   *Greenfield.*
Harper J. H.
Grabill Abraham   *Marshall.*
Keen John M.   *Leesburg.*
Bentley A.
Gish Wm.
Myers James   *Hillsboro'.*
Blount E. J.

Hocking County.

Borland John   *Logan.*
Zimmerman John B.
Hartley Issaac   *Gibisonville.*

Holmes County.

Rowley Mrs. Jane   *Holmesville.*
Jones J. W.
Livensberger J. H.
Keister Shuman   *Millersburg.*

Huron County.

Brewster J. M.   *East Townsend.*
Putnam W. & D.
Stevenson D.   *Clarksfield.*
Wooley A. L.   *Greenwich.*
Knapp A. B.   *Bellevue.*
Strong A.
Howard —,
Sloan Wm.
Eichert J. W.   *Norwalk.*
Poole T.
Dewalctt A. J.
Kirkland G.   *North Fairfield.*

Jefferson County.

Mosegrove Wm., U. S. House *Steubenville*
Boler J., Kossuth   do
Zellers J., Our   do
Roland W. B., Virginia do
North J., Travelers' Hotel
Hunter Saml., Franklin House
Striam John, Black Bear
Earl Wm., Washington Hall

Duey Joseph   *East Springfield.*
McCollough Mrs. D.
Weiser Wm. J.   *Annapolis.*
Hobson John M.   *Mt. Pleasant.*
Hayne J. R.
Dunn Jacob & Son   *Mouth Yellow Creek.*

Knox County.

Kulb A. H., Mansion House   *Mt. Vernon*
Marble J. H., Franklin do
Popham J., Lybrand   do
Winne G., Kenyon   do
Glosser George, Buckeye do *Fredericktown.*
Rigby Wm. H., Rigby do
Riddel John   *Democracy.*
Magers Wm.   *Millwood.*
Vincent S. M.   *Jelloway.*
Phifer F.
Bird C.   *Mt Liberty.*
Crosby J. W.
Hauck Washington   *Bladensburg.*
Atell Thomas

Lake County.

Frank Geo.   *Kirtland.*
Smith L. F.
Burridge S.   *Painesville.*
Stockwell B.
Watson E.
Merriman W.
Rider L.
Duncan Wm.

Lawrence County.

Cochran D. K., Buckeye House   *Ironton.*
Coleman S. H., Ironton House
Parker Samuel, Vernon do
Owen O. D.   *Burlington.*

Licking County.

Starritt James   *Brownsville.*
Davis Wm.   *Jacksontown.*
Headley Uriah
Woodcock R.
Bingham H. & N., Irving House *Newark.*
Davis & Crawley, Davis   do
Tompkins John, U. S. Hotel
Binder A., Giraffe House

Logan County.

Bain E.   *New Richland.*
Erwin & Porter, Slicer's Hotel
                             Bellefontaine.
Harper P. M., Rutan House
Watson P. & Son, American House
Piatt D. P.   *Quincy.*
Park J.
Webb J.

Lorain County.

Norton Rufus   *Rochester Depot.*
Johnston J. J.
Hawn John, American Hotel   *LaGrange.*
Runals J. D., New England do
Plumb Wm. H.   *Oberlin.*
Wack C.

Griffith L., Mansion House   *Elyria.*
Beebe H., Beebe   do
Nelson J. & H. B., Wellington House
                             Wellington.
Tuttle J. M., American House
Oase Thomas H., Huntington House
                              Huntington.

Lucas County.

Clark E., Clark House   *Maumee City.*
Hull A. F., Hull House
Neely John, Eagle House
Langendorffer Joseph, Exchange
Farnsworth J., Mansion House   *Toledo.*
Kingman M., American do
Kingsbury H. D. & Wm. Kingsbury do
Rumsey S., Exchange House
Sellers Wm., Clinton   do
Wheeler L.

Madison County.

Downing F. L., Cowling House   *London.*
Howsman Wm., National do
Jones Wm., Jr., American Hotel   •
Flint Mrs., American do   *West Jefferson.*
Huckill Z., New York House
Mantle B., Jefferson   do

Mahoning County.

Ritter Henry   *Canfield.*
Keck J.
Moore Saml.
Durtman Jacob
Bostwick ——
Thompson J.   *Petersburgh.*
Flemming John
Smith E.   *Youngstown.*
Betts Col.
Ross W. H.
Johnson David   *New Middletown.*
Wisner Robert   *Milton.*
Hudson A.
Smith Nathaniel
McKinsey Thos.
Hadley S. F.   *New Springfield.*
May Wm.

Marion County.

Fostel J.   *Cochranton.*

Medina County.

McClintick John   *Litchfield.*
Butts John   *Wadsworth.*
Hickox R.   *Lodi.*
Stringham & Miller
Davis Wm. T.   *Weymouth.*
Tompkins G. & C.
Wilcox L. W.   *Homerville*
Chidester W. R.   *Medina*
Gilson P. W.
Selkirk H.

Meigs County.

Mathews J. W.   *Salisbury.*
Fultz Jacob

Mercer County.

Prouty Simon	Celina
Allen G.	
Winters Jacob	
Davis Wm. T. R.	Mercer.
Clarke S. H	
Hedges S. P.	Shanesville.
Lipps Henry	Fort Recovery.
Gibson James	
Wurdeman J. H.	Monterey.
Johnson L.	Macedon.

Miami County.

Everett Moses	Fletcher.
Williams J.	
Hoagland A.	West Charleston.
Blair J., Piqua House	Piqua.
Hans D. & Haller, Eagle Hotel	
Carson A. B., City Hotel	
Clark J. S.	
Vandergrift F. H.	Troy.
Hatfield E.	
Firmons G.	
Kleine P. H.	
Fuller W. T.	Casstown.
Murry J.	
Mast J. W.	West Milton.
Kauffman O. M.	Hyattsville.
Whitehead J.	

Monroe County.

Driggs Alfred D.	Woodsfield.
Randolph Joel F.	
Steed John	
Davenport George	Antioch.
Hiddleston James	Plymouth.

Montgomery County.

Clutch S. L.	Centreville.
Watkins Thomas	
Lewis D.	Chambersburg.
Falkner David	Centre.
Chidery J., Third	Dayton.
Dwerf J., Frenchtown Hall, Third	
Edelman J. E., Jefferson House, Jefferson	
Emerick C. C., Union do Third	
Enckenhoffer F., Columbus House, Third	
Forer C., Montgomery do do	
Good H., Pennsylvania do do	
Knecht A., Second	
Knecht C., Canal Hotel, Second	
Leonard & Porter, Phillips' House, Main	
Murry J., Centre House, N. Market	
Musch E., 6th Ward, do Third	
Nauerth J. V., N. Market	
Reid J., Farmers' & Mech. Hotel, Second	
Sage J., Dayton Hotel, Third	
Schutte F., Lafayette House, de	
Smith O., Franklin do Second	
Snyder A., N. Market	
Slaght A., Temperance House, Main	
Spang F. A., Phoenix Hotel, Third	
Swaynie Alex., Swaynie House, de	
Zueisler J., Zueisler do Warren	
Weaver Henry	Little York.
Adams Jacob	New Lebanon.
Garvey Martin	

18

Sneethen Joseph	West Baltimore.
Boner J. C.	Farmersville.
Buls Samuel	
Lutz J. H.	
Catro Z., Germantown Hotel	Germantown.
Eberle ——, Eberle House	
Schaeffar ——, Schaeffer do	
McColly Henry	Miamisburgh.
Method Jonathan	
Zehring Samuel	
Harnest John	Johnsville.
Nicholas John	

Morgan County.

Bumgardner Geo.	Rousseau.
Wilson J. M.	McConnelsville.
McClain, Goodline & McCarver	
Marquis Samuel	
Kraps Jacob	Neelysville.
Neely John	

Morrow County.

Mitchell Wm.	Underwood's.
Norris Daniel	Cardington.
Salsbury G. L.	
Cone A. H.	Shauk's.
Barnhard N.	Nimmon's Cross Roads.

Muskingum County.

Bryant Saml.	Nashport.
Palmer J. K.	
Becker A.	Otsego.
Weaver Saml.	Norwich.
Loyd W. E.	
Norris John	Frazeyburg.
Campbell Mrs.	
Wilsons —,	New Concord.
Grummons —,	
Fulton L.	Fultonham.
Hamilton S.	
Bowers Martin	Gratiot.
Peirce J.	Chandlersville.
Walls J.	
Winslow A. P., Winslow House	Zanesville.
Randolph J., Randolph House	
Stacey & Jones, Stacey's Hotel	
Stenger Jacob, City Hotel	
Goets C., Franklin House	

Noble County.

Bratton E. A., Ohio House	Sarahsville.
Beynier R., Eagle Hotel	
Beynier John, Lion Hotel	

Ottawa County.

Horden A.	Port Clinton.
Robinson J.	

Paulding County.

Tygatt James, American House	Junction.
Columba D., Junction House	
Smith Ezra J.	Paulding.
Thompson James	

Perry County.

Barnd Jacob	New Lexington.

Golborn L. B.   *New Lexington.*
Riley Smith
Carrol John, Carrol House   *Somerset.*
Gordon Saml., American House
Shirley James, Shirley House
Boor George   *Sego.*

Pickaway County.

Boyd Jonathan, National House   *Circle-*
                                 [*ville.*
Rodgers John, American Hotel
Sweyer H. M., Pickaway House
Try Jacob, Farmers & Mech. House
Bidler T. & S. B., Union House   *Tarlton.*
Nye A., Tarlton House
Green C. W. & E.   *Derbyville.*
Stottlemire Joseph

Pike County.

Hadley James   *Jasper.*
Armstrong B. E.   *Piketon.*
Nessler M.
Vallery Jacob

Portage County.

Folger Wm. M.   *Ravenna.*
Adams Hiram
Collins H.
Hillyer D. W.   *Atwater.*
Stannard P.
Hine J.   *Randolph.*
Gray A. T.   *Aurora.*
Latsey Josiah   *Shalersville.*
Miller F. A.
Stowe Eli   *Edinburgh.*
Edson Nehemiah   *Franklin.*
Beardsley E.
Green Benj.   *Suffield.*
Sheakspeare Wm.   *Paris.*
Brown B.   *Mantua.*
Story James
Diver John   *Deerfield.*
Gibbons Peter
Kelso Wm. R.   *Brimfield.*
Barnard John   *Rootstown.*
Dailey J.   *Nelson.*
Lewis Asa
Sackett C.
Lewis F.   *Palmyra.*
Drake O. L.   *Freedom.*

Preble County.

Rice Nathaniel   *Lewisburg.*
Loutzenhiser D. B.   *New Westville.*
Evans Hiram D.   *Fairhaven.*
Campbell & Brasier, Eagle Hotel *Eaton.*
Hulbert James, National Hotel
Place W. J., Eaton House
Tillman R. S.   *New Paris.*
Smith Mrs.

Putnam County.

Armstrong J. S. & J. B., Armstrong House
                                 Medary.
Clutter Jonathan, Medary House
Bell William   *Buckeye.*
Row M.
Bockheld J. G.

Richland County.

Baughman J.   *Shelby.*
Miller D. M.
Cline Jacob   *Shenandoah.*
Cook J. H., Wiler House   *Mansfield.*
Myers P. P., N. American House
Salger J. F., Weldon   do
Smart J., Phœnix Hotel
Spaulding —, Farmers' Hotel   *Lexington.*
Marks Wm.   *Olivesburg.*
Miller David
Farquhar A. Farquhar House   *Belleville.*
Van Buskirk John   *Lucas.*

Ross County.

Pancake Jacob   *Frankfort*
Shanton John
Cormer A. B., Woodbridge House   *Chilli-*
                                 [*cothe.*
Corey Isaac, Corey House
Bader F., Commercial Hotel
Barleon E., Eagle Hotel
Barnes Wm., Main St. Hotel
Maier John, Hydraulic Hotel
Steele J. C., Salem House   *South Salem.*
Satchel J., Clinton House
Lance John   *Gillespieville.*
Tomlinson A.

Sandusky County.

Whicher S. C.,   *Clyde.*
Boyd Wm.
Russell James   *Greensburg Cross Roads.*

Scioto County.

Craig Thos.   *Lucasville.*
Sargent John
Englebrest Wm., White Bear House
                                 Portsmouth.
Graham J. T., United States Hotel
Gilroy Hugh, Swan House
Higgins W., Eagle Hotel
Montgomery R., Franklin Hotel
Myers B. C., Farmers' Hotel
Ramsay S. G., Rail Road House
Welty C., Green Tree House
Coal Jesse   *Scioteville.*
Price Madison

Seneca County.

Miller William   *Attica.*
Shade John
Daymon D.   *Adrian.*
Wing J. W.
Boxer J.   *Tiffin.*
Flanner A., City House
Holt E. M., Holt House
Patterson J. W., Shawhan House
Worthshape G.
Beard Michael   *West Lodi.*
Pierce S. R.   *Republic.*
Kyle Geo. H.
Neikirk S.

Starke County.

Grible H., Navarre House   *Navarre.*
Harter G.

Stahl A..   *Navarre.*
Stahl F.
Hamilton Robert   *Waynesburg.*
Simmon John
Gaddis Henry   *West Brookfield.*
Kreiling Geo.
Drey John, Rail Road House   *Louisville.*
Unkefer S., Union   do
Wyant H., American   do
Raber Leonard   *Lake.*
Unkefer John   *New Franklin.*
Bachtel M.   *Canton.*
Cramer E.
Perrong N.
Shafer Love
Stover S.
Bitzer Michael   *New Berlin.*
Wagner Geo
Cay A. M.,   *New Baltimore.*
Cross Lewis, Franklin House   *Massillon.*
Nutting T. B., Tremont House
Keifer A. J.   *Canal Fulton.*
Shilling John
Morse John G.   *Llansvillé.*
Nixon J. B.   *Mt. Union.*

Summit County.

Barber George   *Middlebury.*
Willard S. W.
Clay D.   *Inland.*
Cobb C. B., Cobb's Exchange   *Akron.*
Fink C., Fink's Hotel
McDonald O. P., Rail Road Hotel
Morse H., Empire Hotel
Weber F., Weber's Hotel
Whitney M. F., Farmer's do
Dennison J. B.   *Richfield.*
Smith Moses
Delany P.   *Montrose.*
Woodard Jehu   *Eden.*
Sour Elhanan   *Summit.*
Chapman George   *Tallmadge.*

Trumbull County.

Anderson James, Anderson House *Girard.*
Leavitt Minerva, Mansion House
Lane Jehiel, Temperance House *Hartford.*
Lane Lester, West Reserve Hotel
Wolcott J. W.   *Farmington.*
Palmer J.
Herner Lewis
Patterson George   *Newton Falls.*
Fulk S.
Watts J.

Tuscarawas County.

Otis Ezekiel   *Winfield.*
Fox Gustavus   *Gnadenhutten.*
Bimeler J. B., A't Zoar Community *Zoar.*
Huston J., Empire House   *Canal Dover*
Kaldenbach J., Liberty Hotel
Wright W. C., Wright House
Herbold John, Dover House
Espich O. F., Exchange Hotel   *New Philadelphia.*

Amspoker J., Gray House

Albert S. J., Lion Hotel   *New Philadelphia.*
Gent C., Union House

Union County.

Snodgrass George, Welch House   *Marysville.*
Wadham M. H., Marysville Hotel
Gamble John   *Watkins.*
Miles George   *Richwood.*

Van Wert County.

Fisher Benjamin   *Van Wert.*
McMullen N. D.
Stake J.
Clark J. R. & Son, American House   *Delphos.*
Phillips J. W., Neil House

Vinton County.

Sisson & Hurlbut   *McArthur.*
Richmond M. & N.
Miller Peter   *Allensville.*
Millet A.
Hampton E.   *Hamden.*
Tissue Wm.
Thompson —   *Wilkesville.*
Chapman Amos   *Mount Pleasant.*

Warren County.

Morrow R.   *Waynesville.*
Yeoman E. P.
Woodruff Mrs.
Harner Peter   *Oregon.*
Haycock W. H.   *Morrow.*
Hatfield & Gustin
Roach S. G.
Shawhan A.
Hasen S.

Washington County.

Lewis J., Mansion House,   *Marietta.*
Watters M., Eagle Hotel
Mosely —, Marietta House
Hart S., Harmar Exchange,   *Harmar.*
Jennings J., Harmar House

Wayne County.

Miller Conrad   *Dalton.*
Ruark T. H.
Wertz J.
Messmore G.   *Edinburgh.*
Crunly J. W.
Meech A.   *Smithville.*
Johnson J.
Secrist W.
Elder Mark   *West Lebanon.*
Steinmetz N.   *Marshallville.*
Wells J.   *Canaan.*
Belnap Wm.   *Wooster.*
Holton S. S.
Howard Horace
Howard Charles
Matthews ——
Winters Henry

Williams County.

Arnold Benj. L.   *Spring Lake.*

Welds Edwin
Barkalow John   *Montpelier.*
Leonard Mary
Barnes G. A.   *Bryan.*
Spiker ——
Eyer A.   *West Unity.*
Rice James
Scannel Wm. O.   *Pulaski.*

Wood County.

Avey G. Z.   *Bowling-Green.*
Thomas Geo. H.
Thustin Alfred

Wyandot County

Pearson C. Y.   *Upper Sandusky.*
Edgington ——
Moore J. B.
Zimmerman ——
Rappee John S.   *Little Sandusky.*
Myers John   *McCutchensville.*
Brackley M.
Bowsher A.
Nichols B. R.   *Carey.*

House Furnishing Warehouses.

Hamilton County.

Maxwell Geo., 26 w. Fifth   *Cincinnati.*
Burnet William, 14 e. Fourth

Muskingum County.

Best, Boyd & Co.   *Zanesville.*

Hub, Spoke, Felloe, and Bow Manufacturers.

Hamilton County.

Royer, Simonton & Co., 3d below Smith   *Cincinnati.*
Byrn & Morris, cor. Park & W. W. Canal

Montgomery County.

Blanchard & Brown, Canal cor. 4th   *Dayton.*

Seneca County.

Berksy & Meyers   *Tiffin.*

Hucksters.

Butler County.

Reister S.   *Bethany.*

Darke County.

Ridenour D.   *Ithica.*
Francis D.
Pickering M.

Gallia County

James Howel   *Anselm.*

Hamilton County.

Farley D. S.   *Montgomery.*

Knox County.

Love & Stephens   *Fredericktown.*

Montgomery County.

Ammon Levi   *Liberty.*
Hollingsworth & Ridgeway   *Centre.*

Ross County.

Heap James   *Hallsville.*
Heap John

Ice Dealers.

Hamilton County.

Spaeth A., 323 Broadway   *Cincinnati.*
Blair Saml. G. & Bro., Plum bet. Wade and Everett
Shute Milton, cor. 12th and Plum
Gandolpho Peter, 375 Elm
Fuller E. E.   *Harrison.*
Hendrickson O. W.

Ink (Printing) Manufacturers.

Hamilton County.

Stearns & Foster, cor. Clay & Liberty sts.,   *Cincinnati.*

Knox County.

Hill Noah   *Mount Vernon.*

Ross County.

Lang A. V. & Co.   *Yellow Bud.*

Ink (Writing) Manufacturers.

Coshocton County.

Elliott William   *Keene.*

Hamilton County.

Titcomb R., 158 w. 5th   *Cincinnati.*
Butler & Brother, 27 Pearl
Fuller E.   *Harrison.*

Jefferson County.

Moodey D. Z.   *Steubenville.*

Ross County.

Lang A. V. & Co.   *Yellow Bud.*

Institutes (Clinical).

Hamilton County.

Newton R. S. & O. E., cor. 7th & John   *Cincinnati.*

Insurance Companies.

Adams County.

U. States Fire Ins. Co., (E. Stevenson, Ag't.)   *Manchester.*
Washington Life Ins. Co., (E. Stevenson, Ag't.)
Washington Union Ins. Co. of Cleveland, (J. W. McFerran, Agent)   *West Union.*

Ashland County.

Ashland County Mutual Ins. Co.,
Ashland.

Ashtabula County.

Washington Life Ins. Co. of Cincinnati,
(Henry Fassett, Agent), *Ashtabula.*
Portage Mutual Fire Ins. Co., Cuyahoga
Falls, O., (H. Fassett, Agent),

Athens County.

Protection Ins. Co. of Hartford, (H. T.
Brown, Agent), *Athens.*

Belmont County.

Ohio Life Ins. Co. of Cincinnati, (M. J. W.
Glover, Agent), *St. Clairsville.*
Protection Ins. Co. of Hartford, Con., (D.
D. T. Cowen, Agent),

Brown County.

Jefferson Life Ins. Co. of Cincinnati, (W.
N. Elliott, Agent), *Higginsport.*
Washington Fire Ins. Co., (Wm. N. Elliott,
Agent),
Farmers' Fire and Marine Ins. Co., (Wm.
N. Elliott, Agent),
Protection Fire Ins. Co., (Wm. F. Wylie,
Agent), *Ripley.*
Hartford Fire Ins. Co., (Wm. F. Wylie,
Agent),
Kentucky Mutual Fire Ins. Co., (Wm. M.
Shan, Agent),
City Ins. Co. of Cincinnati, (Cambers
Baird, Agent),

Butler County.

Dayton Ins. Co. of Dayton, O., (Miller &
Brown, Agents), *Hamilton.*
Protection Ins. Co. of Hartford, Con. (W.
H. Miller, Agent),
Franklin Fire and Marine Ins. Co. of New
York, (John R. Lewis, Agent),
Jefferson Life Ins. Co. of Cincinnati, (A.
F. Hume, Agent),

Clermont County.

Clermont Ins. Co., (P. J. Dunam, Agent),
New Richmond.
Jefferson Life Ins. Co., (W. F. Ballard,
Agent), *Loveland.*

Clinton County.

Protection Ins. Co. of Hartford, (C. M.
Bosworth, Agent), *Wilmington.*
Philadelphia U. S. F. Ins. & Trust Co., (A.
McKay, Agent),

Columbiana County.

Columbiana County Mutual Ins. Co., *New
Lisbon.*
Western Farmers' Ins. Co.

Crawford County.

Summit County Mutual Insurance Co., (J.
Pitezel, Agent), *Poplar.*
Ashland Mutual Ins. Co., (W. R. S. Clark,
Agent), *Bucyrus.*

American Mutual Health Association, (A.
A. Ruhl, Agent), *Bucyrus.*
Knox County Mutual Insurance Co., (John
Sims, Agent),
Portage County Mutual Ins. Co., (C. W.
Butterfield, Agent),
Starke County Mutual Ins. Co., (Aaron
Casey, Agent),
Summit County Mutual Ins. Co., (J. S.
Plants, Agent),
Western Farmers' Mutual Ins. Co. of New
Lisbon, (J. Scroggs, Agent),

Cuyahoga County.

Cleveland Ins. Co., (S. W. Crittenden,
Sec'y), *Cleveland.*
Cleveland Mutual Ins. Co., (S. H. Mather,
Sec'y),
Washington Union Ins. Co., (Geo. B. Sen-
ter, Agent),
New York City Fire and Marine Ins. Co.,
(S. B. Shaw, Agent),
American Fire and Marine Ins. Co., Am-
sterdam, N. Y., (S. B. Shaw, Agent),
Roger Williams Fire Ins. Co., Providence,
R. I., (S. B. Shaw, Agent),
Atlantic Fire and Marine Ins. Co., Provi-
dence, R. I., (S. B. Shaw, Agent),
Rochester Fire and Marine Ins. Co., Ro-
chester, N. Y., (S. B. Shaw, Agent),
Charter Oak Life Ins. Co., Hartford, Con.
(S. B. Shaw, Agent),
Mohawk Valley Farmers' Ins. Co., Scioto,
N. Y., (Levi Martin, Agent),
American and Granite Ins. Co., (Hays &
Moore, Agents),
Atlantic Mutual Ins. Co. of N. York City,
(S. S. Coe, Agent),
Ætna Fire Ins. Co., Hartford, Conn., (C.
C. Carlton, Agent),
Protection Fire Ins. Co., Hartford, Conn.,
(C. C. Carlton, Agent),
Hartford Fire Ins. Co., Hartford, Conn.,
(C. C. Carlton, Agent),
Connecticut Fire Ins. Co., Hartford, Conn.,
(C. C. Carlton, Agent),
Connecticut Mutual Life Ins. Co., Hartford,
Conn., (C. C. Carlton, Agent),
Ætna Life Ins. Co., Hartford, Conn., (C.
C. Carlton, Agent),

Darke County.

New York Union Ins. Co. of Johnstown,
(David Putnam, Agent). *German.*
Protection Ins. Co. of Hartford, Conn.,
(Fire & Marine) (Wm. M. Wilson, Ag't)
Greenville.

Defiance County.

Charter Oak Life Ins. Co. of Hartford,
Conn., (R. H. Gibson, Agent), *Defiance.*
Farmers' Mutual Ins. Co. of New Lisbon,
Ohio, (R. H. Gibson, Agent),
Franklin Fire Ins. Co, of Saratoga Springs,
N. Y., (R. H. Gibson, Agent),
Merchants, Cash and Mutual Ins. Co. of
New Lisbon, O., (R. H. Gibson, Agent),
Protection Fire Ins. Co. of Hartford, Conn.
(R. H. Gibson, Agent),

Union Mutual Life Ins. Co. of Boston,
Mass., (R. H. Gibson, Agent), *Defiance.*
Mutual Life Ins. Co. of Covington, Ky.,
(D. Taylor, Agent),

Erie County.

Sun Mutual Insurance Co. of New York,
(A. Cheesbrough, Agt.), *Sandusky City.*
Equitable Fire Ins. Co. of London and
Jersey City (John W. Godfrey, General
Agent),
N. York City Fire Ins. Co. of N. Y. City
(John W. Godfrey, Gen. Agent),
United States Fire Ins. Co. of West Pots-
dam N. Y. (John W. Godfrey, General
Agent),
National Protection Ins. Co. Saratoga
Spr'gs N. Y. (J. W. Godfrey, Gen. Agt.),
Ætna Fire & Marine Ins. Co. of Utica N.
York (John W. Godfrey, Gen. Agt.),
American Fire & Marine Ins. Co. of Am-
sterdam N. Y. (John W. Godfrey, Gen.
Agent),
Rennselaer Fire Ins. Co. of Lansingburg
New York (John W. Godfrey, General
Agent),
Rochester Fire Ins. Co. of Rochester N. Y.
(John W. Godfrey Gen. Agent),
Ætna Ins. Co. of Hartford (Fire & Marine)
(J. G. & J. A. Camp, Agents),
Hartford Ins. Co. of Hartford (J. G. &
J. A. Camp, Agents),
Portage Mutual Fire Ins. Co. (C. Leonard,
Agent),
Franklin Marine & Fire Ins. Co. of N. Y.
(C. Leonard, Agent),
New York Union Mutual Ins. Co. of
Johnstown, N. Y. (C. Leonard Agt.),
Hudson River Marine & Fire Ins. Co. (C.
Leonard, Agent),
Sandusky City Marine Ins. Co. Sandusky
City (J. A, Pinto, Agent),
Mutual Ins. Co. of Buffalo (R. J. Gibbs,
Agent),
Sandusky Ins. Co. (Marine; R. J. Gibbs,
Agent),
National Loan Fund Life Ins. Co. of Lon-
don and N. Y. City (John W. Godfrey,
Agent),
Hartford Life Ins. Co. of Hartford Conn.
(John W. Godfrey, Agent),
Connecticut Mutual Life Ins. Co. of Conn.
(C. Leonard Agent),
Ætna Life Ins. Co. (J. G. & J. A. Camp,
Agent),
New York Life Ins. Co. (J. G. & J. A.
Camp, Agent),
Pittsburgh Life Ins. Co. of Pittsburgh, Pa.
(R. J. Gibbs Agent),
Manhatten Life Ins. Co. of New York (R.
J. Gibbs Agent),
New England Live Stock Ins. Co. of New
Haven Conn. (John W. Godfrey, General
Agent),

Franklin County.

Ætna Life Insurance Co. of Hartford
(K. H. Vanrenseller, Agt.), *Columbus.*

Ashland Fire Ins. Co. (K. H. Vanrenseller,
Agent),   *Columbus.*
Pittsburgh Life Ins. Co. (K. H. Vanren-
seller, Agent),
Washington Union Ins. Co. (K. H. Van-
renseller, Agent).
New England Live Stock Ins. Co. (Thos.
Stocton, Agent),
Ohio Life Ins. Co, (Thos. Stocton, Agent),
Etna Ins. Co. Utica N. Y. (Warren Jen-
kins, Agent),
Ohio Mutual Ins. Co. (Warren Jenkins,
Agent),
Protection Ins. Co. Hartford (John Pat-
terson Agent),
Manhatten Life Ins. Co., N. Y. (John Pat-
terson, Agent),
Hartford Fire Ins. Co. (Demas Adams, Jr.,
Agent),
Mutual Life Ins. Co. of Hartford (Demas
Adams, Jr., Agt.),

Greene County.

Ashland Mutual Fire Ins. Co. (Francis
Harris, Agent),   *Xenia*
Granite Fire Insurance Co. (Francis Harris,
Agent),
Globe Fire Ins. Co. (Francis Harris, Agt.),
Hartford Life Ins. Co.   "   "   "
Portage Co. Mutual Fire Ins. Co. (Francis
Harris, Agt.),
Penn Life Ins. Co. (Charles R. Merrick,
Agent),
Protection Ins. Co. Hartford (Benoni Nes-
bitt, Agent),
Kentucky Mutual Life Ins. Co. (Benoni
Nesbitt, Agt.),

Hamilton County.

Ætna Ins. Co. of Hartford, Conn (J. H.
Carter Agent), 19 e. Front *Cincinnati*
Ætna Ins. Co. of Utica, N. Y. (A. S. Chew,
Agt.), 14 e. Front
American Union Life Ins. Co. of Cincin.
(Merick B. Dean, Prest.), 14 e. Front
American Mutual Ins. Co. of Amster-
dam, N. Y. (A. S. Chew, Agent), 14 e.
Front
Atlantic Fire & Marine Ins. Co. of Provi-
dence, R. I. (W. T. Phipps, Agent), 4 Col-
lege Buildings
Charter Oak Life Ins. Co. of Hartford,
Conn. (Saml. B. Findlay, Agent), 4 Main
Cincinnati Ins. Co. (John W. Hartwell,
President), 4 e. Front
City Ins. Co. of Cincinnati (E. S. Haines,
President), 8 e. Front
Columbia Ins. Co. of Columbia, S. C. (A.
S. Chew, Agent), 14 e. Front
Commercial Ins. Co. of Charleston, S. C
(A. S. Chew, Agent), 14 e. Front
Connecticut Mutual Life Ins. Co., of Hart
ford, Conn. Joseph J. Davis, Agent),
4 Main
Delaware Mutual Safety Ins. Co. of Phila-
delphia (B. Urner, Agent), 16 e. Front

Eagle Ins. Co. of Cincinnati (Isaac C. Copelen, President), cor. Front & Main *Cincinnati.*

Equitable Life Ins. Co. of London (Geo. W. Copelen, Agent), 9 e. Front

Evansville Ins. Co. of Evansville, Ind. (A. S. Chew, Agent), 14 e. Front

Firemen's Ins. Co. of Cincinnati (H. E. Spencer, President), n. e. cor. Main & Front

Franklin Marine & Fire Ins. Co. of N. Y. (Jos. J. Davis, Agent), 4 Main

Fraternal Mutual Life Ins. Co. of Harrisburg, Pa. (A. Hichenlooper, Agent), Reeder's Building

Globe Ins. Co. of Utica N. Y. (Geo. W. Copelen, Agent), 9 e. Front

Granite, Marine & Fire Ins. Co. of Utica, N. Y. (W. H. Wright, Agent) 8 Main

Hartford Fire Ins. Co. of Hartford, Conn. (J. H. Carter, Agent) 19 e. Front

Howard Life Ins. Co. of N. Y. (W. H. Wright, Agent), 8 Main

Ins. Co. of North America, Phila. (Peter A. White & Co., Agents), 61 Pearl

Jefferson Life Ins. Co. of Cincinnati (Dr. T. O. Edwards, Pres't.), cor. 4th & Vine

Keystone Mutual Life Ins. Co. of Harrisburg, Pa. (A. Hichenlooper, Agent), Reeder's Buildings

Liverpool & London Fire & Life Ins. Co. (Howard Matthews, Agent), s. w. cor. 3d and Main

Long Island Ins. Co. of Brooklyn, N. Y. (Francis Ferry Agent), 19 e. 4th

Manhattan Life Ins. Co. N. Y. (Irwin & Massey, Agents), 8 e. Front

Merchants & Manufacturers' Ins. Co. of Cincinnati (———, President), 11 e. Front

Mohawk Valley Ins. Co. Amsterdam, N. Y. (A. H. Van Buren, Agent), 4 Main

Mohawk Valley Farmers' Insurance Co. of Scioto, N. Y. (S. W. Harris, Agt.), 24 e. Front

National Ins. Co. of Cincinnati (John Burgoyne, President), s. w. cor. Main and Front

National Loan Fund Life Assurance So'ty of London (Geo. W. Copelen, Agent), 9 e. Front

National Life Ins. Co. of Montpelier, Vermont (R. Stewart & Son, Agents), 16 e. Front

New York City Ins. Co. (R. Stewart & Son, Agents), 16 e. Front

Northern Protection Ins. Co. of Camden, N. Y. (T. D. Dobbs, Agent) 8 Main

New York Life Ins. Co. of N. Y. (A. S. Chew, Agent), 14 e. Front

Odd Fellows' Mutual Ins. Co. of Phila. (W. H. Wright, Agent) 8 Main

Ohio Life Ins. Co. of Cincinnati (E. S. Haines, President), 55 w. 3d

Ohio Life Ins. & Trust Co. of Cincinnati (Charles Stetson, President), s. w. cor. 3d and Main

Portage County Mutual Fire Ins. Co. (Jno. B. Moody, Agent), 262 Main *Cincinnati.*

Protection Ins. Co. of Hartford, Conn. (W. B. Robbins, Agent), 6 e. Front

Providence Washington Ins. Co. R. I. (W. T. Phipps, Agent), 4 College Building

Rochester Fire Ins. Co. N. Y. (R. Stewart & Son, Agents), 16 e. Front

Saratoga Ins. Co. N. Y. (Francis Ferry, Agent), 19 e. Front

State Mutual Fire Ins. Co. of Harrisburg, Pa. (G. W. Copelen, Agent), 9 e. Front

The Royal Fire & Life Ins. Co. of Liverpool & London (Dr. J. S. Law, Agt.), cor. 3d & Sycamore.

U. S. Life Ins. Annuity & Trust Co. of Philadelphia (M. L. Knapp, Agent), 30 Third

U. S. Life Ins. Co. of City of New York (Francis Ferry, Agent), 19 e. Fourth

Washington Union Ins. Co. of Cleveland, O. (A. Hichenlooper, Agent), Reeder's Buildings

Western Mass. Ins. Co. of Pittsfield, Mass. (Francis Ferry, Agent), 19 e. Fourth

Western Farmers' Ins. Co. (S. W. Harris, Agent), 24 e. 4th

Washington Fire Ins. Co. of N. Y. City (W. H. Wright, Agent), 8 Main

Harrison County.

Kentucky Mutual Life Ins. Co. (B. W. Phillips, Agent), *Cadiz.*

Ohio Life Ins. Co. (Thomas. C. Bowles, Agent),

Ohio Life Ins. & Trust Co. (Chauncey Dewey, Agent).

Hartford Ins. Co. of Hartford, Conn. (B. W. Phillips, Agent),

Highland County.

Knox Mutual Ins. Co. of Mt. Vernon, O., (James Brown, Agent), *Hillsboro'.*

Franklin Fire Ins. Co. of Saratoga Springs, N. Y., (James Brown, Agent),

Ætna Ins. Co. of Hartford, Conn., (James Brown, Agent),

Huron County.

Hartford Life & Health Ins. Co. of Hartford, Conn., (J. Keuman, Agent), *Norwalk.*

Washington Life Ins. Co. of Cincinnati, O., (G. T. Stewart, Agent),

Portage Ins. Co. of Cuyahoga Falls, O., (John H. Foster, Agent),

Jefferson County.

Jefferson Life Ins. Co. of Cincinnati O., (James Elliot, Agent), *Steubenville.*

American Life & Health Ins. Co., (T. Thompson, Agent),

Jefferson Life Ins. Co., (G. M. Mason, Agent),

Ashland County Mutual Ins. Co., (J. R. Worrell, Agent),

Ætna Ins. Co. of Hartford, Conn., (M. Andrews, Agent),   *Steubenville.*
Protection Ins. Co. of Hartford, Conn., (E. H. McFeely, Agent),

Knox County.

Knox County Mutual Ins. Co., (Wm. Turner, Agent),   *Mt. Vernon.*
Protection Ins. Co. of Hartford, (W. H. Smith, Agent),
Kentucky Mutual Life Ins. Co., (W. H. Smith, Agent),
Ætna Fire Ins. Co. of Hartford, (S. S. Davis, Agent),
New England Mutual Life Ins. Co. of Boston, (Jas. Muenscher, Agent),
Knox County Mutual Ins. Co., (Philo Doolittle, Agent),   *Fredericktown.*
Ashland County Mutual Ins. Co., (Philo Doolittle, Agent),
Zanesville Mutual Ins. Co., (Philo Doolittle, Agent),

Lake County.

Protection Ins. Co. of Hartford, Conn., (Wm. L. Perkins, Agent),   *Painesville.*
Jefferson Life Ins. Co. of Cincinnati, O., (J. G. Moore, Agent),

Lawrence County.

Jefferson Life Ins. Co. of Cincin., (W. W. Johnson, Agent),   *Ironton.*
Protection Ins. Co. of Hartford, (H. S. Neal, Agent),

Licking County.

Grand Life Ins. Annuity & Trust Co., (J. Buckingham, Agent),   *Newark.*
Mutual Benefit Life Ins. Co. of Newark, N. J., (J. Buckingham, Agent),
Mutual Life Ins. Co. of N. York, (J. Buckingham, Agent),
Ætna Life Ins. Co. of Hartford, Conn., (H. B. Ten Eyck, Agent),
Girard Life Ins., Annuity & Trust Co., P'delphia, Pa., (J. Buckingham, Agent),
Ætna Fire Ins. Co. of Hartford, Conn., (H. B. Ten Eyck, Agent),
Hartford Fire Ins. Co. of Hartford, Conn., (H. B. Ten Eyck, Agent),
Ætna Fire Ins. Co. of Utica, N. York, (H. B. Ten Eyck, Agent),
Franklin Fire & Marine Ins. Co., Saratoga Springs, (H. B. Ten Eyck, Agent),
Protection Ins. Co. of Hartford, Conn., (T. H. Woodbridge, Agent),

Lorain County.

Protection Ins. Co. of Hartford, Conn., (S. Bagg, Agent),   *Elyria.*

Lucas County.

Equitable Fire Ins. Co. of London, (A. G. Clark, Agent)   *Toledo.*
New York City Fire & Marine Ins. Co., (A. G. Clark, Agent)
Rochester Fire Ins. Co., (A. G. Clark, Agent),
U. S. Fire Ins. Co. of West Potsdam, N. Y., (A. G. Clark, Agent),

American Mutual Marine & Fire Ins. Co. of Amsterdam, N. York, (A. G. Clark, Agent),   *Toledo.*
Starke County Mutual Fire Ins. Co. of Canton, O., (A. G. Clark, Agent),
National Loan Fund Life Assurance Soc. of London, (A. G. Clark, Agent),
Connecticut Mutual Life Ins. Co. of Hartford, Conn., (A. G. Clark, Agent),
Berkshire County Mutual Life Ins. Co., of Pittsfield, Mass., (A. G. Clark, Agent),
Washington Life Ins. Co. of Cincin. O., (A. G. Clark, Agent),
Washington Union Marine & Fire Ins. Co. of Cleveland, O., (Baker & Latimer, Agents),
American Fire & Marine Ins. Co. of Utica, N. Y., (Baker & Latimer, Agents),
Hudson River Marine & Fire Ins. Co. of Crescent, N. York, (Baker & Latimer, Agents),
Knickerbocker Fire Ins. Co. of Waterford, N. Y., (Baker & Latimer, Agents),
American Mutual Marine & Fire Ins. Co. of Amsterdam, N. Y., (Baker & Latimer, Agents),
Mercantile Mutual Marine Ins. Co. of N. Y. City, (Baker & Latimer, Agents),
New York Mutual Marine Ins. Co. of N. Y. City, (Baker & Latimer, Agents),
General Mutual Marine Ins. Co. of N. Y. City, (Baker & Latimer, Agents),
Union Mutual Marine Ins. Co. of N. Y. City, (Baker & Latimer, Agents),
Connecticut Mutual Life Ins. Co. of Hartford, Conn., (Baker & Latimer, Agents),
Hartford Fire Ins. Co. of Hartford, Conn., (Baker & Latimer, Agents),
Eagle Life Ins. Co. of N. Y. City, (Baker & Latimer, Agents),
Union Mutual Life Ins. Co. of Boston, Mass., (Baker & Latimer, Agents),
New York State Mutual Ins. Co., (E. Bissell, Jr., Agent),
Portage Mutual Fire Ins. Co., (E. Bissell, Jr., Agent),
Franklin Marine & Fire Ins. Co. of N. Y., (Bennett & Nye, Agents),
Ætna Ins. Co. of Hartford, Conn., (Henry E. Eagle, Agent),
North Western Ins. Co. of Oswego, N. Y., (Henry E. Eagle, Agent),
Eagle Ins. Co., of Cincinnati, O., (H. H. Dodd, Agent),

Mahoning County.

Protection Ins. Co. of Hartford, Conn., (John H. King, Agent),   *Canfield.*
Fraternal Mutual Life Ins. Co. of Cincin., (M. Cullation, Agent),   *Youngstown.*

Medina County.

Ohio Farmers' Ins. Co., (B. D. Austin, Agent),   *Leroy.*
New England Live Stock Ins. Co., (H. G. Blake, Agent),   *Medina.*

Miami County.

Franklin Fire Ins. Co. of Saratoga Springs, N. Y., (H. S. Wood, Agent), *Piqua.*
Ashland Mutual Ins. Co., (J. M. Ewing, Agent),
Ætna Ins. Co. of Hartford, (D. Alexander, Agent),
Hartford Fire Ins. Co., (D. Alexander, Agent),

Montgomery County.

Dayton Ins. Co., (Danl. Beckley, Prest.), *Dayton.*

Muskingum County.

Ætna Ins. Co. of Hartford Conn., (Joseph Crosby, Agent), *Zanesville.*
Franklin Marine & Fire Ins. Co. of N. Y., (Bennett & Eaton, Agents),
Hudson River Marine & Fire Ins. Co., (A. W. Perle, Agent),
State Mutual Fire Ins. Co. of Harrisburg, Penn., (J. & J. Crosby, Agents),
Ætna Ins. Co. of Hartford, Conn., (J. & J. Crosby, Agents),
Hartford Fire Ins. Co. of Hartford, Conn., (Isaac Dillon, Agent),

Pickaway County.

Protection Ins. Co. of Hartford, (O. Ballard, Agent), *Circleville.*

Portage County.

Farmers' Mutual Ins. Co. of Portage County, (H. Smith, Agent), *Ravenna.*

Preble County.

Preble County Mutual Fire Ins. Co., (Saml. Collins, Agent), *Camden.*

Richland County.

Starke County Mutual Fire Ins. Co., (Wm. Johnston, Agent), *Mansfield.*
Ohio Life Ins. Co., (Wm. Johnston, Ag't),
Hartford Life Ins. Co., (Wm. Johnston, Agent),
Protection Ins. Co., (D. B. Young, Agent),
Portage Mutual Ins. Co., (D. B. Young, Agent),
Charter Oak Life Ins. Co. of Hartford, (D. H. Young, Agent),
Summit Mutual Ins. Co., (D. A. McQuin, Agent), *Lexington.*
Knox County Mutual Ins. Co., (D. A. McQuin, Agent),
Summit County Mutual Ins. Co., (D. A. McQuin, Agent),
Washington Union Ins. Co., (J. Morrow, Agent), *Belleville.*
Western Reserve Mutual Ins. Co., (Joel Walker, Agent),
Ashland Mutual Ins. Co., (O. Howard, Agent),

Ross County.

National Life Insurance Co. of the U. S., Montpelier, Vermont, (W. H. Safford, Agent) *Chillicothe.*
Eagle Ins. Co., (T. F. Waddel, Agent)
New York City Ins. Co., (Edward Lewis, Agent)
Protection Ins. Co., of Hartford, Conn., (D. A. Schutte, Agent)
Ætna Ins. Co., of Hartford, Conn., (H. M. Pinto, Agent)
Hudson River Ins. Co., of New York, (H. M. Pinto, Agent)
Franklin Ins. Co. of New York, (H. M. Pinto, Agent)
Portage Mutual Fire Ins. Co., (W. H. Safford, Agent)
Summit Ins. Co., (C. W. Gilmore, Agent)

Scioto County.

Kentucky Mutual Life Ins. Co., (L. G. Terry, Agent) *Portsmouth.*
City Fire & Marine Ins. Co., (S. R. Ross, Agent)
Protection Ins. Co., Hartford, (Jas. Lodwick, Agent)
Franklin Ins. Co., (J. McDowell, Agent)
Ætna Ins. Co., Hartford, (Thos. Dugan, Agent)
Granite Ins. Co. of Utica, N. Y., (S. R. Ross, Agent)

Seneca County.

Seneca Mutual Fire Ins. Co. . *Tiffin.*

Summit County.

Portage Mutual Fire Ins. Co., (E. N. Sill, Agent) *Akron.*

Washington County.

Portage Mutual Fire Ins. Co., (Robert Crawford, Agent) *Marietta.*
Ætna Fire & Marine Ins. Co., (W. S. Nye, Agent)
Hartford Fire Ins. Co. of Hartford, Conn., (W. S. Nye, Agent)
Charter Oak Fire Ins. Co., (L. Temple, Agent)
N. York City Fire & Marine Ins. Co., (L. Temple, Agent)
Hudson River Fire & Marine Ins. Co., (L. Temple, Agent)
Franklin Fire and Marine Ins. Co., (L. Temple, Agent)
Rensellaer Fire & Marine Ins. Co., (L Temple, Agent)
American Mutual Fire & Marine Ins. Co., (L. Temple, Agent)
Washington County Mutual Fire Ins. Co. (L. Temple, Agent)
Mutual Life Ins. Co., (S. Shipman, Agent)
Connecticut Mutual Life Ins. Co., (W. S. Nye, Agent)

Wayne County.

Northern Protection Fire & Marine Ins.
Co., Camden, New York, (S. R. Bone-
witz, Agent)   *Wooster.*
Rensellaer Fire Ins. Co. of Lansingburg,
N. Y, (S. R. Bonewitz, Agent)
Medina County Fire Ins. Co. of Medina, O.
(S. R. Bonewitz, Agent)
Western Farmers' Ins. Co. of New Lisbon,
O., (S. R. Bonewitz, Agent)
Cleveland Mutual Fire Ins. Co. of Cleve-
land, O., (Foreman & Johnson, Agents)
Summit County Mutual Fire Ins. Co.,
(Foreman & Johnson, Agents)
Western Reserve Farmers' Ins. Co., Paines-
ville, O., (Foreman & Johnson, Agents)
Mutual Benefit Life Ins. Co. of Newark,
N. J., (S. R. Bonewitz, Agent)
Massachusetts Mutual Life Ins. Co. of
Boston, Mass., (S. R Bonewitz, Agent)
Ætna Life Ins. Co. of Hartford, Conn., (S.
R. Bonewitz, Agent)
American Temperance Life Ins. Co. of
Hartford, Conn., (Foreman & Johnson,
Agents)
Ohio Life Ins. Co. of Cincinnati, O., (Fore-
man & Johnson, Agents)
Eagle Life & Health Ins. Co. of Jersey
city, N. J., (Foreman & Johnson, Agts.)
Connecticut Mutual Life Ins. Co. of Hart-
ford, (Foreman & Johnson, Agents)
Pennsylvania Live Stock Ins. Co. of Pitts-
burgh, (Foreman & Johnson, Agents)
New England Live Stock Ins. Co. N.
Haven, Conn., (S. R. Bonewitz, Agent)

Wood County.

Protection Ins. Co. of Hartford, Conn., (J.
A. Hall, Agent)   *Perrysburg.*
Seneca County Mutual Ins. Co., (A. D.
Wright, Agent)

Iron Fence, and Railing Manufacturers.

Hamilton County.

Baker T. F., 275 w. 5th   *Cincinnati.*
Taylor E. & Co., 275 do
Horton & Macy, 210 and 212 Fifth
Wheeler, Hessle & Magness, Western Row
bet. Laurel & Wade
Horton & Co., 86 Race

Iron Furnaces.

Erie County.

Butman J.   *Milan.*
Burt G.

Gallia County.

Bentley, Campbell & Co. *Gallia Furnace.*
O'Leary & Hartma   *Swan Creek.*

Hardin County.

Bloom E.   *Kenton.*

Hocking County.

Dum J. & Co.   *Logan.*
Dille, Brice & Moore   *Pattonsville.*

Huron County.

Foot Marcus   *North Fairfield.*

Jackson County

Jackson Furnace Co.   *Jackson Furnace.*

Lawrence County.

Campbell. Griswold & Co.   *Coalgrove.*
Kelly Wm. D. & Bro.
Sinton & Means   *Hanging Rock.*
Hamilton, Peebles & Co.
Hamilton Robert B.   *Ironton.*
Culbertson. Means & Co.
Dempsey, Rodgers & Ellison
Dempsey & Co.
Campbell. Ellison & Co.   *Campbell's.*
Seeley, Willard & Co.
Peters J. & Co.

Lake County.

Geauga Furnace Co.   *Painesville.*

Mahoning County.

Wilkeson, Wilks & Co.   *Lowellville.*
Ward, Rice & Co.   *Youngstown.*
Crawford, Morris & Co.
Wood, James & Co

Muskingum County.

Palmer J. E. & Co.   *Zanesville.*

Scioto County.

Campbell, Woodrow & Co.   *Lyra.*
Glidden, Crawford & Co.
Glidden, Murphan & Co.
Cole A. & Co.   *Iron Furnaces.*
Robinson, Glidden & Co.
Eifort H. & S. & Co.   *Sciotoville.*

Trumbull County.

Boardman & Reed   *Newton Falls.*

Iron Manufacturers.

Cuyahoga County.

Spang & Co., 204 River   *Cleveland.*

Hamilton County.

Morrell, Shoemaker & Co., 64 Second
                              Cincinnati.
Patterson N., 13 Public Landing
Phillips & Jordan, 58 and 60 Columbia
Shreve, Steele & Co., cor. Broadway and
Columbia
Worthington & Co., 24 Main
Wolf D., Congress w. of Ludlow

Trumbull County.

Ward James & Co.   *Niles'*
Robeson, Battles & Grist

Iron and Steel Dealers.

Brown County.

Culter, Evans & Co.   *Ripley.*
Debolt J.

Butler County.

Jacoby David   *Rossville.*
Young W. S.   *Middletown.*

Cuyahoga County. ✓

Bingham W. & Co., Superior st., *Cleveland.*
Cary W. F., 96, 97 Dock, 187, 189 River
Clark James F., 4 Superior
Crawford & Reynolds, do
Morley & Raynolds, 8 do
Spang & Co., 204 River

Erie County. ✓

Daniels & Co.   *Sandusky City.*
Whitney J. D. & Co.

Franklin County. ✓

Gere & Abbott, High street, *Columbus.*
Hayden & Baker, Broad
Kilbourne & Kuhns, do
McCune J. M. & Co., do

Geauga County. ✓

Wilber Wm.   *Chardon.*

Greene County.

Carey H. & W. T.   *Xenia.*
McAlpin Henry
Syfers Jacob   *Jamestown.*

Hamilton County.

Cramer & Watson, n. e. cor. W. Row and
    Court streets,   *Cincinnati.*
Monell, Shoemaker & Co., 64 2d
Mitchell & Brother, 395 Main
Neave & Free, 33   do
Patterson N., 13 Public Landing
Phillips & Jorden, 58 and 60 Columbia
Potts J. H., n. w. cor. Walnut and Front
Shoenberger G. & J. H., 15 Front
Shreve, Steele & Co., cor. Broadway and
    Columbia
Worthington & Co., 24 Main
Wenning H. N., 360   do
Wolf D., 379   do

Hancock County. ✓

Spinning & Stansberry   *Finlay.*
Lamb David

Highland County.

Humelly W. C. & Johnson   *Lynchburg.*

Knox County. ✓

McCormick John   *Mount Vernon.*
Minteer John   *Democracy.*
Minteer Wm. M.

Madison County.

McMillan & Webster   *London.*

Miami County.

Fahnestock Jas.   *Covington.*

Montgomery County. ✓

Brown E. & Son, Head Basin   *Dayton.*
Stout D., 3d

Pickaway County. ✓

Groom J. C. & Co.   *Circleville.*

Portage County. ✓

Richardson E. T.   *Ravenna.*
Prentiss C. & J. C.

Preble County. ✓

Marsh & Lockwood   *Eaton.*
Rinehart Perry

Richland County. ✓

Lee J. C.   *Belleville.*

Ross County. ✓

Shutte D. A.   *Chillicothe.*

Shelby County. ✓

Edgar D. & J.   *Sidney.*
Johnston James

Summit County. ✓

Collins C. A.   *Akron.*

Tuscarawas County.

Roby H.   *Rockford.*

Warren County.

Butler Chas. & Co.   *Franklin.*

Wayne County.

Kauke John H.   *Wooster.*

Japanned Cloth, Muslin, Silk & Leather Manufacturers.

Hamilton County.

Heath & Searing, 234 Main   *Cincinnati.*

Japanned Ware Manufacturers.

Hamilton County.

Winchell J. D., cor. Pearl and Walnut
    Cincinnati.

Lamps, Chandeliers, & Burning Fluid Dealers.

Hamilton County.

Starr Chas., Jr. & Co., 165 Walnut *Cincin.*
Baker & Von Phul, 160 Main
Coats Paxson, 6 College Building
Greenough B. F., 46 w. 5th
King & Fairbanks, 103 do

Lard Oil Manufacturers.

Cuyahoga County.

Outhwaite & Blackwell, cor. St. Clair and
　Water　　　　　　　　　*Cleveland.*
Stanley George A., Canal near Weigh Lock

Franklin County.

Buttles, Comstock & Co., Head of Canal,
　　　　　　　　　　　　Columbus.
Fraser D. & Co., Buckeye Block

Geauga County.

Randall, Cook & Co.,　　　　*Chardon.*

Hamilton County.

Skiff J. A., 17 Walnut　　　*Cincinnati.*
Frank F., 19 e. Front
Cheever A. G. & Co., Lock, bet. 3d and 5th
Nye J. O., 21 Canal
Gooch Henry, 130 Columbia
Mitchener J. L. & Co., cor. Plum & Canal
Peebles & Brother, 177 Canal
Wright D. W., 11　　do
Fellow & Armstrong, 61 do
Clark G., 11 Buckeye
Hust J. & Sons, 16 Locust
Bogen G. & P., near Brighton
Meyer F. W., 15 Buckeye

Montgomery County.

Pierce J. H., Canal　　　　*Dayton.*
Stevens John, Main

Muskingum County.

Convers Theodore　　　　*Zanesville.*

Last Makers.

Allen County.

Moore Samuel　　　　*Westminster.*

Hamilton County.

Muhle J. F., 90 Clay　　　*Cincinnati.*

Montgomery County.

Craford O. H. & J., Canal　*Dayton.*

Muskingum County.

Mann S. S. & Co.　　　*Zanesville.*

Warren County.

Jones Jonathan　　　　*Waynesville.*

Lath Manufacturers.

Lorain County.

Ensworth O.　　　　　*Copopa.*

Morrow County.

Nutt & Conklin　　　*Cardington.*

Richland County.

Squire J. D.　　　　*Richland.*

Seneca County.

Foster Charles ·　　　　*Adrian.*

Lead Pipe and Sheet Lead Manufacturers.

Hamilton County.

Worthington & Co., 24 Main　*Cincinnati.*

Lightning Rod (Patent) Manufacturers.

Hamilton County.

Porter A. C., 29 w. Sixth　*Cincinnati.*
Williams Charles　　　　*Springvale.*

Starke County.

Borland John　　　*West Brookfield.*

Lime and Cement Dealers.

Cuyahoga County.

Barrett O. & Co., Merwin　*Cleveland.*
Bradburn O. & Son, 67 River
Clark & Calkins, Canal
Hubby, Hughes & Co.
Rawson L. & Co., near R. R. Depot
Johnson Rowland, Canal

Hamilton County.

Freeman Thomas, 2d bet. Plum & W. Row
　　　　　　　　　　　　Cincinnati.
Marsh & Co., s. w. cor. 4th and Sycamore
McGlincey H., W. Row above 9th
Moore Wm. B., 263 Plum

Lake County.

Hall J. R.　　　　　*Painesville.*
Morrell M.

Portage County.

Kneeland Giles　　　　*Freedom.*
Isbell R.
Dennison E.
Sturtivant O.

Richland County.

Granger W. S.　　　　*Mansfield.*

Linseed Oil Manufacturers.

Ashland County.

Drumb A. & W.　　　　*Ashland.*

Ashtabula County.

Sadd G. F.　　　　*Austinburg.*

Clark County.

Barnet James　　　*Springfield.*
Smith & Boucher

Columbiana County.

Farmer James　　　　*Salineville.*

Erie County.

Meny E.　　　　　*Milan.*

Franklin County.

Yage Frederick　　*Canal Winchester.*

Greene County.

Daugherty M.   *Spring Valley.*

Hamilton County.

McLean & Goodman, cor. Symmes & M.
Canal   *Cincinnati.*

Knox County.

Walters Mahlon   *Levering.*
Pratt J. B.   *Mount Vernon.*

Mahoning County.

Morse H. K.   *Poland.*
Tod J. J.   *Milton.*

Miami County.

Kelly & Field S. & B.   *West Milton.*

Montgomery County.

Harshman & Brothers   *Harshmansville.*
Harris William
Estabrook W., Fifth   *Dayton.*
Gebhart S. & Co., Third
Keifer & Conover, Second
Parrot Thomas, Canal
Cassady & Stewart   *Miamisburgh.*

Muskingum County.

Pratt John R.   *Zanesville.*

Richland County.

Carter Samuel   *Lexington.*

Starke County.

Ware & Logue   *Limaville.*

Summit County.

Bradley L. & Co.   *Cuyahoga Falls.*
Prentiss O.

Trumbull County.

Griswold G. O.   *Warren.*

Tuscarawas County.

Blickensteffer A.   *New Philadelphia.*

Lithographers.

Cuyahoga County.

Brainard & Burridge, Herald Block
     Cleveland.

Hamilton County.

Fleetwood & Son, 200 Walnut   *Cincinnati.*
Mosler G., 177 w. Fifth
Middleton & Wallace, 115 Walnut
Onken Otto, 6th bet. Vine & Race
Anderson Walter, cor. Race & Fourth
Gibson Geo. & Co., 101 Main
Klauprecht & Mensel, s. w. cor. Vine and
  Fifth
McBriar Archibald, 3d opp. O. L. & Trust
  Bank

Live Stock Dealers.

Adams County.

Wilkins E. E.   *Scott.*
Raughley Wm.

Thomas Silas   *Scott.*
Snediker A. R.
Ried W.   *Marble Furnace.*
Sumner J. F.
Gaw E. P. & J. G.   *Lovett's.*
Fulton H.
Hughs P.
Clark P.
Reid G.
Taylor John   *Locust Grove.*
Leedam A.
Fritz A.
George W.
Tener G. P.
McIntyre A.

Allen County.

Getsell M.   *Herring.*
Turner D.   *Dennell's.*

Ashland County.

Beach D. B.   *Ruggles,*
Beach C. S.
Shepard L. A.

Belmont County.

Arrick & Woodmansee   *Saint Clairsville.*
Booker S. F.
Buley S. & C.
Frasier Wm.
Hazlewood Wm.
McMonies Saml.

Butler County.

Elliott Jas. M.   *Darrtown.*
Snyder Philip   *Monroe.*
Fitzgerald P.
Shepard George

Carroll County.

Arbuckle George   *Malvern.*

Clark County.

Baker P. E.   *New Carlisle,*
Cory L. O.
Cory A. H.
Cramer Joseph
Reyburn W. S.
Stafford George J.
Taylor Abijah
Wilson Erastus

Clermont County.

McKeever John D.   *Withamsville.*
Fatman Benjamin
Temple Nathaniel
Bradbury Thos.
McMurchy James   *Bantam.*
Slade Powel
Henderson Wm.
Whitmire A.
Simmons J. R. H.   *Laurel.*

Columbiana County.

Hasson Jonah   *East Palestine.*
Hays John
King E.   *Unity.*

Coshocton County.

Day Stephen   *Tiverton.*
Ravenscroft Wash   *Chili.*
Ringer Joseph
Winkleplecht George
Winkleplecht Jacob
Winkleplecht David
Rodehaver David   *Walhonding.*

Crawford County.

Bebout A.   *Leesville Cross Roads.*
Chambers John A.
Corbit A.
Whitaker Amos
Wiley James
Kirk Samuel   *Bucyrus.*
McLean James
Ward C. K.

Cuyahoga County.

Tousley Wm.   *North Royalton.*
Dunlan Henry   *Brecksville.*
Cooly O.   *Warrensville.*
Gleason L.
Judd O. B.
Welton F.
Brown A. & Co., near R. R. Depot
                                  Cleveland.

Erie County.

Baker J. B.   *Florence.*
Scott L. R.

Fairfield County.

Wylie John   *Amanda.*
Gill John   *Millersport.*
Gill N.
Turner H.
Pearse J. W.
Ketner J.
Olick J.
Fall J.
Cupp V.
Holmes Rezin
Haver Wm.

Franklin County.

Grinnall Wm. H.   *Blendon.*
Grinnall Darwin C.
Phelps Timothy
Phelps P. R.
Thompson & Smiley   *Dublin.*
Brown James
Blue J. W.   *Lockbourn.*
Williams A. K.
Williams Benj.
Williams David
Clark John   *Gahanna.*

Greene County.

Clemens Geo. C.   *New Jasper.*
Levally Wm.
Moore D. D.
Smith James
Thornburg Josiah
Thornburg Joel, Jr.

Folck Bennawell   .   *Byron.*
Routsong John
Ary John   *Paintersville.*
Ary Wm.

Hamilton County.

Calvin R. T.   *Harrison.*
Purcell Thos.

Harrison County.

Welch Rezin   *Cadiz.*
Slemmons Saml.
Moffitt Fulton   *Cold Spring.*
McClarry Ephraim   *Harrisville.*

Hocking County.

Ferne Wm. H.   *Gibsonville.*
Whitcroft Wm.

Logan County.

Edmiston M. S.   *Huntsville.*
Shafer H.

Monroe County.

Clingan John   *Woodfield.*
Kerr John
Neal Isaac N.
Okey John
Okey Woodman
Myers Wm.   *Laing's.*
Barnes C. J.   *Malaga.*
Beardmore Wm.
Beardmore Isaac
Weaver Geo.

Morrow County.

Davis Wm.   *Marengo.*
Doty S. & M.
Johnson Jesse
Noe Wm.
Kreps Wm.   *Woodview.*
Stilts P. N.
Gardner J. L.   *Lincoln.*
Heald Joseph
Heald Joel
Hoffmire Luther
Hoffmire Samuel
Mosher D. W.
Stanley Robert
Starr Timothy
Wood Jonathan
Allison Obadiah   *Vail's Cross Roads.*
Vail B. T.
Turney A. T.
Morris M. T.
Kees Samuel

Noble County.

Burton Joseph   *Kennensburgh.*
Kernet Adam
Ward Edward
Millhore Benj.
Law Robert
Johnson Wm.
Ward John
DePugh Abraham

Cohen Richard   *Kennensburgh.*
Ward William
Kugler Joseph S.
Ward John S.
Johnson Barnet

Pickaway County.

Gamble Samuel   *Darbyville.*
Trego Josiah
Foust Joseph   *Camp Charlotte.*
Halderman George
Winship T. J.

Starke County.

Barber & Oldfield   *Canton.*
Dewalt Daniel
Patterson E. C.
Shorb John S.
Imbaden Jacob   *East Greenville.*
Kanagg John M.

Summit County.

Clay D.   *Inland.*
Babcock L.   *Montross.*
Loomis M.

Trumbull County.

Walker R. H.   *Church Hill.*
Kline Peter
Kline Zenas
Early John
Powers Madison
Powers Wesley
Higgins Wm. H.   *Farmington.*
Loveland R.
Wolcott O. L.
Wolcott T. S.
Wolcott Newton
Wolcott S. H.
Colton U. T.
Goff A. A.
Belden O. H.
Toft Chauncey
Clark A.
Lee Thomas
Waters B. T.
Caldwell James
Campbell Thomas   *Ohltown.*
White John

Tuscarawas County.

Black G. B.   *New Philadelphia.*
Judy D.
Peppers J.

Union County.

Cahill John E.   *Wilkins*
Miller J. G. & J. C.
Newman George W.   *Milford Centre.*
Watson David

Livery Stables.

Ashland County.

Lewis Amos   *Ashland.*

Ashtabula County.

Darkee S. K.   *Ashtabula.*
Fuller Joseph

Belmont County.

Lewis Samuel   *Saint Clairsville.*
Norton John K.

Brown County.

Fulton A.   *Ripley.*

Butler County.

Hazletine & Bonney   *Oxford.*
McCullough Thos.
Harrow J.   *Hamilton.*
Johnson H.
Currie J.
Boatman J.   *Rossville.*

Champaign County.

Van Antwerp D.   *Urbana.*

Clarke County.

Lapp B.   *Springfield.*
Cathgard Joseph
Taylor Abijah   *New Carlisle.*
Weakley R. S.

Columbiana County.

Grafton Thomas   *Wellsville.*
Rowley Theodore   *New Lisbon.*
Watson Franklin W.
Williams Jacob B.

Coshocton County.

Burt Thomas H.   *Coshocton.*

Crawford County.

Kent N.   *Bucyrus.*
Peterman S.

Cuyahoga County.

Adams William K., Superior   *Cleveland.*
Darling S. R., James
Jones John, 77 Public Square
Wells William, 53 Champlain
Folson G. B.   *Ohio City.*
McLean Alexander
Sheldon William B., Detroit
Briggs G. R., Pearl

Darke County.

Hutchins O.   *Greenville.*
Long O. H.

Defiance County.

Whitney Luke   *Defiance.*

Erie County.

Smith W.   *Sandusky City.*
Porter Daniel
Houch H.
Lee & Boylan   *Milan.*
Daniels S.
Hongsinger F.

Franklin County.

Armstrong J. & H.   *Columbus.*

Bagshaw John   *Columbus.*
Bires How
Blake & Williams
Broadrick & Sons
Cadwallader T.
Fairfield & Barker
Mitchell Thos.
Massey Joseph
Taylor Thomas
Worthington A. & S.
Zollinger & Thompson
Kathaway A.   *Canal Winchester.*
Leathers Daniel

Greene County.

Kealhofer H.   *Xenia.*
Webster & Smith
Worden J.

Hamilton County.

Arstingstall G. A., 114 Sycamore *Cincin.*
Brown Geo. & Co., 7 e. 6th
Brown & Brother, cor. Vine and Pearl
Bradley Geo., 214 w. 7th
Buckingham J., 348 W. Row
Bard S. W., s. w. cor. John and Everett
Bohrer G. A. & Co., 506 Elm
Clark Wm. M., 7th near Main
Outter A. 78 6th
Cresin Geo., 216 w. 7th
Cisle T. J., 341 w. 6th
Dickman & Stiens, 627 Race
Frazier Thos., 95 2d
Henry J. & B., 154 Hopkins
Hoffman Wm., 203 W. Row
Hust & Co., 18 Locust
Johnson Isaac D., Walnut bet. 8th and 9th
Leary L. G., 179 Vine
Mors J. A., Hopkins near Linn
Moffatt M., 222 W. Row bet. 6th & Long-
   worth
Mundy & Chambers, 177 w. 6th
Riclag & Schutz, 94 Hunt
Riley D. & P., 6th bet. Main & Syc.
Ruttermiller J., 31 Court
Stegner & Co., Elm bet. 15th and Liberty
Sweeney E., 85 5th
Shepherdson C., Race bet 5th & Centre
Wilson & Brothers, 303 Sycamore
Wood W., cor. Race and Centre
Wood Geo., Race near 5th
Kolb Geo.,   *Harrison.*
Morgan Clark W.

Hardin County.

Kyle James   *Kenton.*
Farrant & Neff

Harrison County.

Houser Wm. L.   *Cadis.*
Howard Joshua & John

Huron County.

Pantlind & McCollough   *Norwalk.*
Jones & Beckwith
Stevens D. S.   *North Fairfield.*

Jefferson County.

Peters R. C.   *Steubenville.*
Repine & Leach
Sharps B. M.
Stoneypher E.
Frye & Dungan
Nichols J.

Knox County.

Bennet Clark L.   *Mount Vernon.*
Coombs William
Crouse George
Rigby W. H.   *Fredericktown.*

Lake County.

Kingsbury H. D. & Co.   *Painesville.*
Stockwell B.
Loomis N.

Licking County.

Shmucker Andrew   *Newark.*
Merchant L.

Lorain County.

Broadwell S.   *Elyria.*
Harkness & Nichols
Mason O. L.

Lucas County.

Cummings D.   *Maumee City.*
Eggleston D.
Ward James H.
Cole James   *Toledo.*
Cole Frederick
Gates Philander
Warren Samuel

Madison County.

Lohr G. W.   *London.*

Medina County.

Knapp H. J.   *Medina.*
Chidester Wm. R.

Miami County.

Ewen John   *Piqua.*
Brooks H.
Boyer A.   *Troy.*

Montgomery County.

Dille & Young, 3d street,   *Dayton.*
Gilbert G., Jefferson
Gillis J. & J. R., do
Heatman Elias, 5th
Westphal J., 2d
Shelebarger J., Jefferson
Caskey J. M.   *Miamisburgh.*
Huber & Cooke

Morgan County.

Bemis S. G.   *McConnelsville.*
Davis S. H.

Pickaway County.

Green Wm. & John   *Circleville*
Skinner Mrs.

Portage County.

Ward Wm.   *Ravenna.*

Robinson John B.   *Ravenna.*
Collins Hiram
Andros A. R. & Co.   *Franklin.*

Preble County.

Perrett Henry   *Eaton.*
Leas Frank

Richland County.

Rossler H. H.   —   *Mansfield.*
Wise David
Cooley Austin   *Belleville.*

Ross County.

Armstrong Geo.   *Chillicothe.*
Ewing A. & Son
Barlern M.

Sandusky County.

Smith Ira   *Fremont.*
Wood R.

Scioto County.

Mitchell & Macklen   *Portsmouth.*
Terry L. G.
White U.

Seneca County.

Lapham John P.   *Republic.*

Starke County.

Barber & Oldfield   *Canton.*
Shorb John S.

Summit County.

Chapman George   *Tallmadge.*

Tuscarawas County.

Grim S. & Co.   *New Philadelphia.*
Wilson R.
Helwig Benj. F.   *Canal Dover.*
Shatter Levi
Sharp Thomas

Warren County.

Rodgers Wm.   *Waynesville.*

Wayne County.

Howard & Belding   *Wooster.*
Hookey Henry

Wyandot County.

Morrison James   *Upper Sandusky.*
Edgington —,

Livery & Sale Stables.

Hamilton County.

Smith M., s. e. cor. 3d and Vine   *Cincin.*
19

Rider Geo. C., 5th bet. Main & Sycamore
Stevens & Cole, 5th   do   *Cincin.*
Bussing & Carney,   do   do
Brown G. & Bro., 7 6th
Hardestay & Dunham, 5th bet. Main and
    Sycamore
Hanner J., 98 Vine
Jennifer B., 411 Walnut
Uphoff Geo. H., 7th bet. Main & Walnut

Lock Manufacturers.

Clark County.

Shaffer L.   *Springfield.*

Franklin County.

Sites Andrew, Friend   *Columbus.*

Hamilton County.

Pfister & Metzger, 30 w. 6th   *Cincinnati.*
McGregor, Lee & Co., Western Row bet.
    6th and 7th
Gott F., 92 Clinton
Aupperle Alex., Ham. Road bet. Main and
    Walnut
Rohrer Geo. B. & Co., s. w. cor. 5th and
    W. Row
Schroders J. B., 3d bet. Main & Walnut

Montgomery County.

Greaz John, Main   *Dayton.*

Ross County.

Dowell Fred.   *Chillicothe.*
Burgline John

Scioto County.

Houck Charles   *Portsmouth.*

Locksmiths & Bell-Hangers.

Crawford County.

Wagoner M.   *Bucyrus.*

Cuyahoga County.

Farnan Walter, Division   *Cleveland.*
Schwartzenburg J., Seneca

Geauga County.

Munsill Wm. G.   *Chardon.*
Parkman E.   *Parkman.*

Hamilton County.

Pfister & Metzger, 30 w. 6th   *Cincinnati.*
Kinnan Wm., 27 e. 4th
Schroders J. B., 3d bet. Main & Walnut
Lehmann M., 544 Vine
Marten B., 577   do
McGregor, Lee & Co., W. Row bet. 6th &
    7th
Gott F., 92 Clinton
Holisel C., 114 Ham. Road

Logan County.

Patterson Thomas   *Huntsville.*

Portage County.

Forker Israel   *Ravenna.*
Rawson S.

Starke County.

Vernier Lewis   *Louisville.*

Looking-Glass Dealers.

Champaign County.

Moore Wm.   *North Lewisburg.*
Townsend Ross

Clark County.

Pittinger A. & Co.   *New Carlisle.*
Baker, Robinson & Co.

Knox County.

Stephens & Shafer   *Fredericktown.*

Trumbull County.

Bridges J. D.   *Johnsonville.*
Langdon Luther
Tyrrel Sherman

Looking-Glass Manufac-
turers.

Cuyahoga County.

Gardner & Vincent, 48 Water   *Cleveland.*
Jones & Co., 58 Superior
Sargeant Saml., 7 Water

Hamilton County.

Wiswell Wm. Jr., 129 Main   *Cincinnati.*
Blakeslee E., 230   do
Hornblow W., 12 6th
Bonte & Moorhead, 159 Vine
Bown & Hartigan, 16 e. Fourth
Burt & Hollowell, 7 Masonic Row 3d

Lumber Dealers.

Adams County.

Stephenson Wm.   *Manchester.*
McConaughy D. M.
James Wm. M.   *Stout's.*
Abbot James   *Wagoner's Ripple.*
Wyckoff Jesse

Athens County.

Brown F. H. & Co.   *Millfield.*

Auglaize County.

Huive, Clemens & Co.   *Minster.*
Deniston L. H. & Wm.   *Kossuth.*

Belmont County.

Dorsey M. & Co.   *Captina.*

Brown County.

Lowry & Cary   *Ripley.*
Evans D. B.
Culter & Evans
Debolt J.
Keethler Danl.   *Puebla.*

Butler County.

McLean John   *Bethany.*
Holcomb C. B.   *Hamilton.*
Miller & Campbell
Sutphin Joseph   *Middletown.*
Hand J. R.   *Contreras.*
Bake P. H.
Stephenson W. F.

Champaign County.

Hill J. H.   *Urbana.*
Snap J. & Co.   *St. Paris.*
Williams Geo.

Clark County.

Truitt Joshua D.   *South Charleston.*

Clermont County.

Horn John   *New Richmond.*
Dunham John   *Nicholsville.*
Sargent J. A.   *Laurel.*
Bainum & Co.

Columbiana County.

Smith John   *Wellsville.*
Smith A. & W.
Bushoney Benjamin   *Columbiana.*
Harrold Jacob
Morris David
Moyer John
Nicols S.
Pyle Isaac

Coshocton County.

Wolf P. O. & Co.   *Evansburgh.*

Cuyahoga County.

Gates O. S.   *Brooklyn.*
Young C. L.   *Brecksville.*
Lawrence Sidney   *Coe Ridge.*
Rice F. J.
Butts, Kendall & Co., cor. Merwin and
   Division   *Cleveland.*
Buttles A. & Sons, Foot of Superior
Dix J. H. & Co.
Fox S. H. & Co., Head of Merwin
Francisco J., Merwin
Holt J.,   do
Hostetter Charles D., cor. M'win & G'rman
Sanford D. & Son, 540 Merwin
Whipple A. & Son
Hurlbut, Star & Stockwell, River
Crapser M. & Co., River near Main   *Ohio*
Butts F.   [*City.*
Foote & King, Water
Whipple A. & Son, Pine
Buttles A. & Sons

Delaware County.

McCollough D. F.   *Delaware.*
Griffin & Penny

Erie County.

McGookey James   *Venice.*
Lea James D. & Co,   *Sandusky City.*
Chapman W. P.
Gilcher Peter
Hubbard K. B. & Co.
Smith W. F. & Co.
Kline & Coon   *Milan.*
Butman & Reed

Fairfield County.

Bennedum P.   *Lancaster.*
Card W. J.
Carter George

Franklin County.

Cloud E., Friend   *Columbus.*
Field & Adams
Zinn Moses   *Groveport.*
Helpman John   *Canal Winchester.*

Gallia County.

Beauman Joseph   *Anselm.*
Kent Milton
Partridge Wm.
Ralph Obadiah
Fisher H.   *Gallipolis.*

Greene County.

Reed Young   *Xenia.*
Swaney & Scarf

Guernsey County.

Wilkin W. & R.   *Londonderry.*

Hamilton County.

Alexander A. J. & Co., n. w. cor. Walnut
   and Liberty   *Cincinnati.*
Ashcraft Richard, 229 e. Front
Baily, Langstaff & Co., Front bet. Mill &
   Wood
Bonsall S. N. & Co., Freeman opp. George
Bateman & Co., cor. Laurel & W. Row
Carson James & Co., Front bet. Mill and
   Wood
Cline John, 161 e. Front
Conn & Brother, east Front near Water
   Works
Cutler & Dunham, 3d bet. Smith & Park
Crowley A. H. & Co., Front near Gas
   Works
Dexter H. & Co., W. Row bet. 12th and
   Elizabeth
Dunlap Jas. & Co., n. w. cor. Plum & 9th
Dunlap James, Vine above 15th
Fay Anthony, 344 Broadway
Fedders B. Henry, Reading Pike near
   Davis Foundery
Fairchild, Asher & Co., 6th opp. C. H. &
   D. R. R. Depot
Goke H. & Co., W. W. Canal and 3d

Goetz A. & Co., cor. Freeman and Clinton
                                 Cincinnati.
Goetz L., west end Everett
Gregory E. M. & Co., n. w. cor. 8th and
   Plum
Hanna James & Co., cor. Linn & Clinton
Higbee Amasa A., n. e. cor. Elm & Water
Hinkle & Guild, Front bet. Smith & Mill
Johnston, Morton & Co., Front bet. Par-
   sons & Whitaker
Jeffries J. C., Plum bet. 12th and Canal
Kilbreth, DeCamp & Co., cor. 12th and
   Plum, and Elm bet. 15th & Liberty
Kimball, Jenks & Co., Junction 3d and
   Front
Longnorth Wm. T., n. e. cor. W. Row &
   Second
Lightfoot J. S., w. 6th bet. Cutter and
   Baymiller
Lilia F. H. & Co., 527 W. Row
Meier H. W., Ham. Road opp. Race
Mitchell J. & Co., 364 Broadway
Mitchell Jethro, 522 Vine
Morgan T. & Co., 521 Elm
Morgan Hugh, s. w. cor. W. W. Canal &
   Smith
Norris & Townly, 445 Vine
Peel Samuel, n. e. cor. Court & Elm
Pearson Daniel B., Plum bet. Court & 12th
Ross Ezekiel, cor. Canal and Plum
Rattermann Francis, 567 Elm
Smith W. F. & Co., Canal bet. Broadway
   and Sycamore
Stewart, Deming & Co., 3d bet. Smith &
   Park
Solar & Vacox, Front bet. Lawrence and
   Pike
Van Dergrift B. B., 139 Water
Ward Wm. W., cor. West Av. and Har.
   Road
Webb Alexander, cor. Park and 4th
Wolfe Geo. & Co., 493 W. Row
Cook H.   *Columbia.*
Vanwickle N.
Weller S. G. & Co.   *Pendleton.*
Wilson J. & Co.   *Fulton.*
Durrell H. C. & Wm., Jr.   *Walnut Hills.*
Hoffner E. W.   *Mt. Healthy.*

Henry County.

Durbin James   *Texas.*

Jefferson County.

Abraham Wm. C.   *Steubenville.*
Copeland John
McKinney J.
Cable & Patterson

Knox County.

Davis Samuel   *Mt. Vernon.*
Smith Russel

Lake County.

Knight D.   *Fairport.*
Wilcox B. O. & Brothers
Root M. L.
McCormick & Pease

Lawrence County.

Mead O.   *Ironton.*
Jones —,

Licking County.

Whipple & Thompson   *Newark.*
Harrison & Son
Warren D. T.   *Croton.*
Spencer O.
Spencer H.

Lucas County.

Cheesbro' Charles & Co.   *Toledo.*
Hall & Smith
Judson & Judson
Raymond W. H.
Rouse B. W. & Co.
Segur Daniel
Smith & Co.
Walterhouse & Co.
Walbridge & Bakewell
Taylor Alfred

Madison County.

Warner John & Eli   *London.*

Mahoning County.

Tod & Smith   *Milton.*

Medina County.

Bradford E. & G.   *Weymouth.*
Potter Isaac B.

Meigs County.

Mank J.   *Silver Run.*
Branch H.   *Langsville.*
Rathburn & Co.

Montgomery County.

Beckel & Spinning, Head Basin,   *Dayton.*
Burroughs Chas., 5th
Gebhart, Brother & Co., Wayne
Gerst D., 3d
Hoglen Jas. R., 5th
Kimbal L., 2d
Owen George, St. Clair
Huiet & Grove   *Miamisville.*

Morrow County.

Smithson & Brocklesby   *Underwood's.*

Muskingum County.

Clark S.   *Zanesville.*

Paulding County.

Shaffer Elias   *Paulding.*

Pickaway County.

Pedrick T.   *Circleville.*

Portage County.

Hazen Wm.   *Atwater.*

Campbell Saml.   *Atwater.*
Russell C. M.
Merrill Wm.   *Randolph.*
Hine Lewis
Ladd H.
Howard C. R.
Elder Saml.   *Aurora*
Burdick O.   *Streetsboro'.*
Dull Noah   *Paris.*
Davis D. J.   *Edinburgh.*
Whittlesey O.
Hall Smith   *Charleston.*
Bonney John   *Freedom.*
Parris S.
Kent M.   *Franklin.*
Sanford B.   *Rootstown.*
Reed, Otis & Co.
Hazen Wm. P.
Denel R.   *Mantua.*
May D.
White & Blake
Sanford E. & Brother
Tappan F. W.   *Ravenna.*
Abels John

Preble County.

Tomson & Cotterman   *Lewisburg.*

Richland County.

Eminger & Sherman   *Mansfield.*

Ross County.

Lewis M.   *Chillicothe.*
Carlisle W. W. & Co.
Bonser J.

Scioto County.

Boynton, White & Co.   *Haverhill.*
Leet D. & R.   *Portsmouth.*
Lodwick James
Rhodes & Martin

Seneca County.

Taylor George   *Tiffin.*

Starke County.

Myers H. H.   *Canton.*
Prince William & Co.
Snider, Mong & Co.   *Massillon.*

Summit County.

Bradley L. & Co.,   *Cuyahoga Falls.*
Holloway T.
Judd S. E. & Co.   *Hudson.*
Carter H. S.   *Tallmadge.*
Filler Charles   *Copley.*
Isbell J. O.
Noble W. & W. A.

Trumbull County.

Ackley D.   *Hartford.*
Brockway Edward
Parsons D. & J.
Snyder George

Hewet George B.   *Hartford.*
Moffit Augustus

Warren County.

Keys Wm.   *Waynesville.*

Washington County.

Towsley & Lord   *Marietta.*
Hall Frank & Co.

Wayne County.

Black Daniel   *Wooster.*

Lumber Manufacturers.

Adams County.

Bradford & Co,   *Manchester.*
McMillan J. B.   *Gustine.*
Holmes John   *West Union.*

Allen County.

Jones E. B.   *Deep Cut.*
McManus D.
Griffith & Scott   *West Newton.*
Crall D.   *Westminster.*
Goble Doub   *Croghan.*
Stump John
Shoemaker John, Jr.

Belmont County.

Branson Joel   *Flushing.*
Clements James
Cordner John, Sen.
Holloway D.
Hollingsworth John
Wright John
Mack Henry   *St. Clairsville.*
McMillen Ira
Duncan John B.   *Belmont.*
Dillon William
McNichols & Curtis
Lamp George
Simpson Geo. T.

Carroll County.

Vail Lewis   *Malvern.*

Clark County.

Black James   *New Carlisle.*
Brubaker J. & H.
Cable Samuel
Kaplinger Isaac
Lowman George
Pumphrey Joseph
Pence Michael
Stafford William
Staley Elias
Smith D. J.
Sprendell Samuel
Voorhis Daniel P.

Clermont County

Goodwin & Gibson   *Bethel.*
Kugler John   *Milford.*
Moore Wm. & Co.   *Moscow.*
Prescott G.   *Rural.*

Columbiana County.

Smith A. & W.   *Wellsville.*

Coshocton County.

Henderson Wm. H.   *Walhonding.*

Crawford County.

Dickson George   *DeKalb.*
Hounstine Peter   *Lykens.*
Wooster & Longwell   *Poplar.*
Wooster, Longwell & Reynolds
Keller & Guiss   *New Washington.*

Cuyahoga County.

Staunton Merril   *Solon.*
Lawrence Sidney   *Cos Ridge.*
Rice F. J.
Cook Hiram & Co.   *Ohio City.*

Defiance County.

Ayres A. A.   *Defiance.*
Bottenberg A.
Deihl, Hepper & Co.
Hopkins E.
Paige C.
Richardson J.
Stevens & Rider
Wisenberger M.
Bell & Peterson   *Ayersville.*
Hilton B.   *Brunersburg.*
Abell B.   *Milldale.*

Fairfield County.

Hamlin & Hedge   *Clear Creek.*
Stukey Solomon   *Sugar Grove.*
Ruble G.
Fatick J.
Stiveson J.
Fink H.

Franklin County.

Lee Theron   *Central College.*
Young John S.   *Hibernia.*
Fisher John   *Canal Winchester.*
Louks Samuel
Rager John
Powell Samuel   *Gahanna*
Hay G. W.

Gallia County

Rose N. D.   *Pine Grove.*
Blazer Joseph   *Raccoon Island.*
Chambers, Clarke & Co.
Payne R.   *Gallipolis.*

Greene County.

Reed Young   *Xenia.*
Boyer Peter   *Yellow Springs.*
Hanstraugh & Swallow
Harlan Aaron

Guernsey County.

Hutchinson H.   *Leatherwood.*
Sherman Levi

Hamilton County.

Ashcraft Richard, 229 e. Front *Cincinnati.*
Baily, Langstaff & Co., Front bet. Mill & Wood
Bateman & Co., cor. Laurel & W. Row
Conn & Brother, east Front near Water Works
Cook H. M., 4th bet. Park & Smith
Cline John, 161 e. Front
Dudley J. M., junction Front and 6th
Fay Anthony, 344 Broadway
Johnston, Morton & Co., Front bet. Parsons & Whitewater
Lape & Gilpin, Canal bet Elm and Plum
Stewart, Deming & Co., 3d bet. Smith and Park
Underwood & Co., 5th bet. Broadway and Pike
Creighton Robert   *Columbia.*
Trimmer A.   *Pendleton.*
Glenn M. & L.   *Fulton.*
Morton J. A. G.
Walden & Vance
Welch C.
Hill & Rogers   *Mt. Healthy.*
Moore R. W.
Prudden J. K.   *Harrison.*
Sefton Harrison
Armstrong M. D.   *Plainville.*
Armstrong Nathl.
Armstrong Thomas   *Newtown.*
Meeker & Myers   *Sharonville.*
Burns T.   *Dunlap.*
Hughes J.
Scott M.
Arnold & Witherby   *College Hill.*
Fithian Joseph   *Cheviot.*

Lawrence County.

Savage & Merrill   *Ironton.*

Hancock County.

Lewis John & Co.   *Van Buren.*
Funk Martin   *Arlington.*
Lee H. K.   *McComb.*

Logan County.

Harrod John & Saml.   *Huntsville.*
Reed Robert L.
Shields James D.
Woodward Jonathan
Pollock M. W.   *Bellefontaine.*
McKee J. W.   *Quincy.*
Patton F.

Lorain County.

Hubbard H.   *La Grange.*
Hill L. M.   *Oberlin.*
Curtis Wm. L.   *Sheffield.*
Day William
Ely Hemon
Reed S., Jr.   *Copopa.*
Bacon & Hawley   *Brownhelm.*
Cooper Geo.

Mors Seth G.   *Brownhelm.*
Miles —,

Lucas County.

Shaffer M.   *Emery.*
Lathrop L. B.   *Riga.*
Wolfinger & Dilgert
Dewey W. F. & Son   *Whiteford.*
Jessup Abram
Pomroy & Delvan

Monroe County.

McConnell Wm. J.   *Laing's.*
Pollock, Suter & Anshutz   *Sunfish.*
Williams J. & Brothers   *Baresville.*

Putnam County.

Kemson W. T.   *Pendleton.*
Krohn S.

Richland County.

Boyd & Co.   *Mansfield.*
Squire J. D.   *Richland.*

Shelby County.

Walker H.   *Sidney.*
Maxwell S.

Stark County.

Groff D.   *Navarre.*
Walton Eli   *New Franklin.*
Coulter Robert   *East Greenville.*
Johnson Josiah
Mohler & Co.   *New Berlin.*
Smith & Shallenberger   *New Baltimore.*
Sluyghter Henry   *Limaville.*
Mounts & Dilworth   *Mt. Vernon.*

Summit County.

Pierson J.   *Montrose.*
Woodard & McDonald   *Eden.*
Wells W.   *Tallmadge.*

Trumbull County.

Burnett S.   *Warren.*
Kinsman & Reeves
Taylor & Hutchins
Van Gorder J. L.
Vaughn & Adams
White U. B.
Fell John   *Orangeville.*
Moffit A.
McCartney Andrew   *Girard.*
Reynolds S.   *Farmington*

Tuscarawas County.

Peter & Demuth   *Gnadenhutten.*
Hansell J. & Co.   *New Philadelphia.*
Talbott J.
Merriman Waters
Wills V.
Kitch J.

Machinists.

Allen County.

Smith A. N. & Co.   *Lima.*
Truesdale George

Ashland County.

Fairchild D. C.   *Jeromeville.*

Ashtabula County.

Sherwood N. B.   *Jefferson.*
Tower Reuben   *Ashtabula.*
Ellis & Cathcart   *Conneaut.*
Smith James
Dibble A. C.
Noble D.

Belmont County.

Davis Gideon   *Loydsville.*

Brown County.

Solonberger Joseph   *Higginsport.*
McKinley A.
Belchambers A.   *Ripley.*
Pindell E. A.   *Ash Ridge.*
Fiscus John
Wemal W.

Butler County.

Owens, Ebert & Dyer   *Hamilton.*

Champaign County.

Castle S. T.   *Urbana.*
Milliturn & Allen
Wilcox & Guinnes
Guinnes & Wilcox

Clark County.

Leffel, Cook & Blakeney   *Springfield.*

Columbiana County.

Cope N. & O.   *Salineville.*
Saffell James   *New Garden.*
Sharp Thomas   *Salem.*
Sharp, Davis & Co.
Taylor Samuel C.
Strickler J. & Co.   *Columbiana.*
Thompson Samuel J   *East Fairfield.*

Coshocton County.

Irwin John   *Chili.*
Shields John   *West Bedford.*
Thompson, Roney & Co.

Crawford County.

Kelly & Thomas   *Bucyrus.*
Wingart J. & H.

Cuyahoga County.

Smith Ira   *Chagrin Falls.*
Craig W. S., Division   *Cleveland.*
Frankland J. & Co., Front
McClelland & Co., Phœnix Foundry
Searls Albert G., River
Cuyahoga Locomotive Works

Darke County.

Avery Daniel   *German.*
Taylor Samuel & John   *Greenville.*

Delaware County.

Bradley, Burnham & Co.   *Delaware.*
Muzzy & Berlew

Erie County.

Griffith & Olds   *Sandusky City.*

Fairfield County.

Devall G. & Co.   *Lancaster.*
Beery & Jenkins
Clark, Wright & Co.
Brown William   *Clear Creek.*

Franklin County.

Ambos & Lennox, National Bridge
    Columbus.
Bickel M.
Butler Edward
Chadwick James
Clarck H. W.
Copeland Geo. M.
Davis L. B.
Deming —, Broadway
Gill John L.
Jelloff A. M.
Krum M.
Lewis C. L.
Lennox John & Wm.
Mills R. L.
Ridgway J., cor. Gay and State
Sylvester B. F.
Ware S. L.
West J. W.
Trumbull H.   *Central College.*
Wright Potter   *Worthington.*

Greene County.

Gowdy John B.   *Xenia.*
McGilligan Peter
Stewart George
Morrell J.

Hamilton County.

Alden John T., Mound, near 7th   *Cin'ti.*
Brown A. C., 37 Walnut
Brown J. & R., Front
Burge & Johnson, Pearl, bet. Elm and Plum
Berckhemer Chas., 62 w. 13th
Donaldson A., cor. 5th and Miami Canal
Greenwald & Bonsall, s. w. cor. 5th and Lock
Gould, Pierce & Co., n. w. cor. 5th and Lock
Holabird A. B. & Co., Front near Smith
Haven James L. & Co., cor. Broadway & Liberty
Kreiger John, W. Row above Liberty
Lyon & Bell, cor. Lock and 3d
Lane & Co., 98 Pearl
Latta, Shawk & Co., Race, bet. 4th & 5th
Martin, Anshutz & Co., e. Front, between Ludlow and Lawrence
Miller H. H., 208 Front
Niles & Co., 222 e. Front
Pollock James S., Columbia, bet. Elm and Race

Powell David A., Butler, bet. Front and
   Congress   *Cincinnati.*
Reynolds, Kite & Tatum, cor. John and
   Water
Robbins & Turner, cor. Fifth and White-
   water Canal
Shield E. M., 75 e. Front
Tuttle John N., W. Row, between Ninth
   and Court
Todd James & Co., cor. Smith and 7th
Wolfington & Budke, Pearl, bet. Vine and
   Race
Bonnel Stephen   *Carthage.*
Burns J. A.

Hancock County.

George Jesse   *Finley.*
Wolf & Wilhelm

Harrison County.

Larkin S. T.   *Harrisville.*

Huron County.

Soyer & McKinney   *Clarksfield.*
Tyler Daniel
Baker J. W.   *Norwalk.*
Perkins N.
Watrous Daniel
Morehouse G.

Jefferson County.

Kenyon Wm.   *Steubenville.*
McDavitt J.
Steele M.
Richardson Wm.

Knox County.

Buckingham C. P. & Co. *Mt. Vernon.*
Cooper C. C. & Co.
Braington, Speakman & Co. *Fredericktown.*
Rarkins D. L.

Lawrence County.

Churchill J. L.   *Ironton.*
Merrill J. M. & Co.

Licking County.

Stewart James   *Jacksontown.*
Armstrong J. T.
McCune & Ebersole   *Newark.*
Hall Henry G   *Kirkersville.*

Logan County.

Davis & Hoyt   *Bellefontaine.*
Humphrey J. A. & R. Y.

Mahoning County.

Hordman Nathan   *Canfield.*
Wells & Hull   *Youngstown.*

Medina County.

Packer R.   *Wadsworth.*

Meigs County.

Dyke B. F.   *Downington.*

Miami County.

Alexander, Rouser & Evans *Piqua.*
Bowdel, Clark & Co.

Curtis B.   *Casstown.*
Kelly John   *West Milton.*

Montgomery County.

McMillen & Son, Third   *Dayton.*
Pease W. H.   "
Smith Jas. M., First
Thompson, Gebhart & Co., Fifth
Westerman & Stout, Canal
Hoover D. H.   *Miamisburgh.*
Hetzel David

Morgan County.

Dawson Geo.   *McConnelsville.*

Muskingum County.

Milhollen John   *New Concord.*
McKinney A. & J.
Ball L. B.   *Putnam.*
Brelsford E.
Taylor H. B.
Douglas, Smith & Co. *Zanesville.*
Hoadley John
Blandy H. & F.

Portage County.

Clute John   *Ravenna.*
Forker Israel
Rawson S.

Richland County.

Hall & Allen   *Mansfield.*
Moody J. W.   *Bellville.*

Ross County.

Keazer John   *Chillicothe.*

Sandusky County.

King J. N.   *Rollersville.*

Seneca County.

Loomis John D. & Co.   *Tiffin.*
Stewart Wm. H.
Hall L. E.   *Republic.*

Starke County.

Allenatz Joseph   *New Berlin.*
Nodle George G.
Walton M. & A.   *Marlboro'.*
Everhart Christian *New Baltimore.*
Russell C. M. & Co. *Massillon.*
Hart & Brown
Partridge H. & R.
Bliler & Helt   *Canal Fulton.*

Summit County.

Bill F.   *Cuyahoga Falls.*
Bills & Chamberlain
Hunt C. & Co.
Webster & Taplin   *Akron.*
Allen, Hall & Co.
Irish, Kent & Baldwin *Middlebury.*

Trumbull County.

Douglass & Madden   *Warren.*
Hull W. H.

Tuscarawas County.

Baker Philip   *Canal Dover.*
English J. (Agent) *New Philadelphia.*

Washington County.
Rolf, Nye & Co.   *Harmar.*
Harmar Manufacturing Co.

Machine and Carriage Bolt Manufacturers.

Hamilton County.
Coleman S. T. J., cor. W. Row and Betts
    Cincinnati.

Montgomery County.
Tucker & Bennet, St. Clair   *Dayton.*

Magic Stain Manufacturer.

Hamilton County.
Baldwin Wm. S., 171 W. Row   *Cincin'ti.*

Magnetic Watergauge Manufacturer.

Starke County.
Faber Geo.   *Canton*

Mahogany Dealers.

Hamilton County.
Carnes Wm. R., 20 e. 3d   *Cincinnati.*
McAlpin A., 103 Walnut
Wayne J. L., 124 Main

Malt (Barley & Rye) Manufacturers & Dealers.

Butler County.
Schelby Geo.   *Hamilton.*

Clermont County.
Kugler John   *Milford.*

Hamilton County.
Wheelwright James, 27 w. Front   *Cin'ti.*

Montgomery County.
Fanning H. & Co., St. Clair   *Dayton.*

Map Dealer.

Hamilton County.
Mendenhall E., 21 e. 4th   *Cincinnati.*

Marble Workers.

Ashland County.
Buck & Ream   *Hayesville.*
McKnight J.

Ashtabula County.
Jones & Co.   *Ashtabula.*
Patterson D. M.   *Conneaut.*
Mayer Lewis

Belmont County.
Evans & Brother   *St. Clairsville.*

Brown County.
Anderson Geo.   *Ripley.*
Harrison Wm. H.

Butler County.
Potter A.   *Hamilton.*

Carroll County.
Amos J. H.   *Hickory.*

Champaign County.
Butler & Emmerson   *Urbana.*

Clark County.
Pierong A.   *Springfield.*

Coshocton County.
Barton & McMain   *Coshocton.*

Crawford County.
Green R. S. & Co.   *Bucyrus.*

Cuyahoga County.
Smith D. E.   *Chagrin Falls.*
Jones T. & Sons, Prospect   *Cleveland.*
Kleeberger Peter, cor. Pittsb'h. & Kinsman
Williams H., Bolivar
Williams J.,   do
Whitman & Cotton, 44 Ontario

Erie County.
Johnson H.   *Sandusky City.*

Franklin County.
Brown C. H., Broad,   *Columbus.*
Strickler Joseph, cor. Gay & Third
Carpenter J. B.   *Ovid.*
Lytle John

Gallia County.
Charlesworth H. R.   *Gallipolis.*

Geauga County.
Rodgers A. L.   *Chardon.*

Greene County.
Bunnell D.   *Xenia.*
Howard & Lloyd

Guernsey County.
Colley Wm.   *Washington.*

Hamilton County.
Bolles David, 210 Vine   *Cincinnati.*
Brookfield Wm. & Son, Broadway above Fifth
Davis, Mason & Co., 249 Walnut
Flagg Wm. J.
Guio E. B., Court, near W. Row
Rule Charles, cor. Broadway & 5th
Smith A. C., 244 Court
Reeves B.   *Fulton.*
Cornulle V.   *Columbia.*

Hardin County.
Louthan Masas, jr.   *Kenton.*
White J. D.
Louthan & Lester
White J.

Highland County.
Devoss J. W.   *Greenfield*
Howard & Lloyd   *Hillsboro'.*

Huron County.
Fisk S.   *Norwalk.*

Jefferson County.
Permar J. M.   *Steubenville.*
Borland J.

Knox County.

Burnes L. C.   *Mt. Vernon.*
Cotton E. W.

Lake County.

Morse Collins   *Painesville.*

Licking County.

Bell J. & R.   *Brownsville.*
Bragg H. W. & G.   *Granville.*
Woodard J.
Nichol R. L. & Wm.
Wissell Edwin   *Newark.*
Glaze —
Mahurin O. F.
Wiswell E. W.

Logan County.

Barnes L. C.   *Bellefontaine.*
Nevin & McClure

Madison County.

Hurley & Hoover   *London.*

Mahoning County.

Woodruff & Osborn   *Cornersburg.*

Marion County.

Conley H.   *Marion.*

Medina County.

Tousley H. G.   *Medina.*

Miami County.

Ludlow & Hamilton   *Piqua.*
Wallace W. W.   *Troy.*

Montgomery County.

Ludlow & Hamilton, Third   *Dayton.*

Morrow County.

Crane & Gunsaula   *Chesterville.*

Muskingum County.

McBride & Bedwell   *Zanesville.*
Darlington & Sutton

Perry County.

Gordon & Fulton   *Somerset.*

Pickaway County.

Taylor W. C. & Co.   *Circleville.*

Pike County.

McBride James   *Cynthiana.*

Portage County.

Arnold C. O.   *Ravenna.*
Hurlbut & Fox
Peyster James D.   *Franklin.*

Preble County.

Miller John D.   *Eaton.*
Whipple Ransom

Richland County.

Dulin G. S. & Co.   *Mansfield.*
Shafer & Meredith   *Belleville.*

Ross County.

Smith C. J.   *Chillicothe.*
Merriam Moses

Sandusky County.

Smith John   *Fremont.*

Scioto County.

Charlesworth H. R.   *Portsmouth.*

Seneca County.

Root T. F.   *Tiffin.*
Ward N. W.

Tuscarawas County.

Myers & Brother   *New Philadelphia.*

Washington County.

Leonard J. D.   *Marietta.*
Murchey John   *Watertown.*

Wayne County.

Hackett & Cox   *Dalton.*
Griffin D. A. & Co.   *Moreland.*

Masons (Stone).

Ashland County.

Cumings Alexander   *Savannah.*
Harvey John

Ashtabula County.

Bates J. D.   *Austinburg.*
Dady L.
Herrick J.
Henry B.
Scofield Frederick   *Jefferson.*
Holbrook H.
Brooks J.   *Ashtabula.*
Pratt D.
Graham H. C.
Avery Jonathan   *Hart's Grove.*
Clemmons Samuel
Gillett L. D.   *Lindenville.*
Leonard S. S.

Athens County.

Boden James   *Lowry.*
Allison Henry
Davis Lewis.
Davis Samuel
Francis Thomas   *Athens.*
Allison W. H.
Paul John

Belmont County.

Bartholomew John   *Uniontown.*
Millburn Mahlon   *Flushing.*
Piggott Joseph
Abel George   *Bellair.*
Roscoe Wm.   *St. Clairsville.*

Brown County.

Calvin Stephen   *Higginsport.*
McWilliams John
Sly John   *Union Plans.*
Kress Henry   *Sardinia.*
Kress Frank
Snider Peter

Carroll County.

Beiter Ignatius   *Oneida Mills.*
Laubender Michael

Clark County.

Barringer Wm.   *Enon.*
Craig John S.

Drummond John   *Enon.*
Grogg George
Davies Henry   *New Carlisle.*
Ritcheson Elijah

Clermont County.

Estell Samuel R.   *Neville.*
Julian Joshua   *Milford.*

Clinton County.

Morgan S.   *Westboro'.*
Fisher J.

Columbiana County.

Crowl George E.   *New Lisbon.*
Gloss Solomon
Huston Jesse
Rummell Jacob
Ward Andrew
Zimmerman John
Bander Fred'k. & Ab'm.   *North Georget'n.*
Fisher Andrew
Fryfogle Benj.
Woolf Peter
Yengling John
Weaver Jacob   *Franklin Square.*
Bricker Reason   *Salem.*
Gonnare Anthony
Lucey George   *Bucks.*
Mires Elias D.
Forney Jesse   *Unity.*
Jenkinson R.
Armstrong Wm.   *Elkton.*
Richardson Harrison
Chamberlain Isaac
Chamberlain John

Coshocton County.

Loveless Thomas A.   *Bakersville.*
Rice Valentine
Davis Thomas   *Keene.*
Davis H.   *Coshocton.*

Crawford County.

Carroll William   *Bucyrus.*
Cunning Wm.
McClure H. W.

Cuyahoga County.

Franks W.   *Chagrin Falls.*
Overton J.
Beebee Sidney   *Coe Ridge.*
Knight R. H.
Dunbar A.   *Bedford.*
Gordon James
Woodworth Theron   *Collamer.*
Woodworth Enoch
McIlrath Alex.
Chapman Wm.   *Berea.*
Knowlton Paul
Pierce J.

Darke County.

Grier Geo.   *German.*

Defiance County.

Allen H.   *Defiance.*
Bridenbaugh F.
Crunkilton A. B.

Delaware County.

Shaver Geo.   *Stratsford.*
Harter John
Young J. L.   *Galena.*
Carey Stephen
Snow Samuel   *Waldo.*

Erie County.

Mears G. W.   *Milan.*
Gardner L. B.
Gorden J. B.
Gardner Geo.
Turner L.
Turner O.
Turner A.
Patch R.

Fairfield County.

Kuhn Michael   *West Rushville.*

Franklin County.

Axe George, Third   *Columbus.*
Kenmacher Geo., do
Kenmacher Jacob, do
Landon Calvin   *Hope.*
Montgomery George
Loomis H.   *Central College.*
Dellinger Jacob   *Canal Winchester*
Myers Ezra
Myer Henry
Woodruff Theodore   *Ovid.*

Geauga County.

Exene F.   *Claridon.*
Fowler E. Z.   *Burton.*
Parks Wyman
Rusk Thomas   *Chardon.*
Huntington D.
Adams E. R.
Abby D.   *Troy.*
Radcliffe Wm.   *Hamden.*
Greene M. S.   *Thompson.*
Schnideker Chas.
Bisbee Asa   *Chester.*
Stafford Stephen   *Auburn.*

Greene County.

Clark R.   *Clifton.*

Guernsey County.

Rossman Edward   *Fairview.*
Carter Wm.
Marshall James
McChan Daniel

Hamilton County.

Sheeley Michael   *Mt. Healthy.*
Auten David   *Pleasant Ridge.*
Smith David
Boganshots Michael   *Harrison.*
Looker Allison
Shubridge Geo.
Liclear Michael   *Mt. Washington.*
Pool —
Baird James H.   *Miami.*
Roberts Wm.
Berwick Martin   *Cheviot.*
Steinman R.

Henry County.

Homan Samuel	Napoleon.
Glass John	

Highland County.

Robbins C.	Highland.
Pine Nathan	Greenfield.
Pine G. & M.	
Extell Lewis	
McClelland James	
Scott James	
Tuttle E.	
Davis S.	
Batton Benj.	Marshall.
Lucas Jacob	

Holmes County.

Piffer John M.	Winesburg.
Hobler S.	
Hinner A.	
Schindler D.	
Blaner C.	
Fought Joseph	

Huron County.

Finch A.	Clarksfield.
Thompson J. R.	
Ivory E.	Norwalk.
Copsey John	
Buck John	
Wilson Joseph	
Buck Chester	

Knox County.

Gardner Joseph	Mt. Vernon.
Jennings John	
Leach L. P. & C.	
Miller V. A.	Monroe Mills.
Tym John	
Hause Samuel	Democracy.
Hause David	
Wright D. P.	
Dailey D. L.	Mt. Liberty.
Hawkins Wm. H.	Milfordton.

Lake County.

Childs R. W.	Madison.
Wayard H.	North Perry.
Mansel Smith	
Wood L. B.	
Wood Q. M.	
Smith Landon	Painesville.
Bacheller J. L.	
Bacheller Chas.	
Morrell J. S.	
Potton R. C.	
Hitchcock L.	

Lawrence County.

Allison T. & J.	Ironton.
Howls Wm.	
Macolroy —	

Licking County.

Johnson John	Newark.
Coffin J.	
Hyrst John	
Boner Jacob	

Vance Benj.	Newark.
Barr Samuel	
Sutton J.	
Peetry Andrew	

Logan County.

Bane & Son	Bellefontaine.
Selden Hugh	
Walters W. W. & Brother	
Watson J. R.	
Courter Alexander	Zanesfield.
Courter George	
McVaugh Jesse	
Reams J. M.	
Chambers Wm.	
Neher M. C.	Quincy.
Neher E.	

Lorain County.

Gerrish N.	Oberlin.
Smith E.	
Hall Orrin	Brighton.

Lucas County.

Barrett Milton	Toledo.
Blodgett Loren	
Boice John, sen.	
Boice John, jun.	
Brigham Loomis	
Corlett Thomas	
Dority John	
Huffman J.	
Rice William	

Mahoning County.

Nogle A.	Petersburgh.
Bush Jacob	Green Village.
Rollins John	
Cole John	Hanna's Mills.
Olinker Reuben	North Lima.
Nagle John	New Springfield.
Spickler David	
Macklen Samuel	

Medina County.

Armstrong A.	Liverpool.
Wilcox Lemuel	Hinckley.
Kentfield E.	
Allen David	Weymouth.
Terrey Wm.	Chatham Centre.
Rounds John	Medina.
Carr A. M.	
Rounds Seth	

Meigs County.

Kennedy Stephen	Pomeroy.
Mieks E.	

Miami County.

Davis J. E.	Casstown.
King B.	Hyattsville.
Hanna James.	

Monroe County.

Brown John	Sunfish.
Lloyd Humphrey	

Morgan County.

Grev Joseph	Meigsville.

Fogle Geo. F.   *McConnelsville.*
Hutchins Thos.
Ougle Wm.
Whitzel George
Sigler George
Jones W. R.
Coulson Jehu   *Pennsville.*
Coulson John

Morrow County.

Ackerman & Crain   *Cardington.*
Kramer C. W.
Morton Lewis   *Nimmon's ⋈ Roads.*
Struble Daniel   *Chesterville.*

Muskingum County.

Boling Wm.   *Fultonham.*
Powell Robert   *White Cottage.*

Ottawa County.

Fratt A.   *Port Clinton.*
Richardson R.
Willet J.

Perry County.

Obineweth A.   *New Richmond.*
La Master John & Son
Miller S.

Pike County.

Sharp Asa   *Cynthiana.*
Earich C. G.   *Waverly.*
Spencer Thos. N.
Dodge Nathan   *Gibson.*
Samson Samuel

Portage County.

Holcomb Samuel F.   *Ravenna.*
Brigham John
Younker Daniel   *Freedom.*
Harmon Jonas   *Deerfield.*
Dodge L. O.   *Franklin.*
Ward Benj.
Morris Henry
Pettibone A.   *Mantua.*
Horton J.
Branch S.   *Shalersville.*
Olmsted Wm.   *Edinburgh.*
Stambaugh M.   *Randolph.*
Allen B. A. & Sons
Lewis A.   *Atwater.*
Horton Z. A.
McNabb A.

Preble County.

Wysing Henry   *Camden.*
Jenkins James
Wilson James
Pierce F.
Brown Chas.
Huzzy Patrick   *New Westville.*
Witchelman J.   *New Paris.*

Ross County.

Thompson & Sons   *Chillicothe.*
Lamhead & Somersett
Stephenson & Doobe
Stagers & Litter

Lister & Brother   *Chillicothe.*
Piper J.
Sawhead Israel   *South Salem.*
Dugleby B.
Hosler George   *Hallsville.*
Brant Oliver

Scioto County.

Bjah —   *Portsmouth.*
Glover A.
Vigres J.
Millirons Samuel   *Iron Furnaces.*
Pinkerman Charles

Seneca County.

Bernard Franklin   *Adrian.*
De Witt Joseph
De Camp Wm.   *Berwick.*
Ramsom George
Dysinger O.   *Bloomville.*
Burns Ervin   *Bascom.*
Gatches Nicholas   *Green Spring.*
Steel A. B.
Strong John M.   *Republic.*
Strong Charles
Rawson James
Porter James

Starke County.

Neregorda Arnold   *Waynesburg.*
Neregorda Peter
Boger John   *New Franklin.*
Coulter Samuel   *East Greenville.*
Kline Henry
Goshart George   *Magnolia.*
Warthorst F.   *Massillon.*
Warthorst E.
Debi J.
Rempis Louis
Powell A.
Jacobs J.

Summit County.

Porter Levi   *Bath.*
Richards Wm.
Richards John

Trumbull County.

Strohm J.   *Farmington.*
Walcott Lewis
Walcott L. B.

Warren County.

Lutalick Wm.   *Waynesville.*
McLoud A.   *Morrow.*
Trapp Caleb
Travillo E.
Miranda John
Dynes J. C.
Everhart Titus   *Mt. Holly.*

Washington County.

Allcock —   *Marietta.*
Sears James   *Harmar.*
Gray M.   *Lower Salem.*
Williams Thos.
Davison A. J.

Wayne County.

Barkley Henry   *Reedsburg.*
Barkley Peter
Hagaman David
Eagle John
Zell A. & Co.   *Smithville.*
McGinnes & Davis
Mickley A.
Peters Geo.
Wolf Geo.

Williams County.

*Fairfield David   *Bryan.*
Rease Lewis

Wood County.

Louzy Frederick   *Bowling-Green.*
Condit James
Condit J. W.   *Weston.*
Vonvolkenburg J. W.

Wyandot County.

Rouk Jacob   *Upper Sandusky.*
Dumm M. S.
Hill James   *Carey.*
Dewitt Chas.
Sabough Jacob
Ingle James   *McCutchensville.*

Masonic and Odd Fellows' Furnishing Store.

Hamilton County.

Addis William, Bacon's Building   *Cin'ti.*

Match (Lucifer) Manufact'rs

Medina County.

Wilson John   *River Styx.*
Syman Geo.   *Wadsworth.*

Montgomery County.

Garst J., Lower Hydraulic   *Dayton.*

Summit County.

Barber George   *Middlebury.*
Honodle Adam
Kent Alison
Aldredge S.   *New Portage.*
Connor E.
Murdock S. M.

Mathematical, Philosophical, and Optical Instrument Makers.

Hamilton County.

Evens P., junr., 187 Walnut   *Cincinnati.*
Foster James, junr., s. w. cor. Race & 5th
Gendon Joseph, 214 Walnut
Hall F., Magnolia Hall, 5th
Isaac M., 285 w. Fifth
Ware Henry, s. w. cor. Syc. and 4th

Medicine (Patent) Dealers.

Crawford County.

Johnston & Fulton   *Bucyrus.*
Peacock & Co.

Defiance County.

Allen O. H.   *Defiance.*
Kintigh Wm. F.   *Evansport.*

Hamilton County.

Meakings B. H. { 10 c. 4th
                 189 Walnut }   *Cincinnati.*
Park John D., cor. 4th and Walnut
Harris J. N. & Co., 7 College Building
Scovill A. L. &' Co., 60 w. Third
Sheppard J. W., 20 w. Fourth
Kohl Wm. M. & Co., cor. 4th and Vine
Kidder & Briggs, Walnut, above 5th
Howe S. D., 1 College Hall
Fuller E. E.   *Harrison.*

Knox County.

White John W.   *Mt. Vernon.*

Perry County.

Coyle Peter   *Chapel Hill.*

Seneca County.

Hamilton William L.   *Republic.*

Medicine (Patent) Manufacturers.

Fayette County.

Ireland M.   *Jeffersonville.*

Knox County.

Campbell J. B. & Co.   *Mt. Vernon.*

Lucas County.

Gregory John S.   *Maumee City.*
Gregory & Moore

Noble County

Fitton J. C.   *South Olive.*

Summit County.

Hard M. K. & S. Ellet   *North Springfield.*

Melodeon Manufacturers.

Cuyahoga County.

Bishop & Child, 64, 66, 68 Ontario
                                 Cleveland.

Hamilton County.

Colburn & Field (Agents) 154 Main
                                 Cincinnati.
Murch & White, 74 w. Fourth

Lucas County.

Butler Derwin E.   *Emery.*

Trumbull County.

Hazeldine Joseph   *Farmington.*

Merchants — Commission and Forwarding.

Athens County.

Williams E. H.   *Hockingport.*

Ashtabula County.

Hubbard H. & Co.   *Ashtabula.*
Seymour L. B.
Humphrey Wm.

Brown County.

King & McConaghay	*Higginsport.*
Jolly & Shaw	*Ripley.*
Hemphill J. & Co.	
Brafford J. W.	

Champaign County.

Magrew & Son	*Urbana.*
Musgrove, Wiley & Winslow	

Columbiana County.

Huffstat & Co.	*Wellsville.*
Lawson & Wells	
Paul, Pritchard & Co.	*New Lisbon.*
McGilvery & Moore	*East Liverpool.*
Icenhour & Allen	*Columbiana.*
Arter & Nicholas	*Hanoverton.*
Arter J. R.	

Coshocton County.

Richmond S.	*Evansburg.*

Cuyahoga County.

Anderson P., Oviatt's Block   *Cleveland.*
Barrett C. & Co., Merwin
Bash J., Canal
Carlisle John, 46 Merwin
Chamberlin & Crawford, Superior and Dock
Clark & Calkins, Canal
Cochran G. W. & Co., near C. C. & C. R. R. Depot
Dickinson C., cor. Front and Dock
Eckhart Wm. R., Oviatt's Block
Eddy D. A. & Co., Front, opp. C. C. & C. R. R. Depot
Fitch & Brown, 38 Dock & 81 River
Forsyth & Camp, do   do
Gillett J., 48 Merwin
Gates H. N. & Co., Oviatt's Block
Goodale, Musgrave & Co., 41 Bank
Gray A. N., Superior
Halliday J. N., 203 River, 102 Dock
Handy, Warner & Co., 73 Dock, 205 River
Hewitt & Tuttle, Merwin
Hickox Charles, 73 Dock
Hubby, Hughes & Co., 93 Dock, 169 & 171 River
Hussey & Sinclair, 70 Dock, 133 River
Johnson Wm. S., Merwin
Lyon R. T., 50   "
Melhinch & Stillman, 32 "
Morgan, White & Co., on Dock
Nims & Tillotson, Merwin
Otis, Knight & Co., River & Front
Oviatt & Holt, Canal & River
Rawson L. & Co., near R. R. Depot
Scott M. B., 45 and 47 River
Russell & Green, 105 Dock, 20 C. and River
Sutliff & Case, near R. R. Depot
Walton T. A., 49 Dock, 97 River
Burton B. & Co.   *Ohio City.*
Guyles W. B.
Mittleberger Edward, River
Burnham T.

Darke County.

Grimes J.	*Greenville.*
Potter D. K.	

Defiance County.

Brown G. R.	*Defiance.*
Evans P. & Lindenberger	
Hilton H.	
Sprage & Warren	
Tuttle J. & Co.	

Erie County.

Stevens & Ryan	*Huron.*
Wright & Sprague	
Chapman W. P.	*Sandusky City.*
Whitney James D. & Co.	
Boalt & Smith	
Hitchcock S. E. & Williams.	
Russell W.	
Pinto A. J., Agent	
Chase H.	*Milan.*
McClure A.	
Skinner C. P.	
Walker & Smith	
Hamilton Thomas	
Stevens J.	
Merrill J.	
Lockwood W. E.	

Franklin County.

Buttles, Comstock & Co., head of Canal   *Columbus.*
Fitch H., Scioto Bridge
Glazier V. R. & Co., cor. Town & 4th
Hale & Tinker, 2 Exchange Buildings
Tuttle & Long, Broad
Watson James W., National Bridge
Eberly Cyrus   *Groveport*
Sharp Abram
Sharp & Paul
Sarber J. A.   *Lockbourne.*

Gallia County.

Guthrie C. L.	*Cheshire.*

Greene County.

Hivling & Williamson	*Xenia.*

Hamilton County.

Campbell, Russell & Co., 3 e. Front   *Cincinnati.*
Eggleston D., Canal, bet. Main & Walnut
Finn Wm., 9th, bet. Main and Syc.
Gilpin & Sherlock, S. Canal
Gilbert, Jones & Ogborn, cor. W. W. Canal & Fifth
Hazard R. F. & W. S., 65 Canal
Hull Julius, Canal, bet. Main & Syc.
Holmes & Conwell, 34 Walnut
Keck George & Co., Canal, bet Main and Sycamore
McCleary Andrew & Co., 19 Canal
Mitchell N., Canal, near Walnut
Porter, Thomas & Sons, 66 Walnut
Taylor E. R. & Co., 5th, w. of Main
Thomas N. W. & Co., s. w. cor. Walnut & Canal

Thayer & Gassaway, n. w. c. 3d & Syc Cin.
Torrance James F., Canal, bet. Wal & Vine
Trowbridge & Beatty, s. w. cor. Canal &
  Race.
Wilson James & Co., Canal, bet. Main &
  Walnut

Holmes County.

Mann T. & J.   *Berlin.*

Huron County.

Amsden & Co.   *Bellevue.*
Harkness & Co.
Chapman & Co.

Jefferson County.

Doyle A.   *Steubenville.*
Frazier & Drennen

Knox County.

Miner M. F.   *Fredericktown.*

Lake County.

Knight D.   *Fairport.*
Wilcox B. O. & Brothers
Root M. L.
McCormick & Pease   *Painesville.*
Wilcox B. O. & Brothers
Root M. L.
Knight D.

Lawrence County.

Murdock & Rodgers   *Ironton.*

Licking County.

Haughey & Byers   *Newark.*
Cooper E.
Warner L. K. & Co.
Vance J. & M.   *St. Louisville.*

Logan County.

Runkle & Shoemaker   *West Liberty.*
Taylor & Miller
Simpson Wm. W.   *New Richland.*
Douglass E.   *Bellefontaine.*
Gardner, McCulloch & Co.

Lucas County.

Dyer E. R.   *Maumee City.*
Smith John
Brown & King   *Toledo.*
Brownlee, Pendleton & Co.
Buckingham P. & Co.
Carpenter Geo. A.
Dodd H. H. & Co.
Godard A.
Hoag, Strong & Co.
Haskell D. & Co.
Hollister & Colter
Johnson E. S.
King C A. & Co.
Morton & Howe
Powers W. G.
Scott & Co.
Scott & Comstock
Smith & Hunt
Smith Platt
Read & Co.

Mahoning County.

Keller P. W.   *Youngstown.*
Warner J. & Co.
Jacobs A. D.
Porter Wm. & Co.   *Milton.*
Tod J. J.

Marion County.

Ault & Gorton   *Marion.*
Brown J. D.

Miami County.

Rogers M. L.   *Piqua.*
Farmington & Ruple
Lawton & Barnett
Dye M.   *Troy.*
Wagner M. S.
Knoop G. P.
Brown & Tilford.

Montgomery County.

Rouser Samuel, N. Market   *Dayton.*
Chambers Robert, Head Basin
Harris W.   "
Rouser & Arnold, Third
Deckert Samuel   *Miamisburgh.*
Hurst & Grove
Peale J. F.

Morgan County.

Russell Geo.   *McConnelsville.*

Morrow County.

Brock & Phelps   *Cardington.*

Muskingum County.

Thompson F. A.   *Zanesville.*
Crosby J. & J.
Monroe J. H.
Spaulding C. W.
Davis W. H. & Co.
Ragut James
Stevens John
Alter John
Smith Perry & Co.
Dixon A.
Graham N. W.

Pickaway County.

Bradford G. G. & N. T.   *Circleville.*
McQueen James & Co.

Portage County.

Prentiss C.   *Ravenna.*
Kent, Grennell & Co.   *Franklin.*
Parmele John

Richland County.

Leyman H.   *Shelby.*
McConnel & Towns
Rowley Geo. P.
Cox J. H. & Co.   *Mansfield.*
Hedges, Weldon & Co.
Robinson J. R. & Co.
Sturges, Tracey & Co.

Ross County.

Clifford J. D. & Co.   *Chillicothe.*

Allston & Peitsmeyer   *Chillicothe.*
Clark Jas. & Son
Smart D.
Allston & Garfield
Madeira & Co.
Searle Geo. C.
Holcomb & Co.
Marfield & Luckett

Scioto County.

Conway B. F. & Co.   *Portsmouth.*
McDowell J. & Co.
Row John & Son
Ross S. R.
Tyrrell W. S.   *Iron Furnace.*
Davis & Smith   *Portsmouth*
Smith J. W.
McDowell & Chandler
Damerin Ch. A. M.

Seneca County.

Cook E. H.   *Adrian.*
Swagart J.
Boyce T. W. & Co.   *Tiffin.*
Shoemaker G. P. & Co.
Walker J.

Shelby County.

Gillespie D. M.   *Lockington.*
Furman G. N.

Starke County.

Faiver L.   *Louisville.*
Lawrence G. W. & Co.
Rodabaugher A. & Co.
Hoffman J. J.   *Massillon.*
Rawson L. & S.
Cummins C. B. & Co.
Atwater D. R.
Pierce Edgar S.   *Limaville.*

Summit County.

Chamberlin J. & Co.   *Akron.*
Sawyer J. & Co.
Stephens J. & Co.
Wheeler D. H.

Trumbull County.

Leffingwell C. E.   *Warren.*
Taylor M. B.

Tuscarawas County.

Fertig Samuel   *Canal Dover.*
Allyn J. W.   *New Philadelphia.*
Patrick J. U.

Van Wert County.

Hollister, Bliss & Lytle   *Delphos.*
McCune & Woolson

Warren County.

Vanhorn W. A. & Co.   *Franklin.*
Barkalow B. B.
Maxwell J.

Washington County.

Hall, Matthews & Co.   *Marietta.*
Finch A.   *Harmar.*

20

Wayne County.

Childs Wm.   *Wooster.*

Wyandot County.

Shawhan R. W.   *Carey.*
Dow, Stephens & Co.
Kiskadden Wm.   *Upper Sandusky.*

Milliners.

Allen County.

Thomas Miss Mary   *Lima.*

Ashtabula County.

Smith Mrs. L. W.   *Ashtabula.*
Dean F. & M.   *Loudonville.*
Day & Ray Misses   *Conneaut.*
Matson L.
Palmer L.
Graham Mrs.

Belmont County.

Dillon Misses   *St. Clairsville.*
Faris Miss Susan
McShaver Mrs.

Brown County.

Hamilton Mrs. Ann   *Higginsport.*
McGinnis Miss   *Ripley.*
Gaddis Mrs.

Butler County.

Temple Mrs. C. W. H.   *Oxford.*
Brott Mrs. R.
Cameron Mrs. M. E.
Rutray Miss E.
Walton Mrs. E.   *Hamilton.*
Williams M. H.
Dellinger Miss A.
Alger Mrs.   *Rossville.*
Jones Mrs. A.   *Middletown.*
Carr Mrs. Eliza   *Monroe.*
Swift Miss H.   *College Corner.*

Champaign County.

Caden Miss R.   *Urbana.*
Laycox Miss S. F.

Clark County.

King Mrs.   *Enon.*
Bascomb Mrs. C.   *Springfield.*
Colt Mrs.
Bancroft Mrs.
Cave Mrs. M. A.
Leedle Miss
Hammond Mrs.

Clermont County.

Castlen Mrs.   *New Richmond.*
Fairchild Mrs. Mary   *Amelia.*
Hopkins Mrs. Caroline
McMahan Miss Rebecca
Edwards Mrs. Emeline

Clinton County.

Nolder M.   *Blanchester.*

Columbiana County.

Averill Miss	Wellsville.
Frazer E. & N.	
Alford Abby	New Lisbon.
Dutch Hannah	
Miller M. A.	
Northcroft —	
Russell & Hamilton Misses	
Starr Sarah	
Watson Mrs.	

Crawford County.

Anderson Miss	Bucyrus.
Lightner Miss	
Morris Miss	

Cuyahoga County.

Jones Mrs.	Coe Ridge.
Weston Miss Celia	Collamer.
Dolman Mrs. C., cor. Superior and Seneca	Cleveland.
Bramley A. B., 11½ St. Clair	
Trimble Miss, 91 Superior	
Manning E.	Ohio City.

Darke County.

Warner M. W.	Fort Jefferson.
Drinkwater L.	

Defiance County.

Ackerman Mrs.	Defiance.
Cole Mrs. E. C.	

Erie County.

Burgess Mrs. & Co.	Sandusky City.
McGraves Miss E.	
Hawley E.	
Taylor Mrs. R. B.	
Humphrey Miss	

Fairfield County.

Reed Mrs. E.	Lithopolis.
Junkurth Miss L.	

Franklin County.

Barker Miss, High	Columbus.
Briggs Mrs. "	
Chears Mrs. "	
Domeny Mrs. "	
Donnell Mrs. "	
Frauenberg Mrs., Third	
Eamon H. & B., High	
Lamport Mrs., Front	
Miner Mrs., cor. High and Rich	
Overmire Mrs.	
Reid Mrs., Rich	
Singer Miss, Third	
Smith Mrs. "	
Rutter Ama, High	
Walter Mrs., Rich	
Watson Mrs., Third	
Winders Mrs., Town	
Vanpoughton Mrs., High	
Searls Miss C.	Groveport.
Shaffer Miss. C.	

Gallia County.

White Mrs. C.	Gallipolis.

Geauga County.

Ford Mrs. B.	Chardon.
Benton Miss A.	
Proctor Mrs. J.	Thompson.
Kelsey Mrs. P.	
Grist Mrs. J. B.	Hamden.

Greene County.

Robison Mrs.	Xenia.
Young Mrs.	
Gleany Mrs. Jane	
Doty Mrs. Lydia	Clifton.
Johnson Miss Alice	
Price Mrs. Ann	
Johns Sarah	Yellow Springs.
Zertman Misses	Jamestown.
Hales Mrs.	
Mead Mrs.	

Hamilton County.

Blong Misses, 96 w. Fourth	Cincinnati.
Bunting Miss P. A., 73 Court	
Baird Misses, 38 e. Fourth	
Berkemeyer H. H., 518 Main	
Cutter Mrs. S., 109 w. Fifth	
Carter Mrs., 26 e. Fourth	
De Young M., 138 w. Fifth	
Dempsey Miss 182 w. Sixth	
Dreifus Mrs. C., 202 w. Fifth	
Feakins Mrs., 24 e. Fourth	
Franklin Mrs., 65 Lower Market	
Grogan Mrs. C., 274 w. Fifth	
Hudson Mrs. W. L., 64 w. Fifth	
Hauserick H., 571	do
Hall Mrs., 389 W. Row	
Jamison Mrs. Mary, 121 w. Fifth	
McLaughlin Misses, 113 " "	
McComas Mrs. J. F. 97 " "	
Massey Mrs. H. J., 298 " "	
Milliner Miss 106 " "	
McNulty E., 343 W. Row	
Morgan Miss, 408 w. Fourth	
Myers Mrs. S., 280 w. Fifth	
Rich Mrs. E. M., 204 w. Fifth	
Richardson Mrs., 83 w. Fourth	
Renans Miss, 591 Main	
Rodefer Mrs. E. J., 152 w. Fifth	
Sattler E , 542 Main	
Simpson Mrs , 156 w. Fifth	
Tiemenn J., 362 Broadway	
Wilson A., cor. Linn and 8th	
Weyland S. H., 103 George	
Weighler Mrs., 5th bet. Smith and Park	
Whitcomb Mrs., 194 Plum	
Wenning Miss Jenny, 201 Elm	
Webb J., 168 w. Fifth	
Burnet Miss S.	Fulton.
Block Hannah V.	Pleasant Ridge.
Hill Rebecca A.	
Penny Mrs. Geo.	Harrison.

Highland County.

Peckhard Lucinda	Leesburg.
Clark Susannah	
Rideings John P.	Hillsboro'.

Holmes County.

Johnson Jane	Benton.

Huron County.

Kinney Miss   *Bellevue.*

Jefferson County.

Houghton Mrs.   *Steubenville.*
Hoobler Miss
Walker Mrs.
Patton M. & S.

Knox County.

Higgins Mrs. E. A.   *Mt. Vernon.*
Trimble Miss Lucinda   *Fredericktown.*
Upson — "
Dalrymple Miss M.   *Bladensburg.*

Lake County.

Beard E. W.   *Painesville.*
Seelay Mrs. L. A.
Seefied Mrs. N. A.

Lawrence County.

Ross Mrs. E. J.   *Ironton.*

Licking County.

Hart Malinda   *Linnville.*
McCandles Miss M.   *Newark.*
Lightbody M.
Spelman Mrs.
Thomas M. J.
Campbell Mrs. H.   *St. Louisville.*

Lorain County.

Rood Miss H.   *Oberlin.*
Smith Miss M.

Madison County.

Arnett Mrs.   *West Jefferson.*
Stevona Miss

Medina County.

Galbraith Miss   *Liverpool.*
Finney Miss Abigail   *Lodi.*
Phelps Miss O.
Minshell & True Misses   *Medina.*
Harris Miss
Garrett Miss
McConnell Miss
Blackford Mrs.

Mercer County.

Armstrong Margaret   *Celina.*

Miami County.

Clinton & McMaise   *Piqua.*
Marshall Mrs.
Ross & Castile M. & E.
Espy A. E.
Mercer M. R.
Irwin M. & J.
Gump Mrs.   *Troy.*
Kreider Mrs.

Montgomery County.

Brown O. R., Main   *Dayton.*
Boyd Miss   "
Columins Mrs. O., Green
Hesse Miss, Third
Howard Mrs., Fourth

Leitz Mrs., Second   *Dayton.*
McCauley Mrs., Main
Moulon & Cox Mrs., Jefferson
Miller Miss H., Third
Oar Mrs., Green
Stark Mrs. S., Main
Stedman Mrs.   "
Warren Mrs. H. L., Main
Wease Mrs. M., Fourth
Wetzel Mrs.

Morgan County.

Sill Mrs. W.   *McConnelsville.*
Nott A. E.
Nott Jemima
Roberts Miss Lavina A.
Martin Mary
Lee Elizabeth

Morrow County.

Thomas Mrs. S.   *Mt. Gilead.*

Muskingum County.

Armstrong Miss & Mrs.   *White Cottage.*

Pickaway County.

Bailey, Mrs. M. E.   *Circleville.*
Sweyer Mrs. S.
Witt Mrs. O.

Portage County.

Collins Mrs. O. M.   *Ravenna.*
Carhart Mrs. D.
Richardson Mrs. E. T.
Dunn Miss
Bradshaw Lucy   *Rootstown.*
Andrews Lucy
Evans Jane   *Palmyra.*
McClenticks Miss   *Nelson.*
Davis Caroline   *Mantua.*
Squires Mrs.
Henry Mrs. W. E.   *Suffield.*
Goddard Mrs. V.   *Edinburgh.*
Strong Martha A.
Spencer Miss   *Aurora.*
Witheral Mary
Travis Mrs. L.   *Franklin.*
Gillett Huldah
Lane Roseth
Stewart Miss Henrietta

Preble County.

McCrillus Mrs. & Paine   *Lewisburg.*
Morgan Miss Julia   *Eaton.*
Grace Mrs. E.
Bruce Miss Melvina
Guild Miss Julia
McGriff Miss
Eidson Miss
Haies Mrs. M.

Richland County.

Wallace Mrs. M.   *Mansfield.*
Wescott Mrs. J. A.
Lavrin Miss J. D.   *Lexington.*
Cooper Miss E. T.   *Bellville.*
Cross Miss Sarah.

Cowan Miss Amanda   *Belleville.*
Kimbal Miss E.

Ross County.

Beyerley Miss E.   *Chillicothe.*
Crawford Mrs. N. A.
Furguson Mrs.
Rinehart Miss
Morse Mrs.

Scioto County.

Adams Mrs. M.   *Portsmouth.*
Currie Mrs.
Davidson Mrs. E.
Montgomery Misses M. & R.
Worcester Mrs. E.
Bennet Miss Mary   *Iron Furnaces.*
Clark Miss M. J.
Cummins Mrs. S. P.   *Wheelersburgh.*
Reed Josephine

Seneca County.

Brown Miss Frances   *Attica.*
Zimmerman M. A.   *Tiffin.*
Allen Mrs. K.   *Republic.*
Bromley Mrs. Jane
Jackson Miss

Starke County.

Griffith Mrs.   *West Brookfield.*
Johnson Catharine   *New Franklin.*
Arbuckle Mrs. D. R.   *Massillon.*

Summit County.

Northrop Mrs. D.   *Copley.*

Tuscarawas County.

Croft Mrs. C.   *New Philadelphia.*
Hellers Mrs. H.
King Mrs. S.

Union County.

Irwin Mrs. A. & Weir   *Marysville.*
Snodgrass Mrs.

Van Wert County.

Lake & Jones Misses   *Delphos.*

Warren County.

Randall Miss R.   *Waynesville.*
Yeo Catharine
Roach Miss E. A.   *Morrow.*
Strader Mrs. H.

Washington County.

Trigler Mrs.   *Marietta.*
Broadhurst Mrs.
Dickey Miss   *Harmar.*

Wayne County.

Firestone J.   *Fredericksburg.*
Wilson Elizabeth
Shilling Mrs. J.   *West Lebanon.*
Babb M. & Co.,   *Wooster.*

Williams County.

Dobbs Mrs. J.   *Bryan.*
Wyatt John R.

Millinery and Fancy Goods Dealers (Retail.)

Defiance County.

Richardson Mrs. E. M.   *Defiance.*

Franklin County.

Miner Mrs., cor. High & Rich   *Columbus.*
Vanboughton Mrs., High
Wagley Mrs.   "
Walter Mrs., Rich

Knox County.

Higgins Mrs. E. A.   *Mt. Vernon.*

Lawrence County.

Ross Mrs. E. J.   *Ironton.*

Morrow County.

Thomas Mrs. S.   *Mt. Gilead.*

Pickaway County.

Bailey Mrs. M. E.   *Circleville.*
Witt Miss C.

Richland County.

Wescott Mrs. J. A.   *Mansfield.*

Scioto County.

Medaugh Mrs. E.   *Portsmouth.*
Montgomery Misses M. & N.
Worcester Mrs. E.

Starke County.

Falke Henry   *Massillon.*
Burgesser S.
Arbuckle Mrs. D. R.

Wayne County.

Babb M. & Co.   *Wooster.*

Mills (Portable) Manufacturer.

Hamilton County.

Burrows J. H. & Co., 23 west Front
       Cincinnati.
Straub Isaac & Co., 19 w. Front
Ward W. & E., n. side Columbia
Cochran Robert, 41 Walnut

Mill-Stone (Burr) Manufacturers.

Hamilton County.

Ward W. & E., n. side Columbia, between
    Walnut and Vine   *Cincinnati.*
Burrows J. H. & Co., 23 w. Front
Bradford Jas. & Co., 65 Walnut
Bradford T. & Co., 59 & 64 "
Cochran Robert, 41   "

Knox County.

Buckingham C. P. & Co.   *Mt. Vernon.*

Montgomery County.

Dacker & Brother, Second   *Dayton.*

Vinton County.

Walden & Ward   *McArthur.*

Millwrights.

Ashtabula County.

Parker S. M.   *Cork.*

Belmont County.

Cordner John, junr.   *Flushing.*
Gallagher John A.   *Bellair.*
Ray Harvey
Workman John
Kirkpatrick John   *Dillies' Bottom.*
Kirkpatrick James A.
Kirkpatrick Wm.

Clark County.

Beack Craver   *Catawba.*
Tussinger G. W.   *New Carlisle.*

Clermont County.

Jones Thomas   *Neville.*
Brunson D.   *Milford.*
Noyes Abner   *Bantam.*

Clinton County.

Straton Levi   *Sligo.*
Newberry Benj.   *Clarksville.*

Columbiana County.

Irwin J.   *West Point.*

Coshocton County.

Sunderlin John   *Evansburg.*
Baumgardner John   *Walhonding.*
McMullen William

Cuyahoga County.

Gates C. & R.   *Brooklyn.*

Darke County.

Carl John   *German.*

Defiance County.

Miller John   *Defiance.*
Myers Benjamin
Waters David

Delaware County.

Knapp S. W.   *Stratsford.*
Blynn John
Powell John   *Waldo.*
Knapp S. W.   *Unison.*

Fairfield County.

Ackers D.   *Sugar Grove.*
Davis Wm.

Geauga County.

Mitchell M.   *Chardon.*
Maltbrie J.   *Thompson.*
Belden Chas.   *Middlefield.*
Hopkins W. A.   *Parkman.*
Hopkins Stephen   *Bainbridge.*

Greene County.

Patterson Thomas   *Xenia.*
Parker Clayton   *Clio.*

Hamilton County.

Greenwald & Bonsall, cor. Lock and 5th
    Cincinnati.

Hesider Wm. C.   *Miami.*
Taylor Wm.

Hancock County.

Pickens Thomas   *McComb.*

Harrison County.

Barrett Albert G.   *Cadis.*

Hocking County.

Conkel Lewis   *Gibisonville.*

Holmes County.

Hurges Samuel   *Benton.*

Huron County.

Petty John   *East Townsend.*
Brownson L. P.
Lester J.
Humphrey H.

Knox County.

O'Bryan Wesley   *Democracy.*

Lawrence County.

Kelly James   *Quaker Bottom.*

Logan County.

Freeman J.   *Bellefontaine.*
Kerr James

Lorain County.

Fuller F. S.   *Amherst.*

Mercer County.

Johnson H. L.   *Celina.*
Hunt W. S.
Hunt Joshua   *Cold Water.*
Hunt David

Miami County.

Elliott J.   *West Charleston.*
Baugh L. K.   *Casstown.*
Jones Hiram   *West Milton.*

Monroe County.

Sloan Wm.   *Malaga.*
Williams Joseph   *Baresville.*
Williams Samuel B.
Williams Robert

Morgan County.

Johnson John K.   *Meigsville.*
Crisman Arthur
Crisman O.
Allen Geo. W.   *McConnelsville.*
Pyle Abner
Tanner David

Muskingum County.

Goshen Henry   *Putnam*
Rankine F.

Pike County.

Johnson John H.   *Waverly*
Lukens Samuel

Preble County.

Hart James M.   *Camden*

Putnam County.

Monroe William   *Vaughnsville.*

Sandusky County.

Holloway Geo. G.   *Rollersville.*
Minker C. G.

Starke County.

Mong Josiah   *Waynesburg.*
Mong John C.
Lindsey Wm.   *Magnolia.*

Summit County.

Bliss A. W.   *Northfield.*
Templeton E.
Noble Washington   *Copley.*
Thayer Wm. W.

Tuscarawas County.

Hornung G. F.   *New Philadelphia.*
Johnston W.
Riggle W.

Van Wert County.

Ross C. & J. W.   *Delphos.*

Warren County.

Middleton Joseph T.   *Harveysburg.*

Washington County.

Michner Ezra   *Watertown.*

Wayne County.

Buffenmayer Peter   *Reedsburg.*
Reed John   *Burbank.*
Walt Daniel   *West Lebanon.*
Keahler Wm.   *Shreve.*
Kealer Eli

Wood County.

Dunfey P. H.   *Weston.*

Money and Loan Brokers.

Hamilton County.

Butler A.,   9 Broadway   *Cincinnati.*
Clark J. W. & C°., 28 do
Gregg & Harvey, s. e. cor 3d & Walnut
Johnson J. W., w. Fifth
Merryweather F., 166 Vine
Powers Samuel, 174 Sycamore
Rohn —, 8 e. Front
Simon J , 201 Vine
Ludden B. M.   *Lockland.*

Monochromatic Artist.

Hamilton County.

Wood S., junr., 21 w. Fourth   *Cincinnati.*

Morocco Dressers.

Geauga County.

Randall, Cook & Co.   *Chardon.*

Hamilton County.

Forbus John H., 254 Main   *Cincinnati.*
Thornton R. & Co., 9   "
Weith Ignatius, 421 Vine

Mouldings and Fine Sawings,

(Manufacturer of).

Hamilton County.

Bechman F. Wm., 86 w. 13th   *Cincinnati.*

Music and Musical Instrument Dealers.

Cuyahoga County.

Brainard S. & Co., 77 Superior *Cleveland.*
Holbrook & Long, Patron's Block
Payne E. A. & Co., 162 Superior

Erie County.

Derby O. L. & Co.   *Sandusky City.*

Franklin County.

Penniman A. W., High   *Columbus.*
Reed & Gillett

Hamilton County.

Colburn & Field, 154 Main   *Cincinnati.*
Peters W. C. & Sons, cor. Fourth and
 Walnut
Lemaire L., 41 Fourth
Truax D., 80 w. Fourth
Schatzman J., cor. W. Row & Fifth
Murch & White, 74 w. Fourth

Knox County.

Cunningham W. M.   *Mt. Vernon.*

Montgomery County.

Jenkins & Deardorf, Third   *Dayton.*
Turpin James

Muskingum County.

Bailey L. P.   *Zanesville.*
Filley M. B.

Portage County.

Hall L. W.   *Ravenna.*

Trumbull County.

Sheppard & Pomeroy   *Warren.*

Musical Instrument Import'rs.

Hamilton County.

Keekeler & Brothers, 38 e. Fourth *Cin'ti*
Wagner Ferdinand, 90 Main (up stairs)

Musical Instrument Manufacturers.

Hamilton County.

Ballhause H., 130 Walnut   *Cincinnati.*
Dubois P., 174 Broadway
Gleich J. F., n. e. cor. Walnut & 9th
Telow E. F., 457 Sycamore

Summit County.

Horton H. B. & Co.   *Akron.*

Mustard and Spice Manufacturers.

Hamilton County.

Dixon & Darst, 243 & 245 Syc. *Cincin'ti.*
Harrison, Eaton & Co., 99 & 101 Walnut

Licking County.

Linnel J. *Granville.*

Montgomery County.

Beatty J. S., Third *Dayton.*

Nails, Rivets, Spikes—
(Wrought)·Manufacturers of.

Hamilton County.

Winslow A. S., 9 and 11 w. Second *Cincinnati.*

Dorrington Wm., Sycamore, on Jail lot

Newspapers.

Adams County.

Adams County Democrat (Weekly) J. M. Smith, Publisher *West Union.*

Scion of Temperance (Weekly) S. Burwell, Publisher

People's Intelligencer (Weekly) H. W. Woodrow, Publisher *Manchester.*

Allen County.

The Lima Argus (Weekly) Cunningham & Tompkins, Publishers *Lima.*

Ashland County.

Ohio Union (Weekly) H. S. Knapp, Publisher *Ashland.*

Ashtabula County.

Ashtabula Telegraph (Weekly) N. W. Hoyer, Publisher *Ashtabula.*

Ashtabula Sentinel (Weekly) J. L. Oliver & Co., Publishers *Jefferson.*

Athens County.

Athens Messenger (Weekly) N. H. & A. J. Van Vorhes, Publishers *Athens.*

Free Presbyterian (Weekly) James Gordon Publisher *Lee.*

Auglaize County.

Auglaize Republican (Weekly) —— Publisher *Wapakoneta.*

Belmont County.

St. Clairville Gazette & Citizen (Weekly) Stephen Gressinger, Publisher *St. Clairville.*

Brown County.

Ripley Bee (Weekly) Campbell & Sniffin Publishers *Ripley.*

Spiritual Era (Weekly) O. Baker, Editor

Butler County.

Hamilton Intelligencer (Weekly) Halsey & McBeth. Publishers *Hamilton.*

Hamilton Telegraph (Weekly) W. R. Kinder, Publisher

Middletown Emblem (Weekly) F. J. Oblinger, Publisher *Middletown.*

Carroll County.

Ohio Picayune (Weekly) F. S. Cable, Publisher *Carrollton.*

Carroll Free Press (Weekly) R. Crosier Publisher

Clark County.

The Republic (Tri-Weekly and Weekly) T. A. Wick & Co., Publishers *Springfield.*

The Springfield Gaz. (Weekly) J. Thomas, Publisher

Clermont County.

Clermont Courier (Weekly) J. R. S. Bond, Publisher *Batavia.*

Clermont Sun (Weekly) —— Publisher

Clinton County.

Clinton Republican (Weekly) Fisher & Russell, Publishers *Wilmington.*

Herald of Freedom (Weekly) J. W. Chaffin, Publisher

Columbiana County.

Aurora (Weekly) —— Publisher *New Lisbon.*

Buckeye State (Weekly) —— Publisher

Ohio Patriot (Weekly) W. H. Gill, Publisher

Western Palladium (Weekly) —— Publisher

Homestead Journal (Weekly) A. Hinchman, Publisher *Salem.*

Anti-Slavery Bugle (Weekly) R. Robinson, Editor

Wellsville Patriot (Weekly) W. L. Clarke, Publisher *Wellsville.*

Coshocton County.

The Coshocton Democrat (Weekly) Rich & Wheaton, Publishers *Coshocton.*

The Coshocton Republican (Weekly) H. A. Guild, Publisher

Crawford County.

Bucyrus Journal (Weekly) —— Publisher *Bucyrus.*

Crawford County Forum (Weekly) —— Publisher

Cuyahoga County.

(DAILY.)

Cleveland Herald, Harris, Fairbanks & Co., Publishers *Cleveland.*

Cleveland Plaindealer, J. W. Gray, Publisher

True Democrat, Thos. Brown, Publisher

Forest City, J. & J. C. Medill, Publishers

(TRI-WEEKLY.)

Cleveland Herald, Harris, Fairbanks & Co. Publishers

Cleveland Plaindealer, J. W. Gray, Publisher

True Democrat, Thos. Brown, Publisher

(WEEKLY.)

Cleveland Herald, Harris, Fairbanks & Co., Publishers

Cleveland Plaindealer, J. W. Gray, Publisher

True Democrat, Thos. Brown, Publisher

Forest City, J. & J. C. Medill, Publishers

Family Visitor, Sawyer, Ingersoll & Co.,
Publishers   *Cleveland.*
The Aliened American, Wm. H. Day, Publisher

(MONTHLY.)

The Golden Rule, David F. Newton, Editor

Darke County.

Greenville Journal (Weekly) J. G. & M.
B. Rees, Publishers   *Greenville.*

Defiance County.

Defiance Democrat (Weekly) J. J. Green,
Editor   *Defiance.*

Erie County.

Commercial Register (Daily, Tri-Weekly
and Weekly) Bill, Cook & Co., Publishers   *Sandusky City.*
Sandusky Mirror (Daily) W. S. Mills,
Publisher
Sandusky Democrat (Weekly) W. S. Mills,
Publisher
Free Press (Weekly) —— Publisher

Franklin County.

(DAILY.)

Ohio Statesman, Smith & Cox, Publishers   *Columbus.*
Ohio State Journal, Scott & Bascom, Publishers
Capital City Fact, John Geary & Co., Publishers

(TRI-WEEKLY.)

Ohio Statesman, Smith & Cox, Publishers
Ohio State Journal, Scott & Bascom, Publishers

(WEEKLY.)

Ohio Statesman, Smith & Cox, Publishers,
Ohio State Journal, Scott & Bascom, Publishers
Columbian, L. L. Rice, Publisher
Der Westbote, Reinbard & Feiser, Publishers
State Capital Fact, John Geary & Co., Publishers

(SEMI-MONTHLY.)

Ohio Cultivator, M. B. Bateman, Editor

(MONTHLY.)

Ohio Journal of Education, A. D. Lord,
Editor
Beauty of Holiness, Scott & Bascom, Publishers
The Ark, A. E. Glenn, Editor

Fulton County.

Fulton Democrat (Weekly) —— Publisher   *Delta.*

Gallia County.

Gallia Courier (Weekly) Vance & Shepard, Publishers   *Gallipolis.*
Gallipolis Journal (Weekly) James Harper, Publisher

Geauga County.

Geauga Republic (Weekly) —— Publisher   *Chardon.*
Free Democrat (Weekly) —— Publisher

Greene County.

Xenia Torchlight (Weekly) Robert Mc-
Bratney, Publisher   *Xenia.*

Hamilton County.

(DAILY.)

The Cincinnati Atlas, John D. Caldwell
& Co., Publishers, 118 Main *Cincinnati.*
The Cincinnati Commercial, Lee & Potter,
Publishers, n. e. cor. Third and Sycamore
The Cincinnati Enquirer, Faran & Robinson, Publishers, 88 Main
The Cincinnati Gazette, Cincinnati Gazette Company, Publishers, 118 Main
The Cincinnati Times, Calvin W. Starbuck, Publisher, 46 Pearl
The German Republican, Schmidt, Storch
& Co., Publishers, e. Third
The Nonpareil, C. D. Millar & Co., Publishers, w. Fifth
The Sun, J. S. McCormick & Co., Publishers, w. Fourth
The Tageblatt, Henry Rœdter, Publisher
The Volksblatt, Stephen Moliter, Publisher, Eagle Buildings
The Volksfreund, Joseph A. Hemann,
Publisher, cor. Vine and Centre

(TRI-WEEKLY.)

The Cincinnati Gazette, Cin. Gazette Co.,
Publishers, 118 Main

(WEEKLY.)

The Dollar Atlas, John D. Caldwell & Co.,
Publishers, 118 Main
The Dollar Commercial, Lee & Potter,
Publishers, n. e. cor. Third and Sycamore
The Dollar Enquirer, Faran & Robinson,
Publishers, 88 Main
The Dollar Nonpareil, C. D. Millar & Co.,
Publishers, w. Fifth
The Dollar Sun, J. S. McCormick & Co.,
Publishers, w. Fourth
The Dollar Times, C. W. Starbuck, Publisher, 46 Pearl
The Liberty Hall and Gazette, Cincinnati
Gazette Co., Publishers, 118 Main
The Tageblatt, Henry Rœdter, Publisher
Volksblatt, S. Moliter, Publisher, Eagle
Buildings
The Wahrheits Freund, J. H. Hemann,
Pulisher, cor. Vine and Centre
The Christian Age, Christian Publication
Society, Publishers, s. w. cor. 8th and
Walnut
The Christian Apologist, Methodist Book
Concern, Publishers, s. w. cor. 8th and
Main
The Christian Press, Rev. C. B. Boynton
Editor, Gazette Buildings

The Catholic Telegraph, Rev. E. Purcell, Editor — *Cincinnati.*

The Central Christian Herald, Rev. C. E. Babb, Editor, Gazette Buildings

The Cincinnati Price Current, Richard Smith, Editor, College Hall

The Letter Sheet Price Current, R. Smith, Editor, College Hall

Genius of Liberty, Mrs. Aldrich, Editress, Gazette Buildings.

Columbian and Great West, W. B. Shattuck, Editor, Gazette Buildings.

Journal and Messenger, Rev. J. L. Batchelder, Editor, 34 w. Fourth

Pen and Pencil, Wm. Wallace Warden, Editor and Publisher, Main

Presbyterian of the West, Rev. A. D. Lord, Editor, 74 w. 4th.

Organ of Temperance Reform, S. F. Cary, Editor, Times Building

Star in the West, Rev. J. A. Gurley, Editor, 52 w. 4th

Weekly Patriot, H. Clay Pate, Editor, 141 and 147 Main

Western Christian Advocate, Methodist Book Concern, Publishers, s. w. cor. 8th and Main

(SEMI-MONTHLY.)

Christian Sunday School Journal, Christian Publication Society, Publishers, s. w. cor. 8th and Walnut

Sunday School Advocate, Methodist Book Concern, Publishers, s. w. cor. 8th & Main

Dye's Counterfeit Detector, John S. Dye, Publisher, s. e. cor. 3d and Walnut

Lord's Counterfeit Detector, T. W. Lord, Publisher, No. 11 Art Union Building

(MONTHLY.)

Buchanan's Journal of Man, Jos. R. Buchanan, M. D., Editor

Eclectic Medical Journal, J. R. Buchanan, M. D., & R. S. Newton, M. D., Editors.

Goodman's Counterfeit Detector, W. McCammon, jun., Publisher, s. e. cor. 3d and Walnut

Ladies' Repository, Methodist Book Concern, Publisher, s. w. cor. 8th and Main

Missionary Advocate, Methodist Book Concern, Publisher, s. w. cor. 8th and Main

National Magazine, Methodist Book Concern, Publisher, s. w. cor. 8th and Main

Masonic Review, J. Ernst, Publisher, 183 Main

Templar's Magazine, J. Wadsworth, M. D., Editor

The Garland, J. C. Richardson & Co., Publishers

Parlor Magazine, Jethro Jackson, Publisher, 180 Walnut

Western American Review, G. W. H. Bickley, Editor, 141 Main

Western Medical News, R. S. Newton, M. D., Editor

Western Magazine, Mr. A. & Mrs. H. G. Moore, Editors — *Cincinnati.*

Investigator, J. R. Payson, Publisher, Times Building

Hardin County.

Kenton Republican, Weekly, J. S. Robinson, Publisher — *Kenton.*

Democratic Expositor, Weekly, Charles Warner, Publisher

Nor Wester, Weekly, Wm. Tomlinson, Publisher

Harrison County.

Cadiz Republican, Weekly, R. Hatton, Editor — *Cadiz.*

Democratic Sentinel, Weekly, Charles N. Allen, Publisher

Henry County.

North West, Weekly, A. M. Hallabaugh, Editor — *Napoleon.*

Highland County.

Highland News, Weekly, J. L. Boardman, Publisher — *Hillsboro'.*

Hillsboro' Gazette, Weekly, J. R. Emrie, Publisher

Greenfield Blade, Weekly, R. J. Strickland, Publisher — *Greenfield.*

Hocking County.

The Hocking Sentinel, Weekly, O. Case, Publisher — *Logan.*

The Hocking County Star, Weekly, J. K. Rochester, Publisher

Holmes County.

Der Deicher, John Raber, Editor — *Holmes.*

Holmes County Farmer and Free Press, Weekly, R. S. McEwing, Publisher — *Millersburg.*

Holmes County Whig, Weekly, J. Casky, Publisher

Huron County.

Huron Reflector, Weekly, Preston & Wickham, Publishers — *Norwalk.*

Norwalk Experiment, Weekly, Joseph M. Farr, Publisher

Jackson County.

Jackson Standard, Weekly, Laird & Mathews, Publishers — *Jackson.*

Jefferson County.

Steubenville Herald, Daily, Tri-Weekly, and Weekly, W. R. Allison, Publisher — *Steubenville.*

Morning Union, Daily, Andrew Stewart, Publisher

American Union, Weekly, Andrew Stewart, Publisher

Steubenville Messenger, Daily, Turner & Co., Publishers

Steubenville Dollar Messenger, Weekly, Turner & Co., Publishers

Knox County.

Ohio State Times, Weekly, Chapman & Thrall. Publishers   *Mt. Vernon.*
True Whig, Weekly, A. Banning Norton, Publisher
Western Home Visitor, Weekly, Higgins & Knox, Publishers
True Whig, Daily, A. Banning Norton, Publisher
Democratic Banner, Weekly, Edmund J. Ellis, Publisher

Lake County.

Painesville Telegraph, Weekly, H. C. Gray & M. R. Doolittle, Publishers   *Painesville.*
Grand River Record, Weekly, ——, Publisher

Lawrence County.

Ironton Register, Weekly, Stimpson & Parke, Publishers   *Ironton.*
Spirit of the Times, Weekly, B. F. Cory, Publisher

Licking County.

Newark Times, Weekly, M. P. Brister, Publisher   *Newark.*
Licking Herald, Weekly, Wm. Parr, Publisher
Newark Advocate, Weekly, B. Briggs, Publisher

Logan County.

Logan County Gazette, Weekly, Hubbard & Brother, Publishers   *Bellefontaine.*

Lorain County.

The Independent Democrat, Weekly, J. D. Baker, Publisher   *Elyria.*
The Elyria Courier, Weekly, ——, Publisher
The Oberlin Weekly Times, Weekly, J. M. Fitch, Publisher   *Oberlin.*
The Oberlin Evangelist, Weekly, J. M. Fitch, Publisher
The Wellington, Journal, Weekly, ——, Publisher   *Wellington.*

Lucas County.

Maumee River Times, Weekly, H. T. Smith. Publisher   *Maumee City.*
Toledo Blade, Daily and Weekly, H. L. Hosmer, Editor   *Toledo.*
Toledo Republican, Daily and Weekly, ——, Editor

Madison County.

Madison Reveille, Weekly, G. W. Spring, Publisher   *London.*

Mahoning County.

Mahoning Free Democrat, Weekly, M. Cullation, Publisher   *Youngstown.*
Republican Sentinel, Weekly, Norris & Webb, Editors   *Canfield.*

Marion County.

Democratic Mirror, Weekly, T. O. Thompson, Publisher   *Marion.*

Medina County.

Democratic Whig, Weekly, John Speer, Publisher   *Medina.*
Medina Democrat, Weekly, F. Harry & Co., Publishers

Meigs County.

Meigs County Telegraph, Weekly, Alf. Thompson, Editor   *Pomeroy.*

Mercer County.

Western Standard, Weekly, ——, Publisher   *Celina.*

Miami County.

Piqua Register, Weekly and Tri-Weekly, Defrees & Jones, Publishers   *Piqua.*
Piqua Enquirer, Weekly, ——, Publisher
Troy Times, Weekly, David Gillis, Publisher   *Troy.*

Monroe County.

Spirit of Democracy, Weekly, James R. Morris, Publisher   *Woodsfield.*

Montgomery County.

Dayton Journal, Daily and Weekly, R. N. & W. F. Conley, Publishers *Dayton.*
Dayton Gazette, Daily & Weekly, D. P. Dubois, Publisher
Dayton City Item, Daily, Schnebly, Davis & Co., Publishers

Morrow County.

Whig Sentinel, Weekly, W. P. Dumble, Publisher   *Mt. Gilead.*
Democratic Messenger, Weekly, G. W. Sharpe, Publisher

Muskingum County.

Zanesville Gazette, Weekly, E. T. & Alex. S. Cox, Publishers   *Zanesville.*
Zanesville Courier, Daily and Weekly, Ball, Buell & Mercer, Publishers
Zanesville City Times, J. Glessner & Brother, Publishers
Zanesville Aurora, Weekly, R. W. P. Muse, Editor

Perry County.

Perry County Democrat, Weekly, E. S. Colburn, Publisher   *Somerset.*

Pickaway County.

The Circleville Watchman, Weekly, Jason Case, Publisher   *Circleville.*
The Circleville Herald, Weekly, G. Scott, Publisher
The Religious Telegraph, Weekly, J. Lawrence, Publisher
Der Frohliche Botschaster, Weekly, H. Straub, Publisher
The Incentive, Monthly, J. Lynch, Publisher

Portage County.

Portage Sentinel, Weekly, S. D. Harris, Editor *Ravenna.*

Portage County Whig, Weekly, J. S. Herrick, Publisher

Ohio Star, Weekly, L. W. Hall, Publisher

Preble County.

Eaton Weekly Register, Weekly, Wm. B. Tizzard, Publisher *Eaton.*

Eaton Democrat, Weekly, Wm. C. Gould, Publisher

Richland County.

Richland Shield and Banner, Weekly, John Y. Glessner, Publisher *Mansfield.*

Mansfield Herald, Weekly, Atthias Day, jr., Publisher

Christian Statesman, Monthly, Rev. E. Smith, Editor

Golden Rule, Monthly, D. F. Newton, Editor

Ross County.

Ancient Metropolis, Daily and Weekly, G. Armstrong, Publisher *Chillicothe.*

Chillicothe Advertiser, Weekly, Eshleman & Bollemeyer, Publishers

Scioto Gazette, Daily, Tri-Weekly, and Weekly, O. Curry, Publisher

Ohio Correspondent, (German) Weekly, W. Raine, Editor

Sandusky County.

Sandusky County Democrat, Weekly, Orton & Dickinson, Publishers *Fremont.*

Fremont Journal, Weekly, S. W. Booth, Publisher

Scioto County.

Dispatch, Daily, Alex. Pearce, Publisher, *Portsmouth.*

Evening Tribune, Daily, John Hanna, Publisher

Portsmouth Enquirer, Weekly, A. Pearce, Publisher

Portsmouth Tribune and Clipper, Weekly, John Hanna, Publisher

Ohio Life Boat, Weekly, J. Miller & Co., Publishers

Scioto Valley Republican, Weekly, S. P. Drake & Co., Publishers

Seneca County.

The Seneca Advertiser, Weekly, John Flaugher, Publisher *Tiffin.*

Tiffin Family Newspaper, Weekly, A. Laubach, Publisher

Shelby County.

Shelby County Banner, Weekly, ———, Publisher *Sidney.*

Shelby County Democrat, Weekly, ———, Publisher

Starke County.

Democratic Transcript, Weekly, — Kleppard, Publisher *Canton.*

Ohio Repository, Weekly, J. Saxton, Publisher *Canton.*

Starke County Democrat, Weekly, A. McGregor, Publisher

Massillon News, Weekly, Logan & Fletcher, Publishers *Massillon.*

Summit County.

The Ohio Observer, Weekly, Sawyer, Ingersoll & Co., Publishers *Hudson.*

The Family Visitor, Weekly, ———, Publisher

The Summit Beacon, Weekly, ———, Publisher *Akron.*

The Standard, Weekly, ———, Publisher

Tuscarawas County.

Dover Citizen, Weekly, McClintock & Bodenhamer, Publishers *Canal Dover.*

Deutscheo in Ohio, Weekly, John J. Robinson, Publisher

Ohio Democrat, Weekly, J. D. Elliott, Publisher *New Philadelphia.*

Uhrichsville Commercial Advertiser, Weekly, Jas. Ilery, Publisher *Uhrichsville.*

Union County.

Marysville Tribune, Weekly, C. S. Hamilton, Publisher *Marysville.*

Union Journal, Weekly, Cassil, Turner & Pollock, Publishers

Van Wert County.

The Delphos Oracle, Weekly, N. L. Perry, Publisher *Delphos.*

The Van Wert Democrat, Weekly, W. Moneysmith, Publisher *Van Wert.*

Vinton County.

Vinton County Flag, Weekly, Hewitt & Bingham, Publishers *McArthur.*

McArthur Republican, Weekly, L. S. & L. W. Bort, Publishers

Warren County.

Miami Visitor, Weekly, J. W. Roberts, Publisher *Waynesville.*

Western Star, Weekly, W. H. P. Denny, Publisher *Lebanon.*

Democratic Citizen, Weekly, J. N. Pepper & G. W. Stokes, Publishers

Washington County.

Marietta Intelligencer, Weekly and Tri-Weekly, B. Gates, Publisher *Marietta.*

Marietta Republican, Weekly, Layman & Lentter, Publishers

Wayne County.

Wooster Democrat, Weekly, Foreman, Johnson & Booth, Publishers *Wooster.*

Williams County.

Williams Democrat, Weekly, ———, Publisher *West Unity.*

Wood County.

North-Western Democrat, Weekly, A. D. Wright, Editor and Pub.   *Perrysburg.*

Wyandot County.

Democratic Pioneer, Weekly, E. Giles, Publisher   *Upper Sandusky.*

Notaries Public.

Adams County.

Dunbar D.   *Manchester.*

Allen County.

Baxter Samuel A.   *Lima.*
Nichols & Waldorf
Lamison C. N.

Ashtabula County.

Turner Asaph   *Geneva.*
Dann S. D.   *Jefferson.*

Athens County.

Fulton L.   *Amesville.*
Brown O. W.   *Athens.*
Wilson John G.   *Hibardville.*

Brown County.

Baird Chambers   *Ripley.*

Butler County.

Wilson John W.   *Hamilton.*
Lewis John R.
Thomas Alfred & John
Smith W. H.   *Oxford.*
Mollyneaux W. J.
Cox A. P.   *West Chester.*
Peck H. P. K.   *Middletown.*

Champaign County.

Jones David N.   *Christiansburg.*

Clermont County.

Tritt J.   *New Richmond.*
Dunam P. J.
Larkin E.   *Neville.*
Sheldon Thomas   *Bantam.*

Columbiana County.

Ambler Jacob W.   *Salem.*
Weaver E. T.

Cuyahoga County.

Johnson Henry N., 10 Seneca Block
    Cleveland.
Mather S. H., Bank
Seymour B., 52 Pearl   *Ohio City.*

Defiance County.

Ingram Wm.   *Defiance.*
Taylor D.
Welle W.
Wilson Geo. H.

Erie County.

Cogswell F. W.   *Sandusky City.*
Leonard Cuyler
Bigelow J. G.
Wildman H.
Sloane Rush R.

Franklin County.

Jenkins Warren   *Columbus.*
Hannum S. B.
Lilly E., High

Hamilton County.

Gibbons Joseph, Law Buildings *Cincin'ti.*
Bryan T. B , 126 w. Third
Miller F. W., Reeder's Building
Van Hamm Alexander, Bacon's Building
Clemmons J. H., cor. Main & 7th
Rands R., cor. Syc. & 8th
Coit D. R , 12 Worthington's Buildings
Brown D. L., 227 Vine
Long A., n. e. cor. 6th & Main
Collet John, 308 Main
Stuart John, cor. 6th & Main
Dana Joseph, 130 Walnut
Hodgson W. Q , 126 "
Graves T. H., 205 W. Row
White J. S., 257 Walnut
Carpenter Sam'l. S., Worthington's Buildings.
Freon J., n. w. cor. Main & 8th
Hartwell Shattuck, 95 Walnut
Vantuyl T. B.   *Springdale.*

Highland County.

Keys J. M.   *Hillsboro'.*

Huron County.

Sawyer Franklin   *Norwalk.*
Sadler Wm.   *Monroeville.*

Jackson County.

Stanley T. R.   *Jackson.*

Jefferson County.

McCleary J. C.   *Warrenton,*

Lake County.

Sterling L.   *Willoughby.*
Doolittle J. T.   *Painesville,*

Logan County.

Strother H. B.   *Bellefontaine.*
Beatty W. W.   *Belle Centre.*

Lorain County.

Burke S.   *Elyria.*
Allen Roswell H.   *Oberlin.*

Mahoning County.

Canfield E. G.   *Canfield.*

Marion County.

Knapp J. R.   *Marion.*

Medina County.

Codding John   *Coddingville.*
Dickenson Abel   *Wadsworth.*

Miami County.

Wood S. H.   *Piqua.*

Morgan County.

Wortley David H.   *McConnelsville.*

Perry County.

Smith Eli   *New Lexington.*
Worley Jesse

Richland County.

Meredith John   *Mansfield.*

Seneca County.

Lee J. C.   *Tiffin.*
Watson O. K.
Pillors J. P.
Lewis P. J.
Tunnison Thos. O.
Keen G. J.

Summit County.

Voris Peter   *Bath.*

Trumbull County.

Jones L. O.   *Hartford.*

Van Wert County.

Huber Noah   *Delphos.*

Vinton County.

Bingham E. F.   *McArthur.*

Nursery, Seedsmen & Florists.

Belmont County.

Askew Wm.   *St. Clairsville.*

Butler County.

Smith P. G.   *Rossville.*

Columbiana County.

Myers Samuel   *New Lisbon.*

Coshocton County.

Mathews James   *Coshocton.*
Humrickhouse Thos. S.

Cuyahoga County.

Stair J. & Son, 6 Ontario   *Cleveland.*
De Witt & Co., cor. West & Merwin

Hamilton County.

Conclin Wm. jr., 26 and 27 5th   *Cinoin'ti.*
Dair John F. & Co., 40 and 42 L. Market
Ernst A. H., Spring Garden
Heaver Wm., Reading Road Nursery
Heaver & Britton, 71 Sycamore
Kelley M. & Co., Hamilton Road
Knott Thomas, Lebanon Turnpike
McCullough J. M., 162 Main
McAvoy D., 11 e. 5th
Mears W. E., 21 Congress
Pfeiffer Anthony, Reading Turnpike
Sayers John, cor. Reading and Mt. Auburn Roads
Thompson F. R., 290 Main
Cook J. S.   *Walnut Hills.*
Howarth James
Craig Edward   *Cheviot.*

Henry County.

Kelley & Mallery   *Napoleon.*

Lorain County.

Wright Wm. W.   *Oberlin.*
Bullock J. W.   *Elyria.*

Lucas County.

Griswold Wm. P.   *Maumee City.*
Maddocks, Perigo & Prentice   *Toledo.*

Montgomery County.

Gunckle Wm.   *Germantown.*
Rhinehart Wm.

Morrow County.

Livesey Wm. B.   *Lincoln.*

Muskingum County.

Iraley Wm. S.   *New Concord.*

Pickaway County.

Tipton W. W.   *Darbyville.*

Portage County.

Brayton Isaac   *Ravenna.*
Harmon John
Tuttle Harvy   *Palmyra.*

Preble County.

Young S. S.   *Eaton.*

Richland County.

Moody M. & J.   *Belleville.*

Summit County.

Johnson Samuel E.   *Middlebury.*

Washington County.

Dana Geo. & Son   *Belpre.*
Stone Francis

Oil-Cloth Carpet Manufacturers.

Cuyahoga County.

Webster & Spencer, Superior   *Cleveland.*

Oil (Lubricating for Machinery) Manufacturer.

Cuyahoga County.

Dean Charles A., 15 Merwin   *Cleveland.*

Omnibus Manufacturers.

Hamilton County.

Bruce W. S., 75 Walnut   *Cincinnati.*
Palmer James R., Bank, bet. W. Row & Linn.

Organ Builders.

Ashtabula County.

Goodrich Wm.   *Jefferson.*
Holt Geo. O.   *Lindenville.*

Hamilton County.

Closs J., 407 W. Row   *Cincinnati.*
Schwab Mathias, n. w. cor. Sycamore and Schiller

Tuscarawas County.

Weber John   *New Philadelphia.*

Wayne County.

Botsford Wm. B.   *Wooster.*

Pail Manufacturers.

Lake County.
Bonsfield John   *Kirtland.*

Muskingum County.
Guthries & Buckinghams   *Putnam.*

Washington County.
Newton John, Agt., Marietta Pail Factory   *Harmer.*
Jewel L. R., Agt, Harmar Pail Manufac'y.

Paint (Ohio Fire Proof) Manufacturers.

Cuyahoga County.
Wilson Wilson   *Brooklyn.*

Paints, Glass, Oils and Dye Stuffs—Dealers in.

Clark County.
Sykes J.   *Springfield.*

Columbiana County.
Walker N. U. & Co.,   *Wellsville.*

Cuyahoga County.
Cary H. G. O., cor. Merwin and Canal,
                                  Cleveland.
Churchill F. E., cor. Euclid and Ontario
Fiske William, 11 Superior
Gaylord & Co., 30   do
Hayward, Woods & Co
Huntington O. E.
Kingsley E., 37 Ontario
Palmer & Sackrider, 73 Superior
Wenham Arthur J., 9 Merwin
Tinker Daniel   *Ohio City.*

Defiance County.
Allen O. H.   *Defiance.*

Hamilton County.
Chrisfield & Peal, 222 Main, *Cincinnati.*
Coolidge & Whetstone, cor. 5th & W. Row
Allen & Co., cor. 5th & Main
Beakirt J. C., Pearl, bet. Main & Walnut
Harrison W. H. & Co., 4th, bet. Main & Walnut
Burdsel & Brother, cor. Front & Main
Eckstein F., cor. 4th & Main
Burdsel O. S., Main, bet. 5th & 6th
Fuller E. E.   *Harrison*

Hardin County.
Bogardus & Rows   *Kenton*

Mercer County.
Williamson E. T.   *Celina*

Portage County.
Hatch Curtis   *Ravenna.*
Swift Isaac
Cone J. W. & Co.   *Franklin.*

Painters—House, Sign and Ornamental.

Adams County.
Cooper John C.   *Eckmansville*

Walker Samuel   *Eckmansville.*

Ashland County.
Crone Benjamin   *Ashland.*
Knoth Charles

Ashtabula County.
Mills John   *Kelloggsville.*
Smith Isaac
Fricker J.   *Jefferson.*
Smalley H. N.
Bishop T. & J. B   *West Williamsfield.*
Judd C. T.   *Cork.*

Athens County.
Selby John J.   *Canaanville.*
Howe James   *Nelsonville.*
Cooper G. J.
Ragner J.   *Athens.*
Howe H.

Brown County.
Casset Dennis   *Higginsport.*
Fawl & Martin   *Ripley.*

Butler County.
Cutler W. T.   *West Chester.*
Kinney W. T.
Brewer Adam P.
Walworth ——   *Hamilton.*
Walton John   *Middletown.*
Layland Wm.   *Somerville.*

Clark County.
Johnson David   *South Charleston.*
Crane Lewis   *New Carlisle.*
Lowman Cyrus

Clermont County.
Towner Abel   *New Richmond.*
Hamrick J.   *Mt. Carmel.*
Miller Owen   *Amelia.*
Stirling Robert
Cheyn J.   *Rural.*

Clinton County.
Harrison J.   *New Vienna.*
Shockley P.
Havens Robert   *Wilmington.*

Columbiana County.
Moore John   *Wellsville.*
Wilson Hugh S.
Shields James H.   *New Lisbon.*
Russell T. J.   *Bucks.*
Russell Joseph
Blythe Andrew   *East Liverpool.*
Beard John   *Columbiana.*
Beard Jacob
Fitzpatrick Albert
Rowe S. O.   *Unity.*

Crawford County.
Zeok John B.   *Bucyrus.*

Cuyahoga County.
Adams George H., 71 Superior, *Cleveland.*
Carson M., 6 Water

Denham Thomas, 60 Public Sq. *Cleveland.*
Downie John, Superior
Proudfoot Wm. & Co., 69 Rockwell
Wadsworth & Akers, Empire Buildings
Worley J., cor. Ontario & Champlain
Steveus C. C. *Ohio City.*
Turton Joseph & Son
Scott D.
Tinker Daniel
Howe & Willard
Preston George *East Cleveland.*
Earl E. *Chagrin Falls.*
Taylor W.
Higgins Wm. *Coe Ridge.*
Huu William
Angel George *Warrensville.*
Robison John
Smith James
Adams E. E. *Colamer.*
Hall Zilea

Darke County.

Fey A. *Fort Jefferson.*
Warner J. W. W.

Defiance County.

Brown Ira *Farmer Centre.*
Clark H. M. *Defiance.*

Delaware County.

Law Edward *Galena.*
Dust John

Erie County.

Barley A. *Huron.*
Anderson L.
Wilkenson O. A.
Ward C. *Sandusky City.*
Huke Wm.
Holland John
Cornell H.
Bangle J.
Gerlash Wm.
Marshall Wm.

Fairfield County.

Reed J. B. *Lancaster.*
Hinkle Charles
Hood C. & G.
Barbinchou F.
Peck Wm. B.

Franklin County.

Deal J., Town *Columbus.*
Jones & Hert. High
Thompson J., do
Mathews J B. *Worthington.*
Olmstead Faran, do

Geauga County.

Redfield Henry *Auburn.*
Scudder C. F.
Gridley George *Hamden.*
Staunton H.
Avery Elias *Chardon.*
Paino J. C.
Rodgers W. T.

Haskill W. *Chardon.*
Parine Charles
Hedges Alfred
Speuce F. *Claridon.*
Gridley C.

Greene County.

Craters Samuel *Xenia.*
Divey Charles *Fairfield.*
Brain H. *Clifton.*

Guernsey County.

Knowlton R. *Cumberland.*
Thomas Samuel *Fairview.*
Querry B. H.

Hamilton County.

Arnan M., No. 56 Findley *Cincinnati.*
Baughman J., 51 Webster
Becker A., 118 Clay
Becker J. C., 105 Bremen
Bogart J., 122 Longworth
Chard C. W., 141 Hopkins
Cummings H., 126 Walnut
Deierlein F., 460 Vine
Flynn J. & Co., 143 Front
Haskell & Estes
Hulse Charles A., n. w. cor. Cutter & Everett
Husten Joseph M., 76 3d
Hargraves J. H., 106 w. 8th
Jewell W. T., 84 Columbia
Jones C, 420 w. 5th
Kenn T., Baymiller, bet. 7th & 8th
Kreyenhagen W., 3d near Sycamore
Koempel H. J., 71 Court
Kelly & Curtiss, 89 Front
Lovell J. D. & Co., 43 Second
Lotz H., 496 Vine
Morris James M., Richmond, bet. Fulton and John
Morris & Looker, 150 w. 3d
McKittrick John, 522 w. 5th
Miller G. P. 295 Elm
Owen J., 139 Front
O'Neil J., 198 Elm
Porter Allen A., 199 Plum
Riggs & Murray, 35 e. Front
Ruffner M., 10 w. 3d
Robinson B., 203 Longworth
Schafer K. H., 549 Elm
Scudder J. W., 224 Betts
Schumard J., 305 w. Sixth
Shulze M., cor. Broadway & Abigail
Schaffer J., 149 Everett
Sexton F, 200 Elm
Saunders & Baldwin, 5th, bet. Elm & Plum
Trener & Misener, 145 Walnut
Venneman H., 23 Woodward
Whitaker Wm, jr., 39 3d
Williams D., 600 e. Front
Worthington J. C., 148 w. 8th
Winder W. W., 252½ W. Row
Kear B. *Fulton.*
LaBoyteaux G. L. *Mt. Healthy.*
Clark Jeremiah M. *Pleasant Ridge.*

Powell William B.   *Harrison.*
Ryan George
Bowlby William
Wiley William
Floro William   *Newtown.*
Freeman William   *Sharonville.*
Firt Daniel   *Cheviot.*
Miller George
Wise John
Price John   *College Hill.*

Hardin County.

Bogardus & Rowe   *Kenton.*
Glenn W. B.
Kennet & Markle

Harrison County.

Simmons John   *Cadix.*

Henry County.

Tyler O. H.   *Napoleon.*

Highland County.

Eyres R. W.   *Greenfield.*
Thompson John
Johnson I.   *Leesburg.*
Pecham William
Grant E. J.   *Hillsboro'.*

Huron County.

Boardman James   *East Townsend.*
Barber S.
Boardman J. I.
Eddinger S.   *Bellevue.*
Ford John

Knox County.

Burns W. M.   *Mount Vernon.*
Ethridge D.
Chamberlain Thomas   *Fredericktown.*
Snow Alvin
Johnson Ephraim   *Millwood.*

Licking County.

Rowe R. T.   *Etna.*
Spelman O.   *Granville.*
Reed James
Fleming G. W.   *Newark.*
Parker J.
Mouell G. W.
Sessor T. F.
Hart W. R.   *Croton.*
Seymour O. F.

Logan County.

Matthews John F.   *Huntsville.*
Robinson Jackson J.   *Bellefontaine.*

Lorain County.

Whiton J. B.   *Huntington.*
Kenaston D.   *Oberlin.*
Smith H.   *Avon Lake.*

Lucas County.

Awl —   *Toledo.*
Lewis David
Miller John
Newcomb Alexander

Nichols —   *Toledo.*
Segur —
Southard Thomas
Weeks J. S.

Madison County.

Oranch S. & Co.   *London.*
Leland A. W.
Gilbert & Cramer

Mahoning County.

Macklin Franklin   *New Springfield.*
Lockhart Joseph

Medina County.

Ellis P. T.   *Leroy.*
Smith A. P.   *River Styx.*
Marsh E. O.   *Lodi.*
Stringham S. L.

Meigs County.

Pugg James   *Letart Falls.*

Miami County.

Dunlap & Richards   *Piqua.*
Bettiton B.
Binkley O.   *Troy.*
Binkley O. A.
Gillson J.   *Casstown.*
Jenks G. W.
Gillson O.
Gillson O.
Boyd M. P. & Co.   *West Milton.*
Falknor & Co.

Montgomery County.

Ayers O. S., 3d   *Dayton.*
Childs O. J., 3d
Hooper A., 5th
Harter P. E., Main
Long James, 3d
McClark, A., Main
More John, 3d
Sullivan A. O., 3d
Theobold H., Ludlow
Wyatt J. J., 1st
Ryson —   *Miamisburg.*
Treon Peter
Heister Cyrus   *Germantown.*
Long Lefevre

Morgan County.

McOarty W. W.   *McConnelsville.*
Stewart James E.   *Pennsville.*

Morrow County.

Pancost J. M.   *Cardington.*

Muskingum County.

Bailey E.   *Zanesville.*

Noble County.

Morrison Kelita   *Sarahsville.*

Ottawa County.

Beck O.   *Port Clinton.*
Schlosser A.

Pickaway County.

McLain & Duff   *Circleville.*

Portage County.

Reeves A.	*Ravenna.*
Russell E. G.	
Brown William	
Gilson Isaac	
Donald Thomas	*Randolph.*
Brocket J.	
Preston Joel	*Shalersville.*
Heighton I. H.	*Edinburgh.*
Allen A.	*Franklin.*
Cook O.	*Mantua.*
McElwaine H.	*Nelson.*
Williams T. R.	*Palmyra.*
Jones E.	
Barlow J. C.	*Rootstown.*
Demming A.	
Carter Henry	
Richardson W.	*Freedom.*

Preble County.

Dunham Asa	*Eaton.*
Sturling William	

Richland County.

Wright Abner	*Mansfield.*
Brown Abner	*Lexington.*

Ross County.

McDowal Alexander	*Chillicothe.*
Mills William	

Sandusky County.

Judson Charles	*Clyde.*
Caul S.	*Fremont.*
Melins Jacob	
Clughern J.	
Niles C. H.	*Rollersville.*
Parker Nathan	
Swingler H.	

Seneca County.

Cox A.	*Bloomville.*
Zimmerman F.	
Spalding Larkin	*Green Spring.*

Starke County.

Zent Jacob	*West Brookfield.*
Doering W. H.	*Marlboro'.*
Coates Hays	*New Baltimore.*
Seaton F. & Co.	*Massillon.*
Snider & Deitz	
McMaster Robert	

Summit County.

Evans E. S.	*Cuyahoga Falls.*
Lawson W. A.	
Lee P. J.	
Russell W.	*Tallmadge.*
Elliott & Colony	*Akron.*
Lane S. A.	
Steinhouse & Wright	
Stripe William	*Inland.*
Mills Sanford	*Copley.*
Bishop Benjamin	*Bath.*
Randall James	

Trumbull County.

Bartlett Lucius	*Johnsonville.*
Winters Ooradon	*Johnsonville*
McNutt C.	*Warren.*
Porter L.	
Long J. H.	
Netterfield William	
Shilling George	
Hall E.	*Orangeville.*
Miller Lent L.	*Girard.*
Colton Edmond	
Bently Martin	*Brookfield.*
Beal John	*Ohltown.*
Turnbull William	

Tuscarawas County.

Miksch Amos	*Gnadenhutten.*
Hall Truman G.	*Canal Dover.*
France Henry	
Stansbury John	
Scott John	
Lahm Frederick	
Williams S.	
Do John	*New Philadelphia.*
Do Joseph	
Carlisle & Son	

Warren County.

Kindal Charles	*Waynesville.*
Grieble Conrad	*Butlerville.*

Washington County.

Sheno Nathan	*Marietta.*
Nesmith J.	
Protsman L.	

Wayne County.

Cheyney J. L.	*Fredericksburg.*
Gragory Charles	*Shreve.*

Williams County.

Miller John M.	*West Unity.*
Norris Peter	*Bryan.*
Kent Sanford	
Wyatt John P.	
Young Charles	

Wood County.

Manson E. H.	*Weston.*
Phillips A.	*Portage.*
Middleton D. C.	*Miltonville.*

Painters—Portrait.

Clark County.

Roberts J. H.	*Springfield.*

Cuyahoga County.

Boisseau A., 111 Superior	*Cleveland.*

Hamilton County.

Aubrey —, 4th	*Cincinnati.*
Beard James H., Hart's building, e. 4th	
Bott E., Art Union building	
Baldwin A., do	
Campbell J., 71 Court	
Cashen —, 61 w. 4th	
Duncanson R. S., do	
Edwards R. C., Hart's building, e. 4th	
Eaton —, 22 w. 4th	
Garret —, 6 do	
Griggs —, 2 do	

21

Johnson J. R., 17 w. 4th   *Cincinnati.*
Noble Miss, Art Union building
Shaw J., 24 w. 6th
Sontag W. L., 76 w. 4th
Van Name G., W. Row
Williams J. Insco, n. w. cor. Walnut & 6th

Licking County.

Godden A.   *Newark.*

Trumbull County.

Merrill F. C.   *Warren.*
Rodden H.

Paper Dealers.

Cuyahoga County.

Sanford A. S., 17 Superior   *Cleveland.*

Hamilton County.

Goodman & Co., 34 Pearl   *Cincinnati.*
Butler & Bro.,   27   do
Nixon & Co., 77 & 79 Walnut
Spear & Stephens, 158 Main
Ross J. L.   386   do
Atkins William & Co., 321 Broadway
Hartwell J. W., 29 Walnut

Paper Manufacturers.

Butler County.

Becket & Rigdon   *Hamilton.*
Shuey & McGuire
Richardson C. H.   *Middletown.*
Erwin J. W. & Bro.
Graham James   *Symmes' Corner.*

Clark County.

Kills J. W.   *Springfield.*

Columbiana County.

Harvey J. & H.   *Little Beaver Bridge.*

Cuyahoga County.

Davis D. A. & Co.   *Chagrin Falls.*

Delaware County.

Howard C. & Co.   *Delaware.*
Williams, Andrews & Co.   *Stratford.*

Gallia County.

Black R. & Co.   *Gallipolis.*
Nash & Parker

Greene County.

Nixon & Co.   *Clifton.*

Hamilton County.

Nixon & Co., 77 & 79 Walnut, *Cincinnati.*
Atkins, William & Co., 321 Broadway
Allen G. W.   . *Lockland.*
Batchelor & Co.
Cecill & McHannan
Friend & Tangenan

Jefferson County.

Thompson, Hanna & Sons   *Steubenville.*

Montgomery County.

Claflin, L. F. & Co., Upper Hydraulic
                     Dayton.
McGrigor T. & D.   do

Muskingum County.

Cox H. I. & Co.   *Zanesville.*

Ross County.

Ingham & Co.   *Chillicothe.*

Summit County.

Peebler R. & Co.   *Cuyahoga Falls.*
Smith J. M. & Co.

Paper-Hangers, Manufactu'rs Importers and Dealers.

Cuyahoga County.

Adams George H., 6 Miller's block *Cleve-*
                           [land.
Carson M., 6 Water
Denham Thomas, 80 Public Square
Downie John, Superior
Worley J., cor. Ontario & Champlain
Jones & Co., 58 Superior

Franklin County.

Burr & Randall, High   *Columbus.*
Riley Joseph H. & Co., High
Aston J. C. & Co.

Hamilton County.

Andress F. & C., 179 Main   *Cincinnati.*
Andress C. S., 163   do
Godman, P. H., 455   do
Hane John, 543 W. Row
Hey James H., 206 Main
Howard L. & Co., 173 do
Knight R., 163 Vine
Kratz Conrad, 184 Walnut
Holmes Southworth, 189 Main
Peter & Sharpless, 24 w. 4th
Smith D. W. C., W. Row above 7th
Williams John S., 85 Main
La Boyteaux G. L.   *Mt. Healthy.*

Pattern Makers.

Franklin County.

Morian David, Broadway   *Columbus.*

Greene County.

Patterson Samuel M.   *Xenia.*

Hamilton County.

Lathrop & Joyce, 121 2d   *Cincinnati.*
Cooke George T., 52 Plum
Harris & Zoiner, cor. Walnut & Canal
Willard Morgan, Lock bet. 4th & 5th

Ross County.

Richie John   *Chillicothe.*

Perfumery. Manufacturers and Dealers.

Franklin County.

Clark & Co., High   *Columbus.*
Denig G. & Sons, cor. High & Rich

Farenholtz William, cor. High and Rich, Columbus.
Little R. P., cor. High and Rich

Hamilton County.

Sleeper Israel, Hammond, next to Henrie House   Cincinnati.
Palmer Solon, 36 w. 4th
Kohl Wm. M. & Co., n. e. cor. 4th & Vine
Coolidge & Whetstone, cor. 5th & W. Row
David Henry, 203 Main

Perfumery and Fancy Goods.
Knox County.

Abernethy M.   Mount Vernon.
Russell W. B.

Physicians and Surgeons.
Adams County.

Stableton D. W. & Joseph   Manchester.
McConaughy D. M.
Adamson T. J.   Stout's.
McFarland John
Grossman J.   Scott.
Miller F. J.
Lewis A. C.
Mason George W.   Dunkinsville.
Coates B. F.   West Union.
Coleman David
Penney B.
Clark J.   Locust Grove.
Richards Newton
Foll Jose
Grear Alexander   Tranquillity.
Hoghland B. V.   Youngsville.
Knight A. F.   Rockville.
Ellis —   Wagoner's Ripple.
Holderney —
Wells —
Fear Franklin   Eckmansville.
Vanmetre E.
Wells Jacob M.   Mahala.
Gustine John   Marble Furnace.
Lewis Samuel   Dunbarton.
McNeil J. W.

Allen County.

Anderson D. H.   Lima.
Hover Newton
Howard N. B.
McHenry & Harper
Kincaid Robert
Sanford Samuel
Matthews V.   Fryburg.
Shepherd Jasper C.   West Newton.
Hartley W. S.   Allentown.
Ward A. B.   Cranberry.
Whitas Uriah
Newell J. A.   Westminster.
Sullivan W.
Sager N.   Herring.
Gates C. W.   Hog Creek.

Ashland County.

Gillett Jacob   Sullivan.
Sampson A. B.
Paxton W. P.   Polk.
Buck H.   Roweburg.

Miller P. McC.   Rowsburg
McHose J.
Deal Josiah   Ruggles.
Parker William W.
Skillinger A. D.
Ewing G. V.   Hayesville.
Glass & Armstrong
Purdy G. L.
Hays James E.   Savannah.
Hays Thomas
Ingram John
Johnston Charles C.   Albion.
McCarty O. C.
Young David
Clark B. B.   Ashland
Clark Henry
Hahn J.
Kellogg Burr
Kineman J. W.
Oesterlin G.
Sampeel David
Sampsel G.
Corran J. P.   Jeromeville.
Palmer J.
Anderson A. R.   Loudonville.
Fuller & Myers.
McBeth J. C.
Smith James
Eagle T. A.   Mohecan.
Moores Thomas
Yocum James M.

Ashtabula County.

Etry A. L.   New Lyme.
Fuller J.
Leslie A.   Cherry Valley.
Henshaw W.
Stephens P. C.   Geneva.
Edson J. J.
Holbrook Stephen   Kelloggsville.
Clark W. W.
Martin S. E.
Stevens E. P.   Windsor.
Pomroy A. L.
Brewster W. W.   Austinburg.
Chester L. L.
Hawley A.   Jefferson.
Richmond B. W.
Harrington S. H.   Ashtabula.
Coleman E.
Hubbard & Grinold.
Prentice O.
Morgan Hiram   Hart's Grove.
Hamilton C.   West Williamsfield
Clark W. W.
Rodgers J. R.   Rome.
Wheeler James   Andover.
Holbrook A. B.
Strickland Wesley
Fobes William   Pierpont.
Judd A. E.   Cork
Ely A. L.   Lindenville.
Wallworth C. B.
Spelman Luther
Bennett L. L.   Harpersfield.
Gist David G.

Athens County.

Earhart W. R.	*Chauncey.*
Dawson ——	
Davis M. P.	*Trimble.*
Derr J. S.	
Reaves Wm.	
Pratt John	*Coolville.*
Brownfield James	
Daily E.	*Calvary.*
Fuller R. N	*Millfield.*
McKitrick James	
Monahan A. B.	*Hockingport.*
Keever J. T.	
Beem George	*Pleasanton.*
Beem E. M.	
Moore & Dodds	*Amesville.*
Fulton L.	
Lindley John N.	*Albany.*
Earhart John	
Harper J. B.	*Nelsonville.*
Aplin Chas.	
Burrel A. H.	
Stinson J. H.	
Moore Joseph	*Shad.*
Wilson M.	
Oamer Abraham	*Canaanville.*
Lively Silas	*Lowry.*
Carpenter E. G.	*Athens.*
Blackstone Wm.	
Carpenter G. H.	
Johnson Wm. P.	
Stimson —— Dr.	
Lindley John N.	*Lee.*
Earhart John	
Townsend Wm.	
Saunders Chas.	*Guysville.*
Campbell Wm.	*Hibardville.*
Martin —— Dr.	*Hulls.*

Anglaize County.

Gibbs William	*Wapakoneta.*
Meyer F. W.	
Meyer E.	
Nichols J. H.	
Underwood —	
Kishler G. W.	*St. Mary's.*
O'Connel ——	
Stearns R. W.	
Cotter James	*Kossuth.*
Tippie Michael	
Schmieder John P.	*Minster.*
Beselai ——	*New Bremen.*
Hoverman ——	
Kisler ——	
Nehat ——	
Shaw John M.	*St. John's.*
Stockdill ——	
Stone E. D.	

Belmont County.

Chapman Patterson R.	*Hendrysburg.*
Oops Caleb	*Colerain.*
Coleman Joseph D.	*Demos.*
McMaster Wm.	
Wilson William	
Davis B. W.	*Somerton.*

Scho ley Addison	*Somerton.*
Schooley Wm.	
Hare William	*Barnesville.*
Hoover Isaac	
Mackall John T.	
Parker Jacob H.	
Williams Ephraim	
Andrews Reuben	*Bellair.*
Birdsong Elijah P.	
Oash J.	
Baily Jesse	*Flushing.*
Bracken John	
Lafferty Joseph	
Voorhies Luke	
Campbell John	*Uniontown.*
Estep William	*Loydsville.*
Jones Y. F.	
Carnes Williams	*Shepherdstown.*
Cash B. F.	*Dillies' Bottom.*
Grimes P. A.	*Lampsville.*
Kemp John A.	
Alexander John	*St. Clairsville.*
Hewetson Joseph	
Walker Joseph	
West Henry	
Gaston E.	*Morristown.*
Hamilton R.	
Dallas L. J.	*Sewellsville.*
Lindsey William	
Lisle Henry	*Hunter.*
Grimes Perry A.	
Reid Moses	*Armstrong's Mills.*
Davis Jacob	*Pilcher's.*
Dean Jacob	
Wright & Schooley	*Belmont.*

Brown County.

Howland John	*Higginsport.*
Smith Fletcher	
Calahan Dennis	
Park Robert	
Evans Dr.	*Lewistown.*
Wylie A. N.	*Ripley.*
Beasley A.	
Beasley N. K.	
Dunlap B. A.	
Thomas T. P.	
Campbel A.	
Wylie Thos. B.	*Decatur.*
Norten G.	
Beance L. L.	
Bailey G. B.	*Georgetown.*
Heterick A. B.	
Salisbury S. S.	
Ellsberry A. M.	
Sidwell J.	
Gorden T. W.	
Gorden G. W.	
Steies J. O.	*Hawesville.*
Maggin J. C.	*Fayetteville.*
Thompson W. B.	
Ederfield W.	
Porter Daniel	
Fee E. B.	*Newhope.*
Ellsberry E. M.	
Gates Wm. M.	
Weaver J. S.	

Moore T. M.	*Aberdeen.*	Webster E.	*Monroe.*
Ellis Samuel		Hawley A. D.	*College Corner.*
Bailey G. B.		Creighton T	*Somerville.*
Sutherland Wm.		Alexander R. P.	
Garwood & Son		Williams D.	*Seven Miles.*
Jennings J. N.	*Puebla.*	Wooley E. C.	
Stevenson & Thompson	*Russelville.*	Heaton J. F.	*Trenton.*
Salisberry J. N.		Eckert A.	
McDonough Geo.	*De La Palma.*	Eckert D.	
Evans J. M.	*Ash Ridge.*	Miller Wm.	*Jacksensburg.*
Gordon G. W.	*Lewis.*		
Beck Oliver C.	*Feesburg.*	**Carroll County.**	
McKee A. B.		Hance J. B.	*Harlem Springs.*
Williams Peter	*Five Mile.*	Moody J. B.	
Glover Zachariah	*Union Plane.*	Ruckenbrod Sol. F.	*Malvern.*
Buchanon John	*Fincastle.*	Stewart Charles	*New Hagerstown.*
Carey S. E.		Vincent James	
Richardson J. T.	*Arnheim.*	Saltsman George H.	*Norristown.*
Beck Isaac M.	*Sardinia.*	Moore Isaiah	*Leavit.*
		West M. C.	
Butler County.		Arter D.	*Carrollton.*
Pennee S. B.	*Bethany.*	Hunter J. S.	
Baxter John M.	*West Chester.*	McMillen C. V.	
Cummins J. P.		Moore Isaiah	
Rowan James L.	*Pisgah.*	Pool W. H.	
Wyman George	*Dartown.*	Todd J. M.	
Carnahan John P.		Phillips Jeremiah	*Leesville.*
McMechan John		Stephenson John H.	
Woolley E. C.	*Collinsville.*	Stephenson James H.	
Auvein J. J.	*Poast Town.*	Sherod David B.	*Sherodsville.*
Huston R. C.	*Oxford.*	Eakin Thomas C.	*Oneida Mills.*
Garver J. A.			
Garver J. S.		**Champaign County.**	
Cory J. M.		Owen E.	*Mechanicsburg.*
Galloway J. S.		Owen T. C.	
McAlister A.		Lawler E. D.	
Fithian J.		Jones J. W.	
Rea R. L.		Jones T.	
Scott F.	*Paddy's Run.*	Wadsworth C. S	
Morris N.		Coliver J.	
Roberts J.		Gill L. C. C.	*Westville.*
Kumber D. C.	*Mellville.*	Brown J. C.	*Urbana.*
Londes Dr.		Howell J.	
Falconer & Smith	*Hamilton.*	Buey H.	
Buckner Wm.		Carter J. S.	
Going W. S. & Rigdon		Houston —— Dr	
Smith L. J.		Howell J. C.	
Routh J. W.		Palmer J. G.	
Hittle J.		Goddard J. W.	
Millikin Samuel		Fyffe E. P.	
Goodall G. C. N.	*Reesville.*	Murdock W.	
Scobey W. H.		Godfrey N. P.	
Millikin R. B.		Mingle T.	*Springhills.*
Ingham Dr.	*Middletown.*	Richards T.	
Wiley J.		Clawson T. S.	
Webster W.		Alsted Wm.	*Careysville.*
Elsworth T. J.	*Princeton.*	Mathews Jacob	
Braden Joseph		McPherson James	*St. Paris.*
Leandis A. H.	*Millville.*	Amison John	
Kumler D. C.		Eversole B.	*Terre Haute.*
Briggs ——			
Marshall J. G.	*Symmes' Corner.*	**Clark County.**	
Brathee C. W.	*Ross.*	Smith H.	*North Hampton.*
Birckhead W. J.		Snodgrass B. D.	
Caldwell W. W.	*Monroe.*	Eakin Thomas C.	*Enon.*
Hayden J. B.		Poage John G.	
Kimball E.		Serviss David	

Cook J. W.	*Selma.*	Kelly M. A.	*Amelia.*
Wilson J. S.		Robinson Wm.	
Ramsey J.	*Springfield.*	White A. B.	
Starr Calvin		Blythe B.	*Owensville.*
Kindleberger T. J.		Coombs John S.	
Winwood ——		Henry William	*Miamisville.*
Buckingham ——		Chatterton E. B.	*Mulberry.*
Rogers ——		Elstune Eli	
Skinner J. A.	;	Leever J. C.	
Foster H. C.		Johnson & Moore	*Moscow.*
Bardridge ——		Murphy C. W.	*Mount Pisgah.*
Hackenberg J. P.		Emory A. B.	*Loveland.*
Bruce A.		Anderson W.	
Noleen J. G.		Mitchell D.	
Fall J. C.		Hatton George	
Cartmell Wm. H.	*Catawba.*	Essex M. D.	*Rural.*
Hunter M. R.		Cline John	*Perin's Mills.*
Helmes Wm. H.	*South Charleston.*	Spence Colton	
Houston & Collins		Simkins Isaac	*Belfast.*
Steele E. W.		Tedrow P. W.	*West Woodville.*
Meranda & Smith	*New Carlisle.*	Pinkham Thos. M.	*Bantam.*
Milot James		Moore A. Canby	
Stockstill J. N.		Simmons W. H.	*Laurel.*
Winans Richard		South S. B	
Shackelford R. J.	*Medway.*		

Clermont County.

		Clinton County.	
Mullen J. T.	*New Richmond.*	Sparks J. K.	*Oakland.*
Garretson J.		Brooke A.	
Rogers J. G.		Hocket D.	*Westboro'.*
Johnson J. T.		Shephard W. W.	*Sligo.*
Robb ——		Richardson J. W.	
Herbert Wm.		Elgin M. B.	*New Burlington.*
Kennedy Philip	*Nicholsville.*	Sprogan D.	
Dennis Franklin		Williams A.	
Sharp E. C.	*Williamsburg.*	Smith J. H.	*Cuba.*
Sharp D. C.		Hunter M. T.	*Port William.*
Pease L. T.		Walker J. C.	
Smith M.		Garland Thomas S.	*Clarksville.*
Faris E. S.		Dakin E. F.	
McChesney A. C.	*Mount Carmel.*	Baugh H. W.	
Thacker J. N.		Morey D. B.	*Lee's Creek.*
Williams Wm.	*Milford.*	Elwood Cyrus	
Brown L. M.		Williams E.	*Blanchester.*
Hendrick L. A., sen.		Ousick W.	
Hendrick L. A., jun.		Oliver S.	
Burnett Elisha	*Withamsville.*	Rannells J. M.	*New Antioch.*
Donham H. L.		Holmes Isaac	
Witham J. Monroe		Quinn J. H.	*New Vienna.*
Ellsberry W.	*Bethel.*	Woodbury E. M.	
Munger H.		Vanterworth Ira	
Thornton S. T.		Dalton J. E.	
Scoville S. S.		Quinn J. W. M.	*Sabina.*
Kincaid W. P.	*Neville.*	Terry D.	
Chase S. H.	*Felicity.*	Tilford J.	
Gibson M.		Parker C. S.	*Martinsville*
Kennedy J. C. & J. W.		Carey Daniel	
Notter & McCaskey		Williams J. C.	*Decatursville.*
Norris O. J.			
Wood A.		**Columbiana County.**	
McFarland ——		Buchanan James G.	*Wellsville.*
Barber Daniel	*Batavia.*	Botsford ——	
McMillan ——		Hill James B.	
Jackson Wm.	*Edenton.*	Leslie Robert	
Hopkins Andrew V.	*Amelia.*	Lucy Jackson	
Hopkins Robert A.		Lyon William	
Hubble Burton		McKenzie N. K.	
		Silver David S.	

Smith J. W.	*Wellsville.*	Beaver J. C.	*Chili.*
Stephens ——		Knight E. N.	
Allen J.	*New Lisbon.*	Conaway John	*Bakersville.*
McCook John		Anderson J.	*Keene.*
Parker W. J.		Howard L.	
Springer Daniel			

Crawford County.

Chamberlain R.	*East Palestine.*	McKane John	*Leesville Cross Roads.*
Sheets S. P.		Rupp P. E.	
Sheets A.		Alvord David	*Poplar.*
Smily J.		Pitezel Joseph	
Arter J. R.	*Salineville.*	Mitchell Thos. A.	*New Washington.*
Farmer William		Wandt A. F. G.	
Hostetler J. C.		Shaffner J. F.	*Wellsville.*
Ball James	*New Garden.*	Keller George	*Liberty Corners.*
Jones E. O.		Squier John B.	*Sulphur Spring.*
Dustan B. W.	*Calcutta.*	Ziegler George L.	
Quigley S.		Zumro Henry S.	
Brenton J. L.	*North Georgetown.*	Applebaugh J. J.	*Bucyrus.*
Dellenbaugh John		Augenstine J.	
Dellenbaugh & Sheets		Byers John	
Sturgeon Eli		Clark W. R. S.	
Andrews ——	*Franklin Square.*	Fulton C.	
McCready R.		Hetich A.	
Manten James	*East Rochester.*	Meyer F.	
Logue M. H.	*New Chambersburg.*	Miller D.	
Swearingen G. W.	*Green Hill.*	Swingley F.	
Graham A. G.	*Bucks.*	Fairbank A. B.	*Chatfield.*
Cary Abel	*Salem.*	Hamon J. M.	*Lykens.*
Coffee J. W.		Bee R. A. N.	*De Kalb.*
Hotchkiss ——			

Cuyahoga County.

Pearson C.		Ruggles P. S.	*Newburgh.*
Schooly R.		Dilla A. L.	*Mayfield.*
Stanton B.		Moore T. M.	*Gates' Mills.*
Forbes J.	*East Liverpool.*	Hopkins L.	*North Royalton.*
Ogden B.		Briegleb G.	*Brooklyn.*
Deemer Daniel	*Columbiana.*	Jauko Vincent	
Estle John A.		Palmer A. S.	
Kyser Jacob		Purple J. G.	
Levis John C.		Turner A. W.	
Metzger George		Day Ezra	*Independence.*
Whealand George		Gleason E. M.	
Mitchell W. H.	*Saint Clair.*	Miner John D.	
Marquis D.	*West Point.*	Foster ——	*Strongsville.*
McDowell James		Leonard H. L. W.	
Shumaker W. J.		Pope Jonathan	
Fisher Amasa	*East Fairfield.*	St. Clair J. J.	
Kay Charles		Trask R.	
Augustine Eli	*Unity.*	Dunham J. W.	
Hindman J. L. D.		Chipman N. G.	*East Cleveland.*
Johnson J.	*Cannon's Mills.*	Streator W. S.	
Robertson James	*Hanoverton.*	Thomas E. C.	
Kuhn J.		Bradley J. M.	*Dover.*
Yates John J.		Bradley Jason	
Atwell A. F.		Butler A. K.	*Chagrin Falls.*
Moore William	*Elkton.*	Curtiss H. W.	
		Hamlin W. S.	

Coshocton County.

Rosenthal J.	*New Bedford.*	Harlow A.	
Fletcher W. B.	*Tiverton.*	Harmon W. S.	
Harrison E. B		Rodgers G. B.	
Barnes David	*West Carlisle.*	Vincent J. H.	
Irvin Thomas		Buck Edward	*Brecksville.*
Smith William	*West Bedford.*	Keys David C.	*Solon.*
Waddell Wm. R.		Thompson Wm.	
Day George	*Evensburgh.*	Fuller George	*Bedford.*
Biach J.	*Clark's.*	Hutchinson B. M.	
Blackburn B. C.	*Chili.*	Robison J. P.	

Streator D. G.   *Bedford.*
Tarbell S. U.
Morrel C. A.   *Warrensville.*
Burton Elijah   *Collamer.*
Burton E. D.
Babcock B. F.
Foster J. N.
Crane J. F.   *Berea.*
Evans Alvah
Kneeland Isaac
McBride Alexander
Parker Henry
Barnum John   *Rockport.*
Hoady O. R.
Barker G. W., 71 Superior   *Cleveland.*
Brooks M. L., 72 Prospect
Czapkay L J., under Forest City House
Cleveland T. G., 1 Seneca Block
Cushing E. & H. K., 52 Public Square
Everett H. & E., cor. Clinton & Prospect
Delamater John, cor. Wood & Rockwell
Gordon P. A., 81 Superior
Keeler C. J., 54 Seneca
Newberry J. S., 2 Kelley's Block
Roeder Philip, 61 Centre
Schueler George, 66 do
Skiles F. W., cor. Superior and Public
  Square.
Sterling E., 2 Kelley's Block
Strong R. S., 46 Seneca
Thrall F. G., 129 Superior
Williams C. D., 111 Superior
Wheeler John, cor. Superior and Pub. Sq.
Gilson E. D.   *Ohio City.*

Darke County.

Paramore & Matchet   *Castine.*
Love Z. P.
Harris William   *Ithica*
Matchet William H.
Long J. K.
Millett J. W.
Williamson J. H.   *Hillgrove.*
McCandliss R. R.
Chew E. C.   *Port Jefferson.*
Miller David   *Abbotsville.*
Gillpatrick R.   *New Madison.*
Blunt James G.
Thomas Isaac H.
Jaqua Charles
Larsh P. H.   *German.*
Woods J. K.
Gard J. N.   *Greenville.*
Otwell Curtis
Koogler Adam
Lynch E.
Messie G.
Serbor Jacob
Ayres —
Cowgill G. J.   *Republican.*
Hostetler Isaac   *Beamsville.*
Hager Samuel D.
Waters John W.   *Seven Mile Prairie*
Waters J. W.   *Mississinawa.*

Defiance County.

Allen O. H.   *Defiance.*
Castlehun —

Colby & Paul   *Defiance.*
Major S.
Porter W. C.
Warren W. P.
Moss George   *Brunersburg.*
Bennett S. G.   *Evansport.*
Mayer John N.
Russell H.
Williams Nathaniel
Colby Levi   *Milldale.*
Thrall M.   *Farmer Centre.*
Rakestraw E.   *Hicksville.*
Clarke Milo
Ladd & Tuple   *Panama.*

Delaware County.

Gerhard M.   *Delaware.*
Hills Ralph
Williams Thomas
Hendrin William
Blymyer A.
Carothers —
Cherry J. M.
Hurd —
Howell D.
Leach William C.
Kinsell D.
Carpenter A.   *Galena.*
Lewis Chancy   *Waldo.*
Slawson A.
Hull E. T.
Budd J.   *Harlem.*
Mercer William B.   *Williamsville.*
Carpenter William B.   *Padnor.*
Black George H.
Cox Joseph
Neilson E.   *Norton.*
McIntyre William   *Delaware.*
Vandeman T. H.
Hudder G. W.
McMillen —   *Sunbury.*
McKinley C. G.
Gregg Henry   *Unison.*
Potter L.   *Kilbourne.*
Carothers John
Morrison John . .   *Bellepoint.*
Hyatt E.

Erie County.

Aikin J. C.   *Sandusky City.*
Austin A.
Blanchard J. A.
Cochran Charles
Delano M. F.
Flehr — Dr.
Gilbert D. H.
Graffs — Dr.
Hargett J. B.
Hoyt M. C.
Kramer T.
Lane E. L.
McMeans — Dr.
Stanley E.
Silva L. A.
Seal — Dr.
Tilden Daniel
Tilden Daniel Jr.

Townsend Charles E.   *Sandusky City.*
Wal-h — Dr.
Caldwell J. S.   *Huron.*
Sanderson C. R.
Parmeter S. H.
Haskins G. S.
.uilo D. H.
Breeman Julius   *Birmingham.*
Eaton C. H.
Griggs Stephen
Trimbley J. B.   *Florence.*
Osburn M. W.
Hill G. S.   *Berlinville.*
Smith L. B.
Barnham N. G.
Kellogg N. G.
Hill B. L.
Carpenter George W.   *Bloomingville.*
Hoyt A. B.
Rogers Isaac
Osborn M. W.   *Furnace.*
Dean E. T.   *Milan.*
Dean W. F.
Horner J.
Galpin H.
Renner — Dr.

Fairfield County.

Baily John D.   *Pickerington.*
Hiland James
Dolison J. F.   *West Rushville.*
Corffman Levi   *Pleasantville.*
Steward W. W.
Armstrong O. S.   *New Salem.*
Brock M. D.
Yontz Joseph
Evans T. W.   *Bremen.*
McCune A.
Hyde S.   *Rushville.*
McFadden Thomas
Turner P. F.
Bugh John W.   *Amanda.*
Dennis A.
Lerch Jared
Boerstler George   *Lancaster.*
Carpenter P.
White James
Kreider M. Z.
Van Fossen —
Biglow J. M.
Effinger M.
Davis O. E.
Davidson A.
Hedges S. A.
Shaw H.
Myers —
Miller George
Shawk C.
Shaffer A. H.   *Clear Creek.*
Drake D. R.   *Lithopolis.*
Eels G. E.
Miner E. L.
Brown B. H.   *Sugar Grove.*
Sharp James
Shrader A. J.
Shumaker H. H.
Tirold M.

Lariuer J. W.   *Millersport.*
Brison J. V.

Fayette County.

Martin E.   *Bloomingburg.*
Stewart H. C.
Stewart William H.
Ray J. D.
Houston J. T.   *Jeffersonville.*
Jones W. H.
Cheever Nathan   *Pancoastburg.*
Wynecoop Lewis
Wilson J. G.   *Washington.*
Williams C. M.
Rush B. H.
Worley Ashbury
Brown A. W.
Littleton T. H.
Allen O. A.
Christy Samuel A.   *Moons.*
McKinney Daniel
McCorkle Thomas J.   *Staunton.*

Franklin County.

Awl W. M., High   *Columbus.*
Barnes Lewis, Town
Broadbelt J. L., Front
Carter F., State
Coulter J. H., Fourth
Denig George, Third
Denig C. E., High
Denig R. M., do
Dow C. L.,   do
Howard R. L., State
Hamilton J. W., do
Jones J. G., Town
Johnson B. F., do
Latham Wm., do
Lazell A. H., do
Lenthstrom C. A., Third
Liebrandt Charles A., High
Longshore F., Rich
Little J. A., Town
Maris George, cor. 3d & Rich
Matthews H., High
Mœler J., State
Morrison John, Town
McMiller William L., State
Parker C. C., High
Reynolds L., Friend
Rashil —, Rich
Sachse George J., Third
Seegar J. R. L, Scioto
Seltzer S. Z., Friend
Silver D. H., High
Schubert M., Friend
Skinner J. S., do
Smith S. M., State
Snow G. R., Town
Spencer E., Rich
Thompson J. B., High
Thompson Robert, Town
Thrall H. L., High
Trevitt William, Broad
Veight T. L., Third
Wormley T. G., 102 High
Dunbar J.   *Central College.*

Chaney H. L.	*Greenvert.*	Leivsey George W.	*Gallipolis.*
Clark A.		Morgan Elisha	
Smith George L.		McSmither John C.	
Carroll F. R.	*Reynoldsburg.*	Sanns John	
Goldrick William		Strong J. S.	*Patriot.*
Langworthy James		Buswell John	*Kyger.*
Bull Thompson	*Clintonville.*	Gardner Perin	
Short A. A.	*Hibernia.*	Pankey James	
Brooks Frank	*Hope.*	Saunders Alonzo D.	
Guerin G. F.		Seigler William	
Goodrich Henry			
Stinson S.		**Geauga County.**	
Woodruff L.	*Alton.*	Hamilton L. A.	*Chardon.*
Helmick J.	*Harrisburg.*	King William	
Helmick G. W.		Bagley A.	
Landon Chauncy P.	*Blendon.*	Sheldon K.	*Welshfield.*
Chapman Albert	*Dublin.*	Bascon J.	
Gabriel R. W.		Foster G. W.	
Pinney E. M.		Brown David	*Claridon.*
Sells Holmes		Cleaveland J. D.	
Sells A. H.		Dowe R.	
Andrus Abner	*Worthington.*	Houghtail John	
Goble Peter		Sumner S. M.	*Burton.*
Gregg Henry		Goodwin E.	
Lewis Jedediah		Bell H.	
Norton W. J.		Calkins A. E.	*Bainbridge.*
Parmeter J. L.		Shepherd David	
Skinner D. W.		Aldrich J. A.	*Munson.*
Davis S. B.	*Lockburn.*	Crane William	*Parkman.*
McLean R. G.		Peabody —	
Marshall J. R.		Fisher O.	*Newburg.*
Blake George W.	*Canal Winchester.*	McHish J.	
Potter Joseph B.		Bellows C. J.	*Huntsburg.*
Talbott William W.		Spencer S. H.	
Kimball David	*Ovid.*	Allen Daniel	*Montville.*
Shafer Jacob		Davidson —	
Baughman John	*Gohanna.*	Atwood J. W.	*Middlefield.*
Williams Isaiah		Miller R.	
		Foster G. W.	*Troy.*
Fulton County.		Bascomb J.	
Winterstein William	*Elmira.*	Sheldon K.	
Lutz Henry		Adams P.	*Chardon.*
Ramsay William	*Delta.*	Lyman —	*Chester.*
Canady S.		Scribner —	*Hamden.*
Odell William		Sadler O. W.	*Auburn.*
Butler M. H.		Tillotson S. & A.	*Thompson.*
Kitridge James J..	*Chesterfield.*		
		Greene County.	
Gallia County.		Bell William	*Xenia.*
Combs A. S.	*Thurman.*	Drake J. S.	
Williams William L.		Engle Nathaniel	
Rathburn James O.	*Rodney.*	Finley R. S.	
Rathburn D. O.		Johnston T. B.	
Eaton H. S.	*Vinton.*	Jewitt John	
Holcomb Ira		Martin Samuel	
Thompson James		Martin Joshua	
Woodworth Z.	*Cheshire.*	McClellan James	
Norton A. L.	*Gallia Furnace.*	Thorp James	
Eaton Henry	*Anselm.*	Dille L. K.	*Cedarville.*
Masterson William F.	*Adamsville.*	Finley Robert	
Sisson N. B.	*Pine Grove.*	Stewart J. M.	
Hannan William F.	*Swan Creek.*	Wilson M. D.	
Shallcross Joseph		Green J. W.	*Fairfield.*
Kenedy A. J.	*Ewington.*	McIlhenny J. J.	
Cromley J. M.	*Gallipolis.*	Reed J. A.	
Frost & Reynolds		Higgins William	*Zimmerman.*
Holt G. H.		Bell J. F.	*Spring Valley.*

Hartman G. O.   *Spring Valley.*
Swain J.
Spahr O. H.   *New Jasper.*
Butler A. B.   *Clifton.*
Newell S. W.
Sagebeil W. F.   *Byron.*
Cheny A.   *Yellow Springs.*
Grimes W. H.
Hall William
Orr D. O.
Stockum —
Thorn —
Johns J. R. B.   *Clio.*
Birdsall G. F.   *Paintersville.*
Watson J. H.
Green Daniel K.
Kile Joseph A.
Hale J. F.
Winans H. O.

Guernsey County.

Welsh D.   *Cumberland.*
Draper C.
McCall J. H.
Foreman William M.   *Washington.*
McConnell M.
Rea F. F.
McFarlin John
Martin J. F.
Chapman C. H.
Patterson A.
Watt J. W.   *Winchester.*
McKinsey M. O.
Stevenson R. G.
Clark J. T.
Weaver E. P.   *Middlebourne.*
Bell William S.
McCall John   *Londonderry.*
Hull James
Gilder George W.   *New Gottingen.*
Warfield J. W.   *Fairview.*
McPherson J. T.
McOlenshan David
Shriver S.   *Dysons.*
Reeder S. B.
Green M.   *Cambridge.*
Haynes V.
Tingle J. P.
Anderson William   *Kimbolton.*
Black William
Moore R. L.
Price C.   *Millersville.*
Whitacer G. W.
Barbor P.
Ferguson V.   *Senecaville.*
Baldridge M. D.
Hill N.
Franklin William A

Hamilton County.

Ames W., Fourth e. of Lytle, *Cincinnati.*
Armstrong N. S., 115 w. 6th
Avery Charles L., 99 w. 7th
Alexander John, n. w. cor. Walnut & 6th
Alexander S., 12th bet. Plum & W. Row
Alden J. M., Catherine bet. W. Row & John

Allen N., Walnut bet. 5th & 6th *Cincinnati.*
Bunchamp H., 31 Elizabeth
Baurippel Henry, 397 Vine
Bradish J. F., 164 Richmond
Betscher O., 423 Walnut
Boyd Charles, 3 Franklin
Branch Charles M., Broadway bet. 2d & 3d.
Brown A., 319 w. 8th
Banes H. O., 24 e. 4th
Bruhl Gustav, 215 Linn
Baker A. H., 316 w. 6th
Borton Jacob, s. w. cor. 8th & John
Buckner Philip J., St. John's Buildings, Walnut
Bauer E. J., 134 w. 6th
Bauer Adolph do do
Barnes O., 116 Vine
Bonner Stephen, 76 w. 8th
Bettmann Abraham, 119 w. Court
Beyer J., 383 Vine
Byrer John, 646 do
Biglar G. W., n. w. cor. College & 6th
Brisbane W. H., 110 w. 6th
Bevan Thomas, 173 W. Row
Carson J., 82 e. 3d
Carson Wm. do
Cobb W. H., do
Cooper L., 407 w. 3d
Cooper J. M., do
Carter R. C., 112 George
Cary M. T., 12th bet. Plum & W. Row
Conner P. S., s. w. cor. 7th & Race
Carrol Thomas, 242 Plum
Curtis A., Walnut bet. 4th and 5th
Cook A. L., 128 Walnut
Cox H., s. e. cor. 12th & Race
Cox J. E., do do
Castlehun —, 666 W. Row
Cameron J. W., 397 do
Carrettson J., 175 Vine
Comegys O. G., 149 w. 6th
Davis John, 435 Vine
Dart J 469 w. Third
Doherty Geo. A., Broadway bet. 6th & 7th
Dodge J. S., 313 Race
Dandridge A. S., n. e. cor. Broadway & 3d
Davis W. B., 435 Vine
Dawson W. W., 25 Broadway
Eversman F. F., 13th bet. Main & Walnut
Ehrman B. & F., 46 w. 7th
Edwards T. O., 97 do
Foster J. B., n. e. cor. Broadway & 3d
Foote H. E., 162 Vine
Fries George, 349 do
Fore P. G., 72 w. 7th
Foster Nathaniel, cor. 3d & Broadway
Foote E., 265 w. 4th
Gotwald G. A., s. w. cor. W. Row & Longworth
Garrettson J., Vine bet. 4th and 5th
Gerwe F. A. J., n. e. cor. Park & Longworth
Graham J., 347 Vine
Grant Charles, 6th bet. Vine & Race
Glass Z. P., 550 W. Row
Hopple James, 151 6th
Hunt J. G., 307 Elm

Homberg T. W., Walnut, bet. 12th & 13th *Cincinnati.*
Hollander E., 10th, bet. Walnut & Vine
Hall L., 134 Walnut
Hussel H. J. C., 6th bet. Race & Elm
Hughes C. B., 292 w. 4th
Helm J. F., n. w. cor. Walnut
Hopple James, 606 W. Row
Junghanns A. V., 349 Walnut
Judkins J. P., 155 w. 4th
Judkins William, n. e. cor. Race & Center
Judkins David, 268 w. 8th
James L. A., 335   do
Judge J. F., e. 3d, near Broadway
Kellogg G. M., Broadway, opp. Franklin
Kyle S., 500 W. Row
Koffman C. S., 349 Vine
Kellough J., 182 Race
Kunz J., 13th, bet. Walnut & Vine
King J., 142 w. 7th
Knese B., 371 w. 5th
Logan C. A., s. w. corner Broadway & Franklin
Laurie George, 160 Vine
Lawson L. M., 31 Ohio Med. Col. building
Langdon O. M., 155 w. sixth
Lawson B. S., 333   do
Longren S. S., cor. 6th & College
Locke J., jun., 128 Walnut
Leinbeber E., Everett, bet. Linn & Cutter
Mendenhall G., 197 w. 4th
Marmet —, s. w. cor. 13th & Jackson
Mudd Jerome, 229 Broadway
Mackenzie J. A., 287 w. 5th
McFeely James, 106 w. Front
Muhl George, 60 w. 6th
Murphy J. A., 443 W. Row
Muller John, 343 Vine
Muscroft Charles S., 447 W. Row
Mier Nathan, s. w. cor. 13th & Clay
Morgan E., Clinton bet. W. Row & John
McCulloch G., s. e. cor. Longworth & John
Murphy R. D., 70 w. 7th
Mussey W. H., do   do
Mussey R. D., do   do
Menzies S. G., 3d, bet. Walnut & Vine
Malone P. W., Broad'y, bet. 3d & L. Mar.
Malone Henry B.,   do   do   do
Mighels J. W., 306 Walnut
Musgrave H. B., 331 W. Row
Newton R. S., 89 w. 7th
Newton O. E., do   do
Norton O. D., 181 W. Row
Norris J., cor. 7th & Broadway
Noyes J. F., 4th bet. Main & Walnut
Oliver James H., 264 Elm
Orr T. J., 9 Ohio Med. Col. building
Owens William 307 Elm
Orr E. M., Walnut, bet. 3d & 4th
Ocheltree John, 435 Vine
Potter J. F., n. w. cor. 4th & Elm
Price William, 106 w. 6th
Perley Thomas F., 53 e. 4th
Park J., 133 Main
Pierson W. H., n. w. cor. 4th & Race
Peck W., 128 w. 8th

Quinn J. J., 123 w. 7th   *Cincinnati.*
Quinn H. R., 210 Sycamore
Rapp F., 455 Vine
Rall —, 537 w. 5th
Rendlen —, Congress, near Lawrence
Richardson B. T., Clinton, bet. W. Row & John
Reddington D., Symmes, bet. Pike & Lawrence
Rives Landon C., 121 Symmes
Rives Landon,   do   do
Richards W., n. w. cor. 4th & Race
   Do   C. A. L. do   do
Ridgely William S., 142 w. 4th
Roelker F., 19 e. 9th
Stites J. J.   *Walnut Hills.*
Saal G., 44 w. 7th   *Cincinnati.*
Slocum A. M., s. e. cor. 7th & Elm
Sanger Wm. W., s. w. cor. 6th & W. Row
Sturm William, 144 w. 7th
Smith S. H., n. w. cor., 6th & Mound
Smith Thomas, 130 Richmond
Sattler G., n. e. cor., Main & Abigail
Smith J. B., 268 w. 6th
Seeger J., n. e. cor. Vine & 13th
Spies A., 434 Vine
Soule N. E., 139 w. 7th
Stockwell E. H., 550 W. Row
Schoenbein John, 477 Elm
Thornton W. P., 292 w. 6th
Terry J. M., 307 Walnut
Trudy D. C., 7th bet. Race & Elm
Talliaferro W. T., Walnut, bet. 6th & 7th
Topp Charles R., 324 Walnut
Tate J. H., n. w. cor. Broadway & 3d
Unzicker J. S., 423 Walnut
Vattier J. L., 349 Vine
Wilt William B., 91 Richmond
Warder J. A., 170 Broadway
Wright C. W., n. e. cor. Race & 3d
Wood William, 99 w. Third
Wright T. J., 8 George
Webb J. T., 141 w. 6th
Webb J. D., do   do
White J. F., 157 w. 4th
Wambaugh P. K., 291 w. 5th
Woodward Chas., 6th bet. Race & Vine
Woodward J.,   do   do
Wilson Israel, 337 Main
Wadsworth Joshua, n. w. cor. W. Row & David
Wilson S. C., 372 w. 7th
Wade D. E., 86 Everett
Walker Jos. P., Broadway, bet. 6th & 7th
Wood T., 7th, bet Walnut & Main
Whipple C. A., 95 w. 7th
Witherill E. C., 44 do
White J., 218 Walnut
Wallace George, n. e. cor. Catherine & John
White —, 234 Main
Williams P. M., W. Row, opp. 12th
Waterman L. D., 382½ w. 7th
Waldo F. A., 4th, opp. post office
Whittemore J. R., 86 Broadway
Bodman H. A.   *Reading.*
Schenck O.

Jones William	*Montgomery.*	Finstone J. B.	*Canonsburgh.*
McGrew John S.		Dean George A.	*McComb.*
Naylor John E.		Turner Samuel M.	
Ludden B. M.	*Lockland.*	Turner George	
Close E. S.	*Springdale.*		
Shepherd Alfred		**Hardin County.**	
Hunt John R.		Rider O. L.	*Kenton.*
Luse A. B.	*Mount Healthy.*	Hance Dr.	
Mead Edward		Kemp G. W.	
Ferre William		Leighton & Munson	
Beattie Thomas	*Harrison.*	Lawrence H.	
Goodheart George S.		Kramer S.	
Hughes J. H.		Rogers J. A.	
Morgan J. C.		Ashton E.	
Saddler J. J.		Holmes M.	
Sweeny Thomas		Jones William, jr.	
West A. E.	*Miami.*	De Long H. P.	*Roundhead.*
Goshorn William	*Cleves.*	Stanley A. F.	*Sylvia.*
Thornton J. H. F.		Brayton B. M.	
Ewing Richard H.			
Cassidy George		**Harrison County.**	
Clarke Walter	*Elizabethtown.*	McBean John	*Cadis.*
Agin Burroughs	*Dent.*	Berkley B. F.	
Brooks J. W.	*Cheviot.*	Wilson Martin	
Cruikshank E. O.		McGrew John B.	
Litzenburgh M. H.		Mager S. R.	*Deersville.*
Miller J. C.	*Cumningsville.*	McNarey A.	
Mount William		Smith Wm.	*Moorefield.*
Smedley Anderson	*Carthage.*	Findley Wm.	*Athens.*
Pease D. E.		McCoy E. H.	*Harrisville.*
Parrish Francis A.	*Madisonville.*	Kennedy Moses	*Green.*
Bishop Preston	*Pleasant Ridge.*	Duffield George W.	*Germans.*
Brown Hope M.	*Newtown.*	Taylor A. H.	
Highlands W. W.		Black J. C.	*Freeport.*
Chatterdon H. M.		Hall Jesse	
Bishop Leonard W.	*Mount Washington.*	Vincent James	*Feed Spring.*
Nicholson H. C.		Worstle Hiram	
Clark Isaac	*Miltonsburgh.*	Mills J. B.	*Updegroff*
Keller C.		Findley James	
		Hewetson John	
Hancock County.		**Henry County.**	
Burson A. F.	*Mount Blanchard.*	Scott R. K.	*Florida.*
Fairchild O. R.		Parry G.	
Haggarty John		Arnold J. L.	
Pickett Samuel		McHenry H.	*Napoleon.*
Adrane R. B.	*Van Buren.*	Patrick L. L.	
Goucher H. B.		Tyler A. M.	
Springer G.		McCann L. M.	
Beach Belizur	*Arlington.*	Adams A. T.	*Texas.*
Ballard T.	*Benton Ridge.*	Blair E. S.	
Siddall John	*Blanchard Ridge.*		
Calihan John	*Cass.*	**Highland County.**	
Engle Manuel	*Ashery.*		
Needles B. J.		Garrett S. P.	*Rainsboro'.*
Wheeler P. J.		Garrett J. M.	
Wilson W. P.		Barrett W. S.	
Armstrong William	*Finley.*	Marshall Peter	*Lynchburg.*
Baldwin Wm. H.		Speece S. S.	
Forman Lorenzo		Pittsor John	
Goucher David		Ayres B.	
Osterlin Charles		Judkins R. P.	*Highland.*
Rawson Bass		Bently Thomas S.	
Rohartch Albert		Drake S. M.	*Priertown.*
Spaythe James		Newcomber — Dr.	*Greenfield*
Cass D. W.	*Canonsburgh.*	Wilson — Dr.	
Cope J.		Dunlap — Dr.	
Ballard F.		Davis — Dr.	

Fillows — Dr.	*Greenfield.*
Dwyre — Dr.	
Hocket Amos	*Belfast.*
McNulty S.	
Sells A. M.	*Dodsonville.*
Grier A.	
Shockey John	*Buford.*
Duvall John	
Mathews C.	
Park R. C.	*Mowrytown.*
Vest J. W. H.	*New Market.*
Wharton J. C. B.	
Dwyer R. A.	
Homes Enos	
Homes Michael	
Meredith T. N.	
Noble David	*Sugartree Ridge.*
McBride Wm.	*Marshall.*
Dunlap A. J.	*Centrefield.*
Taylor David	
Hall J. M.	*Greenford.*
Hulin Smith	
Weikart A.	
Shepherd Wm. A.	*Samantha.*
Hirson N. H.	*Dallas.*
McBride A.	*Leesburg.*
Cunningham T.	
Baker A.	*Hillsboro'.*
Canniff H. J.	
Johnson J. M.	
Kirby Jacob	
Robinson G. W.	
Sams C. C.	
Ayres R. A.	

Hocking County.

Roberts J. F.	*Pattonsville.*
Gardner G. G.	*Rock House.*
Hitt Daniel R.	*Ewing.*
Bishop Gilbert	*Logan.*
Brown & Dalton	
Little David	
Schooley W.	
Brown Frederick	*Gibisonville.*
Williams J. L.	
Green P. J.	*Swan.*
Holland John	

Holmes County.

Smith T. H.	*Holmesville.*
Hoy G. W.	
Tuttle Joel	
Myers D. B.	
Welsh Samuel	
McGee Thos.	*Nashville.*
Jones Samuel & W.	
Harris David	
Soden W. J.	*Benton.*
Baney J.	*Berlin.*
Botts — Dr.	
Peters C.	*Winesburg.*
Woods J. B.	*Killbuck.*
Lippit John R	*Humphreyville.*
Cooper A. H.	

Huron County.

Cook T. M.	*Monroeville.*

Lane John L.	*Monroeville.*
Arnold C. W.	
Olery Wm. J.	
Chamberlin J. N.	*Steuben.*
McCammon Samuel	
Pierce B. G.	*Wakeman.*
Clark H. M.	
Martin A. J. & E.	*East Townsend.*
Staunton J. R.	
Ellis — Dr.	
White H. E.	*Clarksville.*
Kinney C.	
White Wm.	
Segar A. R.	
Campbell J. W.	*Greenwich.*
Haverland S. P.	
Goodson J. W.	*Bellevue.*
Giddings S. B.	
Fray L. W.	
Harts — Dr.	
Stiltson Wm. W.	
Lathrop D. A.	
DeGroff A.	*North Norwich.*
Morrison M. L.	*Centerton.*
White H. E.	*Clarkfield.*
Kenny Chas.	
Sanders & Read	*Norwalk.*
Tifft & Beckwith	
Hull H. L.	
Ingersol E. C.	
Webber W.	
Baker S. W.	*Fitchville.*
Vanvechton D. D.	
Tucker J. A.	
Gibson T.	
Laughlin M. E.	
Palmer M.	

Jackson County.

Williams W. S.	*Oakhill.*
Hurst D. A.	*Allensville.*
McGriffin Samuel	
Wilcox J.	
Hall C. B.	*Keystone.*
Salmans L. W.	*Berlin.*
Isham A. W.	*Jackson.*
Hoffman D. A.	
Mitchell D. H.	
Miller O. C.	
Clewers T. R.	

Jefferson County.

Dorsey D. B.	*Steubenville.*
Harsh L.	
Henning T. S.	
Hamilton Wm.	
Hensaler L.	
Johnson T.	
Mitchell J.	
Paine B. F.	
Rothacker S.	
Sinclair J.	
Stanton Wm.	
Sheets J.	
Tappan B.	
Russell David H.	*Moore's Salt Works.*
Andrews Alex.	

Markle A. T.   *Wintersville.*
Caldwell John   *Warrenton.*
Kelley J. M.
Yost E. B.
Skeggs Thos.
Marsh A. G.   *Richmond.*
Pyle E. M.
Cook Wm. L.   *East Springfield.*
Talbott M.
Parker Isaac   *Mt. Pleasant.*
Finley Robert
Flanner Wm. E.
Flanner Thos. U.
Updegroff J. T.
Drake Wm.
Moon A. C. & Scantling   *Knoxville.*
Hamilton G. D.
Leaslie Robert   *Port Homer.*
Mahan T. S.

Knox County.

Barnes G. W.   *Mount Vernon.*
Burr J. N.
McClelland & Bryant
Officer J. H.
Pumphrey B. W.
Ramsey W. H.
Russell & Thompson
Pazig F.
Shannon D. C.
Turner John J.   *Levering.*
Walters Thos. H.
Berry J. A.   *Danville.*
White John
Kelley Jas. W.   *Millwood.*
Landaker Lewis
McMaken Wm. T.
Moffitt Robert
Rogers M.   *Lucerne.*
Orr Thomas   *Martinsburg.*
Ralston D. H.
Rodman W. F.
Dyer Lewis   *Fredericktown.*
Edwards A.
Potter T. R.
Sapp S. C.
Ramsey C.   *Brandon.*
Shaw M.   *Ankenytown.*
Stough Samuel   *Monroe Mills.*
Pearce John   *Democracy.*
Roberts H. B.
Rogers B. F.
Lawney Henry   *North Liberty.*
McLaughlin Robert
Soller William B   *Jelloway.*
Tawney Henry
Childs H. A.   *Mount Liberty.*
Hildreth J. F.

Lake County.

Gibbs F. C.   *Willoughby.*
Clark E. G.
Storm G. W.
St. John O. S.
Plympton E. L.   *Madison.*
Meriman A.
Holbrook N. B.

Stockton D.   *Madison.*
Nichol John   *Kirtland.*
Webster S.
Whitley Wm.
Gibbs O. O.   *Perry.*
Carpenter J. B.   *Painesville.*
McBride L.
Stibbins L. O.
Gatchel H. P.
Plympton A.
Rosa S. & L. K.
Card G. W.
Palmer B.
Kelley L. H.
Beardsley H. C.

Lawrence County.

Bing T. P.   *Ironton.*
Briggs C.
Edgerton E. P.
Griswold E. M.
Hollingsworth John
Morris J.
Moxley N. K.
Willson Wm. F.
Pringle J.   *Hanging Rock.*
Hall C.   *Burlington.*
Neal D. B.   *Russellaplace.*
Monehan J. T.   *Miller's.*
Paine Wm. V.   *Quaker Bottom.*
McDowell R. M. P.
Trumbo G. W.
Lewis Samuel   *Waterloo.*
Leach M.   *Aid.*
Shattuck G. B.
McGoverney ——   *Campbell's.*
Potter W.

Licking County

Wolf R. S.   *Linnville.*
Johnson G. W.
Rogers J.   *Utica.*
Thrall B. F.   *Brownsville.*
Cassady G. W.
Knight A. W.
Basley & Boyd   *Utica.*
Southard J. M.   *Jacksontown.*
Walker H. J.
Bancroft Wm. W.   *Granville.*
Bryan E. F.
Gilford Chas.
Spencer A. A.
Sennett E.
Stanbury E.   *Newark.*
Marble D.
Pettit D. W.
Kitsmiller — Dr.
Wilson J. N.
Blair A. D.
Blair G. H.
Bird B. W.
Hamill J. J.
Rowe — Dr.
Dickinson J. H.
Andrews E. D.   *Croton*
Allen P. C.
Reynolds S. S.

Yarnell T.	*Croton.*	Day D.	*North Ridgeville.*
Bowers J.		Merriam E. D.	*La Grange.*
Curtis J. Q. A.		Pelton J. K.	
Waters H.	*Perryton.*	Underhill George C.	
McCann S.		Bunce H. A.	*Oberlin.*
Cooley J. B.	*Homer.*	Johnson H.	
Briggs F.		Steele A.	
Fassett Harvey	*Johnstown.*	Wheat J. W.	
Pratt B. W.		Young M. D.	*Pittsfield.*
Hood G. H.		Biglow A.	*Copopa.*
Follett Alfred		Culver A.	
Fassett H. H.		Holcomb R. M.	*Brighton.*
Belt S. J. M.	*Kirkersville.*	Day Edmond A.	*Sheffield.*
Kern J.		Jackson H.	*North Camden.*
Josephs J.		Day Edmond	*Sheffield Lake.*
Palmer Wm.	*St. Louisville.*	Wigton A. E.	*Brownhelm.*
		Willard James H.	

Logan County.

		Griswold L. D.	*Elyria.*
		Parker William	
Ditzler John Y.	*Huntsville.*	Kelley E.	
Seeley S. C.		Strong Jamin	
Snyder Joseph		Chapman Milton	
Allen D. B.	*West Liberty.*	Day D.	
Ayers J. H.		Manter N. H.	
Fuller S. W.		Vincent W.	
Harris D. W.		Peabody O.	*Wellington.*
Taylor J. C.		Meng A. P.	
Leonard B. B.	*Logansville.*	Johns & Smith	
Matson A. F.			
Smith Clinton		**Lucas County.**	
Smyser John	*New Richland.*		
Adams Wm. J.	*East Liberty.*	Burritt H.	*Maumee City.*
Hamilton Jas. W.		Conant H.	
James Spain		Cook Daniel	
Aylworth B. H.	*Bellefontaine.*	Dwight Justice	
Hartley & Lawrence		Hole C.	
McGowen ——		Mason Wm.	
Brown & Williams		Scott D. B.	
Lord & Edmiston		Snell F.	
Pollock J. S.		Spaulding V.	
Penock W. C.		St. Clair Wm.	
Scarf ——		White Oscar	
McCandless ——		Olney S. B.	*Waterville.*
Thomas ——		Pray Welcome	
Blair J. S.	*Zanesfield.*	Gardner J. A.	*Providence.*
Crew James		Houston Wm. W.	*Emery.*
Gee William		Kitridge J. J.	
Holmes Jesse		Pratt D.	*Lyons.*
Robb James S.		Young Joshua	
Moorhead James	*Lewistown.*	Chase James L.	*Manhattan.*
Pollock James S.		Green Joel, junr.	*Whiteford.*
Chambers M.	*Quincy.*	Cosgrove Thos. T.	
Heald A.		Miner Amos	
Leedham S. K.		Bissell A. F.	*Toledo.*
		Clark Jacob	
Lorain County.		Coldham ——	
		Darling William	
Alfred W. N.	*Huntington.*	Fenneburg ——	
Page E. A		Field ——	
Pritchard E. B.		Graham H.	
Brooks Levi	*Grafton.*	Hazlett J.	
Knowlton Cyrus B.		Hobby A.	
Willmot ——		Jones W. W.	
Bunce William	*Rochester Depot.*	Joyce ——	
Bunce Nathaniel		Klawser ——	
Grout William	*North Camden.*	Miner A. E.	
Jackson H.		Forbes ——	
Benham L.	*North Ridgeville.*	Pagin ——	

Scott W. C.	*Toledo.*	Davidson Walter	*Hanna's Mills.*
Timpany R. H.		Hole James M.	*Green Village.*
		Weikart Andrew	
Madison County.		Bronson T.	*Milton.*
Chaney William	*Lafayette.*	Tod Jonathan J.	
Taylor ——	*Midway.*	Ewing Geo.	
Seal John W.	*West Jefferson.*	Turnbull S.	
Stutson J.		Winans Harvey H:	
Crabb B.		Williams Edward	*Damascoville.*
McCullough John		Gruwell John V.	
Johnson N. K.		Hahn Nathan	*North Lima.*
Davis W. B.	*California.*	Entrikin F. W.	
McComb J. J.		Moore J. W.	*New Albany.*
Forsha A. W.		Trago John	*Pottersville.*
Zimmerman G.			
Zimmerman J.	*Rosedale.*	**Marion County.**	
Toland A.	*London.*	Wilkins R.	*Wilson:*
Jones A. T.		Copeland J.	
Strain W. A.		Patton Milton	
Williamson R. A.		Fry S. M.	*Cochranton.*
McMillan D. E.		Tyler Isaac	*Prospect.*
Lemon & Houston	*Midway.*	Bridy V. W.	
Jones A.	*South Solon.*	Blake — Dr.	
Ball J. F.	*West Canaan.*	Oder — Dr.	
Twiford W. H.	*Derby Creek.*		
Elliott D. H.		**Medina County.**	
McCune ——	*Pleasant Valley.*	Alden H.	*Lerna.*
Converse J.		Andrews James	*River Styx.*
McClintic Wm.	*Mt. Sterling.*	Harvy John P.	
McClintie Samuel		Parker L. B.	*Liverpo*
Bodman Elam		Howard O. J.	
Wilson Daniel	*Somerford.*	Willey A. J.	*Sharon Cent.*
		Branch Nathan	*Mallet Creek.*
Mahoning County.		Tiffany H.	
Brooke George W.	*Ellsworth.*	Lyman C. N.	*Wadsworth*
Prentice W. M.	*Canfield.*	Welton W. S. H.	
Fowler C. R.		Simmons A. L.	
Wilson J. W.		Sibley E. H.	*La*
Caldwell J.		Hoag M.	
Foster J.	*Lowellville.*	Painter Wm. H.	*Weymouth*
Loy J.		Laughlin M.	*Hinckle*
Steward J. H.		Peebles Henry	
Casper F.	*Petersburgh.*	Wilcox O.	
Coffin J. D.		Wait E.	
Swisher P. H.		Bell George	
Cook O. O.	*Youngstown.*	Willey A. G.	*Sharon Centre.*
Woodbridge T.		Palmer David	*Chatham Centre.*
Barclay Isaac		Robinson J. N.	
Pasen O. D.		Rose Ezra	*Homersville.*
Manning John			
Manning Henry		**Meigs County.**	
Hughes James W.	*Berlin Centre.*	Lowell M. P.	*Dunnington.*
Davidson Walter	*Frederick.*	Rathburn A.	*Rutland.*
Crable S. H.	*New Middletown.*	Waterman H. C.	
Shannon Thomas J.	*Orange.*	Hoag Wm. G.	
Packard J. A.		Boyd John B.	*Long Bottom*
Hole E. A.	*East Lewistown.*	McClentick J.	*Apple Grove*
Hall James M.	*Greenford.*	Adams Sencer	
Wikart A.		McClintick John	*Letart Fall*
Stewart R. H.	*Coitsville.*	Adams Spencer H.	
Truesdale Jackson	*North Jackson.*	Thomas Chas. F.	*Pomero*
Spears B. W.		Guthrie G. S.	
Truesdale J.	*Poland.*	Knapp Isaac	
Truesdale O.		Rhem Sebastian	
Mygatt E.		Sook Henry L.	
Ewing George	*Hanna's Mills.*	Train Isaac	
Kissel A.		Underwood G.	*Let*

2

Mercer County.

Miller M. M.	*Menden.*
Moncrieff Alex.	
Stearns R. W.	*St. Mary's.*
Bradley J.	
O'Connell A.	
Kishler G. W.	
Hetzler ——	
Gustin W. T.	
Crafford George	*Neptune.*
Sheldon G. J.	*Celina.*
Hutchins B. X.	
Mulligan Samuel	
Harb Wm. B.	*Mercer.*
Curd Silas	*Neptune.*
Sutton Isaac	*Shanesville.*
Burks John	
Judkins & Findley	*Coldwater.*
Milligan Dixon	*Fort Recovery.*
Richardson J. C.	
Fair John S.	
Judkins James	*Coldwater.*
Finley L. C.	
Patty J. L.	

Miami County.

Beamer — Dr.	*Fletcher.*
Roots — Dr.	
dmonds J.	*Piqua.*
i nith J. A.	
t ewart S. L.	
Hall W. P.	
I ee C. G.	
Lee H. A.	
B erger ——	
L eague T.	
F rooks R.	
F sively — Dr.	
Kitsmeller — Dr.	
'orrell — Dr.	
errill A.	
iefer — Dr.	*Troy.*
Tullis J. W.	
Abbot L. J.	
Sabion B. S.	
Hall — Dr.	
Meeks J. S.	*Casstown.*
Darst H. H.	
Potter A.	
Tensy Eli	*West Milton.*
Davis H.	
Parsons J. R.	
Albert J. K.	*Hyattsville.*
Brinkerhoff D. H.	
Furnace Wm.	*Pleasant Hill.*
.ible R. E.	
Bowman J. L.	
Vorth M. H.	
Pond A.	*Brant.*
Shigly Robert	
Smith — Dr.	*Fidelity.*
Hunter — Dr.	
Ct. Clair — Dr.	

Monroe County.

' ook Pardon	*Woodsfield.*
inclair Western T.	

Smith James	*Woodsfield.*
Eddy G. W.	*Sardis.*
McMahon D. S.	
Bowman Jeremiah	*Antioch.*
Covert Abraham B.	
Dowell William W.	
Grimshaw Samuel	*Laing's.*
McMahon John.	
Ashbaugh Frederick	*Masterton.*
Ashley John R.	
Ferrell James P.	
Patterson Wm. L.	
Pierson J. H.	*Rocky Narrows.*
Watkins John	
Ellis Edward	*Stafford.*
Mason George	
Williams J. W.	
Brookover John	*Sunfish.*
Gruber John	
O'Conner J. D.	
McCullough J. G.	*Malaga.*
Judkins H. G.	
Toho A. B.	
Allen J. B.	*Bealsville.*
Gratigny Lewis, senr.	
Githens G. W.	
Grier H. F.	
Clark Isaac A.	*Miltonsburgh.*
Zeller ——	
Bell John	*Lewisville.*
Reed Garrison W.	
Finney T. D.	*Graysville.*
Fogle G. D.	
Boice John A.	*Baresville.*
Henthrom N. E.	

Montgomery County.

Sample ——	*Chamberlain.*
Lucas O. E.	*Vandalia.*
Mullin H. J.	*Alexandersville.*
Taylor J. S.	
Legg Charles	*Liberty.*
Munger J. E.	
Hawkins Samuel	*Union.*
Weybright J.	
Lamme W. H.	*Centreville.*
McCarthy D.	
Strong N.	
Butler Calvin	*Centre.*
Connor J. R.	*Pyrmont.*
Lodders Wm.	
Lefever Alfred	*Little York.*
Basler J.	Main, *Dayton.*
Carey H. G	Ludlow,
Craighead ——	Second,
Cogley ——	"
Crook O. & J.	Third,
Cooms S. A.	Fifth,
Clements ——	Main,
Davis J.	Third,
Egrey W.	"
Gliger ——	Fifth,
Hanlinon ——	Third,
Hoy ——	Jefferson,
Jewett H.	Second,
Jones ——	Third,
James W. P.	Fifth,

Langstedt H.	Third, *Dayton.*	Barnum S. L.	*Iberia.*
Lugal A.	Fifth,	Mills T. S.	
Miller J. V.	Main,	Paxton James	
Newman ——	Upper Hydraulic,	Voorhies L. B.	
Pryor ——	Third,	Randolph Jas. F.	*Morengo.*
Stewart ——	Wilkinson,	Angell & Miller	*Cardington.*
Slubeck ——·	Third,	Resley John	
Vantuyl H.	"	White H. B.	
Wigand ——	First,	Duff H. M.	*Shawk's.*
Wise J.	Third,	Martin O. W.	
Walden ——	Fifth,	Dillon A. G.	*Woodview.*
Donnellan J. E.	*Farmersville.*	Main H. W.	
Carey J.	*West Baltimore.*	Singrey D. M. L.	
Sibley William	*New Lebanon.*	Wadsworth S. Y.	*Vail's ⋈ Roads.*
Wood J. P.		Haswell Charles S.	*Corsica.*
Gish Christopher	*Clayton.*	McFarlin James	
Snevaly John		White Timothy	*Nimmon's ⋈ Roads.*
Comstock James	*Germantown.*	Beebe T.	*Mount Gilead.*
Espich & Donnallan		Cary Z. H.	
Trout Michael		Fisher A.	
Greenwold J.	*Miamisburgh.*	Shaw J.	
Treon John		Brown Wm. S.	*Chesterville.*
Treon Isaac	· ٩	Main H. W.	
Lyons T. V.	·	Swingley D. L.	
Weaver Joseph			
Horubeck R.	*Taylorsville.*	**Muskingum County.**	
Wood J. P.	*Johnsville.*	Trimbly Joseph S.	*Adams Mills.*
		Reader A. J.	
Morgan County.		Wortman E. L.	*Otsego.*
Michener George	*Chester Hill.*	Wortman J. D.	
Huestis Isaac		Jennings Francis H.	*Norwich.*
Branson S.		Mitchell George W.	
Parker Isaac		Pringle G. W.	*New Concord.*
Alexander John	*Morganville.*	Cunningham J. D.	
Sands R.		Carothers — Dr.	
Tinker E. W.	*Malta.*	Peirce David	*Dresden.*
Shock J. G.		Dickinson Chas.	
Ewing A. W.		Lomect Benj. F.	
Plumly A.	*Meigs Creek.*	Cox G. S.	
Cotton E. W.		Safford R.	*Putnam.*
Gray R. J.		Erwin J. B.	
Rusk James	*Triadelphia.*	Farquhar E. A.	
Plumley A.	*Bristol.*	Austin D. A.	
Hudson J. Q. A.	*Deavertown.*	Dillon E.	
Hurd U. K.		Watkins J.	*Fultonham.*
Clark John O.	*Wood Grove.*	Axline J.	
Rush Daniel	*Rousseau.*	Kennedy P.	
Martin Robert		Rankin D.	
Reeves James S.	*Meigsville.*	Spencer Benj. F.	*Gratiot.*
Hogworth W.		McCrary Elias	
Dawes E.	*McConnelsville.*	Green John M.	
Little H. H.		Chambers R.	*Chandlersville.*
Brown J. H.		Howell T. D.	
Robertson Charles		Safford — Dr.	
Hull John		Coverdale L. N.	*Ridgeway.*
Lewis Alex.		Bell A. E.	*Zanesville.*
Edwards Michael		Barr Robert	
Dillenbaugh S.		Ball Alfred	
White J. W.	*Stockport.*	Bond John W.	
Abbott J. S.		Bingle ——	
McNichols Nathaniel	*Pennsville.*	Culbertson H.	
Hambleton Wm. N.		Hildreth Chas. O.	
Atkinson Thomas	*Neelysville.*	Halston J. G. F.	
		Helmick ——	
Morrow County.		Little Lyman	
Black John	*Underwood's.*	McElroy T. O.	
Devore James W.		Moorehead Washington	

Sabin & Macumber	*Zanesville.*	Firor S. V.	*Tarlton.*
Spangler Isaac		Williams Wm.	
Young ——		Allen James	*Darbyville*
		Black F. M.	
Noble County.		Tipton R. H	
Cain R. H.	*Berne.*	Tipton T. C.	
McGany John		Bunch Hilary P.	*Beckett's Store.*
Axtell Jackson	*Mount Ephraim.*	French O. K.	
Keller John		Lewis R. W.	*Williamsport.*
Smith Gustavus A.		Martin D. R	
McKee William	*Olive.*	Smith B. F.	
Melberry J. E.		Houk G. W.	*Palestine.*
Mason F. M.	*Harrietsville.*		
Capell J. F.	*Sarahsville.*	**Pike County.**	
Oconnor R. S.		Bitler Michael	*Cynthiana.*
Hopkins J. Y.		Little Walter S.	
McGarry S.		McBride — Dr.	*Jasper.*
Gibbs Erwin	*Gardner.*	Page J. N.	*Waverly.*
Lingo Benjamin	*Kennonsburg.*	Hutt S. A.	
		Joss Daniel	
Ottawa County.		Lowry Thos.	
Bell F. M.	*Elmore.*	Dunham W. H.	*Beaver.*
Luckey G. W.		Miller Wm. F.	*Byington.*
Luckey W.		Phelps A. & O. J.	*Piketon.*
Parsons E.		Blazer Christian	
Hitchcock James	*Port Clinton.*	Spurck P.	
Green W. G.		Fitzgerald E.	*Omega.*
		Ray J. B.	
Paulding County.			
Woodcock B. B.	*Cranesville.*	**Portage County.**	
Snyder S.	*Junction.*	Wellman John D.	*Ravenna.*
		Wait E. H.	
Perry County.		Collins & Belding	
Flowers & Crosbie	*New Lexington.*	Pratt Henry	
Hamilton T. J.		Hastings Samuel	*Brimfield.*
Smith James		Baily George	*Freedom.*
Vanatta Ezekiel		Smith John	*Palmyra.*
Hood James	*Thornville.*	Bigalow L.	
Shauk William		Cook F.	*Atwater.*
Turner Robert		Bassett G. W.	*Edinburgh.*
Witmer A.		Baldwin G. B.	*Rootstown.*
Tagart William A.	*Rehoboth.*	Bassett A. C.	
Holden William	*Sunday Creek bridge Roads.*	Osborn L. D.	
Lewis William		Price George	*Randolph.*
McQueen C. S.		Day Thos.	
Dorsey George	*Somerset.*	Bean Walter	*Aurora.*
Lynch ——		Coles Isaac	*Palmyra.*
Magruder Edward		Willis J. G.	*Streetsboro.*
McElnee A.		Burlingame H.	
Morris Jesse		Hays J.	*Shalersville.*
Wagenhals P. M.		Jewett M.	*Suffield.*
McGovern C.	*Chapel Hill.*	Knowlton John	*Franklin.*
Ashton Abner	*Straitsville.*	Crane E. W.	
Griffin Henry		Clark W.	
Hufford N. D.		Ward S. J.	*Paris.*
Victor F. P.		Gurley O. V.	
		Squires G. & A. J.	*Mantua.*
Pickaway County.		Ferris O.	
Blake A. M.	*Circleville.*	Curtis J. H.	*Deerfield.*
Hall P. K.		Wagoner J.	
Hankes C. M.		Sherman A. M.	*Nelson.*
Olds Chester		Caine Wm.	*Ravenna.*
Peck W. L.		Sweeney John	*Nelson.*
Ray Kingsley		Barrow P.	*Edinburgh.*
Turner Samuel D.		Cope Fred.	*Randolph.*
Van Harlington R. D.		Haymaker J.	*Franklin.*
Davisson W. W.	*Tarlton.*		

Heath N.   *Nelson.*
Manley Orvil.

Preble County.

Stratton F. J.   *West Alexandria.*
Derrey A. W.
Donnellan A.
Lindsey Wm.
Nesbit R. P.
McKay Isaac   *Lewisburg.*
Bayler Jas. R.
Ford S. J.
Stiles Thos. D.
Dunham L.   *Camden.*
Stephens A. H.
Crews J. H.
Mendenhall E.
Hornsher Robert
Sturr & Son   *Eaton.*
Orume & Helm
Temple J. J.
Brookens J. P.
Stratton — Dr.
Gilmore Eli   - *Fairhaven.*
McDill A. O.
Pinkerton A. W.
Ferris Samuel   *New Westville.*
Hawley Albert   *Gettysburg.*
Sturman G. W.
Boyd E.   *West Florence.*
Beek Joseph   *Hamburg.*
Williams J.
Sloan Richard   *Morningsun.*
Weinland Jacob S.   *West Elkton.*
Cox & Eaton   *New Paris.*
Peck O. W.
Braffett J. L.
Lewis A. B.
Miller V. G.

Putnam County.

Luce H.   *Gilboa.*
Luce R. O.
Moe L. W.
Paul T. E.
Blaker T. H.   *Medary.*
Ward J. W.   *Leipsic.*
De Lacenay Lewis   *Fort Jennings.*
Olds William E.   *Pleasant.*
Weaks J. J.
Allen Edward K.   *Buckeye.*
Pomery C. T.
Godfrey & Thrift   *Kalida.*
Anderson J. J.   *Vaughnsville.*
Robb Vance
Day Hiram   *Pendleton.*
Detwiller A. R.

Richland County.

Bricker W. R.   *Shelby.*
Mack O. H.
Mack J.
McMillin C.
Craig James   *Ontario.*
Hachedorn G. G.
Hachedorn N. E.   •
Jenner A.

Parsons R. F.   *Butler.*
Hahn E. E.   *Shenandoah.*
Dryfoose —
Crabb Jacob   *Olivesburg.*
Starr Michael
Butler S. A.   *West Windsor.*
Hahn H.
Barnes Wm. C.   *Barnet.*
Guthrie A. W.
Reed John
Anderson H. P.   *Lexington.*
Man A.
Miles L. B.
Barber J. K.   *Mansfield.*
Bissel O. J.
Blucker Wm.
Bruck —
Chandler —
Loughbridge & Mowry
Mitchell G. F.
Schallera R.
Southerland —
Todd John J.
Cantwell & Steward
Beach A. J.   *Bellville.*
Eells S. W.
Lee J. C.
Ridnour B.
Smith A.
Smith J. M.
Whitcomb N. D.
Fouts J. T.   *Newville.*
Henderson J. P.
Kinermon D. L.   *Richland.*
Stourtenour J.
Baker Norman   *Lucas.*
Tucker A. C.
Wallace Franklin
Clingan H. B.   *Adario.*
Benschoter Ensign   *Plymouth.*
Bevier Roeliff
Austin Horace
Henderson James
Myers G. H.

Ross County.

Miller Jas. D.   *Bainbridge.*
Green John N.
Morrow C.
Roberts Samuel C.
Philips T. W.
Stiers R. B.
Gillispie J. M.   *Latta's.*
Johnson A. C.
Latta Wm.   *Frankfort.*
Evans & McGarrough
Nye H. S.
Galbreth R.
Guisher A.
Knox J. M.   *Clarksburg.*
Hughey W. F.
Evans J. M.
Wiles David   *Chillicothe.*
Coates John
Fullerton Wm.
Williams W. G.
Zanders F. T.

McAdon Samuel   *Chillicothe.* | Hall O. J.   *Wheelersburgh.*
Waddle Wm. | Moseley T. N.
Foulke L. D. | Mussey F. B.
Miesse J.
Rominger C. L. | **Seneca County.**
Fuller — | Bricker S. & J. W.   *Stoner.*
Baird J. M. | Caples R. C.
McNalley Thomas | Ringler —
Moore James. | Benham A.   *Melmore.*
Hussey Z. | Ladd R. H.
Rehwinkle F. W. | Koons —
Hamilton Samuel C.   *South Salem.* | Gibson R. W. D.
Morton Samuel A. | Graves Theo. P.
Clark Lewis   *Yellow Bud.* | Hutchins W. D.   *Adrian.*
Beidler J. H. | Peters D. N.
Gildersleeve W. C.   *Hallsville.* | Stofer Jacob
Drummonds Josiah   *Gillespieville.* | Furh George   *Berwick.*
Shauk John M. | Martin A.   *Bloomville.*
Jones N. E. | Weeks G. R.
Faraher Thomas | Cessna Joseph P.   *Bettsville.*
Thompson A. W.   *Kingston.* | Norton Rufus
Shannon R. W. | Brickel S. W.   *Tiffin.*
Wilson G. A. | Dresback E.
Litler S. A.   *Bourneville.* | Belars O. B.
Brooks J. | Franklin F.
Deforest S. H. | Heckerman J. U.
                                               | Jeack F.
Sandusky County. | Long A.
Huffman A.   *Woodville.* | Leinecker P.
Treadway H. H.   *Clyde.* | Kuhn H.
Exton G. S. | McFarland J. A.
Searley R. L. | Obermiller N.
Stone & Patterson | Reime E. W.
Ginn John   *Greensburg Cross Roads.* | Sprague G.
Niles Henry   *Rutland Ridge.* | Turley D.
Yates — Dr. | Owen A. G.   *Bascom.*
Rey John   *Townsend.* | Wertz Henry
Thompson John C.   *Rollersville.* | Phiney C. F.   *Reedtown.*
Rousch Chas. A. | Knickerbocker W. B.
Ranson L. Q.   *Fremont.* | Williams B. D.
Beungrand Peter | Frazer R. P.   *West Lodi.*
Ritter M. A. | Finch S. T.   *Green Spring.*
Willmer F. | Kagcy Isaac
Carhner — Dr. | Yates Porter
Soms — Dr. | Hanford William   *Republic.*
Wilson James | Waddle R. N. & J. Mc.
                                               | Hamilton William L.
Scioto County. | Sparks James S.
Johnson Wm. G.   *Haverhill.* | Atwood John
Mitchell T. J.   *Lucasville.* | Smith B. S.
Rouss H. C. | Price William
Smith H. M.
Abernethy A.   *Portsmouth.* | **Shelby County.**
Carson J. | Duer Edwin A   *Montra.*
Dennis J. W. | Houston Levi   *Houston.*
Hempsted G. S. | Mark J. N.
Jones A. B. | Turner Geo. H.   *Wynant.*
Jones H. D. | Baker S. C.   *Pratt.*
Lewis W. H. | Hill John B.
Leiopold — | Hussey S. C.
McDowell W. M. | Musselman S. B.
Schwarb — | Osmond Edmond
Shackleford J. M. | Steely Henry G.   *Valentia.*
Tyrrell William S.   *Iron Furnaces.* | Beeman P.   *Sidney.*
Watts William M. | Conklin H. S.
Wood Alfred L. | Johnston R. C.
Chaffin S.   *Lyra.* | Wilson A.

Steely Henry	*Dinsmore.*
Cowan & Davenport	*Hardin.*
Johnson J. J.	*Lockington.*

Starke County.

Coats J. G.	*Navarre.*
Graves A.	
Leeper J. L.	
Otis J. D.	
Hoke Jacob	*Waynesburg.*
Dibble B. S.	*Minerva.*
Haldermau L.	
Robertson S.	
Hatcher Wm. R.	*Lake.*
Steese Jacob	
Floom J. A.	*Louisville.*
Rahler S.	
Seguin E.	
Beebout Jas. L.	*Paris.*
Guybman G.	
Preston William P.	
Daugherty J. E.	*Greentown.*
Hardman S. D.	*New Franklin.*
Crow S. S.	
Woolf Samuel	*Frease's Store.*
Oleis D.	*Canton.*
Danzinger L.	
Estep J. S.	
Matthews J. H.	
McAbee H.	
Fellows J. K.	
Wernot —	
Whiting L. M.	
Buchanan Robert	*East Greenville.*
Crum P. W.	*New Berlin.*
Bembérger J. F.	
Holtz George	
Gans D. L.	*Magnolia.*
McIlrary Wm. Q.	
Clover Roland	*Marlboro'.*
Lewis George	
Thomas Kersey G.	
Hoffman Daniel	*Hartville.*
Underwood Willen	*New Baltimore.*
Wilcox Allen	
Bacon D. W. C.	*Massillon.*
Shertzer John	
Shertzer J. V.	
Hurxthall F. T	
Shreeve T. C.	
Whiting A. W.	
Barrick J. P.	
Martin A.	
Abbott T. P.	
Slusser Lewis	
Dorband William	
Ziperlin F.	
Musser Jacob	
Houts Abraham	
Bay J. H.	*Limaville.*
Northrop L.	
Jones O.	*Mount Union.*
Lamborn L. L.	
Woodruff E.	

Summit County.

Ewing A. E.	*Richfield.*

Munson W. B.	*Richfield.*
Stephenson N.	
Stock P. C.	
Baker Christopher H.	*Copley.*
Canfield E.	
Chapman B.	
Brown W. H. & Charles	*Eden.*
Biggs Cyrus F. H.	*Summit.*
Wagoner S. W.	
Bliss Hosea	*Northfield.*
Haseltine Moses G.	
Bunn C.	*Bath.*
Curtiss Elijah	*Middlebury.*
Merrill R. S.	
McChesney D. L	
Smith John B.	
Heath Theo. F.	*Cuyahoga Falls.*
Rice C. W.	
Somers P. G.	
Upson George C	
Hand W. S.	*Clinton.*
Caldwell H. W.	
Oberlin O. B.	
Agard A. H.	*Western Star.*
Smith S A.	
Ashmun G. P.	*Hudson.*
Graham J. L.	
Town Israel	
Wright Amos	*Tallmadge.*
Hard M. K.	*North Springfield.*
Perdue Charles A.	*Inland.*
Angel E.	*Akron.*
Bowen William	
Coburn Z. H.	
Cole Joseph	
Fisher & Peck	
Howard E. W.	
King J.	
Munger E. L.	
Scott D. A.	
Stanton J.	
Sisler William	*Nimisilla.*
Sisler Adam	
Dickinson George W.	*Peninsula.*
McNiel R.	*Montrose.*

Trumbull County.

Beebe Robert M.	*Hartford.*
Bushnell George W.	
Jones Allen	
Gilmore Hugh	*Girard.*
Marshall William	
Brown L. C.	*Farmington.*
Bard Isaac	*Church Hill.*
Walker R. H.	
Steuart J. E.	*Brookfield.*
Willis O. L.	
Bronson James	*Newton Falls.*
Earle Homer	
Porter J. F.	
Seaton A. M.	*Ohltown.*
Bowman John C.	*Southington*
Moore Ezekiel	
Rice Milton, jun.	
Metcalf C. T.	*Bristolvih*
Brackin J.	*Mecca*
Powers J. A.	

Bradley M. C.	*Johnsonville.*	Rathbun Charles	*Marysville.*
Fuller J. H.		Owens P. R.	
Kerr Augustus		Kezartee Ira	
Bascom J.	*Greensburgh.*	Marquis J. S.	*Raymond's.*
Ellsworth A. M.		Wilson B. W.	
McBirney T. A.	*Hubbard.*	Heistand H. O. S.	*Richwood.*
McGaughey T. R.		McMillen B. F.	
Bradley L. B.	*Gustavus.*	Munnell William	
Horton T. J.		Ross Joseph N.	
Weibert T.		Fields Erastus	*Jerome.*
McAlpine Samuel	*Mesopotamia.*	Rose E. S.	
Reitter Wm. R.		Baker J.	*Milford Centre.*
Woods D. B. & J. R.	*Warren.*	Mann R. P.	
Loy & Nelson		Mann Fletcher	
Ferrell J. & T.		Smith J. P.	
Paine William		Swain Lafayette	
Townsend E. W.		Sordan S.	*Pharisburg.*
Harmon J. & J. B.		Brees Samuel	*Boke's Creek.*
Van Gorder James.		Davis A. S.	
Brainard A. C.	*Orangeville.*		

Tuscarawas County.

		Van Wert County.	
Burr Joseph S.	*Port Washington.*	Adams J. Q.	*Van Wert.*
Herford —		Blecker J.	
McCall A. R.		Bowland M. J.	
Milligan James	*New Cumberland.*	Coffin T. B.	
Moorehead J. M. C.		Emmerson Charles	
Kurtz Isaac H.	*Cadwallader.*	Hines T. J.	
Willis A. H.		Galleher D. K.	
Trease H. & S.	*Deardorff's Mills.*	Kyle W. H.	
Welty John W.	*Winfield.*	Reid J. L.	
Beebout J.	*Sandyville.*	Ward S. M'C.	
Orellin Wm. K.		Cox James W.	*Delphos.*
Hodge J. M.	*Bolivar.*	Burkholder J. H.	
Sisson J. C.		Reul Rudolph	
Tripp William		Evans C. A.	
Weaver B. H.		Metcalf Z.	
Williams H. W.	*Uhrichsville.*		
Latham William D.	*Peoli.*	**Vinton County.**	
McPherson F. L.		Baird D. M.	
Arnold Robert	*Gnadenhutten.*	Doddridge Joseph	
Gshaway Henry	*Ragersville.*	McGiffin S.	*Allensville.*
Hochli Felix		Wilcox J.	
Simpson J.	*New Philadelphia.*	Keenan J. M.	*Reed's Mills.*
Deal H. P.		Higgins G. W.	
McCoy U. C.		Bishop D.	*Wilkesville.*
Richards D.		Althur G. W.	
Shultz A. W.		Cline —	
McMeal F. D.	*Canal Dover.*	Holland John	*Mount Pleasant.*
Brashear B. B.		Orumit O. K.	*New Plymouth.*
Winhull William		Crawford J. P.	*Prattsville.*
Brisben John			
Slingluff Joseph		**Warren County.**	
Soule James		Baird David	*Franklin.*
Maxwell David		Evans O.	
Schweitzer H.		Haller J.	
Eckman H.	*Tuscarawas.*	McAvoy W. B.	
Seldon O. G.	*Shanesville.*	Schenck W. L.	
it William J.		Evans R. P.	
L ng William		Keever M. H.	*Ridgeville.*
bridge N.	*Rockford.*	Stokes W. H.	
Walker J. D.		Adams T.	*Waynesville.*
vely S.		Stoddard J. C.	
		Wilson W. S.	
Union County.		Anderson W. H.	
sl Jeremiah	*Marysville.*	Martin W.	
nderson David W.		Smizer H.	

Smizer W.	*Waynesville.*	Buchanan C.	*Lowell.*
Ervin Benj.	*Twenty Mile Stand.*	Spooner C.	
Cox Hamilton		Dear R. T.	
Deleplane B. F.	*Oregon.*	Ross Thomas	*Watertown.*
Hart G. D.	*Mason.*	Gillis S. M.	
Steward S. S.		Hardy John R.	*Bonn.*
Nixon J. J.		Lindner E.	
Mitchell R. B.	*Red Lion.*	Warren J. W.	
Crossfield E. D.			
Hill P. W.	*Edwardsville.*	**Wayne County.**	
Waggoner Joseph	*Deerfield.*	Sampson A. S.	*Canaan.*
Curiss J. H.		Nowlan A.	
Bishop N. W.	*Hopkinsville.*	Coulter J. P.	*Wooster.*
Cottle L. A.		Pixley S.	
Taylor J. J.	*Dearfield.*	Thayer R.	
Hunt S. P.	*Morrow.*	Davis M. C.	
Foster C. A.		Harley L. G.	*Dalton.*
Ogden J. T.	.	Snodgrass S. K.	
Stephens J. & B.	*Lebanon.*	Loggert T. M.	
Van Havlingier John		Armstrong A. M.	*Chippewa.*
Drake J. L.		Stedman A. J.	
Scott J.		Adams A.	*Edinburgh.*
Fisher J.		Gorgas C. R.	
Fisher E.		Buckmaster H.	*Fredericksburg.*
Fisher C.		Smally J. W.	
Sellers A.		Miller Lewis	*Big Prairie.*
Harlan Jonathan B.	*Butlerville.*	Willford S. C.	*East Union.*
Johnson Wm. S.		Weyse John	
Scroggs John W.	*Harveysburg.*	Hart George	*Reedsburg.*
Williamson, F. A.		Roberts E. J.	
Roach Geo.		Allen Wm. S.	*Burbank.*
Hormel Milton J.		Rile A. J.	
Dakin Warren		Taggart W. W.	*Smithville.*
		Greenamier Wm.	
Washington County.		Willford Sam'l C.	*East Union.*
Hildreth S. P.	*Marietta.*	Weyse John	
Trevor H.		McMillen J.	*West Lebanon.*
Fuller S.		Scobey John	*Old Hickory.*
Cook P., jun.		Moore J. T.	
Cotton J. D.		Hoopingarner I. J.	*Marshallville.*
Kunckle A. S.		Hyatt Wm. B.	
Hart S.	*Harmar.*	Wilgohs Chas.	
Regnier F.			
Newton Wm. S.		**Williams County.**	
Hart B. F.		Duncher John	*Williams Centre.*
Dana John	*Centre Belpre.*	Ensign A.	
Young John		Pape L. D.	
Veikers Thos.		Dewolf John G.	*Montpelier.*
Gilbert Geo. N.		Picking G. W.	
Gale Geo. W.	*Newport.*	Lang George	
Valentine B.		Finch G. W.	*West Unity.*
Victor Davis,	*Ostend.*	Groves J. W. P.	
Rose Thos.	*Lower Salem.*	Hall W. L.	
Blacklege T. G.		Morrison W. C.	
Gibbs Dennis	*Regnier's Mills.*	Meng A. P.	
Brown Benj.		Kemp John	
Quinby Ephraim	*Fearing.*	Snow Sam'l	
Moor Joseph	*Bartlett.*	Kent Thos.	*Bryan.*
McArthur Dan'l.		Paul Sam'l	
Johnston Wm. S.		Viers Jas. M.	
Bowen George	*Waterford.*	Koonts Henry	*Oak.*
Kelley P. H.		Ransom A.	*Pulaski.*
Reynolds L.	*Beverly.*	**Wood County.**	
Little James			
Parker — Dr.		Robertson Jas.	*Perrysburg.*
Laughlin R. G.	*Jolly.*	Peck E. D.	
Wilson J.		Bowpre Chas.	

Smith Harvey	*Perrysburg.*
Peck Wm. R.	*Bowling Green.*
Rodgers G. J.	
Lamb Wm. G.	
Coss L. H.	*Portage.*
Rogers A.	
Peck — Dr.	
Owings Sam'l B.	*Weston.*
Breese Sam'l M.	*Gilead.*
Mead J. N.	
Bletton John	
Carman T. S.	*Montgomery Cross Roads.*
Gorsuch L. L.	
Wesley — Dr.	
Baird O.	*Woodbury.*
Wylie Wm.	

Wyandot County.

Watson David	*Upper Sandusky.*
Ramsay C.	
McDonald G. T.	
McCannell James	
Ferris O.	
Sigler John	
Kagey Andrew	
Foster J. & T.	*Carey's.*
Wilcox M. W.	
Letson Z.	*McCutchensville.*
Holfhill A.	*Little Sandusky.*
Stephens — Dr.	
McBride — Dr.	*Wyandot.*
Turney J.	
Findley Wm.	
Martin H. B.	*Sycamore.*
Chesney Wm.	*Marseilles.*
Irvine Wm.	
Chesney J. M.	
White S. H.	
Jones J. D.	
Peck T. B.	*Mexico.*
Simpson W. W.	*Belle Vernon.*
Kerr J. J.	

Piano Forte Dealers.
Cuyahoga County.

Brainard S. & Co., 77 Superior *Cleveland.*
Holbrook & Long, Parson's Block
Payne E. A. & Co., 162 Superior

Franklin County.

Reed A., High, 4 doors N. of Neil House
                                    Columbus.

Hamilton County.

Colburn & Field, No. 154 Main *Cincinnati.*
Murch & White, 74 w. Fourth
Smith & Nixon, 76 w. Fourth
Peters Wm. C. & Sons, cor. 4th & Walnut
Niles S. O. O., Agent, Third & Hammond.

Muskingum County.

Bailey L. P.   *Zanesville.*
Filley M. B.

Piano Forte Manufacturers.
Cuyahoga County.

Schneider J., No. 40 Seneca *Cleveland.*

Hamilton County.

Evans L. A., No. 10 e. Fifth	*Cincinnati.*
Schaneul Charles, 333 Walnut	
Dannreuther A., 497	"
Britting J., 74 Canal	
Blackburn T. R., 283 Main	
Brunswick J. M., cor. Court and Walnut.	

Montgomery County.

Barnhart D., Main   *Dayton.*

Muskingum County.

Bailey L. P.   *Zanesville.*

Starke County.

Bushman Adam   *East Greenville.*

Tuscarawas County.

Weber John   *New Philadelphia.*

Pickle Manufacturers and Dealers.
Hamilton County.

Schooley & Thompson, 57 e. 5th *Cin'ati.*
Todd J. & Co., 35 w. Fifth

Pipe (German) Manufactur'rs.
Hamilton County.

Adleta Martin, 473 Walnut   *Cincinnati.*
Seyppel Ferdinand, 427 Vine

Pipe (Steam) Manufacturers.
Hamilton County.

Greenwood & Fifield, corner Walnut and
    Canal   *Cincinnati.*

Plane Manufacturers.
Columbiana County.

Starr James   *New-Lisbon.*

Franklin County.

Ohio Tool Co., State Avenue *Columbus.*

Hamilton County.

Roseboam & Thomas, 519 W. Row *Cin'ati.*
Taylor H. & J. C., 44 & 46 w. 8th
Roseboom & Smith, 208 Main
Seybold C., 267   "
Smith C. J., 206   "
Shaeffer & Cobb, Pearl, b. Main & Walnut
Cunningham & Co., Lock, b. Fifth & Sixth

Montgomery County.

Garrison D. N., Third   *Dayton.*

Trumbull County.

White Charles   *Warren.*

Warren County.

Babbitt J. M.	*Mason.*
Verbryck J. H.	
Hastings S.	
Crawford John	

Planing-Mills.
Brown County.

Collins Thos.   *Ripley.*

Clermont County.

Ward & Ramsay   *Loveland.*

Cuyahoga County.

Hostetter Charles D., corner Merwin and German   *Cleveland.*
Butts C. C., Agent, James

Franklin County.

Field & Adams   *Columbus.*
Neal & Whitman

Hamilton County.

Baily, Langstaff & Co., Front, bet. Mill and Wood   *Cincinnati.*
Bateman & Co., cor. Laurel and W. Row
Cook M. H., Fourth, bet. Park and Smith
Cline John, 161 e. Front
Fay Antony, cor. Broadway and Eleventh
Hinkle & Guild, Front, bet. Smith & Mill
Johnston, Morton & Co., Front, bet. Parsons and Whitaker
Lape & Gilpin, Canal, bet. Elm and Plum
Mitchell J. & Co., 304 Broadway
Smith & Williamson, cor. Third and John
Underwood & Co., Fifth, bet. Broadway and Pike
Creighton Robert   *Columbia.*
Trimmer A.   *Pendleton.*
Glenn M. & L.   *Fulton.*
Morten J. A. G.
Walden & Vance
Welch C.

Highland County.

Gray, Wear & Wilson   *Greenfield.*

Jefferson County.

Manley & Lowe   *Steubenville.*

Mahoning County.

Lynsey Wm.   *Youngstown.*

Miami County.

Vandegrift & Boner   *Troy.*

Pickaway County.

Jewel & Cook   *Circleville.*

Richland County.

Eminger & Sherman   *Mansfield.*

Ross County.

Haskins & Co.   *Chillicothe.*

Scioto County.

Rhodes & Martin   *Portsmouth.*

Planished Ware Manufacturers and Dealers.

Hamilton County.

Brewer A. R., 30 Fifth st.   *Cincinnati.*
Hackman John F., 214 Fifth
Hope, Hopple & Fleming, Front, Cassilly's Row
Thomas G. D., Front, Cassilly's Row
Brittle A. A., opposite S. B. Landing

Payne —, Columbia, bet. Main & Walnut
Horrocks J. R., Commercial Row   *Cin'ti.*

Plaster of Paris Dealers.

Erie County.

Marsh & Co.   *Sandusky City.*

Hamilton County.

Ward W. & E., n. side Columbia, bet. Walnut and Vine   *Cincinnati.*
Marsh & Co., s. w. cor. 4th & Sycamore
Cochran Robert, 41 Walnut
Bradford T. & Co., 59 & 64 Walnut
McGlincey H., W. Row, above Ninth
Burrows J. H. & Co., 23 w. Front
Bradford James & Co., 65 Walnut

Plasterers.

Adams County.

Potts John M.   *Marble Furnace.*
Purcell E. F.

Allen County.

Crayne Joseph   *West Newton.*

Ashland County.

Hammond Philip   *Savannah.*
Harvey John
Rush William   *Mohecan.*

Athens County.

Sims J.   *Athens.*
Fulton Robert

Belmont County.

McCanehan —   *Bellair.*
Bailey Charles H.   *Saint Clairsville.*
Hosleton John

Butler County.

Conklin John   *West Chester.*
Yeargan J.   *Somerville.*

Clarke County.

Holt William   *Selma.*
Murphy J. C.
Harnish J. & Co.   *New Carlisle.*
Sheets & Croney

Clermont County.

Neely J.   *Mt. Carmel.*
Skagg Noble   *Amelia.*
Hitch William   *Neville.*
Talber J. & Scott   *Moscow.*
Ramsey John   *Loveland.*
Clark M.   *Bantam.*
Clark Wm.
Clark Z.
McIntosh Alex.
Smith Wm.

Clinton County.

Dean B.   *New Vienna*
Moon C.
Shockly Milton
Moon A   *Martinsville.*
Pennington Wm. R.

Columbiana County.

Elwell Wm. & Co.	Calcutta.
Dunlap Cyrus	Salineville.
Hunter John	East Rochester.

Crawford County.

Valentine Joseph	Poplar.
Valentine James	

Cuyahoga County.

Spencer J. L.	Coe Ridge.

Darke County.

Ray Stephen	New Madison.
Ray John	
Miller Wm.	
Woods Wm. M.	German

Fairfield County.

Haynes Samuel	Clear Creek.
Heft D.	Sugar Grove.
Matheney James	

Franklin County.

Reed George W.	Groveport.
Yourd John	
Day Lyman	Blendon.
Lewis Elias, jr.	Worthington.
Marlbom S. M.	
McClelland Joseph	Canal Winchester.

Guernsey County.

Burson Joseph	New Gottingen.
Dilley P. A.	

Hamilton County.

Garretson O.	Mt. Healthy.
Hopper Garret	
Johnson Ransaeller	
Spahr Joseph	
Parker J. H.	Mt. Washington.
Rush Joseph	Cheviot.
Craven J.	
McManama A. B.	
Vail Samuel	
Taylor J. F., 140 Vine	Cincinnati.
Bills, Lewis & Co., Court, near Race	
Kirman W., 128 Hopkins	

Highland County.

Robbins O.	Highland.

Hocking County.

Conaway John	Rock House.
Braggs Josiah	Logan.
Funcannon Henry	
Rathburn Wm.	

Holmes County.

Marquis Joseph	Holmesville.
Jackson Silas	
Marquis H.	
McCully Joseph	Benton.

Logan County.

Davis George W.	Huntsville.
Hellings A. J.	
Bush John	Rushsylvania.

Hatcher Daniel	Rushsylvania.
Stilwell Thomas	

Lorain County.

Gerrish N.	Oberlin.
Smith E.	

Monroe County.

Chapman James R.	Woodsfield.
Morrow Marshall	
Brown John	Sunfish.
Lloyd Humphrey	
Lacy James M.	

Montgomery County.

Anderson James	Miamisburg.
Anderson Samuel	

Morgan County.

Pearson David	Chester Hill.
Wells Caleb	Meigsville.
Hawkins John S.	McConnelsville.
Linken Henry	
Sigler L.	
Schriver John	
Wilson Wm.	
Wade Wm.	Pennsville.
Matson Joseph	

Morrow County.

Ackerman & Crain	Cardington.
Kramer C. W.	

Noble County.

Perry J. B.	South Olive.
Webber Ira	

Perry County.

Vanwye William	New Lexington.
Vanwye John N.	
Hewitt D.	Somerset.
Phillips Nathaniel	
Phillips Wingate	
Smith Benjamin	
Smith Charles	
Zane Christian	

Seneca County.

Dysinger C.	Bloomville.

Shelby County.

Steen Thomas	Hardin.

Starke County.

Erskine Robert	Waynesburg.
Gruber Mathias L.	New Franklin.
Miller James	Massillon.
London & Pangburn	
Hoiles Joshua, jun.	Mount Union.

Trumbull County.

Smith P. S.	Brookfield.

Tuscarawas County.

Cummins John	Winfield.
Barthlew B.	New Philadelphia.
Speck L.	

Union County.

Dee Samuel B.	Milford Centre.

Hyland Lewis   *Milford Centre.*

Wyandot County.

Wilson John   *Upper Sandusky.*
Osborn —

Platers, (Silver and Brass.)

Cuyahoga County.

Schwartzenburg J., Seneca   *Cleveland.*

Hamilton County.

Clark P., Third, bet. Main and Walnut
  Cincinnati.
Daniels N. C., 39 w. Fourth
Morrison —, 70 w. Fourth
Wright & Son, 32 w. Sixth

Plow Manufacturers.

Adams County.

Potts Jonas   *Marble Furnace.*

Belmont County.

McLeish James   *Barnesville.*

Brown County.

Thompson Johnson   *Ripley.*

Butler County.

Mills J.   *Rossville.*

Carroll County.

McGuire E.   *Carrollton.*

Clermont County.

Ertel Henry   *West Woodville.*
McSwigart John
Smith D. S.   *Williamsburg.*
Perine James

Clinton County.

Hoover John   *Martinsville.*

Columbiana County.

Nowling Joseph & Co.   *East Fairfield.*

Coshocton County.

Thompson, Roney & Co.   *West Bedford.*
Irwin John   *Chili.*

Erie County.

Burt G.   *Milan.*
Butman J.

Fayette County.

Bastwick Adley.   *Pancoastburg.*

Franklin County.

Gill John L., Broad   *Columbus.*
Roberts & Zingle, High

Geauga County.

Robbinson & Co.   *Auburn.*
Rider William   *Munson.*

Hamilton County.

Garrett & Cottman, corner Seventh and
  Main   *Cincinnati.*
Miller Geo. C. & Co., Seventh near Main
Peacock A., cor. Main and Webster
Hart S., 448 Main

Roberts J. & Co., 614 Main   *Cincinnati.*
Sloop Hiram, Main above Canal
Shepard J. L.   *Columbia.*

Highland County.

Scott G. M.   *Dodsonville.*
Myers J.   *Hillsboro'.*

Huron County.

Skader H. C.   *Four Corners.*
Smith W. E.

Knox County.

Furlong M. C.   *Mount Vernon.*
Rankins D. S.   *Fredericktown.*

Licking County.

Woodcock J. W.   *Brownsville.*
Lennel & Clemons   *Granville.*
Greene Wm. T.   *Perryton.*

Logan County.

Power John   *Bellefontaine.*

Lucas County.

Porter Samuel.   *Toledo.*

Medina County.

Coggahall & Kingbury   *Wadsworth.*
Webber A. A.   *Hinckley.*

Miami County.

Rain F.   *Piqua.*
Wilmington Thomas   *Troy.*

Montgomery County.

Aughe J., Third   *Dayton.*
Kine H., St. Clair

Morgan County.

Geddes John   *Pennsville.*

Pickaway County.

Bright M. & Co.   *Circleville.*

Portage County.

Tilden J. M.   *Nelson.*

Preble County.

Guild & Weist   *Camden.*
Graham & Reinheimer   *New Paris.*

Richland County.

Clark Thomas   *Shelby.*
Liter & Argo   *Mansfield.*
Moody J. W.   *Belleville.*

Ross County.

Allen and Evans   *Chillicothe.*
Ridney John
Gill & Williams

Scioto County.

Murray, Ward & Stephenson   *Portsmouth.*

Seneca County.

Shrider Jacob   *Tiffin.*
Swift & Ogden   *Republic.*

Starke County.

Jones Robert   *Waynesburg.*
Partridge H. & F.   *Massillon.*

Summit County.

Fenton H. C.   *Middlebury.*
Rhoads Matthias

Trumbull County.

Fell N. A.   *Orangeville.*

Union County.

Turner Thomas   *Marysville.*

Washington County.

Harmar Manufacturing Co.   *Harmar.*

Williams County.

Platt Thomas   *Montpelier.*

Wood County.

Brown, Smith & Co.   *Perrysburg.*

Plumbers, Pump and Hydrant Manufacturers.

Cuyahoga County.

Wood and Leland, 28 Superior *Cleveland.*
Smith, Murray & Co., 36 Bank
Parish & Knight, 25 Superior

Hamilton County.

Gibson John B., Walnut bet. Third and
   Fourth   *Cincinnati.*
Eustis S. & H., 244 Main
Borrowman Thos., 283 Walnut
Forbush C & Co., 26 w. Sixth
Brooks G. W., Fifth bt. Main and Syc.
Attlesey James, Vine near Ninth
Johnson Jas. A., 43 East Third
Tatem H. L. & Co., 157 w. Fifth
Moore P. J., 223 w. Fifth
Stacy J. A., Western Row bet. Sixth and
   George
Kirk David, 206 Walnut

Pocket-Book and Porte Monnaie Manufacturers.

Hamilton County.

Strobel Charles, Apollo Building, Walnut
                                Cincinnati.

Potteries.

Adams County.

Parks & Chamberlin   *Manchester.*

Belmont County.

Mehollen & Batson   *Uniontown.*

Butler County.

Osborn J.   *Rossville.*
Eckert Joseph P.   *Trenton.*
Vannath Samuel

Clark County.

Hicks W. J.   *Springfield.*
Foreman Joseph   *New Carlisle.*

Columbiana County.

Philip J. R.   *Wellsville.*
Ridder D.
Croxall & Brothers
Bane Taylor   *New Lisbon.*
Brouse Philip
Russell Wm. E.
Buck Jacob   *Bucks.*
Ball & Morris   *East Liverpool.*
Brunt & Bloor
Goodwin John
Harrison & Brothers
Harvey, Green & Co.
Harker, Thompson & Co.
Larkins, Newell & Co.
Salt & Mear
Walley & Co.
Woodward, Blakeley & Co.
Keister Isaac   *Columbiana.*

Darke County.

Birely William   *Greenville.*

Defiance County.

Speaker Lucas   *Brunersburg.*

Delaware County.

Craner H.   *Norton*

Franklin County.

Jenkins A., Front   *Columbus.*

Greene County.

Nesbitt Nathaniel   *Xenia.*

Hamilton County.

Brumley W., cor. Freeman and Hamilton
   Road   *Cincinnati.*
Eichenlaub V., 649 Vine
Lessell Peter, 99 Hunt
Lewis J. H., 683 Vine
Scott George & Co., w. Front
Seamans & Hainer, 14 and 16 w. Water
Derrough William   *Fulton.*
Jackson J. & E.   *Harrison.*

Highland County.

Jennings Levi   *Greenfield.*
Shafer J. & W.   *Dodsonville.*
Gruber William   *New Market.*

Knox County.

Blue W. H.   *Bladensburg.*
Harris Jesse
Griffith —

Licking County.

Rudoff Jacob   *Etna.*

Lucas County.

French E. P.   *Emery.*

Montgomery County.

Gephart & Isor   *Germantown.*

Winebrenner D.   *Miamisburg.*
Bright Samuel D.   *Liberty.*
Rosa H. J.   *Centreville.*

Portage County.

Loomis Thomas   *Atwater.*
Purdy & Fenton   *Suffield.*

Preble County.

Thomas William   *Gettysburg.*
Crocket David

Pike County.

Bangs B. B.   *Piketon.*

Richland County.

Hisey William   *Shenandoah.*

Ross County.

Clemens T.   *Frankfort.*
Wolfe Jacob   *Chillicothe.*

Starke County.

Ross J. H.   *Waynesburg.*

Tuscarawas County.

Riggs Alfred   *Sandyville.*
Schwendiman John   *Ragersville.*
Gibbs W.   *New Philadelphia.*

Vinton County.

Jefferson Jacob   *Mount Pleasant.*

Wood County.

Klophestein Peter   *Bowling Green.*

Wyandot County.

Breck —   *Upper Sandusky.*

Powder (Wholesale) Dealers.

Hamilton County.

Loomis M. D. W., s. e. corner Main and
  Second   *Cincinnati.*
Donahue J. W., Reeder's Building

Licking County.

Stewart S. M.   *Granville.*
Austin D. H.

Scioto County.

Hall William   *Portsmouth.*
Ross S. R.

Powder Manufacturers.

Cuyahoga County.

Brayton, Wolnorth & Co.   *Newburgh.*

Greene County.

Austin, King & Co.   *Xenia.*

Portage County.

Gilletts & Austin   *Ravenna.*

Printers—Book and Job.

Adams County.

Smith J. W   *West Union*
Burwell S.

Allen County.

Cunningham & Tompkins   *Lima.*

Ashtabula County.

Oliver J. L. & Co.   *Jefferson.*

Athens County.

Van Vorhes N. H. & A. J.   *Athens.*

Belmont County.

Gressinger A.   *St. Clairsville.*
Howard & Cowan

Columbiana County.

Frost John   *New Lisbon.*
Gill Wm. H.
Harthorn R. D.
Wilkinson Joseph

Cuyahoga County.

Sanford A. S., 17 Superior   *Cleveland.*
Smend & Cowles, 17, 19 Water
Ide D. M., 10 Prospect
Gray & Spear, Plaindealer Building
Harris, Fairbanks & Co., Herald Building

Franklin County.

Glover E ,   High   *Columbus.*
Osgood & Blake   "
Riley Joseph H. & Co. "
Scott & Bascom   "
Smith & Cox, Ohio Statesman Office, cor.
  Pearl and State

Geauga County.

Bruce W. W. & E.   *Chardon.*
Wright J. S.

Hamilton County.

Abbott & Bentley, 141 & 147 Main *Cin'ti.*
Clark Charles & Co., 95 Walnut
Dumas & Lawyer, Front, e. of Main
Farran & Robinson, 88 Main
Gazette Co., Main, bet. 3d and 4th
Hart I. & Co., 41 e. 2d
Lee & Potter, cor. 3d and Sycamore
Lowell Benjamin C., Court, bet. Main and
  Walnut
Longley & Brother, Walnut, bet. 4th & 5th
Martin Coll , 41 e. 2d
Marshall & Langtry, Front, e. of Main
McCammau W., jr., cor. 3d and Walnut
McCormick J. S., Fourth, bet. Main and
  Walnut
Morris & Clawson, 103 Walnut
O'Driscoll C. F., Walnut, above Fourth
Pugh Achilles, 12 Lower Market
Schmidt C. F., 21 w. Third
Starbuck Calvin, 95 Walnut
Taggart George, cor. Main and 7th
White & Dorland, cor. Walnut and 5th
Wrightson T. W., 12 w. Second

Hocking County.

Case O.   *Logan.*
Rochester J. K.

Logan County.

Hubbard & Brother   *Bellefontaine*

Lorain County.

Fitch James M.   Oberlin.
Baker J. D.   Elyria.

Mercer County.

Blocher & Snyder   Celina.

Muskingum County.

Church E. C.   Zanesville.
Thomas D. E.

Portage County.

Harris S. D.   Ravenna.
Herrick J. B.
Hall L. M.

Starke County.

Gutshall D. & Son   Canton.
Logan & Fletcher   Massillon.

Trumbull County.

Buttles J. B.   Warren.
Dumars James   .
Howard E. D.

Tuscarawas County.

Elliott J. D.   New Philadelphia.
Patrick A. D.
McClintock & Bodenhamer   Canal Dover.
Robinson John J.

Union County.

Turner, Cassil & Pollock   Marysville.
Hamilton C. S.

Van Wert County

Perry N. L.   Delphos.

Vinton County.

Bort L. S. & L. W.   McArthur.
Hewitt & Bingham

Warren County.

Roberts J. M. & J. A.   Waynesville.

Williams County.

Bays H. B.   West Unity.
Hunter Wm. A.
Hunter John D.
Morrison T. S. C.

Wood County.

Wright A. D.   Perrysburg.
Clark S.

Printers—Steel and Copper-Plate.

Hamilton County.

Middleton E. C., Odd Fellows' Building
                               Cincinnati.
Rawdon, Wright, Hatch & Edson, corner
   Fourth and Main

Printing-Press Manufactur'rs.

Hamilton County.

Foster O. & Brother, s. w. cor. Smith and
   Seventh   Cincinnati.
Wells T., cor. Vine and Center.

Produce Dealers.

Allen County.

Turner D.   Donnell's.
Getsell M.   Herring.

Belmont County.

McCartney James   Uniontown.

Brown County.

Shaw John   Ripley.
Hemphill Samuel M.
Troutman Lewis
Hempfield S. & Co.
Jolly & Shaw
Brafford J. W.
Baker O.
Rickard William   Aberdeen.

Butler County.

Counington T.   Hamilton.
McClearey Andrew
Young Wm. P.
Deuscher H. P.   Trenton.
Carle P.
Potter Wm.
Hunt John & Co.
Feissinger L.
Beall B. O.   Seven Mile.
Watson & Pharis
Landis F. B.

Carroll County.

Hardesty Geo. & Thomas   Malvern.
Hull C. P.   Oneida Mills.

Clark County.

Baker P. E.   New Carlisle.
Cory A. H.
Cory L. C.
Cramer Joseph
Reyburn W. S.
Stafford Geo. J.
Taylor Abijah
Wilson Erastus

Clermont County.

McMurchy James   Benton.
Slade Powell
Henderson William
Whitmire A.
Rush T.   Laurel.

Columbiana County.

Jones William B.   New Chambersburg.

Cuyahoga County.

Bash J., Canal   Cleveland.
Bradburn C. & Son, 67 River
Chamberlain & Crawford, foot of Superior
Denzer & Treat, Vineyard and Champl'n
Eddy D. A. & Co., Front op. C. C. and C.
   R. R. Depot
Fitch & Brown, 38 Dock, 81 River
Gates H. N. & Co., Oviatt's Block
Handy, Warner & Co.
Hanna, Garretson & Co., Merwin & River
Hewitt & Tuttle, Merwin
Johnson Wm. S., Merwin

Mellhinch & Stillman, 32 Merwin
Cleveland.

Nims & Tillotson, 32 Merwin
Rawson L & Co., near R. R. Depot
Reilly Robert, Merwin
Scott M. B., near R. R. Depot
Burton B. & Co. *Ohio City.*
Mittleberger Edward, River
Burnham T.
Gates Haley *Gates' Mills.*
Dunlan Henry *Brecksville.*
Cooly O. *Warrensville.*
Glenson L.
Judd O. B.
Welton F.

Fairfield County.

Gill John *Millersport.*
Gill N.
Turner H.
Pearse J.
Ketner J.
Olick J.
Fall J.
Cupp V.
Holmes Rezin
Haver William

Franklin County.

Buttles, Comstock & Co., head of Canal
Columbus.
Finch Wm. M., Broad
Fisher Isaac & John, High
Hale & Tinker, Broad
Main R., High
Rickly John & Co., High
Stage & Frisbie, cor. High and Friend
Van Sickle E. R., Broad and Gay
Watson James W., National Bridge
Hunter O. S. & Co.
Martin M. D. *Central College.*
Poffenberger R. J.
Comstock H. W. & C. C. *Worthington.*
Bartlitt & Fry *Canal Winchester.*
Benadum A. D. & Co.
Sharp Samuel
Tallman, Stevenson & Co.
Chaney & Son

Gallia County.

Parker & Sons *Cheshire.*

Geauga County.

Wilber William *Chardon.*

Greene County.

Austin & Smith *Xenia.*

Jefferson County.

Hull R. C. & Co. *Steubenville.*
Peters J. B.
Turnbull M.
Orr John
Frazier & Drennen
Mears Robert
Dohrman & Collier

Knox County.

Norton D. S. *Mount Vernon.*
23

Potwin Geo. B. *Mt. Vernon.*
Weaver J.
Miner M. F. *Fredericktown.*

Lake County.

Knights D. *Fairport.*
Wilcox B. O. & Brothers
Root M. L.
McCormick & Pease

Licking County.

Robinson W. A. *Utica.*
Corning S. *Newark.*
Haughey & Byers
Warren L. K. & Co.

Marion County.

Ault & Gorton *Marion.*
Brown J. D.

Miami County.

Rogers M L. *Piqua.*
Farrington & Ruple
Lawton & Barnett

Monroe County.

Okey Jeremiah *Woodsfield.*
Okey Garrison
Smith Isaac
Barnes C. J. *Malaga.*
Beardmore William
Beardmore Isaac
Weaver George

Montgomery County.

Eastbrook & Phillips, First *Dayton.*
Harkman & Brother, Jefferson
Herman Henry, Main
Karr W., First
Chambers Robert, head Basin
Harris W., head Basin
Boyer & Eby *West Baltimore.*
Ketrow Thomas *Germantown.*
Cassaday M. *Miamisburgh.*
Deckert Samuel
Huiet S.
Platt J. F.

Pickaway County.

McQueen James & Co. *Circleville.*

Portage County.

Whittlesey G. B. & Co. *Ravenna.*
Parmele L. & Co.

Richland County.

Cox J. H. & Co. *Mansfield.*
Horton Henry B.
Hedges, Welden & Co.
Robinson J. R. & Co.
Sturges, Tracey & Co.
Moody & Fitting *Belleville.*
Strong & Mickey
Squire & Porter *Richland.*

Ross County.

Madeiry & Co. *Chillicothe.*
Clifford J. D. & Co.
Clemson Wm. P. & Co.

Scioto County.

Conway B. F. & Co.   *Portsmouth.*
Davis James W. & Co.
Damarin Chas. A. M. & Co.
Gilbert M. & G.
Kennedy & Cumming
Martin W. P.
Oakes & Buskirk
Ross S. R.
Smith J. W.
Tillow John

Seneca County.

Simmons William   *Republic.*
Ogden G. M.
Baker B. F.
Harkness & McKee

Starke County.

Pool J. & Co.   *Minerva.*
Rawson L. & S.   *Massillon.*
Lind & Weirick
Sausser & Dangler
Bayliss James
Focke & Brother
Cummins & Co.
Reed T. P. & Co.
Humberger A. & Co.

Summit County.

Brown J. R.   *Hudson.*
Dorr J. C.

Tuscarawas County.

Newburgh Joseph W   *Canal Dover.*
Rupp Lenas
Burnett E.
Beeson H. V.
Welty & Hayden
Walton J. L.

Union County.

Snider P. & Co.   *Marysville.*

Washington County.

Hall, Mathews & Co.   *Marietta.*
Crawford R.
Woodbridge & Westcott
Bowen C. & Co.   *Waterford.*
Hughes George

Provision Dealers.

Cuyahoga County.

Blackmer R. H. & Co., 36 Division
                                      Cleveland.
Cushing & Mead, River and Dock
Gale & Chapin, River
Kyser James, 72 Superior
Miller J. H., 20 Ontario
Mitchell Joseph, Canal Basin
O'Neill John, 121 River, 63 Dock
Penfield A., River
Rose E. & B., 24 Ontario
Ross J. & J., 61 Dock, 119 River
Rouse B. F., 173 Superior
Sanborn C. & G. L., 7 Ontario
Sholl William H.

Stedman B. & Son, Merwin and River
                                      Cleveland.
Sullivan P. O., 94 Water

Franklin County.

Fisher Isaac & John, High   *Columbus.*
Main R., High
Turner W. L., corner Fourth and Town
Van Sickle E. R., Broad and Gay
Frazer D. & Co., Buckeye Block

Hamilton County.

Schooley & Son, 114 Court   *Cincinnati.*
Johnson J., 547 Western Row
Hopkins E., n. w. cor. Hopkins & Cutter
Marshall E. & Co., 202 w. Sixth
Stewart & Hukill, n. w. corner Sycamore
    and Front
Jacob Louis, 222 Walnut
Jacob Charles, 68 Sycamore
Florer N. M., 9 Sycamore
Bender L.   *Harrison*
Bowlby Geo. W.
Daubenheir W. E. & Co.
Hendrickson C. W.
Volk A.
Faudree & Pearson

Hardin County.

Jamison R. G.   *Kenton.*

Highland County.

Allen Richard R.   *Hillsboro'.*

Knox County.

Graff J. A.   *Mt. Vernon.*

Pickaway County.

King C. A. & J. L.   *Circleville.*

Richland County.

Hickox & Kirkwood   *Mansfield.*

Ross County.

Campbell & Wentworth   *Chillicothe.*
Schilder Michael
Cory Isaac
Frazer A. & Co.
Aiken J. & Co.

Union County.

Hawkins & Judy   *Marysville.*

Prussiate of Potash & Chemical Colors—Manufact'rs of.

Hamilton County.

Baum J. C., 53 Dunlap   *Cincinnati.*
Snedewend & Bunce, Miami Canal above
    Liberty

Pump and Block Makers.

Ashtabula County.

Bailey A.   *Jefferson.*

Brown County.

Blair Wm. & Co.   *Newhope.*

Butler County.

Vance & Curtis   *Bethany.*

Cuyahoga County.

Nott William D., 94 Dock, 151 River *Cleveland.*

Defiance County.

Townsend H. A. , *Defiance.*

Franklin County.

Bennet Joshua *Columbus.*

Greene County.

McCarty Andrew *Xenia.*

Guernsey County.

Prouty & Clegg *Cumberland.*
Jeffries D. *Winchester.*

Hamilton County.

Shaw & Welch, 167 Front *Cincinnati.*
Perrine B. T. *Harrison.*

Hardin County.

Kennett Wm. *Kenton.*

Holmes County.

Rutler John *Benton.*

Lake County.

Chase Joseph *Painesville.*

Logan County.

Broaden A. & Co. *Bellefontaine.*

Lorain County.

Smith D. *Oberlin.*

Mercer County.

Rebout — *Celina.*

Miami County.

Haines Samuel *West Milton.*
Irwin Thomas
Pickering B.

Monroe County.

Morrill Jacob T. *Sunfish.*

Montgomery County.

Lehman P., St. Clair *Dayton.*
Ehrstine John *New Lebanon.*
Snyder Adam *Miamisburgh*

Morgan County.

Sherwood R. *McConnelsville.*

Morrow County.

Perry R. S. *Pulaskiville.*

Preble County.

Mitchell Isaac *Camden.*

Seneca County.

Lebel M. *Tiffin.*
Sneath W. O.

Starke County.

Hill Jonathan *Canton.*
Miller Henry

Summit County.

Ohl Jacob *Inland.*
Smith Wm.

Warren County.

Zell George M. *Waynesville.*

Washington County.

Spaulding Isaac *Harmar.*

Wood County.

Cook Chester & Co. *Perrysburg.*

Pump (Chain) Manufacture's.

Cuyahoga County.

Wheeler J. W., Centre Block *Cleveland.*
Low J. J., 132 Superior.

Mahoning County.

Strock A. & Co. *Orange.*

Pike County.

Dewey & Leib *Cynthiana.*
Reed & McCague

Trumbull County.

Langdon Luther *Johnsonville.*
Jackson H. D.

Rake (Horse & Hand) Manufacturers.

Ashtabula County.

Allen Josiah *Plymouth.*

Cuyahoga County.

Colens & Co. *Gates' Mills.*
Blood A. *Chagrin Falls.*

Geauga County.

Sadon Patrick *Russell.*

Licking County.

Wyeth J. B. *Fredonia.*
Orcult Samuel

Lorain County.

Stedman M. W. & C. Sprague, *Huntington.*

Mercer County.

Polm Jacob *Celina.*

Morrow County.

Salsbury G. L. *Cardington.*

Seneca County.

Smith G. G. *Republic.*

Rasp & File Manufacturers.

Hamilton County.

Holmes Benj. & Co., 61 w. Twelfth . *Cincinnati.*

Morris & Reith, 185 Western Row
Timperley Henry, Seventh bet. Western Row and John

Montgomery County.

Wroe Joseph, Fifth *Dayton.*

Restaurants.

Hamilton County.

Alms Henry, 79 w. Third *Cincinnati.*
Canonge Louis, 154 Sycamore

Diserens Frederick, 29 w. Fifth *Cincinnati.*
McLean Nic, 84 Sycamore
Rutherford Thomas, Fifth bet'n Walnut
 Vine
Selves & Roth, Third bet. Main and Syc.
Shafer & Flatch, Court bet'n Main and
 · Walnut
Seitzer G., 336 Western Row
Wilmerton J., s. w. cor. Third and Vine

Riggers.

Hamilton County.

Harcourt Joseph, Landing   *Cincinnati.*
Shaw & Welch

Rolling-Mills.

Franklin County.

Hayden Peter   *Columbus.*

Lawrence County.

Colvin Wm. (Agent Ironton Rolling Mill
 Company)   *Ironton.*
Williams & Co.   *Hanging Rock.*

Mahoning County.

Wick A. B., (Agent Youngstown Iron
 Company)   *Youngstown.*

Meigs County.

Stackpole J. W., (Agent Pomeroy Rolling
 Mill Company)   *Pomeroy.*

Muskingum County.

Palmer J. E. & Co., (Agents Zanesville
 · Rolling Mill Co)   *Zanesville.*

Scioto County.

Gaylord & Co.   *Portsmouth.*
Fox Charles   *Iron Furnaces.*

Rope. Twine, and Cordage—Manufacturers of.

Cuyahoga County.

Church James, cor. Main and ·Pittsburgh
     Cleveland.
Dougherty Robert   *Ohio City.*

Delaware County.

Bills Miles   *Delaware.*
Mead S. L.   *Galena.*
Hinsdale E.   *Waldo.*

Hamilton County.

Bonte John, Main, near Front *Cincinnati.*
Bonte Peter C., 621 W. Row
Gulds Peter, 417 Elm
King Charles C., 218 Main
Links J. A. 520 Vine
Von Der Heide F. & Co., cor. Canal and
 Ann
Hoff T.   *Fulton.*

Hardin County.

Utz Samuel   *Kenton.*

Highland County.

West William   *Marshall.*

Licking County.

Adams G.   ‹   *Granville.*

Miami County.

Kelly J. & D.   *West Milton.*
Chase R. R.

Ross County.

Merritt John   *Chillicothe.*

Tuscarawas County.

Kitch & Himes   *New Philadelphia.*
Robbins & Co.

Union County.

Southwick E. R.   *Pharisburg.*

Saddle-Tree Manufacturers.

Brown County.

Conner S.   *De La Palma.*
Conner Ira

Clark County.

Boyer Samuel   *Springfield.*

Clermont County.

Eder S. W.   *Bethel.*
Hill Theodore
Tice & Still

Franklin County.

Hayden P., Broad   *Columbus.*

Guernsey County.

Ross James   *Senecaville.*

Hamilton County.

Trotman Joseph, w. Sixth op. Cutter
     Cincinnati.
Giles Charles   *Pleasant Ridge.*

Morgan County.

Fortune F. W.   *McConnelsville.*

Saddle, Harness and Trunk Makers.

Adams County.

King & Toner   *Locust Grove.*
Cook George   *Eckmansville.*
Pittinger Wm. P.
Allen W. C.   *West Union.*
Oldson J. R.
Wyckoff Minor   *Dunbarton.*

Allen County.

Baxter George M.   *Lima.*
Dalzell Wm. & Elijah
Mitchel Thornton
Townsend Ira   *Croghan.*

Ashland County.

Smith Samuel R.   *Savannah.*
Swineford John
Hazard Russell   *Ruggles.*
Fox F.   *Hayesville.*
Hull D. K.
Welty S.
Zeigler J.   *Perrysville.*
Boone William   *Mohecan.*

Ashtabula County.

Babcox O. & H.	Geneva.
Hervey J. A. & Co.	Jefferson.
Tombes H. C.	Ashtabula.
Ford George	
Woodworth W. N.	Hart's Grove.
Woodworth C.	
Hyde & Enos	Andover.
Yates Thomas	
Churchill S. R.	Lindenville.
Cummins D.	Conneaut.
Judson J.	
Atwood S. B.	

Athens County.

Andrews M. L.	Millfield.
Cremer A.	Shad
Jewett E. P. & Co.	Athens.
Baverd J. W.	
Billinghurst —	
Palmer A.	Lee.
Buckley A	Guysville.
Bennett G.	

Auglaize County.

McNulty C. J.	Kossuth.

Belmont County.

Foreman R. L.	Demos.
Timberlake T. H.	
Mills Robert	Barnesville.
Patterson Nathan	
Wilson Stephen	
Chambers J.	Bell Air.
Armor Samuel	Uniontown.
Rodgers John	
Purviance Ellis	Flushing.
Ramage John	
Elliott Joel	Loydsville.
Asken Isaac	Saint Clairsville.
Collins Ambrose	
McConnell William	
Ambrose T. S.	Morristown.
Jennings D. J.	
Morrison R.	
Dillon A.	Belmont.

Brown County.

Park Russell	Higginsport.
Snider Z. K.	Ripley.
McClardy & Son	
Smith John S.	Decatur.
Culter A. M.	
Crute J.	Russellville.
McMahan —	
Pillinger John	Sardinia.

Butler County.

Childs J. W.	Bethany.
Apgar G.	West Chester.
Harris Wm. & Antrien W.	Dartown
Bond & Sanders	Oxford.
Irwin W. N.	
Richmond M. B.	Hamilton.
Perryman J. W.	
Morganthaler O.	

Walker P. L.	Rossville.
Kenniker J.	
Meeker E.	Middletown.
Mitchell P.	
Siebert F.	
Rayndill W. V. & Son	Saint Charles.
Allbright James	Symnes Corner.
Linn Joseph	
Waelsmutch H. F.	Ross.
Taulert James	Monroe.
Crane Aaron	
Florer A. M.	College Corner.
Chatten J. E.	
Groonkert A.	
Eichlebarger Joseph	Seven Mile.
Dove H. P.	Somerville.
Miller J.	Jacksonsburg.
Ward John F.	Riley.
Addison L. C.	

Carroll County.

Hardesty H. H.	Malvern.
Maxwell Wm. J.	New Hagerstown.
Perry S. G.	New Harrisburgh.
Allender William	Norristown.
Gladden D. F.	Hickory.
Marquis Wm. C.	Carrollton.
Sterling S. & J.	

Champaign County.

Kelly Wm.	Christiansburg.
McFarland Wm. H.	Westville.
Smith George	
Colwell P. & Co.	Urbana.
Hunter J.	
Glenn W. C.	
Winslow & Whitehead	
Carter J. M.	
Loose D.	
Wilson Joseph	Caryshill.
Rinard Samuel	St. Paris.
Milligan Samuel	North Lewisburg.
Owens Samuel	

Clark County.

Moody P.	Springfield.
Raffensperger A.	
O'Neil H.	
Moody J.	
Paine & Bean	
Sprague R.	
Houston Thomas F.	South Charleston.
Gardner William	New Carlisle.

Clermont County.

Morrin Benj.	New Richmond.
Lee Wm. T.	
Sharp D. H	Williamsburg.
Baker Fergus	Felicity.
Parrish James	
Constant John P.	
Day L. R.	Bethel.
Riley W.	
Boyd Thomas	Batavia.
Harding J.	Mt. Carmel.
Edwards George	Amelia
Kirgan Daniel	

Raney T. J.   *Withamsville.* | Bell & Baker, cor. Ontario and Prospect
Sprong Cornelius | *Cleveland.*
Boys John   *Moscow.* | Christian & Marshall, 22 Ontario
Day M. & Son | Cowan Wm. & Co., 62 Superior
White & Barnhard   *Bantam.* | Goodwin Wm. T., 30 Seneca
Jenkins Joseph W. | Krehbiel D., 76 Public Square
                                             | Moreau L., 3 Ontario
Clinton County. | Whitelaw & Marshall, 36 Superior
Grant John   *New Burlington.*
Dinger J.   *Westboro'.* | ### Darke County.
Jackson J. T. | Engle J. & S.   *Ithica.*
Cornell Wm.   *Lumberton.* | Hinderlight J.
Jones F.   *Blanchester.* | Millett J. W.
Smith M.   *New Vienna.* | McKee J. G.   *Hillgrove.*
Smith J. | Hart Wm.
Huff J. | Brown Wm. B.   *New Madison.*
Way J. | Foster R. C. & H. C.
Grubb Calvin   *Sabina.* | Edwards T. M.   *Fort Jefferson.*
Finley R. P.   *Wilmington.* | Howell J. M.   *German.*
Carpenter J. | Rensnaw Samuel   *Sampson.*
Hogue & Loorish | Vinsen H.   *Republican.*
Outcalt Henry | Tomlinson John   *Greenville.*
                                             | Brown A.
Columbiana County. | Carey S. B.
Moore J. F.   *Wellsville.*
Scott & McCurdy | ### Defiance County.
Craig Robert   *New Lisbon.* | Downs A. L.   *Defiance.*
Richards Wm. M. | Kiser J.
Vaughn Harrison | Richards A.
Barr Mathew   *Salineville.* | Metz Balthazer   *Brunersburg.*
Henderson Samuel
Horner Isaac   *North Georgetown.* | ### Delaware County.
Hime John L.   *New Chambersburg.* | Pettibone Hector   *Delaware.*
Boone Isaac   *Salem.* | Latimer C. F.
Castlebury & Son | Duden Wm. H.   *Galena.*
Weaver George | Bigalow E.
                                             | Crawford —   *Waldo.*
Coshocton County. | Phillips —
Moore Jacob   *Chili.* | Morris J. H.   *Harlem.*
Moore Tobias | Williams Benj.   *Padnor.*
Beall E. T.   *Keene.* | Perry Jacob.
Buckmaster Saul
Stevenson Peter | ### Erie County.
Sprague W. W. | Schmidt G.   *Sandusky City.*
Baker S. F. & R. F.   *Coshocton.* | Partridge & Francis
                                             | McNeil A.
Crawford County. | Williams A.
                                             | Morton P.   *Berlinville.*
Heintz C.   *Leesville ⋈ Roads.* | Beckwith S. P. & J.   *Milan.*
Scott R. W. | Hoys H. E.
Dicks M. A.   *Liberty Corners.*
Good J. G.   *New Washington.* | ### Fairfield County.
Burk J. G.   *Bucyrus.* | Dellinger & Owens   *Pickerington.*
Jones Israel | Kidwell Thomas   *Pleasantville.*
Sims John | Crouch N. H.   *New Salem.*
Yost J. N. | Widner Samuel   *Bremen.*
Jordon J.   *De Kalb.* | Miller D. S.   *Rushville.*
                                             | Little J. N. & Co.   *Lancaster.*
Cuyahoga County. | Young N.
Swift John   *Euclid.* | Shoemaker J.
Ruggles H. C.   *Newburgh.* | Stallsmith W.
Carpenter T. W.   *North Royalton.* | Davis A. J.
Clark M.   *Brooklyn.* | Bergstresser H.   *Lithopolis.*
Guild J. W.   *Dover.* | Drum George
Barrows H.   *Chagrin Falls.* | Noel Jacob
Wickoff J.
Foster J. N.   *Collamer.* | ### Fayette County.
Luster George | Robinson William   *Washington.*
Lindsey Thomas   *Ohio City.* | Cherry H. P.

Campbell L.   *Washington.*
Goolsberry & Millikin
Burgess & Kennedy   *Staunton.*

Franklin County.

Ball Jacob B., 126 High   *Columbus.*
Baylie J. E., 207 High
Breece A. & Co., Town
Cook Robert T., High
Cushman & Howell, 80 High
Dennison James W., High
Kronenberger J., Friend
Reed & Ball, High
Steinmetz William, High
Trannescker & Boehm, High
McBeth Joseph, High
Evans E.   *Reynoldsburgh.*
Fritz J. M.
Howard George
Wright Joseph   *Hope.*
Sheeders J. R.   *Harrisburg.*
Bishop William   *Worthington.*
Bergstresser Daniel   *Canal Winchester.*
Hische Julius W.
Beicher Henry   *Gohanna.*
Young George

Gallia County.

Bell H. R.   *Gallipolis.*
Chopder E. K.
Hampton John   *Kyger.*
Weaver John P.

Geauga County.

Kowles Calvin   *Chardon.*
Smith Charles
Forgison H. L.   *Chester.*
Sallisbury Alex. A.
Hays C. & O.   *Auburn.*
Stone S. S.   *Huntsburgh.*
Gray A.   *Middlefield.*
Stickney S.   *Burton.*
Allen J. A.   *Claridon.*
White A. M.   *Parkman.*

Greene County.

Beale A. B.   *Xenia.*
Fifer Davis
Knox B.
Frick E. H.   *Fairfield.*
Scudder Wm. S.
Breedlove J. W.   *Spring Valley.*
Fury A. Jackson   *Yellow Springs.*
Funk Baylis   *Jamestown.*

Guernsey County.

Johnson William   *Cumberland.*
Hathaway C. & Y.
Boyd John   *Washington.*
Raseman John
Skinner A.
Beymer E.
Copeland Wm. & Samuel   *Londonderry.*
Walker M. M.
Stewart John   *Fairview.*
Griffin James
Bulger Milton

Kennon J.   *Fairview*
Shurb Jacob
Matson M. W.   *Claysville*
Matson J. L.
Bryan Geo. T.   *Cambridge.*
Oldham & Alters
Porter Albert   *Kimbolton.*
Porter E.
McDonald J. & J.   *Buffalo.*
Braniger F.   *Millersville.*
Roseman W. M.
Morrison Geo. W   *Senecaville.*
Wilson D.

Hamilton County.

Blitch —, 665 w. Front   *Cincinnati.*
Clark S. & S. S., 180 Main
Oreiser L., 611 Western Row
Fountain J. S., 242 Main
Graf J., W. Row near Liberty
Greiser John, Ham. Road near Freeman
Hubbert H., 483 Main
Kallmeyer F., 508 Main
Lamin & Brother, 283 Main
Levoy Michael, 305 w. Sixth
Moores & Butterfield, 89 Main
Mushold J. H., 373 Vine
Muller P., 394 Vine
Miller Perry, Ham. Road near Freeman.
Park R. & W. S., 296 Main
Reid John, 318 Main
Roberts D., 216 Western Row
Slocum E. N., 102 Main
Shackelford J. O. & Co., 208 Main
Severns J., 19 Court
Stock J. M., cor. Vine and Ham. Road
Sholl G. W. & Brother, Plum bet. Everett and Mason
Sholl G. W. & Brother, n. w. cor. Walnut and Columbia
Thorten J., 70 Main
Thornhill & Carrick, Third bet. Walnut and Vine
Tennison John R., 94 Fourth
Tucker G. W., 33 Fifth
Weatherby J. S., 158 Main
Wachsmuth F., 62 Hamilton Road
Young —, 166 Main
Zeigler M., 17 Hamilton Road
Dunham J. D.   *Pendleton.*
Rogg J.   *Fulton.*
Holdzcom W.
Crain E.   *Mt. Healthy.*
Perryman J. W.   *Montgomery.*
Constable C.
White Edward   *Harrison.*
Ward John   *Mt. Washington.*
Van Dyke Wm.   *Springdale.*
Marsh Wm. S.   *Cumminsville.*
Disque George   *Newtown.*
Marshall L.   *Sharonville.*

Hancock County.

Taylor Jacob   *Mt. Blanchard.*
Galloway G. W.   *Finley.*
Mefford M. Y.
Westenhaver Peter

Hull J. B.   *Finley.*
Reed John   *McComb.*

Hardin County.

Howell & Mentzer   *Kenton.*
Dean A. & Co.
Gerloch U.
Nevil John L.   *Roundhead.*

Harrison County.

Knox William   *Cadiz.*
Crawford Joseph R.
Hays Levi   *Deersville.*
Morgan Philip   *Short Creek.*
Roberts Ross   *Germano.*

Henry County.

McWilliams C. R.   *Napoleon.*

Highland County.

Swearinger J. W.   *Highland.*
Ellis John
Murrey Samuel C.   *Greenfield.*
Leake R. S.
Douglass D. & W.
McMeekin J.   *Belfast Town.*
Eyler B. F.
Smith James   *New Market.*
Collins J.   *Sugartree Ridge.*
Gray Archibald   *New Petersburg.*
Bayham James   *Marshall.*
Smith Richard
Metzer John L.   *Greenford.*
Glasscock & Lawrence   *Hillsboro'.*
Work John C.
Stuart John C.

Hocking County.

Fenefrock Daniel   *Logan.*
Smith F. A.

Holmes County.

Demmy Martin   *Holmesville.*
Garnes Lewis
Pannel H.   *Benton.*
Gard John   *Walnut Creek.*
Kate William
Gehring John   *Winesburg.*
Blasser G.

Huron County.

Oberer Daniel   *North Fairfield.*
Watrous J. N.
Cleland & Wright   *Steuben.*
Rowley Hiram   *Clarksfield.*
Hoyt S.
Campbell —   *Greenwich.*
Barnes W. S.   *Four Corners.*
Osborne C. J. & Co.   *Norwalk.*
Viebble M.
Hough John   *Clarksfield.*
Smith H. W.   *Fitchville.*

Jackson County.

Rule & Jones   *Oakhill.*

Jefferson County.

Osborn B. F.   *Steubenville.*
Manon George

Callendine D.   *Steubenville.*
McLaughlin Wm. & Son
Gill Daniel   *Warrenton.*
Swart S.   *East Springfield.*
Crabbs George
Powell Wm.   *Annapolis.*
Elliott Geo. D.   *Mt. Pleasant.*
Bing Charles E.

Knox County.

Alling E.   *Mount Vernon.*
Hank G. W.
Lybarger E.
Mifford William
Keish Wm.   *Fredericktown*
Hazelett —
Reed T. A.
Edgar J. K.   *Democracy.*
Fishburn A. M.   *Mount Liberty.*
Daniker John   *Bladensburg.*
Denney Thomas

Lake County.

Wood H.   *Madison.*
Childs Asa   *Painesville.*
Lazelle J. A.
Wilmot A. & A. H.

Lawrence County.

Nixon Wm.   *Ironton.*
Henderson D.   *Russellsplace.*
Reckard William   *Quaker Bottom.*

Licking County.

Hartsell H.   *Etna.*
Lawson M.   *Brownsville.*
Oldham J.
Gilliland Samuel   *Jacksontown.*
Rodgers A. E.   *Granville.*
Beck John
Wilson Henry   *Newark.*
Fry Samuel
Swisher David
Owens W.
Piper J.
Marple J.   *Homer.*
Dunlap Allen
Foot & Atnell   *Croton.*
Shackett J. C.   *Perryton.*
Blizzard M. E.   *Johnstown.*
O'Conner D.
Chircliff E. L.   *Kirkersville.*
Selfridge John
Flinn T.   *Fredonia.*

Logan County.

Jump James E.   *Huntsville.*
Perrin William   *Logansville.*
Smith John
James & Loveless   *East Liberty.*
Wilkins Joseph
Cowman & Obencham   *Bellefontaine.*
Riddle & Rutan
Garwood S. C.   *Zanesfield.*
Stafford S. W.
Dodson P.   *Quincy.*
McClure J.

Lorain County.

Allen R. A. — *Huntington.*
Teachout & Robbins — *La Grange.*
Elmore Wm. & Co. — *Oberlin.*
Goodrich William — *Brownhelm.*
Dibble & Warner — *Elyria.*
Morse Waterman

Lucas County.

Limbrick Wm. — *Maumee City.*
Warren S. G. — *Whiteford.*
Clark J. W. B. — *Toledo*
Redding J.
Unthank Wm. M.
Poe T. L.

Madison County.

Lotspeich Jas. Q. — *London.*
Lehr G. W.
Winchester R. B.
Jones & Snyder — *Pleasant Valley.*
Acton Richard — *West Jefferson.*
Bliss O H. & Co.
Estep William — *California.*
Snyder John — *Mt. Sterling.*
Webster James
Cartmell William — *Midway.*
Hanson A.

Mahoning County.

Mell John H. — *Canfield.*
Weyl Wm. F. — *Petersburgh.*
Lane Caleb
Fuller D. — *Youngstown.*
Marshall John
Ryan Wm. W.
Snider Owen — *North Jackson.*
Swigart Henry — *North Lima.*
Hostettee H.
Wuster John — *New Springfield.*
Fallack H. V. — *Damascoville.*
Thomas J.

Marion County.

Williams W. — *Marion.*
Wilson & James
Beerbower E. J.

Medina County.

Rouse D. W. — *Leroy.*
Vanoradall Wm. — *River Styx.*
Grotz & Furry — *Wadsworth.*
Hulben E.
Mallory C. W. — *Lodi.*
Whitaker A. D.
Root A. R. — *Sharon Centre.*
Beeman C. — *Homerville.*
Hubard & Milestone — *Medina.*
Rettig J. A.

Meigs County.

Wallace Wm. — *Pomeroy.*
Crowfoot L. S.
Chase John

Mercer County.

Ruckman J. M. — *Fort Recovery.*

Miami County.

Mitchell John — *Piqua*
Mitchell Thos.
Mitchell D. A.
Garlick J.
Brown D. — *Troy.*
Pierson & Frealing
Ludlow D. W. — *Casstown.*
Frou & Smelser — *West Milton.*
Aldrich B.

Monroe County.

Cunningham James — *Woodsfield.*
Smith James R.
Armstrong James — *Malaga.*
Coulter Josiah — *Sunfish.*
Wade Peter
Bishop Cam
Meeks Jacob
Brown Hugh — *Stafford*
Ball Joseph

Montgomery County.

Filley Michael — *Centre*
Haas J., Second — *Dayton.*
Haas J., Third
Helfrick A , Second
Kennedy J. F., Third
Kerfoot R. A., Main
Specie A., Third
Ross Robert — *Farmersville.*
Ampt Francis — *Germantown.*
Schaeffer M. N.
Blossom M. S. — *Miamisburgh.*

Morgan County.

Bumgardner Geo. — *Rousseau.*
Searight & Bro. — *Mcigsville.*
Wells James C.
Watkins & McGowan — *McConnelsville.*
Boone John
Dye Enoch

Morrow County.

Dish Mathias — *Shauk's.*
Siminger John
Miles C. — *Cardington.*
Mulford L.
Dicks D. F. — *Vail's ⋈ Roads.*
McCleary R. — *Nimmon's ⋈ Roads.*
Smith Levi
Smith U. B. — *Chesterville.*
Miles J. G.

Muskingum County.

Walker Wm. — *Otsego.*
Webster B. J. — *Norwich.*
Pine E. L. — *Frazeysburg.*
Prior D. D.
Haver S. C. — *Putnam.*
Munch L.
Waters Sampson — *Hopewell.*
Salisbury Thos.
Beaton John — *New Concord.*
Kinkead John S.
Crabb J. — *Chandlersville.*
Hall A. K. — *Zanesville.*
Shaffer Wm.

Noble County.

Laurence & Hiddleston — *Berne.*
Shebel Mathias
Casner John C. — *Sarahsville.*
Watkins & Stotler

Ottawa County.

Graves Henry — *Marble Head.*

Paulding County.

French W. T. — *Paulding.*

Perry County.

Fowler & Trout — *New Lexington.*
McConnel & Chappellaer
McLoy James
McCloy William — *Rehoboth.*
Droegee Edward — *Somerset.*
McNutt John
Overmire Joel
Thompson George — *Chapel Hill.*

Pickaway County.

Ensworth D. — *Circleville.*
Reeder E.
Wolfley J. A. & J.
Wolfley George E.
Kershner, Morris & Co. — *Tarlton.*
Brown & Pickering — *Darbyville.*
Miller J. W.
Beckett H. W. — *Beckett's Store.*
Briggs A. — *South Bloomfield.*

Pike County.

Hagan John D. — *Piketon.*
Sissna & Hempstead
Oissna John

Portage County.

Howe E. B. — *Ravenna.*
Frazer Wm.
Newberry Fred.
Heckman F.
Mason L. — *Atwater.*
Thomas R. — *Streetsboro'.*
Marsh A.
Jewett A. V. & C. — *Aurora.*
Brainard J. C. — *Randolph.*
Foot C. B. — *Shalersville.*
Goddard V. — *Edinburgh.*
Newberry Geo. — *Franklin.*
Rice G. O.
Coon Joseph — *Suffield.*
Allen V. A. — *Mantua.*
Fairchilds J. W. — *Deerfield.*
Roise Joel
Boyd Wm. — *Nelson.*
Lewis John — *Palmyra.*
Payne S. L. — *Rootstown.*
Witter R.
Brown Wm. H. — *Brimfield.*

Preble County.

McLean John — *West Alexandria.*
Long J. W. — *Lewisburg.*
Clark Jackson — *Camden.*
Smith J. E.
Reddish Wm. A.

Martin R. & Son — *Eaton.*
Rossman Wm.
Hice John
Seibert A. A.
Jones S. P. — *Fairhaven.*
Boyse S. M.
Booker F. C. — *New Westville.*
Alcorn P. T. — *West Florence.*
McGriffe A. R. — *Hamburg.*
Graves & Jones — *New Paris.*
Fleming T.
Fleming J. C.
Howell J. W.
Harrison John — *West Elkton.*

Putnam County.

Blodget Salmon — *Buckeye.*
Skinner George — *Kalida.*
Jones John W. — *Vaughnsville.*

Richland County.

May J. — *Shelby.*
Sipe & Strock
McCurdy John — *Butler.*
Mix T.
Welty Henry — *West Windsor.*
Fleming Samuel — *Lexington.*
Guysleman David
Larimore James — *Mansfield.*
McCaslin & Crall
McKellip H.
Thayer & Patterson
Flaherty Perry — *Belleville.*
McIntire William
Walsh James
Huntsman Israel — *Woodview.*
McCully & Frank — *Lucas.*

Ross County.

Harman & Sperry — *Frankfort.*
Blocker D.
Mackey J. S.
Brown Wm. S. — *Clarksburg.*
Pearson Addison — *Chillicothe.*
Peregrine John
Bergerley Wm. H.
White John
Lewis E. T.
Kemery S. & J.
Grim J. A.
Tulleys Wm. A. — *South Salem.*
Laun John — *Gillespieville.*
Baronett J.
Bigger J. W. — *Kingston.*
Noble George.
Acton Jacob L. — *Bourneville.*
Acton Joshua

Sandusky County.

Pillow & Williams — *Woodville.*
Shruder Jacob — *Fremont.*
Raymond —

Scioto County.

Cooly J. — *Portsmouth.*
Neudorfer P.
Salsbury Wm.

Salsbury J.	*Portsmouth.*
Shiery & Barrett	
Wilhelm J. P.	

Seneca County.

Beng Henry K.	*Melmore.*
Youngpeter Michael	*Berwick.*
Geiger J.	*Bloomville.*
Tindall Elijah	*Bettsville.*
Groff H.	*Tiffin.*
Huss G. R	
Poorman, Burkholter & Co.	
Cole L. P.	*West Lodi.*
Antibus John	*Green Spring.*
Herrald William	
Plain M. W.	

Starke County.

Karn Adam	*Waynesburg.*
Wadsworth Jacob R.	
Bouden Joseph	*Minerva.*
Thomas John	
Ritersbaugh Geo.	*Louisville.*
Bridenstine & Slents	*New Franklin.*
Boze C.	*Canton.*
Buckins John	
Reed J.	
Beck Christian	*Paris.*
Heydon Francis	*New Baltimore.*
Wait Nathaniel	
Bell & Wilson	*Massillon.*
Mobley J. & S.	*Canal Fulton.*
Kidney A.	*Limaville.*
Hoiles W. P.	*Mt. Union.*
Walsh W. C.	

Summit County.

Botsford T. A.	*Middlebury.*
Case S. S.	
Heusted G. S.	*Cuyahoga Falls.*
Rockwell E. S.	
Weaver Samuel	*Clinton.*
Beckwith O.	*Akron.*
Bennett P.	
Falor J. M. & H. S.	
Allen P. L.	*Richfield.*
Ellsworth E. T. & Co.	
Miller Benjamin	*Summit.*
Richie Andrew	*Northfield.*
Coulson Orrin	*Bath.*

Trumbull County.

Griffith A.	*Mecca.*
Horton T. G.	*Johnsonville.*
Frederick Wm	*Girard.*
Scaling J. & Co.	*Orangeville.*
Fuller Davis	*Hartford.*
Fuller Alexander	
Scaling John	
Brown J. R. & C. L.	*Warren.*
Patch & Allison	
Lewis A. C.	*Farmington.*
Stow Chester	
Robins Reuben	*Brookfield.*
Simpson Lorin R.	

Tuscarawas County.

Lappin A. W.	*New Cumberland.*

Willer & Culbertson	*New Cumberland.*
Brookens Thomas	*Winfield.*
Bussell & Co.	*Bolivar.*
Frasier J. R.	*Peoli.*
George James	
Dingledine Sebastian	*Ragersville.*
Zimmerman John S.	
Albert & Maisch	*New Philadelphia.*
Blair W.	
Housten S.	
Berndt A.	*Canal Dover.*
Kreiter Jacob	

Union County.

Lee Cyprian	*Marysville.*
Malin & Smith	
Bowen Thos. E. & Co.	*Raymonds.*
Owen Waret	*Watkins.*
Moore Thomas O.	*Milford Centre.*
Case Rufus E.	*Jerome.*
Cary H. H.	*Pharisburg.*
White Benjamin	
Sovern J. Y.	

Vinton County.

McGillivray James	*McArthur.*
Dill Benjamin	*Reed's Mills.*

Van Wert County.

McConaly Grimes	*Van Wert.*
Shupe Frank	

Warren County.

Reeder A. D.	*Franklin.*
Rossman E.	
Thomas J. D.	*Springboro'.*
Clendenen Samuel	*Twenty Mile Stand.*
Jarhitt J. P.	*Mason.*
Crawford S.	
Chandler A.	*Waynesville.*
Satterthwaite George	
Jones A.	*Morrow.*
Snyder Philip S.	*Butlerville.*
Macy David	*Harveysburg.*
Macy Nathan	

Washington County.

Ebinger Jacob	*Marietta.*
Taylor W. H.	
Bosworth, Wells & Co.	
Chambers A. A.	*Harmar.*
Ramsay David	*Bartlett.*
Reed W.	*Lowell.*
Cooksey Levi	*Watertown.*

Wayne County.

Ilgenfritz & Fletcher	*Dalton.*
Bechtel O.	*Edinburgh.*
Ball D.	
Stotler P.	*Chippewa.*
Horn Henry G.	*Reedsburg.*
Young R.	*Burbank.*
Miller John	*Smithville.*
Bickel Jacob	
Bond Peter K.	*East Union.*
Sanderson Jonathan	*Shreve.*
Roch John	*Marshallville.*
Miller M.	
Shults J.	*Wooster.*

Williams County.

Bavers & Evans   *Bryan.*
Albright O.
Patterson H.
Pifer Michael   *West Unity.*
Skinner C. W.
Sawyer O.
McMonegal Wm. H.   *Montpelier.*

Wood County.

Womer Martin   *Weston.*

Wyandot County.

Boond N.   *Upper Sandusky.*
Reynolds T.
Beals Wm.
Harris T. H.   *McCutchensville.*
Hitchew A.
Ward S. M.   *Mexico.*
Seaman S. K.   *Marseilles.*
Kishler John

Safe (Fire-Proof) Manufacturers.

Hamilton County.

Hall, Dodds & Co., 49 Columbia, *Cin'ti.*
Urban Charles, Pearl, w. of Vine

Saleratus Manufacturers.

Cuyahoga County.

Stanley Wm. P. & Co., 54 and 56 St. Clair
        Cleveland.

Fulton County.

Wilden J. G.   *Elmira.*

Hancock County.

Goit E.   *Finley.*

Licking County.

Ourier Samuel   *Fredonia.*

Logan County.

Chapman A. S. & J. O. *New Richland.*
Stevenson Wm.   *Rushsylvania.*

Mercer County.

Pronty Simon   *Celina.*
Collins Moses   *Mercer.*

Union County.

Wood W. W.   *Marysville.*
Raymond N. & Co.   *Raymond's.*
Beach H. D. H.   *Jerome.*

Salt Manufacturers & Dealers.

Athens County.

Ewing, Vinton & Co.   *Chauncey.*
Fuller & Walker
Pruden Samuel B.   *Canoanville.*
Ballard John & Sons   *Athens.*

Columbiana County.

Kirk Isaac   *Salineville.*

Cuyahoga County.

Blossom U. S., (Agent,) cor. Merwin and
James   *Cleveland.*

Hamilton County.

Rogers J. H. (Agent,) 48 Walnut, *Cin'ti.*
Michael D. C. & Bros., (Agents,) 13 w.
  Front
Traber & Aubery, (Agents,)

Meigs County.

Pomeroy C. R., (Agent for Pomeroy Salt
Company,)   *Pomeroy.*

Morgan County.

Havner & Timmons   *Malta.*
Sherwood Wm.   *McConnelsville.*

Sash, Door and Blind Manufacturers.

Ashtabula County.

Powers E.   *Richmond Centre.*
Spencer Joseph   *Windsor.*
Babbet Hiram
Strong George
Wood T. J.   *Jefferson.*
Green H.
Dickinson Moses   *Ashtabula.*

Butler County.

Lighter S. K.   *Hamilton.*

Carroll County.

Hardesty Geo. & Thomas   *Malvern.*

Clark County.

Haskins —   *Springfield.*

Clinton County.

Curl Jesse   *Wilmington.*

Cuyahoga County.

Fisher A.   *Chagrin Falls.*
Abell A. S., 132 Bolivar, *Cleveland.*
Brooks S. C. & E. W. Division
Butts C. C., (Agent,) James
Ransom, Cobb & Co., Columbus
Rudd Chas., cor. Kinsman & Greenwood
Shepard D. A. & Co., 31 Water
Henry J., cor. Kinsman and Cross

Erie County.

Eastman, Oatherman & Co. *Sandusky City.*
Thorpe, Norcross & Thorpe
Stevens D.   *Milan.*

Franklin County.

Remick C. & Co.   *Columbus.*
Whitman E.
Howard H.   *Reynoldsburg.*

Geauga County.

Whitney, Spencer & Hill   *Thompson.*
Parks Nathaniel   *Chardon.*

Guernsey County.

Brown H.   *Winchester*

Hamilton County.

Chivvis D. S., 152 w. Third *Cincinnati*
Cook H. M. & Co., Fourth near Park
De Graw J., Fourth bet. Park and Smith

Hinkle & Guild, Front, op. Gas Works
Cincinnati.

Jaegers —, 505 Elm
Loring A. T., 148 w. Third
Ludlow W. H., Miller, between Main and Walnut
Smith & Williamson, cor. Third and John
Warrington Geo., Third, between Smith and Park
Ludlow G. W. *Pendleton.*
Clark A. *Fu'tin.*
Ross Wm. F. *Harrison.*

Hancock County.

Porter Jonah *McComb.*

Huron County.

Berry A. K. *Norwalk.*

Lake County.

Carter S. C. & S. *Painesville.*

Lawrence County.

Bush, Herd & Co. *Ironton.*

Licking County.

Maxfield Geo. *Etna.*
Davis Titus *Newark.*

Lorain County.

Ellis S. B. *Oberlin.*

Mahoning County.

Routsawn David *Berlin Centre.*

Medina County.

Mack G. A. *Leroy.*

Meigs County.

Townsend C. H. *Downington.*
Townsnell L. S.

Montgomery County.

Rossel J. J., First *Dayton.*
Sheafer R. "
Boyer William *Germantown.*

Morgan County.

Young John L. *Pennsville.*

Portage County.

Bushnell C. & Co. *Franklin.*
McElwaine & Turnham *Ravenna.*

Richland County.

Emminger & Sherman *Mansfield.*

Ross County.

Haskins & Co. *Chillicothe.*

Starke County.

Jarvis Edwin *Massillon.*

Summit County.

Wilcox D. G. *Middlebury.*

Trumbull County.

Spear E. & Son *Warren.*

Saw Manufacturers.

Hamilton County.

Lee & Leavitt, 53 w. Water *Cincinnati*
Siewers C., 5th, bet. Broadway and Canal
Turner & Sons, 7th, bet. John & W. Row
Kimball Isaac, Race, near the Canal
Stringer & King, 3d, bet. Smith & Park.

Saw-Mills.

Adams County.

Bradford & Co. *Manchester.*
McMillan J. B. *Gustine.*
Holmes John *West Union.*

Allen County.

Jones E. B. *Deep Cut.*
McManus D.
Griffith & Scott *West Newton.*
Crall D. *Westminster.*
Goble Doub *Croghan.*
Stump John
Shoemaker John, junr.

Ashland County.

McClain Jacob *Savannah.*
Arthur H. *Ashland.*
McMahan R. & Co. *Jeromeville.*

Ashtabula County.

Herrick Wm. W. *Richmond Centre.*
Sheldon S. C.
Spaulding K. C. & Co.
Brown O. W. *New Lyme.*
Miller J. C.
Howard A. W. *Eagleville.*
Ring E. *Lenox.*
Palmer Wm. D. *Austinsburg.*
Watrous A.
Pierce F. B.
Kingsbury & Gillett *East Plymouth.*
Brown John *Trumbull.*
Sanders John
Foot L. B.
Grant O.
Johnson Hiram
Nelson Wm.
Wright Sylvester
Onvil H. D.
Brazie Nathan *Ashtabula.*
Kingsbury N. K.
Bill E. C. *Hart's Grove.*
Hyde & Loomis
Alderman S. P.
Haskins E. & Son
Johnson E. & Son
Atkins Levi *Cork.*
Hartwell J. W.
Blanchard R. H.
Pool John
Ransom John *Harpersfield.*

Athens County.

Barret Wm. *Canaanville.*
Pruden Samuel B.
Burche Wm.
Kinkead Wm.

Kelley E.   *Shad.*
Stone David
Barnhill —
Stacy & Wilkins   *Hulls.*

Anglaize County.

Huive, Clemens & Co.   *Minster.*
Deniston L. H. & W.   *Kossuth.*

Belmont County.

Branson Joel   *Flushing.*
Clements James
Cordner John, sen.
Holloway D.
Hollingsworth John
Wright John
Mack Henry   *Saint Clairsville.*
McMillen Ira
Dillon William   *Belmont.*
Duncan John B.
McNichols & Curtis
Lamp George
Simpson John T.

Brown County.

Keethler Daniel   *Puebla.*
Laskin Henry   *Maple.*
Kellem & Norris   *Feesburg.*
Weaver & Co.   *Five Mile.*
Webber & Marhoffer   *Union Plane.*

Butler County.

Stephenson W. F.   *Contreras.*
Miller, Campbell & Co.   *Hamilton.*
Barnett J. & O. B.
Wilson & Andrew   *Rossville.*
Barnett J. C. & B.   *Middletown.*
Graham James   *Symmes Corner.*
McKinney J.   *Trenton.*
Spencer O.   *Jacksonburg.*
Sayres A. & Son   *Riley.*
Stevens Wm.
Hand John R.   *Contreras.*
Bake P. H.

Champaign County.

Hunter Lewis   *Urbana.*
James John J.
Smith J. & S.   *Woodstock.*
Buncutter & Baily   *Mutual.*
Snap J. & Co.   *St. Paris.*
Williams Geo.
Andus Wm.   *North Lewisburg.*
Beltz Andrew

Clark County.

Strouss John   *Springfield.*
Leffel James
Warder & Brokaw
Applegate D.   *Catawba.*
Chance Job
Dawson G.
Woodward Wm.
Black James   *New Carlisle.*
Brubaker J. & H.
Cable Samuel
Keplinger Isaac
Lowman George

Pence Michael   *New Carlisle.*
Pumphrey Joseph
Smith D. J.
Sprendell Samuel
Stafford William
Staley Elias
Voorhis Daniel P.

Clermont County.

Goodwin & Gibson   *Bethel.*
Kugler John   *Milford.*
Moore Wm. & Co.   *Moscow.*
Prescott G.   *Rural.*

Clinton County.

Hanes G.   *Westboro'.*

Columbiana County.

Dellenbaugh John   *North Georgetown.*
Fox Jacob
Sisson William
Farmer & Kirk   *Salineville.*
Milbourne Jacob & Co. *New Chambersburg.*
Miller, Ball & Graham   *Green Hill.*
Eaton Samuel   *Saint Clair.*

Coshocton County.

Henderson William H.   *Walhonding.*

Crawford County.

Wooster & Longwell   *Poplar.*
Wooster, Longwell & Reynolds
Keller & Guiss   *New Washington.*
Hounstine Peter   *Lykens.*
Dickson George   *De Kalb.*

Cuyahoga County.

Lawrence Sydney   *Coe Ridge.*
Rice F. J.
Cook Hiram & Co.   *Ohio City.*

Darke County.

Jenkens S.   *New Madison.*
Roberts F.

Delaware County.

Hull Nathaniel   *Waldo.*
Idleman J. J.
Gooding Geo. & Son   *Williamsville.*
Oellar Joseph   *Unison.*

Fairfield County.

Hamlin & Hedge   *Clear Creek.*
Stukey Solomon   *Sugar Grove.*
Ruble G.
Fatick J.
Stiveson J.
Fink H.

Franklin County.

Lee Theron   *Central College.*
Young John S.   *Hibernia.*
Fisher John   *Canal Winchester.*
Louka Samuel
Rager John
Powell Samuel   *Gahanna.*
Hay G. W.

Fulton County.

Johnston Geo. W. *Elmira.*
Wildin J. G. & Lipe

Gallia County.

Rose N. D. *Pine Grove.*
Blazer Joseph *Raccoon Island.*
Chambers, Clark & Co.
Payue R. *Gallipolis.*

Greene County.

Reed Young *Xenia.*
Wolf Simon *Byron.*
Brewer P. J. *Yellow Springs.*
Lannon John

Guernsey County.

Brown, Frame & McCleary *Kimbolton.*

Hamilton County.

Ashcraft Richard, 229 e. Front *Cincinnati.*
.Baily, Langstaff & Co., Front, bet. Mill and Wood
Bateman & Co., cor. Laurel and W. Row
Conn & Bro., e. Front, near Water Works
Cook H. M., Fourth, bet. Park and Smith
Cline John, 161 e. Front
Fay Anthony, 344 Broadway
Johnston, Morton & Co., Front, bet. Parsons and Whitaker
Lape & Gilpin, Canal, bet. Elm & Plum.
Stewart, Deming & Co., Third, bet. Smith and Park
Underwood & Co., Fifth, bet. Broadway and Pike
Creighton Robert *Columbia.*
Trimmer A. *Pendleton.*
Glenn M. & L. *Fulton.*
Morten J. A. G.
Walden & Vance
Welch C.
Hill & Rogers *Mt. Healthy.*
Moore R. W.
Prudden J. K. *Harrison.*
Sefton Harrison
Armstrong M. D. *Plainville.*
Armstrong Nath.
Armstrong Thomas *Newtown.*
Meeker & Myers *Sharonville.*
Burns T. *Dunlap.*
Hughes J.
Scott M.
Arnold & Witherby *College Hill.*
Fithian Joseph *Cheviot.*

Hancock County.

Lewis John & Co. *Van Buren.*
Funk Martin *Arlington.*
Lee H. K. *McComb.*

Hardin County.

White & Nagle *Roundhead.*

Henry County.

Warsner & Parry *Florida.*
Halter Wm. *Napoleon.*
Durbin James *Texas.*

Highland County.

Gray, Wear & Wilson *Greenfield.*
Brackman E. *Dodsonville.*

Huron County.

Tucker U. *Clarksfield.*
Wood W. H.
Hays John
Stiles Benj.

Knox County.

Snyder Henry *Ankenytown.*

Lake County.

Irvin James *Kirtland.*
Pitchers G. S.
Coe J. R.
Williams A.
Turney A. B. *Perry.*
Wires Samuel
Stickney J. *Concord.*
Williams H.
Howe & Curtis
Woodruff D.
Levins W.
Rust T. H.
Brown James.

Licking County.

Rankin & Brown *Brownsville.*
Buskirk Wm. *Newark.*
Wells & Stone *Kirkersville.*
Stone James

Logan County.

Harrod John & Samuel *Huntsville.*
Reed Robt. S.
Shields James D.
Woodward Jonathan
Pollock M. W. *Bellefontaine.*
McKee J. W. *Quincy.*
Patton F.

Lorain County.

Hubbard H. *La Grange.*
Reed S., jun. *Copopa.*
Curtis Wm. L. *Sheffield.*
Day William
Ely Heman
Bacon & Hawley *Brownhelm.*
Cooper George
Mors Seth G.
Miles —

Lucas County.

Shaffer M. *Emery.*
Lathrop L. B. *Riga.*
Wolfinger & Dilgert
Dewey W. F. & Son *Whiteford.*
Jessup Abram
Pomroy & Delevan

Mahoning County.

Cooper & Co. *Coitsville.*

Marion County.

Kinnear, Dickerson & Walters *Marion*

Medina County.

Newton J. R. & E. W.	*Leroy.*
Austin H D.	
Branch & Burt	*Mallet Creek.*
Wooley Isaac	*Sharon Centre.*
Arnold T. O.	*Liverpool.*
Nice A.	*Wadsworth.*
Nash Henry	
Totter John	
Bergy A.	
Brouse William	
Wooley Samuel	*Hinckley.*
Stiles J.	*Weymouth.*
Heacox Wm.	
Dean T.	
Bradford & Cook	

Meigs County.

Hayman J. & Sons	*Apple Grove.*
Jones J. W.	*Salisbury.*
Thompson & Brothers	
Nye N. R.	*Pomeroy.*

Mercer County.

Baker, Hale & Brandon	*Celina.*
Kennedy & LeBlond	
Johnson & Co.	*Montezuma.*
Rantz & Hedricks	*Recovery.*
Rhodes & Gibson	
Laughridge Joseph	*Macedon.*
Buxton G.	*Coldwater.*
Timmonds & Linzee	*Neptune.*
Crow G.	
Hamilton J.	*Mendon.*
Eicher Alex.	*Shanesville.*
Rhodes John	

Miami County.

Shattuck B. F. & Co.	*Fletcher.*
Rite J. W. & B.	*Piqua.*
Bonman & Hillyar	
Young & Yager	
Manning A.	
Mayo Henry	*Troy.*
Kelly Samuel	*West Milton.*
Boggs John	
Tavortle S. D.	*Hyattsville.*
Johns James	

Monroe County.

McConnell Wm. J.	*Laing's.*
Pollock, Suter & Anshutz	*Sunfish*
Williams J. & Brothers	*Barcsville.*

Montgomery County.

Petticrene J. D. C. & Co.	*Vandalia.*
Reichart & Williams	*Centre.*
Longstreet W. &. B. D. & Co., Upper Hydraulic	*Dayton.*
McSherry & Sites	*Farmersvil'e.*
Read & Lasure	*West Baltimore.*

Morgan County.

Taggart A.	*Stockport.*
Beswick S. & W.	
Bingman J.	

Morrow County.

Smithson & Brocklesby	*Underwood's.*
Doty J. & S. & P.	*Merengo.*
Goodman John C. & Co.	*Cardington.*
Allman Silas	*Lincoln.*
Hoffmire S. & L.	

Noble County.

Stoneburner Ren.	*Kennonsburg.*

Ottawa County.

Scott Jacob	*Port Clinton.*
Reynolds & Wright	

Pickaway County.

Hawke & King	*Tarlton.*

Pike County.

Rhea David	*Beaver.*
Slavens Charles	*Pikeston.*
Blosser Joseph	
Sharp David	
Smith Clifford	

Preble County.

Stubbs J. & J. H.	*West Elkton.*

Putnam County.

Kemson W. T.	*Pendleton.*
Krohn S.	

Richland County.

Boyd & Co.	*Mansfield.*
Squire J. D.	*Richland*

Sandusky County.

Farmers' Union Milling Co.	*Rollersville.*
Garns Jacob	

Scioto County.

Boynton, White & Co.	*Haverhill.*
Willcox W. D.	*Sciotoville.*

Seneca County.

Foster Charles	*Adrian.*
Shuler Jacob	*Berwick.*

Starke County.

Groff D.	*Navarre.*
Walton Eli	*New Franklin.*
Coulter Robert	*East Greenville.*
Johnson Josiah	
Mohler & Co.	*New Berlin.*
Doering John C. (Agent)	*Marlboro'.*
Smith & Shollenberger	*New Baltimore.*
Sluyghter Henry	*Louisville.*
Mountz & Dilworth	*Mt. Union.*

Summit County.

Pierson J.	*Montrose.*
Woodard & McDonald	*Eden.*
Wells W.	*Tallmadge.*

Trumbull County.

Burnett S.	*Warren.*
Kinsman & Reeves	
Taylor & Hutchins	
Van Gorder J. L.	
Vaughn & Adams	

White U. B.   *Warren.*
Fell John   *Orangeville.*
Moffit A.
McCartney Andrew   *Girard.*
Reynolds S.   *Farmington.*

Tuscarawas County.

Otis Merrill   *Winfield.*
Peter & Demuth   *Gnadenhutten.*
Hensell J. & Co.   *New Philadelphia.*
Talbot J.
Merriman & Waters.
Wills V.
Kitch J.

Union County.

Cartedaffner J. W.   *Watkins.*
Felkner J. L.
Elwell T. H. & Co.   *Milford Centre.*
Finley James
Scott William

Van Wert County.

Gleason Joseph   *Van Wert.*
Zigler J. & W.

Warren County.

Seigler H.   *Hayesville.*
Spitler Wm.
Galloway J.
Hall J.
Scott J.
Smith D.
McQuiller J.

Washington County.

Boyle Frederick   *Lower Salem.*
Allen A.
Alden & Mathews
Gray Wm. J   *Fearing.*
Launder Henry
Legett & Co.   *Beverly.*
Hildebrand David   *Fillmore.*
Huston S.
Johnson Wm.
Ross James   *Watertown.*
Cook Silas

Wayne County.

Pierson & France   *Dalton.*
Gable Henry   *New Prospect.*
Keeling E. F.
Reed & Reynolds   *Burbank.*
Hurting Geo.   *Smithville.*
Brenizer D.
Burkhalter J.
Fightner S.
Holtzer D.
Kerr Wm.   *Shreve.*

Williams County.

Barber Alonzo   *Oak.*
Boyers Jacob   *Bryan.*
Langle Daniel
Dilman Jacob   *Williams Centre.*
Dusherman & Andrews   *Montpelier.*
Bechtol E.
Miller John

24

Miller Samuel   *Lockport*
Norris P. W.   *West Unity.*
Prickett Joseph

Wood County.

Parks J. J.   *Perrysburg.*
Cook C. & Son
Tift Ezekiel
Wood H. L.   *Stony Ridge.*

Wyandot County.

Carter Wm.   *McCutchenville.*
Galbreth Wm. & John
Downey John

Scale Manufacturers.

Athens County.

Tickley Wm. R.   *Lee.*
Kennedy B. B.

Hamilton County.

Fowler & Ludlow, 10 and 54 w. Second   *Cincinnati.*
Martin & Orr, 40 Columbia
Blundell Joseph M., 6 and 8 Columbia
Colville A. B., n. side Columbia, between
  Sycamore and Broadway
Kempf F., 272 Walnut
Bauman John, 3d, bet. Syc. & Broadway
Huddart Wm., Main, near River

Screw Manufacturers.

Crawford County.

Ludwig Samuel   *Bucyrus.*
Stull John

Scythe Snathe Manufacturers.

Cuyahoga County.

Clark & Brown   *Berea.*

Seal Engravers.

Hamilton County.

Hall C. F., 14 w. Fourth   *Cincinnati.*
Shipley H. H. & Bro., 22 w. Fourth

Seal-Press (Percussion) Manufacturers.

Hamilton County.

Evens Platt, jr., 178 Walnut   *Cincinnati.*

Silesian ware & Candle-Mould Manufacturer.

Hamilton County.

Homan H., 211 w. Fifth   *Cincinnati.*

Shingle Manufacturers.

Ashtabula County.

Fowler Erastus   *Lenox.*
Watrous A.   *Austinburg.*
Bailey A.   *Jefferson.*
Rich Geo. W.
Hunt H.
Adkins M. P.   *Hart's Grove.*

Butler County.
Reed Samuel   *Hamilton.*

Darke County.
Fowler A. & H. B.   *Hillgrove.*

Delaware County.
Martin G. W.   *Waldo.*
Potterfield —

Champaign County.
Wollason Philip   *Christiansburg.*

Cuyahoga County.
Richmond Edmund   *Solon.*
Staunard Walter D.

Huron County.
Odle S. J.   *East Townsend.*
Horner T. R.
Owens O.

Lorain County.
Kennedy R.   *Copopa.*

Morrow County.
Nutt & Conklin   *Cardington.*
Hoffmire L. & S.   *Lincoln.*

Starke County.
Hendershot Samuel   *Limaville.*

Ship Builders.
Ashtabula County.
Thayer G.   *Ashtabula.*
Lockwood E.
Savage —

Columbiana County.
Todd Samuel   *Wellsville.*
Rawson Robert
Rawson Davis

Cuyahoga County.
Treat William   *Euclid.*
Calkus & Sales   *Ohio City.*
Stephens & Presley
Johann & Tisdell

Erie County.
Ritchum F. D.   *Huron.*
Cherry W. H.
Reating J. M.
Bates E.   *Milan.*
Ruggles S.
Shoup J.

Washington County.
Knox Wm.   *Harmar.*

Ship Carpenters and Joiners.
Belmont County.
Gooden Daniel   *Bellair.*
Morton David
Shahan John

Hamilton County.
Fillmore & Lusk, Landing,   *Cincinnati.*

Morton & Co., 61 Front   *Cincinnati.*
Johnson & Morton, 585 e. Front
Hambleton S. F.   *Fulton.*

Lorain County.
Case A. R.   *Avon Lake.*
Griswold Wm.
Shelden Norman
Shelden George
Upham E. S.

Meigs County.
Wadman Benj.   *Pomeroy*
Barclay Peter

Ship Chandlers.
Cuyahoga County.
Barron E. H., Canal Basin   *Cleveland.*
O'Neill John, 121 River, 63 Dock
Ross J. & J., 119 River, 61 Dock

Hamilton County.
Haven, Dean & Clarke, cor. Sycamore and
   Public Landing   *Cincinnati.*
Leidy, Baird & Cassilly, Front bet. Sycamore and Broadway
Isham & Fisher, 47 Front
Hagarty John, 32 Broadway
Barker, Hart & Co., 20 Broadway
Jack, Collier & Co., 46 Public Landing

Shirt & Stock Manufacturers.
Hamilton County.
Lowman J. & Bros., 108 Main, *Cincinnati*
Avis J. J., 146 Walnut
Baker & McCracken, 128 Walnut
Smith R., 58 Broadway
Reynolds Eliza, 258½ e. Main
Richardson James, 4 e. Fourth
Hathaway John A. & Co., 11 w. Sixth
Smith Isaac F., 10 e. Fifth
Martin G. J., 3 w. Fourth
Noon Mrs. E., 241 w. Fourth
Shepherd J., 100 w. Fifth
Leslie James Y., 14 w. Fifth
Boden Mrs. L. H., 242 w. Fifth
Maue F. & Co., 269 Main
Cady Mrs. M., 213 Walnut

Shoe Findings.
Cuyahoga County.
Cook W. P. & Co., Water, near Main
     Cleveland.
Bratenahl, Brothers, Vineyard Block

Franklin County.
Kimball H. H., High   *Columbus.*

Hamilton County.
Flickner J. O., 252 w. Sixth   *Cin'ti.*
Thornton R. & Co., 9 Main
Widmer O. A. & Co., 240 "
Forbies — 254 "
McCabe A. 352 "
Ehlin J. H 356 "
Fells Jacob F. 345 "

Leist John 313 " *Cincinnati.*
Lumsden T. W. 216 "
Veith Iguatz, Vine above 12th
Beitman Charles, w. Sixth

Shoe (Ladies') Manufacturers and Dealers.

Cuyahoga County.

Tuttle E. M., Seneca *Cleveland.*

Hamilton County.

Doerer G. W., Western Row, below Sixth
Cincinnati.
James Robert, 172 w. Fifth
Scott Mrs. 70 w. "
Tresise T., 59 Everett
Webster Mrs. E. G., 102 w. Fifth
Witt George, cor. W. Row and Eighth

Shoe Peg Manufacturers.

Cuyahoga County.

Sturtevant J. T. & Co. *Chagrin Falls.*

Montgomery County.

Crawford O. H. & J., Canal *Dayton.*

Silks and Fancy Goods—Wholesale Dealers.

Hamilton County.

Buchman & Rindskopf, 70 Main *Cin'ti.*
Ogborn W. E. & Co., 35 and 37 Pearl
Brown D. & R., 253 Main
Beal John & Co., 26 Pearl
Fugli C. H., s. w. cor. 3d and Sycamore
Devou & Rockwood, 48 and 50 Pearl
McArthur P. & Co., 20 Pearl

Slaters.

Hamilton County.

Cross Henry, Fifth, between Race and
Elm *Cincinnati.*

Smut Machine Manufact'rs.

Belmont County.

Arrack & Woodmansee *St. Clairsville.*

Logan County.

Reid R. *Bellefontaine.*

Soap (Fancy) Manufacturers.

Hamilton County.

David Henry, 165 Main *Cincinnati.*
Stephens John C., 471 Broadway
Palmer Solon, 36 w. Fourth
Coolidge, Whetstone & Behr, s. w. corner
Fifth and Western Row
Hill Geo. H. & Co., 87 Main

Soap, Candle and Oil Manufacturers and Wholesale Dealers.

Butler County.

Greenham G. *Middletown.*

Cuyahoga County.

Duncan & Ross, Canal *Cleveland.*
Gaul Hugh, Cleveland Centre
Hall & Reid, cor. Canal and Harrison
Outhwait Wm., Cleveland Centre
Patton Alexander " "
Spencer T. P.
Stanley Geo. A., Canal, near Weigh Lock
Wilson, Lee & Stafford, Canal
Huber Francis T. *Ohio City.*

Erie County.

Willard E. H. & Co. *Sandusky City.*
Davis J. T.
Sanderson J.
Johns W.
Pollock J.
Robertson Wm.
Sigenger F. *Milan.*

Franklin County.

Ansell Wm., High *Columbus.*
Funston John "
Remick C. & Co. "
Aston Wm. "
Fraser D. & Co., Buckeye Block

Geauga County.

Randall Cook & Co. *Chardon.*

Hamilton County.

Barkalow Wm. T., 215 Main, *Cincinnati.*
Burkhart F. & Co., n. e. corner Sixth and
Walnut
Chappell W. P., 7 w. Front
Conklin J. L., 109 e. Fifth
Cheever H. G. & Co., Lock, bet. 3d & 4th
Combs A. H., cor. Ninth and Elm
Dean Samuel B., 24 Water
Dole J., cor. Everett and Plum
Donald M. T., Poplar bet. John and Linn
Emery Thomas, 33 Water
Gross & Dietrich, 5 w. Front
Glenn & Co., Water bet. Walnut and Vine
Hill George H. & Co., 87 Main
Nye Joseph T. & Co., 219 Sycamore
Proctor & Gamble, 252 Main
Stephens J. C., 471 Broadway
Tobin W. T. & Co., John bet. Catharine
and Richmond
Wiedemer F. X. & Co., 17 Front
Werk M. & Co., 11 Main
Whetstone R. A., Eighth, e. of Broadway
Purcell & Bloomer *Harrison.*

Jefferson County.

Mendell J. W. & Co. *Steubenville.*
Zellers John
Karum Philip *Annapolis.*

Knox County.

Beebee W. W. *Mount Vernon.*

Muskingum County.

Convers Theodore *Zanesville.*
Barrett J. J. & Co.

Pickaway County.

Hartmayer C. T.   *Circleville.*

Ross County.

Fraser A. & Co.   *Chillicothe.*

Starke County.

Bechell C.   *Canton.*
Winterhatter J.

Tuscarawas County.

Hammond Samuel   *Canal Dover.*

Washington County.

Shepherd & Nye   *Marietta.*

Soda & Mineral Water Manufacturers.

Hamilton County.

Rutherford T. M., Fifth, bet'n Broadway
and Pike   *Cincinnati.*
Herberding Freirz, 106 Walnut
Ritters A., 468 Vine
Nash Hiram, 16 w. Front
Manze & Gottke, Thirteenth bet. Walnut
and Vine
Sleeper Israel, Hammond bet. 3d and 4th

Spoke, Felloe, Hub and Bow Manufacturers.

Hamilton County.

Royer, Simonton & Co., Third, bet. Smith
and Park   *Cincinnati.*
Curtiss & Byrne, n. w. cor. W. W. Canal
and Park
Dillingham John, e. Seventh, near Main

Stair Builders.

Hamilton County.

Smith H. P., Eighth, bet. Cutter and Linn
    Cincinnati.
Cleveland Wm. M.   *Pendleton.*

Seneca County.

Sweatland Joel   *Republic.*

Stamp Cutters, Brands and Branding Plates.

Hamilton County.

Bisbee J., 112 w. Fifth,   *Cincinnati.*

Starch Manufacturers.

Hamilton County.

Proctor Thos. H. & Co., 252 Main   *Cin'ti.*
Everding & Erkenbrecher, Lock, bet. Fifth
and Sixth
Gregory & Turner, 56 w. Third
Fox T. & G., Main, b. Hamburg and Vine
Fox Geo., 18 Findley
Fox F. & G., Hamilton Road, bet. Elm and
Plum

Muskingum County.

Convers Theodore   *Zanesville.*

Stave Manufacturers.

Geauga County.

Smith & Bestwick   *Thompson.*

Knox County.

Harbin E.   *Fredericktown.*

Lucas County.

Johnson & Co.   *Whiteford.*

Mahoning County.

Cooper & Co.   *Coitsville.*

Mercer County.

Frederich Daniel   *Celina*

Ross County.

Jones D. K.   *Chillicothe.*

Steel Manufacturers.

Cuyahoga County.

Cuyahoga Steam Furnace Co.   *Ohio City.*

Erie County.

Steiltz Isaac   *Sandusky City.*

Steel Pen Manufacturers.

Hamilton County.

Lyon & Patterson, 46 Sixth,   *Cincinnati.*

Stencil Cutters.

Hamilton County.

Allen V. R., 141 Walnut,   *Cincinnati*
Power J. S., 9 Canal
Besher J., 112 w. Fifth.

Logan County.

Foster S. B.   *Huntsville.*

Stereotype Founderies.

Hamilton County.

Hart I. & Co., 41 e. Second,   *Cincinnati.*
Morgan C. A. & Co., Hammond b. Third
and Fourth
O'Driscoll C. F., 169 Walnut

Summit County.

Shain Wm. H.   *Hudson.*

Stock and Dye Maker.

Hamilton County.

Thiesing F., 234 Court,   *Cincinnati.*

Stone Cutters.

Ashtabula County.

Harper O. S.   *Hart's Grove.*

Darke County.

Fletcher Charles   *Greenville.*

Delaware County.

Butler J. N.   *Galena.*
Mead Eli
Bancroft Benj.

Columbiana County.

Gardner Lewis   *East Rochester.*

Crawford County.

Green R. S. & Co. — *Bucyrus.*
Lantzenheiser D.

Cuyahoga County.

Ormeston A., jr. — *East Cleveland.*
Plaisted J.
Sherman J.
Brown L. — *Berea.*
Boulton W.
Housman L.
Williams H., Boliver — *Cleveland.*
Williams J.
Murley & Betworth — *Ohio City.*

Fairfield County.

Junkerth J. — *Lithopolis.*

Gallia County.

Campbell R. F. — *Patriot.*

Geauga County.

Rodgers A. L. — *Chardon.*

Hamilton County.

Ahrens J. G., 443 Broadway — *Cincinnati.*
Humble & Co., 290 "
Lawrence J. H., 68 Vine
Guio E. B., Court, near W. Row
Goodall Wm., 236 Court
Dobbeling J. F., 121 w. Court
Graveson —, cor. Linn and Richmond
Thurber S. N., 500 Plum
Elble & McLaghlan, 538 "
Ritter & Hummel, cor. Adams and Miami Canal
De Camp Henry, Freeman, between Front and Sixth

Harrison County.

Quizley A. J. — *Cadiz.*
McPherson — — *Moorefield.*

Lake County.

Stewart G. — *Painesville.*

Logan County.

Coulter David W. — *Huntsville.*

Medina County.

Lemon H. — *Medina.*

Meigs County.

Winget M. — *Downington.*

Monroe County.

Pope Alexander — *Woodsfield.*
Heuthorn Adam R. — *Barnesville.*

Morrow County.

Morton E. M. — *Nimmon's ⅘ Roads.*

Pickaway County.

Landon John — *Circleville.*

Pike County.

Kent & Bennett — *Waverly.*
Bennett Wm. A.
Richie & McCollister

Preble County.

Hathaway E. B. — *Eaton.*
Evading John D.

Ross County.

Gimes J. & Son — *Chillicothe.*
Walter John
Nealey N.
Meach George

Seneca County.

Watt L. W. — *Tiffin.*

Summit County.

Boardman J. C. — *Middlebury.*
Rhoads Abram

Trumbull County.

Gager L. F. — *Warren.*
Howard Charles
Davis Martin — *Ohletown.*
Patterson A. J.

Tuscarawas County.

Kesserman J. — *New Philadelphia.*
Rainsberger G.

Van Wert County.

Engleright Samuel — *Van Wert.*

Vinton County.

Arthur E. — *McArthur.*
Ward B.
Lord John
Robbins James

Washington County.

Wires John — *Centre Belpre.*
Schoonover James
Nelson R.

Stone Pump Manufacturers.

Summit County.

Merrills E. H. & C. J. — *Middlebury.*

Trumbull County.

Callender J. G. — *Newton Falls.*
Loveless Samuel

Stoneware Manufacturers.

Licking County.

Westbrook John — *Brownsville.*

Muskingum County.

Wiles L. & P. — *Putnam.*
Wilbur Thos. & Sons
Richards Lewis — *Hopewell.*
Balson Wm. & Co.
Ensminger A. — *White Cottage.*
Rambo Joseph
Russell G.
Dietrick B. — *Stovertown.*
Dietrick David
Westbrook Peter S. — *Gratiot.*
Harris Wm.

Summit County.

De Haven Abram — *Middlebury.*

Merrill E. H. & O. J.   *Middlebury.*
Rowley Enoch
Atcheson R. L.   *North Springfield.*
Smith P. H.

Stone Water-Pipe Manufacturers.

Summit County.

Hill, Merrills & Co.   *Middlebury.*

Stores (Boat).

Hamilton County.

Barker, Hart & Co., 20 Broadway, *Cin'ti.*
Hagerty John, 32 Broadway
Haven, Dean & Clark, cor. Sycamore and
  Public Landing
Jack, Collier & Co., 46 Public Landing
Isham & Fisher, 47 Front

Stove, Grate and Tinware Dealers.

Ashtabula County.

Crosby J. B.   *Ashtabula.*
Roe Henry A.   *Andover.*

Brown County.

Culter, Evans & Co.   *Ripley.*
Debolt J.
Denis A. P
Blair E. F.   *Georgetown.*
Porter J. H.
Blair & Porter
Shreeve O.   *Russellville.*

Butler County.

Owens, Ebert & Dyer   *Hamilton.*
Enyart T. K.
Webster Wm.   *Middletown.*

Carroll County.

Atkinson Thomas H.   *Carrollton.*

Champaign County.

Helmick & Brother   *Urbana.*
Cavileer & Evans
French S. & Co.
Colwell & Berry

Clark County.

Leffel James   *Springfield.*
Moore William

Columbiana County.

Lider & Morrison   *Wellsville.*

Crawford County.

Picking D.   *Bucyrus.*
Picking J.
Wagoner John

Cuyahoga County.

Wood J. W.   *East Cleveland.*
Bosworth & Mix   *Chagrin Falls.*
Sunderlin S.
Upham A.
Stedman L. T.   *Collamer.*

Lewis Samuel O., 5 Hewitt's Block
                 Cleveland.
Low J. J., 132 Superior,
Marvin Wm. L., 60 Superior
Merchant Silas, Meadow
Tindall & Ernest, 48 Bank
Whitaker S., 29 Superior Lane
Wood & Leland, 28 Superior
Woolson & Hitchcock
Born O., 14 Water
McMillan —, 17 Seneca
Clapt O. R., 1 Exchange Buildings
Wansor Jacob, 17 Superior
Smith, Murray & Co., 36 Bank
Metcalf Horace, 120 Superior
Parish & Knight, 25   do.
White D. P.   *Ohio City.*
Ross J.

Darke County.

Beedle J. N.   *Greenville.*
Danford Wm.

Erie County.

Higgins D.   *Huron.*
Woodworth & Gale   *Sandusky City.*
Flood J.
Bailey J. M.
Dewey W.
Choat C. B.   *Milan.*
Mann M. E.

Fairfield County.

Beery & Jenkins   *Lancaster.*
Green J. A.
McClelland J.
White A.

Franklin County.

Heyl J. K., High,   *Columbus.*
Mason H.,   do.
Rest Jacob, do.
St. Clair & Sheds, High
Armstrong & Gorton, do
Ridgway J., High
Peck Stephen L.   *Worthington.*
Overholser William   *Canal Winchester.*

Gallia County.

McIntyre Alexander   *Gallipolis.*
Mathers F. & Co.

Geauga County.

Marsh & Parks   *Chardon.*
Bruce J. F.

Greene County.

Horn D. L.   *Xenia.*
McAlpin Henry

Hardin County.

Shectala J. A.   *Kenton.*
Holmes George
Thomas A.

Highland County.

Young G. W.   *Greenfield.*
Irwin Wm. T.

Hocking County.

Armstrong Wm.   *Logan.*
Baker T. E.

Holmes County.

Donalson Wm.   *Holmesville.*
McClure Wm.   *Millersburg.*
Bray & Yates

Huron County.

Cline John   *Norwalk.*

Jefferson County.

Sharp & Craig   *Steubenville.*
Lindsey J. H.
Irwin A.

Knox County

Cooper John C. & Co.   *Mt. Vernon.*
Evans Job
Durbin Thomas
Huntaberry James & Son
Rankins D. L.   *Fredericktown.*

Lawrence County.

Campbell, Ellison & Co.   *Ironton.*
Duke & Kingsbury

Licking County.

Jones Lewis   *Granville.*
McCune & Ebersole   *Newark.*
Eddy T. R.

Logan County.

Foster & Frantz   *Huntsville.*
Porter Robert B.   *Zanesfield.*
Nelson & Robinson   *Bellefontaine.*

Lorain County.

Weed & Beckwith   *Oberlin*
Wasson James   *Elyria.*
Crane T.

Meigs County.

Root Peter   *Salisbury.*

Miami County.

Cottingham Wm.   *Troy.*
Eaton Z.
Geyer F.   *Piqua.*

Montgomery County.

Carroll D., Main   *Dayton.*
Genson, Bennet & Co., Third
Greer & Co., Third
Gebhart, Marshall & Co., Main
Lockwood N. S., First
Wiley Orrin   "

Muskingum County.

Hurst P.   *Dresden.*
Silkey J. P.
Potts & Cox   *Zanesville.*

Perry County.

Beckworth Joel K.   *Somerset.*
Maine Frederick
McMan Johnson

Pickaway County.

Bierce W. W. & Co.   *Circleville.*
Hirt L.
Richardson & Trone

Portage County.

Prentiss Cyrus   *Ravenna.*
Rawson S.
Bethel & Dodge   *Franklin.*

Preble County.

McClure Wm. H.   *Lewisburg.*
Fornshell Benj.   *Camden.*
McCabe Walter P.   *Eaton.*
Ecker George
Wilson S. P.

Richland County.

Buttery J. & Co.   *Mansfield.*
Zimmerman Levi
Ebinsther John   *Lexington.*
Pennell James
Howard G. C.   *Belleville.*
Markey & Walker

Ross County.

Gill & Williams   *Chillicothe.*
McAdon J. F.

Scioto County.

Byerly & O'Neil   *Portsmouth*
Grimes James
Smith & Holmes

Seneca County.

White & Holland   *Melmore.*
Searles W. D.   *Tiffin.*
Gross John G. & Co.
Yerk C. M.
Hamilton & McArdle

Starke County.

Buchins H.   *Canton.*
Bucher J. G.
Harman D. H.
Little A.
Stinchcomb W.
Doxee J. N.   *Massillon.*
Partridge H. & R.
Buckins V. S.
Russell C. M. & Co.
Hart & Brown

Trumbull County.

Marsh J. K.   *Mesopotamia.*
Jameson & Fitch   *Warren.*
Morley T. H. & Co.
Burbank R. A.   *Newton Falls.*
Ensign & Co.

Tuscarawas County.

Shriver Peter   *Bolivar.*
Luckenbach John E.   *Canal Dover.*
Rex John
Cummins Samuel
Kunkler P. A.

Vinton County.

Baird W. H.   *McArthur.*

Warren County.

Butler & Meeker　　　　*Franklin.*
Thomas J. S.　　　　　*Waynesville.*

Washington County.

Lammott L. A.　　　　　*Marietta*
Harmar Manufacturing Co.　*Harmar.*
Wheeler W. V. Z.　　　　*Beverly.*

Wayne County.

McDonald, Laughlin & Co.　*Wooster.*
Howard Harvey
Harrison H. R.

Wood County.

Brown & Hunt　　　　　*Perrysburg.*

Stove and Grate Manufacturers and Dealers.

Butler County.

Owens, Ebert & Dyer　　*Hamilton.*

Cuyahoga County.

Merchant Silas, 168 River,　*Cleveland.*
Woolson & Hitchcock

Hamilton County.

Tunnicliffe & Co., e. Front, bet. Pike and
　Butler　　　　　　*Cincinnati.*
Lape, Hopple & Fleming, Front, between
　Broadway and Ludlow
Thomas David G., 7 e. Front
Horrock J. R., 6 Main
Burton S. H. & Co., 13 & 15 w. Columbia
Campbell, Ellison & Co., 21 Columbia
Ball G. W., 36 Main
Resor W. & R. P. & Co., 25 and 27 Main
Childs W. E., 13 and 15 Fifth
Strong & Fine, 5 Fifth
Goodhue & Co., 27 Elm
Buss & French, 28 Fifth
Haller & Young, 228 Elm
Cramer & Watson, n. e. corner Court and
　Western Row
Hollowell & Newhall, cor. Western Row
　and Clinton
Wolf G. & Co., 375 Main
Hollenshade & Mitchell, 395 Main

Lake County.

Geauga Iron Co.　　　　*Painesville.*

Medina County.

Ainsworth J. T.　　　　*Medina.*

Miami County.

Upton M. B. & Co.　　　*Piqua.*
Allen J.
Little D. L.

Montgomery County.

Lockwood N. L., First,　　*Dayton.*

Summit County.

Akron Stove Co.　　　　*Akron.*
Allen Wm. T.

Rockwell J. & Co.　　　　　*Akron.*
Tallman P. & Co.

Straw Goods, Silks, Ribbons, Millinery and Fancy Goods Importers & Wholesale Dealers.

Cuyahoga County.

Dolman Mrs. C., cor. Superior & Seneca
　　　　　　　　　　　Cleveland.
Feedman S. & Bros., 160 Superior
Marchand J., 125 Superior
Slocum L. W., 129　do.
Beebe A. M., 37 Bank
Hoffman & Kupfer, 18 Ontario
Alcot & Horton, 57 Superior
French & Co., 91　do.
Harney T., 164　do.

Hamilton County.

Haseltine S. W. & Co., 62 Pearl,　*Cin'ti.*
Saunders Elisha, 11 w. Fourth
Thayer, Aldrich & Co., 24 Pearl
Forchheimer & Gutman, 60 and 62 Main
Shumard J. & Co., 187 Main
Schlesinger B., 270 w. Fifth
Marks Henry & Co., 12 Pearl
Grogan Mrs. C., 274 w. Fifth
Devou & Rockwood, 48 & 50 Pearl

Jefferson County.

Scott G. & J.　　　　*Steubenville.*

Straw and Fodder Cutter Manufacturers.

Franklin County.

Trumbull H.　　　　*Central College.*

Straw Hat and Bonnet Manufacturers.

Hamilton County.

Haseltine S. W. & Co., 62 Pearl,　*Cin'ti.*
Webb J., jun.,168 w. Fifth
Quinn H., 198 Plum

Sugar Refinery (Steam).

Hamilton County.

McKenzie & Co., Pearl bet'n Plum and
　Western Row　　　　*Cincinnati.*

Surgical & Dental Instrument Manufacturers & Dealers.

Franklin County.

Fenton Joseph, High,　　*Columbus.*
Klott K., Town
Williams D., High
Wolf Francis, do.
Weiler D., 130 do.

Hamilton County.

Brown J. M., n. w. corner Fourth and
　Walnut,　　　　　*Cincinnati.*
Denhard John, (Agent,) Sixth, bet. Walnut and Vine

McCarthy Thomas, 163 w. Fifth,   *Cin'ti.*
Rees William Z., 71 w. Sixth
Daniels D. N., 39 w. Fourth
Wocher Max, College, bet. 6th and 7th
Rogers D.   *Mt. Healthy.*

Montgomery County.

Nafzger C., Fifth,   *Dayton.*

Starke County.

Gammie F.   *Louisville.*
Vernier Lewis

Surgical Splint Manufact'rs.

Franklin County.

Morse Wm. & M. P.   *Worthington.*

Tailors and Drapers.

Adams County.

Flanagan Kaleb   *Manchester.*
Doddridge R. R.   *Stout's.*
Patterson James   *Scott.*
West Wm.
Baker James S.   *Locust Grove.*
Austin Silas P.   *Eckmansville.*
Whipp G. W.   *West Union.*
Moore J.
Coleman S. B.
Gray R.   *Dunbarton.*

Allen County.

Panabaker A. V.   *Westminster.*
Willow W. S.
McDermot Wm. F.   *Croghan.*

Ashland County.

Graver S.   *Rousburg.*
Hettinger J. K.
Henry John H   *Savannah.*
Willtrout Frederick
Leitensnider John
Burgan L.   *Ashland.*
Jones & Brown
Risser Christian
Risser John
Bowers Henry   *Jeromeville.*
Wilson John
Carson J. N.   *Perryoville.*
Weaver J. W.
May Jacob   *Mohecan.*
Moore William

Ashtabula County.

Walding J. S.   *Geneva.*
Hartson A.   *Jefferson.*
Anderson G. C.
Howell E.   *Ashtabula.*
Gifford John
Kincade J. H.   *West Williamsfield.*
Moon J. M.   *South Ridge*
Armstrong J.   *Andover.*
Hanson Philip   *Lindenville.*

Athens County.

Freeman H.   *Chauncey.*
Struter Wm. R.   *Amesville.*
Allison Samuel   *Lowry.*

Winget Isaac   *Pleasanton.*
Frost J. C.   *Athens.*
Davis John
Bellows C. V.   *Lee.*
Terry Wm.   *Guysville.*
Nichols James
Tucker Columbus B.
Pratt H.   *Hebardville.*

Auglaize County.

Baumel C.   *Wapakoneta.*
Martin F.
Eiting John   *Minster.*
Kooper B. A.
Tangemann Henry
Vanderbroek Albert
Vitey —   *New Bremen.*

Belmont County.

McMasters Henry   *Hendrysburgh.*
Reynolds Oliver
Sipe Benjamin
Matson A.   *Demos.*
Jackson E.
King John W.   *Bellair.*
McKown James   *Uniontown.*
Sipe James
Hutchison James P.   *Loydsville.*
Nichols Alfred
Anderson George   *St. Clairsville.*
Frint John L.
Myer Henry
Thomas B.
McMillen Alexander
Davies David M.
Maffit J. S.   *Morristown.*
Sipe J.
McLaughlin Edw'd   *Shepherdstown.*
Reynolds C.   *Sewel sville.*
Ruly H.
Mercer William   *Be'mont.*
Nichols J.
Baty M.
Gregg L.
Russell Reuben   *Hunter.*

Brown County.

Hon Wm.   *Higginsport.*
Menor G.   *Ripley.*
Vansant John   *Dicatur.*
Morgan J. T. & Son   *Georgetown.*
Boyd S. G.
Wilkins S.   *Russellville.*
Crute T. J.

Butler County.

Rolff Nelson   *West Chester.*
Whitlock Derrick
Shears James   *Dartown.*
Hemann E.   *Rossville.*
Presler M.   *Middletown.*
Mitchell J. H.
Wilson H. B.   *Ross.*
Turner Wm.
Creborne P.   *Monroe.*
Roth Adam
Miller Jacob   *Hamilton.*
Brown & Myers

Schober J   *Hamilton.*
Bruck J. P.
McAdams —
Falconer J. H.   *Rossville.*
Becker & Henn
Hunter R.   *College Corner.*
Mee A.
Weider R. M.   *Seven Mile.*
Reed John F.
Grisson J.   *Somerville.*
Fisher E. B.   *Trenton.*
Eckert Jacob
Lissinger Lewis
Dill Andrew
Hoch John
Keepers Wm. H.   *Jacksonsburg.*
Spittle Isaac
Thomas R. E.   *Alert.*
Hazee J. W.   *Reily.*

Carroll County.

Howey E.   *Harlem Springs.*
Thompson T.   *Carrollton.*
Philpot Charles   *Kilgore.*

Champaign County.

Marshal L. A.   *Christiansburg.*
Quick & Berchshire
Evans A   *Urbana.*
Small E. L.
Silvers Richard   *Careyshill.*
Anspaugh Jonathan   *St. Paris.*

Clark County.

Baker Miller   *Enon.*
Robinson John Q. A.
Wallace John
Bruner D.   *Springfield.*
Longnecker J.
Davidson W. H.
Shattler F.
Golden Benjamin   *Catawba.*
Skillman D. C.
Bussard J. & W.   *South Charleston.*
Dooley Greenfield
Sweet Griffith F.
Harr Abraham   *New Carlisle.*
Morehead T. T.
Tilton —

Clermont County.

Layfield & Co.   *New Richmond.*
Powers Samuel
Maise John   *Nicholsville.*
Griffith W. L.   *Bethel.*
Irwin John M.   *Withamsville.*
Test Benj. F.
Krantz S.   *Mt. Carmel.*
McFarland Edward   *Neville.*
Hopkins Joshua H.   *Amelia.*
McLaughlin Samuel
Banister D. A.   *Chilo.*
Shelley A. J.   *Moscow.*
McLaughlin Robert   *Mount Pisgah.*
Carnes Samuel   *Loveland.*
Whitmore S. H.   *Perin's Mills.*

Rice Winslow B.   *West Woodville.*
Brainum J. S.   *Laurel.*

Clinton County.

McIlvain Robert   *New Burlington.*
Curvalt A. R.   *Westboro'.*
McCammon   *New Vienna.*
Howe Abraham   *Sabina.*
Shepherd M. W.   *Martinsville.*
Thompson D. A.
Strattan Charles
Collins Wm. W.   *Wilmington.*
Reed J.
Hammon Wm. H.

Columbiana County.

Blecher & Co.   *Wellsville*
Evans B.
Evans & Co.
Lloyd T.
Williams R.
Arter George   *New Lisbon.*
Dorwart William
Huston & Pitcairn
Maus George
Leibert George   *East Palestine.*
Carpenter Reuben   *Salineville.*
Hepburn John   *New Garden.*
Thornburg Clayton
Ashford Thomas   *Calcutta.*
Grafton Charles
Eckstine David   *North Georgetown.*
Eckstine William
Axe C. L.   *Franklin Square.*
Aulbourne Henry   *New Chambersburg.*
Dillenbach Frederick
Test James D.   *East Rochester.*
Barnaly James   *Salem.*
Sharpnack & McLean
Morgan John
West Wm. P.
Baker H.   *Bucks.*
Hendricks S.
Bucheit George   *East Liverpool.*
Knowles John
Padgett B.   *West Point.*
Augustine Eli   *Unity.*
Forney Levi
Young E. P.
Orr James   *Cannon's Mills.*
Cook John   *Elkton.*
Tullis Henry

Coshocton County.

Conaway Michael   *Bakersville.*
Thomas Adam
Ahom Charles   *   Chili.*
White Thomas   *Evansburg.*
Kinsey Samuel P.   *West Bedford.*
Farwell A.   *Keene.*
Gilchrist Wm.
Brown R. L.   *Walhonding.*
Lemasters M. D.
Cantwell H.   *Coshocton.*
Kahn Joseph
Shaw N. H.
Walmsley B. F.
Shesler L.

Crawford County.

Shoenbach J.   *Leesville Cross Roads.*
Sowers Adam
Feltis Solomon   *Poplar.*
Hollingshead Nathan
Rath Conrad   *New Washington.*
Carr John   *Liberty Corners.*
Cross H. S.
Jones R.   *Lykens.*
Cuplin Samuel   *Sulphur Spring.*
Merriman Samuel
Fenner H.   *Bucyrus.*
Howenstein P.
Scroggs W. M.
Seal G D.
Sheckler E. F.
Worst P.

Cuyahoga County.

Akers W. T.   *North Royalton.*
Eaton P.
Scott T.   *Chagrin Falls.*
Taylor George   *Solon.*
Evans John   *Brecksville.*
Way Wm. H.   *Bedford.*
Quayle T. J.   *Berea.*
Smith Thomas
Houghland Benj.   *Collamer.*
Jared Frederick
Sellers Robert
Reese Nelson
Althen M., 44 Superior   *Cleveland.*
Hancock & Pychon, Weddell House Block
Kenny William, 8 Union
Kuenhold J., 13 Water
Nichols T. H., 24 Superior
Powers S. A. 51 "
Shelly John 27 "
Seaman Henry 40 "
Beverlin John   *Ohio City.*
Wilkinson A.
Mole H.

Darke County.

West A. F.   *Ithica.*
Lockwood E. C.   *Fort Jefferson.*
Thomas Ezra   *New Madison.*
Young Henry   *German.*
Glines John   *Greenville.*
Lavender —

Defiance County.

Weismantle F.   *Defiance.*
Zellers A.
Wymer Wm.   *Brunersburg.*
Matlack J.   *Panama.*

Delaware County.

Brunner & Martin   *Delaware.*
Jones & Dean
Agin James
Reynolds R.
Elridge T. H.   *Galena.*
Cook Wm.
Perfect J. S.
Fleet J. S.
Storer John   *Waldo.*
Elliott D. R. H.

Olds Henry   *Waldo.*
Thompson John   *Norton.*
Griffith David   *Padnor*
Myers Thomas
Price R.
Edwards D. G.

Erie County.

Lytle Isaac   *Sandusky City.*
Knean & Kneale
Deitz Lewis
Predges C.
Haller J. G.
Sanderson Thomas
Bretliger Conrad
Dooner M.
Bradley C. & Co.   *Milan.*
Buck C.

Fairfield County.

Hart Howard   *Pickerington.*
Owens A. J.
Swartz John
Troomger J. K.   *New Salem.*
Fortney Jacob   *Rushville.*
Cunningham C.
Rea D. M.
Bair H. H.   *Amanda.*
Burk B.   *Lithopolis.*
States Emanuel   *Clear Creek.*

Fayette County.

Parvin C.   *Washington.*

Franklin County.

Beck L., Friend   *Columbus.*
Burdell Wm., High
Eldridge Joseph, 106 do.
Pfiefer M., do.
Kacel & Schumacher, do.
Lewis G., do.
McNamer J., Broadway
Millay Wm., Gay
Rose P., 84 High
Rupprecht P. do.
Stewart A. A. do.
Cater William   *Groveport.*
Fearn George W.
Rawn Jacob
Thompson John   *Worthington.*
Thompson Isaac
Wilcox Salmon
Wiley Charles
Dagen Charles   *Canal Winchester.*
Dierling Jacob
McKelva James
Miller Joseph
Sibel Hiram
Bannon James   *Dublin.*
Hays Miller

Gallia County.

McDaniel Mathew   *Kyger.*
Hughes John   *Patriot.*
Carrell & Hibbens   *Gallipolis.*

Greene County.

Osborn & Gibney   *Cedarville.*
Hutchison & Wells   *Xenia.*
Moore John

Kepler & Rogers   *Xenia.*
Smalley James
Sweet Thomas
Dockroy James
Winter William
Griffith William   *Fairfield.*
Horner George
Retter A.
Dill E.   *Spring Valley.*
Tharp W. V. C.
McCarty James   *Clifton.*
Coxler J. M.   *Yellow Springs.*
George Martin
Dodson William   *Jamestown.*
Dingess Peter

Geauga County.

Strohl John   *Chardon.*
Hendryse S. V. R.
Sliter H.   *Burton.*
Hews H.   *Claridon.*
Cleaveland John   *Bainbridge*
Marshall Wm. O.   *Munson.*
Caldwell J. M.   *Parkman.*
Perry Thos.   *Huntsburg.*
Conart J. F.   *Middlefield.*
Griffin John B.   *Montville.*
Heath W. H.   *Newburg.*
Strail J.   *Chardon.*
Myers Lewis   *Chester.*
Redcliffe Wm.   *Hamden.*
Briggs A.   *Bainbridge.*

Guernsey County.

Johnson Samuel   *Cumberland.*
White & Martin   *Washington.*
Cooper & Armor
Gill A. D.   *Londonderry.*
Hossack David   *Kimbolton.*
Braninger D.   *Millersville.*
Gooderl & Rose   *Senecaville.*
Campbell O. H.   *Leatherwood.*
Valiet A.

Hamilton County.

Ahlering & Brummer, 246 Main,   *Cin'ti.*
Ackva & Blickler, 447   do.
Abraham A., 70 Fifth.
Ahlering & Brummer, 39 Broadway
Brugge H. J., 272 Main
Barwise & King, 156 do.
Boyd & Brundrett, 33 e. Third
Brockhoff J. A., 139 Congress
Beesley J. W., 105 Main
Bitter P., 210 Sixth
Billian M., 499 Walnut
Bechman T., Ham. Road bet. Piatt and Freeman
Barger & Sharp, 203 Western Row
Behne Joseph, 221   do   do.
Clark Geo., 6 Pearl
Connelly Edward, 182 Walnut
Dupler Charles, 407 Main
Doepler H., 162 Sixth
Evens P., 127 Main
Frantz & Stimtibee, 98 Hunt
Flour H., 198 Sixth

Falack F., 389 Vine   *Cincinnati*
Felis Peter, Hamilton Road bet. Main and Piatt
Fisher William, W. Row between Everett and Liberty
Flohr J., 276 Western Row
Gunnies D. C., s. w. corner George and Western Row
Greiwe & Putoff, 353 Main
Goodman S., 62 Front
Guthrie A. H. & Co., 34 w. Fourth
Heerdt A., 85 Clinton
Heiddel G., 118 Vine
Heidkamp & Grever, Main above Court
Hostetter & Fuste, 354 Main
Harper A. H., 102 Walnut
Haddix N., 260   do.
Jelliff C. S., W. Row bet. 8th and Kemble
Joring B., cor. Broadway and Woodward
Jost Wm. & Co., 61 Vine
Jinnings Martin C., 139 Main
Johnson William, 190 Walnut
Kramer & Kroger, 262 Main and 62 Broadway
Koch H. & J., 187 Walnut
Kleine Joseph, 40 Fifth
Kauther P. J., 315 e. Front
Kuchler K., 38½ Front
Kolhoff Joseph, Fifth bet. Race and Elm
Kleine H., 477 Main
Keming A., 96, Court
Klome J., cor. Linn and Laurel
Levinson S., 306 Fifth
Logan John, 227 Western Row
Lunings J. & J., 499 Main
Leisant F., cor. Clay and Twelfth
Loos George, 601 Vine
Luhn J. H. & Brother, 8 e. Fifth
Leiter Joseph, 14 e. Front
Lasance A., 120 Front
Luken H. H., 266 Main
Luhin J. B., 285   do.
Lopie & Mass, 219 Walnut
McElevey E., 12 Broadway
Mane Fred., 269 Main
Macke B., 25 Vine
Max Bell, 161 Main
McArdle Edward, n. e. cor. Race & Third
Macke Bernard, 33 Vine
Mority M., 59 Court
Meifeld John G., 147 Fifth
Mooney T., 201 Sixth
Miller P., 483 Vine
Morris J., cor. W. Row and Catharine
McCord William, cor. John and Sixth
Mane F., cor. Vine and Fifteenth
Molenpage P., 495 Race
Nieman H., 546 Main
Niemeyer H., Western Row bet. Everett and Mason
Newbold J. W., 32 Sixth
Northrup W. W., 48 w. Fourth
Ogden & See, 32 w. Fourth
Okeefee & Smallwood, 211 Western Row
Parrett J., 56 Broadway
Purvis A., 111 Fifth
Penny Wm. H., 126 Walnut

Poppe J. D., Front near Vine   *Cincinnati.*
Rieskelman H. H., 335 Western Row
Ranshoff —, 607 Vine
Redman B. F., 1 Burnet House
Shurrager Geo. W., 9 e. Fourth
Stiens John, Front bet. Walnut and Vine
Sullivan J., 248 Vine
Seiter H. H., Walnut bet. Fifth and Sixth
Shafer Wm., 67 Court
Schumaker J. & Co., 549 Main
Schumaker B. H., 463   do.
Stoll W., 84 Court
Surmann A. & Lammers, 32 Court
Schuemacher J. H., 367 Fifth
Schepman J. H., 8 Thirteenth
Stuntebick John H., 360 Broadway
Sebert J., 458 Vine
Swass Lewis, 589 Western Row
Sarle W. R., 219 Main
Thomas S. P., s. e. cor. Walnut & Fourth
Ulmer A., 467 Vine
Vandyke D., 220 Walnut
Westrup Henry, 265 Main
Winabar J. B. J., 205 Walnut
Wrightman B. T., n. w. cor. Vine & Third
Wiggins & Pollock, 34 Fourth
Williams John A., 169 Sycamore
Weiler M., 115 Fifth
Williams J. A., 101 Fifth
Wager W., 24 Thirteenth
Wolf G., 579 Western Row
Woerner L., 281   do.
Koerner Michael   *Newtown.*
Tucker John
Jinkens John   *Sharonville.*
Williamson David
Johnson A. P.   *Carthage.*
McFarland David
Garrison J. O.   *Cheviot.*
Hornour Christian   *Miltonsburgh.*
Sleilein G., 16 Hamilton Road
Lookheat J.   *Columbia.*
Harmer W.   *Fulton.*
Gravy E.
Aldcroft J.   *Walnut Hills.*
Oonk J. G.
Slaback S.   *Montgomery.*
Kitchell C. S.
Saxon Benjamin   *Pleasant Ridge.*
Dobell Joseph   *Harrison.*
Volk William
Thompson Wm.   *Mt. Washington.*
Farmer Henry W.   *Miami.*
Stabin William   *Cumminsville.*
Van Dyke Dominick   *Springdale.*

Hancock County.

Williams R. R.   *Benton Ridge.*
Ford Joseph D.   *Finley.*
Druit James
Youngkin A.
Flenner George
Basolt Anthony
Sours Adam
Baldwin A. J.
Sutherland Wm.
Davis J

Hardin County.

Letson Hugh   *Kenton.*
Fry George
Anderson G. W.
Daugherty Wm.
Johnson J. E.   *Roundhead.*

Harrison County.

Furgason Samuel   *Cadis.*
Hayler Frederick   *Deersville.*
Dickerson J.   *New Athens.*
Day James

Henry County.

Vincent John A.   *Florida.*
Barnitt Thomas   *Napoleon.*
Wells B. S.

Highland County.

Wright David   *Highland.*
Merritt & Hudson   *Greenfield.*
Glasscock H.
Cunningham Wm. L.   *Belfast*
Higgins Wm.   *New Market*
Abors John   *New Petersburg.*
Viers Daniel
Gordon Wm.
Rhonda A. T.   *Sugartree Ridge.*
Griffith Wm. H.   *Marshall.*
Bartley W. F.   *Samantha.*
Lockwood H.   *Leesburg.*
Simpson S.
Wylie Charles   *Hillsboro'.*
Horn Geo. W.
Crosby Isaac

Hocking County.

Jones John   *Logan.*
Meeks J. N.
Moore Harvey

Holmes County.

Griffin Geo. O.   *Holmesville.*
Foster James
Burkholder H. H.   *Benton.*
Lemman John
Lohman R.   *Winesburg.*
Kopp G.
Freuch & Voorhes   *Millersburg.*

Huron County.

Pritts Edwin   *Monroeville.*
Harper & Patterson
Prentiss A. W.
Brown James   *Steuben.*
Todd O. H.   *East Townsend.*
Marshall Henry
Signos G. H.   *Clarkfield.*
Gregory J. L.
Cowle J.   *Bellevue.*
McFadden Samuel   *North Fairfield.*

Jackson County.

Lewis T. W   *Oakhill.*
Evans D. L.
Clemmons J.   *Allensville.*

Jefferson County.

Brashear T.	*Steubenville.*
Keller G.	
Giles W.	
Armstrong J.	
Holton J. L.	
Black Daniel	
Kerman Wm. H.	*Warrenton.*
Hardy James	*Richmond.*
Troter Wm.	
Tiffany A. C.	
Mercer John H.	*Mt. Pleasant.*
Busher Wm.	
Boyles & Brady	*Knoxville.*
Goodlin John	

Knox County.

Clark & Lewis	*Mt. Vernon.*
Singer J. W. F.	
Wolff A.	
Beach John T.	*Fredericktown.*
Greenlee R.	
Roberts T. P.	
Cassil John	*Monroe Mills.*
Phillips Levi	
Miller Michael	*Millwood.*
Spencer William	
Magers L. & John	*Jelloway.*
Richardson John	*Bladensburg.*
Hall Jehu	

Lake County.

Miller D. C.	*Willoughby.*
Clark N.	
Fisher N. M.	*Painesville.*
Wilson D. C.	
Carlin P. S.	
Cain E.	
Powel N.	

Lawrence County.

McCormick E. C.	*Ironton.*
McCune P. & Doyd	
Silverman S. & Bro.	
Wise H. & Bro.	
Patterson James & Geo	*Millers.*

Licking County.

Willey H. F.	*Linnville.*
Bane J. F.	*Brownsville.*
Frymento C.	*Jacksontown.*
Wilson John	
Kirt A. J.	*Newark.*
Buckel J. K.	
Barrick & Carlisle	
Miller Joseph	
Hunt E.	
Walker A.	
Beaty E. A.	*Croton.*
Gray W.	
Landon M.	*Johnstown.*
Greer John	
Gibbouy Samuel	*Kirkersville.*

Logan County.

Bimmell John	*Huntsville.*
Evans Henry T.	

Johnson Almon	*East Liberty.*
Criswell B. F.	*Bellefontaine*
Knapp O. S.	
Mulford D.	
Wilgus & Janney	*Zanesfield.*

Lorain County.

Carpenter R.	*Huntington.*
Ells George W.	*Oberlin.*
Godley Joseph	
Stogell S.	*Copopa.*
Northrop E.	*Elyria.*
Hoyle William	
Norton E. H.	
Merwin & Mason	
Kewley William	
Murphy M. J.	

Madison County.

McCormick & Bates	*London.*
Miller N. H. L.	*West Jefferson.*

Mahoning County.

Kyle John G.	*Canfield.*
Gorside Benj.	
Brainard H. B.	
Hopson Philo	*Petersburgh.*
Acppli G.	
King G.	*Youngstown.*
Theobald David	
Calvin & Fowler	
Armstrong W.	
McGinnis Wm.	*New Middletown.*
Hohn J.	*East Lewistown.*
Buhnalder George	*Orange.*
Koons Cyrus	*North Jackson,*
Fulk Gideon	
Weaver John	
Detrick Peter	*Green Village.*
Swarts George	
Kitsel Fred.	
Morrow Humphrey	*North Lima.*
Golden Jacob	*New Springfield.*
Whalen Wm.	

Marion County

Merrill J. & Co.	*Marion.*
Ulman J.	
Harmon H.	

Medina County.

Cannon J.	*Liverpool.*
Wohlgemuth D.	
Boyer W. F.	*Wadsworth.*
Stickle John	*Lodi.*
Golden Wm. R.	
Washborn C.	*Hinckley.*
Morris J.	*Sharon Centre.*
Rutter S. W.	*Homerville.*
Poe & Musser	*Medina.*
Coppas S. D.	
Brown J.	

Meigs County.

Piper G. L.	*Letart Falls.*
Brading Wm.	*Pomeroy.*
Stivers & Jones	
Cohen Harrison	

Weldon E. S.	*Pomeroy.*	Winfield J.	*Centreville.*
Crosbie James		Michael John	*Chambersburg.*
Atkins H.		Peffley Daniel	*Centre.*
Walker —		Walker Thomas	

Mercer County.

Kable Daniel	*Celina.*

Miami County.

Calpus C.	*Fletcher.*
Kephardt H. G.	
Ferguson R.	*Piqua.*
Legore W. H.	
Kitchen H. A.	*Troy.*
Kitchen J.	
Pettit A. J.	
Hisky R.	*Casstown.*
Montgomery Stephen	*West Milton.*
Folckemmer John	
Gimor Daniel	*Brant.*
Blessinger Geo. W.	

Monroe County.

Burghbacker Mathias	*Woodsfield.*
O'Connor Daniel	
Molden John	*Antioch.*
Loughman Wm.	*Laing's.*
Bowhan Jacob	*Masterton.*
Reynolds John F.	
Walters Joseph	
Dresel Christian	*Miltonsburgh.*
Hosinnoune O.	
Fowler Thomas S.	*Malaga.*
Truax Job	
Cain Milligan	*Sunfish.*
Cox E. B.	
Speelman James	
Rist Paul	*Baresville.*

Montgomery County.

Ahlirs J. H., Wayne,	*Dayton.*
Breeze W. G., Main	
Kissenger H., Second	
Lewis T. M., Third	
McDaniel G. W., Jefferson	
McVicar A. W., Main	
McCann E., Third	
Phillips Thos. H., Jefferson	
Rodenbaugh S., Main	
Stockmyer J., do.	
Thomas S., Fifth	
Wilson D. B., First	
Clayton William	*New Lebanon.*
Archer J.	*Farmersville.*
Schrock D.	
Widman A.	
Coleman W.	*Johnsville.*
Imboden D.	
Gephart A., jun.	*Miamisville.*
Ebole Jacob	
Hoover Simon	
Rice & Solomon	
East & Schaeffer	*Germantown.*
Rowe D. J. & Brother	
Kelly Thomas	*Alexandersville.*
Kiser J.	
Willis & Grauel	*Liberty.*

Morgan County.

Worrell John	*Chester Hill.*
Kerns Isaac	*Meigsville.*
Roland Jacob	*McConnelsville.*
Kirby John	
Hasher Geo.	
Cheadle Thos. D.	
Lamm & Brother	
Zinsmeister D.	
Stedman Eli	
Scott T. P.	*Stockport.*
Harrison Wm.	*Pennsville.*
White Thompson	

Morrow County.

Hutchinson Stephen	*Iberia.*
Bartlett A. W.	*Cardington.*
Prophet H. & A.	
Myers Henry	*Shauk's.*
Murray G. W.	*Woodview.*
Pifer Philip	
Derr G. S.	*Pulaskiville.*
Crane H. P.	*Nimmons' Cross Roads.*
Beach & McEverts	*Chesterville.*
Willets G. W.	

Muskingum County.

Palmer R. A.	*Otsego.*
Whitaker Reuben	*Norwich.*
Henry Peter	
Timms Henry	
Marryman Q. W.	*Frazeysburg.*
Umsted Wm.	*Dresden.*
Henderson Wm. R.	
Wartenbre D. C.	
Johnson Henry	*Gratiot.*
McCutchen P.	*Chandlersville.*
Currier C. K.	*Zanesville.*
Black J. S.	
Keeley W. P.	
Ashmore M. & J.	
Lillibridge Warren	
Crow R. M.	
Clements Z.	

Noble County.

Melton John H.	*Berne.*
Smith Harmon	
Huxley Charles	*Mt. Ephraim.*
Spriggs John P.	
Thomas John	*Kennonsburg.*
Goodhart Daniel C.	*Batesville.*
Sanbower George	

Paulding County.

Savage Bennett	*Paulding.*

Pickaway County.

Black J. O.	*Circleville.*
Gephart G. C.	
Rock Hanson	
Steele J.	
Myers Samuel	*Tarlton.*

Todd & Shappell   *Tarlton.* | Scoven E. C.   *West Florence.*
Walt Ach. | Morrell G. H.   *Morningsun.*
Miller W. A.   *Darbyville.* | Bennett James H.
Tolle E. | Crampton & Davis   *New Paris.*
Campbell Joseph   *Williamsport.* | Purviance & Johnson
                                         | Caughey & Davis
Pike County. | Sites & Swain   *West Elkton.*
Valentine Jacob   *Jasper.*
Vonachen L.   *Waverly.*   **Putnam County.**
Corn G. W. | Tingle Joseph   *Kalida.*
Lorbach Martin   *Beaver.* | Glunny John   *Buckeye.*
Peck & Southworth   *Piketon.* | Gerskin James
Faringer P. | McBride James   *Pendleton.*
Frederick A. | Brandt John

Perry County.   **Ross County.**
Grimsley J. H.   *New Lexington.* | Maule, Martin & Co.   *Chillicothe.*
Sniter A. | Ketner E.
Walker S. H. | Ringson John
Rock Samuel   *Rehoboth.* | Seeauz C. F.
Kenning John   *Mt. Perry.* | Robinson J. W.
Curett Martin   *Somerset.* | Steele C.
Mains John F. | Laird J.
Williams J. L. | Phillips C. J.
                                         | Kutschbach F.
Portage County. | Furry J. M.   *South Salem.*
Sommerville D. M.   *Ravenna.* | Litten N. C.
Dalrymple L. | Jones John   *Hallsville.*
Holt P. | Jones Norman   *Kingston.*
Sutliff M. | Zimmerman J. E.
Alcorn Joseph
Linn P.   **Richland County.**
Stough M.   *Randolph.* | Dougherty J. H.   *Mansfield.*
Witherell N. A.   *Aurora.* | McCullough D.
Parrish Ephraim | Cook John   *Lexington.*
Clutter Edward   *Streetsboro'.* | Cregg Ebin
Clark George   *Shalersville.* | Hartenfelts Justice   *Barnes.*
Kent James | Wagoner John
Fairchilds W.   *Edinburgh.* | Jones George   *West Windsor.*
Davis Wm. D. | Orchard Edmund
Dunbar David   *Franklin.* | Lefevre W.   *Belleville.*
King John T. | Moore Jackson
Stofer Samuel | Dunham J. W.   *Lucas.*
Frost L.   *Mantua.* | McGarey John
Hinckley Wm. A. | Deveney John & Co.   *Plymouth.*
Wilcox Sylvester | Billstun S.
Whitmore Thomas   *Deerfield.* | Burgoyne S. F.
Hale George   *Nelson.*
Foster Wm.   **Sandusky County.**
Evans E. T.   *Palmyra.* | Aris Henry   *Woodville.*
                                         | McMillen Henry   *Clyde.*
Preble County. | Hummell George   *Greensburg & Roads.*
Halinsteger John M.   *West Alexandria.*| Huffman George
Clawson A. J. | Maxwell P.   *Fremont.*
Davis John S. | McElhanie James E.   *Rollersville.*
Spillman T. K.   *Lewisburg.*
Sullivan Samuel   **Scioto County.**
Unger L | McLaughlin Hiram   *Lucasville.*
Sheppard Geo. W. & Son   *Camden.* | Bishop S. D.   *Portsmouth.*
Yoast A. W. | Blankemayer E.
Campbell John H. | Kehrer Charles
Auter A. V.   *Eaton.* | Keogh T. H.
Filbert & Crouse | Miller & Elsas
Mikesel E. | Pelheuk F.
Seackind A. | Rawson S. F.
Kauffman Samuel | Camp John   *Iron-Furnaces.*
Caldwell A. P.   *Fairhaven.* | Cole Alonzo
Lough D. A. | Reed L.   *Wheelersburgh.*

Seneca County.

Feathers Stephen	*Adrian.*
Ragan Daniel	
Wheeler H. A.	
Adam Peter	*Berwick.*
Burnie Alexander	*Tiffin.*
Bloom Andrew	
Backer J. T.	
Knight M.	
Pillars L. W.	
Silvers J.	
Striker & Ross	
Volmer Joseph	
Shotnar George	*Bascom.*
Myers Manassa	*West Lodi.*
Shiltz John	*Green Spring.*
Snatz Philip	

Shelby County.

Munch William	*Pratt.*
Stratham David	

Starke County.

Brenna F.	*Louisville.*
Eisenzimner M.	
Gallagher John	
Kalbaugh Israel	
Boegel H. H.	*Waynesburg.*
Brownwell J. G.	
Rutter J. G.	
Hecker J.	*West Brookfield.*
Rook S. O.	*Minerva.*
Sala B.	
Martin J. & T.	*New Franklin.*
Sleutz E. N.	
Bour N. & P	*Canton.*
Danner John	
Hartman J.	
Kitt A.	
Lemmon W.	
Reehman & Co.	
Rex J. P.	
Rex Jacob	
Stansbury J. C.	*East Greenville.*
Rulfus Wilhelm	*New Berlin.*
Wagner George	
Ream A. J.	*Paris.*
Daniel Simon	*Mapleton.*
White William	*Magnolia.*
Feltz Edward	*Marlboro'.*
McElroy T. C.	
Lee Joseph	*New Baltimore.*
Gidlinger Frederick	*Hartville.*
Hoffman Jacob	
Kitt Joseph	*Massillon.*
Lowe & Crider	
Whitmore & Simon	
Adams A. A.	
Saucerman J.	*Limaville.*
Zarzea J. M.	

Summit County.

Metlin & Boorman	*Middlebury.*
Beebe W. M.	*Hudson.*
King J. B.	
Bender John L.	*Inland.*
Bodner Lewis	

Shaeffer M. W.	*Inland.*
McIntosh Peter	*Clinton.*
Folts A. H.	*Nimishla.*
Weaver Philip	
Shall Robert	*Richfield.*
Kelly E. D.	*Montrose.*
Shook Eli	*Summit.*
Bateman T. E.	*Northfield.*

Trumbull County.

Fredenburgh John	*Johnsonville.*
Carlton Francis B.	*Girard.*
Kyle Oliver	
Goucher W. S.	*Hartford.*
Meikle Thomas	
McNabb H. W.	
McCoy J.	
Morgenstein & Bro.	*Warren.*
Mullin J.	
Weeks & Conn	
Kerr Henry	*Brookfield.*
Shoff Aaron	
Calhoun William	*Church Hill.*
Aydelott Peter Z.	*Ohlstown.*
Dawson B.	*Farmington.*
Brown R. M.	
Mier M. S. B.	
Hofstater J.	*Newton Falls.*
Shell J.	

Tuscarawas County.

Kinney John	*Sandyville.*
Nelson Thomas	
Mumma George	*Winfield.*
Baxter Robert	*New Cumberland.*
Uleman —	*Gnadenhutten.*
Deigh Valentine	*Ragersville.*
Snyder Joseph A.	
Johnson G.	*New Philadelphia.*
Neely W. F.	
Sutton Thomas	
Danforth L.	
Witter J.	
Dougherty G. W.	
Pofer C.	
Law William	*Peoli.*
Olewell C.	*Tuscarawas.*

Union County.

Anderson Levi	*Marysville.*
Brophy Wm. T.	
Geer Leonard	
Hopkins C. G.	*Milford Centre.*
Philips Milford	

Van Wert County.

McCormick H.	*Van Wert.*
Robinson Henry	
Sommers T.	
Lehman G.	*Delphos.*
Murphy Jos. R	

Vinton County.

Caldwell J. W.	*McArthur.*
Elerick J. W.	
Redd Horace	
Allen James	
Ross A.	

25

Lillibridge John   *New Plymouth.*
Vasnotti Jas. R.   *Allensville.*

Warren County.

Walker Wm. B. C.   *Mason.*
Ross D.
McDonough Samuel
Wallace Wm.   *Hayesville.*
Gustor Wm.
Whitmore Thos. H.   *Deerfield.*
Mowen S.
French Uriah   *Waynesville.*
Williams L. W.   *Morrow.*
Compton Alex.
Macombrie Arthur   *Mount Holly.*
Merchant A.   *Harveysburg.*
Smith Benj.

Washington County.

Hasberger T. P.   *Marietta.*
Brookmire O.
Weaver H.
Gruffort Chas.
McCleod J.
Hill E. F.
Higgins Thos.
Edwards W.   *Harmar.*
Fairchild Levi   *Centre Belpre.*
Shepherdson F.   *Newport.*
Parker J.
Sellers G.   *Jolly.*
Brown E. R.   *Lowell.*
Cox G. N.
Bauer J. E.

Wayne County.

Weirick J.   *Dalton.*
Davison John
Albright J. T.
McIntyre A. A   *Chippewa.*
Miller E.   *Fredericksburg.*
Camble R.
Smith J. R.
Kelley J.   *Reedsburg.*
Swartz J.
Bailey R.
Phillips John   *Burbank.*
Peters W. G.   *Smithville.*
Gilbert E. H.
Doersam Geo.   *Number One.*
Zelering A. S.   *West Lebanon*
Haley Peter
Lann Wm.   *Shreve.*

Williams County.

Campbell Michael   *West Unity.*
Bonze C. H.
Peppard H. H.
Sumser John
McLure R.   *Bryan.*
Walt G. W.
Rutter G. N.   *Montpelier.*

Wood County.

Clark George W.   *Perrysburg.*
Houston Wm.
Harrington H. T.
Lee D. H.   *Bowling-green.*

Wyandot County.

Nowell Wm. M.   *Upper Sandusky.*
Depler George
Owen John
Nigh Andrew   *Carey.*
Munger L.   *McCutchensville.*
Finn Chas.
Lappart Wm.   *Sycamore.*
Lumbert J. M.   *Marseilles.*

Tanners and Curriers.

Adams County.

Sparks John   *Stout's.*
Eylor Alfred   *Locust Grove.*
Davidson A.
Reid T. A.   *Marble Furnace.*
Fristoe Joshua   *Dunbarton.*
Kilpatrick Jas. W.
Kilpatrick Samuel P.
McGoveny Adam   *West Union.*

Allen County.

Calwell Nicholas   *Lima.*
Saint Levi
Clippinger D. H.   *Allentown.*
Morris J. J.   *Westminster.*
Stewart John   *Croghan.*

Ashland County.

Fancher Mead   *Savannah.*
Walker Thomas
Davis Hugh   *Ashland.*
Wasson William
Thompson Washington   *Jeromeville.*
Williams James
Coulter T. W.   *Perrysville.*
Bender George   *Mohecan.*

Ashtabula County.

Fairchild John   *Eagleville.*
Spencer N.
Barnum F. G.
Strong A.   *Lenox.*
Hale D. B.   *Geneva.*
Hayward Samuel   *Kellogsville.*
Baker Edward
Shoal Jacob
Rottle John
Carlisle F.
Chase Moses & Son   *Hart's Grove.*
Brooks W. C.   *West Williamsfield.*
Hyde & Enos   *Andover.*
Secheverell H. G.   *Cork.*
Whitney & Kilborn   *Conneaut*
Brown Chauncey
White & Blakeslee
Farnham —

Athens County.

Workman S. D. & Co.   *Chauncey.*
Eskins J.   *Amesville*
Marquis R.
Corner R. M.
McCane N.
Jewett E. P. & Co.   *Athens.*
Carpenter O.
Graham H. L.   *Lee.*

Auglaize County.

Hoerath Henry — *Minster.*
Louge Francis
Carder Edward — *St. John's.*
Neil John F.
Coleman James H.

Belmont County.

Mills Robert — *Barnesville.*
Ramsay & Uncles
Hobson Joseph — *Flushing.*
Parry James
Loyd Joshua — *Loydsville.*
Askew Parker — *Saint Clairsville.*
Collins Charles
Lewis Rezin
Berry G. — *Morristown.*
Holmes & Harris
Hawthorn H. B. — *Shepherdstown.*
White B. — *Belmont.*
Smith Thomas

Brown County.

Shaw F. G. — *Ripley.*
Kirker D. B. & J. H. — *Decatur.*
Purdum Benj. — *Newhope.*
Ross Israel — *Pueblo.*
McKibbon J. T. — *Maple.*
Edwards J. & Son — *Russellville.*
Williams H.
McKibbin John T. — *Feesburg.*
Feike Franz

Butler County.

Parrish J. — *West Chester.*
Cowen Samuel
Sohn J. W. — *Reesville.*
Smiley & Anderson
Smith F. J. — *Middletown.*
Proctor T. — *Saint Charles.*

Carroll County.

Dickey George — *Malvern.*
Hooten Mark M. — *New Hagerstown.*
Perry S. G. — *New Harrisburgh.*

Champaign County.

Darnal W. L. — *Christiansburg.*
Glenn W. C. — *Urbana.*
Winslow & Whitehead
Loose D.
Johnson & Archer — *Woodstock.*
Wilson Benj. — *Careyshill.*
Milligan Samuel — *North Lewisburg.*

Clark County.

Brentney H. — *Springfield.*
Roop Samuel — *New Carlisle.*
Weakley E. T.

Clermont County.

Kinley Thomas — *New Richmond.*
Huber O. B. — *Williamsburg.*
Porter James
Smith C.
Grant J. R. & Co. — *Bethel.*
Lindsey D.

Clare & Wilkinson — *Bethel.*
Iler Jacob T. — *Neville.*
Perin Samuel — *Perin's Mills.*

Clinton County.

Grant John — *New Burlington.*
Furguson S. — *Port William.*
Rester John — *Westboro'.*
Boyd James H. — *Blanchester.*
Betts W. S. — *Martinsville.*
Stephen Evan
Garner Ames
Nicherson Samuel — *Wilmington.*

Columbiana County.

Riddle J. A. — *Wellsville.*
Arter John — *New Lisbon.*
Garretson George
Harbaugh Daniel
Spiker Simon
Meeks W. — *East Palestine.*
Meeks J.
Nixon Henry — *Salineville.*
Nixon John
Bider Sebastian — *North Georgetown.*
Shisler George
Kemp Hercules — *Franklin Square.*
Filson William — *Bucks.*
Glassinger John — *New Chambersburg.*
Hart Samuel — *St Clair.*
Triffinger P. — *West Point.*
Hoffstot A. O. — *Unity.*
Shook C.
Ferrall B. — *East Fairfield.*
Arter A. R. — *Hanoverton.*
Cain Milo.

Coshocton County.

McBride Thomas — *West Bedford.*
Dickey & Russel — *Clark's.*
Wolf Philip — *Evansburg.*
Ax John — *Chili.*
Sprague John — *Keene.*
Lity John & Co.
Johnson Wm. K. — *Coshocton.*

Crawford County.

Jolley Jeremiah — *Lykens.*
Hawk David — *Sulphur Springs.*
Moriarty Patrick
Cary A — *Bucyrus.*
Deardorff E.
Minich H.
Cummins G. — *De Kalb.*
Jordon J.

Cuyahoga County.

Edda Ezra — *Gates' Mills.*
Phinny Edwin — *Dover.*
Vincent & Nash — *Chagrin Falls.*
White R.
Ballow Isaac A. — *Brecksville.*
Higgins Estus
Burton Curtis — *Collamer.*
Luster Samuel

Darke County.

Campbell J. B. & Co. — *Ithica.*
Pence R. K. — *Hillgrove.*

Leas & Mills	*Fort Jefferson.*	Pitner Lewis	*Parkman.*
Snodgrass Robert	*New Madison.*	Baldwin —	*Montville.*
Deem W. C.	*German.*	Gilbert A.	*Newbury.*
Weaver Preston	*Greenville.*	Hitt William	*Thompson.*
Garver Isaac	*Beamsville.*	Cook J. S.	*Burton.*

Defiance County.

Bouton & Robinson	*Defiance.*	Allen John	*Xenia.*
Hilton Brice	*Brunersburg.*	Conwell B. G.	
Olinger Jacob		Comens Charles	*Fairfield.*

Greene County.

		Allen John	*Xenia.*
		Conwell B. G.	
		Comens Charles	*Fairfield.*
		Shaffer H. P.	
		Shaw E. & T. W.	*Spring Valley.*

Delaware County.

Wolfley John	*Delaware.*	Braley George	*Clifton.*
Storm J.		Braley C.	
Brown R. O.		Flint W. W.	
Kurner Chas.		Deaver Benjamin	*Yellow Springs.*
Arnold U.	*Galena.*	Kershner Isaac	
Maxfield D.		Zortman Isaac	*Jamestown.*
Meeker W. C.			
Taylor Arthur	*Waldo.*		

Guernsey County.

Olds Luther		Mead B. L.	*Leatherwood.*
Olosson Luther	*Harlem.*	Lawrence John	*Washington.*
Thompson James	*Norton.*	Ounningham J.	
Peck G. A.	*Sunbury.*	Nace Samuel	
Peck Samuel		Lawrence James	*Londonderry.*
Hughs J. R.		Smith M.	*Antrim.*
		Carlisle G. B.	*Winchester.*
		Ault Daniel	*Fairview.*

Erie County.

Beckwith S. P. & J.	*Milan.*	Saltgaver Jacob	
Hoys H. E.		McCracken Alex.	*Cambridge.*
Keith O. S.		Oldham S. M.	
		Rollstin William	*Kimbolton.*

Fairfield County.

Curtiss John H.	*Pickerington.*	Richey George	*Senecaville.*
Geiger H.	*Rushville.*		

Hamilton County.

Whitmer D.			
Bogle D. S.	*Amanda.*	McCabe A., 352 Main st.	*Cincinnati.*
Shaffer J.	*Lancaster.*	Thornton R. & Co., 9 "	
Pratt James M.		Easton S. 232 "	
Riley William	*Lithopolis.*	Walsh Michael, 9 Walnut	
Brown J.		Swift Alexander, Deer Creek, bet. Fifth	
Stuveson Jacob	*Sugar Grove.*	and Sycamore	
Yonkerman H.		Iliff A., cor. Everett and Plum	
		More A., Plum, bet. Liberty and Findley	

Fayette County.

McIntire L.	*Jeffersonville.*	Ballance J. H., 108 Canal	
		Rasche H., Plum, near Ham. Road	

Franklin County.

		Huber Wm. & Co., 669 Elm	
Kraner G. R., Spring	*Columbus.*	Dickman & Eckert, 349 Main	
Jones John, Rich		Fells Jacob F., 345 do.	
Ridgeway T.		Speigle & Grossman	*Fulton.*
Buchsilb Ludwig, Front		Gaston D. B.	*Mt. Healthy.*
Hulva Josiah	*Lockbourn.*	Keen Wesley	*Harrison.*
Somerville James	*Canal Winchester.*	Mensing & Smith	
Trine Reuben		Howell Arthur O.	*Cleves.*
Naswinder A.	*Ovid.*	Hageman G. W.	*Sharonville.*
McCann J.	*Dublin.*	Lawrence Daniel	*Reading.*

Gallia County.

		Pickett H. C. & Co.	*Mt. Blanchard.*
Mathews M. R.	*Vinton.*	Musgrave Joseph	
Spicer David E.	*Patriot.*	Taylor R. & Co.	
Ravenscroft W. H. & Co.	*Kyger.*	Smith Gideon	*Cass.*
Dages Peter	*Gallipolis.*	Beach R.	*Finley.*
		Hull J. B.	

Geauga County.

Hancock County.

Hardin County.

Parson Norman	*Chardon.*		
Oonverse & Kissock		Smith Edward	*Kenton.*
Trager O. H.	*Clariden.*	Underwood J. E.	*Roundhead.*

Carter J.   *Roundhead.*
Ickes Josiah   *Sylvia.*

Harrison County.

George & Morey   *Cadis.*

Henry County.

Daily & Crosby   *Texas.*

Highland County.

Kelley Thos. & Sons   *Highland.*
Fullerton & Jury   *Greenfield.*
Hays J. G.
Douglass Wm. & D.
Hayton James   *Buford.*
Couch John   *Newmarket.*
Carper Nicholas   *New Petersburgh.*
Amen Noah   *Marshall.*
Hack Geo. & Co.   *Greenford.*
Starr Joseph   *Samantha.*
Kelley R. T.   *Leesburg.*

Hocking County.

Smith John A.   *Logan.*
Gold John   *Gibisonville.*
Phillips Philip

Holmes County.

Hutchison J. P.   *Holmesville.*
Heims M   *Walnut Creek.*
Knee Philip
Kingsley S.   *Winesburg.*

Huron County.

Fisk J.   *Steuben.*
St. John Jasper   *East Townsend.*
Lighter A.   *Bellevue.*
Richards & Zeiner
Baker Theodore & Sons   *Norwalk.*
Peebles A. W.
Robbins S. B.   *Fitchville.*

Jackson County.

Prose & Jones   *Oak Hill.*
Bell John   *Allensville.*
Steele Wm. R. & Co.   *Jackson.*
Walterhouse G. B. & Co.

Jefferson County.

Spencer Joseph C.   *Steubenville.*
Elliott Wm. & Co.
Gray R.   *East Springfield.*
Gruber John   *Annapolis.*
Hogg John   *Mt. Pleasant.*
Day & Clendenning   *Knoxville.*

Knox County.

Hendrick H. & H.   *Mt. Vernon.*
Ogilvie Hugh
Williams Nahum
Penick Wm. & John   *Martinsburg.*
Merring & Morris   *Fredericktown.*
Woodruff T. H. & Co.
Frizzle E.   *Democracy.*
Weirich John
Garrett Jacob & Wm.   *Millwood.*
Frasher Thomas & Henry   *Jelloway.*
Hill & Upfold   *Bladensburg.*
Blue Peter

Lake County.

Wood E.   *Madison.*
Parker L.
Wheeler A.   *Perry.*
Morse A. & J.   *Concord.*
Case Edward   *Painesville.*
Wright G. A.
Taylor J. H.

Lawrence County.

Osner A. & F.   *Burlington.*
Russell Francis   *Russell's Place.*
Keeny William
Stumbo James   *Waterloo.*

Licking County.

Scott John F.   *Linnville.*
Hamilton J.   *Brownsville.*
Hayes C. C. & Co.   *Granville.*
Lantz Michael   *Newark.*
Seymour J. W   *Croton.*
Lemert A.   *Perryton.*
Russell A.
Seaword J. E.
Baker Samuel   *Johnstown.*
Ashbrook A. P.
Wibborn Philip   *Fredonia.*

Logan County.

Badger John C.   *Huntsville.*
Coulter John
Allman & Hiatt   *East Liberty.*
Hatcher Lott J. & Co.   *Rushsylvania.*
Bateman & Stroud   *Bellefontaine.*
Cowman & Obuncham
Runyan P.   *Zanesfield.*
Bell J.   *Quincy.*

Lorain County.

Goodrich Wm.   *Brownhelm.*
Barrow John   *Amherst.*

Madison County.

Long Benjamin   *London.*
Phifer George
Hancock E. S.   *West Jefferson.*

Mahoning County.

Moore Wm.   *Lowellville.*
Wehr Nathan   *Cornersburg.*
Hauser & Auer   *Petersburgh.*
Wilsdorf L. & W.
Moody James   *Boardman.*
Miller Aaron   *New Middletown.*
Justice James
Stewart Wm.   *Coitsville.*
Schwacher Geo.   *North Jackson.*
Johnston Samuel
Hartley J. B.   *Poland.*
Heck Geo.   *Green Village.*
Shull Christian
Olinker S.   *North Lima.*
Showecker C.   *New Springfield.*

Marion County.

Kraner A. & Co.   *Marion.*
Suckle E.
Henderson Thos.

Medina County.

Rice J. A.	*Sharon Centre.*
Rice J. H.	
Wood J.	*Liverpool.*
Trager & Co.	
McMullen Daniel	*River Styx.*
Beck A. C.	*Wadsworth.*
Horner John	*Lodi.*
Griffin Willis	
Welling Wm. T.	*Medina.*

Meigs County.

Miles J. J.	*Pomeroy.*
McQuigg John	

Mercer County.

Huffman D.	*Fort Recovery.*

Miami County.

Geobhardt John	*Fletcher.*
Fergus J.	*West Charleston.*
Jones Wm.	*Piqua.*
Worley Joshua	
Elliott F.	*Troy.*
Huffman Enoch	*West Milton.*
Teague John	

Monroe County.

Lobenstein Charles	*Sunfish.*
Gratigny C. C.	*Bealsville.*
Hutchison A. C.	
Hawkins & Magill	*Stafford.*
Steele W. & Co.	
Black Conrad	*Baresville.*
Bauer J. C.	
Weltschey Henry	
Gitchel Jeremiah	*Grayeville.*

Montgomery County.

Darrow W. S., Fifth	*Dayton.*
Haas & Coughey, Spratt	
Huffman Levi	*Farmersville.*
Thuber J.	*Germantown.*
Staley Israel	*Miamisburgh.*
Urshull L. A.	

Morgan County.

Worrell M.	*Chester Hill.*
Boswell Wm.	
Brownell S. & Co.	*Malta.*
Brownell S. & G.	*McConnelsville.*
Rogers John	*Pennsville.*
Outcalt Hiram	

Morrow County.

Eberhart John	*Underwood's.*
Hatton James	*Shauk's.*
Lamb Philip	
Brown & Gorsuch	*Cardington.*
Roby Thomas	*Lincoln.*
Rambo Edward	*Vail's ⋈ Roads.*
Sears & Struble	*Chesterville.*
Miles J. E.	

Muskingum County.

Caldwell James	*Norwich.*
Clark James	

Nye H.	*Putnam.*
Rutlage George	*Hopewell.*
Voghte F.	*Chandlersville.*
Blue Curren	*Zanesville.*

Noble County

Laurence & Hiddleston	*Berne.*
Steele Henry	*Mt. Ephraim.*
Pool & Baird	*Sarahsvile.*
Eaton Benjamin	*Batesville.*
Frost John	

Perry County.

Fowler D. C.	*New Lexington.*
Grum Jacob	*Rehoboth.*
Webster Joseph	

Pickaway County.

Hayser John	*Circleville.*
Cradlebaugh Jack	*Tarlton.*
Denison James	
Evans Thomas	
Hamilton D. A.	
Mewhorter & Thomas	
Magill James	*Derbyville*
McFarland James	*Williamsport.*
Taylor Edward	*Palestine.*

Pike County.

Havens Chas.	*Gibson.*
Ware David	*Piketon.*

Portage County.

Donalds A. P.	*Randolph.*
Beardsley S. C. & W. E.	*Edinburgh.*
Rockwell D. L.	*Franklin.*
Atchison & Roof	*Suffield.*
Heckman E. & J.	*Brimfield.*
Converse E. S.	*Mantua.*
Kissack John	
Merriman C. & Bro.	*Deerfield.*
Frisby N. T.	*Nelson.*
Baldwin A. T. & Co.	*Palmyra*
Robinson James	*Freedom.*
Heckman F.	*Ravenna.*
Wiggle A. & Co.	
Enos Wm. A.	

Preble County.

Horn Michael	*Lewisburg.*
Hardin —	*Eaton.*
Eidson G.	
Gray Tazewell	*Hamburg.*
Crampton J. C.	*New Paris.*
Graves Milton	
Wright Isaac	*West Elkton.*

Putnam County.

Wilcox R.	*Kalida.*
Williamson Thomas	*Buckeye.*
Curtis E.	*Pendleton.*
Hooper S.	

Richland County.

Kindel Emanuel	*Mansfield.*
Hooker, Horton & Co.	
Ritter Joseph	
Coleman P. T.	*Lexington.*

Whitford Cornelius — *Lexington.*
Graff John — *West Windsor.*
Dean & Bissel — *Belleville.*
Flaherty Nicholas
Rawhouser Peter — *Woodview.*

Ross County.

Lowman Barnett — *Chillicothe.*
Harman O.
Lowe Thos.
Beek Jacob — *Gillespieville.*
Walker Jesse H.
Moms J. H. & Son — *Bourneville.*
May Henry — *Kingston.*
Gay J. H.

Sandusky County.

Gasser John — *Woodville.*
Bartlett Daniel — *Fremont.*
Justice James
Dickinson & Vandivier
Smith Jacob — *Rollersville.*

Scioto County.

Kinney Washington — *Portsmouth.*
Kinney A. & Co.
Bliss T., Sen. — *Wheelersburgh.*
Flanders George W.

Seneca County.

Poorman, Burkholter & Co. — *Tiffin.*
Scott, Denzer & Co.
Rolla —
Wall Michael
Double Christian — *Bascom.*
Bell G. T. — *Green Spring.*
Brestle John
Mansfield O. — *Republic.*
Rhoads F.

Shelby County.

Evans, Wooley & Myers — *Sidney.*
Kennard Garrison — *Hardin.*

Starke County.

Diller M. — *Navarre.*
Gardner J.
Boury Edward — *Waynesburg.*
Young Philip
Lyons Samuel — *West Brookfield.*
Kugal A. — *Minerva.*
Glaser C. F. — *Lake.*
Woods J. B.
Eyster Peter — *East Greenville.*
Eyster Elias
Mohler Jacob — *New Berlin.*
Greenwood J. W. — *Paris.*
Smith Eli — *New Baltimore.*
Snyder Jacob P. — *Hartville.*
Ladue William — *Limaville.*

Summit County.

Potter Theo. — *Middlebury.*
Sill A. H. — *Cuyahoga Falls.*
Spellman H. B. & Co.
Stotler Frederick — *Clinton.*
Seiberling Wm. — *Western Star.*
Ashley A. — *Tallmadge.*

Beltz W. & A. — *Inland.*
Parkin Ira — *Richfield.*
Osborn & Duncan — *Eden.*
Reifschnieder Henry — *Summit.*
Corlett Joseph T. — *Northfield.*
Hollister Enos

Trumbull County.

Dunlap Ames — *Warren.*
Hunt S. L.
Fell Amos D. — *Orangeville.*
Cranden E. — *Girard.*
Richlien William — *Farmington.*
Holmes G. L.
Gaddes James — *Church Hill.*
Chapman A. — *Hartford.*
Wortman Solomon — *Vienna.*

Tuscarawas County.

Tinker J. Y. — *Bolivar.*
Hoopengrue Gabriel — *Winfield.*
Walter Francis — *Gnadenhutten.*
Bimeler J. M., Agent Zoar Community — *Zoar.*
Patterson David — *Ragersville*
Miller Benj. — *Canal Dover.*
Slingluff C. D.
Hildt Francis
Bowers & Bigler — *New Philadelphia.*
Sargeant E.

Union County.

Wiswell Theodore L. — *Raymond's*
Sherwood B. — *Watkins.*
Hill Elijah — *Milford Centre.*
Rose Warren

Vinton County.

Cogswell B. C. — *McArthur.*
Brown L. Green
Bell John — *Allensville.*
Dill Benj. — *Reed's Mills.*
Carr — — *Wilkesville.*
Binkley H. S. — *New Plymouth.*

Warren County.

Clendenen H. — *Twenty Mile Stand.*
Baker M. — *Mason.*
Flick A. J.
Baker D.
Snyder Wm. — *Edwardsville.*
Gibson & White — *Hayesville.*
Henly Moses — *Waynesville.*
Cummins John — *Morrow.*
Kelley James
Spenuell Wm. — *Butlerville.*

Washington County.

Skinner, Rolston & Co. — *Marietta.*
Moss M. C.
Vinton Wm. — *Harmar.*
Goss Daniel — *Centre Belpre.*
Morse M. R. — *Lower Salem.*
Delong Isaac H. — *Regnier's Mills.*
Amoss C. — *Jolly.*
Mills & Deits — *Lowell.*
Kurtz Geo. — *Watertown.*

Wayne County.

Bigler O.	Edinburgh.
Butler A. B. & Co.	Chippewa.
Cromer H.	Fredericksburg.
Robinson A. B.	
Moon Wm. & Josiah	Reedsburg.
Taylor J. & J.	Burbank.
Notestine Henry	
Cramer Michael	West Lebanon.

Williams County.

Booth Eli	West Unity.
Gettle David	Bryan.
Keckler George	
Rowls A. M.	
Carroll John	Montpelier.

Wood County.

Wieland Henry	Perrysburg
North Caleb	Weston.
Miester Chas.	Portage.
Arnold E.	Gilead.

Wyandot County.

Smith Josiah	Upper Sandusky.
Umsted E. & Son	Marseilles.
Long H.	
Mesamore E.	Carey.
Debolt Silas	Mexico.
Pickenbough & Lott	McCutchensville.

Teachers of Music.

Belmont County.

Archer R. W.	Bellair.

Columbiana County.

Frohock —	Wellsville.

Defiance County.

Eldridge Wm.	Defiance.
Taylor R. L.	

Franklin County.

Pinney J. C., High	Columbus.
Saltzer John	

Geauga County.

Collins Norman	Chardon.
Williams F. D.	Parkman.
Clapp Sylvester	Huntsburgh.
Strong A. A.	Thompson.
Utly Alfred	Claridon.

Hamilton County.

Rittor L., 517 Sycamore	Cincinnati.
Thomas E., 74 Centre	
Mein A., 439 Walnut	
Rinbolt F., 38 Jackson	
Nourse S. & A. H. Littlefield, 72 w. 4th	
White S. M., Fifth, bet. Walnut and Vine	
Cook —, Hart's Building, Fourth, bet'n Main and Sycamore	
McKenna J. T., Hart's Building, Fourth, bet. Main and Sycamore	
Wetherbee —, U. S. Hotel, cor. Sixth and Walnut	
Williams Victor, n. e. cor. Elm and 9th	
Lock —, 72 w. Fourth	

Raymond Miss, cor. 3d and Broadway
Cincinnati.
Duval Miss, Centre, bet. Race and Vine
Colliere L. C., 18 Fourth
Sofge H. D., Harrison, s. side
Warner F., Sycamore, bet 4th and 5th
Schuebel L., 336 Vine
Gimble Charles, 460 w. Fifth
Brown Simeon   *Pleasant Ridge.*

Licking County.

Radcliff Mrs.	Newark.

Medina County.

Jones T. W.	Medina.
Milestone Mrs.	

Montgomery County.

Corbet Miss M., Sixth	Dayton.
Schew Jacob	Miamisburg.

Pickaway County.

Ray Miss Elizabeth	Circleville.
Rosenfield —	

Portage County.

Clapp Miss S. M.	Ravenna.
Smead Cora Isabella	
Everett Mrs. E. A.	

Richland County.

Kleeman M.	Mansfield.
Stoumm Mrs.	

Tuscarawas County.

Miller J.	New Philadelphia.

Tea—Importers and Whole-sale Dealers in.

Hamilton County.

Coffin Z. B., 32 w. Fifth	Cincinnati.
Harter L. F., 42 " "	
Moore & Chester, n. e. cor. Walnut & 7th	
Todd J. & Co., 35 Fifth	
Tyson J. W., cor. W. Row and Fifth	
Veasy & Wilder, 32 Main	
White D. A., 34 e. Fifth	
Williamson Samuel, Vine, bet. 4th and 5th	

Telegraph Offices.

Ashtabula County.

Wade's Line, (W. H. H. Potter, Manager,)	Ashland.

Ashland County.

Speed's Line, (N. W. Hoyer, Manager)	Ashtabula.
O'Reilly's Line, (J. M. Allen, Manager)	

Brown County.

New Orleans and Ohio Co., (L. Delleway Manager)	Higginsport

Butler County.

O'Reilly's Line, (J. F. Lawder, Manager	Hamilton
Wade's do. do. do.	

Champaign County.

National Line, (Jas. McCord, Manager)
Urbana.

Clark County.

National Line, (J. B. Miller, Manager)
Springfield.

Clermont County.

New Orleans and Ohio, (S. Reakirt, Manager)
New Richmond.

Clinton County.

Wade's Line, (W. B. Fisher, Manager)
Wilmington.

Columbiana County.

National Line, (— McIntosh, Manager)
Wellsville.
do.   do. (Andrew Huston, Manager)
New Lisbon.

Cuyahoga County.

Speed's Line   *Cleveland.*
Erie and Michigan Co., Ramson's Building, (J. M. Tubbs, Manager)
Cleveland, Warren and Pittsburgh, Ramson's Building, (J. M. Tubbs, Manager)
Cleveland, Wheeling and Zanesville, Ramson's Building, (J. M. Tubbs, Manager)
Wade's Line
Cleveland, Columbus and Cincinnati, Am. Hotel Buildings, (J. Dunham, Manager)
National Line
Lake Erie Co., Ramson's Buildings, (H. S. Bishop, Manager)
House's Line
Printing Telegraph, over Com. Bank, (E. W. Culgan, Manager)

Delaware County.

Wade's Line, (Wm. W. Fay, Manager)
Delaware.

Erie County.

National Line, (A. C. Frey, Manager)
Sandusky City.
Erie and Michigan Line, (J. Downs, Manager)
Wade's Line, (J. L. Downs, Manager)
do.   do. (Geo. Sprague do.) *Huron.*

Fayette County.

National Line, (A. Battelle, Manager)
Washington.
Wade's Line, (N. Blodgette, Manager)

Franklin County.

Wade's Line, (W. H. S. Hyde, Manager,) office High st.   *Columbus.*
House's Line, (C. K. Jones, Manager) office State st.
National Line, (Thos. S. Gates, Manager) cor. High and State sts.

Greene County.

Wade's Line, (J. M. Worden, Manager,)
Xenia.
National Line, (T. L. Tiffany, Manager)

Hamilton County.

Wade's Line, (Charles Davenport, Manager) 5 e. Third   *Cincinnati.*
National Line, (C. S. Holmes, Manager) 7 e. Third
House's Line, (John W. Hurn, Manager) 9 e. Third

Hardin County.

——, (J. S. Root, Manager)   *Kenton.*

Huron County.

Wade's Line, (J. M. Adams, Manager)
Monroeville.

Jefferson County.

National Line, (G. Dean, Manager)
Steubenville.

Knox County.

Wade Line, (John W. White, Manager)
Mt. Vernon.

Licking County.

Wade's Line, (N. Fleming, Manager)
Newark.
do.   do.   (A. P. Prichard, do.)
Granville.
do.   do.   (D. D. Wilson do.) *Hebron.*

Logan County.

O'Reilly's Line, (W. H. Miller, Manager)
Bellefontaine.

Lorain County.

Wade's Line, (J. A. Perkins, Manager)
Wellington.

Madison County.

Wade's Line, (C. P. Matthews, Manager)
London.

Medina County.

Wade's Line, (G. B. Hamilton, Manager)
Medina.

Meigs County.

——, (A. B. Conant, Manager) *Pomeroy.*

Miami County.

O'Reilly's Line, (J. C. Culbertson, Manager)   *Troy.*

Montgomery County.

National Line, (J. H. Keirsted, Manager) Main   *Dayton.*
House's Line, (Dennis Gregg, Manager)
Wade's do.   (J. H. Keirsted   do.)

Morrow County.

Wade's Line, (A. J. Smith, Manager)
Mt. Gilead.
do.   do.   (N. B. Hull, Manager)
Cardington.

Muskingum County.

Wade's Line, (S. H. Kauffman, Manager)
Zanesville.
National Line, (D. S. Brooks, Manager)

Pickaway County.

—— Line, (E. G. Sprague, Manager,) *Circleville.*

Portage County.

——, (Benjamin Little, Manager,) *Ravenna.*

——, (J. W. Cone, Manager,) *Franklin.*

Richland County.

Wade Line, (J. T. Beer, Manager,) *Mansfield.*

Wade Line, (B. F. Abbott, Manager,) *Shelby.*

Wade Line, (Light & Hoffman, Managers,) *Plymouth.*

Ross County.

——, W. D. Wessen, Manager,) *Chillicothe.*

Scioto County.

Morse Line, (V. H. Parker, Manager,) *Portsmouth.*

Scioto Valley Line, (V. H. Parker, Man'r.)

Seneca County.

—— Line, (W. L. Hamilton, Manager,) *Republic.*

Summit County.

Speed's Line, (F. S. Heath, Manager,) *Akron.*

O'Reilly's, (O. S. Bishop, Manager,)

Warren County.

National Line, (J. E. Hunt, Manager,) *Morrow.*

Wade Line, (M. Patton, Manager,) *Lebanon.*

Wayne County.

Wade Line, (Thos. T. Eckert, Manager,) *Wooster.*

Thrashing Machine Manufacturers.

Belmont County.

Taylor & Embree   *Colerain.*
Bales & Bartholomew   *Uniontown.*

Brown County.

McClure William   *Ripley.*

Clark County.

Pitts J. A.   *Springfield.*

Coshocton County.

Thompson, Roney & Co.   *West Bedford.*
Shields John

Franklin County.

Deming —, Broadway,   *Columbus.*

Geauga County.

Merrill Henry   *Munson.*

Harrison County.

Hebuling George   *Short Creek.*
Oogler & Lamb
Larkin T. T.   *Harrisville.*

Knox County.

Buckingham O. P. & Co.   *Mount Vernon.*
Furlong M. C.

Medina County.

Packer K.   *Wadsworth.*

Miami County.

Moffet J. R.   *Piqua.*

Monroe County.

Litten & Horn   *Sunfish.*

Montgomery County.

Prets A. & Co., Second,   *Dayton.*

Morgan County.

Patterson A. H.   *Meigs Creek.*

Richland County.

Moody J. W.   *Belleville.*

Ross County.

Welsh Wm.   *Chillicothe.*

Seneca County.

Stewart Wm. H.   *Tiffin.*

Starke County.

Russell C. M. & Co.   *Massillon.*
Hart & Brown
Partridge H. & R.

Warren County.

Crispen & Kelley   *Waynesville.*

Wayne County.

McDonald, Laughlin & Co.   *Wooster.*

Tin, Copper and Sheet-Iron Workers.

Adams County.

Shriver J. M & W. A.   *Manchester.*
Sparks A. & J. O.   *Scott.*
Boyle Daniel   *West Union.*

Ashland County.

Hohenshill S.   *Roweburg.*
Onstott A.
Schell W. P.   *Hayesville.*
Evers William   *Savannah.*
Zimmerman John   *Ashland.*
Dunham Thomas   *Jeromeville.*
Mayers Henry
Leopold G. G.   *Loudonville.*
Prutsman Daniel

Ashtabula County.

Norris James   *Jefferson.*
Hodge V. J. C.
Roe Henry A.   *Andover.*
Hall L.   *Ashtabula.*
Crosby J. B.

Belmont County.

Hinds Joseph	*Flushing.*
Harris Joseph	*St. Clairsville.*
Yates R. A.	*Morristown.*

Butler County.

Furguson & Matson	*Oxford.*
Enyart T. K.	*Hamilton.*
Owens, Ebert & Dyer	
Menche B.	
Mathias J.	*Rossville.*
Mars S.	
Webster Wm.	*Middletown.*
Stilweg John	*Trenton.*

Brown County.

Blair E. F.	*Georgetown.*
Porter J. H.	
Blair & Porter	
Shreeve C.	*Russellville.*

Carroll County.

Atkinson Thomas H.	*Carrollton.*

Champaign County.

Hare N. H.	*Westville.*
Helmick & Brother	*Urbana.*
Cavalier & Evans	
French S. & Co.	
Winder John	*North Lewisburg.*

Clark County.

Diehl & Baker	*Springfield.*
Caviller A.	
Moore William	
Vance David	*South Charleston.*
Warrington Francis	
Harr Daniel	*New Carlisle.*
Matthews J. W.	

Clermont County.

Hobson John	*New Richmond.*
Zimmerman E.	*Williamsburg.*
Knowly A. L.	*Felicity.*
Shriver A. C.	
Pigman A. S.	*Neville.*
Fairfield Lorenzo D.	*Amelia.*

Clinton County.

Bundle Jacob	*Wilmington.*
Hunt P. H.	*Martinsville.*

Columbiana County.

Transel G. W.	*Wellsville.*
Lider & Morrison	
Baker Jacob	*East Palestine.*
Koll Daniel	*Salem.*
Macalla John	
Miller Julius	*East Liverpool.*
Young W. L.	*East Fairfield.*
Baxter Thomas	*Hanoverton.*

Coshocton County.

Jones E. L.	*Coshocton.*
Bowers Charles & Co.	

Crawford County.

Picking D.	*Bucyrus.*
Picking J.	
Wagoner John	

Cuyahoga County.

Brockett J. W.	*Bedford.*
Stedman L. T.	*Collamer.*
Douglass N.	*Berea.*
Douglass Chas.	
Douglass F.	
Lewis Samuel C., 5 Hewitt's Block,	*Cleveland.*
Low J. J., 132 Superior	
Marvin Wm. L., 60 do.	
Tindall & Ernest, 48 Bank	
Whitaker S., 29 Superior	
Wood & Leland, 28 do.	
Clapt C. R., 1 Exchange Building	
Parish & Knight, 25 Superior	
Metcalf Horace, 120 do.	
Smith, Murray & Co., 36 Bank	
Wansor Jacob, 17 Superior Lane	
McMillan John, 17 Seneca	
Born Charles, 14 Water	
White D. P.	*Ohio City.*
Ross J.	

Darke County.

Beedle J. N.	*Greenville.*
Danford Wm.	

Delaware County.

Williams & Latimer N. & J. F.	*Delaware.*
Evans Thomas	
Bartlett S. C.	*Galena.*
Thrall W.	
Cables G. W.	

Erie County.

Higgins D.	*Huron.*
Fuller T. S.	*Birmingham.*
Woolworth & Gale	*Sandusky City.*
Dewey W.	
Flood Joseph	

Fairfield County.

Green J. A.	*Lancaster.*
Reery & Jenkins	
McClelland J.	
White A.	
Sager Marcus S.	*Clear Creek.*
Willis A.	*Lithopolis.*

Franklin County.

Armstrong, Gorton & Co., High	*Columbus.*
Case O.	
Heyl J. K.	
Mason H.	
Rost Jacob	
St. Clair & Sheds	
Kidd John	*Groveport.*
Bliss M. W.	*Worthington.*
Overholser William	*Canal Winchester.*
Eberly H. T.	*Dublin.*

Gallia County.

Mathers F. & Co.	*Gallipolis.*
McIntyre Alex.	
Bertha Lewis	

Geauga County.

Marsh & Parks	*Chardon.*
Bruce J. F.	

Greene County.

Horn D. L.
Horn J. R.   *Xenia.*
Loy M. B.   *Cedarville.*

Guernsey County.

Tates Thomas   *Cambridge.*
McFarren John
Tucker & Crozier   *Cumberland.*
Rabe William   *Washington.*
Rose & Jorden   *Senecaville.*

Hamilton County.

Brinkman J. C., 564 Elm   *Cincinnati.*
Beekman H., 107 Hamilton Road
Ball G. W., 36 Main
Baxter W. D., 38 "
Burton S H. & Co., 13 & 15 w. Columbia
Britt Nelson A., 40 Public Landing
Beekman A., 566 Vine
Brunne Joseph, 495 Main
Connelly P., 79 Front
Crumpton E., 308 Fifth
Cook C., 365 W. Row
Christopher & Beall, 382 Main
Campbell, Ellison & Co., 21 Columbia
Clements J., 132   do.
Dawson B., 262 Sixth
Dieckemann J., 111 Court
Guine C. F., Ninth, near Elm
Horrocks J. R., 6 Main
Horrocks John & Co., 9 Water
Hoffner Jacob, 28 Lower Market
Lohn J., 533 w. Fifth
Lape, Hopple & Fleming, 9 Water
Lawson Fenton, 178 Main
Lotz A., 217 Walnut
Maear Jacob, 212 Clinton
Maish A., 213 Sixth
Mackelfresh O. W., 302 Fifth
Ornsalt A., 372 Broadway
Peferley J., 29 Ham. Road
Parry & Reckley, 31 Vine
Renor W. & R. P. & Co., 25 and 27 Main
Richard R., 99 Fifth
Rosenbaum & Co., 453 Vine
Smith F., 433 W. Row
Sellew & Co., Main, bet. 5th and 6th
Stephenson Wm. & Son, 164 Main
Stall & McMeekin, 40 Columbia
Schneider Heman, 33 and 59 Court
Shires —, 254 w. 5th. & 36 e. Fourth.
Thomas David G., 7 e. Front
Vance E., 16 Lower Market
Wozencraft J. J., 208 Court
Young Albert K., 77 Front
Zeller M., 529 Vine
Carver Charles   *Cheviot.*
Durham Wm.   *Mt. Healthy.*
Jackson J. & E.   *Harrison.*
McCracken George

Hardin County.

Shectala J. A.   *Kenton.*
Holmes George
Thomas A.

Harrison County.

Cady James   *Cadiz.*
Hoti Aaron
Simonton Findley   *Derrsville.*

Henry County.

McCartney John   *Napolean.*

Highland County.

Young G. W.   *Greenfield.*
Irwin Wm. T.
Couch D. M.   *Sugartree Ridge.*
Mayfield & Luce   *Hillsboro'.*
Shriver E. W.
Kibler Joseph

Hocking County.

Armstrong William   *Logan.*
Baker T. E.

Holmes County.

Hensler G.   *Winesburg.*
Buzzard M.   *Walnut Creek.*

Huron County.

Wakefield N. K.   *Clarksfield.*
Johnson & Co.   *Bellevue.*
Facey Wm. B.
Williams B. H.   *Fitchville.*
Blesh Henry   *North Fairfield.*
Roberts Benj.
Webster & Co.   *Steuben.*

Jefferson County.

Wilson Samuel   *Steubenville.*

Knox County.

Cooper John C. & Co.   *Mount Vernon.*
Evans Job
Durbin Thos.
Huntsberry James & Son
Brentlinger William   *Fredericktown.*
Brentlinger D. F.
Tuttle S. S.

Lake County.

Hayden B. G.   *Madison.*

Lawrence County.

Duke & Kingsbury   *Ironton.*

Licking County.

Rose J. W.   *Brownsville.*
Jones Lewis   *Granville.*
Eddy T. R.   *Newark.*
Schmucker Isaac
Beam H. B. & J.   *Croton.*

Logan County.

Vial James M.   *Huntsville.*
Moore F. O.   *Bellefontaine.*
Nelson & Robinson
Porter Robert B.   *Zanesfield.*

Lorain County.

Lang O. R.   *Huntington.*
Smith & Harmon   *La Grange.*
Weed & Beckwith   *Oberlin.*
Wasson James   *Elyria.*
Crane F.

Lucas County.

Dobson George W.	*Maumee City.*
Durell William	*Toledo.*
Whitney James M.	
Whitaker S. H.	

Madison County.

Dungan & Watson	*London.*

Mahoning County.

French Chas.	*Canfield.*
Lanteuschlager J.	*Petersburgh.*
Hollingsworth Edward	*Youngstown.*
Hollingsworth J. F.	
Holkom J. R. & Son	
Johnson M. C.	
Rowe Joshua	*North Lima.*
Hubbard Henry	*Poland.*
Campbell J. W.	

Marion County.

Gurley John	*Marion.*
Cumming J. B.	

Medina County.

Hickox J. S.	*Sharon Centre*
Borgy & Cassel	*River Styx.*
Kauke & Plow	*Wadsworth.*
Taylor John	*Lodi.*
Warren J.	
Hanville B. F.	*Medina.*
Bostwick C. B.	
Beckwith J. B.	

Meigs County.

Prall Wm J.	*Pomeroy.*
Lowery John M.	

Miami County.

Upton M. B. & Co.	*Piqua.*
Geyer F.	
Allen J.	
Little D. L.	
Cottingham Wm.	*Troy.*
McCullough J.	
Polly A. J.	*West Milton.*
Basson D. R.	*Hyattsville.*

Monroe County.

Jordan William W.	*Woodsfield.*
Jordan John	
Hogan James M.	*Sunfish.*
Atkinson Elijah	

Montgomery County.

Byerly J. K.	*Liberty.*
Boyer & Murphy, Second,	*Dayton.*
Boyer F., Third	
Kelly James, do.	
Roades J. C., Wagon	
Shank W. H., Third	
Wiley Orrin, First	
Yost H., Second	
Emerick Aaron	*Miamisburgh.*
Shock Jacob	
Iler J.	*Germantown.*
Oblinger G.	
Shouk George.	

Morgan County.

Meller & Janeway	*Malta.*
Sill Wm.	*McConnelsville.*
Morris Robert	

Morrow County.

Hall William	*Mt Gilead.*
Kinsell D. B. & D. C.	*Chesterville.*

Muskingum County.

Shinnick W. M.	*Zanesville.*
Dutly W.	
Greenland J. T.	
Langton W. L. & J. T.	
Hurst P.	*Dresden.*
Silkey J. P.	

Perry County.

Smith T. W.	*New Lexington.*
Beckworth Joel K.	*Somerset.*
Mains Frederick	
McMan Johnson	

Pickaway County.

Hirt L.	*Circleville.*
Kinnear Delamar	
Richardson & Trone	

Pike County.

Smith Charles	*Piketon*

Preble County.

Shank John	*West Alexandria.*
McClure Wm. H.	*Lewisburg.*
Fornshell Benj.	*Camden.*
McCabe Walter P.	*Eaton.*
Ecker George	
Hunsacker George	*Fairhaven.*
Underwood J. C.	*New Paris.*

Putnam County.

Stechulte Henry	*Buckeye.*

Richland County.

Roberts Thos.	*Shelby.*
Leyman H.	
Ebinather John	*Lexington.*
Pennel James	
Blymyer B. & Son	*Mansfield.*
Buttery/J. & Co.	
Zimmerman Levi	
Howard G. C.	*Belleville.*
Markey & Walker	
Buzzard Mathias	*Adario.*

Ross County.

Billerson & Sholderer	*Chillicothe.*
Markley Joseph	
McAon James F.	
Gill & Williams	
How W. G.	

Sandusky County.

McLellen & McGee	*Fremont.*
Canfield & Mitchell	

Scioto County.

Grimes James	*Portsmouth.*
Smith & Holmes	

Seneca County.

Harford James D.   *Attica.*
Searles W. D.   *Tiffin.*
Yerk Chas M.
Watrous J. A.   *Green Spring.*
Hamilton & McArdle   *Republic.*

Shelby County.

Bush M.   *Sidney.*
Servis W.

Starke County.

Gaver John   *Minerva.*
Kitsmiller & Co.
Reese Jefferson   *Waynesburg.*
Bauman G.   *Louisville.*
Buchins H.   *Canton.*
Busher J. G.
Harman D. H.
Little A.
Stinchcomb W.
Mohler Jacob   *New Berlin.*
Doxee J. N.   *Massillon.*
Partridge H. & R.
Buckins V. S.
Russell C. M. & Co.
Buckins William   *Canal Dover.*

Summit County.

Weaver Samuel   *Clinton.*
Miller August   *Inland.*
Gilbert Chancey   *Richland.*

Trumbull County.

Jameson & Fifth   *Warren.*
Morley T. H. & Co.
Burbank R. A.   *Newton Falls.*
Ensign & Co.

Tuscarawas County.

Snyder J. S. & Co.   *Ragersville.*
Lane O.   *New Philadelphia.*
Batzly D.
Williams F. P.
Luckenback John E.   *Canal Dover.*
Rex John
Cummias Samuel
Kunkler A. P
Myers Jonathan   *Tuscarawas.*

Union County.

Nettleton —   *Maysville.*
Tomelson John
Thompson Samuel   *Milford Centre.*
Skeels Simeon   *Pharisburg*

Van Wert County.

McKibbin D. D.   *Van Wert.*
Hoover C. H. & Co.   *Delphos.*

Vinton County.

Baird W. H.   *McArthur.*

Warren County.

Duvall J. M.   *Mason.*
Groepper M.   *Morrow.*
Gibson Elias

Esler Jacob   *Butlerville.*
Butler & Meeker   *Franklin.*
Crispen & Kelley   *Waynesville.*

Washington County.

Bacon Isaac   *Marietta.*
Lammot L. A.
Rein A. & Co.
Basworth, Wells & Co.
Wheeler W. V. Z.   *Beverly.*

Wayne County.

Wilson A.   *Dalton.*
Howard Harvey   *Wooster.*
McClure C. & J.
Jacoby Josiah   *Chippewa.*
Miller John P.   *Reedsburg.*
Jason Robert   *Burbank.*
Smith, Simon & Co.   *Marshallville.*

Williams County.

Brainer C.   *Bryan.*
Kent S. M. & S. E.
Garver John & James   *Williams Centre.*
Sauger H. P.   *West Unity.*

Wood County.

Brown & Hunt   *Perrysburg.*
Oribel Grorge   *Gilead.*

Wyandot County.

Anderson & McGill   *Upper Sandusky.*
Snyder D.

Tobacco Dealers.

Brown County.

French & Lion   *Higginsport.*
Lewis & Jennings
Deleway Levi

Clermont County.

Lewis & Simms   *Williamsburg.*
Parker Joseph L.   *Neville.*
Sullivan John T. & Co.   *Rural.*

Fairfield County.

Ijams William   *West Rushville.*
Shaw John
Vansant John W.

Franklin County.

Baldwin L., High   *Columbus.*

Hamilton County.

Kennett & Dudley, 14 Public Landing
                                Cincinnati.
Veasy & Wilder, 32 Main
Hawthorn & Dunn, 50 Pearl
Bodman Chas., 67 Walnut
Skinner & Franklin, 9 w. Front
Rawson, Wilby & Co., 8 "   "
Bates Richard, 43 Walnut
Love Rufus K., cor. Pearl and Race
Porter Thos. & Sons, 66 Walnut

Noble County.

Cooper Charles   *Mt. Ephraim.*
Hance James J.

Morris Isaac Q.   *Mt. Ephraim.*
Ulrich Harmer
Dilley J.   *Sarahsville.*
Fowler J.
Swain H.
Young Wm.
Young T.

Tobacconists.
Ashland County.
Faulk H.   *Jeromeville.*
Hoffman J.

Ashtabula County.
Keys H. P.   *Conneaut*
Cleveland W.
Masters W. G.
Barrett Chas.

Athens County.
Potter Wm.   *Athens.*

Belmont County.
Glover Josiah   *Demos.*
Glover John

Champaign County.
Zink T. F.   *Mechanicsburg.*
Russer Wm. F.   *Urbana.*

Cuyahoga County.
Dietz George, 9 Water   *Cleveland.*
Kepler Frederick A., 20 Superior
Richardson Mark, 10 Miller's Block
Schriber James, Canal
Walter Alexander, 33 Superior
Downing W. W., 19 Seneca.

Fairfield County.
Klatz J. C.   *Lancaster.*
Beery D.   *Sugar Grove.*
Coleus J. A.

Greene County.
Herrit A.   *Xenia.*

Hamilton County.
Aruot B., 25 Ham. Road   *Cincinnati.*
Barnes G. W. 67 Sycamore
Bodman F., 275 Main
Candolpho —, 209 Elm
Carpenter & Ford, 14 Front
Dieckman H., Hughes, near Liberty
Holzman M., 45 Ham. Road
Kirghna John, 88 Court
Knobel C. F. W., 189 Broadway
Klocke Lewis, 427 Main
Koeb B., 76 Buckeye
Lang Louis, 345 Walnut
Marthens & Ordemann, 293 Main
Meyer O. F. & Bro., 70 Court
Miller B., 117 Ham. Road
Massa N., n. e. cor. Race and 8th
Roberts Joseph L., 398 Elm
Schneider J. P., 87 Court
Stomberg P., 187 Walnut
Schechlin G., 14 Ham. Road
Williams Simeon B., 88, 90 & 92 Pearl
Weighel J., 210 and 212 Elm

Lucas County.
Brooks S.   *Toledo.*
Engefer A.
Hide Henry
Quinche O. S.
Hall & Co.   *Waterville.*

Mahoning County.
Cramer A.   *East Lewistown.*

Marion County.
Mohr David   *Cochranton.*

Monroe County.
Gillespie & Mitchell   *Laing's.*
Valentine Nath. & Co.   *Masterton.*
Sanford Samuel   *Sunfish.*

Montgomery County.
Munday & Stomsifer, Jefferson,   *Dayton.*
Munday & Long,   do.
Springer P., Third
Warren H. L., Main

Morgan County.
Cochran H. M. & Co.   *McConnelsville.*

Morrow County.
Page Marcus   *Nimmon's Cross Roads.*

Muskingum County.
Shaw, Hubbell & Co.   *Zanesville.*
Robinson Samuel

Summit County.
McNaughton Benj.   *Akron.*

Tuscarawas County.
Miller F. C.   *New Philadelphia.*
Rickert William

Washington County.
Rossell John   *Bartlett.*
Koons —   *Lowell.*

Toy Manufacturers.
Hamilton County.
Maginnia J., 297 w. Sixth,   *Cincinnati.*
Weisman Wm., 214 w. Fifth

Trunk Manufacturers—
(Wholesale).
Cuyahoga County.
Cleugh R., 100½ Superior,   *Cleveland.*

Franklin County.
Hughes J. R., High,   *Columbus.*

Hamilton County.
Parvin & Johnson, 31 Broadway.   *Cin'i.*
Hise & Williams, 25   do.
Shohl J. W. & Bro., 57 n. w. cor. Walnut and Columbia
Vongenechten M., 55 Broadway, between Columbia and Lower Market
Vandergriff J. A. & W. J., 247 Bacon's Building w. s. Walnut
Grumbine J., Walnut, bet. Fifth & Sixth

Kallmeyer F., 508 Main   *Cincinnati.*
Levoy Michael, 205 Sixth

Truss-Hoop Manufacturers.

Clermont County.

Carr A. & Co.   *West Woodville.*

Turners—(Wood).

Ashland County.

Stem David   *Savannah.*

Brown County.

Day G. W.   *Puebla.*
Kinnett Thos.
Watters James
Holeman James   *De La Palma.*
Holeman Joseph
Watson C.
Weeks Wm.
Moorhead Wm.
Sly Henry   *Union Plane.*
Sly Ambrose
Moore Robert
Malott Theodore

Clermont County.

Ward & Ramsay   *Loveland.*
Hull John K.   *West Woodville.*
Miller John   *Newtonsville.*
Voudegriff T. H.
Clemens John
Wood Stephen

Clinton County.

Harrison Peter   *New Burlington.*

Cuyahoga County.

Bullard O. & Son   *Chagrin Falls.*

Hamilton County.

Stone Henry, Congress bet. Lawrence and Stone,   *Cincinnati.*
Adluta Martin, 473 Walnut
Cameron W. M. & E. D., corner John and Laurel
Fritz Wm., n. w. cor. Western Row and Laurel
Thremdrechsler F., 531 Walnut
Adams Wm., Western Row, bet. Ninth and William
Clark Benjamin, 148 w. Sixth
Stark M., 103 Hamilton Road
Seyppel Ferdinand, 427 Vine
Brandt Charles, Orchard bet. Main and Sycamore
Steigerwaldt Michael, 128 Columbia
Meeks J.   *Walnut Hills.*
Bookwalter Jessie   *Harrison.*
Perry Jackson
Prois L.
Wood Plemon
Ludlum A.   *Carthage.*

Hardin County.

Hoon A. S.   *Kenton.*

Jefferson County.

Priest F. A.   *Steubenville.*

Miami County.

Muchmore R.   *Piqua.*
Denmon & Linon
Hinch & Co.

Montgomery County.

Blanchard & Brown, Canal   *Dayton.*
Colins G., Basin
Mercer R., do.
Shoup Henry   *Miamisburgh.*
Tickle Warner

Morrow County.

Emery S. L.   *Lincoln.*

Preble County.

Gardiner B. F.   *Camden.*
Shaffer J. M.

Richland County.

Lafevre C. A.   *Belleville.*

Seneca County.

Burkie William   *Tiffin.*
Prindle Wm. D.   *Green Spring.*
Haze A. D.
Chamberlin H.   *Republic.*
Kessler George E.

Starke County.

Doering John C.   *Marlboro'.*

Type Founders.

Hamilton County.

Cincinnati Type Foundery, cor. Vine and Center,   *Cincinnati.*
Guilford & Jones, 41 e. Second

Type (Wooden) Manufactu'rs.

Morrow County.

McCreary John   *Chesterville.*

Wayne County.

Doy S. D. & W. T.   *Fredericksburg.*

Umbrella and Parasol Manufacturers.

Cuyahoga County.

McMahon John S., 3 Ontario,   *Cleveland.*

Franklin County.

Smetherst J., High,   *Columbus.*

Hamilton County.

Sleeper Israel & Brother, 167 Main,   *Cincinnati*
Rosental H., 516   do.
Kratz Conrad, 184 Walnut
Kreke M., 207 Vine
Fox Jacob, 9 Western Row
Richard F. R., 14 e. Canal
Mason E. H., 52 w. Fifth

Miami County.

Heifer C.   *Piqua.*

Montgomery County.

Hess Francis, Third,   *Dayton.*

Undertakers.

Clermont County.

Robinson John M.   *Amelia.*

Columbiana County.

Eells Erastus   *New Lisbon.*

Crawford County.

Fulton A.   *Bucyrus*
Lightner D. R.

Cuyahoga County.

Ames John   *Coe Ridge.*
Bauder Levi, 70 Public Square, *Clevel'd.*
Howland J., 19 St. Clair
Strong Homer, 15 Pearl.   *Ohio City.*

Defiance County.

Price Edward   *Defiance.*

Franklin County.

Graver E., High,   *Columbus.*
Williams G. W., High

Hamilton County.

Jenkins John, 138 Sycamore, *Cincinnati.*
Cobb Samuel, 143   do.
Hales Charles, Sixth, bet. Main and Syc.
Uphof Geo. H., 20 Seventh
McGivern David, 128 Water
Sullavan P., 144 w. Third.
Loichenwageu H., 145 Everett
Luhm J. H., cor. Linn and Maple
Pendery Goodloe, n. e. cor. 9th & Main
Epply & Patterson, s. w. cor. Plum & 7th
Dickman Stiens, 627 Race
Tracy M., Catherine, bet. Fulton & John
Rodefer C., 529 Western Row
Myer B. H., 54 w. Twelfth
Soards J. & Son, Sixth w. of Elm
Megrue & Lyon, cor. Plum & Longworth
Hust H. & Co., 18 Locust
Bowen P. M.   *Montgomery.*
Slete & Bonham   *Harrison.*

Jefferson County.

Ammon Daniel   *Steubenville.*
Walker James
Walker R.
Donaldson Alex.
Siddleton H.   *Mt. Pleasant.*
Gill John
McMasters Wm. F.

Medina County.

Davis A.   *Medina.*
Little & Asire

Mercer County.

Hight & Kirkpatrick   *Celina.*

Montgomery County.

Belsuzreser F., Second,   *Dayton.*
Karr Jacob   *West Baltimore.*

26

Scioto County.

Alexander & Co.   *Portsmouth.*

Seneca County.

Chamberlin H.   *Republic.*

Starke County.

Hahn Samuel   *New Franklin.*
Russell C. M. & Co.   *Massillon.*

Upholsterers.

Cuyahoga County.

Bauder Levi, 70 Public Square *Cleveland.*
Berry Geo. W., 27 Superior Lane
De Mortimer E., 59 Water
Wisdom, Russell & Co., 3 Superior
Hart Wm., 59 Water

Erie County.

McNeil A.   *Sandusky City.*
Thorpe, Norcross & Thorpe
Daymond A. J. & Co.
Steitz Jacob

Franklin County.

Baker N. S., Broadway   *Columbus.*
Aston Isaac C. & Co., High

Hamilton County.

Ellis Robert & Co., 133 Sycamore *Cin'ti.*
Orange B.,   87   do.
Hilger F. R.   78   do.
Spring John, Front, bet. Sycamore and
  Broadway
Tompkins, Dayton & Co., 23 & 25 e. 3d
Hall & Prather, Third, bet. Sycamore and
  Broadway
Dickinson J. A. & W. S., 45 Third, bet.
  Sycamore and Broadway
Suydam —, Front, e. of Broadway
Knight B., 23 Front
Jackson F. B. C , Vine, bet. 5th and 6th
Coates J. F., 148 w. Eighth
Barnes S., n. e. cor. Walnut and Court
Hoffman J., 204 Elm
Smith D. W. C., W. Row, below 7th
Whittaker W. H., Fourth, bet. Sycamore
  and Broadway

Holmes County.

Smith O.   *Winesburg.*

Montgomery County.

Corbett Thomas, Sixth   *Dayton.*

Sandusky County.

King John   *Greensburg & Roads.*

Variety Stores.

Clark County.

Mulholland M. S.   *Springfield.*
Fisher & Chausin

Columbiana County

Albert E. P.   *Wellsville*
Riggs T. W.
Brook Samuel   *Salem.*

Cuyahoga County.

Rettberg, Doeltz & Hausman, 166 Superior
              Cleveland.

Erie County.

Engels Jacob   *Sandusky City.*
Bourne & Torrey

Hamilton County.

Berry & Berry, 192 Main st.   *Cincinnati.*
Atkins T.,   102 Fifth
Webb J. & Son, 184   "
Menken S.,   62 "
Webb J. & J.   166 ".
Drowy F., 116 Clinton
Douglass R. N., 64 Front
Vankeuin E., 130 Clinton
Miller R., 49 Wade
Cosgrave J., 242 w. Sixth
McClain P., n. w. cor. Cutter and 7th
Turner S., 356 w. Sixth
Mapes Mrs. E., 273 W. Row
Higgins John   *Cleves.*

Lawrence County.

Nixon D.   *Ironton.*

Montgomery County.

Omer N., Second   *Dayton.*
Swartze A. J. B.   *Germantown.*

Muskingum County.

Merrick, Shaw & Co.   *Zanesville.*
Gingaley & Johnston

Summit County.

Bitman Wm.   *Akron.*
Weibezhan & Brothers

Varnish Manufacturers.
Hamilton County.

Queen City Varnish Company, Walnut,
   bet. Front and Columbia *Cincinnati.*
Price & Pfaff, 95 Walnut
Batchelor S. C., 42 Second
Price H., W. Row

Veneering Mills.
Montgomery County.

Brown J., Lower Hydraulic   *Dayton.*

Venetian Blind Manufactu'rs.
Hamilton County.

Chivvis D. S., 152 w. Third *Cincinnati.*
Cook H. M. & Co., Fourth, near Park
De Graw J., Fourth, bet. Park & Smith
Glasgow Hugh, 169 Vine
Hinkle & Guild, Front, opp. Gas Works
Loring A. T., 148 w. Third
Ludlow W. H., Miller, bet. Main & Waln't
McCord James, 234 Vine
Read Henry, 147 Sycamore
Richards T. J., 82 w. Sixth
Shafer Anthony, 107 Sycamore
Smith & Williamson, cor. 3d and John
Thummel & Veith, Fifth, bet. Sycamore
   and Broadway
Warrington George 3d, bet. Smith & Park

Ludlow G. W.   *Pendleton.*
Clark A.   *Fulton.*
Ross Wm. F.   *Harrison.*

Veterinary Surgeons.
Belmont County.

Neiswanger Isaac   *St. Clairsville.*

Columbiana County.

Bandee A. L.   *North Georgetown.*
Monutz Geo. H.

Cuyahoga County.

Purdy James, Seneca   *Cleveland.*

Greene County.

Allen Davisson   *Clifton.*

Hamilton County.

Collins C. W., 254 Walnut, *Cincinnati.*
Bishop T. B., Race bet. Sixth and Seventh
Kuhlman G., Sycamore bet. 3d and 4th
Gerhard —, Hamilton Road opposite Elm
Sheahon D., Seventh bet. Western Row
   and Plum

Harrison County.

Pitts John, jun.   *Deersville.*

Jefferson County.

Hunter Samuel D.   *Steubenville.*

Montgomery County.

Hindes R. E., First,   *Dayton.*

Perry County.

White & Cadwallader *New Lexington.*

Richland County.

Culbertson A. C.   *Shelby.*
Plummer J. B.   *Mansfield.*

Seneca County.

Bernard F.   *Adrian.*

Van Wert County.

Clark S. D.   *Van Wert.*

Vinegar Manufacturers.
Cuyahoga County.

Lied B., 125 St. Clair, *Cleveland.*

Franklin County.

Seibert S.   *Columbus.*

Hamilton County.

German J. B., 2 Twelfth, *Cincinnati.*
Herbstreet Mathias, 461 Vine
Hummel J., cor. Linn and Hopkins
Durfee Jas. H., cor. Seventh and John
Burkhart A., 430 Plum
Harth M. & Co., 380 Main
Pfirman —, 3 and 4 Canal, (W.)
Nash Hiram, 16 w. Front
Hughes Chas. T., 1 and 4 Hopple's Alley

Wagon Makers.
Adams County.

Freeman James   *Stout's.*
Crawford William   *Dunkinsville.*

Smith Edward T. — *Locust Grove.*
Thomas J.
Walker Joseph — *Eckmansville.*
Potter John — *West Union.*
Emery C.
Wright David — *Dunbarton.*

Allen County.

Mead Stillman — *West Newton.*
Fendal S. — *Allentown.*
Stapleton Andrew — *Middle River.*
Steever Jacob
Murray Joseph A. — *Croghan.*
Bentley Jefferson
Anshuts John

Ashland County.

Scoby Johnson — *Ruggles.*
Scott Moses C. — *Savannah.*
Wickham Jeremiah
Horn Henry — *Jeromeville.*
Hildebrand John W. — *Loudonville.*
Freirmuth Jacob
Shafer Charles
Beard Henry — *Mohecan.*
Chapel R. A. — *Perrysville.*

Ashtabula County.

Webster H. — *Richmond Centre.*
Ritter M.
Bartholomew A. — *Eagleville.*
Bailey J. — *Lenox.*
Alvord D. S. — *Austinburg.*
Calloway C. A.
Nutt E.
Walden H.
Shepard J.
Dady Wm.
Fetch R.
Loomis H. — *Jefferson.*
Amsden P. S.
Johnson H. N.
Blakelee G. — *Ashtabula.*
Benham W. G.
Turner Israel
Phillips J.
Kellogg —
Hubbard E. — *West Williamsfield.*
Rockwell J. R. — *Rome.*
Stage Albert — *Pierpont.*
Young Wm. H.
Dodge H. B. — *Cork.*
McLaughlin Wm. H. — *Lindenville.*
Lillie James
Emig John

Athens County.

Spencer John — *Chauncey.*
Mutchmon J. — *Amesville.*
McDaniel S.
Kigg Wm. N. — *Albany.*
Johnson George
Socie M. D. — *Nelsonville.*
Word Philip — *Shad.*
Horner Henry T. — *Lowry.*
James Richard
Ring J. L. & Co. — *Athens.*

Loresy R. — *Athens.*
Rigg Wm. R. — *Lee.*
Johnson Geo.
Cooley A. — *Athens.*
Cockril Elijah
Durant G. — *Guysville.*
Coe A. S. — *Hibardville.*

Auglaize County

Fritz Alfred — *Kossuth.*
Friederichs J. B. — *Minster.*
Bush William — *St. John.*
Bennett H. S.

Belmont County.

Bernhard J. — *Morristown.*
Sullivan M.
Graham Thos. M. — *Shepherdstown.*
Leslie Thomas — *Hunter.*
Cooper John — *Armstrong's Mills.*
Swann Frederick
Spiker David — *Pilcher's.*
Oller John
Day Henry H. — *Belmont.*
Jones John M. — *Hendrysburgh.*
Lingo William — *Denes.*
Job Allen — *Colerain.*
Oxley John
McLeish James — *Barnesville.*
Krim Simon — *Flushing.*
Walker Isaac
Clark Harrison — *Loydsville.*
Donn Henry
Bales Emmon — *Union.*
Blair William — *Dillies Bottom.*
Byers John
Butler Joseph — *Saint Clairsville.*
Davis Shepherd
Rose George H.

Brown County.

Maxwell Wm. — *Higginsport.*
Gibson H. C. — *Newhope.*
Keethler John — *Puebla.*
Still J. C.
Curren J. — *Russellville.*
Hair Titus — *Five Miles.*
Armstrong Wm.
Reese D. L. & W. — *Feesburg.*
Calvin & Pettijohn — *Sardinia.*
Shubers J.

Butler County.

Kain James — *Bethany.*
Bone Cyrus — *West Chester.*
Kenworthy Thos — *Collinsville.*
Cambers Jas. L. — *Dartown.*
Thomas B. F. & Bro. — *Oxford.*
Wright B.
Smith J.
Kekron P. — *Hamilton.*
Hutchinson E.
Greevy P. M.
Brown J. H. — *Rossville.*
Schlarb J.
Pitman David — *Middletown.*
Schenck Garret

Harris Wm.   *St. Charles.*
Hook J.   *Millville.*
Lowderman J.
Vanlue H.   *Ross.*
Halderman D.
Jotter P.   *Monroe.*
Crume W. R.   *College Corner.*
Howe E.
Rapp F.   *Trenton.*
Yager J. M.
Burk Peter
Bookwalter B. & J.   *Seven Mile.*
Law R.   *Trenton.*
Shafer Samuel   *Jacksonsburg.*
Macy George
Drake Francis   *Alert.*
Applegate M. B. & F. P   *Esely.*
Eberhart F.

Mullen W. E.   *Felicity.*
Phillips E. D.   *Mt. Carmel.*
Dillino Boyd   *Neville.*
Dunton Isaac   *Amelia.*
Short Ephraim
Leming Moses   *Mulberry.*
Picket Levi
Chambers John   *Moscow.*
Hughes Edward & Son
Cornell G.   *Rural.*
Russell John   *Loveland.*
Melvin James W.   *Nicholsville.*
Dickinson Y.   *West Woodville.*
McMurchy John   *Bantam.*
Stellman John
Day T. R.
Long Washington   *Locust Corner.*
Wagner John, jun.

Carroll County.

Lewers Foster   *Harlem Springs.*
Need David   *New Harrisburgh.*
Clark John   *Leesville.*
Clark Grant
Wallace John
Herron Eleazer   *Rose.*
Smith Peter S.   *Oneida Mills.*
Jeune George   *Kilgore.*
Riggle A.

Champaign County.

Rodgers Chas.   *Christiansburg.*
Rodgers John
Frink Samuel   *Urbana.*
Studibocker Wm.
Westfall Jacob   *Mutual.*
Miller John A.   *Careysvhill.*
White David W.   *St. Paris.*
Fronkhovers J.   *Terre Haute.*
Miller David
Jenkins A.
Thompson Wm. D.   *North Lewisburg.*
Startsman Oliver
Startsman Isaac

Clark County.

Baker A. & M.   *Enon.*
Frazer S. C.   *Selma.*
Miller A.
Petticrew D. & J. L.   *Springfield.*
Sheman J.
McManamay Wm.   *Catawba.*
Thacker James   *South Charleston.*
Hamilton Samuel   *New Carlisle.*

Clermont County.

Miller Frederick   *New Richmond.*
Wilson Samuel
Walker William   *Williamsburg.*
McNutt J. D.
Moyer H.
Hall J. H.   *Goshen.*
Gelvin L.
Jones & Wilmington   *Withamsville.*
Thornton C. & Co.   *Bethel.*
Crossly Geo.   *Felicity.*
   ers James

Clinton County.

Wood John N.   *Bloomington.*
Smith & Grant J. & J.   *New Burlington.*
Conklin Thos.   *Lumberton.*
Slack J. W.   *Sligo.*
Longshore J. H.
Frazee Joseph   *Blanchester.*
Taylor Joseph
Luckey J.   *New Antioch.*
Britterson Samuel   *Sabina.*
Puckett Daniel   *Martinsville.*
Smithson John W.
Bilderback Alex.

Columbiana County.

Grimesey John W.   *Salem.*
Iseman Daniel
Kuntz David
Beany Philip   *Bucks.*
Shriher Casper
Young O.
Johnson William   *East Liverpool.*
Nahar John M.   *Saint Clair.*
Ertsinger J.   *Unity.*
Harrold B.
Kugler F.
Stocksberry Wm.   *East Fairfield.*
Eakin Hugh   *Cannon's Mills.*
Mayberry Thomas   *Wellsville.*
Adam Gottlieb F.   *New Lisbon.*
Ells & Myers
Hamilton David
Fording John   *New Garden.*
Liber Charles
Taylor Joel B.
Bowman Henry   *North Georgetown.*
Grass John
Grass John, jun.
Manhill Joseph   *Franklin Square.*
Haldeman Benjamin   *East Rochester.*
Paxson John N.   *New Chambersburg.*
Slents James
Allbright Daniel G.   *Elkton.*
Stiegleman John A.
Baker A. C.

Coshocton County.

Crawford R.   *Clark's.*
Gesse Samuel   *Chili.*

Gonser David	*Chili.*
Walsh William	*Keene.*
Carroll Robert	
Slay George	*Coshocton.*
Tuttle T.	

Crawford County.

Snyder S. R	*Leesville ⋈ Roads.*
Wert Peter	
High Adam	*New Washington.*
Dinkle Lewis	*Bucyrus.*
Miller John	
Norton Jefferson	
Sheckler Hugh	
Trish John	
Yost A.	
Hipp Henry	*Chatfield.*

Cuyahoga County.

Crosier Ira	*Euclid.*
Knapp C. W.	*Gates' Mills*
Bradley Edward	*East Cleveland.*
Brott J. W.	
Martin A. G.	*Independence.*
Perry Wm. H.	
Smith N.	
Pierson C.	*Brooklyn.*
Reeve John	
Wagner N.	
Wood W. C.	
Osborn G.	*Bedford.*
Higgins Wm.	*Coe Ridge.*
Fry J.	*Warrensville.*
Hollister H.	
Smith James	
Hollister George	*Collamer.*
Chester E. F.	*Berea.*
Webster J. H.	
Wiley David	
McMain P.	*Ohio City.*

Darke County.

Thorp A. J.	*Fort Jefferson.*
Davis John	*Tampico.*
Davis D. T.	
Davis E. H.	
Jones W.	*New Madison.*
Weist John	
Thopp S. W.	*German.*
Reed John	
Peden Gibson	*Republican.*

Defiance County.

Corwin J.	*Defiance.*
Dunshee A. E.	
Knowles James	
Thompson George	*Milldale.*

Delaware County.

Cook Henry	*Galena.*
Young A.	
Mossman M.	
Adams J. J.	
Vanfleet H.	
Cook J.	
Cook Nicholas	
Ogden Daniel	*Van's Valley.*
Condit M.	

Lunger John	*Waldo.*
Bishop C.	
Francis M.	
Strong L. C.	*East Orange.*
Deppin Hiram	*Little Mill Creek.*
Brown Wm.	*Norton.*
Brown John N.	
Overshiner P.	
Petticord David	*Padnor.*
Watkins John	
Mentongrave A.	*Sunbury.*
Rineham S.	

Erie County.

Rice C.	*Sandusky City.*
Shanes Geo.	*Bloomingville.*

Fairfield County.

Orain Milton W.	*Pickerington.*
Patterson Wm.	*West Rushville.*
Furry & Yonts	*New Salem.*
Dodson Daniel	*Bremen.*
Book S.	*Rushville.*
Furry H.	
Cross & Smith	*Amanda.*
White W. M.	
Odell R.	*Sugar Grove.*
Hawkins D.	
Philips Joseph	
Oyler J.	*Lithopolis.*
Zonmaster H.	
Hoffman Julius	*Clear Creek.*
Palmer E.	
Shutt William	*Lancaster.*
Deets & McCall	
Zink A.	
Moody W.	
Farrow M.	
Keyser M.	
Hedges S. A.	

Fayette County.

Timmems L. R.	*Pancoastburg.*
Wendel Peter	*Washington.*
Wilson J. N.	
Thompson R.	*Moen's.*
Chambles W.	

Franklin County.

Knoderer V. F., Friend,	*Columbus.*
Knoder Charles, do.	
Luckhaupt A., cor. Broad and Canal	
Marplos J., High	
Miller F., do.	
Morris Dan'l, do.	
Walton Lewis, Rich	
Durant N.	*Central College.*
Dutton R. M.	*Groveport.*
Jones Jacob	
Abbott Ira	*Reynoldsburg.*
Clark J.	
Grimm L.	
Longshore T.	
Norris T.	
Armstrong Thos., jun.	*Hibernia.*
Smith J. R.	*Clintonville.*
Covert S. H.	*Harrisburg.*

Vernon C.	*Harrisburg.*
Weddle Z. G.	
Nicodemus Henry	*Canal Winchester.*
Kendig Jacob	*Gohanna.*
Doty Benjamin	*Dublin.*
Martin & Covey	
Clark W.	*Darby.*

Fulton County.

Harris Wm. H.	*Ottokee.*
Summers John	
Casper Kessler	*Delta.*
Zimmerman Simon	
Hampton Solomon	
Nofsinger Jacob	*Elmira.*
Barr S.	

Gallia County.

Bierly Samuel	*Rodney.*
Ewing George	*Ewington.*
Carter J. L.	*Patriot.*
Kent Calvin	*Kyger.*
Tenney Jonathan	
Vanden James	*Gallipolis.*

Geauga County.

Rodgers Wm.	*Charden.*
McCarty O.	
Parsons George	

Greene County.

Gowdy Alexander	*Xenia.*
Inches Jacob	
Bryan Henry	*Fairfield.*
Lee J. B.	
Boots C.	*Spring Valley.*
Cohegan W.	*Clifton.*
Fitchthorn Isaac	*New Jasper.*
Huffman Josiah	*Cedarville.*
Strasberger William	*Byron.*
Powers Allen	*Paintersville.*
Oglesbee —	
Curl Joel	
Haslet Thos. K.	*Jamestown.*
Zortman Isaac	

Guernsey County.

Davis & Cook	*Cambridge.*
McCune Robert	*Cumberland.*
Conwell J.	*Washington.*
Hurst Wm.	
Maxwell Wm.	*Londonderry.*
Reed John	*Antrim.*
Meridith R. C.	
Johnson J.	*Winchester.*
Hutchison J. C.	*Fairview.*
Williams D. W.	
Chambers J. A.	
Thomas Samuel	
McKee Robert	*Claysville.*
Richey Wm.	
Freeman J. F.	
Klingman H. &	*Cambridge.*
Eberle W.	
Ohaver Isaac	*Kimbolton.*
Beaver Richard	
Secrist Geo. W.	*Senecaville.*
Shadwell J. F.	

Great Milton	*Leatherwood.*
Kuhns Samuel	

Hamilton County.

Crowder J., Front, between Lawrence and	
Pike	*Cincinnati.*
Williams W. & D., Lock, above Sixth	
Neckel & Cockley, 29 Butler	
Stephens J., cor. Canal and Sycamore	
Tillis D., cor. Fourth and Front	
Tebbe Henry, 673 w. Front	
Slater M., 514 w. Fifth	
Pairk J. & T. Simonton, 51 Race	
Wolf M., 604 Walnut	
Schmidtt O., 636 Vine	
Bonte John H., cor. John and Kemble	
Breitenbuch A., Catharine, bet. Brighton	
and Cutter	
Braw Frederick, 189 Linn	
Pugh H., 634 w. Fifth	
Daniel Peter, 524 w. Eighth	
Bockman J., 127 Ham. Road	
Morlim C., 277 " "	
Krazer Jos., 166 " "	
Rutker W., 615 Elm	
Jackson W. R.	*Columbia.*
Iferd A. & Co.	*Pendleton.*
Vinson J. J.	*Fulton.*
Gathers Wm.	*Mt. Healthy.*
Crain Hiram	*Montgomery.*
Bowen P. M.	
Knight Chas.	
Short G. M.	*Mt. Washington.*
Laird John	*Cleves.*
Sparks J.	*Elizabethtown.*
Yanders George	*Miami.*
Earhart Wm.	*Plainville.*
Tozzer William	*Cumminsville.*
Welch James	
Compton Azariah	*Springdale.*
Hough Joseph	
Brown J. H.	*Newtown.*
Lantz Daniel	
Richardson J. D.	
Hageman A. S.	*Sharonville.*
Phillips John R.	
Bonnel John	*Carthage.*
Castner W. H.	
Brinkerhof B.	
Ranceveau R.	
Bish Joseph	*Reading*
Ashley Robert	*Cheviot*
Clark Patrick	
Kreuker Frederick	
Clark James	*Dunlap.*
Benn Benjamin	*Dry Ridge.*
Richardson Joseph	

Hancock County.

May Peter	*Van Buren.*
Liter John	*Ashery.*
Tevinney James	
Bopp Henry	*Finley.*
George Jesse	
Schnyer John	
Harmon & Mull	*Canonsburg.*
Plymie J.	

Hardin County.

Summers Charles	*Roundhead.*
Miller James	*Huntersville.*

Henry County.

Armstrong James	*Napoleon.*
Dier George	*New Bavaria.*

Highland County.

Wright & Hiatt	*Highland.*
Woodmasee G. W. & J.	
Sellers Alex.	*Greenfield.*
Albray Henry	
Baker Ephraim	
Callahan Thomas	
Wegginten P.	
Cunningham J. R.	*Belfast Town.*
Huffman Daniel	
Huggins J. E.	*Buford.*
Scott G. M.	*Dodsonville.*
Haslam J. G.	*Mowrytown.*
Jones J. W.	*New Petersburg.*
Cunningham A.	
James E.	*Sugartree Ridge.*
Taylor Elisha	*Marshall.*
Brady C.	*Centrefield.*
Lawson John	
Chaney R. L.	*Allensburg.*
McDaniel Wm.	*Samantha.*
Bragg Wm.	
Mercer Charles	
Spencer P. F.	*Leesburg.*
Knott O. B.	
Greene J.	
Bonecutter G.	
Myers J.	*Hillsboro'.*

Hocking County.

Frash Frederick	*Logan.*
Gross J. Barnhart	
Hamer B. W.	
Bucher J.	
Hofferbert Jacob	*Gibisonville.*
Moore Michael	
Rambo Moses	*Swan.*

Holmes County.

Young Chas.	*Holmesville.*
Keightly H.	
Alden N.	*Benton.*
Gurwell N.	
Bachtel Jacob	*Winesburg.*
Metzker A.	
Scaar Nicholas	*Walnut Creek.*
Lewis R.	*Nashville.*

Huron County.

Cadiz John	*Bellevue.*
Cook Alfred	*Steuben.*
Burk L. D.	
Cady M.	*East Townsend.*
Lamb Nathan	
Tucker A.	
Hawkins S. S.	*Greenwich.*
Rowcliffe James	*Four Corners.*
Pulver & Furlong	*Clarkfield.*
Rodgers Daniel	

Hadley, Fuller & Co.	*Norwalk.*
Miller & Butts	
Buffington J.	*Fitchville.*

Jackson County.

Jones Wm.	*Oakhill.*
Alexander C. B.	*Allensville.*
McGee John	*McGee's Store.*
Wycoff Henry	
Brown B.	*Jackson.*
Showers M.	

Jefferson County.

Burke D. A.	*Steubenville.*
Stoneypher Ephraim	
Ryan A.	*East Springfield.*
Walker James	
McKenney Eli	*Annapolis.*
Speer M. B.	
Reed Wm.	*Mt. Pleasant.*
Hansberry L.	
Eldridge David	
Dawson Samuel	*Mouth of Yellow Creek.*

Knox County.

Bishop Stephen	*Mt. Vernon.*
Cole Aaron	*Democracy.*
Fults Benjamin	
Kirkpatrick Samuel	
Lybarger Harmon	*Monroe Mills.*
Lybarger Joseph, jr.	
Myers Jacob	*North Liberty.*
Wise John	
Stover Emanuel	*Jelloway.*
Boinhower Peter	*Mt. Liberty.*
Thompson John	*Bladensburg.*
Harris A.	
Lester Samuel	

Lake County.

Hitchcock M.	*Madison.*
Ingersol O. J.	
Gayer A.	
Kellogg J.	
Damon G.	
Turney A. S	
Simons J.	*Perry.*
Foster R.	*Concord.*
Draitt & Brothers	
Morley A.	*Kirtland.*
Morley J.	
Upham B. S.	
Sanborn E. A.	
Wightman C. B.	
Hadden Wm.	

Lawrence County.

Wait & Bushe	*Ironton.*

Licking County.

Wieseman Samuel	*Linnville.*
Fluke J. P.	*Brownsville.*
Ewing Wm.	
Dinsmore Samuel	*Jacksontown.*
Griffith David	
Bedcar Chas.	*Newark.*
Evans H.	*Perryton.*

Hull T. J.	Perryton.
Bush & McLelland	Homer.
Moore John G.	
Wiant James	
Cady C. C.	Johnstown.
Stowell H.	
Gesner W. T.	
Gardner A. A.	
Caper Charles	Fredonia.
Lamson H.	
Arnold Joseph	
Showers Daniel	Etna.
Waite H.	
Rowe R.	

Logan County.

Jackson George W.	Huntsville.
Amspoker Samuel	East Liberty.
Crawford Harvey	
Oglesbie Jacob	Rushsylvania.
Stilwell Stephen	
Emery & Brother	Bellefontaine.
Powers J.	
Brown E. T.	Zanesfield.
Scott B. S.	

Lorain County.

Hubbell P.	La Grange.
Everson Samuel	Rochester Depot.
Gaston R. P.	Oberlin.
Pease H. A.	
Jewitt R.	Copopa.
Lowe T.	
Walkden Wm.	
Fox Joseph	Sheffield.
Washburn F. S.	North Camden.
Bailey Thaddeus	Brownhelm.
Locke Benjamin W.	
Pessley Horace	

Lucas County.

Hubbard Henry	Whiteford.
Jackman Thomas	

Madison County.

Morand John	London.
Nuth A.	Midway.
Brake T.	

Mahoning County.

Whittenberger Adam	New Middletown.
Smith Valentine	
Yoder Tobias	East Lewistown.
Lowry Wm. H.	Coitsville.
Monsell Wm. B.	North Jackson.
Case Stephen	Milton.
Delong James W.	
Wetzler Christian	North Lima.
Peters C.	New Springfield.
Wesh Philip	New Albany.

Marion County.

Pixley B. O.	Cochranton.
Smith Geo.	Prospect.
Canann Joseph	
Hain D.	Marion.
Minceuberger C.	

Medina County.

Sturgges L. B.	Litchfield.
Seldon A. H.	Mallet Creek.
Beach Geo. & Co.	Wadsworth.
Warner J. J.	
Huntsberger E.	
Sims John	Sharon Centre.
Treat J.	
Collins John	Chatham Centre.
Firman Wm.	
White Joel	Leroy.
Rich J. F.	
Baldwin H. J.	
Parker S. S.	Medina.
Drake C. W.	
Kimmell & Baldwin	
Olcott A.	

Meigs County.

Calvert Joseph	Downington.
Stevens A.	
Dike Wm. H.	Pomeroy.

Mercer County.

Downing James	Coldwater.
Winters Jacob	Celina.

Miami County.

Whorten O.	Fletcher.
McClentic Wm.	
Luce John	
Burgman J. F.	West Charleston.
Weaver R.	
Huffman J. N.	Piqua.
Lee Barney	
Keene Wm.	
Winans A.	
Gaskel & Allen	Troy.
Stockton J. C.	
Lewis E. D. & Thos.	Casstown.
Chamberlain A. O. & J.	
Dean John	Brant.
French Jeremiah	
Covert John	West Milton.
Shearer Eli	
Turner Levi	

Monroe County.

Kirkwood Wm. C.	Woodsfield.
St. John Marcus	
Vickers John	
Penn William H.	Antioch.
Berry John A.	Laing's.
Bert Charles	Sunfish.
Clay Loren	
Black John W.	Bealsville.
Gearhart Aaron	
Valentine M. T.	
Johnson William	Miltonsburgh.
Morton William	Stafford.
Noll S. W.	Baresville.

Montgomery County.

Burnett George	Liberty.
Dunwidy J.	Centreville.
Githens J. F.	
Lincoln N. W.	
Rupard Peter	Chambersburg.

Surface Jacob	*Chambersburg.*
Baker David	
Ketters & Thomas	*Centre.*
Boroff Henry	*Harshmansville.*
Isang Jacob	*Little York.*
Bernhard J., 3d	*Dayton.*
Carnell J. do	
Kine H., St. Clair	
Tifferman H., Wayne	
Renner W.	*Farmersville.*
Kilkenny William	*West Baltimore.*
Bandon William	*Clayton.*
Ranch John A.	
May George	*New Lebanon.*
Wyrick S.	*Johnsville.*
Billmire Samuel	*Germantown.*
Schaeffer Geo. W.	
Weaver Daniel	
Hibbart J.	*Miamisburgh.*
McConnell Bookwalter	

Morgan County.

Dike E. C.	*Chester Hill.*
Gray Nelson	
Timberlake Lewis	
Moody S. G.	*Triadelphia.*
Finley David	
Manley James	*Chaneyville.*
Pennel Edward	*Malta.*
Wiseman Joshua	
Dempster David	*Meigs Creek.*
Austin J.	
Dunbar Stephen	*Pleasant Valley.*
Lewis Bernard	*Meigsville.*
Lukens N. C.	*McConnelsville.*
Holbrook David	
Bowers Thomas	
Bingman John	*Stockport.*
McGwigan S.	
Dunn Wm.	*Pennsville.*
Gassage John	

Morrow County.

Brocklesby William	*Underwood's.*
Pim Samuel W	*Shauk's.*
Dennis Emanuel	*Woodview.*
Huffman Samuel	
Hair T. B.	*Pulaskiville.*
Landon J. B.	
Mead Amaziah	*Vail's ⋈ Roads.*
Baker Sigismund	*Corsica.*
Wells A.	*Nimmons' ⋈ Roads.*
Hair N. C.	
Sherman P. T.	
Supples S.	*Chesterville.*
Jeffries George	

Muskingum County.

Dempster John P.	*Norwich.*
Butt M.	*Hopewell.*
Dunlap John	*Shannon.*
Wilking Henry	
Goslin Bernard	*White Cottage.*
Conwell Jonathan	*Gratiot.*
Moore James	*Chandlersville.*
Abbott Joseph.	

Noble County.

Cowan Joseph P.	*Berne*
Hunter Joseph H.	*Mount Ephraim.*
Orr John	*Gardner.*
Gebhart Peter	*Batesville.*

Ottawa County.

Shafer Owen	*Elmore.*

Perry County.

Hunt Hixon	*New Lexington.*
Porter James	
Nyswander Frederick	*Thornville.*
Bateson James	*Rehoboth.*
Brown William	*Somerset.*
Musselman William	

Pickaway County.

Bauman Stephen	*Circleville.*
McCarty John	
Welter Jacob	
Boyer William	*Tarlton.*
Manahan William	
Zechrung T. B.	
Beathard E.	*Darbyville*
Huffmann & Ridgeway	
Vinnatter Jacob	
Burnley Seth	*Beckett's Store.*
Harmount Geo. B.	*Williamsport.*
Loux C.	*South Bloomfield.*
Guseman D. & J. W.	

Pike County.

Beekman B.	*Byington.*
Lindsay James	*Cynthiana.*
Mitchell & Bennett	*Waverly.*
Gikler, Bunahin & Co.	
Stoll Philip	*Beaver.*
Daub Jacob	
Finck F.	
Rockwell Ezra	*Gibson.*
Patterson Thomas	*Pikton.*
Emerich T.	
Bell John	*Omega.*

Portage County.

Hart Henry	*Atwater.*
Bates Lorenzo	
Brocket Albert & Son	*Randolph.*
White L. S.	*Aurora.*
Butler Wm.	
Talbot Robert	*Streetsboro'.*
Boyd Ichabod	
Norway Cha's. H.	*Shalersville.*
Day J. H.	*Edinburgh.*
Christopher J.	*Franklin.*
Miller & Treat	*Suffield.*
Coleman John	
Peck A. C.	*Charleston.*
Sizer L.	*Mantua.*
Wygatt L.	
Purham Cha's.	*Deerfield.*
Day M. L.	
Streeter E.	*Nelson.*
Coolman D. C.	
Tuttle Edgar	*Palmyra.*
Davis George	

Tucker George	*Rootstown.*
Burroughs H.	*Freedom.*
Atwood J.	
Boosinger Philip	*Brimfield.*
Clark N. D. & Co.	*Ravenna.*
Peterson J. H.	
Bond Wm.	
Minard E.	

Preble County.

Smith Wm.	*West Alexandria.*
Smith Stephen	
Guild Chas.	*Camden.*
Kline & Lockwood	*Eaton.*
Fleming & Snow	
Whitfield W. T.	
Clark Michael	*New Westville.*
Collins Charles	*West Florence.*
Collins Luther	
Emans J.	*Hamburg.*
Planks J.	*Enterprise.*
Mattock J.	*New Paris.*
Miller M.	
Patton P. S.	*West Elkton.*
McShane Edward	
Clevinger Wm. L.	*Hagerstown.*

Putnam County.

Krous Wm. & Chas.	*Medary.*
McBride J. G.	*Gilboa.*
Wagner J. H.	
Orum H. F.	*Pendleton.*
Glore Daniel	

Richland County.

Funk D. W.	*Shelby.*
Kerr J.	
Rogers J.	
Garver Jacob	*Butler.*
Robb Elie	
Stoopes Wm	*Ontario.*
Sanker John G.	*Shenandoah.*
Winbaugh John	
Pike John	*Lexington.*
Atkinson Andrew W.	*Barnes.*
Gribling Christian	
Strater Wm.	
Reilly Vincent B.	*West Windsor.*
Buzzard Josiah	*Adario.*

Ross County.

Harrington H.	*Clarksburgh.*
Vorster John	*Chillicothe.*
Fellenstein J. H.	
Bennett Henry	
Brown John	
Wood James	*South Salem.*
Nebergall John	
Reynolds E. D.	*Halleville.*
Ranck John	
Kilburn James	*Gillespieville.*
Griffin Thos. H.	
Hauck Jacob	*Kingston.*
Hunt Wm.	
Rinehart James	
Miller David A.	*Bourneville.*
Browning Joseph	

Walker Samuel	*Bourneville.*
Armsey L. B.	*Richmonddale.*
Dailey Joseph	

Sandusky County.

Myn E. H.	*Woodville.*
Penbaker John	*Greensburg ⋈ Roads.*

Scioto County.

Emory Daniel	*Portsmouth.*
Friday H.	
Smith Jasper	*Sciotoville.*
Gephardt Lewis	*Iron Furnaces.*
McGee James	
McNaughton John	
Mittendorf John F.	
Pool Daniel	
Cahill James	*Friendship.*
Nurse Joshua	
Gibbons G.	*Wheelersburgh.*

Seneca County.

Childs J. A.	*Attica.*
Rehring & Whitman	
Fluber Michael	*Berwick.*
Clahre C.	*Bloomville.*
Isler Henry	*Bascom.*
Kinketer John	
Pierce Joseph	
Bower John	*Tiffin.*
Flaugher Jacob B.	
Gardner Joseph	
Oster Jacob	
Smith F.	
Creque Joseph	*West Lodi.*
Wagoner Ralph	*Green Spring.*
Olds M. T.	*Republic.*
Collins Osborn	

Shelby County.

Jackson Joseph	*Hardin.*
Ruppert Henry	*Sidney.*
Pfiefer Jacob	

Starke County.

Hamilton R. B.	*Waynesburg.*
Pool Samuel	
Richards Samuel	
Bowman Samuel S.	*West Brookfield.*
Crip & Taylor	*Minerva.*
Montgomery Josiah	
Coleman Jonathan	*Lake.*
Wolf A.	
Oddo E.	*Louisville.*
Serheney F.	
Slents Jacob	*New Franklin.*
Gallaher Peter	*East Greenville.*
Allenatz Joseph, senr.	*New Berlin.*
Mercer F. B.	*Paris.*
Smith Gideon	
Lynde Frederick	*Marlboro'.*
Mendenhall Stephen	
Miller David	
Kring George	*Mapleton.*
Loehr Jacob	
Harbraugh Philip	*Hartville.*
Reed John	

Summit County.

Radcliff J. — *Cuyahoga Falls.*
Rumrill Geo.
Blakelee J. — *Tallmadge.*
Boden David — *Inland.*
Ditzler John
Kiplinger Andrew
Canan Hamilton — *Clinton.*
Carr Calvin — *Richfield.*
Cowles Oliver
Huntley Ira — *Mount Rose.*
Alexander T. S. — *Macedonia Depot.*
Seidel George — *Northfield.*
Hennon George — *Eden.*
Lyon Morris — *Copley.*
White Joseph
Porter William
Currier Hiram — *Bath.*
Huntley Benjamin
Jagger Clement N.
White Henry

Trumbull County.

Holcomb L. H. — *Mecca.*
Bradley Albert B. — *Gustavus.*
Brainard Lorenzo D.
Brainard Bud
Gibson Daniel
Miller Lent L. — *Girard.*
Wilson William
Bell James H. — *Church Hill.*
Denison John
Goist Samuel
Hathaway C. — *Farmington.*
Taft Harvey —
Glazier M. C.
Brown N. & J. — *Newton Falls.*
Erwin David — *Ohletown.*
Campbell John
Kenedy Samuel J.
Russell Abraham
Moore James

Tuscarawas County.

Lackey William — *New Cumberland.*
Stoody Daniel
Coffy William — *Winfield.*
Evans E. H.
White John
Swank John — *Sandyville.*
Palmer J. W. — *Peoli.*
White Joseph — *Gnadenhutten.*
Grimm Christian — *Ragersville.*
Seltenright Alex.
Steel D. — *New Philadelphia.*
Granber J.
Brunk Michael — *Canal Dover.*
Yantes A.
Myers Emanuel
Sponsler David
Born David — *Tuscarawas.*
Bears Wm. — *Rockford.*

Union County.

Lee Rolen — *Marysville*
Plum David
Sprague J. G.

Moffit Elias — *Raymond's.*
Mears T. V. — *Wilkins.*
Colver Standish — *Milford Centre.*
Dealing Charles
Sheiderer George
Whitmore Jared

Van Wert County

Strothers A. R. — *Van Wert*

Vinton County.

Gale Wm. D. — *Prattsville.*
Wagner John
Pugh L. B. — *McArthur.*
Swepston J. M. & E.

Warren County.

Conover P. — *Franklin.*
Parker Thos.
Stanton John
Camberlain John — *Oregon.*
Dawson C. — *Mason.*
Stout S.
Waltch Peter
Sides L.
Presby M. — *Red Lion.*
Olinger Samuel
Jarvis R. — *Hayesville.*
McClelan R. & W.
Letchar J.
Frazer J. A. — *Dunlevy.*
Day M. L.
Collett C. — *Waynesville.*
Dillingham Levi — *Hopkinsville.*
Stearns O.
Clise John — *Morrow.*
Messer W.
Chamberlin Lewis — *Lebanon.*
March & Brothers
St. John Hiram — *Butlerville.*
Walters Geo.
Hormel J. H. — *Harveysburg.*
Varner E. F.
Lippincott J. H.

Washington County.

Rouse John — *Centre Belpra.*
Blough J.
Wilson George — *Coal Run.*
Beach J. D.
Campton Robert — *Regnier's Mills.*
Hallett J. H. — *Fearing.*
Bazerr John — *Fillmore.*
Readenbough C. — *Lowell.*
Hadow John — *Watertown.*
Elliott Simpson — *Decaturville.*
Francis Henry
Bosim John

Wayne County.

Tarr G. F. A. — *Edinburgh.*
Baker Geo. — *New Prospect.*
Horn David — *Reedsburg.*
Stouffer Henry — *Burbank.*
Drabenstadt J. — *Smithville.*
Sonders B.
Stainer W.
Sheller D.

Lightfoot Samuel　　　　*Smithville.*
Eyeman Jacob　　　　*Number One.*
Robison Cha's.　　　　*Shreve.*
Berry Isaac
Cryling Henry　　　　*Marshallville.*
Hanna W. W.　　　　*Wooster.*
Wilhelm John
Blackburn J. M.
Lane J. D.　　　　*Canaan.*
Morgan E.

Williams County.

Mowdy Joseph　　　　*West Unity.*

Wood County.

Perrine Christopher　　*Perrysburg.*
Lang Wm.
Reither P.
Oarr E. J.　　　　*Bowling-Green.*
Ketchum A. J.　　　　*Weston.*
Harrison & Besancson　　*Portage.*
Wisler Wm. & Sanderson
　　　　Montgomery Roads.

Wyandot County.

McEwen & Eyestone　　*Sycamore.*
Finch & Berringer　　*Upper Sandusky.*
Hunter Samuel
Myers Wm.　　　　*Carey.*
Parkers Wm.　　　　*Crawfordsvile.*
Houst Thos. & Henry　*McCutchensville.*
Seele Wm.

Washboard (Zinc) Manuf't'rs.

Hamilton County.

Wayne, Baily & Co., cor. 5th & Home
Rice Orrin, 10 Main　　*Cincinnati*
Holmes J. B., 43 7th

Washing Machine Manufacturers.

Brown County.

Venonda S.　　　　*Sardinia.*
Hamilton T. A.

Clermont County.

Dudley C. & P. S. & Co.　*West Woodville.*

Watch-Makers & Jewelers.

Importers, Manufacturers & Dealers in Watches, Jewelry, and Silverware.

Clocks.

Adams County.

Myers Frederick　　　*West Union.*

Allen County.

Salterthal Isaac　　　*Lima.*

Ashland County.

Ralston Wm.　　　　*Ashland.*

Ashtabula County.

Sherwood N. B.　　　*Jefferson.*
Shepherd J. B.　　　*Ashtabula.*
Heele A. W.
Veuen John D.　　　*Conneaut.*
Veuen J. A. & D. P.

Athens County.

Sanderson Robert　　　*Athens.*
Matheny F.
Dewing John　　　　*Lee.*

Auglaize County.

De Witt —　　　　*Wapakoneta.*

Belmont County.

Brown George　　　*St. Clairsville.*
Williams John H.
Allen B.　　　　*Morristown.*
Handy J. J. & Co.

Brown County.

Blanchard J.　　　　*Ripley.*
Daller H.
Snyder C.　　　　*Georgetown.*
Sulenberger E. C.　　　*Feesburg.*

Butler County.

Drayer Wm. E.　　　*Hamilton.*
Rohman B.　　　　*Rossvile.*
Oldein David　　　*Middletown.*

Champaign County.

Thomas Wm.　　　　*Urbana.*
Baxter & Benjamin
Johnson E. D. & Co.

Clark County.

Elliot E. G.　　　　*Springfield.*
Conway Newton S.　　*Catawba.*

Clinton County.

Hinman S.　　　　*Wilmington.*
Baker Joseph
Shepherd —

Columbiana County.

Cooper W.　　　　*Wellsville.*
Benner J. F.　　　　*New Lisbon.*
Custard Joseph
Hewitt & Buck　　　*Salem.*
Pickett J. K.
Wassignara P.　　　*East Liverpool.*

Crawford County.

Feighner H. H.　　　*Bucyrus.*
Huffman John

Cuyahoga County.

Bartholomew H. M.　　*Chagrin Falls.*
Starr L.　　　　*Bedford.*
Cantrovitz & Shrier, 40 Bank　*Cleveland.*
Crittenden N. E., 29 Superior
Cowles & Albertson, 49　do
Deitz & Brother, 22　　do
Field & Gray, 168½　　do
Kidd Wm. & Co., 162　do
Mayer Jacob, 11 Water
Ricaby Wm., 9　　do
Talcott & Co., 2 Ontario
Thiele & Hofer, 36 Seneca
Woolnough J. H., Forest City House
Droz F. Humbert, 26 Detroit　*Ohio City.*

Darke County.

Webb N.　　　　*Greenville.*

Defiance County.

Backus Alex.   *Defiance.*

Delaware County.

Burr R. & Co.   *Delaware.*
Sturdivant & Brother

Erie County.

Dewey R.   *Sandusky.*
Simpson W.
Dewey H. T.
Nusley V.

Fairfield County.

Gates James   *Lancaster.*
Garrahty James
Bininger H.

Fayette County.

Furtwangler D.   *Washington.*

Franklin County.

Blynn & Baldwin, High   *Columbus.*
Buck S., 135   do
Clark & Co.,   do
Dunbar R. D.   do
Kleeman & Brother do
Lesquereux L. & Sons, 179 High
Savage John T.   do
Coppock G. F. & Son   do
Lichtenngger F.   do
Haldy Frederick   do

Gallia County.

Wilkinson Thomas   *Gallipolis.*
Richards Joseph

Geauga County.

Bisbee C. A.   *Chardon.*

Greene County.

Charter D.   *Xenia.*
Feller George
Stark W. T.

Guernsey County.

Boisell Oliver   *Cumberland.*
Murphey H.   *Fairview.*
Madison O. L.   *Cambridge.*
Kelsey Amos   *Leatherwood.*

Hamilton County.

Ange S., No. 203 Elm   *Cincinnati.*
Andrews D. B., 142 w. 5th
Aspinwall & Eyster, 327 W. Row
Atkinson J. V., 343   do
Allen O. & W. H., 117 Main
Berthing E., 426 Walnut
Bliss Henry, 157 Main
Brockman C. F., 309 do
Beggs & Smith, 14 w. 4th
Brownold E., 26 6th
Bush J. H., 12 13th
Carley S. T. & Co., 150 Walnut
Clayton Richard, s. e. cor. Syc. & 2d
Davidson & Clark, 72 w. 6th
Daller J., Vine, bet. Canal & 13th
Duhme & Co., 130 Main

Draper Joseph, 16 w. 4th   *Cincinnati.*
Depperman & Bolmann, 505 Main
Dronseifer H., 445 Main
Grandbeck Daniel, 43 Sycamore
Glatz Henry A., Apollo Building
Grebner W., 433 Vine
Hill E H., 155 Main
Huntington & Laboyteaux, 119 Main
Hollen S. W., Vine, bet. Canal & Court.
Haynes J. R., 40 w. 4th
Isson S., 175 w. 5th
Kinsey E. & D., 32 do
Klausing Clemens, 440 Main
Kent Luke, 234   do
Kleeman, Gertsley & Co., 194 do
Korf Henry, 369   do
McGrew Wilson, 137   do
Martin J. H., 183   do
Oskamp Theodore, 62   do
Oskamp Lewis, 16 Sycamore
Ortman C., 245 w. Court
Palmer & Owen, 135 Main
Rhodes J. F., 103 Main
Rosental S, 190 w. 6th
Reisanthal S. R., 242 do
Solomons S. & Brother, 9 w. 4th
Strueve H. R., 205 Main
Trotter J., 241 w. 5th
Voss J. & Co., 32 e. 5th
Voss J., 276 w. 5th
Wray Henry C., 141 Main
Weming Wm., 291   do
Zumbursch —, 673 Vine
Orr Thomas   *Harrison.*

Hancock County.

Cahill R. F.   *Finley.*
Wilson C. B.

Hardin County.

Chapman & Rogers   *Kenton.*

Harrison County.

Lofland John   *Cadis.*
Shaw T. M.   *Feed Spring.*

Highland County.

Moyers John   *Hillsboro'.*
Sayler Jacob
Picard J. C.   *Mowrytown.*
Wolfram G.   *Dodsonville.*

Hocking County.

Miers —   *Logan.*

Holmes County.

Shrock & Cook   *Millersburg.*
Burger J. & G.   *Winesburg.*
Smith F.

Huron County.

Summers & Weiker   *Bellevue.*
Carter O. G.   *Norwalk.*

Jackson County.

Saylor Samuel   *Jackson.*

Jefferson County.

Spear R.   *Steubenville.*
Sarratt J. H

Knox County.

Brown J. B.   *Mt. Vernon.*
Hyde Joshua
Strieby C. H.

Lake County.

Babcock J. A.   *Painesville.*
Ackley L. W.

Lawrence County.

Weber C. B.   *Ironton.*

Licking County.

Dury M.   *Newark.*
Shrock J. M.
Sprague H. S.

Logan County.

Embry E.   *East Liberty.*
Gudgeon D. L.   *Bellefontaine.*
St. John R. H.
Sargent A. G.

Lorain County.

Ingersol C. F.   *Oberlin.*
Burrell John W. & Co.   *Elyria.*
White D. C.

Lucas County.

Cook H. T.   *Toledo.*
Love & Voight
Reniff T. W.
Stow D. F.

Marion County.

Turney W. A.   *Marion.*
Dickerson T. H.

Medina County.

Whitmore J.   *Medina.*
Coon & Aaron
Ford Daniel   *Abbeyville.*

Meigs County.

Lee George   *Pomeroy.*
Demmet Francis

Miami County.

Thomas A.   *Piqua.*
Julian J. J.

Monroe County.

Adams Thomas J.   *Woodsfield.*
Liniger John
Dungan B. E.   *Sunfish.*

Montgomery County.

Albert Charles, Third   *Dayton.*
Bean R. S., Main
Best H.,   "
Jameson Jacob,   Third
Jenkins & Beardorf   "
Martin Joseph, Second
Reeks H., Main
Reeves E. & Son, Third
Saffee & Allen, Main
Helfrich J., Second.
Kiefer Lewis   *Miamisburg.*

Axman Charles   *Germantown.*
Espich Henry

Morgan County.

Pinkerton D. C.   *McConnelsville.*
Olymer Chas.

Morrow County.

Wilcox John   *Cardington.*

Muskingum County.

Ross Jas. J.   *Zanesville.*
Ross A. C.

Noble County.

Shaw P. & R.   *Sarahsville.*

Perry County.

Johnson W. J.   *Somerset.*
Masterson P.   *Chapel Hill.*

Pickaway County.

Dunkin & McLaughlin   *Circleville.*

Portage County.

Fletcher J. F.   *Ravenna.*
Campbell R. E.
Kingsbury R. R.
Baird R. A.
Parmele John
Stedman Oscar   *Nelson.*

Preble County.

Chambers Jacob   *Eaton.*

Putnam County.

Farver J. K.   *Gilboa.*

Richland County.

Lee John A.   *Mansfield.*
Patterson & Wilkinson
Wilkinson E.
Wiler J. U.
Carey Manson   *Lexington.*
Philpot S.   *Belleville.*
Light & Hoffman   *Plymouth.*

Ross County.

Bangs J. E.   *Chillicothe.*
Pratt E. P.

Sandusky County

Leppelman E.   *Fremont.*

Scioto County.

Coriell A.   *Portsmouth.*
Clugsten J.
Haller L. R. & Son

Seneca County.

Gallup Wm.   *Tiffin.*
Madden James
Sewald P.
Hartman J.
Oram Moses   *Republic*

Shelby County.

Barkdale L. C.   *Sidney.*
Bush M.

Starke County.

Gelier M. — *Louisville.*
Deuble Geo. & Bro. — *Canton.*
Frey S. O.
Rose M.
Withington Martin A. — *Massillon.*
Coleman Joseph
Goodspeed Laban

Summit County.

Sill E. J. — *Cuyahoga Falls.*
Knight C. M. — *Hudson.*
Abbey H. S. — *Akron.*
Gillett J.
McCain Benj.

Trumbull County.

King W. & Son — *Warren.*
Vontrot & Mieksch

Tuscarawas County.

Ricksecker Israel — *Canal Dover.*
Butler M. — *New Philadelphia.*
Kranken E. A

Union County.

Armstrong Joel — *Marysville.*
Lehman Christopher — *Jerome.*

Warren County.

Vandyke D. W. — *Mason.*

Washington County.

Anderson D. B. — *Marietta.*
Baldwin J. W.

Wayne County.

Sheldon & Ewalt — *Wooster.*
Sprague Sindol
Deihl E. H.

Williams County.

Foster Wm. — *West Unity.*
Kissell John G. — *Bryan.*

Wyandot County.

Franklin E. M. — *Upper Sandusky.*

Water-Cure Establishments.

Greene County.

Cheny A. & Co. — *Yellow Springs.*

Hamilton County.

Pease D. A. — *Carthage.*

Lake County.

Mathews D. — *Painesville.*

Medina County.

Beatty Alex. — *Medina.*

Tuscarawas County.

Trease Hiram & Solomon *Deardorff's Mills.*

Wheat-Drill Manufacturers.

Ashtabula County.

Coe Chas. W. — *Ashtabula.*

Medina County.

Cogshall & Kingsbury — *Wadsworth.*
Borst J. A.

Wheelbarrow Makers.

Hamilton County.

Rockey & Co., 97 Eighth — *Cincinnati.*
Purser John, Columbia, bet. Broadway and Sycamore
Hutton J. & R., Front, bet. Elm & Plum
Tebbe Henry, 673 w. Front

Scioto County.

Hall Wm. — *Portsmouth.*
Waite J. H.
Oraine Horace — *Friendship.*
Higgie Thomas

Whips—Wholesale Dealers.

Hamilton County.

Clark S. & S. S., 180 Main — *Cincinnati.*
Dorr & Arnold, 6 w. Sixth
Fountain J. S., 242 Main
Moores & Butterfield, 89 "
Slocum E. N., 102 "
Wilson & Hayden, 17 & 19 w. Columbia

Whip Makers.

Geauga County.

Knowles A. — *Chardon.*

Hamilton County.

Penrose C., 37 Main — *Cincinnati.*

Whitesmiths.

Montgomery County.

Grove Stephen — *Centre.*
Trimback A., Fifth — *Dayton.*

White Lead and Putty Manu-facturers.

Hamilton County.

Conkling R. & Sons, Broadway between Court & Hunt — *Cincinnati.*
Conkling R. & Co., s. s. Court, e. Broad'y
Conkling, Wood & Co., n. s. Court, e. of Broadway
Carneal & Co., 21 Main

Jefferson County.

Means & Scott — *Steubenville.*

Wig Makers and Ornamental Hair Workers.

Cuyahoga County.

Hughes J. G., Melodeon Buildings — *Cleveland.*

Franklin County.

Collier J. W. — *Columbus.*

Hamilton County.

Hart Thomas R., 148 Walnut — *Cincinnati.*
Stembers F., 152 "
Steimberger Henry "

Taylor E. B., 13 w. Third   *Cincinnati.*
Zwick Madame, 28 w. Fourth

Window-Shade and Oil-Cloth Manufacturers.

Hamilton County.

Ernst, Thomas J., No. 2 College Hall, Walnut   *Cincinnati.*
Sawyer M. & Co., 8   do
Schwenker & Gardner, 10 e. Liberty.

Wine (Native) Manufacturers.

Hamilton County.

Corneau & Son, 12 e. 4th   *Cincinnati*
Longworth & Zimmerman, Syc., bet. 5th and 6th.
McConkey & Morsell, 35 3d
Seifert Francis, 72 5th
Zimmerman O., Syc., bet. 5th & 6th
Bogen G. & P., near Brighton

Wine & Liquors — Importers.

Hamilton County.

Abraham Lewis, No. 284 Main *Cincinnati.*
Bepler E. & A., 350   do
Block E. & Co., 34 Sycamore
Daniels & Co., 59 Main
Davis N. H. & G. H., 13 Sycamore
Dexter Edmund, 49 & 51   do
Guiraud & Sarran, 37 Main
Harth M. & Co., 380   do
Hawthorn & Dunn, 50 Pearl
Hoffheimer H. & A., 28 Broadway
Herbstreit M., 461 Vine
Harris T. B., 32 e. Second
Jacob J., 25 Congress
Kellogg & Foote, 17 e. Columbia
Krueskamp & Meyer, Court, near Race
Lehman & Co., 267 Main
Little R. A. & Co., 50 do
Loeb S. & Co., 47 Columbia
Louis Adolph, 22   do
Lewis & Dupuy, 22 Broadway
Mackenzie Robert H., 306 Main
M°pan John M., 346   do
Racine & Constant, 86 & 88 Columbia
Schatzmann Isaac, 233 w. 6th
Sparks & Gogrove, 16 Broadway
Southgate Henry M., 24 Columbia
Seeger Wm. & Co., cor. John & 5th

Wine and Liquors — (Foreign and Domestic — Wholesale and Retail) Dealers.

Belmont County.

Cowan Richard   *Hendrysburgh.*

Clark County.

Dale Geo. W.   *Springfield.*

Cuyahoga County.

Bishop, Remington & Co., 13 Merwin   *Cleveland.*
Beckman H., 84 River
Bloch S. H. & Co., Merwin

Blossom O. S., Ag't., cor. Merwin & Jas.   *Cleveland.*
Cranz C. H., 17 Merwin
Cummings J. M. & Co., 183 & 185 River, 97 & 98 Dock
Denzer & Treat, Vineyard & Champlain
Fortin J. O., 46 Bank
George H. B., Merwin
Gordon W. J., River & Dock
Hayward, Woods & Co.
Kingsley E., 37 Ontario
Lied B., 125 St. Clair
McDowell H. C. & Co., 10 Merwin
Morgan, White & Co., on Dock
Nicola F., 52 Ontario
Palmer & Sackrider, 73 Superior
Parsons H., 2 Columbus Block
Wamelink L. B., 70 & 72 Superior
Wenham Arthur J., 9 Merwin
Sullivan P. O., 94 Water
Williams, Babcock & Hurd, 83 Superior

Darke County.

Funk & Hecox   *Greenville.*

Defiance County.

Kuscmaul Jacob   *Defiance.*

Erie County.

Smith & Parsons   *Sandusky City.*
Porter S. & Co.

Franklin County.

Finch W. M., Broad   *Columbus.*
Rickly John & Co., High
Van Sickle E. R., cor. Broad & Gay.

Greene County.

Warmble W. & Co.   *Xenia.*

Hamilton County.

Adae & Labrot, 16 w. Front   *Cincinnati.*
Armstrong R. G., 29 e. Front
Boss Christian, 72 L. Market
Bender Wm., W. Row, s. of Everett
Bruning A. B., 378 Main
Bunn M., 49 Green
Cody P., 9 & 10 Water
Conklin O. S., n. w. cor. Plum & Water
Dean & Wayne, 51 Second
Duvenech J., 417 Vine
Ficken John, 28 L. Market
Fredeldy John C., 54 & 56 do
Ferguson John, n. e. cor. Ludlow & Front
Fey C. P., 615 Vine
Groene J. H. F., s. e. cor. Race & Colu'a.
Goetz John, 69 Court
Hawthorn & Dunn, 50 Pearl
Hirsch & Strauss, 209 Walnut
Hohenberger Charles, 5 8th
Jacob J., 215 Congress
Kellogg & Foote, 17 e. Columbia
Kelly & Co., 20   do
Krueskamp & Meyer, Court, near Race
King & Dailey, 33 Sycamore
Lenmegher Henrich, cor. Ann & Plum
Loder W. & B., 270 Main
Little R. A., 59   do

Levi S. & Brother, 215 Walnut *Cincinnati.*
Miller & Co., 90 Public Landing
McMillen & Watson, 21 Water
Michael D. C., 5 w. Front
Mills D., jun., 224 Main
Mills J. F., s. w. cor. Main & 6th
Mehner Louis, 34 L. Market
Mueller Ferdinand, 35 & 37 Court
Mackentepe Bernard, n, w. cor. Vine & Columbia
Moore & Beers, 6 Cassilly's Row
Marr J., 475 Walnut
Nathan M., 374 Main
Owen Allison, 29 & 31 e. 3d
Oberhen E. & F., 112 Court
Pürmann Andrew, 15 & 17 Canal
Pearson D., 263 6th
Poland & Henry, 38 & 40 Sycamore
Ross M. B., 19   do
Rauth Francis, 80 L. Market
Rechtin G. H., 70   do
Racine & Constant, 86 & 88 Columbia
Seeger Wm. & Co., n. e. corner Fifth and John
Stockman & Co., s. w. cor. Walnut and Water
Snyder Frederick, 99 Canal Market
Seifert Francis, 72 w. Fifth
Sliter George, Ham. Road, near Freeman
Smith & Winston, 12 w. Front
Smith Holland, 28 Sycamore
Stall & Meyer, n. w. cor. L. Market and Sycamore
Siebern J. N. & Brothers, 8 L. Market
Smielan John, 62   do
Wilcox S. T., n. e. cor. 5th & Broadway
White D. A., 34 e. 5th
Wendland L. C., n. e. cor. Vine & Front
Wenjohan H., 100 Columbia
Wilshire, Bristol & Co., 17 Sycamore
Ward Wm. M., 8 Main
Zimmerman C., Syc., bet. 5th & 6th

Hardin County.

Trager & John   *Kenton.*
Davis A. M.
Frink & Mankle,
Bockway & Shartzer

Holmes County.

Rasp P.   *Winesburg.*

Jefferson County.

Mears Robert   *Steubenville.*

Logan County.

Mills Henry   *Bellefontaine.*

Lucas County.

Brand & Lynx   *Toledo.*
Hine & Dillon
Kraus & Howe
Marx E. & G.
Wheeler L.
Wilder George

Mercer County.

Williamson & Ham   *St. Mary's.*
27

Rich Samuel   *St. Mary's.*
Frontz Geo.
Lakamp H.
Sulter A.
Mervelious H.
House M.

Montgomery County.

Hasselmain & Kurtz, First   *Dayton.*
Kensey J., Second
Viot N., Third,

Muskingum County.

Sheldon N.   *Norwich.*
Bonner G.   *Zanesville.*

Pickaway County.

Heyde Wm. Van   *Circleville.*

Ross County.

Poland Wm.   *Chillicothe.*

Scioto County.

Outler W. S. & Co.   *Portsmouth.*
Hickman Jas. & Co.
Rose & Ormsby

Wayne County.

Keesey E.   *Wooster.*

Wire Manufacturers and Workers.

Hamilton County.

Bromwell & Melish, 181 Walnut,   *Cin'ti.*
Hauselman Wm., W. Row, bet. 3d & 4th
Hanseham J. B., 131 W. Row

Wood & Willow-Ware Manufacturers & Dealers.

Cuyahoga County.

George H. B., 2 Canal Block   *Cleveland.*
Nicola F., Ontario
Smithknight L. & Co., 3 Mechanics' Bl'k.

Geauga County.

Metcalf Thos.   *Chardon.*
Seeland H.   *Munson.*

Hamilton County.

Tylee A. O., 10 Main   *Cincinnati.*
Cryer Thomas, 36 5th
Burnet Wm., 14 e. 4th
Cady & Barlow, n. e. corner Fifth and Walnut

Medina County.

Abbott Wm.   *Medina.*

Warren County.

Holoway & Morgan   *Franklin.*

Wool Carders.

Adams County.

Copes Southy   *Locust Grove.*

Allen County,

Flack Lewis W   *Croghan.*

Ashland County.
Drumb A. & W. *Ashland.*

Ashtabula County.
Palmer Wm. D. *Austinburg.*

Belmont County.
Ewan J. *Morristown.*
Simpson F.
Sweeny E. *Armstrong's Mills.*

Brown County.
Reese Wm. *Higginsport.*
Sayers L. *Ripley.*
Kirkpatrick & West *Decatur.*
West & Son *Russellville.*
Speese Geo. *Feesburg.*

Butler County.
Deevis Richard R. *Middletown.*

Clermont County.
Melvin John W. *Nicholsville.*
Davis Charles *Bethel.*
McLaughlin A. J. *Moscow.*

Coshocton County.
Wirts Geo. D. & Edward *Bakersville.*
Winklepleck David *Chili.*

Crawford County.
Clapper S. *Bucyrus.*
Lantzinheiser H.

Defiance County.
Barnum S. B. *Defiance.*
Stevens & Crosier
Noble G. O. *Panama.*

Delaware County.
Brown E. *Galena.*

Fairfield County.
Fehr H. & F. *Clear Creek.*

Franklin County.
Wright Potter *Worthington.*

Geauga County.
Murphey Thos. W. *Chardon.*
Whitney & Wilcox *Thompson.*
Shaw & Co. *Burton.*

Guernsey County.
Brown, Frame & McCleary *Kimbolton.*
Veitch & Hardin *Senecaville.*
Moore Thomas *Leatherwood.*

Hardin County.
Seaman G. *Kenton.*

Highland County.
McMeekin J. *Belfast Town.*
Bingaman Henry *Mowrytown.*

Lawrence County.
Russell S. *Waterloo.*

Logan County.
Shields James D *Huntsville.*

Mahoning County.
Weikart David & Co. *Green Village.*
Hanna & Brooks *Hanna's Mills.*
Oberlender Jacob *North Lima.*

Medina County.
Sprague & Folger *Wadsworth.*
Palmer H. F. *Lodi.*

Monroe County.
Bridgman Augustus *Antioch.*
Williams J. & Brothers *Baresville.*

Morrow County.
House & Cook *Cardington.*
Dillingham Samuel *Lincoln.*

Muskingum County.
Brown Robert *Duncan's Falls.*
Huston R. *Fultonham.*

Pike County.
Waters Richard *Waverly.*
Slaughter T. *Beaver.*
Lancaster John *Piketon.*

Portage County.
Hoke George *Suffield.*
Kent Marvin *Franklin.*
Elder Samuel *Aurora.*
Wolfindin Thos. *Paris.*

Preble County.
Mills J. & A. D. *Camden.*

Putnam County.
Menham W. M. *Pendleton.*

Richland County.
Wiggins N. S. *Shelby.*

Trumbull County.
McCartney Andrew *Girard.*
Soule H. O. *Newton Falls.*

Union County.
Welsh Rossen *Marysville.*
Elwell T. H. & Co. *Milford Centre.*

Williams County.
Wertz John *Bryan.*
Miller John *Montpelier.*
Bowers Michael
Miller Samuel *Lockport.*

Wyandot County.
Carter Wm. *McCutchensville.*

Wool Dealers.

Ashland County.
Carter Norman *Ruggles.*
Crittenden Medad
Purdy A. W.
Sutton A.
Deming O. R. *Ashland.*

Clark County.
Baldwin Wm. *Selma.*

Columbiana County.

Brown James — *Salem.*

Crawford County.

Holmes Franklin — *Bucyrus.*
Nimmoh George

Cuyahoga County.

Fuller Wm. — *Brooklyn.*
Sutliff & Case, near R. R. Depot *Cleveland.*
Benedict L. & Co., 6 Superior
Roberts Ansel, 26 do.
Goodale, Musgrave & Co., 41 Bank

Fayette County.

Utick Wm. A. — *Bloomingburg.*

Geauga County.

Randall, Cook & Co. — *Chardon.*
Wilkins, Young & Co.
Thompson E. — *Middlefield.*
Parmer C. — *Chester.*
Stephenson & Russell
Field O. C. & C. S. — *Clariden.*
Warner Daniel — *Hamden.*

Hamilton County.

Bailey M. & Son, 61 Walnut — *Cincinnati.*
Bullock A. D., 12 and 14 Columbia
Graham & McCoy, 50 Walnut
McCulloch, Morris & Co., 35 Main.

Harrison County.

Hogge Wm. & Co. — *Cadiz.*
McFadden S. & H.
Grimes Thos. D.
Watson Joshua — *Harrisville.*
Lewis Isaac — *Short Creek.*

Jefferson County.

Dike N. & J. S. — *Steubenville.*
Downes John
Dohrman & Collier

Knox County.

Beebee W. W. — *Mt. Vernon.*
Rogers Thomas — *Martinsburg.*

Licking County.

Johnson G. B. — *Granville.*
Whiting O. L.

Medina County.

Austin B. D. — *Leroy.*
Ellis L. D.
Morton O.
Cook Z. — *Mallet Creek.*
Branch Alfred

Morrow County.

Doty S. & M. — *Morengo.*

Muskingum County.

Darlinton & Metcalf — *Zanesville.*

Portage County.

Gillett S. A. & R. A. — *Ravenna.*
Prentiss O. & J. O.
Earle Thos. — *Franklin.*
Kent M.

Wilson & Gray — *Deerfield.*
Beecher Henry — *Nelson.*
Bradshaw John — *Aurora.*
Coe H. — *Charleston.*
Foster J. W. — *Mantua.*
Bradley & Co.
Adams & Moore — *Suffield.*
Dodge & Collins — *Randolph.*

Seneca County.

Harkness & McKee — *Republic.*
Ogden G. M.
Baker B. F.

Starke County.

Pool John & Co. — *Minerva.*
Elson Reed — *Magnolia.*

Summit County.

Carter H. S. — *Tallmadge.*

Wayne County.

Spink & Robb — *Wooster.*

Woolen Goods Manufactu'rs.

Ashland County.

Reznor, Risser & Co. — *Ashland.*

Ashtabula County.

Palmer Wm. D. — *Austinburg.*
Fitts, Harvy & Co. — *East Plymouth.*
Fitts & Co. — *Ashtabula.*
Rassom & Gibbs — *Harpersfield.*

Belmont County.

Dorsey Michael — *Copting.*
McKay, Langley & Co. — *Barnesville.*

Brown County.

Fox Henry — *Union Plain.*
Kirkpatrick & West — *Decatur.*
West & Son — *Russellville.*

Champaign County.

Winder Rebecca — *North Lewisburg.*

Clark County.

Leffel James — *Springfield.*
Pierce J. L.
Rabbits H.

Clinton County.

Hablit & Clark — *Port William.*

Columbiana County.

Hall Thomas — *Salineville.*
Cook Thomas — *Elkton.*
Farrand David

Cuyahoga County.

Bliss & Pool — *Chagrin Falls.*
Powers S. C. — *Bedford.*

Delaware County.

Cone John — *Pattersonville.*
Hinkle James — *Union.*

Erie County.

Pallit R. — *Milan.*

Fairfield County.

Black John & Co.   *Bremen.*
Teel John   *Lancaster.*

Fayette County.

Missmore John   *Pancoastburg.*
Pursell & McElwaine   *Washington.*

Franklin County.

Columbia Woolen Manufacturing Co.,
  Broad   *Columbus.*
Lee Theron, Central College

Gallia County.

Crouset C. & Co.   *Gallipolis.*

Geauga County.

Murphey Thos. W.   *Chardon.*

Greene County.

Barrett George   *Spring Valley.*
Bradshaw H. & Bomger   *New Jasper.*
Parry W. & D. S.
Lewis & Anderson   *Clifton.*

Hamilton County.

Briggs William   *Harrison.*
Armstrong Thomas   *Newtown.*
Mathon Wm.   *Dunlap.*

Highland County.

Robinson James   *Greenfield.*

Huron County.

Bennett Richard   *Monroeville.*
Mathers S. & Co.   *Steuben.*

Jefferson County.

Woolcott C. C.   *Steubenville.*
Wallace E. J.
Rendyle Benard
Orth George
Hogg John   *Mt. Pleasant.*

Knox County.

Wilkerson Wm.   *Luzerne.*

Lake County.

Madison Woolen Co.   *Madison.*
Howe & Rodgers   *Concord.*

Licking County.

Griffin & Colven   *Newark.*
Evens J. H.   *Parryton.*

Logan County.

Rouse W.   *Zanesfield.*

Madison County.

Fish & Clark   *Landon.*

Mahoning County.

Hanua & Brooks   *Hanua's Mills.*
Wiskart David & Co.   *Green Village.*

Meigs County.

Arnold Thos.   *Downington.*

Hyns Joseph   *Downington.*
Humes S.

Miami County.

Young & Yager   *Piqua.*
Soury Joshua   *West Milton.*
Rutlege Wm.

Montgomery County.

Curtis D. M., Fifth   *Dayton.*
Ellis G. F.   *Miamisburgh.*

Morrow County.

Moore J.   *Mt. Gilead.*
Jarvis Wm.   *Chesterville.*

Muskingum County.

Brown Robert   *Duncan's Falls.*
Rambo L. & Co.   *Dresden.*
Thomas J. R. & Son.   *Putnam.*

Perry County

Pressler C. G.   *Malvern.*

Pickaway County.

Drakeley Thomas   *Circleville.*

Richland County.

Lousde & France   *Lucas.*
Gladhill W.

Scioto County.

Maddock Wm.   *Portsmouth.*
Cranston E. & Son   *Wheelersburgh.*

Seneca County.

Loomis L. M.   *Tiffin.*

Starke County.

Chaddock John   *Waynesburg.*
Cummins & Co.   *West Brookfield.*
Hartzell George   *Canton.*
Robbins John
Skinner A. T. & Co.   *Massillon.*
Hover Elias   *Limaville.*
Alexander Lawrence   *Mahoning.*

Summit County.

Rawson & Goodale   *Middlebury.*
Perkins & Co.   *Akron.*
Raymond J. & Co.
Coffin A. & Co.   *Montreat.*
Pierson Thomas

Trumbull County.

Hurlbutt & Hull   *Orangeville.*

Tuscarawas County.

Bimeler J. M., Agent Zoar Community
                                           Zoar.
Hayden, Harmer & Co.,   *Canal Dover.*
Williams T. K. & Co.,   *New Philadelphia.*

Warren County.

Mayer Jacob   *Hayesville.*

Washington County.

McIntosh Wm. W. & Co.   *Beverly.*

Wayne County.

Grable John   *Dalton.*
Geon M.
Vangilder & Morrow

Evans & McGonigal   *Edinburgh.*
Chidister S. & E.   *Chippewa.*

Worker in Plaster.

Hamilton County.

Fatmy James, No. 16 Art Un. Building
      Cincinnati.

OHIO STATE STOCK BANKS.

NAME.	LOCATION.	PRESIDENT.	CASHIER.	CAPITAL.
Bank of Commerce	Cleveland, Ohio	P. Handy	Sidney Moore, jr.	$25,000
Bank of Marion	Marion	— Bowen	D. Moody	25,000
Citizens' Bank of Steubenville	Steubenville		H. P. Espy	25,000
Champaign County Bank	Urbana	S. A. Winslow	A. W. Brockway	25,000
Forest City Bank	Cleveland	J. O. Hussey	H. M. Grenell	25,000
Franklin Bank of Portage County	Franklin Mills	Z. Kent	James O. Willard	40,000
Iron Bank	Ironton	J. Rodgers	S. Hunt	25,000
Merchants' Bank	Massillon	J. Steese	S. C. Emley	25,000
Miami Valley Bank	Dayton	Daniel Beckel	O. Ballard	25,000
Pickaway County Bank	Circleville	M. Brown	E. P. Grant	25,000
Starke County Bank	Canton	J. S. Saxton	W. M. Means	25,000
Springfield Bank	Springfield	O. Clark	B. F. Sanford	25,000
Saving's Bank	Cincinnati	J. D. Park	S. W. Torrey	25,000
Union Bank	Sandusky City	F. T. Barney		70,900
State Bank of Ohio		G. Swan		

BRANCH BANKS.

NAME.	LOCATION.	PRESIDENT.	CASHIER.	CAPITAL.
Athens Branch	Athens	J. Ballard	J. R. Crawford	$100,000
Akron Branch	Akron	W. A. O. Otis	J. W. McMillen	100,000
Belmont Branch	Bridgeport	Jno. Warfield	John O. Tallman	100,000
Commercial Branch	Cleveland	T. P. Handy		100,000
Commercial Branch	Toledo	Sam Young	M. Johnson	150,000
Chillicothe Branch	Chillicothe	Wm. H. Duglass	J. S. Atwood	250,000
Delaware County Branch	Delaware	H. Williams	B. Powers	93,000
Dayton Branch	Dayton	Peter Odlin	O. G. Swain	200,900

NAME.	LOCATION.	PRESIDENT.	CASHIER.	CAPITAL.
Exchange Branch	Columbus	W. B. Hubbard	H. M. Hubbard	$125,000
Farmers' Branch	Ashtabula	O. H. Fitch	A. F. Hubbard	100,000
Farmers' Branch	Mansfield	James Purdy	H. Colby	100,000
Farmers' Branch	Ripley	T. McCune	Dan'l P. Evans	100,000
Farmers' Branch	Salem	S. Jennings	C. H. Cornwell	100,000
Franklin Branch	Columbus	Sam'l Parsons	James Espy	175,000
Franklin Branch	Cincinnati	J. Kilgore	T. M. Jackson	169,000
Guernsey Branch	Washington	Jno. McCurdy	Wm. Skinner	100,000
Harrison Branch	Cadiz	D. Kilgore	R. Lyons	100,000
Hocking Valley Branch	Lancaster	D. Tallmadge	M. A. Daugherty	100,000
Jefferson Branch	Steubenville	John Andrews	Wm. Spencer	100,000
Knox County Branch	Mount Vernon	H. B. Curtis	J. C. Ramsey	100,000
Licking County Branch	Newark			
Logan Branch	Logan	Reuben Culver	Sam'l P. Officer	99,020
Lorain Branch	Elyria	E. Dewitt	Jno. R. Finn	99,000
Mad River Valley Branch	Springfield	J. Mills	J. T. Claypoole	100,000
Marietta Branch	Marietta	Dr. L'Hommedieu	N. L. Wilson	100,000
Mechanics & Traders' Branch	Cincinnati	T. M. Kelley	S. S. Rowe	125,000
Merchants' Branch	Cleveland	Wm. Barbee	P. Handy	100,000
Miami County Branch	Troy	Joseph Gills	H. S. Mayo	100,000
Mount Pleasant Branch	Mount Pleasant	Wm. Tallant	Jonathan Binns	100,000
Muskingum Branch	Zanesville	T. Baker	H. J. Jewett	125,000
Norwalk Branch	Norwalk	W. Scott	John Gardner	100,000
Piqua Branch	Piqua	R. E. Campbell	J. G. Young	100,000
Portage County Branch	Ravenna	W. Kinney	J. H. Ebbert	103,000
Portsmouth Branch	Portsmouth	John Hunt	E. Kinney	100,000
Preble County Branch	Eaton	O. T. Reeves	Jno. Gray	100,000
Ross County Branch	Chillicothe	E. N. Sill	A. Spencer Nye	150,000
Summit County Branch	Cuyahoga Falls	T. W. Bradley	H. D. Williams	100,000
Toledo Branch	Toledo	M. D. Wellman	B. Bliss	130,500
Union Branch	Massillon		L. Hurxthall	150,000
Wayne County Branch	Wooster		E. Quinby, jr.	115,000
Xenia Branch	Xenia	A. Hivling	A. Trader	150,000

INDEPENDENT BANKS.

NAME.	LOCATION.	PRESIDENT.	CASHIER.	CAPITAL.
Bank of Geauga	Painesville	Dan'l Kerr	S. S. Osborn	$40,000
Canal Bank	Cleveland	Isaac L. Hewitt	T. O. Severance	50,900
City Bank	Cleveland	Lemuel Wick	Wm. H. Stanley	50,000
City Bank of Cincinnati	Cincinnati	J. P. Reznor	T. Heston	139,000
City Bank of Columbus	Columbus	R. W. McCoy	Thos. Moodie	148,000
Commercial Bank of Cincinnati	Cincinnati	Jacob Strader	James Hall	50,000
Dayton Bank	Dayton	J. Rench	J. B. Chapman	91,000
Franklin Bank of Zanesville	Zanesville	Dan'l Brush	John Peters	100,000
Mahoning County Bank	Youngstown	Wm. Raynor	R. W. Taylor	25,000
Sandusky City Bank	Sandusky City	E. Lane	H. S. Flynt	69,500
Seneca County Bank	Tiffin	B. Tomb	Sylvanus Arnold	50,000
Western Reserve Bank	Warren	Geo. Parsons	Geo. Taylor	65,000

OLD CHARTERED BANKS.

NAME.	LOCATION.	PRESIDENT.	CASHIER.	CAPITAL.
Bank of Circleville	Circleville	N. S. Gregg	H. Lawrence	$300,000
Bank of Massillon	Massillon	Chas. K. Skinner	E. F. Platt	200,000
Clinton Bank of Columbus	Columbus	W. S. Sullivant	D. W. Deshler	250,000
Ohio Life Insurance & Trust Company	Cincinnati	C. Stetson	G. S. Coe	2,000,000
Ohio Savings Institute	Tiffin	S. Waggoner		25,000

CITIES AND TOWNS

BUSINESS DIRECTORY
CARDS.

T. W. SPRAGUE & CO.,
MERCHANT
TAILORS
AND
CLOTHIERS,
No. 113 Main Street, Cincinnati, O.

Where can be found at all times

READY-MADE CLOTHING!

Out from the

FINEST GOODS

Made after the **Latest Eastern Styles**! and work warranted equal to the **best Custom Made.** We keep nothing but

FINE GOODS & THE NEWEST STYLES.

The best proof that what we say may be true or false, is to call and examine our stock for yourselves—
should you find it to be a **HUMBUG**, you have the liberty to spread the information, and should do
so; if all should be satisfactory, you will please recommend your friends and acquaintances
to call at **113 Main Street, Cin.**, where you will find **SPRAGUE** in a
prosperous condition, always ready to sell such goods as will recommend themselves.
We have but

ONE PRICE, OUR TERMS ARE CASH.

BOYS' AND YOUTHS'

From 3 to 18 years of age can be accommodated at any time, with all styles
of Clothing ready made.

Clothing made to order, and sent to any part of the West.

HORTON & MACY,

No. 210 Fifth Street, also S. W. Corner of Elm and Pearl Streets, Cincinnati.

MANUFACTURERS OF MARBLEIZED

IRON MANTELS,

TABLE TOPS, COLUMNS, &c.

By this process every variety of Marble is imitated with great perfection. They are more durable than Marble, will resist a much greater degree of heat, and are not affected by acids or oils. Also,

FANCY ENAMELED GRATES.

We are prepared to make to order any kinds of

FINE CASTINGS

IRON RAILING, DOOR SHUTTERS,

BANK VAULTS, &C.

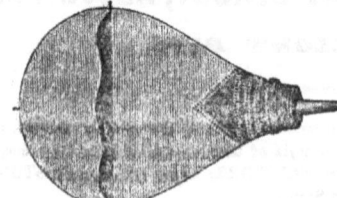

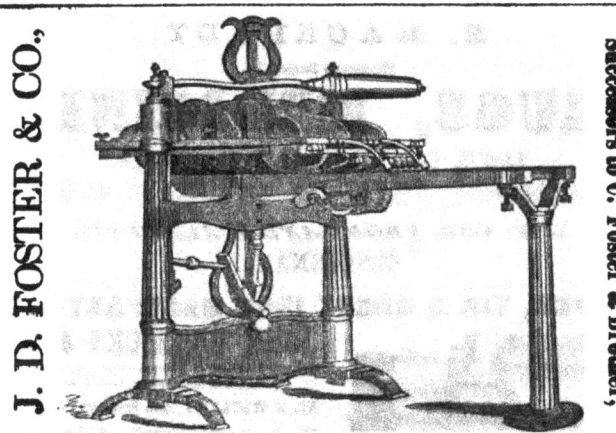

R. MACREADY,

Wholesale Dealers in

DRUGS, MEDICINES,

PAINTS, OILS, VARNISHES, DYES, BRUSHES,

GLASSWARE, PURE WINES AND BRANDIES,

S. W. COR. FRONT AND WALNUT STS.

CINCINNATI

COPPER, TIN & SHEET IRON MANUFACTORY.

JOHN HORROCKS & CO.,

Take this method of informing their friends and the public, that they have opened a store at

NO. 9 WATER ST. bet. Broadway & Ludlow,

Where they are prepared to execute, at the shortest notice, all kinds of

STEAMBOAT WORK,

In either Tin, Copper or Sheet Iron. They will also keep on hand a general assortment of all articles in their line. Also, make to order and keep on hand all sizes of the

Buckeye Cooking Stoves,

FOR STEAMBOATS AND TAVERNS.

All kinds of Jobbing work for Boats attended to with dispatch.

JAMES PAUL.   THOS. MURDOCK.

PAUL & MURDOCK,

STEAMBOAT AGENTS,

AND

Forwarding and Commission Merchants,

No. 7 WATER STREET, SOUTH SIDE,

CINCINNATI, OHIO.

☞ Agents for Bingham's Transportation Line on Pennsylvania Canal and Pittsburgh Packets. ☜

MAHOGANY WAREHOUSE,

ANDREW McALPIN,

NO. 103 WALNUT STREET, CINCINNATI, OHIO,

DEALER IN

MAHOGANY VENEERS,		MAHOGANY LOGS,
WALNUT	DO.	ROSEWOOD DO.
ROSEWOOD	DO.	LIGNUM VITÆ DO.
SATIN	DO.	EBONY DO.
MAPLE	DO.	MAHOG. BOARDS & PLANKS.

☞ Also, Plush, Hair Cloth, Curled Hair, Gimp, Webbing, Cane and Springs. ☜

FRAZER & DENIS,

ENGRAVERS

ON WOOD,

No. 120 Main Street, Gazette Building,

CINCINNATI.

☞ Every description of Engravings executed in the best style. The attention of SHOWMEN in general is called to our Poster work.

Orders from abroad punctually attended to.

SIM COHEN,

260 SIXTH STREET,

CINCINNATI.

S. C. takes this mode of informing his customers that he has located himself as above, and ready to supply the trade with a warranted article equal to any. Begs to observe that no

PENCILS ARE OF HIS MAKE

UNLESS STAMPED

SIM COHEN; or, SIM COHEN & SON,

Which is the present name of the firm.

He wishes it to be known that he is the original SIM COHEN, of New York, who obtained a Premium 16 years ago.

I. F. HOWELLS.   A. PATTON.   M. H. KEEVER.

HOWELLS, PATTON & Co.

Wholesale Druggists,

IMPORT DIRECT FROM EUROPE,

Nos. 16 & 18, East side Main St. between Front and Second.

CINCINNATI, O.

ROBERT MITCHELL.   FRED. RAMMELSBERG.

MITCHELL & RAMMELSBERG,

WHOLESALE AND RETAIL

FURNITURE WARE ROOMS,

Nos. 23 & 25 East Second Street,

BETWEEN MAIN AND SYCAMORE,

CINCINNATI, OHIO.

HENRY CLOSTERMAN,
WHOLESALE

STEAM CHAIR MANUFACTURER,

COR. SMITH & AUGUSTA STS.

BETWEEN FRONT AND SECOND,

CINCINNATI, O.

C. CLAASSEN,
BRUSH MANUFACTURER

East Side Main St., bet. Webster and Orchard,

CINCINNATI, OHIO.

H. PFISTER.   G. METZGER.

PFISTER & METZGER,

BANK,   **HOUSE**

JAIL, SAFE   —AND—

—AND—   **HOTEL**

HOUSE LOCKS   Bells Hung

MANUFACTURERS OF WROUGHT IRON LOCKS,

NO. 30 SIXTH ST., BET. MAIN & WALNUT, CINCINNATI, O.

Latches, Bolts, Door Plates, Butt Hinges, Screws, Pad, Chest and Drawer Locks; also, Fire Grates of every description constantly on hand.

DONALD CAMPBELL.   J. CHAS. RUSSELL.   E. N. FULLER.

CAMPBELL, RUSSELL & CO.,

FORWARDING & COMMISSION MERCHANTS

Front St., one door East of Broadway,

'CINCINNATI.

HERMAN WITTE.   FERDINAND WITTE.

H. & F. WITTE,
BEEF & PORK PACKERS,

AND DEALERS IN

PROVISIONS OF ALL KINDS,

Nos. 15 and 17 East Front Street,

CINCINNATI, OHIO,

Steamboats supplied with Fresh and Salt Meat, and Ice at all times.

J. H. BURROWS.   A. KIMBALL.

J. H. BURROWS & CO.,
COLUMBIA FOUNDRY

Columbia Street, between Elm and Plum.

OFFICE, 23 WEST FRONT STREET, BET. MAIN AND WALNUT, CINCINNATI.

Manufacturers of J. H. Burrows' Patent Grist Mills, French Burr Mill Stones, of all sizes; Steam Engines, Grist and Saw Mill Irons and Castings, of all descriptions; also, dealers in Bolting Cloths, Plaster of Paris, &c.

I. STRAUB. B. HAZLET.

ISAAC STRAUB & CO., Mill Factory,

Corner of Front and John Streets, Cincinnati, O. Warehouse, No. 19 Front Street, between Main and Walnut.

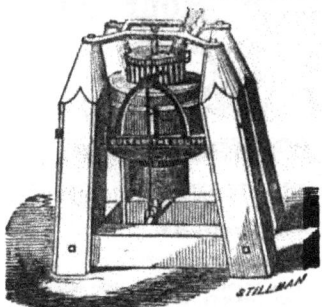

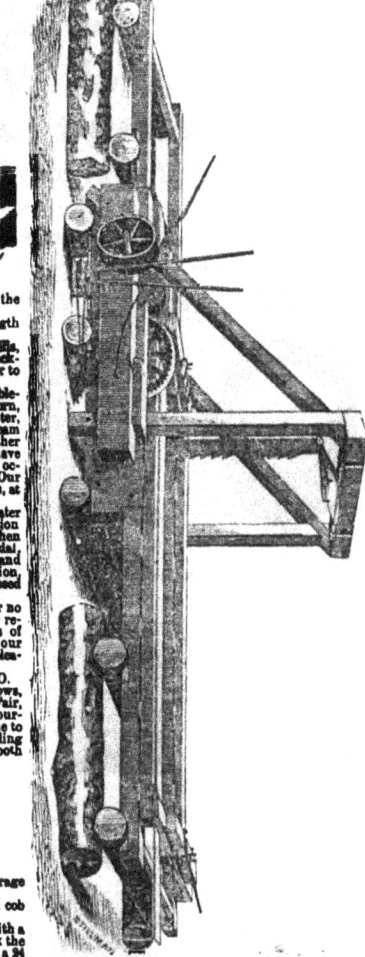

The above is a cut of a single-geared "Queen of the South" Corn Mill and Crusher.

We manufacture a Cob Breaker of great strength and ease of operation.

We place this useful contrivance on all sizes of Mills, by which means we convert a Corn Mill into a Stock-Feed mill, but a few minutes' work to put it on, or to take it off.

We manufacture portable mills, single and double-geared—best quality of French burrs—to grind Corn, Wheat, and Stock Feeds, calculated for steam, water, or horse power. These mills have been run by steam and horse power, in competition against the other make of mills of our city, at our State Fairs, and have never faile' to carry off the first premium—on one occasion was awarded a beautiful silver medal. Our mills also took two first premiums as the best mills, at two Annual Fairs of our Mechanics' Institute.

Also—Portable Saw Mills, to be run by steam, water or horse power. This mill was exhibited in operation by horse power, at the Ohio State Fair, in 1860, when it was awarded a premium and a splendid silver medal.

Also—Different kinds of portable horse power and steam engines. All our articles, for ease of operation, simplicity, usefulness and durability, are surpassed by none now in use.

All our articles are warranted as represented—or no sale—at our cost of transportation, and the money refunded. For a full description and testimonials of merit and usefulness, we refer those interested to our pamphlet, to be had at our factory, where we take pleasure to explain each article.

ISAAC STRAUB & CO.

Note.—Mr. Kimball, the partner of J. H. Burrows, while exhibiting a Burrows' Mill at our State Fair, last fall, was boisterous about his mill, and courageously entered into a verbal agreement with me to grind corn thus. Whoever grinds the most, regarding quality and quantity, was to be the owner of both mills at each and every trial.

FIRST TRIAL.

Straub to run an 18 inch mill.
Burrows & Co. to run a 20 inch mill.

SECOND TRIAL.

Straub to run a 22 inch mill.
Burrows & Co. to run a 24 inch mill.

THIRD TRIAL.

Straub to run a 26 inch mill.
Burrows & Co. to run a 30 inch mill.

When the pinch came, that boisterous courage stepped out.

To the above I now append a challenge to grind cob feed out of whole ears of corn.

I will run my 18 inch "Queen of the South," with a cob-breaker attachment, the same article that took the premium at the Ohio State Fair, last fall, against a 24 inch Burrows' Mill and Wm. Stewart's Ohio and Kentucky Stock Feed Mills, both to be run at once, and if you are apprehensive of a risky business, you have my entire approbation to run Mr. Pomeroy's Corn Crusher as an auxiliary. Should my single article fail to grind equal in quality and quantity to the combined productions of the two or three mills—just as you please—then you can draw a few hundred dollars as stakes put up.

Come boys, don't be cowardly, there is nothing like walking straight into the merits of the things.

To J. H. Burrows & Co., Sept. 29, 1862. ISAAC STRAUB.

T. SMITH,

Dealer in

Eight Day and Thirty Hour Brass

CLOCKS,

AND CLOCK TRIMMINGS,

12 E. FIFTH ST. OPP. DENNISON HOUSE, CIN'TI,

And No. 88 Main St. Saint Louis, Mo.

My assortment consists of every style and variety of Clocks, manufactured by Chauncey Jerome, Seth Thomas, Smith & Goodrich, Wm. L. Gilbert, J. C. Brown, Birge, Peck & Co., Litchfield Manufacturing Co., and others, comprising in all an assortment of some 150 different styles and kinds. Orders from Dealers at a distance filled at prices that will give satisfaction.

No. 1 Octagon 8 day Clocks and Time Pieces.
Height 22 inches.

Paris 8 and 1 day Pearl inlaid.
Height 17 in.

Extra column; 30 hours. Weight and Spring.
He't 25 1-4 & 18 1-4 in.

Octagon 8 day No. 2 Clocks and Time pieces.
Height 24 in.

Kossuth 8 day and 1 day. Pearl inlaid.
Height 19 in.

Victoria 8 day and 30 hour Spring.
Height 15 1-4 in.

Jerome's Union 1 day Spring.
Height 13 1-2 in.

Round top Gothic No. 1 & 2 & with alarm.
He't 19 in.

Round Gilt 8 day time pieces.
3 sizes.

Cottage Time Piece, and with Alarm.
Height 12 inches.

Union 8 and 1 day. Pearl inlaid.
Height 13 in.

Octagon Level Time pieces, 8 day & 30 hour. 6, 8 & 10 in. Dial.

1853. 1853.

BEN FRANKLIN

GREAT STEAM

PRINTING HOUSE

No. 95 WALNUT STREET, NEAR PEARL,
CINCINNATI, O.

The large increase of patronage of this establishment the past year, has rendered it necessary for the Proprietors to add to the already extensive apartments, the four story building fronting on Pearl Street, in the rear of which is located their Steam Power Press Rooms,—and have also made large additions in the way of

TYPE AND PRESSES,

In order to enable them to execute with still more promptness and elegance the heavy contracts for

Plain, Fancy and Ornamental
JOB
PRINTING

They have now in successful operation 1 Super Royal Hoe Cylinder Job Press, 1 Royal Hoe Cylinder Job Press, 2 Adams' Book Presses, 2 Adams' Job Presses, 1 large Double Super Royal Hoe Press, 1 Taylor's Fast Double Cylinder Press, 1 Single Cylinder Press, all of them driven by Steam Power; also 6 Hand Presses, 1 Card Press, 1 Hat Tip Press, and 1 Embossing Press—in all

18 DIFFERENT KINDS OF PRINTING MACHINES.

The Presses and machinery of the BEN FRANKLIN PRINTING HOUSE, for ingenuity of mechanism, strength of construction, and rapidity and elegance of execution, are considered unrivaled by those of any other establishment in the West. The attention of the Proprietors, who are Practical Printers, is exclusively devoted to the

BOOK & JOB BUSINESS,

And not *divided* and *distracted* by the many conflicting interests which beset Daily and Weekly Newspapers.

Especially would they call attention to their increased facilities to execute, in superior style

BOOK WORK OF ALL KINDS.

Their PRICES have been greatly reduced, and will compare with any other Job Office in the West.

O. CLARK & Co. - - - - - Proprietors.

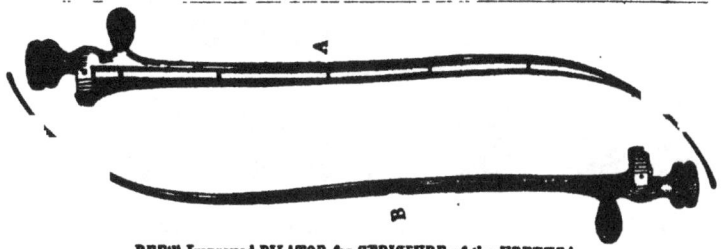

REES' Improved DILATOR for STRICTURE of the URETHRA.

WILLIAM X. REES,

NO. 71 WEST SIXTH STREET.

CINCINNATI, O.

MANUFACTURER OF

Surgical and Dental Instruments,

Such as Amputating, Turphining, Pocket, &c.

Trusses of every Description, to suit the Case, Made, Applied and Warranted.

☞ *Orders Solicited and Promptly Attended to.* ☜

CABINETMAKERS' UNION,

MANUFACTURERS OF

BEDSTEADS, SOFAS, BUREAUS, CARD AND CENTER TABLES.

ALL KINDS OF FURNITURE.

FACTORY: On N. W. Corner of Smith and Augusta Streets,
SALE STORE: No. 217 Walnut, betw. 5th & Sixth Sts.
CINCINNATI, OHIO.

A large assortment of all kinds of Furniture for wholesale or retail, kept on hand. All orders promptly attended to. ☞Always buying Poplar, Sycamore, Walnut, Cherry, &c.

JACOB DIEHL, Agent.

FRANKLIN
FIRE AND MARINE

INSURANCE COMPANY
OF NEW YORK.

Capital Stock, - - - - - $300,000.
Surplus, - - - - - - 62,732,73.
General Agency Office, No. 4 Main Street, Cin.
WM. E. ROLLO, General Agent.
JOSEPH J. DAVIS, Agent at Cincinnati.

JOHN DILLINGHAM,

MANUFACTURER OF

Planed and finished by Mather's Spoke Planing Machine, Patented 1850.

N. S. SEVENTH ST. BET. MAIN & SYCAMORE.

GEO C. MILLER & CO.,

MANUFACTURERS OF STEEL MOULD BOARD PLOWS,

A large assortment of Plows and Steel Mould Boards on hand suitable for Western & Southern agriculture.

SIGN OF THE EAGLE, SEVENTH ST., BET. MAIN & WALNUT, CINCINNATI, O.

H. RASCHE,

TANNER & SKIN DRESSER,

No. 537 MAIN STREET,

WEST SIDE, BETWEEN THIRTEENTH AND ALLISON,

TAN YARD, CANAL ST. NEAR MOHAWK BRIDGE.

CINCINNATI, O.

LONGWORTH & ZIMMERMAN,

NATIVE WINE ESTABLISHMENT, CINCINNATI.

C. ZIMMERMAN,

NATIVE WINE, BRANDY

AND

EXCHANGE BUSINESS,

177 SYCAMORE STREET, CINCINNATI.

QUEEN CITY FOUNDRY.

JAS. L. HAVEN & CO.,

SUCCESSORS TO A. GARDNER & CO.,

IRON FOUNDERS & MACHINISTS,

Foundry, Corner of Broadway & Liberty. Warehouse,
No. 319 Main Street, Cincinnati.

MANUFACTURERS OF

BUTT HINGES & GENERAL HARDWARE,

CHAIN PUMP TRIMMINGS, CASTINGS AND MACHINERY.

☞Agents and Manufacturers of TIMS' PATENT OIL TIGHT
BEARING for Shafting and Machinery, requires oiling but once in ninety days.

CINCINNATI COLLEGE
OF
MEDICINE AND SURGERY,
S. W. Corner of Western Row and Longworth Streets,

FACULTY.

A. H. BAKER, M. D., Professor of Surgery.
B. S. LAWSON, M. D., do of Theory and Practice.
C. B. CHAPMAN, M. D., do of Anatomy.
ELIJAH SLACK, M. D., do of Chemistry.
J. W. MIGHELS, M. D., do of Obstetrics.
G. A. GOTWALD, M. D., do of Materia Medica and Therapeutics.
L. L. PINKERTON, M. D., do of Physiology and Pathology.
W. W. DAWSON, M. D., Demonstrator of Anatomy.

☞Winter Session commences on the first Monday of November. Spring Session on the first
Monday of March.

A. H. BAKER, M. D., President,
Residence, No. 316 West Sixth Street.

STEAM
MARBLE WORKS.
CHARLES RULE,
(LATE LOWRY & RULE,)
COR. BROADWAY AND FIFTH ST. CINCINNATI.

Monuments, Tombs and Grave Stones, Marble Mantles and Statuary, baptismal fonts, urns,
Vases, Garden figures, Cabinet and Counter Slabs, &c., &c., constantly on hand and furnished
to order.

The trade supplied with Marble in Block and Slab, or Sawed to order.

HENRY GOOCH,

LARD OIL MANUFACTURER,

130 COLUMBIA ST.,

BETWEEN RACE AND ELM.

JOLLIFFE & GITCHELL,

Attorneys & Counsellors

AT LAW,

MAIN STREET, BETWEEN THIRD AND FOURTH.

JOSEPH WHITAKER,

DEALER IN

TALLOW, NEATS FOOT OIL,

AND ALL KINDS OF GREASE.

ALSO IN

HOGSHAIR, BRISTLES, SPUN HAIR AND SAUSAGE CASINGS.

Cash paid for the above articles; or, sold at the lowest market price.

(POST BOX 607.)

Establishment, on Deer Creek, near old Corporation Line,

CINCINNATI, O.

WESTERN GLUE FACTORY.

JOHN H. GOAS,

NO. 11 DUNLAP STREET, ABOVE FINDLAY,

BETWEEN MIAMI CANAL AND ELM ST.,

CINCINNATI, O.

N. B.—CASH PAID FOR TANNERS' SCRAPS.

E. G. MEGRUE.   JAMES J. LYON.

MEGRUE & LYON,

SUCCESSORS TO P. RUST & SON,

UNDERTAKERS,

North East Corner Plum & Longworth Sts., Cincinnati.

Burial Cases of all decriptions, Hearse and Carriages furnished. ☞ Particular attention paid to preparing Corpees-

B. D. WHEELER,

SURGEON DENTIST,

OFFICE AND RESIDENCE:

No. 152, North Side of Sixth Street, between Race and Elm,

CINCINNATI, OHIO.

☞ Dr. Wheeler having had long experience in the most difficult operations, and being thoroughly acquainted with all the late improvements in Dentistry, feels confident of being able to give entire satisfaction to all who may favor him with their patronage.

J. H. DETERS,

FASHIONABLE

BOOT MAKER,

NO. 41 THIRD STREET,

CINCINNATI.

SHIRES'

HOUSE FURNISHING ESTABLISHMENT,

AND

TIN, COPPER & SHEET IRON WARE MANUFACTORY,

43 East Fourth and 254 West 5th Sts.

CINCINNATI, OHIO.

J. MULLEN'S

CHAIR & CABINET

WAREROOMS,

No. 132 Sycamore Street, five doors above Fourth,

Opposite the Post Office, Cin.

The Cin'ti Literary & Scientific Institute

PHYSIO-MEDICAL COLLEGE

OF OHIO,

HAVE BEEN REMOVED

From Third Street, East of Broadway, to the splendid and more convenient edifice of the

CINCINNATI COLLEGE,

EAST SIDE OF WALNUT ST., BET. FOURTH AND FIFTH,

Where the Lectures in the Medical Department will be resumed on the First Monday in November, by a full and able faculty. This College has an excellent Library and Anatomical Museum, and is well supplied with apparatus for the illustration of all its teachings; also, with Clinical Practice.

If suitable encouragement be offered, Lectures in some of the Literary Departments and other Sciences not directly connected with Medicine, will be commenced at the same time.   **A. CURTIS, M. D.,**

President of Institute, and Editor of P. M. Recorder,

Office in the College.

THE STONE COMPANY

Whose Yard and Machine Works are located on the

CORNER OF HIGH STREET AND THE MIAMI CANAL,

CINCINNATI,

Have commenced operations in sawing, dressing and polishing stone and marble, for sale to stone cutters. It is their intention to be always provided with a good stock of Italian Marble, Dayton Stone, Free Stone, from Rockville and Buena Vista Quarries; Madison Marble, and to saw and dress it in every required manner. In consequence of their facilities for doing this, they will undertake to furnish the dressed material with a dispatch not hitherto known in the stone business, and which must enable the stone cutter or marble worker to do business more promptly and easily, and with more certainty of quick returns and good profits than has ever been possible under the old system of hand labor. Blocks of marble or stone sent to the yard will be sawed or dressed to dimensions on reasonable terms.

R. P. PENNIMAN.   WILLARD ELMER.

PENNIMAN & ELMER,

RAILROAD IRON FOUNDERS,

CAR WHEELS, SINGLE AND DOUBLE PLATES;

PEDESTALS, OIL BOXES, &c.; BUILDING, DEPOT, BRIDGE AND MACHINERY CASTINGS,

FOUNDRY, ON FIFTH ST.,

Next West of the Cincinnati, Hamilton & Dayton R. R. Depot and W. W. Canal.

WM. LEE & CO.

WEST FOURTH ST., CINCINNATI,

JOBBERS AND RETAILERS OF

DRY GOODS.

THE JOBBING DEPARTMENTS

OF THIS HOUSE OFFER

STRONG INDUCEMENTS TO CLOSE BUYERS

As sales in these departments are made exclusively for cash, and

Prices are made upon the closest Calculations.

THE RETAILING DEPARTMENTS

Afford to persons or families the largest and most varied assortment of

DRY GOODS

IN THE WEST, FROM WHICH TO SELECT THEIR SUPPLIES.

Prices are marked so Low

THAT

NO DEVIATIONS ARE MADE.

☞ Salesmen are not allowed to misrepresent to customers the goods for sale, nor urge them to buy what does not please them.

GEO. S. JENKINS & CO.,
WHOLESALE DEALERS IN

Foreign and Domestic

DRY GOODS,

SOUTH-EAST CORNER PEARL AND VINE STS.,

CINCINNATI.

E. TAYLOR & CO.,
(SUCCESSORS TO BAKER & NORTON,)
MANUFACTURERS OF

Enameled Mantle Grates,

RAILING AND FANCY CASTINGS;
Agents for the Salamander Co.'s Marbleized Cast Iron Mantles,

NO. 275 FIFTH STREET,
SOUTH SIDE, NEAR WESTERN ROW,

CINCINNATI.

 **P. CONNELLY,**

SHEET IRON WORKER

FRONT ST., BET. LUDLOW AND LAWRENCE,

CINCINNATI.

Manufacturer of all kinds of Steamboat, Railroad, Mill and Distillery Works. Jobbing, in all its branches, done at short notice and on reasonable terms. Particular attention paid to building Gasometers.

REFER TO

Cin. Gas Light and Coke Co.   George Shield.   James Todd & Co.   Shreve, Steele & Co.
Anthony Harkness & Son.   James Goodloe.   L. Miami, Hillsborough, and Hamilton and Dayton R. R's.

LAMBE & CO.,

COCOA AND CHOCOLATE

MANUFACTURERS,

180 COLUMBIA ST.,

BETWEEN RACE AND ELM.

OHIO MUSTARD MANUFACTORY

AND

COFFEE AND SPICE MILLS,

Nos. 243 & 245

Sycamore Street, between Seventh & Eighth,

CINCINNATI, OHIO.

DIXON & DARST,

WHOLESALE DEALERS IN

ROASTED & GROUND COFFEE, SPICES, MUSTARD, PEPPER SAUCE,

TOMATO CATSUP, &C.

All Spices put up by us warranted strictly pure.

☞ Silver Medal awarded at the 12th Annual Exhibition of the Ohio Mechanics' Institute, 1852, for the best Mustard and Spices exhibited.

REFERENCES: Springer & Whiteman; Tweed & Andrews; Canfield & Moffett; Thompson & Taaffe; Hosea & Frazer; Thirkield, Thompson & Co.; Raper, Cox & Co.; Bishop, Wells & Co.; Babbitt, Good & Co.; John Swasey & Co.; Poland & Henry; L. L. Harding, Holmes & Co.; Spinning, Wilson & Brown; Brown & Brother; J F. Mills; Jas. B. Bell & Co.; F. R. Thompson; P. Cody; Jones, Lovett & Robbins; Smith & Graham.

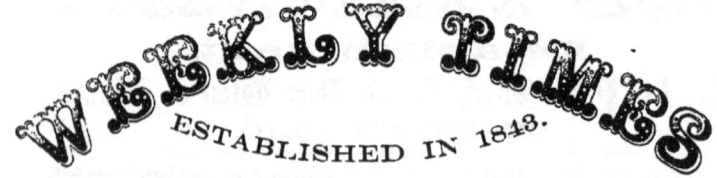

LATIMER, COX, COLBURN & LUPTON,

JOBBERS OF HARDWARE,

No. 74 MAIN STREET,

Near Pearl St.,

CINCINNATI, O.

E. J. LATIMER.   T. M. COX.   CHAS. L. COLBURN.   JAS. LUPTON.

Importers and Wholesale Dealers in every description of Foreign and Domestic
Hardware and Cutlery.

W. S. PEEBLES.   D. M. PEEBLES.

PEEBLES & BROTHER,

MANUFACTURERS OF

LARD OIL AND OPAL CANDLES,

Nos. 177, 179 & 181 Miami Canal,

S. SIDE, BET. ELM & PLUM, CIN'NATI.

CASH PAID FOR LARD.

J. G. DICKSON.   D. LE BETTER.

DICKSON & LE BETTER,

(Successors to Sampson & Andrews,)

Importers and Wholesale and Retail Dealers in

CHINA, GLASS, & QUEENS WARE.

ALSO, LAMPS, CASTORS AND TABLE CUTLERY,

No. 217 Main Street,

Between Fifth and Sixth, Cincinnati.

C. F. ADAE & LABROT,

COMMISSION MERCHANTS,

AND IMPORTERS OF

FOREIGN WINES AND LIQUORS,

Havana Cigars and Havana Goods generally, Dealers in Spanish and
Domestic Leaf Tobacco of every description,

16 W. Front St., N. Side, bet. Main & Walnut, Cincin'ti.

☞ We are prepared at all times to furnish sight or short sight drafts at the lowest rates on
Paris, Strasbourg, Bremen, Hamburg, Osnabrueck, Berlin, Leipsig, Frankfort on the Maine,
Landau, Zweibruicken, (Deuxponts), Mannheim, Carlsruhe, Stuttgart, Nurnberg, Ulm and all
principal points on the European Continent.

ANCHOR LARD OIL WORKS.

OFFICE AND MANUFACTORY
CORNER OF PLUM AND CANAL STREETS,
(Elbow of Miami Canal,)

CINCINNATI, OHIO.

PURCHASERS of LARD OIL, Would do Well to Look after the

ANCHOR BRAND.

J. L. MITCHENER & Co., Manufacturers.

ANDREW C. HERRON,
LAND & GENERAL AGENT,

Fourth st., South side, bet. Walnut and Vine, Cincinnati,

Respectfully informs his friends and the public in general, that he continues to devote his whole attention to the Sale, Exchange and purchase of Real Estate, Merchandise, Goods and Property, valuable Stocks of different kinds, Bonds and Mortgages, negotiating Loans, redeeming Land and paying Taxes; renting Houses, Stores, Country Seats and Farms; writing articles of Agreements, Deeds, Leases, Letters, &c., and executing with despatch and economy, all matters confided to his Agency; wants in general, attended to promptly, and charges will in all cases be reasonable. ANDREW C. HERRON, Land and General Agent, Fourth Street, South side, between Walnut and Vine, Cincinnati, Ohio.

THEODORE ROYER.   JOSEPH SIMONTON.   JOHN YOUNG.

GREAT WESTERN SPOKE MANUFACTORY,
ROYER, SIMONTON & CO.,

Manufacture and keep always on hand, a large supply of SPOKES, HUBS, FELLOES, SHAFTS, BOWS, &c., at their Factory on the

SOUTH SIDE OF THIRD ST., BELOW SMITH,
CINCINNATI, OHIO.

Mr. Simonton being a practical Carriage Maker, our customers may depend upon having their orders filled correctly.

EDWARD KINSEY, 1832.   DAVID KINSEY, 1842.

E. & D. KINSEY,

MANUFACTURERS OF SILVER WARE,

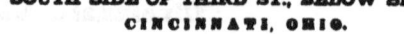

24 West Fifth Street, Cincinnati, Ohio.

Also, Importers of Fine Watches, Jewelry and Sheffield Plate.

KING & FAIRBANK,

WHOLESALE AND RETAIL

LAMP DEALERS,

AND MANUFACTURERS OF

FAIRBANK'S

PATENT VEGETABLE OIL,

A new article for light, recently invented, and is compounded of the extracts of different vegetables, most of which are essential Oils; is much cheaper than Oil or candles, and is free from any danger of explosions.—Also:

Camphene, Spirit Gas & Burning Fluid

OF SUPERIOR QUALITY,

No. 103 Fifth St., bet. Vine and Race,

CINCINNATI, O.

S. M. & C. M. WARREN,

MANUFACTURERS OF

WARREN'S IMPROVED FIRE & WATER-PROOF

COMPOSITION ROOFS;

AND DEALERS IN COMPOSITION ROOFING MATERIALS,

North Side Pearl Street, bet. Vine & Race,

CINCINNATI, O.

The Subscribers, (citizens of Cincinnati and Louisville), having in use Warren's Improved Fire and Water-Proof Composition Roofing, take pleasure in testifying that, thus far, it has sustained the recommendation they have given it, and would cordially recommend it to public favor.

CINCINNATI.	C. W. James,	Horace Wells,	LOUISVILLE.
N. Longworth,	Miles Greenwood,	P. Evans,	Jacob Beckwith,
James Ferguson,	Ephraim Morgan,	Harrison & Eaton,	H. Johnson, M. D.,
Gaylord, Merrell & Co.,	John Slevin,	Shadford Easton,	Thomas McGrain,
Sampson, Lindley & Co.	John W. Ellis & Co.,	John Whetstone,	Cristopher & Stancliff,
Goold & Maccracken,	Gilmore & Smith,	Benjamin Loder,	John B. Semple,
W. B. Smith & Co.,	Eden B. Reeder,	Joseph S. Bates,	Isaac Cromie,
Proctor & Gamble,	John T. Martin,	A. Dudley,	S. Fielder,
Wm. Bromwell,	Peter Gibson,	John Bates,	Schneits & Hewitt,
Richard Miller,	D. A. Powell,	John Lea,	

N. B. Roofing materials constantly on hand, and for sale at lowest prices, with directions for use.

Composition Roofing

J. McGEORGE

McGeorge's improvement in this branch of business, introduced 1847, has given decided character to this style of roofing. The Fire and Water-proof qualities of this Roof, together with its durability, are now no longer doubtful. Experience has proved its utility. He is permitted to refer llowing gentlemen, who have used it:

REFERENCES.

John McCormick,*	Judge Hart.*	Neave & Free.*
Gross & Deitrick,*	Mitchell & Rammelsburg,*	Brunson, Warren & Co.,*
Proctor & Gamble,*	N. Longworth,	T. & J Bradford,
Wm. Glenn & Sons,	A. M. Taylor & Co.,*	Smith, Kinmur & McGill,*
Gardner, Phipps & Co.,	P & T. Gibson,*	Taylor & Odiorne,
S. Davis, Jr , & Co ,*	Sweeny, Walnut St. House,*	John Houte.*
Hosea & Frazer,*	Geffroy, Gibson House,*	Geo. W. Coffin & Co.,
King & Anderson, Esqs.,*	Judge Ed. Woodruff,	John Slevin,*
F. Bodman,	Capt. C. G. Pierce,	Wm. L. Spooner.*

[Those names marked thus * are particularly referred to as having tried both kinds.]
☞ Roofing materials for sale. Orders promptly filled.

WILLIAM B. WOOD.   WILLIAM J DUNLAP.

WOOD & DUNLAP,

BANKERS,

No. 15 West Third Street, Cincinnati, Ohio,

Notes and Drafts collected on all parts of the Union. Time Bills. Stocks, Bonds, etc., bought and sold on Commission. Information furnished as to Exchange, Stocks, Money Market, etc. All Business shall meet with prompt attention.

MARTIN ROBBINS.   WILLIAM D. TURNER.

ROBBINS & TURNER,

MACHINISTS IN WOOD AND IRON,

Fifth St., West of the W. W. Canal and D. & H. R. R. Depot,

CINCINNATI, O.,

Manufacturers of all kinds of Machinery, for Carpenters, Cabinet and Chair Factories, such as Flooring and Molding Machines, etc.

Scroll, Circular, and Concave Saws put up, ready for use, with promptness and dispatch

WM. S MERRELL & CO.,
Wholesale Druggists
AND PROPRIETORS OF THE

UNION DRUG MILLS
AND

MEDICAL LABORATORY,
N. E. cor. Pearl and Vine sts.,

CINCINNATI.

This is the most extensive and complete Depot in the United States, of all

INDIGENOUS MEDICINES
and preparations from them, and, at the same time, embraces the

MATERIA MEDICA
OF

ALL SYSTEMS OF PRACTICE.

The powdered Medicines are prepared at their own Drug Mills, and most of the Medical preparations at their own Chemical Laboratory, and can, therefore, be warranted fresh, pure, and of superior quality. The new concentrated Medical preparations, such as Podophyllin, Leptandrin, etc., (which they were the first to introduce), they now manufacture on a large scale.

WHOLESALE DRUGGISTS, RETAILERS AND PHYSICIANS,
Will each find it to their advantage to give them a call.

N. B. They also manufacture largely. MARBLE DUST. for Soda-Water Makers, and powdered SOAPSTONE, powdered BLACK LEAD, powdered COKE, powdered STONE COAL and CHARCOAL, for Iron Founders' use.

E. G. WEBSTER & CO.,
SHOE AND LEATHER DEALERS,
CORNER OF FIFTH AND LODGE STREETS,
CINCINNATI.

N. B. Manufacturers and Dealers in every variety of Boots and Shoes, French and Philadelphia Calf Skins, Patent Leather, Enameled Leather, Buckskins, Linings, Bindings, Lastings, Galloons and Laces, constantly on hand, and for sale at low prices.

J. N. HARRIS, New London. Ct.	P. DAVIS & SON, Providence, R. I.	T. H. C. ALLEN, Cincinnati, O.

J. N. HARRIS & CO.,
NO. 7 COLLEGE BUILDING, WALNUT ST.,
CINCINNATI, OHIO,
SOLE PROPRIETORS OF
PERRY DAVIS' PAIN-KILLER,
FOR THE
WESTERN AND SOUTHERN STATES.

NEWTON'S CLINICAL INSTITUTE.
Private Medical Instruction.

Having one of the finest buildings in the city, perfectly arranged, in every respect, and capable of accommodating one hundred patients, we propose to form a private class for the vacation between the Spring and Fall Sessions of the E. M. Institute. All Students will have full benefit of the clinical instruction, witness the surgical operations, and the treatment of the various diseases in the Institution Also, there will be from three to five lectures delivered weekly, by the undersigned, and some members of the Faculty, whose services will be obtained This course of instruction and clinical training will embrace the entire round of practical subjects, as taught in the Institute, and will constitute a thorough review of all departments in the prescribed course of recitation and study.

This will facilitate the advancement of the Student, more than any other plan that he can adopt,

Fees for the whole course of Lectures, including clinical advantages, $35.

R. S. NEWTON, M. D.
O. E. NEWTON, M. D.

ATHERTON THAYER.   GEO. GASSAWAY.

THAYER & GASSAWAY,

COMMISSION AND FORWARDING MERCHANTS,

AND

GENERAL STEAM BOAT AGENTS,

Office Second Story, N. W. Corner Front and Sycamore Streets.

Hops, Malt and Grain of every description always on hand.

References.

Henry Thayer, St. Louis,   Trader & Aubery, Cincinnati.
Kennett & Dudley, Cincinnati,   Robt. Getty, Esq.,   "
Wm. Wood, Esq.,   "   Wilshire, Bristol & Co., "

BROADWAY EXCHANGE

HOTEL AND RESTAURAT,

54 Broadway, bet. Columbia and Lower Market Sts.

CINCINNATI, OHIO.

F. PIEPENBRING, PROPRIETOR.

This establishment has recently been enlarged and improved. The main feature is the extensive

RESTAURAT,

All the delicacies of the season, either from home or abroad, are to be found in the Larder.

THE BAR is supplied with the choicest Wines, Liquors, Cigars, &c; persons engaging rooms must settle their bills weekly; meals served only at the Restaurat, at Restaurat prices.

OHIO LIFE INSURANCE COMPANY,

CINCINNATI, O.

INCORPORATED BY THE STATE OF OHIO.

CHARTER PERPETUAL.

CAPITAL STOCK 100,000 DOLLARS.

All paid in and Safely secured.

DIRECTORS.

| E. S. Haines, | G. W. Townley, | Jno. M. Blair, | Jno. W. Donohue, |
| Wm. Burnett, | Eden B. Reeder, | Wm. A. Goodman, | Jas. D. Lehmer. |

OFFICERS.

E. S. Haines, President, Jno. W. Donohue, Vice President, S. W. Reeder, Secretary.
Jacob Sheen, Actuary and General Agent

BOARD OF FINANCE.

Jacob Strader,   Robert Buchanan,   John Kilgore.

MEDICAL EXAMINERS.

W. Richards, M. D., T. O. Edwards, M. D., G. Fries, M. D., J. S. Unzicker, M. D.

Office—South Side Third Street, between Walnut and Vine.

WM. M. KOHL & CO.,

NORTH-EAST COR. FOURTH & VINE STREETS,

CINCINNATI, OHIO,

IMPORTERS, AND WHOLESALE AND RETAIL DEALERS IN

FRENCH, GERMAN, ENGLISH, AND AMERICAN

PERFUMERY,

TOILET ARTICLES, PORTE-MONAIES,
BRUSHES, COMBS, Etc., Etc.
COUNTRY MERCHANTS SUPPLIED AT

IMPORTERS' AND MANUFACTURERS' PRICES.

WHOLESALE WESTERN AGENTS FOR

A. B. L. MYER'S
COMPOUND EXTRACT OF ROCK ROSE,
IN

OHIO, INDIANA, ILLINOIS, TENNESSEE,
KENTUCKY, MISSOURI AND WISCONSIN.

WHOLESALE WESTERN AGENTS FOR

'Wright's Indian Vegetable Pills, Watts' Nervous Antidote, Nuttall's Syringum. M'Lean's Liniment, Clorihugh's Tricopherous, Lyon's Kathairon and Jamaica Ginger, White's Amber Gloss and Jamaica Ginger, Dr. Bright's Corn Plaster, Thurston's Tooth Powder, Da Costa Tooth Wash, Johnson's Tooth Soap, Burgess' Rat and Roach Exterminator, Almond Lotion, Loseek's Wafers, Jew David Paster, spread and in box, etc., etc.,

IN OHIO, KENTUCKY, AND INDIANA.

General Agents for

Barry's Tricopherous, Phalon's Invigorater, Batchelor's, Harrison's, Phalon's. Ballard's, and all celebrated Hair Dyes; Radway's, Swayne's, and all popular Medicines.

GREAT WESTERN AGENCY DEPOT FOR

HARRISON'S COLUMBIAN
PERFUMERY.
ALSO.

BAZIN'S, HAUEL'S, WETHERILL'S, ETC., ETC.

Having made extensive arrangements for importing direct from Europe, as well as to keep persons constantly on the watch at Eastern importing houses and procuring direct from the various American Manufacturers, all articles in our line, we are able to offer inducements to the trade beyond any other similar establishment in the West. We will guarantee to supply all orders at Philadelphia and New York lowest wholesale prices, thus saving expense, to the purchaser, of transportation.

WM. M. KOHL.   **H. W. FOWLER.**

ECLECTIC

MEDICAL INSTITUTE,
OF
CINCINNATI, OHIO.
CHARTERED IN 1845.

TOTAL NUMBER OF MATRICULANTS, 1498.

The Winter Session of this Institution commences every first Monday of November, and continues sixteen weeks, the Spring Session commences every first Monday in March, and continues fourteen weeks, with the following Faculty.

W. SHERWOOD, M. D.
Prof. of Special, Surgical, and Pathological Anatomy;

J. R. BUCHANAN, M. D.,
Prof. of Physiology, and Institutes of Medicine;

R. S. NEWTON, M. D.,
Prof. of Medical Practice, and Pathology;

Z. FREEMAN, M. D.,
Prof. of Surgery;

J. KING, M. D.,
Prof. of Obstetrics, and Diseases of Women and Children;

G. W. L. BICKLEY, M. D.,
Prof. of Materia Medica, Therapeutics and Medical Botany.

J. W. HOYT, M. D.,
Prof. of Chemistry, Pharmacy and Toxicology.

This Institute was chartered in 1845, and has been the most flourishing school in Cincinnati, having already had fourteen hundred and ninety-eight Matriculants. It continues as heretofore, the principal collegiate source of a liberal and progressive system of Medical Science, and has recently adopted the generous measure of dispensing with all charges for the fees of its several professors, leaving only a charge of $15 per session. Graduation fee $20.

Students upon their arrival in the city will call at the office of Prof. R. S. Newton, No. 99 West Seventh Street.

For further information, address Prof. R. S. Newton, or
J. R. BUCHANAN, M. D., Dean.

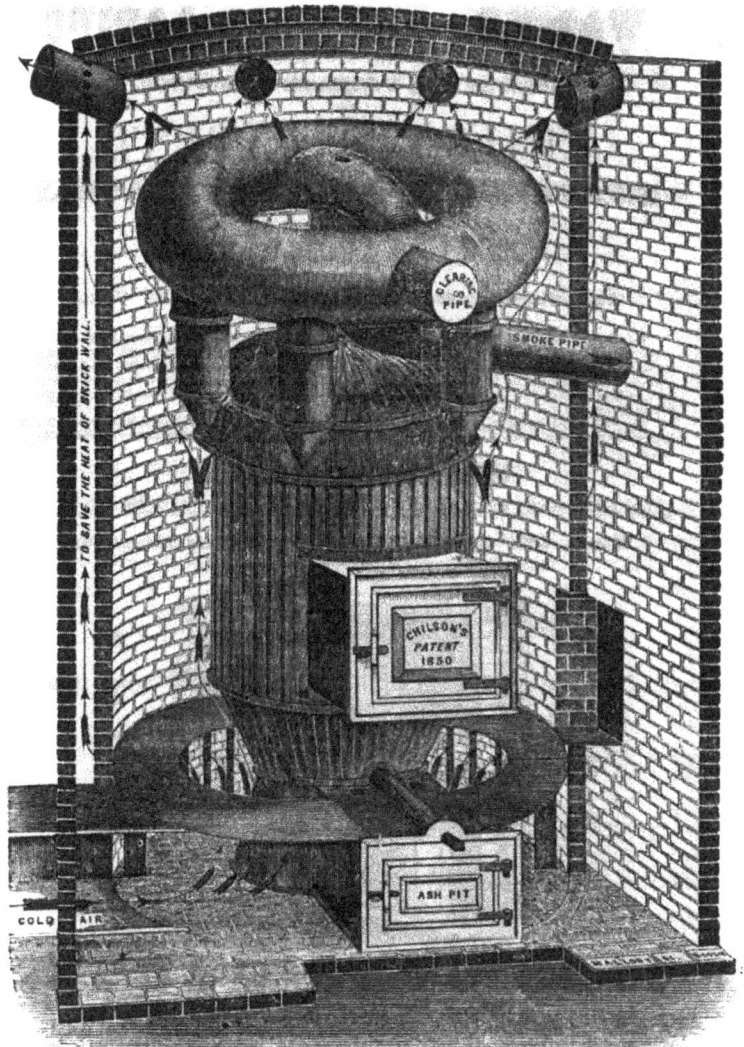

Chilson's Patent Air-Warming and Ventilating

FURNACE. [SEE NEXT PAGE.

THE
Commercial Insurance Company,
OF CHARLESTON, S. C.
FIRE AND MARINE.

Cash Capital, - - - - 300.000.

A. M. LEE, Sec'y. *WM. B. HERIOT, Pres't.*

THE
COLUMBIA INSURANCE CO.,
OF COLUMBIA, S. C.
FIRE AND MARINE.

Cash Capital, - - - - $150.000.

JAS. S. SCOTT, Sec'y. *JAS. V. LYLES, Pres't.*

THE
CONTINENTAL INSURANCE COMPANY,
OF NEW YORK, N. Y.
FIRE.

Cash Capital, - - - - $500.000.

GEO. T. HOPE, Sec'y. *WM. V. BRADY, Pres't.*

THE
EQUITABLE FIRE INSURANCE COMPANY,
OF LONDON.
FIRE.

Authorized Capital, - - - - $2.500.000.
Subscribed Capital, - - - - - 1.000.000.

GENERAL OFFICE, NO. 71 WALL ST., NEW YORK.

The New York Life Insurance Co.
ACCUMULATED CAPITAL, - - - $630.000.

P. FREEMAN, Act'y.   MORRIS FRANKLIN, Pres't.

A. MICHELL HALL, Sec'y.   **A. S. CHEW, Agent,**

Office, No. 14 Front Street, Cincinnati, over Messrs. Kennett & Dudley.

As Agent of the above Companies, I am prepared to issue Policies upon LIVES, or upon any description of PROPERTY against loss or damage by FIRE, OR FROM THE PERILS OF SEA, LAKE OR RIVER TRANSPORTATION.

TEASDALE'S DYE·HOUSE,

KNOWN BY THE NAME OF

NEW YORK DYE-HOUSE,

Has been established nearly 20 years on Walnut street, and for the last 13 years on the

Corner of Gano and Walnut Streets,

Between Sixth and Seventh, opposite the Walnut Street House.

It is a four story building with stone front, which I erected in 1850. Business increased so rapidly, and to meet the demands of a discerning public, last year I erected a five story building in the rear of the one on Walnut street, and am fitting up with all the modern improvements of the age. Continued success is the best proof of true merit, and this house has no parallel in the West in this respect.

Within the last two or three years other New York Dye-Houses have sprung up, they may put out the sign, but they cannot take my ability and skill from me for carrying on the business. A great many have been entrapped by them, and often have they found out their mistake in time; but, behold, they would not give up the goods until they were done by them and paid for. Several have brought them to the Original New York Dye-House to be done over in the usual superior style, which no other New York Dye-House can compe•e with. Be sure and ask for

Teasdale's New York Dye-House,

And see the name for yourself and, don't believe any one until you do see it. We are doing a very heavy business, and this is the only house that does employ hands in the different departments of the business, consequently goods can be done in less time and in a superior manner. This is the original and only responsible New York Dye-House and Steam Dye Works in Cincinnati.

Goods sent to our address by Adams and & Co.'s Express, or Livingston & Fargo's, can have them returned to their satisfaction. We have done considerable business in this way, and in no instance have we ever heard of mistake.

TEASDALE'S NEW YORK DYE-HOUSE.

BURDSAL & BROTHER,

NORTH-WEST CORNER MAIN & FRONT STREETS,

CINCINNATI,

IMPORTERS AND WHOLESALE DEALERS IN

DRUGS, MEDICINES,

AND

CHEMICALS,

PAINTS, OILS, TURPENTINE,

Varnishes, Dye Stuffs, pure Castor Oil,

GLUE, WINDOW GLASS, PUTTY,

VIALS AND BOTTLES,

APOTHECARIES' SHOP FIXTURES,

PERFUMERY, FINE SOAPS,

ESSENTIAL OILS, CONFECTIONERIES,

Fine Tooth & Hair Brushes, Paint Brushes,

AROMATIC SEEDS,

SURGICAL INSTRUMENTS,

CORKS, SNUFFS, PATENT MEDICINES,

Stationery, Superior Inks and Blacking,

ALCOHOL, FREE FROM COLOR,

PURE WINES AND BRANDIES, FOR MEDICAL PURPOSES.

MATCHES, SPICES AND GROCERIES.

We offer goods equally as low, transportation added, as they can be obtained from Eastern Jobbing Houses.

WARRANTED TO BE FRESH, PURE AND GENUINE.

Orders from the country promptly filled and satisfaction guarantied, with regard both to price and quality. Dealers requested to call and examine.

T. F. BAKER,

No. 275 WEST FIFTH ST.

CINCINNATI, OHIO,

MANUFACTURER OF

Wrought and Cast-Iron Railings,

VERANDAS,

BANK VAULTS AND DOORS,

JAIL DOORS & CELLS.

AGENT FOR

DAY & NEWELL'S (Hobb's)

RENOWNED BANK LOCK,

AND FOR

Lilley's Impenetrable

BURGLAR & FIRE-PROOF SAFE,

FOR BANKERS AND OTHERS.

Maish's Patent Refrigerator,

MANUFACTURED SOLELY BY J. & J. M. JOHNSTON,

At their Steam Box Factory, S. Side Third St., bet. Plum & Western Row, Cincinnati.

For the **Improvements** which are found in this **Ice Chest** over all others now in use, LETTERS PATENT were granted April 20, 1859.

In its internal structure, it provides a strong, simple and efficient means of appropriating to cooling purposes, the water from the slowly melting ice, and also, all the condensing moisture of the atmosphere as it accumulates, without wetting the parts of the shelves which come in contact with the articles placed upon them for protection.

One chief advantage is in the shape of the shelves. They are formed of corrugated or crimped sheet metal; the upper angles of which support the dishes, or other articles, above the water which runs in the intervening channels. The ice is contained in a chamber at the top of the Safe. The angular shape of its bottom directs the drip as it falls to one particular point on the upper shelf, the corrugated channels of which are filled to a certain point, and then the water passes down a small pipe at the end, to the next shelf, which is filled in its channels in like manner—it then passes down to the next shelf, and so to the bottom, where it is finally discharged through a small tube, over which there is a cap, while at the same time it lets the water discharge. The angular shape of the bottom of the Ice box allows every drop of water to pass off, as it melts, thereby preserving the ice a longer time than most all other safes.

Uniformity of temperature is secured from top to bottom, and should it be desired at any particular time to lower the temperature, the form of the shelves will safely allow Ice to be placed on any one of the shelves without injury to the surrounding articles. Other safes are made with hollow shelves for the passage of water, but their shelves being double are much heavier, more costly, difficult to clean, and liable to burst from various causes. This one is light, safe, simple and cheap. They are made of all sizes, to accommodate Families, Hotels and Steamers. They can be made ornamental as furniture for dining rooms, or other positions persons may wish them to occupy. We invite all in want of a good and cheap Ice Safe, to call and examine these carefully, confident that they are nearer perfection in their way, than all others now before the public. We are still manufacturing the OLD STYLE of Ice Chests, and are prepared to fill orders for all sizes. **J. & J. M. JOHNSTON, Third Street, Cincinnati.**

LIBERAL DISCOUNT TO THE TRADE.

ISAAC F. SMITH,

No. 10 East Fifth St., bet. Main & Sycamore, Cincinnati,

Would respectfully invite your attention to his Spring Stock of

GENTS' FURNISHING

GOODS,

Having just received all the latest styles and qualities for seasonable wear. We feel confident of pleasing all in price, style and quality, having every facility to purchase low, and from the largest importing houses, enabling us to sell at New York jobbing prices. Therefore, we particularly invite you to call and examine for yourselves, and interest will immediately dictate to you to buy. The following are some of the Goods kept constantly on hand—

Fine Custom Made Shirts, of all qualities and styles.

2 and 3 **Fly Collars,** with and without cording.

Self Adjusting Stocks, with bows and scarf ties.

Neck Ties of every style and description.

Gloves, of Kid, Silk, Lisle, Berlin, Castor, Merino, of every style, color and size. Also, Ladies' and Gents' Driving Gloves.

Under Shirts and Drawers, of Silk, Lisle, Cotton and Merino, all sizes, with every style of Cravat.

Pocket Handkerchiefs.

Money Belts, Dressing Robes, Shoulder Braces, Night Caps, Cravat Stiffners, and every other article in the Gents' Furnishing line. Together with a large assortment of **Umbrellas and Walking Canes,** at manufacturers' prices.

Having just finished the enlargement of my Store, I am enabled to show the Stock with great facility, enabling our customers to see our Goods at a glance.

We solicit Wholesale dealers to call early at our old stand.

FLINT GLASS MANUFACTURERS

Hammond St. bet. 3rd & 4th, Cincinnati,

Keep constantly on hand every variety of

Flint Glassware, Apothecaries' Furniture,

And Chemical Apparatus made to order at the shortest notice. Also, a great variety of

PERFUMERS' WARE, TELEGRAPH GLASSES AND LIGHTNING ROD INSULATORS.

American Express Co.

OFFICES:

10 Wall Street,	- - - - -	**New York.**
Third St., bet. Sycamore and Main,	- - -	**Cincinnati.**

WELLS, BUTTERFIELD & CO., *New York,* } PROPRIETORS.
LIVINGSTON, FARGO & CO., *Cincinnati,* }

N. LATHAM,   **1853.**   L. T. WOODS,
Late Latham & McBurnie, Cin'ti.   *Late S. C. Baker & Co. Wheeling.*

LATHAM & WOODS,

Forwarding & Commission Merchants,

NO. 20 PUBLIC LANDING,

CINCINNATI, OHIO.

AGENTS, BALTIMORE AND OHIO RAILROAD TRANSPORTATION CO.

MELODEONS, MELODEON PIANOS, AND PIANO FORTES.

PATENTED DECEMBER, 1848.   PATENTED, 1850.

BOUDOIR PIANOS.

We are Agents for the sale of the above celebrated Piano Fortes, which for compactness of form, beauty of style, delicacy of touch, power and quality of tone, *surpass all others* ever made in this country.— Their peculiar form and construction render the tone so rich, varied and powerful, as entirely preclude the possibility of being appreciated without being heard.

MELODEONS AND MELODEON PIANOS.

We have on hand a large and splendid stock of Melodeons and Melodeon Pianos and for variety of style and sizes, superior to any stock in the United States. Great improvement has been made upon the original invention, and it is now generally conceded that we make the best reed instruments in the country, both for elegance of finish, and richness and beauty of tone and touch.

DESCRIPTION.—4½ Octaves, with folding scroll legs and Rosewood case, $65. 5 Octaves do., $80.

5 Octaves, in extra Rosewood case, with Patent Mouldings, Plinth running round, Lyric Pedal, Piano style. Price $100.

5 Octaves, in Piano style, with No. 1 Rosewood case, Plinth and Patent Moulding running round, swell Panel and Lyric Pedal, with two sets of reeds or stops. Price $150.

6 Octaves, in Piano style, with No. 1 Rosewood case, Plinth and Patent Mouldings running round, swell Panel and Lyric Pedal. Price $150.

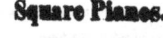

Square Pianos.

We also keep a large stock of square Pianos from the best makers in the country, and and at less price for cash than any other house.

Call and see us before you buy.

The above instruments are intended for Parlors, Lodge Rooms, Churches, and Singing Societies, and are the cheapest and best Parlor instruments extant. We are the only manufacturers of the above instruments West of the mountains, and the only manufacturers who make the Double Reeded and Six Octaves. Orders from a distance faithfully and punctually attended to.

MURCH & WHITE, 74 West Fourth St. Cincinnati.

EDGAR CONKLING.　　WM. WOOD.　　ALFRED WOOD.　　JOHN ELSTNER.

CONKLING, WOOD & CO.,

North Side of Court Street, East of Broadway,

CINCINNATI, O.,

Manufacturers of the following articles, which we warrant to give entire satisfaction in quality and price. Dealers will find it to their interest to buy of us direct as manufacturers. Please examine our list and we trust it will induce your orders.

Castor Oil.
CHINA WHITE, ground in oil, in cans of 10 and 20 lbs. each, a superior article for inside fine painting, retaining its color, and put on with clear turpentine only.
IMPROVED WHITE PATENT DRYER, ground in oil, in cans of 1, 2½, 5, and 10 lb. each, superior to any other patent Dryer in use, drying sooner and whiter, and unlike japan varnish, it does not effect the color of the paint.
Parlor White Lead, in oil.

Pure White Lead, in oil.
No. 1　do　do　do
Pure Dry White Lead.
Putty in bladders, Red Lead and Litharge.
Spanish Whiting, "fire dried."
American Paris white "fire dried."
Paris Green, Premium.
do　do　No. 1.
do　do　No. 2 and 3.
Brunswick Green.
Japanner's Green.
Chrome Red.
do　Green, Premium.

Chrome Green, E. F.
do　do　No. 1.
do　do　P.
do　do　X.
do Yellow Orange and Lemon, pure.
do do　do　do G.
Chinese & Prusian Blue, pure.
do　do　No. 1.
do　do　No. 2.
Celestial Blue, No. 1 and 2.
Boiled Linseed Oil.
Family Cider, and Whisky Vinegar.

PAINTS, ground in Oil, in assorted sized Cans of 1, 2, 3, 5, 10 and 20 lbs.

Red Lead.
Paris Green, Premium.
Do　do　No. 1.
Do　do　No. 2 and 3.
Brunswick Green.
Chrome Green, Premium.
Do　do　E. F.
Do　do　No. 1.

Chrome Green, P.
Do　do　X.
Do　Yellow, pure.
Do　do　G.
Do　Red.
Celestial Blue.
Chinese and Prusian Blue, No. 1.
Verdigris, pure in cans.

Umber, burnt and raw.
Black Paint.
Drop Black.
Yellow Ochre, in kegs.
Spanish Brown.
Venitian Red.
Blake's Patent Fire & Water Proof Paint, in kegs.

ALSO, DEALERS IN COARSE IMPORTED PAINTS.—DRY.

Verdigris, pure.
English Venitian Red.
American do　do
Spanish Brown.
French Yellow Ochre.
Stone Ochre.

Lamp Black, in papers.
Drop Black.
Umber, burnt and ground.
Do　raw lump.
Do　raw fine.
English Rose Pink.

Terra de Sienna, burnt and ground.
Do　do　raw.
Purple Brown, English Paris White.
Blake's Pat. Fire & Water Pr'f Paint.
Chalk by the ton, in bulk, or barrels.
Indian Red, No. 1 and 2.

We are Western Agents for the sale of THEO. SCHWARTZ'S Celebrated New York PARIS GREENS, S brand, which we offer at New York prices and terms, (adding carriage &c.,) in original packages. Those ordering Paris Greens, will please accurately specify the brand and size packages wanted.

SCHWARTZ'S S BRAND.————DRY.

——S grade in English Iron cans, containing 28 and 56 lbs. net.
do　do in Wooden kegs of 112 and 200 lbs. net.
——X　do in Iron cans of 30 and 60 lbs. net.
do　do in Wooden kegs of 130 and 212 lbs. net.
——X-1 do in Iron cans of 33 and 66 lbs. net.

——X—1 grade in Wooden kegs of 130 & 230 lbs. net.
do　2　do　in Iron cans of 35 and 70 lbs. net.
do　do　in Wooden kegs of 140 & 250 lbs. net.
——No 4　do　in 29 lb Iron cans.
do　do　in Wooden kegs of 130 and 235 lbs. net.

☞ Our friends wishing us to buy Oils, Turpentine, and Goods out of our line, requiring CASH to buy with, we expect, will remit the Cash at the time of ordering.

TOMATO PRESERVES
FROM
SCHOOLEY & THOMPSON,
WHOLESALE MANUFACTURERS,

No. 57 Fifth St. between Broadway and Sycamore,

CINCINNATI,

Where may be had all kinds of Pickles, Preserves, Rich Sauces, Ketchups, Jellies, Jams, Lemon Syrup,
&c. fresh Tomatoes and Peaches in cans; Lemon Syrup, &c.

J. M. M'CULLOUGH,
NO. 162 MAIN STREET,
CINCINNATI.

NURSERY AND SEED FARM,

PLEASANT RIDGE.

FRUIT AND ORNAMENTAL TREES,
GARDEN, FIELD & FLOWER SEEDS, HORTICULTURAL & AGRICULTURAL IMPLEMENTS.

MATHEMATICAL AND PHILOSOPHICAL INSTRUMENTS.

HENRY WARE,

S. W. cor. Fourth and Sycamore,

Opposite Post Office, up stairs, entrance on 4th St.

CINCINNATI.

**Keeps constantly on hand Surveyors' Compasses, Levels, Theodo-
lites, Transits, Telegraph Instruments, &c.**

Instruments made to draft per order. Repairing done with neatness and dispatch. Orders from
abroad punctually attended to.

WESTERN TOBACCO MANUFACTORY.

SCHMIDT & SACK,

MANUFACTURERS OF ALL KINDS OF

TOBACCO, SNUFF AND CIGARS,

No. 535 Corner Vine and 15th Streets,

CINCINNATI.

Fine Cut Chewing and Smoking Tobacco.

S. W. HASELTINE & CO.

MANUFACTURERS OF

STRAW BONNETS,

AND IMPORTERS OF

DRESS SILKS, MILLINERY GOODS,

TRIMMINGS, &C.

62 PEARL STREET,

CINCINNATI, O.

H. BAUMER,

Boot & Shoe Manufacturer,

217 SEVENTH ST. BET. PLUM & WESTERN ROW,

CINCINNATI, OHIO.

☞ PRICES LOW. REPAIRS NEATLY EXECUTED.

COLBURN & FIELD,

CINCINNATI MUSIC STORE,

154 MAIN ST.

'J. CHICKERINGS' PIANOS; GEO. A. PRINCE & CO'S MELODEONS.

A. DANNREUTHER,

PIANO MANUFACTORY,

Corner of Walnut and Allison Sts.

CINCINNATI, O.

A constant supply of Boudoir Pianos always on hand.

JACOB KLING,

HAT & CAP MANUFACTURER,

Vine Street, West side, between Fourteenth and Fifteenth,

CINCINNATI, O.

Always keeps on hand a large assortment of fashionable Hats and Caps, at the lowest price, wholesale and retail.

CINCINNATI MUSTARD AND SPICE MILLS.

HARRISON, EATON & CO.,

WHOLESALE DEALERS IN

COFFEE, SPICES & MUSTARD,

99 & 101 Walnut St. bet. Pearl and Third.

CINCINNATI, OHIO.

GREEN COFFEES,	CINNAMON,	PEPPER,	PEPPER SAUCE,
ROASTED do.	NUTMEGS,	ALLSPICE,	RICE-FLOUR,
GROUND do.	MACE.	GINGER.	Roasted PEA NUTS,
Prepared COCOA.	CLOVES,	CAYENNE,	INDIGO.

CINCINNATI AND SAVILL MUSTARD.

**The celebrated "Lighting Yeast," or, Baking Powder, for the imme-
diate production of light and sweet bread, is prepared at this
establishment.**

Grocers and Consumers may rely with entire confidence upon the PURITY of our Spices.
Grocers, Hotels and Steamboats supplied at short notice and on reasonable terms. **Cash paid
for Mustard Seed.**

REFERENCES —Springer & Whiteman, Thompson & Taaffe; J. C. Butler & Co.; Harrison & Hooper;
Minor, Andrews & White; Pullan, Hatfield & Brown, Ross & Ricker; J. & C. Reakirt; Allen & Co.; Babbitt,
Good & Co.; Canfield & Moffitt; Messick & Co.

EDWIN L. MINTZER.   H. B. MALONE.

E. L. MINTZER & CO.

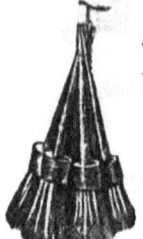

BRUSH MANUFACTURERS,

NOVELTY STEAM BRUSH FACTORY,

NO. 211 WALNUT ST.

CINCINNATI, OHIO.

MACHINE AND FACTORY BRUSHES MADE TO ORDER.

CASH PAID FOR BRISTLES

Medal and Diploma awarded us at U. S. Fairs.

BRIGHTON POTTERY,

WM. BROMLEY,

CORNER FREEMAN & WESTERN ROW,

CINCINNATI, O.

Purchasers will find at our establishment at all times, a large and superior stock of **Yellow Ware,
Rockingham Ware, Chimney Pots, Spittoons,** in every style. We
sell for cash every description of Goods in our line, as cheap as they can
be purchased in the States.

These Restorative Pills have been used in private practice, with unprecedented success, for 20 years, they have never before been offered to the public.   These Pills remove obstructions, open the natural passages of the fluids of the body—as the pores and **lacteal vessels.**

THEY ARE WHOLLY VEGETABLE.

And perfectly harmless in their effects; instead of weakening and debilitating the patient, (as is usually the case with other Pills,) they give **tone** to the **stomach**—strengthening and invigorating both stomach and bowels, and imparting new feeling and energy to every part of the system.

Being wholly vegetable, they are mild in their operation, without griping, or any pain whatever.   They are slow in their movement, but thorough in their renovating and restorative character, and need only to be tried to be approved of by all such as are afflicted with the horrible suffering arising from Dyspepsia, or any of the symptoms of a disordered stomach.

The Stomach is the Centre of Sympathies.

It is principally supplied with nerves by a large pair proceeding directly from the brain, called the Par Vagum.   These, in their course, send branches to the pharynx and larynx, the æsophagus, the vessels of the neck and heart, the lungs, the liver, the spleen, and the diaphragm.

It is unnecessary to go farther than a primary derangement of the stomach, to account for a multitude of distressing symptoms with which many are afflicted, such as Indigestion, Billiousness, Acidity, Palpitation of the Heart, a Sense of Oppression at the pit of the Stomach, an Incapacity for the slightest exertion, Depression of Spirits, Mistiness and Indistinctness of Vision, Cold Hands and Feet, Unpleasant Taste in the mouth, particularly when rising in the morning, Numbness of the Limbs and other parts, Vertigo, Nausea, Dull heavy Pain and sense of weight in the Head, Head-Ache, Extreme Nervous agitation, Difficulty of Respiration, Stupor, a temporary loss of Memory, Irritability, a sense of emptiness, Drowsiness, Pulse less frequent, and more feeble than usual, Debility, extreme Langor and Exhaustion, Despondency, Restlessness, Emaciation and Extreme Debility, Costiveness.

Persons purchasing these Pills will be careful to observe that the name of O. HALSTED, (IN GILT LETTERS, on black paper,) is affixed as a wrapper to each box, and that NONE ARE GENUINE unless labeled in this manner,   For sale by the Druggists everywhere.   Principal depot at

Burnet's, 14 E. Fourth St. Cincinnati.

PRICE FIFTY CENTS.

Persons remitting us $1.00 in cash, or Postage Stamps, will receive (by mail) TWO BOXES of Pills FREE OF EXPENSE,

All who order from seeing this Advertisement, will please notify us of that fact.

Country merchants can purchase these Pills from CINCINNATI DRUGGISTS at Proprietor's prices.

JAMES GILMORE. JAMES H. BROTHERTON.

GILMORE & BROTHERTON,

BANKERS,

31 *MAIN STREET,*

CINCINNATI.

LORD'S CINCINNATI COUNTERFEIT DETECTOR

⌒ A N D ⌒

BANK NOTE REPORTER.

The above named publication has reached its twelfth year; we have not missed, for that period of time, a single issue. It is one of the oldest publications of the kind in the West; it has been the Editor's constant aim to lead off in matters of public utility and reform, and not wait for the movements and opinions of others. Our "DETECTOR" was the first publication in the West to advocate the "Free Banking System," based upon State and United States Stocks, which afterwards passed into a law, and is now in successful operation, not only in Ohio, but has recently been adopted in several other States.

Since we commenced the publication, circumstances have changed and we change with the circumstances. Instead of a monthly, our patrons, which are already numerous, are now calling for a **Semi-Monthly,** we therefore issue our prospectus, and solicit the patronage of a liberal public. The country is being flooded with counterfeit notes and spurious bills of every description, and recent developments show that Cincinnati is the great theatre of action.

Our subscribers to the monthly can take the semi-monthly, to commence at any time, by remitting to us the difference in the price, and we solicit them to do so at once. **It is published upon the 1st and 15th of every month.**

We shall continue to illustrate new and dangerous counterfeits, by engraving parts of the bills, showing the most striking difference.

Each subscriber will be furnished, upon subscribing, with a Gold and Silver Coin Chart, of the various coins now in circulation in the world, free of charge; those who wish will be supplied with a good Magnifying Glass for examining notes, by paying from 25 to 50 cents, according to size and quality.

The publication has recently been re-set in new type of the most approved English style, and enlarged to three columns. It is one of the neatest Detectors extant, and contains nearly one-third more matter than any similar publication in the United States.

We might here insert numerous favorable notices of the press of Cincinnati as well as from various other places; but they are so common that we withhold them, preferring to rest the merits of the publication upon its own established reputation.

Our Detector has been translated into the German language, is now in press, and will be out with all possible dispatch. The first number (German) will be published in July.

TERMS:

English Detector, per annum, Semi-Monthly, - - $2.00

Do. do. do. Monthly, - - - - - 1.25

German do. do. do - - - 1.50

☞ Invariably in advance. Remit, by mail, through your postmaster. **J. T. LORD.**

H. N. WENNING,

IMPORTER AND DEALER IN

IRON, NAILS, STEEL & HEAVY HARDWARE

Warehouse, No. 360 Main St. 3 doors below Ninth,

CINCINNATI, O.

Where will be found a full assortment of the best quality of Iron, Nails, Steel Springs; also, Wagon Boxes, Mould Boards, Anvils, Vices, Bellows, and a full assortment of Wrought and Cast Iron Plows, which I will sell at lowest market prices. Warranted first-rate, or they can be returned at my expense. Stoves of every description; Grates and Hollow-ware.

SAVE YOUR ICE AND DRINK PURE WATER.

ECONOMY, CONVENIENCE,

AND LUXURY COMBINED.

WINCHELL'S OCTAGON
WATER COOLERS
AND FILTERS.

With one of these Coolers you can always have ready for use Water as cold as Ice itself, and as clean as the purest Spring Water. Manufactured by

GEO. D. WINCHELL,
Corner of Pearl and Walnut Streets, Cincinnati.

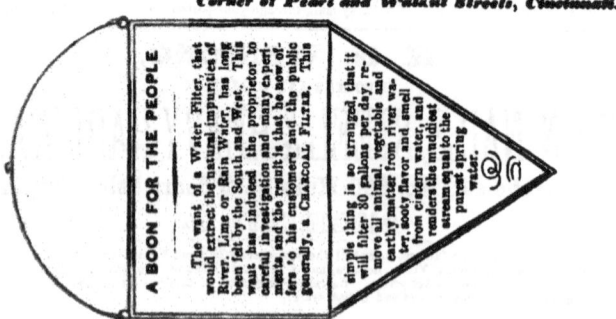

A BOON FOR THE PEOPLE

The want of a Water Filter, that would extract the natural impurities of River, Lime or Rain Water, has long been felt by the South and West. This want has induced the proprietor to careful investigation and many experiments, and the result is that he now offers to his customers and the public generally, a CHARCOAL FILTER. This simple thing is so arranged, that it will filter 30 gallons per day, remove all animal, vegetable and earthy matter from river water, sooty flavor and smell from cistern water, and renders the muddiest stream equal to the purest spring water.

SAVE YOUR ICE.

BURNET'S PATENT WATER COOLER.

We are now prepared to offer our friends and customers a superior article of Water Coolers of entire new styles, at greatly reduced prices. This article is the result of the application of scientific principles to the purpose intended, viz: to keep water *as cool as possible, as long as possible, and with the least possible quantity of ice.*

The proprietor has long devoted his attention to this particular branch of domestic economy, and passing from one improvement to another, has at length arrived as near perfection as it is possible to reach. A proof of this is found in the very general use of these Coolers, in all parts of the country. A simple statement of fact in regard to these Coolers, will satisfy every one of their superiority. First, they are the only *article of the kind ever patented*. They are finished with two distinct non-conducting chambers, by means of which, with two pounds of ice to the gallon, water is kept (at a temperature of 40 degrees above zero, or only 8 degrees from the freezing point) all day. Thus at the cost of some five cents per day, a family of ordinary size can be constantly supplied with water as cold as ice itself; larger numbers in the same proportion. This has been found by actual experiment to be a saving of at least seventy-five per cent. over the earthen jars formerly used for this purpose.

Again, these Coolers NEVER SWEAT, in this way saving much unnecessary waste and trouble.

Being manufactured in the most workmanlike style, and handsomely finished in every respect, they make a very beautiful ornament for the dining-room, hotel or steamboat.

An important improvement has lately been added to the Cooler, viz: a small pan (capable of holding from six to eight pounds of butter) inserted directly under the cover. This quantity of butter can be kept perfectly hard all day, without additional ice, (a very important addition to the economy and comfort of families.)

If desired, the Cooler can also be furnished at a small expense with a **Filtering Apparatus,** which serves the additional purpose of removing all impurities from water, rendering it perfectly clean and wholesome.

The Cooler and Filter may be seen in operation at any time, at

BURNET'S,

NO. 14 EAST FOURTH STREET, CINCINNATI.

For sale by the following persons: Louisville, by John Gill, 45 Main Street; Columbus, by J. K. Hayl, High street, opposite Franklin Bank; Cleveland, by Huntington & Brooks; Indianapolis, by Jacob Lindsley; Frankfort, by Grey & Todd; Nashville, by A. H. Hicks; New Orleans, by J. A. Morton & Co., Tchoupitoulas street; Wholesale and Retail Agent in New York city, J. H. BURNET, No. 61 Wall street.

BEGGS & SMITH,

No. 6 West Fourth Street, Cincinnati,

(One door east of the magnificent First Presbyterian Church,)

DEAL IN ALL KINDS OF FINE

WATCHES, DIAMONDS,

AND THE RICHEST DESCRIPTION OF

JEWELRY.

THEY KEEP A GENERAL ASSORTMENT OF FINE SILVER

Forks, Spoons, Cups, Pitchers, Tea Sets, etc.,

And are Agents for the same style of Articles plated, and varying in price in proportion to the thickness of the Silver. They also have a general assortment of

GOLD, SILVER, & STEEL SPECTACLES,

AND A LARGE VARIETY OF

Fancy Goods,

Such as Gold and Silver head Canes, Fans, Fancy Clocks, Porte Monnaies, Gold Pens, Pocket and Table Knives, Vases, Razors, etc., etc. Those wanting

CHOICE GOODS,

Are invited to call and examine their Assortment.

P. S. Watches, Clocks, Music Boxes and Jewelry, repaired.

6

J. H. HEINSHEIMER & CO.

WHOLESALE DEALERS IN

CLOTHING, CLOTHS, CASSIMERES,

VESTINGS, SHIRTS, AND TAILORS TRIMMINGS,

Nos. 299 and 801 Main Street,
CINCINNATI.

Hat Conformature,
AT

JARVIS & FAIRCHILD'S
100 Main Street,

Second door below Fourth,

CINCINNATI,

WHOLESALE AND RETAIL DEALERS IN
AND MANUFACTURERS OF

HATS,
CAPS,
STRAW GOODS, ETC.
JARVIS & FAIRCHILD

CHARLES JACOB,
CURER OF AND DEALER IN

BACON, HAMS, SHOULDERS, BOLOGNA SAUSAGES,
Dried Beef, and Beef Tongues,
68 Sycamore St. bet. Third and Lower Market, Cincinnati, O.

SIMEON B. WILLIAMS,
MANUFACTURER OF
FINE-CUT CHEWING & SMOKING

TOBACCO
AND DEALER IN
Virginia Manufactured Tobacco,
AND IMPORTED AND DOMESTIC

CIGARS
88, 90, & 92 Pearl St. Cin.

First Premiums awarded, 1852, at
American Institute, N. Y.; Mechanics' In-
stitute, Cin.; Ohio State Fair, Cleveland;
Michigan State Fair, Detroit.

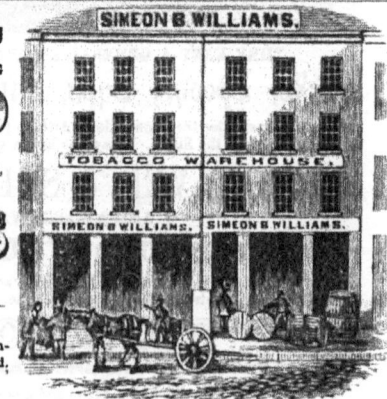

FRANCIS DUNLEVY. J. S. ATWOOD. E. FANSET.

DUNLEVY, ATWOOD & CO.

BANKERS

And Exchange Dealers,

84 THIRD ST.

THORNHILL & CARRICK SADDLE & HARNESS MAKERS, THIRD STREET, BET. WALNUT AND VINE STS., CINCINNATI, OHIO.

Great Western Saddle, Harness and Trunk Manufactory, No. 78 West Third Street.

WILLIAM DUNN,

MANUFACTURER OF ALL KINDS OF

METAL ROOFING

ZINC, COPPER, TIN, AND SHEET IRON,

THIRD STREET, NEAR VINE, CINCINNATI.

Patent Galvanized Iron Cornice and Roofing. Buildings Covered in any part of the
United States, on the most approved plan. All Orders punctually attended to,

AMERICAN VERMICELLI, MACCARONI, AND

CHOCOLATE FACTORY,

BY

J. B. WERNERT & GOETTHEIM,

596 MAIN STREET NEAR LIBERTY, CINCINNATI,

IMPORTERS AND DEALERS IN

SWISS AND LIMBURGH CHEESE, GERMAN PRUNES,

HOLLAND HERRINGS, FARINA, BARLEY, STARCH, ETC.

A FULL STOCK OF BUILDERS' HARDWARE ALWAYS ON HAND.

J. Lawton, DEALER IN FINE CUTLERY, 312 MAIN STREET CINCINNATI, O.

THE Mammoth Knife, 30 INCHES LONG, one of the most *beautiful* SPECIMENS of CUTLERY EVER SEEN VALUED AT $250.00.

A CHOICE SELECTION OF ALL KINDS OF MECHANICS TOOLS ALWAYS ON HAND!

JAMES TODD.   J. R. POINIER.

JAS. TODD & CO.

STEAM ENGINE BUILDERS

AND MACHINISTS,

Corner of Seventh and Smith Sts. Cincinnati, O.

Cotton, Hay, Lard and Tobacco Screws; Portable Corn and Flouring Mills, Threshing Machines and Horse Powers.

ALSO,—PLANING MACHINES OF VARIOUS PATTERNS AND SIZES.

J. EGGERS & WILDE,

WHOLESALE AND RETAIL DEALERS IN

PRINTS AND STATIONERY,

IMPORTERS OF

GERMAN, GREEK, LATIN AND HEBREW BOOKS,

817 MAIN STREET,

CINCINNATI, O.

SHEPHERD'S

CORSET MANUFACTORY,

WHOLESALE AND RETAIL,

NO. 100   FIFTH St. CINCINNATI.

PATENT FRENCH WOVE CORSETS, FRENCH JACKETS,

Ladies' Belts, Shoulder Braces, etc., Corset and other Trimmings.

R. S. SEMPLE & CO.,

STOVE FOUNDERS,

CINCINNATI, O.

G ELLENBECK & DUTMANN, FLOUR DEALERS, No. 426 & 428 Main Street, East side, between Canal and Court, Cincinnati.

Keep constantly on hand the best Family and Baker's Flour, which they will furnish to all who may favor them with a call, Wholesale or Retail.

265. **HENRY WESTRUP,** **265.**

MERCHANT TAILOR,

No. 265 Main Street, between Sixth and Seventh, West side,

CINCINNATI, OHIO.

J. GRUHLER. G. VOLLMER.

O HIO TOBACCO MANUFACTORY.—GRUHLER & Co., Manu- facturers of all kinds of TOBACCO AND SNUFF, French Rapee Macoboy, Scotch, Fine-Cut Cavendish, German and American Smoking Cigars, &c. No. 266, Western Row, bet. 6th and 7th sts., Cincinnati, O.

JULIUS WEDEKIND,

Manufacturer and Dealer in

CIGARS & TOBACCO

No. 55 Fly Market. bet. Plum and Western Row, Cincinnati.

E. BLOCK & CO.,

Importers and Dealers in

FOREIGN LIQUORS AND CIGARS,

'No. 34 Sycamore St., bet. Columbia and Front, Cincinnati, O.

C. H. BENNETT,

W HOLESALE AND RETAIL BAKER, Court Street, South side, six doors East of Vine, Cincinnati, Ohio.

Constantly on hand a good assortment of Bread, Crackers, Cakes, etc.

WILLIAM FISHER,

MERCHANT TAILOR,

No. 663 Western Row between Wade and Liberty Streets

CINCINNATI. OHIO.

M. S. KIMBALL,

CHEAP DRY GOODS STORE,

SOUTH SIDE COURT STREET, ONE DOOR WEST OF VINE.

S. A. REINBERGER,

D EALER IN TOBACCO AND CIGARS; Fine-Cut Chewing and Smoking Tobacco; Imported Cigars, etc.

No. 509 Vine st., bet. 14th and 15th, Cincinnati. One price only.

(Editorial from Cincinnati Gazette, of April 28th, 1853.)

EVENS'
PERCUSSION SEAL PRESS.

" This cut is design
Percussion Seal Press

with any kind of device the purchaser may
select.

Formerly, presses for the same purpose
with this of Mr. Evens, cost from twelve to
thirty dollars. This one is offered complete
for only five dollars, and is in all respects
as perfect in its operations as the most ex-
pensive. Who ever wishes to circulate his
address or his business cards on the paper

man
ment of the press will be found in our business columns."

THE GENERAL AGENCY FOR THE ABOVE PRESS,

U. S. ENGRAVING ROOMS,
14 FOURTH ST., NEXT DOOR WEST OF 1ST PRES. CHURCH, CIN'TI.
C. F. HALL.

Seal Engraving in all its variety. Particular attention given to designing, engraving
and blazoning appropriate coats of Arms, for corporate Bodies, Civil and Ecclesiastic, Crests
and Arms of Ancient families sought and engraved. Copper plate engraving and printing,
such as marriage, business and address Cards, Notes, Drafts &c.

ENVELOPE DIES, Plain and Elaborate.

Self-Sealing advertising Envelopes, Colored embossed Cards, Book Titles, Boot and Hat-
tip stamps, Steel stamps for Silversmiths, Boiler-plate Manufacturers. Carpenters, &c.
Bankers, Post Office and Steam Boat Stamps, with complete inking Apparatus for the same.
Hall's new improved Lever Seal Press. A complete assortment of English. French and
German plain and fancy Billet paper and Envelopes, suitable for Weddings, Balls, Parties &c.
&c., Cake Boxes and every description of Wedding Stationery. Jewelry and Silver plate
marking for the trade.

A. CONSTINE,

MANUFACTURER AND DEALER IN

CABINET WARE

CHAIRS AND UPHOLSTERY GOODS IN GENERAL,

No. 69 FIFTH STREET,

South side, between Walnut and Vine, Cincinnati.

FRANCIS NUELSON,

Successor of NUELSON & FICKE,

IMPORTER AND MANUFACTURER OF

CIGARS TOBACCO & SNUFF

No. 233, MAIN STREET,

Between Fifth and Sixth, Five Doors below the Galt House,

CINCINNATI, OHIO.

H. & F. HELMKAMP,

FASHIONABLE

CABINET, CHAIR AND SOFA

MANUFACTURERS,

No. 13 East Liberty Street, Cincinnati, O.

Frames of Chairs and Sofas always on hand to be finished and to suit customers, at the lowest cash prices. All orders will receive punctual attention at short notice.

BURNET & BROTHER,

MANUFACTURERS OF

HOMINY AND PEARL BARLEY,

Warranted not to be spoiled by change of Climate

Warehouse and Salesroom, South Canal. St. bet. Main and Walnut, Third House from Walnut,

CINCINNATI, OHIO.

MILL, NEAR LOCKLAND, HAMILTON COUNTY,

BOSTON EATING HOUSE,

130 Sycamore opposite Post Office, Cincinnati, O.

Meals at all hours, Bills of Fare of articles, and prices will always be found on the table,

W. H. FALES, & G. W. WHEELER, Proprietors,

N. B.—The traveling community will find here the best of Fare and Rooms, at reasonable prices.

CHARLES SCHANUEL,

PIANO FORTE MANUFACTURER,

Corner Ninth and Walnut Streets,

CINCINNATI, OHIO.

H. DIEGMANN,

TOBACCONIST,

No. 20 Hughes St., East side 3 doors from Liberty,

Cincinnati, Ohio.

Manufacturer, Wholesale and Retail Dealer in all kinds of Cigars, Tobacco, Snuff, and Cut and Dry; also, keeps constantly on hand and for sale a superior quality of Cigar Leaf.

JOSEPH HOW,

INSPECTOR OF LEAF TOBACCO,

For the City of Cincinnati,

OFFICE, SOUTH SIDE PEARL BET. VINE AND RACE.

JAMES THOMSON.

BELT MAKER,

COR. FRONT AND BUTLER STREETS, CINCINNATI.

Keeps ready made Belting always on hand, including Single, Double and Round, from one inch and upwards. These Belts we warrant to be thoroughly stretched and made of the very best material. I have on hand a lot of superior Lace Leather for sale. Orders from the country promptly filled. REFERENCES.—A. M. Taylor, D. A. Powel, E. & W. Cameron, L. H. Fagin, Gould, Pearce & Co., J. Coolidge, George Shields.

P. & H. GOTTMANN,

Main St. bet. Twelfth and Canal, Cincinnati,

PAPER HANGING STORE

AND CARPET WEAVING.

JEFFERSON
LIFE INSURANCE
COMPANY
OF CINCINNATI.

Capital, $100,000; Paid in and Secured.

OFFICE IN BROMWELLS BUILDING,

Corner of Fourth and Vine Streets,

CINCINNATI, OHIO.

TOM. O. EDWARDS, President.   W. W. CONES, Vice President.
H. W. FOWLER, Secretary.

DIRECTORS.

TOM. O. EDWARDS,	W. W. CONES,	H. N. GOODMAN,
S. B. KEYS,	GEORGE CARLISLE,	E. GEST,
WM. M'CAMMON,	CHAS. GOODMAN,	C. CONAHAN,
A. G. BURT,	WILLIAM BURNET.	
D. W. DESHLER, Columbus,		H. B. PAYNE, Cleveland.

Insurance in the "Jefferson" can be effected on the Mutual or Stock plan. Its capital is sufficient to afford a full security to the insured. Its managers are well known. Participation of profits to those insured in the Mutual department. Stock rates reduced to the standard of safety. Policies can be taken in name of the wife, free from any claims of her husband's creditors. Pamphlets furnished gratis, by the agents of the Company, in nearly every town in the State.

PEOPLE'S BANK

OF CINCINNATI,

MANCHESTER BUILDING,

CORNER OF THIRD & SYCAMORE STS.,

P. B. MANCHESTER, Proprietor,

Discounts freely for Customers at all seasons, and pays a LIBERAL INTEREST on money DEPOSITED, payable on demand.

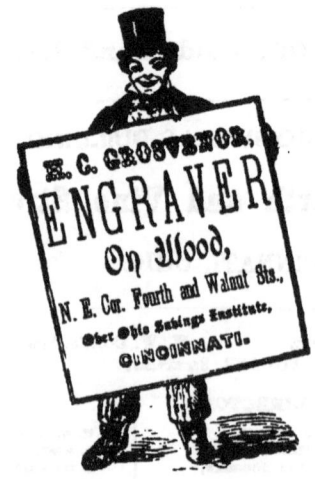

V. SLIKER,

MANUFACTURER AND DEALER IN

BOOTS, SHOES, LEATHER,

AND SHOE LACES,

WHOLESALE & RETAIL,

49 & 82 Lower Market, bet. Broadway & Sycamore,

CINCINNATI, O.

[Henry Clay's Birth Place.]

Every style of Wood Engraving executed with promptness, and for Beauty and Cheapness unequaled in the West.

J. R. TELFER,
Designer and Engraver on Wood,
Third Story Gazette Buildings, Main St., Cincinnati, O.

H. WM. MEIER,

LUMBER MERCHANT,

North side Hamilton Road, opposite Race Street, Cincinnati.

Dealer in all kinds of Lumber for Building, Cabinet, etc., etc.

F. BARTH,

ENGRAVER & GUILLOGEUR,

GOLD AND SILVER SMITH, GILDER AND PLATER,

Vine St., bet. 12th & 13th Sts., east side, Cincinnati.

Good and handsome articles, are warranted and sold low.   Orders in his line will be promptly attended to.

MARTIN AMAN,

GILDER AND PAINTER.

No. 56 Finley street, between Race and Elm streets, Cincinnati.

HENRY ELBREG & C. RUHL.

Manufacturers of Cider & Whisky Vinegar,

NO. 395 BROADWAY, CINCINNATI.

Prof. R. C. CARTER, M. D.,

PRACTITIONER,

ALSO, DEALER IN MEDICINES, MEDICAL BOOKS, PERFUMERY, ETC,

No. 112 George St, N. side, 1 door east W. Row, Cincinnati.

Umbrellas, Parasols, Walking Sticks,
MATTING, CARPETING & OIL CLOTHS,

All of the best qualities and cheapest rates.   Umbrellas and Parasols repaired at short notice.

CONRAD KRATZ,

Walnut street, between Fourth and Fifth, west side, Cincinnati.

WM. WISWELL, Jr.,

LOOKING GLASS AND PICTURE FRAME

MANUFACTURER,

AND STEAMBOAT ORNAMENTER,

No. 129 Main St., bet. Third & Fourth, Cin.

ADAMS & CO'S.

Great Eastern, Western, and Southern

EXPRESS.

OFFICE --- 54 East Third Street, Cincinnati.

Specie, Bank Notes, Jewelry and Packages of every description forwarded with dispatch, to all of the principal cities and towns in the Union.

LEE & LEAVITT,

Manufacturers of every description of

CAST & GERMAN STEEL SAWS

No. 53 Water St., bet. Walnut & Vine, Cincinnati.

☞ Particular attention paid to making Long and Circular Saws for portable saw mills.

A. C. PARRY.   JOHN BECKLY.

PARRY & BECKLY,

Manufacturers and dealers in

TINWARE,

Wholesale and retail,

PLAIN & JAPANNED; STREET LANTERNS, &c.,

No. 31 Vine street, near Front, Cincinnati, O.

N. B. All kind of Job Work in Tin, Sheet Iron and Copper neatly and promptly
executed on reasonable terms. Lantern Glass always on hand.
Orders from a distance promptly attended to.

PHŒNIX BLIND FACTORY,

No. 82 Sixth St., bet. Walnut & Vine,

CINCINNATI, O.

BRANCH FACTORY,

COVINGTON, KY.,

Corner of Craig and Lewis streets.

T. J. RICORDS, - - The Blind Maker.

E. M. SHIELD,

MACHINIST & BRASS FOUNDER,

No. 75 Front St., bet. Ludlow & Lawrence,

CINCINNATI.

Manufacturer of all kinds of Brass and Composition Castings, Pumps of all descriptions, Metallic
Packing and Anti-Friction Metals, and Distillery Work in all its varieties.
Light Machinery of all descriptions built to order.
☞ Agent for BORDEN'S Mercury Steam Guage and FABER'S Water Guage.

Dr. Hall's Medical Office.

Dr. HALL has devoted much time to the pathology and treatment of Private Diseases, and having
permanently located in this city, takes this method of announcing to the citizens and strangers, that he
eradicates this most horrible of all diseases from the system, in an almost incredible short time, without
the use of Calomel, Balsam, Cubebs, or any of the poisonous drugs generally used by others.
   Syphilis, Gonorrhœa, Urethral discharges, Gleet, Stricture, Seminal Weakness, Impotency, Leuch-
orœa, Rheumatism, Disease of the Back and Loins, Inflammation of the Bladder and Kidneys Hydrocele,
Cancers, Ulcers, and the various diseases of the Skin, etc., will be treated in a careful, thorough, and
scientific manner. Also, Coughs, Colds, Bronchitis, Consumption, and all diseases of the Lungs, Dr. H's
knowledge and skill in removing Venereal Diseases has been obtained by much sacrifice, and a long course
of study and practical experience of unlimited extent; therefore it is with pleasure that he can offer to
the unfortunate a sure and safe cure. Ague and Fever cured in 24 hours, warranted. Charges very low.
   N. B. Persons living at a distance, describing their diseases in a letter, and sending a reasonable fee
shall have medicines forwarded to them with directions for use.
Office, No. 134 Walnut street, bet. Third and Fourth, Cincinnati.

DRS. J. ALLEN & G. S. VAN EMON,

DENTISTS,

Fourth Street, 2nd door West of Vine,

CINCINNATI.

A. C. BURBECK,

WHOLESALE CRACKER BAKER,

STORE, NO. 49 CATHERINE STREET,

CINCINNATI.

☞ Every description of Crackers delivered free of charge, to all parts of the city. ☜

McCAMMON & KOLKER,

STAIRBUILDERS, CARPENTERS & JOINERS,

CORNER OF CUTTER AND CLINTON STREETS,

CINCINNATI.

PETER FAIS,

Manufacturer of

Skimmers, Ladles, Fire Shovels, Tongs & Coal Buckets,

CORNER OF VINE AND BUCKEYE STREETS,

No. 190 VINE STREET,

CINCINNATI, O.

AUGUST WAGNER,

Druggist & Apothecary,

Deutsche Apotheke.

CORNER OF MAIN AND WOODWARD STREETS,

CINCINNATI, O.

J. H. FELDWISCH,

WHOLESALE AND RETAIL

GROCERY AND PROVISION STORE,

Nos. 86 & 88 Hughes Street,

CINCINNATI, OHIO.

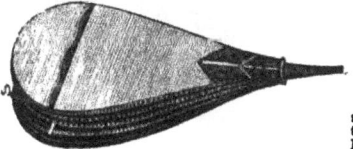

Firemen's Insurance Co.
OF CINCINNATI.

ESTABLISHED IN 1832.

NO AGENCIES.

This Company continues to take Risks, both Fire and Marine at the Lowest Approved Rates.

DIRECTORS.

P. WILSON,
J. T. WARREN,
ROBT. ANDREWS,
EDW'D DODSON,
E. M. BRUCE,
JAS. CALHOUN,
W. B. CASSILLY,

C. W. WEST.

EDMUND DEXTER,
JOHN D. MINOR,
BRIGGS SWIFT,
JOHN P. TWEED,
N. W. THOMAS,
JOHN WHETSTONE,
P. A. WHITE,

HENRY E. SPENCER, Pres't.

L. CLAWSON, Sec'y.

OFFICE, IN THE COMPANY'S BUILDINGS,
NORTH-EAST CORNER MAIN & FRONT STREETS,
SECOND STORY, ENTRANCE ON FRONT STREET.

J. S. CHENOWETH & CO.
Commission and Forwarding Merchants,
NO. 25 EAST FRONT ST.

J. S. CHENOWETH, }
ROSS CHENOWETH, }

CINCINNATI.

☞ Particular attention paid to Filling Orders for Produce, and Forwarding Goods. ☜

ORNAMENTAL PLASTER WORK
IN ALL ITS BRANCHES,
∽BY∽
CYRUS WEST,
No. 130 Vine Street, opposite the Burnet House,
CINCINNATI. O.

Enriched Ceilings of all descriptions; Centre Pieces, Cornice Enrichments; Capitols of all the Orders and Composit, both for Column and Lintel, done to order with accuracy, neatness and dispatch.
N. B.—Orders from abroad will receive prompt attention.

CAMPBELL, ELLISON & CO.

MANUFACTURERS OF

PIG IRON,

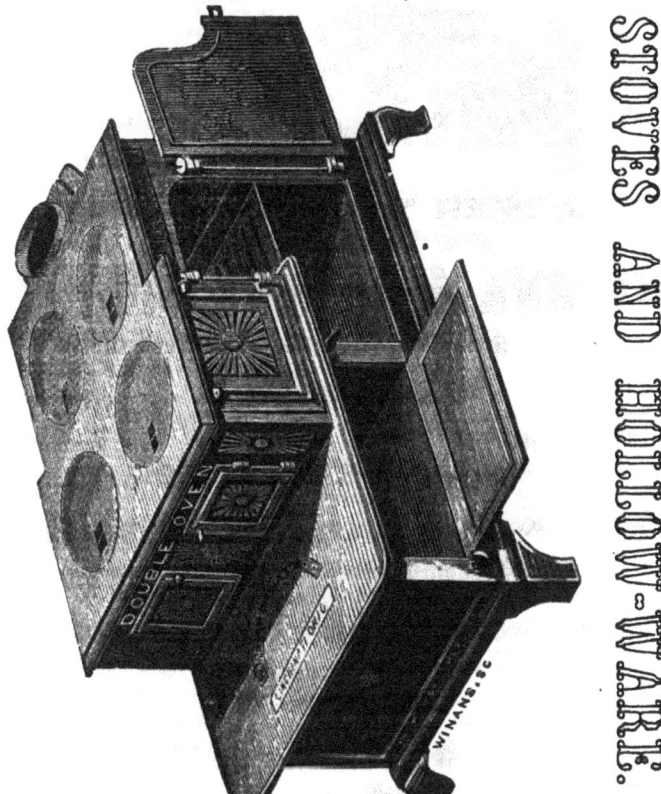

STOVES AND HOLLOW-WARE.

21 COLUMBIA STREET
CINCINNATI, OHIO.

A constant supply of Pig Iron, both cold and hot blast is always kept on hand.

HAY & ORE SCALES,

Of an improved plan, put up in any part of the Country.

☞ REPAIRING done on the shortest notice.

References:

J. S. CHENOWETH & CO.
MINOR, ANDREWS & CO.
BISHOP, WELLS & CO.
R. BUCHANAN,
JOHN SWASEY & CO.
BURDSAL & BROTHER.

Columbia St., North Side,
BETWEEN SYCAMORE AND BROADWAY,
CINCINNATI, O.

E. NEUMANN. H. MOSS.

E. NEUMANN & CO.

IMPORTERS AND WHOLESALE DEALERS IN

HAVANA & GERMAN CIGARS,

No. 128 Sycamore Street, opposite Post Office,

CINCINNATI, O.

JOHN A. DICKINSON. WM. S. DICKINSON.

J. A. & W. S. DICKINSON,

WHOLESALE AND RETAIL

MATTRESS MANUFACTURERS,

No. 45 Third Street, between Broadway & Sycamore,

CINCINNATI, O.

Always on hand or made to order WIRE SPRING, CURLED HAIR, COTTON, MOSS, SHUCK and STRAW MATTRESSES, TARPAULINS, COTTON DUCK, SHEETS, SLIPS, &c. Also, particular attention paid to fitting up Hotels and Steamboats.

Dealers are invited to call and examine our Stock. Orders filled with neatness and dispatch.

J. C. BUCKLES, of Louisville. H. L. JUDGE, of Cincinnati.

J. C. BUCKLES & JUDGE,

Commission & Forwarding Merchants,

AND PRODUCE BROKERS,

NO. 9 EAST FRONT ST., CINCINNATI, O.

☞ Strict attention paid to all consignments for sale of **Produce, &c.** Goods for reshipment to and from the East, forwarded with dispatch.

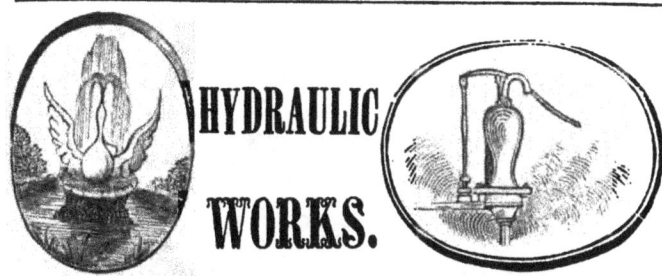

NEWMAN & PRICHARD,

172 Elm Street, between Fourth and Fifth, Cincinnati, Ohio,

Manufacturers of

LIFT & FORGE PUMPS,

Of the most approved styles,

WATER WHEELS AND WIND MILLS,

For supplying Railroad water stations.

Fire Engines, break and horisontal, of all sizes and prices; Hose Reels, Fire Caps, Trumpets, Torches, Copper Riveted Leather Hose, India Rubber Hose of all sizes, etc., Cast Iron Ornamental Fountains, Iron and Brass Castings of all kinds.

We would call the attention of Railroad Companies, Manufacturers and Distillers to our McGowan Double Action Pump, as being particularly adapted to them for its simplicity and certain action.

F. W. MEYER.   J. D. RIEMEIER.

LARD OIL FACTORY

OF

F. W. MEYER & CO.,

NO. 15 BUCKEYE STREET, CINCINNATI, OHIO.

HUST & SONS,

LARD OIL FACTORY,

16 Locust St., bet. Hamilton Road & Buckeye, Cin'ti.

M. DEMAND,

WHOLESALE CANDY MANUFACTURER,

No. 224 Walnut St., bet. 5th & 6th Sts., Cincinnati.

All kinds of Candies kept constantly on hand.

CINCINNATI WATER CURE.

This large and flourishing Institute is open summer and winter, and affords superior advantages for the sick. It is located five miles from the city, on the Cincinnati and Dayton Railway, and but a few rods from the Carthage Depot.

Terms—From eight to ten dollars per week. Extra attention will subject the patient to extra charge. For further particulars address.

D. A. PEASE, M. D.

Carthage, Hamilton Co., O.

FIRE, MARINE AND LIFE INSURANCE.

WASHINGTON FIRE INSURANCE CO.,
Of NEW YORK CITY. CASH CAPITAL - - $200,000.

GRANITE FIRE AND MARINE INSURANCE COMPANY.
Of UTICA, N. Y. CAPITAL, - - $150,000.

ODD FELLOWS' MUTUAL INSURANCE CO.,
Of PHILADELPHIA. CAPITAL, - - - - - - - - - $100,000.

WM. H. WRIGHT, Agent.

As Agent for the above Companies, I am prepared to issue Policies on Buildings, Merchandise, Household Furniture, Produce, &c.; Also, on Steamboats, Freight, Cargoes of Steamboats, Vessels and Flatboats.

OFFICE, No. 8 MAIN STREET,

SECOND DOOR BELOW FRONT, UP STAIRS,   CINCINNATI, O.

G. W. BIGLER, M. D.

HOMEOPATHIST.

Office, N. W. cor. 6th & College Sts., bet. Vine
and Race. OFFICE HOURS—From 7 to 9, A. M.,
and from 3 to 5 and 6 to 8, P. M.

T. SMITH, M. D.

180 Richmond St.

BETWEEN CUTTER & MOUND,

CINCINNATI, O.

S. KYLE,

PHYSICIAN, ELECTIC SURGEON, ETC.

Office & Residence, 500 Western Row,

CINCINNATI, OHIO.

Office Hours, from 10, A. M., to 1, P. M., and
from 3 to 5, P. M.

DR. J. F. WHITE,

South side Fourth St., bet. Mace & Elm,

Cincinnati, Ohio.

WM. HENRY BRISBANE, M. D.

OFFICE AND RESIDENCE,

North West corner of Sixth and College Sts.
CINCINNATI, O.

Dr. J. F. BRADISH,

HOMŒOPATHIST,

No. 164 Richmond Street, Cincinnati, O.

No relief, no pay, if directions are followed.

T. WOOD, M. D.

Seventh St., bet. Main & Walnut, North side,

OFFICE OPPOSITE,

CINCINNATI, OHIO.

Office hours from 1 to 3, & from 7 to 10, P. M.

JESSE GARRETSON, M. D.

HOMŒOPATHIST AND HYDROPATHIST,

NO. 175 VINE STREET,

Offers his services to the citizens of Cincinnati in the practice
of Medicine and Surgery. Persons at a distance addressing him by letter, with a full description of symptoms,
&c., &c., will receive prompt attention. Office Hours,
11 A. M. to 1 P. M., 4 P. M. to 6 P. M.

JOHN M. ALDEN, M. D.

PHYSICIAN AND SURGEON,

Catharine St., bet. Western Row & John,

NORTH SIDE, CINCINNATI.

HUGH RICE QUINN, M. D.

PHYSICIAN & SURGEON

OFFICE & RESIDENCE,

210 Sycamore St., opp. Xavier's College,

Dr. J. P. JUDGE,

OF THE PHYSIO-MEDICAL PRACTICE,

OFFICE—Third St., one door East of Broadway.

Dr J would respectfully tender his professional services
to his friends and the public, whose confidence he shall en-
deavor to secure and sustain by prompt, energetic and faith-
ful attention to his duties.

TALIAFERRO & BUCKNER,

Office, in St. John's College Building, Walnut St.

BET. 6TH AND 7TH, CINCINNATI.

Office Hours, from 7 to 9 A. M. and 1 to 3 P. M.

Dr. J. W. MIGHELS,

PROFESSOR OF MIDWIFERY

And diseases of WOMEN and CHILDREN,
in the Cincinnati College of Medicine & Surgery.

Office, S. E. cor. of 8th & Walnut. Residence
9 Laurel St., Cincinnati.

B. Ahrmann, M. D.   F. Ahrmann, M. D.

Drs. B. & F. EHRMANN,

Homœopathic Physicians and Surgeons,

OFFICE—46 W. Seventh St., North side.

LANDON RIVES, M. D.

SURGEON,

NO. 131 SYMMES STREET, CINCINNATI, O.

ADOLPH BAUER, M. D.

HOMŒOPATHIST,

Office—No. 134 West 6th St., Cincinnati.

JOS. PIERCE WALKER, M. D.

OFFICE AND RESIDENCE,

Broadway, East side, bet 6th & 7th Sts.

J. BORTON, M. D.

PHYSICIAN & SURGEON

Office—S. W. cor. 8th & John Sts.,

CINCINNATI.

OLIVER D. NORTON, M. D.

PHYSICIAN AND SURGEON,

Office, Western Row, bet. 4th & 5th.

OFFICE HOURS—2 to 5 P. M.

R. D. MUSSEY, M. D.   W. H. MUSSEY, M. D.

Drs. MUSSEY,

SURGEONS AND PHYSICIANS,

7th St. N. side, 2 doors East of Vine.

OFFICE HOURS—9 A. M. 3½ P. M.

DENTISTRY.

DR. M. ROGERS,

A Dentist of long experience in this city, has his
Office on the
N. side 4th St., 3 doors west of Main,
Where he will be happy to wait on his customers
in all the various departments of the dental pro-
fession. He is prepared to insert teeth on the
SHORTEST POSSIBLE NOTICE, in the latest and most
improved style of workmanship.

A. R. DUTTON,

Attorney, Counsellor and Solicitor,
No. 13 HOFFLE's LAW BUILDINGS,
CINCINNATI, O.

ALPHONSO TAFT.   THOS M KEY.   PATRICK MALLON.

TAFT, KEY & MALLON,

Attorneys & Counsellors at Law,
1 & 2 MANCHESTER's BUILDING, 3rd St.,
CINCINNATI,

J. FREON,

ATTORNEY AND NOTARY PUBLIC,
N. W. COR. MAIN & EIGHTH STREETS,
CINCINNATI, O.

B. S. HUBBARD,

Attorney at Law and Solicitor in Chancery,
Office — Manchester Buildings, corner
Third & Sycamore, Cincinnati.

SHATTUCK HARTWELL,

ATTORNEY AT LAW, NOTARY PUBLIC,
And Commissioner of Deeds, Depositions, &c., for
Indiana, Kentucky and Massachusetts.
OFFICE — Daily Times Building, 95 Walnut St.,
CINCINNATI, O.

Z. P. GLASS.   E. H. STOCKWELL,

DRS. GLASS & STOCKWELL.

The former devotes his entire attention to the
treatment of Acute Diseases and Obstetrical Practice. The latter to Surgery and Chronic Diseases,
especially Consumption, Asthma, Bronchitis,
Neuralgia, Dropsy, Dyspepsia, Hernia, Fistula,
Cancer, &c.   NO CURE, NO PAY.

Also, dealers in Medicines, Medical Books
and Perfumery,
Office, No. 520 Western Row, near Mason street, Cincinnati.

A. T. BUTLER,   A. N. LEWIS.

LEWIS & BUTLER,

ATTORNEYS AT LAW,

S. E. Cor. 4th & Main Sts., Cincinnati.
REFER TO—Smith, Beadle & Smith, No 255 Pearl
street, N. Y.   Andrew Lester & Co., No. 19
William street, N. Y.   N. Longworth, Cin'ti.

THOMPSON'S

PENMAN'S INSTITUTE,

S. E. COR. WALNUT AND EIGHTH STS., CIN.
Open day and evening.

J ASHCRAFT,

Keeps constantly on hand at the

FRANKLIN COAL YARD

Front St., bet. Lawrence & Pike. Cin.
Youghiogheny Coal, Coke, Fire Brick and Clay.   Hauling
of all kinds done at the shortest notice.

TIMOTHY D. LINCOLN,

Attorney and Counsellor at Law,
AND SOLICITOR IN CHANCERY,
Office, 3 Columbia St, N. S. bet. Main & Syc.
CINCINNATI. O.

Western Button Factory.

S. H. & J. HOOLE,
Pearl St., s. s. bet. Elm & Plum, Cincinnati.
A constant supply of Bone Pantaloon Buttons, always
on hand, at less than eastern prices.

WESTERN FOUNDRY

A. B. HOLABIRD & CO.

STEAM ENGINE BUILDERS,

Saw & Grist Mill Work done with dispatch.
All kinds of Boilers made to order.
Front St., west of Smith street, Cincinnati.

Private Infirmary.

DR. THO'S. J. ORR,
devotes special attention to the treatment of Hernia, (rupture)
Office Rooms— Nos. 9 & 11, in new edifice of
Ohio Medical College, Sixth street.
Refer to, Prof. Avery, Prof. Rives, Prof. Massey, Cincinnati;
Dr. R. Thompson, Columbus; Dr. Joseph N. McDowell,
St. Louis; Dr. Peoton, New Orleans.

JAS. T. MORGAN,

Publisher, Stereotyper,

PRINTER AND BINDER,

111 Main street, Cincinnati.

HOWARD INFIRMARY, COLUMBUS, OHIO.— SEE OPPOSITE PAGE.

JACOB LOWMAN,
CLEVELAND, OHIO,

Corner of Vineyard & Long Streets,

Manufacturer of

Omnibusses, Carriages, Buggys, Rockaways,

Plain and Fancy **WAGONS,** &c., of every description.

All of the most Modern Style, of the best Material and Workmanship. All work warranted.

☞ **Orders respectfully solicited.** ☜

WILLIAMS, BABCOCK & HURD,

Wholesale Dealers in all kinds of

GROCERIES,

Foreign & Domestic Liquors & Wines,

FANCY GOODS, TOYS, &C. &C.

Also—Manufacturers of the best Qualities of

CONFECTIONARIES,

NO. 83. SUPERIOR ST.,

J. B. WILLIAMS,
F. E. BABCOCK, }
N. HURD, JR.,

CLEVELAND, OHIO.

ALCOTT & HORTON,

Wholesale Dealers in

DRY GOODS,

MILLINERY & YANKEE NOTIONS,

NO. 57 SUPERIOR STREET,

CLEVELAND, OHIO.

C. E. FISHER & CO.,

PROPRIETORS OF C. S. EMERSONS'

AMERICAN HAIR RESTORATIVE

No. 57 SUPERIOR STREET,

CLEVELAND, OHIO.

CLEVELAND AGRICULTURAL WORKS.

DEWITT & CO.,

MERWIN STREET, CLEVELAND, OHIO,

Manufacturers & Wholesale & Retail Dealers in

AGRICULTURAL & HORTICULTURAL

IMPLEMENTS & MACHINES

OF EVERY DESCRIPTION,

Would particularly call the attention of dealers to our extensive assortment of Implements, many of which we are manufacturing, aiming to have the best material and workmanship combined. Among our assortment can be found, Steel and Iron Plows, Harrows, Cultivators, Corn Planters, Corn Shellers ; Hay, Straw and Corn Stalk Cutters, Corn and Cob Crushers, Portable Grist Mills, Reaping and Mowing Machines, Horse Powers and Thrashers, Saw Mills, Portable Cider Mills, Seed Drills, Horse and Hand Rakes, Hay and Manure Ferks, Thermometer and Cylinder Churns, Grain Cradles, Scythes and Snaths, Hoes, Wooden Ware, &c. Together with a complete assortment of

GARDENING TOOLS.

ALSO,

FIELD, GARDEN AND FLOWER SEEDS.

☞ Price Lists can always be had on application to us, by letter or otherwise.

Our Motto is, BEST GOODS AND LOW PRICES.

JOHN PARKIN,

FILE MANUFACTURER,

Tracy Street, North corner of Lorain, Ohio City, O.

☞ FILES AND RASPS of every description re-cut, and warranted good as new. ☜

The patronage of Manufacturers and Mechanics is respectfully solicited.

WORK from CITY or COUNTRY PROMPTLY ATTENDED TO.

NEW LISBON, OHIO.

OFFICERS.

JAMES KELLY, President,   JAMES BURBECK, Vice President,
LEVI MARTIN, Secretary and Treasurer.

REFERENCES.

Hon. John Pearce, Ex-President Judge;
Hon. Sam'l B. McKenzie, Ex-Clerk of Court;
William K. Upham, Esq.;
Dr. T. G. Parker;
Nathaniel Mitchel, Post Master;

Hon. Sam'l S. Clarke, Ex-Associate Judge;
Jona. H. Wallace, Prosecuting Attorney;
James Mason, Esq.;
William Hostetter, Esq.;
A. G. McCaskey, Esq.;

Wisdom & Vanatta, Esqs.

CLEVELAND

CURLED HAIR MANUFACTORY,

WISDOM, RUSSELL & CO, PROPRIETORS.

This establishment having been awarded medals and diplomas from the most prominent States in the Union, and after a successful competition with the whole manufacturing world, received the Prize Medal at the World's Fair, London, for the best Curled Hair and Mattresses; with these endorsements we offer to Upholsterers, Cabinetmakers and the trade generally, an article that will always command custom and give entire satisfaction.

Steamboats, Hotels and Public Institutions,

Supplied with Curled Hair Mattresses on the most reasonable terms.

HARRIS & FAIRBANKS.

J. A. HARRIS,   GEO. A. BENEDICT,   A. W. FAIRBANKS,   WM. J. MAY,   JOHN COON,

EDITORS, PUBLISHERS AND PROPRIETORS OF

DAILY HERALD,

CLEVELAND.

An extensive JOB AND BOOK PRINTING OFFICE under the special supervision of Mr. FAIRBANKS is connected with the establishment. The facilities we enjoy, by four steam presses and a very full assortment of Book and Job materials, and the qualifications of those engaged in the various departments, enables us to execute all orders for Railroads, Commercial, Steamboat and other Fine Printing in the best style, and the shortest notice, at very low prices.

MARBLE WORKS!

WHITMAN & COLTON,

No. 44 Ontario Street, a few rods South of the Market,

CLEVELAND, O.

WHOLESALE & RETAIL DEALERS IN

AMERICAN AND FOREIGN

MARBLE.

MANUFACTURERS OF MONUMENTS, &c.

H. SMITH.   C. C. MURRAY.   A. P. PRIOR.

SMITH, MURRAY & CO.,

No. 86 Bank Street, Cleveland, Ohio,

Dealers in and Manufacturers of all kinds of

Tin, Sheet Iron and Copper Work.

Particular attention paid to

PLUMBING, TIN ROOFING,

LOCOMOTIVE & STEAM BOAT COPPER WORK,

Agents for

CULVER'S CELEBRATED HOT AIR FURNACE.

Also, a large variety of

REGISTERS AND WALL VENTILATORS.

Also, Agents for Collins' Ventilator and Chimney Top.

WORK SHOP in the rear of Hilliard & Hayes' Store, on Centre Street. All orders from abroad promptly attended to.

Folsom's Mercantile College

105 Sartwell's Block, N. E. cor. Superior & Seneca Sts. Cleveland, O.

E. G. Folsom, A. B., Principal; H. B. Bryant, Prof. of the Science of Accounts; Chas. Peck, Jun. Tutor in the Initiatory Counting-Room; Willey, Hay, and Palmer, Lecturers on Commercial Law.

The design of this Institution is to be *purely* a Mercantile School, affording to individuals *thorough* and *practical* training (as much so as in actual business) for the duties of the counting-room and the various business pursuits.

As evidence of superior facilities afforded at this institution, attention is called to its very liberal patronage. During the last nine months a *hundred and fifty regular students* have been enrolled, many of whom are from the adjoining States. A large number of its graduates are filling responsible stations in the city and adjoining places.

The course of instruction arranged from transactions drawn from real life, and written out in a good business style, embraces Double Entry Book-keeping, as practically used in the different departments of trade and commerce, including Wholesale, Retail, Commission, Banking, Manufacturing, Shipping and Steamboating, Individual, Partnership and Compound Company Business; also, Mercantile Arithmetic, Correspondence, Penmanship, Political Economy, and Commercial Law.

The average time to complete a course is some eight weeks, and the applicants can enter College at any time, and receive individual instruction. Students are unlimited as to time, and have the privilege of review. Owing to the healthiness of Cleveland, many are induced to take a Mercantile course during summer.

Diplomas awarded to *such,* and *such* only, as complete and understand the entire course. Suitable aid given to graduates to secure good situations.

Terms for the course and diploma, time unlimited, $40.
Stationery costs $3 to $4; board $2.25 to $3 per week.
Business men of all kinds supplied with thoroughly trained accountants.
Cards written to order with genuine Metallic Pencil.

WEDDELL

HOUSE,

C. S. BUTTS & SON,

PROPRIETORS,

Cleveland, Ohio.

C. S. BUTTS.   WM. R. BUTTS.

This Hotel is the best appointed and the largest in the State.

"FOREST CITY"
NEWS, BOOK AND JOB PRINTING
ESTABLISHMENT,
CLEVELAND, OHIO.

DAILY FOREST CITY, $3 per year, in advance, to mail subscribers. **WEEKLY FOREST CITY**, $1 per year, in advance, to mail subscribers.

J. & J. C. MEDILL, Editors and Publishers.

☞ Every description of plain and fancy Job Printing executed with neatness and dispatch, and on reasonable terms.

RUSH R. SLOANE,
Attorney, Counsellor and Solicitor,
SANDUSKY CITY, OHIO.

☞ *Will give particular attention to his Profession in the Northern and Western Counties of Ohio.*

—*REFERENCES:*—

S. W. Torrey, Cashier Union Bank, C. L. Derby & Co., George Reber, Esq., Hon. T. Ewing, Lancaster, O. Henry W. Derby & Co., Cincinnati.	} Sandusky.	Woodburys, Hope & Graydon, Lewis Woodburn, Aldrich & Burton, J. P. Yelverton. Pres't Peoples' Bank, J. W. Blodget & Co., Boston. } N.Y.

C. L. DERBY & CO.,
PUBLISHERS,
WHOLESALE AND RETAIL BOOKSELLERS AND STATIONERS,

Extensive Dealers in Wall Paper, &c. Orders promptly attended to.

Nos. 2 & 3 PHŒNIX BLOCK, SANDUSKY CITY, O.

PREMIUM PIANO FORTES AND MELODEONS, C. L. Derby & Co. North-western Agents for the world-renowned Pianos of Chickering, Gilbert, Bennett and Dunham, warranted, and sold at precisely the factory retail prices. Old Pianos taken in exchange; also, agents for Prince & Co.'s Melodeons, and the newly invented Organ Melodeon for churches. Letters of inquiry promptly attended to. Large discounts made to clergymen. Seminaries and churches. Address C. L. Derby & Co., Sandusky City, O.

WILDER'S CELEBRATED SALAMANDER SAFES, Derby & Co. Agents. The above famous and only reliable Safes, made by Stearns & Marvin, New York, are sold at manufacturers' prices at this agency, and warranted fire and powder proof. Safes of all sizes, patterns and prices, constantly on hand. Price list giving inside measurement, &c., sent on application. Address C. L. Derby & Co., Agents, Sandusky. City, Ohio.

J. J. ROSSELL,

Wholesale & Retail Dealer in

SASH, GLASS, BLINDS & DOORS,

First St. east of Swaynies' Hotel,

DAYTON, OHIO.

N. VIOT,

Importer and wholesale and retail dealer in

FRENCH WINES,

EAST THIRD STREET, DAYTON, OHIO.

M. SCHNEIDER,

Manufacturer and importer of

RIFLES, PISTOLS, SHOT GUNS,

AND ALL KINDS OF SPORTING APPARATUS,

Corner Second & St. Clair streets, opposite the public square, Dayton, O.

G. S. SMITH.   J. B. OLWIN.

SMIT H& OLWIN,

WHOLESALE AND RETAIL

GROCERS,

Main street, Dayton, Ohio.

BARNABY'S MERCANTILE INSTITUTE East Third Street, DAYTON, O. Established 1847. Incorporated 1860. The Institute will be open every DAY AND EVENING, (Saturday excepted.) FROM SEPTEMBER UNTIL MAY. TERMS: One half in advance - - $25.00 Diplomas are awarded the graduates. S. B. BARNABY, Principal.

C. KOERNER,

APOTHECARY AND DRUGGIST,

East second Street, Dayton, O.

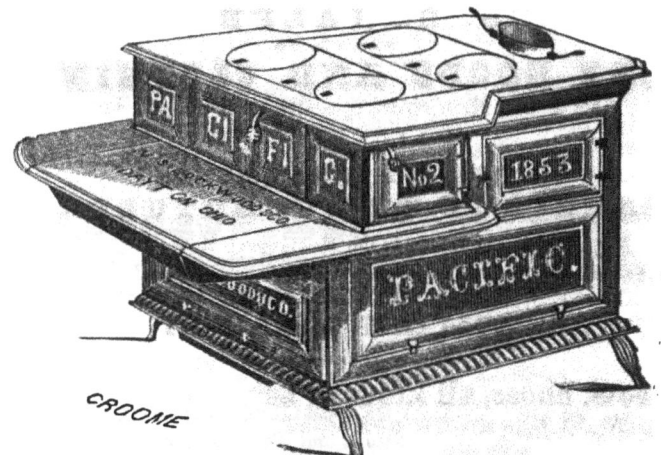

CROOME

N. S. LOCKWOOD & CO,

MANUFACTURERS OF

STOVES & HOLLOW-WARE

2 doors West of Methodist Church, on Third St.

DAYTON, OHIO.

GAZETTE STEAM PRINTING

ESTABLISHMENT,

B. P. DUBOIS & CO., - - - - PROPRIETORS,

DAYTON, O.

The *DAILY GAZETTE* is issued every morning (Sundays excepted) at $5.00 per year. The Weekly Gazette is issued every Saturday morning, at $1.50 per year. The Daily enjoys a large circulation in the city and neighboring towns; the Weekly circulates through the counties of Montgomery, Darke, Clark, Greene, and less numerously in the adjoining counties, each affording an excellent channel for advertising.

BOOK AND JOB DEPARTMENT.

This Department of the Gazette establishment, is one of the most complete in the State. The assortment of type embraces all the newest styles of Wood and Metal Letter, together with Cuts and Ornamental Borders, &c. The Power Presses, Adam's and Hoe's latest improved, are operated by a 12 horse power engine, from Swift's celebrated manufactory, Rochester, N. Y. With these facilities, in addition to Card and Hand Presses, we are able to execute on the shortest notice, and at the lowest rates, Posters, Hand Bills, Circulars, Books, Blanks, Programmes, Show Bills, Cards, Pamphlets, Bill Heads &c., Plain, Fancy, Colored, Shaded, or Bronzed, in the best style of material and workmanship. Address B. P. Dubois & Co.

JOHN BURNS,

DAYTON VENEER MILL.

MANUFACTURER OF

Mahogany, Rosewood and Walnut Veneers.

ALSO, CHAIR STUFF OF ALL KINDS.

☞ ORDERS FROM A DISTANCE PROMPTLY ATTENDED TO.

S. SCHAEFER,

Wholesale Dealer in

DRY GOODS AND CLOTHING,

119 & 121 Main street, opposite the Phillips' House,

DAYTON, OHIO.

GOSLING & HAMMOND,

CARRIAGE MANUFACTURERS,

East Third St., next door to the Montgomery House, Dayton, O.

All kinds of pleasure carriages constantly on hand, and made to order. Repairing of every description done on the shortest notice.

WILLIAM McCAULLY,

Manufacturer of and wholesale and retail dealer in

Boots, Shoes, all kinds of Leather & Findings

No. 89 Main street, between Second and Third, Dayton, O.

Gentleman's fine Boots and Ladies' fine Shoes made on the shortest notice, and latest style.

1853   **WARREN ESTABROOK,**   1853

(Successor to W. & F. C. Estabrook.)

Manufacturer of Linseed Oil,

MILL ON THE OLD HYDRAULIC, DAYTON, O.

☞ Cash paid for Flax Seed.

JONATHAN KENNEY,

Wholesale and retail dealer in

Groceries, Teas, Cigars, Wines & Liquors

OF ALL KINDS,

Cor. of Second & Jefferson streets, Dayton, O,

J. LANGDON & BRO.

Wholesale and retail dealers in

Foreign and Domestic Hardware,

Building Hardware, Nails, Glass, &c. Also, Saddlery Hardware, Carriage and Cabinet Trimmings, Mechanics' Tools, &c,

NO. 91 MAIN STREET, DAYTON, O.

E. BLANCHARD.   S. K. BROWN.

BLANCHARD & BROWN,

Manufacturers of

Turned Spokes, Turned Hubs, Bent Felloes, Bent Bows, Bent Poles, Bent Shafts, Wagon Felloes, Wagon Bows, Wagon Spokes, Wagon Hubs, Plow Beams, Plow Handles; Chair Tops and Banisters. All kinds of Carriage and Wagon Timber Sawed to order.

WANTED,—Black Hickory, Ash, White Oak, Walnut and Poplar Lumber. Also, Hickory and White Oak Spokes.

Factory on Canal, cor. Fourth St., Dayton, O.

DIETRICH & ODLIN,

Dealers in

DRUGS AND MEDICINES

MAIN STREET, DAYTON, OHIO.

They keep constantly on hand a general assortment of Drugs, Paints, Oils, Chemicals, Dye-Stuffs and Putty. All the above Articles warranted pure.

TUCKER & BENNET,

MANUFACTURERS OF

BOLTS OF ALL KINDS,

St. Clair street, between First and Water, Dayton, O.

Are prepared to supply the demand for all kinds of Carriage, Machine, Oar, Bridge and Plow Bolts.

H. FANNING & CO.,

Manufacturers of

Barley & Rye Malt, and Brewers,

DAYTON, OHIO.

L. JOHNSTON,

LEATHER DEALER,

Main, bet. First & Second sts., Dayton, O.

Keeps constantly on hand a full stock of leather of his own manufacture, for Saddlers, Shoe Manufacturers, &c. ☞ N. B —Leather in the rough bought at all times.

JOSEPH SHADE,

Manufacturer of all kinds of Leather,

And wholesale and retail dealer in HIDES and OIL; keeps constantly on hand Calf. Kip. Upper. Sole Leather, Harness and Skirting of his own currying; also a large stock of Eastern and French Calf, Morocco and Linings. ☞ Leather in the rough bought.

Third street, 3 doors west of the Post Office, Dayton, O.

L. F. CLAFLIN & CO.,

Paper Manufacturers, Publishers, Booksellers and Binders,

CLEGG'S BUILDING, THIRD STREET, DAYTON, O.

The highest market price paid for Rags either in cash or trade. Orders promptly attended to.

N. W. Graham & Co.

FORWARDERS & COMMISSION

Merchants,

FOOT OF FIFTH STREET, ON THE CANAL,

Zanesville, Ohio,

Proprietors of Regular Line of Steamers running to Marietta, Wheeling, Pittsburgh and Cincinnati, and regular line of Canal Boats on the Ohio and Hocking Canals.
Through receipts given for all kinds of Produce, to any of the Eastern Cities.

ZANESVILLE ROLLING MILL CO.

"ELKS EYE IRON WORKS."

J. E. PALMER & CO. Agents,

OFFICE, 152 MAIN STREET,

Keep on hand a full Assortment of

BAR IRON, BOILER PLATE AND NAILS,

WROUGHT RAIL ROAD CHAIRS,

Car Axles and Shafting, forged to order, of the best Iron, and warranted.

Muskingum Works.

DOUGLAS, SMITH & CO.

CAR BUILDERS,

GENERAL MACHINISTS

AND

IRON FOUNDERS

Agents and Builders of

BOLLMAN'S PATENT

SUSPENSION IRON BRIDGE,

ALSO,

BOLLMAN'S PATENT IRON & WOOD BRIDGE.

OFFICE AT THE

Muskingum Works,

Corner of Market and Third Streets,

ZANESVILLE, OHIO.

WM. H. HALL,

ATTORNEY, COUNSELLOR AND SOLICITOR,

AND LAND AGENT,

TOLEDO, LUCAS COUNTY,

OHIO.

DENNY HOUSE,

HIGH STREET, NORTH OF MAIN,

HILLSBOROUGH, OHIO.

The proprietor of this House will spare no pains to please those who may favor him with their patronage.

J. W. TUCKER, Clerk.　　　　**E. J. BLOUNT, Proprietor.**

WILSON & JOHNSON,

ATTORNIES,

TIFFIN, OHIO.

J. W. WILSON.　　　　　　　　　　WM. M. JOHNSON.

GIBSON & TUNISON,

Attornies,

TIFFIN, OHIO.

WM. H. GIBSON.　　　　　　　　　T. C. TUNISON, Notary.

PENNINGTON & LEE,

ATTORNIES,

TIFFIN, OHIO.

R. G. PENNINGTON.　　　　　　　　J. C. LEE, Notary.

PHILADELPHIA

BUSINESS CARDS.

UNITED STATES LIFE INSURANCE,
ANNUITY & TRUST COMPANY,
S. E. CORNER THIRD AND CHESTNUT STS.,
PHILADELPHIA.
$806,029,04.

This is quite the only Company, in the City, State, or United States, that proposes to pay its dividends in Cash to its members. This Company do not deal in Scrip dividends, payable when convenient, but make every cent of profits available to its members, if preferred, in Cash on demand.

Assets liable for losses January 1, 1853—$806,029 04.

Premium payments can be made with reference to the convenience of parties opening policies with the Company.

Policies will be issued for the benefit of married women and children, free from the claims of the representatives of husbands, or creditors

Policies may be assigned without the knowledge of the Company.

No policy shall be vitiated through error merely, unless there existed at the time a fraudulent intention.

The original amount of policies will be reduced at any time, to suit the pleasure of insured parties.

Policies of two or more years' standing will be purchased upon surrender.

Policies, with the profits, forfeited by non-payment of premiums, may be renewed at any time by the payment of arrears, with interest provided the health of the party, at the time is unimpaired.

The liberality of the Traveling License is peculiar to this company, permission being granted to cross the Atlantic at any season of the year, in the first-class steamers or sailing packets free of extra charge.

The object aimed at by this Institution, is stability and perpetuity. The rates of premium have been carefully prepared with reference to fluctuations. The first object of the plan presented is to make certain provisions to meet the first motive to insure, and which consideration should be paramount to all others, viz: the prompt payment of losses as they occur; after which, to make such additions of profits to the policy as the progressive gains of the Company will justify, or pay such gains to its members in Cash, on demand.

The plan of operations adopted by this Company is peculiar to itself; no notes are received for premiums. All its operations being based upon cash, its dividends are made available in like manner, or appropriated to the reduction of premiums, at the option of policy-holders. The system is simple and easily understood by all, an important fact (see prospectuses) and for the accommodation of the Company's correspondents, and the numerous persons changing from others to this Institution, the Directors for the convenience of the public throughout the States, have established the following Branch Offices, where all necessary information, prospectuses, annual reports, policies, etc., may be obtained, viz:

HOME OFFICE, S. E. corner Third and Chesnut streets, Philadelphia.
Branch Office, No. 6 Nassau street, New York.
Branch Office, No. 16 Congress street, Boston, Mass.
Branch Office, No. 80 Second street, Baltimore, Maryland.
Branch Office, No. 46 Camp street, New Orleans, La.
Branch Office, Pittsburgh, and Allegheny City.
Branch Office, No. 80 West Third street, Cincinnati, Ohio.
Branch Office, Wheeling, Va.

DIRECTORS:

STEPHEN R. CRAWFORD,
JACOB L. FLORANCE,
LAWRENCE JOHNSON,
BENJAMIN W. TINGLEY,
JAMES DEVEREUX,

AMBROSE W. THOMPSON,
WM. M. GODWIN,
GEORGE McHENRY,
PAUL B. GODDARD,
OCTAVUS A. NORRIS.

STEPHEN R. CRAWFORD, President,
AMBROSE W. THOMPSON, Vice President.

CHARLES G. IMLAY, Secretary and Treasurer.
PLINY FISK, Actuary.

MEDICAL EXAMINERS:

PAUL B. GODDARD, M. D.,   ALEX. C. HART, M. D.,   WILLIAM PEPPER, M. D.

NOTE.—This Company desire to induce business only upon the expectation that policies will be paid when due, after which to return such dividends in cash as the progressive gains of the company will justify. The value of each risk is computed annually by the Actuary of the Company.

MARKET ST.,

NORTH SIDE,

Between 4th and 5th

PHILADELPHIA,

AT THE

RED DOORS.

MARKET ST

NORTH SIDE,

Between 4th and 5th,

PHILADELPHIA.

AT THE

RED DOORS.

    The special attention of dealers in ready made clothing and merchants generally, throughout the United States, is called to this new and extensive ready made clothing establishment, by far the most extensive in the city, and second to none in the Union. The proprietors having secured, at great expense, as superintendant, the services of one of the *best practical tailors in the country. of twenty years experience.* They feel authorized to state that no pains are spared in this establishment to produce garments. which for *cut, style, finish, uniformity of work and durability, is equal, if not superior to any similar establishment in the world.*

    Facilities are offered. to those worthy of credit, to purchase clothing on the usual terms. allowing the regular discount to cash buyers.

REED, BROTHERS & CO., Proprietors,

Nos. 177 & 177½ Market street, Philadelphia.

GREAT CURE

FOR

DYSPEPSIA!

Dr. J. S. HOUGHTON'S

THE TRUE

DIGESTIVE FLUID,

Or, Gastric Juice,

Prepared from RENNET, or the fourth STOMACH OF THE OX.
after directions of BARON LIEBIG, the great Physiological Chemist,
by J. S. HOUGHTON, M. D., Philadelphia, Pa.

This is NATURE'S OWN REMEDY for an unhealthy stomach.
No art of man can equal its curative powers. It contains no ALCOHOL,
BITTERS, ACIDS, or NAUSEOUS DRUGS. It is extremely agreeable
to the taste, and may be taken by the most feeble patients who cannot eat
a water cracker without acute distress. Beware of DRUGGED IMITA-
TIONS. Pepsin is NOT A DRUG.

Call on the Agent, and get a Descriptive Circular, gratis, giving a large
amount of SCIENTIFIC EVIDENCE, from Liebig's Animal Chemistry;
Dr. Combe's Physiology of Digestion ; Dr. Pereira on Food and Diet ;
Dr. John W. Draper, of New York University ; Prof. Dunglison's Physiology; Prof. Silliman, of Yale College ; Dr. Carpenter's Physiology; &c.,
together with reports of CURES from all parts of the United States.

☞ OBSERVE THIS ! — Every bottle of the genuine PEPSIN, bears
the written signature of J. S. HOUGHTON, M. D., sole proprietor, Philadelphia, Pa. Copy-right and Trade Mark secured.

☞ Sold by all Druggists and Dealers in Medicines. Price, ONE
DOLLAR per bottle.

E. DUFRENE,

32 SOUTH SEVENTH ST. BELOW CHESNUT,

Philadelphia,

SCULPTOR & CARVER

Of Ornamental and Agricultural Work;

IMITATION OF MARBLE OR SCAGLIOLA WORK.

Also, Manufacturer of Modern and Antique Figures, in Plaster of Paris Composition. Masks taken from the living or the dead, and Ornaments Repaired in the best manner. Busts Modelled at the shortest notice. A splendid assortment of Medallions. Figures for Churches, Private Dwellings, Gardens, &c., always on hand or made to order from drawings.

A long experience in Paris, London, and other cities in Europe, will guarantee satisfaction to my patrons. Orders from a distance promptly attended to.

N. B. Cisterns, Roofs, Vaults, and Cellars Cemented and warranted to stand. Plaster and Cement for sale Wholesale and Retail.

SHOURDS'
SUPERIOR
EXTRACT OF COFFEE.

The most approved article now in use, put up in square tin packages, suitable for transportation.

In the composition of this valuable and healthy preparation, the manufacturer has sought in a measure to neutralize the ill effects of an excess of strong Coffee, and now offers to the public an article that has

PROVED BY EXPERIENCE

To impart a delicious tone to that much loved beverage. Consumers will find it to their advantage to use this

CELEBRATED ARTICLE,

They will find Coffee made with this extract much more wholesome, perfectly clear without the use of egg or any other article, and in flavor equal to the best Mocha or Java Coffee. Give it a trial; the more you become acquainted with it the better you will like it. Sold by the principal Druggists and Grocers in the United States.

MANUFACTURED BY

WM. C. SHOURDS,

SCHUYLKILL FRONT, BELOW VINE ST., PHILADELPHIA.

DANIEL BOHLER & CO.,

(Successors to G. Hummel, Bohler & Co.,)

MANUFACTURERS OF

GEORGE HUMMEL'S PREMIUM
ESSENCE OF COFFEE,

OLD DEPOT ESTABLISHED IN 1850.

No. 218 Callowhill Street, above Sixth,
PHILADELPHIA.

Four times cheaper than Coffee in the grain!—Two medals and a number of diplomas have already been awarded this Essence, for its fine and delicate flavor, and its clarifying and health giving qualities. Merchants can make a larger profit on it than on Coffee.—Caution: Be careful to purchase G. Hummel's Premium Essence of Coffee, as there are many imitations, and even such as bearing the name of Hummel.

N. B. More Agents wanted.

PRO BONO PUBLICO.

The most popular and efficacious medicine now before the public is

SINES' CELEBRATED COMPOUND SYRUP

of

TAR, WILD CHERRY & HOARHOUND,

FOR THE CURE OF

COUGHS, COLDS, WHOOPING COUGHS, CROUP, BRONCHITIS, ASTHMA, OR PHTHISIC,

Sore Throat, Hoarseness, and all diseases tending to

PULMONARY CONSUMPTION.

It is remarkably pleasant to take, and the sale of which is rapid beyond precedent. No one hesitates to give it a trial, in consequence of the simple fact, that all are familiar with the nature of the specified ingredients, and the price of which is so low that it comes within the reach of all classes. It retails at 22 cents per bottle. Also, SINES' VEGETABLE ANTI-BILIOUS PILLS, which are warranted to be superior to any other Cathartic Medicine in use. Also, SINES' DYSENTERY COMPOUND, for DYSENTERY, CHOLERA, DIARRHŒA, &c., and last but not least SINES' ANTI-RHEUMATIC BALSAM, an internal remedy which is warranted to cure RHEUMATISM, OR THE MONEY REFUNDED.

The Pills retail at 25 cents per box, and the Dysentery Compound and Anti-Rheumatic Balsam 25 cents each per bottle. All orders must be addressed to

CHARLES SINES, PROPRIETOR,

No. 334 North Third Street, below Green, West side,

PHILADELPHIA, PA.

NUTTALL'S

SYRIACUM.

3 Different Preparations for the cure of the

DIFFERENT STAGES OF CONSUMPTION.

FIRST STAGE
INCIPIENT
IN
BLUE WRAPPERS.
} SYMPTOMS.—Cough, pain in the breast, side, head, back, joints and limbs; inflammation, soreness, and tickling in the throat, fever, difficult and quick breathing, *expectoration difficult, slight and frothy.*

SECOND STAGE
CONFIRMED
IN
PINK WRAPPERS.
} SYMPTOMS.—Costiveness, spasmodic cough, violent fever, night, morning and midday sweats, hectic flush in the face and cheeks, burning heat in the palms of the hands and soles of the feet, *expectoration easy, copious and streaked with blood.*

THIRD STAGE
TUBERCULAR
IN
YELLOW WRAPPERS.
} SYMPTOMS.—Diarrhœa, diminished fever, cough, and morning sweats, great and increasing debility, frequent fainting fits, slight delirium and swelling of the extremities.

Each bottle of *NUTTALL'S SYRIACUM* has the SYMPTOMS of the stage for which it is intended printed in front of the wrapper, whereby every invalid knowing his own symptoms can judge for himself *which bottle he requires*, consequently no mistake can occur in selecting THE PROPER MEDICINE.

☞See pamphlet in possession of the Agents, containing Dr. Nuttall's Pathology of Consumption Lectures on the Structure and uses of the Human Lungs, and Certificates of Cures.

☞Prepared only by DR. WM. NUTTALL, Inventor and Proprietor. Price, one dollar per bottle.

PRINCIPAL OFFICE, 263 Race Street, two doors below Eighth, Philadelphia.

JOHN LUCAS & CO.,

PROPRIETORS OF THE

New Jersey Paint and Color Works,

IMPORTERS OF

FOREIGN PAINTS & COLORS,

FRENCH ZINC WHITE,

FRENCH GREENS AND REDS, ENGLISH, FRENCH AND GERMAN BRONZES, BARYTES,
SATIN WHITE, CALCIMINE, PARIS WHITE,
TERRA ALBA, FOSTER'S ENGLISH PATENT DRIERS, GILDER'S WHITING, &c.,
GLAZIERS' DIAMONDS, STEEL GRAINING COMBS, &c.

PAINT MILLS OF ALL SIZES.

N. B. Paints of all colors put up in small cases to the order of Dealers.

PULP COLORS for WALL PAPERS.

STORE AND OFFICE,

38 Arch St., between Front & Second, South side,

PHILADELPHIA.

JOHN LUCAS.   JOSEPH FOSTER.

PAPER HANGINGS.

J. E. VAN METER,

MANUFACTURER AND IMPORTER OF EVERY VARIETY OF

Plain and Decorative Wall Paper,

WHOLESALE AND RETAIL,

No. 149 NORTH THIRD ST., ABOVE RACE,

PHILADELPHIA.

STEPHEN L. ADAMS,

Blank Book Binder & Ruler,

No. 56 NORTH THIRD ST.,

SECOND DOOR ABOVE ARCH, WEST SIDE,

PHILADELPHIA.

Orders also taken at Store N. W. Corner Callowhill and Eighth Streets.
☞ JOBS BOUND; MAGAZINES, &c., BLANK BOOKS, Wholesale and Retail.

Dr. Davis's Depurative:

The Great Purifier of the Blood,

AND CURE FOR

DISEASES OF THE LIVER, KIDNEYS, AND SPLEEN,

SCROFULA,
JAUNDICE,
SCALD HEAD,
TETTER,
RINGWORMS,
BLOTCHES,
AND ALL
SKIN DISEASES,
BOILS,
BRONCHOCELE
OR
GOITRE,
SCURVY,
GOUT,

Cadmus destroying the Dragon.

NEURALGIA,
DYSPEPSIA
OR
INDIGESTION,
SICK HEADACHE,
Habitual
Costiveness,
DIZZINESS,
LUMBAGO,
White Swellings,
General Debility,
NERVOUS
AFFECTIONS,
SPINE DISEASE,
BRONCHITIS,

Chronic Pulmonary Affections, Chronic Rheumatism, Incipient Scirrhus, Incipient Cancer, Chronic Sore Eyes, Chronic Glandular Enlargements, Old and Obstinate Ulcers, Spreading Ulcers of the Throat, Ulcers of the Legs, Mercurial and Syphilitic Affections, Despondency or great Depression of Spirits, Pains and Swellings of the Bones and Tendons, and all Diseases arising from an Impure State of the Blood.

For Diseases peculiar to Females the Medicine is particularly adapted, such as Leucorrhœa

G. W. RIDGWAY.   EDWIN A. DIEHL.

G. W. RIDGWAY & Co.

General Commission Merchants, and Dealers in

SPERM, WHALE, LARD & TANNERS' OILS, RICE,

CANDLES, &c.

No. 37 North Wharves, above Arch Street, PHILADELPHIA.

Are constantly receiving direct and offer at lowest Market Rates, White Winter Sperm Oil, Unbleached Winter Sperm Oil, White Spring Sperm Oil, Unbleached Spring Sperm Oil, Lard Oil, Tanners, Oils, Paint Oils, Extra White Winter Elephant Oil, Extra White Winter Solar Oil, Extra White Winter Whale Oil, Common Whale Oil, Refined Whale Oil, Sperm Candles, &c., &c.

RAIGUEL & CO.,

(Late ECKEL, RAIGUEL & CO.)

IMPORTERS & WHOLESALE DEALERS IN

Dry Goods & Carpeting

Nos. 128 & 130 North Third St. above Race, West side,

PHILADELPHIA.

STEMAN & BAKER,

FORWARDING & COMMISSION

MERCHANTS,

BROAD, ABOVE SASSAFRAS STREET,

(Recently of Front and Willow Streets,)

PHILADELPHIA.

PETER STEMAN.   LAFAYETTE BAKER.

☞ SALT AND PLASTER FOR SALE. ☜

HOLLINGSHEAD, WHITE & CO.

WHOLESALE GROCERS & COMMISSION MERCHANTS,

No. 77 North Water Street, running through to

38 North Wharves,

PHILADELPHIA.

Teas, Wines, Liquors, Tobacco and a general assortment of Groceries.

N. B. Particular attention paid to selling Western Produce.

JOS. M. HOLLINGSHEAD.   PETER SIDES.   JAS. STEVENS.   WM. O. WHITE.

TO DRUGGISTS.

N. SPENCER THOMAS,

MANUFACTURING

PHARMACEUTIST

AND

CHEMIST,

No. 248 New Market Street,

PHILADELPHIA.

Would respectfully call the attention of Druggists to the articles of his manufacture, among which are,

MEDICINAL EXTRACTS,

In all their variety, warranted of superior quality, made according to the best formula, (by the U. S. Pharmacopœia when officinal.) Strict attention is paid to the selection of prime Drugs for their manufacture, as well as to all the minutiæ in the manipulation. They are neatly put up in packages of any description that may be ordered.

GLYCERIN, the valuable article lately brought into use, and so highly prized for its healing power, and great virtue in deafness.

MACHINE SPREAD PLASTERS, superior to any others in the market. These plasters are on the finest lamb-skin, prepared in such a manner as to retain their pliability and freshness of appearance. They are neatly put up in boxes of one dozen each, and are warranted to give satisfaction.

Also, ADHESIVE PLASTER CLOTH, that will compare favorably with any other.

PLASTERS IN ROLLS, of superior quality, believed to be equal to the English Plasters.

BLUE MASS, warranted one-third Mercury, and made in such a way as cannot fail to give satisfaction.

MERCURIAL OINTMENT, of all the various proportions that are in demand, made by a machine that divides the Mercury to the finest possible state, without the aid of any acid or injurious substance.

MERCURY WITH CHALK, of superior quality, pure Powdered Drugs, Spices, &c. Also all the Pharmaceutical Preparations, usually in demand, all of which will be sold on terms which cannot fail to be satisfactory.

☞ He is now prepared to do powdering for the trade on the best terms and in the best manner.

THE PRESBYTERIAN BANNER.

The Banner is published —— Weekly in the city of

PHILADELPHIA,

AND ADAPTED TO GENERAL CIRCULATION IN THE PRESBYTERIAN CHURCH.

Our friends will do us a great favor, and also do their neighbors a kindness, by inducing them to become subscribers. One of the cheapest ways of doing good is to get families to take a good newspaper.

TERMS:

INVARIABLY IN ADVANCE.

TEN SUBSCRIBERS AT THE SAME POST OFFICE,
(their papers to be severally directed,) - - $1.00 each,
FIVE COPIES TO ONE DIRECTION, - - - 1.00 each.
SINGLE SUBSCRIBERS, - - . - - 1.25

POSTAGE ON ALL COMMUNICATIONS TO BE PRE-PAID.

Pastors sending us twenty subscribers and upwards, will be thereby entitled to a paper without charge.
Remit by mail, where no good opportunity is otherwise at hand.

ADVERTISEMENTS

Within eight lines, or not exceeding the space of eight lines—first insertion 50 cents; each repetition 38 cents. Every additional line, first insertion 3 cents; each repetition 2 cents.

DAVID McKINNEY,

NO. 55½ SOUTH FOURTH STREET,

PHILADELPHIA.

SUBSCRIPTIONS TAKEN IN PITTSBURGH BY MR. J. D. WILLIAMS.

N. B.—The above are fair *business* terms, but we do not refuse the Banner to any one who will put us in possession of a dollar.

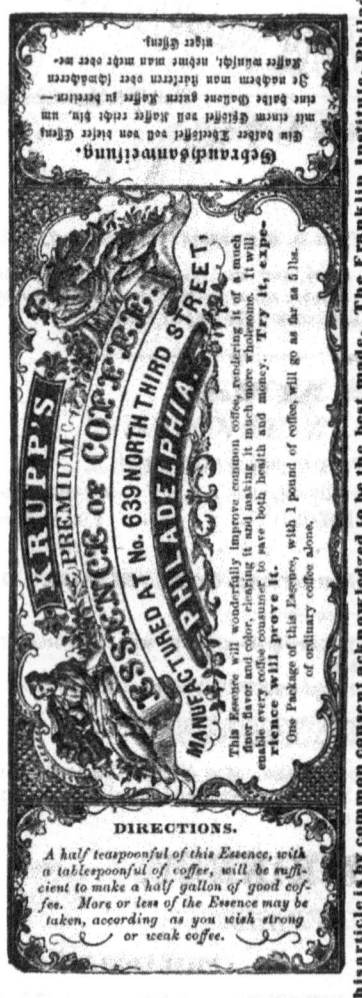

KRUPP'S
PREMIUM
ESSENCE OF COFFEE.
MANUFACTURED AT No. 639 NORTH THIRD STREET,
PHILADELPHIA.

This Essence will wonderfully improve common coffee, rendering it of a much finer flavor and color, clearing it and making it much more wholesome. It will enable every coffee consumer to save both health and money. Try it, experience will prove it.

One Package of this Essence, with 1 pound of coffee, will go as far as 5 lbs. of ordinary coffee alone.

DIRECTIONS.

A half teaspoonful of this Essence, with a tablespoonful of coffee, will be sufficient to make a half gallon of good coffee. More or less of the Essence may be taken, according as you wish strong or weak coffee.

Gebrauchsanweitung.

Ein halber Theelöffel von dieser Essenz, mit einem Eßlöffel voll Kaffee reicht hin, um eine halbe Gallone guten Kaffee zu bereiten.—Je nachdem man stärkeren oder schwächeren Kaffee wünscht, nehme man mehr oder weniger Essenz.

This article is by common consent acknowledged to be the best made. The Franklin Institute, Philadelphia, at its last exhibition pronounced it to be much superior to any exhibited, and composed of materials highly conducive to health. The manufacturer solicits a trial, feeling confident that it will give entire satisfaction.

SPILLIARD & DODGE,

ARCH ST. HALL BRASS FOUNDRY,

AND MANUFACTORY OF

PLUMBERS' AND OTHER BRASS WORK,

PHILADELPHIA,

210 ARCH STREET, □ □ □ □ □ □

We beg to call the attention of Western Merchants to our stock of Water, Steam and Gas Cocks, Basins, Water Closets, Force Pumps, Shower Copper Baths, &c., a great variety of which we have always on hand. Particular attention paid to orders from the country.

N. B.—S. & D. are Agents for Ashcroft's Steam Gauge, of which more than 1500 have been put in use the last year.

THE PENNSYLVANIA INQUIRER,

THE LARGEST DAILY PAPER IN THE STATE.

Devoted to Politics, Literature, News, &c.

TERMS: { DAILY—Payable half yearly in advance, - - **$8 00**
{ TRI-WEEKLY—Payable yearly in advance, -   **5 00**

The Inquirer contains forty columns of matter, printed with clear and distinct type, and on good white paper. It is a Journal suited to both the Counting-house and the Domestic Circle.

While News, Politics, and Business matters take the lead in its columns, Literature, Science, and Art are not overlooked.

JESPER HARDING,
PROPRIETOR AND PUBLISHER,

No. 57 South Third Street, Philadelphia.

☞ A copy of the paper sent gratis, on application.

New and Extensive

Piano-Forte

WARE-ROOMS,

And Wholesale and Retail

Music Publishing House.

J. E. GOULD,

SUCCESSOR TO A. FIOT,

Has rented the new, elegant and spacious building,

No. 3 Swaim's Block, 160 Chesnut St.

And will keep for exhibition and sale one of the largest and most
varied stocks of

PIANO-FORTES, HARPS, GUITARS,

Melodeons, Sheet Music and Music Books,

To be found in the United States. J. E. G. is exclusive Agent for the
sale of Hallet, Davis & Co.'s

CELEBRATED SUSPENSION BRIDGE PIANO FORTES

Unrivalled for distinct and prompt action, clearness of tone, superiority
of finish and durability. These splendid instruments can be furnished at
prices from **Two Hundred to One Thousand Dollars each**, either with or
without COLEMAN'S RENOWNED ÆOLIAN ATTACHMENT.

Also---GILBERT'S BOUDOIR PIANOS,

Well known for their compactness and general good qualities; together with a variety
of Pianos from other celebrated makers. Second hand Pianos taken in part payment
for new. Cash paid for Old Pianos. The largest stock and variety of Sheet Music and
Books in the city. Dealers, Seminaries and Schools supplied on the best terms at
satisfactory prices. All persons interested are requested to call and examine, whether
wishing to make an immediate purchase or not.

J. E. GOULD,

No. 160 Chestnut Street, Philadelphia.

CHOCOLATE,

LUCTOR ET EMERGO.

GERHARD SCHMITZ,

MANUFACTURER OF

Spanish, French, Sweet Spiced Zealand, Homœopathic, Plain

CHOCOLATE AND PREPARED COCOA.

Continues to Manufacture the above articles at the old stand,

185 South Sixth, below Lombard, East side.

THE FRANKLIN INSTITUTE, of the State of Pennsylvania, for the promotion of the Mechanic Arts, have awarded to Gerhard Schmitz, Philadelphia, Penn., this TESTIMONIAL of their approbation, for the skill and ingenuity displayed in Chocolate, deposited by himself at the Thirtieth Exhibition of Domestic Manufactures, held in the city of Philadelphia, on the 17th to the 28th day of October, 1848. *S. V MERRICK, Prest; ISAIAH LUKENS, V. Prest; THOS. FLETCHER, V. Prest A. D. BACHE, Cor Sec'y; J. B. GARRIGUES, Rec Sec'y.*

CRITTENDEN'S POPULAR TREATISE ON BOOK-KEEPING.

E. C. & J. BIDDLE, No. 6 South Fifth St. Philadelphia, publish S. Worcester Crittenden's practical and popular Works on Book-keeping, below named :

Common School Book-keeping, (recently published,) price per copy, 62 cts.		
Blank Books for ditto.	" set 45 cts.	
Key to ditto.	" copy, 20 cts.	
Treatise for High Schools,	" " 90 cts.	
Treatise for the Counting-House,	" " $1.50	

The Treatise for High Schools is an abridgement of that for the Counting-House. In the work for Common Schools the same general plan is pursued to elucidate the science as in that for the Counting House, with such modifications, however, as it is believed, admirably adapt it to the use of Retailers, Mechanics, Farmers, Professional Men, and others whose business renders an acquaintance with only the less complex forms of accounts necessary to them, as well as for the use of schools.

The Counting-House and the High School Editions have had a large sale throughout the United States, which is steadily increasing. The Counting-House edition is pronounced by the Book-keepers of many of the largest and most highly respectable commercial houses of New York, Boston, Philadelphia, Baltimore, New Orleans, St. Louis, and Cincinnati, to be "by far the most complete work we (they) have examined on the subject."

The above named works may be had of H. W Derby & Co., and Moore, Anderson & Co., Cincinnati; J. Kean Jr & Co , Chicago; H. J. Loring, St. Louis; John B. Steel, New Orleans; and of Booksellers generally.

11

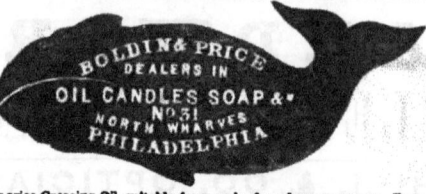

PENNSYLVANIA

RAILROAD

Notice to Eastern Travelers.

A continuous Railroad from Cincinnati, Cleveland, Wooster, Massillon, Alliance, O. and Chicago, Ill. to Philadelphia, via. Pennsylvania Railroad from Pittsburg to Philadelphia,

Through from Cincinnati to Philadelphia in 36 hours;
" " Cleveland to Philadelphia in 26 "
" " Pittsburg to Philadelphia in 19 "

Being the shortest and quickest route from the Great West to the Atlantic cities.

Fare, from Cincinnati to Philadelphia, by Railroad, ... $16 50.
" Cleveland " " . . . . 10 00.
" Massillon " " . . . . . . 10 00.
" Pittsburg " " . . . . . . 9 50.
" Cincinnati to Philadelphia, (Cincinnati to Pittsburg by steamboat,) . 11 00.

Tickets from Cincinnati to Philadelphia or Baltimore, by Railroad, can be purchased of P. W. STRADER, Ticket Agent, Cincinnati. And by the Steam Packet Line, to Pittsburg. and thence by Railroad to Philadelphia, from the Captains on board. And from Cleveland, via. the Cleveland and Pittsburg Railroad, and of the Ohio and Pennsylvania Railroad, of D. HORTON, Ticket Agent, at the Weddell House, in Cleveland, O.

On or about the middle of February the road will be opened from Crestline to Wooster, and the time between Cincinnati and Philadelphia reduced to 34 hours.

NOTICE:—In case of loss, the Company will hold themselves responsible for personal baggage only, and for an amount not exceeding one hundred dollars. THOS. MOORE, Pass'r Ag't Phila

J. MESKIMEN, Pass'r Ag't, Pittsburgh.

PENNSYLVANIA RAILROAD.

This road being now complete, it opens a communication between PITTSBURG AND PHILADELPHIA, or PITTSBURG AND BALTIMORE, by which Freight from the West can reach an Eastern market quicker and cheaper than by any of the present rival routes They connect with the

DAILY PACKETS AT PITTSBURG FROM

ST. LOUIS, LOUISVILLE, CINCINNATI, WHEELING,

And all the different points on the Western waters, and with the CLEVELAND AND PITTSBURG Rail Road, and the OHIO AND PENNSYLVANIA Rail Road, at Pittsburg. Cars run through between Pittsburg and Philadelphia without transhipment of Freight, an advantage that can be appreciated by all shippers In case of obstruction of navigation. by ice or low water, Freights Westward can be forwarded from Pittsburg to Cincinnati or towns in the interior by Rail Road.

Rates of Freight between Pitt-burg and Philadelphia or Baltimore.

	Winter Rates.	Summer Rates.
FIRST CLASS.		
Dry Goods, Books and Stationery, Boots, Shoes, Hats and Carpeting, Furs and Peltries, Feathers, Saddlery, etc. }	$1	75c.
SECOND CLASS.		
Brown Sheetings and Shirtings in bales, Drugs, Glassware, Groceries, except Coffee, Hardware, Hollowware, Machinery, Oil Cloth, Wood, etc. }	85c.	60c.
THIRD CLASS.		
Butter, in firkins and kegs, Candles, Cotton, (in Winter,) Queensware, Tallow, Tobacco, in leaf or manufactured, (Eastward.) etc. }	75c.	50c.
FOURTH CLASS.		
Bacon, Cotton. (in Summer.) Coffee, Lard and Lard Oil, (through,) Pork, fresh, in full car loads, at owners' risk, }	65c.	40s.

GEO. C. FRANCISCUS, Frt. Agt . Pittsburg.
E. J. SNEEDER, Frt. Agt. Philadelphia
MAGRAW & KOONS, Frt. Agts altimore.
J. L. ELLIOTT Frt. Agt. No 7 West St N. Y.
H. H. HOUSTON, General Frt. Agt. Philadelphia

A. G. VAN WALTERSDORFF,

DEALER IN

CIDER & WINE VINEGAR,

No. 170 North Fifth St. near Vine, Philadelphia,

Keeps constantly a good supply of the best Vinegar. Dealers from the country, and shippers, supplied at the shortest notice.

BATES & COATES,

AGENTS FOR J. W. COATES'

SIX CORD SPOOL COTTON,

COATES' PATENT THREAD,

AND A GENERAL ASSORTMENT OF FOREIGN DRY GOODS,

No. 9 Church Alley, Philadelphia.

DELAWARE LOTTERIES

Are Drawing daily in the town of Wilmington.

CAPITAL PRIZES FROM $40,000 TO $80,000,

TICKETS FROM $1 TO $20.

Orders including cash or prizes, will meet with prompt attention, and the official drawings forwarded to any part of the United States by

G. B. GLAZIER, Agent,

WILMINGTON, DEL.

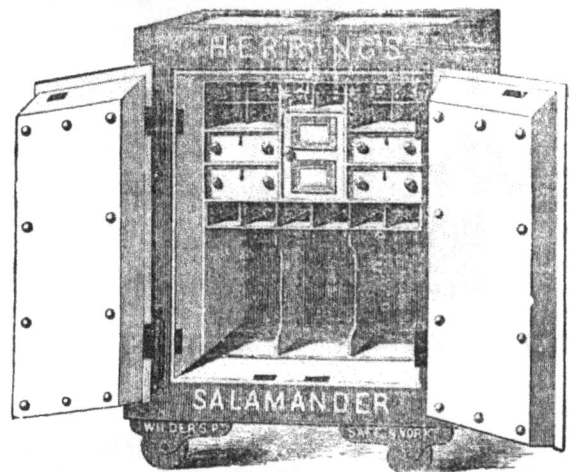

ROBINSON, LORD & CO.,

Manufacturers and

Wholesale Dealers in

WOODEN WARE, BRUSHES,

CORDAGE, CHAIRS, ETC.,

And Importers and Dealers in

French, English, German & American

FANCY GOODS,

Nos. 108 & 110 Lombard Street,

(BET. LIGHT AND CALVERT STS.,)

BALTIMORE, MD.

G. W. ROBINSON, CH'S W. LORD, E. ESTABROOK.

BONN, NEIMYER & CO.,

(LATE BONN, BRO. & CO.,)

North-East Corner of CHARLES and LOMBARD S.

BALTIMORE,

WHOLESALE DEALERS IN LEAF AND MANUFACTURED

TOBACCO,

CIGARS AND SNUFFS.

A. BONN,   R. BONN,   JNO. H. NEIMYER,   JOHN FOWLER.

J. & H. WARDEN,

FLOUR AND GENERAL

PRODUCE COMMISSION MERCHANTS,

NO. 26 COMMERCE ST., BALTIMORE, MD.

REFER TO Messrs. Reynolds & Smith, Balt, Md, Mr Jas George, Balt. Messrs Alex & Jas Laughlin Brown & Kirkpatrick, James Dalzell, Pittsburg, Pa, Messrs R Crangle & Co, Wheeling, Va

J. M'CULLOGH.   C. D. CULBERTSON.

M'CULLOGH & CULBERTSON,
COMMISSION,
PROVISION AND PRODUCE MERCHANTS,

No. 2 Western Row—Exchange Place, Baltimore.

REFERENCES:—John Swasey & Co., and McKeehan & Evans, Cincinnati.

MICHAEL HERR & CO.,
COMMISSION MERCHANTS,
FOR THE SALE OF
AGRICULTURAL PRODUCE &c.,

Nos. 88 and 90 SPEAR'S WHARF, AND

Herr's Depot, adjoining. Calvert Station, North St,

MICHAEL HERR, }
O. A. ZANE. }   **BALTIMORE.**

B. T. ELDER & CO.,
Late, Elder, Gelston & Co.,
PRODUCE
COMMISSION MERCHANTS,
AND FORWARDING AGENTS,

Corner Pratt and Commerce Streets, Baltimore.

Our attention is strictly devoted to the sale of Pork, Bacon, Lard, Flour, Feathers, Cheese, Candles, and Western Produce generally. N. B.—Sole agents for Dupont's Gunpowder.

A. SCHULLER & SON.
Commission Merchants,
AND DEALERS IN LEAF & MANUFACTURED
TOBACCO, CIGARS, SNUFF, &C.,
44 LOMBARD STREET, BALTIMORE.

Keep constantly on hand, a large and well selected stock, to which they desire to call the atten tion of Western buyers.

WM. WILKENS'
STEAM
CURLED HAIR MANUFACTORY
Frederick Road, above the Cattle Scales, Baltimore.

New York Depot, 14 and 16 Division St. near Bowery and Chatham Square.

Baltimore Depot, Cor. North and Fayette Sts. formerly "Old Post Office."

Constantly on ha d the finest quality of pure Curled HORSE and CATTLE HAIR also, MIXED and HOGS' HAIR at the lowest prices. All orders received through the Post Office will be punctually attended to. N. B.—The highest prices paid for raw Cattle and Horse Hair, &c.

OBER & CO.
WHOLESALE DRUGGISTS
N. E. Corner of Hanover and Lombard Streets,

GUSTAVUS OBER,
JOHN LEARY. } **BALTIMORE.**

Always on hand a general Assortment of

DRUGS, MEDICINES, PAINTS, OILS, DYE-STUFFS,
SPICES, PERFUMERY, WINDOW GLASS, ETC.

E. KIMBERLY & BRO.
BEEF AND PORK PACKERS
AND BACON CURERS,
S. W. CORNER OF PATTERSON AND PRATT STREETS,

E. KIMBERLY,
W. H. KIMBERLY. } **BALTIMORE,**

KEEP CONSTANTLY ON HAND

Barrel Beef, Barrel Pork, Smoked Beef, Smoked and Pickled Tongues, Hams, Sides, Shoulders, Lard, Joles. &c.

JOHN JOHNSON & SON,
Forwarding and Commission
MERCHANTS,
NO. 68 NORTH STREET, BALTIMORE.

REFERENCES.

David R. Porter, Esq., James McCormick, Esq., J. W. Weir, Esq., R. J. Ross, Esq., Harrisburg, Pa.; Simon Cameron, Esq., Middletown, Pa.; A. L. Boggs & Sons, W. T. Walters & Co., J. C. Wilson & Co., McCullough & Culbertson, Michael Herr, Esq., Baltimore.

R. & W. W. ISAAC,
LEAF TOBACCO
And General Commission Merchants,
No. 91 Light Street Wharf,
BALTIMORE.

LEW'S H. COLE.   ISAAC SHIRK.   HIRAM D. MUSSELMAN.

COLE, SHIRK & CO.,
TOBACCO
COMMISSION MERCHANTS,
NO. 330 BALTIMORE STREET,
(SECOND DOOR WEST OF HOWARD,)
BALTIMORE, MD.

MARTIN & HOBSON,
FLOUR AND GENERAL
COMMISSION MERCHANTS
Corner Eutaw and Baltimore Streets,
BALTIMORE, MD.

READ! READ!! READ!!!

RELIEF FOR MAN AND BEAST.

THE
HORSEMAN'S HOPE,

OR
FARMER'S FRIEND.

Arrangements are now made for supplying the Public with this

GREAT REMEDY,

Which has been used with wonderful success by those who have had an opportunity of testing its virtues No family should neglect to have a supply, and all persons would do well to keep some by them, to be used in case of accident to Man or Horse.

For Horses, etc.

For the Cure of

Sprains,
Bruises,
Saddle and Collar Galls,
Swelled Joints,
Stiffness and Weakness of the Legs,
Old Sores,
Scratches, etc., etc.

For Man.

For the Cure of

Rheumatism,
Lumbago,
Sprains,
Swellings,
Bruises,
Sciatic Pains,
Stiffness and Weakness of the Limbs.

And other Accidents and Afflictions to which Men and Animals are liable.

This Preparation has been before the Public a sufficient time to have its merits fairly tested, and the reports received from various parts of the country prove it to be one of the most valuable Remedies ever offered, both for Man and Horse

A gentleman from Rapahannock co., Va., states that he has found it a first rate remedy for Rheumatism: One from Gloucester county, Va , has used it both for Rheumatism in Man and Lameness in Horses, with great success.

Another from Rapahannock county says that he used it on one of his men, whose hand was severely crushed in blasting rocks; and that he was speedily cured.

A distinguished gentleman, formerly State Senator, from Rockingham co , Va , used it on one of his servants, whose hand was badly wounded in a threshing machine, and he was restored very soon.

A gentleman in Augusta county, Virginia, cured his horse of Fistula, and also used it in his family with great success for Rheumatism.

One in Carolina co , Va , says it has been found to be very valuable for horses troubled with the scratches. A gentleman of high standing of Frederick co., Md., says he considers it the best thing ever used on a horse.

A distinguished gentleman, formerly Sheriff of Jefferson county, Va , says that he has tried it, both for Man and Horse, and that he finds it first rate for either.

Where this preparation is known, it has attained a deservedly high reputation. The Proprietors have in their possession a number of letters, from different parts of the country, bearing testimony to its great value and they confidently CHALLENGE THE WORLD to produce any thing superior to it as a Remedy, in those cases for which it is recommended.

Prepared only by
SMITH & ATKINSON,
288 Baltimore Street, Baltimore,
And for sale by Storekeepers and Druggists throughout the Country.

12

F. SULLIVAN.   F. H. SULLIVAN.   JOHN J. SULLIVAN.   JAMES H. BARNEY.

JOHN SULLIVAN & SONS,

COMMISSION MERCHANTS,

For the Sale of

TOBACCO,

COTTON, FLOUR, PROVISIONS, etc., etc.,

Camden St., near Light,

BALTIMORE, MD.

The Warehouses just erected by us are admirably situated, and are within three blocks of the new Depot of the Baltimore & Ohio Railroad Co. They are the most extensive, commodious, and conveniently arranged buildings in the country, having been built in the strongest manner, expressly for the prosecution of a

WESTERN PRODUCE BUSINESS.

They are four stories high, with a front of 177 feet on Camden street, by a depth of 85 feet, metal roof, and fire proof.

FRED. SCHUMACHER,

Dealers and Planters' Agent

FOR THE SALE OF

WESTERN

LEAF TOBACCO,

NO. 81 LIGHT STREET WHARF,

BALTIMORE.

REFERENCES:

C. R. Taylor, Esq., Wm. Robinson, Esq., Messrs. Bonn, Neimyer & Co., Baltimore ; Messrs. K. Hager & Sons, John Bradfield, Esq., Barnesville, O.; Messrs. Mott, Fordyce & Co., Calais, O.; Messrs. Wm. Ijams & Co., Logan, O.; John A Collins, Esq., Lancaster, O.; George Irwin, Esq., Fredericktown, O.; Messrs. Bent, Durall & Co., Louisville. Ky.; R. Brook Blakemore, Esq., Oakgrove, Kentucky.

Will be pleased, at all times, to furnish his Western friends with every information relative to current rates, and prospects for TOBACCO in this Market. Personal and particular attention given to all consignments to his care, and liberal advances made.

HENRY TOWNSLEY & CO.,
GENERAL COMMISSION MERCHANTS,
NO. 78 BOWLY'S WHARF,
BALTIMORE.

REFERENCES.

Messrs. F. W. Brune & Sons, Ballard, Chadbourn & Co., Robinson, Lord & Co., J. Hall Pleasants, Esq., Col. Geo. P. Kane, Baltimore ; Messrs. Lord, Warren, Salter & Co., C. P. Peck & Co., C. S. Martin, Esq., A. Sidney Baxter, Esq., New York ; Messrs. G. Townsley & Co., Albany ; Messrs. Whitney, Fenno & Co., Emmons Raymond, Esq., Samuel L. Harding, Esq., Henry Dean, Esq., Boston ; Jas. R. Bailey, Boston ; J. S. Hamlin, Esq., Portland ; Messrs. Bauld & Gibson, John Tobin, Esq., Halifax, N. S.; Messrs. Massey & Caldwells, Pittsburg ; Messrs. Wheat & Chaplin, Wheeling ; Geo. Carlisle, Esq., Pres. Lafayette Bank, Cincinnati ; Jas. D. Lehmer, Esq., A. G. Taylor, Esq., John T. Martin, Esq., Cincinnati ; Messrs. Darrah & Pomeroy, St. Louis ; Messrs. Woodruff & Huntington, Mobile ; Messrs. Ellis, Russell & Co., Wilmington, N. C.

F. NEALE.   JAS. H. LUCKETT.

NEALE & LUCKETT,
COMMISSION MERCHANTS
151 WEST PRATT STREET, BALTIMORE,
Give their exclusive attention to the sale of

Tobacco, Flour, Grain, Bacon, etc., etc.
REFER TO THE FOLLOWING GENTLEMEN:

C. C. Jamison, Esq., Cash. Bank Balt., D. Spriggs, Esq., Cash. Merch. Bk., James W. Alnutt, Esq., Cash. Mechanics' Bank, Messrs. Wm. Woodward & Co., Hare, Pierson, Holiday & Co., A. S. Davidson & Harris, Murdoch, Duer & Evans, Harvey, Carson & McKnight, Cole, Howard & Co., Baltimore ; Gallager & Ronold, E. Wibb, Rowland & Co., Rowland & Green, Louisville.

BROWN, JONES & CO.,
Produce & General
COMMISSION MERCHANTS,
No. 15 Bowly's Wharf,
BALTIMORE.

BROWN & GODWIN,   T. B. JONES,
Philadelphia.   Baltimore.

W. M. STARR.   G. D. TEWKSBURY.

WESLEY STARR & SONS,
TOBACCO & GENERAL
COMMISSION MERCHANTS,
No. 4 Light St. Wharf, Baltimore,

Attend to the SALES OF TOBACCO, and all kinds of WESTERN PRODUCE, PROVISIONS, etc:

JOHN D. HAMMOND,
SADDLE, HARNESS, AND TRUNK
MANUFACTURER,
WHOLESALE AND RETAIL

359 Baltimore St. opposite the Eutaw House,
BALTIMORE.

Manufactures and keeps constantly on hand every description of Harness, Trunks, Valises, Carpet Bags, Collars, and every other article in his line.

All Orders executed with neatness and despatch.

JOHN B. TIDY,
COACH AND HARNESS
MANUFACTURER,
N. E. corner of Howard and Franklin Sts.

BALTIMORE.

All orders promptly attended to, and all new work warranted for six months.
TRADE FURNISHED WITH HARNESS AT SHORTEST NOTICE.

H. F. ALBERTI & CO.
IMPORTERS OF
GERMAN, FRENCH, & ENGLISH
FANCY GOODS

And wholesale Dealers in all kinds of

YANKEE NOTIONS
Nos. 6 and 8 South Liberty St. cor. of German,
BALTIMORE.

DAGUERREOTYPISTS, ARTISTS, AND
PAINTERS' DEPOT,
WILLIAM A. WISONG,
No. 2 N. Liberty St. Baltimore.

The subscriber keeps constantly on hand a full assortment of

CAMERAS, FIXTURES, CASES, PLATES, CHEMICALS, &c. FOR

Daguerreotypists' Use.

Every variety of Material for Artists' use, with a full Stock of Glass, Paints, Oils, Varnishes, Brushes, etc. for Painters, all of which are offered at wholesale and retail, at the lowest market rates.

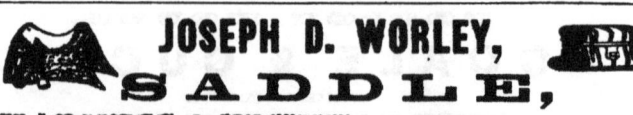

BOOKS AND STATIONERY.

NEW YORK
BUSINESS CARDS.

GEO. W. & JEHIAL READ,

MANUFACTURERS AND WHOLESALE DEALERS IN

HATS, CAPS AND STRAW GOODS,
FURS AND BUFFALO ROBES,
100 CHAMBERS STREET,

NEAR THE IRVING HOUSE AND WEST OF BROADWAY,

NEW YORK.

Keep one of the largest stocks of the above goods in the city of New York, which they offer at low prices for cash or approved credit. Buyers would do well to examine their stock before purchasing elsewhere. PARTICULAR ATTENTION PAID TO ORDERS.

C. P. & E. WILLIAMS,

WHOLESALE DEALERS IN

TEAS & GROCERIES,
No. 192 Front street, near Fulton,
NEW YORK.

LITCHFIELD & CO.
OIL & CANDLE MANUFACTURERS,
No. 154 Front street, corner of Maiden Lane,
NEW YORK.

Sperm, Whale and Lard Oils, Patent Sperm & Adamantine Candles

NUKERCK, ROOT & CO.

Produce Commission Merchants,

NO. 1 WATER STREET, NEW YORK.

C. C. NUKERCK.   CHANDLER ROOT.   WM. CLARK.

REFERENCES:

Messrs. E. FISH & Co. - New York,   J. C. DANN, Esq., Cashier of Sacketts Harbor Bank.
"   LANE & MANGAM,   "   H. SCOTT, Esq.,   Cashier of Otsego Co. Bank.
SWIFT, WALDRON & Co.   "   H. DOOLITTLE, Esq.   Cashier of Agricultural Bank.
C. ROOT & Co., Cooperstown, "   CLARK & HOFFMAN,   - - - - Fort Plain, N. Y.

CLARK & BEATTY,

COMMISSION MERCHANTS,

AND DEALERS IN

Butter, Cheese. Provisions, English Salt, &c.

65 DEY STREET, NEW YORK.

JOHN M. CLARK.   WM. C. BEATTY.

PAINE & FISHERS,

MANUFACTURERS AND JOBBERS OF

STRAW GOODS,

HATS, CAPS, FURS, UMBRELLAS AND PARASOLS,

No. 30 Dey Street, near Broadway, New York.

J. L. PAINE.   E. C. FISHER.   C. W. FISHER.

BABCOCK & CO.

WHOLESALE GROCERS & COMMISSION MERCHANTS,

Nos. 65 & 67 Water Street, New York.

JOHN D. PHŒNIX.   FRANCIS M. BABCOCK.   JOHN BABCOCK.

JAMES & HENRY McBRIDE,

Wholesale Grocers & Commission Merchants,

No. 102 BROAD, corner Pearl St., New York.

DARLING, ALBERTSON & ROSE,

PRODUCE COMMISSION MERCHANTS.

13 FRONT STREET, NEW YORK.

LEANDER DARLING.   D. T. ALBERTSON.   MARTIN H. ROSE.

FENNER, McMILLAN & ARTHUR,

WHOLESALE

GROCERS & COMMISSION MERCHANTS,

No. 90 Broad Street,

NEW YORK.

KENDALL & CO.

GENERAL COMMISSION MERCHANTS,

75 Pearl Street, New York.

REFER TO

Messrs. BURGOYNE & PLUME, Bankers, } —NEW YORK.— { Messrs. SPOFFORD, TILESTON & CO.
" HUSSEY, BOND & HALE, } { JOHN JOHNSON, Esq.

Messrs. BRADLEY & CO., Dunkirk, New York.

LIBERAL CASH ADVANCES MADE ON CONSIGNMENTS.

J. & RILEY CARR,

Manufacturers of

CAST, SHEAR, GERMAN & BLISTER STEEL,

OF ALL DESCRIPTIONS, WARRANTED GOOD,

Baily Lane Works, - - - SHEFFIELD.

R. S. STENTON, Agent,

No. 20 CLIFF STREET, NEW YORK.

Also, manufacturers of FILES and SAWS, COMPOSITION and STEEL DOCTORS, Spring Beds, Tools for Planing, &c by Engine Power, Paper Maker's Knives and Tools, Cloth Manufacturer's Ledger Blades and Spiral Cutters; and Patentees of the Double Edged Spiral Cutter.
ALL WARRANTED OF THE VERY BEST QUALITY.

WM. STENTON & SON,

Foreign Hardware Commission Merchants,

No. 20 CLIFF STREET, NEW YORK.

R. S. STENTON, especial Agent for J. & Riley Carr's Steel Files, &c. John Rommer & Son's Drilled Eyed Needles. C. T. BINGHAM, late F. Fenney's Tally Ho Razors. W. Nicholson's Spring and Table Cutlery. J. Cutler's Edge Tools. J. Wilson & Co., Saws. And for others, Manufacturers of

Table Cutlery, Joiners' Tools, &c., &c.

10,000 PACKAGES

BROWN AND BLEACHED

SHEETINGS,

~AT~

65 Liberty Street, near Broadway,

FOR CASH OR APPROVED PAPER.

Also, Grain Bags, (sewed and seam'ess, of all descriptions); Southern Cotton Yarn; white and col'd Carpet Warp; Batting, Wicking, Wadding, Bagging, &c.

☞ COUNTRY MERCHANTS visiting New York for supplies, are invited to examine the above stock, comprising every variety of style and quality, and satisfy themselves that this is the place to purchase

DOMESTIC GOODS LOW FOR CASH.

CHAS. H. PARSONS, 65 Liberty St., Up Stairs.

A. B. & D. SANDS,

WHOLESALE DRUGGISTS,

No. 141 William Street, corner of Fulton,

NEW YORK.

Offer for sale, for CASH, or on approved credit, at the LOWEST MARKET PRICES, a large and well selected assortment of EAST INDIA, MEDITERRANEAN and EUROPEAN

DRUGS AND MEDICINES,

FRENCH, ENGLISH AND AMERICAN CHEMICALS OF ALL KINDS,

Perfumery, Fancy Articles, Fancy Soaps, Brushes, Paints and Oils, Dye-Stuffs, Druggists' Labels, Window Glass. Extracts, Bronzes, Trusses, Le-ches, Surgical Instruments, Druggists' Glass Ware, Hatters' Goods, Shakers' Herbs and Roots, together with

Every Article Comprising the Stock of a Druggist or Physician.

SWAIM'S
CELEBRATED PANACEA,

FOR THE CURE OF

INCIPIENT CONSUMPTION,

Scrofula, General Debility, White Swelling, Rheumatism, Diseases of the Liver and Skin, and all Diseases arising from Impurities of the Blood and the Effects of Mercury.

SWAIM'S PANACEA has been for more than thirty years celebrated in this country and in Europe for its extraordinary cures—for the certificates for which reference is made to the directions and books (which may be had gratis) accompanying the Panacea. Some of which give the particulars of cases too frightful for general publication, where the patients had been almost eaten up with Scrofula, and were deemed incurable by Physicians.

It has been used in hospital and private practice, and has had the singular fortune of being recommended by the most celebrated physicians and other eminent persons. Among others by—

W. GIBSON, M. D , Professor of Surgery, Pa. University.
VALENTINE MOTT, M D., Professor of Surgery, N. Y. University.
W. P. DEWEES, M D., Professor of Mid., Pa. University.
N. CHAPMAN, M D., Professor of Phys·c, Pa. University.
T. PARKE, M. D., President College of Physicians, Phila.
DR. DEL VALLO, Professor of Medicine, Havana.
JOSE EOURENCO DE LUZ, Professor of Surgery, Lisbon.
J. CHIPMAN, Member Royal College Surgeons, London.
G. W. ERVING, late Minister to Spain.
SIR THOMAS PEARSON, Major General British Army.
GILBERT ROBERTSON, British Consul, &c , &c.

And also, the wonderful cures effected by Swaim's Panacea have for many years made it an invaluable remedy. The Panacea does not contain mercury in any form, and being an innocent preparation, it may be given to the most tender infant.

The retail price has been reduced to $1 50 per bottle, (containing three half pints) or three bottles for $4.

BEWARE OF IMPOSITION.

Swaim's Panacea is in round bottles, fluted longitudinally, with the following letters blown on the glass :—"SWAIM'S—PANACEA—PHILADA." and having the name of JAS. SWAIM stamped on the sealing wax, and written on the label covering the cork, and a splendid engraving for the side of the bottle composed of geometric lathe work, comprising nine different dies, which have been turned for the exclusive use of the proprietor, by Draper & Co., bank note engravers, of Philadelphia. In the centre is a portrait of the late Wm. Swaim, copyright secured.

ALSO, SWAIM'S VERMIFUGE.

A valuable Family Medicine, being a highly approved remedy for all diseases arising from debility of the digestive organs, such as Worms, Cholera Morbus, Dysentery, Fever and Ague, Bleeding Piles, Sick Headache, &c. See the Pamphlet (which may be had gratis) accompanying the Vermifuge.

Prepared only at SWAIM'S LABORATORY, THE OLD STAND, Seventh street, below Chesnut, Philadelphia, and sold by all the respectable Druggists in the United States.

CAUTION TO THE PUBLIC.

Persons wishing to obtain the genuine SWAIM'S PANACEA and SWAIM'S VERMIFUGE should be careful to observe that the name SWAIM is spelled correctly on the bottles and labels, or they may be imposed on by medicines made in imitation of them, by a person bearing a somewhat similar name, well calculated to dece've. General Agents for the United States,

SCHIEFFELIN BROTHERS & CO.,
104 and 106 John Street, New York.

GUNPOWDER,

MANUFACTURED BY

E. J. DU PONT de NEMOURS & CO.

```
6.000 kegs Du Pont's Rifle, FFFG, 25 lbs. each;
5 000 ½ do   do      do    FFFG, 12½ lbs. do;
5.000 ¼ do   do      do    FFFG,  6¼ lbs. do;
4.000  do    do      do    FFG,  25 lbs. do;
3.000 ½ do   do      do    FFG,  12½ lbs. do;
3.000  do for sea shooting,   FG, 25 lbs. do;
2.000  do Rough Powder,  FFFR, 25 lbs. do;
2.000  do do      do    FFR, 25 lbs. do;
1.000  do do      do·    FR, 25 lbs. do;
5.000  do A. F. & Co. Glazed FFF, 25 lbs. do;
3.000 ½ do   do      do    FFF, 12½ lbs. do;
5.000  do    do      do    FF, 25 lbs. do;
3.000 ½ do   do      do    FF, 12½ lbs. do;
5.000  do    do      do    F, 25 lbs. do;
5.000  do    do·     do    C, 25 lbs. do;
5 000  do Blasting & Shipping Pow. 25 lbs. do;
3.000  do High Glased    FFF, 25 lbs. do;
1.0 0 ½ do do    do    FFF, 12½ lbs. do;
3 000  do do      do    FF, 25 lbs. do;
1.000 ½ do do    do    FF, 12½ lbs. do;
1.500 ½ do Duck Shooting,    12½ lbs. do;
1.000 ¼ do Rifle    "     6¼ lbs. do;
1.000  do MealedPowder, Pyrotechnists.
```

CANISTER POWDER.

10.000 canisters Eagle Rifle, oval canisters, 1 lb. each; 8 000 canisters FFFG, round canisters 1 lb. each,
5.000   do   do   do round do   1 lb. do; 5.000   "   FFFG, do   do   ½ lb. do,

The above Powder is from the celebrated manufactory of Messrs. Du Pont, and is greatly superior to
any other made in the United States. It will be sold on reasonable terms in lots to suit purchasers.
Also, **Safety Fuse.**

F. L. KNEELAND,

Agent for the sale of Du Pont's Powder, 168 Front street, New York.

For Fever and Ague, Chagres Fever, and other Bilious Diseases,

Principal Office, No. 98 Broadway,

NEW YORK CITY.

SOLD BY THE PRINCIPAL DRUGGISTS THROUGHOUT THE U. STATES.

SEE THE FOLLOWING CERTIFICATES:

ANN ARBOR, Feb. 16, 1853.

This is to certify that I have been afflicted with Fever and Ague for the last eighteen months, and having tried everything I could think of but all to no purpose, until I was recommended to take Dr. E. Bleecker's Stampede Mixture, which I commenced taking and found immediate relief, and am now enjoying good health.
JOHN ARMSTRONG.

YATESBURGH, MICH., Dec. 20, 1853.

This is to certify that I have been afflicted with Fever and Ague for the last eighteen months, during that time have used different medicines recommended to me, without obtaining any relief; one bottle of Bleecker's Stampede Mixture completely cured me of the disease, and I do most cordially recommend those who are afflicted with ague to make use of this invaluable medicine.
GEORGE WHITNEY.

PORT HURON, March 2, 1853.

This is to certify that I was taken with the Fever and Ague in the month of July, 1852, and immediately looked for something to cure me, as my business was such that my time was worth too much to loose in my circumstances, and found nothing to benefit me until I happened to be at Mr. L. S. Noble's store where I heard Bleecker's Stampede Mixture highly recommended. I there purchased a bottle and used it three times from which time I have been well, and I will here state for the benefit of the public, that I immediately went to work on the marsh where my feet were wet from morning till night without having any return of ague.
IRA PARKER.

XENIA, OHIO, March 16, 1853.

The Stampede Mixture has not failed to cure in any instance that I have sold it up to this time.
C. S. VIGER.

SANDWICH, CA., September, 1852.

I do hereby certify that I have been afflicted with Fever and Ague, and having heard of Bleecker's Stampede Mixture, obtained a bottle which has effected a perfect cure and I cheerfully recommend it to those who are suffering with Fever and Ague as a most invaluable remedy.
ABNER E. ELLIS.

SANDWICH, CA., Sept., 1852.

This is to certify that having had the Fever and Ague for some time, and having tried many remedies without effect, I procured one bottle of Dr. Bleecker's Stampede Mixture which has completely cured me of that dreadful disease, and I recommend his remedy to the public as a safe and sure cure
HUGH C. GOURLAY.

SANDWICH, CA., Sept., 1852.

Having been informed by the agents in the town of Sandwich, of Dr. Bleecker's Stampede Mixture for the cure of Fever and Ague and other bilious diseases, and having been suffering for some time with the Fever and Ague, I procured a bottle which has entirely cured me, and I hereby certify it to be the best medicine I ever used for that purpose, and I strongly recommend it to the afflicted.
FRANZ BLOSSEVNEIR.

STEBBINS, MORGAN & BUTLER,

46 CLIFF STREET,

BETWEEN FULTON & BEEKMAN,

NEW YORK.

Importers, Wholesale and Jobbing Dealers in

DRUGS, CHEMICALS,

PAINTS, PERFUMERY, &C.

Having extensive connections in Europe, they are prepared to furnish the choicest goods to be found in

FOREIGN OR DOMESTIC MARKETS

In quantities to suit the purchaser, and on terms as favorable as any similar house in the United States.

S., M. & B. are the regularly appointed agents for the following European Manufactories, viz:

Walker Alkali Co., Sup. Carb. Soda, Sal Soda & Chloride Lime Makers,
Mander, Weaver & Co, the old established Chemists.
A. Rowland & Sons, whose elegant Toilette requisites are so popular.
Ede & Co, old and highly celebrated Perfumers.
Robt. Low & Son, whose Celebrated Brown Windsor Honey and other Soaps, are so well known.

ALSO--

Cox's Celebrated Sparkling Gelatine,

BROWN'S BLISTERING & DRESSING TISSUE,

MURRAY'S FLUID MAGNESIA,

And other standard preparations of the highest celebrity.

We respectfully request you to examine our stock and prices before purchasing elsewhere.

STEBBINS, MORGAN & BUTLER,

46 Cliff Street, New York.

FOWLERS & WELLS,

PHRENOLOGISTS.

THE PHRENOLOGICAL CABINET,

CLINTON HALL, 131 NASSAU STREET,

NEW YORK,

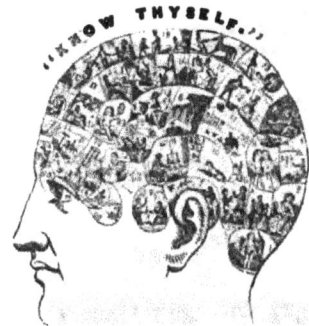

Contains Portraits, Busts and Casts, from the most distinguished men that ever lived; also, skulls from all parts of the globe, including Egyptian Mummies, pirates, robbers, murderers, and thieves living and dead; and is always open and FREE to visitors.

PROFESSIONAL EXAMINATIONS given when desired, including directions as to the most suitable occupations, to self-improvement, and advice relative to the cultivation of all the Faculties of the mind, all of which will be found most valuable, as well as exceedingly interesting.

FOWLERS & WELLS,
Clinton Hall, 131 Nassau St, New York.

Office of the Illustrated Phrenological Journal, The Water Cure Journal, and The Student, each published monthly at one dollar a year. Address

FOWLERS & WELLS,
Clinton Hall, 131 *Nassau St., New York.*

W. M. TIERS & CO.,

Importers and Dealers in

TOYS, FANCY GOODS,

YANKEE NOTIONS, &C.,

NO. 31 CORTLANDT STREET, (second floor,)

NEW YORK.

N. B.—W. M. TIERS & Co. having had a long experience in the above line, would call the attention of dealers to their large and varied assortment which are offered at prices that cannot fail to suit—all of their Foreign Goods being imported direct from the manufacturers.
W. M. T. & Co are agents for the manufacturers of FIREWORKS, and can execute orders with dispatch.

S. & E. WILLETS,

DEALERS AND IMPORTERS OF

CHINA, GLASS & EARTHENWARE

No. 113 Water street, one door below Wall Street, New York.

PRATT, HARDENBERGH & CO.,

MANUFACTURERS AND IMPORTERS OF

PAPER HANGINGS,

No. 360 Broadway, between Leonard and Franklin streets, New York.

HUESTIS & LEVY,

Manufacturers of

SINGLE & DOUBLE HEAD

PLAYING CARDS,

OF

Every description known in the United States.

Spanish Cards of superior qualities.

HUESTIS & LEVY,

UNION CARD MANUFACTORY,

177 & 179 Grand St., near the Odd Fellows Hall, N. Y.

HAWES & GRAHAM,

DEALERS & IMPORTERS OF

MAHOGANY & ROSEWOOD,

Nos. 176 & 178 Centre Street, New York.

Their stock embraces the most extensive
variety of finely Figured Woods,
to be found in the United States, viz :—

MAHOGANY,
ROSEWOOD,
SATIN, ZEBRA,
EBONY, OAK,
SPANISH AND RED CEDAR,
WHITE HOLLY,
WALNUT,
MAPLE AND SPRUCE,

—CONSISTING OF—

LOGS, BOARDS,

PLANKS and VENEERS.

Also, Newels, Balusters, Chair Tops, and a
large assortment of Glue, Sand Paper, Bench and
Hand Screws, together with 500 different patterns of "Wiler's celebrated Piano and Cabinet
Mouldings."

L. P. HAWES.   JNO. R. GRAHAM.

KUMBEL'S

PATENT MACHINE STRETCHED

LEATHER BANDING

THE ONLY PATENTED BAND IN THE UNITED STATES.

THEY ARE MADE FROM THE

BEST OAK LEATHER,

Are thoroughly Stretched, Cemented and Riveted together, and made to
run straight,

And can be furnished of any length or width,

FROM ONE TO THIRTY INCHES WIDE,

Single, double or round, by addressing

WM. KUMBEL, Patentee,

38 FERRY STREET, NEW YORK.

CYRUS W. FIELD. JOSEPH F. STONE.

CYRUS W. FIELD & CO.,

COMMISSION MERCHANTS,

IMPORTERS & WHOLESALE DEALERS IN

Paper and Paper Manufacturers Materials.

Office 11 Cliff Street,

NEW YORK.

Warehouses 11 & 58 Cliff & 94 Beekman Streets.

ARE SOLE AGENTS IN THE UNITED STATES FOR

Muspratt's Superior Bleaching Powder.
Victoria Mills Celebrated Writing Papers.
Russell   "   Superior   "   "
Genesee   "   "   Printing   "
Rawlins & Sons' English Tissue.
Cowan & Co.'s English and Scotch Writing do.

They are also Agents for the principal Paper Manufacturers in this country, and offer for sale by far the most extensive and desirable stock of PAPER and Paper Manufacturers' Materials that can be found in this or any other country.

They occupy the large and commodious Warehouses, No. 11 Cliff Street, No. 58 Cliff Street, No. 94 Beekman Street, and the Lofts over the large Iron Stores, 7 and 9 Cliff Street.

THEIR BUSINESS IS STRICTLY WHOLESALE.

WRITING PAPERS ARE SOLD BY THE CASE ONLY.

Their extraordinary facilities enable them to offer all Goods, both

FOREIGN AND DOMESTIC,

At the LOWEST POSSIBLE PRICES.

PAPER MADE TO ORDER, ANY SIZE OR WEIGHT.

Liberal advances made on consignments of Paper.

PAPER MAKERS' STOCK & OTHER MERCHANDISE.

The highest Market Price paid in Cash for all kinds of Rags.

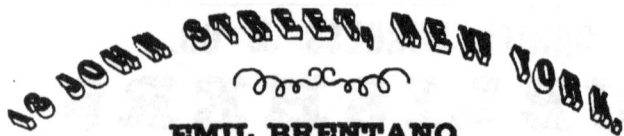

PETER MURRAY,

—IMPORTER OF—

FRENCH, ENGLISH AND GERMAN

FANCY GOODS,

85 MAIDEN LANE,

NEW YORK.

J. H. BATES,   ALFRED TAYLOR,   ANDREW DICKSON,   H. A. GRAVES.

BATES, TAYLOR & CO.

Manufacturers and wholesale dealers in

CLOTHING,

NOS. 23 & 25 DEY ST., (up stairs.)

NEW YORK.

C. B. HATCH & CO.,

Importers and Manufacturers of

GENTLEMEN'S FURNISHING GOODS,

97

WILLIAM ST., NEW YORK.

P. & J. DEVLIN,

MANUFACTURERS OF AND DEALERS IN

CLOTHING,

WHOLESALE AND RETAIL.

83 & 85 JOHN ST. CORNER OF NASSAU,

NEW YORK.

THE

Hazard Powder Company

MANUFACTURERS AND DEALERS IN

GUNPOWDER,

Office---89 Wall, corner of Water St.,

NEW YORK.

A. E. DOUGLASS, Sec'y.   A. G. HAZARD, Pres't.

GUNS   RIFLES
AND   AND
PISTOLS,   REVOLVERS,

B. J. HART & BROTHER,

74 MAIDEN LANE,

NEW YORK.

Importers of English, French and German double and single barrel Fowling and Ducking Guns, from the lowest to the finest qualities. Manufacturers of Rifles and Revolvers.
A large assortment of Pistols, embracing 100 different patterns.
United States' Muskets, Rifles and Holster Pistols.
Flasks, Pouches, Caps, Wads, &c., &c. Every article connected with the trade offered at very low prices.

E. B. BLEASBY,

IMPORTER OF AND DEALER IN

LONDON & DURHAM MUSTARDS,

SAUCES, CATSUPS, PICKLES, &C.

No. 196 Fulton street, late 2 St. Peter's Place, New York.

N. B. Premium 'Sun-Bleached' Wax Tapers of every description and Night Lights constantly on hand.

TRUSSES, ELASTIC SHOULDER BRACES,

(For expanding the chest.)

LADIES' BELTS AND SUPPORTERS,

Instruments for Club-Foot, Knock-Knees, Bow-Legs, Weak Ankle Joints, Curvature of the Spine, Piles and Prolapsus. Also a very superior Elastic Stocking for enlarged veins of the leg, Elastic Knee Caps, Children's Trusses, and every kind of Surgical Belt and Bandage, Wholesale and Retail, at

R. GLOVER'S, M. D.,

No. 19 Ann street, near Broadway, New York.

☞ Entrance for Ladies through the entry. Office hours, Sunday, from 10 A. M. to 4 P. M.

DR. S. P. TOWNSEND'S

SARSAPARILLA,

Established in the City of New York in 1840.

DR. TOWNSEND'S
COMPOUND EXTRACT OF SARSAPARILLA,

Improved and manufactured under the supervision of Dr. JAMES R. CHILTON, the celebrated Chemist of

NEW YORK.

Many valuable Improvements have been made by Dr. CHILTON in the mode of preparing this popular medicine. Under his skilful hand its sanative powers have been so much increased, that only one or two tea-spoonsful of the extract are required for a dose which is an important item to those using Compounds of Sarsaparilla, as this fact alone proves it to be the STRONGEST and CHEAPEST medicine ever invented to **Purify the Blood,** and permanently cure

Stubborn Ulcers,	*Ringworm, or Tetter,*	*Rheumatism,*	*Scrofula,*
Erysipelas,	*Effects of Mercury,*	*Pimples on the Face,*	*Dropsy,*
Dyspepsia,	*Costiveness and Piles,*	*Heart Disease,*	*General Debility,*
Female Debility,	*Coughs, Colds &c.,*	*Ulcers Fever Sores,*	*Liver Complaint,*
Neuralgia,	*Enlargement of the Joints,*	*Palpitation of the Heart,*	*Nervous Debility.*

TO THE PUBLIC.

The public are hereby notified that the preparation extensively known as DR. S. P. TOWNSEND'S COMPOUND EXTRACT OF SARSAPARILLA, is now manufactured under my direction and supervision, from the original recipe obtained from Dr. S. P. Townsend; and I certify that it is composed of ingredients PURELY VEGETABLE, and WITHOUT MERCURY; and also that the ingredients are judiciously compounded, so as to obtain from them their greatest medicinal effect.

JAMES R. CHILTON, M. D., Chemist.

Dr. Chilton's name is surety that the elements of this Extract are combined in the most correct and scientific manner, and that it is adapted to the wants of the invalid, with the highest professional ability. This we hope will be sufficient GUARANTEE to the public and to those purchasing Dr. S. P. Townsend's Compound Extract of Sarsaparilla. Such may have no fear of getting one of the spurious and baneful mixtures which fill the channels of trade and are concocted without any KNOWLEDGE either of the nature of REMEDIAL AGENTS, or the WANTS OF THE HUMAN SYSTEM when LABORING UNDER DISEASE.

DR. S. P. TOWNSEND'S SARSAPARILLA

IS WARRANTED TO

Keep for any lenghth of time, in all Climates.

CAUTION.

To avoid IMPOSITION it will be necessary to see that the following certificate of Dr. JAMES R. CHILTON is printed on green paper, and pasted on the outside wrapper; as also the signature of "S. P. Townsend" at foot of the steel plate label of each bottle.

THIS IS TO CERTIFY, that the *Compound Extract of Sarsaparilla* contained in this bottle, is prepared under my direction and supervision from the *original recipe* of *Dr. S. P. Townsend,* and that it is composed of ingredients *purely vegetable,* and *without mercury.*

JAMES R. CHILTON, M. D., Chemist.

Without this all others are Counterfeits.

Sold by all the Principal Druggists and Country Merchants throughout the United States, Canadas, &c.

PROPRIETORS' OFFICE,

82 NASSAU STREET, NEW YORK.

GOOD NEWS TO THE AFFLICTED!

DR. S. D. CORNELL'S

PAIN EXPELLER

Is a remedy that stands unequaled amidst the many Pain Destroying medicines of our age, and has come into use on its own intrinsic merits, and enjoys a reputation for its promptness in removing Pain, that has never been awarded to any similar preparation. It is emphatically the great Remedy for removing Pain — it having been demonstrated in thousands of families with perfect success.

MANUFACTURERS & PROPRIETORS

DR. S. D. CORNELL,

93 John Street, New York;

AND S. D. FULLER & CO.,

3 TREMONT TEMPLE, BOSTON.

All genuine Dr. S D. Cornell's Pain Expeller has on the label of each bottle his figure-head, as represented above, with a fac-simile of his handwriting, thus —

Stephen D Cornell

BALL, BLACK & CO.,

(SUCCESSORS TO MARQUAND & CO.,)

IMPORTERS & MANUFACTURERS OF

SILVER & PLATED WARE,

DIAMONDS, WATCHES, JEWELRY, &c., &c.,

SIGN OF THE GOLDEN EAGLE,

247 BROADWAY,

South corner of Murray Street, Opposite the City Hall,

HENRY BALL,
WM. BLACK,   }   NEW YORK.
EBENAZER MONROE,

Diamonds, Pearls, and every variety of Precious Stones, unset,

Which at very short notice can be set in any style or pattern on the premises.

Constantly on hand a very large assortment of Silver Ware, and Plated Goods, consisting of Tea Sets, Urns, Waiters, Goblets, Communion Sets, Dish Covers, Pitchers, Forks Spoons, &c. to which the attention of Ship Owners, Hotel Proprietors, Steamboat owners and Committees on Presentation are particularly requested, as they will here find one of the largest assortments of the above goods in the United States or world.

Agencies having been established throughout Europe, by which means all the new styles of goods both rich and rare are obtained direct from the manufactories before they are offered in the European market.

FANCY GOODS

Of every description, comprising in part, Papier Mache Goods, Pearl and Ivory Goods, Porte-Monnaies, Fans, Combs, China and Briquet Ornaments, Parian and Porcelain Ware, &c., &c.

OIL PAINTINGS.

A very choice collection of Oil Paintings of the old and modern schools.

STATUARY

Of the most choice description.

PARISIAN BRONZES

A beautiful assortment, consisting of Clocks, Candelabras, Figures, Ornaments, Gas Fixtures, Chandeliers, large and elegant Figures for fountains and gardens, halls, &c. These goods need no comment, as they are of the finest bronze and will bear a close inspection.

FINE WATCHES,

Of all the celebrated manufacturers of London Germany, Switzerland and France, a very large assortment of every style, from plain silver to the very richest of Gold, Enameled, Diamond and Ruby settings.

☞ With an experience of over thirty years, and the investment of an amount of capital unequalled by any other firm in the same department of business, are enabled to offer inducements to purchasers, that few can surpass.

A. K. WARNER & CO.,

IMPORTERS AND JOBBERS OF

WATCHES AND WATCH MATERIALS,

AND

Manufacturers of Jewelry & "Eagle" Gold Pens,

No. 10 CORTLANDT ST, /up stairs,/

OPPOSITE THE WESTERN HOTEL,

A. K. WARNER,
FRED'K COOK.

NEW YORK.

Calling the attention of the TRADE to our card above, we beg leave to say, we we have a handsome stock of goods suitable for the Watch and Jewelry Retail Trade, embracing particularly the

FINEST OF ENGLISH AND SWISS WATCHES,

ALSO,

JEWELRY OF OUR OWN MANUFACTURE,

And the Superior Gold Pen known as "Warner & Co's Eagle Pen."

And will sell at very low Prices on the Usual Terms.

Our Mr. Warner, who, from 16 years' experience in this business, is fully acquainted with all the wants of the trade, will pay special attention to orders. and those favoring us with orders may rely on prompt attention, and also be assured that goods and prices shall be satisfactory.

NOTICE.

We are in the Second Story, at low Rent, and Sell at small Profits.

We solicit your orders, and respectfully invite you to see our Stock before buying elsewhere, on your visit to New York City.

A. K. WARNER & Co.

PEARL STREET HOUSE,

PORTER & CUMMINGS,

No. 88 PEARL STREET, NEW YORK.

The Subscribers having recently taken the above favorite Hotel, and having refitted it in a neat and comfortable manner, would respectfully solicit a share of the business Travel. It being in the immediate vicinity of Broadway, Wall Street and the Battery. ☞Travelers and Strangers, will find it a convenient and quiet stopping place, combining all the advantages of a House, and at the same time all the luxuries of a good Hotel

SOLOMON S. REILLY,

CAMPHENE & LAMP

MANUFACTURER,

135 CANAL STREET, CORNER OF LEIGHT.

51 CARMINE, CORNER BEDFORD.

167 GREENWICH, COR. CORTLANDT.

218 CANAL ST. NEAR HUDSON, N. Y.

T. THOMAS & CO.

MANUFACTURERS OF

BLOCK TIN WARE,

OF EVERY VARIETY,

BRASS, IRON, WIRE & BRONZED FENDERS, ANDIRONS SHOVELS & TONGS,

Suitable to the Southern and Western Markets,

No. 63 Nassau Street, near Maiden Lane,

T. THOMAS.
E. C. FRAZYER. } **NEW YORK.**
B. W. FAIRBANKS.

☞Hotels and Steamboats fitted out with Copper Dishes, Stands, Covers, Urns, &c., of every size.☜

GWYNNE'S CENTRIFUGAL PUMP,

For Manufactories. Paper Mills, Tanneries, Drainage and Irrigation, Coffer Dams Dry Docks, Mines Quarries, Railroad Water Stations, and for supplying Canals or Water Works for large Cities, this Pump has no equal. Sizes capable of discharging from 25 to 10 000 gallons per minute kept constantly on hand, larger sizes capable of discharging up to 100,000 gallons per minute. furnished on reasonable notice. All Pumps Warranted. From the many Testimonials of their superiority we have only room for the following:

MR. J. S. GWYNNE, New York,

DEAR SIR: We take great pleasure in recommending your Patent Centrifugal Pump. We put one into our Brewery in February last which throws sixty gallons per minute, and do not hesitate on all accounts to recommend it as the best Pump we possess any knowledge of. Yours very, Respectfully, &c.

Point Brewery, Pittsburgh, May 16th, 1853.   GEO. W. SMITH & CO.

The above Pumps are Manufactured and Sold by the

THE UNION POWER CO. of U. S.

Office & Warehouse—49 Dey Street, New York.

SEWING MACHINES,

Patented February 11th, 1851; June 22nd, 1852; February 22nd, 1853.

GROVER, BAKER & Co.

Patentees & Proprietors.

Machines of every variety adapted to all kinds of work, with any kind of Thread, wholly unlike all others rightfully in use, Sewing without a Shuttle, from stationary spools of any size desired, and forming a new and fast stitch, which for beauty and strength is unequalled. The threads are securely tied at each stitch, and the seam, unlike that formed by any other machine, will not rip, but remain firm where every third stitch is cut.

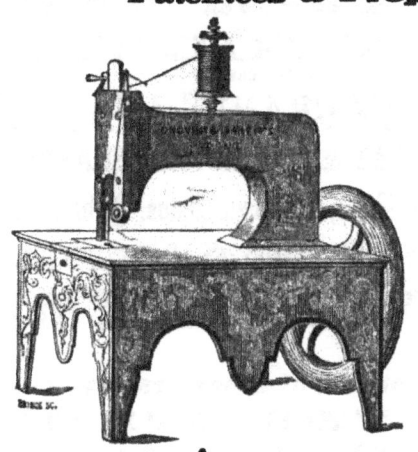

A.

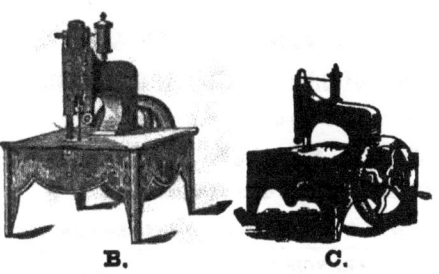

B.   C.

These Machines make with the same facility, straight, curved and irregular seams in fabrics and leather of any thickness, and are the only Machines which make a fast and fine stitch. Our patents all are upon the stitch itself, and all modes of making it, and all persons are cautioned against making, using, or vending any machine making a fast and fair stitch with two needles from spools, as all such infringe directly our patents, and will be dealt with accordingly. Descriptive pamphlets containing evidence from persons using hundreds sent to all who wish.

PRICES FOR SINGLE MACHINES

WITH RIGHT TO USE.

Machine,	A	$150 00
"	B	125 00
"	C	100 00
	D	80 00
	E	60 00

PITTSBURGH
BUSINESS CARDS.

WEST POINT FORGE.
JOHN RIDALL,

MANUFACTURER OF

LOCOMOTIVE CRANKS AND AXLES,

STEAMBOAT & SUGAR MILL SHAFTS,

Cranks, Piston Rods, Pittman Jaws, Levers, Wrists,

SCREW MOULDS & ANCHORS,

WROUGHT PITTMAN

AND

Heavy Forging of every description,

51 WATER STREET,
PITTSBURGH, PA.

JOS. P. HAIGH.   A. HARTUPEE.   JOHN MORROW.

HAIGH, HARTUPEE & CO.

STEAM ENGINE BUILDERS AND IRON FOUNDERS,

PATENT HOT PRESSED

NUT AND WASHER

Manufacturers.

Corner of First & Short Streets, Pittsburgh, Pa.

N. G. MURPHY.   FRANCIS TIERNAN.   MORRIS JONES.

MURPHY, TIERNAN & CO.

IMPORTERS AND WHOLESALE DEALERS IN

FOREIGN AND DOMESTIC

DRY GOODS

No. 48 WOOD STREET,

PITTSBURGH, PA.

DUFF'S MERCANTILE COLLEGE,
PITTSBURG, PA.
ESTABLISHED IN 1840.

Incorporated by the Legislature of Pennsylvania, with a perpetual Charter.

Board of Trustees—Hon. James Buchanan, late Secretary of State; Hon. Wm. Wilkins, late Secretary of War; Hon. Moses Hampton; Hon. Walter H. Lowrie; Hon. Charles Naylor; Gen. J. K. Moorhead.

Faculty:—P. Duff, Principal, author of the "North American Accountant," Professor of the theory and practice of Double Entry Book-Keeping, and Lectures on Commercial Sciences. J. D. Williams, Professor of Mercantile and Ornamental Penmanship. N. B. Hatch, Esq. of the Pittsburg Bar, Professor of Mercantile Law.

This Institution occupies five spacious apartments and employs three assistants in the Book-Keeping department, and is now considered the most extensive and perfectly organized Commercial college in the United States. Eighteen years' experience in extensive Eastern business enables the principal to train his pupils in many important business matters, not attempted in any other establishment of the kind in the country. The American Institute and Chamber of Commerce, of New York, have sanctioned DUFF'S NEW SYSTEM OF BOOK-KEEPING, as the most perfect combination of science and practice published. The Collegiate course comprehends Double Entry Book-Keeping, in its application to the most extensive Inland and Maritime Commerce, Penmanship and Commercial Computations. Daily Lectures on Commercial Law, Political Economy and Commercial Sciences, &c.

Duff's Book-Keeping, pp 192, Royal Octavo, Harpers. Price $1 50, postage 24 cts. "The most perfect combination of instruction and practice published." Duff's Western Steamers' Accountant—Price $1, postage 9 cts. "A perfect system fo keeping such books & accounts. Steamboats & steamers supplied with thoroughly trained accountants. Send by mail for circular

JOHN FLEMING.   COCHRAN FLEMING.

FLEMING BROTHERS,

(Successors to J. Kidd & Co.)

PROPRIETORS OF

M'LANE'S CELEBRATED

VERMIFUGE

LIVER PILLS

AND

LUNG SYRUP,

No. 60 WOOD STREET, PITTSBURG, PA.

The late firm of **J. KIDD & CO.** Druggists, having been dissolved by the death of Jonathan Kidd, and the surviving partner, JOHN FLEMING, having purchased the entire interest of the deceased in said firm, including proprietorship of

M'LANE'S CELEBRATED MEDICINES,

Has associated with him his brother, COCHRAN FLEMING, and will continue the business at the old stand, corner of Wood and Fourth Streets, Pittsburg, Pa. under the name and style of

FLEMING BROTHERS,

Where they will be happy to see the friends and customers of the late firm, and all others desiring articles in their line. Country Merchants and Druggists will find it to their interests to call and examine their goods and prices before purchasing elsewhere.

The business of the late firm will be closed by JOHN FLEMING; and all persons knowing themselves indebted to said firm will please settle by remitting or otherwise, at their earliest convenience, and those having claims against said firm will please present the same for payment.

ISAAC JONES.   JOHN F. QUIGG.

JONES & QUIGG,

Manufacturers of

SPRING & BLISTER STEEL,

Plow Slab Steel, Steel Plow Wings, Coach and Eliptic Springs, Brass Nut Taper, Half Patent,
Mail Screw and Hammered Iron Axles.   Corner of Ross and First Streets, Pittsburg, Pa.

JONES & QUIGG.   D. B. ROGERS.

D. B. ROGERS & Co.

MANUFACTURERS OF ROGERS' PATENT

IMPROV'D STEEL CULTIVATOR TEETH

Corner of Ross and First Streets, Pittsburg.

A. A. MASON & CO.

HAVING REMOVED TO THEIR NEW STORE,

No. 25 FIFTH STREET,

Between Market & Wood, opp. the Iron City Hotel,

Would solicit the attention of their friends and the public, to their
New and Extensive Stock of Rich and Fashionable

DRY GOODS

Embracing every variety of

Dress Goods, Linen do. White do. Hosiery & Gloves,
HOUSE KEEPING GOODS, GENTS' FURNISHING GOODS,
SUMMER STUFFS, SHAWLS, LACE AND SILK MANTILLAS,
EMBROIDERIES, LACES, AND TRIMMINGS,
RIBBONS AND BONNETS, MILLINERY GOODS,
BROADCLOTHS & CASSIMERES, ALL KINDS OF DOMESTICS.

All of which will be offered at the lowest possible price.   New Goods will be opening and
exhibiting almost daily.

Pittsburg, April 6, 1853.   A. A. MASON & CO.

S. C. TIERNAN.   JNO. K. TIERNAN.

TIERNAN & CO.

BANKERS

AND EXCHANGE BROKERS,

NO. 95 WOOD STREET, PITTSBURG,

LARGEST ESTABLISHMENT OF THE KIND

IN THE WEST.

HENRY STIMPLE,

NOS. 17 & 23 STEVENSON ST., PITTSBURG, PA.

TANNER!

And Manufacturer of all kinds of

LEATHER,

Enamelled Hides,

GRAIN DASH JAPANNED SKIRTING, SHOE, OIL & BELT

Leather. Sheep—Moroccos of all kinds, and every description of Fancy Colored Leather.

CHARLES E. LOOMIS,

STOCK & BILL BROKER,

Office, 75 Fourth St. bet. Market and Wood, opp. Bank of Pittsburg, Pittsburg.

Particular attention paid to the purchase and sale of Stocks.

D. & J. LITTLE,
MANUFACTURERS OF

RIFLE BARRELS

Office and Stock at Fahnestock & Bro's Hardware Store,

247 LIBERTY STREET, PITTSBURG.

IOWA FOUNDRY, PITTSBURG, PA.

JOHN C. PARRY,

103 WOOD STREET, MANUFACTURER OF

ROLLING MILL AND OTHER MILL AND MACHINERY CASTINGS,

PATENT CHILLED ROLLS, PATENT KETTLES,

A superior article for Manufacturers of Cane Sugar, Soda, Potash and Soaps

Iowa Foundry Cooking Stoves, Highest Prize taken at the Allegheny County Fair.

☞ Coal and Cooking Stoves, Hollow-ware and Castings of every description; Kitchen Ranges, with or without boilers for baths; Tin and Sheet Iron always on hand or made to order; Enamelled Parlor Grates and Fenders, of beautiful designs and superior finish; Improved Corn Shellers, Plows, and Plow Castings; Patent Ornamental Railing, for Cemetery and other enclosures.

M. GRAFF.   D. REISINGER.

M. GRAFF & CO.

MOULDERS' UNION FOUNDRY,

NO. 194 WOOD STREET, PITTSBURG.

Manufacturers of Cooking Stoves, Coal and Wood Stoves, Parlor Stoves, Hollow-ware, Plain and Fancy Grates, Plain and Fancy Fenders Sad and Dog Irons.
Platform and Counter Scales, Sugar Kettles, Tea do. Bark Mills Wagon Boxes, etc.

SAM'L P. SHRIVER.   JOSEPH DILWORTH.   JOHN S. DILWORTH.

SHRIVER, DILWORTH & CO.

WHOLESALE GROCERS & COMMISSION MERCHANTS

Nos. 130 and 132 Second Street, between Wood and Smithfield,
PITTSBURG.

M'KELVY & BLAIR'S EAGLE STEEL WORKS,
Office, No. 57 Water Street, Pittsburg.

Manufacturers of Cast, Shear, German, and Blister Steel.

Keep constantly on hand, or manufacture to order, all shapes and sizes of Round, square, Flat Octagon, Plate, and Sheet Steel, for the Hardware Trade. Shovel, Hoe, Fork, Saw, File, Plow, and Spring Steels. Drills, Cast Steel Crow Bars, &c. for R. R. Work. Special Sizes for Nailors' Knives and Dies. All warranted qualities subject to return, at our expense, if not equal to any imported.

GEO. WILSON.   WM. GORMAN.

WILSON & GORMAN,

MANUFACTURERS of SOAP & CANDLES

No. 16 Fourth Street, Pittsburg, Pa.

N. B.—MINING CANDLES. The attention of Copper Miners is particularly requested to a very superior article of Candles, manufact'd expressly for their use. Refer to DR. C. G. HUSSEY, JOSHUA HANNA, Esq.

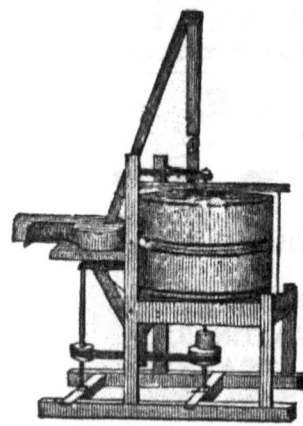

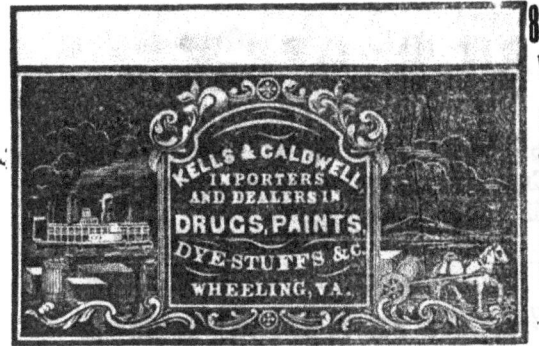

83 MAIN ST.,
WHEELING, VA.

Having superior advantages in their purchases, they are confident of successful competition with the Eastern Market, with addition of transportation, & pledge themselves to sell goods lower than ever before offered in this City.

All goods warranted.

JOHN E. BOYD,

No. 10 South side Monroe Street, Wheeling, Va.

Wholesale Dealer in

FOREIGN AND DOMESTIC
DRY GOODS AND YANKEE NOTIONS.

The Subscriber respectfully invites the attention of Merchants and Pedlars, and he says without any hesitancy, that he can furnish a Country Merchant or Pedlar with a better assortment of goods, than is kept by any other house of the same description, and pledges himself to sell for cash or approved paper, as cheap as can be bought West.

SWEARINGEN & TAYLOR,

PUBLISHERS AND PROPRIETORS OF

THE WHEELING INTELLIGENCER,

PLAIN & ORNAMENTAL PRINTERS,

No. 21 WATER ST., WHEELING, VA.,

NEAR THE BALTIMORE AND OHIO RAIL ROAD DEPOT.

A. C. PARTRIDGE,
PREMIUM DAGUERREOTYPIST,

And Daguerreotype Stock Dealer,

36 Monroe, between Market & Main St., Wheeling, Va.

☞ Likenesses, either single or in groups, from the smallest to the largest size taken in all kinds of weather.

A. A. QUARRIER.   A. M JACOB.   L. H. PATTERSON.

UNION GLASS WORKS.

QUARRIER, JACOB & CO.

MANUFACTURERS OF

VIALS, BOTTLES, &C.,

Black and Green Wines, Porter and Ale Bottles,

Office 33 Monroe Street,

WHEELING, VA.

ROB'T. FORSYTH.   JNO. F. HOPKINS.   JAS. H. FORSYTH, Jr.

FORSYTH'S & HOPKINS,

Forwarding and Commission Merchants,

AND PRODUCE DEALERS,

WHEELING, VA.

Our House is the largest in the Country, covering an aria of an Acre and one-third on the two floors, with track from Rail Road on each floor, offering our friends superior facilities for handling Freight and Storage.

JOSHUA BODLEY.   T. M. GALLY.

S. BODLEY & CO.

MANUFACTURERS OF

WAGONS, CARTS AND IRON AXLETREES,

Corner of Fourth and Clay Sts., Wheeling, Va.

Also, all kinds of Iron Work for Wood or Wire Suspension Bridges. Bridge, Telegraph, Fencing, Cable and Market Wire, and all kinds of Machinery.
The Wire in the Wheeling and Nashville Wire Suspension Bridges was made at this Establishment.

LLOYD LOGAN.   J. G. BAKER.   W. CARR.   H. H. CARR.

LOGAN, CARR & CO.

Wholesale Dealers in all kinds of

TOBACCO, SNUFF AND SEGARS,

No. 81 Main St., Wheeling, Va.

C. S. LAMBDIN.   R. C. BONHAM.   F. W. BASSETT.

LAMBDIN, BONHAM & CO.

VIRGINIA, WHEELING & PHŒNIX

PAPER MILLS,

WHEELING, VA.

JOHN McCAULRY,

WHOLESALE AND RETAIL

CONFECTIONER,

MARKET ST., 1 DOOR EAST OF THIRD,

STEUBENVILLE, O.

MEANS & CO.
IRON FOUNDERS, MACHINISTS
AND
RAIL - ROAD - CAR
MANUFACTURERS.
STEUBENVILLE, O.

D. A. SMITH,

DEALER IN

Country Produce, Dry Goods and Groceries,

CORNER THIRD AND NORTH STREETS,

STEUBENVILLE, O.

Our stock being entirely new, dealers would find it to their interest to call and examine our stock and prices for themselves. All kinds of Produce taken in exchange.

JOHN COCHRAN & BRO.

WHOLESALE DEALERS IN

Dry Goods, Watches,

JEWELRY AND NOTIONS,

FOURTH STREET,

STEUBENVILLE, O.

WILSON'S
AMERICAN HOTEL.

WELLSVILLLE, OHIO.

☞ The public are hereby informed that every thing will be done at this establishment to insure the comfort of all those favoring me with their patronage. All information as to traveling routes, &c., can be obtained. Conveyance of Luggage, &c., from the Boats and Cars Free.

W WILSON.

P. F. GEISSE,
ENGINE, CAR BUILDER AND FOUNDER,

WELLSVILLE, OHIO.

Steam Engines of all sizes and descriptions built to order on most favorable terms. Also, Machinery of all kinds made to order. Castings, such as Mill Gearing, Stoves Ploughs, Hollow Ware, Chilled Froggs for Rail Roads. Car Wheels superior to any thing offered heretofore they being cast in Dry Sand Moulds and of the most superior Chill, and combine more strength for the weight than any other wheels now used. Gravel, Platform, House and Passenger Cars, made to order, of the best quality and at reasonable Rates and Terms. Reference for Cars and Wheels, at the C. & P. R. R. Co.

P. F. GEISSE.

A. F. SCOTT.   D. M'CURDY.

SCOTT & M'CURDY,
MANUFACTURERS OF
SADDLES, BRIDLES, HARNESS, TRUNKS, &C.
Collars, Wholesale & Retail.

Location, Lisbon St., Wellsville, Ohio.

T. M'COLLISTER,
(Formerly of Pittsburgh,)
STEAM ENGINE BOILER MAKER,

WELLSVILLE, OHIO.

Is now prepared to make or repair all kinds of High and Low Pressure Boilers, Salt Pans and other Sheet Iron work at low rates. Office opposite the "Fulton Foundry."

OSCAR STODDARD,

Wholesale Dealer in

DRY GOODS, CLOTHING, PEDLARS' GOODS

CROCKERY, GLASSWARE AND GROCERIES,

SUMMIT ST. NEXT DOOR TO JOHNSON'S BLOCK AND THE EXPRESS OFFICE,

TOLEDO, OHIO.

CHARLES D. WOOD & CO.

MANUFACTURERS AND WHOLESALE AND RETAIL DEALERS IN

CLOTHING & GENT'S FURNISHING GOODS,

SUMMIT STREET,

TOLEDO, OHIO.

O. MATHER,

DEALER IN ALL KINDS OF

LUMBER, SHINGLES AND LATH,

CORNER OF LOCUST AND WATER STS.

TOLEDO, O.

☞ Shipping done on reasonable terms.

BYE & JOHNSON,

DEALERS IN

BOOKS, STATIONERY, WALL PAPER, BLANK BOOKS,

Writing and Printing Paper and Printing Inks, at Wholesale & Retail,

D. N. BYE,   }   COR. SUMMIT & MADISON STS.
J. N. JOHNSON,   TOLEDO, CHIO.

B. F. STOW,

Wholesale and Retail Dealer in

CLOCKS, WATCHES, SPECTACLES, JEWELRY,

MUSICAL INSTRUMENTS, FINE CUTLERY, FANCY GOODS AND GERMAN TOYS,

CORNER OF SUMMIT AND JEFFERSON STREETS,

TOLEDO, OHIO.

Looking Glasses, French English and Italian Violin Strings, Porcelain Ornaments. Watches cleaned and repaired in the best manner, on short notice.

JOHN B. CLARK, JR.

BUCKEYE

Saddle, Harness and Trunk Manufacturer,

AND CARRIAGE TRIMMER AND UPHOLSTERER,

Whips at Wholesale and Retail.

Smith Street, one door East of Mack & Thorner's Clothing Store, Toledo, O.

☞ All work warranted to do good service. ☜

C. E. WINANS & CO.,

Wholesale and Retail Dealers in

CHEMICALS, MEDICINES, GROCERIES,

Drugs, Paints, Oils, Dye-Stuffs, Window Glass,

DRUGS STS' GLASSWARE, TOBACCO, CIGARS, &C.

COR. SUMMIT & JEFFERSON STS. TOLEDO, O.

Z. HUSSEY, M. D.

PHYSICIAN AND SURGEON,

SECOND ST., NEAR WALNUT, CHILLICOTHE, O.

Inventor of a recently Patented Apparatus for adjusting Club feet. With this apparatus, and the inventor's method of applying it, a restoration is effected in a few weeks, with almost absolute certainty, which it is doubtful about accomplishing in twice as many months, under other methods of treatment. Dr. H. is also inventor of the **Perfect Adjuster** for fractures and dislocations.

WILLIAM WELSH,

CHILLICOTHE, OHIO.

Foundry and Machine Shop, ON SECOND ST. AND OHIO CANAL,

Warehouse, and Copper, Tin and Sheet Iron Ware Manufactory,

ON PAINT ST. NORTH OF SECOND,

STEAM ENGINE BUILDING,

General Machinery, Mill and Railroad Work,

STOVES, GRATES, HOLLOW-WARE, PLOWS, HOUSE FRONTS,

CAST & WROUGHT IRON RAILING, &C.

Copper Smithing, Tin Plate and Sheet Iron Working carried on in all its various branches.

R. W. DENNING.   F. CAMPBELL.   JNO. HARPER.   R. HARTLEY JORDAN.

DENNING, CAMPBELL & CO.,

IMPORTERS, WHOLESALE AND RETAIL DEALERS IN

ENGLISH, GERMAN AND AMERICAN HARDWARE, CUTLERY,

SADDLERY AND CARRIAGE TRIMMINGS, IRON, NAILS,

Glass, Sash, Oils, Paints, Cordage, Wooden Ware and Baskets, Vulcanized Rubber Belting, Hose and Packing, Oil Cloth and Window Shades, Mechanics' & Farmers' Tools and Building Materials, and all kinds of Agricultural Implements.

AT THEIR NEW ROOM, SIGN OF THE GILT ANVIL,

On the East side of Paint Street, between Water and Second,

CHILLICOTHE, OHIO.

GEO. ARMSTRONG,

BOOK AND JOB PRINTER,

And Editor and Proprietor of the

DAILY & WEEKLY ANCIENT METROPOLIS,

CHILLICOTHE, OHIO.

WERDEN HOUSE.

SPRINGFIELD, O.,

G. FERREE, Proprietor.

PASSENGERS CONVEYED TO AND FROM THE CARS

FREE OF CHARGE.

ETNA

IRON FOUNDRY,

MANUFACTURE

RAIL ROAD CARS,

Mill Gearing & Castings in general.

MAUMEE CITY, O.

LEFFEL, COOK & BLAKENEY,

SPRINGFIELD, OHIO,

PROPRIETORS OF THE

Buck Creek Iron and Brass Foundries,

AND MACHINE SHOP,

Manufacturers of every description of Mill Gearing, Steam Engines, Horse Powers, Threshing Machines, Water Wheels,
Cooking and Heating Stoves, Hollow Ware, Sad Irons,
Potash and Sugar Kettles, and Castings in General,
of Iron and Brass.

RALSTON'S PATENT IMPROVED GRAIN THRESHER
SEPERATOR AND CLEANER.

The subscriber has been engaged in manufacturing the above machines for a number of years, and has introduced them in all the Western grain growing States & along-side of the most popular machines in use, and has taken the preference in all cases.

The advantage this machine has over all other Machines yet introduced, is—First: It will thresh more grain in a given length of time, with less power, than any other machine in use. Second: The simple construction and durability of the Machine makes a very important item to inexperienced hands. Third: In the chafing riddle, it being made of perforated sheet iron, so there is no possibility of choking in damp grain as is the case in other Machines. Fourth: In the elevating of the grain, after being separated and screened, and the second operation of screening and fanning. which leave no possibility of any dirt remaining. and discharges the tailings back to the cylinder. Fifth: The advantage of having the clean grain elevated so it can be discharged some distance from the machine by a close spout into a box or bag ready for market. Sixth: In the open straw carrier and the trunk, so there is no waste by carrying grain with the straw. Seventh: The advantage of attaching the tumbling shaft in three different places on either side or end as the ground or barn suits best.

The power is simple, strong, and but little gearing, consequently the friction is small, and takes less power to drive it. there being but four wheels o the power. Being convinc d that this machine has all the advantages claimed for it, and having spent much time in examining all the various machines throughout the east and west, have become satisfied that it is unequaled, and the best evidence can recommend it. Having taken pains in selecting the l est material and workmen can give entire satisfaction.

Also: Four Horse Threshers, without the Cleaner, Machine Castings, Sausage Grinders, etc., constantly on hand and for sale.

References can be had, with satisfactory evidence from men that have used my machines and the various others.

☞ For further information apply by letter or at my Shop on Second Street, Ripley Brown County, Ohio.
WILLIAM M'CLURE.

ALEX. JOLLY.   W. M. SHAW.

JOLLY & SHAW,
GROCERS AND COMMISSION MERCHANTS,
Corner Main and 4th Sts., RIPLEY, OHIO.

WALLACE POPE & CO.

GENERAL COMMISSION MERCHANTS,

Dealers in Flour and Clover Seed,

Second Street, between Main and Market, Louisville, Kentucky.

BRINKMAN'S HOTEL,

MAIN, BET. 7TH & 8TH, LOUISVILLE, KY.

JOHN BRINKMAN, Proprietor.

MIAMI WORKS,

Hamilton, Butler County, Ohio.

J. T. MURDOCK,

Has obtained the premium for, and manufacturer

FILES, RASPS, BUTCHER KNIVES,

SHOE KNIVES AND RAZORS.

N. B.—The above articles are of the most superior workmanship, and constantly on hand to supply dealers at the very lowest cash prices.

WM. E. DRAYER,

DEALER IN

WATCHES, CLOCKS, JEWELRY, SILVER WARE & FANCY GOODS,

Also, Dealer in Perifocal Spectacles, &c.,

CORNER OF FRONT AND HIGH STREETS,

HAMILTON, OHIO.

M. P. ALSTON,

DRY GOODS AND GROCERIES,

FORWARDING AND COMMISSION MERCHANT,

HAMILTON, OHIO.

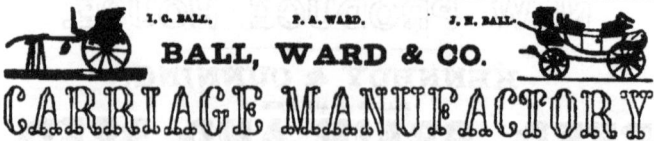

I. C. BALL.   P. A. WARD.   J. N. BALL.

BALL, WARD & CO.

CARRIAGE MANUFACTORY

North-east corner of First and Church streets,

NEWARK, OHIO.

Where carriages of every description are built to order and for sale, which for style, durability and finish cannot be surpassed by any in the western country.   Clarence Coaches & Omnibuses built to order.

A. THOMA,

DEALER IN

WATCHES AND JEWELRY,

CLOCKS & FANCY GOODS,

NO. 197 MAIN STREET,

PIQUA, OHIO.

A. C. ALEXANDER.   H. ROUZER.   J. M. EVANS.

UNDER THE FIRM OF

ALEXANDER & CO.

Piqua Foundry and Machine Shop,

North End of Main Street,

PIQUA, OHIO.

N. B. Steam Engines, Mill Gearing, Machinery and Castings of all kinds made and fitted up to order.

J. D. HOLTZERMANN,

WHOLESALE DEALER IN

FOREIGN AND DOMESTIC LIQUORS,

VINEGAR, CIDER, &C.,

Corner of Main and Water Streets,

PIQUA, OHIO.

PIQUA SASH FACTORY,

North End of the City, on the Canal,

PIQUA, OHIO,

W. O. DILLS, ... PROPRIETOR.

SASH OF ALL SIZES AT WHOLESALE & RETAIL.

Also, Doors and Blinds made to order. Dressed Flooring always on han

E. H. & W. S. BARTON,

Wholesale and Retail

GROCERS AND COMMISSION MERCHANTS,

Dealers in Foreign and Domestic Liquors, Cotton Yarns, Batting, Nails, and Notions of all descriptions.

No. 140 Main Street,

PIQUA, OHIO.

CLARK & ZOLLINGER,

WHOLESALE AND RETAIL

GROCERS AND COMMISSION MERCHANTS,

No. 94 Border Hall, Building fronting on Main and Canal Streets,

PIQUA, OHIO.

A. C. & B. ALEXANDER,

MANUFACTURERS

Of all Descriptions of

RAIL ROAD CARS,

Piqua, Ohio.

CITY HOTEL,

CORNER OF MAIN AND ASH STREETS,

PIQUA, OHIO.

A. B. Carson, Proprietor.

S. H. WOOD,

ATTORNEY AT LAW,

AND

GENERAL COLLECTING AGENT,

PIQUA, MIAMI COUNTY, OHIO.

Collections made in the Counties of Miami, Montgomery, Darke, Mercer, Allen, Auglaize, Shelby, Champaign, and Logan.

M. J. BROWN,

WHOLESALE

GROCER, LIQUOR & COMMISSION MERCHANT,

170 Main Street, Piqua, Ohio.

The subscriber would respectfully call your attention to his stock of OLD BOURBON, MONONGA-
HELA and RYE WHISKEYS, WINES and LIQUORS, and as he buys directly from first hands in bond,
he can warrant to sell as cheap, and on as good terms as they can be bought in Cincinnati, or any other
place. He would call particular attention to his large stock of **Wines, Brandies, Gin, Tea,
Tobacco, Cigars and Double Rectified Whiskey**, which cannot be excelled.
He also keeps on hand a general assortment of Groceries, consisting, in part, of Sugar, Molasses,
Rice, &c., &c. Tavern keepers and Country Stores would do well by calling on him, as he will sell
as low as they can be bought at any other place. **M. J. BROWN.**

JOSEPH M'KNIGHT,

DRY GOODS MERCHANT,

AND DEALER IN GROCERIES, PRODUCE & NOTIONS.

199 Main Street,

PIQUA, OHIO.

J. B. LARGER,

DRY GOODS MERCHANT,

And Dealer in

GROCERIES, PRODUCE & NOTIONS,

196 MAIN STREET,

PIQUA, OHIO.

Hueston & Lklicired,

DRY GOODS MERCHANTS,

AND DEALERS IN

GROCERIES, PRODUCE AND NOTIONS,

Parties purchasing will find it to their advantage to examine our Stock, as all our Goods are new and
of the best quality.

Central Hall Building, South East corner Market Street,

PIQUA, OHIO.

COOLIDGE, ADAMS & BOND,

SUCCESSORS TO H. WINCHESTER & CO.,

WHOLESALE BOTANIC DRUGGISTS,

NO. 108 JOHN STREET,

NEW YORK.

Dealers in Concentrated Medicines, Essential Oils, Shaker Herbs, Extracts, Ointments, Syrups, and every variety of simple and compound Vegetable Medicines, Medical Books, Druggists' Glassware, Syringes, Surgical Instruments, &c. Wholesale Agents for Pettit's American Eye Salve; also, for Garden Seeds put up by the United Society of Shakers, of Enfield, Conn. All goods sold by us warranted strictly pure and of the best quality.

ESSENTIAL

OILS

Foreign and Domestic.

The following articles
crude and in powder :

AFRICAN

BIRD PEPPERS.

ALEX. SENNA.

Rhubarb E. J.

Do. Turkey,

Gum Myrrh,

Do. Arabic,

Do. Aloes cope,

Do. do. Soi,

Do. Guaiacum,

Do. scammony,

Do. Gamboge,

PERUVIAN

Bark,

BAYBERRY

BARK,

&c., &c., &c.

MONUMENT FOUNDRY.

A. & W. DENMEAD & SON,

CORNER NORTH & MONUMENT STREETS,

BALTIMORE.

HAVING THEIR

IRON FOUNDRY & MACHINE SHOP

IN COMPLETE OPERATION,

Are prepared to execute, faithfully and promptly, orders for

**Locomotive or Stationary and Marine Steam Engines,
Woolen, Cotton, Flour, Rice, Sugar, Grist or Saw Mills,
Machinery for Cutting all kinds of Gearing,
Hydraulic, Tobacco, and other Presses,
Car and Locomotive patent Ring-Wheels, warranted,
Bridge and Mill Castings, of every description,
Gas and Water Pipes, all sizes — warranted,
Railroad Wheels, with best Fagoted Axle, Furnished
and Fit up for use, Complete.**

Being provided with Heavy Lathes for Boring or Turning Screws, Cylinders, &c., &c., we can furnish them of any pitch, length or pattern.

Old Machinery Renewed or Repaired and Estimates for Work, in any part of the United States, furnished at at short notice.

EDMUND SNOWDEN,

ATTORNEY AT LAW

AND

NOTARY PUBLIC,

NO. 142 FOURTH STREET,

PITTSBURGH, PA.

M. M. SHIRK.   D. FITZSIMONS.

M. M. SHIRK & CO.,

Copper, Sheet Iron, and Tin Plate Worker,

NO. 8 MARKET STREET, PITTSBURGH, PA.

Keeps on hand and makes to order, Sheet Iron Cooking Stoves for steamboats and hotels; Cast Iron Cooking Stoves for families; and every variety of Tin, Copper and Sheet Iron work for Steamboats, Salt Wells, &c.

N. B. Repairing and Jobbing done at the shortest notice, and in the most substantial manner.

WM. H. DAVIS,

DEALER IN

SALT AND CAUSTIC ALKALI,

CANAL BASIN, LIBERTY STREET,

PITTSBURGH, PA.

GLOBE LARD OIL WORKS.

G. & P. BOGEN,

MANUFACTURERS OF NO. 1

LARD OIL,

NEAR BRIGHTON, CINCINNATI, O.

ALSO:

Curers of Fancy Sugar Cured Hams,

AND MANUFACTURERS OF

SPARKLING CATAWBA AND STILL CATAWBA,

From their own vineyards near Brighton, Cincinnati, and near Carthage, O.

All orders from abroad for either of the above articles promptly attended to.

PETER GRIFFIN,

MANUFACTURER OF CUSTOM-MADE

BOOTS AND SHOES,

OF EVERY STYLE AND FINISH,

126 Vine Street, east side, two doors below Fourth,

NEARLY OPPOSITE BURNET HOUSE,

CINCINNATI.

DAN'L KELLY & CO.

WHOLESALE DEALERS IN

FOREIGN & DOMESTIC LIQUORS,

20 Columbia street, bet. Main & Sycamore,

CINCINNATI, O.

Constantly on hand, a large assortment of the choicest wines and Brandies; also, a few hundred barrels domestic brandy and gin ; sweet Malaga and Muscat wines by the hundred barrels.

Orders from a distance promptly filled, (the qualities being clearly designated,) at the same prices as if purchasers were present.

E. O. GOODMAN & CO.

WHOLESALE

PAPER WARE-HOUSE,

NO. 84 PEARL ST.

CINCINNATI.

We have now on hand and are receiving weekly, the largest and best selected stock of

PAPER, of every description,

Ever offered in Cincinnati. Our recent arrangements with the best

EASTERN MANUFACTURERS,

Enables us to sell as low as the same classed articles can be had in the East. We have the exclusive sale of

Owen & Hurlbut's, Platner & Porter's and Laflin Brothers, Laid and Wove Caps Letters, Packet, Commercial and Bath Posts and Folio Posts;

L. L. Brown & Co.'s Bay State Mills, and Jessup & Laflin's

Demys, Mediums, Royals and Super Royals and Flat Caps, which Papers will please any and every body who may use them; they excel in color, texture, style and finish. We have the agency of **Lightbody's** News, Book and Colored Inks; also, *McCreary's* Colored Inks. Our stock of

CARDS, CARD BOARDS, ILLUMINATED BORDERS,

COLORED AND FANCY PAPERS,

Are of the finest quality and greatest variety in the market.

BOOK BINDERS' STOCK.

We have a full supply of Fleshers, Skivers, Law Sheep, Russia Leathers, Colored Skivers, Turkey Morocco, Imitation Turkey, Muslin, Plow Knives, Straw and Tar Boards, &c.

We have the agency of the **Dayton Mills** Book and News **Paper,** the best made in the West. All regular sizes on hand, and any size and weight made to order on short notice.

ALL ORDERS PROMPTLY ATTENDED TO.

N. B.—HIGHEST PRICE IN CASH PAID FOR RAGS.

GOODLOE PENDERY,

UNDER TAKER,

AND SOLE AGENT

For the Manufacturers and sale of

FISK'S PATENT METALIC BURIAL CASES,

Of this city and vicinity. Undertakers and others having use for the articles, can be supplied at all times. Orders received by telegraph or otherwise, promptly attended to. Also, am prepared to furnish Funerals with Hearses and Carriages and other equipments belonging to the undertaking business.

Office, corner Ninth and Main Streets,

CINCINNATI, O.

BERNARD VEERKAMP,

COACH AND CARRIAGE BUILDER,

Walnut St., east side, bet. 13th & Allison Sts.,

CINCINNATI, O.

N. B. — Ready built coaches, carriages, barouches, buggys, &c., constantly on hand and made to order in a prompt, elegant and durable manner.   Repairing done cheap and all work warranted.

DR. J. M. YOUART,

OFFICE:

SOUTH SIDE OF SEVENTH STREET, BET. RACE AND ELM,

CINCINNATI, O.

Cancers, Ulcers, Tumors, Chronic and Surgical Diseases generally ; treated with success. Address

JOHN YOUART, M.D.

S. WICKERSHAM,

DENTIST,

NO. 317 EIGHTH STREET, SOUTH SIDE, BET. JOHN & MOUND STREETS,

CINCINNATI.

VERTICAL VACUUM FAN AND SMUT MACHINE COMBINED.

The object of the Vacuum Fan and Smut Machine combined was (simply) to arrange and combine a suction fan with an improved Smut Machine, in such a manner as to render the combined machine capable of performing the work that has hitherto required two machines, to wit :

1st. To separate the chaff, smut balls, &c., &c., from the wheat, preparatory to the commencement of the scouring process.

2nd. To thoroughly scour with the least liability to breaking the wheat.

Reference being had to the subjoined certificates.

This certifies that we have used Mr. Lewis Fagin's Vacuum Fan and Smut Machine combined, and can safely say that it cleans wheat decidedly better than any thing of the kind we ever saw. In fact it is the only machine we know of that takes out the smut, chaff, &c., before the scouring is commenced. It not only does this effectually, but it thoroughly scours the fuzz from the grain and is not half so liable to break wheat, as machines do that rely upon the beating process, its operation is that of pearling rather than beating, and is so arranged and ventilated as to draw the dust out at intervals during the scouring process ; (a great advantage this over other machines) it is very durable, cleans fast with little power and room, and gives no trouble, and will, as we believe, more than meet the expectation of those who try them, and therefore we cordially recommend them as a valuable machine possessing all the advantages claimed by the inventor.

Practical Millers, { H. C. HAYMAN, JOSEPH H. FAGIN, JOHN NAIRN.

VERTICAL VACUUM FAN AND SMUT MACHINE COMBINED.—This certifies that we are using Mr. Lewis Fagan's Vertical Vacuum Fan and Smut Machine combined, which performs its work most admirably. This machine not only separates the smut and other foul substances from the grain, before the scouring process is commenced, (an important item,) but it thoroughly scours the same, and further, the dust is immediately drawn out as soon as scoured loose from the grain. We consider that this machine richly deserves all the merit that Mr. Fagin claims for it, and that it will fully meet the expectations of those who try it, therefore we heartily recommend its adoption.

STILES & ROMINE.

ROCKPORT, Nov. 20th, 1852.

LEWIS FAGAN,

LOCK, BETWEEN SYMMES AND FIFTH STREETS,

CINCINNATI, O.

H. M. COOK & CO.

Fourth St., near Park,

CINCINNATI, OHIO.

DEALERS IN LUMBER OF ALL KINDS, AND MANUFACTURERS OF SASH, DOORS, BLINDS, FLOORING, PARTITION BOARDS, SHELVING, WEATHER BOARDS, ETC., ETC.

Having constantly on hand from one to two million feet of the best pine lumber that can be procured, we are prepared to fill all orders for any of the above named articles, or lumber, at short notice,—pledging ourselves that our work shall not be surpassed (if equalled) by that of any other establishment in the west.

WILLIAM F. THORNE,

Wholesale Dealer in LEATHER, and Manufacturer of

GENTLEMEN'S FINE PEGGED BOOTS & SHOES

ALSO, EVERY VARIETY OF

Ladies', Misses', & Childrens' Sewed & Pegged Bootees & Shoes,

No. 74 Lower Market Street,

CINCINNATI, OHIO.

HENRY DAVID,

MANUFACTURER AND IMPORTER OF

FANCY SOAPS, PERFUMERY, &C.

165 Main Street,

BETWEEN FOURTH AND FIFTH, WEST SIDE,

CINCINNATI, OHIO.

PREMIUM PERFUMERY.

REPORT.

We hereby certify that we have examined the FINE SOAPS AND PERFUMERY exhibited at the Annual Fair of the Ohio Mechanics' Institute, and decide that the Soaps manufactured by HENRY DAVID are superior to any offered by his competitors, and the Perfumery exhibited by Mr. David is not surpassed either in quality or style of putting up, by any which we have seen manufactured in the United States.

WM. S. MERRILL, } Judges.
J. A. WARDER, }

STRONG & FINE,

MANUFACTURERS OF

STOVES & HOLLOW-WARE,

Ware-Rooms, No. 5 Fifth street, near Main,

CINCINNATI, O.

E. K. STRONG.   T. B. FINE.

QUEEN CITY LARD OIL FACTORY.

F. FRANK,

19 EAST FRONT STREET, ABOVE BROADWAY,

CINCINNATI, O.

This is one of the oldest establishments in the West and sells at lowest rates.

PENSYLVANIA HOUSE,

Corner of Front and Pike streets,

CINCINNATI, O.

KEPT BY J. H. HULLMAN.

WM. P. DEVOU.   CHAS. A. ROCKWOOD.

W. P. DEVOU & ROCKWOOD,

IMPORTERS AND JOBBERS IN

Silk, Straw and Millinery Goods, Laces,

IRISH LINENS, JACONETS, CAMBRICS,

HANDKERCHIEFS, TRIMMINGS, ETC.

NO. 46 & 50 PEARL STREET,

CINCINNATI, O.

SKIFF & TRAYSER,

MANUFACTURERS OF TRAYSER'S PATENT

Large Grand Boudoir Piano Fortes,

Fine Small do do, Fine Square 7---6¾ and 6½ do.

By this new principle the peculiar form and construction render the tone more rich, varied and powerful than any other made before.

J. A. SKIFF, General Agent, Cin., O.

H. STEGNER.   G. A. BOHRER.

STEGNER & CO.,

Undertakers and Livery Stable Proprietors,

ELM ST., BETWEEN FIFTEENTH & LIBERTY STS.,

CINCINNATI, OHIO.

Burial Cases of every description, Hearse and Carriages furnished in the best style and at the lowest possible rates.

JOHN MITCHELL.   WM. F. MITCHELL

MITCHELL & BROTHER,

Wholesale and Retail Dealers in

POMEROY IRON,

Nails, Steel, Springs, Axles, &c., &c.

They also keep on hand a large variety of

COOKING AND PARLOR STOVES.

No. 395 Main Street, West Side, three doors below Court,

CINCINNATI, OHIO.

M. RICHEIMER,

WHOLESALE & RETAIL

CANDY MANUFACTURER

AND FANCY CAKE BAKER,

No. 295 Main Street, between Sixth and Seventh,

CINCINNATI, OHIO.

THE

CINCINNATI GAZETTE COMP'Y,

NEWSPAPER

～AND～

JOB PRINTING

Establishment.

A FURTHER ENLARGEMENT--EXTRA MAMMOTH SIZE!

The largest & best Daily & Weekly Paper printed in the West.

COMMENCED THE FIRST WEEKLY IN CINCINNATI,

COMMENCED THE FIRST DAILY IN THE NORTH-WEST.

Weekly commenced 1793. Daily, 25 June, '27.

EACH WEEKLY EQUAL TO 250 PAGES OF A CURRENT NOVEL

The Company has again been compelled to enlarge to an *Extra Mammoth Size.* They wish to give more and better reading than any other, and to issue the cheapest Paper. They say unhesitatingly, that as their papers are the oldest, so they are determined they shall be the largest, best and cheapest papers. No expense has been spared. They have many editors—have the largest force—and publish the most selected news, telegraph, and commercial. It has the largest business patronage, and has always increased in circulation and advertising.

SEVEN POWER PRINTING PRESSES

Are kept running day and night on NEWSPAPER, BOOK AND JOB PRINTING. They have every facility for doing all kinds of BOOK AND JOB PRINTING, in the quickest time and on the most reasonable terms.

WOODRUFF HOUSE.

WETHERBEE, BLEDSOE & Co.
Proprietors.

THIS IS A NEWLY ERECTED EDIFICE, LOCATED ON

SYCAMORE STREET,

BETWEEN THIRD AND FOURTH,

Fronting on both Sycamore and Hammond Streets.

It has been recently leased by the above firm, and newly fitted and furnished throughout. Its location being so central, renders it a desirable place for those visiting the City on business. Being but a short distance from the principal Wholesale and Retail Stores, convenient to the Post Office, Rail Road Depots and Ohio River, besides containing all the new and modern Hotel conveniences.

GEORGE WHITE,

WHOLESALE & RETAIL DEALER IN

SILKS, SHAWLS, CLOAKS, MANTILLAS,

FINE DRESS GOODS,

EMBROIDERIES, LACES, GLOVES,

HOSIERY, LINENS, RIBBONS AND DOMESTICS,

56 & 58 FIFTH STREET,

CINCINNATI, OHIO.

MEAD, SELDEN & CO.

Importers and Wholesale Dealers in

Foreign & Domestic

HARDWARE,

NO. 15 PEARL STREET,

CINCINNATI.

BAKER & VON PHUL,

MANUFACTURERS AND IMPORTERS OF

GAS FIXTURES,

Lamps, Gerandoles and Fancy Articles.

Also, Western Agents for the sale of

WROUGHT IRON STEAM & GAS PIPES, METERS, &C.

AT MANUFACTURERS' EASTERN PRICES.

GAS PIPES introduced into dwellings, churches, stores, &c., in the best and most approved manner, at the lowest rates.

BAKER & VON PHUL,

160 Main st. above 4th, & No. 60 4th st. West of Walnut,

CINCINNATI.

M. HERBSTREIT,

WHOLESALE

WINE & CIDER VINEGAR DEPOT,

Importer and Dealer in

WINES AND LIQUORS,

481 VINE STREET, NEAR 13TH,

CINCINNATI.

WILLIAM HOLMES,

GILDER, LOOKING GLASS & PICTURE FRAME

MAKER,

119 Fifth street, South side, between Vine and Race,

CINCINNATI.

Mirrors, Plain and Ornamental Portrait, Picture and Looking Glass Frames, Window Cornices of every description.
Prints and Maps Mounted and Varnished. Old Frames re-gilt—Old Paintings carefully cleaned and backed on the most approved principle.

ADAM KUHN.   ALFRED BUCHANAN.

KUHN & BUCHANAN,

DEALERS IN

YOUGHIOGHENY AND OTHER COALS,

EIRE BRICK AND CLAY,

Also--McKeesport, Connellsville & Manufacturers City Coke,

COR. SECOND & ELM STREETS,—AND FRONT ST. WEST OF SMITH ST.,

CINCINNATI, OHIO.

ELISHA SAUNDERS,

IMPORTER AND JOBBER OF

SILK AND STRAW GOODS,

No. 11 west Fourth St., bet. Main & Walnut sts.,

CINCINNATI, OHIO.

Ribbons, Silks, Velvets, Flowers, Bonnets, Mantillas, Shawls, &c., Cheap for Cash.

J. & R. HUTTON,

WAGON MANUFACTURERS,

Front Street, between Elm and Plum,

CINCINNATI, O.

Wagons, Carts, Drays and Wheelbarrows kept constantly on hand and made to order.
Also, a superior article of hames.

THOS. TURNER.   JAS. TURNER.

TURNER & SON,

FIRST PREMIUM SAW MANUFACTORY,

Manufacturers of Saws of every description, warranted and made of the best material.

No. 238 Seventh St., north side. bet. Western Row & John St.,

CINCINNATI, OHIO.

J. SIMON,
FURNITURE & CABINET WAREROOMS,
No. 444 Walnut St., 3rd door South of Thirteenth, Cin.

☞Always on hand a large assortment of House Furniture, Matrasses, Beddings, &c., at the lowest Wholesale and Retail Prices.

ALLISON OWEN,
Wholesale Dealer in
Fine Groceries and various Foreign Delicacies, &c.
Manchester Buildings, Nos. 29 and 31 Third Street, between Main and Sycamore Streets, Cincinnati, Ohio.

LOUIS JACOB,
WHOLESALE AND RETAIL DEALER IN
BACON, HAMS, SHOULDERS, DRIED BEEF,
BEEF TONGUES AND BOLOGNA SAUSAGES,
Walnut Street, between 5th and 6th, East Side, Cincinnati.

J. KLING & THEIS,
Fashionable Hat and Cap Manufacturers,
No. 260 MAIN ST., BETWEEN SIXTH & SEVENTH, EAST SIDE, CINCINNATI.

H. BALLHOUSE & HAMMER,
Manufacturers, Importers and Dealers in
MUSICAL INSTRUMENTS,
No. 130 Walnut St., East Side, between 3rd and 4th, Cincinnati.

Accordeons, and all kinds of Musical Instruments, neatly repaired, on the most reasonable terms.

CHEAP SHOE STORE!
J. WALLWORK,
Manufacturer of Boots and Shoes, Wholesale and Retail,
No. 214 Sixth Street, North Side, Cincinnati.

N. PATTERSON,
No. 18 Public Landing, Cincinnati,

Manufacturer of all sizes Bar, Rounds, Squares and Hoop Iron, and wholesale dealer in Nails, Steel, Grindstones, &c. Also, manufactures the Bay State, Halcyon, Old Kentucky, Queen City, Prize Premium and Ohio Premium Cooking Stoves, Etna Parlors, N. Y. Parlors, Six Plate, Seven and Ten Plate and Common Stoves, Plain and Ornamental GRATES, SAD IRONS, DOG IRONS, WAGON BOXES, MOULD BOARDS, and every description of HOLLOW WARE and CASTINGS.

M. VONGENECHTEN,
TRUNK & CARPET BAG MANUFACTURER
No. 55 Broadway, bet. Columbia and Lower Market,
CINCINNATI, O.
WHOLESALE AND RETAIL.
Particular attention will be paid to all orders from any part of the counter
At the most reasonable terms.

H. & J. O. TAYLOR,
WHOLESALE AND RETAIL

Plane Manufacturer,
Eighth st, bet. Broadway & Sycamore,
CINCINNATI.
Carpenters' and Coopers' Tools always on hand.   Punctual attendance given to all Jobbing
and repairing.

GEO. BROWN & Co.
LIVERY STABLE KEEPERS
NO. 7 SIXTH ST. BET. MAIN & SYCAMORE,
CINCINNATI.

J. F. GLEICH,
MUSICAL INSTRUMENT MAKER,
N. E. corner Walnut and Ninth Streets,
CINCINNATI.
ALL KINDS OF REPAIRING DONE AT THE SHORTEST NOTICE.

H. H. HUTTE,
MANUFACTURER OF FASHIONABLE

BOOTS & SHOES
No. 235 Walnut St.
WEST SIDE, 1 DOOR BELOW U. S. HOTEL
CINCINNATI.
Repairing done in a style equal to any in the city.

CUTLER'S

PURIFYING SYRUP

FOR THE CURE OF

Liver Complaint, Asthma, Breast Complaint, Spitting of Blood, Night Sweats, Fever and Ague, &c., &c.

This Medicine can be had at Mr. Geo. B. Rohrer's Hardware store, south-west corner of Fifth and Western Row; and at Dr. Pease's Drug Store, north-west corner Western Row and Richmond; and on Catharine street, first brick house west of Cutler, south side; and at the proprietor's place, south-east corner of Chesnut and Fulton streets, No. 192.

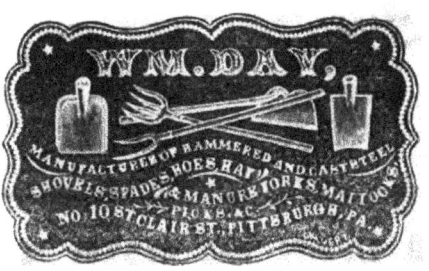

R. S. NEWTON, M. D.   O. E. NEWTON, M. D.

R. S. & O. E. NEWTON,

PHYSICIANS AND SURGEONS,

OFFICE—COR. SEVENTH & COLLEGE, STS,

CINCINNATI, O.

I. H. BALLINGER,

ECLECTIC PHYSICIAN,

May be consulted on all diseases to which the human family is subjected.

ROSSVILLE, BUTLER CO., O.   OFFICE -- ON MAIN STREET, OPP. BUTLER HOUSE.

CINCINNATI COLLEGE

OF

MEDICINE AND SURGERY,

South-west cor. of Western Row and Longworth streets.

FACULTY:

A. H. BAKER, M. D.,
Professor of the Principles and practice of Surgery.

B. S. LAWSON, M. D.,
Professor of the Theory and Practice of Medicine.

C. B. CHAPMAN, M. D.,
Professor of Anatomy.

ELIJAH SLACK, A. M., M D.,
Professor of Chemistry and Pharmacy.

J. W. MIGHELS. M D,
Professor of Obstetrics and Diseases of Women and Children.

G. A. GOTWALD, M. D.,
Professor of Materia Medica and Therapeutics.

L. L. PINKERTON, M. D.,
Professor of Physiology and Pathology.

EDWARD MEAD, M. D.,
Professor of Insanity and Medical Jurisprudence.

W. W. DAWSON, M. D..
Demonstrator of Anatomy.

FEES,—Professors' Tickets, $90; Matriculation Tickets, $5; Dissecting Ticket, $10; Hospital Ticket, 5; Graduation Fee, $25.

Students by calling at the College Building on their arrival, will be conducted to places of boarding and furnished with all necessary information.

For further particulars address, by letter or otherwise, the President or Registrar.

S. B. LAWSON, REGISTRAR.   A. H. BAKER, PRESIDENT.
Residence 533 west Sixth street.   Residence 316 west Sixth street.

CINCINNATI MARINE HOSPITAL,

AND

INVALID'S RETREAT,

South-west corner of Western Row and Longworth sts.

This institution is attached to the Cincinnati College of Medicine and Surgery, and is under the care of the Professors of Medicine and Surgery, as above; and the patient will have the benefit of the advice of the Faculty generally.

The Invalid can be accommodated here, on such terms as may suit his circumstances. 1st If unable to pay for Professional Services, he can receive all necessary medical and surgical attention gratis, by submitting his case for Clinical Instruction, in the College; for Board, Nursing, &c., he will be charged from four to six dollars per week. Patients may bring their own nurses, but must submit to the rules of the house.

Patients able to pay for Professional services, will be charged for the same.

For further particulars address DRS. BAKER & LAWSON,

{ A. H. BAKER,
{ B. S. LAWSON.

INDEX TO BUSINESS MEN'S CARDS.
CINCINNATI.

COLUMBUS CARDS.

CLEVELAND CARDS.

PHILADELPHIA CARDS.

WHEELING CARDS.